The Corsini Encyclopedia of Psychology and Behavioral Science

Third Edition

The Corsini Encyclopedia of Psychology and Behavioral Science

Third Edition

VOLUME 2

Co-Editors

W. EDWARD CRAIGHEAD
University of Colorado
Boulder, CO

CHARLES B. NEMEROFF
Emory University School of Medicine
Atlanta, GA

Editorial Board

JOHN WILEY & SONS
New York • Chichester • Weinheim • Brisbane • Singapore • Toronto

ISBN 0-471-24096-6 (Volume 1)
ISBN 0-471-24097-4 (Volume 2)
ISBN 0-471-24098-2 (Volume 3)
ISBN 0-471-24099-0 (Volume 4)
ISBN 0-471-23949-6 (Four-volume set)

Printed in the United States of America
10 9 8 7 6 5 4 3 2 1

Preface

This revision of Raymond J. Corsini's successful *Encyclopedia of Psychology* is based on the need to update and expand the previous edition. Because of the advances in behavioral science and the relationship of those advances to psychology, this edition has been renamed to reflect the inclusion of those advances.

The major purpose of these volumes is to make the current knowledge in psychology and behavioral science available to the community at large. It is hoped that they will constitute a concise and handy reference for individuals interested in these topics. Each entry is designed to inform the reader on its particular topic; of necessity, however, an entry in an encyclopedia can be only a succinct summary of that topic. Cross-references are provided for the entries so that the reader can easily make his or her way to related topics for more detail.

In order to keep the encyclopedia to four volumes and still be inclusive of contemporary topics, several now-outdated topics were dropped from the prior edition. We updated about two-thirds of the prior edition, and replaced the remaining one-third with new topics. We have sought to keep the international flavor that Corsini had employed in the original encyclopedia; thus, we selected our contributors from an international list of scholars on the chosen topics.

Coordinating a publication of this magnitude is a formidable task, particularly when undertaken within the framework of one's regular job. Thus, we are extremely appreciative of those who have been so helpful in making this project possible. We are deeply grateful to the more than 1,000 authors who contributed to this encyclopedia; without them, these volumes would not have been. Our greatest appreciation is expressed to Alinne Barrera, Benjamin Page, and Fiona Vajk, who have served as managing editors for this project. We also express our gratitude to Nancy Grabowski (administrative assistant to W. Edward Craighead), who provided necessary support to the editors and managing editors. It is hard to imagine a better or more efficient working team than Kelly Franklin and Jennifer Simon at John Wiley & Sons. Even though many of us involved in this project have experienced numerous, and at times unbelievable, life events during the development and production of these volumes, the project has been brought to a successful and timely completion. We are happy and grateful to have been surrounded by such a fine group of wonderful and dedicated individuals.

In the final analysis, production of these volumes has allowed us to continue a warm friendship and professional collaboration begun about 15 years ago at Duke University Medical Center—a friendship and collaboration that have survived the selection, coordination, and editing of the contributions of well over 1,000 authors on more than 1,200 topics. We have treated patients together; we have conducted collaborative research; we have published together; we have presented together at professional meetings; and we have laughed and cried together in good times and bad. It has been a satisfying experience to edit these volumes together. We trust they will be useful to you, the reader.

W. Edward Craighead, PhD
Boulder, Colorado

Charles B. Nemeroff, MD, PhD
Atlanta, Georgia

Contributors List

NORMAN ABELES
Michigan State University

L. Y. ABRAMSON
University of Wisconsin

ROSEMARY C. ADAM-TEREM
Kapiolani Medical Center, Honolulu, HI

HOWARD S. ADELMAN
University of California, Los Angeles

BERNARD W. AGRANOFF
University of Michigan

LEWIS R. AIKEN
Pepperdine University

ICEK AJZEN
University of Massachusetts

GEORGE W. ALBEE
Florida Mental Health Institute

LYNN E. ALDEN
University of British Columbia

THERON ALEXANDER
Temple University

MARY J. ALLEN
California State College

LAUREN B. ALLOY
Temple University

G. HUGH ALLRED
Brigham Young University

NANCY S. ANDERSON
Emory School of Medicine

JOHN L. ADREASSI
City University of New York-Baruch College

J. E. ALCOCK
The Australian National University

L. B. AMES

RICHARD S. ANDRULIS
Andrulis Associates, West Chester, PA

HYMIE ANISMAN
Carleton University, Ottawa

H. L. ANSBACHER

RUBEN ARDILA
National University of Colombia

E. Ö. ARNARSON
University of Iceland

MARK ARONOFF
State University of New York, Albany

RICHARD M. ASHBROOK
Capital University

J. WILLIAM ASHER
Purdue University

J. A. ASTIN
University of Maryland School of Medicine

CAROL SHAW AUSTAD

ROBERT M. DAVISON AVILES
Bradley University

K. W. BACK

ALBERT BANDURA
Stanford University

DAVID H. BARLOW
Boston University

AUGUSTINE BARÓN, JR.
University of Texas, Austin

DANIEL BAR-TAL
Tel Aviv University

S. HOWARD BARTLEY
Memphis State University

VALENTINA BASSAREO
University of Cagliari, Italy

B. M. BAUGHAN
University of Colorado, Boulder

ANDREW SLATER BAUM
University of Pittsburgh Cancer Institute

ALAN A. BAUMEISTER
Louisiana State University

RAMÓN BAYÉS SOPENA
Universidad Autónoma de Barcelona

STEVEN BEACH
University of Georgia

AARON T. BECK
Beck Institute for Cognitive Therapy and Research

GARY S. BELKIN
Brown University

ALAN S. BELLACK
University of Maryland

JOEL B. BENNETT
Texas Christian University

THOMAS S. BENNETT
Brain Inquiry Recovery Program, Fort Collins, CO

HEATHER A. E. BENSON
University of Manitoba

P. G. BENSON
New Mexico State University

SHERI A. BERENBAUM
Southern Illinois University

S. BERENTSEN

LEONARD BERGER
Clemson University

JOANNE BERGER-SWEENEY
Wellesly College

GREGORY S. BERNS
Emory University

G. G. BERNTSON
Ohio State University

MICHAEL D. BERZONSKY
State University of New York, Cortland

SIDNEY W. BIJOU
University of Nevada

AIDA BILALBEGOVIC
Tufts University, Medford, MA

JEFFREY R. BINDER
Medical College Of Wisconsin

JERRY M. BINDER
Behavioral Health Consultant, Corona Del Mar

NIELS BIRMBAUER
University of Tübingen, Germany

D. W. BLACK
University of Iowa

THEODORE H. BLAU

BERNARD L. BLOOM
University of Colorado

MILTON S. BLOOMBAUM
Southern Oregon University

JODI L. BODDY
Simon Fraser University, British Columbia

C. ALAN BONEAU
George Mason University

EDWARD S. BORDIN
University of Michigan

EDGAR F. BORGATTA
University of Washington

P. BOSE
University of Florida

DALE E. BOWEN
Psychological Associates, Grand Junction, CO

A. D. BRANSTETTER

C. REGINALD BRASINGTON
University of South Carolina

MARGARET BRENMAN-GIBSON
Harvard Medical School

RONAL BRENNER
St. John's Episcopal Hospital, Far Rockaway, NY

WARRICK J. BREWER
The University of Melbourne & Mental Health Research Institute of Victoria

SARA K. BRIDGES
Humboldt State University

ARTHUR P. BRIEF
Tulane University

R. W. BRISLIN
University of Hawaii

GILBERTO N. O. BRITO
Instituto Fernandes Figueira, Brazil

DONALD E. BROADBENT
University of Oxford

J. D. BROOKE
Northwestern University

FREDERICK GRAMM BROWN
Iowa State University

ROBERT TINDALL BROWN
University of North Carolina, Wilmington

SHELDON S. BROWN
North Shore Community College

J. BROZEK

MARTIN BRÜNE
Ruhr University, Germany

B. R. BUGELSKI
State University of New York, Buffalo

GRAHAM D. BURROWS
University of Melbourne

JAMES M. BUTCHER
University of Minnesota, Minneaplois

ANN B. BUTLER
George Mason University

REBECCA M. BUTZ
Tulane University

J. T. CACIOPPO
University of Chicago

SHAWN P. CAHILL
University of Pennsylvania

JOHN B. CAMPBELL
Franklin & Marshall College

N. A. CAMPBELL
Brown University

TYRONE D. CANNON
University of California, Los Angeles

SAMUEL S. CARDONE
Illinois Department of Mental Health, Chicago

BERNARDO J. CARDUCCI
Shyness Research Institute, Indiana University Southeast

MARK CARICH
Adler School of Professional Psychology

PETER A. CARICH
University of Missouri

JOHN G. CARLSON
University of Hawaii, Honolulu

J. DOUGLAS CARROLL
Rutgers University

GIOVANNI CASINI
Tuscia University, Italy

T. CASOLI
I.N.R.C.A., Italy

LOUIS G. CASTONGUAY
Pennsylvania State University

CARL ANDREW CASTRO
Walter Reed Army Institute of Research

FAIRFID M. CAUDLE
College of Staten Island

JOSEPH R. CAUTELA

STEPHEN J. CECI
Cornell University

JAE-HO CHA
Seoul National University

PAUL F. CHAPMAN
University of Minnesota, Minneaplois

U. CHARPA
Cologne University, Germany

GORDON J. CHELUNE
The Cleveland Clinic Foundation

GLYN CHIDLOW
University of Oxford

IRVIN L. CHILD
Yale University

MARGARET M. CLIFFORD
University of Iowa

RICHARD WELTON COAN
Retired, University of Arizona

KIMBERLY PEELE COCKERHAM
Allegheny Ophthalmic and Orbital Associates, Pittsburgh

MARK S. COE
DePaul University

NORMAN J. COHEN
Baylor State University

P. COHEN-KETTENIS
Utrecht University, The Netherlands

RAYMOND J. COLELLO
Virginia Commonwealth University

GARY R. COLLINS
Trinity Evangelical Divinity School

MARY BETH CONNOLLY
University of Pennsylvania

M. J. CONSTANTINO
Pennsylvania State University

GERALD COOKE
Plymouth Meeting, PA

JEREMY D. COPLAND
Columbia University College of Physicians and Surgeons

STANLEY COREN
University of British Columbia

GERALD F. COREY
California State University, Fullerton

JOHN F. CORSO
State University of New York, Cortland

ERMINIO COSTA
University of Illinois, Chicago

JOSEPH T. COYLE
Harvard University

BENJAMIN H. CRAIGHEAD
Medical College of Virginia

W. EDWARD CRAIGHEAD
University of Colorado

PAUL CRITS-CHRISTOPH
University of Pennsylvania

ARNOLD E. DAHLKE
Los Angeles, CA

JOHN G. DARLEY
University of Minnesota, Minneaplois

WILLIAM S. DAVIDSON II
Michigan State University

EDWARD L. DECI
University of Rochester

CRISTINA MARTA DEL-BEN
Universidade de São Paulo, Brazil

H. A. DEMAREE
Kessler Medical Rehabilitation Research and Education Corporation

FLORENCE L. DENMARK
Pace University, New York

M. RAY DENNY
Michigan State University

DONALD R. DENVER
Quebec, Montreal, Canada

NORMAN K. DENZIN
University of Illinois, Urbana

SARAH E. DEROSSETT

FRANCINE DEUTSCH
San Diego State University

DAVID L. DEVRIES
Kaplan DeVries Institute

DONALD ALLEN DEWSBURY
University of Florida

ESTHER E. DIAMOND

MILTON DIAMOND
University of Hawaii, Honolulu

R. DIAZ-GUERRERO
University of Mexico

MANFRED DIEHL
University of Colorado

VOLKER DIETZ
University Hospital Balgrist, Zurich

R. DILLON

RAYMOND DINGLEDINE
Emory University School of Medicine

JOHN W. DONAHOE
University of Massachusetts

NICK DONNELLY
University of Southampton, UK

SYLVAIN DORÉ
Johns Hopkins University

MICHAEL G. DOW
University of South Florida

PETER W. DOWRICK
University of Hawaii, Manoa

JURIS G. DRAGUNS
Pennsylvania State University

CLIFFORD J. DREW
University of Utah

D. A. DROSSMAN
University of North Carolina

PHILIP H. DUBOIS

HUBERT C. J. DUIJKER
University of Amsterdam

BRUCE R. DUNN
The University of West Florida

M. O. A. DUROJAIYE
University of Lagos, Nigeria

TERRY M. DWYER
University of Mississippi School of Medicine

G. D'YDEWALLE
University of Leuven, Belgium

BARRY A. EDELSTEIN
West Virginia University

THOMAS E. EDGAR
Idaho State University

WILLIAM E. EDMONSTON, JR.
Colgate University

C. L. EHLERS
University of California, San Diego

HOWARD EICHENBAUM
Boston University

ROGER E. ENFIELD
West Central Georgia Regional Hospital, Columbus, GA

JOHN WILLIAM ENGEL
University of Hawaii, Honolulu

FRANZ R. EPTING
University of Florida

ANGELICA ESCALONA
Nova Southeastern University

DAVID RICHARD EVANS
University of Western Ontario

FREDERICK J. EVANS
Reading Hospital

ROBERT B. EWEN
Miami, FL

CORA E. EZZELL
Medical University of South Carolina

CLARA C. FAURA-GINER
Universidad Miguel Hernandez, Spain

HERMAN FEIFEL
Veterans Administration Outpatient Clinic, Los Angeles

LAURIE B. FELDMAN
State University of New York, Albany

EVA DREIKURS FERGUSON
Southern Illinois University

JOSEPH R. FERRARI
Depaul University

MICHAEL A. FIEDLER
University of Alabama, Birmingham

FRANK W. FINGER
University of Virginia

S. FINGER
Washington University

HAROLD KENNETH FINK
Honolulu, HI

NORMAN J. FINKEL
Georgetown University

CHET H. FISCHER
Radford University

DAVID A. FISHBAIN
University of Miami

DENNIS F. FISHER
U.S. Army Human Engineering Laboratory

DOUGLAS A. FITTS
University of Washington

REIKO MAKI FITZSIMONDS
Yale School of Medicine

DEBRA A. FLEISCHMAN
Rush-Presbyterian St. Luke's Medical Center

EDNA B. FOA
University of Pennsylvania

JAMES L. FOBES
Army Research Institute for the Behavioral Sciences

JOHN P. FOREYT
Baylor College of Medicine

BARBARA L. FORISHA-KOVACH
University of Michigan

GEORGE FOURIEZOS
University of Ottawa

MARCI GITTES FOX
Beck Institute for Cognitive Therapy and Research

NATHAN A. FOX
University of Maryland

J. FRANKENHEIM
National Institutes of Health

CALVIN J. FREDERICK
University of California, Los Angeles

MATS FREDERICKSON
Uppsala University, Sweden

C. R. FREEMAN
McGill University

W. O. FRIESEN
University of Virginia

ROBERT H. FRIIS
California State University, Long Beach

KARL J. FRISTON
Institute of Neurology, UK

BENJAMIN FRUCHTER
University of Texas, Austin

ISAO FUKUNISHI
Tokyo Institute of Psychiatry

TOMAS FURMARK
Uppsala University, Sweden

PAUL A. GADE
U. S. Army Research Institute

SOL L. GARFIELD
Washington University

G. GASKELL
University of York, UK

STEVEN J. GARLOW
Emory School of Medicine

TIMOTHY L. GASPERONI
University of California, Los Angeles

JEAN S. GEARON
University of Maryland

NORI GEARY
Weill Medical College of Cornell University

K. F. GEISINGER
Le Moyne College

MARK S. GEORGE
Medical University of South Carolina

T. D. GIARGIARI
University of Colorado, Boulder

KAREN M. GIL
University of North Carolina, Chapel Hill

RITA T. GIUBILATO
Thomas Jefferson University

THOMAS A. GLASS
Honolulu, HI

WILLIAM GLASSER
The William Glasser Institute, Chatsworth, CA

J. M. GLOZMAN
Moscow University

CHARLES J. GOLDEN
Nova Southeastern University

ROBERT N. GOLDEN
University of North Carolina School of Medicine

ARNOLD P. GOLDSTEIN
Syracuse University

JEFFREY L. GOODIE
West Virginia University

G. KEN GOODRICK
University of Houston

LEONARD D. GOODSTEIN
Washington, DC

BERNARD S. GORMAN
Nassau Community College

GILBERT GOTTLIEB
University of North Carolina, Chapel Hill

DONALD L. GRANT
Roswell, CTA

J. W. GRAU
Texas A & M University

MARTIN S. GREENBERG
University of Pittsburgh

W. A. GREENE
Eastern Washington University

SHELLY F. GREENFIELD
McLean Hospital, Belmont, MA

JAMES LYNN GREENSTONE
Southwestern Academy of Crisis Interveners, Dallas

WILLIAM EDGAR GREGORY
University of the Pacific

SEBASTIAN P. GROSSMAN
University of Chicago

AMANDA J. GRUBER
McLean Hospital, Belmont, MA

ROBERT M. GUION
Bowling Green State University

LAURA GULI
University of Texas, Austin

G. GUTTMANN
University of Vienna

RUSSELL A. HABER
University of South Carolina

HAROLD V. HALL
Honolulu, HI

KATHERINE A. HALMI
Cornell University Medical Center

MARK B. HAMNER
Medical University of South Carolina

GREGORY R. HANCOCK
University of Maryland

FOREST W. HANSEN
Lake Forest College

J. M. HARPER
Brigham Young University

JOSEPH T. HART
University of Colorado

ALISHA B. HART
Kupat Holim Klalit, Tel Aviv

E. I. HARTLEY

SCOTT HARTMAN
Center for Marital and Family Studies, University of Denver

DAVID B. HATFIELD
Eastern Washington University

ELAINE HATFIELD
University of Hawaii, Manoa

ROBERT P. HAWKINS
West Virginia University

STEPHEN N. HAYNES
University of Hawaii, Manoa

N. A. HAYNIE

DONALD A. HECK
Iowa State

S. R. HEIDEMANN
Michigan State University

J. HEIMAN
University of Washington

LYNNE M. HENDERSON
The Shyness Institute, Stanford

GREGG HENRIQUES
University of Pennsylvania

P. P. HEPPNER
University of Missouri, Columbia

GREGORY M. HEREK
University of California, Davis

EDWIN L. HERR
Pennsylvania State University

ALLEN K. HESS
Auburn University

ERNEST R. HILGARD
Stanford University

JEANNE SWICKARD HOFFMAN
Honolulu, HI

RALPH E. HOFFMAN
Yale School of Medicine

CHRISTINE HOHMANN
Morgan State University

P. Y. HONG
University of Kansas

B. HOPKINS
Seattle University

RONALD R. HOLDEN
Queen's University, Ontario

DAVID L. HOLMES
The Eden Institute, Princeton

DAVID SHERIDAN HOLMES
University of Kansas

WAYNE H. HOLTZMAN
University of Texas, Austin

BURT HOPKINS
Seattle University

J. HOSKOVEC

ARTHUR C. HOUTS
University of Memphis

ROBERT H. HOWLAND
University of Pittsburgh School of Medicine

C. H. HUBER
New Mexico State University

BRADLEY E. HUITEMA
Western Michigan University

LLOYD G. HUMPHRIES
University of Illinois, Champaign

MAX L. HUTT

G. W. HYNDE
University of Georgia

JAMES ROBERT IBERG
Chicago, IL

S. S. ILARDI
University of Kansas

DANIEL R. ILGEN
Michigan State University

Y. IWAMURA
Toho University, Japan

I. JACKSON
Brown University

L. JANOSI
Exponential Biotherapies, Inc.

ARTHUR R. JENSEN
University of California, Berkeley

QICHENG JING
Chinese Academy of Sciences, Beijing

DAVID W. JOHNSON
University of Minnesota, Minneaplois

JAMES H. JOHNSON
University of Florida

ORVAL G. JOHNSON
Centennial BOCES, La Salle, CO

ROGER T. JOHNSON
University of Minnesota, Minneaplois

EVE S. JONES
Los Angeles City College

LASZLO JANOSI
Exponential Biotherapies, Inc.

JON H. KAAS
Vanderbilt University

ROBERT B. KAISER
Kaplan DeVries Institute

AKIRA KAJI
Exponential Biotherapies, Inc.

JAMES W. KALAT
North Carolina State University

P. W. KALIVAS
Medical University of South Carolina

TOMOE KANAYA
Cornell

SAUL KANE
Queens College, City University of New York

BARRY H. KANTOWITZ
Battelle Institute, Seattle

RICHARD PAUL KAPPENBERG
Hawaii Professional Psychology Group, Honolulu

WERNER KARLE
Corona Del Mar, CA

NADINE KASLOW
Emory School of Medicine

A. J. KASTIN
University of New Orleans

BOJE KATZENELSON
University of Aarhus, Denmark

TERENCE M. KEANE
Boston University

A. J. KEARNEY
Behavior Therapy Institute

E. JAMES KEHOE
University of New South Wales

TIMOTHY KEITH-LUCAS
The University of the South

SALLY KELLER
Adelphi University

THOMAS M. KELLEY
Wayne State University

CAROLIN S. KEUTZER
University of Oregon

GREGORY A. KIMBLE
Duke University

JAMES E. KING
University of Arizona

BRENDA J. KING
University of Tennessee

DANIEL N. KLEIN
State University of New York

WALTER G. KLOPFER

MAX J. KOBBERT
Hochschule for Beildende Künste, Münster

ALBERT T. KONDO
University of Houston

S. J. KORCHIN

WILLIAM J. KOROTITSCH
University of North Carolina, Greensboro

SURESH KOTAGAL
Mayo Clinic

G. KOVACS
Dalhousie University

LEONARD KRASNER
Stanford University School of Medicine

DAVID R. KRATHWOHL
Syracuse University

ALAN G. KRAUT
American Psychological Society, Washington, DC

STEFAN KRUEGER
Yale School of Medicine

STANLEY KRIPPNER
Saybrook Graduate School, San Francisco

SAMUEL E. KRUG
MetriTech, Inc., Campaign, IL

CAROL LANDAU
Brown University Division of Medicine

PHILIPPE LANDREVILLE
Laval, Sainte-Foy, Quebec

TED LANDSMAN
University of Florida

CHRISTOPH J. G. LANG
University of Erlangen-Buremberg, Germany

GEORGE M. LANGFORD
Dartmouth College

KEITH LANGLEY
University of Strasbourg, France

E. K. LANPHIER
Pennsylvania State University

V. W. LARACH
Univerdidad de Chile

DAVID G. LAVOND
University of Southern California

ARNOLD A. LAZARUS
Center for Multimodal Psychological Services, Princeton

RICHARD S. LAZARUS
University of California, Berkeley

THOMAS H. LEAHEY
Virginia Commonwealth University

ROBERT A. LEARK
Pacific Christian College

ARTHUR LERNER
Los Angeles City College

RICHARD M. LERNER
Tufts University

L. S. LEUNG
University of Western Ontario

ALLAN LEVEY
Emory University

HARRY LEVINSON
The Levinson Institute

SHARON C. LEVITON
Southwestern Academy of Crisis Interveners, Dallas

EUGENE E. LEVITT
Indiana University School of Medicine

P. M. LEWINSOHN
Oregon Research Institute, Eugene

RONALD T. LEY
State University of New York, Albany

ANDRE L'HOURS
World Health Organization, Geneva

KAREN Z. H. LI
Max Planck Institute for Human Development

SHU-CHEN LI
Max Planck Institute for Human Development

P. E. LICHTENSTEIN

CAROL SCHNEIDER LIDZ
Touro College

SCOTT O. LILIENFELD
Emory University

G. LIN
National Institutes of Health

HENRY CLAY LINDGREN
San Francisco State University

RONALD LIPPITT

MARK W. LIPSEY
Vanderbilt University

A. LLOYD

JOHN E. LOCHMAN
University of Alabama, Tuscaloosa

JOHN C. LOEHLIN
University of Texas, Austin

JANE LOEVINGER
Washington University

DONALD N. LOMBARDI
Seton Hall University

WOLF-EKKEHARD LÖNNIG
*Max Planck Institut fur
    Züchtungsforschung, Köln, Germany*

JOSEPH LOPICCOLO
University of Missouri

JEFFREY P. LORBERBAUM
Medical University of South Carolina

O. IVAR LOVAAS
University of California, Los Angeles

ROBERT E. LUBOW
Tel Aviv University

J. O. LUGO
Fullerton, CA

K. LUKATELA
Brown University

ROBERT W. LUNDIN
Wheaton, IL

DAVID T. LYKKEN
University of Minnesota, Minneapolis

BRETT V. MACFARLANE
University of Queensland

ROBIN M. MACKAR
*National Institute on Drug Abuse, Bethesda,
    MD*

S. MADHUSOODANAN
*St. John's Episcopal Hospital, Far
    Rockaway, NY*

MICHAEL P. MALONEY
Pasadena, CA

HOWARD MARKMAN
*Center for Marital and Family Studies,
    University of Denver*

RONALD R. MARTIN
West Virginia University

C. MARTINDALE
University of Maine

P. MARUFF
La Trobe University, Australia

ROBERT C. MARVIT
Honolulu, HI

MELVIN H. MARX
N. Hutchinson Island, FL

JOSEPH D. MATARAZZO
Oregon Health Sciences University

BARBARA B. MATES
City College, NY

RYAN K. MAY
The University of Memphis

FAUZIA SIMJEE MCCLURE
University of California, San Diego

BARBARA S. MCCRADY
Rutgers University

JANET L. MCDONALD
Louis State University

JENNIFER J. MCGRATH
Bowling Green State University

JOHN PAUL MCKINNEY
Michigan State University

KATHLEEN MCKINNEY
University of Wisconsin

C. M. MCCLEOD
University of Toronto

JAMES H. MCMILLAN
Virginia Commonwealth University

PATRICK MCNAMARA
Boston University

NEIL MCNAUGHTON
University of Otago, New Zealand

JANICE MCPHEE
Florida Gulf Coast University

PAUL W. MCREYNOLDS
University of Nevada

HEATHER MEGGERS
University of Missouri

RICHARD MEILI
University of Bern, Switzerland

RONALD MELZACK
McGill University, Montreal

P. F. MERENDA
University of Rhode Island

STANLEY B. MESSER
Rutgers University

CINDY M. MESTON
University of Texas, Austin

JAMIE L. METSALA
University of Maryland

ANDREW W. MEYERS
The University of Memphis

K. D. MICHEVA
Stanford University

DAVID J. MIKLOWITZ
University of Colorado

STANLEY MILGRAM

MARK W. MILLER
Boston University

NEAL ELGAR MILLER
Yale University

RALPH R. MILLER
State University of New York, Binghamton

THEODORE MILLON
University of Miami

HENRYK MISIAK
Fordham University

AKIRA MIYAKE
University of Colorado

TAE-IM MOON

STEWART MOORE
University of Windsor, Ontario

JAMES A. MORONE
Brown University

DANIEL G. MORROW
University of New Hampshire

F. MUELLER
*Forschungszentrum Juelich GmbH,
    Germany*

K. L. MULLER
Rutgers University

R. MURISON
University of Bergen, Norway

FRANK B. MURRAY
University of Delaware

ANNE MYERS
St. Jerome Convent, Philadelphia

FRANCIS A. NEELON
Duke University

ROBERT A. NEIMEYER
University of Memphis

J. NEISEWANDER
Arizona State University

A. NELSON

ROSEMARY O. NELSON-GRAY
University of North Carolina, Greensboro

CORY F. NEWMAN

DAVID G. NICKINOVICH
University of Washington

PHILIP T. NINAN
Emory School of Medicine

J. T. NOGA
Emory University

TREVOR R. NORMAN
University of Melbourne

M. S. NYSTUL

WILLIAM H. O'BRIEN
Bowling Green State University

WALTER EDWARD O'CONNELL
Natural High Center, Bastrop, TX

W. O'DONOHUE

K. DANIEL O'LEARY
State University of New York, Stony Brook

G. A. OLSON
University of New Orleans

R. D. OLSON
University of New Orleans

MARLENE OSCAR-BERMAN
Boston University

THOMAS M. OSTROM
Ohio State University

J. BRUCE OVERMIER
University of Bergen, Norway

B. D. OZAKI
Honolulu Waldorf School

DANIEL J. OZER
University of California, Riverside

K. PACAK
National Institutes of Health

DAVID C. PALMER
Smith College

EDWARD L. PALMER
Davidson College

LOREN D. PANKRATZ
Oregon Health Sciences University

C. PANTELIS
University of Melbourne, Australia

WILLIAM M. PARDRIDGE
University of California School of Medicine, Los Angeles

ALAN J. PARKIN
University of Sussex, England

E. J. PARKINS
Nottingham University, England

H. MCILVANIE PARSONS
Human Resources Research Organization, Alexandria, VA

R. PATUZZI

PAUL PAULI
University of Tübingen, Germany

V. PEČJAK

PAUL PEDERSON
University of Alabama, Birmingham

T. M. PENIX

HAROLD BRENNER PEPINSKY
Ohio State University

KATHERINE L. PETERS
University of Alberta

C. PETERSON
University of Michigan

DONALD R. PETERSON
Rutgers University

CHARLES S. PEYSER
The University of the South

E. JERRY PHARES
Kansas State University

D. PHILIP
University of Florida

JESSICA M. PIERCE
Boston University

AARON L. PINCUS
Pennsylvania State University

LUIGI PIZZAMIGLIO
Universita Degli Studi di Roma, Italy

J. POIRIER
University of Washington

R. E. POLAND
University of California, Los Angeles

H. G. POPE, JR.
McLean Hospital, Belmont, MA

R. M. POST
National Institute of Mental Health

BRUNO POUCET
Centre National de la Recherche Scientifique, France

A. R. PRATKANIS
University of California, Santa Cruz

ANN B. PRATT
Capital University, Columbus, OH

ROBERT ALAN PRENTKY
Justice Resource Institute, Bridgewater, MA

AINA PUCE
Swinburne University of Technology, Australia

S. J. QUALLS
University of Colorado

MARK QUIGG
University of Virginia

KAREN S. QUIGLEY
Pennsylvania State University

RÉMI QUIRION
Douglas Hospital Research Center, Canada

ALBERT ISRAEL RABIN
Michigan State University

M. K. RAINA
Sri Aurobindo Marg, India

K. RAMAKRISHNA RAO
Duke University

U. RAO
University of California, Los Angeles

J. RAPPAPORT
University of Illinois, Chicago

MARK D. RAPPORT
University of Central Florida

RICHARD L. RAPSON
University of Hawaii, Manoa

NATHANIEL J. RASKIN
Northwestern University Medical School

R. L. RASMUSSON
Allegheny University of Health Sciences

A. RAVIV
Tel Aviv University

W. J. RAY
Pennsylvania State University

HERB REICH

ANTHONY H. REINHARDT-RUTLAND
University of Ulster

J. M. REINISCH
Indiana University

DANIEL REISBERG
Reed College

MAURICE REUCHLIN
Institute Nationale D'Orientation Professionale, Paris

MARY E. REUDER

G. R. REYES

CECIL R. REYNOLDS
Texas A&M University

GEORGE F. RHOADES, JR.
Ola Hou Clinic, Aiea, HI

ALEXANDER RICH
University of South Florida

DAVID C. S. RICHARD
Southwest Missouri State University

EDWARD J. RICKERT
University of Alabama, Birmingham

L. RIES

Y. RINGEL
University of North Carolina

ARTHUR J. RIOPELLE
Louisiana State University

CHRISTIE RIZZO
New York State Psychiatric Institute

DONALD ROBBINS
Fordham University

GARY JEROME ROBERTSON
Wide Range, Inc., Tampa

GEORGE H. ROBINSON
University of North Alabama

RONALD ROESCH
Simon Fraser University, British Columbia

MICHAEL J. ROHRBAUGH
University of Arizona

STEVEN PAUL ROOSE
Columbia University

R. ROSENBERG
Sleep Disorders Center, Evanston, IL

ROBERT ROSENTHAL
University of California, Riverside

SAUL ROSENZWEIG
Washington University

HELEN WARREN ROSS
San Diego State University

WILLIAM H. ROSS
University of Wisconsin

J. S. ROSSI
University of Rhode Island

B. O. ROTHBAUM
Emory University

DONALD K. ROUTH
University of Miami

PETER ROY-BYRNE
Harborview Medical Center, Seattle

MARK A. RUIZ
Pennsylvania State University

ROGER WOLCOTT RUSSELL
University of California, Irvine

J. J. RYAN
Central Missouri State University

DEBORAH SADOWSKI
Tufts University

W. S. SAHAKIAN

WILLIAM SAMUEL
University of California, San Diego

T. SAND
*Norwegian University of Science and
  Technology*

WILLIAM C. SANDERSON
Rutgers University

JEROME SANES
Brown University

LAWRENCE J. SANNA
Washington State University

C. SANTERRE
University of Arizona

JOHN WYNNE SANTROCK
University of Texas-Dallas, Richardson

EDWARD P. SARAFINO
The College of New Jersey, Ewing

WILLIAM IRVIN SAUSER, JR.
Auburn University

ALICE D. SCHEUER
University of Hawaii, Honolulu

K. SCHMIDTKE
University of Frieberg, Germany

DAVID A SCHULDBERG
University of Montana

ALEXANDER JULIAN SCHUT
Pennsylvania State University

JULIE B. SCHWEITZER
Emory School of Medicine

D. L. SEGAL
University of Colorado

SAUL B. SELLS
Texas Christian University

J. SHANTEAU

D. H. SHAPIRO
University of California, Irvine

KENNETH JOEL SHAPIRO
*Psychologists for the Ethical Treatment of
  Animals*

S. L. SHAPIRO
University of Arizona

J. A. SHARPE
University of Toronto

Y. SHAULY
Allegheny University of Health Sciences

ROBERT A. SHAW
Brown University

GLENN D. SHEAN
College of William and Mary

STEVEN D. SHERRETS
Maine Head Trauma Center, Bangor

EDWIN S. SHNEIDMAN
*University of California School of Medicine,
  Los Angeles*

VARDA SHOHAM
University of Arizona, Tucson

BERNARD H. SHULMAN
Northwestern University Medical School

JULIE A. SHUMACHER
State University of New York, Stony Brook

M. SIGUAN
Barcelona, Spain

ELSA A. SIIPOLA
Smith College

ALCINO J. SILVA
University of California, Los Angeles

HIRSCH LAZAAR SILVERMAN

L. SILVERN
University of Colorado, Boulder

HERBERT A. SIMON
Carnegie Mellon University

ALAN SIMPKINS
University of Hawaii, Honolulu

M. BREWSTER SMITH
University of California, Santa Cruz

WILLIAM PAUL SMITH
Vanderbilt University

DAWN SOMMER
University of Texas, Austin

SUBHASH R. SONNAD
Western Michigan University

PETER W. SORRENSEN
University of Minnesota, St. Paul

JANET TAYLOR SPENCE
University of Texas, Austin

DANTE S. SPETTER
New England Medical Center, Boston

ROBERT P. SPRAFKIN
*Veterans Administration Medical Center,
  Syracuse*

SCOTT STANLEY
*Center for Marital and Family Studies,
  University of Denver*

KEVIN D. STARK
University of Texas, Austin

STEPHEN STARK
University of Illinois, Champaign

TIMOTHY STEENBERGH
The University of Memphis

ROBERT A. STEER
*University of Medicine and Dentistry of
  New Jersey*

A. STEIGER
*Max Plank Institute of Psychiatry,
  Germany*

ROBERT M. STELMACK
University of Ottawa

ROBERT H. STENSRUD
University of Northern Iowa

R. J. STERNBERG
Yale University

GERALD L. STONE
University of Iowa

WILLIAM S. STONE
Harvard University

HUGH A. STORROW
University of Kentucky

EZRA STOTLAND
University of Washington

GEORGE STRICKER
Adelphi University

RICHARD B. STUART
Weight Watchers International

D. I. SUCHMAN
University of Florida

ARTHUR SULLIVAN
Memorial University, Newfoundland

S. W. SUMERALL
William Jewell College

NORMAN D. SUNDBERG
University of Oregon

J. T. SUPER

ROBERT J. SUTHERLAND
University of New Mexico

H. A. SWADLOW
Brown University

SUSAN SWEARER
University of Texas, Austin

JULIAN I. TABER
Veterans Administration Medical Center, Reno

ANA TABOADA
University of Maryland

YASUMASA TANAKA
Gakushuin University, Tokyo

JAMES T. TEDESCHI
State University of New York

J. A. TESTA
University of Oklahoma

ALEXANDER THOMAS
New York University School of Medicine

S. M. THOMPSON
University of Maryland

BEVERLY E. THORN
University of Alabama, Tuscaloosa

B. MICHAEL THORNE
Mississippi State University

DAVID F. TOLIN
University of Pennsylvania

ELEANOR REARDON TOLSON
University of Washington

JOE TOMAKA
University of Texas, El Paso

LOUIS G. TORNATZKY
National Science Foundation, Washington, DC

DANIEL TRANEL
University of Iowa

FREDERICK TRAVIS
Maharishi University of Management, Fairfield, IA

WILLIAM T. TSUSHIMA
Straub Clinic and Hospital, Inc., Honolulu

LEONARD P. ULLMANN
Incline Valley, Nevada

E. ULVESTAD

RHODA KESLER UNGER
Montclair State College

SUSANA PATRICIA URBINA
University of Northern Florida

T. BEDIRHAN ÜSTÜN
World Health Organization, Geneva

A. L. VACARINO
University of New Orleans

P. VALDERRAMA-ITURBE
Mexico

P. VANDEL
Hospital Saint-Jacques, Bensancon, France

R. D. VANDERPLOEG
University of South Florida

KIRSTEN M. VANMEENAN
University of Maryland

ANTHONY J. VATTANO
University of Illinois, Champaign

FRANCES E. VAUGHAN
California Institute of Transpersonal Psychology, Menlo Park

P. E. VERNON

WILLIAM F. VITULLI
University of Southern Alabama

N. J. WADE
University of Dundee, Scotland

REX ALVON WADHAM
Brigham Young University

E. E. WAGNER
Forest Institute of Professional Psychology

RICHARD D. WALK
George Washington University

ARLENE S. WALKER-ANDREWS
Rutgers University

PATRICIA M. WALLACE
University of Maryland

ROGER N. WALSH
University of California, Irvine

ZHONG-MING WANG
Zhejiang University, China

WILSE B. WEBB
University of Florida

JOEL LEE WEINBERGER
Adelphi University

ARNOLD D. WELL
University of Massachusetts

W. W. WENRICH
University of North Texas

MICHAEL WERTHEIMER
University of Colorado

DONALD L. WERTLIEB
Tufts University

IAN Q. WHISHAW
University of Lethbridge, Alberta

M. A. WHISMAN
University of Colorado, Boulder

SARAH WHITTON
Center for Marital and Family Studies, University of Denver

ERIKA WICK
St. John's University

DELOS N. WICKENS
Ohio State University

RICHARD E. WILCOX
University of Texas, Austin

SABINE WILHELM
Massachusetts General Hospital, Charlestown

DOUGLAS A. WILLIAMS
University of Winnipeg

RICHARD H. WILLIS
University of Pittsburgh

J. WILSON
University of Minnesota, Duluth

MARGARET T. T. WONG-RILEY
Medical College of Wisconsin

MICHAEL L. WOODRUFF
East Tennessee State University

D. S. WOODRUFF-PAK
Temple University

MARGARET P. WOODS

T. E. WOODS
University of Wisconsin School of Medicine

ROBERT L. WOOLFOLK
Rutgers University

ANTHONY WRIGHT
University of Manitoba

TRISTAM D. WYATT
University of Minnesota, St. Paul

R. C. WYLIE

LARRY J. YOUNG
Emory University

L. M. YOUNGBLADE
University of Colorado

ZAHRA ZAKERI
Queens College, City University of New York

O. L. ZANGWILL
Cambridge, England

JOHANNES M. ZANKER
The Australian National University

PATRICIA A. ZAPF
University of Alabama

W. ZHANG
New York Medical College

DANIEL J. ZIEGLER
Villanova University

PHILIP G. ZIMBAROO
Stanford University

M. ZUCKERMAN
University of Delaware

FIONA VAJK: MANAGING EDITOR
BENJAMIN PAGE: MANAGING EDITOR
ALINNE BARRERA: MANAGER EDITOR

The Corsini Encyclopedia of Psychology and Behavioral Science

Third Edition

E

EARLY CHILDHOOD DEVELOPMENT

Childhood is a culturally defined period in human development between infancy and adulthood, and, in historical perspective, is a relatively recent social construction. Only in the past 400 years or so has the idea of childhood been a part of Western culture, with the recognition of this special class of people and special phase in the growth of each individual (French historian Philippe Aries analyzes the emergence of these ideas in *Centuries of Childhood*). Early childhood, as a special and important sub-period of childhood, most often refers to the months and years between infancy and school age or middle childhood: age 2 to 5 years.

These preschool years, sometimes extended to include infancy and toddlerhood or even lengthened into middle childhood to about age 8 years, are a time of significant and complex advances and reorganizations in behavior, and thus figure centrally in most theories of human development. Learning, perception, reasoning, memory, and social relations undergo important changes and progressions in early childhood.

Many complex milestones and achievements have been described by numerous researchers. Gesell and his colleagues described the steps of development across domains, including physical growth, motor behavior, adaptive responsiveness, language, and personal/social behavior in their classic book, *The First Five Years of Life*. Language is among the most impressive achievements in early childhood as the infant's babbling transforms itself into the very sophisticated language of the youngster at age 5. White describes the physical, emotional, and intellectual growth of preschool children in *The First Three Years of Life*. Similarly, other authors have described the equally remarkable complex of behavioral development and reorganization between ages 5 and 7.

Psychoanalytic developmental psychology posits early childhood as the critical period in development during which major personality orientations emerge that will continue into childhood, adolescence, and adulthood, forming boundaries and constraints on later modifications of intrapsychic organization, interpersonal relationships, and ego development. A person's sense of self and his or her gender identity are formed during this period of development. Freud's theory of psychosexual development describing the oral, anal, and phallic/Oedipal phases of early childhood development, and Erikson's theory of psychosocial development describing the tasks and crises of early childhood—trust versus mistrust, autonomy versus shame and doubt, initiative versus guilt, industry versus inferiority—are among the most influential psychoanalytic contributions toward understanding early childhood development. Bowlby's theory of attachment, further elaborated by Ainsworth, Harlow, and others, applies Erikson's theory to the special relationship between parent or primary caregiver and the developing child. These writers suggest that successful negotiation of the early parent-child relationship has lifelong implications for successful personality development, interpersonal relationships, and mental well-being.

In addition to learning to get along with others, a young child must learn to regulate his or her own behavior. Self-regulation refers to the capacity to monitor and direct one's activities in order to achieve goals or meet demands imposed by others. Self-control is the ability to regulate oneself even when the caregiver is absent, and may be considered a sign of emerging moral development. Learning to use a toilet or refraining from grabbing toys are examples of emerging self-regulation and self-control skills.

Cognitive developmental theories espoused by the Swiss psychologist Jean Piaget and his followers (Piaget & Inhelder, 1969) also emphasize early childhood development as a period of major steps in a child's construction of his reality and knowledge. The infant in the sensorimotor stage of intelligence develops knowledge of self and the world through a complex series of interactions with the environment that emphasize sensory and motor experience. In early childhood the child achieves preoperational and then concrete operational thinking. With the increase in a child's capacity for imaginative and logical thought, important levels of symbolic and representational thinking develop as a basis for classification and categorization of information, essential to appreciation of important rules about the physical and interpersonal world. Recent controversies regarding the validity of children's memories of either traumatic or routine events are partly based on Piaget's descriptions of the limitations in reasoning skills during this stage of development and subsequent extensions of his theory.

Changes in family structure in the United States have dramatically altered the way many young children are raised. Mothers of young children are more likely to work outside the home for a variety of reasons, and both mothers and fathers are working longer hours. While some lay-people worry about the long-term implications of extensive out-of-home care during early childhood, accumulating evidence suggests that good, high-quality day care with appropriate ratios of staff to children can actually enhance some aspects of cognitive and social development. Increasing awareness of the influence of diverse family structures and multicultural family contexts for the multivariate processes of early childhood development characterizes contemporary research and practice.

The theoretical centrality of early childhood as a critical period in human development is applied in early childhood education and intervention. Great teachers and theorists such as J. A. Comenius (1592–1670), Jean-Jacques Rousseau (1712–1778). J. H. Pestalozi (1746–1827), Friedrich Froebel (1782–1152), John Dewey (1859–1952), Maria Montessori (1870–1952), and Anna Freud (1895–1982) long ago recognized the importance of learning and development in early childhood. Nursery schools, kindergartens, and early intervention programs such as Headstart are manifestations of an appreciation of early childhood development, not only in education and psychology, but also in social reform and public policy. With increases in the number of children and the number of hours spent in structured day-care settings, opportunities to observe and apply the knowledge gleaned from the study of early child development have expanded in the past two decades.

SUGGESTED READING

Aries, P. (1962). *Centuries of Childhood.* NY: Knopf.

Damon, W., & Lerner, R. (1997). *Handbook of child psychology.* New York: Wiley.

Gessel, A. (1940). *The first five years of life.* NY: Harper

Piaget, J., & Inhelder, B. (1969). *The psychology of the child.* NY: Basic Books.

White, Burton. (1975). *The first three years of life.* Englewood Cliffs, NY: Prentice Hall.

D. S. SPETTER
New England Medical Center, Boston

D. L. WERTLIEB
Tufts University

CHILD PSYCHOLOGY
EARLY CHILDHOOD DEVELOPMENT
INFANT DEVELOPMENT

EATING DISORDERS

Several defined disorders in humans are related to eating behavior and behavior immediately following eating. The most common of these, obesity, is discussed in a seperate entry under that name.

Pica is the eating of substances that provide no nutrition by individuals over the age of approximately 18 months. Although it is clearly most common in childhood, statistics concerning its prevalence tend to be unreliable because they are largely based on individuals seeking or being brought for treatment. Behavior therapy would seem to be an appropriate treatment, but outcome data are scanty.

Rumination is chewing and swallowing food that was previously eaten and then regurgitated. The condition is rare, occurs mostly in infants, and affects both sexes equally. Some reports of success with behavioral treatments can be found in the literature, but no convincing outcome statistics are available.

ANOREXIA NERVOSA

Anorexia nervosa is characterized by the refusal to maintain a normal minimal weight in proportion to height, intense fear of obesity, and a distorted self-image (perceiving oneself as heavier than one really is). In women, the constellation of symptoms often includes amenorrhea. Much more common in females, who comprise 94 to 95% of those afflicted, it usually has its onset during the second or third decade of life. No longer considered rare, anorexia nervosa is more common in the middle and upper socioeconomic strata. Theories as to etiology vary from primarily psychological to essentially biological; none at this time finds universal acceptance.

Typically, the disorder's onset is abrupt and may coincide with a significant life change such as the beginning of menses or moving from one school to another. A key feature of the disorder is severe food restriction, often accompanied by bizarre patterns of food intake such as eating only alone, refusing all but a narrow range of foods, secretly throwing food away, squirreling away small amounts of food for later consumption, and compulsive arranging of food on the plate. There is an obsessive preoccupation with the exact quantity of food consumed and with its caloric value. Liquids too are often restricted. Diuretic and laxative abuse is common, as is forced vomiting. This vomiting may follow binges during which a large amount of food is consumed within a brief period. Hunger is typically denied, although the patients' intense preoccupation with food—collecting recipes, cooking for others—tends to indicate that this denial is false. Vigorous exercise is often part of the pattern.

The underlying personality structure is often compulsive, with patients tending toward perfectionism and rigidity. Suppression and denial of negative affect, especially anger, are frequently found. Typically, there is great fear of loss of control in any area—not only relative to food. In many cases there seems to be a rejection of adult heterosexuality coupled with a desire to remain prepubertal, protected, and unchallenged by the stresses of adult life. Depression is often apparent.

Symptoms are typically denied, and resistance to treatment is often powerful. Frequently the disorder is brought to the attention of the clinician only at the insistence of relatives or close friends. There is much debate concerning what constitutes effective treatment, with verbal psychotherapy and behavior therapy (operant conditioning) programs being the most popular.

Psychotherapy, usually conducted on an outpatient basis, risks allowing prolonged malnutrition. Behavioral methods are usually effective over the short term, but tend to be associated with high relapse rates. Drug therapies have also had some success, including tricyclic antidepressants and antipsychotics. Yet none of the therapies mentioned has yet proven to be the answer; anorexia nervosa remains one of the few psychological disorders with a sometimes fatal outcome.

BULIMIA

Bulimia is an eating disorder characterized by rapid ingestion of large portions of food in a brief time span. This binge eating is usually done surreptitiously and is interrupted by self-induced vomiting, use of laxatives, abdominal distress, sleep, or by being caught by others. Binges are often followed by stringent dieting in an effort to keep weight within normal limits. Patients express fear of losing control and being unable to restrain themselves. Bingeing is often followed by guilt, shame, and depression.

Like anorexia nervosa, bulimia is more common in females and in higher socioeconomic classes. Unlike anorexics, however, bulimics are not usually emaciated, are not amenorrheic, and are overtly interested in sex. The age of onset tends to be higher—in the 20s. Etiology is unknown, but the disorder appears to be linked to depression.

Since this disorder is clearly associated with abnormal overt behavior, operant conditioning would appear to be applicable and has met with some success in the form of contingency contracting. All forms of psychotherapy, however, tend to be stormy and difficult.

Drug treatments have also been employed with varying success. Often recommended are diphenylhydantoin (Dilantin), an anticonvulsant, and tricyclic antidepressants. Drug treatments are best seen as adjuncts to psychotherapy or behavior therapy.

SUGGESTED READING

Bruch, H. (1979). *Eating disorders: Obesity, anorexia nervosa, and the person within.* New York: Basic Books. (Original work published 1973)

Cooper, M. (1957). *Pica.* Springfield, IL: Thomas.

Geffen, N. (1966). Rumination in man. *American Journal of Digestive Diseases, 11,* 963.

Herzog, D. B. (1982). Bulimia: The secretive syndrome. *Psychosomatics, 23,* 481–484.

Milman, D. H. (1981). When thin is not beautiful: Anorexia nervosa. *Resident and Staff Physician,* 47–54.

H. A. STORROW
University of Kentucky

BORDERLINE PERSONALITY
OBESITY
OBSESSIVE-COMPULSIVE PERSONALITY

EBBINGHAUS, HERMANN (1850–1909)

Hermann Ebbinghaus studied at the universities of Bonn, Halle, and Berlin and received his degree in philosophy in 1873. He continued his study independently in Berlin, England, and France, where his interest shifted to science.

Ebbinghaus, the first psychologist to investigate learning and memory experimentally, invented the nonsense syllable which revolutionized the study of association and learning. After his appointment to an academic position at the University of Berlin, he continued his research on memory and published his findings in *Memory* in 1885. In 1894 he moved to Breslau where he worked until 1905 developing the sentence completion test, probably the first successful test of higher mental abilities.

Ebbinghaus's research methods were objective, experimental, and quantified through meticulous attention and recordings. His procedures have laid a foundation of data on the study of association and learning that has stood the test of time. The Ebbinghaus curve of retention or forgetting demonstrated that material is forgotten rapidly in the first few hours after learning, and more and more slowly with the passage of time. He founded the *Journal of Psychology and Physiology of the Sense Organs* in 1890. Ebbinghaus also published two successful textbooks, *The Principles of Psychology* and *A Summary of Psychology,* which appeared in several editions and revisions.

N. A. HAYNIE

ECLECTIC PSYCHOTHERAPY

Surveys of modern therapists have shown that the majority tend to be eclectic in their theories and techniques, rather than identifying with a single school or orientation (Garfield & Kurtz, 1976; Larson, 1980; Swan, 1979). This trend represents a shift from the 1940s and 1950s, when most therapists identified with either pro- or antipsychoanalytic approaches. There are a great number of psychotherapists who call themselves eclectics, ranging all the way from the pragmatic eclectic who simply uses anything that works, to the systematic eclectic who attempts to identify underlying principles and methods that all effective therapies have in common.

Two textbooks that take the approach of systematic eclecticism are Garfield's *Psychotherapy: An Eclectic Approach* and Palmer's *A Primer of Eclectic Psychotherapy.* Garfield defines his orientation thus: "I have tried to present a view of psychotherapy . . . that includes emphases and procedures drawn from a variety of approaches. This being essentially what most psychotherapists appear to do in practice" (1980, p. vii). Palmer's definition is: "I call this selection of the essential features of the various theories about human behavior and their integration into a comprehensive theory *eclecticism*" (1980, p. 6). Systematic eclectics try to find the common theory of practice which underlies differences in language, style, and historical affiliation.

Goldfried asked leading representatives from different orientations (humanistic-existential, analytic, and behavioral) to respond in depth to clinical questions such as "What is the role played by new experiences in facilitating change?" and "In what way do you see the therapist-client relationship as contributing to the change process?" He found strong agreement on several points:

1. The importance of new experiences
2. The significance of the therapeutic interaction
3. The emphasis on a caring, trustworthy, and confident attitude by the therapist

Goldfried (1980) suggests that common principles relevant to all therapies can be found by focusing on strategies or principles of change that lie between the highest level of abstraction (the philosophy of each therapy) and the lowest level of abstraction (the particular techniques of each therapy). These strategies are said by Goldfried (1980, p. 11) to function as "clinical heuristics that implicitly guide our efforts during the course of therapy." The task of systematic eclectic therapy could be described as making the implicit explicit.

FREDERICK THORNE'S SYSTEMATIC ECLECTIC THERAPY

One of the first modern efforts to formulate a systematic eclecticism was undertaken by Frederick Thorne (1909–1978), who spent his entire career developing, reformulating, and expostulating an eclectic approach to psychotherapy and counseling. In 1945 he founded the *Journal of Clinical Psychology* as an outlet for eclectic contributions to the field. In *Principles of Personality Counseling* (1950, p. i), Thorne, in his own words, "attempted to make an eclectic presentation of all known methods of counseling and psychotherapy." He believed that psychotherapy should model itself after clinical medicine and "relate therapy to diagnosis with a clear statement of the indications and contraindications for use of all methods" (p. i). He took as his professional ideal Sir William Osler, the founder of the modern system of eclectic medical practice.

One of Thorne's last books was entitled *Psychological Case Handling: An Eclectic System of Counseling and Psychotherapy* (1968). "Case handling" for Thorne was a broader term than "therapy." He defined "psychological case handling" as "a generic term referring to all the operations conducted by competent psychologically-trained personnel in helping clients to get along better in life" (p. 23). Thorne recognized that psychotherapy was only one among several choices the therapist might use; in his discussion he included chapters on "Symptomatic therapy," "Supportive therapy," "Reassurance," "Conditioning and behavior therapies," "Suggestion," "Persuasion," "Pressure," "Coercion and punishment," and "Life management analysis."

Although Thorne greatly admired the medical model, he broadened it far beyond the narrow objectivist forms it is sometimes given when applied to psychology. The first postulate among the 97 that constitute Thorne's book *Personality: A Clinical Eclectic Viewpoint* is: "Personality is a clinical concept which has no valid meaning apart from the actual status of what a person is at specific moments and in specific situations of existence. . . . This specific study of *personality statuses* can be accomplished only by appropriate clinical methods of which trained introspection and the direct personal encounter are the most important" (1961, p. 1). Thorne's medical eclecticism was further broadened by an emphasis on psychological health. In a monograph entitled *Tutorial Counseling: How to Be Psychologically Healthy* (1965), Thorne argued that personality growth must be a goal of all people and that psychologists need to develop skills and theories that promote psychological health. Thorne went beyond the medical model of the psychotherapist as physician to the fitness-coaching model, arguing that psychological fitness requires diligent exercise and conditioning just as does physical fitness. He proposed a very broad view of psychological health that "depends upon the degree to which any person succeeds in actualizing his potentials in learning to cope with all the standard situations of life, living actively and creatively, and acting out many roles well" (*Tutorial Counseling,* p. 155).

HISTORICAL BASIS OF SYSTEMATIC ECLECTICISM

J. T. Hart in *Modern Eclectic Therapy* argues that there is a historical basis to modern eclecticism. He claims that Thorne in the 1950s and 1960s, and Goldfried, Palmer, and Garfield of the 1970s and 1980s, are all actually drawing upon a theoretical orientation derived from the late 1800s. Hart identifies that orientation as functionalism and traces it back to the theories of William James, John

Dewey, Pierre Janet, and Morton Prince, as well as other functionalists.

In a 1981 article Hart asserts that James was the primary source for systematic eclectic therapy: "Although William James was not a clinician and is not usually cited for his contributions to psychotherapy . . . his 'functional psychology' is the greatest single unrecognized influence on the attitudes of the majority of today's psychotherapists and counselors" (1981, p. 88).

James' special position in the history of psychology is due to his theory of consciousness, which includes a concern about subconscious processes. His *Principles of Psychology* began: "Psychology is the science of mental life, both of its phenomena and their conditions" (James, 1890/1950, p. 1). By "phenomena" James meant "feelings, desires, cognitions, reasonings, decisions, and the like" (p. 3), and by "conditions" he referred to any influences which could alter the phenomena. "The quest of conditions becomes the psychologist's most interesting task" (p. 3). Within the Jamesian formulation, psychotherapy becomes a practical search for the conditions that bring about individual changes in conscious functioning.

Functional eclectic therapy provides a theoretical connection between behavior therapy, humanistic-existential therapy, and analytic therapy. Hart sees all functional eclectic therapists as sharing seven points:

1. The immediate moment is the focus of clinical concern, with gaps in consciousness considered to be of special significance.

2. Feelings are regarded as conscious regulators of behavior; regulation is achieved through expression of feelings, not merely insight about feelings.

3. The self-concept and related self-images are always carefully examined.

4. Willful choices, plans of action, and philosophical and moral concerns are included within the purview of therapy.

5. Models of growth and health are given at least as much weight as models of psychopathology.

6. Conscious, subconscious, and unconscious processes are considered, but in that order.

7. A pragmatic attitude toward the tools of therapy is endorsed; a great variety of techniques and strategies are used.

For Hart, the psychological basis of eclecticism, which both therapy and art have in common, is the bisociation of images, thoughts, and actions at the level of feeling expressiveness. The artist uses an external medium of expression (painting, sculpting, playing the piano), while the client uses the interaction with the therapist (see Koestler, *The Act of Creation,* for the bisociative theory of creativity.)

EXAMPLES OF ECLECTIC APPROACHES

The social-skills training program developed at Livermore Hospital between 1968 and 1976 by Trower, Bryant, and Argyle is described in their book (with Marzillier) *Social Skills and Mental Health.* The authors combined ideas and methods from drama, social psychology, communication and linguistics, psychiatry, plus experimental and clinical psychology. They also cite the specific influence of Eric Berne, Carl Rogers, Carl Jung, Sigmund Freud, J. L. Moreno, cognitive behavior therapy, and mileu therapy upon their program.

Despite this eclectic variety, the Livermore researchers devised a coherent, repeatable program that was applied to both inpatients and outpatients. They used as their unifying model the image of the therapist as a teacher whose function is not mainly diagnosing, prescribing for, and curing abnormality, but identifying areas of life dissatisfaction, setting goals, and teaching skills.

The authors describe their program thus (Trower et al., 1978, p. 5):

The form of social skills training we recommend is different, in practice, from the procedures developed by some others, but the basic idea is usually the same. That is that patients or others deficient in skills can be taught directly a new and more socially accepted repertoire of skills, which will enable them to influence their environment sufficiently to attain basic personal goals. This *training* approach stands in contrast to other therapies, aimed at eradicating or inhibiting maladaptive behaviour or symptoms, or changing underlying defenses or conflicts. Training does not preclude these other approaches, and our purpose is partly to explore fruitful combinations.

The eclectic emphasis on creative borrowing and practical synthesis is evident.

A similar eclectic program of social-skills training, directed more to nonpatients, was described by Zimbardo (1977), who drew upon survey research with more than 5,000 people conducted by the Stanford Shyness Clinic to construct a program that could be both self-applied and applied by therapists. Zimbardo stressed the value of both understanding shyness and its causes and of undertaking specific, measurable, graded steps toward overcoming it. He made use of self-testing, journal-keeping, relaxation, guided imagery, role playing, and mutual-help groups in guiding people to overcome unwanted shyness.

A different kind of eclectic approach, based upon the medical model, is reported in *The Nature and Treatment of the Stress Response* by Everly and Rosenfeld. These authors present both a multilevel analysis of the stress response which includes chemical, psychophysiological, and psychological measurements, and a multimodal treatment approach that includes client education in self-responsibility, various relaxation techniques, dietary recommendations, pharmacological treatment, biofeedback techniques, hypnosis, and physical exercise. Their stated goal is "to present a unique and clinically useful discussion of numerous and diverse treatment options" (1981, p. 59).

In *The Skilled Helper* and *Exercises in Helping Skills,* Egan presents an eclectic developmental model for the counselor or trainer that covers specific techniques for responding to the clients' self-explorations, techniques for integrative self-understanding, and methods for facilitating actions. He draws heavily upon ideas and methods from humanistic therapy and group therapy, but also makes use of techniques from cognitive behavior therapy. The basic contention of Egan's approach is that both clients and beginning counselors can learn from modeling and supervised practice.

What seems clear from these examples is that many different role models (educator-trainer, coach, clinician, and counselor) can be used to generate useful therapeutic programs. The truly eclectic practitioner must be prepared to utilize not only combinations of ideas and methods but also combinations of role models.

REFERENCES

Everly, G. S., & Rosenfeld, R. (1981). *The nature and treatment of the stress response.* New York: Plenum.

Garfield, S. L. (1980). *Psychotherapy: An eclectic approach.* New York: Wiley.

Garfield, S. L., & Kurtz, R. (1976). Clinical psychologists in the 1970's. *American Psychologist, 31,* 1–9.

Goldfried, M. R. (1980). Toward the delineation of therapeutic change principles. *American Psychologist, 35,* 991–999.

Hart, J. T. (1981). The significance of William James' ideas for modern psychotherapy. *Journal of Contemporary Psychotherapy, 12,* 88–102.

Hart, J. T. (1983). *Modern eclectic therapy.* New York: Plenum.

James, W. (1950). *The principles of psychology.* New York: Dover. (Original work published 1894)

Koestler, A. (1964). *The act of creation.* New York: Macmillan.

Larson, D. (1980). Therapeutic schools, styles, and schoolism: A national survey. *Journal of Humanistic Psychology, 20,* 1–20.

Palmer, S. (1980). *A primer of eclectic psychotherapy.* Monterey, CA: Brooks/Cole.

Swan, G. E. (1979). On the structure of eclecticism: Cluster analysis of eclectic behavior therapists. *Professional Psychology, 10,* 732–734.

Thorne, F. C. (1950). *Principles of personality counseling.* Brandon, VT: Journal of Clinical Psychology Press.

Thorne, F. C. (1961). *Personality: A clinical eclectic viewpoint.* Brandon, VT: Journal of Clinical Psychology Press.

Thorne, F. C. (1965). Tutorial counseling: How to be psychologically healthy. *Clinical Psychology Monograph, 20,* 1–157.

Thorne, F. C. (1968). Psychological case handling: An eclectic system of counseling and psychotherapy. Brandon, VT: *Clinical Psychology.*

Trower, P., Bryant, B., Argyle, M., & Marzillier, J. (1978). *Social skills and mental health.* Pittsburgh, PA: University of Pittsburgh Press.

Zimbardo, P. G. (1977). *Shyness: What it is, what to do about it.* Reading, MA: Addison-Wesley.

SUGGESTED READING

Karasu, T. B. (1979). Toward unification of psychotherapies: A complementary model. *American Journal of Psychotherapy, 23,* 555–563.

Lazarus, A. A. (1976). *Multi-modal behavior therapy.* New York: Springer.

Silverman, L. H. (1974). Some psychoanalytic considerations of non-psychoanalytic therapies. *Psychotherapy, 11,* 298–305.

Strupp, H. H. (1973). *Psychotherapy: Clinical research, and theoretical issues.* New York: Aronson.

J. T. HART
Kupat Holim Klalit

COUNSELING
COUNSELING PSYCHOLOGY
PSYCHOANALYSIS
PSYCHOTHERAPY

ECOLOGICAL PSYCHOLOGY

Application of the ecological viewpoint to psychology has significantly broadened the discipline's focus of analysis and its understanding of the determinants of human behavior. While psychology has nominally acknowledged the importance of molar and social system variables in understanding behavior, the thrust of most psychological theorizing and research has been concentrated on the single person or organism responding to a single stimulus.

The contribution of the ecological perspective to psychology has been to consider individual behavior as inseparable from its context, including the interpersonal, social, and physical aspects. The early classic work in ecological psychology was performed by Roger Barker and Herbert Wright of the University of Kansas. Much of this work focused on detailed analysis of public behavior in two small towns, one in Kansas and one in England. In 1955 Barker and Wright published *Midwest and Its Children: The Psychological Ecology of an American Town,* one of the first major presentations of the ecological approach.

For Barker and his followers the basic unit of analysis was the *behavior setting,* conceived as a bounded social and physical system which has a function or program to perform. Each behavior setting has its participants, its range of normative activities, and various physical artifacts that guide the flow of behavior. For example, a credit union office might constitute a behavior setting, as might a fast food restaurant or a newspaper stand.

Much of the work of Barker and his associates involved creating comprehensive base-line descriptions of behavior settings. In contrast to other branches of psychology, little use was made of measurement devices that could conceivably intrude on the setting, such as questionnaires, interview guides, and the like. The method was basically ethnographic in nature, involving laborious and lengthy direct observation of behavior settings, and the compiling of specimen records of behavior. Measurement domains of interest have included the demographic mix of participants, the nature of the program or function being carried out, time and place boundaries, and what generic types of behavior occur. However, in the early work of Barker and associates there was very little attempt to aggregate descriptors on the basis of any a priori conceptual model: More than 200 data points were recorded for any behavior setting!

One exception to this atheoretical bent has been the interest of ecological psychologists in the extent to which behavior settings are adequately manned, so that there are enough participants to carry out the setting program. For example, a crowded restaurant with insufficient help would represent a behavior setting that is undermanned. According to Barker, undermanned settings will generate activities to rectify the situation.

From a conceptual perspective, the variables of interest to Barker-style ecological psychology are midrange between traditional psychology and sociology. The array of variables is obviously much wider than in the discrete, single-stimulus orientation of psychology. Yet while Barker's ecological psychology deals with operating social systems, as does sociology, the level of conceptual and empirical aggregation is much less than in that discipline. For example, by focusing on an ethnographic level of detail, behavior setting descriptions rarely use concepts such as group cohesion, bureaucratic structure, and the like. As a qualification, there has been some recent multivariate statistical work to empirically aggregate the many descriptors used by Barker. Describing the physical artifacts of behavioral settings is also not a strong tradition in either psychology or sociology.

A recent development emanating from an ecological perspective has been the intentional manipulation of behavior settings. For example, one ecological psychologist studied a busing program in a national park that had experienced crowding, shoving, and inefficient boarding. An experiment was designed in which a passenger queuing system was established, and significant improvements over baseline were noted in passenger boarding.

Another line of work in psychology from an ecological perspective has placed an even heavier emphasis on the experimental production and evaluation of social innovations, and has virtually ignored the ethnographic method and conceptual nomenclature of Barker and his followers. The program of ecological psychology research and training at Michigan State University established by Fairweather has also focused on units of analysis at the social system level, but it has largely borrowed its conceptual framework and nomenclature from the existing literature in social psychology, sociology, and other social science disciplines. The major importance of this work has been in extending experimental approaches to the field setting, as a way of systematically developing what are, in Barker's terminology, new behavior settings. Fairweather and Tornatzky's *Experimental Methods for Social Policy Research* is a description of this version of ecological psychology.

It should also be noted that other ecological perspectives on behavior can be found outside the psychology field. Some organizational researchers have concentrated on the physical and technological artifacts of work settings, and attempted to intervene in both social and technical systems to produce desired behavioral outcomes. This field of sociotechnical design has many affinities with ecological psychology as described here, although most research has been conducted in industrial settings.

In summary, the ecological perspective on psychology provides a way of keeping the discipline in touch with some of its core concepts. That behavior is a function of both intrapersonal and environmental factors has long been a premise presumably accepted by all psychologists, yet significant portions of the physical and social environment are ignored in traditional psychological research. The ecological perspective provides a way of maintaining a conceptual and empirical bridge to those important aspects of the environment.

REFERENCES

Barker, R. G., & Wright, H. F. (1971). *Midwest and its children.* Evanston, IL: Row, Peterson. (Original work published 1955)

Fairweather, G. W., & Tornatzky, L. G. (1977). *Experimental methods for social policy research.* Oxford: Pergamon.

SUGGESTED READING

Barker, R. G. (1968). *Ecological psychology: Concepts and methods for studying the environment of human behavior.* Stanford, CA: Stanford University Press.

Davis, L. E., & Taylor, J. C. (1972). *The design of jobs.* London: Penguin.

Tornatzky, L. G., Fairweather, G. W., & O'Kelly, L. I. (1970). A Ph.D. program aimed at survival. *American Psychologist, 25,* 884–888.

Wicker, A. W. (1979). Ecological psychology: Some recent and prospective developments. *American Psychologist, 34,* 755–765.

L. G. TORNATZKY
National Science Foundation

CROWDING

ECOLOGICAL VALIDITY

The concept of ecological validity pertains mainly to the areas of comparative psychology and animal learning, but it can apply to any research activity to determine whether its findings have any relevance to real-life situations or habitats for the class of subjects involved, including humans. It refers to the fact that an organism is genetically or environmentally prepared to exhibit different behaviors in different contexts or environments. The organism performs well at one time and place but not so well, or at all, in others.

When species-specific attributes involved in the species' adaptation to its environment are fully considered, then the research is assumed to be ecologically valid. Put more generally, it is important to know and appreciate the particular responses that are in an animal's repertoire for the situation at hand whenever research is conducted. For example, assigning a pigeon the arbitrary instrumental response of pecking a key to avoid electric shock was wholly unsuccessful, whereas treadle depression, which is in part similar to a locomotor flight response, was readily learned.

By and large, ecological validity appears in the literature as a criticism of animal learning studies and comparative psychology because most animal behavior studies in the United States from 1930 through the 1970s were conducted in the laboratory with the white rat or pigeon as the usual subject. The whole approach was quite narrow; not only was the subject pool limited but the problems, situations, and responses were sorely circumscribed. There were clear exceptions, of course, with Schneirla's (1972) research in the field with army ants and other animals and Carpenter's (1964) work with nonhuman primates in Central America leading the way. And a few isolated views of learning were aware of these strictures against the prevailing zeitgeist quite early (e.g., Breland & Breland, 1961; Ratner & Denny, 1964).

However, the bulk of the research published in the *Journal of Comparative and Physiological Psychology* through the early 1970s was concerned with basic principles of learning from a standpoint that largely ignored the nature of the organism being studied. For the most part, the rat and pigeon were seen as animal models of human behavior. Later, psychological investigators emphasized ecological relevance and the importance of breadth in the study of behavior, as, for example, Kamil's (1987) study of foraging behavior and Barash's (1974) study of the social behavior of marmots. In fact, the range of behaviors studied subsequent to early experimenters attests to the ecological relevance of orientation, hoarding, nest building, exploration, ingestive behavior, play, tonic immobility, hibernation, predation, thermoregulation, elumination, care of body surfaces (grooming, dust bathing, etc.), dominance, social organization and facilitation, mimicry, aggression, cooperation, competition, avoidance, limitation, courtship and mating, parental behavior, tool use, and abnormal behavior. Timberlake's (1983) work represents an attempt to incorporate the ecological demands of different species into learning theory.

Boice (1977) has reviewed the literature on surplusage, a sidelight to the notion of ecological validity, which notes that animals have evolved a greater ability to learn and remember than seems useful in the natural habitat. This is probably not too surprising and says little that contradicts ecological relevance.

An illustration of ecological validity is a study by Seyfarth and Cheney (1992) on vervets. These monkeys make different alarm calls for three different predators: leopards, eagles, and pythons. The monkeys decode the meaning of each signal to arrange their escape route to fit the predator. For example, they climb trees to leopard calls, search the sky or run into the bushes for eagle calls, and stand on their hind legs and search the grass for snake calls. Using recordings of the alarm types these investigators have demonstrated that the vervets respond selectively to the sound of the calls rather than to any visual cues.

In addition, Seyfarth and Cheney have determined that vervets are probably responding to the meaning of the calls not just the acoustic signals. The investigators exploited an habituation-dishabituation technique and the monkeys made two quite different sounds to convey the same message: a loud trill, or *wrr,* and a harsh raspy chutter. Both *wrr* and chutter occurred when neighboring groups of vervets had been seen. They habituated monkeys to *wrr* and found chutter was also habituated and vice versa, but if the monkeys were responding to the sound of the call rather than its meaning, dishabituation should have occurred. With two different calls with different meanings habituation did not transfer from one to the other. Ecologically oriented research can alter our ideas about other animals' capabilities.

REFERENCES

Barash, D. P. (1974). The social behavior of the hoary marmot (*Marmota caligata*). *Animal Behavior, 72,* 1–6.

Boice, R. (1977). Surplusage. *Bulletin of the Psychonomics Society, 9,* 452–454.

Breland, K., & Breland, M. (1961). The misbehavior of organisms. *American Psychologist, 16,* 681–684.

Carpenter, C. R. (1964). *Naturalistic behavior of nonhuman primates.* University Park: Pennsylvania State University Press.

Kamil, A. C. (1987). *Foraging behavior.* New York: Plenum.

Ratner, S. C., & Denny, M. R. (1964). *Comparative psychology.* Homewood, IL: Dorsey.

Schneirla, T. C. (1972). In L. R. Aronson, E. Tobach, J. S. Rosenblatt, & D. S. Lehrman (Eds.), *Selected writings of T. C. Schneirla.* San Francisco: Freeman.

Seyfarth, R. M., & Cheney, D. L. (1992). Meaning and mind in monkeys. *Scientific American, 267,* 122–128.

Timberlake, W. (1983). The functional organization of appetitive behavior: Behavior systems & learning. In M. D. Zeiler & P. Harzem (Eds.), *Awareness in the analysis of behavior: Vol. 3. Biological factors in learning.* Chichester, UK: Wiley.

M. R. Denny
Michigan State University

ANIMAL COMMUNICATION
COPING
ECOLOGICAL PSYCHOLOGY
ETHOLOGY
FIELD RESEARCH
HERITABILITY OF PERSONALITY
INSTINCT
SPECIES-SPECIFIC BEHAVIOR

EDUCATIONAL MAINSTREAMING AND INCLUSION

Earlier advocacy for mainstreaming in education has become increasingly focused on inclusion, with frequent confusion and failure to distinguish between the two. While at times used synonymously, *mainstreaming* refers most frequently to the return of children from special education to regular education. *Inclusion* refers to meeting the needs of children within the regular classroom setting without assignment to a special education setting. In the case of the use of support services, inclusion implies the provision of services within the classroom or on a consultative basis to the teacher (push in), in contrast to pull out, where children are removed from the classroom. Both mainstreaming and inclusion reflect the federal mandates concerning placement of children with special needs in the least restrictive environment (IDEA, PL101-476, Sec 612(5) (B)), with the arguable assumption that increasing distance from full-time special education placement toward full-time participation in regular education represents a continuum of decreased restrictiveness. Inclusion has been most strongly advocated for children with mildly handicapping conditions, though it has been proposed for those with the most severe conditions as well. The meaning of inclusion in fact may vary from full- to part-time, and from applying to some or all children with disabilities. The move toward mainstreaming was given impetus by the landmark article by Dunn in 1968, and the move toward inclusion by the Regular Education Initiative proposed by Madeleine Will (e.g., 1986) and the Heller, Holtzman, and the Messick report in 1982.

Success of students with disabilities in regular education relies to a great extent upon introduction of a number of curriculum modifications and supports such as cooperative learning (Slavin, 1990), reciprocal teaching (Palinscar & Brown, 1983), educational collaboration (Idol & West, 1991), team teaching (Bauwens, Hourcade, & Griend, 1989), peer tutoring (Cook, Heron, & Heward, 1983), computerized learning (Gardner & Edyburn, 1993), and curriculum-based assessment (Fuchs, Fuchs, & Hammlett, 1990). Classroom size and the degree of disruptiveness and depth of need of the included students are likely to impact the success of inclusion as well. It is clear that merely placing students with special needs in regular education settings is an insufficient intervention. Mere proximity of handicapped and nonhandicapped children does not result in a successful mainstreaming experience (Allen, 1980; Guralnick et al., 1992; Zigmond & Baker, 1990). Children need to interact in order to modify their attitudes (Voeltz, 1980; Weinberg, 1978). Teachers need to intervene both personally and programmatically, and, to do so effectively, requires supportive consultative services and training experiences.

Teachers need staff development opportunities, consultative support, and in-class help in order to address the needs of these students (Johnson & Cartwright, 1979; Naor & Milgram, 1980; Sloper & Tyler, 1992), but it is not clear that teachers are being provided with sufficient training and supportive experiences to enable them to accommodate exceptional children placed in their classrooms. The attitudes of teachers toward mainstreaming appear to reflect their feelings of their ability to succeed with teaching students with special needs, and success with this requires adequate support services (Galis & Tanner, 1995; Larrivee & Cook, 1979).

Evidence regarding the effectiveness of inclusion depends upon the population and the nature of the variables studied. Carlberg and Kavale (1980) and Baker, Wang, and Walberg (1995) conducted meta-analyses documenting small to moderate positive effects for children with special needs in favor of inclusion, with no significant negative effects on students without disabilities. The effectiveness of inclusion as an educational intervention remains to be seen and may in fact vary, depending upon the student and the attitudes, experience, and practices of the teaching and support staff (Galis & Tanner, 1995). Parents and educators, as well as individuals with the disabilities themselves, seem to have very different points of view about their preferences for settings (Vaughn & Klingner, 1998). The most valid conclusion appears to be that assignments to educational treatments and settings need to be carried out in a highly individualistic way that takes into consideration evidence of effectiveness, the needs of the learner, and the preferences of the family and student.

REFERENCES

Allen, K. E. (1980). Mainstreaming: What have we learned? *Young Children, 35,* 54–63.

Baker, E. T., Wang, M. C., & Walberg, H. J. (1995). The effects of inclusion on learning. *Educational Leadership, 42,* 33–35.

Bauwens, J., Hourcade, J., & Griend, M. (1989). Cooperative teaching: A model for general and special education integration. *Remedial and Special Education, 10,* 17–22.

Carlberg, C., & Kavale, K. (1980). The efficiency of special versus regular class placement for exceptional children: A meta-analysis. *Journal of Special Education, 14,* 295–309.

Cohen, O. P. (1995). Perspectives on the full inclusion movement in the education of deaf children. In I. B. Snider (Ed.), *Conference proceedings: Inclusion? Defining quality education for deaf and hard-of-hearing students.* Washington, DC: College of Continuing Education, Gallaudet University (800 Florida Avenue, NE, 20002).

Cook, N. L., Heron, T. E., & Heward, W. L. (1983). *Peer tutoring: Implementing classroom wide programs.* Columbus, OH: Special Press.

Dunn, L. M. (1968). Special education for the mildly retarded—Is much of it justifiable? *Exceptional Children, 35,* 5–22.

Fuchs, L. S., Fuchs, D., & Hammlett, C. L. (1990). Curriculum-based measurement: A standardized, long-term goal approach to monitoring student progress. *Academic Therapy, 25,* 615–632.

Galis, S. A., & Tanner, C. K. (1995). Inclusion in elementary schools: A survey and policy analysis. *Education Policy Analysis Archives, 3,* http://olam.ed.asu.edu/epaa.v3n15.html

Gardner, J. E., & Edyburn, D. L. (1993). Teaching applications with exceptional individuals. In J. D. Lindsey (Ed.), *Computers and exceptional individuals* (pp. 269–284). Austin, TX: Pro-Ed.

Guralnick, M. J., Connor, R. T., Hammond, M., Gottman, J. M., & Kinnish, K. (1996). Immediate effects of mainstreamed settings on the social interactions and social integration of preschool children. *American Journal on Mental Retardation, 100,* 359–377.

Heller, K., Holtzman, W., & Messick, S. (1982). *Placing children in special education: A strategy for equity.* Washington, DC: National Academy of Science Press.

Idol, L., & West, J. F. (1991). Educational collaboration: A catalyst for effective schooling. *Intervention, 27,* 70–78.

Johnson, A. B., & Cartwright, C. A. (1979). The roles of information and experience in improving teachers' knowledge and attitudes about mainstreaming. *Journal of Special Education, 13,* 453–462.

Larrivee, B., & Cook, L. (1979). Mainstreaming: A study of the variables affecting teacher attitude. *Journal of Special Education, 13,* 315–324.

Naor, M., & Milgram, R. M. (1980). Two preservice strategies for preparing regular class teachers for mainstreaming. *Exceptional Children, 47,* 126–129.

Palinscar, A., & Brown, A. L. (1983). *Reciprocal teaching of comprehension-monitoring activities.* Technical Report No. 269. Champaign, IL: Center for the Study of Reading, University of Illinois.

Slavin, R. E. (1990). *Cooperative learning: Theory, research, and practice.* Englewood Cliffs, NJ: Prentice-Hall.

Sloper, T., & Tyler, S. (1992). Integration of children with severe learning difficulties in mainstream schools: Evaluation of a pilot study. *Education & Child Psychology, 9,* 34–45.

Vaughn, S., & Klingner, J. K. (1998). Students' perceptions of inclusion and resource room settings. *Journal of Special Education, 32,* 79–88.

Voeltz, L. M. (1980). Children's attitudes toward handicapped peers. *American Journal of Mental Deficiency, 84,* 455–464.

Weinberg, N. (1978). Modifying social stereotypes of the physically disabled. *Rehabilitation Counseling Bulletin, 22,* 114–124.

Will, M. C. (1986). Educating children with learning problems: A shared responsibility. *Exceptional Children, 52,* 411–415.

Zigmond, N., & Baker, J. (1990). Mainstream experiences for learning disabled students (Project MELD): Preliminary report. *Exceptional Children, 57,* 176–185.

SUGGESTED READING

Fuchs, D., & Fuchs, L. (1994). Inclusive school movement and the radicalization of special education reform. *Exceptional Children, 60,* 294–309.

Lewis, R. B., & Doorlag, D. H. (1995). *Teaching special students in the mainstream* (4th ed.). Englewood Cliffs, NJ: Merrill.

National Education Association. (1992). *The integration of students with special needs into regular classrooms: Policies and practices that work.* Washington, DC: National Education Association.

Saleno, S. J. (1994). *Effective mainstreaming: Creating inclusive classrooms* (2nd ed.). New York: Macmillan.

Smith, T. E. C., Polloway, E. A., Patton, J. R., & Dowdy, C. A. (1995). *Teaching children with special needs in inclusive settings.* Boston: Allyn and Bacon.

Stainback, S., Stainback, W., & Forest, M. (Eds.). (1989). *Educating all students in the mainstream of regular education.* Baltimore: Brookes.

Wolery, M., & Wilbers, J. S. (Eds.). (1993–1994). *Including children with special needs in early childhood programs.* Washington, DC: National Association for the Education of Young Children.

C. S. Lidz
Touro College

SCHOOL LEARNING

EDUCATIONAL PSYCHOLOGY

To understand educational psychology, one must recognize its origins. Educational philosophy and practice have served as its major foundations (Trow, 1977). In the first half of the 19th century, educational philosophers expressed increased concern for the quality of education as well as teacher preparation programs. In due time such concerns became a focal point for many educational psychologists. Johann Pestalozzi (1746–1827), the Swiss educator known as the "father of modern pedagogy," was among the first to emphasize the need for instructing teachers. His philosophical contributions, including the importance of stressing human emotion and kindness in the teaching of children, led to the establishment of normal schools to prepare teachers. Johann Herbart (1776–1841) enunciated the doctrine of apperception and emphasized the need to relate new with old experiences, and to attend to the sequencing of instructional units. The Herbartian movement resulted in marked changes in educational methods. A third educational philosopher, Friedrich Froebel (1782–1852), is credited with establishing the kindergarten movement in Germany in 1837, and with popularizing such concepts as self-activity, continuity, self-expression, creativity, and physical and mental growth and development. While these three pioneers were at times criticized for the methods they used (McKeag, 1910), they are given credit for stressing development as an essential part of the psychology of education.

The quality and theoretical bases of education continued to preoccupy educational leaders during the latter part of the 19th century. Concern for these dimensions was evidenced in written works as well as new practices. *Lectures on Pedagogy, Theoretical and Practical* by Compayré (1879/1887) was an elementary manual on teaching; it was divided into a treatise on the child and one on methods of instruction. It represented one of the earliest expressions of concern for the role of education in fostering the child's psychological development. Sully's *Outlines of Psychology with Special Reference to the Theory of Education* (1884) was another early publication juxtaposing psychology and education. Sully identified the two methods of psychology as introspection and observation—methods to be vehemently debated by educational psychologists at the turn of the century. In 1899 William James (1842–1910) published *Talks to Teachers on Psychology: And to Students on Some of Life's Ideals.* In this work he emphasized the pragmatic aspects of psychology, while simultaneously cautioning teachers against expecting too much from this scientific discipline: "I say, moreover, that you make a great, a very great mistake, if you think that psychology, being the science of the mind's law, is something from which you can deduce definite programmes and schemes and methods of instruction for immediate schoolroom use" (1899/1962 p. 3). James devoted much of his career to serving as an intermediary between psychology and education.

Early in the 20th century Maria Montessori implemented her program of education, which combined work and play for young children. At approximately the same time John Dewey, at the University of Chicago, established his experimental school with its student-centered curriculum. These were some of the major educational and philosophically related events that served as the backdrop and "stage props" for the debut of educational psychology.

SCIENTIFIC AND APPLIED FOCUS

The scientific, experimental dimension characterizing educational psychology, although traceable to Wilhelm Wundt (1832–1920) and the establishment of the first psychological laboratory in 1879, is more traditionally and immediately attributed to Edward L. Thorndike (1874–1949), who earned the title "father of educational psychology." Thorndike, more than any other single individual, determined educational psychology's early development. Though he may not have been the first to use the term, he was the first to publish a text entitled *Educational Psychology,* thereby providing the first operational definition of this discipline. As evidenced by the original edition of this text (1903), and even more emphatically by the three-volume edition (1913–1914), Thorndike viewed educational psychology as the experimental study and measurement of "the inherited foundations of intellect, morals, and skills," "the improvement of mental functions," and the examination of "individual differences and their causes." He stated unambiguously that his objective was to apply "methods of exact science" to educational problems, and that he "paid no attention to speculative opinions and very little attention to the conclusions of students who present data in so rough and incomplete a form that accurate quantitative treatment is impossible" (1903, p. v).

Method of study—including the nature and function of measurement—would prove to be a dimension of this new discipline that provoked continual controversy. It was the focal point of most of Thorndike's work, and his research laboratory clearly reflected his preoccupation with the scientific measurement of observations. The value of Thorndike's brand of educational psychology, with its conditioning, animal research, and measurement emphases, did not go unquestioned. Powell (1971) claims that James E. Russell, dean of Teachers College (where Thorndike pursued his interests) was not convinced that Thorndike's research would ever affect education. In appreciation for the prestige Thorndike brought to the institution, however, Russell apparently "acquiesced to his growing requests for withdrawal from participation in the general life of the College" (Powell, 1971, p. 409).

It is unfair, however, to present Thorndike as one so enthralled with laboratory science that he ignored or overlooked the real world of education. In the lead article of the first issue of the *Journal of Educational Psychology,* Thorndike (1910, p. 12) commented on the contribution of psychology to education as well as the contribution of education to psychology:

The science of education will itself contribute abundantly to psychology. Not only do the laws derived by psychology from simple, specially arranged experiments help us to interpret and control mental action under the conditions of schoolroom life. Schoolroom life itself is a vast laboratory in which are made thousands of experiments of the utmost interest to "pure" psychology. . . . Indeed I venture to predict that this journal will before many years contain a notable proportion of articles reporting answers to psychological questions got from the fact of educational experience, in addition to its list of papers reporting answers to educational questions got from the experiments of the laboratory.

Thorndike, it would appear, rejected not so much the school as a data source, but rather, the unscientific, unsystematic data-gathering techniques then associated with that data source.

Charles Hubbard Judd (1873–1946), a contemporary of Thorndike, is also recognized as a chief contributor to the early development of educational psychology. Van Fleet (1976) points out that Judd, a student of Wundt, provided a marked contrast to Thorndike. While Thorndike and his students were preoccupied with learning theories, animal experiments, and the quantification of data, Judd and his students focused on transforming the educational scene—its content, organization, policies, and practices. This concern for school organization led to Judd's recommending the establishment of junior high schools as well as junior colleges, and to his concentrating on ensuring smooth transitions between elementary school and secondary school, and between secondary school and college. Judd also stressed the need to democratize education: During his professional career, the percentage of youth attending secondary school increased from 7 to 75%. As director of the School of Education at the University of Chicago, he formulated and publicized his psychology of schooling, and completed such works as *Genetic Psychology for Teachers* (1903/1909), *Psychology of High School Subjects* (1915), *Psychology of Secondary Education* (1927), and *Educational Psychology* (1939). Judd focused both his experimental and his theoretical work on school subjects and the best ways to teach them. He was highly critical of research not directly applicable to learning as it occurred in the school (Van Fleet, 1976).

Thorndike and Judd provided a contrast that was to characterize subsequent movements and leaders of educational psychology. While the approaches of these two founders of educational psychology might well have complemented each other, there is no reason to believe that either Judd or Thorndike worked to that end. Bingham (1910) reported on an exchange between the two at the 61st meeting of the American Association for the Advancement of Science. Thorndike reported on a research project "designed to perfect a scale of merit in children's handwriting." Following Thorndike's detailed report of this scale, including its "eleven degrees of excellence," Judd made a presentation of "the application of the experimental method to problems in education." He took the occasion to comment on Thorndike's "non-psychological" scale and argued that the development of such scales, in contrast to the study of mental *processes* and the *improvement* of learning, explained why "mental tests have proven futile and valueless for education." Bingham (1910) goes on to say:

At the conclusion of Professor Judd's paper, Professor Thorndike took his adversary into camp by granting all that had been said regarding the need for the study of mental processes, and then calling attention to the fact that any study of mental development presupposes a comparison of products of some sort, which ought to be accurately measured. The attack was quickly renewed by Professor Judd, and the audience had the keen pleasure of hearing the rapid give-and-take of a brief but brilliant *Auseinandersetzung. (pp. 160–161)*

Thus the measurement and learning theory movements with their laboratory origins, and the school and curriculum movements with their classroom orientation, moved forward with greater independence and less integration than desirable. Evidence of this independence was observed not only in publications and formal presentations, but also in relationships among schools of education, departments of psychology, and educational psychology units. Ironically, the discipline which professed to be concerned with the integration of psychology and education was often physically isolated from faculty in psychology and philosophically rejected by faculty in schools of education. The consequence for educational psychology tended to be a narrow concept of learning that was challenged, if not rejected, by educators and psychologists. The consequence for educational practice was a preoccupation with credentialing, professionalism, and curriculum development, with all too little concern for theoretical or psychological foundations.

While the physical location and the administration of academic units may partially explain the isolation-rejection phenomenon, there were at least two other contributing factors. First, educational psychology programs differed markedly in terms of the academic backgrounds required or recommended for aspiring students (Hall-Quest, 1915). While many programs presumed a general foundation in psychology, others emphasized a background in education and teaching. Second, the course offerings making up these newly established programs were as varied as the prerequisites. This made the nature and identity of the new discipline at best difficult to detect, and at worst easy to ignore.

The study of human development—today widely recognized as a major component of educational psychology—is most directly traceable to G. Stanley Hall (1846–1924), who focused his efforts on the study of adolescence, and to Arnold Gesell (1880–1961), who explored and explained the early years of childhood. Their writings reflected a dependency upon field observations, survey responses, and interpretations of nonexperimental data. Hall and Gesell were far more committed to gaining practical insights than to generating scientific theories. Because of the unscientific nature of their works and that of most of their colleagues, the field of child study was subject to much criticism. Even Jean Piaget (1896–1980), the most recent of the developmental theorists—and one sure to have a long-lasting effect on educational psychology—was initially criticized by many and ignored by others because of his method of study. Development was not even mentioned as a topic of study in either edition of Thorndike's text on educational psychology.

Not until the 1930s did development become a major part of educational psychology texts (Gates, 1930; Sandiford, 1938), and even then some authors gave it only passing recognition. The intertwining of the scientific and the applied, theory and practice, testing and teaching, psychology and education has proven to be a never ending challenge for educational psychologists. Fortunately, however, it is a challenge that has been acknowledged and addressed with gradually increasing commitment and confidence.

RECURRING ISSUES: CONTENT AND NATURE

Debate regarding the proper content of courses and texts within the field of educational psychology began before Thorndike's edition was off the press. Over the years, numerous reviews and surveys have been conducted in an effort to identify the boundaries of this discipline. Among the earliest efforts was that of Hall-Quest (1915). In an effort to distinguish educational psychology in general, he surveyed "all teachers of educational psychology included in the membership of the Society of College Teachers of Education." Based on 53 responses, Hall-Quest (1915, p. 613) stated the following as his first two conclusions:

1. There is no general agreement on terminology or on the structure of courses in educational psychology. There should be some standardizing agency to bring about uniformity in these respects.

2. In general, courses include the study of the learning process with special attention to instinct, habit formation, imaging [sic] with particular reference to memory, association, thinking [sic]. School subjects are being analyzed psychologically. "Individual differences" are receiving much attention in connection with the study of exceptional children and the problem of retardation. The science of measurements is included as the sine qua non of accuracy in experimentation and investigation.

In 1941 Blair completed an analysis of the technical language used in eight texts published between 1937 and 1941. Based on an examination of every odd page in each of these texts, Blair reported marked differences among books. Upon identifying the 15 most commonly used terms in each of the eight texts, he observed that the only word common to all the resulting lists was "psychology". While he predicted that standardization of terminology and content would increase with the development of the discipline, he found little evidence of that when he reassessed the situation eight years later (Blair, 1949). The fact is, of the numerous studies designed to assess the content of courses and texts in educational psychology over the past 70 years, all have revealed marked diversity within this discipline (Hall-Quest, 1915; Worcester, 1927; Seagoe, 1960; Nunney, 1964; Yee, 1970; Englander, 1976; Feldhusen, 1977). The content issue, as reflected in journal publication, has also been reviewed.

An analysis of the articles printed in the *Journal of Educational Psychology* was conducted by Ball (1981), who identified 13 content categories judged to be all-inclusive of the studies reported in the journal from its beginning. Ball systematically sampled issues published between 1910 and 1980 and, using titles, categorized each entry. Learning-memory research—a major focus of Thorndike's first text—never accounted for more than 11% of the sampled journals' publications, and at times, dropped below 5%. On the other hand, measurement-evaluation articles—also a major focus of Thorndike's—accounted for 9 to 48% and ranked first in topic frequency for all but two of the eight time periods Ball sampled. While several new topics emerged beginning with the 1930s (special education, sex-race, media, creativity), none had worked its way to the top five rankings. However, the topic of motivation-affect, which tied for last place in the 1910 rankings, held second place for the 1979 through 1980 rankings.

An issue related to diversity of content—and one just as old (and new)—is whether educational psychology is a discipline in its own right. In 1915, Hall-Quest wrote:

To call educational psychology a distinct discipline or science is therefore looked upon by many as arrogant presumption.

But the fact that education forms one of the many fields of specific application of psychological truth and one of the most significant in the life of individuals and nations is reason enough to emphasize educational psychology as worthy of a distinct title. (p. 602)

Fifty-four years later Ausubel reaffirmed this position and argued that, despite the fact and misfortune that many educational psychology textbooks contained little more than "watered-down miscellany of general psychology," educational psychology was indeed a discipline in its own right. He viewed it as "that special branch of psychology concerned with the nature, conditions, outcomes, and evaluation of school learning and retention" (1969, p. 232), and included among the special subject matters of this discipline all cognitive, developmental, affective, motivational, personality, and social variables manipulable by educators and curriculum developers. He recognized educational psychology as an applied discipline and contended that it was distinct from psychology in terms of its specific school-classroom focus. Ausubel further argued that classroom learning problems could not be solved by merely extrapolating from "basic science laws that are derived from the laboratory study of . . . learning." This was compatible with Spence's view (1959). But while Spence acknowledged that psychology in its then current form could offer little to education, he predicted that education and its related concerns would be subsumed by psychology in due time.

Others have contended that educational psychology amounts to little more than psychological theories placed in the context of education. Keats states: "As a distinctive area of study, as a distinctive method of approach, as a distinctive focus of research, the term educational psychology eludes definition" (1976, p. 37). Wolfle (1947), after comparing educational psychology and general psychology textbooks and being somewhat dismayed by their similarity, offered the following formula for writing an education psychology text:

. . . start with a good average introductory [psychology] text. Remove the chapters which deal with the nervous system and sense organs and write three new chapters to use up the space. These three new chapters will have such titles as *Learning in the Schoolroom, Measuring Student Progress,* and *Social Psychology of the Schoolroom.* (p. 441)

More recent critics, while recognizing the potential for an independent discipline focused on learning in applied settings, contend that educational psychology in its present form serves as little more than an inept translator of pure psychology (Hargreaves, 1978). However, the recency of such criticisms, coupled with the promptness and vehemency of the rebuttals elicited (Burden, 1979), is evidence that the validity of this discipline is not a settled matter.

Issues associated with the measurement of learning, which captured the interest of Edward L. Thorndike and provoked criticism from such men as Charles H. Judd, are sure to help keep the field of educational psychology alive and vibrant. The similarity of the exchange between Thorndike and Judd, reported by Bingham in the *Journal of Educational Psychology* in 1910, and the exchange between Ebel (1982) and Fenstermacher (1982), reported in the *Phi Delta Kappan* 72 years later, attests to the fact that the value and function of psychological measurement for educational purposes have remained central issues of contention.

In 1982 nearly 14% of the members of the American Psychological Association identified themselves as educational psychologists and held membership in Division 15 (Educational Psychology) within the national association. The history of this division presents a picture of the struggle, controversy, and resiliency that has characterized educational psychology (Grinder, 1967). While members of Division 15 are primarily affiliated with universities and research centers, a large group of educational psychologists is to be found in settings more directly related to the teaching and learning activities of schools.

REFERENCES

Ausubel, D. P. (1969). Is there a discipline of educational psychology? *Psychology in the Schools, 4,* 232–244.

Ball, S. (1981, December). *Educational psychology as an academic chameleon: An historical survey of published research and some thoughts on the future.* Presented at the University of Iowa.

Bingham, W. V. (1910). Educational psychology at the Boston meeting of the American Association for the Advancement of Science. *Journal of Educational Psychology, 1,* 159–167.

Blair, G. M. (1941). The vocabulary of educational psychology. *Journal of Educational Psychology, 32,* 365–371.

Blair, G. M. (1949). The content of educational psychology. *Journal of Educational Psychology, 40,* 267–273.

Compayré, G. (1887). *Lectures on pedagogy, theoretical and practical.* Boston: Heath. (Original work published 1879)

Ebel, R. L. (1982). Three radical proposals for strengthening education. *Phi Delta Kappan, 63,* 375–378.

Englander, M. E. (1976). Educational psychology and teacher education. *Phi Delta Kappan, 57,* 440–442.

Feldhusen, J. (1977). Issues in teaching undergraduate educational psychology courses. In D. J. Treffinger, J. K. Davis, & R. E. Ripple (Eds.), *Handbook on teaching educational psychology.* New York: Academic.

Fenstermacher, G. D. (1982). Three nonradical proposals for strengthening Ebel's argument. *Phi Delta Kappan, 63,* 379–380.

Gates, A. I. (1930). *Psychology for students of education* (rev. ed.). New York: Macmillan.

Grinder, R. E. (1967). *A history of genetic psychology: The first science of human development.* New York: Wiley.

Hall-Quest, A. L. (1915). Present tendencies in educational psychology. *Journal of Educational Psychology, 6,* 601–614.

Hargreaves, D. (1978). The proper study of educational psychology. *Association of Educational Psychologists Journal, 4*(9), 3–8.

James, W. (1899). *Talks to teachers on psychology: And to students on some of life's ideals.* New York: Holt.

Judd, C. H. (1909). *Genetic psychology for teachers.* New York: Appleton. (Original work published 1903)

Judd, C. H. (1915). *Psychology of high school subjects.* Boston: Ginn.

Judd, C. H. (1926). *Psychology of social institutions.* New York: Macmillan.

Judd, C. H. (1927). *Psychological analysis of the fundamentals of arithmetic.* Chicago: University of Chicago.

Keats, D. M. (1976). Psychologists in education. *Australian Psychologist, 11,* 33–42.

McKeag, A. J. (1910). The use of illustrative experiments in classes in education. *Journal of Educational Psychology, 1,* 467–472.

Nunney, D. H. (1964). Trends in the content of educational psychology. *Journal of Teacher Education, 15,* 372–377.

Powell, A. G. (1971). Speculations on the early impact of schools of education on educational psychology. *History of Education Quarterly, 11,* 406–412.

Sandiford, P. (1938). *Foundations of educational psychology.* New York: Longman, Green.

Seagoe, M. V. (1960). Educational psychology. In C. W. Hams (Ed.), *Encyclopedia of educational research.* New York: Macmillan.

Sully, J. (1884). *Outlines of psychology with special reference to the theory of education.* New York: Appleton.

Thorndike, E. L. (1910). The contribution of psychology to education. *Journal of Educational Psychology, 1,* 5–12.

Thorndike, E. L. (1913–1914). *Educational psychology* (3 vols.). New York: Teachers College, Columbia University. (Original work published 1903)

Trow, W. C. (1977). Historical perspective. In D. J. Treffinger, J. K. Davis, & R. E. Ripple (Eds.), *Handbook on teaching educational psychology.* New York: Academic.

Wolfle, D. (1947). The sensible organization of courses in psychology. *American Psychologist, 2*(10), 437–445.

Worcester, D. A. (1927). The wide diversities of practice in first courses in educational psychology. *Journal of Educational Psychology, 18,* 11–17.

Van Fleet, A. A. (1976). Charles Judd's psychology of schooling. *Elementary School Journal 76,* 455–463.

Yee, A. H. (1970). Educational psychology as seen through its textbooks. *Educational Psychologist, 8,* 4–6.

M. M. CLIFFORD
University of Iowa

PYGMALION EFFECT
SCHOOL LEARNING

EDWARDS PERSONAL PREFERENCE SCHEDULE (EPPS)

The Edwards Personal Preference Schedule (EPPS) is a self-report personality inventory that measures 15 needs and motives: abasement, achievement, affiliation, aggression, autonomy, change, deference, dominance, endurance, exhibition, heterosexuality, intraception, nurturance, order, and succorance—all derived from Murray's theory of personality (Murray1938/1962). The test is designed for college students and adults.

The EPPS consists of 210 items, each one containing two self-descriptive statements. Statements are matched on their social desirability but measure different needs. Test takers are to select the item in the pair that best describes them. This forced-choice format is used because Edwards found that the probability of endorsing statements was dependent on their social desirability scale value (Edwards, 1957). By using a forced-choice format, test takers must respond on the basis of the item content (that is, the need or motive), rather than on the basis of the statement's social desirability.

The use of a forced-choice format results in ipsative scores—that is, scores indicating the relative strengths of the various needs within the individual. This presents some problems in interpretation of scores and in validity studies, as two test takers can obtain the same score on a test but differ in their absolute strength of the need or motive.

REFERENCES

Edwards, A. L. (1957). *The social desirability variable in personality assessment and research.* New York: Dryden.

Murray, H. A. (1962). *Explorations in personality: A clinical and experimental study of fifty men of college age.* New York: Oxford University Press. (Original work published 1938)

SUGGESTED READING

Edwards, A. L. (1959). *Manual for the Edwards Personal Preference Schedule* (Rev. ed.). New York: Psychological Corp.

Edwards, A. L. (1966). Relationship between probability of endorsement and social desirability scale values for a set of 2,824 personality statements. *Journal of Applied Psychology, 50,* 238–239.

Edwards, A. L. (1970). *The measurement of personality traits by scales and inventories.* New York: Holt, Rinehart & Winston.

F. G. BROWN
Iowa State University

MULTIDIMENSIONAL SCALING
PERSONALITY ASSESSMENT

EFFERENT

Axons leaving the neuronal soma are often referred to as efferents. The observations made on the efferents of alpha spinal motoneurons have contributed to our understanding of motor control. In natural recruitment of motoneurons, Ohm's law applies, so neurons with the smallest-diameter somas are recruited first. In contrast, electrical stimulation of a mixed nerve results in the largest-diameter axons being activated at the lowest threshold, that is, first if stimulation current is gradually increased. The diameters of the largest-diameter axons of alpha motoneurons are similar to those of Ia afferents, although the largest of the latter are usually slightly larger than the largest motoneuronal axons.

M WAVES IN EMG FROM MOTONEURONAL AXON STIMULATION

When motoneuronal axons are stimulated, an M wave results in the EMG after the brief interval required for nerve conduction from the stimulus site to the muscle electrodes. This wave appears before the H reflex waveforms that result from stimulating Ia afferents, as the effects of the latter must be exerted over a longer path, through the synapse with motoneurons in the spinal cord (Brooke et al., 1997). The similarity in diameter of alpha motoneuronal axons and Ia axons results in the constancy of the M wave magnitudes being used as a bio-calibration of the stability of stimulating Ia axons in reflex studies. Using this technique during passive movement-induced attenuation of H reflexes, Misiaszek, Cheng, and Brooke (1995) showed that the attenuation occurred over all stimulus strengths, from that at the threshold for M waves to that eliciting Mmax. It was inferred that the same afferent group, likely Ia, was involved in the expression of the reflex over the range of stimulation.

The M wave is the orthodromic outcome of stimulating motoneuronal axons. However, there is also an antidromic action potential set up at that time. This potential may collide with antidromically proceeding motoneuronal action potentials resulting from H reflex activation. Accordingly, as M wave magnitudes rise, H reflex magnitudes diminish. A further nuance results when alpha motoneuronal action potentials for voluntary movement are occurring. Then, (a) M waves may be diminished due to refractory motoneuronal axons; (b) H reflexes may be diminished due to antidromic activation of alpha efferents and/or to refractory motoneuronal somas and dendrites; and (c) H reflexes or M waves may be maximized under a recently-cleared-line principle. Thus, a series of samples involving the combination of maximal muscular contraction and high stimulus intensity to elicit Mmax results in distributions of M wave and H reflex magnitudes that range from zero to maximal (Brooke & McIlroy, 1985). It is noteworthy that with normal stimulus recruitment curves, the maximal H reflexes obtained seem to actually be maximal, as the collision technique described in the previous sentence does not appear to produce any larger H reflexes. This collision technique has the potential to describe the ongoing ebb and flow of temporal recruitment of motoneurons over time.

CLINICAL EVALUATION USING EFFERENT STIMULATION

M waves are used for assessment of the number of motor units in a muscle, and thus, for estimation of the number of alpha motoneurons serving a muscle (the motoneuronal pool for that muscle). When the intensity of transcutaneous electrical stimulation of a mixed nerve is gradually increased, a current is reached at which the first small M wave is seen at the appropriate latency in the EMG. This M wave represents the muscular result of activation of the axon of a motoneuron. If the current is then gradually increased, at a certain point the M wave will become larger and its shape will alter. The muscular response to the axonal response of a second motoneuron has been added to the first. This process and identification in the M wave shape can be continued for a number of motoneurons. If the current is reduced, the M wave decreases in discreet steps. At a high current, the maximum M wave is obtained, and further increases in current elicit no further increase in M wave magnitude. These phenomena have been combined by McComas and colleagues (McComas, 1996) to estimate the number of motoneurons in a pool. In principle, the mean M wave magnitude (mV) from a small sample of early recruited motoneurons is divided into the magnitude of Mmax (mV), the result being the estimate of the number of motoneurons serving the muscle. The procedure now is computerized. The technique has revealed the very large losses of motoneurons with advanced aging and during diseases such as amyotrophic lateral sclerosis (McComas, 1996).

F waves in the EMG are used to establish motoneuronal integrity (Ma & Liveson, 1983). With high intensities of transcutaneous stimulation of motoneuronal efferents, antidromic activation can produce action potentials that, arising from the soma, course orthodromically back down the axon to lead eventually to excitation of the muscle fibers. These F waves have latencies very similar to H reflexes. Separation from H reflexes usually relies on the high variability in being able to produce F waves, compared to H reflexes, and the high stimulation intensity required for the former compared to the latter. Morphological differences in wave forms of reflex and F wave may also help.

Completeness of maximum voluntary contraction can be established using the sequelae of Mmax stimulation. The resulting muscle-twitch from such stimulation should not be observable if all muscle fibers are voluntarily activated while the patient is asked simultaneously to make a maximum voluntary contraction (McComas, 1996).

In some diseases, such as myasthenia gravis, the adequacy of release of acetylcholine (the neurotransmitter at the myoneuronal junction) is compromised. In diagnosing this deficiency, it is common to test with a series of four or five Mmax stimuli closely spaced in time (interstimulus rate can range from 3–50 Hz; Walton, 1987). The later stimuli in the time series result in markedly reduced M waves in the EMG in the patient with transmitter deficiency, compared to the healthy person. This contrasts with the availability of glutamate at the Ia-motoneuronal synapse. In that case, even as few as two closely spaced stimuli will result in the second H reflex's being much reduced in magnitude or even nonexistent, the phenomenon of homosynaptic depression (Capek & Esplin, 1977).

SUMMARY

Transcutaneous electrical stimulation of efferents from alpha motoneurons leads to M waves in the EMG of the muscle served by those motoneurons. These M waves are useful in the neurophysiological investigation of humans in the performance of tasks:

- They act as a biocalibration of the activation of large-diameter afferents in mixed nerves.

- Their use suggests that the maximal reflex EMG response, seen as the H reflex, is obtained when increasing currents of stimulation are used to eventually activate all available Ia afferents.

- Combination of maximum voluntary contraction and electrical stimulation for Mmax produces curves of distribution of magnitudes of M waves and H reflexes that reflect the ongoing temporal recruitment of motoneurons serving the autogenic muscle.

M waves also have numerous clinical uses, such as the study of diseases and trauma leading to motoneuronal loss and the estimation of the number of motoneurons in a pool; and in closely-spaced series of stimuli, they are useful in identifying inadequate transmitter release at the myoneuronal junction.

REFERENCES

Brooke, J. D., & McIlroy, W. E. (1985). M wave distribution shift and concomitant H reflex increase with contraction efference. *The Physiologist, 28,* 282.

Brooke, J. D., Cheng, J., Collins, D. F., McIlroy, W. E., Misiaszek, J. E., & Staines, W. R. (1997). Sensori-sensory afferent conditioning with leg movement: Gain control in spinal reflex and ascending paths. *Progress in Neurobiology, 51,* 393–421.

Capek, R., & Esplin, B. (1977). Homosynaptic depression and transmitter turnover in spinal monosynaptic pathway. *Journal of Neurophysiology, 40,* 95–105.

Ma, D. M., & Liveson, J. A. (1983). *Nerve conduction handbook.* Philadelphia: Davis.

McComas, A. J. (1996). *Skeletal muscle: Form and function.* Champaign, IL: Human Kinetics.

Misiaszek, J. E., Cheng, J., & Brooke, J. D. (1995). Movement-induced depression of soleus H-reflexes is consistent in humans over the range of excitatory afferents involved. *Brain Research, 702,* 271–274.

Walton, J. (1987). *Introduction to clinical neuroscience* (2nd ed., p. 91). London: Balliere Tindall.

J. D. BROOKE
Northwestern University Medical School

ACETYLCHOLINE

EGO DEVELOPMENT

The term "ego development" is used in different ways by different authors. Most psychoanalysts use it in one of three ways: (a) to describe the period of formation of the self or ego in the first two or three years of life; (b) to describe the development of all ego functions, including what Hartmann in *Ego Psychology and the Problem of Adaptation* called the "conflict-free ego sphere," that is, locomotion, speech, and so on; or (c) to describe aspects of ego development such as those described by Erikson in *Childhood and Society* as psychosocial tasks, entwined with psychosexual development (i.e., the development of drives and drive derivatives) and tied to age-specific life tasks. In clinical psychoanalytic usage, as in Blanck and Blanck's *Ego Psychology: Theory and practice,* disorders of ego development usually refer to problems arising in the period of ego formation; they are likely to lead to profound maladjustment or to so-called borderline personality types. Among some clinical psychologists and social workers, there is a somewhat careless usage in which the term "immature", implying ego immaturity, is synonymous with "maladjusted."

Psychologists have delineated a different conception that has roots in Sullivan's *Interpersonal Theory of Psychiatry,* of which Loevinger's *Ego Development* will serve as an example. This conception, in addition to being a developmental sequence, is a dimension of individual differences that applies in principle at any age, though higher stages are never found in early childhood, and the lowest stages are rare in maturity. Terms such as "moral development," "interpersonal relatability," and "cognitive complexity" have been used for aspects of the sequence. Descriptions of stages under these headings are not identical, but they are too much alike to refer to independent sequences. The topic is a major aspect of personality development, possibly correlated with but not reducible to either psychosexual development or intellectual development.

STAGES

The earliest stage (or stages)—the *period of ego formation*—is shrouded in the mists of infancy. This stage is presocial, at first autistic, later symbiotic with the mother or mother figure. Mahler has described the problems of separation and individuation characteristic for the period in *On Human Symbiosis and the Vicissitudes of Individuation.* Acquisition of language is believed to be an important factor in bringing the period to an end.

The *impulsive stage* is next: The child confirms a separate existence from the mother by willfulness and is dependent on others for control of impulses. Persons at this stage are preoccupied with their own needs, often bodily ones, and see others as a source of supply. They live in a universe conceptually oversimplified, at least as to its interpersonal features. Rules are seen as specific prohibitions or as frustration of wishes rather than as a system of social regulation.

Growth at first is in terms of ensuring more certain gratification by tolerating some delay and detour, which leads to the *self-protective stage.* Children at this stage will often assert some degree of autonomy to free themselves from excessive dependence; however, their interpersonal relations remain exploitative. They are concerned with power and control, dominance and submission. In early childhood this period is normally negotiated with the help of rituals; when a person remains at this stage into adolescence and adult life, there may be a marked opportunism. Rules are understood, but are manipulated to the person's advantage.

Normally in late childhood there is a sea-change. One identifies oneself and one's own welfare with that of the group. Rules are partly internalized, are adhered to precisely because they are group-accepted and endorsed. This is the *conformist stage,* which

has been widely recognized and described as a personality type. Conformity is valued for its own sake, and people tend to perceive others and themselves as conforming—a tendency that, in relation to performance on psychological tests, is labeled "social desirability." People at this stage perceive others in terms of stereotypes; they typically tend to be nice, friendly, and helpful, and to value such virtues, though niceness may be limited to those seen as part of the in-group. Interpersonal relations are seen in terms of reciprocity, not the primitive reciprocity of tit-for-tat that characterizes the self-protective stage, but the reciprocity of mutual trust. Interpersonal relations are still understood in a somewhat superficial manner—in terms more of actions than of feelings and motives. The person is concerned with belonging, with appearances, and with reputation.

Many people seem to advance beyond the conformist stage by perceiving that they themselves do not always live up to the high standards of conduct that society endorses, and do not always have the approved emotions in some situations. This period is called the *conscientious-conformist level,* or the *self-aware level.* Whether it is a transition between the conformist stage and the conscientious stage or a true stage is an unsettled point. The person at this level sees multiple possibilities as appropriate, where those at lower levels tend to see one possibility as right always and for everyone. Holt (1980), based on a survey by Daniel Yankelovitch, has shown that this is the modal level for the young adult population of the United States.

At the *conscientious stage* rules are truly internalized. The person obeys rules not just because the group approves, but because they have been self-evaluated and accepted as personally valid. Interpersonal relations are understood in terms of feelings and motives rather than merely actions. The person has a richly differentiated inner life and—in place of stereotyped perceptions of others—a rich vocabulary of differentiated traits with which to describe people. Thus their parents are described as real people with both virtues and failings, rather than as idealized portraits or as entirely hateful persons. Self-descriptions are also modulated; the person does not describe the self either as perfect or as worthless, but sees circumscribed faults that he or she aspires to improve. Achievement is valued, not purely as competitive or as social recognition, but as measured by the person's own standards. Persons at this stage may feel excessively responsible for shaping the lives of others—for instance, their own children.

In moving beyond the conscientious stage, the person begins to appreciate individuality for its own sake; thus this transitional level is called *individualistic.* It is characterized by increased conceptual complexity: Life is viewed in terms of many-faceted possibilities, instead of diametrically opposed dichotomies. There is spontaneous interest in human development and an appreciation of psychological causation, as for example that one's current problems or traits may reflect problems or traits of one's mother or father years ago.

At the *autonomous stage* the characteristics of the individualistic level are developed further. The name "autonomous" is somewhat arbitrary, as are all the stage names. No aspect of behavior arises suddenly in one era and perishes immediately on passage to the next. What characterizes this stage particularly is respect for the autonomy of others. A crucial case is the subject's own children, especially acknowledging their right to make their own mistakes. The person at this stage is often aware of functioning differently in different roles. One copes with inner conflict such as that between one's own needs and duties. Conflict is viewed as an inevitable part of the human condition rather than as a failing of self, other family members, or society.

Beginning at the conscientious stage and especially characteristic of higher stages is seeing oneself in a larger social context. This is particularly true of persons at the *integrated stage,* who are able to unite concern for society and for self in a single complex thought. Maslow's description of the self-actualizing person in *Toward a Psychology of Being* applies to those at the integrated stage. Such persons are rare, accounting for less than 1% of the adult population.

RELATED DOMAINS

Many authors have sketched stages of development closely related to the foregoing sequence. Sullivan, Grant, and Grant (1957) refer to their stages as "interpersonal integration." Their conception has been used in studies of differential treatment of different subtypes of delinquents.

Kohlberg has developed a system of stages for the development of moral judgment; his ideas, delineated in *The Philosophy of Moral Development,* have been widely applied. In schools they have been the basis for curricula to encourage moral development, including the forming of alternative schools on the model of "just communities." Experiments with just communities in prison settings are recorded in Hickey and Scharf's *Toward a Just Correctional System.*

Selman labels his stages "interpersonal perspective taking" in *The Growth of Interpersonal Understanding.* He has studied school-age children, thus his work applies chiefly to early stages. He has also studied a small clinical sample.

Perry's study, *Forms of Intellectual and Ethical Development in the College Years,* was based on research with Harvard students through their college careers. Thus his sequence corresponds to some of the higher stages. Broughton (1980) covered a wide age range. He was concerned with development of "natural epistemologies"—conceptions of mind, self, reality, and knowledge.

Justifying the inclusive label "ego development" is the similarity in the sequences under the above and related headings. Nothing less than the ego—or, if one prefers, the self—encompasses that broad range of functions.

METHODS OF STUDY

Although the idea of character development goes back at least to Socrates, modern study begins with Jean Piaget's *The Moral Judgment of the Child.* Kohlberg, Selman, and others have adapted Piaget's method of clinical interviewing. Kohlberg presents his subjects with an unfinished story ending in a moral dilemma. When the subject finishes the story, there follows a probing interview during which reasons for choices are explored; the stage assigned depends on the reasoning. Rest, in *Development in Judging Moral Issues,* has evolved an objectively scored test that is an adaptation of

Kohlberg's instrument. Broughton and Perry have worked out interviews beginning with broad, unstructured questions.

Loevinger, Wessler, and Redmore's *Measuring Ego Development* is a scoring manual for a sentence completion test; it is sufficiently detailed as to be semi-objective and includes self-teaching exercises. Marguerite Warren (formerly Grant) and others working with the interpersonal integration system of Sullivan and colleagues have used a variety of instruments including interviews, sentence completion tests, and objective tests.

THEORIES

There are two major theoretical issues: Why is the ego (or self) as stable as it is? How and why does it manage to change at all?

The theories of ego stability are all variations of Sullivan's anxiety-gating theory. What Sullivan calls the self-system acts as a kind of filter or template or frame of reference for one's perception and conception of the interpersonal world. Any observations not consonant with one's current frame of reference cause anxiety. However, the main purpose of the self-system is to avoid or attenuate anxiety. Therefore such perceptions are either distorted so as to fit the preexisting system, or—in Sullivan's phrase—they are "selectively inattended to." Thus the theory states that because the self-system or ego is a structure, it is self-perpetuating.

Kohlberg has a structural theory of change. When a person at one stage repeatedly encounters and grapples with reasoning and arguments just one stage higher, conditions are optimal for assimilating the reasoning and hence advancing toward that stage. (A full stage change takes 3 or 4 years.) This is the rationale for the use of the constitutional democracy format in Kohlberg's "just communities." Teachers (or prison guards) are theoretically given no special status, but they are expected to ensure that some attention is focused on discussions that represent a slightly (but not greatly) higher level than that of most participants.

An early psychoanalytic theory of ego development is given by Ferenczi (1913/1950). Ferenczi maintained that the ego develops not because of spontaneous striving for development—an idea associated with Alfred Adler's then recent apostasy—but because it is compelled to develop by frustration of drives in reality. This version has become obsolete with the development of psychoanalytic ego psychology, beginning with Sigmund Freud's essay "On narcissism: An introduction."

Identification is the key to the current psychoanalytic theory of ego development. One moves ahead in part because one identifies with some admired model who is (or is perceived as being) at a slightly higher level. Although Kohlberg's theory is primarily cognitive and the psychoanalytic theory is effective, both imply a Piagetian model of equilibrium, disequilibration, re-equilibration. Both are, in effect, "social learning" theories, though they differ radically from what is usually called social learning theory.

There is another element in the psychoanalytic theory that originates as social learning but becomes wholly internal to the individual. The ideal or model toward which the person strives or aspires need not be embodied in the environment. The capacity for constructing one's own model is what is called the ego ideal. Freud's essay on narcissism is a dynamic explanation of this developmental achievement, which is itself a milestone of ego development and also an explanation of how further development can be partially independent of environmental models. This point is elaborated by Loewald (1960), but it was anticipated by Baldwin in *Social and Ethical Interpretations in Mental Development.*

In *Ego Development and the Personality Disorders,* Ausubel presents another theory of some aspects of ego development. Infants believe themselves omnipotent because their wishes are magically realized. (Here Ausubel is following Ferenczi's essay.) As children learn of their total dependence on their parents, they face a catastrophic loss of self-esteem. To escape that fate, they assign their former omnipotence to their parents and so become their satellites, shining in their reflected glory. In late childhood and early adolescence one should desatellize—should learn to derive self-esteem from one's own achievements. Satellization and desatellization may miscarry at several points, resulting in various patterns of psychopathology.

Perry depicts many factors as contributing to both stability and change in the college years. His model of change has implications for a dynamic explanation. The student whose world view is, say, dualistic (right vs. wrong, us vs. them) at first learns to perceive some special field as more complicated and multiplistic (many possibilities, everyone has a right to his or her own opinion). As the fields of application for the multiplistic view increase, those where the dualistic view apply correspondingly shrink, until the multiplistic view becomes the predominant one, with only isolated areas of life still seen in dualistic terms. The same paradigm applies for the transition from multiplistic to relativistic thinking (some views are better because they are grounded in better data or sounder reasoning). One of the generally accepted aims of a liberal education is to encourage acceptance of the relativistic nature of all knowledge. In Perry's view, relativism should be followed by acceptance of some commitments. Such commitments differ from unquestioning acceptance of parental or other unexamined commitments in the same way that Marcia (1966) differentiates "identity achieved" from "identity foreclosed," based on Erikson's theory of ego identity.

REFERENCES

Ausbel, D. P. (1952). *Ego development and the personality disorders.* New York: Grune & Stratton.

Baldwin, J. M. (1973). *Social and ethical interpretations in mental development: A study in social psychology.* New York: Arno. (Original work published 1897 [New York: Macmillan])

Blanck, G. & Blanck, R. (1979). *Ego psychology: Theory and practice.* New York: Columbia University Press.

Broughton, J. M. (1980). Genetic metaphysics: The developmental psychology of mind-body concepts. In R. W. Rieber (Ed.), *Body and mind.* New York: Academic.

Erikson, E. H. (1963). *Childhood and society.* New York: Norton. (Original work published 1950)

Ferenczi, S. (1950). Stages in the development of the sense of reality. In S. Ferenczi (Ed.), *Sex in psychoanalysis* (Vol. 1). New York: Basic Books. (Original work published 1913)

Freud, S. (1957). On narcissism: An introduction. In *The standard edition of the complete psychological works of Sigmund Freud* (Vol. 14). London: Hogarth. (Original work published 1939)

Hartmann, H. (1964). *Ego psychology and the problem of adaptation.* New York: International Universities Press. (Original work published 1939)

Hickey, J. E., & Scharf, P. L. (1980). *Toward a just correctional system.* San Francisco: Jossey-Bass.

Holt, R. R. (1980). Loevinger's measure of ego development: Reliability and national norms for male and female short forms. *Journal of Personality and Social Psychology, 39,* 909–920.

Kohlberg, L. (1981). *The philosophy of moral development.* San Francisco: Harper & Row.

Loevinger, J. (1976). *Ego development: Conceptions and theories.* San Francisco: Jossey-Bass.

Loevinger, J., Wessler, R., & Redmore, C. (1970). *Measuring ego development* (Vols. 1, 2). San Francisco: Jossey-Bass.

Loewald, H. W. (1960). On the therapeutic action of psychoanalysis. *International Journal of Psycho-Analysis, 41,* 16–33.

Mahler, M. S. (1968). *On human symbiosis and the vicissitudes of individuation:* Vol. 1. *Infantile psychosis.* New York: International Universities Press.

Marcia, J. E. (1966). Development and validation of ego-identity status. *Journal of Personality and Social Psychology, 3,* 551–558.

Perry, W. G., Jr. (1970). *Forms of intellectual and ethical development in the college years.* New York: Holt, Rinehart & Winston.

Piaget, J. (1965). *The moral judgment of the child.* New York: Free Press. (Original work published 1932)

Rest, J. R. (1979). *Development in judging moral issues.* Minneapolis: University of Minnesota Press.

Selman, R. L. (1980). *The growth of interpersonal understanding: Developmental and clinical analyses.* New York: Academic.

Sullivan, H. S. (1968). *The interpersonal theory of psychiatry.* New York: Norton. (Original work published 1953)

Sullivan, C., Grant, M. Q., & Grant, J. D. (1957). The development of interpersonal maturity: Applications to delinquency. *Psychiatry, 20,* 373–385.

J. LOEVINGER
Washington University at St. Louis

ANALYTICAL PSYCHOLOGY
ARCHETYPES
ERIKSONIAN DEVELOPMENTAL STAGES
IDENTITY FORMATION
SELF

ELECTROCONVULSIVE THERAPY

Electroconvulsive shock therapy, abbreviated as ECT or EST, is a controversial treatment applied to a small percentage of emotionally disturbed people, mostly those suffering from endogenous depression. Its origin was in the observation that people suffering from a combination of schizophrenia and epilepsy often experience a reduction of their schizophrenic symptoms following an epileptic seizure. At first, insulin and other chemicals were used to induce epileptic seizures. This procedure was supplanted by the use of electrically induced seizures, first introduced by Ugo Cerletti (1950) in the 1930s, after years of animal experimentation.

In subsequent years psychiatrists experimented with the use of ECT for a wide variety of disorders. The treatment developed a bad reputation, partly because of people's associations with the terms "shock" and "convulsion," and partly because on occasion it was used carelessly or punitively. The treatment was sometimes repeated hundreds of times per patient. Side effects included a confused state, both retrograde and anterograde amnesia, cardiac complications, and even physical injury. With the advent of antidepressant and antipsychotic drugs, the use of ECT became much less common.

Beginning in the 1970s the treatment made a partial comeback as "modified ECT" (Weiner, 1979). It can now be given only with the informed consent of the patient. The electrical intensity is lower than before, and the number of repetitions is ordinarily limited to six to eight, on alternate days. The ECT is preceded by muscle relaxants such as methylscopolamine or anesthetics such as methohexital, to minimize discomfort and the threat of injury. Unilateral ECT, usually over the right hemisphere of the brain, can be therapeutically effective with a minimum of memory impairment and other side effects (Miller et al., 1981). Side effects are usually mild, unless ECT is combined with lithium (Small et al., 1980).

In this modified form ECT has some demonstrable benefits for limited patient categories. It is strongly therapeutic for many endogenous depressed patients who fail to respond to antidepressive drugs (Paul et al., 1981). For depressed patients with psychotic thoughts, ECT is more effective than either antidepressive or antipsychotic drugs alone (Minter & Mandel, 1979). Because ECT takes effect more rapidly than drugs, it is often recommended for depressed patients who are actively suicidal. Some authorities favor using it for a broader range of depressive conditions and even for mania, some subtypes of schizophrenia, and other disorders; the empirical support for these latter applications is, however, much weaker (Scovern & Kilmann, 1980). For any application, the benefits of ECT are temporary. A relapse can be prevented by sustained use of antidepressant drugs.

The mechanism of ECT's therapeutic action is not known. The memory deficit that often occurs is not essential, and probably not even helpful, to the therapeutic effect. ECT has been found to increase norepinephrine turnover in the brain, to alter receptor sensitivity to monoamine synaptic transmitters, to increase the release of pituitary hormones, and to weaken the blood-brain barrier (Kalat, 1981). Any or all of these effects may contribute to the antidepressant action.

Much interest has focused on the memory deficits that often result from ECT. Both anterograde and retrograde amnesia are demonstrable, to declining degrees, for about the first month after ECT. Patients continue to complain, however, about memory problems for another six months or so (Squire, Wetzel, & Slater, 1979).

It is possible that small but real deficits persist this long, which do not show up in formal testing. It is also possible that the memory difficulty that patients experience soon after ECT sensitizes them to pay more attention to minor, normal episodes of forgetfulness.

REFERENCES

Cerletti, U. (1950). Old and new information about electroshock. *American Journal of Psychiatry, 107,* 87–94.

Kalat, J. W. (1981). *Biological psychology.* Belmont, CA: Wadsworth.

Miller, M. J., Small, I. F., Milstein, V., Malloy, F., & Stout, J. R. (1981). Electrode placement and cognitive change with ECT: Male and female response. *American Journal of Psychiatry, 138,* 384–386.

Minter, R. E., & Mandel, M. R. (1979). The treatment of psychiatric major depressive disorder with drugs and electroconvulsive therapy. *Journal of Nervous and Mental Disease, 167,* 726–733.

Paul, S. M., Extein, I., Calil, H. M., Potter, W. Z., Chodoff, P., & Goodwin, F. K. (1981). Use of ECT with treatment-resistant depressed patients at the National Institute of Mental Health. *American Journal of Psychiatry, 138,* 486–489.

Scovern, A. W., & Kilmann, P. R. (1980). Status of electroconvulsive therapy: Review of the outcome literature. *Psychological Bulletin, 87,* 260–303.

Small, J. G., Kellams, J. J., Milstein, V., & Small, I. F. (1980). Complications with electroconvulsive treatment combined with lithium. *Biological Psychiatry, 15,* 103–112.

Squire, L. R., Wetzel, C. D., & Slater, P. C. (1979). Memory complaint after electroconvulsive therapy: Assessment with a new self-rating instrument. *Biological Psychiatry, 14,* 791–801.

Weiner, R. D. (1979). The psychiatric use of electrically induced seizures. *American Journal of Psychiatry, 136,* 1507–1517.

J. W. KALAT
North Carolina State University

DEPRESSION

ELECTROENCEPHALOGRAPHY

Many of the chemical events occurring in the individual neurons of the brain generate electrical signals. In 1875 Caton published *The Electric Currents of the Brain,* which documented the first recording of electrical activity from outside the brain of animals. Similar electrical activity of the human brain was successfully recorded from the scalp surface by an Austrian psychiatrist, Anton Berger, in 1924 and was reported by him in 1929. The record of these fluctuating electrical signals emanating from the brains of humans and other animals is called the electroencephalogram (EEG). The considerable technical advances made since Caton's and Berger's studies have provided a technique for unobtrusively measuring brain activity for experiments on the relationship between brain and behavior, and for assessing various clinical conditions such as epilepsy and brain damage.

Nearly all EEG procedures involve electrodes—most commonly, metal discs pasted onto the scalp or wires placed in contact with the skull, or with the brain itself after a hole has been made through the skull. The EEG electrode can also be lowered into the brain to record the activity of deeper structures, although this is not a common clinical practice. In addition, an indifferent electrode is placed on some presumably neutral spot such as the ear. For most human applications, scalp recording is used. The tiny electrical signals picked up by the electrodes must be amplified to be useful, and a trace of the fluctuations in voltage is recorded on paper using an ink-writing system, or by an oscilloscope and tape recorder.

The recorded EEG is actually a reflection of the activity of many millions of neurons located in a large volume of tissue in the brain. It has been suggested that electroencephalographic waves are nothing more than the vibration of the brain's movement caused by heartbeat, respiration, and body movement. This "jiggling of the jelly" hypothesis is not taken seriously, because it has been shown that an electrode implanted inside a single brain neuron is able to record the slow waves of that neuron, which are correlated with the slow waves of the EEG, thus proving that the activity is produced by electrochemical events around the cell membrane. The major contributors to EEG are the excitatory and inhibitory electrical potentials generated at synapses between neurons. The electrical currents that are generated at synapses are conducted through a considerable volume of tissue, before being all summed together at the site of the recording electrode. This fact makes it difficult to locate specific generators of a particular electrical pattern.

EEG characteristically has a wavelike or rhythmical quality. The two basic dimensions for quantifying the EEG signal are the frequency of the waves (measured in cycles/second [cps]) and the size or amplitude of the waves (measured in millivolts [mV] or microvolts [μV]). The EEG observed in scalp recording from awake, alert subjects is typically composed of desynchronous, fast waves of low amplitude (see Figure 1). Often when the subject is awake, but quite relaxed with eyes closed, a pronounced, relatively synchronized 8 to 12 cps rhythm is present, called the alpha rhythm. During normal sleep the EEG shows large, irregular, slow waves with occasional bursts of rapid, high-amplitude waves called sleep spindles. Several clinical conditions such as coma, general anesthesia, and the period following an epileptic seizure are also associated with large, irregular, slow waves, reminiscent of slow-wave sleep. Periods of paradoxical or REM sleep (dream sleep) are marked in the EEG by a pattern of activity that closely resembles the pattern observed in the awake, alert person.

A large number of studies have documented the correlation between EEG activity and states of arousal, but more recently investigators have discovered correlations between EEG patterns and specific behaviors. Penfield and Jasper (1954) demonstrated relations between EEG and movement in man. They placed an electrode on the exposed motor cortex of a patient and observed that,

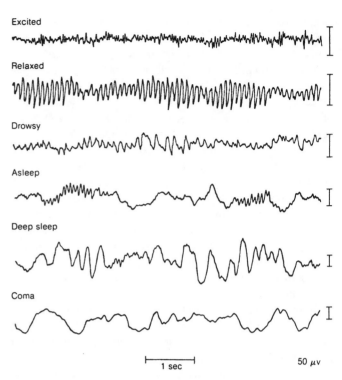

Figure 1.   Characteristic EEG recorded during various behavioral states in man. From *Epilepsy and the Functional Anatomy of the Human Brain* by W. Penfield and H. H. Jasper, 1954, Boston: Little, Brown & Co. Reprinted with permission.

when the patient moved an arm, the characteristic beta pattern was blocked; that is, the amplitude became smaller and the wave frequency became faster. The patient's imagining the movement did not cause blocking; blocking only occurred in the motor area of the brain. Similarly, the alpha wave, which is prominent over the posterior visual cortex when the eyes are closed, is blocked when the eyes open. A dramatic relation between patterns of EEG and movement has been demonstrated for EEG activity in the hippocampus of many animals (see Figure 2).

Clinically, EEG recording is often useful in diagnosing certain pathological conditions involving the cerebral cortex, such as epilepsy, certain tumors, and strokes. Tumors composed of tissue which does not generate electrical activity, and cortical regions not functioning properly because of disruption of blood supply or some other trauma, can often be detected through scalp recordings. Pathology involving structures underneath the cortex is more difficult to detect by using scalp-recording techniques. However, depth EEG recordings obtained by lowering an electrode into the brain through a hole drilled in the skull can sometimes locate subcortical pathology. The EEG recorded from epileptics will occasionally display large-amplitude, fast waves called spikes, which are probably generated by the synchronous excitation of millions of neurons. Often these spikes are followed by an absence of high-frequency activity. During a grand mal seizure the EEG is composed of continuous large-amplitude, fast waves.

Several authors have suggested that EEG be used to establish brain death: many patients, even though their hearts continue to beat, have no detectable EEG activity. However, it is almost cer-

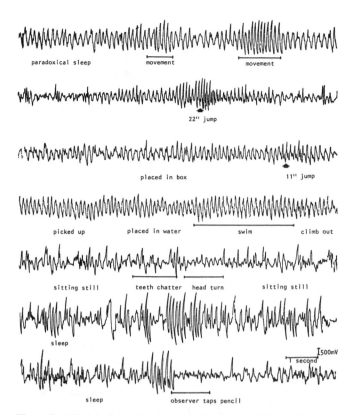

Figure 2.   Electrical activity at a single hippocampal site during sleep and various behaviors in the rat. Note the following: RSA (rhythmical slow activity) during paradoxical sleep, while struggling when held in the hand, and during swimming and head movement; large-amplitude irregular activity when sitting still while alert and while chattering the teeth; irregular slow activity and spindling during slow-wave sleep, and small-amplitude irregular activity when the rat awakens but does not move about. Note also the following: increased RSA frequency and amplitude associated with twitching during paradoxical sleep, and with jumping in avoidance tasks; different frequencies and amplitudes of RSA associated with head movements, swimming, and jumping 11 in. (27.9 cm) and 22 in. (55.9 cm). From "Hippocampal EEG and behavior: Changes in amplitude and frequency of RSA (theta rhythm) associated with spontaneous and learned movement patterns in rats and cats," by I. Q. Whishaw and C. H. Vanderwolf, 1973, *Behavioral Biology, 8,* pp. 461–484. Reprinted with permission.

tainly the case that people who have displayed long periods with little or no detectable EEG activity have shown striking recovery, while on the other hand some profound comas are associated with cortical EEG composed of the low-amplitude, fast activity characteristic of the alert, awake pattern. Cortical EEG can also be recorded from fetuses in the uterus by means of electrodes on the surface of the mother's abdomen. Sometime between the second and third month after conception, fetal brain waves can be detected using this method. However, studies of development of EEG have shown that the typical adult pattern does not fully appear until 11 to 14 years of age.

As a research tool, EEG has been used to assess the effects of a vast number of drugs. Many investigators have used EEG to discern specialization of behavioral functions within different parts of the cortex and subcortical structures. This has been accomplished by studying changes in EEG pattern during specific movements (movement-related potentials), or during presentation of specific sensory events (sensory evoked potentials).

REFERENCES

Berger, A. (1929). Über das Elektroenzephalogramm des Menschen. *Archiv für Psychiatrie und Nervenkrankheiten, 87,* 527–571.

Penfield, W., & Jasper, H. H. (1954). *Epilepsy and the functional anatomy of the human brain.* Boston: Little, Brown.

Whishaw, I. Q., & Vanderwolf, C. H. (1973). Hippocampal EEG and behavior: Changes in amplitude and frequency of RSA (theta rhythm) associated with spontaneous and learned movement patterns in rats and cats. *Behavioral Biology, 8,* 461–484.

R. J. SUTHERLAND
University of New Mexico

I. Q. WHISHAW
University of Lethbridge

NEUROPSYCHOLOGY
SPLIT-BRAIN RESEARCH

ELLIS, ALBERT

Albert Ellis is president of the Albert Ellis Institute in New York City, where he does individual, family, and group therapy; supervises therapists; and gives many workshops and lectures. He received a PhD in clinical psychology from Teachers College, Columbia University; was chief psychologist of the New Jersey State Diagnostic Center; and was chief psychologist of the New Jersey Department of Human Services and Agencies. He founded rational emotive behavior therapy, the first of the cognitive-behavior therapies, in January 1950, and has given many lectures and workshops on it throughout the world. He has received the highest awards for distinguished professional contributions to knowledge from the American Psychological Association, the Association for the Advancement of Behavior Therapy, the American Psychopathology Association, as well as from several other leading associations and universities. He was voted the second most influential psychotherapist (to Carl Rogers) by the clinicians of the American Psychological Association and the most influential one by Canadian clinicians. He has published over sixty books, 600 papers, and 200 recordings for the psychological profession and the public.

STAFF

ELLIS, HAVELOCK (1859–1939)

The English psychologist Henry Havelock Ellis was raised by his mother in a climate of Victorian asexuality. He credited this lack of information with spurring him to study the typical sexual behavior of humans.

Ellis's first work was the 1897 sexual inversion volume of his *Studies in the Psychology of Sex.* He concluded that homosexual behavior was congenital and a statistical anomaly, rather than a disease. He presented some 80 cases of quite successful males who either accepted this feature of their personalities or tried to minimize its effects; none had sought professional counseling. Two years later he published the volume on auto-erotism. Masturbation, he stated, did not inevitably lead to serious illness but rather was a legitimate source of mental relaxation. In adults, he observed, masturbation was more frequent in women.

In all his work he challenged the typical approach to sexual behavior in which the individual took as his reference point his own behavior and the behavior of friends and neighbors. Ellis stated that it was vital to remember that one was not necessarily like one's acquaintances, and that one's acquaintances were probably not as much alike as one might suppose. He objected to Freud's application of adult sexual terms to infants. Infants surely had an erotic life, but it certainly should not be conceptualized in language designed to apply to adult behavior. Unlike writers such as Krafft-Ebing and Freud, Ellis was interested in normal human sexuality, not in pathology; thus his work was an important forerunner of both the surveys of Kinsey and the experimentation of Masters and Johnson.

Ellis described the essential characteristic of human coitus as the face-to-face position. When human coitus occurred in other positions, notably rear entry, it thereby took on some of the flight/pursuit characteristics of animal coitus.

Ellis also wrote on such diverse topics as eugenics and manners. He reported on his own experiences with the hallucinogen mescal around the turn of the century. He wrote about the "literature of life," including that of such authors as Nietzsche, Casanova, Zola, and Huysmans. Life *is* an art, he said, but only some literature actually deals with the important questions of life.

C. S. PEYSER
The University of the South

EMOTION AND MEMORY

Early memories have a strong emotional component. An autobiographical memory study by Wagenaar and Groeneweg (1990) of concentration camp survivors indicates that events that happened 50 years ago are well remembered, but there also is evidence of repression of intensely emotional experiences unique to them, namely details related to witnessing torture and murder and being the victim of brutal maltreatment. In other words, intensity is not a safeguard against forgetting.

For the more ordinary levels of arousal autobiographical data are in keeping with experimental studies in which emotional words and pictures of sufficient intensity are recalled better than nonemotional materials (Blum, 1961; Evans & Denny, 1978; Strongman & Russell, 1986), and with the theoretical suggestion by Posner (1978) that emotion increases the level of alertness, as well as

Walker's (1958) view that high arousal during the associative process produces greater permanent memory. Presumably, better retention can be due to better learning, better storage, or both.

Walker's hypothesis includes the notion of temporary inhibition of recall right after high arousal, and Kleinsmith and Kaplan (1963) obtained results that support Walker's view. Eight words that produced different arousal levels as measured by skin resistance (GSR)—for example, "rape," vomit," "dance," and "swim,"—were used as stimuli for digit responses of 2 through 9. Low arousal words were recalled better than high arousal words immediately following the study trial, but 45 minutes later and thereafter, high arousal words were recalled much better. Several similar studies confirmed better recall with high arousal and long retention intervals, but some did not find poorer recall with high arousal and very short intervals. As with the life experiences mentioned earlier, the source of emotion or arousal was the stimulus to which something was being recalled. But much the same results were obtained by Weiner and Walker (1966) using electric shock as a negative incentive or money as a positive incentive for correctly responding to a paired associates list. That is, retention was better with incentives than without incentives, increasing with incentive value and showing an even greater difference in favor of increased affect with a longer retention interval. Berlyne (1966) also manipulated arousal with a completely independent agent by using white noise and found that white noise presented over ear phones during training improved recall, especially with longer retention intervals.

Uehling and Sprinkle (1968) examined the effects of arousal at time of recall only, using a serial list of adjectives and either white noise or muscle tension to induce arousal. Only white noise increased recall significantly and only at the longer retention intervals. There is little research on this topic or related topics such as repression or mood dependence. It seems clear, however, that the presence of emotion during learning and probably-increased arousal during recall facilitate remembering.

Bower and associates have studied the phenomenon of mood-dependent memory retrieval extensively. In essence, retrieval is supposed to be better if the subject's mood at retrieval matches his or her mood at learning. After conducting a few successful experiments in which subjects who felt happy at both learning and recall (or felt sad both times) recalled more than subjects tested in a mood opposite of the one during learning, they had a number of failures, which prompted Bower and Mayer (1985) to conclude that mood-dependent retrieval is an unreliable phenomenon, at least in the laboratory.

Blaney (1986) in a review of affect and emotion distinguishes between mood-dependent memory and mood congruence, which states that material is better learned and retained if the material has emotional tone congruent with the subject's mood at acquisition and/or recall. The evidence for mood-congruent memory is much stronger than for mood-dependent memory, which is not too surprising theoretically, because a cue that is clearly relevant for the material to be recalled is supplied by the congruent mood present at recall. In autobiographical memories, according to Blaney, these two effects are often confounded, which, in part, may account for the easy access to autobiographical memories. In general, the mood studies seem to work better if the induced moods are intense.

A rather forgotten area of research has been testing the psychoanalytic theory of repression—whether unpleasant events or materials are forgotten more than pleasant items. By and large the results are inconclusive. There is usually no difference in recall as a function of type of affective response; rather intense experiences, whether pleasant or aversive, are recalled better than neutral events, as is the case of the research reported earlier. Klugman (1956) found no difference in the retention of pleasant and unpleasant materials in both normal and neurotic subjects, which would seem to run counter to Freud's notion. Normals in particular retained more intensely toned material. Holmes and Schallow (1969) indicate that a true test of repression must involve an ego threat and designed their study accordingly. Their results showed that poorer performance on a test could readily be attributed to response competition (worrying about test feedback and its implications) instead of repression. Other studies involving ego threat that had positive results also seem to support response competition.

Finally, an even clearer example of an inhibitory effect of emotion on test performance is the phenomenon of test anxiety (Sarason, 1980). For those who are most susceptible to worry and emotionality during a school test, the following seems to be true: the range of cues attended to is reduced; processing emphasizes the physical stimulus rather than semantic content; there is a slightly shorter digit span in highly anxious subjects; deficit is present for both recall and recognition tests; and the highly anxious benefit more from relaxed retest conditions and memory supports (such as open-book tests) than do less anxious subjects.

REFERENCES

Berlyne, D. E. (1966). Curiosity and exploration. *Science, 153,* 25–33.

Blum, G. S. (1961). *A model of the mind.* New York: Wiley.

Bower, G. H., & Mayer, J. D. (1985). Failure to replicate mood-dependent retrieval. *Bulletin of the Psychonomic Society, 23,* 39–42.

Evans, T., & Denny, M. R. (1978). Emotionality of pictures and the retention of related and unrelated phrases. *Bulletin of the Psychonomic Society, 11,* 149–152.

Kleinsmith, L. J., & Kaplan, S. (1963). Paired-associate learning as a function of arousal and interpolated interval. *Journal of Experimental Psychology, 65,* 190–193.

Klugman, S. F. (1956). Retention of affectively toned verbal material by normals and neurotics. *Journal of Abnormal and Social Psychology, 53,* 321–327.

Posner, M. I. (1978). *Chronometric explorations of mind.* Hillsdale, NJ: Erlbaum.

Strongman, K. T., & Russell, P. N. (1986). Salience of emotion in recall. *Bulletin of the Psychonomic Society, 24,* 25–27.

Uehling, B., & Sprinkle, R. (1968). Recall of a serial list as a function of arousal and retention interval. *Journal of Experimental Psychology, 78,* 103–106.

Wagenaar, W. A., & Groeneweg, J. (1990). The memory of concentration camp survivors. *Applied Cognitive Psychology, 4,* 77–87.

Walker, E. L. (1958). Action decrement and its relation to learning. *Psychological Review, 65,* 129–142.

Weiner, B., & Walker, E. L. (1966). Motivational factors in short-term retention. *Journal of Experimental Psychology, 71,* 190–193.

SUGGESTED READING

Blaney, P. H. (1986). Affect and memory: A review. *Psychological Bulletin, 22,* 229–246.

Weiner, B. (1966). Effects of motivation on the avialability and retrieval or memory traces. *Psychological Bulletin, 65,* 24–37.

M. R. DENNY
Michigan State University

ATTITUDES
DEFENSE MECHANISMS
EMOTIONS
MEMORY
PSYCHOANALYSIS
PUNISHMENT

EMOTIONAL CONTAGION

Emotional contagion has been defined as "the tendency to automatically mimic and synchronize expressions, vocalizations, postures, and movements with those of another person and, consequently, to converge emotionally" (Hatfield, Cacioppo, & Rapson, 1993).

The Emotional Contagion Scale (Doherty, 1997) was designed to measure the extent to which men and women tend to "catch" expressions of joy, love, anger, fear, and sadness from others. Theoretically, emotions can be caught in several ways. Some researchers have argued that conscious reasoning, analysis, and imagination can account for the phenomenon; some (Aronfreed, 1970) contend that people must learn to share others' emotions, that contagion is a conditioned emotional response. Most, however, assume that emotional contagion is an even more primitive process, that it happens automatically, outside conscious awareness. Hatfield and her colleagues (1993), for example, argue that the process of emotional contagion operates as follows:

- *Proposition 1.* In conversation, people automatically and continuously mimic and synchronize their facial expressions, voices, postures, movements, and instrumental behaviors with those of others.

- *Proposition 2.* Subjective emotional experience is affected moment-to-moment by the feedback from such mimicry/synchrony.

Theoretically, emotional experience could be influenced by either (a) the central nervous system commands that direct such mimicry/synchrony in the first place; (b) the afferent feedback from such facial, verbal, or postural mimicry/synchrony; or (c) conscious self-perception processes, wherein individuals draw inferences about their own emotional states on the basis of the emotional expressions and behaviors evoked in them by the emotional states of others. Consequently,

• *Proposition 3.* People tend, from moment to moment, to catch others' emotions.

Researchers have collected considerable evidence in support of these three propositions.

PROPOSITION 1
Researchers have found evidence that people do tend to imitate the facial expressions, postures, voices, and instrumental behaviors of others. Facial mimicry is at times almost instantaneous. People seem able to track the most subtle of moment-to-moment changes. Haggard and Isaacs (1966) observed that emotional experiences and their accompanying facial expressions may change with surprising speed—within a span of 125–200 ms. Social psychophysiological investigations have found that emotional experiences and facial expressions, as measured by electromyographic (EMG) procedures, tend to mimic the changes in emotional expression of those they observe, and that this motor mimicry can occur at levels so subtle that they produce no observable facial expressions (Cacioppo, Tassinary, & Fridlund, 1990). When subjects observe happy facial expressions, they show increased muscular activity over the zygomaticus major (cheek) muscle region. When they observe angry facial expressions, they show increased muscular activity over the corrugator supercilli (brow) muscle region (Dimberg, 1982).

Such mimicry begins almost at birth. Haviland and Lelwica (1987) found that 10-week-old infants could and would imitate their mothers' facial expressions of happiness, sadness, and anger. Mothers mimicked their infants' expressions of emotion as well. There also is voluminous evidence that people mimic and synchronize their vocal utterances. Communication researchers have found interspeaker influence on utterance durations, speech rate, latencies of response, and a host of other speech characteristics. People have been found to mimic and synchronize their postures and movements with others as well.

PROPOSITION 2
Researchers have found that emotions are tempered to some extent by somatic and skeletal feedback. Those researchers interested in testing the facial feedback hypothesis have employed a variety of different strategies for inducing subjects to adopt various emotional expressions. Sometimes they simply ask subjects to fake an emotional expression. Sometimes they ask subjects to exaggerate or to hide any emotional reactions they may have (see Lanzetta, Biernat, & Kleck, 1982). Sometimes they try to trick subjects into adopting various facial expressions (Laird & Bresler, 1991), or to arrange the setting/circumstance so subjects will unconsciously mimic others' emotional and facial expressions (Hsee, Hatfield, Carlson, & Chemtob, 1991). In all cases, scientists have found that

the emotional experiences of subjects are affected by feedback from the facial expressions they adopt. An impressive array of evidence supports the proposition that people's subjective emotional experiences are affected, moment-to-moment, by feedback from facial, vocal, postural, and movement mimicry.

PROPOSITION 3
Researchers from a variety of disciplines have provided evidence that emotional contagion exists. The majority of such work has come from animal researchers (Miller, Banks, & Ogawa, 1963); child psychologists interested in primitive emotional contagion, empathy, and sympathy; clinicians exploring the process of transference and countertransference; social psychologists (Hatfield et al., 1993; and historians.

REFERENCES
Aronfreed, J. (1970). The socialization of altruistic and sympathetic behavior: Some theoretical and experimental analyses. In J. Macaulay & L. Berkowitz (Eds.), *Altruism and helping behavior* (pp. 103–126). New York: Academic.

Cacioppo, J. T., Tassinary, L. G., & Fridlund, A. J. (1990). Skeletomotor system. In J. T. Cacioppo & L. G. Tassinary (Eds.), *Principles of psychophysiology: Physical, social, and inferential elements* (pp. 325–384). New York: Cambridge University Press.

Dimberg, U. (1982). Facial reactions to facial expressions. *Psychophysiology, 19,* 643–647.

Doherty, R. W. (1997). The emotional contagion scale: A measure of individual differences. *Journal of Nonverbal Behavior, 21,* 131–154.

Haggard, E. A., & Isaacs, F. S. (1966). Micromomentary facial expressions as indicators of ego mechanisms in psychotherapy. In C. A. Gottschalk & A. Averback (Eds.), *Methods of research in psychotherapy* (pp. 154–165). New York: Appleton-Century-Crofts.

Hatfield, E., Cacioppo, J. T., & Rapson, R. L. (1993). *Emotional contagion.* New York: Cambridge University Press.

Haviland, J. M., & Lelwica, M. (1987). The induced affect response: 10-week-old infants' responses to three emotional expressions. *Developmental Psychology, 23,* 97–104.

Hsee, C., Hatfield, E., Carlson, J. G., & Chemtob, C. (1991). The effect of power on susceptibility to emotional contagion. *Cognition and Emotion, 4,* 327–340.

Laird, J. D., & Bresler, C. (1991). The process of emotional feeling: A self-perception theory. In M. Clark (Ed.), *Review of Personality and Social Psychology.*

Lanzetta, J. T., Biernat, J. J., & Kleck, R. E. (1982). Self-focused attention, facial behavior, autonomic arousal and the experience of emotion. *Motivation and Emotion, 6,* 49–63.

Miller, R. E., Banks, J. H., & Ogawa, N. (1963). Role of facial expression in "cooperative-avoidance conditioning" in monkeys. *Journal of Abnormal and Social Psychology, 67,* 24–30.

SUGGESTED READING

Bernieri, F. J. (1988). Coordinated movement and rapport in teacher-student interactions. *Journal of Nonverbal Behavior, 12,* 120–138.

E. HATFIELD
R. L. RAPSON
University of Hawaii

EMOTIONS
EMPATHY

EMOTIONS

Emotions are a basic component of human experience, but their exact nature has been elusive and difficult to specify. This is due to a number of causes, including the fact that so many systems of the body are involved in emotion. A second problem has been the tendency to separate emotion from cognition or rational thought processes. The physiological and psychological processes involved in emotion are, however, most likely interrelated. As a result, separation of emotion from these other aspects of experience may not be productive.

Emotions are generally thought of as strong mental states, usually involving excitement or high energy, that give rise to feelings and passions. There is also usually a valence or direction to this state: Emotions are generally positive or negative. Thus surprise, euphoria, anger, or fear, while varying in how positive or negative they are, are strong, energetic feelings.

Early depictions of emotion focused on their high-energy quality: Emotions were physical stirrings or excited mental states. Subsequently, the physical energy involved in emotion was seen as being controlled by the brain. Finally, integration of the psychological and physiological realms was achieved.

One of the most influential theories of emotion—developed independently by William James and Carl Lange—is usually referred to as the James-Lange theory of emotion. Basically, it postulated that emotions are made up of bodily changes (e.g., arousal) and a mental event or feeling. This in itself was not new. However, prevailing views of emotion at the time argued that an emotion-causing event was perceived, a feeling arose from that perception, and bodily expression of that feeling then followed. In other words, the mental state involved in emotion was determined directly by the event; physiological aspects were secondary. But James and Lange disagreed. In his *Principles of Psychology* (1890), James argued that the mental state or feeling, which was the emotion proper, followed from bodily changes. In essence, he was reversing the sequence generally believed to be true. According to James, an event was perceived, physiological changes occurred as a result of this event, and the feelings that one had as a result of physiological change was the emotion.

Emotion, then, was a mental feeling-state that followed directly from bodily changes. Different events were thought to cause different bodily changes and thus different emotions. Sad events caused bodily changes that led to sorrow, while frightening events led to a different type of bodily change that gave rise to fear. Most people believed that laughter was the result of being happy and crying was attributable to sadness. James and Lange argued the converse: laughter gave rise to happiness, crying gave rise to sadness, and trembling gave rise to fear.

The James-Lange theories have generated a great deal of response. Research and theory followed the publication of their theories and have continued to the present. One of the more far-reaching of these responses was provided by Cannon, who observed a weakness in the James-Lange formulation and proposed a theory of emotions based on their evolutionary value.

Cannon (1927) noted that the James-Lange theory implied that there was a specific pattern of bodily changes associated with each emotion. Since there were many different emotions, there must therefore be a large number of different patterns of bodily change. He then argued that research evidence did not support this, and focused his theory on a unitary pattern of bodily change.

According to Cannon, events that caused emotions gave rise to arousal of the sympathetic nervous system. This arousal involved secretion of epinephrine by the adrenal glands and included changes such as increased heart rate, increased respiration, and increased muscle tone. Cannon argued that the function of this arousal was to prepare the organism to deal with the event—to fight or flee, for example. In other words, an event that could cause harm generated arousal—an emergency response—that prepared the organism to cope with the event. Increased heart rate, respiration and so on, enabled the organism to respond more quickly, more alertly, and with greater strength, increasing its chances of survival.

Emotional states, Cannon argued, are related to this arousal, but they are not completely determined by one another. Bodily changes are constant; the same changes are involved in different emotional states. Feelings, on the other hand, vary from situation to situation. He saw the hypothalamus as the seat of both arousal and feeling states, and emotion as the product of these states as integrated by the central nervous system.

Several theories or criticisms have appeared in response to this model. Some, including Duffy's notion (1934) based on the concept of energy mobilization and Lindsley's activation theory (1951), focused on the role of arousal in emotion. Others focused on the role of the central nervous system in emotion. Papez (1937) reported that specific areas of the brain were associated with emotion, and subsequent work has identified the reticular formation, extending from the thalamus to the brain stem, as the center of activation or arousal. Research also suggests that electrical stimulation of specific areas of the brain causes a general emotional pattern classifiable as rage or fear. However, despite the fact that areas of the brain are necessary for emotional expression, there do not appear to be specific locations in the brain for each emotion.

Much modern research on emotion has focused on the interplay between bodily changes and feeling states. Arnold (1960) argued that mental evaluations of events determine emotional response, including bodily changes and feelings. Part of this determination involves evaluation of sensations: Feelings are based partly on interpretation of events and partly on interpretation of bodily changes. Others have argued for more or less emphasis on evaluation of bodily changes, with the issue of primacy left unsettled.

The primacy issue is, on the surface, relatively straightforward, and in many ways reflects the differences between the James-Lange and Cannon approaches. On the one side are those who, like James and Lange, believe that specific bodily changes are associated with specific emotions. These theorists suggest that the brain simply recognizes different physiological changes and thereby gives rise to the appropriate emotion. In this tradition, physiological changes are the primary determinant of emotion. On the other side are theorists who believe that bodily changes are fairly similar from situation to situation, and that the most important aspect of emotion is the way in which these changes are interpreted.

Research supports both positions to some extent. Several studies have reported evidence suggesting that specific emotions can be reliably associated with specific patterns of physiological changes. Ax (1953) found that changes in blood pressure, heart rate, and skin conductance were somewhat different when subjects were angry than when they were afraid. Other studies have found the same thing, but only a few emotions have been found to be associated with specific bodily changes. Consistent with Cannon's point that there were not enough different patterns of change to account for all emotions, research has identified only two or three different physiological precursors of emotion.

Schachter and Singer (1962) reported a study that provided evidence for the opposite view. Their study led to the formulation of a two-factor theory of emotion. According to this theory, emotion is based on both physiological changes and cognitive interpretations of the environment. Arousal is viewed as more or less unitary. Like Cannon, Schachter and Singer believe that emotion is based on a physiological state of arousal. This arousal is the same for different emotions, and serves primarily to motivate the individual to attempt to explain or label it. These labels are derived from the situation. In some cases they are fairly easy to derive. Upon confronting a bear, an individual experiences arousal and seeks to explain it. If the bear is wild, the arousal may be interpreted as fear, but if the bear is tame, arousal can be labeled excitement. The same cues in the situation are seen as the most important determinants of which emotion is experienced.

Not all theories of emotion focus on the relationship between bodily changes and mental activity, although the idea that emotions involve both is widely held. Some attention has been focused on understanding the dimensions of emotion. There are hundreds of different emotional states, many of which are subtle shades of others. To understand all these states, researchers have attempted to identify basic dimensions along which they can be placed. These continue to range from one extreme to another. For example, the most common dimension ranges from pleasant to unpleasant. Most emotions can be placed somewhere along this dimension: love and happiness are pleasant, and anger and fear are unpleasant. Somewhere in between these extremes one would find most emotions. Disgust is not as unpleasant as anger, but more unpleasant than surprise.

REFERENCES

Arnold, M. B. (1960). *Emotion and personality* (2 vols.). New York: Columbia University Press.

Ax, A. F. (1953). Physiological differentiations between fear and anger in humans. *Psychosomatic Medicine, 15,* 433–442.

Cannon, W. B. (1927). The James-Lange theory of emotions: Critical examination and an alternative theory. *American Journal of Psychology, 39,* 106–124.

Duffy, E. (1934). Emotion: An example of the need for reorientation in psychology. *Psychological Review, 41,* 184–198.

James, W. (1890). *The principles of psychology.* New York: Holt.

Lindsley, D. B. (1951). Emotion. In S. S. Stevens (Ed.), *Handbook of experimental psychology.* New York: Wiley.

Papez, J. W. (1937). A proposed mechanism of emotion. *Archives of Neurology and Psychiatry, 38,* 725–744.

Schachter, S., & Singer, J. E. (1962). Cognitive, social and physiological determinants of emotional state. *Psychological Review, 69,* 379–399.

A. S. BAUM
University of Pittsburgh Cancer Institute

ANXIETY
SURPRISE

EMPATHY

Empathy is generally understood to refer to one person's vicariously experiencing the feelings, perceptions, and thoughts of another. Some early European and American psychological and philosophical thinkers such as Scheller and McDougall viewed empathy as the basis of all positive social relationships.

Within the context of this broad definition, various theorists and researchers have defined the term quite differently, each emphasizing different aspects or implications of this overall definition. Clinical psychologists and others doing research on therapeutic situations, such as Truax, have tended to define the term most broadly, incorporating the therapist's intellectual understanding of the client, the therapist's sharing of the client's feeling, the ease and effectiveness of communication, and the therapist's positive attitude toward the patient. It is assumed that therapists' empathy is desirable, although some therapists have cautioned that a therapist who empathizes too much runs the risk of drowning in the same sea of anxiety or depression as the patient he or she is trying to rescue. Scales—among them Truax's (1961)—have been developed to measure such multifaceted empathy. Such a broad definition of empathy is intuitively attractive, but the mélange of several aspects and implications of empathy leads to theoretical confusion, since it is unclear which aspect is at the core, either definitionally or causally, with the other aspects being effects or derivatives. For example, one might ask: Is intellectual understanding—however cold and unfeeling it might in some instances be—the core of empathy?

Other psychologists such as Dymond (1949) have emphasized the cognitive aspects, focusing on the ability of one person to understand intellectually the inner experience of another. The significance of cognitive empathy appears to be the probable facilitation of communication between the two persons. Also implied is that the empathizer will tend to like, to help, to accept the other more as a consequence of this empathy. However, the consequences of intellectually understanding another who has a repugnant inner life are usually ignored. Furthermore, an individual who can understand others may not necessarily use this ability in relationships with particular others; the motivation to empathize is assumed, but is not dealt with theoretically. Cognitive empathy has been measured primarily by the prediction or postdiction of another person's responses to some attitudinal or personality questionnaire. This method has been shown by Cronbach (1955) to be replete with problems of multidetermination of the accuracy of the prediction, such as the empathizer's generalizing from his or her own responses to the other's. Thus if the other happens to be a person similar to the empathizer, the latter scores high on empathy. Or the empathizer may simply use his or her stereotype about the type of person the other is; then, to the extent that the other conforms to this stereotype, the empathizer is accurate. Despite these and other problems, this approach has encouraged more attention to the processes involved in perceiving and understanding others.

A third approach to empathy defines it as the empathizer's experiencing a given emotion because he or she perceives that the other is experiencing that emotion. Some developmentally oriented theorists maintain that such direct sharing of feelings between parent and infant is a key step in the maturation process. This definition has been used by a number of experimental social psychological researchers, of whom Berger (1962) was the first to report that empathy does in fact occur in laboratory experiments under conditions controlled for possible nonempathetic sources of emotional arousal. Empathetic emotional arousal has been reflected both in self-reports and in physiological changes.

Stotland, Shaver, and Sherman report in *Empathy and Birth Order* on some of the conditions leading to the occurrence of empathy, including perceived similarity to the other, the empathizer and the other having interacted, and so forth. (Some researchers have generated empathy by making the others' experiences serve as a signal to the potential empathizers about their own future welfare. As Berger pointed out, such methodology trivializes the studies.)

Stotland and his colleagues found, however, that the key antecedent condition for empathy appears to be the empathizer's imagining himself or herself as having the same experience as the other—thus imaginatively taking the role of the other. This mental process contrasts with viewing the other in more objectified or intellectualized ways. An empathizing adult is in some sense temporarily regressing to an earlier state by imagining herself or himself in the place of the other, and may have the ability to empathize only because of earlier experiences. As Hoffman (1977) points out, empathy in adults may have a long developmental history, since infants at first do not distinguish between self and other, and therefore empathize readily. Only gradually do they come to learn that self and other are distinct entities.

Empathetic imagining has been both induced experimentally and measured as an individually characteristic way of reacting to others, as reported by Stotland and others in *Fantasy, Empathy, and Helping*. This approach to empathy overlaps with the cognitively oriented one described above, to the extent that it is based on a cognitive or mental process of imagining. However, unlike the purely cognitively oriented approach, this cognitive process does not have to be veridical, so that the persons can empathize with an actor or a fictional character. Imagining the other person's experience appears to be based primarily on attributive projection, since persons appear to empathize more with others who are in the same situation that the empathizer has experienced, observed closely, or previously imagined himself or herself experiencing.

Since empathizing involves projective attribution and appears to be a conscious, voluntary process, it is not surprising that empathizers are aware of the empathetic basis of their emotions. Furthermore, the dependence of empathy on the process of projective attribution indicates that the person may be led to empathize by any information or stimulus providing some basis for inferring the other's state, whether this information consists of knowledge of the other's situation, perception of facial expressions or bodily movements, verbal reports, and so forth.

The linkage between the process of imagining and the processes involved in physiologically or behaviorally manifest emotion may be complex. This linkage may occur as a result of direct, past association through a process involving subtle liminal or subliminal muscular movements, or it may occur in a direct neural fashion.

Philosophers and social theorists have long assumed that empathizing leads to greater helpfulness and even altruism. This simple relationship has been demonstrated empirically when empathy has been induced by instructions, as reported by Toi and Batson (1981). Stotland and his colleagues have shown that empathizing, when measured as an individual characteristic, also leads to altruism, especially when the helpful actions are easily taken. Hoffman and Saltzstein (1967) report that if parents have a warm relationship with their children and call their attention to the consequences of their behavior for the welfare of others, the children are more likely to treat others well than if these conditions are lacking. In laboratory studies by Aronfreed, described in *Conduct and Conscience*, children who are more likely to aid an adult have apparently learned to empathize with the adult through a series of associations between their own welfare and that of the adult.

On the other hand, Stotland and his colleagues found that in situations in which help for a suffering other is not easy or even possible, the empathizer may attempt to escape the unpleasantness either physically or psychologically by "freezing" himself or herself. If the other's pain is extreme or manifest in great agony, an empathizing person may flee physically or psychologically from the situation. Batson and Coke (1981) report that this escape from unpleasant empathizing is less likely to occur if the person does not just empathize, but also sympathizes with the other—that is, reports feeling emotionally impelled to aid the other, feeling compassionate, sympathetic, and kind. In factor analyses of self-reports, such sympathy/empathy has been distinguished from empathy, which as defined above is limited to experiencing the same type of emotion as the other. The latter form of empathy has been found in at least some studies not to lead to altruism. Curiously, instructing a person to imagine another's experiences has been found to generate self-reports of sympathy. This sympathy approach to empathy comes close to demonstrating that people who report they are motivated to help actually do so. Such a finding or interpretation would be more relevant for the validity of attitude scales than for the consequences of empathizing. Hoffman has shown that regardless of which of the approaches has been taken to empathy, self-reports have shown higher scores among females than males. When children were asked by Feshback and Roe (1968) how they felt while observing another experience various emotions, girls showed more empathy than boys.

Most of the theorizing and research on empathy has been predicated on the empathizer sharing either the identical emotion or one that is of the same general type, positive or negative. Some scholars such as Berger have extended the definition to include contrasting emotions, as in the instance of sadism or envy. Little research, however, has been done on this problem.

REFERENCES

Aronfreed, J. (1968). *Conduct and conscience: The socialization of internalized control over behavior.* New York: Academic.

Batson, D., & Coke, J. (1981). Empathy: A source of altruistic motivation for helping. In *Altruism and helping behavior.* Hillsdale, NJ: Erlbaum.

Berger, S. (1962). Conditioning through vicarious instigation. *Psychological Review, 69,* 450–466.

Dymond, R. (1949). A scale for measurement of empathetic ability. *Journal of Consulting Psychology, 14,* 127–133.

Feshback, N. & Roe, K. (1968). Empathy in six- and seven-year-olds. *Child Development, 39,* 133–145.

Hoffman, M. (1977). Empathy, its development and prosocial implications. *Nebraska Symposium on Motivation, 25,* 169–211.

Hoffman, M. L., & Saltzstein, H. D. (1967). Parent discipline and the child's moral development. *Journal of Personality and Social Psychology, 5,* 45–57.

Stotland, E., Shaver, K., & Sherman, S. (1971). *Empathy and birth order.* Lincoln, NE: University of Nebraska Press.

Stotland, E., Mathews, K., Sherman, S., Hansson, R. & Richardson, B. (1978). *Fantasy, empathy, and helping.* Beverly Hills, CA: Sage.

Toi, M., & Batson, D. (1981). *More evidence that empathy is a source of altruistic motivation.* Unpublished manuscript. University of Kansas.

Truax, C. (1961). A scale for the measurement of accurate empathy. *Psychiatric Institute Bulletin 1,* 12.

E. STOTLAND
University of Washington

EMOTIONS
IMAGERY

EMPIRICISM

Empiricism is one of several rival doctrines in the philosophical field of epistemology, the study of knowledge. Epistemology's main concern is how to establish the truth of knowledge claims. If someone advances a proposition or group of propositions—for example, a scientific theory—how are we to determine that it is true? Empiricism holds that knowledge arises from and is to be justified by perceptual experience. Although empiricism seems straightforward enough, it faces challenges that have created its epistemological competitors.

Plato offered the first influential critique of experience as the basis for knowledge claims, pointing out that experience is frequently mistaken. If one person enters a room from a blizzard and another enters it having stoked a fire, they will disagree about whether the room is hot or cold. Perception is a source only of opinions, of beliefs that might be true or false. Knowledge, Plato said, must be absolutely and demonstrably true for all times and all places. Plato advanced two important alternatives to empiricism: rationalism and nativism. Rationalism locates the truth of knowledge claims in logic. Plato was influenced by Pythagoras and his followers, who created the notion of logical proof. When one works through the proof of the Pythagorean theorem, for example, one arrives at a truth that cannot be doubted because it has been formally proved. Mathematical proofs derive their authority from reason, not experience, and Plato hoped to extend a similar level of provable certainty to all knowledge claims.

Plato was also influenced by the Eastern religions infiltrating Greece from the fifth century B.C.E. onward. These religions taught that humans had immortal souls; some taught that a soul went through a cycle of reincarnations. Plato taught that, while out of the body, the soul sees eternal, transcendental Forms, heavenly prototypes of the objects of ordinary experience. Thus, a cat is a cat because it resembles the Form of the Cat, while a dog resembles the Form of the Dog. Knowledge of the Forms remains latent in the soul upon reincarnation and is merely awakened by perceptual experience. In Plato's philosophy, right use of reason makes knowledge demonstrably true, while existence of the Forms makes knowledge true eternally and transcendentally.

Plato's student, Aristotle, defended the validity of experience. He advanced a version of perceptual realism, asserting that we perceive things as they really are. Error arises from mistaken judgments we make about our experience, not from experience itself. Seeing a man on the street, one might mistake him for a friend, but the error impugns the viewer's judgment, not his or her perception. In a broad sense, Aristotle was an empiricist because he said that knowledge arises from experience; but in the modern sense, he was not an empiricist because he did not share its representational theory of perception.

Modern empiricism in philosophy and psychology began with Locke and Descartes. Because of Descartes' emphasis on reason and his belief in innate ideas he is typically lumped together with Plato as a rationalist and nativist, but his theory of perception is also the starting point for modern empiricism as developed by Locke. Descartes proposed that we do not experience the world directly, but through a veil of ideas that represent objects. In this representational theory of perception, one does not directly perceive the book he or she is now reading (as Aristotle taught), but only a representation of it, an idea held in consciousness. Locke's empiricism held that knowledge is the mind's acquaintance with its ideas.

Unfortunately, representational empiricism runs up against the problem that, because one does not perceive things directly, one cannot be certain—cannot *know*—that one's ideas are, in fact, accurate copies of things outside consciousness, raising the possibility that the world is very different than it seems to be, or even that the external world is a dream or hallucination. In the 17th and 18th centuries, different philosophers responded to the shortcomings of empiricism in different ways. Hume developed the skeptical possibilities in empiricism, concluding that knowledge is, in fact, never provably true, thus anticipating the American philosophy of pragmatism. Other Scottish philosophers attempted to revive realism and a new form of nativism. They taught that God endowed us with mental powers—faculties—enabling us to perceive and know His creation as it really is.

Perceptual realism, however, remained a minority viewpoint, surfacing in the philosophy of Brentano and American Neorealism and in Gestalt and Gibson's ecological theory of perception. Nativism was slain by evolution—that is, innate ideas and faculties, if they exist at all, are implanted not by God but by the vagaries of natural selection. In psychology, nativism has returned in Noam Chomsky's linguistics and in evolutionary psychology, but researchers in these fields seek in the genes, not truth, only certain mental dispositions we inherit from our hominine ancestors.

Empiricism became and remains the dominant epistemology in Great Britain and in the United States. The most important alternative to empiricism, idealism, arose with Kant, and it exerted great influence in 19th- and early 20th-century Germany. Kant was shocked by Hume's conclusion that all knowledge claims are fallible, and attempted to synthesize empiricism and rationalism into an epistemology more worldly than the former but more certain than the latter. Kant thought of science as the paradigm of human knowledge, and acknowledged that it begins with and systematizes experience. However, Kant held that human experience is shaped by logically necessary (not God-given) characteristics of the human mind, which yield the orderly phenomena studied by science. Science therefore rests on a rationally provable foundation that is inherent in the mind, and therefore exists prior to experience. Kantian idealism affected the psychology of Jean Piaget, who proposed that formal logical structures of the mind determine how children and adults perceive and think about the world.

T. H. LEAHEY
Virginia Commonwealth University

FACULTY PSYCHOLOGY
LOGICAL POSITISM
OPERATIONALISM
POSITISM

EMPLOYMENT TESTS

Employment tests include all psychological assessment procedures used in selection and classification of personnel by employers. As such, nearly every type of psychological test can and has been used in making occupational decisions. Interest inventories may be used as employment tests, but are more commonly applied in vocational or educational counseling centers as aids in choosing a particular training program prior to employment. Objective tests of personality, and occasionally even projective scales, are used in personnel selection for jobs that entail substantial stress (e.g., corporate executive vice-president or certain safety monitoring positions in nuclear energy or fuel plants), though this practice has lessened in recent years.

The most frequently used employment tests are now tests of aptitude, both general and specific. In the earlier stages of employment testing, general aptitude tests predominated the field, the most notable being the Army Alpha and the nonverbal Army Beta examinations. General aptitude measures continue to be used successfully as employment tests in a variety of settings. One of the major stock brokerage firms in the United States currently requires an individually administered test of intelligence prior to hiring a new account executive. Intelligence testing prior to employment is justified by this corporation on the basis of their belief that a highly successful broker must be able to hold a myriad of complex facts in mind and be able to manipulate this information quickly and accurately. General ability tests designed specifically for industrial settings, such as the Wonderlic Personnel Test and the Thurstone Test of Mental Alertness, remain in active use today, despite a strong push toward more specific tests of aptitude in the 1960s and 1970s.

Tests of special aptitude are designed, as their name implies, to assess narrow slices of any individual's ability spectrum. While a certain level of intelligence may be necessary to perform a given job, this may be insufficient in and of itself. Assembling a complex piece of machinery requires a certain level of general intellectual prowess but, given two individuals of sufficient general intelligence, can likely be performed better by a person with superior psychomotor speed, coordination, and manual dexterity. In such an instance it may be appropriate to administer a test like the Crawford Small Parts Dexterity Test prior to making a hiring decision. The most common tests of special aptitudes in use in employment testing include measures of psychomotor skill, clerical ability, and mechanical aptitude, though measures are available in such diverse areas as artistic and musical aptitude.

Until recently, conventional wisdom in employment testing held that the more specific the job, the more specific the test should be to predict performance on the job. Thus task differences were believed to moderate the validity of employment tests. Recent work by Schmidt and colleagues (1981) has generally refuted this doctrine, as considerably wider generalizability of validity across jobs and tests has been found than was previously believed to exist.

The validity of employment tests is a major issue in the field and not infrequently a bone of contention between management and employees and their representatives. Valid selection procedures in employment are important to the economy, however, and in this sense to the entire work force. Choosing individuals correctly for the correct job has an impact measured annually in billions of dollars of the gross national product (GNP) of the United States, according to recent work by Hunter and Schmidt (1981).

Employment tests can also be abused and misused. For these reasons the U.S. Equal Employment Opportunity Commission maintains a set of guidelines for employment testing. To promote the proper use of employment testing at a professional level, the Division of Industrial and Organizational Psychology of the American Psychological Association publishes a set of principles in personnel selection. Further information on employment tests may be found in Dunnette (1976), Dunnette and Fleishman (1981), and most major texts on psychological testing (e.g., Anastasi, 1982).

REFERENCES

Anastasi, A. (1982). *Psychological testing* (5th ed.). New York: Macmillan.

Dunnette, M. D. (Ed.). (1976). *Handbook of industrial and organizational psychology.* Chicago: Rand McNally.

Dunnette, M. D., & Fleishman, E. A. (1981). *Human performance and productivity.* (Vol. 1). Hillsdale, NJ: Erlbaum.

Hunter, J. E., & Schmidt, F. L. (1981). Fitting people into jobs: The impact of personnel selection on national productivity. In M. D. Dunnette & E. A. Fleishman (Eds.), *Human performance and productivity* (Vol. 1). Hillsdale, NJ: Erlbaum.

Schmidt, F. L., Hunter, J. E., & Pearlman, K. (1981). Task differences as moderators of aptitude test validity in selection: A red herring. *Journal of Applied Psychology, 66,* 166–185.

C. R. REYNOLDS
Texas A&M University

JOB EVALUATION MEASUREMENT

ENCOPRESIS

Encopresis is generally regarded as a disorder of childhood. The term refers to repeated fecal soiling. The fourth edition of the *Diagnostic and Statistical Manual of Mental Disorders* (*DSM-IV;* American Psychiatric Association, 1994) gives four criteria for diagnosis of Encopresis: repeated passage of feces into inappropriate places; the occurrence of this behavior at least once a month for at least three months; a chronological age of the child of at least four years, or if there has been a developmental delay, a mental age of at least four years; and an inability to attribute the fecal incontinence to a general medical condition (except constipation) or to the effects of substances (e.g., a laxative).

The *DSM-IV* recognizes that fecal soiling may be voluntary or involuntary, but many family physicians and pediatricians would not diagnose voluntary fecal soiling as Encopresis, and would most often diagnose Encopresis as a consequence of constipation. The *DSM-IV* defines two subtypes of Encopresis. The first is with constipation and the inappropriate passage of feces due to overflow of fecal matter. About 80% of cases of Encopresis fall into this category, which may be called *Retentive Encopresis.* It is often the case that a child suffering from Retentive Encopresis has experienced pain or discomfort associated with bowel movements, leading to voluntary retention of stool. As large amounts of fecal material are retained the rectum stretches to accommodate the increased mass. The larger the mass the more painful the elimination, and the greater the motivation to hold the stool. Ultimately, the mass becomes large enough that the rectum is stretched to the point that the sensation of needing to have a bowel movement disappears. Indeed, the abdominal mass that results from this series of events is large enough to externally palpate in about half of the children with Encopresis (Loening-Baucke, 1994). The inappropriate soiling in Retentive Encopresis occurs as fecal matter leaks around the mass and escapes from the anus without the child's knowing that this has occurred.

The second form of Encopresis occurs without constipation and overflow incontinence (APA, 1994) and accounts for about 20% of all cases of Encopresis (Kuhn, Marcus, & Pitner, 1999). It may be called *Nonretentive Encopresis.* Nonretentive Encopresis is usually associated with other behavioral problems, such as Oppositional Defiant Disorder or Conduct Disorder (DSM-IV, 1994).

In addition to the distinction between Retentive and Nonretentive Encopresis, this disorder is further defined as being either primary or secondary. If a child has not been continent of stool for at least one year the disorder is referred to as *Primary Encopresis.* If a 1-year period of continence can be documented, the disorder is classified as *Secondary Encopresis.* Fifty to 60% of all children with Encopresis have Secondary Encopresis (Howe & Walker, 1992). Secondary Encopresis may be traced to a significant change in the life of the child, such as the birth of a sibling, a move to a new house, or beginning school.

The prevalence of Encopresis varies by age and by sex. Boys are three to four times more likely than girls to develop Eencopresis and, not surprisingly, the frequency decreases with age. Between the ages of 4 and 5 years about 3.5 to 4% of boys and 1 to 1.5% of girls are encopretic, whereas by age 8, the frequency is about 2.3% in boys and 0.7% in girls. By age 12 the frequency is 1.3% in boys and 0.3% in girls (Kaplan & Sadock, 1991). In rare cases, Encopresis may continue into adulthood.

In making the differential diagnosis of Encopresis it is important to distinguish the disorder from others caused by organic pathology. Hirschprung's disease, or aganglionic megacolon, is chief among the organic disorders that may be confused with functional Encopresis. Aganglionic megacolon is a congenital disorder in which the colon becomes dilated due to lack of neural supply. The patient may have an uncontrollable overflow of feces, but the rectum will often be empty. One of the symptoms of other medical disorders, including hypothyroidism, diabetes insipidus, and early inflammatory bowel disease also may mimic some aspects of Encopresis, but the other signs and symptoms associated with these conditions make differential diagnosis relatively easy.

Because Encopresis is probably caused by the interaction of a number of variables, including physiological predisposition, pain upon defecation, and difficulties in toilet training, treatment will often be multifaceted (Levine & Bakow, 1976). The family as well as the child should be involved in the treatment. Family counseling and therapy directed toward reducing conflict between the parents and child is advised. Family therapy sessions may also be useful in identifying precipitating factors within the child's psychosocial milieu and changing attitudes toward toilet training, if the problem is Primary Encopresis and the child has not been continent for an extended period of time.

In addition to family counseling therapy and a full developmental and behavioral analysis of the child, the treatment strategy should take into account the type of Encopresis. For example, treatment of Nonretentive Encopresis will primarily utilize behavioral therapies, with the use of laxatives only if the stool is not soft enough to produce comfortable bowel movements. Daily, scheduled, positive toilet sits should then be conducted and reinforcement given for successful defecation during these sits (Kuhn et al., 1999).

In treating cases of Retentive Encopresis medical treatment is employed on a regular basis. This treatment involves using enemas for disimpaction and laxatives to promote bowel movements. However, relying on medical intervention alone diminishes the success rate of treatment of Encopresis. Cox and colleagues (1998) compared the effectiveness of (a) three months of treatment for Retentive Encopresis by medical treatment alone (enemas and laxatives); (b) medical treatment and enhanced toilet training employing reinforcement, scheduled toilet sits, and instruction and modeling to promote appropriate straining; or (c) medical treatment, toilet training, and biofeedback directed at relaxing the external anal sphincter during attempted defecation. They found that medical care alone reduced soilings per child by 21%, whereas enhanced toilet training and medical treatment caused a 76% reduction and biofeedback and medical treatment yielded a 65% reduction. Additionally, Cox and colleagues reported that enhanced toilet training significantly benefitted more children than either of the other two treatment regimens and that fewer laxatives and fewer training sessions were necessary. The results of this study of 87 children are in general agreement with many other studies that behavioral therapy is a necessary addition to medical therapy in treating Retentive Encopresis.

REFERENCES

American Psychiatric Association. (1994). *Diagnostic and Statistical Manual of Mental Disorders* (4th ed.). Washington, DC: Author.

Cox, D. J., Sutphen, J., Borowitz, S., Kovatchev, B., & Ling, W. (1998). Contribution of behavior therapy and biofeedback to laxative therapy in the treatment of pediatric encopresis. *Annals of Behavioral Medicine, 20,* 70–76.

Howe, A. C., & Walker, C. E. (1992). Behavioral management of toilet training, enuresis, and encopresis. *Pediatric Clinics of North America, 39,* 413–432.

Kaplan, H. I., & Sadock, B. J. (1991). *Synopsis of psychiatry* (6th ed.). Baltimore: Williams & Wilkins.

Kuhn, B. R., Marcus, B. A., & Pitner, S. L. (1999). Treatment guidelines for primary nonretentive encopresis and stool toileting refusal. *American Family Physician, 59,* 2171–2178.

Levine, M. D., & Bakow, H. (1976). Children with encopresis: A study of treatment outcome. *Pediatrics, 58,* 845–852.

Loening-Baucke, V. (1994). Assessment, diagnosis and treatment of constipation in childhood. *Journal of the WOCN, 21,* 49–58.

M. L. WOODRUFF
East Tennessee State University

BEHAVIOR MODIFICATION
BIOFEEDBACK
ENEURESIS
IRRITABLE BOWEL SYNDROME (IBS)
TOILET TRAINING

ENDLER, NORMAN S. (1931–   )

Norman Solomon Endler is Distinguished Research Professor in the department of psychology at York University, Toronto, Ontario. Endler is one of the leading authorities in the world on the interaction model of personality psychology. Other research areas of interest include anxiety, stress and coping, depression, and ECT.

Endler was born in Montreal, Quebec on May 2, 1931. He married Beatrice in 1955 and has two children, Mark and Marla, and three granddaughters. Endler received both his BS (1953) in mathematics and psychology and his MS (1954) in psychology from McGill University (Montreal) and his PhD (1958) in clinical psychology from the University of Illinois, Urbana. Endler taught at Pennsylvania State University and worked in their division of counseling before coming to York University in 1960 as a research associate, lecturer, and founding member of the department of psychology. At York University, he was the first director of the Student Counselling Service (1960–62), now called the Counselling and Development Centre. He became assistant professor in 1962, associate professor in 1965, professor of psychology in 1968, and distinguished research professor in 1995. Endler was the director of the graduate programme at York University from 1968 to 1971 and chair of psychology from 1974 to 1979.

While Endler has spent most of his professional career as a leading scholar at York University, he has also consulted at many other institutions, including the Toronto East General Hospital (1964–1984) and the Clarke Institute of Psychiatry (1972–1981). He has also held visiting professorships at many universities in Europe and North America, including the University of Stockholm (1973–1974), Oxford University (1978; 1993), the University of Florence (1985–1986), Stanford University (1979–1980; 1986), and the University of Santiago de Compostela (1996).

Additionally, Endler has impacted the community through his continuing work on the Council of Suicide Prevention and his contributions to public education. He is a founding member of the Council of Suicide Prevention, established in 1975 to facilitate suicide prevention in Toronto through public education, research, advocacy, and professional development. Endler chaired the Board of Directors in 1992–1993 and continues to serve on the board today. Endler has also given many public educational addresses to various organizations (e.g., Manic-Depressive Associations, Friends of Schizophrenics) and has been interviewed extensively in the major newspapers, and on radio and television, providing information and support for those suffering from mental illness.

Endler is a prolific scholar, having well over 200 publications (journal articles, books, chapters in books), plus over 100 technical reports. He has eight single or joint-author books, eight edited books, 173 articles in refereed journals published or in press, 66 book chapters, seven test manuals, and five psychometric tests. He has received significant funding from the Social Sciences and Research Council of Canada (SSHRC; 1979–1980; 1985–1986; 1991–1994; 1994–2001) and its predecessor, the Canada Council. Endler was a member of the Fellowship Selection Committee for Psychology and Education (Canada Council; 1970, 1971) and served as chairman of that committee (1972–1973). He has also chaired the Research Grants Adjudication Committee of SSHRC for psychology for two consecutive years (1997–1999) and was a member of the Killam Research Fellowship Selection Committee (Canada Council; 1982–1985). Endler has also received several Sabbatical Leave Fellowships throughout his career from Canada Council (1967–1968), SSHRC (1979–1980; 1985–1986) and York University (1993–1994; 1999–2000).

Endler's early experiments were on conformity, and made important contributions to social psychology. His subsequent studies in the person/social interaction were exciting investigations which signaled Endler as a leader in the field of social psychology. Following these seminal contributions, Endler's research expanded to cover aspects of clinical psychology and normal personality theorizing, including theoretical issues in depression and coping. Furthermore, Endler's clinical work extended to applied aspects of treatment (including electroconvulsive therapy) and assessment.

Endler and his colleagues have developed measures to assess both anxiety and coping. The Endler Multidimensional Anxiety Scales (EMAS) assess state anxiety, trait anxiety, and the perception of the situation. The Coping Inventory for Stressful Situations (CISS) assesses task-oriented, emotion-oriented, and avoidance-oriented coping. The CISS-Situation Specific Coping (CISS-SSC) measure assesses coping with specific stressful situations. Most recently, the Coping with Health Injuries and Problems (CHIP) scale has been developed. The CHIP assesses distraction, palliative, instrumental, and emotional preoccupation coping. Among his many books is *Holiday of Darkness: A Psychologist's Personal Journey Out of His Depression.* Additionally, Endler coedited the *Handbook of Coping* with M. Zeidner.

Endler's approach to research has been varied and integrative. Through his work in interactionist approaches to how people deal with environmental changes and stressors, Endler has argued for the explicit and systematic consideration of biological factors to be integrated with siuationism in psychological models in order to explain behavior and personality. As a result of Endler's approach, insight, and talent, his work is held in the highest esteem internationally, and he is among the world's top researchers in these areas.

In recognition of these outstanding achievements, Endler has received many awards and honors. In 1977, Endler received the Queen Elizabeth II Silver Jubilee Medal. He has been an editorial consultant or board member of nearly all of the national and international journals of social psychology. He became a fellow of the Royal Society of Canada in 1986 and is also a fellow of the Canadian Psychological Association and of the American Psychological Association. During 1987–89, Endler was a Killam Research Fellow, Canada Council. In 1988, Endler received an Award of Merit from the Ontario Psychological Association. He received the title of distinguished research professor at York University in 1995. In 1997, he received the Innis-Gérin medal for Distinguished and Sustained Contribution to the literature of the social sciences, including psychology, from the Royal Society of Canada. Also in 1997, Endler received the Donald O. Hebb Award for Distinguished Contribution to Psychology as a Science from the Canadian Psychological Association. In 2000, Endler received the Deans Award for outstanding research.

STAFF

ENDORPHINS/ENKEPHALINS

During the late 1970s and early 1980s, component parts of the polypeptide β-lipotropin began to receive a great deal of attention. Besides the adrenocorticotropic hormone (ACTH), which was already known as an adrenal gland stimulant involved with physiological arousal states, β-lipotropin includes a sequence of 30 amino acids called β-endorphins. Enkephalin is a small segment of this sequence. Endorphins are found in the pituitary gland and parts of the brain. While animal studies have allowed direct access to brain tissue, human research has primarily been limited to the measurement of blood plasma endorphin levels.

Endorphins are similar to the opiate morphine in both chemical structure and effect. Hence, the contraction "endogenous" + "orphine" = endorphin. The primary effect of endorphins appears to be analgesic. The similar analgesic effects of morphine and endorphins are blocked by naloxone, a well-known opiate antagonist. Enkephalins also produce analgesic effects, but the effect is weaker and of shorter duration than that of endorphins. This, together with some evidence (Pert, 1981) that the brain consumes endorphins in response to pain, has contributed to speculation that enkephalins may simply be by-products of incompletely consumed endorphins.

In addition to their analgesic properties, endorphins have been linked to thermoregulation, appetite, memory, lipolysis, reproduction, pleasure experiences, fat breakdown, antidiuresis, depression of the ventilatory response to carbon dioxide, and inhibition of thyrotropin and gonadotropin. There is also some evidence that endorphins are responsible for some of the pain relief attributed to the placebo effect. One theory holds that acupuncture stimulates endorphin secretion.

Stress—both physical (e.g., exercise, pain) and psychological (e.g., conditioned fear) seems to stimulate endorphin secretion. One form of physical stress that has been linked to endorphins is aerobic exercise, particularly running. Carr and associates (1981), as well as several other researchers, have found increased endorphin levels in individuals who have recently exercised at what was considered an intense level, given their level of conditioning. Although plasma endorphin levels usually return to baseline within 30 min of the completion of exercise, Appenzeller (1981) suggested that endorphins are responsible for the so-called runner's high and exercise addiction described by some frequent exercisers. Others (Moore, 1982) have speculated that endorphins play a role in the lessened sensitivity to pain reported by many athletes who are injured while performing. There is further speculation that the successful use of exercise in treating some mildly depressed individuals may be related to abnormal endorphin levels sometimes found in psychiatric patients.

REFERENCES

Appenzeller, O. (1981). What makes us run? *New England Journal of Medicine, 305,* 578–580.

Carr, D. B., Bullen, B. A., Skrinar, G. A., Arnold, M. A., Rosenblatt, M., Bettins, I. Z., Martin, J. B., & McArthur, J. (1981). Physical conditioning facilitates the exercise-induced secretion of beta-endorphin and beta-lipotropin in women. *New England Journal of Medicine, 305,* 560–563.

Moore, M. (1982). Endorphins and exercise: A puzzling relationship. *The Physician and Sports Medicine, 10*(2), 111–114.

Pert, A. (1981). The body's own tranquilizers. *Psychology Today, 15*(9), 100.

SUGGESTED READING

Bolles, R. C., & Faneslow, M. S. (1982). Endorphins and behavior. *Annual Review of Psychology, 33,* 87–101.

Hughes, J., Smith, T. W., Kosterlitz, H. W., Fothergill, L. A., Morgan, B. A., & Morris, H. R. (1975). Identification of two related pentapeptides from the brain with potent opiate agonist activity. *Nature, 258,* 577–579.

J. R. CAUTELA
Boston College

A. J. KEARNEY
Behavior Therapy Institute

CENTRAL NERVOUS SYSTEM
HOMEOSTASIS
NEUROCHEMISTRY
PSYCHOPHARMACOLOGY

ENGINEERING PSYCHOLOGY

Though perhaps several thousand psychologists in the United States and as many elsewhere call their subdiscipline "engineering psychology," the term is both unclear and somewhat of a misnomer, persisting through tradition and organizational inertia; Division 21 of the American Psychological Association until 1983 was "The Society of Engineering Psychologists," and its hybrid composition long frustrated efforts to adopt a more suitable name. The field might better be named "psychology for modern technology." It is that branch of psychology that examines human behavior as it relates to the equipment, computer software, environments, and human-machine systems that characterize modern technology. Primarily, it has asked: What are the capabilities and limitations of human performance in using technology and its products? How should people and machines be shaped to fit each other? Here machines must be interpreted to include the creations not only of engineers but also of computer programmers and analysts, architects, training developers, and planners.

Clearly, engineering psychologists often find themselves closely associated with these other disciplines, as well as with physical anthropology and physiology. The title of this article reflects an initial and continuing association with engineering, the principal source of technology, and the subdiscipline's vocabulary has drawn on engineering for such terms as input, output, coding, feedback, and information channel. Within psychology, engineering psychologists border not only on experimental psychology, in which most early engineering psychologists were trained, but also on organizational and industrial, personnel, and operant subdisciplines. They are distinguished by their emphasis on the physical features of technology as the sources of inputs to human behavior and the recipients of outputs. Because technology so greatly influences modern life, engineering psychology would seem to have considerable significance. Its growth is tied to that of the multidisciplinary field of human factors (overseas, "ergonomics"). Many, if not most, American engineering psychologists identify themselves also as human factors scientists, and some who engage in applications as human factors engineers.

HISTORY

Conventionally, the origin of engineering psychology is placed in World War II, with its major technological innovations in weaponry, aircraft, submarines, and radar. The demands these innovations imposed on psychomotor skills and information processing seemed at times to exceed human capabilities. As a result, lives might be lost—and worse, the battle. Things had to work right the first time; traditional trial-and-error development was not enough. With such a driving influence, military organizations began to foster engineering psychology to find out what operators of such new equipment could actually accomplish with it—where they might succeed or fail. Problems lay not only in the designs of displays and controls but in the workloads operators confronted and the environments in which they functioned. Tasks had to be accomplished within certain time limits and as free of error as possible. Past laboratory studies of psychophysics and psychomotor activity did not disclose enough about what people can and cannot do; investigations had to be directed toward special, more complex sensing, processing, and control activation, involving particular inputs from equipment to operators and their outputs to manage it. Because some of the new technological marvels had to be operated in high-altitude and undersea environments hostile to human beings, it became necessary to find out how their performance was affected by increased or reduced atmospheric pressures, increased or reduced accelerations, noise, heat, cold, and vibration. The biological impacts of these conditions were studied by medical investigators and psychophysiologists such as Ross McFarland, who was also a distinguished engineering psychologist.

With the advent of space missions, such inquiry became even more urgent. Equipment had to be designed (with engineering psychologists' support) to allow for human inadequacies, then tested (again with such support) to see whether it did the job. Combinations of humans and machines—especially air defense centers, shipboard combat information centers, and ballistic missile complexes—were called human-machine systems. Engineering psychologists helped engineers design and test these systems—a far cry from the knobs and dials focus with which engineering psychology started. Later such involvement in system design extended to other human-machine complexes, such as air-traffic control centers and power plants; the driving force behind the development was again life and death—as well as financial loss.

Military support continued for engineering psychology in a number of ways after World War II. For example, the Office of Naval Research funded a substantial research program led by Alphonse Chapanis at Johns Hopkins University, also an early one at New York University and later ones at many other universities and locations. The Army established a Human Engineering Laboratory that employed many engineering psychologists. The Air Force's Aerospace Medical Research Laboratory conducted extensive research itself and supported it elsewhere. When the Air Force began to require its contractors to conform to new requirements for human factors engineering in system and equipment design, contractors formed human factors groups in their engineering departments that included engineering psychologists. The first was at Hughes Aircraft under the aegis of Alexander Williams; other major aerospace concerns followed: Lockheed, Douglas, McDonnell (becoming McDonnell Douglas), Boeing, and Honeywell. The Navy and Army established similar requirements, which became consolidated in Department of Defense regulations and standards.

Given such employment opportunities, experimental psychologists moved into engineering psychology, and graduate courses were established. Some engineering psychologists worked in laboratory research, some in development or applications, some in both. Military aircraft absorbed most of the effort, though engineering psychologists worked on almost all new equipment and systems. When the National Aeronautics and Space Administration was established, it also supported research and development by engineering psychologists. A large number of consulting companies were formed, funded largely by Department of Defense or NASA contracts. Although a National Academy of Sciences report urged more support for engineering psychology, it received very little assistance from the National Science Foundation, perhaps because its orientation seemed too applied.

Engineering psychology had actually begun before World War II—on a very small scale—with the printed word. Though printing as a technological development had been with us for a long time, experimental psychology had not. Early in the 20th century a few psychologists sought to apply the experimental method to printing to make print easier to use—that is, read—in work described by Paterson and Tinker in *How to Make Type Readable,* and

by Tinker in *Legibility of Print.* Some research on legibility and readability continued over the years, involving not only books and media but also highway signs, instruction manuals, license plates, and cathode ray tubes. More recently engineering psychologists have investigated comprehension of printed commands, data, error messages, and the like in interactive computer systems. Since a purchaser might prefer the interactive system that was more comprehensible, financial motivation invigorated this field of research and application.

Although military work has been given the credit for the growth of engineering psychology since World War II, some commercial support also developed early, first at the Bell Telephone Laboratories, then at International Business Machines and other large corporations. In subsequent years nonmilitary research, development, and applications increased, as evidenced in the number and size of in-house human factors groups as well as human factors consulting organizations, though often it was difficult to sort out what proportions could be claimed by engineering psychology. Product effectiveness for the user resulting from engineering psychology has seldom been an outstanding advertising feature in the competition for sales, though it might become so if prospective purchasers were more aware of it. However, product hazard has indeed become a driver, and engineering psychologists have been testifying more and more as expert witnesses in product liability litigation.

Product effectiveness is not the concern of engineering psychologists alone. Engineers can design automobiles to brake better or accelerate faster without their help. However, the threat to life and limb in motorcars fostered some engineering psychology as early as 1928, as reported by Lauer in *The Psychology of Driving: Factors of Traffic Enforcement,* and as subsequently recorded by Forbes in *Human Factors in Highway Traffic Safety Research.* Thanks in part to Ralph Nader, the Federal government eventually established the National Highway Traffic Safety Administration, which along with the Federal Highway Administration employs a number of engineering psychologists, as do the major automobile manufacturers—General Motors, Ford, and Chrysler. The Federal Aviation Administration has also made use of engineering psychology. Roscoe's *Aviation Psychology* described a substantial body of technology-oriented research in commercial aviation. The National Institute of Occupational Health and Safety and the Bureau of Mines have also turned to engineering psychology for help in reducing occupational accidents and loss of life, limb, or money. But engineering psychology has rarely penetrated the factory. The work-related design of industrial machinery was preempted early by industrial engineers, while industrial psychologists concerned themselves with organizational and personnel problems. Eventually, however, engineering psychologists began to investigate robotics as a significant form of automation still requiring human involvement. They also studied quality control, since human error is a major target of engineering psychology—and an important factor in productivity.

For more complete accounts of engineering psychology's history, the reader can consult chapters on engineering psychology in the *Annual Review of Psychology* (1958, 1960, 1963, 1966, 1971, 1976) and articles or chapters by Fitts (1951, 1963), Taylor (1957, 1963), Grether (1968), and Christensen (1971).

FOCAL POINTS IN REAL-WORLD APPLICATIONS

Outside academia, engineering psychology has concentrated on some particular aspects of human performance as dependent variables, and on various categories of equipment, environments, and systems as independent variables affecting these performance aspects. Its work has been applied to diverse human-machine aggregates. The dependent variables have largely though not exclusively consisted of: the time needed and accuracy attained in a particular performance; components of human information processing, decision making, monitoring and vigilance; inspection and signal detection accidents, auditory communication, psychomotor skills and skill acquisition; continuous manual control (tracking); reading, stress and fatigue; and various kinds of workload capacity. Categories of independent variables include: systems, automation, tasks, controls and control devices; displays (including print); equipment and tool design; workload (mental and physical); work-rest cycles; procedures, maintenance activities and information feedback; training techniques and devices; and ambient conditions (illumination, glare, noise, temperature, vibration, acceleration, and atmospheric pressure).

Among the human-machine aggregates have been aircraft (military and commercial), submarines, spacecraft, radar, sonar, undersea habitats, air-traffic control, highway transportation, automobiles, urban transportation, postal operations, residential environments, offices, telephonic and radio communications, nuclear power plants, mining, interactive computers, missile systems, command and control systems, health care delivery, and law enforcement.

UNIVERSITIES

Despite overlaps, engineering psychology has had a somewhat different role within American university psychology departments than elsewhere. For one thing, engineering psychologists in universities teach graduate students (who subsequently receive essential on-the-job training in industry or government, if they enter these to make a living). A number of American universities have graduate curricula and give graduate degrees in engineering psychology, and some (for example, the Air Force Academy) teach it to undergraduates. However, the number has been shrinking for several reasons: (a) Graduate work in human factors, including much of engineering psychology, has been shifting to engineering departments, notably industrial engineering; (b) employer needs have emphasized training in cross-disciplinary applications rather than in experimental research, though quite a few employers still regard the latter as an important qualification; (c) psychology departments dominated by experimental psychologists tend to derogate engineering psychologists on the grounds that their research is too mundane—that is, insufficiently theoretical (though at the same time, ironically, experimental psychologists have been exploring potentials in applied research so their students can obtain employment after graduation).

Most university research in engineering psychology tries to be basic—that is, abstract or highly generalizable—although some is applied—applicable to the processes and products of modern technology. Strong views have been expressed on behalf of each emphasis. A major research interest is human information processing, which largely originated in engineering psychology in the United States and Great Britain, in dealing with technological problems. But human information processing has also become a major focus of experimental psychology, which takes it as a virtual synonym for cognition. Where, then, is the dividing line in research between engineering and experimental psychology?

In human information processing, "information" seems to be a newer term for stimuli—inputs into an individual's sensory apparatus; processing involves what might earlier have been subsumed under perception, attention, memory, and choice or discrimination. Reaction time is a favorite dependent variable. A number of examples illustrate the difference between applied (engineering) and basic (experimental) research. Applied research showed that if an actual switch, knob, or stick on a console were moved to the right, the indicator or signal it controlled should appear or be moved to the right—not to the left—so as to reduce errors and reaction times. Further research with synthetic stimulus and response arrays of pushbuttons and lamps in a variety of spatial arrangements further demonstrated stimulus-response compatibility. Conducted in a laboratory, this early research was published in an experimental, not an applied, journal (but probably would not have been later). More recently, research under the joint label of human information processing and experimental psychology has sought to identify some theoretical stage of in-the-head processing to explain S-R compatibility.

In another illustration, a British investigator studied air-traffic controllers receiving coinciding messages from pilots over the same loudspeaker. Success in getting clearer messages with a loudspeaker for each sound source led to research in processing stimuli close to each other or coinciding in time, and to models or theories of human channel capacity and filtering. The visual and auditory stimuli were simpler and thus more abstract—they were no longer pilots' messages. Together with its modeling and theorizing, this research has come to be viewed by some as experimental rather than engineering.

In still another example, engineering psychologists have employed extraneous secondary tasks to increase the workload faced, for instance, by a pilot operating a cockpit simulator; the purpose can be to determine maximum capacity on the primary task, when any reserve capacity is exhausted. Such time sharing has been investigated in experimental psychology laboratories to find out how different kinds of nonpilot primary and secondary tasks interact, and to construct theoretical models of information-processing capacities.

Whatever it is called, such basic research in academia may be able to guide engineering psychologists facing practical problems, such as helping an engineer design a complex display panel in a nuclear power plant, so an operator will not be overloaded with information and can filter out data of less importance. But such translations may not be easy, if the information (the stimulus) is very different in the laboratory from that in the power plant. On the other hand, if the translation is too easy, the laboratory research risks being called engineering rather than experimental, and the investigator receives less credit as a scientist from departmental colleagues. Similar dilemmas have marked interfaces between other basic and applied sciences.

Theorizing, to which many experimental psychologists appear partial, comes more easily when variables seem unrelated to some technological problem. Thus color discrimination in coding for a display belongs to engineering psychology, but experimental psychology examines its theoretical basis. "Coding" means some way of representing the external world. Such representation in a machine, for operator processing, has been a major interest in engineering psychology; information is coded. When the machine is a computer, most of such coding is alphanumeric (including language). With an increasing focus on computers, engineering psychology has been investigating language as an information-processing medium—but so has experimental psychology, or at least it has been investigating information processing with language as the medium. Thus the difference between them has become blurred; inputs as well as outputs are much alike in each, in contrast to the marked differences when engineering psychology was oriented more toward psychomotor skills.

TECHNIQUES

Experimentation has been the primary investigative technique of both university and nonuniversity engineering psychology—one reason that academic training in experimental psychology has been useful. Experiments are conducted in laboratories, in field settings, and in mixes of the two. Some experiments outside academia are oriented toward general problems but most have some particular goal, such as to evaluate how well an operator performs with some specific equipment, or to compare alternative displays or machines when operated by humans. The dependent variables are not necessarily the same in these two kinds of particular experiments. In the former, the time an individual takes or the errors the individual makes in reacting to a component can (but may not) be isolated, so only human performance is being measured—although, as Taylor, an early engineering psychologist, pointed out, it is often difficult to exclude that of the machine component entirely. In the latter kind of experiments—the comparison of alternative devices—the investigator measures the joint output of the device and the operator. It has been questioned whether the study of such combinations constitutes psychology. One reason justifying a psychologist's participation is the relative unfamiliarity of most engineers with experimental design, especially with respect to human variables.

When combinations of human operators and machines become large and complex, experiments evaluating them have been called human-machine system experiments, and the investigators, system psychologists. Such experiments are similarly large and complex, and experimental subjects function as teams or crews. Investigators have made comparisons between two designs for an operations center; have assessed system capabilities, as for example how many aircraft an air control center can bring into an airport in an hour; and have diagnosed problems, such as which system components or subsystems (including operators) should be held responsible for some particular level of system performance. In addition to design factors, such system experiments have investigated procedures, skill levels, and training methods. Generally they simulate parts of the system or its environment. Though such research

rarely gets reported in journals, more than 200 experiments in approximately 50 programs between 1950 and 1970 were described by Parsons in *Man-Machine System Experiments;* the most cited investigator was Sinaiko.

Most nonacademic experimentation in engineering psychology takes place, however, on components within a system—on display design, maintenance procedure, skill requirement, or training device. Here, too, simulation is one of the principal tools, often created for the study. It consists, for example, of a mockup or of signals seen on a cathode ray tube. Some experimentation is exploration for discovery; some is verification for certainty. Experimental designs have been developed to combine these stages by putting all seemingly important independent variables into an experiment at the start, screening them by means of fractional factorials with only two states per variable, then sequentially refining the design with fewer variables and more replication. "Response surface methodology," adapted by Charles W. Simon, has exemplified such approaches, as has central composite design described by Williges (1981).

Engineering psychology employs additional ways to gather data such as observations of real-world operations, examination of archival sources, and systematic querying of operators and maintainers to obtain their self-reports. Such self-report data from interviews or questionnaires are particularly useful in providing insights into problems that can then be studied more objectively. For example, an operator is asked to recall critical incidents resulting from a design flaw, a faulty procedure, or inadequate training. Operators are not too reliable in reporting their own levels of performance or the relative advantages of two different equipments; however, if they have been trained to become experts and are furnished well-tested rating scales, their self-report data may be better than no data at all.

A number of analytic techniques are used by engineering psychologists. Foremost is task description and analysis. This technique sets forth in detail what a person does step by step in operating or maintaining some equipment, relating each action to some input (e.g., from a display), to some control device, perhaps to some choice or decision, and to any feedback. In a sense, such analysis constitutes a verbal simulation of performance. When added to such a description, the time taken for each action, the probability of error, and the skill level needed furnish a substantial basis for equipment design, procedure development and documentation, skill requirements, and the development of training methods and equipment. However, it is often difficult to provide reliable time and error data before equipment is built, since there has been no comprehensive task taxonomy or accompanying data base. A related technique is computer modeling of human and machine performance. Data similar to those for task analysis are programmed into a computer, which can then be used to vary nontask factors such as workload, design changes, or procedural differences, to determine how these alter the time and accuracy of a task. The computer model's findings are reliable, however, only to the extent that the inputs it gets are reliable.

On the basis of their data gathering, experimentation, and analysis, engineering psychologists produce reports, briefings, and face-to-face consultation with system developers, design engineers, and others. Reports contain generalizable knowledge or specific findings. They may be transformed into presentations at professional gatherings or journal articles, or may remain reports with little circulation, possibly for proprietary or security reasons. Briefings and consultation are more effective methods of getting recommendations adopted, but are evanescent. As a result, much of what engineering psychologists accomplish in the actual design of some equipment or system remains unknown to other psychologists and to the public. (In that sense they resemble clinical psychologists in private practice.) Further, their individual contributions may not be apparent within a team effort. It is difficult to determine from the published word what engineering psychology has actually done to shape technology.

ORGANIZATIONS AND PUBLICATIONS

Engineering psychologists make up a division of the American Psychological Association and participate in that association's annual meetings. Without a technical journal of their own, they generally publish in *Human Factors,* the journal of the Human Factors Society to which many or most belong, or in *Ergonomics,* the journal of the Ergonomics Society (in England) and the International Ergonomics Association. The APA Division of Applied Experimental and Engineering Psychology is an amalgam of varied professionals, some from universities, some from government, some from industry; some concentrate on research, some on development or applications; some identify more as experimental psychologists, some as human factors engineers. One of its members, Conrad Craft, was the first recipient of the American Psychological Association's annual Distinguished Scientific Award for Applications of Psychology. Chapanis and Fleishman were later winners of the award.

Outside the United States, engineering psychology occupies a strong position in many states of the former Soviet Union, where it is a well-supported field of psychology with considerably more public recognition than in the United States. At least one of its leading investigators and teachers, Boris Lomov, is also prominent in the Academy of Science of the former U.S.S.R. (Two American psychologists who worked in engineering psychology have belonged to the National Academy of Sciences, though their work in engineering psychology was apparently not the primary basis for such recognition.) Great Britain and various continental nations have produced distinguished engineering psychologists as well, such as Broadbent and Bartlett.

PROSPECTS

As long as technology continues to evolve and produce new processes in which humans participate or new products they use, there will be a continuing need for engineering psychology, or at least for psychologists concerned with the interactions between technology and people. The term "engineering psychology," however, may not survive, nor the separate identity of such psychologists in universities. For those elsewhere, their continuity and growth will depend on various factors: involvement in new technological innovations such as robotics, interactive computers, and office automation; ex-

tending their interests beyond skilled performance; and the driving factors (such as life and death and financial gain or loss) that make their contributions to a technological world seem important to those who create it. (In the absence of such factors, for example, work in environmental design as a facet of engineering psychology has languished for lack of funding, despite much intellectual interest.)

The outstanding development in technology is automation—in the factory and office as well as in various products. Of increasing uncertainty is the extent to which something can or should be automated—an industrial process, paperwork, transportation, teaching, a toothbrush, or the game of chess. To proponents of artificial intelligence there appear to be no limits technically—at least, in the future. Presently, human beings remain in the act. But what should their roles be? What will they continue to do that intelligent machines cannot? Engineering psychologists can help resolve that issue, by continuing to reveal human capabilities and limitations (especially cognitive) in technology-related performance, at the same time examining with some skepticism what intelligent machines can and cannot do. Adopting Licklider's notion of man-machine symbiosis, engineering psychology can investigate how humans and machines can best work together to cope with the complexity and variety that characterize our world, which neither humans nor machines can comprehend alone.

But engineering psychology is also challenged to broaden its perspective. There is more to the impact of technology on human behavior than skilled performance. How people feel, why they act as they do, their relationships with others—these emotional, motivational, and social variables are also influenced by technology, and in turn influence the shape it takes. Because these considerations demand systematic inquiry into the physical world of technology, virtually all psychologists have left them unattended, or attended only superficially. Engineering psychology—or psychology for modern technology—seems the logical candidate to fill this void. Indeed, one of its pioneers, Paul Fitts, once said it should encompass stressors, motivation, and social consequences. In this way it can orient technology to human advantage.

REFERENCES

Christensen, J. M. (1971). The emerging role of engineering psychology. In W. C. Howell & I. L. Goldstein (Eds.), *Engineering psychology: Current perspectives in research.* New York: Appleton-Century-Crofts.

Fitts, P. M. (1951). Engineering psychology and equipment design. In S. S. Stevens (Ed.), *Handbook of experimental psychology.* New York: Wiley.

Fitts, P. M. (1963). Engineering psychology. In S. Koch (Ed.), *Psychology: A study of a science* (Vol. 5). New York: McGraw-Hill.

Grether, W. F. (1968). Engineering psychology in the United States. *American Psychologist, 23,* 743-751.

Lauer, A. R. (1960). *The psychology of driving: Factors of traffic enforcement.* Springfield, IL: Thomas.

Parsons, H. M. (1972). *Man-machine system experiments.* Baltimore: Johns Hopkins Press.

Paterson, D. G., & Tinker, M. A. (1940). *How to make type readable.* New York: Harpers.

Roscoe, S. N. (1980). *Aviation psychology.* Ames, IA: Iowa State University Press.

Taylor, F. V. (1957). Psychology and the design of machines. *American Psychologist 12,* 249–258.

Taylor, F. V. (1963). Human engineering and psychology. In S. Koch (Ed.), *Psychology: A study of a science* (Vol. 5). New York: McGraw-Hill.

Tinker, M. A. (1963). *Legibility of print.* Ames, IA: Iowa State University Press.

Williges, R. C. (1981). Development and use of research methodologies for complex system/simulation experimentation. In M. J. Moraal & K. F. Kraiss (Eds.), *Manned system design.* New York: Plenum.

SUGGESTED READING

De Greene, K. B. (1970). *Systems psychology.* New York: McGraw-Hill.

Howell, W. C., & Goldstein, I. L. (Eds.). (1971). *Engineering psychology: Current perspectives in research.* New York: Appleton-Century-Crofts.

Kantowitz, B. H. (1982). Interfacing human information processing and engineering psychology. In W. C. Howell & E. A. Fleishman (Eds.), *Human performance and productivity: Information processing and decision making* (Vol. 2). Hillsdale, NJ: Erlbaum.

Parsons, H. M. (1976). Psychology for engineering and technology. In P. J. Woods (Ed.), *Career opportunities for psychologists: Expanding and emerging areas.* Washington, DC: American Psychological Association.

H. M. Parsons
Human Resources Research Organization

INFORMATION PROCESSING
PSYCHOPHYSICS
TASK DESIGN

genetic or constitutional factors such as delays in maturation of bladder control or neurological sleep disturbances, failures in toilet training, disturbed intrafamily relationships, and acute stress of life changes such as the birth of a sibling or the loss of a parent. Most cases of functional enuresis spontaneously remit. The need for treatment typically results from the unpleasantness of the disorder and its implications for the child's interpersonal functioning (e.g., disapproval from family members and ridicule from peers).

Treatment of enuresis depends upon the presumed etiology. The most common medication used is imipramine (Tofranil). After gradual withdrawal of imipramine, many children remain dry through the night, as reported by Rapoport and colleagues (1980). Psychological approaches have included bladder control training by practicing the retention of fluids and increasing the child's sensitivity to changes in bladder distension (Kimmel & Kimmel, 1970); bell-and-pad devices for the bed that emit an auditory signal when moisture completes the circuit in an electrical grid (Taylor & Turner, 1975); and awakening the child during the night to urinate (Samaan, 1972).

REFERENCES

Kimmel, H. D., & Kimmel, E. (1970). An instrumental conditioning method for the treatment of enuresis. *Journal of Behavior Therapy and Experimental Psychiatry, 1,* 121–123.

Rapoport, J. I., Mikkelson, E. J., Zavadil, A., Nee, L., Gruenau, C., Mendelson, W., & Gillin, C. (1980). Childhood enuresis. *Archives of General Psychiatry, 37,* 1146–1152.

Samaan, M. (1972). The control of nocturnal enuresis by operant conditioning. *Journal of Behavior Therapy and Experimental Psychiatry, 3,* 103–105.

Taylor, P. D., & Turner, R. K. (1975). A clinical trial of continuous, intermittent and overlearning "bell-and-pad" treatments for nocturnal enuresis. *Behavior Research and Therapy, 13,* 281–293.

T. S. Bennett
Brain Inquiry Recovery Program

FAMILY THERAPY
TOILET TRAINING

ENURESIS

Enuresis is involuntary urination beyond the age at which one is expected to have learned bladder control. Functional enuresis is the term applied when the disorder is presumed not to have a primary physical cause. While enuresis can occur during waking hours, it is more common during sleep. Minimum numbers of episodes per month for different age groups have been established arbitrarily for the diagnosis to be made. The incidence of enuresis is higher among boys than girls (*DSM-III*).

There are multiple etiologies of enuresis. Factors that may contribute to the development of enuresis are genitourinary disorders,

ENVIRONMENTAL PSYCHOLOGY

Environmental psychology is a specialized area that studies the relationships between behavior and the environmental context in which it occurs. Behavior here refers to both overt and covert acts, and includes thoughts, emotions and so on. The environment refers to one's physical surroundings. Although environmental psychologists incorporate aspects of social environment in their work (e.g., family, reference groups), their primary focus is the influence of the physical environment. Thus much of the research subsumed under environmental psychology deals with the influences of noise, air pollution, extreme temperatures, and the ways in which architectural designs structure space.

Although environmental psychology did not develop into a coherent subdiscipline until the late 1960s, there has been some recognition of the importance of the environment in determining behavior for many years. The roots of experimental psychology were in controlled investigations of light, pressure, and other environmental events. Unfortunately, this interest was in discrete stimuli, so that studies of light were nothing like real-life exposure to varying intensities of light. Instead, they were studies of human sensation of isolated physical stimuli. Later, behavioral psychology recognized the importance of the environment in controlling behavior, but the environment as defined usually consisted of reinforcement schedules or isolated elements pulled out of an environmental setting. Although use of the word "environment" was common by the 1950s, it was used somewhat differently from how modern environmental psychology uses it.

The first approximation of this modern use of "environment" was provided by Lewin (1951), who believed that behavior (B) is determined by personality (P) and environment (E). Hence the equation $B = f(P,E)$. Even though Lewin's use of environment was largely social, it was a whole environment rather than a small piece of a setting pulled out of context and administered in controlled trials. With Lewin came an initial expression of the notion that the environmental context of behavior is an important determinant of it.

In the years between 1950 and 1970, the concept of environment grew slowly toward the rich contextual role in behavior that Lewin had envisioned. Festinger, Schachter, and Back (1950) conducted studies of friendship formation and group development in the physical context of a housing project. They reported clear influences of the layout of the project on these social processes. Subsequently, human factors researchers began considering technological environments such as an airplane cockpit, and applied psychology toward determining how different designs influenced human response.

By 1970 there were researchers calling themselves environmental psychologists and studying environmental contexts and consequent behavior. Proshansky, Ittelson, and Rivlin (1970) studied the ways in which the physical design of psychiatric wards affected the behavior of patients and staff. Sommer (1969) conducted research on the ways in which people use space to regulate the intensity and appropriateness of their interactions with other people. He found, for example, that the space people maintain between themselves and others with whom they are interacting varies with a number of factors. People increase the amount of space between themselves and others when the others are of higher status, are unfamiliar or unknown, are stigmatized, and so on. Research also suggested that physical barriers or architectural features that increased or decreased the impact or prominence of others' presence (e.g., walls, decor that hides other people, etc.) also influenced the ways in which people use space in interaction (Baum, Riess, & O'Hara, 1974; Desor, 1972).

Environmental psychology views the environment as a whole rather than as a bundle of stimuli. A traditional psychologist interested in the effects of noise, for example, would study noises by exposing subjects to sounds under "sterile" laboratory conditions. The environmental psychologist would argue that responses to noise in a laboratory could very well be different from those in the real world, where noise occurs in its natural context. The laboratory would not be abandoned, but supplemented with field research.

Glass and Singer (1972) conducted an extensive series of studies on the effects of urban stress. Most of their research dealt with noise exposure and was conducted in the laboratory. This approach allowed them to identify effects of noise and revealed that control and predictability reduced the effects. However, it did not provide tests in real-world settings. Subsequent research applied these laboratory findings to field settings. Cohen, Glass, and Singer (1973) studied the effects of highway noise in a New York City apartment complex, and Cohen, Evans, Krantz, and Stokols (1980) examined the effects of aircraft noise on children attending school near the Los Angeles International Airport. These studies provided information about naturalistic exposure to noise. The laboratory finding that having control over the environment reduces the impact of stressful events was extended to conditions other than noise. Control was found to reduce stress on crowded commuter trains and in high-pressure work settings (Frankenhaeuser & Gardell, 1976; Singer, Lundberg, & Frankenhaeuser, 1978).

A somewhat different example is provided by research on crowding and architectural design in college dormitories (Baum & Valins, 1977). This research found that, given comparable amounts of space and identical numbers of people, different architectural arrangements of space were associated with different levels of crowding. One type of design housed people in relatively large groups and engendered more crowding than did designs that clustered students in smaller groups. Initial observation of students in crowded dormitories suggested that they were relatively withdrawn. Subsequent laboratory research substantiated this and further suggested that students were actively avoiding social contact with people who were not personal friends. Moving back to the field, Baum and Valins found this to be true in the dormitory as well as in the laboratory, and also identified the development of learned helplessness among some crowded students. Subsequent laboratory research substantiated and refined these findings as well.

The use of the laboratory to substantiate and/or refine findings from field settings was more deliberate in the program of research discussed than is usually the case. Environmental psychologists generally prefer to move freely among several research approaches. Laboratory findings must also be studied under the harsh light of the real world. However, since it is often difficult to maintain good experimental procedures in the field, laboratory work is often needed to eliminate alternatives and to refine concepts. These problems result in pressures to abandon experimental rigor for mundane realism, but for the most part they have been resisted in favor of a more balanced approach.

Another characteristic of environmental psychology is its emphasis on the interrelatedness of environment and behavior. The environment clearly constrains behavior, provides varying options in some instances, and influences behavior more subtly at other times. However, people also cope by changing their environments. In an office, a particular arrangement of space may affect employee social interaction. One means of changing interaction is to change the furniture arrangement, which of course changes the environment's effect on the employees. Environment-behavior relationships are more or less in flux continuously.

Research in environmental psychology tends to be problem-oriented. Most work is directed toward solving problems, as for example ameliorating the effects of environmental stressors. Few, if any, theoretical orientations guide research across problem areas. Conceptual frameworks have been proposed for a number of problem areas, but they are secondary to work directly applied toward understanding or solving problems. Those theories that do exist are rarely used to explain more than one or two areas within environmental psychology.

There are, of course, exceptions. One is the stress model, which has been used to integrate research on a number of environmental stressors, including crowding, noise, and temperature. Basically, this approach posits that all stressors have similar effects. Generally this is meant to include psychological and physiological specific coping mechanisms. This is because many coping behaviors are specific to the event evoking the stress response. For example, one might cope with noise by closing one's window, turning up the stereo, inserting ear plugs, and the like. One should not expect to find these same coping responses in a crowded setting or during a summer heat wave.

The notion of nonspecific stress response—that people respond to all stressors in much the same way—is derived from the work of Selye (1956), who identified common responses to many different noxious agents and formulated a general adaptation syndrome to explain response to these agents.

Subsequent elaboration of the stress concept has identified appraisal as an important mechanism, explaining specific coping responses (Lazarus, 1966). In addition, differences in response to different stressors have been found (Mason, 1975). By and large, however, research has found that common responses to different stressors outweigh these differences, and at least two environmental events, noise and crowding, appear to influence behavior in a similar manner (Baum, Singer, & Baum, 1981; Cohen, 1980).

A more general orientation within environmental psychology is called *determinism*. Although not particularly popular, it has characterized a great deal of work on the effects of architecture on behavior. Its lack of popularity is due to its emphasis on environmental effects on behavior and its refusal to acknowledge the give-and-take between the two. In its most extreme form, this position argues that the environment causes certain behaviors, denying any interaction between environment and behavior. Architectural determinism poses the idea that people can adapt to any arrangement of space and that behavior in a given environment is caused entirely by the characteristics of the environment. Most theories of environment and behavior do not concur with this position.

Another perspective used by environmental psychologists is centered on the construct of arousal. Because arousal is one aspect of stress, this model is similar to the stress model. However, this one differs in that arousal, defined as increased brain activity and autonomic responding (e.g., heart rate, respiration), can be associated with events that do not cause stress. Pleasant stimuli as well as negative ones can elicit arousal, and research has suggested that any environment can be described in part in terms of its arousal-evoking properties (Mehrabian & Russell, 1974).

Environmental load is yet another perspective used to study environment and behavior, focusing on attention as a key variable in the person-environment relationship. When the amount of information provided by an environment is greater than an individual's ability to process it, overload occurs. The converse, in which there is too little information, results in underload. Overload has been used to explain problems of city life and crowding, while underload has been used to describe monotonous settings and the effects of isolation (Milgram, 1970; Frankenhaeuser, 1978).

Altman (1975) has proposed an organizing model of environmental phenomena that attempts to explain spatial behavior, territoriality, and crowding. Centered around the notion of privacy, his approach argues that crowding and isolation are extreme instances of the same dimension: Too little privacy results in crowding, while too much leads to isolation. This dimension works much like an equilibrium system; when there is too little privacy, pressures act to increase it, and when there is too much, they act to decrease it. Spatial behavior is a primary mechanism of adjusting or optimizing privacy.

Another orientation toward environment-behavior relationships is Barker's ecological psychology (1968). Barker is concerned primarily with the integrity of the context of behavior. Each instance of behavior has a spatial and temporal context and this three-part unit, the behavior setting, is the proper level of analysis for environmental research. A number of processes operate to maintain these settings, and these can provide alternative perspectives on various environmental problems. For example, a behavior setting analysis of crowding would focus not on the number of people present but on the relationship of this number to the opportunities and options provided by the setting. If the number exceeds these options or roles, overstaffing occurs and people become more withdrawn from involvement in the setting.

There are other theories and orientations in environmental psychology, but to a large extent the field remains relatively atheoretical. Theories that try to arch over all aspects of environment-behavior interchange become complex and burdensome. Instead, the field has evolved a set of smaller areas of investigation, each with models and literatures of its own.

Most fields can be defined by what is done within them, and environmental psychology is no different. Proshansky, Ittelson, and Rivlin (1970) defined the field as what environmental psychologists do, perhaps because of the character of the field. These smaller areas within environmental psychology all have basic and applied aspects. Briefly, they include crowding, spatial behavior, architecture and behavior, environmental cognition, environmental education, environmental stress, and to a limited extent, technological environments.

REFERENCES

Altman, I. (1975). *The environment and social behavior.* Monterey, CA: Brooks/Cole.

Barker, R. G. (1968). *Ecological psychology: Concepts and methods for studying the environment of human behavior.* Stanford, CA: Stanford University Press.

Baum, A., Riess, M., & O'Hara, J. (1974). Architectural variants of reaction to spatial invasion. *Environment and Behavior, 6,* 91–100.

Baum, A., Singer, J. E., & Baum, C. S. (1981). Stress and the environment. *Journal of Social Issues, 37,* 4–35.

Baum, A., & Valins, S. (1977). *Architecture and social behavior: Psychological studies in social density.* Hillsdale, NJ: Erlbaum.

Cohen, S. (1980). Aftereffects of stress on human performance and social behavior: A review of research and theory. *Psychological Bulletin, 88,* 82–108.

Cohen, S., Evans, G. W., Krantz, D. S., & Stokols, D. (1980). Physiological, motivational and cognitive effects of aircraft noise on children: Moving from the laboratory to the field. *American Psychologist, 35,* 231–243.

Cohen, S., Glass, D. C., & Singer, J. E. (1973). Apartment noise, auditory discrimination, and reading ability in children. *Journal of Experimental Social Psychology, 9,* 407–422.

Desor, J. A. (1972). Toward a psychological theory of crowding. *Journal of Personality and Social Psychology, 21,* 79–83.

Festinger, L., Schachter, S., & Back, K. (1950). *Social pressures in informal groups: A study of human factors in housing.* New York: Harper.

Frankenhaeuser, M. (1978). *Coping with job stress: A psychobiological approach.* Reports from the Department of Psychology, University of Stockholm (532).

Frankenhaeuser, M., & Gardell, B. (1976). Underload and overload in working life: Outline of a multidisciplinary approach. *Journal of Human Stress, 2,* 35–46.

Lazarus, R. S. (1966). *Psychological stress and the coping process.* New York: McGraw-Hill.

Lewin, K. (1951). *Field theory in social science.* New York: Harper.

Mason, J. W. (1975). A historical view of the stress field. *Journal of Human Stress, 1*(2), 22–36.

Mehrabian, A., & Russell, J. A. (1974). *An approach to environmental psychology.* Cambridge, MA: MIT Press.

Milgram, S. (1970). The experience of living in cities. *Science, 167,* 1461–1468.

Proshansky, H. M., Ittelson, W., & Rivlin, L. G. (1970). Freedom of choice and behavior in a physical setting. In H. M. Proshansky, W. H. Ittelson, & L. G. Rivlin (Eds.), *Environmental psychology.* New York: Holt, Rinehart & Winston.

Selye, H. (1956). *The stress of life.* New York: McGraw-Hill.

Singer, J. E., Lundberg, U., & Frankenhaeuser, M. (1978). Stress on the train: A study of urban commuting. In A. Baum, J. E. Singer, & S. Valins (Eds.), *Advances in environmental psychology* (Vol. 1). Hillsdale, NJ: Erlbaum.

Sommer, R. (1969). *Personal space.* Englewood Cliffs, NJ: Prentice-Hall.

A. S. BAUM
University of Pittsburgh Cancer Institute

APPLIED RESEARCH
CROWDING
GENERAL ADAPTATION SYNDROME
INDUSTRIAL PSYCHOLOGY
WORK EFFICIENCY

EPILEPSY

The term "epilepsy" comes from the Greek word meaning "to seize"; hence the word seizure is used to describe an epileptic attack. A seizure is described by Hughes in "Epilepsy: A medical review" (p. 3) as an "excessive, disorderly, neuronal discharge, characterized by discrete attacks, tending to be recurrent, in which there is a disturbance of movement, sensation, perception, behavior, mood, or consciousness." Contrary to popular beliefs, epilepsy is a symptom, not a disease, and is best understood in terms of *seizure threshold.* We all probably inherit a certain seizure threshold, but if it is sufficiently high, our threshold for seizures will never be reached. However, for individuals with low thresholds or whose threshold has been lowered by a neurological disorder, a minimal amount of activation is needed to elicit an epileptic seizure. It is estimated that one to four million Americans fall into this latter category.

ETIOLOGY

Epilepsy can develop at any age and may or may not be associated with a specific neurological disorder or identifiable precipitating factor. Those seizures that appear to be spontaneous and of unknown etiology are referred to as *idiopathic*—a term generally applied to seizures that appear to have an inherited basis, or for which the exact cause of the abnormal neural discharge eludes identification.

Seizures that develop secondarily to known causes are called *symptomatic.* The most common causes of symptomatic seizures include head injuries, febrile seizures, brain tumors, encephalitis, cerebral vascular disease and malformations, hypoxia, drug and alcohol withdrawal, and metabolic disorders. While each of these etiologies affect the brain in its own unique way, the common denominator is that they all irritate or damage brain cells in such a way as to lower the individual's seizure threshold. For example, head injuries resulting from significant trauma, depressed skull fractures, or penetrating head wounds often damage brain tissue and result in local proliferation of the brain's glial cells, forming an irritative scar; because of the sharp bony processes of the middle fossa, the temporal lobe is often the site of such damage irrespective of the point of impact. On the other hand, the physiological events associated with infection or inflammation of brain cells (e.g., brain abscess or encephalitis) can also set up sufficient irritation of those cells to later result in epileptic seizures.

CLASSIFICATION OF SEIZURES

Since the causes, areas of brain involvement, and clinical symptomology of epilepsy are as varied and complex as the nervous system itself, the terminology and criteria for classifying seizures has varied widely. The recent International Classification of Epilepsy system now lists four major classes of epilepsy: generalized, unilateral, partial (focal), and unclassified. These classes generally correspond to whether the whole brain (generalized), one hemisphere (unilateral), or a specific area within a hemisphere (partial) is involved. Specific types of seizures within each of these classifications have also been differentiated on the basis of clinical features and EEG characteristics.

The two most common types of generalized seizures are *tonic-clonic* (grand mal) and absence (petit mal) attacks. Tonic-clonic attacks occur in approximately 60% of epileptics and have distinctive stages. In the first or tonic stage, the muscles become rigid, consciousness is lost, and breathing stops. The tonic phase lasts for 10 to 15 sec and gives way to the clonic stage, in which there are generalized muscle spasms and twitching, lasting another 45 to 50 sec. After about a minute, the person relaxes and drifts into a deep sleep or comatose state called the postictal stage. Prior to these stages, but still part of the seizure itself, there may be a warning or aura stage in which the person experiences a strange sensation such as a peculiar noise, smell, or numbness.

The other common form of generalized seizure is the *absence attack,* which typically occurs in childhood and usually disappears by adulthood. The typical or simple absence attack involves only a diminution of consciousness rather than a complete loss, and muscle responses may consist of only slight facial twitching or rapid eye blinking. Ordinarily, the person is unaware that anything unusual has happened and resumes whatever she or he was doing before the attack. More complex absence attacks may involve what Hughes (p. 14) calls automatisms, "automatic kinds of movements, especially fingering of clothes, and various types of movement of the mouth, especially chewing." Other forms of generalized seizures include tonic and clonic seizures, infantile spasms, and myoclonic seizures.

As the name implies, *unilateral seizures* involve only one side of the brain, and the types of seizures manifested are the same as those presented above. However, because only one hemisphere is involved, only one side of the body is affected and there is usually less impairment of consciousness and fewer changes in autonomic functioning.

Partial (focal) seizures appear primarily in adults and can have elementary or complex symptomology. The elementary type of partial seizure usually involves either the motor or sensory systems on one side of the body. In some cases the symptoms may begin in a discrete body area like the thumb and then spread or march to adjacent body regions like the hand or arm. This progressive involvement of successive body areas is called a *Jacksonian seizure,* after Hughlings Jackson, who first reported the phenomenon.

Complex-partial seizures (previously called temporal-lobe or psychomotor seizures) present a complex symptom picture. Usually there is some impairment of consciousness or cognitive ability, and the individual may engage in complicated but typically nonpurposive movements like walking in circles. Changes in the perception of time or sounds, illusions, and feelings of déjà vu or *jamais vu* are often associated with complex partial seizures.

TREATMENT AND PROGNOSIS

Anticonvulsant medications have been found to be effective in reducing both the number and severity of epileptic seizures in most individuals. The most commonly prescribed drugs are Dilantin, Phenobarbital, Mysoline, Tegretol, Zarontin, and Clonopin. Other forms of treatment include cerebellar stimulation, surgery, biofeedback, and ketogenic diets. Based on the findings of the Epilepsy Foundation of America, it is estimated that with good medical care and appropriate drug therapy 50% of epileptics can live free of convulsions and another 30% can have their seizures reduced to a minimum. However, psychological and neuropsychological investigations have found that, while there is no epileptic personality or characteristic pattern of deficit, individuals with symptomatic epilepsy are generally more impaired than those with idiopathic seizures. Also, people with generalized tonic-clonic attacks fare less well than those with complex-partial seizures. Within a given seizure type, an early age of onset and higher frequency of seizures have been associated with increased mental impairment.

REFERENCES

Hughes, J. R. (1980). Epilepsy: A medical overview. In B. P. Herman (Ed.), *A multidisciplinary handbook of epilepsy.* Springfield, IL: Thomas.

SUGGESTED READING

Boll, T. J. (1978). Diagnosing brain impairment. In B. B. Wolman (Ed.), *Clinical diagnosis of mental disorders.* New York: Plenum.

Herman, B. P. (1980). *A multidisciplinary handbook of epilepsy.* Springfield, IL: Thomas.

Howell, L. (1978). Epilepsy. In R. M. Goldenson, J. R. Dunham, & C. S. Dunham (Eds.), *Disability and rehabilitation handbook.* New York: McGraw-Hill.

G. J. CHELUNE
The Cleveland Clinic Foundation

BRAIN INJURIES
BRAIN WAVES
CENTRAL NERVOUS SYSTEM DISORDERS
NEUROSURGERY
PSYCHOPHARMACOLOGY
SPLIT-BRAIN RESEARCH

ERIKSON, ERIK H. (1902–1994)

Erik H. Erikson was psychoanalyzed by Anna Freud. After completing training at the Vienna Psychoanalytic Society in 1933, he left for Boston, became that city's first child psychoanalyst, and served as consultant to the Judge Baker Guidance Center and the Massachusetts General Hospital. In 1936 he did research at Yale's Institute for Human Relations and instruction at its medical school. In 1939, while associated with the Institute of Child Welfare at the University of California (Berkeley), he opened a private practice. Believing psychoanalysis should be an instrument for coping with the "vicissitudes of normal life," during the 1950s Erikson was on the Senior Staff of the Austen Riggs Center in Stockbridge, Massachusetts, where he treated youth with emotional problems. During the 1960s he served as professor of human relations at Harvard University until his retirement (in 1970).

Erikson is known for his work in developmental psychology. He coined the term "identity crisis," and described the human life cycle as comprised of eight stages: (a) the oral-sensory stage; (b) the muscular-anal stage; (c) the locomotor-genital stage; (d) the latency period; (e) puberty or adolescence; (f) young adulthood; (g) adulthood; and (h) maturity and old age. Each stage has its accompanying psychosocial identity crisis, with its desired developmental outcome. For example, the desired outcome of the trust versus mistrust crisis of the oral-sensory stage is hope.

Erikson's books included two psychobiographies, *Young Man Luther* and *Gandhi's Truth,* which show how emotional conflicts can be utilized toward constructive social ends. He is best known, however, for his *Childhood and Society,* in which human life cycles are described. In *Identity: Youth and Crisis* he elaborates on the life stages of the individual and the identity crisis.

STAFF

ERIKSONIAN DEVELOPMENTAL STAGES

The developmental theory of Erik Erikson builds upon and extends Sigmund Freud's account of psychosexual development in significant ways. (Erikson was trained and analyzed by Freud's daughter, Anna, at the Vienna Psychoanalytic Institute.) According to classical Freudian theory, development is completed by at least adolescence and is relatively independent of environmental influence. Moreover, ego development is defensive in nature; the ego emerges in order to control and regulate the id—biologically determined instincts, urges, needs, and the like. Erikson (1950, 1968) provides a life-span theory of psychosocial development that emphasizes the autonomous or conflict-free development of an adaptive ego. Erikson postulates that human beings have a need to categorize and integrate their experiences, as well as a need to satisfy their basic biological needs. A consolidated sense of ego identity—a perceived sense of personal wholeness and "continuity of experience"—must be achieved for optimal personal functioning.

The building and integrating of personality follows an eight-stage, life-span sequence governed by what Erikson, in *Identity: Youth and crisis,* calls the epigenetic principle: "this principle states

that anything that grows has a ground plan, and that out of this ground plan the parts arise, each part having its time of special ascendancy, until all parts have arisen to form a functioning whole." Each stage, from birth to old age, is marked by a normative crisis that must be confronted and negotiated. These bipolar crises may stem from intrapsychic conflicts (the first five parallel the Freudian psychosexual stages), but the quality of the social context within which resolutions are attempted may vary; the crises are psychosocial in nature. Crisis resolutions have residual effects on the developing person, with each contributing to the totally formed personality. Ideally, however, resolutions should not be completely one-sided; too much trust or naivete, for instance, can be maladaptive. A blend or positively balanced ratio of the two poles indicates optimal progress.

The stages are assumed to be interdependent and to build upon one another in a cumulative manner; personality becomes increasingly differentiated and hierarchically organized. According to Erikson (1964), each stage contributes a unique personal quality of strength or virtue, such as hope or faith, to the evolving personality. The achievement of ego identity during adolescence is the central concept in this developmental scheme; it entails the synthesis and integration of prior experiences and developments, and serves as the foundation upon which future progress occurs. The name of each stage signifies the psychosocial crisis that is involved.

1. *Trust versus mistrust (infancy).* At birth, infants are dominated by biological needs and drives. The reliability and quality of their relationships with caregivers will influence the extent to which they develop a sense of trust (or mistrust) in others, themselves, and the world in general. The virtue of *hope* is associated with this stage.

2. *Autonomy versus doubt and shame (early childhood).* Social demands for self-control and bodily regulation (toilet training) influence feelings of self-efficacy versus self-doubt. The quality of *will,* the willful self-discipline to do what is expected and expectable, emerges at stage two.

3. *Initiative versus guilt (preschool age).* Here children actively begin to explore and intrude upon their environment. Will they sense guilt about these self-initiated activities or will they feel justified in planning and asserting control over their activities? The virtue of *purpose*—the courage to pursue personally valued goals in spite of risks and possible failure—now ascends.

4. *Industry versus inferiority (school age).* The societal context in which the first three psychosocial conflicts are negotiated is predominantly the home and immediate family. In stage four, however, children begin formal instruction of some sort. Mastery of the tasks and skills valued by their teachers and the larger society now becomes focal. The quality of *competence* (with the implements and ways of the adult world) is said to develop.

5. *Identity versus diffusion (adolescence).* This is the linchpin in Erikson's scheme, the stage when adolescents actively attempt to synthesize their experiences in order to formulate a stable sense of personal identity. Although this process is psychoso-

cial in nature—a social fit or "solidarity with group ideals" must occur—Erikson emphasizes reality-testing and the acquisition of credible self-knowledge. Individuals come to view themselves as products of their previous experiences—despite a lifetime of changes, they experience a unified sense of temporal self-continuity. Positive resolutions of prior crises—being trusting, autonomous, willful, and industrious—facilitate identity formation, whereas previous failures may lead to identity diffusion. *Fidelity,* the ability to maintain commitments in spite of contradictory value systems, is the virtue that emerges during adolescence.

In Erikson's theory, development continues throughout life. The three adult stages, however, are directly affected by the identity achieved during adolescence.

6. *Intimacy versus isolation (young adulthood).* In this stage, one must be able and willing to unite his or her identity with another's. Since authentic disclosure and mutuality leave people vulnerable, a firm sense of identity is prerequisite. The quality that ascends during this stage is *love.*

7. *Generativity versus stagnation (middle adulthood).* This is the time in the life span when one strives to actualize the identity that has been formed and shared with select others. The generation or production of offspring, artifacts, ideas, products, and so forth is involved. The virtue of *care* emerges: generative adults care for others through parenting, teaching, supervising, and so forth, whereas stagnating adults are self-absorbed in immediate personal needs and interests.

8. *Integrity versus despair (maturity).* The final Eriksonian stage focuses on the perceived completion or fulfillment of one's life cycle. When individuals become aware that death may be imminent, do they feel despair—either fearing or welcoming death—or do they perceive the order and meaningfulness of their one and only life within a larger perspective? *Wisdom* is the last virtue to emerge. A wise person understands the relativistic nature of knowledge and accepts that her or his life had to be the way it was; this final reckoning permits no might-have-been's.

As a heuristic scheme, Erikson's theory has had a profound impact on contemporary psychology, especially adolescent development. Despite the theory's popularity and apparent face validity, critics have argued that the empirical foundation for the overall stage theory is relatively weak. Erikson's insightful interpretations were based primarily on information that he gleaned from case studies, play therapy, and psychohistorical analyses. However, the imprecise nature of the theoretical constructs—for instance, hope or wisdom—as defined by Erikson has made it difficult for researchers to independently test specific predictions derived from the theory. Another obstacle is that prohibitive, long-term longitudinal studies are needed to evaluate Erikson's claims about the sequential nature of psychosocial stages and the processes responsible for life-span personality development. Nonetheless, productive lines of research based on and generally consistent with Erikson's views relevant to particular stages have emerged. The voluminous body of research on identity formation (Marcia, 1993),

inspired by the identity-status paradigm developed by James Marcia (1966), is particularly noteworthy (Berzonsky & Adams, 1999). Research on other stages—for instance, intimacy (Orlofsky, 1993) and generativity (McAdams, Ruetzel, & Foley, 1986)—also tends to be consistent with Erikson's theory.

REFERENCES

Berzonsky, M. D., & Adams, G. R. (1999). Reevaluating the identity status paradigm: Still useful after 35 years. *Developmental Review, 19,* 557–590.

Erikson, E. H. (1950). *Childhood and society.* New York: Norton.

Erikson, E. H. (1964). *Insight and responsibility.* New York: Norton.

Erikson, E. H. (1968). *Identity: Youth and crisis.* New York: Norton.

Marcia, J. E. (1966). Development and validation of ego identity status. *Journal of Personality and Social Psychology, 3,* 551–558.

Marcia, J. E. (1993). The status of the statuses: Research review. In J. E. Marcia, A. S. Waterman, D. R. Matteson, S. L. Archer, & J. L. Orlofsky (Eds.), *Ego identity: A handbook for psychosocial research* (pp. 22–41). New York: Springer-Verlag.

McAdams, D. P., Ruetzel, K., & Foley, J. M. (1986). Complexity and generativity at mid-life: Relations among social motives, ego development, and adults' plans for the future. *Journal of Personality and Social Psychology, 50,* 800–807.

Orlofsky, J. L. (1993). Intimacy statuses: Theory and research. In J. E. Marcia, A. S. Waterman, D. R. Matteson, S. L. Archer, & J. L. Orlofsky (Eds.), *Ego identity: A handbook for psychosocial research* (pp. 111–133). New York: Springer-Verlag.

M. D. Berzonsky
State University of New York at Cortland

ADOLESCENT DEVELOPMENT
IDENTITY FORMATION

ERON, LEONARD D. (1920–   )

Leonard D. Eron is Professor of Psychology and Research Scientist at the Research Center for Group Dynamics of the Institute for Social Research, University of Michigan, and a Research Professor Emeritus at the University of Illinois at Chicago. Born on April 22, 1920, in Newark, New Jersey, he received a BS degree in psychology in 1941 from City College of New York, where he was elected to Phi Beta Kappa. After one semester of graduate work at Columbia University he was drafted into the army, serving in the campaigns of North Africa, Sicily, and Italy and attaining the rank of 1st lieutenant. In 1946 he completed his MA in Psychology at Columbia, followed by a PhD from the University of Wisconsin in 1949. Since that time he has served on the faculties of Yale University, the University of Iowa, and the University of Illinois at

Chicago—where at various times he was chair or director of clinical training and was named Research Professor of the Social Sciences in Psychology in 1970. He joined the Michigan faculty in 1992.

He is a diplomate of the American Board of Professional Psychology and a fellow of the Academy of Clinical Psychology. He has served as editor of the *Journal of Abnormal Psychology* and as associate editor of the *American Psychologist;* he has also been president of the Midwestern Psychological Association and of the International Society for Research on Aggression. He is a fellow of APA, APS, and AAAS. In 1980 he received the APA award for Distinguished Professional Contributions to Knowledge, and in 1995 the American Psychological Foundation Gold Medal Award for Life Contribution to Psychology in the Public Interest. He was a member of the National Research Council panel on Understanding and Control of Violence, and Chairman of the American Psychological Association Commission on Violence and Youth.

His early research was concerned with the reliability and validity of projective techniques and clinical interviews. Later he turned his attention to longitudinal research, following a class of first-year medical students through their graduation. He found that, over the course of four years, the students increased in cynicism and decreased in humanitarian attitudes. This was not true of a class of law students and a class of graduate nursing students followed during the same time. The findings had some influence on the reorganization of medical curricula at the time.

Since about 1960 he has done research on the learning of aggression in children. This research has included laboratory studies as well as field investigations. Of critical importance is a longitudinal study begun in 1960 (the Columbia County Longitudinal Study). The subjects included 856 children (the entire 3rd grade population of a semi-rural county in New York State) and 80% of their mothers and fathers. The purpose of the study was to relate the aggressive behavior of children in school to the child-rearing practices of their parents. The original subjects were seen again at age 19 and then again at age 30. At that time 75% of the subjects' spouses and 81 of their children between ages 6 and 8 were also seen. Currently a 40-year follow-up is underway in which the subjects and their spouses, children, and in some instances, grandchildren, are also being interviewed, providing data on four generations. To date the most significant findings have to do with the stability of aggressive behavior over time and across generations and how its development is affected by observational learning (including both the media and family and neighborhood violence) and parental patterns of punishment and nurturance. This has been one of the first studies to document the causal relation between viewing TV violence, subsequent aggressive behavior in children, and the cumulative effect over time of continued observation. What is learned by observation and reinforcement is not only the actual behaviors that are copied, but attitudes about he appropriateness of such behaviors, their efficacy and their normativeness. These findings have now been replicated in other areas of the United States and a number of European countries.

Dr. Eron is the author of nine books and approximately 150 articles in edited journals. He has testified numerous times before the United States Senate, the United States House of Representatives, and various state legislatures on the effects of violence in the media and on the implementation and evaluation of violence prevention programs.

STAFF

ERRORS (TYPE I AND TYPE II)

Statistical tests, which attempt to infer whether or not variables appear related in a population by evaluating data from smaller samples, are by no means foolproof. Occasionally sample information would seem to imply that variable X is related to variable Y in the population, when in fact no such population relation exists. Such an inaccurate inference is termed a Type I Error (or "alpha error"). On the other hand, sample data may seem to imply that X and Y appear unrelated, when indeed those variables do have a relation in the population. This inaccurate inference is termed a Type II Error (or "beta error"). These two types of errors are discussed in the context of an illustrative research example.

Consider a biofeedback technique claiming to reduce anxiety in academic testing situations. A researcher randomly samples 200 subjects with acute test anxiety, all college seniors registered to take the Graduate Record Examinations (GRE) General Test. The researcher randomly assigns 100 participants to learn how to employ the biofeedback method in an academic testing situation, while the other 100 participants are given a placebo experience consuming comparable time but unrelated to test anxiety or test performance. Both groups of students then take the GRE as originally intended; for simplicity we will only consider scores from one section (e.g., quantitative). The specific question of interest is whether or not, in the population, average performance for test-anxious students using biofeedback differs from that of test-anxious students not using biofeedback; information from the two samples is used to facilitate the population inference. Put another way, the relation arising from the sample information between the biofeedback variable (present/absent) and the academic test performance variable (GRE score) will be used to make an inference about the existence and nature of that relation at the population level.

For the current example, one can think of two possible truths existing at the population level, and two possible conclusions derived from the sample information. For the populations, either biofeedback has some average effect or it has none. This latter notion, that there is no average difference between scores from a population of test-anxious students using biofeedback and scores from a population not using the technique, is termed the "null hypothesis" (symbolized H_0). Thus, a biofeedback treatment that affects test performance means that H_0 is false. As for conclusions drawn from samples, if the two sample means are relatively similar (i.e., not differing "statistically significantly") the guarded inference would be made that H_0 remains tenable. One need not actually believe that biofeedback is completely ineffective in the population; one may merely feel that sufficient evidence has not been gathered to the contrary, thus retaining H_0 as a tenable explanation for the lack of statistical significance associated with the observed difference between the two sample means. Conversely, if the two sample means are statistically significantly different, then one would infer that H_0 is false and that biofeedback has some effect. Specifically, if the biofeedback sample's mean is statistically significantly higher than that for the control sample, then one would infer that the treatment has a positive effect; alternatively, if the biofeedback sample's mean is statistically significantly lower than that for the control sample, then one would infer that the treatment actually has a negative effect.

Crossing the two population and two sample conditions outlined above defines four possible outcomes of a research endeavor, two representing accurate inference and two representing inaccurate inference (i.e., Type I and Type II errors). These are depicted in Figure 1. Consider first the cells on the left side of the figure, representing the condition in which H_0 is true; in the context of the example, these cells represent a population truth in where biofeedback has no effect on test performance. The top left cell results when the observed sample relation between biofeedback (presence/absence) and test performance is not statistically significant; that is, the observed difference between sample means falls in the realm of what one would comfortably expect by chance if two population means truly do not differ. In this situation the study would lead one to infer that H_0 remains tenable, and in fact the inference would be accurate because H_0 is true. In short, the study would have gathered no evidence that biofeedback is effective, and in truth it has no effect in the population.

The bottom left cell, on the other hand, results when the observed sample relation between the variables of interest is statistically significant; that is, the observed difference between sample means falls outside the realm of what one would comfortably expect by chance when two population means truly do not differ. In this situation the study would lead one to infer that H_0 should be rejected as false; however, the inference would be inaccurate because H_0 is true, and is thus labeled a Type I error. Such an event would be an unfortunate random occurrence, in which two samples happened to be selected whose quantitative ability was extremely disparate, but this disparity was merely a random occurrence and in no way reflective of any beneficial or detrimental effect of biofeedback.

Now consider the right column of the figure, in which H_0 is false; in the context of the example, these cells represent a population truth in which biofeedback has some effect on test performance. The bottom right cell results when the observed sample relation between the variables of interest is statistically significant; that is, the observed difference between sample means falls outside the realm of what one would comfortably expect by chance if two population means truly do not differ. In this situation the study would lead one to infer that H_0 should be rejected as false, and in fact the inference would be accurate because H_0 is false. Thus, the study would have gathered evidence that the biofeedback is related to test performance, and in truth such a relation does exist in the population.

The top right cell, on the other hand, results when the observed sample relation between biofeedback and test performance is not statistically significant; that is, the observed difference between sample means falls in the realm of what one would comfortably expect by chance if two population means truly do not differ. In this

Truth in population

	H_0 is true (X and Y unrelated) Inference	H_0 is false (X and Y related)
X and Y sample relation not statistically significant; retain H_0 as tenable	accurate inference	inaccurate inference (Type II error)
X and Y sample relation statistically significant; reject H_0	inaccurate inference (Type I error)	accurate inference

Figure 1

situation the study would lead one to infer that H_0 remains tenable; however, the inference would be inaccurate because H_0 is false, and is thus labeled a Type II error. Such an event would be an unfortunate random occurrence, in which two samples happened to be selected whose quantitative ability was not particularly disparate, but this lack of disparity was not reflective of the actual effect of the biofeedback treatment.

Now looking at the figure from the sample perspective, a study will leave a researcher in either the top row or the bottom row. In the bottom row the variables of interest appear to be related on the basis of the sample information; the researcher infers that a relation exists in the population, thereby rejecting H_0. This is either an accurate inference or a Type I error, and the researcher never knows which is the case without having direct information about the relevant population(s). Thus, in order to minimize the occurrence of Type I errors, researchers often try to choose a fairly small region (alpha region; critical region) in which statistical significance will be proclaimed and H_0 rejected. This will help to avoid inferring the existence of a population relation where none truly exists. Choosing too small a region, however, will hinder the researcher from proclaiming statistical significance when the H_0 is false. A common choice is to deem statistically significant a sample relation that is so unlikely as to be observed only 5% of the time or less just by chance (i.e., when no such relation exists in the population). This is reflected in common language as, "the alpha level was set at .05".

In the top row of the figure the variables of interest do not appear related on the basis of the sample information; the researcher infers (albeit guardedly) that the hypothesis of no relation in the population remains tenable. This is either an accurate inference or a Type II error, and again the researcher never knows which is the case without having direct population information. Thus, in order to minimize the occurrence of Type II errors, and thereby increase the chance of inferring the existence of relations in the population when they truly exist (i.e., increase the statistical power), researchers are encouraged to take several preventative steps. Among the many ways to help avoid Type II errors are using the most reliably measured variables possible, using statistical techniques that help to control for extraneous variability in scores, and, perhaps most importantly, to use samples of adequate size. The reader is referred to any introductory social science statistics text for further discussion of these and related issues.

G. R. HANCOCK
University of Maryland, College Park

HYPOTHESIS TESTING, POWER
MEASUREMENT
RESEARCH METHODOLOGY

ESQUIROL, JEAN ÉTIENNE (1772–1840)

A successor to Philippe Pinel, who first started reforms in mental asylums in France about 1793 by allowing the chains to be cast off patients at La Bicêtre hospital in Paris, the French psychiatrist Jean Étienne Esquirol instituted further humanitarian reforms and founded 10 new mental hospitals in various parts of France, each based on the humane and rational treatment developed by Pinel.

Esquirol was one of the first, if not the first, to apply statistical methods to clinical studies of the mentally ill. His book *Les Maladies Mentales* (*Mental Maladies*), begun in 1817, reported his results. Unlike his predecessors, he looked for psychological causes for mental diseases such as dissatisfaction in love, financial loss, or other kinds of failures. He also distinguished various kinds of depression from other forms of mental illness, and introduced the term "hallucination," giving it the clear-cut definition of today. Further, he defended criminals who were mentally ill. Prior to Esquirol's work, the physicians of the time had presumed some kind of physical or physiological causes for mental illness, but Esquirol was inclined toward more psychological interpretations.

R. W. LUNDIN
Wheaton, Illinois

ESTES, WILLIAM K. (1919–   )

William K. Estes earned the BA and PhD (1943) from the University of Minnesota, where he studied under B. F. Skinner. Estes was considerably influenced, however, by the theories of C. L. Hull and especially E. R. Guthrie, and brought statistical (probability) theory to bear upon Guthrian learning theory. Estes's career began at the University of Indiana in 1946, where he remained until 1962, when he left for Stanford University. From Stanford he went to Rockefeller University, where he has been professor of psychology since 1968.

Known for his stimulus sampling theory, Estes developed a statistical theory of learning predicated on the principle of contiguity.

Learning, complete in one trial, is a learned response, a conditioning which is a sample of all possible stimulus elements reaching the individual on subsequent trials.

Estes served as editor of the *Journal of Comparative and Physiological Psychology*, was a fellow of the Center for Advanced Study in Behavioral Sciences (1955–1956), and won the Warren Medal in 1963. His principal book (written with others) is *Modern Learning Theory*.

STAFF

ETHICAL TREATMENT OF ANIMALS

In the quarter century since the publication of Peter Singer's *Animal Liberation* (1976) reopened discussion of our use of animals other than humans (hereafter, animals) in scientific research, three major developments have occurred.

First, within moral philosophy, several theories have been expounded regarding the ethics of this use. In addition to Singer's utilitarian ethic, Regan's eponymous rights theory ("animal rights movement"), and, more recently, feminist, communitarian, and contractarian theories, each answered with formal treatises by their detractors, together have assured a secure and dynamic place for this topic in courses and texts on moral philosophy.

The theories all attempt to answer the question of the moral considerability of animals and to infer the policy and practices that follow from the standing claimed for them. For example, beyond that moral consideration due a sentient being, some thinkers argue that some animals (the Great Apes) are persons and obligate us to give them legal as well as ethical standing.

Among the concepts being explicated is the putative foundational notion of inherent value (Dol et al., 1999; Vilkka, 1997). Beyond any instrumental value for people, do beings other than humans—nonhuman animals, but also plants and ecosystems—have intrinsic value?

Second, in the area of institutional self-regulation and governmental regulation, following the passage of federal legislation in 1966 and subsequent amendments, review committees now oversee almost all laboratories engaged in animal research. Although modeled after the successful institutional review boards for research involving human subjects, the adequacy of this mechanism is hotly debated. Do the preponderance of animal researchers on these review boards and the exclusion of rodents and birds (the most frequent objects of study in psychological animal research) from the committees' purview undermine effectiveness and credibility? Or does the exercise of requirements such as the search for alternatives that replace animals, or at least reduce their numbers and extent of suffering, and the provision that both husbandry and procedures ensure the "well-being of primates" constitute adequate policing and reforming practices?

ANIMAL STUDIES

Symbolized by Singer's acceptance of the position of DeCamp Professor of Bioethics at Princeton University, the third development is the emergence of a field of Animal Studies, which provides academic foundation to a progressive social movement. A core of scholars in the social and natural sciences, as well as, the humanities apply the methods of their respective disciplines to the study of nonhuman animals and human-animal interfaces. Books published by major publishing houses; book series; journals; and university programs, courses, and chairs devoted to animal studies constitute a robust intellectual infrastructure. The defining feature of Animal Studies is the shift from the study of nonhuman animals as representative objects—models, cultural artifacts, and symbols of human phenomena—to subjects in the full sense of that term. From their traditional position on the margins, they become focal objects of study in and of themselves.

PSYCHOLOGY'S AMBIVALENCE

The role of psychology in these three developments has been mixed. A major study of the attitudes of psychologists provides evidence of this ambivalence on an individual level. The study found a high level of support for research involving observation and even confinement (Plous, 1996). However, when asked about research involving pain or death to primates and rats, many psychologists (62.1% and 44.4%, respectively, for the two animal groups) indicate that such research is unjustified—even when the research is described as "institutionally approved and deemed of scientific merit" (p. 1171).

On the negative side of psychology's role, several writers, including Singer, single out psychological research for criticism beyond its proportionate share of the research enterprise, citing the allegedly high level of suffering involved and questioning the quality of the research as science. Psychology also contributed a cause célèbre of abuse (the Silver Spring monkeys) as a psychology laboratory had its major federal support grant suspended. The animal rights movement frequently criticized another prominent psychologist, Harry Harlow, for his involvement in highly invasive nonhuman primate research. Regarding the field's general response to the issue of psychological animal research, two psychologists chided the field for adopting a "strategic defensive posture" (Gluck & Kubacki, 1991, p. 158).

More positively, two British psychologists contributed conceptual advances in the debate: Ryder coined the term "speciesism," while Heim articulated the notion that there are ethical limits on our use of animals that are independent of any beneficial ends. Although generally dragging its feet on the issue, the American Psychological Association did publish guidelines for the care and use of animals that were as progressive as those of other professional societies. A number of psychologists have conducted noninvasive animal research with primates and other animals that demonstrate the sophisticated capabilities of these animals, such as communication, self-reflection, and attribution of mind. The findings have raised the ethical bar to the use of animals in invasive research.

Psychologists also have contributed to the critique of animal research by adding science-based evidence and argument to the debate within ethics (e.g., Shapiro, 1998). They also have developed scales to measure degree of pain and harm, and provided empirical studies demonstrating the link between violence toward humans and other animals.

Increasingly, clinical psychologists are capitalizing on the empirically demonstrated social support, interpersonal facilitation, and other beneficial and therapeutic effects of involvement in a compassionate and respectful human-animal relation. Therapists use animals as adjuncts in individual therapy (animal-assisted therapy). Residential group settings also use caring for animals as a vehicle for developing mutual, responsible relationships. A number of psychologists have chosen careers working in organizations in which the mission is the abolition or reform of invasive animal research, and one group of psychologists has organized as animal advocates. Through these and other avenues, psychology is moving from a defensive to a constructive and progressive position on the issue of the ethical treatment of animals.

REFERENCES

Dol, M., Van Vlissingen, M. J., Kasanmoentalib, S., Visser, T., & Zwart, H. (Eds.). (1999). *Recognizing the intrinic value of animals.* Assen, The Netherlands: Van Gorcum.

Gluck, J. P., & Kubacki, S. R. (1991). Animals in biomedical research: The undermining effect of the rhetoric of the besieged. *Ethics & Behavior, 1*(3), 157–173.

Plous, S. (1996). Attitudes toward the use of animals in psychological research and education: Results from a national survey of psychologists. *American Psychologist, 51,* 1167–1180.

Regan, T. (1983). *The case for animal rights.* Berkeley: University of California.

Shapiro, K. (1998). *Animal models of human psychology: Critique of science, ethics, and policy.* Gottingen, Germany: Hogrefe and Huber.

Singer, P. (1975). Animal liberation: A new ethic for our treatment of animals. New York: Avon.

Vilkka, L. (1997). *The intrinsic value of nature.* Amsterdam: Rodapi.

K. J. SHAPIRO
Psychologists for the Ethical Treatment of Animals

ANIMAL COMMUNICATION

ETHNOCENTRISM

The term "ethnic" has been in use in the written English language at least since the fifteenth century and was derived from the Greek "ethnos," which was interpreted variously as people, race, culture, or nation. The term was also used by the Greeks to denote heathens, as the term "ethnos" itself was derived from "ethnikos." The term "ethnocentric" was used in the literature as early as 1898, though the term "ethnicity" is believed to have been introduced in the 1940s (Sollors, 1996). The concept of ethnocentrism as introduced by Sumner in 1906 was "this view of things in which one's own group is the center of everything, and all others are scaled and rated with reference to it. . . . Each group nourishes its own pride and vanity, boasts itself superior, exalts its own divinities, and looks with contempt on outsiders. . . ." (Sumner, 1959). Sumner used ethnocentrism as one of the terms to describe intergroup attitudes, such as we-group, ingroup, and outgroups. He gives many examples of ethnocentrism, such as the name "Kiowa" that meant "real or principal people," and that the Greeks and Romans considered all outsiders "barbarians." Ethnic groups are not limited to racial factors, as they are based on many other social, cultural, and linguistic factors including nationality, national origins, and geographical boundaries as well. Ethnicity is often subjective in nature and based on the claims of the members of a group as well as the perception, recognition, attribution, and designation from other groups. Thus, the subjective perceptions of a distinct ethnicity by members of a particular ethnic group have to be corroborated and confirmed by one or more groups in terms of their "otherness." The group boundaries are not always clearly demarcated in the absence of geographic boundaries or other demarcating features. There are different levels of ethnocentricity, and some researchers have indicated that the extent of ethnocentrism varies considerably (Brewer & Campbell, 1976). Ethnocentrism or ethnocentric attitudes may or may not result in discrimination, conflict, or violence.

The concept of ethnocentrism has been supplemented and extended by other concepts in the literature such as "the stranger" and "marginal man" introduced by Simmel. These concepts provide a bridge between the ingroup and outgroup. The concept of social distance introduced in the 1920s enabled researchers to measure the extent of perceived distance from other ethnic groups. Though the concept of ethnocentrism was originally used as a group-based concept, it is now also widely used to measure individual views and perspectives. The authoritarian personality studies have addressed the problems of relationship between ethnocentrism and discernible personality traits and characteristics such as authoritarian personality, and postulated that to understand fully the nature of ethnocentrism and nationalism, they need to be studied in the context of the psychology of the person for whom such attitudes have a special appeal (Forbes, 1985). The attitude scales used by psychologists and social psychologists, starting with the F scale, provide other examples of measurement of personality characteristics that are authoritarian and ethnocentric (Brewer & Campbell, 1976).

Sumner's use of the term "ethnocentrism" has also been interpreted more broadly as an ethnocentric syndrome with three facets. The first meaning is the inclusion of a cluster of social attributes that coexist simultaneously, the second characteristic is that this syndrome is functionally associated with group cohesion and intergroup competition, and the third interpretation is that these characteristics are common to all groups (Le Vine & Campbell, 1972). In recent years the concept of ethnocentrism has been further expanded to the use of terms such as Eurocentricity. Such terms refer to perceptions based on the expansion of the original concept of ethnocentrism to include multiple ethnic groups and nationalities that have one or more common characteristics. Eth-

nocentrism needs to be clearly distinguished from xenophobia, jingoism, and chauvinism, though ethnocentric views can be indoctrinated and harnessed in the development of other prejudicial views and attitudes.

REASONS AND CONSEQUENCES OF ETHNOCENTRISM

The causes and manifestation of ethnocentrism can take different forms. The first type of explanation would be based on personality factors of individuals. Research in this area can be interpreted to support the argument that some types of personalities tend to be more ethnocentric than others. This was evident in the case of authoritarian personality studies and social distance scale studies. The second form of ethnocentric behavior is contextual or situational. It can be attributed to a situation where external conditions impact on the attitudes of a group member, such as the loss of jobs due to competition from a neighboring state or neighboring group. In such situations, the perceptions of groups may change as one group or nation can be transformed from a friend to an enemy and vice versa, as in the case of allies and enemies during a war. The third form is a manifestation of ethnocentrism among nations, tribes, or groups with different subcultures. This is the form of ethnocentrism encountered by most. The reasons for this type of ethnocentrism vary from mistrust of the stranger and self-aggrandizement of a group, and extend to aims of conquest and subjugation of a group. This type of ethnocentrism often involved hostility and distrust among the groups involved.

Ethnocentrism has been utilized also as a means to bolster the ingroup feelings and group solidarity built along ethnic lines. Terms of reference such as "brother" and "sister," or use of one's own ethnic group as a positive reference group, or concepts such as a "white man's burden" that is to be endured because of a sense of noblesse oblige, are examples of such efforts. The development of ethnic literature, theaters, clubs, and distinct costumes or modes of dressing are examples of activities undertaken by ethnic groups to maintain and continue their separate identity and self-respect. Socialization through the family, schools, media, peer groups, and religious teaching are the major avenues of ethnocentric indoctrination.

The negative aspects of ethnocentrism have often manifested themselves as violent conflicts or battles or wars throughout history. The proto-historical accounts of warfare were based on tribal affiliations. The Crusades in the Middle Ages, conflict in Northern Ireland, Arab-Israel conflict in the Middle East, and the holocaust were based on religious differences. In the case of Native Americans, more than one ethnic factor was involved. More new nations have been created along ethnic lines during the decade of the 1990s than any other decade in history. Usage of terminologies such as ethnic cleansing, ethnocide, and ethnic nationalism or ethnonationalism is another indication of the ethnocentric basis of conflicts and cleavages between different ethnic groups. However, all ethnic conflicts are not necessarily violent, as they may just consist of peaceful demonstrations or marches.

In addition to tribal and religious basis of ethnocentric behavior illustrated above, two other types of ethnocentrism based on "race" and colonial rule have had widespread and serious consequences. Prejudice, segregation, and other discriminatory behavior among Whites and African Americans in the United States are examples of ethnocentrism based on racial lines. The apartheid practices in South Africa constitute one example of colonial ethnocentrism. However, it is based on race as well. In most of the relationship between the colonizer and the colonized, racism was a concomitant factor. In addition, the minority groups also had a lower class status. Even though many colonies were constituted of multiracial or multicultural groups, the primary White and non-White dichotomy persisted along with the master and the subjugated categories because of the convergence of power, color or race, language, and social class differences. The colonial perspective was thus unavoidably ethnocentric, with hierarchical and discriminatory lines drawn between the colonizer and the colonized. The perceived distinctions of superiority and inferiority of groups became a self-fulfilling prophecy. The minority ethnic groups are often disrespectful of their own ethnicity in contrast with the ethnic group that is in power, a phenomenon often noticed in the colonial context. Ethnocentrism based on race as in the United States has often been described as internal colonialism by Marxists and non-Marxists alike. Segregation, denial of voting rights, and race riots can be traced back to ethnic perspectives of the Whites and the non-Whites. It was easy to deny the demands for equality and equity because of the ethnocentric views of basic differences between the two or three groups in the United States.

Ethnocentrism is a learned behavior, and thus can be unlearned. Cultural contact has been suggested and tried as one of the approaches to reduce ethnocentrism. Another solution suggested is the submerging of the local ethnic groups into a larger collective, such as a nationality. This was the assumption made in the case of development of many African countries with intertribal or intergroup conflicts or rivalries, such as Nigeria. It was believed that these conflicts would be subordinated or submerged in the superordinate collective such as that of nationhood. One of the reasons for the low level of intensity of ethnocentric views is crosscutting boundaries or loyalties. Two groups may be sharing a common linguistic orientation but belong to different religious groups. In such cases, the boundaries of the ingroup and outgroup get shifted depending on the context, resulting in a lack of convergence. Socialization of children in schools through the emphasis on multicultural perspectives is another technique used to reduce ethnocentric biases. Socialization, however, can be used with the opposite effect as well, in order to germinate ethnocentric values. The Olympic Games, for example, were established to promote multinationalism and reduce ethnocentric ideologies, and they have not always worked uniformly in that direction. Legal measures have often been effective in reducing discriminatory behavior in an intranational context in some cases, but ethnocentric attitudes and prejudices are not likely to be significantly affected, especially in cases of long-standing distrust or animosities. Social changes are likely to reduce ethnocentrism between two groups. For example, the conflict and rivalry between two immigrant groups living in one neighborhood would get shifted toward a third group with the influx of a large number from this new group into the neighborhood, as it often happened in the case of new waves of immigrants from different nationalities, different religions, and different linguistic groups. The research on this important topic is surprisingly sparse.

REFERENCES

Brewer, M. B., & Campbell, D. T. (1976). *Ethnocentrism and intergroup attitudes: East African studies.* New York: Sage.

Forbes, H. D. (1985). *National ethnocentrism and personality: Social science and critical theory.* Chicago: University of Chicago Press.

LeVine, R. A., & Campbell, D. T. (1972). *Ethnocentrism: Theories of conflict, ethnic attitudes, and group behavior.* New York: Wiley.

Sollors, W. (Ed.). (1996). *Theories of ethnicity: A classical reader.* New York: New York University Press.

Sumner, W. G. (1959). *Folkways.* New York: Dover.

SUGGESTED READING

Forbes, H. D. (1997). *Ethnic conflict: Commerce, culture, and the contact hypothesis.* New Haven: Yale University Press.

Guibernau, M., & Rex, J. (1997). *The ethnicity reader: Nationalism, multiculturalism, and migration.* Cambridge: Polity.

Memmi, A. (1965). *The colonizer and the colonized.* Boston: Beacon.

S. R. SONNAD
Western Michigan University

INGROUPS/OUTGROUPS

ETHOLOGY

Ethology is most simply defined as the study of animal behavior in its natural environment, including its physical, biological, and social aspects. Ethology is also concerned with the role of Darwinian natural selection in shaping animal behavior. This implies that the behavior is related to genotypes that are in turn a product of the species' evolutionary history. This further implies that gene selection has been influenced by the consequences of naturally occurring behaviors. Jaynes (1969) has written a comprehensive review of ethology's origins.

CONCEPTS IN CLASSIC ETHOLOGY

The usual starting point for ethological study has been ethograms, which are extensive, highly detailed descriptions of a species' behaviors in its natural environment. They originated in the work of European naturalists such as Heinroth, Fabre, and Spaulding during the latter nineteenth and early twentieth century. These early ethologists were impressed by the constant, stereotyped nature of many adaptive behaviors that were often labeled as innate or instinctive. The ethological conceptualization of these behaviors was refined in a classic paper on egg retrieval by greylag geese written by Lorenz and Tinbergen (1938). If an egg is presented to an incubating goose, it will immediately fix its gaze on the egg. It will then approach the egg, place its head and bill over it, and begin pulling the egg back to the nest. When Lorenz and Tinbergen removed the egg before the bird reached its nest, the bird persisted in its egg-retrieving movements all the way back to its nest. It was as if the goose had a preset neurological program that, once initiated, continued to completion although the original eliciting stimulus was absent. Behaviors of this type were termed fixed-action patterns. However, Lorenz's German word *Erbkoordination* (inherited coordination) more accurately conveys the meaning of the concept.

Fixed-action patterns are specific, stereotyped behaviors characteristic of a species. Fixed-action patterns are so constant that they have been used as criteria for taxonomic classification of species (Hinde, 1970/1966). Furthermore, fixed-action patterns are usually elicited by specific stimuli (called releasers or sign stimuli) and are assumed to continue in the absence of the original releaser. Lorenz and Tinbergen assumed that for each fixed-action pattern, an animal had an innate neural program that responded only to stimuli resembling the usual sign stimulus found in the natural habitat. This innate program was called an innate-releasing mechanism (IRM). The releasing stimuli were thus likened to triggers that set off an IRM (Eibl-Eibesfeldt, 1975). Occasionally, an artificial stimulus is more effective than the naturally occurring one in releasing a fixed-action pattern. For example, Tinbergen showed that geese would retrieve a volleyball in preference to one of their own eggs. These highly effective artificial releasers are "supranormal stimuli." A further important characteristic is that fixed-action patterns are highly specific behaviors. Nest building, maternal behavior, and mating may include several fixed-action patterns, but are too global to be considered fixed-actions by themselves.

A drive system accompanied classic ethological theory. Action-specific energy was assumed to build up in the animal if it did not find an appropriate releasing stimulus. If sufficient energy accumulated, the threshold for elicitation of the behavior decreased and eventually reached a point where the behavior appeared in the absence of the usual releasing stimuli (vacuum activity).

A classic experiment by Spaulding (1873) demonstrated another characteristic of fixed-action patterns and was an early example of a basic type of ethological experiment. Spaulding raised a group of swallows in small cages that prevented the birds from flapping their wings. When the swallows reached the age at which they would normally fly, they were released. The liberated swallows flew off, apparently suffering no ill effects from the early environmental restriction. Clearly, practice at flying movements was not necessary for development of flying capability.

Spaulding's demonstration was an ethological deprivation experiment, a type of restriction differing from the typical deprivation experiment in American experimental psychology. In the ethological deprivation experiment, only a small, carefully chosen set of stimuli are withheld from the subjects. The deprivation is simply intended to prevent the animal from displaying or practicing some target behavior. The ethologist makes a point of imposing no more deprivation than necessary to prevent the occurrence of the fixed-action pattern. If, following the deprivation, the animal shows the full fixed-action pattern in response to the appropriate releasing stimulus, then the behavior did not depend on previous practice. Early ethologists further concluded that the behavior was innate and did not depend on any prior learning, an inference that is not necessarily justified.

The deprivation experiment has been extensively used in ethological research, sometimes with striking results. Eibl-Eibesfelt (1975) raised a group of squirrels on a liquid diet in isolation cages with solid floors. The squirrels never saw another squirrel burying a nut nor did they practice food burying. When a large quantity of nuts was then given for the first time to the mature squirrels, they took some and promptly went through all the typical stereotyped burying movements of squirrels. It was as if the nuts released a pre-programmed behavioral sequence.

LATER DEVELOPMENTS IN ETHOLOGY

Following Lorenz and Tinbergen's establishment of a basic theoretical foundation for ethology in the 1930s, several major changes occurred in the theoretical and empirical approaches of ethologists to animal behavior. The ethological mechanism, in which action-specific energy accumulates until a sign stimulus releases a fixed-action pattern through operation of the IRM, resembles other early drive-reduction theories ranging from Hull's to Freud's. And like these theories, the original IRM theory is deficient as an exploratory system because of an inherent circularity: the only way of measuring the action-specific energy is through the behavior that it is intended to explain. Furthermore, there is no evidence of a separate neurological subsystem corresponding to each presumed IRM of an animal.

The classic IRM theory does have some virtue as a descriptive device. Many different behaviors are released by relatively specific sign stimuli. Furthermore, many of these behaviors acquire lowered thresholds for elicitation with the passage of time (Eibl-Eibesfeldt, 1975).

A major change in classic ethological theory has been an increasing awareness of the strong influence of learning in animal behavior, including many fixed-action patterns. The best known example is imprinting, which was initially regarded by Lorenz as an innately released following behavior in recently born or hatched animals of some species. Later research showed that a simple and rapid conditioning probably underlies imprinting (Moltz, 1963). Even Lorenz ultimately acknowledged that conditioning is involved in imprinting.

The sophistication of ethological research has increased dramatically during the past 20 years. One facet of modern ethological research is a focus on quantification of the adaptive value of behavior. The study of territoriality in golden-winged sunbirds (Gill & Wolf, 1975) showed how territorial defense could be predicted by analysis of calories expended in foraging or defending territories and caloric values of food sources in alternative territories. This was an early example of the use of optimality theory in understanding animal behavior. Optimality theory assumes that natural selection has adjusted animal behavior such as foraging for food in the natural habitat so as to achieve an optimum balance between costs and benefits (Krebs & Davis, 1993).

The field of behavioral ecology has also emerged from classic ethology. Behavioral ecology is focused on the interactions of animals within their entire ecological communities including the inorganic environment, plants, other animal species, and their own species (Krebs & Davis, 1993). Feeding, predator-prey relationships, and population regulation have been frequent issues addressed by behavioral ecologists.

One of the most dramatic findings to emerge from recent ethological research is the increasingly abundant evidence of evolved behavioral dispositions that promote group cohesion and reduce aggression (de Waal, 1996). These processes include reconciliation, reciprocity of both positive and negative acts, consolation, as well as processes having some resemblance to sympathy and altruism. The power of these prosocial processes was shown by the observation that when the population density of rhesus monkeys was increased by a factor of 646 there was no increase in aggression but marked increases in appeasement and submissive gestures (de Waal, 1996).

Ethological studies in recent years have also overlapped with the domain of sociobiology wherein a large variety of behaviors are explained in terms of an expanded definition of evolutionary fitness that includes natural selection for benefits accruing to all genetic relatives (kin selection; Trivers, 1985). For example, the old evolutionary dilemma seemingly posed by castes of sterile workers in eusocial insects was explained by this approach.

Elements of game theory have been introduced in ethology based on evidence that the old idea of single set of species-specific behaviors characterizes all species is incorrect. In fact, behavioral polymorphism (distinctly different types of behaviors in different animals within the same species) has been identified in several species. These polymorphisms may be determined by an animal's social and environmental circumstances or may be genetically determined. Behaviors displaying polymorphic variation are often different reproductive strategies, each of which is assumed to have the same evolutionary fitness.

REFERENCES

Eibl-Eibesfeldt, I. (1975). *Ethology: The biology of behavior.* New York: Holt, Rinehart & Winston.

Gill, F. B., & Wolf, L. L. (1975). Economics of feeding territoriality in the golden-winged sunbird. *Ecology, 56,* 333–345.

Hinde, R. A. (1966/1970). *Animal behavior: A synthesis of ethology and comparative psychology.* New York: McGraw-Hill.

Jaynes, J. (1969). The historical origins of "ethology" and "comparative psychology." *Animal Behavior, 17,* 601–606.

Krebs, J. R., & Davis, N. B. (1993). *An introduction to behavioral ecology.* Boston: Blackwell Scientific Publications.

Lorenz, K. Z., & Tinbergen, N. (1938). Taxis und Instinkhandlung in der Eirollbewegung der Graugans. *Zeitschrift für Tierpsychologie, 2,* 1–29.

Moltz, H. (1963). Imprinting: An epigenetic approach. *Psychological Review, 70,* 123–138.

Spaulding, D. A. (1873). Instinct with original observation on young animals. *Macmillan Magazine, 27,* 282–283.

Trivers, R. (1985). *Social evolution.* Menlo Park, CA: Benjamin/Cummings.

de Waal, F. B. M. (1996). *Good natured: The origins of right and wrong in humans and other animals.* Cambridge, MA: Harvard University Press.

SUGGESTED READING

Dawkins, R. *The extended phenotype: The gene as the unit of selection.*

Gould, J. L. *Ethology: The mechanisms and evolution of behavior.*

Hinde, R. A. *Ethology, its nature and relations with other sciences.*

McFarland, D. *Animal behavior: psychobiology, ethology, and evolution.*

J. E. KING
University of Arizona

ANIMAL COMMUNICATION
ECOLOGICAL PSYCHOLOGY
INSTINCTIVE BEHAVIOR
SOCIOBIOLOGY

EVANS, DWIGHT L.

Dwight L. Evans is the Ruth Meltzer Professor, chairman of the Department of Psychiatry, and professor of psychiatry, medicine, and neuroscience at the University of Pennsylvania School of Medicine. He was formerly professor and chairman of the Department of Psychiatry at the University of Florida College of Medicine, and held professorships in the Departments of Medicine and Neuroscience. Prior to this, at the University of North Carolina School of Medicine, he was professor of psychiatry and medicine, associate director of the National Institute of Mental Health (NIMH) Clinical Research Center, director of the Psychoneuroimmunology Laboratory, and chief of the inpatient division. Evans is a former clinical scholar in the Robert Wood Johnson fellowship program at the University of North Carolina. He is the author of over 300 articles, chapters, and abstracts and serves on the editorial boards of a number of professional journals, including *Psychoneuroendocrinology; Depression; Seminars in Clinical Neuropsychiatry;* and *Journal of Clinical Psychiatry and Neurosciences.*

Evans is a fellow of the American College of Psychiatrists, the American Psychiatric Association (APA), and the American College of Neuropsychopharmacology. He has served on numerous national committees, including those for APA, the Society of Biological Psychiatry, and the Cancer and Leukemia Group B. He has also served as chairman of the NIMH Mental Health AIDS/Immunology Research Review Committee and as a member of the National Advisory Board of the Robert Wood Johnson Clinical Scholars Program. Evans is a member of the Scientific Advisory Board of the National Depressive and Manic Depressive Association (NDMDA) and is a senior examiner of the American Board of Psychiatry and Neurology. He has received numerous awards for teaching and research, including the Gerald L. Klerman Lifetime Research Award from NDMDA. Evans has had a long-standing clinical and research interest in depression. He is currently principal investigator on several NIMH grants studying the neurobiology of stress and depression, and conducts clinical drug trials specializing in depression and related mood disorders.

STAFF

REFERENCES

Darwin, C. (1859). *On the origin of species.* London: John Murray.

Denny, M. R. (1980). *Comparative psychology: An evolutionary analysis of animal behavior.* New York: Wiley.

Stanley, S. M. (1981). *The new evolutionary timetable.* New York: Basic Books.

Wilson, E. O. (1975). *Sociobiology: The new synthesis.* Cambridge, MA: Harvard University Press.

M. R. DENNY
Michigan State University

COMPARATIVE PSYCHOLOGY

EVOLUTION

Evolution is generally assumed to account for the variety of species on earth today. The changes that have taken place over millions of years are presumably due to (a) variation in the genes of a population and (b) survival and transmission of certain variations by natural selection.

Variation in the genes may occur through mutation, but more often by genetic recombination through bisexual reproduction. According to Darwin (1859), natural selection interacts with genetic variation so that the fittest members of the population (those producing the most viable offspring) contribute most to the gene pool of subsequent generations. Chance is responsible for gene mutations and the juggling of genes in the population, but success in survival determines the perpetuation of genetic changes. Rate of evolutionary change is thus determined by rate of advantageous mutations and intensity of selection pressures.

Evolution produces *speciation,* the origin of new species, when two or more populations of a species become insulated from each other in different environments. They evolve differently and eventually these populations become different species. *Adaptation* occurs when the environment remains fairly constant and the entire species through natural selection becomes better suited to the environment. Behaviors, as well as anatomical structures, evolve through natural selection (Darwin, 1859). Behavior can be adaptive or maladaptive in the evolutionary sense: Much of the study of comparative psychology, modern population ecology, and ethology consists of describing the adaptive value or origin of certain behavior patterns (Denny, 1980). When the adaptive behavior is social, the discipline is called sociobiology (Wilson, 1975).

Presumably, evolutionary change does not have to be slow, gradual, and continuous. There are not necessarily any so-called missing links in the fossil record of the evolution of Homo sapiens (Stanley, 1981), and all aspects of an animal do not need to have evolutionary usefulness. Many changes may be accidentally linked to changes that are adaptive. There is no gene for one's thumb and another for the big toe; when the thumb enlarged, the big toe did also.

Although evolution is a theory, it is a well-established one; it is not a hypothesis. Theory is the end product of an empirical science that rests on masses of accumulated data. Nothing is absolutely certain in science.

EXCITATORY AND INHIBITORY SYNAPSES

Chemical synapses—that is, synapses that use a chemical neurotransmitter to transfer information from one neuron to another—can be excitatory or inhibitory, depending on their effects on the postsynaptic neuron. Synapses releasing a neurotransmitter that brings the membrane potential of the postsynaptic neuron toward the threshold for generating action potentials are said to be excitatory. Alternatively, inhibitory synapses drive the membrane potential of the postsynaptic neuron away from the threshold for generating action potentials. The effect of a synapse is determined by its neurotransmitter content and the properties of the receptors present on the postsynaptic membrane. For example, in the adult mammalian brain, glutamate synapses are known to be excitatory, while GABA synapses are inhibitory. Meanwhile, synapses containing acetylcholine can be either excitatory or inhibitory, depending on the type of receptors present at a given synapse. Thus, at the neuromuscular junction, acetylcholine produces synaptic excitation by acting on a nicotinic receptor, while in the heart it acts on the inhibitory muscarinic receptor, resulting in slowing of the heart rate. Moreover, acetylcholine can have both excitatory and inhibitory effects in the same region, as described in the hippocampus (Ben-Ari, Krnjevic', Reinhardt, & Ropert, 1981; Dodd, Dingledine, & Kelly, 1981).

Interestingly, in many instances excitatory and inhibitory synapses appear also to differ morphologically. In the cerebral cortex, Gray (1959) described two morphological types of synapses, type 1 and type 2, which were later correlated to excitatory and inhibitory synapses, respectively (Eccles, 1964). Type 1 synapses have a prominent postsynaptic density and a synaptic cleft about 20 nm wide. They are also called asymmetric synapses, because the postsynaptic membrane specialization is thicker than the presynaptic one (Colonnier, 1968). Most type 1 or asymmetric synapses contain round synaptic vesicles, so they are also termed S-type, (S for Spheroid vesicles). The great majority of type 1 synapses in the cerebral cortex use glutamate as a neurotransmitter and are excitatory. Type 2 synapses are characterized by a less pronounced postsynaptic density and a narrower synaptic cleft of about 12 nm.

They are also known as symmetric, because the pre- and postsynaptic membrane specializations have a similar appearance. These synapses contain both round and flat synaptic vesicles after aldehyde fixation; hence the term F-type, (F for flat vesicles). In the cerebral cortex, the vast majority of type 2 or symmetric synapses contain GABA as a neurotransmitter and are inhibitory. Glycine, another major inhibitory neurotransmitter of the brain, is found in symmetric synapses in the spinal cord and the cochlear nucleus.

While this correlation between morphology and function essentially holds true for the synapses in the adult cerebral cortex, this is not always the case during development or in all other regions of the brain. For example, in the very young cerebral cortex, GABA cannot be detected by immunocytochemistry in as many as three-quarters of the symmetric synapses (Micheva & Beaulieu, 1996). In some regions of the brain, such as the spinal cord, basal ganglia, and inferior olive, GABA terminals have been observed to also form asymmetric synapses. Thus, while the correlation between the two morphological types of synapses and their functions holds true in a significant number of cases, it must be viewed with caution, and always in conjunction with an immunocytochemical identification of the neurotransmitter type.

The excitatory and inhibitory synapses have been the object of many studies in different regions of the brain. For example, in the cerebral cortex, it was found that these two types of synapses differ both in quantity and distribution. The excitatory synapses represent the majority of synapses (more than 80%), and contact predominantly distal parts of the neuron, such as dendritic spines (i.e., the protoplasmic protrusions extending from the dendrites of some cells). Inhibitory synapses, meanwhile, are much less numerous and are most often found on proximal parts of the neuron such as dendritic shafts and cell bodies (for example, Beaulieu, Kisvarday, Somogyi, Cynader, & Cowey, 1992). These morphological data appear to contradict physiological studies indicating the existence of a balance between the excitatory and inhibitory neurotransmissions in the cortex. However, even though the excitatory connections are much more abundant, the cortical inhibitory neurons fire at much higher rates than the excitatory pyramidal neurons (reviewed in Connors & Gutnick, 1990). The fact that inhibitory neurons make many more contacts on or near the cell bodies is also important because the spatial location of a synapse determines its relative contribution to the electrical state of the cell—that is, the closer the synapse to the site of generation of action potentials (presumably the axon hillock) the greater its effect. Therefore, the inhibitory system, by way of its distribution and pattern of activity, can efficiently balance excitatory neurotransmission in the cerebral cortex. The inhibitory system is also in a position to exert a very focused effect on a single excitatory input, since some dendritic spines receive both an excitatory and an inhibitory synapse (Jones & Powell, 1969; Qian & Sejnowski, 1990). In this case, the interaction between the two synaptic inputs would occur locally, at the level of the dendritic spine that is relatively isolated from the rest of the neuron.

It thus becomes clear that studying the distribution and physiology of the excitatory and inhibitory synapses, as well as their development and plasticity, is essential for understanding the overall organization and functioning of the brain.

REFERENCES

Beaulieu, C., Kisvarday, Z., Somogyi, P., Cynader, M., & Cowey, A. (1992). Quantitative distribution of GABA-immunopositive and -immunonegative neurons and synapses in the monkey striate cortex (area 17). *Cerebral Cortex, 2,* 295–309.

Ben-Ari, Y., Krnjevic', K., Reinhardt, W., & Ropert, N. (1981). Intracellular observations on the disinhibitory action of acetylcholine in the hippocampus. *Neuroscience, 6,* 2475–2484.

Colonnier, M. (1968). Synaptic patterns on different cell types in the different laminae of the cat visual cortex: An electron microscope study. *Brain Research, 9,* 268–287.

Dodd, J., Dingledine, R., & Kelly, J. S. (1981). The excitatory action of acetylcholine on hippocampal neurones of the guinea pig and rat maintained in vitro. *Brain Research, 207,* 109–127.

Connors, B. W., & Gutnick, M. J. (1990). Intrinsic firing patterns of diverse neocortical neurons. *Trends in Neuroscience, 13,* 99–104.

Eccles, J. C. (1964). *The physiology of synapses.* Berlin: Springer-Verlag.

Gray, E. G. (1959). Axo-somatic and axo-dendritic synapses of the cerebral cortex: An electron microscope study. *Journal of Anatomy, 93,* 420–433.

Jones, E. G., & Powell, T. P. S. (1969). Morphological variations in the dendritic spines of the neocortex. *Journal of Cell Science, 5,* 509–529.

Micheva, K. D., & Beaulieu, C. (1996). Quantitative aspect of synaptogenesis in the rat barrel field cortex with special reference to GABA circuitry. *Journal of Comparative Neurology, 373,* 340–354.

Qian, N., & Sejnowski, T. J. (1990). When is an inhibitory synapse effective? *Proceedings of the National Academy of Science, U.S.A., 87,* 8145–8149.

K. D. MICHEVA
Stanford University

ACTION POTENTIAL
NEUROTRANSMITTER

EXECUTIVE SELECTION

There is a long history of efforts to select managers, and many studies on leadership. Prominent among the former are the long-term management selection programs at Sears Roebuck and American Telephone and Telegraph Company. Historically, studies by the Institute for Social Research at the University of Michigan, those undertaken at Ohio State and summarized by Stogdill in his *Handbook of Leadership,* and those by Fiedler reported in *A Theory of Leadership Effectiveness,* have exemplified the efforts to learn what qualities make a good manager and a good leader. However, the prediction of successful managerial behavior does not necessarily apply to executive behavior. As Zaleznik has pointed out (1977), being an executive involves a higher level of complexity and risk taking than does being a manager. Selecting executives, therefore, is an area unto itself.

There are no scientifically validated predictors of successful executive behavior. Different people succeed in different companies or leadership roles at different times under different circumstances. Entrepreneurs are psychologically different from the heads of more established companies. The heads of small companies operate differently from the heads of large companies. The behaviors required of executives seem to change decade by decade, as new and different problems become dominant.

Unlike in studies of managers, where significant numbers are drawn from and followed in the same company, or where representative samples are easy to obtain, there is no general population from which to predict who will achieve executive success. While some potential executives may come from among managers, others may come from other professions such as law or accounting. Some may be fortunate enough to be in the right place at the right time. Some may have been well tutored, others may be so-called favorite sons.

Almost all the criteria for selection are derived from informed opinion. Authorities usually infer from the behavior of successful prominent executives the personal qualities that enabled those executives to succeed. To be successful usually means that the executive has strengthened the organization's capacity for perpetuation, while simultaneously sustaining its values and economic viability. Henry (1949) concluded that his subjects had strong mobility drives. They saw authority as controlling but helpful. They had a high ability to organize unstructured situations and were able to decide among several optional courses of action. They tended to be firm in their sense of self-identity and to know where they were headed in life. They were active and aggressive, and feared failure. Strongly reality-oriented, they had severed the ties with their parents and were free to pursue life on their own.

These characteristics of successful executives recur in many other reports. All writers recognize the strong need to achieve high goals that motivate the executive and his or her organization, as well as the need for dominance, power, and self-assertion, and the willingness to take risks. Successful executives must be flexible, must be able to change course readily when it becomes necessary to do so. They must face up to difficult situations, while simultaneously maintaining self-control under the most adverse circumstances, and must be able to integrate and use a great store of information which is then translated into product or service. Executives must view the world broadly in economic and sociological terms, as well as with an understanding of historical and political forces and cultural and ethnic considerations.

To be an executive of a contemporary organization requires a high level of intelligence, a wide range of information from many different sources. Successful executives are well read and thoughtful, and as a consequence are sagacious. They have quick intellectual perceptions, can penetrate a mass of material to discern important issues. They are able to judge people and methods well. They have an intuitive understanding that also gives them a humanitarian quality.

Successful executives must have a sensitivity to their political and social environments, as well as to the natural environment, and have a social responsibility and social awareness. Increasingly, students of the subject agree on these issues. They agree also on the need for successful executives to motivate people, to capture their creative energies, and direct those energies into problem-solving activity. The successful executive creates the conditions for identification with himself or herself, enhancing the capacity of subordinates as they work with the executive to master reality problems, to learn from those experiences, and thereby increase their own adaptive capacities. Executives must accept the support of others in their role. To do that, however, means they must also be willing to risk losing the approval of others when disappointment or failure occurs. Also, they must receive ideas, analyze them, consolidate them into a position or stand, pursue them, enunciate them articulately, and support others in carrying them out.

Executives have to represent their organization not only among its many publics, but particularly in its relationship with the government. In "The new class of chief executive officer," Steiner emphasizes the need for executives to be articulate in these growing interactions.

A particular competence of the successful executive is the capacity to balance political forces both inside and outside the organization. Such leaders must absorb hostility from their many constituencies—some of it unfair and some of it exploitative—and deflect that hostility without letting it destroy them.

Psychologically speaking, successful executives are akin to parental figures in a given culture. Unconsciously, people attribute to those who have power over them characteristics of parental figures. They expect those who have executive power to behave toward them as parents in that culture ideally behave toward their children. This requires that executives be sensitive to others' feelings. Such sensitivity may also arouse feelings of guilt. Frequently, successful executives find it difficult to face up to the limits and deficiencies of subordinates.

Good executives are able to take charge of their organizations, set goals and directions, compel attention to them, and maintain those boundaries which channel organization efforts in specific, as contrasted with diffuse, efforts. They can "see over the hill," being not necessarily prescient, but able to project anticipated consequences of present forces and directions and to act on those projections. Their capacity for taking risk means also that they are able to admit mistakes. Their capacity for compassion also means that they take their public responsibility seriously. The best executives are mentors who develop successors who are better than they. They are held together by their integrity. They are significantly motivated by conscience and recognize the multiple obligations to a range of constituencies. The successful executive has a coherent and solid sense of self, good relationships with both subordinates and superiors as well the external environment, and can manage stress well, which means flexibility and a sense of humor.

Summarizing the present characteristic behavior of executive candidates and juxtaposing it against the required behavior is as close as we can come to prediction. While the approximation may be crude, it permits flexibility of thinking about the behavioral requirements of each situation at any given point in time, and lets us assess a range of candidates for the likelihood of success in that role at that time.

REFERENCES

Fiedler, F. E. (1967). *A theory of leadership effectiveness.* New York: McGraw-Hill.

Henry, W. E. (1949). The business executive: The psychodynamics of a social role. *American Journal of Sociology, 54,* 286–291.

Stogdill, R. M. (1974). *Handbook of leadership.* New York: Free Press.

Zaleznik, A. (1977). Managers and leaders: Are they different? *Harvard Business Review, 55,* 67–78.

SUGGESTED READING

Maccoby, M. (1981). *The leader.* New York: Simon & Shuster.

McClelland, D. C. (1975). *Power: The inner experience.* New York: Irvington.

Zaleznik, A., & Kets de Vries, M. R. F. (1975). *Power and the corporate mind.* Boston: Houghton Mifflin.

H. LEVINSON
The Levinson Institute

INDUSTRIAL PSYCHOLOGY
JOB ANALYSIS
LEADERSHIP STYLES
MANAGEMENT DECISION MAKING

EXIT INTERVIEWS

Exit interviews are used in employment settings, focusing specifically on those employees who are leaving the organization. Two distinct purposes can be identified for such an interview: information gathering and information giving (Downs, Smeyak, & Martin, 1980). In addition, the exit interview can be a good way to show support for the departing employee's decision (Finney, 1999), or to stay in touch with an employee after he or she leaves (Brotherson, 1999).

Information gathering is an attempt to curb financial losses associated with excessive turnover, and to collect diagnostic information regarding organizational functioning. Why are employees seeking other jobs? Are departing employees the best or worst workers? In contrast, information given to the employee helps smooth his or her transition. What is the status of the employee's benefits? Has the employee checked in all keys and other company property? Maintaining good relations with past employees is a more recent consideration in the literature on the exit interview, but in an era of declining employee loyalty to organizations, it is always possible to have an employee work in or around the organization again, either as a rehire or as an employee of an organization that does business with the former employer.

The value of exit interviews is open to question. Research by Joel Lefkowitz and Myron Katz (1969) showed that a later follow-up questionnaire resulted in different reasons for leaving than the earlier exit interview did, with questionnaire results being more negative toward the company. The same general results were found by John Hinrichs (1975) in a study comparing exit interviews to results obtained by an interview with an outside consultant. Perhaps the best time to collect information is either before the decision is made to leave (i.e., "What would it take to get you to consider employment elsewhere?" "Why do you stay here?"), or six months after the employee has left (Finney, 1999). At the actual time of departure, the employee may well not give accurate or honest information, as he or she is emotionally elsewhere—the new job. In short, employees may be reluctant to help the employer.

In spite of such problems, exit interviews should be used. To be effective, the organization should carefully consider the information to be gathered, who should be doing the interview, how that interviewer should be prepared for the task, and what kinds of organizational support are required (Finney, 1999). Furthermore, interpretation of any information obtained should carefully consider biases.

REFERENCES

Brotherton, P. (1999). Staying in touch with past employees. *Employment Management Today, 4*(2), 45–48.

Finney, M. (1999). Debriefing departing employees: Tips on conducting exit interviews. *Employment Management Today, 4*(2), 22–27.

Hinrichs, J. (1975). Employees going and coming: The exit interview. *Personnel, 48,* 30–35.

Lefkowitz, J., & Katz, M. (1969). Validity of exit interviews. *Personnel Psychology, 22,* 445–455.

SUGGESTED READING

Downs, C. W., Smeyak, G. P., & Martin, E. (1980). *Professional interviewing.* New York: Harper and Row.

Dunnette, M. D., Arvey, R. D., & Banas, P. A. (1973). Why do they leave? *Personnel, 50,* 25–39.

P. G. BENSON
New Mexico State University

EXORCISM

An exorcism is a ritual, formalized by the Catholic Church during the seventeenth century, performed on a person exhibiting signs of demonic possession. This ritual, described in the *Ritual romanum* in 1614 and still accepted as the official procedure, was directed at the Devil or "unclean spirit" assumed to inhabit the body of the possessed (Hoyt, 1981). Historically, demonic possession, one of the most popular and dramatic explanations of disordered behavior, was mentioned only once in the Old Testament. Possession, however, is referred to frequently in the New Testament. Four complete cases of exorcism were performed by Jesus Christ (McCasland, 1982). Oesterreich, in his classic book *Possession and Exorcism* (1974), asserts that explanations relying on demonic possession have been reported in most countries at various times throughout history.

Accepted signs of demonic possession may include any of the following: an offensive stench, tight lips, inability to pray, vomiting strange objects, rolling of the eyes, exhibiting powers beyond one's physical capacity, shouting obscenities, personality changes, prophetic wisdom, convulsions, speaking or understanding a strange language, repulsion by the sight of the cross, repelled by holy water, and the refusal to enter a sanctified place of worship (Neaman, 1975; Richards, 1974). Most of those persons found possessed were women (Hoyt, 1981).

During the early Christian era, exorcistic skills were considered to be a special talent. Later, during the middle of the third century, the Catholic Church created the position of exorcist. The exorcist was typically a minor cleric. The exorcism procedure consisted of two parts (Neaman, 1975). First, the exorcist strengthened himself by praying, and then the Devil was attacked, insulted, and commanded to leave the body of the possessed. Second, recovery was assumed to have occurred when the person returned to a prepossessed state. Contemporary Roman Catholic belief distinguishes between major and minor exorcisms, depending upon the degree of possession (Richards, 1974). A brief exorcistic rite is often included in the baptismal ceremony of the Catholic church (McBrien, 1994). The Catholic church updated the guidelines for exorcism in 1999. The new guidelines encourage a thorough medical and psychological evaluation before recommending an exorcism. The psychological literature regarding exorcisms is limited primarily to case studies and anecdotal reports (Pfeifer, 1994).

REFERENCES

Hoyt, C. (1981). *Witchcraft.* Carbondale, IL: Southern Illinois Press.

McBrien, R. (1994). *Catholicism: A new study.* San Francisco: Harper.

McCasland, S. (1982). *By the finger of God: Demon possession and exorcism in early Christianity in light of modern views of mental illness.* New York: Macmillan.

Neaman, J. (1975). *Suggestions of the devil: The origins of madness.* New York: Doubleday.

Oesterreich, T. (1974). *Possession and exorcism: Among primitive races in antiquity, the middle ages and modern times.* New York: Causeway.

Pfeifer, S. (1994). Belief in demons and exorcism in psychiatric patients in Switzerland. *British Journal of Medical Psychology, 4,* 247–258.

Richards, J. (1974). *But deliver us from evil: An introduction to demonic dimensions in pastoral care.* London: Darton, Longman & Todd.

C. H. FISCHER
Radford University

RELIGION & PSYCHOLOGY

EXPECTANCY THEORY

The concept of expectancy is central to much of mammalian and avian behavior. When a naive, hungry rat, for example, is first placed in the start box of a maze, it typically resists by spreading its legs so that one has to turn the rat on its side to get it through the opening. After a number of reinforced trials the rat eagerly leaps into the start box, may even try to claw open the start box door or take off over the top of the maze toward the goal box, if it is a complex maze. It makes sense to say that the rat now expects to find food when at first it did not.

Tolman (1932) can probably be considered the main exponent of the expectancy theory although the importance of expectation to behavior has several long-standing roots. For Tolman, cognitive expectation of a goal is established with experience and is one of the principal things learned by an animal in its habitat or in the laboratory. He called it a sign-Gestalt expectation or a "what-leads-to-what" sign–significate relation in which the sign is like a cue and the significate is usually some sort of goal. Tolman cited a number of experiments to support the notion of specific expectancies in rats and monkeys. For example, when a rat that has been running a complex maze under thirst motivation and water reward is made hungry, there is a momentary disruption of performance on the transitional day, when it has no basis for expecting food. But on the next day with expectancy for the food reward established, the rat's performance is back to the previous level.

One of the more striking observations of expectancy behavior is reported by Tinklepaugh (1928). In a delayed response situation, a piece of banana was hidden under one of two containers while a monkey watched. After a short delay, during which time a screen hid the containers, the screen was removed and the monkey was allowed to choose and typically chose correctly. On a later trial, the experimenter substituted a less-preferred piece of lettuce for the banana. When the monkey turned over the correct container, revealing lettuce instead of banana, there was definite disruption of behavior. The monkey showed surprise and emotion, rejected the lettuce, and searched all around for the expected banana. Similar observations have been made, for example, with rats when sunflower seeds were substituted for preferred bran mash and in recent experiments with chimpanzees. Animals other than humans clearly have some sort of expectancy for specific goal objects, but whether these expectancies are the sign–significate (S–S) type of Tolman, the fractional anticipatory goal response (R–S) of Hull, or something else is still a theoretical question. Human expectancies, of course, have a strong language component.

In one sense most classically conditioned responses qualify as expectancies, because the conditioned response (CR) when elicited by the conditioned stimulus (CS) comes forward in the behavior sequence and anticipates the unconditioned stimulus (US). Thus when a dog is conditioned to salivate to a bell, it can be said that the dog now expects food when the bell rings, and when a rat is shocked when a light goes on, the resulting conditioned fear means it expects shock or pain with light onset and behaves accordingly.

Such expectancies also engender new behavior or new expectations when not realized. Without an expectation for a particular goal object, there can be no thwarting or frustration of behavior toward that goal. The responses elicited by thwarting or frustrative nonreward are usually antagonistic to the original response to the goal, for example, escape, withdrawal, and aggression. Or if an animal no longer receives shock when the light goes on, it could relax or undergo relief or, put another way, expect safety. But the expectancy for shock or pain must exist first. Simple absence of shock is not safety, just as simple absence of a goal (food) is not frustrating.

Bolles's (1975) expectancy theory of avoidance learning, with roots in Tolman's work, emphasizes the idea that learning involves the acquisition of information about the environment rather than the acquisition of S–R bonds. According to Bolles, there is no reinforcement or punishment mechanism operating in avoidance learning. The animal behaves appropriately (avoids) because it expects shock, say, in the shock chamber and expects safety elsewhere.

Expectancy is an integral part of instrumental appetitive learning, as illustrated by the differential outcome effect (DOE; Trapold, 1970). In early DOE experiments, it was clearly demonstrated that expectancies based on different reinforcers (e.g., solid food versus liquid sucrose) have different stimulus consequences, to which different instrumental responses can be conditioned. This was shown, for example, in a two-choice conditional discrimination study in which R_1 was reinforced to S_2 with food and R_2 was reinforced to S_2 with sucrose.

According to expectancy theory, the use of differential reinforcers should condition different expectancies to S_1 and S_2 whereas using the same reinforcer for both S_1–R_1 and S_2–R_2 would condition the same expectancy to S_1 and S_2. If the expectancies E_1 and E_2 for two different reinforcers have distinctive stimulus properties, then the unique interoceptive properties of E_1 and E_2 augment the exteroceptive differences between S_1 and S_2 and more precisely elicit the correct response (R_1 or R_2). In contrast, a single reinforcer would retard learning, because the same expectancy would be conditioned to both R_1 and R_2. Trapold not only demonstrated faster learning with different reinforcers (DOE) but also found that cue-reward pretraining that was the reverse of the pairings during training interfered with final learning. That is, incorrect expectancies had to be extinguished before the correct expectancies became operative.

Differential outcome effect has been found by numerous investigators using a variety of different outcomes: food versus water, food of different quality or quantity, different delays of the same reinforcer, one a reinforcer and the other a neutral stimulus like a tone, and so forth. To the extent that there is a delay between S_1 or S_2 and the availability of R_1 and R_2, then E_1 and E_2 as intervening and long-lasting stimuli can mediate correct responding and enhance conditional discrimination learning even more than without such a delay.

Differential expectancies can probably be conceived of as images, emotional responses, or R_g–S_g and R_f–S_f in the Hull–Spence–Amsel tradition. The rather precise nature of two expectancies has been identified by Brodigan and Peterson (1976) in the pigeon in a conditional discrimination with three keys in an operant chamber. They found that the pigeon responds to the conditional cue (central key) with a response topography appropriate to the reinforcer that would be available for a correct response on the subsequent choice trial (side keys). For example, pigeons gave food-type pecks (i.e., sharp, open-beak pecks to the central key) when followed by a food reinforcement trial and water-type pecks (i.e., slower, more sustained key contacts) when it was given a water reinforcement trial. Such expectancies are very much like Hull's R_g–S_g and are consistent with elicitation theory.

The expectancy concept seems to relate to conditioning in another different but basic way. When Kamin (1969) discovered the phenomenon of blocking, he posited that a CS becomes strongly associated with a US only if the US is unexpected or surprising. Supposedly, surprising events are more likely to be rehearsed and retained than expected events. In the blocking experiment, stimulus A is the CS for a number of trials, then stimulus B is added so that the CS is an AB compound for many trials. Finally, when tested alone, B shows hardly any conditioning compared with A alone. Presumably, B is presented after the subject already expects the US, and without a surprising US, B is not well conditioned. To handle this aspect of conditioning, Rescorla and Wagner (1972) formulated an equation for Pavlovian conditioning in which they quantified and ojectified surprisingness so successfully that it has flourished for 20 or more years.

Expectancy theory as explicitly applied to humans is best exemplified in the area of industrial-organizational behavior as a motivational manipulation (Vroom, 1964). Here the important source of motivation is the specific expected outcome for the work effort expended. That is, a positively valued incentive or outcome functions selectively on actions that lead to it. This is in contrast to a drive notion in which energizing has a generalized effect. In brief, the theory has three parts: (a) an expectancy that work effort, including equipment, training, and skills, will accomplish the behavior (performance); (b) instrumentality, the means that connect behavior to outcomes such as recognition, awards, advancement, bonuses, co-worker involvement, and pay; and (c) valence, the attractiveness of a particular outcome. The worker's motivation to perform may not necessarily be fully conscious. For all practical purposes the theory predicts that the greater the value of the outcome and the higher the perceived probability that effort will lead to the reward, the greater the effort expended.

In the area of organizational psychology, expectancy theory engendered considerable research, but the results were only moderately supportive. And managers did not accept expectancy theory to any extent, because they had to do something that influenced many workers at once rather one worker at a time. Goal-setting theory, which ignores individual differences in motives, has largely replaced expectancy theory for researchers of worker motivation.

REFERENCES

Bolles, R. C. (1975). *Learning memory.* New York: Holt, Reinhart, & Winston.

Brodigan, D. L., & Peterson, G. B. (1976). Two-choice discrimination performance of pigeons as a function of reward expectancy, pre-choice delay, and domesticity. *Animal Learning and Behavior, 4,* 121–124.

Kamin, L. J. (1969). Predictability, surprise, attention and conditioning. In B. Campbell & R. Church (Eds.), *Punishment and aversive behavior.* New York: Appleton-Century-Crofts.

Tinkelpaugh, D. L. (1928). An experimental study of representative factors in monkeys. *Journal of Comparative Psychology, 8,* 197–236.

Tolman, E. C. (1932). *Purposive behavior in animals and men.* New York: Appleton-Century-Crofts.

Trapold, M. A. (1970). Are expectancies based upon different positive reinforcing events discriminably different? *Learning and Motivation, 1,* 129–140.

Vroom, V. H. (1964). *Work and motivation.* New York: Wiley.

M. R. Denny
Michigan State University

ATTITUDE THEORY
ECOLOGICAL VALIDITY
ETHOLOGY
IMAGERY
INSTINCT
MEMORY
SURPRISE
WORK EFFICIENCY

EXPERIENTIAL PSYCHOTHERAPY

Experiential psychotherapy refers to a way of performing therapy, rather than to a therapy specific to one theory of persons or personality. Experiential therapy is a method of methods, and is in this way metatheoretical.

THE TOUCHSTONE OF THE EXPERIENTIAL METHOD

A central focus in conducting therapy experientially is the client's moment-to-moment experiencing. Experiencing is seen as the entry point to the processes of personality change and psychological improvement. It is the primary navigational aid regarding the productive course of therapeutic interaction.

Therapeutic moves (empathic response, interpretation, suggestion, question, confrontation, chair-work, psychoeducation, etc.) may be immediately evaluated by their effect on client experiencing: when experiencing becomes more closed, defensive, abstract, or out of control for the client, the move has had an experiential effect of dubious value. When experiencing becomes more open, complex, intricate, sensation-based, and accurately expressible in words or other symbols, the move has had a desirable experiential effect.

Attending to this experiential feedback protects the therapist against the pitfall of selectively perceiving data anticipated by the therapist's particular theoretical or personal expectations. The experiential therapist may thereby quickly correct unhelpful moves, rather than persisting with faulty plans and generating problems in the therapeutic relationship.

References to the experiential way of performing therapy are found in the works of many major early psychotherapists: Sigmund Freud, Rank, Ferenczi, Reich, Fromm-Reichmann, Sullivan, and Horney (Friedman, 1976). Rogers (1951, 1961) was perhaps the first to develop a method of psychotherapy in which the client was explicitly designated to be the proper guide of the course of therapy, as opposed to the doctor's being the proper guide. Whitaker and Malone (1969) may have been the first to use the term "experiential psychotherapy" to describe their approach. Gendlin, who worked closely with Rogers, developed the philosophical basis for the experiential method (Gendlin, 1962), and cites the existential and phenomenological philosophers Kirkegaard, Dilthey, Husserl, Heidegger, Buber, Sartre, and Merleau-Ponty as precursors of his experiential philosophy (1979).

The proponents of as many as four dozen later-generation psychotherapies have called their approaches experiential (Mahrer, 1998), but in five of these the experiential method receives major and central emphasis: client-centered, existential, Gestalt process-experiential, and focusing-oriented (Watson, Greenberg, & Lietaer, 1998; Gendlin, 1996).

The theorists in these therapies all drew on Goldstein's (1939) observation and conceptualization of an actualizing tendency. This is the tendency found in any living organism to behave in ways that fulfill and further perfect the capacities, according to its nature, of the organism as a whole.

The client's moment-to-moment experiencing is seen as the real-time expression of the actualizing tendency. Experiencing is held to be wider and deeper than conscious experience; it is considered inherently life-promoting for both the individual and the social group, and generally more so with more awareness. As Greenberg and Van Balen put it:

A general principle that has united all experientially/phenomenologically oriented theorists is that people are wiser than their intellects alone . . . tacit functioning is an important guide to conscious experience, is fundamentally adaptive, and is potentially available to awareness . . . interpersonal safety and support are viewed as key elements in promoting an increase in the amount of attention available for self-awareness and self-exploration . . . an active, integrating self [is a] . . . dynamic system . . . in which healthy functioning results when as many parts as possible are integrated in awareness . . . the integration of ever-developing facets of experience, including polar aspects . . . as well as different levels and types of experience. (1998, p. 29)

The actualization of healthy potentials implicit in experiencing does not depend on the individual alone, but is seen as highly dependent on the interpersonal conditions with which it interacts currently and with which it has interacted historically.

THE NEED FOR THERAPY

Things go awry when factors in a person's environment interfere with healthy awareness of and symbolization of experiencing, especially if the interference is systematic over a long time. Certain patterns of relating to experiencing (or avoiding it) may result; these shape the positive potentials of experiencing into negative forms of expression. "The source of evil and antisocial behavior lies much more in factors that prevent full, accurate, ongoing symbolization of experiencing than it does in the individual personality" (Iberg, 1990, p. 101).

Gendlin (1999) makes interactions rather than units (such as atoms or personality traits) the basic building block in his philosophy. Thus, experiential therapies pay a great deal of attention to interactions, both interpersonal and intrapsychic. Maintaining an empathic climate has long been recognized as a way of interacting that facilitates personal growth and development, both in therapy and in the normal course of development (Rogers, 1957; Brazelton, 1992; Watson, Goldman, & Vanaerschot, 1998). Reflexive attention to the patterns of interaction between client and therapist is one thing that makes the therapy interaction different from (and more change-promoting) than other relationships the client may have (van Kessel & Lietaer, 1998).

Intrapsychically, psychological problems are seen by Greenberg and Van Balen (1998) as involving

... the inability to integrate aspects of functioning into coherent, harmonious internal relations. ... At another level ... the inability to symbolize bodily felt constituents of experience in awareness, or symbolizing them in restricted or rigid ways, [is] another source of dysfunction. ... A third major source ... involves the activation by minimal cues of core maladaptive emotion schemes. (p. 50)

On a more phenomenological level, these things involve problematic relationships to one's bodily felt sense—Gendlin's (1996) carefully defined, more everyday term for experiencing when focused upon.

Movement Toward Healthy Psychological Functioning

Therapy is then very much about correcting problematic attitudes toward experiencing (Cornell, 1996; Gendlin, 1996). Leijssen's (1998) characterization of the generic therapeutic attitude for relating to one's experiencing is as follows:

[It] requires an attitude of waiting, of quietly ... remaining present with [and being friendly to] the not yet speakable, being receptive to the not yet formed. To achieve this, it will be necessary to suspend temporarily everything that the person already knows about it and to be cognitively inactive. This kind of attention can also be found in Zen meditation and Taoism, but in therapy it is directed toward a specific object, the felt sense. ... The therapist interacts with the client in an attitude of acceptance and empathy; gradually, in the corrective therapeutic milieu the client learns to adopt ... [this] focusing attitude by interacting with the bodily felt experience (the client's inside) in the same friendly and listening way. (Leijssen, 1998, p. 123)

Arriving at the capacity to relate to one's experiencing in this way is not a short-term or trivial matter for many people, especially for those with troublesome psychological issues. The therapeutic relationship establishes a climate within which, aided by the expertise of the therapist, the client can begin to adopt healthier attitudes toward experiencing. The process of doing this takes time, and involves many little successes before major and lasting change is accomplished. The little successes involve "felt shifts":

When the right symbols that fit the experience are found, the client feels a satisfying sense of rightness. This is a 'felt shift': a physical sensation of something moving in the way the problem is experienced. There are many kinds of shifts. . . . On the continuum of *intensities* at the low end there are small shifts which may be very minimal, very subtle; one could easily skip over them if one didn't know about them. At the high end the shift is intense, dramatic, obvious. . . . There are also different *kinds* of shifts: sometimes the client feels a release or a relief in the body (e.g., a sigh, tears); sometimes it is a sharpening of some vague experience or the sense becomes stronger (e.g., a general feeling of confusion becomes a clear feeling of anger); sometimes the client feels something moving from one location in the body to another (e.g., a choking sensation in the throat becomes a warm feeling around the heart); sometimes it is an experience of more energy, excitement, enthusiasm, personal power, or new life awakening and stirring in some parts of the body or the whole body; at other times it's a feeling more of peace, clarity, groundedness, a warm spacious sense of well-being. The client might also have a new insight about an issue, but we consider this only as a felt shift or a new step if the insight doesn't happen only in the mind but is also in some way a bodily felt resolution. (Leijssen, 1998, p. 138)

When a person regularly and reliably relates to experiencing so as to achieve felt shifts, he or she is said to have a high level of experiencing. There is some evidence that a high-experiencing way of working with one's feeling about a traumatic experience has a positive effect on physical health, in the form of improved immune function (Lutgendorf, Antoni, Kumar, & Schneiderman, 1994). Many studies have found psychological benefits associated with high levels of experiencing (Hendricks, in press; Orlinsky, Grawe, & Parks, 1994).

THEORETICAL AND PRACTICAL DEVELOPMENTS

Recent developments by experiential theorists have pursued the specification and differentiation of types of problematic ways of relating to one's experiencing that correspond to various contemporary diagnostic categories. Although there remains much further work to be done, the theorists have begun to identify and empirically test some typical processing problems as listed in Table 1. Implications for corresponding differential therapist responses are also being articulated.

The experiential therapies look for structure in repeated pat-

Table 1. Some Diagnostic Categories and Associated Processing Difficulties*

Category	Processing Difficulties
Major depression	Excessive self-criticism; unacknowledged emotions; over-regulated feelings
Posttraumatic Stress Disorder	Under-regulated bodily experiencing in need of accurate symbolization
Psychosomatic gastrointestinal tract disorders	Tendency to avoid acknowledging and coping with negative self-image inconsistent with aspects of self.
Anxiety disorders	Tendency to interrupt the coming into awareness of bodily experiencing; hyperinclination to reflexivity of attention

*Source: Greenberg, Lietaer, & Watson, 1998, ch. 20

terns of experiencing and interaction, rather than in the contents of awareness or self-concept or in physical structures. One development along this line has been the identification of "markers" indicating recognizable types of processing difficulty to which the experiential therapist may differentially respond. Some examples are: (a) problematic reactions, in which the person's current view of an experience and his or her emotional reaction to it don't match; (b) self-evaluative splits, in which one part of a person negatively evaluates another part; (c) unfinished business, in which there are unresolved emotional memories; and (d) a generally vulnerable, fragile sense of self (Greenberg, Rice, & Elliott, 1993). The experiential therapies take pains to minimize the diagnostic categorization of the individual client, concerned to maintain respect for and the dignity of the person:

Focusing on the state or processes a person is currently engaged in with the therapist in the session allows one to identify blocks to healthy functioning without categorizing the person as a whole as dysfunctional. Thus we need to talk about depressive, anxious, and borderline processes, not people. This would acknowledge that all people engage in processes such as self-criticism, catastrophic expectation, and splitting the good and the bad, and that all have to find ways of dealing with these. People can become more or less repetitive and rigid in the processes they engage in both internally and interactionally. To the degree that people lose flexibility their behavior and experience is restricted into a narrow range of options. Thus they become predictable. New episodes produce repetitive experience and behavior that can become maladaptive patterns. Treatment ought to help melt rigidity and restore people's ability to make more flexible contact with the world. (Greenberg, Lietaer, & Watson, 1998, p. 463)

Recent developments in experiential therapies have moved them from extreme positions toward the middle. The earlier Rogerian position of nondirectivity was one in which therapists studiously avoided guiding clients in any way. The earlier Gestalt position involved a heavy portion of encounter-group-like confrontation (Yontef, 1998). The more modern position is one of guiding the process but not the content of the client's experiencing. Watson, Goldman, and Vanaerschot (1998) convey the spirit of this kind of guiding: "Clearly the art of experiential therapy is one of achieving a fine balance between leading and following, knowing when clients need a gentle nudge or when they need to be nurtured and bathed in compassion" (p. 75). The main new element in the experiential therapies is process diagnosis: specifically defined types of inner relationship. Once a therapist perceives distinctive features of a client's process that are unhealthy and that are likely to benefit from certain therapeutic procedures, it would be insincere for the therapist to keep silent with this knowledge. "In this approach the therapist uses process diagnosis as a key tool and is seen as an expert not on what a client experiences but on how to differentially facilitate optimal client process at particular times" (Greenberg, Lietaer, et al., 1998, p. 456). As always, the client's experiencing is the safeguard against problems: If the therapist's proposal of or attempt at a therapeutic procedure does not have a desirable experiential effect, the therapist returns to empathically responding to locate a course the client experiences as helpful.

Regardless of his or her theoretical training, the experiential

therapist remains alert for the words, images, behavioral strategies, or situational changes that have a positive resonating power with the client's bodily felt sense. Thus, many different approaches to helping the client are useful, limited only by what the therapist knows and can apply skillfully. Therapist and client both rely on their body senses of the steps of therapeutic interaction to guide the way toward improvement—a reliance that both is uniquely right for the client and is a step in the theoretically and interpersonally desirable direction.

REFERENCES

Brazelton, T. B. (1992). *On becoming a family: The growth of attachment.* New York: Delta/Seymour Lawrence.

Cornell, A. W. (1996). *The power of focusing: A practical guide to emotional self-healing.* Oakland, CA: New Harbinger.

Friedman, N. (1976). From the experiential in therapy to experiential psychotherapy: A history. *Psychotherapy: Theory, Research and Practice, 13,* 236–243.

Gendlin, E. T. (1962). *Experiencing and the creation of meaning.* New York: Free Press.

Gendlin, E. T. (1979). Experiential psychotherapy. In R. J. Corsini (Ed.), *Current psychotherapies* (pp. 340–373). Itasca, IL: Peacock.

Gendlin, E. T. (1996). *Focusing-oriented psychotherapy: A manual of the experiential method.* New York: Guilford.

Gendlin, E. T. (1999). *The process model.* On-line: <http://www.focusing.org/process.html>.

Goldstein, K. (1939). *The organism: A holistic approach to biology derived from pathological data in man.* New York: American Book.

Greenberg, L., Lietaer, G., & Watson, J. (1998). Experiential therapy: Identity and challenges. In L. Greenberg, J. Watson, & G. Lietaer, (Eds.), *Handbook of experiential psychotherapy* (pp. 461–466). New York: Guilford.

Greenberg, L., Rice, L., & Elliott, R. (1993). *Facilitating emotional change: The moment-by-moment process.* New York: Guilford.

Greenberg, L., & Van Balen, R. (1998). The theory of experience-centered therapies. In L. Greenberg, J. Watson, & G. Lietaer, (Eds.), *Handbook of experiential psychotherapy* (pp. 28–57). New York: Guilford.

Hendricks, M. N. (in press). Research basis of experiential/focusing-oriented psychotherapy. In D. Cain (Ed.), *Research bases of humanistic psychotherapy.* Washington, DC: American Psychological Association Press.

Iberg, J. R. (1990). Person-centered experiential psychotherapy. In J. K. Zeig & W. M. Munion, (Eds.), *What is psychotherapy? Contemporary perspectives* (pp. 97–102). San Francisco: Jossey-Bass.

Leijssen, M. (1998). Focusing microprocesses. In L. Greenberg, J. Watson, & G. Lietaer (Eds.), *Handbook of experiential psychotherapy* (pp. 121–154). New York: Guilford.

Lutgendorf, S., Antoni, M., Kumar, M., & Schneiderman, N. (1994). Changes in cognitive coping strategies predict EBV-antibody titre change following a stressor disclosure induction. *Journal of Psychosomatic Research, 38,* 63–78.

Mahrer, A. (1998). How can impressive in-session changes become impressive postsession changes? In L. Greenberg, J. Watson, & G. Lietaer, (Eds.), *Handbook of experiential psychotherapy* (pp. 201–223). New York: Guilford.

Orlinsky, D., Grawe, K., & Parks, B. (1994). Process and outcome in psychotherapy: Noch einmal. In A. Bergin, & S. Garfield, (Eds.), *Handbook of psychotherapy and behavior change* (4th ed., pp. 270–376). New York: Wiley.

Rogers, C. R. (1951). *Client-centered therapy.* Boston: Houghton Mifflin.

Rogers, C. R. (1957). The necessary and sufficient conditions of therapeutic personality change. *Journal of Consulting Psychology, 21,* 95–103.

Rogers, C. R. (1961). *On becoming a person.* Boston: Houghton Mifflin.

van Kessel, W., & Lietaer, G. (1998). Interpersonal processes. In L. Greenberg, J. Watson, & G. Lietaer, (Eds.), *Handbook of experiential psychotherapy* (pp. 155–177). New York: Guilford.

Watson, J., Goldman, R., & Vanaerschot, G. (1998). Empathic: A postmodern way of being? In L. Greenberg, J. Watson, & G. Lietaer, (Eds.), *Handbook of experiential psychotherapy* (pp. 61–81). New York: Guilford.

Watson, J., Greenberg, L., & Lietaer, G. (1998). The experiential paradigm unfolding: Relationship and experiencing in therapy. In L. Greenberg, J. Watson, & G. Lietaer, (Eds.), *Handbook of experiential psychotherapy* (pp. 3–27). New York: Guilford.

Whitaker, C., & Malone, T. P. (1969). Experiential or nonrational psychotherapy. In W. Sahakian (Ed.), *Psychotherapy and counseling: Studies in technique* (pp. 416–431). Chicago: Rand McNally.

Yontef, G. (1998). Dialogic gestalt therapy. In L. Greenberg, J. Watson, & G. Lietaer, (Eds.), *Handbook of experiential psychotherapy* (pp. 82–102). New York: Guilford.

SUGGESTED READING

Iberg, J. R. (1981). Focusing. In R. J. Corsini (Ed.), *Handbook of innovative psychotherapies.* New York: Wiley.

Klein, M., Mathiew, P., Kiesler, D., & Gendlin, E. (1970). *The Experiencing scale: A research and training manual.* Madison, WI: University of Wisconsin.

Rogers, C. R. (1980). *A way of being.* Boston: Houghton Mifflin.

J. R. Iberg
Chicago, Illinois

PSYCHOTHERAPY
PSYCHOTHERAPY TECHNIQUES

EXPERIMENTAL CONTROLS

Edwin G. Boring (1954) developed three meanings in psychology for the word *control:* (a) a check, in the sense of verification; (b) a restraint, in the sense of maintaining constancy; and (c) a guide or direction. Controlled observations or checks on observations, and controls on experimental variables, are as old as science. The use in psychology, however, of an experimental control group as such—a separate group of individuals against which observations of the experimental group are compared—has happened only since the start of the 20th century.

Since people not in psychological experiments do learn, mature, and change from experiences in daily living, experimental control groups for comparison purposes are valuable, almost necessary, in most of psychology, in order to have a context in which to interpret meaningful research findings. In addition, the lack of ability to measure with precision in psychology has a decided influence on changes in observations over time. The research context in which the observations are made, the possible reaction of participants in the somewhat unusual conditions of the psychological research study, and motivational differences between the experimental and control groups, can also reduce the quality of the comparisons needed for interpretation. These concerns are also the subject of experimental design and research methodology.

Attempts to develop experimental controls in psychological research include the effort to hold all variables constant except those being deliberately manipulated. This is difficult to do with human participants, can be done only within rather broad limits, and often makes the experimental conditions so artificial that generalizations to the everyday psychological world are difficult.

Participants in psychological research are sometimes used as their own experimental controls: they are observed, an experimental condition is applied, then they are observed again. This method is useful if a large number of observations are made prior to the experimental condition. Such observations can be used to establish the stability of the participant's behavior and the behavior's typical range. When the experimental treatment can be applied and withdrawn over time—again, with many observations made in each interval between conditions—the experimental control is better. If a stable change can be observed after each of the conditions, then good comparisons and interpretations can be made.

In psychology, experimenters often match participants on one or more variables, or group participants by characteristics or prior conditions. Some of these groups will have the experimental treatment and some will not. If the groups are matched on variables such as gender, residential area, or other accurately observed characteristics, the method is acceptable. If the matching or grouping can be followed by a chance allocation of participants (i.e., at random) to experimental and control groups, the resulting experimental controls and comparisons are quite good. If not, major errors may result.

Sometimes statistical adjustments are attempted as a control method in psychological research. Unless accompanied by allocation of participants to experimental and control groups by chance, these methods often are less than adequate to obtain good research comparisons.

During this century psychology has developed a rather mature, rigorous, and sometimes elaborate set of experimental controls for its research methodology, taking into account the special characteristics and problems associated with human participants and psychological variables. Its research methodology is still growing, however, and undoubtedly more and better experimental controls will be developed.

REFERENCES

Boring, E. G. (1954). The nature & history of experimental control, *American Journal of Psychology, 67,* 573–589.

J. W. ASHER
Purdue University

CONTROL GROUPS
RESEARCH METHODOLOGY
SAMPLING

EXPERIMENTAL DESIGNS

Experimental designs guide researchers in performing an experiment. Experiments involve the planned introduction of a factor into a situation with the intent of associating it with a change in that situation. The introduced factor is usually called an intervention, treatment, or independent variable; the change is the measure of the dependent variable. Experimental designs are plans that detail what groups shall be established and how important plausible alternative explanations shall be eliminated. The linking of the intervention to effect, and the elimination of all other explanations for the observed change are the major purposes of experimental design.

The simplest experimental designs involve an intervention given to a single subject or group of subjects with observations before and afterward to determine the change in their condition. For example, if the use of a color display is expected to enhance skill in playing a computer game, observations of the skill of a player or group of players with a black and white display would be followed by observations of that skill with a color display, the intervention. Presumably, any change is due to the introduction of color.

But is it? Experimental designs serve not only to relate variables to their effects, but also to rule out alternative explanations. An obvious alternative explanation is that skill level improved with practice! Both increased practice and the color display occurred in the latter part of the study, so we cannot separate their effects. When this occurs, the variables are said to be confounded.

Only as we separate these effects can we attribute the change to the intervention (color in the display), or to the confounded alternate explanation (practice). In the language of experimental design, we would say we are controlling the confounded variable. How could we do so? There are four common control methods: (a) eliminating the confounded factor; (b) measuring the effect of the confounded factor and correcting for it; (c) comparing equivalent situations, one of which is affected by the confounded variable

and treatment, while the other is affected only by the confounded variable; and (v) varying the treatment but not the confounded variable to see if effect follows the treatment pattern. While there are other methods of control as well, these are the ones most commonly used.

We can illustrate these four ways of controlling confounding variables with our computer game example. We could eliminate the effect of practice by starting the subject with a color display and then removing it. There should be a drop in skill, if color has a stronger effect than practice on performance (experiment 1).

As suggested by method 2, we could plot increasing skill with a black and white display, measuring the rate at which it is increasing, so as to predict its increase over the period when color is introduced. Then we can introduce the color and see if performance is higher than predicted (experiment 2). This design is called the regression discontinuity design, since a statistical method known as regression analysis is used to predict performance; if there is an effect, it shows as a discontinuity from predictions based on preintervention performance.

Using the third method, we could randomly divide our subjects into two equal groups by flipping a coin. Beginning both groups with a black and white display to assure they have started at comparable levels of skill, we would then introduce color to only one of them (experiment 3). This is a control group design, since the control group provides a base in terms of which other influences one wishes to control can be measured. It assumes that the groups are equivalent in every relevant way except for the intervention. Variations on this logic inspire many common designs.

Finally, using method 4, one might start with a black and white display (condition A) for a group, introduce a color (condition B), then revert to black and white (condition A). The pattern of skill level should follow the ABA pattern in which the conditions were applied, even though the general level of skill increases with practice (experiment 4). This is called an ABA design after the pattern of conditions. To be still more certain of the association, color (condition B) might be reintroduced a second or third time (an ABAB or ABABAB design).

THE LOGIC UNDERLYING DESIGNS

The preceding examples illustrate the logic from which most designs are constructed:

1. Hold a situation constant, introduce the treatment, observe the change.

2. If a situation cannot be held constant but is changing, observe the pattern of change, introduce the treatment, determine whether the pattern of change has been disturbed.

3. Hold two or more equivalent situations constant, keep one situation like the others in all ways but the treatment, introduce the treatment to the other (or its variations to still others), and observe the differences.

4. Relate the pattern of treatment application-withdrawal to the pattern of change; if there is a measure of treatment or intervention strength, relate the strength or intensity of the intervention to a relevant aspect, such as size or strength of change.

(This works only if the change reverts back when the intervention is removed. It will not work with changes like learning, which persist.)

Designs are more complex today than when John Stuart Mill first published *A System of Logic* in 1843, yet his attempts to state the logic that undergirded the burgeoning effort called "science" has repeatedly been cited as a basic formulation. He noted in his method of difference that if two circumstances in which a phenomenon does not occur and one in which it does occur "have every circumstance in common save one . . . the instance in which alone the two circumstances differ is the effect, a cause or an indispensable part of the cause of the phenomenon" (Mill, 1843, p. 391).

Experiment 1 involves the application of an intervention to a single set of circumstances. This preintervention-postintervention similarity satisfies the condition of having "every circumstance in common save one." Experiment 3 is a little more complex, yet is more commonly used. It presumes two different groups or sets of circumstances that have "every circumstance in common"— hardly likely, since every person is unique. Mill recognized this and talked about two situations "resembling one another in every other respect" (p. 391). But how shall we interpret "resemble"? One answer is that they are enough alike so that differences in a factor which might otherwise provide an alternative explanation of the effect could not be presumed to be the cause in this instance. But this requires our knowing the relevant variables and knowing when a difference is large enough to make a difference.

Given our relatively weak knowledge base in psychology, in most instances we cannot be sure we know all the variables on which we make sure the groups are equated. Our best protection, then, is random assignment of subjects to groups.

Random assignment to experimental and control groups* (e.g., flipping a coin to assign subjects randomly selected from a population or pool of subjects) assures that the groups on the average "have every circumstance in common," both those suspected as being involved in the phenomenon as well as unsuspected variables, even irrelevant ones like number of skin pores and length of finger nails. Indeed, Campbell and Stanley (1963) believe random assignment sufficiently important because of this protection for "hidden" variables that they label designs which *do not* use it "quasi-experimental designs," and those which do, "true experimental designs." This is somewhat too drastic a distinction, since "quasi" designs are both useful and popular, and the label "true" designs seems to suggest one need not worry about alternative explanations, a condition Campbell and Stanley recognize is false. Nonetheless, random assignment is clearly an important tool.

But there are instances where we do not wish to leave to chance the equating of the groups on variables we are sure are important. Factors such as level of education, learning ability, motivation, and socioeconomic status are often alternative explanations we wish to rule out by assuring equivalence of groups. We do this by stratifying or blocking or matching on measures of these variables, and then randomly assigning subjects to experimental and control groups.

The logic of keeping all circumstances common save one is also employed in more complex designs such as factorial designs. These simultaneously examine the effect of several variables, yet there is always one (or more) group of subjects that differs from another group (or groups) by only one circumstance or variable.

The logic underlying experiments 2 and 4 was formulated by Mill as the method of concomitant variation. He noted that when one phenomenon varies as another does, then either one is cause and the other is effect or vice versa, or both are related to a common cause. Both the regression discontinuity design (experiment 2) and the ABA or ABAB type of design (experiment 4) depend on this logic. So do correlational studies which examine how closely the size of one variable—college grades, for example—is related to the size of another, such as high school grades. In this instance, we would be examining the relation of high school preparation to college success. But is it causally related? Except where an experimental intervention occurs, inference of causation from correlation is fraught with difficulty, since the covariation may be due to a third variable. For instance, success in both high school and college grades could be best explained as a function of student motivation rather than because high school success leads to college success.

CRITERIA OF GOOD DESIGN

A good design should reduce whatever uncertainty one has that the variables under study are related. In some studies, researchers may also intend the results to generalize to other instances of the phenomenon. The design should do these things with the best use of one's resources, time, and energy, and within resource and time limits. It should fit an appropriate formulation of the problem rather than investigating the problem in too limited circumstances, cutting the problem to fit design requirements, or investigating a peculiar or atypical form of the question. Finally, the choices made in design formulation must be such that they build maximum confidence in the audience that the study was well done, and that it was done with appropriate regard for ethical standards and institutional constraints. This is a large set of criteria, but to be realistic, this is what a researcher confronts.

It is difficult to maximize all these criteria simultaneously. Consider the inference that the variables are related, and that their relationship can be generalized. It is easier to demonstrate that variables are related when one can eliminate all explanations, as is most easily accomplished in a carefully controlled laboratory setting. But results from a laboratory setting lack generality in the real world. So one trades off the ability to clearly associate the variables for generality of the results, or vice versa. It is possible, therefore, only to optimally fit the criteria as a set rather than to maximally fit each individual criterion. One does this with numerous trade-offs to get the balance deemed best for a particular study and a particular audience.

The terms "internal validity" and "external validity" were used to describe certain aspects of these criteria by Campbell and Stanley in 1963. These terms were later refined by Cook and Campbell in *Quasi-experimentation* (1979/1966). The capacity of a study to

---

*For simplicity, throughout this discussion, the comparison is between experimental and control groups. Many experimental studies, however, compare the effects of different treatments, so there may be two or more experimental groups and possibly no control group, the weakest treatment serving as the basis of comparison.

associate variables in the form in which they are represented in a study is referred to as the *internal validity* of a study. In particular, this refers to the capacity of the design to reject alternative explanations of the phenomena other than the intended one. *Construct validity* is the extent to which the form in which the variables are represented or measured in the study correspond to what was intended in the problem's original formulation. *Statistical conclusion validity* designates the proper use of statistics to infer that a relationship exists. *External validity* refers to the generalizability of the findings to other persons, settings, and times.

Finding the appropriate balance between internal and external validity is important. In researching a new field, we are usually first concerned with whether a relationship between the variables exists under some especially favorable conditions. Later we check generality over more normal conditions. For example, a special phonetic alphabet has helped bright children to read (internal validity), but will it help all children, especially less bright ones (external validity)?

ALTERNATIVE EXPLANATIONS

A prime function of design is the elimination of alternative explanations that could otherwise explain the effect as readily as the presumed cause, the treatment. Each study probably has alternative explanations unique to its particular situation, but there are certain common ones that Cook and Campbell (1979/1966) and Campbell and Stanley (1963) described. These they called "threats to validity," since they reduce internal or external validity. We can only discuss a few of them here.

History

History refers to events other than the treatment that occur during the study and might cause the effect. For example, consider an experiment testing the effectiveness of signs warning against shoplifting placed next to commonly stolen items. During a study of their effectiveness, a television program is aired indicating how shoplifting raises the prices of products and seeking community reporting of shoplifters. Reduced shoplifting could be due to history, the television program, or the signs. A control group—in this instance, similar stores in the same neighborhood where the shoppers would be equally affected by the television program—would control history.

Maturation

Subjects may get older, wiser, or more experienced or skillful during the study, though this is not related to the treatment of interest—a development labeled "maturation." For example, subjects practicing with a black and white computer game display get increasingly skilled. A control group protects against maturation, since both groups will increase in skill with practice and the control group will provide a measure of that increase.

Testing

Subjects do better the second time a test is administered because they are familiar with it, more relaxed, and so forth. Repeated testing lets factors affect the score that were not present at the first testing. A control group can provide a measure of the increase in test scores with which the experimental group's gain may be compared.

Testing by Treatment Interaction

As a result of a pretest, a student may be forewarned as to what parts of an experimental curriculum he or she must study harder. The student's performance on the posttest is improved over what it would have been without the pretest; pretest and treatment interacted. Since a control group, by definition, receives no treatment, it can provide no protection, but elimination of the pretest will.

Instrumentation or Instrument Decay

The way an observation or measuring instrument is used or interpreted may change during the study. For example, Mary becomes discouraged by the poor scores her students are getting on the individually administered reading test, so she begins to drop hints and coax answers. The scores of students tested later then differ from what they would have been if they had been tested earlier.

THE RELATIONSHIP OF DESIGN TO STATISTICS

There is some confusion about the role of design in relation to statistics, design often being seen as following whatever path statistics permit. In part, this can be traced to the work of Fisher, who in the first edition of *Design of Experiments* (1935) developed the intimate relationship between analysis of variance and experimental design. Indeed, many designs—especially those involving analysis of variance—are popular because their relation to statistics has been so completely explored, and remedies for contingencies and aberrations so well developed.

For most studies, statistics, besides describing the data, serve mainly to eliminate only one alternative explanation of the effect—namely, the probability that the result is simply an aberration resulting from the cumulated errors or random "noise" that exists in any study (sampling error, measurement error, etc.). In those instances where the effect—the "signal"—is very clear, the effect is so much larger than the "noise" that there is no question about it being a chance occurrence, so that inferential statistics become unimportant. But few psychological phenomena produce so strong an effect. If inferential statistics are to be used, there must be a working relationship between statistics and design, since it is quite possible to devise designs for which known statistical models are a poor fit. But the demands of the problem should be the determining factor in choosing a design. Only when no statistical model fits the design should trade-offs be explored, to determine how much problem definition has to give to fit a statistical model.

In some studies with complex designs, statistics permit measurement and removal of the impact of one or more confounded variables which might otherwise provide alternative explanations of the effect. *But for all designs, the main protection against the whole range of possible alternative explanations must be provided by the design itself, rather than by statistics.* The traditional emphasis on training in statistics is misplaced unless design is equally emphasized. With strong effects, good design is the critical factor in inferring that one has isolated the cause. Design must be supplemented by inferential statistics for weak effects.

THE DEVELOPMENT OF DESIGNS

The design for a simple study is primarily a matter of translating one's hypothesis or question into certain choices: (a) suitable *subjects;* (b) an appropriate *situation* or location; (c) the way the *treatment* variable will be administered; (d) how one *measures or observes* the effect; (e) the *basis of comparison*—how one assures that an effect occurred and that it was due to the treatment; and (f) the *procedure:* who gets what treatment and measures of effect, and when they get them. For example, given the hypothesis that color enhances novices' ability to play a computer game, one must: (a) find a representative sample of novices; (b) decide on the setting (a laboratory or arcade); (c) choose the computer game to be used and decide how color will enhance learning it; (d) decide on a measure of "ability to play" the game, such as time required to reach a certain skill level; (e) determine whether to use an AB or ABAB design or a control group design; and (f) decide on the timing and procedure to be followed in running subjects through the study. These six aspects represent the categories of choices required to specify a design.

SOME SAMPLE DESIGNS

The possible combination of the six characteristics above is extremely large. By concentrating on such general characteristics as when and to whom observations and treatments will be given, we can describe some design patterns that are widely used and note some strengths and weaknesses. To do so, let us establish that "X" stands for treatment and "O" for an observation or measurement. Elapsed time during the study is portrayed from beginning to end by the distance of events from each other from left to right. "R" indicates that individuals were randomly assigned to groups.

Pretest-Posttest Design

Individuals randomly assigned to the experimental and control groups are tested before and after the treatment is administered:

$$R\ O\ X\ O$$
$$R\ O\ \ \ \ O$$

This widely used design controls for a large number of alternative explanations, including the repeated effect of testing, since both groups are tested twice. But treatment by testing interaction is an uncontrolled alternative explanation.

Posttest Only

The previous design, minus the pretest, controls for both testing and testing by treatment interaction. But one has to assume

$$R\ \ \ X\ O$$
$$R\ \ \ \ \ \ O$$

that the randomization has worked and the groups were equal at the beginning.

Solomon Four Group

Solomon and Lessac (1968) combined the features of the previous two designs so that comparisons permit assessment of testing by treatment interaction (OXO versus XO) and randomization is working (OXO versus O O), but it requires four groups and thus a larger number of subjects.

$$R\ O\ X\ O$$
$$R\ O\ \ \ \ O$$
$$R\ \ \ \ X\ O$$
$$R\ \ \ \ \ \ O$$

Designs Controlling Initial Levels of Groups

While random assignment of individuals from a pool of subjects to experimental and control groups will, on the average, equate the groups on all variables, this is of little comfort if the groups happen not to be equivalent on an important variable. In a comparative study of two training procedures, one would want to make sure that the groups were of equal learning ability. In a *matched pairs design,* one might use results of an intelligence test to match individuals in pairs, assigning a member of each pair at random to the experimental or control group. This assumes considerable accuracy on the part of the test and, where individuals have nobody near them in score, can result in unmatched discarded cases. Such discarded cases might obviously limit the generality of the results, especially if, as is likely, scores at one or both extremes are underrepresented.

More common is the technique of blocking or stratifying, as in a *randomized block design.* Instead of pairing subjects, they are categorized (e.g., as high, middle, and low on an IQ test), and a randomly selected half of the individuals within each block is randomly assigned to experimental groups, the rest assigned to the control group.

Factorial Designs

Factorial designs permit consideration of the effects of two or more variables simultaneously. Groups are provided to measure the influence of all possible combinations of the variables. For example, in examining the effect of reducing room temperature 5° below a normal 68° on ability to attend to a set of radar patterns on men ($\male$) versus women ($\female$) of heavy (H), normal (N), or thin (T) physique using a posttest-only design, one would block the subjects by sex and physique (see Figure 1). Then one would randomly assign half the subjects in each cell to the experimental treatment, thus creating twelve groups (see Figure 2). In the previous section, we discussed blocking before random assignment to assure comparability of groups. This factorial design example il-

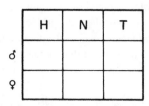

Figure 1.   Factorial design blocking the subjects by sex and physique.

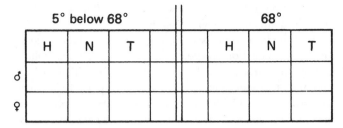

Figure 2.   Random assignment of half the subjects in each cell to the experimental treatment.

lustrates blocking followed by random assignment on sex and body type.

Such designs are designated by the number of categories for each variable, or in this instance a $2 \times 2 \times 3$ factorial design (high/low temperature, boys/girls, heavy/normal/thin). The product of the number categories (12) indicates the number of groups required. If a pretest as well as posttest were given, this would be termed a *repeated measures* $2 \times 2 \times 3$ factorial design.

Factorial designs permit one to examine whether variables like sex or body type alone have an effect on attending to radar patterns; whether any combination of these with the lower temperature have enhanced or reduced the effect; and whether all three together have an enhanced or reduced effect. The effects of combinations are called interaction effects.

Latin Square Design

A Latin square design permits one to control for two or more variables much like the factorial design. It trades fewer groups for information which may not be needed. It takes its name from an ancient puzzle in which Latin letters were arranged in a table so that a given letter, which here represents a treatment or variable condition, appeared once in a row or column. In a 3×3 Latin square, each of three versions of a training program (A, B, C) might be assigned at random to a combination of ability level (high, middle, low) and motivation (high, middle, low), such that each training program is tried out once with each ability level and each motivation level:

			Motivation	
		High	Middle	Low
	High	A	B	C
Ability level	Middle	C	A	B
	Low	B	C	A

This requires only nine groups in comparison to the $3 \times 3 \times 3$ or 27 required by a factorial design. But it would not supply all the information that a factorial design would give regarding the possible heightening or depressive effect (interaction) of a particular level of ability or motivation with a particular training version.

Time Series Designs

The ABA and ABAB experiments described earlier are time series designs. Time series designs follow an individual or group with re-

peated observations and repeated interventions or treatments. Sometimes the same treatment is used in the repetitions, sometimes different ones. A change should be observed following the intervention if it is effective, so that each person or group acts as their own control group. Where the effect of treatments persists, as in learning studies, subsequent interventions may be affected by the effects of earlier ones, therefore this "multiple treatment effect" needs to be anticipated as a possible confounding and contaminating factor. By contrast, certain tranquilizers that are excreted rapidly would show immediately in a set of time-series observations. Without further doses their effect would dissipate, but would reappear when dosage is resumed. Being able to show that the pattern of effect coincides with the pattern of times of intervention and its cessation, is very convincing evidence that a cause-and-effect relationship exists.

Multiple Baseline Designs

These are time series designs that measure one or more behaviors over time to establish baselines and then apply an intervention to one of the behaviors. If the intervention is effective, one notes a change in it, but not in the others. Allowing the pattern to return to stability, one then intervenes in a second baseline behavior, noting change in it but not in others, and so on. For example Liberman and Smith (1972), studying desensitization to fear through relation training in the real or imagined presence of feared stimuli, targeted four of them: being alone, menstruation, chewing hard foods, and dental visits. Working with a 28-year-old female, they established baselines on all four behaviors. Sequential application of desensitization to each of the four affected the particular phobias being treated with no change in the other baselines, hence no generalization to the others.

There are many more designs and design types than even hinted at here (see Cook and Campbell, 1979/1966). Other references are listed below.

REFERENCES

Campbell, D. T., & Stanley, J. (1963). Experimental and quasi-experimental designs for research. In N. L. Gage (Ed.), *Handbook of research on teaching.* Chicago: Rand McNally.

Cook, T. D., & Campbell, D. T. (1979). *Quasi-experimentation: Design and analysis issues for field settings.* Chicago: Rand McNally. (Original work published 1966)

Fisher, R. A. (1966). *Design of experiments.* Edinburgh, Scotland: Oliver & Boyd. (Original work published 1935 [New York: Hafner.])

Liberman, R. P., & Smith, V. (1972). A multiple baseline study of systematic desensitization in a patient with multiple phobias. *Behavior Therapy, 3,* 597–603.

Mill, J. S. (1973). A system of logic ratiocinative and inductive. In J. M. Robson (Ed.), *Collected works of John Stuart Mill* (Vol. VII). Toronto: University of Toronto Press. (Original work published 1843)

Solomon, R. L., & Lessac, M. S. (1968). A control group design for experimental study of developmental processes. *Psychological Bulletin, 70,* 145–150.

SUGGESTED READING

Box, G. E. P., Hunter, W. G., & Hunter, J. S. (1978). *Statistics for experimenters: An introduction to design, data analysis, and model building.* New York: Wiley.

Cochran, W. G., & Cox, G. M. (1957). *Experimental designs* (2nd ed.). New York: Wiley.

Collier, R. O., & Hummel, T. J. (1977). *Experimental design and interpretation.* Berkeley, CA: McCutchan.

Hersen, M., & Barlow, D. H. (1976). *Single-case experimental designs: Strategies for studying behavioral change.* New York: Pergamon.

Keppel, G. (1982). *Design and analysis* (2nd ed.). Englewood Cliffs, NJ: Prentice-Hall.

Kirk, R. E. (1968). *Experimental design: Procedures for the behavioral sciences.* Belmont, CA: Brooks/Cole.

Kratochwill, T. R. (Ed.). (1978). *Single-subject research: Strategies for evaluating change.* New York: Academic.

Winer, B. J. (1971). *Statistical principles in experimental design* (2nd ed.). New York: McGraw-Hill.

D. R. KRATHWOHL
Syracuse University

CONTROL GROUPS
DEPENDENT VARIABLES
HYPOTHESIS TESTING
PARAMETRIC STATISTICAL TESTS
RESEARCH METHODOLOGY
SAMPLING
SCIENTIFIC METHOD
STATISTICS IN PSYCHOLOGY

EXPERIMENTAL METHODS

Experimental methods are among the scientific methods used in psychological research. True experiments involve the careful observation of the effects of one or more variables (independent variables) on one or more outcome variables (dependent variables) under carefully controlled conditions with subjects randomly assigned to treatments. For example, the effect of adrenaline on activity level could be studied by randomly assigning subjects to an experimental group (who receive adrenaline) or to a control group (who receive an inert substance—a placebo) and then recording their activity levels in an objective way. The independent variable (drug dosage) has two levels (drug vs. placebo), and the dependent variable (activity level) is measured by an operational definition (a description of how scores on activity level are assigned). More levels of the independent variable could be used; for example, subjects might be given 0, 3, 10, or 25-mg doses of adrenaline, so that the independent variable would have four levels.

The experiment could be made more complex by the addition of more independent or dependent variables. For example, time of day may be used as a second independent variable with three levels (morning, afternoon, evening), so that subjects might be randomly assigned to any of 12 different conditions (0 mg in the morning, 10 mg in the evening, etc.). It is clear that the number of subjects required for more complex designs would be greater than for simpler designs, since the number of subjects under each condition (e.g., 10 mg in the afternoon) must be sufficient for generalizations about each event.

Although other scientific methods exist, the true experiment is the only method that allows researchers to make conclusions about cause-and-effect relationships. In the simple experiment with one independent variable (drug dosage) with two levels, if subjects in both the experimental and the control groups are treated in identical ways (except for the independent variable), and if subjects are randomly assigned to treatment conditions (drug vs. placebo), then any differences between the activity level scores must be due to the independent variable. If differences are observed, they must be caused by the difference in drug dosage. To infer causation, it is essential that the subject groups not differ with respect to anything other than the drug dosage. For example, if only men were in the experimental group and only women were in the control group, observed differences might reflect gender rather than dosage differences.

Experimenter bias may create subtle differences between groups and confound the results of the experiment, making interpretations in terms of the independent variable less trustworthy. For example, researchers who are eager to have their theories supported may unintentionally treat subjects differently in different conditions, creating the desired effects. Robert Rosenthal and his colleagues have documented the strong effect that experimenter bias can produce in Rosenthal's *Experimenter Effects in Behavioral Research,* and in Rosenthal and Jacobson's classic work on how teacher expectations can affect children's class participation and development, *Pygmalion in the Classroom.*

Any differences between conditions can confound results. If different researchers handle the different stimuli, they, rather than the independent variable, may cause the results. Subjects may be more cooperative for an attractive researcher and less cooperative for an unattractive one, or the different researchers may score responses in different ways. Similarly, data-gathering locations may affect results: Interviews in a comfortable, quiet room may differ from interviews in a crowded, noisy room. If, by chance, a disproportionate number of interviews for one level of the independent variable occur under different physical conditions, interpretation of the results cannot be clear.

The demand characteristics of the study's conditions—cues to the subjects about appropriate responses to the stimuli—can also confound results. For example, behaviors of other subjects in response to the stimuli may influence subjects who are tested in the same group, or unintentional smiles by the researcher may reinforce subjects who respond in the desired manner. One method to reduce experimenter and subject bias effects is to use "blind" research strategies in which subjects (single blind), or both subjects and researchers (double blind), do not know which experimental condition each subject is in. Thus, in the drug dosage study, coded pill containers could be used to create a double-blind study, ensuring that subtle expectations based upon knowledge of drug dosage could not influence results.

Sometimes independent variables cannot be manipulated by the researcher. For example, a researcher who uses gender, race, political party, frequency of marijuana use, or educational level as an independent variable cannot randomly assign subjects to levels of independent variables. Such variables sometimes are called nonmanipulated variables. Such variables are not of use in a true experiment, but they are frequently studied in quasi-experiments. Interpretation of results for nonmanipulated variables is complicated, since various additional variables generally are confounded with them. For example, social class and race are confounded in the United States, so that race differences in test scores may reflect social class differences, rather than any inherent or genetic race differences. Similarly, social class, intelligence, and a number of personality variables are confounded with educational level, so that observed differences between high school and college graduates may reflect these confounded variables, rather than the effect of education.

One way to facilitate interpretation of nonmanipulated independent variables is to match subjects on relevant confounding variables. For example, each high school graduate could be paired with a college graduate who matches in age, gender, social class, intelligence, and personality measures. The more complete the matching, the more comfortable the researcher can be in interpreting the effects of the independent variable. An alternative is to hold such variables constant (for example, restrict the research to middle-class male subjects of average intelligence and personality), so that the confounded variables cannot affect results; however, this practice would limit the researcher's ability to generalize results. A third alternative is to use a more complex design, with gender, age, and so forth used as additional independent variables.

Sometimes research strategies involve repeatedly testing the same subjects: a longitudinal study of human development may test the same group of children at ages 2, 5, 10, and 20, or a learning study may test subjects after every stimulus presentation. This introduces another complication that reflects an order effect: If level 1 of the independent variable is always tested before level 2, different results may reflect not only the effect of the independent variable, but may also reflect practice, fatigue, or maturation. Thus, if subjects are asked to rate the physical attractiveness of 10 people, and slides showing the stimuli are presented to all subjects in the same order, the rating of the third slide may reflect the stimulus, as well as an order effect. If the second slide, for example, is of a particularly attractive person, the third slide may be undervalued because of a contrast effect. If the third slide were in a different ordinal position, ratings would be different. Clearly, the solution to such problems involves manipulation of the order, so that different subjects receive the stimuli in randomly selected sequences. This is the technique of counterbalancing.

When more than one independent variable is studied, interpretation of the results may become complicated. Analysis of variance is the statistical technique most commonly used in the analysis of experimental studies. Key words in this analysis are *main effect* and *interaction*. A main effect occurs if, on average, scores for the levels of the independent variable are significantly different from one another. For example, if independent variable A has three levels (A_1, A_2, A_3), the average dependent variable scores for A_1, A_2, and A_3 are compared. If at least one of them is significantly different from another, a main effect for variable A has occurred. If additional independent variables—perhaps called B and C—are also studied, then additional tests are conducted to see if there is a significant main effect for either B or C. If an independent variable has only two levels, a significant main effect indicates that the two levels led to significantly different scores on the dependent variable. However, if there are three or more levels, a main effect indicates that at least one pair of levels is significantly different, although it is possible that every pair of levels is significantly different (that is, A_1 and A_2 are different, A_1 and A_3 are different, and A_2 and A_3 are different, etc.). In such a case, appropriate post hoc analyses are used to interpret the main effect and discover which pairs or subsets of levels are different from one another.

If more than one independent variable is examined, the independent variables may interact in such a way that the effect of one or more variables depends upon the level of one or more other variables. If there are three independent variables—A, B, and C—then there are four possible interactions: A with B, A with C, B with C, and A, B, and C together. Usually these interactions are labeled AB, AC, BC, and ABC, respectively. The first three are two-way interactions, involving two independent variables; ABC is a three-way interaction. A separate statistical test is performed for each main effect and interaction, so that complex designs involve many statistical tests; if significant results are obtained, numerous post hoc analyses may be needed to explore results. For example, a study with four independent variables would test for four main effects (A, B, C, D), six two-way interactions (AB, AC, AD, BC, BD, CD), four three-way interactions (ABC, ABD, ACD, BCD), and one four-way interaction (ABCD)—a total of fifteen tests. Any significant result generally would be followed by post hoc analyses.

Experimental designs vary across experiments and depend upon a number of factors: the number of independent and dependent variables; whether independent variables are manipulated or nonmanipulated; whether subjects are matched or tested once or repeatedly; and how subjects are assigned to experimental conditions.

The number of independent and dependent variables relates to the complexity of the design. An n-way design has *n* independent variables. The simplest design involves one independent and one dependent variable. Multiple independent variables, as noted earlier, lead to more statistical tests and to tests that involve both main effects and interactions. Multiple dependent variables require more advanced statistical procedures, such as multivariate analysis of variance.

Two major types of independent variables are between-group and within-subject variables. Between-group variables have different subjects for each level, so that comparisons of levels involve comparisons between independent groups of subjects. Within-subject variables have the same (or matched) subjects at more than one level, so that comparisons of levels involve comparisons of the same (or matched) subjects' performance. In general, the statistical tests for within-subject variables are more powerful (more likely to find significant results), if there are large individual differences among subjects on the dependent variable. The effect of matching subjects depends upon how accurately the matching can control for confounding variables; careless matching can lead to less powerful tests.

Subjects can be assigned to experimental conditions in a number of ways. For a one-way design, subjects can be randomly assigned to different levels (a between-group design) or can be tested at each level (a within-subject design). For a two-way design, either or both independent variables can be within-subject or between-group variables. The most simple two-way design is a completely randomized factorial design, with subjects randomly assigned to only one level for each variable, with treatment conditions including all possible combinations of levels. If the first variable has p levels and the second variable has q levels, there are pq conditions and the design would be called a "p by q" factorial design. A three-way factorial design would have pqr conditions and would be a "p by q by r" factorial design, where r is the number of levels for the third independent variable.

A design with at least one between-group and at least one within-subject variable is a mixed design. A subject (or set of matched subjects) generally is called a "block" (a term adopted from earlier agricultural work), and observations within a block are expected to be identical (within measurement error), unless the independent variables affect performance.

In their 1963 classification of research designs, Campbell and Stanley describe four major categories: preexperimental, true experimental, quasi-experimental, and correlational and ex post facto designs. *Preexperimental designs* include the one-shot case study (one independent variable with one level), the one-group pretest-posttest design (each subject measured twice, before and after an intervention occurs), and the static-group comparison (two preexisting groups are compared, one being the control and the other differing with respect to the independent variable). Preexperimental designs are marked by extensive confounding variables that make clear interpretation of results very difficult, and are used more often in applied than in theoretical research.

Campbell and Stanley (1963) describe three *true experimental designs:* the pretest-posttest control-group design (two groups, each tested twice, with only one group receiving the intervention before the posttest); the Solomon four-group design (the preceding design plus two more groups of subjects, one that receives the intervention and is given only the posttest, and one that is given only the posttest), and the posttest-only control-group design (the experimental and control groups are given only postintervention tests, with placebo intervention for the control group). Each of the true experiments requires random assignment of subjects to conditions and has sufficient controls that cause-effect inferences can be made with more confidence than in other designs. Multiple independent variables can be added through factorial methods.

Quasi-experimental designs involve variables that cannot be manipulated or controlled by the researcher, such as gender or block membership (without control groups). Such designs include the time-series experiment (a single subject or group of subjects is repeatedly measured, with one or more intervening conditions between measurements); the nonequivalent control-group, pretest-posttest design (like the pretest-posttest control group design, but without random assignment to conditions); and the multiple time-series design (a combination of the two preceding designs). Quasi-experimental designs are used when ethical or practical considerations preclude true experimental designs, and represent a compromise that allows some inference about cause-effect relationships.

Correlational and *ex post facto designs* do not allow inferences about cause-and-effect relationships, but may have heuristic value (value in generating hypotheses for further research). Ex post facto designs compare preexisting groups, and may use retrospective data (data collected now, based upon memories about the past) and match subjects on the basis of archival or retrospective variables. Retrospective data are open to serious validity problems, because people tend to re-create memories so that they are consistent with current views. Such designs are weaker than true experiments, but may be more ethical or practical.

All experimental methods must be used carefully and cautiously, with attention to ethical, practical, and statistical considerations. Scientific theory is built upon repeated, consistent research results; a single study represents only one piece of information for scientific evaluation.

REFERENCES

Allen, M. J. (1995). *Introduction to psychological research.* Itasca, IL: Peacock.

Campbell, D., & Stanley, J. (1963). *Experimental and quasi-experimental designs for research.* Washington, DC: American Educational Research Association.

Rosenthal, R. (1966). *Experimenter effects in behavioral research.* NY: Appleton-Century Crofts.

Rosenthal, R., & Jacobson, L. (1968). *Pygmalion in the classroom: Teacher expectations and student intellectual development.* New York: Holt, Rinehart, & Winston.

M. J. ALLEN
California State University, Bakersfield

ANALYSIS OF VARIANCE
CONTROL GROUPS
DOUBLE BLIND RESEARCH
RESEARCH METHODOLOGY

EXPERT TESTIMONY

It has been over a century since lively debate began in scientific journals and law reviews on the psychology of testimony and the value of psychology to the judicial process (Goldofski, 1904; Jaffe, 1903; Lobsien, 1904). Hugo Munsterberg brought together a number of essays on psychology and crime, first publishing these in the

New York Times magazine and then as the book *On the Witness Stand* (1908). In his enthusiasm Munsterberg stated, "my only purpose is to turn the attention of serious men to an absurdly neglected field which demands the full attention of the social community." He then presented a series of essays on illusions, the memory of witnesses, the detection of crime, untrue confessions, hypnotism and crime, and the prevention of crime.

Munsterberg's effort was interesting, enthusiastic, and predictive of the increasing overlap of psychology and law. It was, unfortunately, somewhat premature, but it did not go unnoticed. John H. Wigmore, professor of the Law of Evidence at Northwestern University, wrote a scathing parody of *On the Witness Stand* that was published in the *Illinois Law Review* in 1909. The critique reported a mythical suit filed in the city of "Windyville, Illiania" against Munsterberg for having "caused to be printed, published, and circulated in Illiania and throughout the country . . . [a book that] contained . . . certain assertions, erroneous, incorrect and untrue concerning the said plaintiffs, in their capacity as members of the bar."

Wigmore confronted Munsterberg with the lack of published evidence to support the claim that the law was ready for psychology, as Munsterberg had cited no references in his pioneer text. The mock complaint cited 127 learned treatises to justify the proceedings. The mock trial ended with a finding against Munsterberg, the jury assessing damages of one dollar.

Wigmore's attack was telling: few references to psychologists as expert witnesses appeared for a quarter of a century. Then in 1931 Lewis M. Terman, a professor of psychology at Stanford University, appeared before the Los Angeles Bar Association to present an address, "Psychology and the Law." Terman took pains to refer to Munsterberg's *On the Witness Stand* and Wigmore's scathing response. He suggested that Munsterberg's error was in exaggerating the importance of psychology's contributions based on the then-existing research. Termin indicated, however, that the ultimate significance of psychology for the legal profession could hardly be overstated considering the scientific advances made during the first quarter of the century. Terman emphasized the value of experimental psychology in clarifying errors of testimony He suggested psychology may be useful in developing, researching, evaluating, or clarifying lie detection, eyewitness testimony, the vagaries of the insanity plea, and jury selection. Terman ended his presentation with a critique similar to that presented by Hugo Munsterberg nearly a quarter of a century before: "Our law, like our proverbs and adages, are the product of folk-thinking and like those, they are a mixture of shred wisdom, childish error, superstition, and folly" (Terman, 1935).

By this time, Wigmore's *On Evidence* was considered the definitive work, as it was being used and cited by attorneys and judges throughout the United States. Yet psychology's most bitter critic in the law at that time modified his position in the last edition of his master work: "Both law and practice permit the calling of any expert scientist whose method is acknowledged in his science to be a sound and trustworthy one. Whenever the Psychologist is ready for the Courts, the Courts are ready for him" (Wigmore, 1937). Clearly, Wigmore was demonstrating the flexibility, awareness, and practicality psychologists are likely to find among lawyers and

judges when presented with psychological data, techniques, and methods generally acceptable to colleagues and concordant with the standards of the profession.

One of the earliest reviews of the legal and psychological literature regarding the psychologist as expert witness was published by D. W. Louisell in 1955. An appendix to this article presented the testimony of Dr. Kenneth E. Clark in the trademark infringement case of *Robinsdale Amusement Co. v. Warner Brothers Pictures Distributing Corp. et al.;* Clark testified as an expert in public opinion techniques.

During the 1950s psychologists were sometimes qualified as experts and sometimes dismissed by the judge. In 1954, Dr. Michael H. P. Finn, then chief psychologist at the Springfield State Hospital, appeared in *Hidden v. Mutual Life Insurance of New York.* The judge refused to allow Finn to testify. On appeal, the U.S. Court of Appeals reversed this decision on the ground that Finn was qualified to give expert testimony.

In the earliest formal text on private practice in clinical psychology, T. G. Blau (1959) included a chapter entitled "The Clinical Psychologist and the Legal Profession." Blau suggested psychologists would do well to prepare themselves to be competent expert witnesses within their field. Several court transcripts were included to illustrate direct examination and cross-examination of psychologists in personal injury and competency cases.

The role of the psychologist as expert witness in matters of mental disease or defect was addressed in considerable detail in the landmark case of *Jenkins v. United States* in 1962. After indictment for housebreaking with intent to commit an assault, assault with intent to rape, and assault with a dangerous weapon, Jenkins was committed to a hospital in Washington, D.C., for a mental examination on 4 September 1959. The purpose of the examination was to determine his competence to stand trial and his mental state at the time of the alleged offense. Jenkins was given a series of psychological tests by staff psychologists under the supervision of Bernard I. Levy. Jenkins was also examined by several psychiatrists, who informed the District Court that he was incompetent. He was then committed to St. Elizabeth's Hospital until mentally competent to stand trial. At S. Elizabeth's he was tested extensively by Lawrence Tirnauer, PhD, who concluded Jenkins was schizophrenic. Two other psychiatrists found "no evidence of mental disease or defect." Margaret Ives, PhD, administered additional tests and concluded Tirnauer's diagnosis was correct. The trial court, *sua sponte* (on its own motion), instructed the jury to disregard the testimony of the three defense psychologists' opinions that the defendant had had a mental disease when allegedly committing the crimes.

On appeal, Judge Bazelon of the U.S. Court of Appeals held that the lower court had erred on several points, including rejection of qualified psychologists as experts on the presence or absence of mental disease. This decision was rendered in spite of an *amicus curiae* brief submitted by the American Psychiatric Association, urging the court not to allow psychologists to qualify as experts. Bazelon's scholarly opinion defined the fully trained psychologist. In a rare concurrence, Judge Warren Burger (who later became a Chief Justice of the U.S. Supreme Court) agreed with Bazelon. Since the *Jenkins* decision, the rejection of psychologists by the court as experts in their fields of specialization has been considered trial error.

Not all psychologists are likely to be accepted by the court as expert witnesses in all areas of psychological practice. The psychologist must be qualified before the court as an expert in the area about which he or she will testify. Furthermore, as legal scholars have pointed out, the issue must be such that the expert may answer by giving an opinion that is a reasonable probability, rather than conjecture or speculation (Ladd, 1952).

The credibility of any expert's testimony in some jurisdictions continues to follow the admonition delineated in *Frye v. United States* (1923), in which the court reasoned:

Just when a scientific principle of discovery crosses the line between the experimental and demonstrable stages is difficult to define. Somewhere in this twilight zone the evidential force of the principle must be recognized, and while courts will go a long way in admitting expert testimony deduced from a well-recognized scientific principle or discovery, the thing from which the deduction is made must be sufficiently established to have gained general acceptance in the particular field which it belongs.

The admissibility of expert testimony was predicted to change drastically subsequent to the 1993 case *Daubert v. Merrell-Dow Pharmaceuticals.* A majority opinion by the U.S. Supreme Court indicated the *Frye* test was too austere and that a new standard based on the Federal Rules of Evidence should be adopted. Admissibility of testimony based on the Federal Rules of Evidence tended to be more flexible than the *Frye* rule. It indicated a qualified expert could provide scientific, technical, or specified knowledge that would assist the trier of fact or law in determining an issue that was based on material that was reliably accepted by the scientific community. The *Daubert* ruling basically made the trial judge the gatekeeper to the admissibility of expert testimony. Several criteria were enumerated by Justice Blackman for trial judges to use in determining the admissibility of testimony, and include: (1) whether the hypothesis that formed the basis for the testimony was testable (falsifiability), (2) whether it had been published, (3) whether there was a known error rate for the procedure, (4) whether it has been peer-reviewed, and (5) whether it was generally accepted in the field. Interestingly, the *Frye* test of whether a particular scientific principle is "generally accepted in the relevant scientific community" bears considerable similarity to the last criteria enumerated in *Daubert* regarding whether such a principle is generally accepted in the field.

In 1999, the trial judge's gatekeeper status was reaffirmed by the U.S. Supreme Court in the case of *Kumho Tire Company v. Carmichael.* The Supreme Court upheld exclusion of testimony based on the unreliability of the methodology.

The Revised Ethical Principles of Psychologists and Code of Conduct (American Psychological Association, 1992) addresses forensic activities. Specialty guidelines for forensic psychologists published in 1991 by the Committee on Ethical Guidelines for Forensic Psychologists more specifically address ethical obligations of psychologists providing expert testimony.

Since the *Jenkins* decision, psychologists have appeared more frequently in the courts as experts. Most published reports of psychologists as expert witnesses involve competency evaluations and

the sanity plea. In this narrow area of expert testimony, psychologists have entered into a domain once belonging exclusively to psychiatrists. Data suggest that psychologists are successful and well-regarded as expert witnesses in matters of competence and sanity (Perlin, 1980). Psychologists testify in civil matters, including personal injury, wrongful death, trademark infringement, product liability, and other issues. Psychologists have testified in criminal courts in matters of change of venue, death-qualified juries, prison conditions, and capacity to form criminal intent.

Judges are increasingly aware of the potential of psychologists to assist the courts. Patricia McGowan Wald (1982), circuit judge for the U.S. Court of Appeals, District of Columbia, has stated: "I find that after a decade or more of increasing awareness among psychologists and lawyers about what litigation can and cannot accomplish, the era of their most productive relationships built on mutual respect and realistic idealism may be only just beginning."

More graduate and postgraduate training is being offered to prepare psychologists to function as expert witnesses in the courts. Psychologists who currently expect to function in this role must acquire education, training, and experience *ad lib,* or more appropriately, from continuing education at the postdoctoral level. Interest in this area is burgeoning; it seems likely that doctoral students in professional training programs will, in the future, have a greater opportunity to prepare to function as experts for the courts. Joint PhD/JD programs are producing psychologists/lawyers who hopefully will bridge the gap of knowledge and issues of mutual distrust between the two professions (Wolinksy, 1982).

One way to assess the importance of appropriately given expert testimony is by the number of books and chapters dedicated thereto. The interested reader is referred to the Suggested Reading section that follows.

REFERENCES

American Psychological Association. (1992). Ethical principles of psychologists and code of conduct (Rev. ed.). *American Psychologist, 47*(1), 1597.

Daubert v. Merrell-Dow Pharmaceuticals, Inc. 509 U.S. 579 589 (1993).

Frye v. United States, 293 F. 1013 (DC 1923).

Goldofski, O. B. (1904). The psychology of testimony. *Vyestnik Prava,* No. 16–18, 185.

Hidden v. Mutual Life Insurance Co., 217F. 2d 818, 821 (4th Cir. 1954).

Jaffe, S. (1903). Ein psychologisches experiment in Kriminalistischen seminar der universitaet Berlin [A psychological experiment in criminality seminar at the University of Berlin]. *Beitraege zur Psychologie der Aussage, mit besonderer Bereuecksrchitigung der Rechtspflege, Paedogogik, Psychiatrie und Geschichtsforschung, 1,* 79.

Jenkins v. United States, 307 F. 2d 637 (1962).

Kumho Tire Company v. Carmichael, 67 U.S. L.W. 4179 (1999).

Ladd, J. (1952). Expert testimony. *Vanderbilt Law Review, 5,* 414, 419.

Lobsien, M. (1904). Veber psychologie der aussage. *Zeit schrift feur Paedagogische Psychologie, VI,* 161.

Louisell, D. W. (1955). The psychologist in today's legal world. *Minnesota Law Review, 39*(3), 235–272.

Munsterberg, H. (1908). *On the witness stand.* New York: Doubleday.

Perline, M. L. (1980). The legal status of the psychologist in the courtroom. *Mental Disabilities Law Review, 3*(4), 194–200.

Robinsdale Amusement Co. v. Warner Brothers, Civil #4584 (4th Division, Minneapolis).

Terman, L. M. (1935). Psychology and the law. *Commercial Law Journal, 40,* 639–646.

Wald, P. M. (1982). Become a real "friend of the court." *APA Monitor, 13*(2), 5.

Wigmore, J. H. (1909). Professor Munsterberg and the psychology of testimony. *Illinois Law Review, 3*(7), 399–445.

Wigmore, J. H. (1940). On evidence (3rd ed., pp. 367–368). Boston: Little, Brown.

Wolinksy, J. (1982). Programs join "distrustful" disciplines. *APA Monitor, 13*(2), 15.

SUGGESTED READING

Blau, T. H. (1998). *The psychologist as expert witness* (2nd ed.). New York: Wiley.

Brodsky, S. L. (1991). *Testifying in court: Guidelines and maxims for the expert witness.* Washington, DC: American Psychological Association.

Hess, A. K., & Weiner, I. B. (Eds.). (1999). *The handbook of forensic psychology* (2nd ed.). New York: Wiley.

Lubet, S. (1998). *Expert testimony: A guide for expert witnesses and the lawyers who examine them.* Chicago: National Institute for Trial Advocacy.

Melton, G. B., Petrila, J., Poythress, N. G., & Slobogin, C. (1997). *Psychological evaluations for the courts: A handbook for mental health professionals and lawyers* (2nd ed.). New York: Guilford.

T. H. Blau
J. T. Super

FORENSIC PSYCHOLOGY

EXTRASENSORY PERCEPTION (ESP)

Awareness of information that occurs independently of known sensory channels such as sight, hearing, taste, smell, or touch is referred to as extrasensory perception (ESP). Examples of ESP claims include the detection of hidden objects (clairvoyance), thought transference between people (telepathy), and knowledge of future events (precognition). While people have made these anomalous claims for centuries, a useful distinction exists between extrasensory *experience* and extrasensory *phenomena*. Some experiences may give the appearance of extrasensory awareness, yet ESP phenomena require scientific support to verify their authenticity (Irwin, 1999). Historically, anecdotes of "spontaneous cases" of anomalous experiences constituted the basis of ESP claims. Spontaneous cases are subjective reports of everyday-life experiences categorized in terms of clairvoyance, telepathy, or precognition (Rhine, 1953). The validity of such spontaneous reports used as evidence for the existence of ESP phenomena is limited by possible inaccuracies of memory and misperceptions of ambiguous situations. Attempts to conduct objective research on ESP experiences began in 1882 in England by the Society for Psychical Research (SPR; Irwin, 1999).

GENERAL EXTRASENSORY PERCEPTION (GESP)

When distinctions between clairvoyance, telepathy, and precognition became ambiguous, the concept known as "general extrasensory perception (GESP)" was proposed by Joseph B. Rhine (1948), an American pioneer in conducting research on ESP. GESP refers to explanations of laboratory data or spontaneous-case reports that could have been due to a confluence of two or more elements of ESP. Beyond GESP is the term *psi*, which embraces both ESP and psychokinesis (PK), that is, mental influence on physical events ("mind over matter"; Schmidt, 1973). *Psi* refers to any paranormal element, such as ESP or PK, suggested by data not explainable by known causes. Concerns over the precision and proliferation of terminology in ESP have persisted for over a century (Zingrone & Alvarado, 1987).

RHINE'S RESEARCH EFFORTS AT DUKE UNIVERSITY

Joseph Banks Rhine was a botanist who joined the faculty at Duke University in 1927. In 1934, based on his laboratory studies, Rhine published a monograph entitled *Extra-Sensory Perception,* in which he claimed overwhelming statistical evidence for the existence of ESP. The design of Rhine's research consisted of the use of five symbols—circle, star, three wavy lines, cross, and square—which served as hidden targets. Professor K. E. Zener of the Duke psychology department suggested these symbols to Rhine, and with Rhine's approval Zener created a deck of 25 cards, five of each symbol. Subjects in Rhine's research attempted to guess the identity of the Zener cards' symbols, which were ostensibly hidden from view, under several procedures according to the methods and location of presentation. Target cards were placed face down, and sometimes they were located in a different room from the subject, or even in a different building. Moreover, on some tests an "agent-sender" viewed each symbol to enhance telepathy for the subject. By chance alone, a subject, called percipient, has a probability of one out of five to guess correctly ("hit") resulting in an average of five likely hits in a deck of 25 ESP cards. Scores above eight on one run of 25 trials resulted in statistically significant "hitting," yet averages as low as 5.3 hits per 25 trials over 690 runs would occur only one time in a million by chance (Hansel, 1980). These lab studies conducted by Rhine were empirical in design and his data were statistically analyzed, which provided greater objectivity than the spontaneous-case approach. Yet, Rhine's observations were not experimental in the technical sense, because his research did not employ control groups or conditions. Control tests would include the use of blank target cards, that is, no Zener symbols, to serve as a basis of comparison with an experimental subject's guesses of the Zener targets.

ESP research continued at Duke until 1962, when Rhine reestablished his laboratory, independently of Duke University, also in Durham, North Carolina close to the Duke campus. Rhine called his new location the Foundation for Research on the Nature of Man (FRNM), now referred to as the Rhine Research Center. The Center houses the publication facilities for the *Journal of Parapsychology*. It contains an extensive library in parapsychological literature, and serves as a focal point for ongoing research projects in ESP claims (Mauskopf & McVaugh, 1981).

COMPUTERIZED TESTING OF ESP

Attempts to automate ESP research designs and rid them of extraneous physical cues called "sensory leakage" prompted the use of computers. Randomizing and presenting sequences of targets, tabulating and analyzing data, and storing cumulative data sets for later reference are appropriate tasks for the capabilities of a computer (Broughton, 1982). Moreover, useful control tests can be done with a computer. For example, the matching of two nonrandom series of 37,100 digits one through five by a computer showed 529 more hits than chance expectation. The odds against such an occurrence by chance are 10^{10} to one. This finding created serious doubts among some researchers that any anomalous element such as human ESP is responsible for significant results in subjects whose scores reach statistical significance in the laboratory. That is, the mere nonrandomness of the distribution of human guesses may be sufficient to explain significant scoring (Gaither & Zusne, cited in Zusne & Jones, 1982).

LEARNING TO USE ESP

Principles of conditioning and learning models in psychology have been applied toward the possibility of teaching people to increase their ESP skills. Giving immediate feedback to subjects after each trial has led to a reduction in the "decline effect." The decline effect is a reliable finding in ESP research in which subjects with no feedback per trial about the accuracy of their guesses typically show a gradual decrease in the number of hits over many series of tests. Controlled studies in the lab have shown increases in ESP test scores with trial-by-trial feedback compared to no feedback, even though the scores for subjects with feedback are not consistently above chance (Tart, 1976).

REMOTE VIEWING EXPERIMENTS

The Stanford Research Institute (SRI) conducted a series of experiments to determine whether subjects could accurately describe a randomly selected outdoor location, which was at a distance and not visible from the subject's laboratory room. A coinvestigator was concurrently situated in the target area to serve as an agent-sender. The researchers reported "extra-chance" correspondence between the subjects' imagery and the outdoor targets under the remote viewing procedures (Targ & Puthoff, 1978). Consequently,

the Central Intelligence Agency financed an independent study of possible uses of remote viewing such as for governmental spying, only to abandon this program in the late 1970s in the absence of encouraging findings (Hyman, 1996). Suggestions of methodological and statistical flaws and concerns that the judges of subjects' reports were not totally "blind" to the identity of the target locations cast doubt on the validity of remote viewing data (Irwin, 1999).

BELIEFS IN THE EXISTENCE OF ESP

The term "sheep" was chosen to refer to people who believe in the possibility of ESP, while "goats" refers to those who doubt or deny its existence (Schmeidler & McConnell, 1958; Thalbourne & Delin, 1993). Persistence of belief in the existence of ESP despite only occasional hits compared with the many trials of failure reported in controlled lab research has been analyzed. Rationales for such tenacity of belief include the cognitive need for people to structure many puzzling events in life so that they appear comprehensible (Irwin, 1999), or the "partial reinforcement effect," in which occasional hits of ESP hidden targets compared to numerous misses result in a strong "resistance to extinction" of ESP beliefs (Vitulli, 1997).

FUTURE STATUS OF ESP THEORY

Scientific theories are characterized as having aesthetic value or beauty in rough proportion to the degree of empirical data in support of that theory (McAllister, 1998). Theoretical assumptions underlying the existence of ESP have been compared often with assumptions of quantum mechanics in physics. For example, quantum theory was regarded at one time as "aesthetically repulsive" by Albert Einstein, because it was not compatible with laws of determinism (McAllister, 1998). Yet, quantum theory gained considerable empirical support, eventually, which bolstered its theoretical status. Conversely, the assumptions underlying the existence of ESP have not received the same degree of empirical verification. The absence of reliable demonstrations, upon demand, of the existence of ESP leaves this area of inquiry in a state of limbo. Nevertheless, the spirit of human curiosity serves as a beacon for scientific progress. Despite paranormal claims, research in anomalous experiences such as ESP continues to occur for the sake of knowledge, regardless of where it may lead.

SELECTED JOURNALS DEDICATED TO ESP-RELATED RESEARCH

European Journal of Parapsychology
Journal of Parapsychology
Journal of the American Society of Psychical Research
Journal of the Society for Psychical Research
Skeptical Inquirer
Zetetic Scholar

REFERENCES

Broughton, R. S. (1982). Computer methodology: Total control with a human face. *Parapsychology Review, 13*, 1–6.

Hansel, C. E. M. (1980). *ESP and parapsychology: A critical reevaluation.* Buffalo, NY: Prometheus Books.

Hyman, R. (1996). Evaluation of the military's twenty-year program on psychic spying. *Skeptical Inquirer, 20,* 21–23.

Irwin, H. J. (1999). *An introduction to parapsychology* (3rd ed.). Jefferson, NC: McFarland.

Mauskopf, S., & McVaugh, M. (1981). Obituary: Joseph Banks Rhine (1895–1980). *American Psychologist, 36,* 310–311.

McAllister, J. W. (1998). Is beauty a sign of truth in scientific theories? *American Scientist, 86,* 174–183.

Rhine, J. B. (1934). *Extra-sensory perception.* Boston: Boston Society for Psychic Research.

Rhine, J. B. (1948). *The reach of the mind.* London: Faber & Faber.

Rhine, L. E. (1953). Subjective forms of spontaneous psi experiences. *Journal of Parapsychology, 17,* 77–114.

Schmeidler, G. R., & McConnell, R. A. (1958). *ESP and personality patterns.* New Haven, CT: Yale University Press.

Schmidt, H. (1973). PK tests with a high-speed random number generator. *Journal of Parapsychology, 37,* 105–118.

Targ, R., & Puthoff, H. (1978). *Mind reach.* London: Granada.

Tart, C. T. (1976). *Learning to use extrasensory perception.* Chicago: University of Chicago Press.

Thalbourne, M. A., & Delin, P. S. (1993). A new instrument for measuring the sheep-goat variable: Its psychometric properties and factor structure. *Journal of the Society for Psychical Research, 59,* 172–186.

Vitulli, W. F. (1997). Beliefs in parapsychological events or experiences among college students in a course in experimental parapsychology. *Perceptual and Motor Skills, 85,* 273–274.

Zingrone, N. L., & Alvarado, C. S. (1987). Historical aspects of parapsychological terminology. *Journal of Parapsychology, 51,* 49–74.

Zusne, L., & Jones, W. H. (1982). *Anomalistic psychology.* Hillsdale, NJ: Lawrence Erlbaum Associates, Inc.

W. F. VITULLI
University of South Alabama

PARAPSYCHOLOGY
PSEUDOPSYCHOLOGY

EXTRAVERSION AND INTROVERSION: CONCEPT OF

The words "extraversion" and " introversion" have been in use for several centuries. Considered etymologically, they may be construed respectively as an "outward turning" and an "inward turning." They have been used, in fact, with essentially those meanings, both in a physical sense and in a psychological sense. The psychological usage can be found in writings dating as far back as the seventeenth century, where extraversion referred to the turning of thoughts toward outer objects and introversion referred to the turning of thoughts inward to one's own mind or soul or to the spiritual realm.

The work of Jung (1921/1976) is largely responsible for directing the attention of psychologists to these concepts. Jung viewed extraversion versus introversion as the most basic dimension of human temperament and believed many major fluctuations and controversies in Western thought could be understood in terms of a clash between these opposing outlooks. He also believed that Western thought on the whole, in comparison with that of the Orient, stressed extraversion.

Jung defined extraversion as an outward turning of libido, or psychic energy. This is equivalent to saying that extraversion means a directing of interest toward objects (other people or things) in the environment and functioning in relation to those objects. In an extraverted state one perceives, thinks, feels, and acts in relation to the object. We might also say that action and experience are determined directly by the object. Introversion is defined as an inward turning of libido. This implies a directing of interest away from the object toward the subject—toward the individual's own conscious experience. In an introverted state, perception, thinking, feeling, and action are determined more directly by subjective factors than by the object. The extravert, the individual who is habitually in an extraverted state, tends to respond immediately and directly to stimuli from without. Habitually in an introverted state, the introvert tends to withhold immediate responses and act on the basis of subjective considerations that follow the external stimulus.

Jung (1921/1976) reviewed a variety of earlier dichotomous typologies and concluded that many of them represented equivalent expressions of the same basic dimension. He regarded hysteria and psychasthenia respectively as extraverted and introverted forms of psychoneurosis, and he suggested that manic-depressive psychosis and schizophrenia represented a similar parallel in the realm of psychosis. He also concluded that the polarity of tough-minded versus tender-minded, which James (1907) applied to a basic division within the field of philosophy, was basically the same as his own dimension. It can be argued, however, that James's dimension is more concerned with ingredients of the psychic function dimensions described by Jung (thinking versus feeling and sensation versus intuition). There is evidence that the most basic division of perspectives evident in the histories of both philosophy and psychology is better characterized by the dimension postulated by James than by that of Jung (Coan, 1979). Many other theorists have proposed dichotomous typologies that involve some sort of inner-outer contrast, but it is a mistake to assume that these all involve the same underlying temperament dimension.

The dimension of extraversion versus introversion itself has been subject to a variety of interpretations. Upon learning of Jung's use of these terms, Freud concluded that extraversion was the healthy condition, while introversion constituted a predisposition to psychopathology. To Freud, an "inward turning of libido" implied narcissism, while an "outward turning of libido" implied the possibility of forming a true object-cathexis, hence the achievement of the genital level of development. Jung, however, did not construe extraversion and introversion in quite this way and considered neither to be preferable to the other. The Freudian perspective tends to prevail in any society, such as the United States, that favors extraversion over introversion.

There has been a tendency among American psychologists and educators to view extraversion as preferable and to reinterpret the dimension in terms of social behavior. Thus, extraversion has often been understood in terms of sociability, while introversion has been regarded as a tendency to withdraw from social contacts. Jung thought of the dimension primarily in terms of modes of experience or consciousness, and the behavioral definition itself reflects a more extraverted approach to psychology. Most efforts to construct questionnaire scales for the dimension reflect this shift in orientation, for the items have often contained extraversive scale content that pertains to sociability and introversive scale content that pertains to shyness, reserve, and anxiety. Even scales purported to measure the Jungian dimension usually focus on social behavior, because it is more difficult to formulate items that will evoke self-descriptions that directly express the variables conceptualized by Jung (Coan, 1978). A different method of assessment may be needed.

Murray (1938/1962) contended that Jung's concepts encompassed a number of component variables that might be distinguished and separately assessed. He suggested a component dimension of exocathection versus endocathection, which is concerned with the extent to which the individual attaches value to either the outer world or the inner world. He also posited a component dimension of extraception versus intraception. This is concerned with the extent to which perception, judgment, and action are governed either by observable, physical conditions or by subjective factors (feelings, fantasies, speculations, and aspirations).

Murray offered a rational analysis of Jung's concepts, but the work of some of the major factor-analytic researchers—including Cattell, Guilford, and Eysenck—indicates that semi-independent components of the extraversion-introversion dimension can be distinguished by statistical methods. These researchers concur in finding evidence for a broad general dimension of this sort, a dimension that enters into a large number of the specific individual differences we find in human personality. They differ in their identification and labeling of the components, but in the research findings of all three there is evidence of constituents of extraversion entailing such things as high activity level, sociability, impulsiveness, dominance, and dependence on the group. In contrast, such features as low activity level, deliberateness, and self-reliance are found to be associated with the introversive end of the dimension. Since the bulk of relevant factor-analytic research has focused on questionnaire responses, it is not surprising that the most obvious ingredients of the dimension lie in the realm of social behavior. In contrast, Murray's analysis remained closer to the polarity conceptualized by Jung.

Eysenck (1967) devoted particular attention to this dimension and, in interpreting it, borrowed a couple of physiological concepts from Pavlov. While studying temperamental variations among dogs, Pavlov concluded that some animals were characterized by a predominance of excitatory cortical processes, while others were characterized by a predominance of inhibitory cortical processes. Pavlov suggested a relationship between these processes and the four classical temperament types of Hippocrates and Galen. Eysenck rejected Pavlov's rationale for this relationship, but he felt the process concepts could be used to explain the extraversion-introversion dimension. According to Eysenck, introverts are characterized by very sensitive cortical excitation processes. They tend, therefore, to feel intellectually and emotionally overwhelmed by moderate social and physical stimulation, and they are relatively prone to the experience of anxiety and despair. As a consequence, they often resort to a self-protective retreat from their surroundings and may limit interaction by means of self-control or behavioral inhibition. Extraverts are characterized by less sensitive cortical processes or by a predominance of inhibitory cortical processes. Consequently, they require more stimulation from the social environment and may actively seek it to overcome their own cortical inertia.

REFERENCES

Coan, R. W. (1978). Myers-Briggs Type Indicator. In O. K. Buros (Ed.), *The eighth mental measurements yearbook* (Vol I.) Highland Park, NJ: Gryphon.

Coan, R. W. (1979). Psychologists: Personal and theoretical pathways. New York: Irvington.

Eysenck, H. J. (1967). *The biological basis of personality.* Springfield, IL: Thomas.

James, W. (1907). *Pragmatism: A new name for some old ways of thinking.* New York: Longman Green.

Jung, C. G. (1976). *Psychological types.* Princeton, NJ: Princeton University Press. (Original work published 1921)

Murray, H. A. (1962). *Explorations in personality: A clinical and experimental study of fifty men of college age.* New York: Oxford University Press. (Original work published 1938)

R. W. COAN
University of Arizona

INTROVERSION-EXTRAVERSION
PERSONALITY TYPES

EYE

The eye performs three fundamental functions. Its optical components collect light energy. Its neural components transduce that light energy into electrochemical events and use these electrochemical events to produce meaningful neural signals that become the subjective sense of sight when further processed by the brain. Each of the structures that make up the eye either contribute in some way to these functions or provide protection to the eye.

The protective tissue of the eye includes the lids, and the transparent epithelial membrane known as the conjunctiva that lines the lids and continues to cover the white (sclera) of the eyeball. The tear or lacrimal glands and the fatty tissue of the orbit, which acts to absorb shock, also contribute protection to the eye.

The optical tissues of the eye include the cornea, the lens, the aqueous humor, and the vitreous humor or body. The cornea is the main structure responsible for refraction of light as it enters the eye. It normally does not have a blood supply. In addition to its refractive function, the cornea acts to protect the other optical structures of the eye and aids the sclera in giving the eye form and rigidity. The sclera is the tough white coat that forms the posterior four-fifths of the eye. The cornea is continuous with the sclera and when the two structures are subjected to routine histological staining, the anatomical appearance of the cornea does not differ markedly from that of the sclera. The transparent quality of the cornea is due to a continual pumping of interstitial fluid across the cell surfaces, which prevents the cornea from becoming cloudy.

The lens of the eye lies behind the cornea and the pigmented iris. The lens is held in place by suspensory ligaments called the zonule fibers. The zonule fibers are connected to the ciliary body containing the ciliary muscle. When the ciliary muscle contracts, the lens bulges, thereby increasing the refraction of light. This happens, along with pupillary constriction and convergence of the eyes, as part of the accommodation reflex that occurs when an object close to the eyes is viewed. The image focused on the retina by the cornea and lens is upside down and reversed right to left.

The aqueous humor is secreted into the posterior chamber of the eye by epithelial cells that cover the ciliary body. Aqueous humor flows through the pupil to the anterior chamber of the eye, where it can exit the eye through the canals of Schlemm. Schlemm's canals are located in the angle of the anterior chamber where the iris contacts the cornea.

Both the posterior and anterior chambers of the eye lie in front of the lens and zonule fibers. The zonule fibers that encircle the lens consist of individual strands of connective tissue, and for this reason the fluid in the posterior chamber is in contact with the gelatinous substance called vitreous humor that fills the area of the eyeball between the lens and the retina. If the aqueous humor cannot drain through Schlemm's canals the resulting accumulation increases pressure within the eye and this pressure is transmitted by the vitreous humor to the retina. This condition is called glaucoma and the pressure on the retina can cause blindness.

The uvea, or vascular tunic, of the eye is composed of the iris, the ciliary body, and the choroid. The choroid is vascularized and pigmented. It lies between the retina and the sclera. Its pigmentation prevents the scattering of light in the eye. The iris lies posterior to the cornea and anterior to the lens. Light causes the iris to constrict. This reduces the amount of light that enters the eye, but also enhances the depth of focus when the eye focuses on a near object. Thus, the iris constricts not only in response to increases in light, but also as part of the accommodation reflex.

The retina is the photoreceptive and integrative portion of the eye. Embryologically, it is an outpouching of the surface of the brain. At the retina a light stimulus is converted into a neural code and transmitted over the optic nerve and tract to the brain. The neural organization of the retina is sufficiently complex to allow a fair amount of integration of visual information. The rods and cones are the photoreceptive cells of the retina and are located at the very back of the retina (i.e., in its most posterior aspect). The cones function during daylight and are responsible for color vision. The rods function best in dim light and present the world in shades of gray. Rods are most numerous in the periphery of the retina, while cones are concentrated toward the focal center. The fovea, or macula, is found in the focal center of the retina and contains only cones. The rods and cones make contact with the bipolar cells. In turn, the bipolar cells of the retina synapse with the ganglion cells. The ganglion cells give rise to axons which form the optic nerve. The point where all of the ganglion cell axons come together and leave the eye is called the papilla or optic nerve head. Because there are no receptors at this point, the papilla is a "blind spot" in the retina. Other neurons in the retina are associated with the bipolar layer and perform associative functions; they are known as horizontal and amacrine cells. The photoreceptive rods and cones are located behind the other retinal cells and the axons of the ganglion cells, such that light must pass through the axons, nonphotoreceptive neurons, and supporting glial cells before reaching the rods and cones.

The process of visual perception is initiated when light is absorbed by the photopigments contained within the outer segment of the rods and cones. Rhodopsin is contained within rods. The cones appear to utilize at least three separate photopigments which have peak absorptions at wavelengths of light corresponding to the colors blue, green, and yellow. There is, however, considerable overlap in absorption among these pigments. Chemical changes initiated in the photopigments of the rods and cones when light is absorbed produce the rod and cone generator potentials.

SUGGESTED READING

Geneser, F. (1986). *Textbook of histology.* Copenhagen, Denmark: Munksgaard.

Hutchins, J. B., & Corbett, J. J. (1997). The visual system. In D. E. Haines (Ed.), *Fundamental neuroscience* (pp. 266–271). New York: Churchill Livingstone.

Koretz, J. F., & Handelman, G. H. (1988). How the human eye focuses. *Scientific American, 259,* 92–99.

May, P. J., & Corbett, J. J. (1997). Visual motor system. In D. E. Haines (Ed.), *Fundamental neuroscience* (pp. 399–416). New York: Churchill Livingstone.

M. L. WOODRUFF
East Tennessee State University

ACCOMMODATION
COLOR VISION
VISUAL ACUITY

EYE MOVEMENT DESENSITIZATION AND REPROCESSING (EMDR)

DESCRIPTION AND BACKGROUND

Eye Movement Desensitization (EMD; Shapiro, 1989) or, as it is currently known, Eye Movement Desensitization *and Reprocessing* (EMDR; 1995), is a relatively new psychotherapy technique that has inspired both great enthusiasm and great skepticism. The enthusiasm, based on the initial empirical evaluation of EMDR followed by numerous case studies, was for a simple treatment that promised rapid relief from Posttraumatic Stress Disorder (PTSD). The skepticism resulted from a number of subsequent studies that failed to replicate the early findings, and several review articles that identified serious methodological shortcomings in many of the studies in support of EMDR (e.g., Acierno, Hersen, Van Hasselt, Tremont, & Meuser, 1994; Lohr, Kleinknecht, Conley, Dal Cerro, Schmidt, & Sonntag, 1992). More recent research has addressed many of the methodological weaknesses of earlier studies, the results of which indicate that EMDR can be a beneficial form of psychotherapy (Cahill, Carrigan, & Frueh, 1999).

EMDR was first developed as a treatment for posttraumatic stress reactions, including PTSD. It has since been applied to a range of psychological problems and disorders including other anxiety disorders (e.g., Panic Disorder, fear of public speaking, other specific phobias), grief and bereavement, depression, substance abuse, and dissociative disorders. However, the published outcome research is limited to posttraumatic stress reactions and a few other anxiety problems.

Treatment with EMDR is formally described as consisting of eight phases (e.g., Shapiro, 1995, 1999; see Table 1). However, as the name implies, EMDR may be viewed as comprised of two major components: (a) structured imaginal exposure to trauma-related memories, thoughts, and feelings (desensitization); and (b) a form of cognitive restructuring (reprocessing). Both imaginal exposure and cognitive restructuring have been found to be effective in treating PTSD (Foa, Rothbaum, Riggs, & Murdock, 1991; Foa, Dancu, Hembree, Jaycox, Meadows, & Street, 1999; Marks, Lovell, Noshirvani, Livanou, & Thrasher, 1998), although the combination of these two procedures has not been found to be any more effective than either individual procedure (Marks et al., 1998). Although the form which exposure and cognitive restructuring take in EMDR is different from more standard variations of these techniques, what is most unique about EMDR is that both of these components are accompanied by therapist-induced rapid eye movements.

During the desensitization phase of EMDR, clients are instructed to generate an image that represents the targeted traumatic event and to think about a specific trauma-related negative cognition that they currently hold but would like to change (e.g., "I am worthless"). The client then tracks the therapist's fingers as the therapist moves them rapidly back and forth across the client's visual field at a rate of approximately two complete left-right cycles per second for approximately 24 cycles. In between sets, the client is instructed to "blank out" the image and to take a deep breath, after which the client is asked, "What do you get now?" The client's response to this question forms the content for the next set of imagery plus eye movements. This process is repeated until there is a

Table 1.   The Eight Phases of EMDR

Phase	Description
1. Client History and Treatment Planning	The therapist assesses the client's appropriateness for treatment, readiness for change, and motivation to not change (e.g., secondary gain); evaluates the client's symptoms, dysfunctional behaviors, and personal characteristics; works to identify and prioritize targets for treatment.
2. Preparation	The therapist works to establish a therapeutic relationship and set appropriate expectations, provides psycho-education and instruction in coping and self-control skills.
3. Assessment	The client and the therapist identify the specific image and associated thoughts (negative and positive), emotions, and somatic sensations to serve as the initial targets in treatment. Baseline SUDs and VoC ratings are obtained.
4. Desensitization	The client is instructed to hold the trauma image in mind, along with the relevant negative cognition. The therapist then induces a series of rapid eye movement, approximately 24 complete left-to-right cycles, by instructing the client to track the therapist's fingers as they are moved back and forth across the client's visual field at a rate of two cycles per second. At the end of the set, the client is instructed to "Blank it out and take a deep breath." The client is then asked, "What do you get now?" The information elicited by this question provides the content for the next set of imagery plus eye movements. Intermittently, the client provides additional SUDs ratings. When SUDs have declined to 0–1, the desensitization phase is terminated.
5. Installation	The client is instructed to hold the trauma image in mind, along with the new positive cognition they would like to believe. The therapist then induces rapid eye movements as in the desensitization phase. This continues until the new cognition receives a VoC rating of 6–7.
6. Body Scan	When the new cognition has achieved a VoC rating of 6–7, the body scan is conducted. The client is instructed to hold the target image in mind along with the positive cognition and then to mentally scan their body for any signs of residual tension in the form of body sensations, which are then targeted with additional sets of eye movements.
7. Closure	Closure occurs at the end of each treatment session. The goal is to help the client achieve "emotional equilibrium by the end of each session, whether or not the reprocessing is complete" (Shapiro, 1995, p. 73). This is done through normalizing the client's experiences and instructing the client in the use of self-control procedures, such as journal writing and positive imagery.
8. Reevaluation	The final stage, reevaluation, occurs at the beginning of each subsequent session by reviewing the thoughts, feelings, and images worked on in the previous session and discussing any issues that arise between sessions. The purpose of this review is to help the therapist to make decisions as to what to target in the current session. Thus, EMDR is designed to be flexible in meeting the client's needs as they alter during the course of therapy.

Note: SUDs = Subject Units of Discomfort; participants rate how much anxiety, fear, or discomfort they feel on a scale from 0 (none) to 10 (greatest possible). VoC = Validity of Cognitions scale; participants rate how strongly they believe in or how valid they find a specified belief or cognition to be on a scale from 1 (completely untrue) to 7 (completely true).

significant decline in self-reported fear or anxiety, as measured by the client's Subjective Units of Distress (SUDs; see Table caption for further explanation of SUDs). Once SUDs levels have declined to a zero or one, the client is again instructed to imagine the trauma memory, but this time while holding an alternative positive cognition in mind the client would prefer to believe (e.g., "I am a good person") and the therapist again induces rapid eye movements. This process is then repeated until the client reports a high level of belief in the new cognition, as measured by the Validity of Cognitions (VoC) scale (see Table caption for further explanation of VoC). This constitutes the reprocessing or installation phase.

Discovery

The inspiration for this treatment was a chance observation made by Francine Shapiro, the technique's originator, while walking through a park one day and noticing that some disturbing thoughts she had been thinking suddenly disappeared. When she subsequently retrieved the earlier disturbing thoughts, she found them to be less upsetting than before. This lead to more detailed introspection of this process:

Fascinated, I started paying very close attention to what was going on. I noticed that when the disturbing thoughts came into my mind, my eyes spontaneously started moving very rapidly back and forth in an upward diagonal. Again, the thoughts disappeared, and when I brought them back to mind, their negative charge was greatly reduced. At that point I started making the eye movements deliberately while concentrating on a variety of disturbing thoughts and memories, and I found that these thoughts also disappeared and lost their charge. (Shapiro, 1995, p. 2)

Shapiro subsequently went on to apply the eye movement technique to other people, such as friends, colleagues, and psychology workshop participants, until she developed a procedure that appeared reliably to produce improvement. She then formally tested the efficacy of her new treatment in a randomized outcome study (Shapiro, 1989), the results of which were significant changes in SUDs and VoC ratings in the direction of improvement among a group of trauma victims. Treatment consisted of a single session in which the technique was applied for between 15 and 90 minutes. In comparison, a control group that briefly talked about their trauma, while periodically providing SUDs ratings, showed little or no improvement. However, when the control participants were later provided with the same treatment, similar improvements were observed. In addition, these positive treatment gains were maintained up to three months after treatment.

Further Developments

At the time of the first publication on EMDR (Shapiro, 1989), the technique was viewed as a variant of Wolpe's systematic desensitization, and there was a clear emphasis on the eye movements serving to produce reciprocal inhibition of the traumatic memory. However, this view was rapidly expanded to emphasize accelerated information processing (Shapiro, 1995). Moreover, the procedure expanded to include a variety of different types of rhythmic laterally alternating stimuli, such as alternating audio cues or hand taps. An additional development has been a more complex form of cognitive restructuring, called the cognitive interweave, that therapists

may use when a client's progress appears to be blocked. As noted, the range of problems targeted for treatment has also substantially expanded.

CRITICAL EVALUATION OF EMDR OUTCOME AND DISMANTLING STUDIES

Shapiro's (1989) initial study has been critiqued as suffering from numerous serious methodological shortcomings (e.g., Acierno et al., 1994; Lohr et al., 1992). These include failure to establish the PTSD diagnosis prior to treatment; failure to use standardized measures of known reliability and validity to assess outcome; failure to obtain outcome assessments by an evaluator blind to the clients' experimental condition; and the author serving as the sole therapist. Several more recent studies have been conducted addressing these limitations, focussing on three important questions: (a) Is EMDR more effective than no treatment? If so, (b) how does EMDR compare to other forms of treatment, particularly those that are more commonly known or have been empirically validated? Finally, if EMDR works, (c) what components of the treatment (e.g., imaginal exposure, cognitive restructuring, eye movements) contribute to outcome?

Comparison with No Treatment

Comparison of a treatment with a no-treatment group controls for a number of important variables including the effects of repeated measurement, such as regression to the mean, and natural fluctuations in symptom severity over time. In addition, it is important that (a) participants be randomly assigned to treatment conditions, (b) researchers use reliable and valid measures, and (c) people conducting the outcome evaluations be blind to the clients' treatment condition. These steps are taken to minimize the effects of experimenter bias. There are now a growing number of studies on EMDR that meet these rigorous methodological standards, the results of which have found EMDR to be more effective than no treatment for posttraumatic stress reactions, including PTSD (e.g., Carlson, Chemtob, Rusnak, Hedlund, & Muraoka, 1998; Rothbaum, 1997; Wilson, Becker, & Tinker, 1995). In addition, EMDR appears more effective than no treatment for panic disorder (Feske & Goldstein, 1998) and fear of public speaking (Foley & Spates, 1995), although these results await replication.

Comparisons with Other Treatments

By some estimates, there are currently more than 400 "name brand" forms of psychotherapy (Karasu, 1986). Therefore, when developing a psychological treatment, it is typically not enough to show that the new treatment works better than nothing. Rather, it is important to determine how well it works compared to other treatments for the same problem. This information helps therapists offer the best available treatment and not spend their time and effort learning new treatments that are not more effective than what they already use.

EMDR has been directly compared to a number of different treatments. In the treatment of posttraumatic stress reactions, EMDR has been found to be as effective as, or slightly more effective than, relaxation (Carlson et al., 1998; Vaughan, Armstrong, Gold, O'Connor, Jenneke, & Tarrier, 1994), a form of self-administered exposure therapy called Image Habituation Training (Vaughan et al., 1994), and Active Listening (Scheck, Schaeffer, & Gillette, 1998). However, none of these treatments have been independently validated for the treatment of posttraumatic stress reactions. One study found that EMDR administered by one group of therapists was more effective for PTSD than "treatment as usual" administered by a different group of therapists (Marcus, Marquis, & Sakai, 1997). Unfortunately, the design of this study confounded potential therapist effects with the type of treatment. Another concern is that treatment as usual consisted of a variety of interventions such as medications, group therapy, and different types of individual therapy, some of which may have been more effective than others. Therefore, it is not clear what EMDR was found to be more effective than. A more recent study compared EMDR to routine individual therapy (Edmond, Rubin, & Wambach, 1999), in which the same therapists administered both forms of therapy, thereby eliminating the confounding of therapist and type of therapy. The result of this study indicated that both treatments were more effective than no treatment and there were no statistically significant differences between groups immediately after treatment. However, at a follow-up assessment three months later, clients treated with EMDR had better long-term outcomes than treatment as usual on two of the four measures administered. The reason for the group difference at follow-up was that clients treated with EMDR continued to improve on measures of depression and general anxiety even after treatment was completed. In contrast, clients who received treatment as usual maintained their treatment gains at follow-up but did not show any further improvement. Thus, EMDR may have some long-term benefits over regular counseling. However, the treatment as usual condition was not comprised of a specific alternative therapy. Rather, therapists were free to choose from a range of interventions, such as cognitive restructuring, ego strengthening, problem solving, various forms of visualization, and relaxation exercises. Because some of these interventions may have been more effective than others, it is again difficult to know which of the various techniques EMDR was found to be better than.

Other, more standard forms of cognitive-behavior therapy have also been found to be effective for the treatment of PTSD, particularly Prolonged Exposure and Stress Inoculation Training. These two treatments tend to produce similar outcomes, and their combination is no more effective than either of the individual treatments (Foa et al., 1991; Foa et al., 1999). Indeed, the American Psychological Association Division 12 (Clinical Psychology) Task Force on Psychological Intervention Guidelines recently listed Prolonged Exposure and Stress Inoculation Training as "probably efficacious for PTSD" and listed EMDR as "probably efficacious for civilian PTSD" (Chambless et al., 1998). How does EMDR compare with these treatments? At present, only one relevant study has been published. Devilly and Spence (1999) compared twelve sessions of EMDR with twelve sessions of a treatment called Trauma Treatment Protocol that, based on the work of Foa and her colleagues (1991), combined Prolonged Exposure with elements of Stress Inoculation Training and additional cognitive therapy intervention. The results revealed that participants receiving the Trauma Treatment Protocol were significantly better off than those

treated with EMDR, both immediately after treatment and at a three-month follow-up assessment. However, this study lacked random assignment and the results therefore await replication.

Three studies have compared EMDR for treating spider phobia with a form of exposure therapy called Participant Modeling (Muris & Merckelbach, 1997; Muris, Merckelbach, Holdrinet, & Sijsenaar, 1998; Muris, Merckelbach, van Haaften, & Mayer, 1997). Participant modeling for spider phobia involves graduated *in vivo* exposure to feared, but otherwise safe, spiders. In addition, the therapist models techniques for effectively handling spiders and assists the client in their use. Participant modeling is extremely effective in helping individuals rapidly overcome a variety of specific phobias (e.g., spiders, snakes, dogs, heights) and is more effective than passive *in vivo* exposure and forms of imaginal exposure (e.g., Bandura, Blanchard, & Ritter, 1969; Williams, Dooseman, & Kleifield, 1984). All three studies utilized designs in which treatment outcome was evaluated by assessing the effects of prior treatment with EMDR on subsequent treatment with Participant Modeling. In all three studies, EMDR resulted in decreased SUDs and increased VoC ratings. However, EMDR had little effect on direct testing with spiders, in that participants continued to avoid contact with the spiders. In contrast, subsequent treatment with Participant Modeling was found to rapidly reduce behavioral avoidance.

The authors of these studies openly acknowledged that they truncated the EMDR phobia protocol by not including some of the components. The reason for this was to equate the duration of treatment with EMDR to that of treatment with Participant Modeling. Although the authors have been criticized for this decision (e.g., Shapiro, 1999), until there is further research, treatment with Participant Modeling should be preferred to EMDR for specific animal phobias. Even if it were to be shown that the full EMDR treatment protocol would have produced comparable outcomes to Participant Modeling on the behavioral test, the Participant Modeling protocol would still have been more efficient, as it can be administered in less time.

Why Does EMDR Work?

EMDR is a multicomponent treatment that appears to be effective in reducing symptoms of PTSD and possibly other anxiety disorders and problems, such as Panic Disorder and fear of public speaking. Many critics of EMDR view it as little more than a variation of exposure therapy with some cognitive restructuring. Dismantling studies address the question, "What are the effective components of a multicomponent therapy?" by comparing the full treatment with variations in which one or more of the components have been eliminated. As reviewed by Cahill et al. (1999), a number of dismantling studies have evaluated the role of eye movements and other laterally alternating stimuli, such as alternating sounds and alternating hand taps. Several of these studies have also included a condition in which there were no laterally alternating stimuli.

The majority of these studies have found that replacing the eye movements with other forms of laterally alternating stimuli or completely eliminating the eye movements does not reduce the efficacy of the treatment. However, there are a few notable exceptions. For example, Boudewyns, Stwertka, Hyer, Albrecht, and

Sperr (1993) found that, compared to a no eye movement condition, EMDR resulted in greater within-session SUDs reduction and a greater proportion of participants rated by their therapist as being a "treatment responder." However, there were no differences between these groups at the final outcome assessment on any measure, including SUDs in response to tape-recorded descriptions of target memories. For example, Wilson, Silver, Covi, and Foster (1996) found that eye movements, but not alternate thumb tapping, resulted in decreased within-session SUDs and skin conductance activity, and increased VoC. However, no posttreatment measures of psychopathology were obtained and all control participants but one immediately received treatment with EMDR. Therefore, it is impossible to determine whether the within-session changes that were observed for EMDR translated into meaningful changes in client outcome following treatment. Feske and Goldstein (1997) reported another exception. They found that EMDR resulted in significantly better outcome than a treatment that included all elements of EMDR except eye movements immediately after treatment for panic disorder. However, the group difference was no longer statistically significant at the three-month follow-up assessment.

One recent study (Cusack & Spates, 1999) investigated the role of cognitive restructuring in EMDR. It compared the full EMDR treatment with a condition in which the installation phase was replaced by additional desensitization trials to equate the groups for the total number of sets of imagery plus eye movements. Results revealed that both groups showed improvement, with no differences between the groups on any outcome measure.

Taken as whole, the outcomes of dismantling studies suggest that eye movements or other laterally alternating stimuli and cognitive restructuring are not necessary for treatment with EMDR to be effective. In some cases, it may be that eye movements facilitate within-session fear reduction (e.g., Boudewyns, et al., 1993; Wilson et al., 1996) and possibly produce a modest improvement over treatment without eye movements shortly after treatment (Feske & Goldstein, 1997). However, there is no evidence from these studies that eye movements contribute to the long-term resolution of psychopathology outcomes. There are still other components of EMDR, including the cognitive interweave, that have yet to be evaluated. As the data currently stand, however, they lend support to the idea that the primary active ingredients in EMDR consist of several nonspecific variables that are common to most therapies (e.g., meeting with an acknowledged expert for the purpose of solving one's problems, talking with a caring and empathic listener) and/or exposure to trauma-related thoughts and feelings. Further research is needed to further clarify problems for which EMDR may be helpful, how well EMDR compares to other treatments for particular problems, and what elements of the EMDR protocol are responsible for good clinical outcomes.

REFERENCES

Acierno, R., Hersen, M., Van Hasselt, V. B., Tremont, G., & Meuser, K. T. (1994). Review and dissemination of eye-movement desensitization and reprocessing: A scientific and ethical dilemma. *Clinical Psychology Review, 14,* 284–299.

Bandura, A., Blanchard, E. B., & Ritter, B. (1969). The relative efficacy of desensitization and modeling approaches for inducing behavioral, affective, and attitudinal changes. *Journal of Personality and Social Psychology, 13,* 173–199.

Boudewyns, P. A., Stwertka, S. A., Hyer, L. A., Albrecht, J. W., & Sperr, E. V. (1993). Eye movement desensitization for PTSD of combat: A treatment outcome pilot study. *The Behavior Therapist, 16,* 29–33.

Cahill, S. P., Carrigan, M. H., & Frueh, B. C. (1999). Does EMDR work? And if so, why? A critical review of controlled outcome and dismantling research. *Journal of Anxiety Disorders, 13,* 5–33.

Carlson, J. G., Chemtob, C. M., Rusnak, K., Hedlund, N. L., & Muraoka, M. Y. (1998). Eye movement desensitization and reprocessing for combat-related posttraumatic stress disorder. *Journal of Traumatic Stress, 11,* 3–24.

Chambless, D. L., Baker, M. J., Baucom, D. H., Beutler, L. E., Calhoun, K. S., Crits-Christoph, P., Daiuto, A., DeRubeis, R., Detweiler, J., Haaga, D. A. F., Bennett Johnson, S., McCurry, S., Mueser, K. T., Sanderson, W. C., Shoham, V., Stickle, T., Williams, D. A., & Woody, S. R. (1998). Update on empirically validated therapies, II. *The Clinical Psychologist, 51,* 3–16.

Cusack, K., & Spates, C. R. (1999). The cognitive dismantling of eye movement desensitization and reprocessing (EMDR) treatment of posttraumatic stress disorder (PTSD). *Journal of Anxiety Disorders, 13,* 87–99.

Devilly, G. J., & Spence, S. H. (1999). The relative efficacy and treatment distress of EMDR and a cognitive-behavior trauma treatment protocol in the amelioration of posttraumatic stress disorder. *Journal of Anxiety Disorders, 13,* 131–157.

Edmond, T., Rubin, A., & Wambach, K. G. (1999). The effectiveness of EMDR with adult female survivors of childhood sexual abuse. *Social Work Research, 23,* 103–116.

Feske, U., & Goldstein, A. J. (1997). Eye movement desensitization and reprocessing treatment for panic disorder: A controlled outcome and partial dismantling study. *Journal of Consulting and Clinical Psychology, 65,* 1026–1035.

Foa, E. B., Dancu, C. V., Hembree, E. A., Jaycox, L. H., Meadows, E. A., & Street, G. P. (1999). A comparison of exposure therapy, stress inoculation training and their combination for reducing PTSD in female assault victims. *Journal of Consulting and Clinical Psychology, 67,* 194–200.

Foa, E. B., Rothbaum, B. O., Riggs, D. S., & Murdock, T. B. (1991). Treatment of posttraumatic stress disorder in rape victims: A comparison between cognitive-behavioral procedures and counseling. *Journal of Consulting and Clinical Psychology, 59,* 715–723.

Karasu, T. B. (1986). The specificity versus nonspecificity dilemma: Toward identifying therapeutic change agents. *American Journal of Psychiatry, 143,* 687–695.

Lohr, J. M., Kleinknecht, R. A., Conley, A. T., Dal Cerro, S. Schmidt, J., & Sonntag, M. E. (1992). A methodological critique of the current status of eye movement desensitization.

Journal of Behavior Therapy and Experimental Psychiatry, 23, 159–167.

Marcus, S., Marquis, P., & Sakai, C. (1997). Controlled study of treatment of PTSD using EMDR in an HMO setting. *Psychotherapy, 34,* 307–315.

Marks, I., Lovell, K., Noshirvani, H., Livanou, M., & Thrasher, S. (1998). Treatment of posttraumatic stress disorder by exposure and/or cognitive restructuring. *Archives of General Psychiatry, 55,* 317–325.

Muris, P., & Merckelbach, H. (1997). Treating spider phobics with eye movement desensitization: A controlled study. *Behavioural and Cognitive Psychotherapy, 25,* 39–50.

Muris, P., Merckelbach, H., Holdrinet, I., & Sijsenaar, M. (1998). Treating phobic children: Effects of EMDR versus exposure. *Journal of Consulting and Clinical Psychology, 66,* 193–198.

Muris, P., Merckelbach, H., van Haaften, H., & Mayer, B. (1997). Eye movement desensitization and reprocessing versus exposure in vivo: A single-session crossover study of spider-phobic children. *British Journal of Psychiatry, 171,* 82–84.

Rothbaum, B. O. (1997). A controlled study of eye movement desensitization and reprocessing for posttraumatic stress disordered sexual assault victims. *Bulletin of the Menninger Clinic, 61,* 317–334.

Scheck, M. M., Schaeffer, J. A., & Gillette, C. (1998). Brief psychological intervention with traumatized young women: The efficacy of eye movement desensitization and reprocessing. *Journal of Traumatic Stress, 11,* 25–43.

Shapiro, F. (1989). Efficacy of the eye movement desensitization procedure in the treatment of traumatic memories. *Journal of Traumatic Stress, 2,* 199–223.

Shapiro, F. (1995). *Eye movement desensitization and reprocessing: Basic principles, protocols, and procedures.* New York: Guilford Press.

Shapiro, F. (1999). Eye movement desensitization and reprocessing (EMDR) and the anxiety disorders: Clinical and research implications of an integrated psychotherapy treatment. *Journal of Anxiety Disorders, 13,* 35–67.

Vaughan, K., Armstrong, M. F., Gold, R., O'Connor, N., Jenneke, W., & Tarrier, N. (1994). A trial of eye movement desensitization compared to image habituation training and applied relaxation in post-traumatic stress disorder. *Journal of Behavior Therapy and Experimental Psychiatry, 25,* 283–291.

Williams, S. L., Dooseman, G., & Kleifield, E. (1984). Comparative effectiveness of guided mastery and exposure treatments for intractable phobias. *Journal of Consulting and Clinical Psychology, 52,* 505–518.

Wilson, D., Silver, S. M., Covi, W., & Foster, S. (1996). Eye movement desensitization and reprocessing: Effectiveness and autonomic correlates. *Journal of Behavior Therapy and Experimental Psychiatry, 27,* 219–229.

Wilson, S. A., Becker, L. A., & Tinker, R. H. (1995). Eye movement desensitization and reprocessing (EMDR) treatment for psychologically traumatized individuals. *Journal of Consulting and Clinical Psychology, 63,* 928–937.

SUGGESTED READING

Acierno, R., & Cahill, S. P. (Eds.). (1999). Advances in conceptualization and research on the efficacy and mechanism of EMDR [Special Issue]. *Journal of Anxiety Disorders, 13,* (1–2).

Lohr, J. M., Kleinknecht, R. A., Conley, A. T., Dal Cerro, S. Schmidt, J., & Sonntag, M. E. (1992). A methodological critique of the current status of eye movement desensitization. *Journal of Behavior Therapy and Experimental Psychiatry, 23,* 159–167.

Lohr, J. M., Kleinknecht, R. A., Tolin, D. F., & Barrett, R. H. (1995). The empirical status of the clinical application of eye movement desensitization and reprocessing. *Journal of Behavior Therapy and Experimental Psychiatry, 26,* 285–302.

Lohr, J. M., Tolin, D. F., & Lilienfeld, S. O. (1998). Efficacy of eye movement desensitization reprocessing: Implications for behavior therapy. *Behavior Therapy, 29,* 123–156.

Shapiro, F. (1995). *Eye movement desensitization and reprocessing: Basic principles, protocols, and procedures.* New York: Guilford Press.

S. P. CAHILL
University of Pennsylvania

PSYCHOTHERAPY
PSYCHOTHERAPY TECHNIQUES

EYELID CLASSICAL CONDITIONING

Classical conditioning is one of the most important tools for behavioral and neural scientists. Classical conditioning as Pavlov discovered it involves the creation of an association between a previously neutral stimulus (a bell, a lab coat) and a reflex-evoking stimulus (meat powder) which causes an unconscious reflexive response (salivation). With repeated pairings, the neutral stimulus (becoming the conditional stimulus as Pavlov termed it or the conditioned stimulus as we know it today) comes to evoke a learned response (the conditioned response) which is similar to but not exactly like the reflexive response elicited by the meat powder (the unconditioned stimulus). Pavlov's salivating dogs are common enough images to the public in cartoons and science fiction. Strictly speaking, Pavlovian conditioning is classical conditioning of an autonomic or visceral response.

In contrast, classical conditioning of a somatic response involves a striated muscle reflex rather than smooth or cardiac muscles. The classic example is Twitmeyer's patellar tendon reflex, familiar to most of us from physical exams: A tap to the knee with a physician's hammer (the unconditioned stimulus) causes a knee-jerk reflex (the unconditioned response). The conditioning situation is similar to Pavlov's autonomic conditioning, with a previously neutral stimulus (such as a sound) acquiring the eliciting properties of the unconditioned stimulus—the sound alone comes to elicit a knee jerk. The difference from Pavlov is that somatic conditioning of the patellar tendon reflex is a skeletal muscle response. For various reasons mostly related to its application, the patellar tendon reflex is awkward to implement. Theoretically, however, any reflexive motor response can be classically conditioned. The eyelid reflex provides a convenient, easily accessible, easily implemented means of studying classical conditioning of a somatic muscle response. First widely used in studies of classical conditioning in humans, an eye blink response is typically elicited with a puff of air directed at the cornea (the unconditioned stimulus) or shock to the face. Either stimulus reliably elicits an eye blink. Animal studies of eye blink conditioning often use an air puff when the subject is restrained, but under conditions where the animal is freely moving a face shock may be used instead. Studies using human eye blink conditioning favor using an air puff.

It is important to note that Pavlov's classical conditioning paradigm using salivation and the eye blink paradigms are structured in the same way and have the same essential properties found in all classical conditioning. That is, in each paradigm there are identifiable conditioned and unconditioned stimuli, unconditioned reflexes and learned conditioned responses. The relationships between these stimuli and responses are also the same. Thus, for example, the conditioned stimulus must precede the unconditioned stimulus (forward conditioning) by at least about 100 msec. The learned conditioned response is very similar to but not identical with the evoked reflexive response. In both types of classical conditioning, acquisition shows a typical sigmoid curve and reaches an asymptotic level. In general, strong stimuli result in faster learning. Subsequent training where the unconditioned response is withheld (extinction procedure) causes diminution of the learned response, spontaneous recovery at the beginning of subsequent days of testing, and eventually the absence of conditioned responses. Additional training that pairs the conditioned and unconditioned stimuli rapidly restores the conditioned response. These are only a few of the salient properties that are shared in both types of classical conditioning.

In studies with animals, optimal learning is usually reached in about 130 trials when each trial has the onset of tone (conditioned stimulus) preceding the onset of the air puff (unconditioned stimulus) by 250 msec. The interval between trials might average 30 sec. Intertrial intervals of 9 sec or less do not support conditioning. In studies with humans, optimal learning is usually reached in about 50 trials when each trial has the onset of the tone (conditioned stimulus) preceding the onset of the air puff (unconditioned stimulus) by 500 msec. The interval between trials might average 60 sec. Humans must additionally be distracted during conditioning, by watching silent movies, for example. Recent studies show, however, that humans who learn can accurately describe the stimulus contingencies.

Learned responses are defined as eye blinks that occur after the onset of the tone and before the air puff on paired trials. A further criterion is that the response must be 0.5 mm or larger to be counted as a response. On test trials where only the tone is given, conditioned responses are defined as any 0.5 mm or larger response after the tone until the end of the trial, usually a period of 250 msec after the air puff would have begun. In both cases, reflexive alpha responses that occur too quickly after the tone should be excluded as not being true conditioned responses. For rabbits, any response less than 25 msec is considered to be an alpha response. For humans, any response less than 100 msec might be considered to be an alpha response. The usual criterion for learning is the first time that 8 conditioned responses occur in 9 trials (89% responding). An additional criterion for stable performance (overtraining) requires continued performance at some level, for example, 70% responding with learned responses. With rabbits 100% responding is often achieved, but with humans the rate is usually not perfect. Once learned, the association shows good retention over months and sometimes years.

Traditionally, the unconditioned response was thought to be stable and impervious to influence by the training stimuli. However, reflex facilitation is seen before conditioned responses appear. Reflex facilitation occurs when the size of the reflexive response to the air puff increases in the presence of the tone. It has also been shown that there is sensitization of the eye blink. This sensitization is seen as an increase in the size of the eye blink after repeated exposure to a tone and air puff that have never been presented together.

The fact that the motor response is so well defined is one of the distinguishing features between operant and classical conditioning. The actual motor response in eye blink conditioning involves sensations of the air puff from receptors on the cornea and the region of the face around the eye. This sensation involves the trigeminal nerve (cranial nerve V) and its projections to the trigeminal nuclei. The trigeminal nuclei most involved are the principal (sensory) and descending (inferior or spinal) trigeminal nuclei. The former is characterized as being involved in the sense of touch and position, while the latter is characterized as being involved in light touch and pain, although these designations overlap. The reflex arc involves projections from the trigeminal nuclei to cranial motor nuclei that project motor neurons to the muscles involved in the eye blink. In its simplest terms, the principal motor nucleus for the eye blink is the facial cranial nucleus (cranial nerve VII) which innervates the orbicularis occuli muscles that effect the eye blink. The eye blink involves more than just this connection, but in humans this is the pathway usually considered. In animals other pathways may receive most of our attention. In common experimental subjects like the rabbit and cat which have a "third eyelid"—the nictating membrane—the cranial motor nuclei most involved are the abducens (cranial nucleus VI) and the accessory abducens nuclei, which innervate the rectus bulbus muscle. The nictitating membrane response for the rabbit involves retraction of the eyeball into the orbit, which presses Hardner's gland, which in turn causes nictitating membrane extension. In the rabbit, nictitating membrane movement is a passive phenomenon. In the cat, nictitating membrane extension is an active process, where there is a projection to the superior oblique muscles that control the nictitating membrane. In addition to these connections, the eye blink response (especially in the case of the nictitating membrane in the rabbit) involves cranial projections to the extraocular eye muscles through the oculomotor (cranial nucleus III), trochlear (cranial nucleus IV), and abducens (cranialnucleus VI) innervations. Simultaneous activations of these extraocular muscles pull the eye ball into the socket.

From the above it should be obvious that there are several ways to measure the response to a puff of air directed at the eye. The most direct method is to measure the movement of the eyelids or nictitating membrane. This is accomplished by using a transducer—a device to translate movement into an electronic signal. Most commonly, this is accomplished with a minitorque potentiometer with a lever attached to the axel. Although it has been done, researchers are generally hesitant to directly attach a potentiometer lever to the eyelids of human subjects, for fear of poking the subject in the eye. This is especially a concern when the subject's movements are unpredictable, as in Alzheimer's patients. In animal subjects this measurement is made by placing a small loop of suture into the eyelid or nictitating membrane for attachment of the potentiometer lever or by temporarily gluing the potentiometer lever directly to the eyelid. The great advantage of using a potentiometer is that the actual movement is recorded. Because an eye blink presumably performs a protective feature, monitoring the actual eyelid movement gives an indication of its functionality.

An alternative to directly measuring the movement is to record (EMG) activity from the eyelid. This can be done directly, by inserting recording electrodes into the orbicularis muscles, or indirectly, by placing surface electrodes over the skin of the muscles. Both methods have been used in animals, but in humans surface electrodes are favored because they are noninvasive. It should be noted, however, that surface electrodes also pick up information about eye position because the anterior chamber of the eye is charged. In any event, the signal obtained through EMG measurements is imprecisely related to the actual movement. One method is to treat EMG as if it were a neural signal and to send it through a height discriminator. The actual shape of the eye blink is surprisingly reasonable with such a crude measure. The greatest advantage, however, is that the latency of the eye blink is very accurate. However, since movement is easier for us to relate to, EMG signals are usually converted electronically into signals that mimic the output of the potentiometer. The advantage is that the measurement appears to be more familiar. The disadvantage is that the electronics involved in the conversion delay the latency measurement depending on the speed of the eye blink (and therefore it is not a constant delay) and the overall travel of the blink is distorted by the filtering characteristics of the conversion.

Probably the most favored method for recording eye blinks in humans involves an indirect measure. Here, a light is reflected off the eye, and the returning signal gives an indication of the position of the eyelid. Two methods are commonly employed. The first method uses visible light emissions from an incandescent source (for example, a flashlight bulb) or a light emitting diode (LED). The advantage of using visible light is that it can be used to continuously monitor the position of the eyelid. The one drawback of this method is that it is affected by ambient light. In particular, 60 Hz noise from fluorescent lighting can be picked up with the light detector. The second method uses infrared (IR) emissions from an IR-LED. The advantage of infrared emissions is that they are little affected by ambient light. The disadvantage of infrared emissions is that infrared emission is heat, which can be uncomfortable or

even harmful to the eye. To counteract the heating problem, infrared emissions are typically turned on and off rapidly to limit the buildup of heat. This technique requires electronic circuitry to only measure eyelid activity during the period when the infrared device is turned on, a technique which introduces higher frequency noise problems. There is no perfect measure of the eye blink response. The methods outlined here indicate some of the trade offs that must go into making a decision, about acquiring the data.

One of the old issues about conditioning is whether the subject needs to make the actual physical response in order to make the association. At one time there were reports in the autonomic conditioning literature that paralyzing the skeletal muscles with curare did not prevent the formation of learning, but this could not be replicated later. Instead, somatic mediation (voluntary skeletal movements or relaxation) is the prime factor in supposedly autonomic conditioning. Recently, however, experiments with reversible inactivation of the cranial motor nuclei show that classical conditioning is learned without the subject actually making the eye blink response during acquisition training.

Pavlov himself appreciated the advantages of classical conditioning for studies of the neural bases of learning and memory. The advantages include the experimenter's control over the stimuli for the association and the experimenter's ready identification of the motor responses. Classical conditioning is a model system for understanding the biology of learning. Unfortunately, Pavlov failed to localize learning and memory, in large part because he took a "top-down" approach, starting with cerebral cortex, which most people incorrectly assume is the repository of even the simplest of memories. The detached spinal cord is capable of forming primitive associations that are classically conditioned. Recently, studies that have taken a "bottom-up" approach, starting with the circuitry for the basic reflexive response, have shown that the association for classical conditioning of the somatic muscle response involved in eyelid conditioning is localized to the cerebellum as a type of motor learning.

Today, classical conditioning of the eyelid response is increasingly favored for providing a quick, reliable test of cognitive functioning in human clinical settings. The reasons for this include the clear structure of the paradigm with identifiable control over the stimuli and responses, the extensive behavioral studies on the properties of classical conditioning, and recent advances in identifying neural structures responsible for or participating in classical conditioning.

SUGGESTED READING

Gormezano, I., Prokasy, W. F., & Thompson, R. F. (Eds.). (1986). *Classical conditioning: III. Behavioral, neurophysiological, and neurochemical studies in the rabbit.* Hillsdale, NJ: Erlbaum.

Pavlov, I. P. (1927). *Conditioned reflexes.* Oxford: Oxford University Press.

Prince, J. H. (Ed.). (1964). *The rabbit in eye research.* Springfield, Illinois: Charles C. Thomas.

Schneiderman, N., Fuentes, I., & Gormezano, I. (1962). Acquisition and extinction of the classically conditioned eyelid response in the albino rabbit. *Science, 136,* 650–652.

Thompson, R. F., Bao, S., Berg, M. S., Chen, L., Cipriano, B. C., Kim, J. J., Thompson, J. K., Tracy, J. A. & Krupa, D. J. (1997). Associative learning. In J. D. Schmahmann (Ed.), *The cerebellum and cognition.* San Diego: Academic.

Woodruff-Pak, D. S. & Steinmetz, J. E. (Eds.). (in press). *Eyeblink classical conditioning, Vol. 1 (Animal) and 2 (Human).* Norwell, MA: Kluwer.

D. G. LAVOND
University of Southern California

CLASSICAL CONDITIONING
SIMULTANEOUS CONDITIONING

EYEWITNESS TESTIMONY

Eyewitnesses to an event report what they had perceived; such reports also are limited to what the witnesses remember about the event. Hence both perception and memory are relevant in evaluating the completeness and veracity of testimony. (Kassin, Ellsworth, & Smith, 1989; Lloyd-Bostock & Clifford, 1983; Loftus, 1979, 1986; Wells & Loftus, 1984; Williams, Loftus, & Deffenbacher, 1992.) Eyewitness testimony is highly persuasive for juries, more than other forms of evidence (Loftus, 1974; Wells, Lindsay, & Ferguson, 1979; McCloskey & Egeth, 1983).

MEMORY FOR FACES

Eyewitnesses are often called on to identify or to describe perpetrator(s), making face memory important for eyewitness research. In general, memory for faces is quite good, with accuracy high even at long retention intervals (Bahrick, Bahrick, & Wittlinger, 1975). However, memory for faces is far from perfect, and large-scale errors have been documented (Baddeley, 1982). A number of factors can erode the accuracy of face memory, including such expected factors as brief exposure and long delay between the exposure and the subsequent identification. It also is well documented that individuals are far better in remembering faces from their own race than remembering faces of other races (Brigham, 1986; Deffenbacher & Loftus, 1982; Shapiro & Penrod, 1986).

In addition, subjects are much better at remembering that a face is familiar than they are at remembering why a face is familiar. For example, Brown, Deffenbacher, and Sturgill (1977) had subjects observe an event. Several days later, they showed the subjects mugshots of individuals who supposedly had participated in the event. The people in the photos were different from the people who had actually been on the scene. After some more days, subjects were shown a lineup of four individuals and were asked to select the individuals seen in the original event. Subjects often selected individuals who had been seen in the mugshots; that is, they correctly realized that these individuals were familiar, but then misattributed this familiarity to the original event.

This experiment illustrates *photo-biased* identification (Brigham & Cairns, 1988). Related effects have been documented in which a person encountered in one circumstance is remembered (falsely) as having been encountered in some other circumstance, a confusion often referred to as *unconscious transference* (Loftus, 1979; Read, Tollestrup, Hammersley, & McFadzen, 1990). In these cases, subjects are again correct in remembering that a face is familiar; their error arises when they attribute this familiarity to some specific prior episode.

Some strategies and some sorts of training can improve witness's memory for faces. For example, deep processing of faces (e.g., thinking about the personality of the person, rather than about the size of specific features) leads to better memory (Bloom & Mudd, 1991; Shapiro & Penrod, 1986; Sporer, 1991). However, this is probably due to the number and variety of features attended to while doing deep processing. Thus face memory may be best if, when a face is being observed, one pays attention to many and diverse aspects of the face.

Eyewitness memory for individuals is often assessed via a lineup, in which the witness must select from a group of people the person observed during the original event. Many studies have examined the factors that influence lineup identifications and have sought ways to determine when a lineup identification should be trusted. For example, it appears that identification is equally accurate from a live or from a videotaped lineup (Cutler, Fisher, & Chicvara, 1989) and the likelihood of correctly identifying a culprit also is largely unaffected by clothing or disguise (Lindsay, Wallbridge, & Drennan, 1987). However, an *innocent* suspect is more likely to be misidentified as the culprit if he or she is wearing clothes similar to those the witness remembers the suspect wearing (Lindsay et al., 1987).

The other individuals in the lineup are termed the foils, or distractors. Lineups without foils (with the question "Was this the culprit?") entail considerable risk of misidentification. It also is crucial that the foils be of the same age, race, height, and weight as the suspect. If the eyewitness has verbalized other features of the culprit (e.g., that he or she was attractive or looked fierce), the foils must be matched on these features as well. In fact, it seems more important that the foils resemble the witnesses' *descriptions* of the culprit, rather than resembling the suspects themselves (Loftus, 1979; Luus & Wells, 1991).

Given these considerations, researchers have distinguished the functional, or effective, size of a lineup (i.e., the number of people among whom the witness is plausibly choosing) from the lineup's nominal size (the actual number of people). If several individuals in the lineup are rather dissimilar from the suspect, then the functional size may be considerably smaller than the nominal size. In fact, the nominal size of the lineup plays relatively little role in witnesses' identifications (Loftus, 1979; Nosworthy & Lindsay, 1990), but having an adequate functional size is crucial for identification accuracy. Consequently, researchers have developed a number of ways to quantify a lineup's functional size (Brigham, Ready, & Spier, 1990; Loftus, 1979).

Lineup identifications are strongly influenced by the instructions given to the witness as well as the format of the lineup itself. Instructions explicitly acknowledging that the culprit may be absent from the lineup (making "none of these" a plausible response) tend to decrease the number of false identifications, while having little impact on the overall identification accuracy (Malpass &

Devine, 1981; Warnick & Sanders, 1980; Köhnken & Maas, 1988). Likewise, instructions can influence the likelihood of selecting any particular person from the lineup, emphasizing the importance of unbiased instructions. In addition, identifications seem more accurate when the members of the line-up are viewed one at a time, rather than simultaneously (Cutler & Penrod, 1988; Lindsay, Lea, & Fulford, 1991; Lindsay, Lea, Nosworthy, et al., 1991; Lindsay & Wells, 1985). Accuracy can also be improved by allowing witnesses to hear the suspects' voices, to view the suspects in their customary postures and gaits, and, it seems, to see them in three-quarter profile (Cutler & Penrod, 1988).

EMOTION AND WEAPON FOCUS

Eyewitnesses are likely to be afraid or angry during the crime; this is particularly likely if the eyewitness is physically threatened during the crime. In general, high levels of stress at the time of the event impair the accuracy of testimony. In contrast, low to moderate levels of stress may actually improve memory, yielding a relation between arousal and memory accuracy that can be depicted as an inverted U shape. This inverted U is generally described as the Yerkes-Dodson function (Deffenbacher, 1983; Eysenck, 1982).

Research also has examined claims about *weapon focus,* a pattern alleged for eyewitnesses in which their attention is focused on the threatening weapon, to the exclusion of all else. Consequently, the weapon (and perhaps details of the hand holding the weapon) will be well remembered, but little else. This is similar to a pattern resulting from emotional arousal, even in the absence of a weapon: According to the Easterbrook hypothesis, emotional arousal also narrows the focus of attention, so that one is less sensitive to many cues in the environment when one is emotionally aroused; as a result, one is likely to remember well the focus of one's attention during an emotional event but to remember other aspects of the event less well.

Many studies have documented the weapon focus and Easterbrook patterns (Heuer & Reisberg, 1992; Williams et al., 1992). Emotions also shape memory in several other ways. For example, there is some suggestion that emotion serves to slow the process of forgetting more slowly than for unemotional events (Burke, Heuer, & Reisberg, 1992). In addition, if events are experienced while in an emotional state, there is some indication that these events will be better remembered if, at the time of remembering, one is in the same emotional state (Blaney, 1986; Ellis & Ashbrook, 1989; Parrott & Sabini, 1990). Emotion also may lead to specific types of memory errors (Reisberg & Heuer, 1992). In short, emotion has multiple effects on memory, adding complexity to the evaluation of eyewitness testimony.

POSTEVENT LEADING AND MISLEADING QUESTIONS

Eyewitness accounts can be affected by the phrasing of questions. In one study, subjects were asked to estimate how quickly two cars were moving when they *hit* each other; other subjects were asked how quickly the cars were moving when they *smashed into* each other. Subjects in the "hit group" gave appreciably lower estimates than subjects in the "smashed group" (Loftus & Palmer, 1974). In a different study, subjects were less likely to recall seeing a broken

headlight if asked "Did you see a broken headlight?" than if they were asked "Did you see the broken headlight?" This subtle change, from *a* to *the,* doubled the likelihood of reporting the target object (Loftus & Zanni, 1975).

Leading questions also influence how an event is subsequently remembered. For example, in the hit versus smashed experiment, subjects also were asked, one week later, whether any broken glass was visible in the scene. (None was visible.) Subjects who had been asked the "smashed question" were far more likely to report (falsely) that they had seen glass, compared with subjects who had been asked the "hit question." In the same vein, subjects asked about a stop sign, right after viewing an event, are subsequently likely to report that they had in fact seen a stop sign, even though a yield sign was plainly visible, and so on.

Similar results are observed when postevent misinformation is delivered in narrative form, rather than in questions. For example, subjects in many studies have witnessed an event, and then read a description of the same event (analogous to reading a newspaper account, or hearing reports from other witnesses). If this description contains false elements—for example, mentions objects or actions that actually were not part of the original event—these false elements will often be reported subsequently by the eyewitness, as part of the remembered sequence. Misinformation introduced in this fashion is capable of changing how people's appearances are remembered (in terms of age, or weight, or facial characteristics), what objects are remembered as being present in the scene, the colors of objects on the scene, and so on. In sum, a wide range of false memories can be planted in this fashion.

Related effects are observed if subjects are asked to recall an event soon after it occurred and then to recall it again some time later. If errors occur in the initial recollection, they seem to become interwoven with the initial memory, and so subjects are likely to repeat the errors in subsequent testing (Bartlett, 1932; Belbin, 1950; Burke, Heuer, & Reisberg, 1992). This resembles the postevent misinformation paradigm, except that in these studies the misinformation is provided by subjects' own initial recall.

There is little doubt that postevent misinformation can change how subjects later describe the initial event. Postevent misinformation can cause minor alterations in subjects' reports (e.g., substituting a yield sign for a stop sign), but in some studies, it also has been shown to cause larger-scale changes in the recollection. The false memories created by postevent misinformation are typically reported with confidence and without hesitation, suggesting that subjects genuinely believe the veracity of these false reports. (Belli, 1989; Lindsay, 1990; Loftus, 1979; Loftus & Hoffman, 1989; Williams et al., 1992; Zaragoza & McCloskey, 1989). There is controversy, though, over the mechanisms behind these misinformation effects. One proposal is that the postevent misinformation literally replaces the initial memory, an effect called *destructive updating.* As a different possibility, subjects may remember both the original event and the postevent information, but may be confused about which information came from which source, for example, they may not remember which details they saw in the original videotape and which details they merely read about in a subsequent narrative; this is called *source confusion.* As another possibility, subjects may not have noticed the key information in the original event and so have no basis for doubting the (false) postevent information, which has been called *misinformation acceptance.* Similarly, subjects may remember both the original and postevent information. Subjects may presume that the postevent information is correct and, as a result, may doubt their own memories about the original. This also would be misinformation acceptance.

Studies indicate that all of these mechanisms may contribute to the effects of postevent misinformation. These various mechanisms clearly have different implications for memory theory and for the possibility of recovering the memory of the original event. However, these mechanisms converge in leading subjects to report, as a bonafide memory, false information planted in their memories by the experimenter.

MEMORY ACCURACY AND MEMORY CONFIDENCE

Eyewitnesses are more persuasive when their testimony is delivered with confidence than when testimony is hedged with hesitation and expressed uncertainty (Brigham & Wolfskiel, 1983; Cutler, Penrod, & Stuve, 1988; Loftus, 1979; Wells, Lindsay, & Ferguson, 1979). That is, juries seem to assume a positive relationship between confidence and memory accuracy and so grant more credibility to confident witnesses. But, in fact, many studies have observed low or zero correlations between accuracy and confidence; some studies have documented negative correlations, with subjects more confident in their wrong answers than their right ones (Bothwell, Deffenbacher, & Brigham, 1987; Loftus, 1979). On the other hand, some studies have observed positive correlations between confidence and accuracy, with more confident subjects being more accurate. This suggests that there are circumstances in which confidence is predictive of memory accuracy and other circumstances in which it is not. Specifically, confidence expressed after a lineup selection seems to be more closely associated with accuracy than confidence expressed before the lineup (Cutler & Penrod, 1989). Likewise, confidence is more closely associated with accuracy if the suspect is distinctive in appearance (Brigham, 1990). Other related studies have been reported, in each case asking what variables moderate the relation between accuracy and confidence (Cutler & Penrod, 1989; Deffenbacher, 1980; Fleet, Brigham, & Bothwell, 1987; Kassin, 1985).

The association between accuracy and confidence is never strong, and studies rarely document correlations greater than 0.30 or 0.40. Some studies have documented large errors even in memories reported with total confidence; the rememberer is completely convinced of the veracity of a memory that happens to be false (Neisser & Harsh, 1990). Juries rely on confidence in evaluating a witness and so overuse confidence in assessing evidence.

OVERALL ACCURACY OF EYEWITNESS TESTIMONY

Eyewitnesses may overlook many aspects of an event if a weapon is present or if the eyewitness is emotionally aroused. False memories may be planted after the event has occurred. Eyewitness confidence in a recollection is no guarantee of memory veracity. To what extent do these concerns undermine the credibility of eyewitness testimony?

A number of studies have assessed the overall accuracy of subjects' event memory, often focusing on flashbulb events: singular and surprising events that occur in one's life, often with considerable emotional impact (Winograd & Neisser, 1992). Subjects recall flashbulb events in considerable detail and with impressive confidence, but on close examination, many of these recollections turn out to be incorrect, often in important ways. This underscores the possibility of large-scale memory errors and the dissociation between confidence and memory accuracy.

Recall of flashbulb events is often rather accurate, overall, with subjects, remembering many details even months after the event. Yuille and Cutshall (1986) examined memory for an actual crime witnessed by 13 bystanders, assessing eyewitnesses' memory 4 to 5 months after the event. In evaluating the memories, Yuille and Cutshall employed strict criteria; for example, reported ages had to be within 2 years to be counted as correct and reported weights, within 5 pounds. Even with these criteria, witnesses were correct in 83% of the details reported about the action itself, 76% correct in their descriptions of people, and 90% in descriptions of objects on the scene.

CHILDREN AS EYEWITNESSES

Children's reports of an event are often incomplete, children also tend to have little idea about which aspects of the event are relevant to the courts. In addition, children's memory for events is often limited by their poor understanding of the event's causal structure (Pillemer, 1992) or by their ignorance about various memory strategies. Despite these limitations, evidence indicates that reasonably full and accurate reports can be elicited from children, even children as young as 3 or 4 years old. Children's recall, although sparse, tends to be accurate, and fuller reports can be obtained through the use of props and appropriate questioning (Fivush, 1992). Special care must be taken, however, to minimize the possibility of leading or misleading questions, because children seem at least as vulnerable as adults to the effects of postevent information, in regard to this information's impact on immediate testimony and the subsequent memory consequences from this information. Finally, concern is often expressed that children's memories indiscriminately mix imagined and actual events. However evidence indicates that this mixing is less common than is widely thought. For broad reviews of the evidence on child testimony, see Ceci, Toglia, and Ross (1987), Davies and Drinkwater (1988), Doris (1991), and Goodman and Bottoms (1992). Research also has examined the quality of testimony by the elderly; for a review, see Williams and colleagues (1992).

TECHNIQUES FOR IMPROVING EYEWITNESS RECOLLECTION

Police officers and other trained observers seem no more accurate than untrained individuals as eyewitnesses (Yuille, 1984), although most people expect a memory advantage for law-enforcement professionals (Deffenbacher & Loftus, 1982). Geiselman and colleagues have developed an approach for questioning eyewitness (Fisher, Geiselman, & Amador, 1989; Fisher, Geiselman, Raymond, & Jurkevich, 1987; Geiselman, 1984). Their cognitive interview employs several strategies to aid witnesses in retrieving information from memory. For example, witnesses are encouraged to recount the event in more than one sequence (i.e., from first to last and from last to first) and from more than one perspective; witnesses also are led to reconstruct the environmental and personal context of the witnessed event. Evidence indicates that this technique is useful for improving both adult and child testimonies (Geiselman & Padilla, 1988; Geiselman, Saywitz, & Bornstein, 1991).

For many years, hypnosis was widely believed to enhance eyewitness testimony, with the hypothesis that hypnotized witnesses would provide more complete accounts of the remembered event. Research has cast considerable doubt on this hypothesis. In general, hypnosis does not improve memory. Hypnosis does render the subject quite compliant and suggestible, leading hypnotized subjects to report more about the remembered event. But in the absence of any memory facilitation, this report may include some amount of confabulation, that is sincere but false reconstruction of the target event, often incorporating details suggested by the questioner (Dywan & Bowers, 1983; Geiselman & Machlovitz, 1987; Hilgard, 1968; Orne, Soskis, Dinges, & Orne, 1984; Sanders & Simmons, 1983; Smith, 1982). Given this, most psychologists (and most courts) are skeptical about the value of hypnotically induced testimony.

REFERENCES

Baddeley, A. (1982). *Your memory: A user's guide.* New York: Macmillan.

Bahrick, H. P., Bahrick, P. O., & Wittlinger, R. P. (1975). Fifty years of memory for names and faces: A cross-sectional approach. *Journal of Experimental Psychology: General, 104,* 54–75.

Bartlett, F. C. (1932). *Remembering: A study in experimental and social psychology.* Cambridge, UK: Cambridge University Press.

Belbin, E. (1950). The influence of interpolated recall upon recognition. *Quarterly Journal of Experimental Psychology, 2,* 163–169.

Belli, R. F. (1989). Influences of misleading postevent information: Misinformation interference and acceptance. *Journal of Experimental Psychology: General, 118,* 72–85.

Blaney, P. H. (1986). Affect and memory: A review. *Psychological Bulletin, 22,* 229–246.

Bloom, L., & Mudd, S. (1991). Depth of processing approach to face recognition: A test of two theories. *Journal of Experimental Psychology: Learning, Memory, and Cognition, 17,* 556–565.

Bothwell, R. K., Deffenbacher, K. A., & Brigham, J. C. (1987). Correlation of eyewitness accuracy and confidence: Optimality hypothesis revisited. *Journal of Applied Psychology, 72,* 691–695.

Brigham, J. (1990). Target person distinctiveness and attractiveness as moderator variables in the confidence-accuracy relationship in eyewitness identifications. *Basic and Applied Social Psychology, 11,* 101–115.

Brigham, J. C. (1986). The influence of race on face recognition. In H. D. Ellis, M. A. Jeeves, F. Newcombe, & A. Young (Eds.), *Aspects of face processing* (pp. 170–177). Dordrecht, Netherlands: Martinus Nijhoff.

Brigham, J. C., & Cairns, D. L. (1988). The effect of mugshot inspections on eyewitness identification accuracy. *Journal of Applied Social Psychology, 18,* 1394–1410.

Brigham, J. C., Ready, D., & Spier, S. (1990). Standards for evaluating the fairness of photograph lineups. *Basic and Applied Social Psychology, 11,* 149–163.

Brown, E., Deffenbacher, K., & Sturgill, W. (1977). Memory for faces and the circumstances of encounter. *Journal of Applied Psychology, 62,* 311–318.

Burke, A., Heuer, F., & Reisberg, D. (1992). Remembering emotional events. *Memory & Cognition, 20,* 277–290.

Ceci, S. J., Toglia, M. P., & Ross, D. F. (1987). *Children's eyewitness memory.* New York: Springer-Verlag.

Cutler, B. L., Fisher, R. P., & Chicvara, C. L. (1989). Eyewitness identification from live versus videotaped lineups. *Forensic Reports, 2,* 93–106.

Cutler, B. L., & Penrod, S. D. (1988). Improving the reliability of eyewitness identification: Lineup construction and presentation. *Journal of Applied Psychology, 73,* 281–290.

Cutler, B. L. & Penrod, S. D. (1989). Forensically relevant moderators of the relation between eyewitness identification accuracy and confidence. *Journal of Applied Psychology, 74,* 650–652.

Davies, G., & Drinkwater, J. (Eds.). (1988). The child witness: Do the courts abuse children? *Issues in Criminological and Legal Psychology No. 13.* Leicester, UK: The British Psychological Association.

Deffenbacher, K. A. (1980). Eyewitness accuracy and confidence: Can we infer anything about their relationship. *Law and Human Behavior, 4,* 243–260.

Deffenbacher, K. A. (1983). The influence of arousal on reliability of testimony. In S. M. A. Lloyd-Bostock & B. R. Clifford (Eds.), *Evaluating witness evidence* (pp. 235–251). Chichester, UK: Wiley.

Deffenbacher, K. A., & Loftus, E. F. (1982). Do jurors share a common understanding concerning eyewitness behavior? *Law and Human Behavior, 6,* 15–30.

Dywan, J., & Bowers, K. (1983). The use of hypnosis to enhance recall. *Science, 222,* 184–185.

Ellis, H. C., & Ashbrook, P. W. (1989). The "state" of mood and memory research: A selective review. *Journal of Social Behavior and Personality, 4,* 1–21.

Eysenck, H. J. (1982). The psychophysiology of intelligence. In C. D. Spielberger & J. N. Butcher (Eds.), *Advances in personality assessment* (Vol. 1). Hillsdale, NJ: Erlbaum.

Fisher, R. P., Geiselman, R. E., & Amador, M. (1989). Field test of the cognitive interview: Enhancing the recollection of the actual victims and witnesses of crime. *Journal of Applied Psychology, 74,* 722–727.

Fisher, R. P., Geiselman, R. E., Raymond, D. S., & Jurkevich, L. M. (1987). Enhancing enhanced eyewitness memory: Refining the cognitive interview. *Journal of Police Science & Administration, 15,* 291–297.

Fivush, R. (1992). Developmental perspectives on autobiographical recall. In G. Goodman & B. L. Bottoms (Eds.), *Understanding and improving children's testimony.* New York: Guilford.

Fleet, M. L., Brigham, J. C., & Bothwell, R. K. (1987). The confidence-accuracy relationship: The effects of confidence assessment and choosing. *Journal of Applied Social Psychology, 17,* 171–187.

Geiselman, R. E. (1984). Enhancement of eyewitness memory: An empirical evaluation of the cognitive interview. *Journal of Police Science and Administration, 12,* 74–80.

Geiselman, R. E., & Machlovitz, H. (1987). Hypnosis memory recall: Implications for forensic use. *American Journal of Forensic Psychology, 5,* 37–47.

Geiselman, R. E., & Padilla, J. (1988). Cognitive interviewing with child witnesses. *Journal of Police Science & Administration, 16,* 236–242.

Geiselman, R. E., Saywitz, K., & Bomstein, G. (1991, April). *Enhancing children's eyewitness memory: A test of the cognitive interview with children.* Paper presented at the annual meetings of the Society for Research on Child Development, Seattle, WA.

Hilgard, E. R. (1968). *The experience of hypnosis.* New York: Harcourt, Brace, Jovanovich.

Kassin, S., Ellsworth, P., & Smith, V. (1989). The "general acceptance" of psychological research on eyewitness testimony: A survey of the experts. *American Psychologist, 44,* 1089–1098.

Kassin, S. M. (1985). Eyewitness identification: Retrospective self-awareness and the accuracy-confidence correlation. *Journal of Personality and Social Psychology, 49,* 878–893.

Kohnken, G., & Maas, A. (1988). Eyewitness testimony: False alarms on biased instruction? *Journal of Applied Psychology, 73,* 363–370.

Lindsay, D. S. (1990). Misleading suggestions can impair eyewitnesses' ability to remember event details. *Journal of Experimental Psychology: Learning, Memory and Cognition, 16,* 1077–1983.

Lindsay, R. C., Lea, J. A., & Fulford, J. A. (1991). Sequential lineup presentation: Technique matters. *Journal of Applied Psychology, 76,* 741–745.

Lindsay, R. C., Wallbridge, H., & Drennan, D. (1987). Do the clothes make the man? An exploration of the effect of lineup attire on

Lindsay, R. C., Lea, J. A., Nosworthy, G., Fulford, J., Hector, J., LeVan, V., & Seabrook, C. (1991). Biased lineups: Sequential presentation reduces the problem. *Journal of Applied Psychology, 76,* 796–802.

Lloyd-Bostock, S., & Clifford, B. (Eds.). (1983). *Evaluating witness evidence: Recent psychological research and new perspectives.* New York: Wiley.

Loftus, E. (1986). Ten years in the life of an expert witness. *Law and Human Behavior, 10,* 241–262.

Loftus, E. F. (1974). Reconstructing memory: The incredible eyewitness. *Psychology Today, 8,* 116–119.

Loftus, E. F. (1979). *Eyewitness testimony.* Cambridge, MA: Harvard University Press.

Loftus, E., & Palmer, J. C. (1974). Reconstruction of automobile destruction: An example of the interaction between language and memory. *Journal of Verbal Learning and Verbal Behavior, 13,* 585–589.

Loftus, E. F., & Hoffman, H. G. (1989). Misinformation and memory: The creation of new memories. *Journal of Experimental Psychology: General, 118,* 100–104.

Loftus, E. F., & Zanni, G. (1975). Eyewitness testimony: The influence of the wording of a question. *Bulletin of the Psychonomic Society, 5,* 86–88.

Luus, C. E., & Wells, G. L. (1991). Eyewitness identification and the selection of distractors for lineups. *Law & Human Behavior, 15,* 43–57.

Malpass, R. S., & Devine, P. G. (1981). Eyewitness identification: Lineup instructions and the absence of the offender. *Journal of Applied Psychology, 66,* 482–489.

McCloskey, M., & Egeth, H. (1983). Eyewitness identification: What can a psychologist tell a jury? *American Psychologist, 38,* 550–563.

Nosworthy, G. J., & Lindsay, R. C. (1990). Does nominal lineup size matter? *Journal of Applied Psychology, 75,* 358–361.

Orne, M. T., Soskis, D., Dinges, D., & Ome, E. (1984). Hypnotically induced testimony. In G. Wells & E. Loftus (Eds.), *Eyewitness testimony: Psychological perspectives* (pp. 171–213). New York: Cambridge University Press.

Parrott, W. G., & Sabini, J. (1990). Mood and memory under natural conditions: Evidence for mood incongruent recall. *Journal of Personality and Social Psychology, 59,* 321–336.

Pillemer, D. (1992). Preschool children's memories of personal circumstances: The fire alarm study. In E. Winograd & U. Neisser (Eds.), *Affect and accuracy in recall: The problem of "flashbulb" memories.* New York: Cambridge University Press.

Read, J. D., Tollestrup, P., Hammersley, R., & McFadzen, E. (1990). The unconscious transference effect: Are innocent bystanders ever misidentified? *Applied Cognitive Psychology, 4,* 3–31.

Reisberg, D., & Heuer, F. (1992). Remembering emotional events. In E. Winograd & U. Neisser (Eds.), *Affect and flashbulb memories.* New York: Cambridge University Press.

Sanders, G., & Simmons, W. L. (1983). Use of hypnosis to enhance eyewitness accuracy: Does it work? *Journal of Applied Psychology, 68,* 70–77.

Shapiro, P. N., & Penrod, S. (1986). Meta-analysis of facial identification studies. *Psychological Bulletin, 100,* 139–156.

Smith, M. (1982). *Hypnotic memory enhancement of witnesses: Does it work?* Paper presented at the meetings of the Psychonomic Society, Minneapolis, MN.

Sporer, S. (1991). Deep-deeper-deepest? Encoding strategies and the recognition of human faces. *Journal of Experimental Psychology: Learning, Memory and Cognition, 17,* 323–333.

Warnick, D. H., & Sanders, G. S. (1980). Why do eyewitnesses make so many mistakes? *Journal of Applied Psychology, 10,* 362–366.

Wells, G. L., Lindsay, R. C. L., & Ferguson, T. J. (1979). Accuracy, confidence, and juror perceptions in eyewitness identification. *Journal of Applied Psychology, 64,* 440–448.

Wells, G. L., & Loftus, E. F. (Eds.). *Eyewitness testimony: Psychological perspectives.* New York: Cambridge University Press.

Williams, K. D., Loftus, E. F., & Deffenbacher, K. (1992). Eyewitness evidence and testimony. In D. K. Kagehiro & W. S. Laufer (Eds.), *Handbook of psychology and law* (pp. 141–166). New York: Springer-Verlag.

Winograd, E., & Neisser, U. (Eds.). (1992). *Affect and accuracy in recall: The problem of "flashbulb" memories.* New York: Cambridge University Press.

Yuille, J. C. (1984). Research and teaching with police: A Canadian example. *International Review of Applied Psychology, 33,* 5–23.

Yuille, J. C., & Cutshall, J. L. (1986). A case study of eyewitness memory of a crime. *Journal of Applied Psychology, 71,* 291–301.

Zaragoza, M. S., & McCloskey, M. (1989). Misleading postevent information and the memory impairment hypothesis: Comment on Belli and reply to Tversky and Tuchin. *118,* 92–99.

D. REISBERG
Reed College

CHILD PSYCHOLOGY
CRITICAL INCIDENT TECHNIQUE
EXPERT TESTIMONY
FORENSIC PSYCHOLOGY
HYPNOSIS
IMPRESSION FORMATION
LIFE EVENTS
PEAK EXPERIENCES
POLICE PSYCHOLOGY
SELECTIVE ATTENTION
WORKING MEMORY

EYSENCK, HANS J. (1916–1997)

Educated in Berlin, Hans J. Eysenck left Germany in 1934 for political reasons (opposition to the Hitler regime) to study in Dijon, France, and Exeter, England, before enrolling in a psychology course at the University of London in 1935. He obtained the BA and the PhD in 1940, and then joined the Maudsley Hospital and later the Institute of Psychiatry, which is part of the University of London. In the newly formed Institute he founded the Department of Psychology, becoming a professor at the University and psychologist to the Maudsley and Bethlem Royal Hospitals. He was given the task of starting clinical psychology as a profession in the United Kingdom, and his newly created department was the first to train clinical psychologists and to use the newly developed methods of behavior therapy.

Eysenck's main research was in the areas of personality theory and measurement, intelligence, social attitudes and politics, behavioral genetics, and behavior therapy. He viewed psychology from a natural science approach, and was hostile to so-called humanistic, psychodynamic, and other literary and subjective approaches. He published some 600 scientific papers in psychological, biological, genetic, and other journals, and published three dozen books. His autobiography has been published in *A History of Psychology in Autobiography,* and a book-length biography was published by H. B. Gibson.

Eysenck's view of man, which had always governed his thinking and the direction of his research, was that of a biosocial organism whose actions are determined equally by biological (genetic, physiological, endocrine) factors and social (historical, economic, interactional) factors. He believed that a one-sided stress on either biological or social factors impeded the development of the science. This insistence on seeing man as a product of evolution, still bearing the traces of millions of years of development from earlier life forms, was not always popular with social scientists more inclined to stress social factors, but was regarded by Eysenck as essential for a proper understanding of man.

STAFF

F

FACE RECOGNITION

Face recognition is an important and arguably unique ability critical to social interaction. Some researchers assert that face recognition in humans represents action of a specific, neurally encapsulated mechanism (Fodor, 1983) or special type of processing (e.g., Ellis & Young, 1989), whereas others view face recognition as simply an example of a perceptual skill in which humans become expert given constant practice (e.g., Bushnell, 1998). Although face recognition is rapid and seemingly effortless in most cases, it is a complicated process involving several levels of analysis. In addition, differences may exist between the processing of familiar and unfamiliar faces (Bruce & Young, 1986). Numerous studies have been completed detailing the workings of this process, its failure, and its development in both human and nonhuman primates.

ACCURACY IN FACE RECOGNITION

Face recognition is highly skilled in adulthood. Bahrick, Bahrick, and Wittlinger (1975) documented that individuals could distinguish the faces of their high school classmates from other faces long after graduation. Even 50 years later, participants recognized three quarters of the faces shown. Even brief exposures to faces leads to extremely accurate recognition, although documented errors in studies of eye witness testimony indicates that recognition is not perfect. Specific modifications in face recognition tasks clearly affect performance as well. For example, recognition accuracy is decreased significantly when faces are presented in an inverted orientation relative to pictures of objects or animals, such as houses or dogs (Scapinello & Yarmey, 1970). Speed and accuracy of face recognition may also be affected by the context in which the face is presented.

PROSOPAGNOSIA

The failure to recognize faces, or prosopagnosia, is a rare but fascinating disorder that yields information about the mechanisms responsible for face recognition. Individuals with prosopagnosia do not visually recognize faces of individuals they have known before onset of the disorder, nor the faces of those they encounter frequently afterwards, although they typically recognize facial expressions. The source of the disorder appears to be damage to the occipito-temporal regions of the central visual system, especially in the right hemisphere. Although the term prosopagnosia ("agnosia for faces") is meant to describe a specific inability to recognize faces, individuals with the disorder may have difficulty with any stimulus that requires specific and context-related recognition (Damasio, Damasio, & Van Hoesen, 1982). In addition, prosopagnosic patients may show variations in their performance, with one patient unable to identify faces only, and another patient items from a given class. It is possible, however, that the lesion responsible for prosopagnosia in some individuals is larger than required for producing the deficit so that it affects other abilities as well.

FACE RECOGNITION IN PRIMATES

Nonhuman primates also show face recognition, for both human and nonhuman primate faces. For example, both humans and squirrel monkeys recognize upright human faces and great ape faces better than inverted faces (Phelps & Roberts, 1994). Gross, Rocha-Miranda, and Bender (1972) discovered that some cells in the temporal cortex of the monkey were selectively responsive to stimuli such as hands and faces. Moreover, single neurons in the primate temporal lobe visual cortex respond primarily to faces and differentially to familiar faces (Rolls, Treves, Tovee, & Panzeri, 1997). Such evidence suggests that facial configurations are such biologically important stimuli for primates that mechanisms have evolved allowing for early steps in a facial recognition process without extensive learning.

DEVELOPMENT OF FACE RECOGNITION

Initially, human infants attend preferentially to faces. Goren, Sarty, and Wu (1975) discovered that newborns would follow facelike images farther with their eyes than they would similar images that contained facial features but in noncanonical patterns. Furthermore, newborns also have been shown to recognize their mothers' faces. Infants ranging in age from 12 to 36 hours produced more sucking responses when viewing an image of their mothers' faces rather than an image of a stranger's face that was comparable in terms of eye color, hair color, complexion, and hairstyle (Walton, Bower, & Bower, 1992).

One question regarding the development of face recognition is whether infants and children process a face as a set of independent features or as a unified whole. Carey and Diamond (1977) reported that children do not encode the configurations of upright faces until almost adolescence. Studies of face perception during infancy, however, suggest that an ability to process configurations occurs much earlier. Cashon and Cohen (1999) have found that after repeated exposure to two unfamiliar faces, 7-month-old infants will treat a composite face that combines the internal features of the two faces as novel, rather than as merely a collection of now-familiar features. This effect disappears when infants are presented the composite face in an inverted position, suggesting that infants (like adults) process an inverted face as a set of features.

SUMMARY

The ability to detect, discriminate, and recognize facial information is highly developed in human adults. Moreover, human infants show similar skills even as newborns—recognizing their mothers' faces after only a few hours and using configurational information to discriminate faces by 7 months. Unequivocal evidence that face recognition is special or simply expert is not yet available, although findings from neurophysiological studies are becoming increasingly useful.

REFERENCES

Bahrick, H. P., Bahrick, P. O., & Wittlinger, R. P. (1975). Fifty years of memory for names and faces: A cross-cultural approach. *Journal of Experimental Psychology: General, 104*, 54–75.

Bruce, V., & Young, A. (1986). Understanding face recognition. *British Journal of Psychology, 77*, 305–327.

Bushnell, I. W. R. (1998). The origins of face perception. In F. Simion & G. Butterworth (Eds.), *The development of sensory, motor and cognitive capacities in early infancy* (pp. 69–86). Hove, UK: Psychology Press.

Carey, S., & Diamond, R. (1977). From piecemeal to configurational representation of faces. *Science, 195*, 312–314.

Cashon, C. H., & Cohen, L. B. (April 1999). Infant face perception: Do infants process independent features or the face as a whole? Poster presented at the meetings of the Society for Research in Child Development, Albuquerque.

Damasio, A. R., Damasio, H., & Van Hoesen, G. W. (1982). Prosopagnosia: Anatomic basis and behavioural mechanisms. *Neurology, 32*, 331–341.

Ellis, H. D., & Young, A. W. (1989). Are faces special? In A. W. Young & H. D. Ellis (Eds.), *Handbook of research on face processing*. Amsterdam: North Holland.

Fodor, J. A. (1983). *The modularity of mind.* Cambridge, MA: MIT Press.

Goren, C. C., Sarty, M., & Wu, P. Y. K. (1975). Visual following and pattern discrimination of face-like stimuli by newborn infants. *Pediatrics, 56*, 544–549.

Gross, C. G., Rocha-Miranda, C. E., & Bender, D. B. (1972). Visual properties of neurons in inferotemporal cortex of the macaque. *Journal of Neurophysiology, 35*, 96–111.

Phelps, M. T., & Roberts, W. A. (1994). Memory for pictures of upright and inverted primate faces in humans (Homo sapiens), squirrel monkeys (Saimiri sciureus), and pigeons (Columba livia). *Journal of Comparative Psychology, 108*, 114–125.

Rolls, E. T., Treves, A., Tovee, M. J., & Panzeri, S. (1997). Information in the neuronal representation of individual stimuli in the primate temporal visual cortex. *Journal of Computational Neuroscience, 4*, 309–333.

Scapinello, K. I., & Yarmey, A. S. (1970). The role of familiarity and orientation in immediate and delayed recognition of pictorial stimuli. *Psychonomic Science, 21*, 329–330.

Walton, G., Bower, N. J. A., & Bower, T. G. R. (1992). Recognition of familiar faces by newborns. *Infant Behavior and Development, 15*, 265–269.

A. S. WALKER-ANDREWS
Rutgers University

EYE-WITNESS TESTIMONY
INFANT DEVELOPMENT
MEMORY

FACE VALIDITY

Face validity refers to a characteristic associated with a psychological test and its individual items. Distinct from more technical types of validity, face validity is the appropriateness, sensibility, or relevance of the test and its items as they appear to the person answering the test. Do a test and its items look valid and meaningful to the individual taking the test? More formally, face validity has been defined as the degree to which a test respondent views the content of a test and its items as relevant to the situation being considered (Wiggins, 1973).

Three factors are important in the definition of face validity. First, face validity is not based on the judgments of psychologists or experts, but rather on the opinions of test-takers who may be quite naive about the domain being assessed by the test. Second, face validity depends on the obviousness of the test item content (e.g., the test items may imply that a personality trait, such as neatness, is being measured). Third, the situation in which a test is given will influence face validity. Most important, however, is the combination of these three factors in determining the face validity of a test or test item. Consider the statement, "Trying something new is scary," to which a test-taker must answer either true or false. If this item appeared on an employment test being given to job candidates who were applying to work for a manufacturing company, the applicants might feel that the test item is irrelevant or inappropriate for that testing situation (i.e., the item is not face valid). Further, if the entire employment test consisted of statements with similar content, then the test as a whole might be viewed as lacking face validity. Now, consider the same item being given on a test to patients newly admitted to a psychiatric hospital. For test-takers in such a mental health setting, the test item might well seem to be quite appropriate and situationally relevant (i.e., the item is face valid).

Should test developers strive to construct tests that are face valid? The answer to this question depends on the test developer's theoretical orientation as well as on considerations of technical validity, public relations, and possible litigation.

The content of face valid tests is readily identifiable by test-takers and is susceptible to faking, either consciously or unconsciously. Test developers who have a theoretical orientation emphasizing test respondent defensiveness (e.g., psychoanalytically oriented test developers), or test administrators who are employed in defensiveness-inducing situations (e.g., personnel or forensic settings) in which there is an assumption that individuals will not present themselves openly and honestly, believe that face valid tests will result in inaccurate responses and, consequently, that such tests should be avoided. Alternatively, test constructors who possess the theoretical perspective that people will present themselves openly and honestly believe that direct, transparent (i.e., face valid) tests are those of choice.

Research on technical validity has shown significant positive associations between face validity and test item accuracy (Holden & Jackson, 1979). Test items having face validity, on average, tend to be more technically valid or accurate (i.e., they are better items because they tend to be more strongly associated with a relevant criterion) than those items not possessing face validity. Further, research also indicates that, in circumstances under which test-takers have been asked to fake, face valid items (which are supposedly more susceptible to faking) are no less accurate than items that are not face valid (Holden & Jackson, 1985). Although the positive association between face validity and technical validity is significant and stable, it is not perfect, and consequently, cautions are warranted. Face validity may be related to better test items, but it does not guarantee other, more technical and desirable forms of validity. Thus, the mere appearance of relevance or face validity (e.g., as regularly found in tests published in popular magazines) fails to ensure a test's accuracy. Furthermore, the absence of face validity does not necessarily mean that a test or its items are inaccurate.

The face validity of a test is an important factor for issues of public relations and litigation (Nevo, 1985). Psychological testing should not be an antagonistic and seemingly irrelevant exercise for test respondents. Cooperation and good rapport between testers and test-takers is sound practice in all assessment circumstances. The presence of face validity enhances the perceived relevance of a psychological test and reduces the likelihood of feelings of depersonalization and resentment in the individual being tested. The absence of face validity (regardless of technical validity or accuracy) may result in feelings of anger and frustration and of being cheated. Such feelings may well be acted on, resulting in negative media publicity, public demands for the cessation of testing programs (e.g., in schools), labor-management conflict, or even costly legal proceedings.

REFERENCES

Holden, R. R., & Jackson, D. N. (1979). Item subtlety and face validity in personality assessment. *Journal of Consulting and Clinical Psychology, 47,* 459–468.

Holden, R. R., & Jackson, D. N. (1985). Disguise and the structured self-report assessment of psychopathology: I. An analogue investigation. *Journal of Consulting and Clinical Psychology, 53,* 211–222.

Nevo, B. (1985). Face validity revisited. *Journal of Educational Measurement, 22,* 287–293.

Wiggins, J. S. (1973). *Personality and prediction: Principles of personality assessment.* Reading, MA: Addison-Wesley.

R. R. HOLDEN
Queen's University, Ontario

CULTURE FAIR TESTS
TEST ANXIETY

FACTITIOUS DISORDERS

"Factitious" means arising from an artificial or manufactured source. Any medical or psychological symptom may be called factitious if it develops or persists outside its natural course. Some factitious symptoms may be ignored, such as the appearance of a fever produced by the manipulation of a thermometer. On the other hand, some factitious symptoms can be serious, such as a physical fever induced through self-injection of a toxic substance. Both are factitious, but management varies accordingly.

Just as depression can be either a symptom or a disorder, factitious symptoms may rise to the level of being considered a disorder. The *DSM-IV* suggests that a Factitious Disorder diagnosis can be made when the patient produces (or feigns) symptoms in order to assume the sick role, not simply for an obvious external incentive as in malingering. Malingering, it should be noted, is not a psychiatric disorder, and symptoms of the malingerer do not arise from a psychiatric disorder. Therefore, a Factitious Disorder should be considered whenever symptoms become excessively costly, bizarre, painful, or life-altering. The malingerer wants to appear sick, but the patient with Factitious Disorder wants to be sick, or to appear sick even when no one is watching (Pankratz, 1998).

The medical literature describes an enormous spectrum of symptoms that have been imitated or induced (Feldman & Eisendrath, 1996; Reich & Gottfried, 1983). Injuries may be surreptitiously self-inflicted, and many natural disorders can be self-maintained in ways that keep the patient unnecessarily in a sick role (Pilowski, 1994). The diagnosis is best revealed by carefully reading all the medical records, interviewing family members, and monitoring compliance.

The disorder experienced by patients who travel from hospital to hospital and make dramatic presentations of their symptoms is sometimes given the label "Munchausen Syndrome" (Asher, 1951; Pankratz & Jackson, 1994). This syndrome can be viewed as the extreme end of the Factitious Disorder spectrum. The syndrome was named in whimsical honor of Baron von Münchhausen, a German traveler who told outlandish tales about his hunting and military exploits.

Factitious Disorder by Proxy (also called Munchausen Syndrome by Proxy) is an unusual form of abuse in which a careprovider creates an illness (or the appearance of an illness) in another person under the individual's care (Meadow, 1977). Mostly this syndrome has focused on mothers who abuse their children. The *DSM-IV* lists Factitious Disorder by Proxy in Appendix B, among the criteria sets proposed for further study. The diagnosis is appropriate when the perpetrator intentionally produces symptoms (or falsely reported symptoms) in the victim with the motivation of assuming the sick role by proxy. Unfortunately, many mothers have been entangled with this proxy label because of doctor shopping, noncompliance, over-monitoring, and various troublesome behaviors that should be clinically treated and not thrown into the legal arena (Pankratz, 1998; Rand & Feldman, 1999).

REFERENCES

Asher, R. (1951). Munchausen's syndrome. *Lancet, 1,* 339–341.

Feldman, M. C., & Eisendrath, S. J. (1996). *The spectrum of factitious disorders.* Washington, DC: American Psychiatric Press.

Pankratz, L. (1998). *Patients who deceive: Assessment and management of risk in providing benefits and care.* Springfield, IL: Charles C. Thomas.

Pankratz, L., & Jackson, J. (1994). Habitually wandering patients. *New England Journal of Medicine, 331,* 1752–1755.

Pilowsky, I. (1994). Abnormal illness behaviour. A 25th anniversary review. *Australian and New Zealand Journal of Psychiatry, 28*, 566–573.

Rand, D. C., & Feldman, M. D. (1999). Misdiagnosis of Munchausen syndrome by proxy. A literature review and four new cases. *Harvard Review of Psychiatry, 7*, 94–101.

Reich, P., & Gottfried, L. A. (1983). Factitious disorders in a teaching hospital. *Annals of Internal Medicine, 99*, 240–247.

SUGGESTED READING

Meadow, R. (1977). Munchausen syndrome by proxy: The hinterland of child abuse. *Lancet, 2*, 343–345.

Pankratz, L. (1999). Factitious disorders and factitious disorder by proxy. In S. Netherton, D. Holmes, & C. E. Walker (Eds.), *Child and adolescent psychological disorders: A comprehensive textbook*. New York: Oxford University Press.

L. D. Pankratz
Clinical Professor, Oregon Health Sciences University

MALINGERING
SOMATO PSYCHICS

FACTOR ANALYSIS

Factor analysis is a general label applied to a set of statistical procedures designed to identify basic dimensions or *factors* that underlie the relationships among a large number of variables.

Historically, factor analysis began with the seminal ideas of Francis Galton (1888), who was concerned with the relationships between intelligence and anthropometric data, and Karl Pearson (1901), who developed mathematical techniques for portraying points in space by lines and planes. In essence, the work of Galton suggested the concept of "latent factors" to account for the interrelated variables, while Pearson provided the earliest mathematical tools for constructing models to identify them.

The most recognized beginning of modern factor analytic techniques is the work of Charles Spearman (1904), who attempted to account for the correlations among various aptitudes in the hope of measuring general intelligence. He proposed that those correlations could be generated by the combination of a single general-intelligence factor and secondary or specific factors that reflect the unique qualities of individual aptitude measures. Subsequent investigators enlarged Spearman's model of a general factor linearly combined with specific factors by adding the concept of common or group factors. Thurstone (1947), in proposing his "centroid method," particularly championed extended factor models, which he referred to as "multiple factor analysis."

Over the years, investigators have developed a wide diversity of factor analytic techniques and mathematical models for factor analysis. Different approaches are currently valid for different research problems, depending on both the goal of the research and the underlying assumptions made by the researcher about the basic nature of human attributes. Harman (1960/1976) has compiled a comprehensive text on factor analysis in which he compares the most popular procedures and mathematical solutions.

The increasing availability and convenience of computers during the past two decades has inspired numerous articles and books describing and comparing a wide variety of specialized approaches. Before computers, unique factor solutions could be arrived at only through laborious visual and hand-calculator procedures. Computers have given the researcher a very rapid and efficient tool for greatly expanded multivariate approaches.

In conducting a factor analysis, variables such as scores on psychological tests, responses to questionnaire items, or quantified biographical data are correlated with one another. The resulting correlations are arrayed in an *intercorrelation matrix,* which is a chart displaying each of the correlation coefficients for every possible pair of variables being analyzed. Then, using one of a variety of specific factor analytic techniques, the relationships among the variables in the matrix are accounted for by mathematically reducing them to a number of basic dimensions or factors. If the correlations among the variables in the intercorrelation matrix are close to zero, then no factors will emerge from the factor analysis. On the other hand, the higher the correlations among variables—that is, the more they are interrelated—the more likely it will be that one or more factors will result from the analysis.

Although factor analysis includes a diversity of mathematical models and statistical approaches, the following concepts are common to all procedures: (a) factor structure; (b) common factors; (c) specific factors; (d) factor loading; (e) communality; and (f) specificity.

The term "factor structure" essentially refers to the set of factors derived from a factor analysis. Some of those factors are *common factors,* or factors that are shared to varying degrees among the variables, and some of them are *specific factors,* or factors that are specific or unique to individual variables. Each variable in the analysis is accounted for by a linear combination of common and specific factors.

In describing the results of a factor analysis, each variable in the matrix is numerically expressed in terms of its *factor loading,* which refers to the extent to which that variable is loaded onto a given factor. Factor loadings vary between minus one and plus one, since they are actually correlation coefficients between the factors mathematically derived in the analysis and the variables in standardized form. Thus, for example, if a particular intelligence test has a factor loading of 0.80 on a factor labeled as "verbal ability," the test is said to be highly loaded on verbal ability.

In any group of variables subjected to factor analysis, many variables share something in common with one another. That shared something is referred to as the *communality* of a given variable. It, like the factor loading, is expressed numerically, varying from zero to one. It represents the proportion of variability among the variables that is accounted for by a shared factor. (Mathematically, it is calculated by adding up the squares of each of the factor loadings for a particular variable.)

The proportion of variability left over after the communality is called *specificity.* Specificity reflects the uniqueness of a given variable. (Mathematically, it is calculated by subtracting the communality from one.)

Factors are actually hypothetical variables or constructs that portray the degree of interrelationships among the variables being analyzed. The meaning of a given factor is summarized from the attributes of those variables highly loaded on that factor. Thus, factor analysis enables the researcher to explore hypotheses regarding the basic dimensions underlying collections of related variables. It is an important technique for determining the minimum number of such dimensions needed to account for the variability among those variables.

REFERENCES

Galton, F. (1888). Co-relations and their measurements, chiefly from anthropometric data. *Proceedings of the Royal Society, 45,* 135–140.

Harman, H. H. (1976). *Modern factor analysis.* Chicago: University of Chicago Press. (Original work published 1960)

Pearson, K. (1901). On lines and planes of closest fit to systems of points in space. *Philosophical Magazine, 6,* 559–572.

Spearman, C. E. (1904). "General intelligence," objectively determined and measured. *American Journal of Psychology, 15,* 201–292.

Thurstone, L. L. (1947). *Multiple-factor analysis: A development and expansion of the vectors of the mind.* Chicago: University of Chicago Press.

A. E. Dahlke
Los Angeles, California

CLUSTER ANALYSIS
EXPERIMENTAL METHODS

FACTORIAL DESIGNS

A factorial design is one in which the effects of two or more factors are studied simultaneously. Because the factors are considered in the same design, both their individual effects (called main effects) and their joint effects (called interactions) on the dependent variable can be assessed.

SINGLE-FACTOR DESIGNS

To better understand the previous definition, one should first consider a design that is not factorial, namely, a one-factor design. Suppose an investigator wishes to assess the effects of fatigue on test performance by using three groups of subjects: a low fatigue group, a moderate fatigue group, and a high fatigue group. Because fatigue level is the variable manipulated by the investigator, it is referred to as the independent variable or factor in the design. In this design, the fatigue factor is said to have three levels, one for each of the fatigue groups used. More generally, the single factor in this experiment may be referred to as "A," and the levels of the factor as A_1, A_2, and A_3.

Test performance is measured for each subject and is referred to as the dependent variable. The goal of the study would be to determine whether the dependent variable varied as a function of the level of factor A. Even if the fatigue factor had no effect, we would not expect the mean test performance to be exactly the same at each level

Table 1.   A 3 × 2 Factorial Design

Test Difficulty	Level of Fatigue		
	Low	Medium	High
Low			
High			

Table 2.   A 3 × 2 Factorial Design with No Interaction

Test Difficulty	Level of Fatigue			
	Low	Medium	High	
Low	80	70	60	70
High	60	50	40	50
	70	60	50	

of fatigue, because of random variability. If, however, performance differed across levels of fatigue by more than would be expected on the basis of within-level variability, we would say that the fatigue factor was statistically significant. Analysis of variance (ANOVA) is a general statistical procedure for testing the null hypothesis that there is no difference in the means at each level of a factor.

TWO-FACTOR DESIGNS

In a factorial design, more than one factor is employed. We can change the one-factor design previously discussed into a factorial design by adding a second factor, for example, test difficulty, with both low and high levels; that is, a second factor B with levels B_1 and B_2 has been added to the design (see Table 1).

In this 3 × 2 factorial design (so called because factor A has three levels and factor B has two), the effects of fatigue and test difficulty can be studied as well as their joint effects. This design has six combinations of levels of fatigue and difficulty, each corresponding to a cell in Table 1. Now consider some idealized data presented in Table 2. We assume that there are equal numbers of subjects in each condition, and that there are no effects of random variability or measurement error, so that any differences obtained among groups will be due to real effects of the factors. With real data, any true effects would be obscured by random error, and statistical tests would be performed to determine whether it was likely that real effects existed.

In Table 2, the number in each cell represents the mean test score for subjects at the corresponding combination of levels A and B—for example, the mean score for medium fatigue and low test difficulty is 70. The numbers outside the table are called marginal means, and represent the means of rows and columns of the table. For example, the mean of all scores in the high difficulty test condition, averaging across levels of fatigue, is 50.

MAIN EFFECTS

If there is no error variability, we say that a factor has a main effect if the means of the levels of the factor are not all the same (for real data, there will always be error variability, and a statistical test would be performed to determine if the differences were larger

Table 3.   A 3 × 2 Factorial Design with An Interaction

Test Difficulty	Level of Fatigue			
	Low	Medium	High	
Low	75	70	65	70
High	65	50	35	50
	70	60	50	

than would be expected solely on the basis of error variability). In our example, there are main effects of both fatigue and test difficulty. For test difficulty, the mean score for the low difficulty test condition, 70, is 10 points higher than the average (60) of the combined low and high difficulty levels, whereas the mean score in the high difficulty test condition is 10 points lower than that average. Therefore, the effects associated with the low and high difficulty conditions are +10 and –10. The corresponding effects for the low, medium, and high fatigue conditions are +10, 0, and –10.

INTERACTIONS

In Table 2, the data are additive; that is, the effect of being in the A_1B_1 cell is the sum of the effects of being at level A_1 of A and level B_1 of B. For example, the effect of high fatigue is –10, the effect of the high difficulty condition is –10, and the effect being in both the high difficulty and high fatigue conditions is –20 (that is, 40 – 60). However, in many cases particular combinations of levels of factors may have joint effects that are not obtainable by simply adding the main effects of the factors. In Table 3 the marginal means, and hence the main effects for both factors, are exactly the same as in Table 2. However, some of the cell means are different. The effect of the combination of high fatigue and high test difficulty (35 – 60 = –25) is not the same as the sum of the high fatigue and high test difficulty effects (–10 and –10). In this case there is a nonzero joint effect, and we say that there is a Difficulty × Fatigue interaction. A useful way to think of interactions is in terms of differences of differences. There would be no Difficulty × Fatigue interaction if the differences between the low and high difficulty condition were the same for each level of fatigue. In Table 3 these differences are 10, 20, and 30 for the low, medium, and high fatigue conditions, respectively.

Interactions and main effects are logically independent. Knowing whether there are A and B main effects does not tell us anything about whether there is an A × B interaction. It is therefore possible to investigate interactions among factors only if they are considered in the same design.

HIGHER-ORDER FACTORIAL DESIGNS

In designs with more than two factors, there may be different kinds of interactions. If we have a design with three factors A, B, and C, we could have three first-order interactions, A × B, A × C, and B × C. If we wished to consider, say, the A × B interaction, we could average over the levels of C. Similarly, if we wished to investigate the B × C interaction, we could average over levels of A, and so on. Higher-order interactions involve more than two factors. With fac-

tors A, B, and C it would also be possible to have a second-order interaction, A × B × C. This would occur if, for example, the simple A × B interactions at each level of C were not all the same (or equivalently, if the simple A × C interactions were not the same at each level of B, or the simple B × C interactions were not all the same at each level of A). Usually it is difficult to interpret interactions involving more than two or three factors.

SUGGESTED READING

Keppel, G. (1991). *Design and analysis: A researcher's handbook.* Englewood Cliffs, NJ: Prentice Hall.

Myers, J. L., & Well, A. D. (1995). *Research design and statistical analysis.* Hillsdale, NJ: Erlbaum.

A. D. WELL
University of Massachusetts

EXPERIMENTAL DESIGNS
RESEARCH METHODOLOGY
STATISTICS IN PSYCHOLOGY

FAMILY THERAPY

The field of family therapy began in the 1950s, partly because those who were to become the early pioneers were not satisfied with the slow progress made when doing individual therapy. They recognized that the impact of changes in the patient on family members could be great, and that if families had no place to discuss what was occurring and their reactions to it, they might sabotage treatment, so that it would be better if they were part of the process. Finally, these pioneers were aware of the huge waiting lists at agencies after World War II. Administrators and therapists alike realized that they could not accommodate on an individual and long-term therapy basis all of the returning servicemen and their family members who were requesting treatment. Seeing all of the members of the nuclear family conjointly seemed a viable alternative. It meant more people could be seen in the same number of hours without adding extra staff—and since budgets were limited, this seemed like a cost effective route to pursue.

Earlier roots of what became the family therapy movement existed in the child guidance movement, even though in child guidance clinics a psychiatrist usually saw the child while a social worker saw the parent concurrently—not conjointly, as was to be the model in the emerging field of family therapy. Another tributary was the early approach to social work with troubled, multi-problem families (Richmond, 1917). Such work often entailed home visits rather than having the whole family come to the therapist's office, which was to evolve as the most frequent practice in the ensuing 40-plus years. (For histories of the field of family therapy see Guerin, 1976; Kaslow, 1982, 1987; and Kaslow, Kaslow, Farber, 1999). Interestingly, since the 1990s there has been a resurgence of the practice of home-based treatment (both in the United States and other countries) with poor and multi-problem families who are unable or unwilling to go to therapists' offices (Sharlin & Shamai, 1999).

The fact that the field of family therapy had come into its own was marked by the birth of the journal *Family Process* in 1961, and solidified by the subsequent inauguration of at least a half dozen other major family journals in the United States (and several dozen additional ones in other countries) in the 1970s and 1980s. The number of books on this vast topic has also proliferated exponentially. The United States has spawned two major organizations dedicated to the field of family therapy: the American Association for Marriage and Family Therapy (AAMFT) which began in 1942 with the name "American Association of Marriage Counselors," reflecting its focus at the time (it was not changed to AAMFT until the late 1970s); and the American Family Therapy Academy (AFTA), which began in the mid-1970s as the American Family Therapy Association. Both the American Psychological Association (APA) and the American Psychiatric Association (ApA) have separate units focused on the family—the APA's unit is the Division of Family Psychology. Other countries have established similar national and regional organizations.

There are also two international organizations—the International Family Therapy Association (IFTA), started in 1987, and the International Academy of Family Psychology (IAFP), inaugurated in 1990. Using organization memberships, journal subscriptions, and the number of books published annually as a quantitative measure of the field's importance and stature, it is indeed thriving.

Some of the basic tenets of family therapy that have evolved and survived include the following:

1. The members of a family constitute a system, with all parts interdependent and inter-related.

2. Change in any part (member) of the system causes corresponding changes in all other members of the system.

3. Families range on a continuum from dysfunctional, through mid-range, to quite functional and healthy.

4. Some members of families seek to retain the existing homeostatic balance or equilibrium, while other members, usually the younger ones, try to alter that balance.

5. Many dysfunctional families are characterized by rigid alliances, schisms, and secrets.

6. Healthy families exhibit good problem-solving skills and open communication styles.

7. Boundaries between generations should be clear and should not be crossed inappropriately.

8. Some patterns are transmitted intergenerationally and can be detrimental or healthy, depending on the pattern.

There are more basic principles, these merely constitute a representative sample of some of the core tenets.

Over the years numerous theories of family therapy have emerged (Becvar & Becvar, 1996). Each theory or school has had its major progenitor(s) and its second-, third-, and fourth-generation leaders and staunch followers. Each theory promulgates a somewhat different approach to the way therapy should be conducted—that is, the process and techniques the theory advocates. Each theory is predicated upon ideas about what makes change occur and holds that interventions should be consonant with these underlying assumptions and beliefs (Goldenberg & Goldenberg, 1996, Nichols & Schwartz, 1995).

The following is one possible way to divide and classify these theories, subsuming the most prominent of the contemporary approaches under the heading that seems most appropriate. The various theories have waxed and waned in popularity, although, having waned, they sometimes experience a resurgence of interest and once again come to occupy a central position within the range of available theories of family dynamics, structure, and functioning. Different theories have adherents in different countries, depending on where the theories originated, which leaders have been to those countries to conduct workshops on their approaches, and which therapeutic styles and methodologies are most compatible with each country's cultural contexts. Our classification schema is as follows (Kaslow et al.):

I. Transgenerational schools
   Psychodynamically informed (including object relations approaches)
   Bowenian
   Contextual/relational
   Symbolic/experiential

II. Systems models
   Communications
   Strategic
   Structural
   Systemic
   Brief and solution-focused

III. Cognitive and behavioral models
   Behavioral (including functional)
   Cognitive behavioral
   Functional

IV. Miscellaneous
   Psychoeducational
   Social constructionist (including postmodern linguistic approaches)
   Integrative (including comprehensive and multi-modal models)

The field to date has witnessed the ascendance of a plethora of charismatic leaders, some of whom attain the status of gurus around whom disciples gather. However, in the last two decades at least some members of the field, noticeably the more research-trained psychologists, have pushed for analysis and validation of what works using both qualitative and quantitative research on process and outcome variables, reaching beyond beliefs that are based only on clinical evidence and personal testimonials.

Among current debates in the field is the issue of whether graduate and professional students should be trained broadly first, learning many of the theories, and then go on to gain greater knowledge and competence in one or several theories they believe have greatest efficacy; or whether they should learn one theory and its accompanying techniques in depth, and then be exposed to the other approaches. Although some see the latter training model as akin to indoctrination, many others deliberately select such a curriculum (even though the curriculum may be viewed as ethnocentric).

Theoreticians, practitioners, supervisors, and researchers continue to be drawn from the fields of psychology, psychiatry, social work, counseling and guidance, nursing, and specialty programs in marriage and family therapy. Such diversity enriches the field, yet it also contributes to interdisciplinary discord and conflicts around licensing—that is, who may use the title and practice marriage and family therapy. These turf battles are apt to continue.

Since we are born into families, grow up in our family of origin or in an adoptive or foster family, and then move on to create our own families, the fascination with the family as a system and as a unit worthy of professional and societal attention no doubt will continue unabated in the new century. Therapists of all disciplines and theoretical persuasions share this fascination and find family therapy to be challenging, stimulating, frustrating, and ultimately, rewarding.

REFERENCES

Becvar, D. S., & Becvar, R. J. (1996). *Family therapy: A systemic integration* (3rd ed.). Needham Heights, MA: Allyn & Bacon.

Goldenberg, I., & Goldenberg, H. (1996). *Family therapy: An overview* (4th ed.). Pacific Grove, CA: Brooks Cole.

Guerin, P. J. (1976). Family therapy: The first twenty-five years. In P. J. Guerin (Ed.), *Family therapy and practice,* pp. 2–22. New York: Gardner Press.

Kaslow, F. W. (1982). History of family therapy in the United States: A kaleidoscopic overview. In F. W. Kaslow (Ed.), *The international book of family therapy,* pp. 5–40. New York: Brunner/Mazel.

Kaslow, F. W. (1987). Marital and family therapy. In M. B. Sussman & S. K. Steinmetz (Eds.), *Handbook of marriage and the family,* pp. 835–860. New York: Plenum.

Kaslow, N. J., Kaslow, F. W., Farber, E., (1999) (in press). Theories and techniques of marital and family therapy. In M. B. Sussman, S. K. Steinmetz, & G. W. Peterson (Eds.), *Handbook of marriage and the family* (2nd ed.). pp. 767–793. New York: Plenum.

Nichols, M. P., & Schwartz, R. C. (1995). *Family therapy: Concepts and methods* (3rd ed.). Boston, MA: Allyn & Bacon.

Richmond, M. (1917). *Social diagnosis.* New York: Russell Sage Foundation.

Sharlin, S. A., & Shamai, M. (1999). *From distress to hope: Intervening with poor and disorganized families.* New York: Haworth.

F. W. KASLOW
Florida Couples & Family Institute

FAMILY CRISIS
PSYCHOTHERAPY
SYSTEMS THEORY

FAST AXOPLASMIC TRANSPORT

Fast axoplasmic transport (also known as fast axonal transport) is defined as the movement of vesicles in the axons of nerve cells at speeds that range between 200 and 400 mm/day. Vesicle transport occurs in both directions along the axon. The fast speed of movement distinguishes vesicle transport from the transport of soluble protein-complexes that move along the axon at speeds of 0.5 to 3 mm/day (slow axonal transport). Schematically, a nerve cell can be subdivided into a cell body (perikaryon), short-branched dendrites, and a long axon. The diameter of the axon is small compared to the diameter of the cell body, and the axon can reach a length of many centimeters. Therefore, the end of the axon or axon terminal is often located a long distance from the cell body. The membrane proteins of axoplasmic vesicles are synthesized in the cell body where the rough endoplasmic reticulum (ER) and Golgi apparatus reside. Thus, transport of vesicles into the axon is required to supply synaptic vesicles at the axon terminal and for axon survival and regeneration. Fast axonal transport is also the mechanism by which membrane components are returned to the cell body for degradation.

The diameters of vesicles that are transported in the axon range in size from very small (50 nm; e.g., synaptic vesicles) to very large (1,000 nm; e.g., multivesicular bodies). The transport of vesicles originating in the cell body and traveling toward the axon terminal is defined as anterograde transport. The transport of vesicles originating at the axon terminal and traveling toward the cell body is defined as retrograde transport. The vesicles in transit along the axon represent the cargo transported by molecular motors as they travel on filaments of the cytoskeleton. There are three types of cytoskeletal filaments in neurons: neurofilaments (10 nm in diameter), microtubules (25 nm), and actin filaments (6 nm). Only the latter two types of filaments are known to function as tracks or rails on which molecular motors transport cargo. Molecular motors require chemical energy in the form of adenosine triphosphate (ATP) to transport vesicles, and therefore the proteins are called ATPases. A given motor is filament-type specific. Kinesin and cytoplasmic dynein are the molecular motors that transport vesicles along microtubules (Hirokawa, 1998) and myosin is the motor that transports vesicles on actin filaments (Mermall, Post, & Mooseker, 1998; DePina & Langford, 1999).

Microtubules are usually long filaments (>25 µm) and have an intrinsic polarity due to the identical orientation of the tubulin subunits within the filaments. To distinguish the two ends of the microtubule, one is called the plus end (fast growing) and the other the minus end (slow growing). All microtubules in the axon are aligned parallel to the long axis of the axon with their plus ends distal relative to the cell body. The molecular motor kinesin is a plus-end directed motor; that is, it transports vesicles toward the plus end of the microtubule or away from the cell body (anterograde transport). Cytoplasmic dynein is a minus-end directed motor and is responsible for vesicle transport from the axon terminal (retrograde transport). The specific type of motor attached to a vesicle determines the direction in which it will be transported in the axon. Kinesin has been shown to be associated with synaptic vesicles, synaptic precursor vesicles, mitochondria, multivesicular bodies, and presynaptic membrane precursor vesicles. Cytoplasmic dynein has been shown to be associated with retrogradely transported vesicles in axons including early and late endosomes and lysosomes.

Actin filaments in the axon are short (1 μm) compared to the length of microtubules (Fath & Lasek, 1988), and they too have an intrinsic polarity due to the identical orientation of the actin subunits that make up the filaments. As with the microtubules, the two ends of the actin filaments are distinguish with the use of the terms "plus end" and "minus end"; these two ends are also sometimes referred to as barbed (plus) and pointed (minus) ends, as with the two ends of an arrow. The orientation of actin filaments in the axon is not uniform, and actin filaments are sometimes cross-linked into bundles and cables. The plus ends of some actin filaments are attached to the plasma membrane or to the surfaces of vesicles. Most actin filaments co-align with microtubules in the axon. Myosin is a plus-end directed motor; therefore, transport is toward the plus end of actin filaments.

The transport of vesicles on microtubules is designed for movement over long distances in the axon; the movement of vesicles on actin filaments is postulated to serve a different function (Langford & Molyneaux, 1998), which appears to be to produce fine and precise movements required to position vesicles at specific locations in cells. Thus the short-range movements that occur on actin filaments function to transport vesicles to membrane sites for capture, docking, and fusion (DePina & Langford, 1999). Examples of vesicles that may require precision movements on actin filaments for localization are synaptic vesicles at the presynaptic terminal of the axon (Prekeris & Terrian, 1997), and smooth ER vesicles within the spines of neuronal dendrites and along the axon membrane (Tabb, Molyneaux, Cohen, Kuznetsov, & Langford, 1998; Dekker-Ohno et al., 1997). Myosin has been shown to transport endoplasmic reticulum (ER) vesicles in the squid giant axon (Tabb et al., 1998), and to be associated with synaptic vesicles (Prekeris & Terrian, 1997) and the ER in the spines of Purkinje cell dendrites (Dekker-Ohno et al., 1996; Takagishi et al., 1996). The interrelationship between microtubules and actin filaments and the motors that move cargo on them are active areas of research in the study of axonal transport.

REFERENCES

Dekker-Ohno, K., Hayasaka, S., Takagishi, Y., Oda, S., Wakasugi, N., Mikoshiba, K., Inouye, M., & Yamamura, H. (1996). Endoplasmic reticulum is missing in dendritic spines of Purkinje cells of the ataxic mutant rat. *Brain Research, 714,* 226–230.

DePina, A. S., & Langford, G. M. (in press). Vesicle transport: The role of actin filaments and myosin motors. *Microscience Research Techniques, 47,* 93–106.

Fath, K. R., & Lasek, R. J. (1988). Two classes of actin microfilaments are associated with the inner cytoskeleton of axons. *Journal of Cell Biology, 107,* 613–621.

Hirokawa, N. (1998). Kinesin and dynein superfamily proteins and the mechanism of organelle transport. *Science, 279,* 519–526.

Langford, G. M., & Molyneaux, B. (1998). Myosin V in the brain: Mutations lead to neurological defects. *Brain Research Review, 28,* 1–8.

Mermall V., Post, P. L., & Mooseker, M. S. (1998). Unconventional myosins in cell movement, membrane traffic, and signal transduction. *Science, 279,* 527–533.

Prekeris, R., & Terrian, D. M. (1997). Brain myosin V. is a synaptic vesicle-associated motor protein: Evidence for a Ca2+ dependent interaction with the synaptobrevin-synaptophysin complex. *Journal of Cell Biology, 137,* 1589–1601.

Tabb, J. S., Molyneaux, B. J., Cohen, D. L., Kuznetsov, S. A., & Langford, G. M. (1998). Transport of ER vesicles on actin filaments in neurons by myosin V. *Journal of Cell Science, 111,* 3221–3234.

Takagishi, Y., Oda, S., Hayasaka, S., Dekker-Ohno, K., Shikata, T., Inouye, M., & Yamamura, H. (1996). The dilute-lethal (dl) gene attacks a Ca2+ store in the dendritic spine of Purkinje cells in mice. *Neuroscience Letters, 215,* 169–172.

G. M. LANGFORD
Dartmouth College

NEURONAL CELL BODY

FATIGUE

A major problem area in understanding the human is *demand* and *ability to meet it.* Demand originates at one of two places—outside the individual, or within the individual. Demand from within may originate in local tissue, or may be attributed to the individual as a person. External demands may be of two sorts—one social, the other purely physical, as when temperature makes demands on the thermoregulating mechanism of the body.

In everyday speech, fatigue is generally defined as inability to meet demand. But to be precise, only those cases in which the organism at the personal level is unable to meet demand should be called fatigue. The tissue changes themselves that reduce ability to function are more appropriately called *impairment.* When this impairment causes the organism at the personal level to become less able to function, the result is fatigue. If the impairment in any tissue is permanent, it is termed *injury.*

Mere maintenance of some fixed body posture can be a demand, as can expectation expressed verbally by another person. Remembering something that one ought to do is another form of demand, as is having to sit and listen to a speech.

A demand may bring on any or all of three things: impairment, fatigue, tiredness. Impairment is a cellular state: a reversible, reduced, or otherwise modified ability of a cell or group of cells to function. Oxygen lack, for example, brings about such a state. Impairment is distinguishable from injury since it is reversible, whereas injury is not. (Impairment can also be used to label a situation when a nonbiological system fails to meet the usual demand put upon it, as in the so-called fatigue of metals.)

The nervous system is made up of various cells working together and the pattern of this interaction may change. The changed pattern may constitute fatigue, in relation to the task at hand. This definition makes fatigue an inability to meet task demand; a fatigued person need not be aware of it. When awareness does occur, the person is *tired*. Tiredness and fatigue are not synonyms, though used as such in everyday speech. Using these words as indicated deals with aspects of human existence with relation to demand and disentangles them in an appropriate way.

The term "fatigue" is commonly misused for cases where *work decrement*—the slowing down of work—is in evidence, but the reason for work decrement often lies outside the workers themselves. To define fatigue, we can say that: (a) something may happen to cells as cells; (b) something may happen to cell groups in some restricted parts of the body; and (c) something may happen whereby the organism as a person may not be able to function. Bartley and Chute, in *Fatigue and Impairment in Man,* reserved the term "fatigue" for labeling the person's own realization of inadequacy, and "impairment" for what happens to cells, as in the case of oxygen deficit, where a general shift in cell functions takes place, although some cells may be affected more critically than others. Bartley and Chute recognized that fatigue was the outcome of a form of disorganization within the tissue systems of the body involving the brain in a specific way. That is, it was a form of disorganization of function that produced discomfort and a self-realization of inadequacy.

Extreme impairment can reduce ability to meet demand without bringing about self-realization. This is the case in oxygen lack (anoxemia). McFarland (1932) found that when he greatly reduced the available oxygen supply for his subjects, there were four different outcomes: (a) some subjects became extremely amused and exhibited fits of laughter; (b) some reacted with extreme irritation and mishandled the apparatus they were using; (c) some reacted with sustained persistence in their assigned tasks, while evidencing little concern for their ineffective performances; and (d) some immediately abandoned the tasks assigned them.

REFERENCES

Bartley, S. H., & Chute, E. (1947). *Fatigue and impairment in man.* New York: McGraw-Hill.

McFarland, R. A. (1932). The psychological effects of oxygen deprivation (anoxemia) on human behavior. *Archives of Psychology, 145,* 1–35.

S. H. BARTLEY
Memphis State University

RELAXATION TRAINING
WORK EFFICIENCY

FEAR

Historically considered one of the primary emotions along with joy, anger, and grief, *fear* is the emotion of avoidance of a consciously recognized, usually external, eminent danger. *Anxiety,* on the other hand, is the emotion of avoidance to perceived but largely unrecognized dangers, whereas *phobias* are irrational obsessions and intense avoidance of specific objects or situations. Fear, anxiety, and phobias are terms inappropriately used, when inter-

changed. In some respects their confusion is understandable, since all three represent a state of arousal that results when an individual recognizes a lack of power or capability to handle some threatening situation, and all three have similar physiological states.

PHYSIOLOGICAL CHANGE

Concomitant aspects of fear are physiological changes primarily induced by the biochemical arouser adrenalin. Adrenalin basically prepares the skeletal muscles for great strain as might occur in running to escape (flight) or in protecting self and property (fight). In fact, if the individual does not engage in vigorous physical activity of some sort following arousal, uncomfortable physiological changes such as trembling in arms and legs, general weakness, and heightened awareness of breathing and heart rate occur. Heart rate, systolic blood pressure, and respiration rate increase in the body's effort to divert blood flow from digestive areas, head, neck, and face to areas like musculature that are in need of it. If the diversion from the cortex is too swift, there is inhibition of voluntary cortical function and the individual faints into unconsciousness. This results in vastly reduced heart and breathing rates—not unlike the freezing posture witnessed in animals.

ORIGINS OF FEAR

Experientially everyone knows fear, but applying scientific rigors to aid understanding has not proved productive. In the 1880s William James and Carl Lange independently arrived at the conclusion that the experienced somatic state is the emotion—in short, we are afraid because we tremble. After rigorous physiological monitoring of individuals experiencing fear and anger, Ax in 1953 concluded that, except for slight increases in muscular tension during anger and slight increases in respiration rates during fear, the two physiological responses were identical. Since the mid-1950s cognitive theorists have challenged the James-Lange notion by demonstrating that thoughts can elicit the same physiological change as evidenced in an actual fear situation.

Confusion and loss of control such as that which occurs when an individual does not know how to ward off a life threat—upon seeing an escape route blocked, for instance, or upon experiencing unexpected and unexplained alterations in familiar settings—can lead to feelings of fear. Such a formulation of fear was provided by Hebb in 1946 in "On the Nature of Fear," along with an account of the resultant "profound disorganization of cerebral process."

The notion that fear is learned is not new, but this does not distract from its popularity. Early in the 20th century, John B. Watson (Watson & Rayner, 1920) provided some very potent demonstrations of the conditioning or learned aspects of fear. That is, a neutral or even previously pleasurable object would elicit a fear reaction after it was combined with a noxious conditioning stimulus: A child, for instance, might refuse to touch a previously huggable teddy bear, after it had appeared in close temporal contiguity with a loud, annoying buzzer. Though such learning may be more typical of phobic reactions, it is not unusual to witness similar associations in true fear.

Fear, as a means of self-preservation, seems most frequently to be inspired by the unknown and ultimately by death. Zilboorg, in an article entitled "Fear of Death," wrote that "there always lurks the basic fear of death, a fear which undergoes most complex elaborations and manifests itself in many indirect ways. . . . No one is free of the fear of death . . . the anxiety neurosis, the various phobic states . . . amply demonstrate the ever-present fear of death" (1943, pp. 465–66). For Zilboorg, fear of death is pervasive—constantly present in mental functioning; only through repression can we achieve any degree of comfort. As with all forms of repression, it requires constant monitoring, effort, and a determination to "never relax our watchfulness." As a result, our normal experience is without fear of death, but when it is expedient to self-preservation, the fear returns.

Questions of whether the fear of death is natural as a preservation/reproduction force or whether it is unnatural and dependent upon maternal attitudes, perceived security, or some irrational notion of the importance of each individual in society, will be argued for a long time. It is perhaps more important to raise the issue of the utility, rather than that of the innateness, of the fear of death.

The most common usefulness of the fear of death is the avoidance of life-threatening situations. Yet those who confront dangerous situations and attempt to save others are revered. Heroic gestures represent the first and foremost reflex to the terror of death. Christianity also utilized the fear of death as a means of encouraging commitment to correct present lifestyles with the promise of being born again, modeled after Christ's rising from the grave, and of receiving salvation and eternal life.

REFERENCES

Ax, A. F. (1953). Physiological differentiations between fear and anger in humans. *Psychosomatic Medicine, 15,* 433–442.

Hebb, D. O. (1946). On the nature of fear. *Psychological Review, 53,* 259–276.

Watson, J. B., & Rayner, R. (1920). Conditioned emotional reactions. *Journal of Experimental Psychology, 3,* 1–14.

Zilboorg, G. (1943). Fear of death. *Psychoanalytic Quarterly, 12,* 465–475.

SUGGESTED READING

Becker, E. (1973). *The denial of death.* New York: Free Press.

Rachman, S. J. (1978). *Fear and courage.* San Francisco: Freeman.

D. F. Fisher
U.S. Army Human Engineering Laboratory

ANXIETY
EMOTIONS

FECHNER, GUSTAV THEODOR (1801–1887)

Gustav Theodor Fechner began his medical studies at the University of Leipzig in 1817. He remained there for the rest of his life, pursuing careers in physiology, physics and mathematics, psy-

chophysics, and philosophy. He was appointed professor at Leipzig in 1833; however, because of severe ill health over a number of years, he was pensioned in 1844. He then recovered his health and every year thereafter made a serious contribution to his work.

Fechner is best remembered for his development of psychophysics, a study of the relationship between mind and the material world. "On the morning of October 22, 1850—an important date in the history of psychology—Fechner had an insight that the law of the connection between mind and body can be found in a statement of quantitative relation between mental sensation and material stimulus" (D. Schultz, 1975/1981, p. 52). The relationship between the two is stated in the equation: $S = K \log I$. As the stimulus intensity increases in geometrical series, the mental sensation increases in arithmetical series. In the early part of the century, Immanuel Kant had predicted that psychology could never become a science, because it would be impossible to experimentally measure psychological processes. Because of Fechner's work, for the first time scientists could measure the mind; by the mid-19th century the methods of science were being applied to mental phenomena.

Fechner systematized three fundamental methods of psychophysics: (a) the method of average error, or calculating the mean to represent the best approximation of a large number of measures; (b) the method of constant stimuli, or finding the amount of difference in stimulation needed to identify that difference, which has been useful in measuring sensory thresholds and aptitudes; and (c) the method of limits, originally called the method of JND (just noticeable differences), for determining the thresholds of visual and temperature stimulations.

Although Ernst Weber's work on the method of just noticeable differences had preceded Fechner's, Fechner found a mathematical statement of the relationship between the mental and the physical worlds. He used and built upon Weber's work, with insights that revealed the implications and consequences of the work in application to psychology as an exact science. Later, Wilhelm Wundt would take these original and creative achievements and organize and integrate them into a founding of psychology.

Fechner published the *Elements of Psychophysics* in 1860. It is considered one of the original contributions to the development of psychology as a science. Wundt, who developed psychophysics into experimental psychology, recognized the book's importance to his own work. Hermann Ebbinghaus, chancing upon a second-hand copy of the book in Paris about 1876, was inspired to apply the mathematical approach and method to his study of higher mental processes in the field of memory and learning.

N. A. Haynie

FECHNER'S LAW

Gustav T. Fechner (1801–1887), professor of physics at the University of Leipzig, sought to measure the mind quantitatively. In approaching this task he studied stimuli and the sensations they aroused. His interest was in ascertaining how sensations changed with changing stimulation. While lying in bed on the morning of October 22, 1850, he conceived the essential idea of what was later to be called Fechner's law. In his subsequent derivation of the law, he began with Weber's law (that the just noticeable difference in stimulation is a constant proportion of the stimulus magnitude, or $JND = kI$) and the assumption that the sensation (R) of a stimulus is the cumulative sum of equal sensation increments. Translating this into differential form, he started with $dR = dI/I$ and integrated, under the assumption that $R = 0$ at absolute threshold (I_0), to get the equation $R = c \log (I/I_0)$. This equation is Fechner's law, where R is the sensation magnitude, c is a constant (which depends on the logarithmic base and the Weber ratio), I is the stimulus intensity, and I_0 is the absolute threshold intensity. The law states that sensations follow a negatively-accelerated increasing (logarithmic) curve. For example, the increase in brightness experienced in going from one to 10 lamps would be the same as the increase in brightness in going from 10 to 100 lamps. Sensation increases arithmetically when stimulus magnitudes increase geometrically.

SUGGESTED READING

Boring, E. G. (1942). *Sensation and perception in the history of experimental psychology.* New York: Appleton-Century-Crofts.

Fechner, G. T. (1964). *Elemente der psychophysik.* Amsterdam: E. J. Bonnet. (Original work published 1860)

Fechner, G. T. *Elements of psychophysics. Vol. I.* (D. H. Howes & E. G. Boring, Eds.; H. E. Adler, Trans.). New York: Holt, Rinehart and Winston. (Original work published 1860)

Uttal, W. R. (1973). *The psychobiology of sensory coding.* New York: Harper & Row.

G. H. ROBINSON
University of North Alabama

PSYCHOPHYSICS
WEBER'S LAW

FEMALE SEXUAL DYSFUNCTION

Scientific interest in female sexuality is relatively recent, and dialogue continues concerning the nature and etiology of female sexual dysfunction. For example, much of what is considered "dysfunction" is predicated on a Western, heterosexual notion of sexuality, which some would argue exists primarily through our construction of it (Teifer, 1995). Moreover, though the research in this area often includes lesbian, bisexual, and heterosexual women as subjects, studies often do not address issues related to sexual orientation (Leiblum & Rosen, in press). However, most in the field would agree that two major components of female sexual dysfunction include: (a) some aspect of a woman's sexual life either differing from a culturally defined norm or having changed from previous functioning; and (b) that this difference or change causes the woman distress or interpersonal difficulty (American Psychiatric Association [APA], 1994).

Epidemiological data suggest that female sexual problems are widespread. In a random sample of U.S. women who were asked to report on "sexual problems experienced in the last year for several months or more," researchers (Laumann, Gagnon, Michael, & Michaels, 1994) found that 14.4% reported pain during sex; 18.8% reported difficulty with lubrication; 21.2% reported sex was not pleasurable; 24.1% indicated a lack of orgasm; and 33.4% reported a lack of interest in sexual activity. Clinical samples usually include even higher levels of dysfunction.

Many factors, including intrapersonal, interpersonal, medical, hormonal, and developmental aspects of a person's life are thought to play a role in causing and maintaining sexual dysfunction, though few have been systematically studied. From correlational studies, there is evidence that both historical and current factors play a role (e.g., Heiman, Gladue, Roberts, & LoPiccolo, 1986), and that etiological factors vary by dysfunction.

There are six sexual dysfunction disorders described by the American Psychiatric Association's (APA) *Diagnostic and Statistical Manual,* fourth edition (*DSM-IV*) that are applicable to women: Hypoactive Sexual Desire, Sexual Aversion Disorder, Female Sexual Arousal Disorder, Female Orgasmic Disorder, Dyspareunia, and Vaginismus. In addition, each sexual dysfunction can be categorized as either lifelong or acquired and global or situational (APA, 1994).

HYPOACTIVE SEXUAL DESIRE DISORDER

Hypoactive Sexual Desire Disorder (HSD) is defined as a low level of interest in sexual activity, often indicated by persistent or recurrent lack of sexual fantasies and desire, that causes the woman distress (APA, 1994). Etiological factors found to be associated with decreased desire include: medical illness, depression, stress, interpersonal conflict, hormonal imbalance, and the use of certain medications (e.g., many antidepressants) or recreational drugs. Global and lifelong dysfunction are more suggestive of a physical problem, such as an endocrine disorder, an illness, or long-term medication use. Treatment is dependent on the physical and psychosocial issues that underlie the disorder, and can include psychotherapy, androgen administration, or a change in medication (Leiblum & Rosen, in press). There are no controlled treatments documented to be effective in treating HSD, though there is evidence that testosterone can be helpful for women with low levels of bioavailable testosterone (Davis, 1998; Sherwin, Gelfand, & Brender, 1985).

SEXUAL AVERSION DISORDER

Sexual Aversion Disorder is an extreme aversion to, and avoidance of, all genital sexual contact with a partner. This diagnosis is rare. Physical factors, such as illness or medications, are rarely contributory; negative interpersonal or intrapersonal factors such as extreme negative thoughts about intercourse or a painful, phobia-inducing sexual experience more often play a causal role. Psychotherapy, either couples or individual, can be useful in resolving the aversion. Most often, therapy includes cognitive-behavioral techniques, desensitization, and, when appropriate, working through issues of past sexual assault (Heiman & Meston, 1997a).

FEMALE SEXUAL AROUSAL DISORDER

Female Sexual Arousal Disorder (FSAD) is marked by the lack of physical (e.g., vasocongestion and lubrication of the genitals) and subjective psychological sexual response. This disorder has unknown prevalence and etiology, though it appears to be an unusual disorder in women unless it is concomitant with dyspareunia, anorgasmia, or menopausal changes; to date, there is no clear evidence that FSAD is a distinct sexual disorder. Treatment should first examine physical factors (Goldstein & Berman, 1998), and may possibly include discussion of topical lubricants or hormonal agents. Current research is examining pharmacological agents which may help alleviate the physical symptoms of this disorder. Whether these agents will also change subjective perceptions of arousal remains to be seen. Additionally, psychotherapy, with a focus on issues such as worries about contraception, inadequate stimulation, or lack of attraction to a partner may be useful, though as yet has not been adequately researched for this disorder.

FEMALE ORGASMIC DISORDER

Female Orgasmic Disorder is defined as a frequent delay in or lack of orgasm. Lack of orgasm during intercourse is not considered to be a dysfunction if the woman can reach orgasm through other means. Psychological and interpersonal factors often contribute to lack of orgasm, such as believing that sex is shameful or having a history of unpleasant sexual experiences (Heiman, in press). Physical factors more rarely play a role, although there are a substantial number of women who complain of orgasmic delay secondary to taking a specific serotonin reuptake inhibitor (SSRI) or other antidepressants (Heiman in press). Depending on the type of SSRI, delayed orgasm tends to occur in 40–60% of women (Rosen, Lane, & Menza, 1999).

For orgasmic disorders that are not medication-induced, treatment can include bibliotherapy, brief therapy with a clinician trained in sex therapy, masturbation, or a combination of these modalities. When treatment is performed by a trained professional, success rates are in the 88–90% range for becoming orgasmic during masturbation and around 25–75% for becoming orgasmic with a partner (Heiman & Meston, 1997b).

DYSPAREUNIA

Dyspareunia is a recurrent genital pain that occurs before, during, or after intercourse. Similar to HSD, this diagnosis is heterogeneous and common: both physical (e.g., injury, endometriosis, scarring) and psychological (e.g., guilt and shame, relationship difficulties) factors may play an etiological role. Lack of lubrication may be a contributing factor to painful intercourse. If physical etiologic factors are found, they may or may not be responsive to treatment. In conjunction with any physical treatment, or when physical treatment is not indicated, psychotherapy may help the woman deal with feelings and behavioral interactions associated with the sexual pain. One subcategory of dyspareunia, vulvar vestibulitis, has been shown to be helped by surgery, and to some extent by behavioral interventions (Schultz et al., 1996). Although tricyclic antidepressants (TCAs) have been shown to help alleviate pain associated with intercourse, their use must be decided upon judiciously, given their potential for causing decreased desire and difficulty with orgasm (Heiman & Meston, 1997b).

VAGINISMUS

Vaginismus is the recurrent, involuntary spasming of the muscles of the outer third of the vagina. The response is usually triggered by a fear that accompanies the anticipation of penetration of the vagina. Vaginismus is less common than dyspareunia, and is often secondary to an association between vaginal penetration and a negative or painful experience. Etiological factors are primarily psychological, and can include: sexual inhibition, sexual trauma, negative feelings toward sexual partner, and phobia about sexual response or intercourse. Treatment requires both physical and psychological approaches, in which the cycle of anxiety is slowly broken down by pairing relaxation with the use of a series of dilators (Leiblum et al., 1989). Genital/perineal biofeedback is also promising, but no controlled studies of its efficacy have been published.

REFERENCES

American Psychiatric Association. (1994). *Diagnostic and statistical manual of mental disorders* (4th ed.). Washington, DC: Author.

Davis, S. R. (1998). The role of androgens and the menopause in the female sexual response. *International Journal of Impotence Research, 10*(Suppl. 2), S82–S83.

Goldstein, I., & Berman, J. R. (1998). Vasculogenic female sexual dysfunction: vaginal engorgement and clitoral erectile insufficiency syndromes. *International Journal of Impotence Research, 10*(Suppl. 2), S84–S85.

Heiman, J. R. (in press). Female orgasmic disorder. In S. R. Leiblum & R. C. Rosen (Eds.), *Principles and practice of sex therapy* (3rd ed.). New York: Guilford.

Heiman, J. R., Gladue, B., Roberts, C., & LoPiccolo, J. (1986). Current factors discriminating sexually functional from sexually dysfunctional married couples. *Journal of Marital and Family Therapy, 12,* 163–174.

Heiman, J. R., & Meston, C. M. (1997a). Evaluating sexual dysfunction in women, *Clinical Obstetrics and Gynecology, 40*(3), 616–629.

Heiman, J. R., & Meston, C. M. (1997b). Empirically-validated treatment for sexual dysfunction. *Annual Review of Sex Research, 8,* 148–157.

Laumann, E. O., Gagnon, J. H., Michael, R. T., & Michaels, S. (1994). *The social organization of sexuality: Sexual practices in the United States.* Chicago: University of Chicago Press.

Leiblum, S. R., & Rosen, R. C. (Eds.). (1988). *Sexual desire disorder.* New York: Guilford.

Leiblum, S. R., Pervin, L. A., & Campbell, E. H. (1989). The treatment of vaginismus: Success and failure. In S. R. Leiblum & R. C. Rosen (Eds.), *Principles and practice of sex therapy* (2nd ed.). New York: Guilford.

Leiblum, S. R., & Rosen, R. C. (Eds.) (in press). *Principles and practice of sex therapy.* 3rd Edition. New York: Guilford.

Rosen, R. C., Lane, R., & Menza, M. (1999). Effects of SSRI on sexual dysfunction: A critical review. *Journal of Clinical Psychopharmacology, 19,* 67–71.

Schultz, W. C. M. W., Gianotten, W. L., van der Meijden, W. I., van de Wiel, H. B. M., Blindeman, L., Chadha, S., & Drogendijk, A. C. (1996). Behavioral approach with or without surgical intervention to the vulvar vestibulitis syndrome: A prospective randomized and non-randomized study. *The Journal of Psychosomatic Obstetrics and Gynecology, 17,* 143–148.

Sherwin, B. B., Gelfand, M. M., & Brender, W. (1985). Androgen enhances sexual motivation in females: A prospective, crossover study of sex steroid administration in the surgical menopause. *Psychosomatic Medicine, 47*(4), 339–351.

Teifer, L. (1995). *Sex is not a natural act and other essays.* Boulder: Westview Press.

J. POIRIER
J. HEIMAN
University of Washington

MALE SEXUL DYSFUNCTION
SEX THERAPY

FERSTER, CHARLES B. (1922–1981)

Charles B. Ferster received the BS from Rutgers University, and the PhD in 1950 from Columbia, where he studied under such well-known behaviorists as Fred S. Keller and William N. Schoenfeld. He served as research scientist at Harvard University and the Indiana University School of Medicine. He then became professor of psychology at Georgetown University and finally at the American University in Washington, D.C., until his death.

Throughout his career he was dedicated to a behavioristic approach to psychology. His writings and research ranged from basic behavioral research to the applications of a behavioral approach to such areas as education and clinical psychology. With B. F. Skinner, Ferster published the results of a long research project in *Schedules of Reinforcement* (1957). This work demonstrated the powerful control that various schedules of positive reinforcement could have over the behavior of lower animals such as the pigeon. With Mary C. Perrott he published *Behavior Principles,* which involved the application of the principles of operant conditioning to various species of animals, including man. Other applications of operant conditioning principles involved the modification of the behavior of autistic children.

In the 1950s researchers in operant conditioning often had difficulty in getting their research published in the current journals of experimental psychology, because their methodology involved using small numbers of subjects rather than large groups. As a result, in 1958 Ferster was one editor of *The Journal of the Experimental Analysis of Behavior,* which was devoted to the publication of research using operant conditioning techniques. Following its founding, Ferster became the journal's first editor.

R. W. LUNDIN
Wheaton, Illinois

FESTINGER, LEON (1919–1989)

Leon Festinger received the bachelor's degree from the College of the City of New York. He then attended the State University of Iowa, receiving the MA, and PhD in 1942. There Festinger came under the influence of Kurt Lewin's theories and developed them further, earning a reputation in social psychology.

Lewin's theories, oriented from Gestalt principles, include cognitive dissonance theory and social comparison theory. According to cognitive dissonance, people whose behavior is in discord with their thoughts will either structure their thoughts to comport with behavior, or vice versa. Because of psychological pressures toward uniformity, individuals compare their cognitions with others, seeking to convince others of their own position or abandoning their own thoughts for the views of the others. A person, for example, who feels hot in a room and wonders whether it is due to a fever or the room temperature, will inquire of others (provided there is no thermometer in the room). Thus social comparison drives us to convert others to our own opinions, or else yield to theirs.

Festinger's books include his classic *A Theory of Cognitive Dissonance: Conflict, Decision, and Dissonance; Theory and Experiment in Social Communications* (with others); *Research Methods in the Behavioral Science* (with D. Katz); *Deterrents and Reinforcement* (with D. H. Lawrence); *When Prophecy Fails* (with H. W. Riecken and S. Schachter); and *Social Pressures in Informal Groups* (with S. Schachter and K. Back).

Before going to the New School for Social Research in 1968, Festinger was at the University of Rochester (1943–1945), M.I.T. (1945–1948), the University of Michigan (1951–1955), and Stanford University (1965–1968).

STAFF

FETAL ALCOHOL SYNDROME: BACKGROUND, TREATMENT, AND PREVENTION

HISTORICAL BACKGROUND

Although authors have claimed to find ancient reference to damaging effects of maternal alcohol consumption, Abel (1984) suggested that those claims rest on erroneous secondary sources or mistranslations. Abel does report suggestions of adverse effects of maternal drinking in seventeenth-century England and that several writers observed during the "gin epidemic" in the early eighteenth century that children of mothers who drank heavily were small, sickly, and mentally slow. Further, a number of nineteenth-century reports linked stillbirth, infant mortality, and mental retardation to maternal drinking during pregnancy.

But studies in the twentieth century failed to find a link between maternal drinking and adverse effects on offspring. Elderton and Pearson (1910) reported no relationship between parental drinking and intelligence or appearance of children, and suggested that children of alcoholics might have problems because parents and children shared "defective germ plasm" (as quoted by Abel, 1984, p. 18) or because the parents provided a poor home environment. Although their claim was much criticized, it was later supported by Haggard and Jellinek (1942), who denied that prenatal alcohol produced malformations. Thus, however inaccurate from our perspective, Montagu's (1965, p. 114) conclusion was apparently well-founded at the time: "Unexpectedly, alcohol in the form of beverages, even in immoderate amounts, has no apparent effect on a child before birth. . . . [I]t now can be stated categorically . . . that no matter how great the amount of alcohol taken by the mother—or the father, for that matter—neither the germ cells nor the development of the child will be affected." The date of Montagu's publication has a certain irony, appearing at about the time Lemoine, Harousseau, Borteryu, and Menuet began their study of the offspring of 127 alcoholic parents. In 1968, they reported that several of the children had such characteristic anomalies that maternal alcoholism could be inferred from them. The abnormalities were in the three areas now associated with FAS: growth retardation, low intelligence, and facial anomalies. Their paper, published in French (although with an English abstract), had little impact (Abel, 1984; Rosett & Weiner, 1984), and was unknown to Jones and Smith and their colleagues at the time of their initial reports in 1973 (Abel, 1984). Those reports brought the effects of maternal alcohol to international attention, in part by providing a name, fetal alcohol syndrome (FAS), that "dramatically refocused interest on an important perinatal risk" (Sokol et al., 1986, p. 88).

INCIDENCE AND RISK FACTORS

As might be expected given sampling error, use of different diagnostic criteria, and actual national/regional differences, incidence estimates vary across study and country. Estimates of full FAS generally fall within the 0.5 to 3.0 cases per 1,000 births range given by the Institute of Medicine (IOM) (Stratton, Howe, & Battaglia, 1996), but studies summarized in Streissguth, Barr, Kogan, & Bookstein (1997) had incidence estimates of 1.3 to 4.8 per 1,000 births. Applying the IOM's criteria, Sampson and colleagues (1997) estimated that the combined incidence of FAS and alcohol-related neurodevelopmental disorder (ARND) is about 9 per 1,000 births. Even the lowest estimates confirm that prenatal alcohol exposure is a major cause of birth defects.

As would be expected, incidence varies most with degree of prenatal maternal drinking. Full-blown FAS appears to be associated only with heavy maternal drinking; no cases have been reported among moderate drinkers (Abel & Sokol, 1987; Abel, 1998). FAS

may occur in 30 to 50 percent, and fetal alcohol effects (FAE) in 50 to 70 percent, of offspring of truly alcoholic women who consume eight or more drinks daily (Little, Snell, Rosenfeld, Gilstrap, & Gant, 1990). Some studies report incidence as high as 80 percent in low SES samples (e.g., Bingol et al., 1987).

Incidence of human newborns with some features of FAS also increases with amount of prenatal maternal alcohol consumption (e.g., Streissguth, Landesman-Dwyer, Martin, & Smith, 1980). Degree of physical growth retardation is also dose-related (e.g., Abel, 1984). A dose-response curve is found in virtually all animal studies: The number and the severity of offspring anomalies both increase with amount of prenatal exposure to alcohol (see Abel, 1984, for a summary). Well-controlled animal studies have confirmed that the damage is from prenatal alcohol and is not secondary to some other effect (e.g., Abel, 1984, 1998; Streissguth et al., 1980).

Some effects of prenatal alcohol appear to occur only above a certain threshold level of exposure (e.g., Ernhart, Sokol, Ager, Morrow-Tlucak, & Martier, 1989; Streissguth, 1986). For example, Ernhart and colleagues (1989) reported that women who drank small amounts of alcohol early in pregnancy had children with no incidence of FAS-related neonatal physical anomalies above that of a control group. However, teratogens typically have neurobehavioral effects at levels below those at which physical defects are shown (e.g., Abel, 1989). Indeed, Mattson and Riley (1998) report that groups of FAS children and alcohol-exposed children who had no characteristic physical features of FAS showed significant and largely similar deficits in IQs relative to normal children. One of the controversies mentioned at the beginning of this entry concerns the extent to which prenatal alcohol exposure has either threshold or linear effects. Abel (1998) has recently claimed that: (a) prenatal alcohol exposure generally is associated with a threshold effect; (b) a "unifying principle" is that "it is alcohol abuse, and not simply alcohol, that causes *alcohol-abuse-related birth effects*" (p. 13, italics in original); and (c) FAS would more appropriately termed "fetal alcohol abuse syndrome." Abel (1998) particularly focuses on the role of binge drinking as a cause of prenatal-alcohol induced defects. In response, Bookstein (1999, p. 1078) bluntly states that the claim of a threshold effect is "factually an error." Indeed, several studies and reviews (e.g., Goldschmidt, Richardson, Stoffer, Geva, & Day, 1996; Streissguth & Kanter, 1997) report relatively linear relationships between degree of prenatal exposure and degree of some adverse postnatal effects.

Of importance, FAS is seen much more commonly in offspring from lower SES mothers (Abel, 1984, Abel & Hannigan, 1995, Bingol et al., 1987). A variety of possible reasons exist for this relationship, including the fact that alcoholism is inversely related to SES status. Equating alcohol intake in different SES women, however, Bingol and colleagues (1987) found a 71 percent incidence of FAS/FAE in offspring of heavy drinking low SES mothers and only 4.6 percent in offspring of heavy drinking middle/upper SES mothers. SES was confounded with ethnicity, complicating interpretation, but Abel and Hannigan argue persuasively that SES is the major factor. SES is a marker variable, leaving open the question as to what underlies the SES differences. Abel (1998) suggests that the pattern, more than the amount, of prenatal alcohol intake is important, with binge drinking being a particular problem. Other factors increasing the adverse of prenatal alcohol exposure include minority ethnic status, smoking, maternal age, and under-nutrition (Abel, 1998; Abel & Hannigan, 1995).

Both human and nonhuman research suggests that some of the variability in incidence of FAS/FAE stems from genetic factors. Clinical reports indicate that dizygotic (fraternal) twins of alcoholic mothers show differential development and performance (e.g., Streissguth, 1986). Maternal factors are implicated in research by Chernoff (1977, 1980): Pregnant mice from two different strains given comparable doses of alcohol had different blood-alcohol levels, and the strain with higher levels had offspring with higher incidence of anomalies.

FAS EFFECTS FROM CHILDHOOD TO ADULTHOOD

FAS has effects that last into adulthood in modified form. Longitudinal studies (e.g., Streissguth, 1986; Streissguth, Aase, Clarren, Randels, LaDue, & Smith, 1991; Streissguth, Clarren, & Jones, 1985) reveal that FAS/FAE adolescents and adults were about two standard deviations below the mean in height and head circumference, although variability was high; little overall catch-up growth had occurred. The characteristic low weight of FAS/FAE children had largely disappeared, although weight/height ratios were even more variable than other measures.

The facial dysmorphologies characteristic of FAS children became less distinctive with age. Although some features (such as short palpebral fissure length) remained, growth in a number of facial areas reduced the extent of the overall abnormal appearance.

The average IQ of the 61 FAS/FAE adolescents and adults reported by Streissguth and colleagues (1991) was 68, just into the mild retardation level. The FAS mean was 66 and the FAE was 73. Variability was again high, with IQ ranging from 20 to 105; no FAS individual's IQ was above the low 90s. Those with the most severe growth retardation and facial dysmorphologies in childhood continued to have the lowest later IQ scores. Only six percent of the 61 were in regular classes and not receiving special help; 28 percent were in self-contained special education classes, 15 percent were neither in school nor working, and nine percent were in sheltered workshops. Although academic deficits were broad, arithmetic deficits were particularly large. Academic performance had not improved since childhood.

Children and adolescents with FAS/FAE show a number of additional behavioral deficits and excesses that present serious educational and other challenges (Carmichael & Burgess, 1997; Mattson & Riley, 1998). Among the more common features are hyperactivity, inattention, impaired learning but not memory of verbal material, a wide variety of receptive and expressive language problems, and fine motor coordination impairments. Of particular concern are reports of temper tantrums in younger affected children and serious conduct disorders in older ones. Not surprisingly, FAS children have difficulty conforming to social norms.

In Streissguth and colleagues' (1991) study, even FAS/FAE adolescents and adults who were not mentally retarded showed poor socialization scores and an unusually high level of maladaptive be-

haviors, including poor concentration and attention, sullenness, impulsivity, lying, and cheating. However, their family environments were highly unstable, making difficult the determination of whether many of these effects owed to prenatal alcohol exposure, postnatal environment, or an interaction between difficult infants and inadequate parenting. Only nine percent were still living with both parents; the mothers of 66 percent had died, many from alcohol-related causes. More recently, Streissguth and colleagues (1997), in a large sample study of 415 FAS/FAE children and adults, identified six "secondary characteristics" that develop after birth and might be reduced with appropriate intervention. The six effects (and the percent of cases each) are: mental health problems serious enough to have resulted in consultation with a mental health professional (90% of subjects 6 or older); disrupted school experience (60% of subjects 12 or older); trouble with the law (60% of subjects 12 or older); confinement in inpatient units for mental health or substance-abuse problems, or imprisonment for crime (50% of subjects 12 or older); inappropriate sexual behavior (50% of subjects 12 or older); and alcohol or drug problems (30% of subjects 12 or older).

ENVIRONMENTAL FACTORS PROTECTING AGAINST BEHAVIORAL PROBLEMS

Streissguth and colleagues (1997) also identified several "protective factors" that reduce the incidence or degree of secondary characteristics. In order of importance, they may be summarized as: living in a stable and nurturant home; diagnosed before age six; not having been abused (72% of their subjects had been abused in some way); staying in living situations for extensive periods; being in a good quality home from eight to 12 years of age; having a diagnosis of FAS rather than FAE (apparently paradoxically, lower IQ was associated with fewer of some secondary characteristics); and having basic needs met for at least 13% of life.

TREATMENT

A variety of pharmacological and behavioral interventions have been used with FAS/FAE children and adults with varying degrees of success, many of which are presented in Carmichael and Burgess (1997) and Streissguth and Kanter (1997). Of particular importance is a highly structured and relatively low-stimulation environment, which improves attention and reduces problem behavior in both adults and children (e.g., Dyer, Alberts, & Niemann, 1997; Tanner-Halverson, 1997). Given the high level of ADHD characteristics in FAS/FAE individuals, stimulant medication would appear to be the preferred treatment. However, in an admittedly small sample of a well-controlled study, Snyder, Nason, Snyder, and Block (1997) found mixed effects of various stimulants. Generally, relative to placebo control, stimulants reduced hyperactivity but did not increase attention. Additionally, subjects showed high variability in their response to medication. Given the variety and extent of problems manifested by FAS/FAE individuals and the effect of these problems on others, Clarren and Astley (1997) suggest that clinics specifically devoted to FAS/FAE individuals may be needed.

PREVENTION

Although 100 percent preventable theoretically, FAS may prove resistant to reduction efforts in practice. Alcohol abuse is notably resistant to treatment, and relapse rates are as high as 75 percent 12 months after treatment (e.g., Tucker, Vuchinich, & Harris, 1985). Thus, education programs on the adverse effects of prenatal alcohol may lower alcohol consumption of moderately drinking women during pregnancy, but are unlikely to affect alcohol-abusing or alcoholic women, whose infants are most at risk. Although a variety of general approaches are available (e.g., Cox, 1987; Milkman & Sederer, 1990), treatment and prevention programs targeted specifically at women (e.g., Kilbey & Asghar, 1992; National Institute on Alcohol Abuse and Alcoholism, 1987) may be necessary if we wish to decrease the incidence of this tragic condition.

For more information contact the National Organization on Fetal Alcohol Syndrome on line at www.nofas.org/what.htm.

REFERENCES

Abel, E. L. (1984). *Fetal alcohol syndrome and fetal alcohol effects.* New York: Plenum.

Abel, E. L. (1989). *Behavioral teratogenesis and behavioral mutagenesis.* New York: Plenum.

Abel, E. L. (1998). *Fetal alcohol abuse syndrome.* New York: Plenum.

Abel, E. L., & Hannigan, J. H. (1995). Maternal risk factors in fetal alcohol syndrome: Provocative and permissive influences. *Neurotoxicology and Teratology, 17,* 445–462.

Abel, E. L., & Sokol, R. J. (1987). Incidence of fetal alcohol syndrome and economic impact of FAS-related anomalies. *Drug and Alcohol Dependence, 19,* 51–70.

Bingol, N., Schuster, C., Fuchs, M., Iosub, S., Turner, G., Stone, R. K., & Gromisch, D. S. (1987). The influence of socioeconomic factors on the occurrence of fetal alcohol syndrome. *Advances in Alcohol and Substance Abuse, 6*(4), 105–118.

Bookstein, F. L. (1999). Review of Abel's *Fetal alcohol abuse syndrome. Addiction, 94,* 1078–1079.

Carmichael, O. H., & Burgess, D. M. (1997). Early intervention for children prenatally exposed to alcohol and other drugs. In M. J. Guralnick (Ed.), *The effectiveness of early intervention* (pp. 109–145). Baltimore: Brookes.

Chernoff, G. F. (1977). The fetal alcohol syndrome in mice: An animal model. *Teratology, 15,* 223–230.

Chernoff, G. F. (1980). The fetal alcohol syndrome in mice: Maternal variables. *Teratology, 22,* 71–75.

Clarren, S., & Astley, S. (1997). Development of the FAS diagnostic and prevention network in Washington State. In A. Streissguth & J. Kanter (Eds.), *The challenge of fetal alcohol syndrome: Overcoming secondary disabilities* (pp. 40–51). Seattle, WA: University of Washington Press.

Cox, W. M. (Ed.). (1987). *Treatment and prevention of alcohol problems.* New York: Academic.

Dyer, K., Alberts, G., & Niemann, G. (1997). Assessment and treatment of an adult with FAS: Neuropsychological and behavioral considerations. In A. Streissguth & J. Kanter (Eds.), *The challenge of fetal alcohol syndrome: Overcoming secondary disabilities* (pp. 52–63). Seattle, WA: University of Washington Press.

Elderton, E. M., & Pearson, K. (1910). A first study of the effect influence of parental alcoholism on the physique and ability of the offspring. *Eugenics Laboratory Memoir, 10,* 1–46. (As described in Abel, 1984)

Ernhart, C. B., Sokol, R. J., Ager, J. W., Morrow-Tlucak, M., & Martier, S. (1989). Alcohol-related birth defects: Assessing the risk. In D. E. Hutchings (Ed.), Prenatal abuse of licit and illicit drugs (pp. 159–172). *Annals of the New York Academy of Sciences, 592.*

Goldschmidt, L., Richardson, G. A., Stoffer, D. S., Geva, D., & Day, N. L. (1996). Prenatal alcohol exposure and academic achievement at age six: A nonlinear fit. *Alcoholism: Clinical and Experimental Research, 20,* 763–770.

Haggard, H. W., & Jellinek, E. M. (1942). *Alcohol explored.* Garden City, NJ: Doubleday.

Kilbey, M. M., & Asghar, K. (Eds.). (1992). *Methodological issues in epidemiological, prevention, and treatment research on drug-exposed women and their children.* Research monograph 117. Rockville, MD: National Institute on Drug Abuse.

Lemoine, P., Harousseau, H., Borteryu, J. P., & Menuet, J. C. (1968). Les enfants de parents alcooliques: Anomalies observees a propos de 127 cas. *Ouest Medical, 21,* 476–482. (As described in Abel, 1984)

Little, B. B., Snell, L. M., Rosenfeld, C. R., Gilstrap, L. C. III, & Gant, N. F. (1990). Failure to recognize fetal alcohol syndrome in newborn infants. *American Journal of Diseases in Children, 144,* 1142–1146.

Mattson, S. N., & Riley, E. P. (1998). A review of the neurobehavioral deficits in children with fetal alcohol syndrome or prenatal exposure to alcohol. *Alcoholism: Clinical and Experimental Research, 22,* 279–294.

Milkman, H. B., & Sederer, H. B. (Eds.). (1990). *Treatment choices for alcoholism and substance abuse.* New York: Lexington.

Montagu, A. (1965). *Life before birth.* New York: Signet.

National Institute on Alcohol Abuse and Alcoholism. (1987). *Program strategies for preventing fetal alcohol syndrome and alcohol-related birth defects.* Rockville, MD: National Institute on Alcohol Abuse and Alcoholism.

Rosett, H. L., & Weiner, L. (1984). *Alcohol and the fetus.* New York: Oxford University Press.

Sampson, P. D., Streissguth, A. P., Bookstein, F. L., Little, R. E., Clarren, S. K., Dehaene, P., Hanson, J. W., & Graham, J. M. Jr. (1997). Incidence of fetal alcohol syndrome and prevalence of alcohol-related neurodevelopmental disorder. *Teratology, 56,* 317–26.

Snyder, J., Nason, J., Snyder, R., & Block, G. (1997). A study of stimulant medication in children with FAS. In A. Streissguth & J. Kanter (Eds.), *The challenge of fetal alcohol syndrome: Overcoming secondary disabilities* (pp. 25–39). Seattle, WA: University of Washington Press.

Sokol, R. J., Ager, J., Martier, S., Debanne, S., Ernhart, C., Kuzma, J., & Miller, S. I. (1986). Significant determinants of susceptibility to alcohol teratogenicity. In H. M. Wisniewski & D. A. Snider (Eds.), Mental retardation: Research, education, and technology transfer (pp. 87–100). *Annals of the New York Academy of Sciences, 477.*

Stratton, K., Howe, C., & Battaglia, F. C. (1996). *Fetal alcohol syndrome: Diagnosis, epidemiology, prevention, and treatment.* Washington, DC: National Academy Press.

Streissguth, A. P. (1986). The behavioral teratology of alcohol: Performance, behavioral, and intellectual deficits in prenatally exposed children. In J. R. West (Ed.), *Alcohol and brain development* (pp. 3–44). New York: Oxford University Press.

Streissguth, A. P., Aase, J. M., Clarren, S. K., Randels, S. P., LaDue, R. A., & Smith, D. F. (1991). Fetal alcohol syndrome in adolescents and adults. *Journal of the American Medical Association, 265,* 1961–1967.

Streissguth, A. P., Barr, H., Kogan, J., & Bookstein, F. (1997). Primary and secondary disabilities in fetal alcohol syndrome. In A. Streissguth & J. Kanter (Eds.) *The challenge of fetal alcohol syndrome: Overcoming secondary disabilities* (pp. 25–39). Seattle, WA: University of Washington Press.

Streissguth, A. P., Clarren, S. K., & Jones, K. L. (1985). Natural history of fetal alcohol syndrome: A 10-year follow-up of eleven children. *Lancet, 2,* 85–91.

Streissguth, A., & Kanter, J. (Eds.). (1997). *The challenge of fetal alcohol syndrome: Overcoming secondary disabilities.* Seattle, WA: University of Washington Press.

Streissguth, A. P., Landesman-Dwyer, S., Martin, J. C., & Smith, D. W. (1980). Teratogenic effects of alcohol in humans and laboratory animals. *Science, 209,* 353–361.

Tanner-Halverson, P. (1997). A demonstration classroom for young children with FAS. In A. Streissguth & J. Kanter (Eds.), *The challenge of fetal alcohol syndrome: Overcoming secondary disabilities* (pp. 78–88). Seattle, WA: University of Washington Press.

Tucker, J. A., Vuchinich, R. E., & Harris, C. V. (1985). Determinants of substance abuse relapse. In M. Galizio & S. A. Maisto (Eds.), *Determinants of substance abuse* (pp. 383–421). New York: Plenum.

R. T. Brown
University of North Carolina, Wilmington

ALCOHOLISM TREATMENT
FETAL ALCOHOL SYNDROME: DESCRIPTION AND DIAGNOSIS
SUBSTANCE ABUSE

FETAL ALCOHOL SYNDROME: DESCRIPTION AND DIAGNOSIS

Fetal alcohol syndrome (FAS) is a complex of physical anomalies and neurobehavioral deficits that may severely affect offspring of heavy-drinking mothers. Apparently the leading type, above Down Syndrome and Fragile X Syndrome, of mental retardation in the Western world (e.g., Abel & Sokol, 1987), FAS is the most prevalent environmentally-based and preventable form of mental retardation. In 1987, Abel and Sokol estimated that as much as 11 percent of annual cost of mental retardation in the United States might be devoted to FAS cases and that the annual cost of treatment of all FAS-related effects was 321 million dollars. In its 1996 report (Stratton, Howe, & Battaglia), the Institute of Medicine (IOM) stated:

> The costs of FAS and related conditions can be quite high—for the individual, for the family, and for society. Rates of FAS in several of the most complete studies are similar—on the order of 0.5 to 3 cases per 1,000 births. Assuming an annual birth cohort of approximately 4 million, this translates into 2 to 12 thousand FAS births per year in this country. These incidence figures are offered not as established facts but to emphasize the magnitude of a problem that has serious implications—for the individual and for society. (p. 1)

The subject of some 4,000 scientific reports since its first description in 1973 (Jones & Smith; Jones, Smith, Ulleland, & Streissguth), FAS is still accompanied by some uncertainty and controversy. Certain and uncontroversial is that alcohol in heavy consumption is a teratogen that produces lifelong impairments. Prenatal exposure to alcohol has a range of adverse effects, and FAS comprises the most serious. Less serious sequelae occurring in children exposed to alcohol who do not show facial dysmorphologies are termed by various groups fetal alcohol effects (FAE), alcohol-related neurodevelopmental disorder (ARND; Batshaw & Conlon, 1997), alcohol-related birth defects (ARBD), or prenatal exposure to alcohol (PEA; Mattson & Riley, 1997).

DIAGNOSTIC CRITERIA AND COMMON CHARACTERISTICS

FAS in its full manifestation is associated with three major effects, known as "the triad of the FAS" (Rosett & Weiner, 1984, p. 43): (1) growth retardation of prenatal origin; (2) characteristic facial anomalies; and (3) central nervous system dysfunction. Several sets of diagnostic criteria are now available. They virtually all include the three major effects, but differ in detail and approach. The Fetal Alcohol Study Group of the Research Society on Alcoholism (Rosett, 1980) established the first and most widely cited set of minimal criteria for diagnosis of FAS, based largely on Clarren and Smith's (1978) summary of 245 cases. It specifies that FAS should be diagnosed only when the following three criteria are met:

1. Prenatal and/or postnatal growth retardation (below 10th percentile for body weight, length, and/or head circumference, when corrected for gestational age). Growth retardation has been viewed as the most common characteristic of FAS, but some suggest that it may not be a primary feature and perhaps not a defining characteristic (Carmichael-Olson & Burgess,

1997). Although low birthweight is associated with other maternal factors (several of which, including smoking, malnutrition, and drug abuse, are also associated with alcohol abuse), two lines of evidence suggest that alcohol induces prenatal growth retardation: (1) The other maternal factors are rarely associated with other defining features of FAS (Rosett & Weiner, 1984); and (2) Offspring of pregnant animals given alcohol show both growth retardation and virtually all other physical and neurobehavioral features of FAS (e.g., Abel, 1984; Riley & Barron, 1989).

2. Central nervous system dysfunction (neurological abnormality, developmental delay, or mental impairment below the 10th percentile). As West (1986b, p. vi) has observed, "Central nervous system dysfunction is the most devastating and one of the more consistently observed clinical abnormalities in surviving offspring of mothers known to have consumed large amounts of alcohol during pregnancy." Prenatal alcohol has a variety of adverse effects on the developing CNS (see Abel, 1984, 1998; Phelps, 1995; Stratton et al., 1996; Streissguth & Kanter, 1997; West, 1986a for reviews). Mental retardation or subnormality is the most common CNS indicator associated with FAS (see Streissguth, 1986, for a detailed review). Variability of affected children's IQ is high within and across studies. Average IQ across studies is estimated at about 65 (Mattson & Riley, 1997), but has been as high as 79 (Streissguth, Barr, Kogan, & Bookstein, 1997). Children with the most severe morphology and growth indicators have the most severe intellectual and other CNS deficits. Affected infants and children may also show failure to thrive, poor sucking, retarded speech and motor development, fine-motor dysfunction, repetitive self-stimulating behaviors such as head rolling or head banging, auditory deficits, and seizures. Symptoms of Attention-Deficit/Hyperactivity Disorder (ADHD) are common and associated with school problems. Seizures occur in about 20 percent of cases, but are not considered characteristic of FAS.

3. Characteristic facies (at least two of the following three facial dysmorphologies: (a) Microcephaly [head circumference below the third percentile]; (b) Microphthalmia or short palpebral fissures; (c) Poorly developed philtrum, thin upper lip, and flattening of the maxillary area. The importance of facial appearance is clear in the Institute of Medicine's (Stratton et al., 1996) statement: "At present, the facial features observed in FAS remain the most unique feature of the disorder. . . . No one can receive an FAS diagnosis without an experienced clinician's assertion that the face, *taken as a whole,* appears to be the FAS face" (p. 72, italics in original).

A history of drinking during pregnancy should be present for confident diagnosis, since no individual feature is specific to prenatal exposure to alcohol (Sokol et al., 1986). However, Streissguth, Sampson, Barr, Clarren, and Martin (1986, p. 64) have suggested that " . . . FAS and alcohol teratogenicity are reciprocal terms. . . . [I]dentifying a child with all the features of FAS strongly suggests that the child was affected by alcohol *in utero.*" Of impor-

tance, they also stated (p. 64) that although alcohol teratogenicity may cause a "milder" FAS or FAE phenotype, such milder phenotypes should not be inferred to result necessarily from alcohol: "[O]ther environmental or genetic problems could produce similar manifestations. . . . When examining the individual patient, the examiner cannot be sure that alcohol produced a 'possible' fetal alcohol effect, even when a maternal history is positive for alcohol." An important attributional implication is that women who have occasionally consumed small amounts of alcohol during pregnancy and have slightly deformed infants should not be made to feel guilty or that alcohol caused the deformities. Women should certainly take precautions during their pregnancy, but do not have control over everything that may affect their babies (Rosett & Weiner, 1984). Although a number of quantitative diagnostic systems have been proposed (e.g., Burd & Martsolf, 1989), diagnosis apparently can be made more validly on the basis of an overall clinical evaluation that emphasizes facial features as a whole—"the facial gestalt of FAS" (Stratton et al., 1996, p. 72).

The IOM (Stratton et al., 1996) has proposed defining criteria for five disorders associated with maternal alcohol consumption. Three categories of FAS are defined: Category 1, FAS with a history of maternal alcohol exposure; Category 2, FAS without a history of maternal alcohol exposure; and Category 3, partial FAS with a history of maternal alcohol exposure. Category 2 permits a diagnosis of FAS based on clinical signs alone, permitting diagnosis of FAS in infants or children who have been adopted shortly after birth and for whom maternal drinking data are not available. IOM (Stratton et al., 1996) intends for Category 3:

to include people with signs and symptoms attributable to significant prenatal alcohol exposure and who need medical, social services, and other attention. . . . Category 3 allows an FAS diagnosis to be given to someone who would not receive a Category 1 diagnosis. . . . [It] could be particularly useful, for example, for some patients who present for diagnosis as an adult . . . [since] some of the "hallmark" indicators used in infancy or childhood are not maintained into adolescence or adulthood.

It can also be used temporarily until additional data indicate whether or not a Category 1 diagnosis is justified. The two other categories "are intended to represent some degree of uncertainty whether prenatal alcohol exposure caused the adverse effects documented in an individual patient, or whether other factors were causative" (Stratton et al., 1996, p. 3): Category 4, alcohol-related birth defects (ARBD; physical anomalies only), and Category 5, alcohol-related neurodevelopmental disorder (ARND). The ARND criteria are essentially equivalent to those used to diagnose FAE and provides a diagnostic category for children adversely affected by prenatal alcohol who do not meet criteria for mental retardation (Streissguth et al., 1997). They include adverse effects associated with maternal alcohol intake in either clinical or animal research. The two categories may occur together, and IOM states that both should be diagnosed if criteria for both are met. A highly condensed version of IOM's diagnostic criteria is in Table 1. Of importance, IOM (Stratton et al., 1996, p. 5) provides an operational definition of "maternal alcohol exposure":

Table 1.   Summary of IOM's (1997) Diagnostic Criteria for Fetal Alcohol Syndrome (FAS) and Alcohol-Related Effects

Category 1. FAS with Confirmed Maternal Alcohol Exposure

   A. Confirmed maternal alcohol exposure

   B. Characteristic pattern of facial anomalies such as short palpebral fissures and abnormalities in the premaxillary zone (e.g., flat upper lip, flattened philtrum, and flat midface)

   C. Growth retardation as indicated by at least one of the following: low birth weight for gestational age; decelerating weight over time not due to nutrition; disproportional low weight to height

   D. CNS neurodevelopmental abnormalities, including at least one of the following: decreased cranial size at birth; structural brain abnormalities (e.g., microcephaly, partial or complete agenesis of the corpus callosum, cerebellar hypoplasia); neurological hard or soft signs (as age appropriate), such as impaired fine motor skills, neurosensory hearing loss, poor tandem gait, poor eye-hand coordination

Category 2. FAS without Confirmed Maternal Alcohol Exposure

   B (Characteristic pattern of facial anomalies), C (Growth retardation), and D (CNS neurodevelopmental abnormalities) as in Category 1

Category 3. Partial FAS with Confirmed Maternal Alcohol Exposure

   A. Confirmed maternal alcohol exposure

   B. Some components of B (Characteristic pattern of facial anomalies), as in Category 1

   Either C (Growth retardation) and D (CNS neurodevelopmental abnormalities), as in Category 1, or

   E Complex pattern of behavior or cognitive abnormalities that is inconsistent with developmental level and cannot be explained by familial background or environment alone, such as learning difficulties; deficits in school performance; poor impulse control; problems in social perception; deficits in higher level receptive and expressive language; poor capacity for abstraction or metacognition; specific deficits in mathematical skills, or problems in memory, attention, or judgment

Alcohol-Related Effects

   Alcohol-related Birth Defects (ARBD): Presence of a subset of an extensive list of congenital anomalies, including cardiac, skeletal, renal, ocular, auditory, and numerous other malformations and dysplasias

   Alcohol-related Neurodevelopmental Disorder (ARND). Presence of CNS neurodevelopmental abnormalities, as indicated by any one of 1D, above, and/or the Complex pattern of behavior or cognitive abnormalities, as in Category 3E

A pattern of excessive intake characterized by substantial, regular intake or heavy episodic drinking. Evidence of this pattern may include frequent episodes of intoxication, development of tolerance or withdrawal, social problems related to drinking, legal problems related to drinking, engaging in physically hazardous behavior while drinking, or alcohol-related medical problems such as hepatic disease.

The definition specifies excessive intake and has criteria that reflect such intake. It appears to exclude occasional social drinking and is thus similar to Abel's (1998) proposal that FAS should more accurately be described as fetal alcohol abuse syndrome. These proposals, however, are controversial, as explored in the entry "Fetal Alcohol Syndrome: Background, Treatment, and Prevention."

Underdiagnosis, recently thought to be a problem (Little, Snell, Rosenfeld, Gilstrap, & Gant, 1990), is now unlikely, owing to increased knowledge of FAS (Abel & Hannigan, 1995). Indeed, IOM's Category 2 could potentially lead to overdiagnosis in an attempt to gain services for children who would not otherwise qualify.

REFERENCES

Abel, E. L. (1984). *Fetal alcohol syndrome and fetal alcohol effects.* New York: Plenum.

Abel, E. L. (1998). *Fetal alcohol abuse syndrome.* New York: Plenum.

Abel, E. L., & Hannigan, J. H. (1995). Maternal risk factors in fetal alcohol syndrome: Provocative and permissive influences. *Neurotoxicology and Teratology, 17,* 445–462.

Abel, E. L., & Sokol, R. J. (1987). Incidence of fetal alcohol syndrome and economic impact of FAS-related anomalies. *Drug and Alcohol Dependence, 19,* 51–70.

Batshaw, M. L., & Conlon, C. J. (1997). Substance abuse: A preventable threat to development. In M. L. Batshaw (Ed.), *Children with disabilities* (4th ed., pp. 143–162). Baltimore: Brookes.

Burd, L., & Martsolf, J. T. (1989). Fetal alcohol syndrome: Diagnosis and syndromal variability. *Physiology & Behavior, 46,* 39–43.

Carmichael-Olson, H., & Burgess, D. M. (1997). Early intervention for children prenatally exposed to alcohol and other drugs. In M. J. Guralnick (Ed.), *The effectiveness of early intervention* (pp. 109–145). Baltimore: Brookes.

Clarren, S. K., & Smith, D. W. (1978). The fetal alcohol syndrome. *New England Journal of Medicine, 298,* 1063–1067.

Jones, K. L., & Smith, D. W. (1973). Recognition of fetal alcohol syndrome in early infancy. *Lancet, 2,* 999–1001.

Jones, K. L., Smith, D. W., Ulleland, C. N., & Streissguth, A. P. (1973). Pattern of malformation in offspring of chronic alcoholic mothers. *Lancet, 1,* 1267–1271.

Little, B. B., Snell, L. M., Rosenfeld, C. R., Gilstrap, L. C. III, & Gant, N. F. (1990). Failure to recognize fetal alcohol syndrome in newborn infants. *American Journal of Diseases in Children, 144,* 1142–1146.

Mattson, S. N., & Riley, E. P. (1998). A review of the neurobehavioral deficits in children with fetal alcohol syndrome or prenatal exposure to alcohol. *Alcoholism: Clinical and Experimental Research, 22,* 279–294.

Phelps, L. (1995). Psychoeducational outcomes of fetal alcohol syndrome. *School Psychology Review, 24,* 200–212.

Riley, E. P., & Barron, S. (1989). The behavioral and neuroanatomical effects of prenatal alcohol exposure in animals. In

D. E. Hutchings (Ed.), Prenatal abuse of licit and illicit drugs (pp. 173–177). *Annals of the New York Academy of Sciences, 592.*

Rosett, H. L. (1980). A clinical perspective of the fetal alcohol syndrome. *Alcoholism: Clinical and Experimental Research, 4,* 119–122.

Rosett, H. L., & Weiner, L. (1984). *Alcohol and the fetus.* New York: Oxford University Press.

Sokol, R. J., Ager, J., Martier, S., Debanne, S., Ernhart, C., Kuzma, J., & Miller, S. I. (1986). Significant determinants of susceptibility to alcohol teratogenicity. In H. M. Wisniewski & D. A. Snider (Eds.), Mental retardation: Research, education, and technology transfer (pp. 87–100). *Annals of the New York Academy of Sciences, 477.*

Stratton, K., Howe, C., & Battaglia, F. C. (1996). *Fetal alcohol syndrome: Diagnosis, epidemiology, prevention, and treatment.* Washington, DC: National Academy Press.

Streissguth, A. P. (1986). The behavioral teratology of alcohol: Performance, behavioral, and intellectual deficits in prenatally exposed children. In J. R. West (Ed.), *Alcohol and brain development* (pp. 3–44). New York: Oxford University Press.

Streissguth, A. P., Barr, H., Kogan, J., & Bookstein, F. (1997). Primary and secondary disabilities in fetal alcohol syndrome. In A. Streissguth & J. Kanter (Eds.), *The challenge of fetal alcohol syndrome: Overcoming secondary disabilities* (pp. 25–39). Seattle, WA: University of Washington Press.

Streissguth, A., & Kanter, J. (Eds.). (1997). *The challenge of fetal alcohol syndrome: Overcoming secondary disabilities.* Seattle, WA: University of Washington Press.

Streissguth, A. P., Sampson, P. D., Barr, H. M., Clarren, S. K., & Martin, D. C. (1986). Studying alcohol teratogenesis from the perspective of the fetal alcohol syndrome: Methodological and statistical issues. In H. M. Wisniewski & D. A. Snider (Eds.), Mental retardation: Research, education, and technology transfer (pp. 63–86). *Annals of the New York Academy of Sciences, 477.*

West, J. R. (Ed.). (1986a). *Alcohol and brain development.* New York: Oxford University Press.

West, J. R. (1986b). *Preface.* In J. R. West (Ed.), *Alcohol and brain development.* New York: Oxford University Press.

R. T. Brown
University of North Carolina, Wilmington

FETAL ALCOHOL SYNDROME: BACKGROUND, TREATMENT & PREVENTION
INFANT DEVELOPMENT

FIELD RESEARCH

Field research consists of the application of scientific methodology to the study of organisms in their natural (real-world) environments. Field research is typically neither as contrived nor as controlled as laboratory-based research, but it is more generalizable. As defined by Campbell and Stanley (1966), the results of field research tend to have lower internal validity, that is, less control over extraneous variables, but higher external validity, or generalizability beyond the immediate situation, than those of laboratory research. However, it is possible to conduct field experiments in which control over extraneous variables approaches that attained in the laboratory. Likewise, it is possible to conduct realistic laboratory research in which consideration of the effects of numerous variables leads to highly generalizable results.

The principal method employed in field research is objective observation of ongoing behavior, but interviews, psychological testing, and even experimentation may also be employed. In observing humans, observations made in the field should be as unobtrusive as possible so the observer and the observational process do not influence the observed behaviors. This usually means that the observer must remain out of sight, recording his or her observations without the awareness of those who are being observed. There are, however, ethical questions concerning the surreptitious or secretive observation of people under certain circumstances. Allegations of invasion of privacy may occur when researchers are too "underhanded" in observing and recording the actions of people in private domains.

In certain observational research situations, the observer interacts with those who are being observed in such a way that he or she is accepted as part of the situation or scene and does not interfere with the naturalness of their behavior. Such is the case in participant observation of the sort employed by cultural anthropologists and others who wish to study the customs and other social behaviors of groups of people at close range. Participant observation is, of course, not limited to cultural anthropology, but may also be employed by social psychologists, developmental psychologists, clinical psychologists, and other behavioral researchers whose research interests may be more suitable for exploration in the field than in the laboratory.

The term "field research," also known as action research, cooperative action research, and operational research, is also used to refer specifically to practical applications of the scientific method to human problems in organizational contexts. As enunciated originally by Corey in 1953, the field research movement in education was stimulated by the perceived gap between educational research findings and educational practice, and it attempted to bring about a closer cooperative interaction between researchers and practitioners. Corey maintained that practical decisions involving school matters would be much sounder if teachers and school administrators became involved in both the idea-generation and research phases of the scientific process as applied to educational problems.

The purpose and sequence of steps in field research in business and industrial organizations are similar to those in educational contexts. Research data pertaining to a system problem are collected, changes are made in the system based on the data, and the consequences of these changes are evaluated by collecting more data. Thus, the field research model is a dynamic, informational feedback procedure based on an immediate practical concern in a human group or organization.

Critics of the field research model point out that scientists do not subscribe to a naive here-and-now empiricism, but rather base their efforts on a knowledge of previous research and some kind of theoretical framework. Field research is also said to suffer from problems of control over extraneous variables and from a lack of generalizability of the findings from one group or situation to another. On the positive side, although almost a half-century of field research conducted in schools has not completely closed the gap between research and practice, it has made educational practitioners more aware of and knowledgeable about research methods and findings. The field research model encourages teachers to ask questions about the effects of particular teaching methods in specific educational contexts and with children of different abilities, motivations, and backgrounds, and to exercise their creativity in answering those questions. More teachers and other practitioners in educational and other organizations are conducting field research, but such research is typically of the survey or quasi-experimental type rather than controlled experimentation.

REFERENCES

Campbell, D. T., & Stanley, J. C. (1966). *Experimental and quasi-experimental designs for research.* Chicago: Rand-McNally.

Corey, S. M. (1953). *Action research to improve school practices.* New York: Bureau of Publications, Teachers College, Columbia University.

L. R. AIKEN
Pepperdine University

EXPERIMENTAL METHODS
OBSERVATIONAL METHODS
RESEARCH METHODOLOGY

FISHER, RONALD A. (1890–1962)

Sir Ronald A. Fisher was educated at Cambridge. His early career was spent as a statistician at Rothamsted Experimental (agricultural research) Station in Hertfordshire. He was the second holder (after Pearson) of the Galton chair in eugenics and biometry at University College, London, and finished his career in the Balfour chair of genetics at Cambridge. Clearly the most creative statistician of modern times, Fisher gave psychology (a) the analysis of variance, (b) analysis techniques for small samples, (c) the concept of null hypothesis, and (d) the notion of significant/insignificant as a continuum rather than a dichotomy.

Fisher's work at Rothamsted led to his *Statistical Methods for Research Workers* (1925), which presented for the first time precise inference based on small data samples and precise tests of statistical significance (theoretical chances of obtaining the same results if the study were repeated). He wrote extensively on the need to develop statistics that showed sufficiency—that exhausted all information in the sample in arriving at the conclusion. He also developed the idea of the unbiased estimator—a measure that becomes more accurate as more observations are made.

Later at Rothamsted he turned to the more complex experimental situations, developing the notion of analysis of variance based on the classical least squares theory. For the first time it was possible to deal meaningfully with more than one manipulated variable at a time; his *Design of Experiments* (1935) became the researcher's Bible. He later extended his work to multivariate procedures, permitting multiple outcome measures as well as multiple manipulations. With Yates (1938), he collected the statistical tables needed to perform the various inferential techniques.

C. S. PEYSER
The University of the South

THE FIVE-FACTOR MODEL OF PERSONALITY

INTRODUCTION

Personality traits describe individual differences in human beings' typical ways of perceiving, thinking, feeling, and behaving that are generally consistent over time and across situations. Beginning with the work of Allport and Odbert (1936), trait psychologists have attempted to identify a set of basic traits that adequately describe variation in human personality. This effort has employed two strategies: the analysis of descriptive adjectives across human languages (the lexical approach) and the measurement of various traits derived from personality theories (the questionnaire approach). For nearly 50 years competing sets of fundamental traits set forth by various psychologists (e.g., Cattell, Eysenck, Guilford) and typically derived through factor analysis created disagreement about which traits were basic. However, in the 1980s, a convergence of the lexical and questionnaire strategies generated a consensus among many trait psychologists that five basic, broad traits provided an adequate description of individual differences (McCrae & John, 1992). This set of basic traits is referred to as the Five-Factor Model of Personality (FFM).

Additional support for the FFM was found when trait psychologists rediscovered earlier factor analytic studies that consistently reported variations of these five basic traits underlying observer ratings of personality (Norman, 1963). Contemporary factor analytic investigations have recovered the FFM traits in diverse languages spoken around the world (McCrae & Costa, 1997) and demonstrated that most traits assessed by personality questionnaires, regardless of their original theoretical roots and applied purposes, can be subsumed by the FFM (McCrae, 1989). The major advantages of this consensus include the provision of a common language for psychologists of different traditions to use in describing individual differences, and the ability to focus research on the roles traits play in diverse human phenomena rather than on endless debates over which traits are basic (Wiggins, 1992).

DESCRIPTION

Although opinions differ as to the names of the five basic traits, the most popular articulation of the FFM involves the following labels (Costa & McCrae, 1992).

Neuroticism vs. Emotional Stability

High neuroticism suggests a proneness to psychological distress and emotional reactivity reflected in chronic experiences of anxiety, depression, self-consciousness, low self-esteem, and ineffective coping. Low neuroticism does not guarantee psychological health, but does suggest a calm, even-tempered emotional style.

Extraversion vs. Introversion

High extraversion suggests an interpersonal style marked by preferences for social interaction, high activity levels, and the capacity to experience positive emotions. Low extraversion suggests a preference for solitude, and a reserved, quiet, and independent interpersonal style, but not an inherently unhappy or unfriendly individual.

Open to Experience vs. Closed to Experience

High openness suggests an active pursuit and appreciation of experiences for their own sake, reflecting curiosity, imagination, tolerance of diverse values and beliefs, novelty-seeking, and attraction to aesthetic experiences. Low openness suggests a preference for conventional attitudes, conservative tastes, dogmatic views, and little interest in the unfamiliar or markedly different.

Agreeableness vs. Antagonism

High agreeableness suggests a friendly, cooperative, trustworthy, and nurturant interpersonal style. Low agreeableness suggests a cynical, rude, abrasive, suspicious, uncooperative, and irritable interpersonal style.

Conscientiousness vs. Unconscientiousness

This trait describes individual differences in the degree of organization, persistence, control, and motivation in goal-directed behavior. High conscientiousness reflects a tendency to be organized, reliable, hard-working, self-directed, deliberate, ambitious, and persevering. Low conscientiousness reflects a tendency to be disorganized, aimless, lazy, careless, lax, negligent, and hedonistic.

THEORY

Although the FFM is empirically derived through factor analytic investigations of language and personality questionnaires, it would be erroneous to conceive of the FFM as atheoretical. The emerging consensus regarding the five basic traits led to the question, "*Why* are these traits universal descriptors of human individual differences?"

Several theoretical perspectives have arisen to answer this question. The lexical hypothesis (Saucier & Goldberg, 1996) suggests that (a) observable individual differences will be encoded in human language; (b) important individual differences will have a correspondingly larger number of descriptive words in a particular language; and (c) universal individual differences should be recovered across all human language systems.

The dyadic-interactional perspective (Wiggins & Trapnell, 1996) examines the FFM from the perspective of interpersonal personality theory (Pincus, 1994). This view places conceptual priority on the interpersonal traits (extraversion and agreeableness) as represented by the more finely grained interpersonal circumplex model (Wiggins, 1979) and a theoretical emphasis on social exchange and the metaconcepts of agency and communion.

McCrae and Costa (1996) provide a metatheoretical framework for personality theories that includes basic tendencies, characteristic adaptations, self-concept, objective biography, and external influences. Basic tendencies refer to the universal raw material of personality—the basic capacities and dispositions of the individual. The FFM traits are among the basic dispositional tendencies that influence, and are influenced by, the other elements of their framework throughout the lifespan.

Hogan (1996) has combined psychoanalytic theory and symbolic interactionism into his socioanalytic personality theory. He suggests that trait terms reflect observers' views of the social reputation of individuals, and the FFM traits that describe reputation have been historically important for achieving the fundamental goals of getting along and getting ahead in human social organization.

Finally, Buss (1996) has argued that the FFM traits have evolutionary significance by contributing to the social (as opposed to the environmental) adaptive problems faced by humans and the strategic adaptive solutions employed by humans to achieve important evolutionary goals.

ASSESSMENT

The FFM can be assessed through self-reports, observer-ratings, and a structured interview. Inventories that closely correspond to the lexical tradition employ adjective ratings to assess FFM dimensions. Lexical FFM inventories include the Standard Markers (Goldberg, 1992) and the Interpersonal Adjective Scales—Big Five (Trapnell & Wiggins, 1990). Some psychologists suggest that adjectives do not provide much context for the rater to make judgments about the self, whereas phrases provide more context and allow for more precise judgments. The Hogan Personality Inventory (Hogan & Hogan, 1992) and the NEO Personality Inventory—Revised (Costa & McCrae, 1992) are widely used FFM inventories employing descriptive phrases. The NEO inventory also has an observer-rating format, and adjectival inventories can be easily modified for observer ratings. Finally, Trull and Widiger (1997) developed the Structured Interview for the Five-Factor Model. Individuals interested in assessing the FFM should consider important differences among instruments and methods (Widiger & Trull, 1997).

APPLICATIONS

The FFM has been widely applied in diverse domains of psychological science and practice. Clinical psychologists have demonstrated the advantages of using the FFM for treatment planning and understanding the psychotherapy process (Miller, 1991). The

FFM has also been linked to both symptom-based psychopathologies (Ruiz, Pincus, & Ray, 1999) and the personality disorders (Costa & Widiger, 1994). Beyond clinical psychology, the FFM has been widely used in industrial/organizational psychology, where it has been applied to topics such as employee performance and job satisfaction (Barrick & Mount, 1991). The FFM has also demonstrated promising connections in the areas of cross-cultural psychology, health psychology, social psychology, developmental psychology, counseling, and close relationships. Finally, the FFM dimensions are likely to be reliable and valid predictors of many everyday behaviors of potential interest to investigators.

CRITICISMS

Although the FFM has been successfully applied in diverse areas of psychology, criticisms of the model have been raised (Block, 1995; McAdams, 1992; Westen, 1995). Methodological criticisms focus largely on the use of factor analysis and its inherent vulnerabilities or the lack of validity scales in most FFM inventories. Ontological criticisms focus on the model's contemporaneous and descriptive nature, and suggest the scope of the FFM is limited and fails to account for complex developmental and intrapsychic personality processes. Finally, some critics suggest it is unlikely that universal traits encoded in natural language are sensitive enough to capture the pathological nuances of human personality.

REFERENCES

Allport, G. W., & Odbert, H. S. (1936). Trait names: A psycholexical study. *Psychological Monographs, 47,* (1, Whole no. 211).

Barrick, M. R., & Mount, M. K. (1991). The big five personality dimensions and job performance: A meta-analysis. *Personnel Psychology, 44,* 1–26.

Block, J. (1995). A contrarian view of the five-factor approach to personality description. *Psychological Bulletin, 117,* 187–215.

Buss, D. M. (1996). Social adaptation and the five major factors of personality. In J. S. Wiggins (Ed.), *The five-factor model of personality: Theoretical Perspectives* (pp. 180–208). New York: Guilford.

Costa, P. T., Jr., & McCrae, R. R. (1992). *NEO-PI-R/NEO-FFI professional manual.* Odessa, FL: Psychological Assessment Resources.

Costa, P. T., Jr., & Widiger, T. A. (1994). *Personality disorders and the five-factor model of personality.* Washington, DC: American Psychological Association.

Goldberg, L. R. (1992). The development of markers for the big five factor structure. *Psychological Assessment, 4,* 26–42.

Hogan, R. (1996). A socioanalytic perspective on the five-factor model. In J. S. Wiggins (Ed.), *The five-factor model of personality: Theoretical Perspectives* (pp. 163–179). New York: Guilford.

Hogan, R., & Hogan, J. (1992). *Hogan Personality Inventory Manual.* Tulsa, OK: Hogan Assessment Systems.

McAdams, D. P. (1992). The five-factor model in personality: A critical appraisal. *Journal of Personality, 60,* 329–361.

McCrae, R. R. (1989). Why I advocate the five-factor model: Joint analyses of the NEO-PI and other instruments. In D. M. Buss & N. Cantor (Eds.), *Personality psychology: Recent trends and emerging directions* (pp. 237–245). New York: Springer-Verlag.

McCrae, R. R., & Costa, P. T., Jr. (1996). Toward a new generation of personality theories: Theoretical contexts for the five-factor model. In J. S. Wiggins (Ed.), *The five-factor model of personality: Theoretical Perspectives* (pp. 51–87). New York: Guilford.

McCrae, R. R., & Costa, P. T., Jr. (1997). Personality trait structure as a human universal. *American Psychologist, 52,* 509–516.

McCrae, R. R., & John, O. P. (1992). An introduction to the Five-Factor Model and its applications. *Journal of Personality, 60,* 175–215.

Miller, T. R. (1991). The psychotherapeutic utility of the five-factor model of personality: A clinicians experience. *Journal of Personality Assessment, 57,* 415–433.

Norman, W. T. (1963). Toward an adequate taxonomy of personality attributes: Replicated factor structure in peer nomination personality ratings. *Journal of Abnormal and Social Psychology, 66,* 574–583.

Pincus, A. L. (1994). The interpersonal circumplex and the interpersonal theory: Perspectives on personality and its pathology. In S. Strack & M. Lorr (Eds.), *Differentiating normal and abnormal personality* (pp. 114–136). New York: Springer.

Ruiz, M. A., Pincus, A. L., & Ray, W. J. (1999). The relationship between dissociation and personality. *Personality and Individual Differences, 27,* 239–249.

Saucier, G., & Goldberg, L. R. (1996). The language of personality: Lexical perspectives on the five-factor model. In J. S. Wiggins (Ed.), *The five-factor model of personality: Theoretical Perspectives* (pp. 21–50). New York: Guilford.

Trapnell, P. D., & Wiggins, J. S. (1990). Extension of the Interpersonal Adjective Scales to include the big five dimensions of personality. *Journal of Personality and Social Psychology, 59,* 781–790.

Trull, T. J., & Widiger, T. A. (1997). *Structured Interview for the Five-Factor Model of Personality: Professional Manual.* Odessa, FL: Psychological Assessment Resources.

Westen, D. (1995). A clinical-empirical model of personality. Life after the Mischelian ice age and the NEO-Lithic era. *Journal of Personality, 64,* 495–524.

Widiger, T. A., & Trull, T. J. (1997). Assessment of the five-factor model of personality. *Journal of Personality Assessment, 68,* 228–250.

Wiggins, J. S. (1979). A psychological taxonomy of trait descriptive terms: The interpersonal domain. *Journal of Personality and Social Psychology, 37,* 395–412.

Wiggins, J. S. (1992). Have model, will travel. *Journal of Personality, 60,* 527–532.

Wiggins, J. S., & Trapnell, P. D. (1996). A dyadic-interactional perspective on the five-factor model. In J. S. Wiggins (Ed.), *The five-factor model of personality: Theoretical Perspectives* (pp. 88–162). New York: Guilford.

A. L. Pincus
M. A. Ruiz
Pennsylvania State University

EXTRAVERSION + INTROVERSION: CONCEPTS OF INTROVERSION-EXTRAVERSION PERSONALITY TYPES

FLAVELL, JOHN H. (1928–   )

John Flavell was born on August 9, 1928 in Rockland, MA. He and his sisters, Constance and June (now both distinguished artists), were raised there by his mother, Anne, and his father, Paul, a civil engineer. Although the Great Depression caused his parents considerable anxiety and financial hardship, they somehow managed to shield their children from its worst effects, and the Flavell's home environment was stable, secure, and caring.

After graduating from high school in 1945, Flavell spent two years in the Army, following which he entered Northeastern University. Upon receiving his AB in psychology in 1951, he enrolled in the clinical psychology training program at Clark University, earning his MA in 1952 and his PhD in 1955. The dominant intellectual figure at Clark in those days was the developmental theorist H. Werner. From Werner and his colleagues, Flavell learned much Werner, some Piaget, and—above all—a sense of what cognitive development might be like and how one might do research on it. It is hard to think of another graduate program during the behavioristic 1950s that could have provided that sense. It was during the Clark years that Flavell met Eleanor Roberts, who became his wife and research collaborator, and they began to live happily ever after. The couple have two grown children, Beth and Jim, of whom they are very fond.

After completing his doctoral dissertation in late 1954, Flavell became a staff clinical psychologist at a Veterans Administration hospital in the arid plains of eastern Colorado. In 1955 he accepted a teaching position at the University of Rochester, happy to exchange clinical practice and dust storms for academic life and snow. Believing that only assistant professors who write books ever get to be tenured associate professors, Flavell set out to write a small book summarizing the work of the major developmental theorists of the day. He soon discovered that adequate summaries already existed for all the theorists except one—Piaget. Although by 1956, Piaget had written what seemed to Flavell to be an infinite and rapidly growing number of books and articles, most of them available only in French, no one had summarized his theory and research. So Flavell abandoned a small book on several theorists for a large book on only one, eventually entitled *The Developmental Psychology of Jean Piaget*. The change of plan was undoubtedly predestined, given the fact (which Flavell discovered only later) that he and Piaget shared the same birthday. To Flavell's great surprise and pleasure, the book became very widely read and cited.

It was during the Rochester years, also, that Flavell began investigating the growth of children's role-taking and communication skills and their developing use of memory strategies. He was initially interested in studying the development of private speech, not memory strategies. However, the kind of private speech he chanced to select for study was semicovert verbal rehearsal of to-be-remembered object names. What transformed Flavell's private speech work into a program of research on memory strategy development was the discovery that, although clearly capable of this kind of private speech, young children did not think to engage in it on their own. Flavell spent the academic year 1963–1964 in Paris at the Laboratoire de Psychologie Génétique, where he began a book summarizing the role-taking and communication research.

In 1965, Flavell left the University of Rochester to take a position at the University of Minnesota's Institute of Child Development. Flavell's research on memory strategy development went into high gear at Minnesota and evolved into the study of metamemory and other areas of metacognition (knowledge/regulation of cognition). Similarly, his work on role-taking evolved into the study of young children's knowledge about perception, also conceptualized as a form of metacognition. Flavell spent the academic year 1969–1970 as a fellow at the Center for Advanced Study in the Behavioral Sciences at Stanford. Stanford rapidly joined Paris in Flavell's pantheon of very agreeable places to live and work, a fact he did not forget when he was later invited to come to Stanford for a much longer stay. At the Center, he wrote theoretical articles on the nature of developmental stages and sequences, problems he had begun to work on earlier with J. Wohlwill. After returning to Minnesota, Flavell continued his empirical research and also began to write a textbook on cognitive development. No such textbook had been written—a rather surprising state of affairs, in view of the rapidly growing popularity of the field.

In 1976 Flavell joined Stanford University's superb department of psychology. Since coming to Stanford, Flavell has been busy doing developmental research on children's knowledge about the mind.

Flavell received the American Psychological Association's Distinguished Scientific Contribution Award and the G. Stanley Hall Award of the Association's Division of Developmental Psychology. He is also a past president of that division and of the Society for Research in Child Development. He is a member of the National Academy of Sciences and the American Academy of Arts and Sciences, and the recipient of honorary degrees from the Universities of Paris, Rochester, and Thessaloniki. The citation for the first-listed award summarizes his scientific contributions:

"For outstanding contributions to the study of cognitive development. As a theoretician, his brilliant book on Piaget opened American psychology to the power of the structural descriptive approach to children's thinking; his theoretical essays have continued to make him the seminal thinker in the field. Empirically, he has been a ground-breaking researcher in four different domains—children's memory, metacognitive development, role taking, and communication skills. In each empirical domain he asked fundamental questions, offered creative hypotheses, invented many novel experimental tasks, and inspired others to follow his lead. His scholarship has a fresh, constantly evolving quality, and his writing is lucid and engaging."

FOA, EDNA B.

Edna B. Foa is a professor of clinical psychology and psychiatry at the University of Pennsylvania, and director of the Center for the Treatment and Study of Anxiety. She received her BA in psychology and literature from Bar Ilan University, Israel, in 1962; her MA in clinical psychology from University of Illinois in 1970; and her PhD in clinical psychology and personality from University of Missouri in 1970. Foa devoted her academic career to studying the psychopathology and treatment of anxiety disorders, primarily Obsessive-Compulsive Disorder (OCD), Posttraumatic Stress Disorder (PTSD), and Social Phobia, and is currently one of the world's leading experts in these areas.

Foa began her research career by examining the efficacy of behavioral treatments for anxiety disorders and identifying the active processes involved in these treatments. She soon discovered the limitations of behavior therapy: Not all patients were helped and many remained quite symptomatic. This realization motivated her to examine the failures carefully. Consequently, Foa embarked on an inquiry into treatment processes that distinguishes patients who benefit from behavior therapy from those who do not. This interest has led her to edit a book entitled *Failures in Behavior Therapy* (1983), which has been quite influential in drawing researchers' attention to exploring variables that predict success and failure in behavior therapy. As a natural sequel, Foa extended her interest from the study of treatment processes to the study of what it is that treatment should correct. Hence she has been conducting studies that aim to elucidate the mechanisms involved in pathological fear and anxiety. Her work emphasizes the relationship among three areas of research: therapy outcome, therapy processes, and psychopathology.

Foa's research on therapy outcome with OCD, described in many publications (e.g., Foa & Wilson, *Stop Obsessing,* 1991) has been influential both in clinical psychology and in psychiatry. Among psychologists, it has helped establish exposure and response prevention as the treatment of choice for OCD while fostering the awareness that certain drugs are helpful, and sometime necessary. Among psychiatrists, it prompted the realization that psychosocial treatments can be at least as effective as medication. Her role in the field was recognized by her appointment as chair of the *DSM-IV* Subcommittee for OCD. The influence of her research is reflected in the fact that *Experts' Treatment Guidelines* for OCD recommended exposure combined with response prevention as the treatment of choice.

As with her work in OCD, Foa has been developing short-term cognitive behavior therapy programs for PTSD and conducting empirical studies to evaluate their relative efficacy in ameliorating the severity of the disorder. The results of these studies have influenced the field to such an extent that exposure therapy, alone or in combination with other cognitive behavioral techniques, is considered by many experts to be the treatment of choice for PTSD. As a result, many researchers and clinicians have adopted this treatment in their work with various trauma victims. Again, this research has been disseminated in journal articles, book chapters, and many lectures and workshops, both in the United States and abroad. The treatment has also been published in a book that presented the theory and practice of cognitive behavior therapy for PTSD (Foa & Rothbaum, *Treating the Trauma of Rape,* 1998). Foa co-chaired the *DSM-IV* Subcommittee for PTSD, and most recently, chaired the Taskforce for Treatment Guidelines for PTSD of the International Society for Traumatic Stress Studies.

As a complement to her interest in developing effective treatments for pathological anxiety, Foa has been continuously concerned about understanding the processes that make the treatment work. In this endeavor, she was first influenced by conditioning theory and later on by the conceptual framework of information processing. In addition to her research on outcome and processes of treatment, Foa has been investigating the mechanisms underlying pathological anxiety. Here she has been interested in applying methods of experimental psychology to clinical research, as well as in conducting descriptive psychopathology studies. Additional contributions of Foa include the development of measures for OCD, PTSD, and social phobia, as well as new methodology for studying narratives of trauma victims.

Foa's interest in the psychopathology of anxiety and its treatment has produced a number of theoretical papers that have received much attention and have become classics in the field. These include: "Emotional processing of fear: Exposure to corrective information" (*Psychological Bulletin,* 1986), on the processes involved in pathological anxiety and its treatment; "Behavioral cognitive conceptualizations of post-traumatic stress disorder" (*Behavior Therapy,* 1989); and "Uncontrollability and unpredictability in post-traumatic stress disorder: An animal model" (*Psychological Bulletin,* 1992).

Foa has published several books and over 250 articles and book chapters, and has lectured extensively around the world. Her work has been recognized with numerous awards and honors. Among them are the Distinguished Professor Award under the Fulbright Program for International Exchange of Scholars; the Distinguished Scientist Award from the American Psychological Association, Society for a Science of Clinical Psychology; the first annual Outstanding Research Contribution Award presented by the Association for the Advancement of Behavior Therapy; the Distinguished Scientific Contributions to Clinical Psychology Award from the American Psychological Association; and the Lifetime Achievement Award presented by the International Society for Traumatic Stress Studies.

FORENSIC PSYCHOLOGISTS: ROLES AND ACTIVITIES

Forensic psychology deals with the interface of psychology and the law, and with the application of psychology to legal issues. This specialty includes a wide range of clients and settings, including individuals of all ages, couples, groups, organizations, industry, government agencies, schools, universities, inpatient and outpatient mental health settings, and correctional institutions. Forensic psychologists may become involved in such diverse areas as criminal competency and responsibility, tort liability and damages, product liability, mental hospital commitment and treatment, divorce and custody litigation, treatment of offenders, rights of patients and offenders, special education, eyewitness identification, jury selection, police selection and training, employment practices, workers' compensation, and professional liability. While few forensic psychologists are qualified in all these areas, all are expected to have a basic knowledge of certain "core" areas as well as a thorough knowledge of their specialization.

Though psychiatry has had a role within the legal system for many years, it was not until Judge Bazelon's decision in *Jenkins v. United States* (307 F2d, 637, D.C. Cir., 1962) that psychology obtained firm legal status. In *Jenkins*, a criminal case, the trial judge had ordered the jury to disregard the psychologist's testimony regarding mental disease. He did so on the basis that a psychologist is not qualified to give a medical opinion. The Court of Appeals ruled that the judge was in error and stated that "some psychologists are qualified to render expert testimony in the field of mental disorder." The court went on to suggest criteria for qualifying a psychologist as an expert. In the years since that decision, other cases have substantially broadened the issues included within the psychologists' legally defined expertise. Today, though there are some differences among states and between the state and federal governments, psychologists are regularly accorded expert status in practically every area of criminal, civil, family, and administrative law. The parameters of expert testimony have been further defined by the Federal Rules of Evidence and The Daubert case (Daubert v. Merrell Dow Pharmaceuticals, Inc., 113 S. CT. 2786 [1993]) (Bronstein, 1999).

The growth of forensic psychology has been manifested in a variety of other ways. Some interdisciplinary programming between law schools and psychology departments began in the 1960s. The early 1970s witnessed the development of joint PhD-JD degree programs and psychology PhD programs with a specialty in forensic or correctional psychology. Today there are four joint degree programs. Most psychology graduate schools include law-related courses in the curriculum. There are ten programs offering postdoctoral fellowships and roughly half of internships offer forensic rotations.

A number of professional organizations have also emerged. In 1980, the American Psychological Association membership approved the creation of a Division of Psychology and Law (Division 41). The American Board of Forensic Psychology (ABFP) was established in 1978. Its purpose is to identify qualified practitioners to the public and to promote forensic psychology as a recognized discipline. Applicants for diplomate status must, among other criteria, have at least 1000 hours of experience in a minimal five-year period in forensic psychology to qualify. They then must submit a work sample which, when approved, allows them to take a three-hour oral peer-review examination. As of 1999 there are 181 Diplomates of the ABFP, which is now a part of the American Board of Professional Psychology.

Another manifestation of growth is the publication of journals and books specific to the field. Among the important journals are *Law and Human Behavior, Criminal Justice and Behavior, American Journal of Forensic Psychology, Behavioral Sciences and the Law,* and *Psychology, Public Policy and Law.*

SPECIFIC ISSUES ADDRESSED BY FORENSIC PSYCHOLOGISTS

Three types of cases will be discussed: criminal, civil damage, and child custody. While these are not necessarily the most frequent or most important issues addressed by forensic psychologists, they illustrate some major aspects of forensic practice.

In most forensic cases the questions that the psychologist is called upon to answer fall into three categories: (a) diagnostic questions: personality dynamics, presence of psychosis or organicity, evidence of malingering, and so forth; (b) questions involving inference from the diagnostic level to opinions regarding specific legal questions: competency to stand trial, the relationship of a psychological disorder to an accident, the best interests of the child, and so forth; and (c) questions regarding disposition: need for treatment and prognosis, potential for future dangerous behavior, and so forth. To address these questions, the forensic psychologist must not only possess the usual evaluation skills, but must also be aware of special screening instruments and relevant case law. Also, there are important confidentiality issues which vary from situation to situation. The psychologist must be aware of these and take the necessary steps to protect clients. The psychologist must also work with attorneys prior to the evaluation to determine the questions to be addressed and to help them understand what the evaluation can and cannot do. For example, an attorney may incorrectly request that the evaluation answer the question of whether the person is telling the truth regarding the commission of a crime. The attorney must also understand that the payment of a fee is for the evaluation only, and that there is no commitment on the part of the psychologist to testify on behalf of the client. Whether this occurs depends on the findings of the evaluation.

It is also necessary for the psychologist to take a "forensic history," which is more comprehensive than the usual one and is likely to include such information as hospital records, school records, police reports, and the statements of witnesses. These sources of information will then be referenced in the report generated by the psychologist.

A Criminal Case

The attorney for Mr. A has called the forensic psychologist, requesting an evaluation of a client, who is charged with homicide. The forensic psychologist asks for basic details of the crime and requests all records relating to the present offense and to past criminal behavior and past evaluation or treatment for emotional problems. In determining what questions need to be answered, the psychologist asks whether Mr. A admits to committing the crime and whether he has given a statement to the police. If Mr. A's ability to understand and to waive his Miranda rights is an issue, a copy of the statement is requested. Other questions will be defined as well. For example, if the attorney is interested in pursuing an insanity defense, then witness and police statements are also requested. The evaluation itself, which may have to take place in a prison or a hospital, is then scheduled.

Usually an evaluation in a prison or hospital will require a court order instructing the personnel at the institution to allow the evaluation. The attorney should notify the client, so the client will understand who the evaluator is and will cooperate with the evaluation. When possible, records should be reviewed prior to the evaluation, but they must always be reviewed prior to the preparation of the report. In choosing the tests to be used, the psychologist will generally use a battery that includes both objective and projective personality tests and intelligence tests. The choice of tests should be made with reliability, validity, and applicability in mind, as this choice may have to be defended later on the witness stand. Regarding the question of applicability, many offenders have minority class status and educational or socioeconomic deprivation. It is important to know what effects these factors have on test results, and to interpret the test findings accordingly.

In addition to the testing, the psychologist must, in the interview, ask questions specifically related to the offense and to the legal issues. For example, if there is a Miranda issue, Mr. A's IQ reading level, and level of verbal comprehension will have to be evaluated. In addition, the psychologist will have to determine whether Mr. A demonstrates an understanding of the specific terminology involved in the warnings. If Mr. A admits to committing the crime and the attorney is considering an insanity defense, Mr. A must be questioned closely about his feelings and behavior prior to, during, and after the act, in order for the evaluator to offer opinions on intent, knowledge of the "nature and quality of the act," and so forth. If competency to proceed legally is an issue, the psychologist must question Mr. A regarding the functions of the principals in the court process (judge, etc.), the relationship with his attorney, the range of pleas, and the possible consequences.

Following the evaluation, the psychologist communicates the findings to the attorney, and usually at this point the attorney decides whether or not to pursue certain legal strategies and whether or not to call the psychologist to testify. The psychologist may be called to testify at pretrial hearings, at the trial itself, and/or at sentencing. Considerable time may elapse between the initial evaluation and the scheduling of testimony. If this is the case, the psychologist may want to conduct a follow-up evaluation prior to giving testimony.

A Civil Case

Mrs. B was involved in an automobile accident in which she sustained head and back injuries. Since the accident, which occurred a year ago, she has been complaining of pain, anxiety, and memory difficulty. Mrs. B's attorney requests an evaluation to determine her present mental status, its relationship to the accident, her need for treatment, her prognosis, and the damages in terms of her future potential for functioning in the occupational and home situation. If past medical evaluations have indicated the absence of a physical basis for her complaints of pain, the attorney may also wish to know the extent to which psychological factors are contributing to these complaints.

The psychologist's request for records includes discharge summaries (and in some cases, daily progress notes) from her hospital-izations related to the accident, any records of prior physical or emotional problems, and records that provide information on her premorbid functioning, such as school or work records. The symptoms described may be due only to psychological factors. However, if there is a question of organic brain damage raised either by the nature of the injuries or by preliminary test findings, further testing will be required. Specialized test batteries such as the Halstead-Reitan Neuropsychological Battery may be used to evaluate the presence of organic brain damage. In addition, a comparison should be made between present test findings and the indications from the records of premorbid intellectual functioning. If the psychological and/or organic deficit requires the giving up of a prior occupation, vocational interests and abilities testing may also be required to generate recommendations for further training or placement.

The opinion on the relationship between the accident and the present symptoms will depend largely on historical data. Also important in evaluating this relationship is the consistency between the nature of the trauma and the symptoms as revealed by current test findings. In some instances a person with preexisting emotional problems may indicate that the accident caused these problems. This may be done to gain compensation or it may be the product of an unconscious process. In the latter case, the accident may provide a psychologically acceptable reason for the patient's difficulties. The forensic psychologist must be aware of all these possible bases for the current symptoms.

A Child Custody Case

Mr. and Mrs. C are involved in a custody action for their two children, ages 12 and 7. While criminal and civil damage cases are often, though not always, performed as part of the adversary system, in child custody cases it is often the court, and not the individual attorney, that requests the evaluation, and the forensic psychologist is considered to be an independent evaluator. That is the situation in the case of Mr. and Mrs. C: evaluation is required of all parties. This includes the new partners of the separated or divorced parents, and may even include grandparents. The standard for the custody recommendation is what is in the best interest of the child, though this encompasses many factors, including the psychological fit between parent and child.

In addition to the usual testing considerations, several additional aspects are usually involved in such cases. First, because a child's behavior is more variable than an adult's and more reactive to situational factors, the evaluation usually requires at least two contacts with the child. In evaluating the children, their mental and emotional maturity will contribute to the weight given their verbalized preference. In most cases, the court will respect the preference of a child over the age of 12. However, for children 12 and under the court is likely to give considerably less weight to the stated preference for either parent. How much weight is given may well depend on the evaluation of the psychologist.

A second special aspect in custody evaluations is that each of the parents is likely to make accusations about the other which may be relevant to the custody issues. These accusations need to be explored and compared with other sources of data.

A third special aspect is a visit to each of the homes while the children are present. It is helpful if this is the first contact with the children, as it is less formal and occurs on their "territory," thus perhaps decreasing their anxiety about the evaluation. Observation in the home setting can provide information about the parent-child relationship, the degree of the home's orientation toward children, and the home's physical characteristics, such as adequate privacy. In the case of Mr. and Mrs. C, where all parties are evaluated, an opinion on the best interests of the children can be offered. However, if the evaluation is conducted at the request of one attorney as part of the adversary process, and only one parent and the children are assessed, only descriptive information can be provided. In this situation a final statement regarding the best interests of the children cannot ethically be made, because the entire family has not been evaluated.

Emerging Issues in Forensic Psychology

The issues that attract the most attention in forensic psychology change over time as a function of changes in the law, changes in the level of knowledge, and changes in patterns of behavior. Within liability law, two areas have become more important recently than in the past. One of these resulted from changes in the law in the early 1990s that allowed victims of harassment or discrimination to be awarded damages for psychological injuries. An area in which a change in the level of knowledge has been a factor is forensic neuropsychology. Much has been learned regarding the impact on an individual's cognitive, emotional, and behavioral status as a result of Mild Traumatic Brain Injury (MTBI) that can result from motor vehicle accidents (Sweet, 1999).

Within the criminal area, changes in patterns of behavior have led to considerable clinical and research activity in two areas: violence in the workplace (Hall, 1996) and violence by students within the school setting. The patterns associated with these types of aggression raise prediction and prevention issues that differ from these previously associated with aggressive behavior. Increases in knowledge about children's memory and their susceptibility to influence have led to increased attention to children's credibility as witnesses in criminal cases, particularly where the children are allegedly the victims of sexual offenses (Ceci & Bruck, 1995).

Within family law, changes in both the law and patterns of behavior have resulted in far more cases where geographical relocation is a major issue. Another area of increased concern and attention is the rights of grandparents.

A general issue that cuts across all these areas is the issue of assessment of malingering. More sophisticated tests have been developed to assess malingering on psychological and neuropsychological measures. Numerous books have been published regarding clinical and test approaches to the assessment of malingering.

TESTIFYING IN COURT

In some cases the report of the forensic psychologist will be accepted without an appearance in court. At other times, however, the psychologist may be called to testify. Giving testimony can be a traumatic experience; the key to minimizing difficulties is thorough preparation. This preparation takes place on several levels. The first level involves a thorough knowledge of the relevant law, the tests used, and the test findings. The psychologist must also be able to express the test findings without using excessive jargon and by

utilizing behavioral examples that will illustrate the statements made. The second level of preparation involves meeting with the attorney. The forensic psychologist must abide by ethical principles and must retain personal integrity. However, the psychologist also has the responsibility to present the findings as effectively as possible. The attorney, on the other hand, is required to advance the client's interests. The attorney has been taught never to ask a witness a question to which the attorney does not already know the answer. Preparation, therefore, includes an agreement between the psychologist and the attorney on the order in which the findings will be presented, on what questions will be asked, and on what the psychologist's answers will be. It is also helpful to review likely cross-examination questions so that the psychologist can indicate what the answers would be.

The credibility of the psychologist in the courtroom will depend on several factors. The first of these is credentials: the psychologist should provide the attorney with a curriculum vitae, which the attorney can use when presenting the psychologist's qualifications. The credibility of the psychologist will also depend on courtroom demeanor. The psychologist on the witness stand must remember that the cross-examining attorney is only doing a job when questioning the credibility of the psychologist and of the findings. The cross-examination is not a personal attack, though if one loses perspective, it is easy to feel personally attacked. Also, the courtroom situation often is not as formal as expected, and the judge is usually helpful to an expert witness. In giving testimony, the psychologist should not hesitate to say that he or she did not understand the question or does not know the answer, or that there is insufficient information to answer the question.

FORENSIC TREATMENT

Forensic treatment covers as wide a range of cases as forensic evaluation. In criminal cases, treatment may consist of therapy focused on returning an incompetent individual to competency, or it may provide emotional support to the person who must face imprisonment. Treatment in criminal cases sometimes includes therapy focused on personality problems or on aggressive or sexual behavior, either while the individual is incarcerated or when outpatient therapy is required as a condition of probation or parole. Treatment of offenders requires special knowledge about the criminal justice system, the nature and the effects of the prison environment, the probation-parole system, and the personality characteristics and/or behavior frequently observed in offenders. Group therapy or behavioral therapy techniques are often valuable in treating sexual offenders, offenders with alcohol problems, and others.

In a civil damage situation, treatment may consist of insight-oriented or supportive psychotherapy. In addition, special methods such as behavior therapy, biofeedback, or cognitive therapy may be used to treat anxieties, phobias, depression, or cognitive deficits. The therapist must be aware that testimony may be required in court, and this may at times influence both the mental status of the client and the course of therapy. Often in such cases the therapist will find the legal situation to be at odds with the therapeutic situation. For example, it is often therapeutic for a patient who has been unable to work to return to work as soon as possible. However, this is often inconsistent with the approach being taken by the attorney. In such cases, the therapist has a responsibility to make the patient and the attorney aware of the recommendations, but the final decision as to whether to proceed on those recommendations lies with the patient.

In the child custody situation, treatment is often ordered by the court either to avoid full custody litigation or as part of the resolution of the conflict. The focus of treatment is to help the child make a positive adjustment, and this, of course, requires treatment of the child. However, treatment of the parents is almost always required as well. The treatment of the parents focuses on such issues as communication processes in dealing with the child to enhance co-parenting, unconscious or conscious derogation of the other parent to the child, and resolution of conflicts between the parents. Conflicts often arise over visitation issues, so that the child becomes the focal point of overt conflict between the parents. Resolving such issues often requires joint sessions with the parents which, though often explosive, may be necessary and productive.

RESEARCH IN FORENSIC PSYCHOLOGY

Many of the questions asked of the forensic psychologist require only a description of the present status of an individual. But other questions make an explicit or implicit request for a prediction of future behavior. For example, the answers to such questions as the probability of future dangerous behavior, response to treatment, or the adjustment of a child under various possible living situations require not only thorough clinical evaluation, but a knowledge of relevant research. The research may often reveal that clinical lore is incorrect. The state of the art is such that it is often difficult to support a clinical opinion within the framework of available research findings. It is therefore incumbent on the forensic psychologist to be both the recipient and the provider of research on these questions. The psychologist may not be called upon to provide research support for clinically based opinions, but should be prepared to do so if necessary.

The forensic psychologist must keep abreast of new information that emerges from research. Such effort, along with up-to-date knowledge of the law and modifications of the law by new cases, provides a perspective which, when combined with a thorough clinical approach, allows the forensic psychologist to be of greatest service to the legal system.

REFERENCES

Bronstein, D. A. (1999). *Law for the expert witness.* Boca Raton: CRC Press.

Ceci, S. & Bruck, M. (1995). *Jeopardy in the courtroom, a scientific analysis of children's testimony.* Washington DC; American Psychological Association.

Hall, H. V. (1996). *Lethal violence 2000.* Kamuela, HI: Pacific Institute for the Study of Conflict and Aggression.

Sweet, J. J. (1999). *Forensic neuropsychology.* Lisse, The Netherlands: Swets & Zeitlinger.

G. COOKE
Private Practice, Plymouth Meeting, PA

EXPERT TESTIMONY
EYEWITNESS TESTIMONY
FORENSIC PSYCHOLOGY
PSYCHOLOGY AND THE LAW

FORENSIC PSYCHOLOGY

Forensic psychology refers to the burgeoning field in which psychology and law share interests. While called "psycho-legal studies," "psychology and law," or "criminal and legal psychology," among other terms, forensic psychology encompasses three basic and overlapping areas of collaboration between psychology and law. These are psychology in the law, psychology and the law, and psychology by the law.

Psychology in the law refers to the ways that psychology has been used by the law to solve problems. Traditionally these problems include determining sanity, assessing competency in both civil court (e.g., assessing the ability to take care of one's affairs or providing child custody recommendations in divorce proceedings) and criminal matters (e.g., the ability to defend oneself at trial or the modification of sentencing upon conviction), classifying prisoners' risks in determining level of custody, assessing whether educational and employment practices are discriminatory, determining disability, recommending probation and parole suitability, and assisting in child custody determinations. When people think about psychologists in forensic matters, they are typically considering how psychologists work in the law.

While psychologists have traditionally testified on questions involving the above topics, as forensic psychology has grown, novel applications of psychological expertise have developed. For example, in determining whether a company infringed upon another company's trademark when advertising their logo, a cognitive psychologist's testimony would be most helpful in seeing whether targeted consumers would show trademark confusion. When determining whether a highway sign was appropriately placed so drivers could process information, an experimental psychologist would be most helpful. Psychologists assess community attitudes in determining whether a fair trial can be conducted, and they measure juror attitudes in helping attorneys select jurors during *voir dire*. An attorney might use psychologists to conduct focus groups to see how a jury might consider different legal arguments when confronting the facts of a case. These innovative applications of psychology are helping fuel the growth in this area of forensic psychology.

Psychology of the law is centered on research about legal issues and how the law functions. For example, psychologists have determined that the usual way of conducting lineups (that is, the simultaneous display of six people for an eyewitness to view) is inferior to the sequential lineup, in which the eyewitness makes individual judgments about one person at a time in making an identification. This results in fewer errors with no loss of accuracy detecting the guilty parties. Psychologists have also studied how people view privacy. While the law will recognize that anyone in a home, including a person painting the house or repairing a refrigerator, may grant entry to a police officer, most people think that only the owner or renter can grant entry and allow seizure of items the police may want. Interestingly, the police typically view privacy, not as the law regards, but as citizens think.

Psychology of the law involves studying the decision-making processes of litigants (e.g., should I sue, and should I settle?), criminals (e.g., what makes a target vulnerable?), victims (e.g., have I been the victim of a crime and is it worth pressing charges?), police (e.g., should I ticket or arrest this person?), prosecutors (e.g., is this crime worth prosecuting?), judges and juries (e.g., determining liability in civil cases and guilt in criminal cases, and setting awards or sentences), and corrections (e.g., what degree of security is needed for this convict, and when should parole be granted?). Recent innovative research includes examination of how jury instructions affect awards in tort cases. If the results of this research are applied, then we may not need legislatures to reform tort law. Psychology of the law concerns applying behavioral research strategies to legal phenomena in order to increase the administration of justice in our society.

Psychology by the law refers to the laws, statutes, regulations, and ordinances that affect the practice of psychology. The psychologist who teaches must be aware of organizational procedures for handling such matters as student cheating, so the student receives a fair hearing, and must know the proper way to recruit research participants. Recently, the privacy of research data has come under attack, so that psychologists conducting research need to know what they can or cannot promise in terms of the confidentiality of data gathered in research. The psychologist in practice needs to know about licensing and about confidentiality and privilege, as well as understanding the limits of each of these (e.g., most states have mandatory child abuse reporting statutes and require warning a third party of a patient's homicidal threats if such threats present an imminent danger to an identifiable third party). Psychologists who hire other professionals and staff need to know about employment and personnel law, and if services are rendered to the public, psychologists need to provide reasonable accommodations to people with disabilities.

Each of these three areas has grown explosively in recent years. The growth in the subscriptions to psychology journals, the popularity of forensic psychology forensic workshops, the development of forensic psychology graduate programs, the diplomate in forensic psychology and the publication of the second edition of *The Handbook of Forensic Psychology* (Hess and Weiner, 1999) are signs of the interest in this area.

REFERENCES

Hess, A. K., & Weiner, I. B. (1999). *The handbook of forensic psychology, second edition.* New York: John Wiley & Sons, Inc.

A. K. HESS
Auburn University at Montgomery

EXPERT TESTIMONY
FORENSIC PSYCHOLOGISTS: ROLES AND ACTIVITIES
PSYCHOLOGY AND THE LAW

FORGETTING

Forgetting is the loss of information from any point in the memory process or memory system. James in *Principles of Psychology* suggested that in real life, in spite of occasional surprises, most of what happens is actually forgotten. Bartlett in *Remembering* indicated that memory was hardly ever exact.

Forgetting occurs because information is lost from, or in the process of, memory storage. Baddeley in *The Psychology of Memory* outlined and described many theories of forgetting, including Freud's ideas based on the concept of repression; Gestalt trace theory; trace decay theory; and displacement and interference theories. The latter theories, according to Crowder in *Principles of Learning and Memory,* are the most comprehensive theoretical systems in the field of human learning and memory. Summaries of those theories are given by Underwood (1957) and Postman and Underwood (1973).

Ebbinghaus in *Memory* (1885/1964) described three major theories of forgetting: one in which the earlier images are more overlaid and covered by later ones; a second in which the persisting images suffer changes; and a third in which the images crumble into parts, with a resultant loss of separate components instead of general obscuration.

Different methods of learning and memory measurement have been used to evaluate the amount and/or rate of forgetting. Ebbinghaus used the number of trials to relearn items as a percentage of the number of trials required to learn the material originally. The difference between this percentage and 100% was called the rate of forgetting. Crowder indicated that the assessment of forgetting by a cognitive stage analysis tries to separate information that is lost during acquisition, retention, or retrieval processes. Application of this stage analysis to losses of memory or forgetting during amnesia has not isolated the loss to only one stage or supported a single theory of forgetting. Furthermore, impaired memory performance or forgetting during aging is sometimes attributed to slower or imperfect acquisition, or on the other hand, to losses in retrieval. In summary, forgetting is the rule, not the exception; theoretical approaches have produced research results which only in part explain the losses from memory.

REFERENCES

Baddeley, A. D. (1976). *The psychology of memory.* New York: Basic Books.

Bartlett, F. C. (1932). *Remembering: A study in experimental and social psychology.* Cambridge, England: Cambridge University Press.

Crowder, R. G. (1976). *Principles of learning and memory.* Hillsdale, NJ: Erlbaum.

Ebbinghaus, H. (1964). *Memory: A contribution to experimental psychology.* New York: Dover. (Original work published 1885)

James, W. (1950). *The principles of psychology.* New York: Dover. (Original work published 1894)

Postman, L., & Underwood, B. J. (1973). Critical issues in interference theory. *Memory and Cognition, 1,* 19–40.

Underwood, B. J. (1957). Interference and forgetting. *Psychological Review, 64,* 49–60.

SUGGESTED READING

Craik, F. I. M. (1979). Human memory. In M. R. Rosenszweig & L. W. Porter (Eds.), *Annual review of psychology* (Vol. 30). Palo Alto, CA: Annual Reviews.

N. S. Anderson
University of Maryland

ATTENTION
MEMORY
SHORT-TERM MEMORY

FORM/SHAPE PERCEPTION

Form/shape perception refers to how figure (as distinct from background) information is specified so that object recognition and shape matching are possible and object-oriented actions can be made accurately. Generally, the terms "form" and "shape" are used synonymously; here, the term "shape" will be used to refer to both form and shape. Shape information is available from vision and touch, although most research has focused on shape perception in vision.

As shape can readily be seen in monochrome line drawings and silhouettes, shape can be established without reference to color, motion, or depth information. Consequently, most research on shape perception has concentrated on how shape can be computed from edge-based stimuli. However, it is important to know that shape can also be computed from patterns of motion (shape-from-motion) by using Gestalt principles such as common fate (Johansson, 1973). Given certain constraints, shape can also be perceived from shadow (e.g., Ramachandran, 1988). Therefore, how we perceive shape in the real world will be determined from at least three sources of visual information: edge, movement, and shadow.

COGNITIVE PROCESSES

Processes of shape representation are usually thought to operate in a bottom-up or data-driven fashion (e.g., Marr, 1982; Biederman, 1987). Particular attention has been given to understanding whether shapes are processed as global entities or broken down into parts and shape constancy.

Although some have claimed that the global aspects of a shape are most important for understanding its structure (e.g., Cave and Kosslyn, 1993), most authors believe that shapes are usually described in terms of parts and the relationships among parts. Specifying what the constituent parts' shapes are has been a theoretical challenge. Some authors have suggested a role for stored primitives or templates (Marr, 1982; Biederman, 1987), while others have suggested that parts are computed on-line using physical properties of the image (Hoffman & Richards, 1985). The weight of evidence is currently in favor of the latter approach with segmentation between parts being made at boundary cusps. The rule describing the places where shapes are divided into parts is called the minima rule (see Hoffman & Richards, 1985).

The representations of three-dimensional shapes must exhibit constancy such that their perceived shapes do not change with viewpoint. The mechanisms through which shape constancy is achieved have been the subject of intensive research. Various computational schemes have been proposed. Some schemes rely, for example, on global computations, whereby objects are described with reference to their principle axes (e.g., Marr, 1982); while others suggest the information specifying constancy is directly available in image features (e.g., Biederman, 1987). In the latter case, these aspects of images are described as an object's non-accidental properties, and they allow a single interpretation to be placed on an object irrespective of its current position with respect to a viewer.

Not all shape processing can be bottom-up, as recent studies have shown that object recognition affects figure-ground segmentation (e.g., Peterson & Gibson, 1991) and the perception of ambiguous and incomplete figures (Rock, 1983). Therefore, top-down processing is also likely to be critical for shape perception. However, exactly which top-down information is used in shape perception and the mechanisms through which this information is exploited remain unknown.

NEUROPSYCHOLOGY OF SHAPE PERCEPTION

Patients exhibiting failure to specify shape information are said to suffer from apperceptive agnosia. In such cases, sensory loss either is absent or is unable to account for their perceptual loss. It is also critical for the diagnosis of apperceptive agnosia that patients are shown to have retained stored knowledge of object form and function. The classic test of shape perception is the Efron test (Efron, 1968). In the Efron test, patients must judge whether two orthogonally oriented rectangles, matched for overall flux (luminance and area), have the same or different dimensions. Failure on this test can be due only to an inability to compute shape information. The type and locus of brain damage usually considered sufficient to produce apperceptive agnosia is diffuse injury to the parieto-occipital cortex of the right hemisphere.

The failure to perceive shape consciously does not necessarily imply that shape is not computed. There is good evidence that the conscious experience of shape is doubly dissociated from the ability to reach and grasp appropriately for objects. Patients with optic ataxia cannot reach and grasp objects, but they can report accurately the shape of a stimulus along with the shape's location, size, and orientation (Perenin & Vighetto, 1988); patients with visual form agnosia, on the other hand, cannot report accurately the shape, size, or orientation of an object. Nevertheless, they can reach and grasp for objects automatically and without error (Goodale, Milner, Jakobsen, & Carey, 1991). Therefore, a failure to perceive shape consciously does not mean that it has not been processed.

NEUROANATOMY OF SHAPE PERCEPTION

The cortical loci responsible for shape analysis have also been studied using functional imaging. The critical design for such a study must ensure that shape analysis is isolated from feature processing and activation of semantic memory, using a subtractive methodology (see Peterson, Fox, Snyder, & Raichle, 1990). In studies in which these conditions have been met, the cortical areas activated only during shape analysis are on the inferolateral surface of the brain near the junction of occipital and temporal lobes in both the right and left hemispheres (e.g., Kanwisher, Woods, Iacoboni, & Mazziotta, 1997).

In conclusion, shape perception refers to a complex set of processes through which two- and three-dimensioinal figures come to be represented in order that recognition, matching, and actions can be supported. These processes are mostly driven by bottom-up considerations such that part decomposition and shape constancy can be achieved. However, shape processing is also affected by top-down factors, as evidenced in their role in figure-ground segmentation and the perception of ambiguous figures. Shape processing can break down following brain damage to posterior regions of the right hemisphere, and the awareness of shape can be lost even if shape processing still allows accurate grasping of objects. Functional imaging studies concur with the studies of brain-damaged patients in highlighting the role of the posterior cortex in shape perception, but suggest a role for both the right and left hemispheres.

REFERENCES

Biederman, I. (1987). Recognition-by-components: A theory of human image understanding. *Psychological Review, 94,* 115–147.

Cave, C. B., Kosslyn, S. M. (1993). The role of parts and spatial relations in identification. *Perception, 22,* 229–248.

Efron, R. (1968). What is perception? *Boston Studies in Philosophy of Science, 4,* 137–173.

Goodale, M. A., Milner, A. D., Jakobsen, L. S., & Carey, D. P. (1991). A neurological dissociation between perceiving objects and grasping them. *Nature, 349,* 154–156.

Hoffman, D. D., & Richards, W. A. (1985). Parts of recognition. *Cognition, 18,* 65–96.

Johansson, G. (1973). Visual perception of biological motion and a model for its analysis. *Perception and Psychophysics, 14,* 210–211.

Kanwisher, N., Woods, R. P., Iacoboni, M., & Mazziotta, J. C. (1997). A locus in human extrastriate cortex for visual shape analysis. *Journal of Cognitive Neuroscience, 9,* 133–142.

Marr, D. (1982). *Vision.* San Francisco: Freeman.

Perenin, M-T., & Vighetto, A. (1988). Optic ataxia: A specific disruption in visuomotor mechanisms. *Brain, 111,* 643–674.

Peterson, S. E., Fox, P. T., Snyder, A. Z., & Raichle, M. E. (1990). Activation of extrastriate and frontal cortices by visual words and word-like stimuli. *Science, 249,* 1041–1044.

Ramachandran, V. S. (1988). The perception of shape from shading. *Nature, 331,* 163–166.

Rock, I. (1983). *The logic of perception.* Cambridge, MA: MIT Press.

SUGGESTED READING

Peterson, M. A., & Gibson, B. S. (1991). The initial organization of figure-ground relationships: Contributions from shape recognition processes. *Bulletin of the Psychonomic Society, 29*(3), 199–202.

N. DONNELLY
University of Southampton, U.K.

FOWLER, RAYMOND D.

Raymond D. Fowler is executive vice president and chief executive officer of the American Psychological Association (APA). Founded in 1892, APA is the primary scientific and professional association for psychologists in the United States. With over 155,000 members and affiliates, APA is the largest and oldest of the world's psychological societies. It is a major publisher of psychological books and journals. The chief executive officer is responsible for overseeing both the corporate and professional management of the association and for supervising a staff of 500.

Fowler received his PhD in psychology with a specialization in clinical psychology from the Pennsylvania State University in 1957 and joined the faculty of the University of Alabama in Tuscaloosa, where he remained until 1987, when he was appointed professor emeritus. From 1965 to 1983, he served as department chairperson. In 1987, Fowler was appointed professor and head of the psychology department at the University of Tennessee in Knoxville, where he served until June 1989, when he assumed his current position at APA.

Fowler has contributed to the research literature in psychology with over 70 articles, books, chapters, and other publications, especially in the areas of substance abuse, criminal behavior, and personality assessment. He is the recipient of over a dozen research and training grants. He pioneered the development of programs to reduce juvenile delinquency, and the development of classification systems for juvenile justice and prison programs. In recognition of his expertise in the area of criminology, he was appointed in 1976 by Federal District Judge Frank M. Johnson, Jr. to direct a court-ordered prison reform program that involved evaluating every prisoner in the Alabama prison system and developing rehabilitation programs for them.

Fowler is recognized for his work in the area of personality assessment. In the early 1960s, he developed an innovative method of computer interpretation for the Minnesota Multiphasic Personality Inventory. His system was translated into most major European languages, has been used to generate personality reports on almost two million individuals in the United States and abroad, and became the prototype for hundreds of other computer-based systems now used in psychological testing in the United States and abroad.

Fowler has served in a variety of leadership roles in professional psychology. He was president of the Alabama Psychological Association and was a member of Alabama's first psychology licensing board. He served as president of the Southeastern Psychological Association (SEPA) and subsequently as director of the SEPA Workshops Program, which provided continuing education to thousands of psychologists in this country and abroad and has sponsored meetings and conferences between U.S. psychologists and psychologists in other parts of the world. In 1979, he was the first U.S. psychologist invited to visit the Chinese Institute of Psychology in Beijing, and he has returned to China on five occasions to lecture and to lead two joint conferences between U.S. and Chinese psychologists.

Fowler has been actively involved in the American Psychological Association since 1965, and has served as a member or liaison to most of APA's major boards and committees. In 1978, he was elected president of the Division of Consulting Psychology. He was elected three times to the APA council of representatives and twice to the board of directors, and served as treasurer from 1983 to 1987. In 1988, he served as the 97th president of APA.

Fowler's distinction in psychology has been recognized by a number of awards: Award for Outstanding Contributions to Academic Psychology (Alabama Psychological Association, 1979); Southeastern Psychological Association Distinguished Speaker (1982, 1987); and Pennsylvania State University Alumni Fellow (Life Appointment). In 1988, he received the Significant MMPI Contribution Award from the University of Minnesota, and in 1989, he was the first recipient of the Raymond D. Fowler Award for Contribution to the Professional Development of Students, an annual award named in his honor by the APA Graduate Students Association. Fowler is a diplomate of the American Board of Professional Psychology and a distinguished practitioner of the National Academies of Practice.

He has been elected fellow of 23 APA divisions (General, Teaching, Behavioral Neuroscience and Comparative Psychology, Clinical, Consulting, School Psychology, Counseling, Psychologists in Public Service, Adult Development and Aging, Experimental Analysis of Behavior, History of Psychology, Community, Psychotherapy, State Psychological Affairs, Humanistic, Health, American Psychology-Law Society, Independent Practice, Family Psychology, Media Psychology, Exercise and Sport Psychology, Addictions, and International Psychology). He is also a fellow of the Society for Personality Assessment. He is a member for Psi Chi, the psychology honorary society, and served as a member of Phi Kappa Phi (scholastic honorary), Sigma Xi (scientific honorary), and Omicron Delta Kappa (leadership honorary).

At the state and national level, Fowler has been a member of the National Advisory Committee on Alcoholism of the Department of Health, Education and Welfare. He was a task force member of the President's Commission on Mental Health, and was an invited participant to the White House Conference on Health and the National Conference on Criminal Justice Standards and Goals. He has been a consultant to the director of the Law Enforcement Assistance Administration, the Veterans Administration, and the National Institute of Alcohol Abuse and Alcoholism.

In addition to his service to psychology organizations, Fowler has been a chapter president of the American Association of University Professors, chairperson of the Southern School of Alcohol Studies, and a director of the Alcohol and Drug Problems Association of North America. From 1965 to 1968 he was vice president of the Council on Human Relations, the first biracial human rights group in Alabama. He has testified extensively in civil rights– and

mental health–related court cases, and he served as a special consultant to the estate of the late Howard R. Hughes, Jr.

Fowler is married to Sandra Mumford Fowler, an organizational psychologist who consults with government and business organizations on cross-cultural issues and adaptation to overseas living. They live in Washington, DC, and have five adult children and three grandchildren.

STAFF

FRAGILE X SYNDROME

Fragile X [fra(X)] is a chromosomal abnormality that is the most common heritable cause, and second only to Down syndrome as a genetically-based cause, of mental retardation. (Down syndrome generally arises through nondisjunction of chromosome pair 21 during meiosis and is thus genetic but not inherited.) Fra(X) was little known until the 1980s, when a new technique facilitated its identification; since then it has been the topic of thousands of research articles. Based on a weak or fragile site on the X chromosome, fra(X) is sex-linked and thus expressed more frequently in males. It is the only one of the more than 50 X-linked disorders associated with mental retardation that occurs frequently (e.g., Brown, et al., 1986) and is largely responsible for the higher prevalence of mental retardation in males than females. Although estimates vary across studies, incidence is about 1 in 1500 in males and 1 in 2000 in females (Fryns, 1990). Fragile X may account for over five percent of retarded males and about 0.3 percent of retarded females (Jones, 1997). Of males with mental retardation serious enough to require extensive support, 6 to 14 percent have fra(X), as do three to six percent of individuals with autism (Batshaw, 1997). Individuals with mental retardation of unknown cause are now routinely screened for fra(X). With the discovery of the responsible gene, described below, DNA testing has become available, which is both more effective and less expensive than the previous cytogenetic testing (Hagerman & Lampe, 1999). DNA testing identifies not only affected individuals, but also carriers, facilitating genetic counseling.

HISTORY

From the beginning of the twentieth century, researchers have noted a considerable excess of males, frequently about 25 percent, with mental retardation. Martin and Bell in 1943, and others after them, described families in which mental retardation was inherited in an X-linked pattern. Although Lubs first described the fragile X site in 1969, his description drew little interest until Sutherland (1977) reported that some fragile sites were expressed only if lymphocytes were grown in a culture medium that lacked folic acid. The discovery of folic-acid sensitivity of fra(X) and some other fragile sites led to more accurate diagnosis, which in turn led to the discovery of the high incidence of fra(X) and an exponential growth of interest generally in X-linked mental retardation (e.g., Fryns, 1990; Sutherland & Hecht, 1985). Retesting has indicated a fra(X) basis for the retardation in the family studied by Martin and Bell, and Martin-Bell Syndrome is a term occasionally used instead of Fragile X.

GENETICS OF FRA(X)

Fra(X) is genetically unusual in several ways. In typical X-linked disorders, a carrier female who expresses no characteristics of the disorder passes the defective gene, on average, to half of her children. Of those children who inherit the defective gene, males will express any effects, whereas females will be unaffected but carriers. In fra(X), however, the situation is more complicated. Heterozygotic (carrier) females, who have one normal X chromosome and one with the fragile site, may manifest some fra(X) characteristics, including impaired intelligence and specific learning disabilities. About 20 percent of males who inherit the fragile site show no apparent physical or psychological effects and no evidence of fragility. They do, however, pass the X chromosome on to their daughters who may have affected sons (Brown, 1990). As a further complication, repeated cytogenetic testing fails to reveal the fragile site in more than 50 percent of unaffected carrier females.

Since the discovery of the underlying mutated FMR1 gene in 1991, research has clarified the basis and inheritance patterns of fra(X) and its precursors. The description that follows is closely modeled after Batshaw's (1997) exposition. Initially, the specific defective gene, the FMR1 gene (fragile X mental retardation gene) was found in all males who expressed the fra(X) syndrome. The defective gene was later found to interfere with a particular protein apparently important in brain development. Normally, the genetic code shows some perseveration, or repetition in three nucleotide base pairs. These triplet repeats may expand abnormally into fragile sites, which occur on many chromosomes. The expansion of the triplet repeat is likely to increase over generations. The fragile X site (FRAXA) normally contains some 6 to 50 repeats of the cytosine-guanine-guanine (CGG) triplet base pair sequence. Asymptomatic transmitting males and carrier females have 50 to 90 and 50 to 200 CGG repeats, respectively; do not show a fragile X site; and are said to have a premutation. Such premutations are relatively common, occurring in about 1 in 500 males and 1 in 250 females. Males and females who have the full mutation of 200 to 3000 CGG fragile X repeats have observable fragile X sites and show various symptoms. All males and 50 percent of females will show mental retardation.

The increased expansion of the CGG repeats over successive generations leads to increased fra(X) symptomatology over the same generations. Premutations of more than 100 CGG repeats almost always expand into full mutation range in the next generation. Transmitting males usually have less than 100 CGG repeats, so their daughters will tend also to have premutations and be asymptomatic. Since these daughters will likely have CGG repeats expanded into the 90 to 200 range, their male and female offspring who inherit the fra(X) site are likely to have CGG repeats of over 1000. That, of course, is in the full mutation range, and they will display fra(X) symptoms. As Batshaw (1997, p. 379) observed, "Thus, transmitting males tend to have grandchildren manifesting fragile X syndrome, a very unusual pattern for an X-linked disorder!"

CHARACTERISTICS OF AFFECTED MALES

About two-thirds of affected adult males show a "clinical triad": (a) moderate to severe mental retardation; (b) characteristic craniofacial features, including large forehead, protruding chin, coarse facial features, long face, macrocephaly, and elongated ears; and, (c) large testes (macroorchidism; e.g., Curfs, Wiegers, & Fryns, 1990; Fryns, 1990; Sutherland & Hecht, 1985). However, affected individuals show such a variety of characteristics that diagnosis can firmly be based only on cytogenetic analysis. Females and prepubertal males are even more variable. Although most males show an "overgrowth syndrome" from birth, with head size, fontanel, and body measurements exceeding the 97th percentile, macroorchidism and craniofacial features are much less distinct in prepubertal boys (Curfs et al., 1990). The following summary of characteristics of affected individuals is based on information in Batshaw (1997), Bregman, Dykens, Watson, Ort, and Leckman (1987), Brown et al. (1986), Curfs et al. (1990), Dykens and Leckman (1990), Fryns (1990), and Hagerman (1990).

Physical Features

In addition to the characteristic craniofacial features, macroorchidism, and overgrowth described above, males with fra(X) may show a variety of other features, such as hyperextensible joints, high arched palate, mitral valve prolapse (a form of heart murmur), flat feet, scoliosis, and low muscle tone. Female carriers, particularly those with subnormal intelligence, may also show facial features, including high broad forehead and long face, and hyperextensibility.

Cognitive Features

Approximately 95 percent of affected males have mild to profound mental retardation; a small percentage is in the low normal range of intelligence. Males frequently show a decline in intelligence quotient, but not absolute intelligence, with age. Affected males have particular difficulty with sequential processing and short-term memory for information presented serially, performing poorly on tasks requiring recall of series of items or imitation of a series of motor movements. This deficit in sequential processing differentiates fra(X) individuals from those with other forms of mental retardation (Zigler & Hodapp, 1991). Affected males perform relatively well on tasks requiring simultaneous processing and integration, such as block design. Auditory memory and reception is poor.

Language

About 95 percent of affected males show some form of communication disorder. Language development in general is delayed beyond their mental retardation. Additionally, specific problems such as perseverations, repetitions, echolalia, cluttered speech, and dysfluencies are often shown, some of which may stem from general deficits in sequential processing. Word-finding problems and irrelevant associations are exacerbated by anxiety.

Behavioral Characteristics

About 75 percent show serious behavior problems, including ADHD (hyperactivity and attention deficits), stereotyped self-stimulatory behaviors, and aggression. About 60 percent show some degree of autistic features, discussed in a separate section below, and 20 percent have seizures. The combination of features leads many to be diagnosed with pervasive developmental disorder (Batshaw, 1997). Many affected individuals are also socially withdrawn, show gaze aversion, and engage in self-injurious behavior, particularly self-biting.

CHARACTERISTICS OF AFFECTED FEMALES

About 70 percent of carrier females show no clear physical, cognitive, or behavioral problems. The remaining 30 percent show a variety of symptoms, less severe than in males. About 10 percent show mild mental retardation, 20 percent show learning disabilities, 30 percent show communication problems, and 30 percent show emotional disturbances. Frequent learning disabilities include problems in visual-spatial skills, executive function, and simultaneous processing. Language problems, similar to males, include cluttered and perseverative speech. Some evidence suggests that, unlike males, intelligence quotient of affected carrier females increases with age.

RELATIONSHIP TO AUTISM

Many of the behavioral characteristics of fra(X), including mental retardation, gaze aversion, self-stimulation, and echolalia, are similar to those of autism. Indeed, many studies report fra(X) in males, but not females, diagnosed with autism. For example, in a fairly large sample study of autistic children, Blomquist and colleagues (1985) identified fragile X in 13 of 83 boys (16%) but in none of 19 girls. More recently, Bailey and colleagues (1998) found that 14 of 57 boys with fra(X) scored above the criterion for autism on the Childhood Autism Rating Scale (CARS). The overlap is sufficient that boys diagnosed with autism are now routinely screened for fra(X). However, the disorders appear to be separate and that the overlapping of symptoms implies neither that the disorders are the same or that they have a common causal basis. Twelve of Bailey and colleagues' (1998) 14 autistic fra(X) boys were mildly or moderately autistic, suggesting that severe autism rarely occurs with fra(X). More directly, a recent molecular genetic study (Klauck et al., 1997) of a large sample of autistic boys found no true association between fra(X) and autism and that the Xq27.3 fra(X) site is not causal for autism.

TREATMENT

Due to the variety and variation in problems exhibited by those with fra(X), a team approach is recommended for treatment (e.g., Hagerman, 1990; Hagerman & Lampe, 1999). The information in this section is largely based on Hagerman and Lampe (1999); that volume should be seen for more detail.

Medical Treatment

Pharmacological treatment is frequently used for behavioral problems. Stimulant medications, clonidine, and folic acid are commonly used to reduce ADHD symptoms and temper tantrums. Owing to differential response to medications and dosages, no one drug regimen is seen as appropriate. Folic acid is an often-used remedy that has effects similar to those of mild stimulants, and other medications may often be more effective. Antiseizure medications may be effective in controlling not only seizures but also mood swings and aggression. Given the common side effects of such medications, however, their use must be carefully monitored. Among the most effective treatments for mood swings, anxiety, and aggression in fra(X) individuals are the SSRIs, which also have the benefit of relatively slight side effects.

Therapeutic and Educational Interventions

Given the variety of speech problems which fra(X) children commonly manifest, speech/language therapy is almost always helpful. Physical and occupational therapy can help overcome motor and other dysfunctions. Fra(X) children respond well to computer-assisted instruction that provides immediate and multimodal feedback. Psychological approaches are of importance in dealing with fra(X) for at least two reasons (Curfs et al., 1990): (1) The diffuse and variable physical effects of fra(X) in children place additional significance on the role of psychological assessment in identifying potentially fra(X) children for DNA testing; and (2) Cognitive characteristics of those with fra(X) have important implications for treatment and educational programs. Of particular importance are behavioral therapy programs for managing problem behaviors.

THEORETICAL IMPLICATIONS

The clear distinction between characteristics of those with fra(X) and those with Down syndrome indicates heterogeneity among groups with organic retardation and suggests that they cannot be accurately characterized as a single type (e.g., Burack, Hodapp, & Zigler, 1988; Dykens & Leckman, 1990; Zigler & Hodapp, 1991).

Among several reviews of information on fragile X are Batshaw (1997), Davies (1990), and Hagerman and Lampe (1999). Numerous websites are available. One site particularly useful for genetic information is www3.ncbi.nlm.nih.gov:80/htbin-post/Omim/dispmim?309550.

REFERENCES

Bailey, D. B. Jr., Mesibov, G. B., Hatton, D. D., Clark, R. D., Roberts, J. E., & Mayhew, L. (1998). Autistic behavior in young boys with fragile X syndrome. *Journal of Autism and Developmental Disorders, 28,* 499–508.

Batshaw, M. L. (1997). Fragile X syndrome. In M. L. Batshaw (Ed.), *Children with disabilities* (4th ed. pp. 377–388). Baltimore: Brookes.

Blomquist, H. K., Bohman, M., Edvinsson, S. O., Gillberg, C., Gustavson, K.-H., Holmgren, G., & Wahlstrom, J. (1985). Frequency of the fragile X syndrome in infantile autism: A Swedish multicenter study. *Clinical Genetics, 27,* 113–117.

Bregman, J. D., Dykens, E., Watson, M., Ort, S. I., & Leckman, J. F. (1987). Fragile-X syndrome: Variability of phenotypic expression. *Journal of the American Academy of Child and Adolescent Psychiatry, 26,* 463–471.

Brown, W. T. (1990). Invited editorial: The fragile X: Progress toward solving the puzzle. *American Journal of Human Genetics, 47,* 175–180.

Brown, W. T., Jenkins, E. C., Krawczun, M. S., Wisniewski, K., Rudelli, R., Cohen, I. R., Fisch, G., Wolf-Schein, E., Miezejeski, C., & Dobkin, C. (1986). The fragile X syndrome. In H. M. Wisniewski & D. A. Snider (Eds.), Mental retardation, research, education, and technology transfer (pp. 129–149). *Annals of the New York Academy of Sciences, 477.*

Burack, J. A., Hodapp, R. M., & Zigler, E. (1988). Issues in the classification of mental retardation: Differentiating among organic etiologies. *Journal of Child Psychology and Psychiatry, 29,* 765–779.

Curfs, L. M. G., Wiegers, A. M., & Fryns, J. P. (1990). Fragile-X syndrome: A review. *Brain Dysfunction, 3,* 1–8.

Davies, K. E. (Ed.). (1990). *The fragile X syndrome.* Oxford, UK: Oxford University Press.

Dykens, E., & Leckman, J. (1990). Developmental issues in fragile X syndrome. In R. M. Hodapp, J. A. Burack, & E. Zigler (Eds.), *Issues in the developmental approach to mental retardation* (pp. 226–245). Cambridge, UK: Cambridge University Press.

Fryns, J.-P. (1990). X-linked mental retardation and the fragile X syndrome: A clinical approach. In K. E. Davies (Ed.), *The fragile X syndrome* (pp. 1–39). Oxford, UK: Oxford University Press.

Hagerman, R. (1990). Behaviour and treatment of the fragile X syndrome. In K. E. Davies (Ed.), *The fragile X syndrome* (pp. 66–75). Oxford, UK: Oxford University Press.

Hagerman, R. J., & Lampe, M. E. (1999). Fragile X syndrome. In S. Goldstein & C. R. Reynolds (Eds.), *Handbook of Neurodevelopmental and Genetic Disorders of Children* (pp. 298–316). New York: Guilford.

Jones, K. L. (1997). *Smith's recognizable patterns of human malformation* (5th ed.) Philadelphia: Saunders.

Klauck, S. M., Munstermann, E., Bieber-Martig, B., Ruhl, D., Lisch, S., Schmotzer, G., Poustka, A., & Poustka, F. (1997). Molecular genetic analysis of the FRM-1 gene in a large collection of autistic patients. *Human Genetics, 100,* 224–229.

Lubs, H. A. (1969). A marker X chromosome. *American Journal of Human Genetics, 21,* 231–244.

Martin, J. P., & Bell, J. (1943). A pedigree of mental defect showing sex-linkage. *Journal of Neurology, Neurosurgery, and Psychiatry, 6,* 154–157.

Sutherland, G. R. (1977). Fragile sites on human chromosomes: Demonstration of their dependence on the type of tissue culture medium. *Science, 197,* 265–266.

Sutherland, G. R., & Hecht, F. (1985). *Fragile sites on human chromosomes.* New York: Oxford University Press.

Zigler, E., & Hodapp, R. M. (1991). Behavioral functioning in individuals with mental retardation. *Annual Review of Psychology, 42,* 29–50.

R. T. Brown
University of North Carolina, Wilmington

CHROMOSOME DISODERS
MENTAL RETARDATION

FRANCE, PSYCHOLOGY IN

It is difficult to present in a limited space an accurate picture of current psychology in France, and so the main focus here will be on the research topics pursued at some of the French laboratories of psychology or psycho-physiology. It is hoped thereby to strengthen the links between French researchers and English-speaking researchers. As this choice prevents a detailed description of other aspects of psychology in France, these are introduced briefly in the following.

THE INSTITUTIONS

Teaching of Psychology

Psychology is offered in 28 French universities. After receiving the baccalaureate (the diploma certifying completion of secondary education), students study for at least two years for the *diplôme d'études universitaires généráles* (DEUG) de psychologie, up to one year for the *licence* (bachelor's degree), and up to one year for the *maîtrise* (master's degree). They may then earn, in one year, a *diplôme d'études supérieures spécialisées* oriented toward professional life, or in approximately three years, a *diplôme d'études approfondies,* along with a *doctorat de troisième cycle*. The *doctorat d'Etat* is the highest French degree, and it requires many years of preparation. Up to the bachelor's degree, the greater part of the curriculum is the same for all students. At the master's level, students are divided among the following specialities: clinical psychology, differential psychology, experimental psychology, developmental psychology, pathological psychology, and social psychology.

Research in Psychology

There are laboratories at the universities in which instructors and advanced students pursue research. Other laboratories are called the "Great Institutions," such as the Collège de France, the Ecole Pratique des Hautes Etudes, and the Conservatoire National des Arts et Métiers. Many of these laboratories receive part of their funding from the Centre National de la Recherche Scientifique (CNRS). The involvement of CNRS in French scientific research (notably in psychology) is of three types. It organizes and manages the institutes or laboratories that it has established, and which are its proper concern. It allocates funds to outside laboratories, for the most part university laboratories independent of CNRS administratively, but with which it is associated. And it promotes research undertaken in common by several laboratories (cooperative research programs) and influences on the program that make it possible to provide impetus in well-defined areas.

PROFESSIONAL ACTIVITIES OF PSYCHOLOGISTS

Teaching

Instructors specializing in psychology are found only at the university level. They include assistants, master assistants, and professors. In 1979, there were approximately 500 teachers of psychology and psychophysiology. Part of the teaching is provided by assistants who are employed part-time and are paid by the hour.

Research
Research is carried out by instructors and specialized researchers, most of whom are affiliated with the CNRS. There are approximately 200 researchers in psychology and psychophysiology. The CNRS also employs an approximately equal number of technicians.

Psychology in Education
Some psychologists work in the "crêches," institutions that admit children of preschool age. They take part in detecting problems of development, giving advice to parents, and organizing the activities of the crêche.

School psychologists are generally assigned to primary educational institutions. They identify children presenting a variety of problems and propose appropriate treatment. In general, their function is to promote the adjustment of the students to school life and to make scholastic life better fit the personality of the child. They work closely with teachers and have frequent contact with the families of the students. There are about 2,000 school psychologists in France.

Guidance counselors are not connected with scholastic institutions, but rather with centers of information and guidance. They work in close partnership with schools, especially the colleges, in which the first four years of secondary education take place. They also try to facilitate the adjustment of each child to learning. In addition, they help students and their families to make decisions concerning school and professional placement. There were about 3,000 guidance counselors as of 1982.

Psychology in the Field of Health
Clinical psychologists work in a variety of institutions (hospitals, medicopsychopedagogic centers, institutions for the handicapped, etc.). They serve in many functions, principally diagnosis (with the aid of appropriate psychological examinations) and psychotherapy. In the public sector, these psychologists may be civil servants or may be paid for a period of service. In the private sector, mutual agreements determine the working conditions and compensation.

Psychology in the World of Work
In the area of work, psychologists serve quite diverse functions: selection of workers and employees, recruitment of officials, placement or classification of personnel, participation in training, study of problems relating to communications or conflicts in the company, study of accidents, and ergonomics. If an employee of the company, the business psychologist's position is that of an officer. There are also outside agencies capable of carrying out certain tasks for businesses that call on them.

Other Professional Activities
Psychologists also work with judicial institutions (juvenile delinquency), in the commercial sector (publicity), in opinion polling, and in the army, among other fields.

LA SOCIÉTÉ FRANÇAISE DE PSYCHOLOGIE
The Société Française de Psychologie, founded in 1901, had about 1,450 members as of 1982. It is comprised of nationwide sections that include psychologists in the same specialty, and of regional sections covering psychologists practicing in the same region. Its goals are to promote the study and resolution of theoretical and practical problems to further the progress of psychology and its applications, to maintain among its members the highest level of qualification through exchanges and continuous training, to contribute to public awareness concerning the goals and methods of scientific psychology, and to take a position or become involved in questioning the scientific and professional qualifications of psychologists, as well as their ethics. The Société Française de Psychologie is affiliated with the Union Internationale de Psychologie Scientifique. It hosted the 21st International Congress of Psychology in Paris in 1976. It also publishes a review, *Psychologie Française.*

Publications
Several reviews devoted to psychology are published in France. These include *L'Année Psychologique,* the *Journal de Psychologie, Le Travail Humain,* the *Cahiers de Psychologie Cognitive, Enfance, L'Orientation Scolaire et Professionelle,* and the *Revue de Psychologie Appliquée.* An international review in English, French-Language Psychology, regularly furnishes analyses of French articles and books on psychological topics.

SOME LABORATORIES OF PSYCHOLOGY
The following outlines the research being carried on at just a few of the many psychology laboratories in France; all are associated with CNRS.

Hearing Research Group, Collège de France. Studies of the mechanisms of auditory fatigue; of relations between the nonlinearity of microphonic responses and their fatigability with regard to noise; of the interaction between frequencies at the level of microphonic responses and of neural responses.

Laboratory of Sensory Psychophysiology, Université Pierre et Marie Curie, Paris. Studies of the mechanisms of release and of a new model of oculomotor rhythmicity; of the accessory optical system of birds and nystagmus; of albinism, hypodactyly, and perturbations of the electroretinogram; psychophysical analysis of the visual performance of the pigeon.

Laboratory of Psychophysiology, Université de Paris XI. Research on the neurophysiological mechanisms of memory—cerebral mechanisms of the processing of information previous to its storage and mechanisms conditioning its restitution; electrophysiological study of the process of acquisition in the cat; comparative study of the effects on training of central stimulation of three subcortical structures.

Laboratory of Psychophysiology and Neuroethology, Université Paul Sabatier, Toulouse. General theme—the preparation for action in animal and human behavior: genetic aspects of preparation for action; epigenetic aspects of preparation for action; habituation, cardiac responses, and preparation for action in insects; determination of the preparation for action in insects and in human beings at work.

Laboratory of Psychophysiology, Université de Bordeaux. Behavioral, electrophysiological, neurochemical, and neuroanatomical approach to the role of the hippocampus in the process of training and memorization; amelioration of training capacities several weeks after electrical stimulation of certain aminergic systems; study of the approach and flight responses induced by stimulations of the lateral hypothalamus or of the central gray matter of the midbrain of the mouse.

Laboratory of Psychophysiology, Université de Provence, Marseille. General theme—functional continuity between simple sensory-motor reflexes, automatisms, and cognitive activities: activities of perceptive structuration; models and simulation of networks of neurons; sensory-motor control and adaptive control; proprioception, perception, and regulation of movement in humans; reticulated formation, cerebrum, and motor function; postlesional restoration of motor functions; motor commands and controls; relations between voluntary commands and automatisms.

Neuropsychological and Neurolinguistic Research, Ecole des Hautes Études en Sciences Sociales, Paris. Studies on motor aphasia and verbal behavior in the course of anterior lesions; conductive aphasia and sensory aphasia; study of syntactical and semantic verbal comprehension; disorders in reading and writing; nonverbal communication; disorders of taste; disorders of visual perception; studies of cerebral dominance.

Laboratory of Experimental Psychology, Universite de Paris V and Ecole Pratique des Hautes Études (3ème section). Cognitive development of the child; sensory psychophysics; phonological coding, effects of recency, and memorization by the subject of verbal production; perception and comprehension of language; elementary operations in the visual field; methodological research in experimental psychology; processing of information and the process of control; mechanisms of evaluative judgment; access to repertories; acquisition of reading; automatism and control.

Laboratory of Experimental Psychology, Université des Sciences Sociales, Grenoble. Manual-tactile representation and visual-tactile representation; encoding and retrieval in human memory; genetic and differential aspects of natural thought.

Psychology and Psychopedagogy of Language, Université de Poitiers. Functioning of memory—semantic memory as a generative system, operations in the memory of work; comprehension and production of statements by children; construction and functioning of semantic representations in the comprehension and memorization of texts; perception and language in the situation of communication; activities and training in the school setting.

Study of Learning in Man, Université de Paris VIII. Processing of information in human instrumental conditioning; comparison of phrases and patterns; different attitudes in regard to language; processing, commitment to memory, and conservation of information; comprehension and memorization of texts; identification of concepts and resolution of problems; studies of strategies of processing and retrieval of information.

Laboratory of Differential Psychology, Université de Paris V. Influence of certain environmental factors on the intellectual development of children in the course of elementary education; relationship between structure and functioning in cognitive behaviors; motivations of French-speaking black Africans working in the Paris region; psychosocial development between 12 and 18 years; self-esteem in elementary school students; individual differences in conditioning in humans; genetic etiology of psychoses; the perceptions of the professor in the area of educational objectives; mathematics and psychological development; motivation to pursue higher studies; schooling and guidance of children of migrant workers; clinical operation of judgment; methodology of investigations.

Laboratory of the Neuropsychology of Development, Collège de France. Spontaneous movements in the first two months of life; the parent-child relationship following birth; study of precocious interactions between the newborn and the mother; study of the language of parents in interaction situations; development of exchanges between children during the first two years; child-to-child interrelations from the ethological point of view.

Laboratory of the Psycho-biology of the Child, Ecole Pratique des Hautes Études (3éme section), Paris. Role of visual information in the postural control of the head in the nursling; visual-motor coordination in the appropriation of bidimensional space in the child of school age; the development of intermodal transferences in learning by "modeling"; the role and longterm effects of precocious stimulation; models of psychological development and simultaneous activities in the child; functions of imitative behaviors; ontogenesis of the sensation of taste; study of the sexuality of the adolescent; the development of communication behaviors in the baby.

Laboratory of Genetic Psychology, Université de Paris V. Research on the sign language of the deaf; development of communication; development of memory in the child; functional studies on the ontogenesis of imitation; attitude with regard to marginality and deviation.

Laboratory of Psychology, Université de Provence, Aix-en-Provence. Analysis of the structures of social perceptions; cognitive process related to space; resolution of problems; judgment and evaluation; origin of the cognitive process and functioning of the subject; cognitive origin and functioning; history of the division of mental work; analysis of educative interaction; perception of the school and its partners.

Laboratory of Social Psychology, Université de Paris VII. Risk, anxiety, motor function; intergroup phenomena; general mechanisms of psychosocial action; experimental and quasiexperimental research; methodological, epistemological, and theoretical works; language, subject, sense; theory and analysis of discourse.

Group for the Study of Psychological Incidences of Linguistic Settings and Cultural Complexes, Université Louis Pasteur, Strasbourg. Study of psychological motivations and social functions in the use of the Alsatian dialect, of French, and of German; linguistic settings and cultural complexes outside of France; the teaching of French in the world; notion of a "regional language" in France.

Psychology of Culture, Université de Paris X. Continuity and change in the organization and decoration of living quarters; physiological mechanisms of musical perception and appreciation; the role of oculary movements in the perception of texture; the effects of noise on children at school; preferential choices of simple colors and of color harmonies.

Personalization and Social Change, Université de Toulouse-Le-Mirail. Study of the psychological determinants of behaviors in their cultural interstructure; formation of the cognitive process in connection with the formation of differentiated language according to social class as well as the pedagogies of knowledge; relationships among educational, professional, political, and cultural institutions; regulation of behavior and process of subjectivation.

Laboratory of the Psychology of Work, Ecole Pratique des Hautes Études (3éme section), Paris. Elaboration of a pluralistic model of cognitive functioning permitting study of the adult; representation of space—displacement and movements; interindividual coordination in group work; organization of activity by social influences; biotechnological studies; studies on the training of adults.

M. Reuchlin
Institute Nationale d'Orientation Professionelle, Paris

FRANK, JEROME D. (1909–   )

Jerome D. Frank was born in New York City on May 30, 1909. After graduating from Horace Mann School in Fieldston, NY, he received a bachelor's degree from Harvard, *summa cum laude,* in 1930, and a PhD in psychology from Harvard in 1934. He earned his MD degree, *cum laude,* from the Johns Hopkins University in 1939. He received his psychiatric training at the Johns Hopkins Hospital from 1940 to 1943. He spent the rest of his career climbing the academic ladder in psychiatry at Johns Hopkins, from which he retired in 1974 as a professor of psychiatry.

During the 1960s and 1970s Frank was prominent in the peace movement, and was an active member of organizations including the Council for a Livable World, the National Peace Foundation, the Federation of American Scientists, SANE, Physicians for Social Responsibility, and Psychologists for Social Responsibility. He was a member of the Social Science Advisory Board of the US Arms Control and Disarmament Agency from 1963–73 and testified by invitation before the US Senate Foreign Relations Committee in May of 1966.

Through Frank's articles in psychiatric journals and books, he was instrumental in shifting the emphasis in research on psychotherapy from determining which form of psychotherapy was "better" to establishing the therapeutic factors they all have in common; this thesis was expressed in his book *Persuasion and Healing: A Comparative Study of Psychotherapy,* first authored by Frank alone in 1961, and starting with the third edition in 1991, in collaboration with his psychiatrist daughter Julia B. Frank, MD. He believes that the essence of the healing power of all forms of psychotherapy, individual and group, is to transform the meanings of the signs and symptoms of psychiatric illnesses from pessimistic to hopeful. This is accomplished through 1) a confiding relationship between the patient and a healer or a healing group in a healing setting; 2) a rationale that provides a plausible explanation for the patient's symptoms; 3) prescribing a ritual or procedure for resolving them; and 4) the active participation of both patient and therapist.

To be effective in any culture, the worldview and ethics on which the therapy is based must be compatible with those of the surrounding culture; for example, in many Asian cultures, therapies based on meditation are more effective than those based on deconditioning exercises.

His other publications include *Group Psychotherapy: Studies in Methodology of Research and Therapy,* with Florence Powdermaker and others; *Sanity and Survival: Psychological Aspects of War and Peace,* reissued as *Sanity and Survival in the Nuclear Age; Effective Ingredients of Successful Psychotherapy* (with Rudolf Hoehn-Saric, Stanley D. Imber, Bernard L. Liberman, and Anthony R. Stone); and *Psychotherapy and the Human Predicament: A Psychosocial Approach* (edited by Park E. Dietz). He is the author or coauthor of over 250 articles.

Jerome Frank's involvement with professional associations included serving as president of the Society for the Psychological Study of Social Issues (1965–66), vice-president (1974–76) and councillor (1976–79) of the American Association for Social Psychiatry, and president of the American Psychopathological Association (1963–64). He served on many national advisory committees, among them the National Institute of Mental Health; the Psychiatry and Neurology Service, Department of Medicine and Surgery, Veterans Administration Central Office; and the Office of Technology Assessment, Congress of the United States. He held a fellowship from the Center for Advanced Study in the Behavorial Sciences at Stanford in 1958–59, and received a special research fellowship from the National Institute of Mental Health, sponsored by the Center for the Study of Democratic Institutions in Santa Barbara in 1966.

Frank's many academic positions and awards include:

- Praelector in Psychiatry, Faculty of Medicine, University of St. Andrews, Dundee, Scotland, September, 1967.

- Tenth Emil A. Gutheil Award of the Association for the Advancement of Psychotherapy for 1970.

- H. B. Williams Travelling Professorship in Psychiatry, Australia and New Zealand, July–August, 1971.

- 1972 Kurt Lewin Memorial Award of the Society for the Psychological Study of Social Issues.

- Litchfield Lecturer, Oxford University, May, 1977.

- Honorary Professor, Universidad Nacional Mayor de San Marcos, Lima, Peru, 1978.

- Honorary Doctor, Universidad Peruana "Gaetano Heredia," Lima, Peru, 1978.

- 1979 Blanche Ittleson Award of the American Orthopsychiatric Association.

- 1980 Holmes Center Annual Award of the Holmes Center for Research in Holistic Healing.

- Special Research Award of the Society of Psychotherapy Research, 1981.

- Honorary Fellow, Royal College of Psychiatrists, 1981.

- McAlpin Research Achievement Award of the National Mental Health Association, 1981.

- First annual Oskar Pfister Award of the American Psychiatric Association, 1983.

- Honorary Member, Polish Psychiatric Association, 1983.

- American Psychological Association Award for Distinguished Contribution to Psychology in the Public Interest, 1985.

- McKerracher Lecturer, University of Saskatchewan, 1985.

- Thomas W. Salmon Medal of the New York Academy of Medicine, 1986.

- Harold D. Lasswell Award of the International Society of Political Psychology, 1987.

- Honorary doctorate in psychology from the State University of New York at Binghamton, 1991.

- Special Award of the American Psychological Association, Division of Psychotherapy, 1992.

- Award from American Psychological Association, Division of Peace Psychology, 1993.

- Distinguished Service Award of the American College of Psychiatrists, 1995.

- Honorary doctorate in psychology from Saybrook Graduate School, 1997.

STAFF

FRANKL, VIKTOR E. (1905–1997)

Founder of logotherapy and *Existenzanalyse,* Victor E. Frankl saw his system designated as the Third Viennese School of Psychotherapy, the first two being Freud's and Adler's. In the mid-1920s, Frankl's earliest publications appeared: the first in Freud's *International Journal of Psychoanalysis* and the second in Adler's *International Journal of Individual Psychology,* the former by Freud's invitation and the latter by Adler's. Because of his unorthodox views, however, Frankl was expelled from Adler's Society of Individual Psychology. Frankl subsequently came under the influence of Oswald Schwarz and Rudolf Allers, both disenchanted Adlerians. The phenomenologist Max Scheler also influenced him.

Frankl's psychotherapy, designated logotherapy, was predicated on "man's search for meaning"—accordingly, Frankl had entitled the book for which he is best known, *Man's Search for Meaning.* The book opens with Frankl's three-year experience in Nazi concentration camps, including the notorious Auschwitz. The remainder of the book outlines the theory and practice of logotherapy, a psychiatry spawned from his concentration camp experience. His later works—*The Will to Meaning, The Unconscious God, The Unheard Cry for Meaning, Psychotherapy and Existentialism,* and *The Doctor and the Soul*—elaborate and expand his logotherapy.

Frankl's university affiliations included the University of Vienna, where he received the MD and the PhD in 1949; a distinguished professorship at the United States International University; and visiting professorships at Harvard, Stanford, Duquesne, and Southern Methodist universities. Over the years he served as head of the Department of Neurology at the Poliklinik Hospital of Vienna.

STAFF

FREUD, ANNA (1895–1982)

Known particularly for being the daughter of Sigmund Freud, but also in her own right a specialist in children's psychoanalysis, Anna Freud championed the needs of children.

She graduated from Vienna's Cottage Lyzeum in 1912. After the Nazis took over Austria in 1938, she accompanied her father to London, where she became a practicing psychoanalyst.

Deeply interested in the growth of personality, Anna Freud invested 50 years applying her father's psychoanalytic theories to children. Her writings, including collected papers, fill seven volumes under the title *The Writings of Anna Freud.* The books for which she is best known are *The Ego and Mechanisms of Defence* and *Psychoanalysis for Teachers and Parents.* The former discusses essentially the nonsexual mechanisms of the mind. The ego, in dealing with repressed impulses, resorts to defense mechanisms.

Clark University in Massachusetts, which had given her father an honorary degree when Freud delivered a series of lectures there in 1909, also gave Anna Freud an honorary doctorate in 1950. Her father's alma mater, the University of Vienna, conferred on her an honorary MD in 1972.

W. S. SAHAKIAN

FREUD, SIGMUND (1856–1939)

Sigmund Freud moved from Moravia to Vienna at age 4, and lived there for nearly 80 years. He demonstrated an unusual intellectual ability early in life and was encouraged by his family. Freud graduated with distinction from the Gymnasium at age 17 and entered the University of Vienna to study medicine and scientific research. Because of his diversified interests in biology, physiology, and teaching, as well as medicine, Freud spent 8 years at the University. Finally persuaded to take his medical examinations, he entered private practice as a clinical neurologist in 1881.

Freud's interest in what was to become psychoanalysis began and developed during his associations with Josef Breuer in 1884. From Breuer he learned about the "talking cure" and the use of hypnosis for hysterical neuroses. In 1885, Freud spent 4½ months in France studying hypnosis with Jean Charcot, from whom he heard about a sexual basis for patients' problems. The idea stayed in his mind, and by the mid-1890s Freud was convinced that the dominant difficulty in neurosis was inadequate sexual development.

In 1895 Breuer and Freud published *Studies on Hysteria,* often noted as the formal beginning of psychoanalysis. In 1897 Freud undertook the task of self-analysis. He diagnosed his own neurotic difficulties as anxiety neuroses, which he claimed were caused by an accumulation of sexual tension. The method of self-analysis that Freud used was dream analysis. This was both a creative period of his life and a time of intense inner turmoil. The analysis continued for about 2 years and was reported in The Interpretation of Dreams, now considered Freud's major work.

By 1902 Freud had become interested in promoting psychoanalytic theory and practice. A small number of colleagues, including Alfred Adler, joined him in a weekly discussion group at his home. These early discussions on the problems of neurosis were important to the development of the different theoretical beliefs and applied techniques of the four pillars of depth psychology: Freud, Adler, Otto Rank, and Carl Jung. The group became known as the Vienna Psychological Society; later, Freud expanded his efforts to promote psychoanalysis and formed the Vienna Psychoanalytical Association. In 1905 Freud published Three Essays on the Theory of Sexuality. In 1909 he was invited to America by G. Stanley Hall of Clark University; in this, his first international recognition, he was awarded an honorary doctorate.

As Adler, Jung, and Rank developed their own theories and style, the original psychoanalytic group was disrupted with conflict and disagreement. Adler left the group in 1911; Jung, in 1914. The height of Freud's fame was from 1919 to his death in 1939. In the 1920s Freud developed a personality theory and system for all human motivation that expanded his influence beyond a method of treatment for the disturbed.

Freud's method of treatment in psychoanalysis identified resistances as a form of protection from pain, and repression as the way of eliminating that pain from conscious awareness. Repression became the fundamental principle of psychoanalysis. Repressed material was uncovered through free association and dream analysis in a long, intensive course of therapy lasting months or years. Effective therapeutic work depended on the personal relationship developed between client and therapist, or transference. Freud believed that transference of the client's emotional attitudes from parent figures to the therapist was necessary for curing the neuroses.

The personality system of psychoanalysis dealt with the driving forces or energies that have been called instincts in English translation, but that could also be called drives. The life instincts or urges for self-preservation and creative forces were called libido. The death instincts were energies directed either inward toward self-destruction, or outward in aggression and hatred. Freud divided psychic mental life of the personality into id, ego, and superego. The id, corresponding to the unconscious, included sexual and aggressive instincts, no value judgments, and energies directed toward immediate satisfaction and tension reduction; it obeyed the pleasure principle. The ego, commonly known as reason or rationality, mediated between the id and the external world, holding under control the pleasure-seeking demands of the id; it obeyed the reality principle. The superego—the conscience developed in early childhood—worked toward inhibiting the id completely, and toward actualizing the ego ideal to a state of perfection. Anxiety resulted whenever the ego became too overburdened with the triple impact of the psychic energies of the pleasure-seeking id, the need to manipulate reality for tension reduction, and the perfectionistic superego.

Freud's theories and methods have been criticized on several grounds: (a) unsystematic and uncontrolled data collection and interpretation; (b) overemphasis on biological forces, particularly sex, as the primary influence on personality development; and (c) a deterministic view of the influence of past behavior, with a denial of free will and the role of future goals, dreams, and hopes in personal growth.

Schultz has written on the contributions of psychoanalysis to the field of clinical psychology and psychiatry: "Certain Freudian concepts have gained wide acceptance and been assimilated into the mainstream of contemporary psychology. These include the role of unconscious motivation, the importance of childhood experiences in shaping adult behavior, and the operation of defense mechanisms. Interest in these areas has generated much research" (1981, pp. 338–339).

Psychoanalysis retains its particular identity today, not having been absorbed into the mainstream of general psychological thought. Freud was an originator, a pioneer in new techniques and understandings of human nature, a great contributor to the history of psychology.

N. A. HAYNIE

FROMM, ERICH (1900–1980)

Erich Fromm received the PhD at Heidelberg in 1922. He later studied at the Berlin Psychoanalytic Institute. In 1934 he immigrated to the United States. He taught at many schools in North America, including the New School for Social Research, Columbia, Yale, Michigan State, and the National University of Mexico.

In his system of personality Fromm acknowledged man's biological past but stressed his social nature. In his first book, *Escape from Freedom*—considered by many to be his best—Fromm departed from the standard Freudian theory in stressing the effect of social forces on personality. The main theme involved human loneliness. As we evolved from early times, we gained greater independence from nature and social institutions (such as the medieval church), but in so doing became isolated and lonely. Freedom, then, became a condition from which to escape. There were two solutions: either to join with others in a spirit of love and social productivity, or to submit to authority and conform to society. The general theme of productive love permeates much of Fromm's writings.

In *The Sane Society* Fromm envisioned an ideal solution in which there is equality for all, in which each person has the opportunity of becoming purely human, and in which individuals relate to one another in a loving way. In *Man for Himself* he developed various personality or character types that emerged as we reacted to social influences and were related to the methods of escape from the basic problem of loneliness. He designated five, four of which were undesirable. The *receptive character* demands all that it can get and is willing to take but not give. The *hoarding character* sees the outside world as a threat, therefore tries to keep all that it has and not share. The *exploitative character* satisfies its desires through force and cunning. The *marketing character* considers itself a commodity that can be bought or sold. Finally, the *productive character* is the desirable one. Being productive means realizing one's potentialities, and in so doing, devoting oneself to the welfare and well-being of all mankind.

R. W. LUNDIN
Wheaton, Illinois

FRUSTRATION-AGGRESSION HYPOTHESIS

The frustration-aggression hypothesis is a model originally proposed by Dollard, Doob, Miller, Mowrer, and Sears in their classic book *Frustration and Aggression* (1939), which attempted to explain human aggression in terms of a few basic concepts. While rejecting the Freudian notion of innate and accumulating aggressive energy, the model proposed that there is an inborn tendency to respond aggressively after being frustrated. According to their hypothesis, frustration always leads to aggression and aggression is always caused by frustration. Frustration is defined as interference with behavior directed toward a particular goal, and it leads to a latent aggressive state, which they referred to as *instigation.* The degree of frustration and the strength of the instigation depend on the strength of the goal-seeking behavior (how strongly motivated is the individual to achieve the goal), the extent of the interference (whether goal seeking is merely delayed or completely blocked) and the number of goal-directed behaviors subjected to interference (aggressive inclinations that will be summated over repeated frustrations).

This model also incorporates the concept of inhibition. Inhibition is proportionate to the anticipated likelihood and severity of punishment for aggressive behavior. When the instigation is greater than the inhibition, then aggressive behavior toward the frustrating agent is produced. If the inhibition is greater than the instigation, then aggression will be displaced to alternative targets. However, if frustration is ongoing, eventually instigation will exceed inhibition, and aggression toward the frustrating agent will occur.

This classic version of the frustration-aggression hypothesis has not been substantiated by empirical research, although in some circumstances frustration does lead to aggression. However, numerous laboratory and field studies have demonstrated that while frustration may lead to aggression, it does not do so invariably, and it can also produce withdrawal and other behaviors. Moreover, not all aggression is preceded by frustration, for it is often used instrumentally to obtain a particular goal.

Although the failure to produce adequate empirical support for the frustration-aggression hypothesis led many psychologists to abandon it, Berkowitz (1962, 1969) reformulated the hypothesis in such a way as to account for the finding that frustration does not always lead to aggression while at the same time acknowledging the important role played by situational factors. He proposed that frustration produces only a *readiness* to act aggressively, but to produce aggression, appropriate environmental cues, or "releasers," are usually necessary to trigger it or to indicate that it is allowable or appropriate.

More recently, Berkowitz (1983, 1989) has proposed a further reformulation of the frustration-aggression hypothesis in terms of aversively stimulated aggression. (Instrumental aggression, which is deliberately directed at attaining some goal, is excluded from the realm to which this hypothesis applies.) He argues that the reason that frustrations give rise to aggressive tendencies is because they are aversive to the individual, producing negative affect, and it is this negative affect that produces aggressive tendencies. Thus frustration is not a necessary condition for aggression to occur, because other aversive events also can produce negative affect, which in turn can produce aggressive tendencies.

Aversive events can be of either a physical nature (e.g., pain and excessive heat) or a psychological nature (e.g., frightening information). Although there is a defensive component to the resultant aggressiveness, insofar as the individual attempts to remove the source of the unpleasantness, there also is an active inclination to harm available targets. Social learning factors, based on reinforcement history, will either increase or decrease the likelihood of aggression as well as determine the target and form of the aggression.

Cognitive factors play an important role as well, according to this revised model. Cognitive appraisal of a situation will influence the extent to which frustrations elicit negative feelings—annoyance, sadness, pain, or other unpleasantness. Once such negative affect is stimulated, it elicits an experience of anger. Subsequent cognitive activity will either lead to the expression of that anger through aggressive behavior or can nullify its effects altogether. For example, anticipated failure to attain a goal will be less unpleasant than unanticipated failure. People also are more likely to be upset and to attack their frustrators if they believe that the frustration was deliberate and directed at them (Berkowitz, 1969).

Social learning theorists (e.g., Bandura, 1973) dispute the frustration-aggression hypothesis and argue that frustration (and aversive stimulation in general) only produces generalized arousal and that social learning determines how this arousal will influence behavior. According to this view, aggressive responses are acquired because they are effective. Thus people learn to perform aggressive actions and learn the circumstances under which aggressive behavior is likely to be rewarded.

It is a little over a half century since the frustration-aggression hypothesis was first formulated. In the years following its presentation, it generated considerable research and stimulated a great deal of theoretical discussion. Because of the continuing work of its supporters, and especially the recent work of Berkowitz, it will undoubtedly, in one form or another, continue to generate research and theoretical controversy for the next half century as well, as psychologists continue to struggle to understand human aggression.

REFERENCES

Bandura, A. (1973). *Aggression: A social learning analysis.* Englewood Cliffs, NJ: Prentice-Hall.

Berkowitz, L. (1962). *Aggression: A social psychological analysis.* New York: McGraw-Hill.

Berkowitz, L. (1969). The frustration-aggression hypothesis revisited. In L. Berkowitz (Ed.), *Roots of aggression: A reexamination of the frustration-aggression hypothesis* (pp. 1–28). New York: Atherton Press.

Berkowitz, L. (1983). Aversively stimulated aggression: Some parallels and differences in research with humans and animals. *American Psychologist, 38,* 1135–1144.

Berkowitz, L. (1989). Frustration-aggression hypothesis: Examination and reformulation. *Psychological Bulletin, 106,* 59–73.

Dollard, J., Doob, L. W., Miller, N. E., Mowrer, O. H., & Sears, R. R. (1939). *Frustration and aggression.* New Haven, CT: Yale University Press.

J. E. ALCOCK
York University, Toronto

AGGRESSION
COOPERATION-COMPETITION
CROWDING
DEPRESSION
EMOTIONS
MOB PSYCHOLOGY
OBEDIENCE
PUNISHMENT
REWARDS
SADOMASOCHISM
SOCIAL EXCHANGE THEORY

FUNCTIONAL ANALYSIS

DEFINITION

Functional analysis is a strategy for the assessment and treatment of mental health problems. It has origins in radical behaviorism and applied behavioral analysis and is generally viewed as a subset of the larger realm of behavioral assessment. Functional analysis is a set of procedures that attempts to identify important variables that help to cause or maintain problematic behaviors or behavior-environment interactions. The goal of functional analysis is to effectively identify targets of intervention that are changeable so that appropriate treatments may be rapidly implemented and evaluated through concentrated intervention efforts.

CAUSAL RELATIONSHIPS

Functional analysis derived from basic behavioral principles and is most associated with Skinner and behavior analysts. It attends to the antecedents, stimuli, responses, consequences, and contingencies that produce or maintain effective or ineffective behaviors. Functional analysis attempts to identify pertinent, controllable variables in this sequence and to treat those variables to produce more positive outcomes. Skinner advocated that the scientist or clinician should find which variables are functionally related to the variable desired to be changed (e.g., yelling). The researcher or clinician does this by conducting a single-subject research design in which one variable is systematically manipulated to determine its effects on the outcome variable of interest. It has been argued that the concept of cause, as in, "the ball hitting the window caused the window to break," is un-

clear. Hume pointed out that cause is unobservable. All one actually sees is concomitant variation. When X happens, so does Y. Mach was among the first to argue that cause can be captured by a functional relation, y f(x) = g, which is often depicted on Cartesian coordinates. One systematically manipulates a single variable to see its effects (if any) on another variable. If some systematic relationship is found, one variable is said to be a function of the other. This view dovetails nicely with modern scientific research methods and has been said to allow valid causal inferences.

BEHAVIORAL ASSESSMENT

Assessment is an enterprise as old as psychotherapy itself. When a client presents with a problem, the obvious questions are "What created the problem?" and "How can the problem be resolved?" Assessment investigates the first question and attempts to inform the second one. Assessment is sifting through the multitude of facts that comprise a person's life and determining which aspects are relevant to the development or maintenance of the problem: that is, what is causing the problem. Historically this process has resulted in classifying individuals, based on commonalities in apparently relevant variables, into a diagnostic category.

Behavior therapists have questioned the usefulness of diagnosis and syndromal classification systems such as the *Diagnostic and Statistical Manuals* of the American Psychiatric Association. New approaches to assessment have been called for that consider the function of behaviors (i.e., a panic attack impacts the environment and the person having the attack in observable ways), over the topographical form of the behaviors (i.e., that a panic attack occurs), and that attend more closely to individual differences in behavior. One product of this desire to understand behavior functionally and idiographically is functional analysis.

"Functional analysis" is a term that has been used interchangeably with several others in the behavioral literature, including "behavioral analysis," "behavioral assessment," "functional behavioral analysis," and "behavioral case formulation." Compounding the confusion, "functional analysis" is used to refer to a diversity of procedures in the literature. This phrase has been used to describe any part or the entirety of discovering the variables of which behavior is a function, designing an intervention for the environment or behaviors, implementing the intervention, reevaluating the case conceptualization based on response to treatment, and recycling the process until the problem subsides. While some behavior analysts focus exclusively on the assessment portion of this intervention process, others consider the whole process to be the functional analysis.

PROCEDURES

The basic form of a functional analysis is as follows.

1. Identify aspects of the client, his environment, or history that may be relevant to the problem.

2. Organize information about possibly relevant variables according to behavioral principles in order to hypothesize possible causal relationships among variables.

3. Collect additional information about potential causal variables in order to complete the analysis.

4. Identify or create a treatment by systematically manipulating one variable at a time based on the case conceptualization.

5. Implement the intervention and observe any change in the problem.

6. If the problem is not sufficiently solved, return to the case conceptualization to identify alternative variables that may be pertinent or alternative causal relationships and continue with the steps of the functional analysis.

7. Continue to revise the conceptualizations and interventions until the problem is solved.

STRENGTHS AND WEAKNESSES

Strengths

The strengths of functional analysis are the precision with which cases may be conceptualized and the direct link to treatment implementation. Instead of relying on imprecise diagnostic categories as heuristics to guide conceptualizations of the problem, the unique aspects of the particular problem are the foci of case conceptualizations and treatment planning. These unique aspects of the problem are the points of customized clinical interventions instead of a generic syndrome level intervention.

Weaknesses

The weaknesses of functional analysis stem from its lack of specificity. Communication and replication are impeded by the imprecision of functional analysis language and procedures. When different terms are being used for functional analyses, relevant information may not be shared because it is not identified as belonging to the functional analysis category. Similarly, when the term "functional analysis" is being used to refer to overlapping or altogether different procedures, miscommunications can occur because the discussants are working from different assumptions about the procedures that are involved. Moreover, as communication is increasingly removed from direct observations of client behaviors, there are greater opportunities for miscommunications to arise. Clinicians that are familiar with functional analysis have difficulties communicating effectively; it is much more difficult to create and maintain clear lines of communication with administrators and insurance representatives.

A related problem is replication. Functional analysis currently refers to a range of assessment and intervention procedures. Without the specificity in the field of what a functional analysis is, clinicians may perform different sets of procedures and call each of them a functional analysis. As a result, there is no guarantee that one clinician's conclusions are going to match another professional's conclusions in the same case. This lack of replication distills confidence from the assessment procedures, which is in opposition to their purposes. Furthermore, if a functional analysis cannot be replicated, doubt is cast on the ability to reliably study the phenomenon. This replicability problem ironically renders untestable any assessment and intervention procedure that developed from the behavioral empirical literature.

FUTURE DIRECTIONS

The field of behavior analysis acknowledges the strengths and weaknesses of functional analysis, and improvements on functional analysis are being proposed. Suggestions have been made regarding standardizing the definition of functional analysis and the procedures that comprise such an analysis in order to advance communication and replication. Additional proposals have been made to strengthen the communication aspect of the procedure. The development of a nomothetic classification system that is based on functional analysis has been put forth. Possibilities for this system include expert systems, logical functional analytic systems, or functional diagnostic systems, each based on functional analyses.

In addition, while functional analysis has been viewed primarily as a clinical assessment strategy, researchers have proposed an increased use of functional analysis as a research strategy. Compiling and analyzing functional analytic data within and across clients may contribute to the basic understanding of many behaviors and behavior-environment interactions.

SUGGESTED READING

Cone, J. (1997). Issues in functional analysis in behavioral assessment. *Behaviour Research and Therapy, 35,* 259–275.

Hayes, S., & Follette, W. (1992). Can functional analysis provide a substitute for syndromal classification? *Behavioral Assessment, 14,* 345–365.

Haynes, S., & O'Brien, W. (1990). Functional analysis in behavior therapy. *Clinical Psychology Review, 10,* 649–668.

Kanfer, F., & Saslow, G. (1969). Behavioral diagnosis. In C. M. Franks (Ed.), *Behavior therapy: Appraisal and status.* New York: McGraw-Hill.

Sturmey, P. (1996). *Functional analysis in clinical psychology.* Chichester, UK: Wiley.

W. T. O'DONOHUE
T. M. PENIX

CLINICAL ASSESSMENT
DEPENDENT VARIABLES
IDIODYNAMICS

FUNCTIONALISM

As a school or system of psychology, functionalism had its roots in Darwin's theory of evolution as well as in the psychology of William James. Darwin's doctrine of natural selection stated that those variations of a particular species best able to adapt to a particular environment would survive and perpetuate themselves, while those variations less able to adapt would die off. Darwin also believed that the mind evolved along with the body, so the whole process of adaptation could apply to the mental as well as the physical.

The ideas set forth in the psychology of William James constituted a more immediate influence on functionalism. In an informal sense, it could be said that James was really the functionalism's founder. James stressed psychological adaptation and adjustment. Sometimes the mind aided the body in its survival. In the case of reason and problem solving, mental activity was preeminent and promoted survival. Yet reason had its seat in the machinery of the brain and operated, in part, to help fulfill bodily needs. At other times, as in the case of habit, traces left in the brain governed the habit, leaving the mind free for more useful endeavors.

A second aspect of James's psychology which influenced functionalism was his pragmatism. Ideas had value only if they were useful. The pragmatism that James fostered was taken up by John Dewey, the first of the functionalists to apply it to social problems and education.

As was often the case when a new school of psychology emerged in the early 20th century, functionalism arose as a protest against existing systems. Its main protest was against structuralism, which had begun in Germany with Wilhelm Wundt and was brought to America by Edward B. Titchener. For the functionalists, the subject matter of psychology was mental processes or functions and *not* the study of the contents of consciousness, as the structuralists had stated. Furthermore, functionalism was concerned with utilitarian, common-sense issues in psychology. It was not the pure ivory-tower psychology of structuralism. Finally, the structuralists had maintained that mental functions were not subject to introspective analysis; it was the *contents* of the mind that could be analyzed. The functionalists disagreed, believing they could study mental functions if the proper methods were applied.

Although functionalism was less organized and less closely knit than structuralism, certain tenets characterized the system: (a) Psychology should deal with mental functions rather than contents; (b) psychological functions were adjustments to the environment; (c) psychology should be utilitarian, allowing for practical applications; (d) mental functions were a part of the whole world of activity, which included the mental and the physical; and (e) psychology was very closely related to biology: An understanding of anatomy and physiology would help in the understanding of mental activity.

The development of functionalism as a school of thought was the result primarily of three men, all at the University of Chicago: John Dewey (1859–1952), James Angell (1867–1949), and Harvey Carr (1873–1954).

Dewey's main contribution to functionalism is to be found in "The Reflex Arc Concept in Psychology" (1896). To make his point, he used the simple example of a child who saw a flame, reached into the fire, and burned his fingers. This was not to be analyzed separately as perceiving, reaching, and being burned. After the experience, the flame that at first attracted the child became something from which to withdraw. Thus this experience was a unitary act that had adaptive value: In the future, the child would avoid the flame so as not to be burned again. Not only did the act have adaptive value, but it was a practical matter as well.

James Angell further promoted the functionalist movement in *Psychology: An Introductory Study of the Structures and Functions of Human Consciousness* (1904). The book was an assemblage of what was known about psychology at the time, but it did contain a flavor of functionalism. His best statement of the functionalist position was in his 1906 presidential address to the American Psychological Association, published the following year as "The Province of Functional Psychology," in which he made the following points: (a) Functional psychology was the study of mental operations or functions, as opposed to contents; (b) functional psychology was the study of the fundamental utilities of consciousness; and (c) functional psychology had to be concerned with the entire psychophysical relationship between the organism and its environment: Mind and body could not be separated, as there was a constant interaction between the two.

Harvey Carr organized the functionalist ideas in the most coherent fashion in *Psychology: A Study of Mental Activity* (1925). Although the term "mental activity" appeared in the title, the stress was more on behavioral adaptation. The Core of Carr's Psychology was to be found in his description of the adaptive act, which had three separate but interrelated aspects. First, there was a motivating stimulus, which remained relatively persistent until the organism acted in such a way as to satisfy it. The motive aroused and directed the activity. Second, there was the sensory stimulus, which acted as an incentive or goal. Finally, there was the activity or responding, which continued until the motivating stimulus was satisfied. Thus a hungry person (motivating stimulus) looks for and finds (activity) the goal of food (sensory stimulus). It should be noted that the adaptive act was a function of the whole situation: One would react differently upon seeing a bear in the zoo, as compared to one in the wild. In the case of the hungry man looking for food, the consequences of the adaptive act involved the satisfaction of the hunger need as well as the survival value it achieved.

The adaptive act obviously involved learning. Association was extremely important. Carr distinguished between descriptive and explanatory laws of association. Association by similarity fell under the descriptive laws. Explanatory laws included association by contiguity (coming together in space and time), which explained the origin of the association. Strength resulted from continued repetition. The law of frequency applied here: The more often an act was performed, the stronger it would become.

Carr interpreted emotions as organic adjustments or readjustments. In anger, persons exhibited an increase of energy, allowing them to overcome obstacles. The energy came from internal physiological processes. In fear, likewise, a person was energized to flee from enemies. These emotions were biologically useful. But other emotions such as sorrow or envy did not seem to have utilitarian value. Emotions arose when other avenues or adaptation seemed to be lacking. Carr supported the more classical theory of emotion in which a person saw a dangerous object, became afraid, and consequently ran. The fear energized the biological functions allowing him to run. This was in opposition to the James-Lange theory of emotion, whereby the emotion was the result of biological and motor adjustments.

Carr supported experimentation and common observation as the methods of psychology. He stressed the value of experimentation, but since in human studies proper experimental controls might be difficult to achieve, common observation was acceptable in the discovery of knowledge of a particular psychological event.

Carr did not make an issue of the distinction between the mental and the physical. Angell had talked about the interaction between mind and body, but for Carr the mental and physical were simply two different aspects of the same event.

Like structuralism, functionalism no longer exists as a distinct psychological system. Some psychologists maintain a kind of functionalist position in stressing adaptation of an organism to its environment. We speak of adjustment and maladjustment: A maladjusted person may be having trouble in interacting with other people, or fails to work efficiently, or cannot satisfy needs. Generally speaking, functionalism has fallen into the mainstream of psychology.

One of the difficulties of functionalism was its vagueness. In *The Scientific Evolution of Psychology,* Kantor states that the functionalist position was so formless that the historian of psychology is hard put to set down its basic principles in any orderly fashion. Furthermore, functionalism has always been rather eclectic. Eclecticism involves the patching together of a little from one system and a little from another. It tries to reconcile conflicting viewpoints, but in so doing it ends up as nondescript. Yet functionalism added a good bit to psychology: It broadened its scope to include behavior as well as experience, and extended it to a wide range of areas including adjustment, intelligence testing, learning, and child, abnormal, and animal behavior. Functionalism faded not because its principles were rejected as incorrect, but because it became absorbed into the general fabric of American psychology.

REFERENCES

Angell, J. R. (1904). *Psychology: An introductory study of the structures and functions of human consciousness.* New York: Holt.

Carr, H. A. (1925). *Psychology: A study of mental activity.* New York: Longman, Green.

Dewey, J. (1896). The reflex arc concept in psychology. *Psychological Review, 3,* 357–370.

Kantor, J. R. (1969). *The scientific evolution of psychology* (Vol. 2). Chicago: Principia.

SUGGESTED READING

Henle, M. (1957). Some problems of eclecticism. *Psychological Review, 64,* 296–305.

James, W. (1950). *The principles of psychology.* New York: Dover. (Original work published 1894)

Lundin, R. W. (1979). *Theories and systems of psychology.* Lexington, MA: Heath. (Original work published 1972)

Titchener, E. B. (1899). Structural and functional psychology. *Psychological Review, 8,* 290–299.

R. W. LUNDIN
Wheaton, Illinois

PSYCHOLOGY, HISTORY OF STRUCTURALISM

FUNDAMENTAL ATTRIBUTION ERROR

"Folk explanations of behavior guide people's perceptions, attitudes and actions toward each other, they affect impressions, sway sympathies, and alter the paths of relationships. By explaining behavior, people make sense of the social world, adapt to it, and shape it." (Malle, 1999, p. 23). Attribution theory is concerned with the various causes that people assign to behavior in their attempts to explain it. The inferences about causation of a person's actions fall into two broad categories—internal (characteristics of the person) and external (characteristics of the environment and nonpersonal forces).

The fundamental attribution error (FAE), sometimes called actor-observer asymmetry or overattribution, is the general tendency of an observer to perceive another person's behavior as caused by internal, personal characteristics or dispositions, rather than external or situational influences. Conversely, the behaving person (the actor) tends to see his or her own behavior as caused by the situation. The concept of FAE grew out of an extensive body of research on social perception and cognition, and in turn the idea has stimulated much research. Premack and Woodruff (1978) gave evidence of attributional thinking even in primates. In human beings, this well-established observer overemphasis on personal traits and underemphasis on context raises serious questions about bias in many situations in which people judge other people, such as clinical assessment or treatment, voting for political candidates, and jury decisions.

Weary, Stanley, and Harvey (1989), in their book on attribution, noted that this prominent tendency to overattribute internal causes had been recognized by such early social psychologists as Heider (1958). Jones and Nisbett (1972) described this actor-observer effect, and in further research Ross (1977) gave FAE its name. In typical experiments subjects judge statements allegedly made by persons under various conditions, or compare subjects' explanations for their own choices and the choices of others. Subjects might report causes of actions while viewing themselves or another person on videotapes. The FAE process is so strong that even when the observer is told something about the situational conditions of the actors, there is a tendency to attribute others' actions to personal traits. In daily life, this seems related to "blaming the victims" of rape, poverty, and other social problems. In organizations, people may overattribute responsibility to individuals, such as leaders, when there are structural or system faults (Martinko, 1995). Since psychology in general focuses on individual variables, there is a strong likelihood that psychologists will overattribute observed results to individual dispositions.

There are several approaches to explaining FAE. Baron, Graziano, and Stanger (1991, p. 145) stated, "The best current explanation involves differences in the amount and type of information most available to actors and observers. . . . When people inspect their own behavior as actors, they have a lifetime of previous behavior against which to compare it. When they make attributions to others, however, they almost never have the same amount or quality of information available." Also, actors and observers differ in information that is salient or striking to them—what is figure and what is ground.

The application of attribution theory to counseling and clinical work is of considerable importance. Some studies (e.g., Batson, O'Quin, & Pych, 1982) have shown that a dispositional bias may exist among professional helpers, but this bias has not been clearly proven. Since, however, the tendency to overattribute problems to personal characteristics is common in the general population, it would seem important in clinical training to help student professionals examine their explanations of clients' feelings and behaviors. Conversely, counselors and clinicians may use FAE as part of "attribution therapy" to help the client reframe self-attributions. Depressed patients tend to use self-blame much more than others. Some studies (e.g., Hollon, DeRubeis, & Seligman, 1992; Ramirez, Maldonado, & Martos, 1992) have shown that cognitive therapeutic instructions to decrease overattribution of negative events helps to reduce depression or "immunize" people against a sense of helplessness. Some measures of individual differences are available, for example the Attributional Style Questionnaire (Peterson et al., 1982) and the Causal Dimension Scale (Russell, McAuley, & Tarico, 1987).

Other interesting areas of application of the FAE principle are in legal and international situations. Questions such as the following arise: What was the intent of an individual alleged to have committed a crime? What does he or she see as reasons or causes for doing the deed? How about witnesses and attribution errors? Tetlock, McGuire, and Mitchell (1991), in discussing the security problems of nations, noted that FAE exacerbates attribution of hostile intentions to others and leads even peaceful states to arm excessively. Policymakers see arming themselves as defensive and assume that others' military buildups are aggressive. McDonald (1995) pointed out that social identity theory suggests that observers will tend to perceive ingroup members as similar to themselves and therefore give situational explanations for discrepant behavior but will attribute outgroup responsibilities differently.

There are several cautions and limitations about the FAE bias. It is important to note that FAE refers to a relative tendency of observers to attribute to the actor more responsibility for behavior than does the actor; it does not say anything about accuracy of causal claims. There are few research attempts to determine the reality or "truth" of attributions; questions may be raised about the accuracies of the observer, the actor, or both. Another caution is that observers may make personal attributions because of efficiency; if information about the actor's situation is not available, it may not be possible or practical to take the complexity of the actor's view into account. Attitudes in the attributional process are also important; the actor-observer differences may be diminished by an observer's empathic attitude or personal acquaintance with the actors and their situations. There seem to be cultural differences in the FAE tendency; North Americans may have a bias toward blaming the individual, in contrast with people from India (Miller, 1984) and China (Anderson, 1999) or other collectivist cultures.

Considerable work must be done to clarify the theoretical confusions about how FAE relates to similar concepts such as theories of mind, self-efficacy, and internal and external locus of control

(Peterson & Stunkard, 1992). Malle (1999) added important theoretical elements and showed the difference between a person giving "mere causes" for behaviors as compared with reasons which involve intentionality Malle argued for a more detailed conceptual and linguistic analysis of folk explanations.

REFERENCES

Anderson, C. A. (1999). Attributional style, depression, and loneliness: A cross-cultural comparison of American and Chinese students. *Personality and Social Psychology Bulletin, 25,* 482–499.

Baron, R. M., Graziano, W. G., & Stangor, C. (1991). *Social psychology.* Fort Worth: Holt, Rinehart & Winston.

Batson, C. D., O'Quin, K., & Pych, V. (1982). An attribution theory analysis of trained helpers' inferences about clients' needs. In T. A. Wills (Ed.), *Basic processes in helping relationships.* New York: Academic.

Heider, F. (1958). *The psychology of interpersonal relations.* New York: Wiley.

Hollon, S. D., DeRubeis, R. J., & Seligman, M. E. P. (1992). Cognitive therapy and the prevention of depression. *Applied and Preventive Psychology, 1,* 89–95.

Jones, E. E., & Nisbett, R. E. (1972). The actor and the observer: Divergent perceptions of the causes of behavior. In E. E. Jones, D. E. Kanouse, H. H. Kelley, R. E. Nisbett, S. Valins, & B. W. Weiner (Eds.), *Attribution: Perceiving the causes of behavior* (pp. 79–94). Morristown, NJ: General Learning Press.

Malle, B. F. (1999). How people explain behavior: A new theoretical framework. *Personality and Social Psychology Review, 3,* 23–48.

Martinko, M. J. (Ed.). (1995). *Attribution theory: An organizational perspective.* Delray Beach, FL: St. Lucie Press.

McDonald, D. M. (1995). Fixing blame in n-person attributions: A social identity model for attributional processes in newly formed cross-functional groups. In M. J. Martinko (Ed.), *Attribution theory: An organizational perspective* (pp. 273–288). Delray Beach, FL: St. Lucie Press.

Miller, J. G. (1984). Culture and the development of everyday causal explanation. *Journal of Personality and Social Psychology, 46,* 961–978.

Peterson, C., Semmel, A., von Baeyer, C., Abramson, L. Y., Metalsky, G. I., & Seligman, M. E. P. (1982). The Attributional Style Questionnaire. *Cognitive Therapy and Research, 6,* 287–300.

Peterson, C., & Stunkard, A. J. (1992). Cognates of personal control: Locus of control, self-efficacy, and explanatory style. *Applied and Preventive Psychology, 1,* 111–117.

Premack, D., & Woodruff, G. (1978). Chimpanzee problem-solving: A test for comprehension. *Science, 202,* 532–535.

Ramirez, E., Maldonado, A., & Martos, R. (1992). Attributions modulate immunization against learned helplessness in humans. *Applied and Preventive Psychology, 1,* 139–146.

Ross, L. (1977). The intuitive psychologist and his shortcomings: Distortions in the attribution process. In L. Berkowitz (Ed.), *Advances in experimental social psychology* (Vol. 10, pp. 174–221). New York: Academic.

Russell, D., McAuley, E., & Tarico, V. (1987). Measuring causal attributions for success and failure: A comparison of methodologies for assessing causal dimensions. *Journal of Personality and Social Psychology, 52,* 1248–1257.

Tetlock, P. E., McGuire, C. B., & Mitchell, G. (1991). Psychological perspectives on nuclear deterrance. *Annual Review of Psychology, 42,* 239–276.

Weary, G., Stanley, M. A. & Harvey, J. H. (1989). *Attribution.* New York: Springer-Verlag.

N. D. SUNDBERG
University of Oregon

ACTOR/OBSERVER DIFFERENCES
ATTRIBUTIONS
BATTERED PEOPLE
COGNITIVE DETERMINANTS OF BEHAVIOR
PERSON ATTRIBUTION
SITUATION ATTRIBUTION

G

GABA RECEPTORS

It is now universally recognized that γ-aminobutyric acid (GABA), synthesized by the two molecular forms of glutamic acid decarboxylase (GAD 65 or 67) expressed in neurons, functions as a key neurotransmitter in the crustacean to mammals speciation.

GENERAL INFORMATION

GABA$_A$ Receptors

In the brains of vertebrates, GABA mediates synaptic inhibitory events by binding to specific recognition sites located in various members of a pentameric protein family, including a transmembrane anion channel which is termed GABA$_A$ receptor (Macdonald & Olsen, 1994). When two molecules of GABA bind to a GABA$_A$ receptor molecule, the opening frequency of the anionic channels increases and most of the time Cl$^-$ ions flow inwardly. In 1952 Hodgkin and Huxley suggested that in voltage-operated Na$^+$ and K$^+$ channels, the gating and its ion permeation are two independent processes. The idea that the gating opens and closes the channels but pays scant attention to the behavior of fully activated channels might apply also to the GABA$_A$ gated receptor channels. The binding of two GABA molecules to a GABA$_A$ receptor molecule activates the Cl$^-$ channel; in contrast, the binding to positive or negative allosteric modulatory sites of hormones (neurosteroids) or endogenous modulatory ligands (endozepines) affects the ohmic behavior of the channel by changing either the open time duration or the opening frequency of the Cl$^-$ channels gated by GABA. Some of these modulatory sites also function as the high-affinity binding sites for important drugs used during surgery to induce anesthesia (barbiturates) or in psychiatry for the treatment of anxiety or mood disorders [benzodiazepines (BZ), Costa & Guidotti, 1996; Guidotti & Costa, 1998]. Both drugs amplify the GABA-gated Cl$^-$ current intensity and thereby decrease retention of recent memories, reduce learning speed, and induce sedation. Anesthesia is induced by barbiturates and not by BZs because only barbiturates can gate the GABA$_A$ receptor channels in absence of GABA.

In GABA$_A$ receptors the anion flux direction depends on many factors, including the Cl$^-$ equilibrium potential of neuronal membranes, which in part relates to the expression level and relative intrinsic activity of a K$^+$/Cl$^-$ cotransporter that changes in relation to various factors, including patterns of ontogenetic neuronal maturation (Rivera et al., 1999). During embryonic corticogenesis, pioneer GABAergic neurons termed Cajal-Retzius (CR), which also express GABA$_A$ receptors (Mienville, 1998), are located in the marginal zone of the developing cortex. CR cell expression occurs before the neurons proliferating from the ventricular zone initiate their migration on radial glia toward the marginal zone. Before birth, GABA application to CR neurons elicits a Cl$^-$ efflux which is associated with depolarization. This in turn increases Ca^{2+} influx and triggers the extracellular secretion from CR of several proteins,

including Reelin, a secreted protein which binds to extracellular matrix proteins and very likely is operative in terminating neuronal migration and guiding cortical neurons to their final position in the pyramidal layers (D'Arcangelo et al., 1995).

In the adult brain, the GABA-gated Cl$^-$ influx increases neuronal membrane polarization which functions as a hindrance to the excitatory depolarization mediated by glutamate activation of specific ionotropic receptors (NMDA, KAINATE or AMPA selective). The intensity of the GABA-gated Cl$^-$ currents is inhibited by bicuculine, a drug that causes convulsions by specifically antagonizing the increased polarization of neuronal membranes induced by GABA when acting at GABA$_A$ receptors (Macdonald & Olsen, 1994). A similar hyperpolarization can also be elicited by muscimol, a drug acting as a specific agonist of GABA$_A$ receptors; when injected into rodents, it causes a dose-dependent reversible loss of the righting reflex (Enna & Bowery, 1997).

GABA$_B$ Receptors

This family of metabotropic GABA receptors (Hill & Bowery, 1981) was identified after the ionotropic GABA$_A$ receptor family. The activation of GABA$_B$ receptors by GABA decreases the rate of cAMP formation, and this metabotropic function differentiates these receptors from ionotropic GABA$_A$ receptors (Vojcik & Neff, 1982). The GABA$_B$ receptors were further characterized by their insensitivity to bicuculine inhibition and muscimol stimulation (typical of GABA$_A$ receptors), by a specific inhibition by a number of selective antagonists inactive on GABA$_A$ receptors, and by their selective stimulation by baclofen, which does not stimulate GABA$_A$ receptors. Confirmation of the metabotropic nature and of their functional association to G proteins has been accomplished by cloning two specific DNA sequences (each encoding for a slightly different 7 transmembrane domain protein) which, functioning as dimers, inhibit adenylate cyclase or gate K$^+$ channels using various G protein subtypes as second messengers.

The complete structural and functional distinction between GABA$_A$ (ionotropic) and GABA$_B$ (metabotropic) receptors has a clear parallel to that between nicotinic (ionotropic) and muscarinic (metabotropic) acetylcholine receptors and ionotropic and metabotropic receptors for the transmitter glutamate.

GABA$_C$ Receptors

This third family of ionotropic receptors ligated by GABA is insensitive to bicuculine inhibition, baclofen or muscimol stimulation, and positive allosteric modulation by BZs (Sivilotti & Nistri, 1991).

The ionotropic responses elicited by GABA acting on GABA$_C$ receptors are also of the fast type associated with an opening of an anion channel. The GABA$_C$ receptor structure results from homomeric assembly of ρ (ρ$_1$, ρ$_2$, ρ$_3$) subunits. The only organ that expresses ρ subunits in both rat and human is the retina. Since these ρ subunits have a 27% homology to GABA$_A$ receptor subunits,

Table 1.   Ligands of BZ Recognition Sites on GABA$_A$ Receptors and Their Pharmacological Profile

Class	Chemicals and generic names	Tolerance Liability (Intensity)	Flumazenil precipitated withdrawal (intensity)
Full positive allosteric modulators or *full agonists*	Classical 1, 4 BZs (alprazolam, clonazepam, diazepam, flunitrazepam, lorazepam, midazolam, triazolam)	+++	+++
Selective positive allosteric modulators or *selective agonists*	Triazolopyridazines (Cl218872) Pyrazolopyridines (CGS20625, ICI190622) Thienoopyrimidines (NNC14–0590) Imidazoquinazolines (NNC14–0185, NNC14–0189) Imidazopyridines (zolpidem) β-carbolines (abecarnil) 1,4 BZ (2-oxoquazepam)	++	++
Partial positive allosteric modulators or *partial agonists*	Imidazobenzodiazepine carboxamines (imidazenil) Imidazobenzodiazepinones (bretazenil, FG8205) Benzoquinolizones (RO19–8022)	+/–	–
Antagonists Devoid of intrinsic activity	1,4 BZ (flumazenil, ZG63, RO147437) β-carbolines (ZK93426) pyrazoloquinolinines (CHS8216)	–	–

they have been considered a subgroup of these receptor subunits. However, unlike GABA$_A$ receptors, when ρ subunits combine to form GABA$_C$ receptors they form only homomeric receptors. Thus, the function of homomeric ρ receptors sharply differs from that of GABA$_A$ receptors because ρ subunits lack the regulatory sites that are expressed in α, β, and γ subunits. The resistance of GABA$_C$ receptors to bicuculine inhibition or muscimol stimulation and the absence of allosteric modulation sites for barbiturates and BZs justify maintaining a functional distinction between GABA$_C$ and GABA$_A$ receptors.

THE STRUCTURE OF THE GABA$_A$ RECEPTOR SUBUNIT FAMILIES

Although the BZs were first introduced into clinical practice between 1959 and 1960 and soon became the most-sold drugs, it was not until 1975 that BZs were recognized to exert their action as specific amplifiers of the GABA-mediated inhibitory synaptic activity in the brains of the crustacean and of the speciation to human primates (Costa et al., 1975; Haefely et al., 1975). In 1977, Squires and Braestrup independently from Mohler and Okada and vice versa demonstrated the presence of high-affinity binding sites for BZs in the mammalian brain. It was recognized successively that the brain expresses two types of high-affinity recognition sites for BZs which differ in their affinity for selective BZs: One located in mitochondria is selectively activated by 4-Cl-diazepam and its function is associated with the regulation of the access of cholesterol into mitochondria where cholesterol is enzymatically (P450scc) converted into pregnenolone. This receptor is considered to define the rate-limiting event in the biosynthesis of steroid hormones in endocrine glands. In brain glial cells, this event is rate-limiting for the biosynthesis of pregnenolone, the parent compound of progesterone which in the brain can be converted to allopregnanolone (which has a limited genomic action and a very strong ability to positively modulate GABA action at GABA$_A$ receptors (Guidotti & Costa, 1998). The other BZ recognition site is specifically located in neuronal membranes and was putatively associated to a specific site expressed by GABA$_A$ receptors, which selectively binds BZs

(Haefely et al., 1975; Costa et al., 1975). Several investigators, however, subsequently postulated that BZs specifically bind to an unknown receptor for another neurotransmitter, and various lines of independent investigation were directed to validate this proposal. The interest for such a line of research greatly diminished when it was shown that the apparent molecular mass of the brain protein including the BZ recognition site, mediating the anxiolytic and anticonvulsant action of several drugs (Table 1), was identical to that including the GABA recognition site expressed by GABA$_A$ receptors. In fact, it was the availability of a BZ affinity column that allowed the isolation from preparation of brain GABA$_A$ receptors of a protein including a BZ and a GABA recognition site which allowed obtaining the first amino acid sequences for the cloning of the first two GABA$_A$ receptor subunits (Schofield et al., 1987). Various successive cloning attempts from cDNA libraries have identified 19 genes encoding for 19 subunits included in the pentameric structure of GABA$_A$ and GABA$_C$ receptors (Figure 1). These genes encode 6α, 4β, 3γ, 1δ, 1ε, and 1π subunits, which have better than 70% intrasubunit family homology. We have discussed earlier that the ρ subunits, which have 27% homology with the subunit families of GABA$_A$ receptors, by this criterion, but not by functional considerations, qualify as GABA$_A$ receptor subunits.

The database accession numbers for these subunits are: α$_1$ = P18504; α$_2$ = P23576; α$_3$ = P20236 α$_4$ = P28471; α$_5$ = P19964; α$_6$ = 30191; β$_1$ = P15431; β$_2$ = P15432; β$_3$ = P15433; δ = P18506; ε = U66661; γ$_1$ = P23574; γ$_2$ = P18508; γ$_3$ = P28473; π = U95368; ρ$_1$ = P50572; ρ$_2$ = P47742; ρ$_3$ = P50573. The chromosomal clustering for GABA$_A$ and GABA$_C$ receptor subunit genes is reported in Table 2. Unfortunately, there are not appropriate methods to analyze the stoichiometry and degree of isomerism of the subunits of various natural or recombinantly assembled GABA$_A$ receptor subtypes (Costa, 1998). Moreover, we are not yet able to decipher the molecular language of a presumed code regulating the assembly sequence order of the subunits that form a given natural or GABA$_A$-recombinant receptor subtype. Hence a subunit stoichiometry- and sequence-based classification of GABA$_A$ receptors expressed in various neurons is not possible at this time. The most frequent subunit assembly number expressed in $GABA_A$ or $GABA_C$ receptors appears to be pentameric (Nayeem et al., 1994).

A study (Ducik et al., 1995) of the GABA ED_{50} (µM) of 19 recombinant $GABA_A$ receptor subtypes in the HEK (293) cell line has revealed that the highest affinity (2.4) is for $\alpha_5 \beta_1 \gamma_2$ and the lowest (15) is for $\alpha_3 \beta_1 \gamma_2$. However, because we do not know whether a cDNA transfection in a given cell culture yields a uniform receptor assembly population, we have to assume that the ED_{50} mentioned above could be an average value of different clusters of $GABA_A$ receptors subtypes in which the repetition of two identical subunits or the order of subunit assembly may be different.

CHARACTERIZATION OF $GABA_A$ RECEPTOR FUNCTIONAL MODIFICATIONS BY VARIOUS ANXIOLYTIC DRUGS ACTING ON THE BZ RECOGNITION SITE

There is a considerable interest in the availability of an effective $GABA_A$ receptor-acting anxiolytic drug which will not share the problems of presently available medications. These problems are tolerance, dependence liability, and several inconvenient side effects such as sedation, induction of recent memory deficit, barbiturate or ethanol potentiation, and ataxia.

The overall intrinsic activity of these anxiolytic drugs that bind with high affinity to the $GABA_A$ receptor recognition site specific for BZs has been ranked in terms of the drugs' amplification modes of GABA-gated Cl^- current intensities (see Table 1) as following:

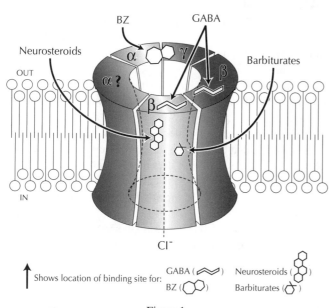

Shows location of binding site for: GABA ( ) Neurosteroids ( )
BZ ( ) Barbiturates ( )

Figure 1

1. Full positive allosteric modulators that maximize GABA-gated Cl^- current intensities at several $GABA_A$ receptor subtypes. These compounds have also been termed full agonists.

2. Partial positive allosteric modulators that partially amplify GABA-gated Cl^- current intensities at several $GABA_A$ receptor subtypes. These compounds have also been termed partial agonists.

3. Selective positive allosteric modulators of GABA-gated Cl^- current intensities at one or few selected $GABA_A$ receptor subtypes. These drugs have been termed selective agonists.

4. High-affinity ligands of BZ recognition sites that are devoid of intrinsic activity but antagonize the actions of BZs belonging to above groups 1, 2, and 3. These compounds have been termed antagonists (see Table 1).

The high-affinity binding site for BZs located in $GABA_A$ receptors has specific structural features. It consists of a binding pocket formed by the contiguity of an α subunit (not present in α_6 and with low intrinsic activity in α_5) with a γ_2 or a γ_3 subunit (which is not expressed by a γ_1 subunit). These requirements specify that, in order to predict which $GABA_A$ receptors are susceptible to positive allosteric modulation by ligands to the BZ recognition sites, we must know subunit isomerism and sequence (Costa, 1998). Unfortunately we do not have suitable methods to fulfill either task. It is presently believed that BZs amplify the actions of GABA by facilitating the opening of channels in monoligated $GABA_A$ receptors, which, to open the channel in absence of BZs, require two molecules of GABA bound to the receptor.

DEPENDENCE AND TOLERANCE TO PROTRACTED TREATMENT WITH ANXIOLYTIC DRUGS THAT BIND TO BZ RECOGNITION SITES

As shown in Table 1, full agonists have the highest incidence of tolerance and dependence liability. In various animal species, the degree of dependence liability is estimated by the severity of a withdrawal syndrome triggered by abruptly stopping a long-term administration of BZ recognition site ligands in animals that become tolerant to the anxiolytic or anticonvulsant actions of these drugs. In order to precipitate the withdrawal syndrome, some investigators have also used the administration of BZ recognition site antagonists (see Table 1) to animals tolerant to anxiolytic ligands for these sites. During protracted administration of a full agonist of BZ recognition sites, tolerance to each behavioral response elicited by this ligand (i.e., sedative, anticonvulsant, amnesic, anxiolytic) occurs after a well-defined latency time which is characteristic for

Table 2. Chromosome Clustering of $GABA_A$ and $GABA_C$ Receptor Subunits

Chromosome #	1	4	5	6	15	X
Subunits	δ	$\alpha_2 \alpha_4 \beta_1 \gamma_1$	$\alpha_1 \alpha_6 \beta_2 \gamma_2$	$\rho_1 \rho_2$	$\alpha_5 \beta_3 \gamma_3$	$\alpha_3 \varepsilon_1$
Chromosomal Subunit Clustering site	(1q)	(4q13–q11)	(5q34–q35)	(6q14–q21)	(15q11–q13)	(Xq 28)

each response. It is believed that the mechanism underpinning the tolerance to each of the actions of BZs is due to an adaptive response of $GABA_A$ receptors to the protracted continuous occupation of the BZ recognition sites. This adaptation very likely results in changes in the subtype of $GABA_A$ receptors which are expressed, leading to the formation of $GABA_A$ receptors with a lower intrinsic affinity and activity for the BZ recognition site ligands that have been administered. According to mechanistic tolerance studies of full agonist BZs (Impaganatiello et al., 1996), it has been concluded that the intensity of amplification of $GABA_A$ receptor Cl^- currents plays a role in triggering the adaptive response to the persistence occupation of the BZ recognition site. In fact, full agonists (see Table 1), but not partial agonists, have a high liability to the expression of tolerance and dependence.

Imidazenil, the prototype of a partial agonist (see Table 1) fails to cause tolerance or dependence to the anticonvulsant action in animals that are tolerant to the anticonvulsant action of diazepam. In addition, in nonhuman primates imidazenil fails to impair cognitive functions which are disrupted by a full BZ agonist and, when a partial agonist (see Table 1) is injected simultaneously with a full BZ agonist, it prevents the onset of tolerance to the latter. The compensatory changes of $GABA_A$ receptor structure expressed during tolerance to protracted administration of a full agonist BZ recognition site ligand consist in a decrease in the mRNA encoding for α_1 and γ_2 subunits while the expression of the α_5 mRNA subunit increases. Similar changes were also detected in the expression of the corresponding subunits (Impagnatiello et al., 1996; Pesold et al., 1997). In contrast, a protracted treatment with the partial agonist imidazenil, with doses multiple to those that cause an anxiolytic and anticonvulsant action similar to that elicited by doses of full agonist that cause tolerance and dependence, failed to cause tolerance liability. The interpretation of these findings is that a maximal amplification by BZs of GABA-gated Cl^- currents is not necessary to cause their anticonvulsant or anxiolytic action, but it is required to elicit a high liability to their tolerance and dependence.

REFERENCES

Costa E. (1998). *Annu. Rev. Pharmacol. Toxicol. 38*, 321–350.

Costa E., & Guidotti, A. (1996). *Trends Pharm. Sci., 17*, 192–200.

Costa E., Guidotti A., & Mao, C. C. (1975). *Adv. Biochem. Psychopharmacoal., 14*, 113–130.

D'Arcangelo G., Miao, G. G., Chen, S. C., Soares, H. D., & Morgan, J. I., et al. (1995). *J. L. Nature, 374*, 719–723.

Ducic, I., Caruncho, H. J., Zhu, W. J., Vicini, S., & Costa, E. (1995). *J. Pharmacol. Exp. Ther. 272*, 438–445.

Enna, S. J., & Bowery, N. G., (1997). The GABA receptors. /edited by S. J. Enna, G. Bowery. Totowa, NJ: Humana Press.

Guidotti, A., & Costa, E. (1998). *Biol. Psychiatry 44*, 865–873.

Haefely, W., Kulesar, A., Mohler, H., Pieri, L., & Pole, P., et al. (1975). *Adv. Biochem Psychopharmacol., 14*, 131–151.

Hill, D. R., & Bowery, N. G. (1981). *Nature, 240*, 149–152.

Impagnatiello, F., Pesold, C., Longone, P., Caruncho, H. J., Fritschy, & J. M., et al. (1996). *Mol. Pharmacol., 491*, 822–831.

Macdonald, R. L., & Olsen, R. W. (1994). *Annu. Rev. Neurosci., 17*, 569–602.

Mienville, J. M. (1998). *J. Physiol., 512*, 809–817.

Mohler, H., & Ohada, T. (1977). *Science, 198*, 849–851.

Nayeem, N., Green, T. P., Martin, I. L., & Barnard, E. A. (1994). *J. Neurochem., 62*, 815–818.

Pesold, C., Caruncho, H. J., Impagnatiello, F., Berg, M. J., Fritschy, & J. M., et al. (1997). *Neuroscience, 79*, 477–487.

Rivera, C., Voipio, J., Payne, J. A., Ruusuvuori, E., & Lahitinen, H., et al. (1999). *Nature, 397*, 251–255.

Schofield, P. E., Darlison, M. G., Fujita, N., Burt, D. R., & Stephenson, F. A., et al. (1987). *Nature, 328*, 221–227.

Sivilotti, L., & Nistri, A. (1991). *Prog. Neurobiol., 36*, 35–92.

Squires, R. E., & Bestrup, C. (1977). *Nature, 266*, 732–734.

Vojcik, W. J., & Heff, N. H. (1984). *Mol. Pharmacol., 25*, 24–28.

E. Costa
University of Illinois, Chicago

GAGE, PHINEAS

On September 13, 1998, a group of brain scientists, including neurologists, neuropsychologists, and neurosurgeons, gathered in Cavendish, Vermont to commemorate a bizarre anniversary: that of an accident in which a young man named Phineas Gage had suffered a brain injury when an iron bar was shot through the front part of his head. The accident itself was remarkable enough: immediately afterward, despite a gruesome wound to the front of his head and brain, Gage was conscious, alert, and talkative, and it seemed rather a miracle that he had even survived. But what followed over the next few decades, and then over the many years since, is what put Cavendish, Vermont, on the scientific map, and the reason why scientists traveled there to commemorate the anniversary of Gage's accident.

On September 13, 1848, Gage was laboring with coworkers to blast a bed for railroad tracks through the rugged, rocky terrain of southern Vermont. While setting an explosive, Gage prematurely triggered an explosion with his tamping iron. The iron was propelled through the front part of his head, entering his left cheek just under the eye, piercing the frontal lobes of his brain, and exiting through the top front part of his head. In light of the comparatively primitive state of medicine in the mid-nineteenth century, Gage's medical recovery was nothing short of astonishing—he survived this massive onslaught with normal intelligence, memory, speech, sensation, and movement. Following his surprising physical recovery, however, Gage displayed a profound change in personality and social conduct. Before the accident, he had been responsible, socially well-adapted, and well-liked by his peers and supervisors. Afterwards, Gage proved to be irresponsible, untrustworthy, irreverent, and capricious, demonstrating markedly unreliable behavior and little regard for social convention; in short, he was no longer *Gage*.

Gage's physician, John Harlow, speculated (highly accurately, as it turned out) that there was a causative relationship between the damage to the front part of Gage's brain and the profound change in his personality and social conduct (Harlow, 1868). Harlow's observations, although never fully appreciated by his contemporaries, hinted at a conclusion that was both radical and prescient: There are structures in the front part of the human brain that are dedicated to the planning and execution of both personally and socially adaptive behavior and to the aspect of reasoning known as rationality. Case reports published over the first several decades of the twentieth century supported Harlow's contention, and modern neuropsychological investigations have documented that the prefrontal region is crucial for social conduct, planning, and decision making.

Recently, the tools of modern neuroscience have allowed scientists to perform a careful reconstruction of the injury to Gage's brain (Damasio, Grabowski, Frank, Galaborda, & Damasio, 1994). Using measurements of Gage's skull and the tamping iron (which are part of the Warren Anatomical Medical Museum at Harvard University), scientists were able to reproduce the precise path the tamping iron traversed through Gage's brain. (The skull and iron, which were on display at the anniversary celebration in 1998, are remarkably well preserved to this day.) This reconstruction confirmed that the damage included the left and right prefrontal regions, anterior to structures required for motor behavior and speech, in precisely the location that modern studies have highlighted as the key neural underpinning of social conduct and rational decision making.

The importance of the Gage case can be more fully appreciated when one considers just how difficult it has been to unravel the cognitive and behavioral functions that are subserved by the prefrontal region of the human brain. The prefrontal sector, situated anterior to the motor/premotor cortices and superior to the Sylvian fissure, comprises an enormous expanse of the brain, forming nearly half of the entire cerebral mantle. In humans in particular, this region has expanded disproportionately. Throughout the history of neuropsychology, the psychological capacities associated with the prefrontal region have remained enigmatic and elusive. Beginning with the observations of Gage, however, the special significance of this region began to be appreciated.

Following Harlow's prescient writings regarding Gage, other investigators have called attention to the often bizarre development of abnormal social behavior that can follow prefrontal brain injury (e.g., Eslinger & Damasio, 1985; Stuss & Benson, 1986). The patients have a number of features in common (Damasio & Anderson, 1993): inability to organize future activity and hold gainful employment, diminished capacity to respond to punishment, a tendency to present an unrealistically favorable view of themselves, and a tendency to display inappropriate emotional reactions. Making this profile especially puzzling is the fact that most of these patients, like Gage, retain normal intelligence, language, memory, and perception.

Other scientists have called attention to the striking characteristics of patients with prefrontal lobe brain injury, especially damage to the ventral and lower medial portions of this region (the "ventromedial prefrontal" sector). Blumer and Benson (1975) noted that the patients displayed a personality profile (which the authors termed "pseudo-psychopathic") featured by puerility, a jocular attitude, sexually disinhibited humor, inappropriate and near-total self-indulgence, and complete lack of concern for others. Stuss and Benson (1986) emphasized that the patients demonstrated a remarkable lack of empathy and general lack of concern about others. The patients showed callous unconcern, boastfulness, and unrestrained and tactless behavior. Other descriptors included impulsiveness, facetiousness, and diminished anxiety and concern for the future.

This personality profile is strikingly similar to that characterized in clinical psychology and psychiatry as psychopathic (or sociopathic; American Psychiatric Association, 1994). In fact, Tranel and colleagues have designated this condition as "*acquired* sociopathy," to emphasize the fact that patients with prefrontal injuries often have personality manifestations that are quite reminiscent of those associated with sociopathy (Tranel, 1994). The qualifier *acquired* signifies that in the brain-damaged patients, the condition follows the onset of brain injury and occurs in persons whose personalities and social conduct were previously normal (as in the case of Gage). Patients with acquired sociopathy have a proclivity to engage in decisions and behaviors that have negative consequences for their well-being. They repeatedly select courses of action that are not in their long-term best interests, making poor decisions about interpersonal relationships, occupational endeavors, and finances. In short, the patients act as though they have lost the ability to ponder different courses of action and then select the option that promises the best blend of short- and long-term benefit.

To investigate the decision-making defect of prefrontal lobe patients, Bechara developed a paradigm known as the Gambling Task, in which participants play a card game that contains complex, implicit trade-offs between immediate and long-term rewards and punishments (Bechara, Damasio, Damasio, & Anderson, 1994; Tranel, Bechara, & Damasio, 1999). Participants must learn to accept lower immediate rewards in order to maximize long-term gains, because the task is set up so that higher immediate rewards are accompanied by higher long-term losses. To play the Gambling Task successfully (and to navigate successfully in the real world), one must develop a notion as to the relative merits and hazards of one's decisions, in regard to both immediate and long-term consequences of behavior, a capacity that appears to depend critically on structures in the ventromedial prefrontal cortex. Patients with ventromedial prefrontal lobe injuries play the game in a manner which suggests that they are insensitive to the future consequences of their behavior; that is, they opt repeatedly for higher short-term reward, even if this leads eventually to long-term punishment. These observations highlight the fact that the ventromedial prefrontal region also plays a key role in emotional behavior, particularly the link between emotions and reasoning. Our studies suggest that reasoning with too little emotion can be as detrimental for good decision making as reasoning with too much emotion.

As it turned out, the misadventures of Phineas Gage provided crucial early clues about the importance of the prefrontal sector of the brain for social behavior, reasoning, decision making, and what can generally be called "personality." Gage's accident was bizarre, to be sure, but its important place in neuroscientific history is firmly secure.

REFERENCES

American Psychiatric Association (1994). *Diagnostic and statistical manual of mental disorders* (Fourth Edition). Washington, DC: Author.

Bechara, A., Damasio, A. R., Damasio, H., & Anderson, S. W. (1994). Insensitivity to future consequences following damage to human prefrontal cortex. *Cognition, 50,* 7–15.

Blumer, D., & Benson, D. F. (1975). Personality changes with frontal and temporal lobe lesions. In D. F. Benson & D. Blumer (Eds.), *Psychiatric aspects of neurologic disease* (pp. 151–169). New York: Grune & Stratton.

Damasio, A. R., & Anderson, S. W. (1993). The frontal lobes. In K. Heilman & E. Valenstein (Eds.), *Clinical neuropsychology* (3rd Ed.; pp. 409–460). New York: Oxford University Press.

Damasio, H., Grabowski, T., Frank, R., Galaburda, A. M., & Damasio, A. R. (1994). The return of Phineas Gage: Clues about the brain from the skull of a famous patient. *Science, 264,* 1102–1105.

Eslinger, P. J., & Damasio, A. R. (1985). Severe disturbance of higher cognition after bilateral frontal lobe ablation: Patient EVR. *Neurology, 35,* 1731–1741.

Harlow, J. M. (1868). Recovery from the passage of an iron bar through the head. *Publications of the Massachusetts Medical Society, 2,* 327–347.

Stuss, D. T., & Benson, D. F. (1986). *The frontal lobes.* New York: Raven.

Tranel, D. (1994). "Acquired sociopathy": The development of sociopathic behavior following focal brain damage. In D. C. Fowles, P. Sutker, & S. H. Goodman (Eds.), *Progress in experimental personality and psychopathology research,* Vol. 17 (pp. 285–311). New York: Springer.

Tranel, D., Bechara, A., & Damasio, A. R. (1999). Decision-making and the somatic marker hypothesis. In M. S. Gazzaniga (Ed.), *The Cognitive Neurosciences,* 2nd edition. Cambridge, MA: The MIT Press.

SUGGESTED READING

Bigelow, H. J. (1850). Dr. Harlow's case of recovery from the passage of an iron bar through the head. *American Journal of the Medical Sciences, 39,* 13–22.

D. TRANEL
University of Iowa College of Medicine

BRAIN INJURIES

GALL, FRANZ JOSEF (1757–1828)

Franz Josef Gall was a German physician who believed a correlation existed between mental abilities and the formation of the skull. Because he held that skull formation determines personality and behavior, he was charged with fatalism and hence with subverting religion. Consequently he was forced to leave Vienna, where he had settled in 1785, after completing medical studies at Strasbourg and Vienna.

His lectures in phrenology began in 1796, but by 1802 the Austrian government prohibited them. In 1805 he left Austria for an extended lecture tour to Germany, Holland, Sweden, and Switzerland. His fame peaked in Paris, where he settled as a physician in 1807. With his associate J. G. Spurzheim, he delivered an account of their research to the Institute of France, but that august body (which included Philippe Pinel and other notables) repudiated their report.

In the history of psychology, Gall is credited with being a pioneer in brain mapping or brain localization. Brain localization became accepted in psychology in 1861, when Paul Broca found the speech center in the brain. Phrenology's basic premise, however, was invalidated when it was discovered that the skull and the brain's topographies do not accord, because the skull's thickness varies. Gall did, however, correctly identify the brain's gray matter with neurons and its white matter with ganglia or connective tissue.

Six volumes of Gall's writings were published as *Works: On the Functions of the Brain and Each of its Parts.* With Spurzheim, he published *Researches on the Nervous System,* and *Anatomy and Physiology of the Nervous System.* His medical practice and research continued until his death at Montrouge, a suburb of Paris.

W. S. SAHAKIAN

GALTON, FRANCIS (1822–1911)

The father of differential psychology and one of the foremost progenitors of psychometrics, Francis Galton was born into a wealthy English family, a half-cousin of Charles Darwin. Galton was a prodigy who could read and write at the age of 3, but a problem pupil in school. After attending medical school and earning a degree in mathematics at Cambridge at 21, Galton fell heir to a family fortune that allowed him to pursue freely his scientific interests the rest of his long life, without need to earn a living. Strictly speaking, he could be regarded as a lifelong amateur inventor and scientist, but because he was also an authentic genius he made seminal contributions in a variety of fields: exploration and geography (of Africa), meteorology, photography, classification of fingerprints, genetics, statistics, anthropometry, and psychometry. His prodigious achievements and prolific publications brought him worldwide recognition and many honors, including knighthood, being named a Fellow of the Royal Society, and gold medals awarded by various scientific bodies in England and Europe.

Galton's contributions to differential psychology reflected his conviction that all human characteristics, both physical and mental, could ultimately be described quantitatively. This he believed a necessary condition for achieving a science of humanity. His motto was, "When you can, count." To promote quantitative thinking in the biological sciences, Galton and his disciple Karl Pearson founded the journal *Biometrika,* which continues to the present day.

Galton's long-term investigations of heredity culminated in *Natural Inheritance,* in which he anticipated the polygenic theory of inheritance of continuous characteristics later developed by Sir Ronald Fisher. But it was *Hereditary Genius: An Inquiry into Its Laws and Consequences,* that became Galton's best-known work and the one most relevant to psychology. He was the first scientist to formulate clearly the nature-nurture question—that is, the relative contributions of heredity and environment to individual and group differences in human traits, abilities, and talents. He was also the first to note the methodological importance of monozygotic and dizygotic twins for estimating the relative effects of genetic and environmental factors in human variation.

As intelligence tests had not yet been invented, in *Hereditary Genius* Galton studied the inheritance of general mental ability by looking at nearly 1,000 men who had achieved intellectual eminence and tabulating the frequency of eminent men among all their relatives. He found that as the degree of genetic kinship decreased, the percentage of eminent relatives also decreased in a markedly stepwise fashion, as one should predict from Galton's model of genetic inheritance, which also explained similar effects for indisputably hereditary traits such as stature and fingerprints, which Galton also investigated. From this, Galton argued that mental ability is inherited in the same fashion, and to much the same degree, as many physical traits. Stature, for example, also displayed Galton's law of filial regression: The offspring of a deviant parent are, on average, less deviant from the mean of the population than is the parent regarding the trait in question.

Galton invented a number of sensory and motor tests, described in *Inquiries into Human Faculty and Its Development,* and he tested thousands of the general public in his laboratory in the South Kensington Science Museum. He was the first clearly to put forth the idea of general ability and specific abilities later developed by Charles Spearman, and held that general ability was by far the more important influence on a person's life achievements. He viewed general ability as largely hereditary, with its distribution in the population following the normal or Gaussian curve.

Galton's contributions to statistics and psychometrics include formulations of regression and correlation, the bivariate scatter diagram, multiple correlation, standardized or scale-free scores, percentile ranks, the use of the median and geometric mean as measures of central tendency, and rating scales.

Galton devoted his last years to championing eugenics, and wrote a Utopian novel, *Kantsaywhere* (unpublished), based on eugenic principles. In 1904 he founded and endowed the Galton Laboratory at the University of London, which, under the directorship of such luminaries as Karl Pearson and Sir Ronald Fisher, has been a leading center for research in genetics and statistics.

A. R. JENSEN
University of California at Berkeley

GAMBLER'S FALLACY

The gambler's fallacy, or the Monte Carlo fallacy as it is also known, reflects a common misconception of chance events, one that often misleads the unsavvy gambler. For example, suppose that a coin is tossed a number of times in succession. If a string of, say, 10 heads is produced and if the coin can be presumed to be fair, it would seem intuitively likely to most people that a tail is overdue. And if gambling on the outcome is involved, the careless gambler might bet heavily that this inference is correct and that a tail must come up. However, the inference is false, for the coin has no memory, and the likelihood of a tail appearing on the next toss is exactly the same as it was for any previous toss.

This fallacy is technically referred to as a negative recency effect: the tendency is to predict that the event that has recently been occurring with the greatest frequency will soon stop occurring. It is based in a belief in local representativeness, i.e., that a sequence of randomly produced events will represent the characteristics of the random process even when the sequence is short (Tversky & Kahneman, 1982). Thus a random generator such as a coin toss should, according to this misconception, produce outcomes that appear—even over the short run—to give no particular preference to one or the other of the possible outcomes. If a string of a particular outcome is produced, then the chance sequence is expected to have to correct itself in the near future, and a deviation in one direction thus needs to be balanced by a deviation in the other. In reality, however, randomly generated strings, especially if they are relatively short, often appear quite unrepresentative of the random process producing them.

The gambler's fallacy is more than a reflection of the statistical ignorance of laypeople, for it can be observed even in the private lives of the statistically sophisticated. It reflects two aspects of human cognitive function: (a) the strong and automatic motivation that people have to find order in what they observe around them, even should it happen to be a series of outcomes from a random process; and (b) the all-too-human predilection to ignore base-rate probabilities while giving in to intuition. While logic may persuade us that a chance process does not keep track of its outcomes, our intuitive reaction can be powerful and can sometimes overwhelm logic. Reed (1984) examined the relative impacts of logical and intuitive thought and argued that the latter often seems more compelling than the former, probably because such inferences simply spring to mind, therefore defying logical analysis, and are often accompanied by a strong feeling of being correct. Although it is not possible to see the process by which such intuitive "conclusions" are found, the process of logical reasoning is open for examination and critique. People are thus in control of logical thought, while they merely receive the outcomes of intuitive thought, imbuing the latter with a powerful sense of feeling right. As a consequence, most people believe that their intuitive judgments about probabilistic processes are more accurate than conclusions based on logic and probabilistic reasoning (Kleinke, 1978).

The gambler's fallacy is most likely to occur when chance alone produces the outcomes. When some skill is involved, a positive recency effect is more often observed. The observer is likely to see a string of successes by, e.g., a billiards player, as indicative of a hot streak and will bias his or her predictions of the next outcome in a positive rather than a negative direction. Even the tossing of dice can lead to a positive recency effect, to the extent that the individual believes that the outcome is in some manner influenced by the thrower's "skill."

REFERENCES

Kleinke, C. L. (1978). *Self-perception.* San Francisco: Freeman.

Reed, G. (1984, August 28). *Superstitious beliefs and cognitive processes.* Paper presented at the Symposium on Anomalistic Psychology, annual meeting of the American Psychological Association. Toronto.

Tversky, A., & Kahneman, D. (1982). Judgment under uncertainty: Heuristics and biases. In D. Kahneman, P. Slavic, & A. Tversky (Eds.), *Judgment under uncertainty: Heuristics and biases* (pp. 3–22). Cambridge, UK: Cambridge University Press.

J. E. ALCOCK
York University, Toronto

EMPIRICISM
GAMBLING BEHAVIOR
SAMPLING

GAMBLING BEHAVIOR

In "Gambling," his introduction to the *Psychology of Gambling,* a book edited by Jon Halliday and himself, Peter Fuller defined gambling as a redistribution of wealth on the basis of chance and risk, an event that always involves loss to one party and gain to another. In some gambling games, such as poker and blackjack, elements of skill combine with chance to influence the outcome of each play. In addition, basically nonrecreational activities such as stock and commodities transactions may serve on the one hand as vehicles of prudent investment, or on the other hand as outlets for irrational risk taking. Whether participation in events involving chance outcomes is simple recreation, reasonable risk taking, or irrational gambling seems to depend not so much on the nature of the game or transaction itself as upon the motivations and personality characteristics of the participant. The attention of behavioral scientists has focused on gambling because of the significant social, legal, and economic complications created both by widespread recreational gambling and by the development of compulsive or pathological gambling in a significant number of individuals.

HISTORICAL AND SOCIAL ASPECTS OF GAMBLING

Popular literature on gambling tends to focus on entertaining tales of legendary gamblers and on the various techniques of gambling. The psychologist Clemens J. France was one of the first professionals to publish in the field; his essay "The Gambling Impulse" (1902) reviewed evidence that gambling was popular and often posed a problem in ancient civilizations. Gambling seems to have been an obsession at times at the imperial court of China and at the royal courts of all European countries. France noted a tendency for

gambling to wax and wane in popularity over the centuries, with periods of excess alternating with periods of suppression—a finding that is perhaps suggestive of the mixed attitudes toward gambling created by the intense pleasure and complex problems it entails. As some theorists were later to argue, France suggested that gambling might be a healthy release for pent-up forces within the personality.

In his 1979 review of state-conducted lotteries, Blakey found that governments over the centuries have frequently sponsored public lotteries to raise funds for a variety of special projects such as military campaigns and harbor improvements. Such lotteries, however, have frequently failed to produce the hoped-for revenues and have often ended in corruption. Further, government lotteries generally turn out to be forms of regressive taxation by taking proportionately more money from the poor than from the well-to-do.

The Organized Crime Control Act, passed by the U.S. Congress in 1970, mandated among other actions the creation of a Commission on the Review of the National Policy Toward Gambling. The Commission was to deal with such complex problems as the lax enforcement of antigambling laws, gambling and organized crime, the effects of legalized gambling, and the impact of gambling on the character of American life. *Gambling in America,* the final report of the Commission published in 1976, stated that 61% of the population engaged in some kind of gambling and that 80% of Americans approved of gambling in some form. The report also included an estimate that there were approximately 1.1 million compulsive gamblers in the country and that the increasing availability of gambling might pose significant problems. In Nevada, where casino gambling was legalized in 1931, the commission found measurably higher rates of gambling by local residents than in other areas of the country. Proportionately more low- than high-income family members gambled on a regular basis in Nevada. The Commission also concluded that many antigambling laws were simply impossible to enforce. In 1979 much of the research for the Commission done by social scientists was summarized in a special issue of the *Journal of Social Issues,* in which Kallick-Kaufman and Reuter urged that government policy be based on scientific research, but pointed out that funding for research on gambling had been meager and that, when available, research findings were often ignored in favor of political considerations in formulating policy.

The cultural impact of legalized gambling has been further documented by the sociologist Jerome Skolnick (1979). He argued, as have others, that legalized gambling might only add to problems of street crime, drug trafficking, and illegal gambling. Skolnick argued that gambling has a differential impact on social classes, pointing out that in the European model of legalized casino gambling, local blue-collar citizens were usually excluded from casinos. That gambling can have negative effects even on casino workers has been documented by Smith and his associates (1976). They found greater feelings of powerlessness, meaninglessness, social isolation, and self-estrangement among dealers.

As a measure of increasing social awareness of the problems introduced by gambling, it should be noted that in 1979 the state of Maryland passed legislation to create a treatment facility for pathological gamblers. New York and Connecticut did the same in 1981.

RECREATIONAL GAMBLING

Although gambling is a problem for some, it is often viewed as a normal, natural, and healthy recreation for the majority. In the early paper by France mentioned above, gambling was held to increase metabolism, heighten sensations of reality, and produce a beneficial intensity of emotion. In interviews with retired persons and industrial workers in southern Nevada, Campbell (1976) found that gambling increased worker productivity and gave meaning to the lives of people in retirement. The psychologist Igor Kusyszyn (1976) presented evidence that gamblers are more emotionally stable, more secure, and more dominant than nongamblers. Ashton (1979) agreed that gambling is a normal and healthy pastime that can produce peak experiences through arousal and stimulation. Ashton reviewed several of Kusyszyn's unpublished papers which argue strongly for the positive aspects of recreational gambling. With the legalization of casino gambling in New Jersey by popular referendum in 1976, and with widespread legalization of various other forms of gambling in many other states, gambling has become a readily available recreation for Americans, as it has long been in many other countries. The public appetite for gambling has been welcomed by state governments eager to enhance revenues with what may be called painless taxation.

RISK TAKING AND UTILITY THEORY

Apart from psychoanalytic theories of gambling behavior, there has been relatively little psychological theory building to explain the attractiveness of gambling. Several attempts have been made to include gambling in a general theory of risk taking. Bern (1971) wrote that willingness to take reasonable risk is a valuable characteristic. The motivation to achieve, he said, is positively correlated with realistic risk taking, while fear of failure may be associated with foolish or excessive risk taking. Knowles (1976) pointed out that there is great difficulty in defining risk taking as a specific class of behaviors, and that there are few common elements in different situations. To explain gambling by saying that it is a special case of risk taking is therefore difficult.

Economic utility theory attempted to explain how the subjective value of a given risk to an individual could outweigh the objective value of a possible pay off. In reviewing the basic assumptions of utility theory, Elmore (1979) held that the subjective value of a bet does not have a linear relationship with the objective probability of payoff. The willingness to assume gambling risks varies, depending on the relative wealth of the individual, psychological factors, and the hope of gaining an otherwise impossible financial goal. Thus, although objectively not a good investment, a bet involving a potentially high payoff may have greater utility to the bettor than the amount that could be lost.

THE GAMBLING LIFESTYLE

For some individuals gambling has become the central organizing theme in life, and several have left fascinating accounts of the agonizing growth of the obsession. Fyodor Dostoyevsky, in his classic short story, *The Gambler,* gave an essentially autobiographical account of personal destruction through extended bouts of gambling. Dostoyevsky himself seems to have been able to turn away from gambling and resume writing only when he had lost all his money and come near to total ruin. Robin Moore has given a highly detailed modern account of the gambling lifestyle in his autobiography *Compulsion: The True Story of an Addictive Gambler,* which contains a commentary by psychiatrist Robert Custer. Jay Livingston entered the world of the chronic gambler by attending Gamblers Anonymous meetings and gathering the stories of the gamblers he met. In *Compulsive Gamblers* he traced the development of gambling from its first challenge as an adventure to its final compulsive stage in which borrowing, stealing, and lying inevitably led to alienation and desperate attempts to stop. Henry R. Lesieur interviewed gamblers and members of Gamblers Anonymous, and in *The Chase* described how gamblers acquire a chase philosophy in which they endlessly try to win back what was lost in defiance of laws of probability, thinking that gambling, which caused their problems in the first place, is the only solution; thus the alternatives to gambling are limited by gambling itself. This is not to say that all frequent gamblers are compulsive; the majority probably are not. The work of Campbell (1976) mentioned above also contains reports of her participant observer studies of casino gambling in which she clearly sees a majority of frequent gamblers as noncompulsive pleasure seekers.

THE PSYCHOANALYTIC APPROACH

In "Dostoyevsky and Parricide" Sigmund Freud used the life of Fyodor Dostoyevsky to illustrate how the psychodynamic view might explain adult addiction to gambling by childhood sexual conflicts. Dostoyevsky's father was actually murdered, thus fulfilling for Fyodor the universal childhood wish for the father's death—an event which Freud supposed was longed for since it would, in fantasy, permit the boy child a free sexual reign with the mother. Lindner (1950) pointed out the gambler's dilemma: Winning is desirable since it fulfills the childish wish for omnipotence and is a symbolic approval of incestuous urges, but losing is also desirable since it provides punishment for forbidden incestuous acts and thus removes the pain of guilt. Since winning produces intolerable guilt while losing proves the lack of omnipotence, the gambler is caught in an endless, repetitive search for a solution. Perhaps the best-known psychoanalytic study of gambling is Edmond Bergler's *The Psychology of Gambling,* which traces the roots of gambling to childhood rebellion, oral and anal sexual investment, and the forbidden act of masturbation.

The psychoanalytic theorists saw in gambling a reenactment of such conflict-filled acts as autoeroticism, a situation filled with tension, pleasure, fear, and guilt. Because there were symbolic thematic elements in common in both childish sex play and gambling, these theorists assumed a causal relationship. But convincing objective evidence is scarce; the burden of proof lies on the interpretation of case histories.

THE MEDICAL MODEL OF PATHOLOGICAL GAMBLING

Many psychoanalytic theorists, including Freud, were psychiatrists trained initially in medicine, so it is understandable that they came to accept compulsive gambling as a disease or sickness of the mind. In 1960 E. M. Jellinek published a landmark book, *The Disease*

Concept of Alcoholism, which quickly won wide acceptance for the view that alcohol dependence is a chronic, progressive, and sometimes fatal illness that prevents the victim, once addicted, from ever resuming the role of a social or moderate drinker. Total abstinence was viewed as the only way of arresting the illness. Alcoholics Anonymous, and its 1957 offshoot Gamblers Anonymous, adopted this view and incorporated the disease model into their literature. Bolen and Boyd (1968) used the term "pathological gambling" to describe cases they had seen in psychiatric practice, but held that gambling was symptomatic of a wide variety of specific mental disorders and not an illness in its own right. Moran (1975) argued convincingly that gambling could be a primary diagnostic entity and gave a detailed, objective description of the syndrome. Symptoms included preoccupation with gambling, an overpowering urge to gamble, tension, inability to control gambling, chronic shortage of money, family conflict, and loss of employment due to gambling.

Robert Custer, who was the first to treat gamblers in a hospital program, further refined the diagnostic criteria for pathological gambling and was primarily responsible for the inclusion of the illness in the 1980 edition of the American Psychiatric Association's *Diagnostic and Statistical Manual of Mental Disorders* (3rd ed.). In "An overview of compulsive gambling" Custer reviewed in detail the course of the disease, its social and legal complications, and various treatment methods.

By no means has the medical model of pathological gambling gone unchallenged. Behaviorists saw gambling not as sickness but as a simple behavioral phenomena resulting from conditions of learning. In offering critical comments (contained in the Custer paper cited above) on the medical model, Hankoff argued that the idea of gambling as a disease is circular reasoning, since the presence of the symptom of gambling is the only proof the disease exists. Hankoff argued that the disease model might absolve the gambler from responsibility for doing something about the problem: In calling it a disease, physicians were guilty of serving their own interests. Herman (1976) also examined and rejected a medical model, saying that assigning labels to people might actually make the problem worse. Nevertheless, at least one strictly medical solution has been found to help some pathological gamblers: Joel Moskowitz used lithium in three cases and found significant improvement, possibly because these patients also had manic tendencies.

It is yet to be resolved whether chronic gambling is best viewed as a disease, an addiction, a learned habit, an excessive behavior, or a symptom of deeper illness.

THE BEHAVIORAL VIEW

Although the literature flowing from experimental psychology contains few studies of gambling behavior, the theoretical framework developed from the analysis of behavior offers unique insight into the causes of risk taking. Knapp (1976) employed basic principles of operant behavior to explain persistent gambling, saying for example that since betting is only occasionally reinforced by winning, gambling represents the result of intermittent or partial schedules of reinforcement. Such schedules are known to produce behaviors which are extremely resistant to extinction. Knapp's behavioral view rejected personality variables as causal, arguing that gambling is shaped and maintained by discriminative stimuli in the gambling environment and by the individual's history of reinforcement. Frank (1976) further pointed out that gambling leads to adaptation or desensitization to the punishment of losing. Losing, in fact, may become a positive discriminative stimulus to bet again, since losing is often followed by winning. Frank suggested, as have others, that gamblers seem to have an external locus of control: They do not view their own behavior as responsible for winning or losing and attribute results to chance or luck.

Behavioral psychologists, in rejecting a strictly medical model of pathological gambling, have sometimes settled on an addictive behavior model in which gambling is seen as one of many similar dependencies or abuse patterns. Victor (1981) argued that addictive gambling resulted from an interaction between certain personality characteristics and contingencies of reinforcement, thus suggesting the possibility of compromise between medical and behavioral views.

THE TREATMENT OF PATHOLOGICAL GAMBLING

The chronic or compulsive gambler has long been recognized in history and literature, but humane treatment and professional recognition of the problem began only in 1964 when the Rev. Gordon Moody in England helped to start an English branch of Gamblers Anonymous and opened a halfway house for destitute gamblers (Anita, "Gamblers Anonymous"). Gamblers Anonymous began in the United States in 1957; professional treatment began in 1972 at the Veterans Administration hospital in Brecksville, Ohio (Alsop, 1977).

Custer's 1982 paper and Alsop's 1977 article describe modern treatment techniques. These include heavy emphasis on group psychotherapy, education, activities therapy, and plans for restitution of money owed because of gambling. Lester (1980) reviewed other behavioral treatments such as pain aversion, in which electric shock is associated with betting, and paradoxical intention, in which the therapist orders the patient to gamble according to a strict schedule that the therapist devises. But pathological gambling is often highly resistant to all forms of treatment. There is little doubt that the encouragement and availability of gambling poses a serious threat to the mental health of a significant percentage of the population.

REFERENCES

Alsop, R. (1977, July 8). Hospital pays ante for gamblers trying to shake the habit. *The Wall Street Journal,* 1, 13.

American Psychiatric Association. (1980). *Diagnostic and statistical manual of mental disorders* (3rd ed.). Washington, DC: Author.

Ashton, N. (1979). Gamblers: Disturbed or healthy? In D. Lester (Ed.), *Gambling today.* Springfield, IL: Thomas.

Bem, D. J. (1971). The concept of risk in the study of human behavior. In R. C. Carney (Ed.), *Risk-taking behavior.* Springfield, IL: Thomas.

Bergier, E. (1970). *The psychology of gambling.* New York: International Universities Press.

Blakey, G. R. (1979). State conducted lotteries: History, problems, and promises. *Journal of Social Issue, 35,* 62–86.

Bolen, D. W., & Boyd, W. H. (1968). Gambling and the gambler. *Archives of General Psychiatry, 38,* 617–630.

Campbell, F. (1976). Gambling: A positive view. In W. R. Eadington (Ed.), *Gambling and society.* Springfield, IL: Thomas.

Dostoyevsky, F. (1971). *The gambler.* New York: Penguin Books.

Elmore, E. (1979). Economic aspects of gambling. In D. Lester (Ed.), *Gambling today.* Springfield, IL: Thomas.

France, C. J. (1975). The gambling impulse. In J. Halliday & P. Fuller (Eds.), *The psychology of gambling.* New York: Harper & Row.

Frank, M. L. (1976). Why people gamble: A behavioral perspective. In D. Lester (Ed.), *Gambling today.* Springfield, IL: Thomas.

Fuller, P. (1975). Gambling: A secular "religion" for the obsessional neurotic. In J. Halliday & P. Fuller (Eds.), *The psychology of gambling.* New York: Harper & Row.

Herman, R. D. (1976). *Gamblers and gambling.* Lexington, MA: Heath.

Jellinek, E. M. (1960). *The disease concept of alcoholism.* New Haven, CT: Hillhouse.

Kallick-Kaufman, M., & Reuter, P. (1979). Introduction. *Journal of Social Issues, 35,* 1–6.

Knapp, T. J. (1976). A functional analysis of gambling behavior. In W. R. Eadington (Ed.), *Gambling and society.* Springfield, IL: Thomas.

Knowles, E. S. (1976). Searching for motivations in risk-taking and gambling. In W. R. Eadington (Ed.), *Gambling and society.* Springfield, IL: Thomas.

Kusyszyn, I. (1976). How gambling saved me from a misspent sabbatical. In W. R. Eadington (Ed.), *Gambling and society.* Springfield, IL: Thomas.

Lesieur, H. R. (1979). The compulsive gambler's spiral of options and involvement. *Psychiatry, 42*(1), 79–87.

Lester, D. (1980). Choice of gambling activity and belief in locus of control. *Psychological Reports, 47,* 22.

Lindner, R. M. (1950). The psychodynamics of gambling. *Annals of the American Academy of Political and Social Science, 268,* 93–107.

Livingston, J. (1974). *Compulsive gamblers.* New York: Harper & Row.

Moore, R. (1981). *Compulsion: The true story of an addictive gambler.* New York: Doubleday.

Moran, E. (1975). Pathological gambling. *British Journal of Psychology* [Special Publication no. 9], 416–428.

Skolnick, J. H. (1979). The social risks of casino gambling. *Psychology Today, 13,* 52–58, 63–64.

Smith, R. W., Preston, F., & Humphries, H. L. (1976). Alienation from work: A study of casino card dealers. In W. R. Eadington (Ed.), *Gambling and society.* Springfield, IL: Thomas.

Victor, R. G. (1981). Gambling. In S. J. Mulé (Ed.), *Behavior in excess.* New York: Macmillan.

SUGGESTED READING

Arcuri, A. F. (1979). Illegal gambling. In D. Lester (Ed.), *Gambling today.* Springfield, IL: Thomas.

Barker, J. C., & Miller, M. (1968). Aversion therapy for compulsive gambling. *Journal of Nervous and Mental Disease, 146,* 285–302.

Bruns, B. P. (1973). *Compulsive gambler.* New York: Stuart.

Dickerson, M. G. (1979). FI schedules and persistence at gambling in the U.K. betting office. *Journal of Applied Behavior Analysis, 12,* 315–323.

Diehman, T. E. (1979). Gambling: A social problem? *Journal of Social Issues, 35,* 36–42.

Eadinton, W. R. (Ed.) (1976). *Gambling and society.* Springfield, IL: Thomas.

Fink, H. K. (1961). Compulsive gambling. *Acta Psychotherapeutica, 9,* 251–261.

Gamblers Anonymous. (1977). *Gamblers Anonymous.* Los Angeles: Author.

Greenson, R. R. (1975). On gambling. In J. Halliday & P. Fuller (Eds.), *The psychology of gambling.* New York: Harper & Row.

Haller, M. H. (1979). The changing structure of American gambling in the twentieth century. *Journal of Social Issues, 35,* 87–114.

Miller, M. E., & Barker, J. D. (1968). Aversion therapy for compulsive gambling. *Nursing Mirror, 18,* 21–25.

Moran, E. (1970). Clinical and social aspects of risk-taking. *Proceedings of the Royal Society of Medicine, 63,* 41–44.

Moran, E. (1970). Varieties of pathological gambling. *British Journal of Psychiatry, 116,* 593–597.

Suits, D. B. (1979). Economic background for gambling policy. *Journal of Social Issues, 35,* 43–61.

Victor, R. G., & Krug, C. M. (1967). Paradoxical intention in the treatment of compulsive gambling. *American Journal of Psychotherapy, 21,* 808–814.

J. I. TABER
Veterans Administration Medical Center, Reno

ALCOHOLISM TREATMENT
BEHAVIOR MODIFICATION
CRISIS INTERVENTION
DRUG REHABILITATION

GAMBLING, PROBLEM

INTRODUCTION

Gambling and the consequences associated with it have been with us for millennia. The nineteenth-century Russian writer and philosopher, Dostoevsky was among the well-known historical figures who gambled excessively and experienced the negative consequences of his gambling behavior. Dostoevsky wrote about this experience in his novel *The Gambler.* For Dostoevsky, the opportunity to "beat the system" seemed to draw him toward gambling. He believed that he had "devised a system of playing" which had produced large winnings. In 1892, he wrote to his brother and alluded to his passion for gambling, ". . . how could I help being carried away after this, how could I help believing that if I followed my system strictly I would have a fortune in my hands." Inevitably, Dostoevsky's system failed and he had to turn to his family for money.

INCREASES IN GAMBLING OPPORTUNITIES AND ASSOCIATED PROBLEMS

The 1980s and 1990s have witnessed a massive increase in legalized gambling opportunities in the United States. Currently 48 states, with the exceptions of Utah and Hawaii, have some form of legalized gambling. Record levels of gambling expenditures have accompanied the increase in gambling opportunities. For example, in 1996 Americans wagered $586.5 billion (Christiansen, 1997), an increase of 3,300% over 1974 expenditures. With the increase in gambling availability, there has been a concomitant increase in the opportunity for problem gambling behavior. Numerous studies have attempted to estimate the number of individuals who experience gambling problems; however, these estimates have varied considerably. A recent quantitative review of 120 prevalence studies of problem gambling revealed that approximately 5.5% of the adult population have experienced significant problems related to gambling at some point during their lifetime (Shaffer, Hall, & Vander Bilt, 1997). Higher rates of problem gambling have been reported among youth, college students, and residents of some states, such as New York (7.3%), Mississippi and Louisiana (Shaffer et al., 1997). Males and African-Americans are also more likely to experience gambling problems.

Gambling legislation has been proposed as a "pain free" form of taxation. However, economic appraisals have suggested that this taxation is regressive in nature. For example, a study of Mississippi residents found that those in low to middle income levels tended to gamble more often and spend a greater percentage of their income on casino gambling than those in the higher income levels (Rivenbark & Slabach, 1996). These data suggested that casino gambling was a regressive form of taxation because those in the lower income levels paid a disproportionately higher tax relative to those with a high level of income. There is evidence that state lotteries may be an even more regressive tax strategy than casino gambling.

PROBLEMS ASSOCIATED WITH EXCESSIVE GAMBLING

A number of concerns associated with problem gambling have been identified. The most basic consequence of excessive gambling is financial difficulty. Those with serious gambling problems spend more than their discretionary income on gambling and, as a result, are unable to meet their basic financial responsibilities. To deal with their debts, problem gamblers often must turn to other sources for money, including family, friends, or criminal activities such as embezzlement. As a result of insufficient financial resources, many gamblers file for bankruptcy. Arrest and incarceration due to illegal activities aimed at securing more money with which to gamble are also common.

In addition to financial difficulties, problem gamblers are likely to experience a variety of other problems. Epidemiological data has suggested that problem gamblers are over three times more likely to suffer from major depression or alcohol abuse or dependence (Cunningham-Williams, Cottler, Compton, & Spitznagel, 1998). Problem gamblers reported greater rates of psychological distress and more use of psychiatric treatment than nonproblem gamblers (National Opinion Research Center [NORC], 1999). Too much time spent gambling, coupled with financial complications, can also lead to serious relationship difficulties for problem gamblers. Spouses and family members of problem gamblers must cope with the consequences of the gambler's behavior, including absence from the home, distrust of the gambler, and stress over family finances. As a result of these strains, divorce rates are higher among problem gamblers (NORC, 1999).

ASSESSMENT AND DIAGNOSTICS

A number of labels have been used to identify those who experience problems due to their gambling behavior, including "problem," "compulsive," "pathological," and "disordered" gambler. The American Psychiatric Association (APA) officially recognized pathological gambling as a disorder in 1980 when it classified pathological gambling as an impulse control disorder. Since its introduction, pathological gambling disorder has been studied extensively using the South Oaks Gambling Screen (SOGS; Lesieur & Blume, 1987), a measure based on the *DSM-III* criteria. However, this measure has received much criticism. More recent measures of pathological gambling have been based on revised criteria outlined in the *DSM-IV.* These criteria include: (a) preoccupation with gambling; (b) wagering larger amounts of money to experience excitement; (c) feelings of withdrawal when trying to stop or control gambling; (d) gambling to escape problems or feel better; (e) chasing losses, or betting more money in an attempt to recoup losses; (f) lying to others to conceal gambling involvement; (g) committing illegal acts to obtain money to gamble; (h) jeopardizing important relationships or other opportunities because of gambling; (i) relying on financial assistance from others to pay for gambling debts; and (j) unsuccessful efforts to limit or stop gambling. These criteria were fashioned, to a large degree, after the criteria for substance use disorders, and are based on the assumption that gambling may be similar to other addictive behaviors, such as alcoholism and smoking.

MODELS OF PROBLEM GAMBLING

Medical Models

A variety of explanatory models for problem gambling have been developed. One very common view of problem gambling is that it is a disease. This theory views problem gambling like a medical illness, such as heart disease or cancer. Excessive gambling behavior is considered to be a chronic condition that manifests itself in clear signs and symptoms. Explanations for the actual "cause" of the disease have been offered by a variety of theorists. For example, psychodynamic theorists have explained that gambling may fulfill an individual's instinctual drives. A number of other psychodynamic theories of gambling behavior have been offered. Unfortunately, the natures of these theories have not allowed researchers to either support or refute them.

Recent efforts have attempted to understand the role of biological factors in problem gambling. Some evidence has suggested that problem gamblers may inherit a genetic predisposition to gamble excessively (Eisen et al., 1998). However, genetic factors appear to be only one of the important components related to the development of gambling problems.

Psychological Models

Psychologists have attempted to understand the role of psychological factors in the development of gambling problems. Personality theorists have examined the relationship between personality traits (such as sensation-seeking, extroversion, and locus of control) and gambling behavior. However, these investigations have generated only limited support for the role of personality in gambling.

Behavioral theorists have used learning models to explain how individuals develop gambling-related problems. According to operant conditioning theory, individuals gamble because they have been reinforced on a variable ratio schedule. Although each bet does not lead to the acquisition of money, occasional wins serve to maintain the gambling behavior. These behavioral theories have some difficulty explaining the seemingly irrational basis of gambling behavior, as well as accounting for individual differences in the development of gambling problems after exposure to gambling.

In recent years, models of problem gambling have increasingly focused on the role of cognition. Cognitive models of problem gambling are based on empirical evidence that irrational or maladaptive beliefs are related to gambling behavior. According to this theory, many gamblers hold beliefs that lead them to continue to gamble, despite the odds and their mounting losses. Belief in luck, the ability to control chance events, and the notion that gambling will likely lead to financial wealth are examples of irrational beliefs that may lead to problematic gambling behavior.

While there are many theoretical models that have been used to explore problem gambling behavior, at the core of this behavior is a lack of self-regulation. Problem gamblers fail to control their gambling behavior and experience the consequences that result from their unregulated behavior. Although early treatment models were based on medical models of problem gambling, more recent treatment strategies have shifted to cognitive and behavioral perspectives that attempt to understand and improve the self-regulatory skills of the gambler.

Treatment of Problem Gambling

As few as 4% of those who experience gambling problems actually seek treatment (Feigelman, Wallisch, & Lesieur, 1998). For those who do seek treatment, the most readily available option is Gamblers' Anonymous (GA), which began in 1957 and was fashioned after Alcoholics Anonymous (AA). GA is a self-help group that is based on the disease model of problem gambling. Like AA, the GA model focuses on a 12-step program that emphasizes group support, faith, and commitment. As part of the GA program, members share with the group their unique stories about how excessive gambling led to problems. In the GA model, complete abstinence from gambling is considered the only viable treatment goal. Members are encouraged to be actively involved in the program even after extensive periods of abstinence, because relapse into problematic gambling is just one bet away. Available evidence has suggested that GA is beneficial for a small percentage of those who attend. However, for the majority of problem gamblers, GA does not appear to be effective (Stewart & Brown, 1988).

A variety of behavior therapy strategies have been administered to problem gamblers including aversion therapy, in vivo desensitization, imaginal desensitization, and cue exposure and response prevention. Although most of these programs were conducted with individual problem gamblers or lacked stringent methodologies, outcome data has generally supported their effectiveness.

More recent therapy developments have focused on contemporary understandings of addictive behaviors. For example, Ladouceur and his colleagues (Sylvain, Ladouceur & Boisvert, 1997) have designed a cognitive-behavioral treatment program that is based on cognitive models of problem gambling and addiction. This program is unique because of its focus on cognitive restructuring techniques designed to change gamblers' irrational beliefs about gambling. Problem-solving skill training and training to identify and cope with situations that present a high risk of relapse are also used in this treatment strategy.

Much of the treatment literature for problem gambling parallels the early research on interventions for problem drinking. It is likely that future treatment strategies for problem gambling will build on more contemporary models that have been developed in the alcohol treatment field or models that are specific to problem gambling. For example, brief, motivation-based treatment programs, which have received empirical support as an effective alternative to traditional abstinence-based interventions for alcohol problems, are now being adapted and tested to help problem gamblers. The growing availability of gambling, the recognition of individual and societal problems associated with excessive gambling, and the increasing attention of scientists and clinicians suggest that the area of problem gambling will be a dynamic one in years to come.

REFERENCES

Christiansen, E. M. (1997). The U.S. 1996 gross annual wager. *International Gaming and Wagering Business* (Special Supplement).

Cunningham-Williams, R. M., Cottler, L. B., Compton, W. M., & Spitznagel, E. L. (1998). Taking chances: Problem gamblers and mental health disorders—Results from the St. Louis Epidemiological Catchment Area Study. *American Journal of Public Health, 88,* 1093–1096.

Eisen, S. A., Lin, N., Lyons, M. J., Scherrer, J. F., Griffith, K., True, W. R., Goldberg, J., & Tsuang, M. T. (1998). Familial influences on gambling behavior: An analysis of 3359 twin pairs. *Addiction, 93,* 1375–1384.

Feigelman, W., Wallisch, L. S., & Lesieur, H. R. (1998). Problem gamblers, problem substance uses, and dual-problem individuals: An epidemiological study. *American Journal of Public Health, 88,* 467–470.

Lesieur, H. R., & Blume, S. B. (1987). The South Oaks Gambling Screen (SOGS): A new instrument for the identification of pathological gamblers. *American Journal of Psychiatry, 144,* 1184–1188.

National Opinion Research Center. (1999). *Gambling impact and behavior survey.* Final report to the National Gambling Impact Study Commission.

Rivenbark, W. C., & Slabach, D. E. (1996, July). *Who pays to play? Voluntary tax incidence and Mississippi gaming.* Starkville, MS: John C. Stennis Institute of Government, Mississippi State University.

Shaffer, H. J., Hall, M. N., & Vander Bilt, J. (1997). *Estimating the prevalence of disordered gambling in the United States and Canada: A meta-analysis.* Boston, MA: Harvard Medical School, Division on Addictions.

Stewart, R. M., & Brown, R. I. (1988). An outcome study of Gamblers Anonymous. *British Journal of Psychiatry, 152,* 284–288.

Sylvain, C., Ladouceur, R., & Boisvert, J. M. (1997). Cognitive and behavioral treatment of pathological gambling: A controlled study. *Journal of Consulting and Clinical Psychology, 65,* 727–732.

T. A. STEENBURGH
A. W. MEYERS
University of Memphis

ADDICTION
GAMBLING BEHAVIOR

GARCIA, GUILLERMO DAVILA (1902–1968)

Guillermo Davila Garcia was a Mexican psychiatrist and neurologist whose fundamental research and teaching interest was in psychopathology. His dedication as a teacher, administrator, and advocate for the profession and science of psychology is legendary. Many generations of students and some of the most distinguished Mexican psychologists of today were his disciples.

Garcia obtained the MD from the National University of Mexico (UNAM) in 1925 with a dissertation on schizophrenia. From this date until 1951, he worked at the state asylum (*La Castaneda*), the penitentiary, the *Tribunal de Menores* (children's court), and at the Mexican Social Securities System (IMSS) in addition to running his own private practice. Garcia also promoted vocational and professional guidance programs.

From 1951 to 1957, Garcia was head of the department of psychology at UNAM where he had taught since 1947. He remained at UNAM until his death.

Garcia was one of the leaders of a group that invited Erich Fromm to Mexico. In 1951, with Werner Wolf, O. Robles, R. Falcon, and R. Diaz-Guerrero, Garcia founded the Interamerican Society of Psychology and the Mexican Society of Psychology. As a major leader in Mexican psychology in the 1950s, he began contacts with W. Holtzman, R. Peck, and P. Worchel at the University of Texas. With Cuban J. A. Bustamante and Peruvian C. A. Seguin, Garcia founded the first Latin American group of cross-cultural studies.

P. VALDERRAMA-ITURBE
Mexico

GATE CONTROL THEORY OF PAIN

The theory of pain which we inherited in the twentieth century was proposed by Descartes three centuries earlier. Descartes' specificity theory of pain proposed that injury activates specific pain fibers which, in turn, project pain signals through a spinal pain pathway to a pain center in the brain. The psychological experience of pain, therefore, was virtually equated with peripheral injury. In the 1950s, there was no room for psychological contributions to pain, such as attention, past experience, and the meaning of the situation. Instead, pain experience was held to be proportional to peripheral injury or pathology. Patients who suffered chronic pain syndromes without presenting signs of organic disease were labeled as "crocks" and sent to psychiatrists. The picture, in short, was simple. However, to thoughtful clinical observers, it was clearly wrong (Livingston, 1943; Noordenbos, 1959).

In 1965, Melzack and Wall proposed the gate control theory of pain, based on the following propositions:

1. The transmission of nerve impulses from afferent fibres to spinal cord transmission cells is modulated by a spinal gating mechanism in the dorsal horn.

2. The spinal gating mechanism is influenced by the relative amount of activity in large-diameter and small-diameter fibres: Activity in large fibres tends to inhibit transmission (close the gate) while small-fibre activity tends to facilitate transmission (open the gate).

3. A specialized system of large-diameter, rapidly conducting fibres (the central control trigger) activates selective cognitive processes that then influence, by way of descending fibres, the modulating properties of the spinal gating mechanism.

4. When the output of the spinal cord transmission cells exceeds a critical level, it activates the action system—those neural areas that underlie the complex, sequential patterns of behavior and experience characteristic of pain.

When the gate control theory was published, it generated vigorous (sometimes vicious) debate as well as a great deal of research to disprove or support the theory. It was not until the mid-1970s that the gate control theory was presented in almost every major textbook in the biological and medical sciences. At the same time there was an explosion in research on the physiology and pharmacology of the dorsal horns and the descending control systems.

The theory's emphasis on the modulation of inputs in the spinal dorsal horns and the dynamic role of the brain in pain processes had both a clinical and a scientific impact. Psychological factors, which were previously dismissed as "reactions to pain," were now seen to be an integral part of pain processing, and new avenues for pain control were opened. Similarly, cutting nerves and spinal pathways was gradually replaced by a host of methods to modulate the input. Physical therapists and other health-care professionals, who use a multitude of modulation techniques, were brought into the picture. The current status of pain research and therapy has recently been evaluated (Melzack & Wall, 1996) and indicates that, despite the addition of a massive amount of detail, the theory has remained basically intact up to the present time.

The gate control theory's most important contribution to pain research and therapy is its emphasis on the central, rather than peripheral, nervous system (Melzack & Wall, 1996; Melzack, 1998, 1999). The great challenge at present is to understand brain mechanisms. Melzack and Casey (1968) made a start by proposing that specialized systems are involved in the sensory-discriminative, motivational-affective, and evaluative dimensions of pain. The McGill Pain Questionnaire, which taps into subjective experience, is widely used to measure pain (Melzack & Torgerson, 1971; Melzack, 1975). We have also begun to understand the different pathways and neural mechanisms that underlie acute and chronic pain—again, by invoking complex spinal and brain mechanisms—and we have gained a far better understanding of analgesic drugs (Wall & Melzack, 1999).

In 1978, Melzack and Loeser described severe pains in the phantom body of paraplegics with verified total sections of the spinal cord, and proposed a central "pattern generating mechanism" above the level of the section. They focused more powerfully than ever before on CNS mechanisms. Recent studies have explored new theoretical concepts to explain phantom body experiences—from pain to orgasm—in people with total spinal sections (Melzack, 1989). These experiences reveal important features of brain function, because the brain is completely disconnected from the cord. Psychophysical specificity, in such a concept, makes no sense, and we must explore how patterns of nerve impulses generated in the brain can give rise to somesthetic experience.

REFERENCES

Melzack, R. (1989). Phantom limbs, the self, and the brain (The D. O. Hebb Memorial Lecture). *Canadian Psychology, 30,* 1–14.

Melzack, R. (1998). Pain and stress: Clues toward understanding chronic pain. In M. Sabourin, F. Craik, & M. Robert (Eds.), *Advances in psychological science: Volume 2, Biological and cognitive aspects.* Hove: Psychology Press Ltd.

Melzack, R. (1999). Pain and stress: A new perspective. In R. J. Gatchel & D. C. Turk (Eds.), *Psychosocial factors in pain* (pp. 89–106). New York: Guilford.

Melzack, R., & Wall, P. D. (1965). Pain mechanisms: A new theory. *Science, 150,* 971–979.

Melzack, R., & Wall, P. D. (1996). *The challenge of pain* (2nd ed.). London: Penguin.

Wall, P. D., & Melzack, R. (Eds.). (1999). *Textbook of pain* (4th ed.). Edinburgh: Churchill Livingston.

SUGGESTED READING

Livingston, W. K. Pain Mechanisms. Macmillan, New York, 1943.

Noordenbos, W. Pain. Elsevier Press, Amsterdam, 1959.

Melzack, R., & Casey, K. L. Sensory, motivational, and central control determinants of pain: a new conceptual model. In D. Kenshalo (ed.), The Skin Senses. Thomas, Springfield, Ill., 1968, pp. 423–443.

Melzack, R., & Torgerson, W. S. On the language of pain. Anesthesiology, 34, (1971) 50–59.

Melzack, R., & Loeser, J. D. Phantom body pain in paraplegics: evidence for a central "pattern generating mechanism" for pain. *Pain, 4* (1978) 195–210.

Melzack, R. (1975). The McGill Pain Questionnaire major properties and scoring methods. *Pain, 277–299.*

R. MELZACK
McGill University

AMPUTEES AND PHANTOM LIMB PAIN
PAIN
PAIN: COPING STRATEGIES

GENERAL ADAPTATION SYNDROME

The General Adaptation Syndrome (GAS) is a cluster of bodily responses to severe, prolonged stressors that was described by Selye. Selye observed that rats exposed to a wide variety of noxious agents exhibited a nonspecific syndrome consisting of enlargement of the adrenal gland; shrinkage of the thymus, spleen, and lymph glands; and the emergence of ulcers in the stomach and small intestine. This response was seen in animals exposed to extreme cold and heat, intense sound or light, forced exercise, injections of various organ extracts or formalin, or a variety of other intense biological challenges to normal homeostatic function. Selye suggested that the GAS consisted of three phases of response to a stressor. The initial stage consisted of an alarm reaction, during which the adrenal cortex enlarged and released large amounts of the antiinflammatory hormone cortisol into the bloodstream, the lymphatic tissues shrunk, the number of white blood cells declined, the gastrointestinal tract developed ulcers, heart rate and blood pressure increased, and the animals lost weight. During the second stage, the stage of resistance, the adrenal cortex remained enlarged, but instead of releasing cortisol, the gland retained the hormone; other tissues and physiological functions appeared relatively normal and the body weight returned to near normal levels. With continued application of the severe stressor, the animals eventually entered a third stage, called the stage of exhaustion. Here again, similar to the body's responses during the alarm reaction, substantial amounts of cortisol were released into the blood, lymphatic tissues shrank, and body weight again fell. This stage ended with the animal's death.

Selye's GAS, and the research that followed from this early notion of a nonspecific response to challenges from the environment, was an important idea that launched the study of biological stress. Indeed, Selye himself used the term "stress", which he had borrowed from physics, to refer to this syndrome of responses to a noxious agent. However, more recent studies of the concept of stress have broadened the definition of stressors to include less potent challenges to an organism's normal function, including psychological presses. Thus, it is now clear that the GAS does not occur following all events that one would reasonably consider stressors, and does not occur in all individuals. As Selye himself noted, organisms may not incur all three stages of the GAS, and stressors sometimes may produce only limited features of the alarm reaction (e.g., cortisol release without gastric ulceration). Thus, the GAS does not appear to generalize to all, or perhaps any but the most intense, prolonged, and painful physical stressors. Despite these criticisms, Selye's GAS was an important concept in the history of research on stress because it suggested that in addition to the specific, finely tuned bodily changes induced by aversive physical challenges to homeostasis, there was also a more generalized bodily response elicited by any one of a diverse array of intense stressors that threatened the organism's survival.

SUGGESTED READING

Selye, H. (1936). A syndrome produced by diverse nocuous agents. *Nature, 138*, 32.

Selye, H. (1956). *The stress of life.* New York: McGraw-Hill.

Weiner, H. (1992). *Perturbing the organism: The biology of stressful experience.* Chicago: Chicago University Press.

K. S. QUIGLEY
Pennsylvania State University

ADRENAL GLANDS
HOMEOSTASIS
STRESS

GENETIC APPROACHES TO MEMORY

There is a long history documenting the usefulness of genetic approaches in studies of brain function, including learning and memory. These approaches fall into two general categories: forward and reverse genetics. Forward genetics is concerned with the identification of genes involved in biological processes such as learning and memory. The starting point of these studies is usually the identification of mutant organisms with interesting phenotypic changes, and their goal is to identify the mutations underlying these changes. In reverse genetic studies, the gene is already at hand, and the goal is to define its role in biological processes of interest. This normally involves the derivation and study of organisms with defined genetic changes. Although the principal purpose of genetic approaches is to study how genetic information determines biolog-

ical function, recently animals with genetically engineered mutations have been used to develop and test multidisciplinary theories of learning and memory that go well beyond gene function.

THE ROLE OF GENETICS IN BIOLOGY

To explore the role of genetics, it is important to place it in the large context of biological investigations. The ultimate goal of biological research is to develop and test explanations of complex phenomena such as learning and memory. At the heart of this process is the establishment of causal connections between phenomena of interest, such as changes in synaptic function and learning. There are four complementary general strategies that science uses to make causal connections between phenomena of interest. One of these strategies is the lesion strategy. Thus, pharmacological and genetic lesions of calmodulin-induced kinase II (CaMKII) are known to result in deficient long-term potentiation (LTP) of synaptic function, suggesting a connection between the activation of this synaptic kinase and LTP (Silva et al., 1997). It is noteworthy that genetics and pharmacology are the only two approaches to interfere with molecular function in biology. The second strategy that science uses to make causal connections between phenomena of interest is the direct observation of these phenomena in their natural context. For example, the induction of LTP is accompanied by observable increases in CaMKII activity. The third strategy involves the induction of one phenomenon by the other. For example, injection of activated CaMKII into pyramidal neurons in hippocampal slices induces an LTP-like phenomenon. Finally, modeling plays a critical role in making causal connections between phenomena of interest. To assert that two natural phenomena are connected, it is essential to understand something about the mechanism that links them. Thus, CaMKII activation is thought to trigger LTP by phosphorylating and thus enhancing the function of synaptic glutamate receptors. Each of the strategies mentioned above is insufficient to connect two phenomena of interest. Instead, convergent evidence from all four strategies is needed. Therefore, since genetics is one of only two general molecular-lesion approaches available, it is easy to see why it has played a key role in biology. Besides its key role in testing hypothesis (i.e., CaMKII is required for LTP induction), it can be argued that the principal role that genetics has played in biology has been to suggest possible hypotheses or explanations of natural phenomena. Indeed, forward genetic screens have allowed biologists to make major discoveries, even in the absence of a well-delineated hypothesis.

FORWARD GENETICS

Long before we had the ability to directly manipulate genes in animals, such as flies and mice, geneticists were busy using chemical mutagens to alter genetic information in living systems (forward genetics). The goal of classical or forward genetics, which continues to be used extensively, is to identify the genes critical for biological processes of interest. The idea is that study of those genes is often a critical first hint for unraveling underlying biological processes. In forward genetic screens, animals are first exposed to a mutagen, (for example, the DNA-altering compound ethylnitroso-urea), mated, and the progeny are screened for phenotypic changes of interest. The phenotype of a mutant is the sum total of observed biological changes caused by a genetic manipulation. Recent application of this approach in the study of mammalian circadian rhythms resulted in the identification of *clock,* a crucial link in the cascade of transcriptional events that marks molecular time in organisms as diverse as *Drosophila* and mice (Wilsbacher and Takahashi, 1998). Other molecular components of this pathway, such as *per,* were isolated in mutagenesis screens in *Drosophila.* By identifying novel and unexpected molecular components of biological processes of interest, forward genetics has often reshaped entire fields of research. At times, science can go in circles, obsessively chasing its own tail of half-truths, incapable of escaping the gravitational pull of its worn-out paradigms. Forward genetics, in the hands of masters such as Lewis (developmental mutants) and Benzer (learning mutants), has the ability to turn paradigms upside down, and initiate new lines of scientific inquiry. The key to the success of forward genetics is the design of biological screens with which the randomly mutagenized animals are tested. If the screens are too stringent, or if the fundamental biological insights underlying the screen's design are off-mark, one runs the risk of ending up with empty hands, or even worse, with a number of misleading mutants. In contrast, nonstringent designs lead to overwhelming numbers of nonspecific mutants that are essentially useless.

THE FIRST SCREENS FOR LEARNING AND MEMORY MUTANTS

Benzer and colleagues, working with *Drosophila* at the California Institute of Technology, designed the first successful screen for learning and memory mutants in the seventies (Dudai, 1988). Benzer and colleagues developed a behavioral procedure with operant and Pavlovian components. During training the flies were allowed to enter two chambers (each with a different odorant), but they only got shocked in one of the chambers. During testing, approximately 2/3 of the trained flies avoided the chamber with the odorant that previously had been paired with shock. With this procedure, Benzer and colleagues tested a number of *Drosophila* lines derived from flies treated with ethylmethane sulfonate (EMS). The first mutant line isolated from this screen was *dunce* (Dudai, 1988).

Remarkably, three out of the four learning and memory mutations, first discovered in genetic screens in *Drosophila,* code for members of the cAMP-signaling pathway. For example, *dunce* lacks a phosphodiesterase that degrades cAMP. Importantly, these findings have recently been extended into vertebrates, where electrophysiological and behavioral studies have confirmed the critical importance of cAMP signaling to learning and memory (Silva et al., 1998). Remarkably, in the early seventies Kandel and his colleagues at Columbia University also found evidence for the importance of cAMP signaling in learning and memory with a completely different approach. They used a reduced cellular preparation to study sensitization, a nonassociative form of learning, in the sea snail *Aplysia* (Byrne & Kandel, 1996). They also found that sensitization depends on cAMP signaling. This is a fascinating example of convergent evidence in science, but it also serves to illustrate that genetics, like any other tool in science, is most successful when used in parallel with other approaches. The persuasive power of convergent evidence cannot be overemphasized. Besides identifying new genes, genetics can also be used to test hypothesis about the function of cloned genes (reverse genetics).

REVERSE GENETICS

In classical genetics an interesting phenotype is usually the driving force behind the molecular experiments required to identify the underlying mutant gene(s). In contrast, in reverse genetics, the interesting molecular properties of a gene usually drive the generation and study of the mutant animal (hence the word "reverse"). It is now possible to delete and add genes to many species, ranging from bacteria to mice. For example, mice can be derived with the deletion (knock-outs) or overexpression (transgenics) of almost any cloned gene. These manipulations can involve whole genes, or they can target specific domains or even single base pairs.

To generate knock-out mice, the desired mutation is engineered within the cloned gene, and this mutant DNA is introduced into embryonic stem (ES) cells. Since ES cells are pluripotent, they can be used to derive mice with the genetically engineered lesion. For that purpose, they are injected into blastocysts (early embryos), and the blastocysts are implanted in host mothers. The resulting chimeric (having mutant and normal cells) offspring are then mated to obtain mutant mice. In contrast, transgenic mice are derived by injecting the pronuclei of fertilized eggs with a DNA construct carrying a gene of interest under the regulation of an appropriate promoter. The injected eggs are transplanted into pregnant females, and some of the resulting progeny will have the transgenic construct inserted randomly in one of its chromosomes.

With classical knock-out and transgenic techniques it is not possible to regulate the time and the regions affected by the mutation/transgene. However, recent techniques promise to circumvent these limitations with a variety of techniques. For example, the expression of the gene of interest can be regulated by gene promoters that can be controlled by exogenously provided substances, such as tetracycline derivatives (Mayford et al., 1997). Alternatively, it is also possible to regulate the function of a protein of interest by fusing it with another protein that can be regulated by synthetic ligands, such as tamoxifen (Picard, 1993). For example, our laboratory has recently showed that a transcriptional repressor called CREB can be activated at will when fused with a ligand-binding domain (LBD^m) of a modified estrogen receptor. Addition of tamoxifen (the ligand of the modified receptor) activates the CREB^r/LBD^m fusion protein. It is important to note that irrespective of the exact method used, the general idea of reverse genetic studies is that the function of a gene can be deduced from the phenotype of the mutant animal.

KNOCK-OUTS, TRANSGENICS, AND LEARNING

The first knock-out/transgenic studies of learning and memory analyzed mice with a targeted mutation of the α isoform of CaMKII (Grant & Silva, 1994). Pharmacological studies had previously shown that this family of calcium calmodulin-induced kinases present in synapses were required for LTP, a stable enhancement in synaptic efficacy thought to contribute to learning and memory. Remarkably, deleting αCaMKII resulted in profound deficits in hippocampal LTP and in hippocampal-dependent learning and memory. Additional studies showed that either the overexpression of a constitutively expressed form of the kinase or a mutation that prevented its autophosphorylation also disrupted LTP and learning. Importantly, studies of hippocampal circuits that fire in a place-specific manner (place fields) showed that these CaMKII genetic manipulations disrupted the stability of these place-representations (but not their induction) in the hippocampus. Altogether, these studies suggested the provocative hypothesis that this kinase is important for the induction of stable synaptic changes, that the stability of synaptic changes is crucial for the stability of hippocampal circuits coding for place, and that these circuits are essential for spatial learning (Elgersma & Silva, 1999). Even this very abbreviated summary demonstrates that these studies went well beyond gene function. Instead, they used mutations to test hypotheses that connected molecular, cellular, circuit, and behavioral phenomena. Although it is reasonable to claim that the αCaMKII has a direct role in the regulation of synaptic function (for example, by phosphorylating glutamate receptors), it is more problematic to argue that the kinase is regulating spatial learning. There are a lot more phenomenological steps between kinase function and the animal's ability to find a hidden platform in a water maze than between the biochemical properties of this kinase and its role in synaptic plasticity. By comparison, it is easier to see how the stability of place fields in the hippocampus could be an important component of hippocampal-dependent spatial learning.

COMMON CONCERNS WITH THE INTERPRETATION OF TRANSGENIC/KNOCK-OUT STUDIES

Despite the power of genetics, there are a number of concerns that must be kept in mind when using genetic approaches. One of the most commonly discussed is the possibility that developmental effects or any other change caused by the mutation preceding the study could confound its interpretation. Another pertains to the possible effects of genetic compensation. Since proteins do not work alone, but instead function in highly dynamic networks, it is often observed that specific genetic changes lead to alterations or compensations in the function of other related proteins. A related concern pertains to genetic background. Extensive studies have shown that the genetic background of a mutation has a profound effect on its phenotype. The concerns listed above are not limitations of genetics, but simply reflect the properties of the biological systems that genetics manipulates. At the heart of many of the concerns described above are two misconceptions concerning the nature and organization of biological systems.

First, genetics is essentially a lesion tool. As other lesion tools it cannot be used in isolation. To establish causal connections between any two phenomena (A and B) in science, it is never enough to lesion A and document the alteration of B. As described above, it is also critical to fulfil three other criteria: first, A must be observed to precede B; second, triggering A should result in B; and finally, it is essential to have a clear hypothesis of how and why A triggers B. Fulfilling only one or two of those four criteria is simply not enough to establish a causal connection between A and B. Therefore, although studying the effects of a deleted protein is an important component in determining its function, it is by no means sufficient.

Second, biological systems are dynamic and adaptive, and

therefore, the lesion of any one component is always followed by changes in several other components. Although it is often a helpful simplification to think of biological components as independent functional units, it is important to remember that they are not. Thus, it is hardly surprising that the effect of a mutation is dependent on biological variables such as genetic background.

THE FUTURE OF GENETIC MANIPULATIONS

In the near future, it will be possible to delete or modify any gene, anywhere in most organisms of interest, and at any time of choice. Additionally, more powerful forward genetic strategies will allow the isolation of entire pathways of genes involved in any neurobiological phenomenon of interest, including learning, attention, emotion, addition, and so on. In parallel with expected advances in genetics, there will also be advances in the methods used to analyze mutants. These advances are just as critical to genetic studies as advances in genetic methodology. For example, imaging the brains of mutant mice may yield insight into how molecular lesions affect the function of brain systems. Most genetic studies of learning and memory in mice have focused on the relationship between cellular phenomena (i.e., LTP) and behavior. Advances in small animal magnetic resonance imaging (MRI) may enable the kind of functional system analysis in the brains of mutant mice that have so far only been possible in large primates. Similarly, multiple-single unit recording techniques are starting to yield system-wide snapshots of circuit activity in the brains of mutant mice. At a molecular level, small-size positron emission tomography (PET) devices will allow the imaging of molecular function in living animals such as mice. For example, it may be possible to image the activation of a receptor, such as the dopamine receptor, during learning or memory. Micro-array techniques and other molecular cloning approaches will allow the identification of gene profiles in mutant mice. These molecular profiles will be critical to delineating the molecular changes behind the expression of a mutant phenotype. It is important to note that genetics allows us to reprogram the biology of organisms. The finer and more sophisticated the phenotypic and genotypic tools that we have at our disposal, the deeper we may be able to probe the magical natural programs embedded in our genes.

REFERENCES

Byrne, J. H., & Kandel, E. R. (1996). Presynaptic facilitation revisited: State and time dependence. *Journal of Neuroscience, 16*(2), 425–435.

Dudai, Y. (1988). Neurogenetic dissection of learning and short-term memory in *Drosophila*. *Annual Review of Neuroscience, 11,* 537–563.

Elgersma, Y., & Silva, A. J. (1999). Molecular mechanisms of synaptic plasticity and memory. *Current Opinions in Neurobiology, 9*(2), 209–213.

Grant, S. G., & Silva, A. J. (1994). Targeting learning. *Trends in Neurosciences, 17*(2), 71–75.

Mayford, M., Mansuy, I. M. (1997). Memory and behavior: A second generation of genetically modified mice. *Current Biology, 7*(9), R580-R589.

Picard, D. (1993). Steroid-binding domains for regulating functions of heterologous proteins in cis. *Trends in Cellular Biology, 3,* 278–280.

Silva, A. J., & Kogan, J. H. (1998). CREB and memory. *Annual Review of Neuroscience, 21,* 127–148.

Silva, A. J., & Smith, A. M. (1997). Gene targeting and the biology of learning and memory. *Annual Review of Genetics, 31,* 527–546.

Wilsbacher, L. D. & Takahashi, J. S. (1998). Circadian rhythms: Molecular basis of the clock. *Current Opinion in Genetics and Development, 8*(5), 595–602.

A. J. SILVA
University of California, Los Angeles

MEMORY

GENETIC DOMINANCE AND RECESSIVENESS

Genetics is the study of heredity. Ironically, we know a good deal more about the inheritance of dogs, cats, horses, cows, and other domestic animals, as well as corn, wheat, and other crops—and even about insects such as *Drosophila melanogaster,* the common fruitfly that hovers over aging bananas and oranges—than we do about humans. We cannot cage humans and breed them in research studies as we do rats or rabbits. The life cycle of humans is so long that we can get genetic information (genealogies) for only a few generations in the lifetime of one researcher.

Inheritance results from gene combinations. Genes are biochemical entities in chromosomes which determine the potential for sex and other characteristics at conception. Chromosomes come in pairs in the nucleus of the sperm and the nucleus of the egg. A half century ago, genetics textbooks listed the number of human chromosomes as 24 pairs, or 48 in all. As proved later by more powerful and efficient microscopes, there are only 23 pairs or 46 chromosomes in human beings, of which one pair is called the sex chromosomes because they determine the sex of the future organism. Females bear two X chromosomes, whereas males possess an X and a Y. The Y chromosome is smaller and contains fewer genes along its surface. Some XXY males were discovered and the extra X chromosome was first thought to cause criminality, but this theory was blasted when many normal, law-abiding citizens were found to have the same extra chromosome.

As a result of ovarian cell division, all eggs contain one X chromosome, while the sperm cells from the male testes contain either an X or a Y. Thus there is a 50% chance of a human ovum being fertilized by either an X- or a Y-bearing sperm, so that the babies born in the population should be 50% female and 50% male. (Actually, slightly more male infants appear, but they die more readily, so that the ratio of male to female becomes equalized; then, as children grow older, the ratio changes to favor female survivors, because of women's greater resistance to disease.) An X-bearing sperm cell that fertilizes the egg will create a female, while a Y-bearing sperm cell will produce a male.

Although little is known about gene location along the sex (X and Y) chromosomes and along the autosomal (body characteristics, exclusive of sex) chromosomes, there must be innumerable genes along each chromosome, given the complexity of the makeup of humans and what is known about inheritance in other animals. A gene is the biochemical location of an influential determinant that causes a particular trait or condition (such as blue eyes or hemophilia) or a part of the body (e.g., the thumb epidermis) to develop.

The map of the genes along the chromosomes is called the individual's *genotype,* while the *phenotype* is the expression of these genes in the flesh of the body. A dominant gene can cause its effect in haploid (single) number, because it is stronger than a recessive allele (the gene in the same location in the opposite chromosome of a pair). When a trait comes from a recessive gene, the diploid number (both alleles or genes at the same locus on a pair of chromosomes) is necessary to create the trait or defect in the phenotype. A person having the recessive gene for some inherited deficiency or disease on one chromosome, but having the normal allele on the other chromosome, is called a carrier, because this potential parent carries the defective gene in haploid form but cannot give expression to it, unless it joins with another defective recessive in the other parent to produce an affected infant. The exception to this rule is a sex-linked recessive on the X chromosome of a female carrier. When this recessive joins with the husband's Y chromosome, the XY son will exhibit the disease as if the Y chromosome did not exist (since there is usually no corresponding allele on the Y to dominate the X's defective gene).

In sum, a dominant gene always overrules a recessive gene, but two recessives at the same locus on a pair of chromosomes are strong enough to allow the trait or defect to show in the phenotype, and a recessive on the X chromosome of a male will also usually show up in the phenotype or body of the child.

Dominant traits in humans include dark and curly hair; white hair patch; male baldness; brown, hazel, or green eyes; normal pigmented skin; fused fingers or toes, or extra digits; shorter fingers (because of a missing finger joint); dwarfed limbs; double-jointed body; poison ivy immunity; Rh positive factor; normal blood-clotting factors; and blood types A, B, and AB. *Recessive traits* include straight, light, or red hair; female baldness; blue or gray eyes; lack of skin pigment (albinism); normal digits; susceptibility to poison ivy; night- and color-blindness; deaf-mutism; Rh negative factor; hemophilia; and blood type O.

SUGGESTED READING

Evans, I. M., & Smith, P. A. (1970). *Psychology for a changing world.* New York: Wiley.

Krech, D., Crutchfield, R. S., et al. (1969). *Elements of psychology.* New York: Knopf. (Original work published 1958)

H. K. FINK
Honolulu, Hawaii

GERIATRIC PSYCHOLOGY

While the scientific body of knowledge pertaining to aging is called gerontology, I. L. Rascher in 1914 coined the term "geriatrics" for that branch of medicine dealing with the health problems of the aged. Rascher declared that medicine's challenge is to restore a diseased organ or tissue to a state that is normal in senility, not to a state that is normal in maturity; the ideal, in other words, is adding life to years rather than merely years to life.

Interdisciplinary in nature and process, geriatric psychology is the science of the behavior of the aged. Geriatric psychology, with its medical, neurological, psychiatric, and psychological emphases, involves the behavioral, biological, and social sciences. The importance of cross-cultural and cross-national studies in geriatric psychology is increasingly patent in research.

Geriatric psychology is a rather new area of interest: Experimental studies of aging became a matter of concern only in the last fifty years. In 1947 G. Lawton wrote comprehensively on a philosophy for maturity, proposing a bill of rights for old age. There are now delicate interpersonal situations in the multigeneration family in which the older group, conventionally defined as 65 years and older, increasingly calls for the attention, interest, and commitment of mental health workers. Geriatric psychology must be concerned with the terrors of loneliness in old age, worry about illness or shelter, anxiety over finances, or the unhappiness which results when one generation infringes on the life of another. Geriatric psychology must deal with the fact that aging is not synonymous with disease; that aging is not a state of ill health; and that a disabling, lengthy sickness is not an inevitable part of growing old. It must, however, promote understanding of the mental and emotional problems of life, because accumulated physical handicaps, plus a general deterioration in bodily functions, superimpose a heavier burden in whatever emotional traumas may have developed earlier within the individual.

Atchley (1999) uses the term "continuity" to explain the ability of older persons to maintain a strong sense of purpose and self in the face of the changes associated with aging. He points out that continuity can help individuals evolve psychologically and socially in the presence of life events such as retirement, widowhood, and physical disability. In "Concepts and Issues of Mental Health and Aging," Birren and Sloane (1980) wrote, "Despite the fact our knowledge about the biological, psychological, and social processes associated with growing old has greatly increased, . . . our understanding of the mental health problems of aging remains diffuse, particulate, and uncoordinated" (pp. 3ff).

Geriatric psychology recognizes that the outstanding sign of aging is found in body tissues, where *stroma* (connective tissue, or nonfunctional elements) increases while *parenchyma* (functional tissue) decreases. The geriatric psychologist knows that every organ of the human body pursues its individual pattern of aging, and that, neuropsychologically, a decrease in hormones may be as important in aging as a flagging vascular system. A full understanding of the entire relationship between glands and aging still awaits experimental findings.

The Task Panel on the Elderly of the President's Commission on Mental Health (1979) reported that the graying of America is one of the most significant demographic trends of this century.

Every day over 5,000 Americans join the ranks of those over 65, while only 3,600 die—a net gain of at least 1,400 elderly a day. The total number of older Americans is expected to increase from 23 million to 55 million by 2030 (US Census Bureau, 1977). The 75-plus age group is the fastest growing segment of the population.

Mental illness is more prevalent in the elderly than in younger adults. An estimated 15 to 25 percent of older persons have significant mental health problems. Psychosis increases after age 65, and even more so beyond age 75. Twenty-five percent of all reported suicides in this country are committed by elderly persons. The chronic health problems that afflict 86 percent of the aged, and the financial difficulties faced by many, clearly contribute to increasing stress (Cohen, 1977). The stresses affecting the mental health of the elderly are multiple and pervasive.

Silverman (1996) suggests various psychotherapeutic interventions in dealing with personality problems in individuals of whatever age. He writes: "One sees psychotherapy as a process: as a kind of conditioning to a certain type of behavior. . . . By separating the past from the present, healthier, interpersonal relationships may be constructed" through the appropriate use of therapy psychologically. Poe and Holloway (1980, p. 147) quote Hayflick:

. . . If zero population growth can be achieved, it can be predicted that by 2025 ad those over 65 will number nearly 40 million and will constitute more than 20 percent of the total population. The inevitable consequence would be a further acceleration of current trends in which the government would be providing more health care, food, housing, recreation, and income to the elderly. Since it could safely be assumed that the proportion of those in government over 65 would also increase, the closest thing to a gerontocracy could prevail in 2025.

Sierles (1982, p. 206) wrote, "Aging (senescence) is a gradual decline in physiological functioning as the years progress. It is debatable whether it begins with birth or in adulthood, and its causes are not known for sure. The decline in function varies in degree from individual to individual, and competence or excellence in behavior or other physiological functioning can be maintained by some at any age. For example, Vinci, Titian, Durer, Michelangelo, Voltaire, Goethe, Verdi, Renoir, and Picasso are examples of artistic genius that continued to flower in old age."

Crook and Cohen (1981, p. 43) of the National Institute of Mental Health point out, "Although many individuals remain physically and emotionally healthy into and beyond the seventh and eighth decades of life, the prevalence of a broad range of physical and emotional disorders is increased in these years. Persons over age 65 account for a disproportionate number of visits to primary care physicians, for example, more than 30% of visits to specialists in internal medicine, and a substantial proportion of the prescriptions written for a number of drugs, including many psychotherapeutic compounds."

A basic geriatric problem of a psychological nature concerns elderly individuals who share households with kin. Mindel's study (1979) indicated that while there has been a definite decline in the number and proportion of multigenerational households, the decline has been greater for the "young-old" (65–74) than the "old-old" (75+), with only slight differences in the proportion of "single" elderly males and "single" elderly females living in multigenerational families. In spite of the decline, the multigenerational household is still viable for approximately 2 million elderly persons.

Reever, Beck-Peterson, and Zarit (1979) reported on the impact of the elderly on relatives in a family constellation. The principle reason for institutionalizing cognitively impaired older persons is the caregivers' inability to continue providing help, and not the severity of deficits. Feelings of burden were significantly correlated with the frequency of visits made by others, but not with other variables such as the severity of cognitive impairment and frequency of memory and behavior problems. These findings suggest the importance of facilitating natural support systems as an essential part of providing services to the families of the impaired elderly. To be sure, the physical manifestations of aging are only a small part of the process of growing old. Changing attitudes, behavior, and overall personality—often the results of societal pressure—are now recognized as equally important considerations in the study of geriatric psychology.

In their *Handbook of Mental Health and Aging,* Birren and Sloane (1980) write: "A national health problem which is most severe in terms of its prevalence and cost is a group of mental disorders and dysfunctions which are associated with aging. . . . More important, perhaps, is a cost that cannot be measured or tabulated: the loss of human potential and of the affected person's capacity for adaptation and ability to contribute to human welfare."

Geriatric psychology also concerns itself experimentally and theoretically with the signs and symptoms of disease processes. Widespread inflammation, muscular rigidity, cough, pain, and fever in the elderly are not minor but acute processes. Senile persons cannot bear extremes such as heat, cold, overeating, starvation, and dehydration. The older individual has accumulated many scars from the hazards of life, injurious habits, poor nutrition, intoxications, infections, and actual injuries, including the psychological traumas incident to a long life. Given the complexity of actual situations in the application of geriatric psychology, Moody (1996) points out that abstract notions of rights and autonomy cannot alone be relied on for satisfactory analyses. There is a formidable, wide-ranging panorama on the myriad ethical problems that confront us all in our rapidly aging society.

Steury and Blank (1981, p. 105) write on retirement state:

In contrast to the popular view of the post-menopausal, empty-nest phase of a woman's life, it is typically experienced as a productive period with increased levels of satisfaction. Retirement in men is often considered an equivalent of menopause and may be viewed as marking the end of a productive life. Retirement is a new phenomenon in the history of man. In preindustrial societies men continued to work until poor health or death intervened. Some persons view work and satisfactions derived from work—apart from the income itself—as the raison d'être for men, such as they do childbearing for women. For many men, however, work is not the central life concern by middle age. Its meaning varies substantially by occupational level. For many men retirement is not feared but anticipated.

Another important aspect of geriatric psychology is the sexuality of the older person. Ludeman (1981) reports that research refutes the pervasive cultural myth of a sexual old age. Men and women continue to be physiologically capable of sexual functioning, although in most older persons interest in sexual activity and actual performance decline with age. Older men are more interested in sex and more active sexually than older women.

Parron, Solomon, and Rodin (1981) emphasize the need to direct the behavioral sciences toward a wider range of health problems than the mental health issues with which they have traditionally been concerned: to link the biomedical and behavioral sciences, and to stimulate interdisciplinary clinical and basic research. They point out that new research initiatives should be undertaken with respect to the changing vulnerabilities of the elderly to disease; and the relationships of the health care provider to the elderly patient.

No less should appropriate attention be given by mental health practitioners to the immunologic status of the elderly, as for example the impact of behavioral processes of adaptation on immune function, the impact of age-related changes in immunologic competence on behavior, and the role of the immune system in mediating relationships between behavioral processes of adaptation and the maintenance of health and the development of disease.

Suicide among the elderly is a major problem especially in America, according to Osgood (1988). She points out that suicide prevention to reduce the rate of suicide in this high-risk group depends on accurate knowledge of major factors in late-life suicide, perceptive reading of suicidal clues and warning signs, and effective application of appropriate intervention techniques.

The keynote in geriatric psychology is individualization. Each elderly person must be separately assessed and inventoried. The changes psychologically produced by old age are many: changes in emotional reactions, in intellectual functioning, response to stress, immunity, biochemical equilibrium, metabolism, structure, and so forth. In fact, recognition of "abnormal" mental and emotional features in persons of advanced years still remains one of the real perplexities of medical practice. Nowhere in the fields of psychiatry, neurology, and geriatric psychology are holistic principles of practice more meaningful than in treating geriatric individuals, for the aged person's mental condition will always be complicated by organic disorders of some kind.

Studies of health behavior in the elderly must take into account the social conditions as well as the underlying physical and psychologic changes that occur with age. These changes function as a substrate for the influence of age and the presentation of disease, response to treatment, and complications that ensue. The same is true for the study of alcohol and drug use in the elderly. Of particular interest in both domains is the variability of physiological changes within and among individuals. Understanding the relationship among central nervous system, endocrine, and immune function may help in identifying one of the bases for the variability.

Research is needed to determine how adaptation to environmental situations may be interrelated with psychological defenses, coping, and social supports, since these factors affect health and disease in older persons. Geriatric psychologists should look at specific components of the immune response and at substances such as thymic factors—especially important because they change with aging—that have powerful influences on immune function. Many of the important questions concerning the effects of aging on the interaction of health and behavior demand multidisciplinary research. Whitehouse, Maurer, and Ballenger (2000) interpret and conceptualize dementia as a complex process involving psychiatry, neurology, molecular biology, sociology, ethics, and health policy, as a multifactorial and multifaceted matter, in geriatric psychology and gerontology.

One of the major problems in the work of the geriatric psychologist is that of chronic "degenerative" diseases which include gout, arthritis, arteriosclerosis, high blood pressure, inadequate or poorly functioning metabolism, and nutritional disorders such as diabetes, anemia, and gonadal deficiency. Most of the disorders of old age are of doubtful etiology. They usually arise from factors within the patient, are highly variable, and are in operation years before they are overtly manifested. Unless and until the causative factors are unequivocally established, geriatric psychology must aim at control rather than cure, and at prevention through better supervision and living. Brussel (1967), writing on environmental stress in later years, quotes Bernard, the father of modern physiology: "Health comes from harmony between the external environment and the internal milieu." This implies that geriatrical and gerontological knowledge, if it is to be truly scientific, must embrace all aspects of the process of aging.

"The study of aging", writes Birren (1996b), "has come to be one of the more important areas of interest because of its implications for the well-being of individuals and society." Man's attitudes toward morality are changing rather radically. Youngner, Arnold, and Schapiro (1999) indicate that, while death is a familiar collective destiny of the human race, there are aspects of death that are themselves challenging for investigation: medical, philosophical, legal, and religious problems of our times.

Pardes wrote, "It is the challenge, and often the quandary, of behavioral scientists to assimilate a vast variety of influences and forces into a coherent portrayal of the whole person. A comprehensive model for studying and understanding the process of human development across the lifespan is essential for progress in all areas of understanding mental health and illness" (Pardes, 1981). Knaus, Wagner, and Portnoi (1982) refer to the need for improved systematic data collection on acute and chronic health status, to help make the intricate relationships among age, intensive care, and outcome easier to investigate and thereby improve.

REFERENCES

Atchley, R. C. (1999). *Continuity and adaptation in aging: Creating positive experiences.* Baltimore, MD: The Johns Hopkins University Press.

Birren, J. E. (1996b). Preface. In Birren, J. E. (Ed.), *Encyclopedia of gerontology: Age, aging, and the aged* (Vol. 1). New York: Academic.

Birren, J. E. (Ed.), (1996a). *Encyclopedia of gerontology: Age, aging, and the aged.* New York: Academic. Volumes 1 and 2, particularly sections "Ageism and discrimination", by T. G. Gowan (71–81); "Autonomic nervous system", by S. Borst (141–149); "Cognitive-behavioral interventions", by H. M. DeVries (289–299); "Creativity", by D. K. Simonton (341–353); "Epidemiology", by K. G. Manton (493–505), of Volume 1; and

"Memory", by A. D. Smith (107–119); "Personality", by J. E. Ruth (281–295); "Psychological well-Being", by C. D. Ryff (365–371), of Volume II. See also: Academic American Encyclopedia (1995). Danbury, CT: Grolier. Section on Geriatrics, 122ff.

Birren, J. E., & Sloane, R. B. (Eds.). (1980). *Handbook of mental health and aging.* Englewood Cliffs, NJ: Prentice Hall.

Brussel, J. A. (1967). *The layman's guide to psychiatry* (2nd edition). New York: Barnes and Noble.

Cohen, G. D. (1977). Mental health and the elderly. Unpublished paper, National Institute of Mental Health. Bethesda, MD.

Crook, T., & Cohen, G. D. (Eds.). (1981). *Physicians' handbook on psychotherapeutic drug use in the aged.* New Canaan, CT: Pawley.

Knaus, W. A., Wagner, D. F., & Portnoi, V. A. (1982). Intensive treatment for the elderly. *Journal of the American Medical Association, 247* (23), 3185–3186.

Lawton, G. (1947). *Aging successfully.* New York: Columbia University Press.

Ludeman, K. (1981). The sexuality of the older person: Review of the literature. *The Genrontologist, 21*(2), 203–209.

Mindel, C. H. (1979). Multigenerational family households: Recent trends and implications for the future. *The Gerontologist, 19* (5), 456–463.

Moody, H. R. (1996). *Ethics in an aging society.* Baltimore, MD: The Johns Hopkins University Press.

Osgood, N. J. (1988). Suicide in the elderly: Clues and prevention. *Carrier Foundation Letter, 133,* 1–2.

Pardes, H. (1981). Concepts of the Aging Process. In S. I. Greenspan & G. H. Pollock (Eds.), *The course of life: Volume III: Adulthood and the aging process.* Adelphi, MD: U.S. Department of Health and Human Services, National Institute of Mental Health.

Parron, D. L., Solomon, F., & Rodin, J. (Eds.). (1981). *Health, behavior and aging.* Interim Report, Number 5. Washington, D.C.: National Academy Press.

Poe, W. D., & Holloway, D. A. (1980). *Drugs and the aged.* New York: McGraw-Hill.

President's Commission on Mental Health (1979). Task Panel on the Elderly. Washington, D.C.

Reever, K. E., Beck-Peterson, J. M., & Zarit, S. H. (1979). Relatives of the impaired elderly. In *32nd Annual Scientific Meeting Program,* Part II. Washington, D.C.: Gerontological Society.

Sierles, F. (Ed.). (1982). *Clinical behavioral science.* New York: Spectrum.

Silverman, H. L. (1996). On the meaning of psychotherapy: A survey and evaluation. *PAMA Journal,* Vol. 1, No. 1, 32–39.

Steury, S., & Blank, M. L. (Eds.). (1981). *Readings in psychotherapy with older people.* Rockville, MD: National Institute of Mental Health, U.S. Department of Health and Human Services.

U.S. Census Bureau (1977). *Report.* Washington, D.C.

Whitehouse, P. J., Maurer, K., & Ballenger, J. F. (2000). *Concepts of Alzheimer disease.* Baltimore, MD: The Johns Hopkins University Press.

Youngner, S. J., Arnold, R. M., & Schapiro, R. (1999). *The definition of death: Contemporary controversies.* Baltimore, MD: The Johns Hopkins University Press.

H. L. SILVERMAN

AGING: BEHAVIOR CHANGES
AGING: PHYSIOLOGICAL AND BEHAVIOR CONCOMITANTS

GERMANY, PSYCHOLOGY IN

Most psychology textbooks do refer to psychology in Germany, mainly in sections about the history of psychology (e.g., Bourne & Russo, 1998). Ernst Weber and Gustav Fechner worked between 1830 and 1860 in Leipzig, Germany, founding psychophysics, and Wilhelm Wundt established in 1879 in Leipzig, Germany, the first research laboratory in experimental psychology. Other German-speaking scientists who significantly contributed to psychology were Hans Ebbinghaus, with his studies about memory; Sigmund Freud, founder of psychoanalysis; Max Wertheimer, K. Koffka, and Wolfgang Köhler, founders of Gestalt psychology; Karl Bühler, pioneer of cognitive and language psychology; and Hans Berger, who performed the first EEG registration.

In the first third of the 20th century, Germany was among the leading nations in scientific psychology, and German was an important language for psychological publications. Today, the impact of German psychology on the scientific community is rather small (Keul, Gigerenzer, & Stroebe, 1993; Montada, Becker, Schoepflin, & Baltes, 1995). First, reasons for the decline of German psychology will be discussed; and second, the status of German psychology today will be outlined.

DECLINE OF PSYCHOLOGY IN GERMANY

The obvious cause of the decline of German psychology was the Nazi regime (1933–1945). Most eminent psychologists, mainly Jews, were harassed, fired, and either emigrated, committed suicide, or were killed. One hundred thirty psychologists from German universities emigrated, including 29 full professors (Geuter, 1986). After the war, only a few of the emigrated scientists (14 according to Geuter, 1986; e.g., Bondy and Düker) returned to Germany, and only one full professor in psychology was explicitly invited to return to his previously held chair (Rohracher offered to resign and invited Bühler to his previous chair, but Bühler declined the invitation). Simultaneously, 79 psychology professors employed at the German universities during the Nazi regime remained in their university positions after 1945 (Geuter, 1986), in spite of the fact that most of them received their positions because of political loyalty to the Nazis and not because of scientific excel-

lence. In 1947, half of the West German professors were former members of the Nazi party (Strobl, 1998). These remaining political appointments caused ongoing scientific mediocrity in German psychology after the Third Reich (Birbaumer, in press; Birbaumer & Flor, in press). In addition, no effort was undertaken to rejuvenate the field. For example, the study guidelines for psychology that were developed in 1941 were not substantially changed. Only recently did German universities seek to atone for the Nazi past (Strobl, 1998).

Initial restructuring of the German university system and German psychology was triggered by the student revolts of 1968. German universities became open to a larger number of students, and the number of employed scientists in psychology increased about tenfold. However, only a few well-trained and internationally competitive psychologists were available in Germany, Austria, or Switzerland. A large part of the hiring was politically motivated and scientific scholarship was frequently a selection criterion of minor importance. As a consequence, the scientific output and the international reputation of German psychology did not improve.

GERMAN PSYCHOLOGY TODAY

In Germany, about 50 university departments or institutes of psychology exist, with somewhat more than 400 professors (full professors and *habilitierte* associate professors) holding research and teaching positions. In addition, there are about 30 departments or institutes of medical psychology belonging to the medical faculty where about 90 professors work. Altogether more than 5000 psychologists hold positions devoted to research and teaching (full- or part-time positions; see Psychologen-Kalender, 1999). The curriculum is tightly regulated by nationwide study and examination guidelines, and therefore universities do not differ in teaching and examination topics. The student has limited possibilities to study psychology at the university of his or her choice, since distribution of students is regulated by a national agency mainly on the basis of high school grades. This distribution process was established for psychology and medicine since both have far more applicants than openings. The nationwide selection process allows universities and professors no opportunities to select students, and does not allow students to choose departments with proven excellence. As a consequence, competition between universities for students and state money until now was weak. Only recently have rankings (although of questionable validity) of universities and study subjects been published, and only recently have the states started to distribute research money on the basis of proven scientific scholarship.

Most recent reviews uniformly conclude that the research resources for psychology in Germany are comparable or even better than those in the United States, Britain, Canada, Australia, France, Netherlands, or Israel. However, the scientific output, the international reputation, and the reception of German psychology were found to be comparatively mediocre. Further facts about psychology in Germany include:

- Physics and chemistry in Germany contribute about 3–4% of the publications in international journals, while the corresponding number for psychology is below 0.5% (Keul et al., 1993).

- Forty-two percent of the German professors in psychology did not publish within a five-year period (1986–1990) any article that was listed in the SSCI (Keul et al., 1993).
- Of the psychologists who publish, a considerable number never or rarely publish in English (Basler & Schieferbein, 1995; Keul et al., 1993; Montada et al., 1995). German academic psychologists seriously discussed between 1975 and 1990 whether it is necessary to publish in English (*Sprachenstreit*). Now it is increasingly recognized that reception and citation rates for publications in German are 5–10 times lower than the rates for publications in English.
- An evaluation of *Psychological Review* and *Psychological Bulletin* articles between 1975 and 1992 revealed that German contributions are rare compared to those of the Netherlands, Israel, and Sweden, although these latter countries have substantially smaller populations, fewer full professorships, and fewer research resources (Keul et al., 1993). In addition, most publications of German psychologists in APA journals come from just a few institutes (Montada et al., 1995).

These problems are mainly acknowledged now, and several proposals were made regarding how to improve scientific output as well as the international reception and citation of German psychology (e.g., Birbaumer, in press; Gigerenzer et al., 1999).

The slow but continuous increase in the proportion of publications by German psychologists in international journals, driven mainly by a subgroup of productive psychologists, indicates progress (Becker, 1994). In particular, German psychophysiologists and social psychologists have received international acknowledgment in their fields (Keul et al., 1993). For example, German psychophysiologists or psychobiologists are among the responsible chairs for neuroimaging centers. In addition, in Germany are three MEG systems and two functional MRIs allocated at psychological institutes.

An asset of the German science system that greatly helped to overcome the decline of psychology in Germany after the war and to improve the reputation of German psychology is the German Research Foundation (DFG, Deutsche Forschungsgemeinschaft). According to the lessons learned during the Nazi regime, the peer review process and the rules for grant application do not allow any political or economic influences or pressures. Grant award decisions are based on peer review and scientific reputation only. The allocated money to a particular discipline, such as psychology, depends entirely on the number of awarded grant proposals in that particular discipline (NieBen & Rosler, 2000). The grant money awarded to psychology continuously increased within the last years, a sign that the quality and international reputation of psychology in Germany is improving.

REFERENCES

Basler, H.-D., & Schieferbein, J. (1995). Zur wissenschaftlichen Produktivität in der Medizinischen Psychologie. *Psychologische Rundschau, 46*, 36–41.

Becker, J. H. (1994). Publizieren produktive deutschsprachige Psychologen zunehmend in englischer Sprache? *Psychologische Rundschau, 45*, 234–240.

Birbaumer, N. (in press). Psychologie 1933 bis heute. *Zeitschrift für Psychologie* (*Sonderband: Deutschsprachige Psychologie im 20. Jahrhundert edited by F. Klix*).

Birbaumer, N., & Flor, H. (in press). Deutsche Psychophysiologie 2000. *Zeitschrift für Psychologie* (*Sonderband: Psychologie2000 edited by F. Klix*).

Bourne, L. E. J., & Russo, N. F. (1998). *Psychology.* New York: Norton & Company.

Geuter, U. (1986). *Daten zur Geschichte der deutschen Psychologie.* Göttingen: Hogrefe.

Gigerenzer, G., Rösler, F., Spada, H., Amelang, M., Bierhoff, H. W., & Ferstl, R. (1999). Internationalisierung der psychologischen Forschung in Deutschland, Österreich und der Schweiz: Sieben Empfehlungen. *Psychologische Rundschau, 50,* 101–113.

Keul, A. G., Gigerenzer, G., & Stroebe, W. (1993). Wie international ist die Psychologie in Deutschland, Österreich und der Schweiz? Eine SCCI-Analyse. *Psychologische Rundschau, 44,* 259–269.

Montada, L., Becker, J. H., Schoepflin, U., & Baltes, P. B. (1995). Die internationale Rezeption der deutschsprachigen Psychologie. *Psychologische Rundschau, 46,* 186–199.

Strobl, M. (1998). Universities seek to atone for Nazi past. *Nature, 391,* 112–113.

P. PAULI
N. BIRMBAUER
University of Tuebingen

GESELL, ARNOLD L. (1880–1961)

Arnold L. Gesell received the BPhil from the University of Wisconsin. He received the PhD from Clark University in 1906. While at Clark he was heavily influenced toward the study of child development by G. Stanley Hall. His first position was at the Los Angeles State Normal School. He soon moved to Yale University as assistant professor of education. His early work focused on retarded children, but he soon broadened his approach to normal children as well. Gesell obtained the MD from Yale in 1915 and remained associated there for the remainder of his career. The clinic he founded is known as the Gesell Institute of Child Development.

Gesell put the study of child development on a sound methodological base with his system of observing and measuring behavior. He was the first to use photographic techniques and observation through a one-way mirror. He concentrated on the extensive study of a small number of children. Gesell's method was published in *The Mental Growth of the Pre-School Child.* He later extended his work to children aged 5 to 10 (1946) and to youth aged 10 to 16.

Gesell's *Infant and Child in the Culture of Today,* coauthored with his colleague Frances Ilg, had great influence on child rearing practices in the 1940s and 1950s. Gesell took a strictly constitutional or physiological approach in which the cultural or learning factors played little part. As a result, he is more known for his methodological advances and inspiration to his students than for his theoretical explanations of development of behavior.

C. S. PEYSER
The University of the South

GESTALT PSYCHOLOGY

At the time when Watson founded behaviorism in the United States, Gestalt psychology began to emerge in Germany. While behaviorism was concerned with stimulus and response, Gestalt psychology focused on interconnected psychical organization and experience.

HISTORY

About 1900, there were two competing theories in the natural sciences: atomic theory and holistic field theory. In psychology, the theory of psychical elements and their associations corresponded with the atomic conception. In contrast to this, a holistic view was developed for the psychical sector. Von Ehrenfels' paper on *Gestaltqualitäten* in 1890 proved to be a breakthrough within the German-speaking countries. Alongside other holistic schools it was, above all, the concept of Gestalt psychology that became successful. After fundamental investigations in 1912, Wertheimer first introduced the Gestalt concept and became the founder of the Berlin school alongside Köhler and Koffka. They began to analyze cognitive and learning processes as well as perceptual and psychophysical problems. Lewin applied the concept to the psychology of action. Further representatives of the Gestalt school were Arnheim, Metzger, and Rausch. It was significant for the psychophysical theory that Wertheimer was a friend of Einstein and that Köhler studied physics with Planck (both Planck and Köhler were heads of scientific institutes and as such opposed the Nazis).

With the rise of Nazism, the hitherto successful development of Gestalt psychology suffered a setback. Koffka had already emigrated to the United States in 1927, and was followed by Wertheimer, Köhler, Lewin, and Arnheim in the 1930s. Despite the American predominance of behaviorism, Koffka was met with approval in the sector of developmental psychology and Lewin in social psychology; Arnheim was acknowledged for his works on the psychology of art.

After World War 11, new centers of Gestalt psychology were established in Italy and Japan, while in Germany the theory was further developed by Metzger, Rausch, Witte, and Gottschaldt.

EPISTEMOLOGY

To a naive realist, the world exists as he perceives it. In 1933, Köhler pointed out that the characteristics of objects correlate with the observer's inner processes. Köhler's epistemology has come to be known as critical realism: He differentiates between two kinds of realities, conscious experience and physical reality. Reality, as perceived by the individual, is connected with physical reality via the organism's receptors and effectors, yet these realities are not identical. For instance, electromagnetic waves of a specific frequency are different from what we experience as the color red. It seems to be paradoxical that although every individual develops a certain awareness of reality, he has the impression that he exists within the world. However, all experienced relations of reality arise from the connections between the models of the world and of the self represented within the individual.

METHODOLOGY

The methods of Gestalt psychology are partly derived from the epistemological position. The phenomenological analysis of experienced reality in psychological experimentation is the predominant method. The term "introspection" is inappropriate, since the phenomenological approach is not primarily aimed at what people may discover in themselves, but at the way they experience the world.

The Gestaltists' methodological criticism was particularly directed towards behaviorism. They argued that in the field of learning, one does not acquire associations of absolute stimuli and rigid responses, but instead learns patterns of relationships. According to the Gestaltists, it is one's personal insight and not the process of trial-and-error that often yields creative solutions to problems. From their point of view, the inappropriateness and artificiality of scientific analysis has prevented the behaviorist approach from recognizing these factors.

THEORETICAL ESSENTIALS

It is hardly possible to translate the German word Gestalt. There are, however, similar terms such as "holistic structure" or "form of organization". Gestalt conveys the idea of an integral whole, which is not to be regarded as the sum of separate parts but as an item of Gestaltqualitäten of its own. A tune, for example, has its individual character which cannot be explained as an aggregate of every individual note. Being transposed into another key, the tune remains the same, although the entire range of acoustic stimuli has been altered. This transferability is one of the chief properties of *Gestalten* besides their "non-summativity." The holistic structure assigns to each of its components a specific function, which the component does not possess by itself. Such terms as "center," "function," and "role" are only significant in relation to the structure in its entirety.

Gestalten are dynamic systems. The dynamics, which is determined by the reciprocity of the components, is directed towards homeostasis. Any kind of influence via external stimuli is processed in a fashion that manifests itself as Prägnanztendenz or minimum principle: the tendencies of simplification, emphasizing, and completion. These self-organizing tendencies can be observed in the areas of perception, learning, thinking, ontogenesis, and role-specific behavior. As a result of the interplay of external stimuli and the autonomous tendencies of self-organization, the *Gestalten* gradually adopt a greater complexity.

The term "isomorphism" denotes the relation between items of the same Gestalt, such as the transposed melody above. Isomorphism is of central importance to Köhler's Gestalt theory: it attempts to overcome the Cartesian dualism of body and soul by means of an interdisciplinary theory. By pointing at self-organizing processes in physics, Köhler presumed that electromagnetic field processes in the brain correlate on a "psychophysical level" with the autonomous organization of *Gestalten* in conscious experience. The idea of the conformity of psychical and physical dynamics was put forward by Arnheim.

However, antinomies remain, such as the spatiotemporal continuity of experience and the spatiotemporal discontinuity of neural processes. It is true that dualism has nearly disappeared and, in the domain of neuroscience, has been replaced by monism, a concept which is based on the assumption that psychical and cerebral processes are identical from different perspectives. But the theory of monism can only be maintained if one succeeds in finding the organizational level of cerebral processes that correlate with the phenomenological *Gestalten,* their characteristics, and their dynamics.

THE CURRENT SIGNIFICANCE OF GESTALT PSYCHOLOGY

The theory of Gestalt psychology has never really recovered from its disruption during the Nazi regime. Behaviorism had a strong impact, even in Germany, and continued to disregard phenomenological approaches. On the part of the neo-Marxists in the 1960s, the conception of autonomous processes was dismissed due to its incompatibility with environmentalism. Information theory and computer technology have revived an elementaristic way of thinking. In various statistical methods, the phenomenological mode of argumentation has been renounced.

Nevertheless, Gestalt psychology has by no means lost its influence. The concept has become an integral part of the sciences, even where its sources are not expressed in obvious terms. The "cognitive turn" of American behaviorism in the 1970s was prepared by those *Gestaltists* who had emigrated to the United States, especially so by Köhler and Arnheim. Similarly, Duncker and Wertheimer had laid the groundwork for the psychology of creativity that was developed in the 1950s.

It is not possible to regard a work on perceptual psychology as complete without references to Gestalt psychology. In the neurosciences, Köhler's critical realism has contributed considerably to differentiating the relationship between experienced and physical reality. Critical realism even anticipated central aspects of Maturana's and Varela's constructivism without the paradoxical argument that all types of reality are constructions of the brain. Self-organizing processes, as they are described by the theory of dynamical systems, have already been found as an essential ingredient in Köhler's Gestalt theory.

Gestalt psychology does not merely answer questions of psychological interest and those about the mind-brain problem of the neurosciences. Wertheimer, for example, also applied the Gestalt concept to ethical and social problems. Gestalt psychology today is represented in various efforts to confront the consequences of fragmentarization, hyperspecialization, and egocentricity in the realms of sciences and society, and it is utilized to create new frames of references.

REFERENCES

Arnheim, R. (1954). *Art and Visual Perception.* Berkeley.

Arnheim, R. (1982). *The Power of the Center.* Berkeley.

Ash, M. G. (1995). *Gestalt Psychology in German Culture.* Cambridge.

Ehrenfels, Christian von. (1890). Über Gestaltqualitäten Vierteljahresschrift für wissenschaftliche Philosophie 3.

Ertel, S., Kemmler, L., Stadler, M. (Eds.). (1975). *Gestalttheorie in der modernen Psychologie.* Darmstadt.

Kobbert, M. (1986). *Kunstpsychologie.* Darmstadt.

Köhler, W. (1933). *Psychologische Probleme.* Berlin.

Köhler, W. (1928). *Gestalt Psychology.* New York.

Koffka, K. (1935). *Principles of Gestalt Psychology.* London.

Lewin, K. (1936). *Principles of topological psychology.* New York.

Metzger, W. (5. Aufl. 1975). *Psychologie.* Darmstadt.

Metzger, W. (Ed.). (1966). *Handbuch der Psychologie, Bd. I.1 Wahrnehmung und Bewußtsein.* Göttingen.

Rausch, E. (1952). *Struktur und Metrik figural-optischer Wahrnehmung.* Frankfurt.

Sader, M., & Stadler, M. (1983). Auswahlbibliographie der Gestaltpsychologie. 1. Einführungstexte. *Gestalt Theory, 5,* 125–129.

Stadler, M. (1981). Feldtheorie heute - von Wolfgang Köhler zu Karl Pribram. *Gestalt Theory, 3.*

Tholey, P. (1986). Deshalb Phänomenologie! Anmerkungen zur experimentell-phänomenologischen Methode. *Gestalt Theory, 8.*

Wertheimer, M. (1911). Experimentelle Studien über das Sehen von Bewegung. *Z. Psychol., 60.*

Wertheimer, M. (1924). Über Gestalttheorie. *Philosophische Zeitschrift für Forschung und Aussprache, 1,* 1925.

Wertheimer, M. (1945). *Productive thinking.* New York.

Witte, W. (1952). Zur Geschichte des psychologischen Ganzheits- und Gestaltbegriffes. *Studium generale, 5.*

M. J. KOBBERT
Hochschule für Bildende Künste
Münster, Germany

GESTALT THERAPY
PSYCHOLOGY: HISTORY

GESTALT THERAPY

Gestalt therapy is an existential and phenomenological approach emphasizing the principles of present-centered awareness and immediate experience. To discover how one blocks one's flow of awareness and aliveness, the individual in therapy is directed to fully experience current thoughts, feelings, and body sensations. By assuming greater responsibility for experience, one learns to trust one's own resources and to become less dependent and manipulative in relating to others. Gestalt therapy is nonanalytical and noninterpretive, encouraging patients to find their own meanings, set their own goals, and make their own choices.

ORIGINS

Gestalt therapy was developed by Frederick S. (Fritz) Perls, who was trained in classical Freudian psychoanalysis in Europe in the

1920s and emigrated to the United States following World War II. Perls's broad interests in existentialism, Eastern religions, and Gestalt psychology led him away from the Freudian viewpoint toward his own theory and method of therapy. Influenced by the work of Kurt Goldstein, Perls saw the human being as a unified organism, an integration of mental, physical, emotional, and sensory processes expressed in the present moment. Wulf (1998) notes that together with Perls, two other co-founders, Laura Perls and Paul Goodman, were instrumental in creating the new synthesis out of existing concepts of the time.

"Gestalt" is a German word with no exact English equivalent. It means a configuration or whole, an entity that is more than the sum of its parts. In his first book, *Ego, hunger, and aggression,* published in the United States in 1947, Perls presented the preliminary outlines of his approach. Later works elaborated and extended these early formulations (Perls, Hefferline, & Goodman, 1951; Perls, 1969; Perls, 1973).

MAJOR THEORETICAL CONCEPTS

Gestalt theory suggests that the natural tendency of the organism is toward growth and the satisfaction of basic needs. The healthy individual is responsive to inner urges and trusts them as a basis for choices and decisions. If one denies aspects of one's being by blocking awareness or attempting to live up to a rigid set of "shoulds," one loses the capacity to support oneself adequately and becomes alienated from inner strivings and resources. A continuing flow of needs and wishes comes into awareness; each can be thought of as a Gestalt, a figure or focus that emerges from an undifferentiated background of experience. In healthy functioning, the organism mobilizes to meet each need, making contact with aspects of the environment appropriate to need satisfaction. In this manner the equilibrium of the organism is restored.

For this self-regulating process to function, it is essential that the organism has sufficient awareness—that is, that it be in touch with thoughts, feelings, and sensations as they occur from moment to moment. Present, here-and-now experience constitutes the only reality, whereas memories of the past and expectations of the future are considered fantasies. Since awareness can be focused on only one place at a time, the person occupied with either the past or the future is not aware of what is happening in the present. As Polster and Polster put it, "only the present exists now and . . . to stray from it distracts from the living quality of reality" (1973, p. 7).

Perls emphasized the importance of accepting responsibility for one's own behavior. Instead of denying, blaming, projecting, and displacing responsibility for one's experience, the individual is encouraged to accept thoughts, feelings, and actions as parts of the self. Attributing responsibility to scapegoats—parents, childhood traumas, spouse, and the like—leaves the individual powerless and dependent. Instead of blaming the environment for what we imagine we cannot do for ourselves, we must each of us do our own work, take our own risks, and thereby discover who we are and of what we are capable.

In Gestalt theory a key concept is that of unfinished business: incomplete situations from the past, accompanied by unexpressed feelings never fully experienced or discharged. Carried into present life, these incomplete experiences interfere with present-centered awareness and authentic contact with others. Perls believed that unexpressed resentments were the most frequent source of unfinished business. Unfinished business can be resolved by reenacting (either directly or in fantasy) the original situation and allowing the associated emotions to be experienced and expressed. In this way completion is achieved, preoccupations with the past dissipate, and the individual can redirect attention and energy to new possibilities.

THERAPEUTIC GOALS AND ROLE OF THE THERAPIST

In Gestalt therapy the goal is not mere symptom relief, but rather, personal growth. The therapist assists the patient to achieve greater self-acceptance, to assume more personal responsibility, to reintegrate disowned or split-off aspects of the personality, and to be more authentic and less manipulative in relating to others. Noting discrepancies between what the patient is saying and what the patient is doing, the therapist makes interventions based on the patient's present behavior. Interventions tend to be descriptive rather than interpretive.

The therapist not only observes the patient's process, but also brings his or her own individuality into the encounter. The Gestalt therapist believes that she or he is as much a part of the therapeutic interaction as is the patient, and takes responsibility for being present in a direct, spontaneous, and self-disclosing manner. According to Kempler, "No behavior is the exclusive property of the patient alone. If the patient-therapist process is to be kept alive it depends as much on the full participation of the therapist as it does on his demand for the patient's full commitment" (1973, pp. 270–271). Simkin characterizes his therapeutic role as that of the "midwife": "Having been present at many 'births' of new attitudes, feelings, conceptualizations, behavior and the like (including my own), I can facilitate acceptance (re-owning) . . . on the part of the patient through my acceptance of where the patient and I are at the moment" (1974, p. 14). Perls summed up the relationship between therapist and patient succinctly in his dictum, "I and Thou, Here and Now." (Yontef 1993).

TECHNIQUES OF GESTALT THERAPY

Gestalt therapists have described a variety of techniques—some of them powerful and dramatic—that they use to sharpen direct experience, heighten conflicts and polarities, foster freer expression, or bring into awareness blocks and avoidance mechanisms. Perls cautioned therapists, however, not to become technicians depending on a bag of tricks or gimmicks. Naranjo writes, "Practically every technique in Gestalt therapy might be seen as a particularized embodiment of the broad prescription: 'be aware.' This prescription, in turn, is an expression of the therapist's belief and experience that only with awareness can there be true living" (1973, p. 4).

Continuum of awareness, is a technique that encourages the patient to focus on the now, the ever-shifting midpoint of experience. The Gestalt therapist will ask questions that begin with "what" (What is your present awareness?) and "how" (How do you experience this?), avoiding "why" questions, which encourage theorizing, rationalizing, and justifying. If the patient attempts to diminish feelings (sadness, anger, fear) through deflection, intellectualizing, or other avoidance mechanisms, the therapists may encourage the patient instead to stay with whatever is in the foreground and bring full awareness to the experience. The resolution of an unpleasant situation lies in experiencing it fully, not trying to avoid it. In *Awareness*, Stevens offers an extensive compendium of Gestalt awareness exercises for individuals, pairs, and groups (Stevens, 1971).

In addition to awareness, experimentation is encouraged so as to make sufficient contact with the environment to determine the suitability of a contemplated action. For example, when a patient avoids being critical of others for fear of rejection, the Gestalt therapist may suggest he experiment by making critical statements and noticing the results. The patient can then discover how this feels to him and what responses he actually gets from others.

In Gestalt therapy as practiced by Perls, taking the so-called hot seat, indicated a person's willingness to engage with the therapist. In this case, the hot seat was a chair facing the therapist. An additional empty chair next to the patient might be used to imagine the presence of a significant other or disowned part of self for the purpose of initiating a dialogue. The technique of dialogues is helpful in identifying projected and denied parts of the personality. If, for example, a patient is conflicted between one part of herself with high expectations for achievement and another part that procrastinates, making promises and excuses—a particular personality split that Perls labeled "top dog/underdog"—the therapist might suggest a dialog between these two parts. By using two chairs and moving back and forth between them, the patient carries out a conversation by speaking alternately from each position. As the interplay between these polar opposites is heightened and more fully experienced, integration through greater self-acceptance becomes possible.

The Gestalt therapist attends to the full range of a patient's expression, not just the words. Nonverbal cues such as body posture, gestures, or tone of voice often reflect an aspect of functioning outside the patient's awareness. The therapist may ask a patient to exaggerate or repeat a gesture, for example, and through this intensification allows the patient to discover its function or significance.

The Gestalt method of dream-work grew out of Perls's belief that dreams are among our most spontaneous productions. Each dream is thought to contain an existential message—an expression of aspects of the dreamer's present state of being. By becoming every object and character in the dream (both animate and inanimate), the dreamer can identify with and thereby re-own projections, conflicts, and unfinished situations reflected in the dream. Some excellent examples of Gestalt dream-work can be found in verbatim transcripts of Perls at work with patients on their dreams (Perls, 1969).

APPLICATIONS OF GESTALT THERAPY

As originally practiced by Perls, Gestalt therapy was primarily an individual form of treatment, carried out privately or in the presence of others in workshops or training groups. Other Gestaltists have applied the principles to group therapy in a way that encourages more interaction among group members (e.g., Glass, 1972;

Feder & Ronall, 1980). Going beyond Perls's unique personal style of therapy, they have extended the work to a broad spectrum of client populations and settings. Lederman (1969), Brown (1975), and Oaklander (1978) have described Gestalt work with children and adolescents. Theory and methods of Gestalt family therapy are presented in the works of Kempler (1981) and Resnikoff (1995). Rhyne's art therapy work (1973) and Herman and Korenich's applications to management (1977) further extended the breadth and scope of Gestalt theory and practice.

EVALUATION AND CURRENT STATUS

Gestalt therapy at its best can be energizing and enlivening through its emphasis on direct contact, expressiveness, focus on feelings and body experience, and minimal theorizing and interpreting. Critics, however, have pointed out that this approach can be anti-intellectual, technique-dependent, overly confrontive, and suitable only to well-motivated, verbal clients. Since Gestalt techniques can release intensive affect, Shepherd (1970) expressed concern about the appropriateness of their use with severely disturbed patients and those who lack impulse control. There is general agreement that negative consequences can be minimized by the mature, well-trained therapist who is adequately grounded in the conceptual framework of Gestalt therapy, and who works with a client population with which he or she is experienced and comfortable.

In the fifty years since its inception, Gestalt therapy has undergone considerable evolution. Yontef (1999) describes a growing movement toward a more relational trend in Gestalt therapy characterized by increased support, kindness, and compassion, and away from the confrontation, catharsis and dramatic emphases of the 1960s and 1970s. There is also an increasing acknowledgment of gender and cultural issues as they are reflected in the therapeutic relationship.

Gestalt therapy has become truly international, with active practitioners, institutes, training centers, and university-based programs throughout the United States and in many other countries. The Center for Gestalt Development (Highland, New York) publishes *The Gestalt Journal,* a scholarly periodical of Gestalt theory and practice, as well as *The Gestalt Directory* (1996), an international guide to practitioners of Gestalt therapy and to institutes and centers offering training in Gestalt therapy. The Center also sponsors international conferences, and through The Gestalt Journal Press publishes books related to Gestalt Therapy.

Diversity in therapeutic styles, adaptations to varied client populations, and a burgeoning literature all point to Gestalt therapy's continuing vitality and development, as it finds its place in the mainstream of contemporary psychotherapy.

REFERENCES

Brown, G. I. (1975). *The live classroom: Innovation through confluent education and gestalt.* New York: Viking.

Feder, B., & Ronall, R. (Eds.). (1980). *Beyond the hot seat: Gestalt approaches to group.* New York: Brunner/Mazel.

The Gestalt Directory. (1996). Highland, NY: Center for Gestalt Development.

Glass, T. A. (1972). *The gestalt approach to group therapy.* Paper presented at the 80th annual convention of the American Psychological Association, Honolulu, HI.

Herman, S. M., & Korenich, M. (1977). *Authentic management: A gestalt orientation to organizations and their development.* Reading, MA: Addison-Wesley.

Kempler, W. (1973). Gestalt therapy. In R. Corsini (Ed.), *Current psychotherapies* (pp. 251–286). Itasca, IL: F. E. Peacock.

Kempler, W. (1981). *Experiential psychotherapy within families.* New York: Brunner/Mazel.

Lederman, J. (1969). *Anger and the rocking chair: Gestalt awareness with children.* New York: McGraw-Hill.

Naranjo, C. (1973). *The techniques of gestalt therapy.* Berkeley, CA: SAT Press.

Oaklander, V. (1978). *Windows to our children.* Moab, UT: Real People Press.

Perls, F. S. (1947). *Ego, hunger, and aggression.* New York: Vintage.

Perls, F. S. (1969). *Gestalt therapy verbatim.* Lafayette, CA: Real People.

Perls, F. S. (1973). *The gestalt approach and eye witness to therapy.* Ben Lomond, CA: Science and Behavior.

Perls, F. S., Hefferline, R. F., & Goodman P. (1951). *Gestalt therapy: Excitement and growth in the human personality.* New York: Julian.

Polster, E., & Polster, M. (1973). *Gestalt therapy integrated: Contours of theory and practice.* New York: Brunner/Mazel.

Resnikoff, R. (1995). Gestalt family therapy. *The Gestalt Journal, 18* (2), 55–75.

Rhyne, J. (1973). *The gestalt art experience.* Monterey, CA: Brooks/Cole.

Shepherd, I. L. (1970). Limitations and cautions in the gestalt approach. In J. Fagan & I. L. Shepherd (Eds.), *Gestalt therapy now: Theory, techniques, applications* (pp. 234–238). Palo Alto, CA: Science and Behavior Books.

Simkin, J. S. (1974). *Mini-lectures in gestalt therapy.* Albany, CA: Wordpress.

Stevens, J. O. (1971). *Awareness: Exploring, experimenting, experiencing.* Layfayette, CA: Real People.

Wulf, R. (1998). The historical roots of Gestalt therapy theory. *The Gestalt Journal, 21* (1), 81–92.

Yontef, G. (1999). Preface to the 1998 edition of *Awareness,* dialogue and process. *The Gestalt Journal, 22* (1), 9–20.

Yontef, G. (1993). *Awareness, dialogue and process: essays on gestalt therapy.* Highland, NY: The Gestalt Journal Press (p. 66).

T. A. GLASS
Honolulu, HI

GESTALT PSYCHOLOGY
PSYCHOTHERAPY
PSYCHOTHERAPY TECHNIQUES

GODDARD, HENRY H. (1866–1957)

An early student of the causes of mental retardation, Henry H. Goddard argued for hereditary intelligence and was an early advocate of eugenics.

Goddard was professor of abnormal and clinical psychology at Ohio State University, and served for many years as director of the research laboratory at the training school at Vineland, New Jersey. He is best known for *The Kallikak Family,* in which he traced two branches of a family, one of which was largely mentally deficient. In *Feeblemindedness: Its Causes and Consequences,* he classified cases of retardation by cause, finding between one-half and two-thirds to be hereditary. This conclusion led him to advocate preventing reproduction by individuals judged to be feebleminded.

Goddard also helped popularize the Binet test of intelligence in the United States and introduced the term "moron." His very simple theory of inherited intelligence finds little support today.

T. KEITH-LUCAS
The University of the South

GOLDMAN EQUATION

In 1943, the chemist David Goldman studied salt flow through artificial membranes and described his results with an equation now known as the Goldman equation. His work remains important in psychology because the difference between sadness and happiness, good mood and bad, and even sanity and mental illness depends on the flow of charged salts (ions) through the protein channels puncturing neural membranes. For example, cocaine opens some Ca^{+2} channels; a mutation in some K^+ channels is thought to be associated with schizophrenia; and general anesthetics keep GABA-sensitive Cl^- channels open longer.

Much of any cell's function is controlled by changes in the voltage across its ultra-thin insulating wall. For a typical voltage of 100 mV across the 10 nm-thick membrane, the electric field strength is about 10 million V/m (about ten million volts across a doorway!). It should not be surprising, then, that small voltage changes can alter cell function by contorting the charged channel proteins. This is particularly true of voltage-controlled channels. Similarly, changes in the local electric field within stretch-sensitive channels due to slight membrane stretch alters ion flow through them, making them useful in cell volume regulation and detection of atomic movements throughout the body (in the ear, skin, muscle spindles, joints, etc.). For ligand-mediated channels, ion flow is altered by changes in the local electric field caused by bound hormones, drugs, or neurotransmitters. Because all of these channels are crucial in the electrical and chemical communication within and between cells, we clearly need to understand how channels open and close, how membrane voltages determine ion flow, and how ion flow determines membrane voltage.

EQUILIBRIUM

If an ion x (say, Na^+, K^+, or Cl^-) passes through a particular type of channel, the electrochemical potential energy difference (μ_x) driving the ion through the channel is given by $\mu_x = z_x V + E_{10} \log_{10}(x_o/x_i)$, where V is the voltage across the membrane, z_x is the ion's charge, and x_o and x_i are its concentrations, or activities, inside and outside the cell. $E_{10} = (2.303 kT/q)$, where q is the proton charge in Coulomb, k is the Boltzmann constant, and T is absolute temperature in degrees Kelvin (Adamson, 1973; Hille, 1992). At 38°C, $E_{10} = 60$ mV. Diffusion of ion x is equal in both directions (equilibrium occurs) when $\mu_x = 0$ for $V = E_x = (E_{10}/z)\log_{10}(x_o/x_i)$, where E_x is the equilibrium voltage for x.

NON-EQUILIBRIUM

While important, this last Nernst equation has limited practical application because ions are not often at equilibrium (except after death). Most often $V \neq E_x$, and there is a net ion flow or current through channels, approximated by the modified Goldman-Hodgkin-Katz (GHK) current equation

$$I_x = (n_x g_x p_o)[(z_x^2 q/E_{10}) V (x_i - x_o 10^{-z_x V/E_{10}})/(1 - 10^{-z_x V/E_{10}})]$$
$$= P_x \text{GHK}_x$$

where n_x is the number of channels in the membrane, with a probability of opening of p_o and a single-channel conductance of g_x. The product $P_x = (n_x g_x p_o)$ is the membrane's permeability to ion x.

GRAPHICAL INTERPRETATION

While the GHK equation appears daunting, it is most easily appreciated in its graphical form, in which it describes the current-versus-voltage (IV) curve for the ion/channel combination. As shown in Figure 1.1, the shape of the IV curve is defined by the complex term within square brackets (GHK_x) and varies with the concentration ratio (x_o/x_i), and the magnitude of the current is scaled by the permeability P_x (Figure 1.2). The IV curve passes through the ordinate ($I_x = 0$) at equilibrium, where $V = E_x$. As for P_x, the channel density n_x is determined genetically, is often up- and down-regulated during cell function, and may also be altered with drugs; and the channel conductance g_x may change with drugs or a genetic mutation (e.g., cystic fibrosis or schizophrenia). For voltage-controlled channels, p_o often follows a simple Boltzmann function $p_o = 1/[1 + 10^{(V-V_{1/2})/V_{11}}]$, where $V_{1/2}$ is the voltage at which $p_o = 1/2$, and V_{11} is the voltage change from $V_{1/2}$ required to increase p_o from 1/2 to 10/11, or decrease it from 1/2 to 1/11 in the other direction. Because p_o is a strong function of V for voltage-controlled channels, their IV curve can take on complex shapes, often either N-shaped (Figure 1.3) or L-shaped (Figure 1.4). For stretch-sensitive channels, p_o is often described by a Boltzmann function, with $p_o = 1/[1 + 10^{(d-d_{1/2})/d_{11}}]$, where d is the membrane deformation, $d_{1/2}$ is the membrane deformation at which $p_o = 1/2$, and d_{11} is the displacement away from $d_{1/2}$ required to increase the opening probability from 1/2 to 10/11, or from 1/2 to 1/11 if the displacement is in the other direction. For ligand-mediated channels the opening probability is often a saturating function of the concentration (C) of the molecular ligand, and if n (the Hill coefficient) ligand molecules must bind to the channel receptor to open the channel, the opening probability is given by $p_o = [C/(C + K_{sat})]^n$, where K_{sat} is a binding parameter that determines the onset of saturation, and n is the Hill coefficient.

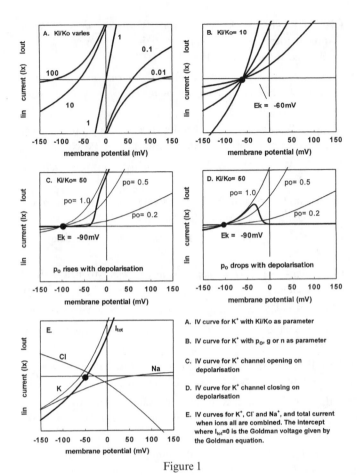

Figure 1

ALL IONS COMBINED

Of course, the parameters are different for different channel types, and different values of z_x, x_o, and x_i apply to each ion x. Nevertheless, if all ions flowing through a membrane share the same V (assuming no local charge screening), and we ignore ionic currents through membrane pumps and carrier molecules, then the total current is the sum of all channel currents, and the total IV curve is the vertical sum of each separate IV curve. Assuming only one type of fixed channel for each major ion (Na^+, K^+, and Cl^-), with permeabilities P_{Na}, P_K, and P_{Cl}, the total current would be $I_{tot} = P_{Na}\text{GHK}_{Na} + P_K\text{GHK}_{Na} + P_{Cl}\text{GHK}_{Cl}$ (Figure 1.5), and the net current is zero at a particular voltage, V_m, which is not necessarily equal to E_{Na}, E_K, or E_{Cl}. This resting membrane voltage is important because it is the only voltage that is stable: When $I_{tot} = 0$, the membrane is neither charging nor discharging, and the voltage remains constant as long as the concentrations remain fixed. It can be shown that $I_{tot} = 0$ for a value of V_m given by the Goldman equation $V_m = E_{10}\log_{10}[(P_{Na}Na_i^+ + P_K K_i^+ + P_{Cl}Cl_o^-)/(P_{Na}Na_o^+ + P_K K_o^+ + P_{Cl}Cl_i^-)]$ Clearly the resting membrane voltage changes with the concentration ratios (as in sensory cells, like Na^+ detection on the tongue), or permeabilities (as in sensory cells, in neurotransmission, and during drug action).

PROBLEMS WITH THE GOLDMAN EQUATION

While useful as a first approximation, the Goldman equation is not applicable when cells or their environments are asymmetrical, because different permeabilities and ion concentrations apply around the cell's perimeter. The equation is also inappropriate when significant current flows through membrane pumps or carriers, as in salt transport epithelia. Nevertheless, in symmetric cells dominated by channel currents, the Goldman equation estimates the membrane voltage. If ion x dominates because of its large concentration or high permeability, the Goldman equation simplifies to the Nernst equation, and V_m tends to E_x. Finally, if an ion is not being pumped through a membrane, it ultimately distributes passively across the membrane according to its charge and the membrane voltage, and cancels itself out of the Goldman equation. It is common, then, for such passive ions to be excluded from the equation at the outset. This is problematic, because the passive redistribution of passive ions takes time, and passive ions can still modify rapid voltage changes such as action potentials or postsynaptic potentials.

R. PATUZZI

GORMAN, JACK M.

Jack M. Gorman is the first Lieber Professor and Vice Chair for Research in the Department of Psychiatry at the College of Physicians and Surgeons, Columbia University in New York, New York. As part of his responsibilities at Columbia, he serves as the director for the Lieber Center for Schizophrenia Research, one of the most advanced collaborations of scientists in the area of schizophrenia. In addition to his busy teaching schedule, he also is the director of the Mental Health Clinical Research Center for Schizophrenia Studies at the New York State Psychiatric Institute's Research Foundation for Mental Hygiene, and the scientific director of the Phobia, Anxiety, and Stress Disorders Clinic at Long Island Jewish Medical Center's Hillsides Division.

Gorman earned his medical degree at the College of Physicians and Surgeons, Columbia University. He then interned in pediatrics at Babies Hospital in New York city, and completed a residency in psychiatry at the New York State Psychiatric Institute and Columbia-Presbyterian Medical Center. He also completed a fellowship in psychiatric research and psychopharmacology at Columbia University.

In addition to his two books, both for the general audience (*The Essential Guide to Psychiatric Drugs* and *The Essential Guide to Mental Health,* both published by St Martin's Press), he is the author of more than 270 journal articles and several textbook chapters. *Treatment That Works, Prenatal Exposures in Schizophrenia,* and *Treating Mental Disorders* are just a few of many other books to which he has contributed. Gorman also serves as the editor of *CNS Spectrums,* the deputy editor of the *American Journal of Psychiatry,* and reviews for several other psychiatric journals. His research interests include the neuroanatomy and neurotransmitter function in panic disorder, the neuroendocrinology of depression, and the neuroimmunology of schizophrenia.

STAFF

GRACE, ANTHONY A.

Anthony A. Grace received his BS degree in 1977 from Allegheny College in Meadville, PA, with a double major in psychology and biology and a minor in chemistry. He attended the graduate program at Yale University in the department of pharmacology, where he began to study the pharmacology of dopamine system regulation under the mentorship of B. S. Bunney. His dissertation work led to an impressive series of groundbreaking studies on the physiology of midbrain dopamine neurons, resulting in the publication of 29 papers and book chapters during his graduate career. He received his PhD in pharmacology from Yale in 1983. In order to further his background in cell biophysics, Grace completed postdoctoral training in the department of physiology and Biophysics at New York University under the mentorship of R. Llinas, where he learned cell staining techniques and in vitro electrophysiological recordings from mammalian brain slices. In 1985 Grace accepted a position as an assistant professor of psychology and psychiatry in the psychobiology program at the University of Pittsburgh. He is currently a professor of neuroscience and psychiatry at the University of Pittsburgh.

Over the past 20 years, Grace's research has focused on the physiology and anatomy of the dopaminergic system and its postsynaptic targets in the basal ganglia, thalamus, and cortex, with an emphasis on the system's role in schizophrenia and other psychiatric disorders. These efforts have spanned four major interrelated topics, each of which has proven relevance to schizophrenia in humans: (a) the biophysical regulation of DA-containing neurons and their postsynaptic targets; (b) the mechanism of action of antipsychotic drugs; and (c) the gating of information flow within the limbic and thalamocortical systems, including developmental disruption as a model of schizophrenia pathophysiology; and (d) the plasticity of the limbic system in response to repeated administration of drugs of abuse. In each of these areas, Grace's seminal observations and intriguing analyses have not only advanced our understanding of basic phenomena involving dopamine action but also have stimulated the field in many directions. Further, Grace has consistently gone beyond empirical data to articulate the theoretical impact of his work, with data-based, credible, falsifiable, and heuristic models. Accordingly, his research papers, reviews, and theoretical articles are among the most widely quoted in the field of neuropsychopharmacology and have driven the field in new directions. Most importantly, his work provides a model of translational research by extrapolating direct clinical implications from his research findings. These implications have had a powerful impact not only on the advancement of knowledge but on the practical matter of screening drugs in the pharmaceutical industry for the ultimate benefit of patients suffering from major psychiatric disorders.

Grace's first major contribution to the field of schizophrenia research was the discovery of antipsychotic drug-induced depolarization block in dopamine cells. This response provided an explanation for the delayed therapeutic action of antipsychotic drugs, and furnished a model system used by pharmaceutical companies in the development and screening of potential antipsychotic drugs. Grace developed the technique of in vivo intracellular recordings from dopamine-containing neurons, which enabled him to be the first to directly identify these neurons electrophysiologically, and to contribute the definitive work that describes the physiology of dopamine neuron regulation in the brain. Investigations into the plasticity of the nervous system and gap junction communication opened up new avenues in our understanding of the long-term sequalae of therapeutic drugs as well as how drugs of abuse can produce persistent alterations in the nervous system of mammals, contributing to addiction and craving. His work on the regulation of basal ganglia function led to the development of a new model of dopamine system dynamics, whereby small changes in extracellular dopamine levels lead to substantial alterations in synaptic dopamine transmission. This tonic/phasic model of dopamine system function had a major impact in the interpretation of functional imaging data and has been cited in numerous research articles and textbooks. By investigating neuronal interactions at a systems level within the brain, Grace discovered basic properties of the gating of information flow within the limbic system, which he used to develop a model describing the physiological bases of multiple symptom clusters in schizophrenia. A recent line of Grace's investigation employed a developmental disruption model of psychiatric disturbances, which has been found to emulate many aspects of the pathophysiology of schizophrenia. Such a model system has proven invaluable in examining how early developmental insults may cause the brain to rewire, leading to the emergence of limbic system dysfunction in the adult organism.

Grace has published more than 120 papers and book chapters during his career. The impact that this body of work has made on the field can be assessed by his numerous highly cited manuscripts. He has received numerous recognitions for his research endeavors. These include a Research Scientist Development Award from the National Institute of Mental Health, a Chancellor's Distinguished Research Award from the University of Pittsburgh, the Judith Silver Award from the National Alliance for the Mentally Ill, a Distinguished Investigator Award from the National Alliance for Research in Schizophrenia and Depression, and the Daniel H. Efron Award for Excellence in Research in Neuropsychopharmacology from the American College of Neuropsychopharmacology. He has received support for his research from the Sloan Foundation, the Scottish Rite Foundation for Schizophrenia Research, the National Institute of Mental Health, and the National Institute for Neurological Disorders and Stroke. Grace is an associate editor for the *Journal of Pharmacology and Experimental Therapeutics,* and is on the editorial board of *Synapse, Neuropsychopharmacology, and Biological Psychiatry.* He is regularly asked to participate on NIH and VA study sections and special review panels, and is on the Scientific Advisory Board for the International Congress on Schizophrenia Research.

Grace's exceptional research accomplishments are derived from his widely acclaimed technical skills in neurophysiology, his extensive knowledge of the relevant scientific literature that spans several disciplines, and his unique ability to integrate this information to develop novel and highly original hypotheses regarding the basic neurobiological underpinnings of major psychiatric disorders, including schizophrenia, Parkinson's disease, and drug abuse. As a result, even though his research work is in the basic neurosciences, he has achieved leadership status in the clinical research literature, as substantiated by his numerous invited speaking engagements and awards. He has been invited to give numerous talks at universities and international symposia throughout the world, based on his leadership role in two very competitive disciplines: schizophrenia research and drug abuse. For someone to be considered an expert in either of these fields is quite an accomplishment, but to achieve international notoriety in both is truly unique.

In summary, it is clear that Grace has had a substantial impact on the field of neuropsychopharmacology. His work is unique in that he uses a basic science cellular approach to investigate systems and phenomena related to major psychiatric disorders, but also is very talented in incorporating his findings into highly original, testable models of system function and pathophysiology. As a result, both his basic neurophysiological work and his theoretical constructs have been very widely cited in both the basic science and clinical literature.

STAFF

GRADUATE RECORD EXAMINATIONS (GRE)

The GRE are graduate-school aptitude and achievement tests and the associated testing program, conducted by the Educational Testing Service (ETS) for the Graduate Record Examinations Board. Originated in 1939 by the Carnegie Foundation for the Advancement of Teaching and several Eastern universities, and since expanded and revised, the program is long-lived, widely used by graduate institutions, and respected among psychometricians for its technical quality. An applicant takes the aptitude test and an advanced test in the field of the undergraduate major. All scores are reported on a 500 ± 100 standard-score scale. A composite score is based on the aptitude and advanced score.

The *aptitude test* includes items on verbal reasoning, verbal comprehension, mathematical reasoning, and data interpretation that are suited to advanced undergraduates; it yields verbal (V) and quantitative (Q) scores. A new section added in 1977 and revised by 1981 gives an analytical (A) score, based on analytical-reasoning items and logical-reasoning items (revised version). Data on the predictive utility and meaning of A scores are expected to accumulate, as they have for V and Q (Conrad, Trismen, & Miller, 1977; *Guide to the Use of the Graduate Record Examinations,* 1981).

The *advanced tests* are available in 20 fields: biology, chemistry, computer science, economics, education, engineering, English literature, French, geography, geology, German, history, mathematics, music, philosophy, physics, political science, psychology, Spanish, and sociology. Some tests yield a total score; others include part scores for subdivisions of the field as well.

V, Q, and A aptitude scores and all total scores for advanced tests have consistently met professional standards for reliability. Among criterion measures used in predictive-validity studies have been graduate school grade point averages, attainment versus nonattainment of the PhD within 10 years, and performance on departmental comprehensive exams. In general, combining undergraduate grade point averages with GRE scores has given the highest validities, and the GRE composite score alone has predicted criterion better than undergraduate GPA alone (Anastasi, 1988). Because the range of academic aptitude among graduate-school applicants is narrower than among applicants to college, GRE validities are necessarily lower than validities for tests such as the Scholastic Aptitude Test. GRE validities vary somewhat with institution, area, and applicant group, making local or departmental validity studies desirable. Since percentile norms differ by major field, interpreting applicant scores in terms of specific norms (and if available, local norms) is suggested. The ETS publications previously cited describe appropriate versus inappropriate use and interpretation of scores, the evolution of the testing program, associated services, and related publications. ETS also publishes sample items from previously administered tests.

REFERENCES

Anastasi, A. (1988). *Psychological testing* (6th ed., pp 318–321). New York: Macmillan.

Conrad, L., Trismen, D., & Miller, R. (Eds.). (1977). *GRE technical manual.* Princeton, NJ: Educational Testing Service.

Guide to the use of the Graduate Record Examinations (1981). Princeton, NJ: Educational Testing Service.

A. B. PRATT
Capital University

INTELLIGENCE MEASURES
PSYCHOMETRICS

GRAHAM, FRANCES (1918–   )

Graham, née Keesler, received the BA from the Pennsylvania State University and, as an advisee of Clark L. Hull and Donald G. Marquis, the PhD from Yale University (1942). Except for 3 years at Barnard College, she was associated with the Washington University School of Medicine until 1957 and the University of Wisconsin at Madison until 1986. In 1986, she joined the University of Delaware psychology faculty.

Graham has related physiological changes in autonomic and brain activity to perceptual-cognitive function, especially during early development. Contributions include the Graham-Kendall Memory-for-Designs Test; the St. Louis prospective study of perinatal anoxia; delineation of the nature of startle, orienting, and defense reflexes; and the design of a reflex probe technique that demonstrates selective attentional effects on sensory input. Her work has been published in a number of monographs and in psychology, medical, and interdisciplinary journals.

She was president of the Society for Psychophysiological Research (SPR), Society for Research in Child Development (SRCD), APA Division of Comparative and Physiological Psychology, and chair of the Psychology Section of the American Association for the Advancement of Science. She also served on the NIMH Board of Scientific Counselors and the President's Commission on Ethics in Medicine and Biomedical and Behavioral Research. Honors include distinguished scientific contribution awards from SPR, SRCD, and APA, the G. Stanley Hall medal from APA's Division on Developmental Psychology, and election to the National Academy of Sciences.

STAFF

GREAT BRITAIN, PSYCHOLOGY IN

The academic discipline of psychology, as separate from philosophy and physiology, came later to Great Britain than to Germany or to the United States, and developed at first along rather different lines. For some reason, British culture was unsympathetic to the kind of careful analysis of experience that characterized both German and American work. E. B. Titchener, though British, developed his systematic analyses of introspection on the more sympathetic soil of the United States after studying at Leipzig. Equally, work on animal conditioning was less influential in Britain, so that the behaviorist movement started by J. B. Watson left the country almost untouched. There were, however, three local influences which had a large impact on British psychology until fairly recently, and which can still be seen, to some extent, at work. The first was the tradition of statistical analysis and correlation; the second, neurology and neurophysiology; and the third, general biology and field naturalism.

As far as the first is concerned, the notion of correlation was first advanced by Francis Galton toward the end of the 19th century, and the mathematics developed in essentially their modern form shortly afterward by Karl Pearson. The obvious power of the correlational approach had a considerable influence on thinkers in Britain at the time, particularly in London. The second noticeable influence was that of neurology and neurophysiology. The British were fortunate in the 19th century in possessing physicians concerned with the effect of brain injury who were very alert to the broader implications of the defects they observed; they included Ferrier, Hughlings, Jackson, and Head. More academic physiologists, such as Sherrington, and later Adrian, also exercised considerable influence. Last, the influence of general biology was bound to be enormous in the country of Charles Darwin. He placed some emphasis on the evolutionary significance of behavior, and he was followed by investigators of animal behavior such as Lloyd Morgan, who did much to clarify concepts of instinctive behavior.

These influences, however, did not lead to the establishment of academic teaching in psychology as quickly as in other countries. By 1939 there were only six professors of psychology in Britain—three in London, and one each at Manchester, Cambridge, and Edinburgh. The number of graduates in psychology remained extremely small until the 1960s; however, some important intellectual developments did take place, and the foundation was laid for the development of the contemporary profession. The intellectual developments can be seen, without too much forcing, as following the three lines of influence already mentioned.

LINES OF INTELLECTUAL ADVANCE

The Correlational Tradition

C. S. Spearman of University College, London, is noted for his establishment and development of the technique of factor analysis. He drew attention to the fact that most measures of ability are positively correlated, and that the pattern of the correlation coefficients is such that one can represent them as due to an underlying single factor together with other, more specific factors. The possibilities opened up by these methods occupied Spearman and many other British psychologists, such as Godfrey Thomson, throughout the first half of this century. Spearman was succeeded in his professorship at London by Cyril Burt, who continued a similar tradition, and large areas of contemporary psychometrics are based originally upon the concepts of this school. More generally, the use of multivariate analysis of measurements is a method of increasing importance outside the particular field of psychometrics, and has expanded well beyond the original national boundaries that produced it.

It is worth noting that the reputation of this school has suffered in recent years through its association with a belief in very strong genetic influences on behavior. In the case of Burt, it is for all practical purposes certain that he published false data concerning this problem, though it is also fair to say that he did so as a very old man a number of years after retirement. Whatever one's views on this issue, however, the fact remains that the techniques developed at London are a major weapon in the armory of all modern psychologists, including those most committed to environmental determination. Furthermore, the widespread replicability of factorial analyses of abilities poses a still unanswered question regarding the way in which general problem-solving, mathematical, and verbal performance are interrelated.

In more recent years, psychometric analysis of abilities has become of less interest in Britain. It has been succeeded by factor analysis of personality tests, in which the most notable development is H. J. Eysenck's establishment of two orthogonal factors as describing a large number of measurements of temperament. One of these factors can be described as neuroticism and one as introversion. Such an analysis is widely replicated, though some investigators would prefer to use a larger number of correlated factors rather than two independent ones.

The Neurological Tradition

As noted previously, the distinguished work of neurophysiologists such as Sherrington and Adrian had established, by World War II, the broad concept of the nervous system as an integrated assembly of separate pathways, each transmitting information in an all-or-none manner. At the same time, the thinking of neurologists such as Head had considerable influence on the concepts employed by psychologists such as Bartlett. With the onset of World War II, a large number of head injuries were observed, and the resulting deficits in performance were studied by O. L. Zangwill and his successors, with increasingly sophisticated methods. In 1952, Zangwill became a professor at Cambridge. Influenced by the experiments of Karl Lashley in the United States, popular opinion at that time was skeptical of the possibility of drawing any links between injury to particular parts of the brain and deficits of particular kinds of function. This concept of mass action, however, had been pushed too far, as could be seen at an early stage by the differences in deficits found in the right and left hemispheres, as well as, increasingly, a function of parietal, frontal, and temporal lesions. A tradition of laboratory experiment in examination of neurological patients was established, particularly at the National Hospital for Nervous Diseases, and increasingly throughout the country. This tradition is now one of the strongest in British psychology. (It is, of course, reinforced by corresponding traditions in other countries, such as the work in Montreal of Brenda Milner, herself British by origin, and at a number of centers in both North America and Europe.) At the same time, experimental studies of animal behavior following lesions to the brain developed both at Cambridge and, more recently, at Oxford.

The Tradition of General Biology

Because of the tradition of observing animal behavior in the wild, Britain formed a receptive environment for the resurgence of ethology from Europe in the 1950s: N. Tinbergen came to work at Oxford, and flourishing studies of animal behavior developed both at Oxford and at Cambridge, under W. H. Thorpe. The significance of behavior for general evolution has been increasingly emphasized, through work such as that of Maynard Smith. Briefly, the behavior of an individual may or may not lead to survival, depending on the behavior of other individuals; it may be very desirable to act aggressively if all individuals in the neighborhood are relatively passive, but beyond a certain point aggression ceases to pay if the costs in conflict and damage are too great. Thus there will be certain mixtures of behavior that form stable strategies from an evolutionary point of view, as the probabilities of such behavior can be tracked in a population.

Studies of animal learning based on the model of American learning theory were not established in Britain to any great extent, partly because of the differences in tradition already noted, but also because of the practical difficulties of keeping animals during the disturbed period of World War II and its aftermath. When animal work did begin, with studies such as those of J. A. Deutsch and N. S. Sutherland, the theories being put forward involved fairly complex models of internal processes, rather than simple stimulus-response links. This development is, of course, parallel to the one that has occurred in the United States.

The effect of relatively complex theorizing about behavior can be seen most clearly in a psychologist who never worked with animals at all—F. C. Bartlett of Cambridge. Bartlett is a major figure in the development of psychology in Britain, both because of his own research, and because, with very few university departments in existence, he was responsible for training a large number of those who developed the new departments of psychology that grew up in Britain after World War II. As already noted, Bartlett's thinking was influenced by neurology and general biology, which conceived of the nervous system as carrying out fairly elaborate processes, organized in an integrated fashion through a number of levels of function, and performing tasks that are adaptive, directed, and describable as homeostatic. The biological approach tended to regard S-R theorizing as unduly simple. Consequently, when Bartlett undertook experiments on perception and memory in human beings, he used very naturalistic situations rather than the laboratory tasks of Wundt and Titchener, and his theorizing was in terms of complex process rather than the reflex arc concepts of Ivan Pavlov and Watson. At the empirical level, he demonstrated that memory was often creative and constructive rather than the restoration of a past sensory impression, and that the reconstruction tended to follow lines of probability in the person's experience, and also motivational lines corresponding to the interests of the particular individual. Bartlett's theoretical concepts, therefore, suggested that each event in a person's history is not stored individually, but by changing a general framework of action, which he called the *schema,* following a term introduced by Head in neurology. The schema would determine the particular way an event was perceived; and when later recall took place, the person would reconstruct the event using schematically derived probabilities and a few details rather than perfect storage of the original experience. In 1932, when Bartlett's major book appeared, it was difficult to find terminology to express such concepts; but the general framework of ideas can be fairly clearly understood and it is interesting to note that similar concepts very recently have been found necessary by investigators working in the field of artificial intelligence.

The use of mechanical and computational analogies became possible about a decade later, with the development of more complex systems of engineering control, largely for military purposes. Bartlett welcomed and strongly encouraged the thinking in this area of K. J. W. Craik, an investigator who, during World War II, put forward the declared aim of understanding human behavior by analogy with these more complex models from engineering. Thus he was, by a few years, the earliest proponent of cybernetic or information-processing approaches to psychology. He died very young, in 1945, but his ideas had been taken up enthusiastically by Bartlett, and he left a small number of writings and a group of people who had been strongly influenced by him. Consequently, from 1945 to 1952, there developed at Cambridge an extremely active group of investigators who applied engineering analogies in their theoretical approaches to behavior; these included Welford, Hick, and Mackworth. Mackworth succeeded Bartlett as director of the research unit founded by Craik; this unit became separate from the University of Cambridge in 1952, when Zangwill succeeded Bartlett in his university post. The unit continued active experimental work on problems of perception, memory, motor control, and the effects of environmental stress; to understand these problems, they found it necessary to reinvestigate topics such as attention, which other traditions in psychology had found difficult to handle. The staff in the 1950s included such names as Broadbent, Poulton, Conrad, and Gregory, and it is widely held that their publications were instrumental in establishing current interest in the problems of cognitive psychology.

INSTITUTIONAL AND PROFESSIONAL DEVELOPMENT

Given the small number of graduates in psychology up to World War II, a profession of psychology could hardly be regarded as existing. The research unit founded by Craik and Bartlett, however, did form part of a long-standing tradition of applied work, funded for the most part by the Medical Research Council. (The body roughly corresponds to the U.S. National Institutes of Health, but it supports work more through grants and staff based at university departments than in its own laboratories.) The tradition goes back to 1918, when a Committee on the Health of Munition Workers was established, and during the period between the two world wars, a number of important investigations of problems in occupational psychology were conducted by the Industrial Health Research Board. These included problems of job design, environmental factors, selection, training, and vocational guidance, but also more general problems in stress and neurosis. During the same period, a private organization (the National Institute of Industrial Psychology) was working in similar fields under C. S. Myers. The work of these investigators created considerable appreciation of the value of psychology. This was reinforced during World War II by the work of psychologists in the armed forces, and particularly by such people as Alec Rodger and P. E. Vernon. This laid the basis not only for occupational psychology, but also for the much wider field of educational psychology. In the latter area, it is also fair to record that Burt had demonstrated the possibilities of professional educational psychologists in his work on educational problems at London. Thus, after World War II, the stage was set for the establishment of a much larger profession. On the clinical side, a beginning was made in the training of clinical psychologists by the appointment of Eysenck as a professor in the Institute of Psychiatry at the University of London; quite apart from his intellectual contributions, he played a large part in putting the training of clinical psychologists on a sound basis. Again, the wider society was more inclined to accept this because of the work of pioneers such as May Davidson and Grace Rawlings.

In the 1960s, British universities expanded suddenly and very substantially, and at the same time psychology departments were increased in size in those universities where they already existed. The numbers graduating, therefore, increased from approximately 200 to several thousand each year. This has allowed the appearance of strongly organized professions of clinical and educational psychology, with recognized qualifications and standards. In the British educational system, the normal qualification is not usually an academic doctorate, but a specialized bachelor's degree in psychology followed by a master's course in the particular specialization, and relevant experience. (Educational psychologists, for example, must normally be qualified as teachers.) Since Britain has a national health service, the employment of clinical psychologists is generally within that service, and private practice is very rare. Similarly, educational psychologists usually work for the local education authorities in their geographical area. As yet, there is no registration of professional psychologists, although the matter is under discussion; most professional affairs are managed by the British Psychology Society. This society was originally founded in 1901 at University College, London, as a largely academic society. For a period, it admitted anybody interested in the subject regardless of qualifications, and this was for a time, a strength; in the period between the world wars, it became a forum where psychoanalytically interested doctors could discuss analysis. During the period since World War II, however, academic qualifications have been introduced as a necessity for membership, with higher qualifications needed for the higher grades; for the divisions governing particular professional specializations, specialized qualifications are also necessary. For example, members of the Division of Occupational Psychology must have qualifications and experience in the areas of both personnel psychology and job design. Since the mid-1960s, the society has held a Royal Charter, which, in Britain, is a mark of a body regarded as making a general contribution to the welfare of the community rather than simply being a private association for mutual benefit.

In addition to the British Psychological Society, there are smaller, more specialized societies concerned with particular academic or applied problems—for example, the Experimental Psychology Society, which corresponds roughly to the Psychonomics Society in the United States, and the Ergonomics Society, corresponding roughly to the Human Factors Society.

THE PRESENT INTELLECTUAL POSITION

The very large expansion of universities, and the greater freedom of international movement in the last 20 years, mean that no two or three intellectual movements dominate British psychology now as they could be said to do 40 years ago. There are still recognizable influences from the past: For example, the current professor at University College, London, is R. J. Audley, and while he is not active in psychometrics, he has developed, and has stimulated others to develop, an area of research in the mathematical modeling of decision times. This approach supposes that decisions are made through the accumulation of probabilistic evidence rather than by determinate logical sequences, and has affinities with signal detection theory in the United States. Like that theory, it carries implications concerning the ways in which human error may occur, and the way in which motivation will affect performance. As yet, its influence has been greater in Britain and Australia than in North America, but this may well change in the coming years.

The strongest development academically has been in neuropsychology, which is now occupying the position of prominence that psychometrics did in Britain in the 1920s or information processing did in the 1950s. In the work of Weiskrantz and his collaborators, for example, both animal and human patients have been found to react to light when the normal route from the eye to the visual projection areas is destroyed. Quite apart from their clinical relevance, these results provide data on the organization of the visual system. Amnesia and aphasia have been extensively studied by Warrington, Baddeley, and Coltheart; it is particularly gratifying that investigations of reading by cognitive psychologists have proved to be very useful tools for the investigation of brain injury. For example, it is possible to discriminate dyslexic patients who are disturbed on the reading of irregular words but can read nonwords and patients who can read irregular words but not nonwords. These seem to correspond to the mechanism of accessing the utterance from the sequence of letters, on the one hand, or from the lexical entry corresponding to the word, on the other.

It is particularly interesting and significant of the interaction between areas that the major successor to Eysenck's tradition of dimensional analysis of personality is J. A. Gray, who has, in recent years, worked mostly on physiological structures in relation to behavior, and particularly on the role of the hypothalamus. The connection he makes is between the role of hypothalamic structures in response to punishment or failure of anticipated reward and those features of Eysenck's system that emphasize anxiety. Clearly this linkage of physiological and psychometric traditions can only be profitable.

On the more general biological front, R. A. Hinde continues the ethological tradition, studying effects of attachment and breaking of attachment in monkeys, as well as a variety of other problems. Again, the growing convergence between animal studies and human ones is evident, as it is in the development of animal learning theory by N. Mackintosh at Cambridge. In Mackintosh's approach to animal learning, the rat is seen as selecting some aspects of the environment for learning, and as establishing contingencies between experienced stimuli, or between action and outside events, in a fashion more comparable to the theories of human cognitive psychology than to those of animal psychologists of past generations.

Human cognitive psychology as such continues to be active; the unit founded by Craik is now directed by Baddeley, who has developed a major program of research on "working memory," the use of temporary or short-term memory to hold information during the performance of some task. This approach has considerably changed attitudes toward short-term memory, and seems to be very widely supported. Work on attention also continues, in the tradition of Broadbent, and of A. Treisman whose theory was, in the 1960s, a very dominant one in the field. Since her departure to Canada, younger investigators in the Cambridge unit and elsewhere in Britain are continuing to contribute to that field.

Two areas in which British psychology was slow to develop are now beginning to become very important—the fields of developmental and social psychology. Apart from the pioneering work of Valentine, Britain did not have a tradition of developmental psychology comparable to that started by Stanley Hall. In recent years, however, and with a helpful stimulus from the presence of J. S. Bruner as a professor at Oxford during the 1970s, an impressive body of investigation has now been undertaken. Its main strength is perhaps that it acts as a bridge between the relatively vigorous American approach and the very subtle, but less experimental, continental tradition derived from Piaget; the work of Donaldson, Bryant, and Schaffer suggests that a position at the junction of these traditions is likely to be very fruitful.

The other area of past weakness was that of social psychology. Despite the fact that T. H. Pear was the first professor at Manchester, the topic was slower to develop than other areas of psychology have been. Under the guidance of Argyle at Oxford and of the late Henri Tajfel at Bristol, there are now a number of indigenous British social psychologists. One could characterize the Oxford-trained ones as interested in relationships, social skills, and interactions, while those from Bristol are concerned with the properties of group membership, and with sociolinguistics. Both developmental and social psychology appear to have much of the vigor of relatively newly established fields.

In clinical psychology, a number of international movements are reflected in Britain, particularly the successive movements toward behavior modification, the use of personal construct theory, and, perhaps particularly, cognitive therapy.

The dominant theme of contemporary psychology, however, is

the integration of different specialist topics, and the gradual merging of distinctively British psychology into a larger and more powerful international discipline. As a last instance, one may take the links between cognitive, occupational, and clinical psychology that are appearing in a number of centers. Thus Baddeley's unit, which has always included both cognitive and occupational psychology, now includes clinical work as well. Another MRC unit at Sheffield, under Professor Warr, is studying clinical implications of occupational changes and of unemployment. Broadbent (who retired as director of the Cambridge unit in 1974 and moved to Oxford) is similarly studying the relationships between job stress, cognitive performance as measured by the ability to deploy attention, and the development of neurotic symptoms. In the linking of originally separate traditions lies the future course of both British and international psychology.

D. E. BROADBENT
University of Oxford, England

GREENOUGH, WILLIAM T.

William T. Greenough, Swanlund and Center for Advanced Study professor of psychology, psychiatry and cell and structural biology, at the University of Illinois, Urbana Champaign is a leading authority on the effects of experience (including physical exercise) and learning on the structure and function of the developing and adult mammalian brain. He received a BA degree from the University of Oregon in 1964 and a PhD from the University of California, Los Angeles, in 1998, and has been at the University of Illinois since then.

Greenough's research ranges from behavioral to cell biological studies of learning and memory. He is generally regarded as the major figure in the research that concluded that the formation of new synaptic connections between nerve cells was a fundamental aspect of memory storage in the brain. Currently, he is also studying molecular and cellular substrates of memory and of developmental brain organization processes, and has made major breakthroughs in understanding the molecular neurobiology of fragile-X mental retardation syndrome.

Greenough has held elected office in the Society for Neuroscience, the Winter Conference on Brain Research, the Society for Developmental Psychobiology, and the Federation of Behavioral, Psychological and Cognitive Societies; has served on the advisory committee of the Biological Sciences Directorate of the National Science Foundation; and was a member of the OSTP Forum on Science in the National Interest that helped to lay out the Clinton administration's science policy document released in 1994. He is a member of the National Academy of Sciences and a fellow of the American Association for the Advancement of Science, the American Psychological Association (APA), the American Psychological Society, and the Society for Experimental Psychology. In 1996, he received the American Psychological Society's William James Award in recognition of distinguished achievements in psychological science, and in 1998 he received APA's Distinguished Scientific Contribution Award "for pioneering seminal contributions to un-

derstanding how experience alters the structure of brain." He edits the journal *Neurobiology of Learning and Memory* and has served on the editorial boards of numerous other journals. He currently directs the University of Illinois Center for Advanced Study and co-directs the Beckman Institute Main Research Theme Group on Biological Intelligence.

STAFF

GROUP DYNAMICS

The importance of groups has long been recognized by students of society, but the study of groups as a special topic began only in the 1930s and 1940s. Several sources are responsible for the beginning of this specialty: (a) the increased importance of small groups in a labile society; (b) the increased effectiveness achieved by using group techniques in such disparate fields as industry, group therapy, and adult education; and (c) the development of experimental techniques for studying conditions and processes of small groups. Thus three sources—social importance, practical use, and scientific understanding—have been the joint foundation of group dynamics; they have also contributed to a fragmentation of interests up to the present time.

BACKGROUND

The definite establishment and naming of the field of group dynamics is due to Kurt Lewin (*Resolving Social Conflicts, Field theory in Social Science*). Lewin had established a psychology of personality using geometrical forms, which employed such social concepts as boundaries, specialization, direction, and planning to explain the actions of the person (topological psychology). This theory could then be transformed back to an interpretation of groups. For instance, one could give the different subfields of a person a natural interpretation of roles and statuses, and view the boundaries between them—as well as their strengths—as obstacles to social mobility.

This theoretical model turned out to be applicable to a set of experiments which had already been performed on groups. These included Lewin's own—particularly those with Lippitt on autocratic and democratic group atmosphere—as well as Mayo's and Roethlisberger's experiments on groups in a factory, Sherif's on group conflicts in a camp group and on the development of group standards, and Moreno's on sociometric study in residential groups. These forerunners showed different techniques and possible sites for group experiments. An additional feature was that they could be performed under the abstract conditions of laboratory experiments as well as in actual life situations or field experiments.

The question of applicability relates to the social context in which group dynamics arose: the heightened mobility and weakening of established social structure in the wake of the Depression and World War II. Small groups were used by government agencies for reeducation and community planning; groups were seen to be instrumental as starting points for conflict moderation in industry and community; and families and intentional communities were seen as focal points for new starts after violent disruption. The common theme of beneficial action of the group could be recognized; it was taken as an established dimension for the study of groups, investing it with a kind of messianic flavor. This interest led to a split in the meaning of group dynamics, as a science of groups and as a program on the value of groups. All these trends combined in the formulation of group dynamics. Lewin's relevant theoretical and practical works are collected in *Field Theory in Social Science* and *Resolving Social Conflicts*.

THE NATURE OF GROUP DYNAMICS

Theory

The theory of group dynamics looks at a small person-to-person group as a unit. A group can be defined as an association of persons small enough that all can stay in personal contact with one another. This procedure implies the primary reality of the group; statements can then be made like "the group has aims," "the group exerts power over its members," or "a group rejects outsiders" without committing a false concretization or anthropomorphization.

In common with Lewin's general program of science, the concepts of group dynamics represent structural and dynamic aspects. The structural aspects are represented by simple graphic representations of an oval divided into subregions. They exhibit simple relationships such as adjacency of subregions, the shortest path from one to another, accessibility from outside, and centrality—in short, all those relations which can be obtained by visual inspection of pictures. The strength of a boundary can be represented by weaker and heavier lines. Inspection can describe all the structural effects within a group, which can be interpreted as stratification, articulation, peripheral and central positions, and the features of groups.

Parts of the group picture can be seen as individuals, but these parts can also be defined as functions or roles within the group, as possible places for individuals which may stay unfilled at any time. The nature of this subdivision is not given, but depends on the particular use to which the parts are put. Roles may be defined by the nature of the task (e.g., occupational roles), by conditions of group functioning (functional roles), or by a theoretical scheme imposed as leader, resource person, or opposition. The spatial arrangement of the roles can indicate mobility, the ability of an individual to move from one role to another, or communication or other interactions. If the subdivision of the group means particular individuals, then the arrangement of the subregions would mean interaction or influence of some kind between these individuals. This ambiguity is but one indication that group dynamics is less a definite theory with rigid empirical interpretations, and more a way of approaching groups with a certain set of general concepts. This status has also prevented it from becoming a definite theory in sociology or psychology, although its general approach is listed under field theory in discussions of theory in social psychology.

The dynamic concepts have a rough analogy to mathematical concepts, principally with those of applied mechanics. They include locomotion, vectors, forces, tension, goals, power, and power fields. All these concepts invest the group with change or at least the possibility of change. Change may involve the whole group, in which case the group is seen as embedded in some other structure through which it is traveling. If the group is trying to complete some task, the field is the steps leading to this completion. Forces are then inferred as directing the group toward the goal region, which represents completion of the task; this region is then said to have valence for the group. However, the group may have an additional goal, or may be able to use different paths to complete the goal, or may have a negative valence (or abhorrence) of a region which has been crossed in search of the goal, in which case conflicts will be created. The path indicated by the resultant of the forces will then be the preferred path to be taken by the group.

The intent to reach a group goal is also seen as a tension within the group—a condition which is unpleasant to the group or the subregions affected, and which is relieved by the attainment of the goal. Tensions are generalizations of drives, but they can be set up simply by a wish or instruction to attain a certain goal. Thus interruption of a task can lead to an increase in tension; attempts to release this tension will result in appropriate actions, either in reality by trying to complete the task, or in fantasy, as seen in group discussions or imagination productions of the group.

While the dynamic concepts discussed up to now refer to action of the group in its environment, power and its associated concepts link the group to its members. Power differentiates the subregions or individuals within the group: one region has power if its movements or changes will result in corresponding changes in other regions. One can assign a certain degree of power to each region and in this way describe a power field to the whole group. If one wants to be more specific, one can assign power relations pairwise between members of the group; the description of power fields then becomes more complex, especially if the power relations are not consistent. In addition, power may be specific, dependent on certain issues. In their elaborate study, "The bases of social power" (Cartwright & Zander, 1968/1953), French and Raven have identified five bases of power which might lead to different power relationships: legitimacy, coercion, expert knowledge, attraction, and reward. Depending on the issue before the group, different power relations may prevail. In any particular analysis, any relevant refinement will be taken into consideration.

In addition to power exerted by individuals, the group as a unit is capable of exerting power. In fact, investigations of the power of the group over its members have realized some of the most important research and applied achievements in the field. Again, one must associate a certain measure with each subfield, indicating the amount of power the group exerts in these parts. The variation will then explain differences in the possibility of power and influence over certain members and also may lead to a hypothesis on the cause of different strengths of power. Multiple membership will lead to conflicts within individuals, correlated with the variations in power; these may lead to stress as well as changes in group membership, if the stress becomes intolerable.

The theoretical base of group dynamics described an abstract, geometrical mechanical system. It tried to make mathematical predictions which only in some cases were built on a definite algorithm. Success would have led to an exact science, given suitable empirical interpretation. This was the goal of the theoretical program, but in fact the geometrical system was used as an aid to visual intuition for specific problems, and no overarching, real mathematical system was ever attempted. However, even these partial insights and intuitive derivations led to important advances in research and practice.

Research

The reputation of group dynamics rests particularly on its creations of new research traditions in experimental social psychology. A comprehensive summary of this research in Cartwright and Zander's *Group Dynamics* lists six fields: groups and group membership, pressure for conformity, power and influence, leadership and performance, motivational processes, and structural processes. Each of these topics depends on some combination of the theoretical concepts and represents innovative research traditions; the arrangement of Cartwright and Zander is followed here, and most studies referred to are presented in their anthology.

The study of *group membership* deals with the creation of group boundaries and the bases of the power of the group over its members. The empirical question is then to define the boundaries and strengths of membership of the group's cohesion. Fortunately, it was found that artificial groups formed by individuals brought together for experiments could produce viable conditions of group membership. Experiments could then show a variety of conditions for the existence of a group and also these consequences. Groups can be created by giving a common task, creating friendship among members, showing similarity in background or attitudes, making membership an honor or something difficult to achieve, having frequent interaction, or having a common negative fate. Depending on the strength of any of these factors, people will discriminate between insiders and outsiders, make entry and exit easy or difficult, and resist pressure to dissolve the group.

Pressure for conformity represents the power of the group over its members. In translating the abstract concept of power into the operation of creating conformity, a variety of factors had to be considered in experimental as well as field studies. The stress toward conformity is not equal in all members, nor is it expressed equally for all attitudes and behaviors. Thus leaders are given leeway to break rules and are even required to be innovative ("idiosyncracy credit"), and a long-established group will attain power over its members and tolerate diversity over many issues, as long as crucial issues are accepted. In the main, though, adherence to group standards is a function of the cohesion of groups. This relationship and its specific limitations have been explored in laboratory experiments, as well as in studies in industrial, electoral, and community settings.

Under the heading of *power and influence* the dynamic relationships of group members have been explored. These studies have usually specified the techniques used to increase compliance with influence. Deriving from the conditions of social power, techniques can be identified which rely on general social conditions such as appeals to legitimacy or expertise, or which use purely interpersonal processes such as flattery (ingratiation or augmentation), or which are based on exchange or possible future interaction. Thus experiments on the manifestation of social power can show how leadership positions are maintained, but also treat mechanisms which maintain a group by mutual influences of members, including the establishment of trust.

Although the differentiation of the group is important in all studies, the conditions and functions of *leadership* form a special topic in itself. Indeed, an important beginning of group dynamic experiments was the study of autocratic/democratic and laissez-faire leadership, and the exact definition of these three terms has occupied much of its development. Studies of leadership as a function have been concerned with its effect on the group's achieving its goals, which can be measured as group productivity. The study of leadership tries to demonstrate the relation of power within the group to group locomotion in the group's environment.

The last two topics are concerned with dynamics and structure within the group. Tension within the group, just as in the individual, can be identified with *motivation*. In groups we sometimes find formal records of goal setting and of efforts to reach the goals. Observation of groups in action would measure the creation of the tension and differentiation of tension within the group, in the same way in which individual tension systems were studied; to some degree this was even easier to do, as the conceptual differentiations within the person are visually present in a group as leaders, discussants, or actors. Experiments paralleling those with individuals could be performed, showing again the persistence of tension, and its effects on recall and resumption of interrupted tasks.

Group structure and its effects represent the topological aspect of the theory. Here again the theoretical abstractions of the topological theory of personality could be made concrete in a group context by either studying or controlling the patterns of contiguity. The study of communication and control in task-oriented groups, and of sociometric patterns in existing groups, is one of the most intensive research areas in the field. It is also the one in which the most consistent mathematical practices have been used, in the application of matrix and graph theory.

The research activities in group dynamics included some striking studies in all fields and showed a way toward the general understanding of groups. They were less concerned with application to specific natural groups such as family, friendship groups, community, and association, however, and the link between the general work in group dynamics and the specific social groups is still tenuous.

Practice

Applications of group dynamics had a distinctive development. Lewin and his associates created workshops—training institutes lasting from a weekend to several weeks—where participants learned skills in working with groups, and where the teaching technique used an application of group dynamics in inducing influence, assigning roles, and establishing group goals. The first efforts in this direction were made in the late 1940s in workshops in New London, Connecticut, and Bethel, Maine. In these precursors the basic format of the workshop, which would be called sensitivity training, was established. The content was mainly concerned with group process and involved the following: examples taken widely from current interaction and participants' backgrounds; observation of the process and "feedback" (interpretive descriptions of participants' actions by group leader and surrogate); use of both positive and negative affect to create an intensive emotional atmosphere; and emphasis on the value of personal and organizational change.

Applied group dynamics mentioned for some time a program for training professionals in varied fields such as education, the military, administration, management, labor, and the ministry. The experience made it possible to adapt the training to specific organizations (it became a specialized profession of group trainers). Several major corporations were involved, most notably the National Training Laboratory, which kept several centers, among them the original one at Bethel. The history of the movement was traced by K. W. Back in *Beyond Words*.

Group training proper was partly superseded in the 1960s and early 1970s by the human potential movement. Here the emphasis was on the individual and personal growth. The basic techniques were the same, but the emphasis changed subtly toward self-expression, physical manipulation, and even more intense emotional experience; the groups were now called encounter groups. Just as sensitivity training was centered in Bethel, so encounter groups were centered in Esalen, California. This center, with its combination of Eastern mysticism and Western psychology, communal bathtubs, and intricate massage techniques, combined applied group dynamics with the social turmoil of the 1960s.

At this point applied group dynamics almost became a social movement, more ideological than professional or scientific. However, this aspect of group dynamics declined with the general change in social trends. Applied group dynamics is now more cautiously reviewed, especially because of the test of proven results for enduring change, but it keeps up a steady stream of instruction, written and personal, in transmitting certain basic elements of effective action in groups.

OUTLOOK

The self-conscious movement of group dynamics, both scientific and applied, seems to have subsided in the 1970s. Little is being added to the general theory of groups, and research has diverged to either the individual (or at best dyadic) situation or to a more sociological investigation of larger units. In the same way, the hope of reconstructing society through small groups has lost its ideological foundation, though it may be revived in specific contexts and in communes or group therapy. The contributions have been absorbed into the general field of social psychology by accepting a variety of concepts, by bolder experimentation in social situations, and even by introducing some aspects of applied group dynamics into the general culture. A symposium arranged by Leon Festinger reviewing 40 years of this work (*Retrospections in Social Psychology*) found little direct use of the original theory, but instead a wide range of topics in social psychology inspired by it.

REFERENCES

Back, K. (1973/1972). *Beyond words: The story of sensitivity training and the encounter movement.* New York: Russell Sage Foundation.

Cartwright, D., & Zander, A. (1968/1953). *Group dynamics: Research and theory.* New York: Harper & Row.

Festinger, L. (Ed.). (1980). *Retrospectives in social psychology.* New York: Oxford University Press.

Lewin, K. (1948). *Resolving social conflicts.* New York: Harper.

Lewin, K. (1951). *Field theory in social science.* New York: Harper.

SUGGESTED READING

Lakin, M. (Ed.). (1979). What's happened to the small group? (entire issue) *Journal of Applied Behavioral Science, 15,* [3].

Shaw, M. (1981/1971). *Group dynamics: The psychology of small group behavior.* New York: McGraw-Hill.

K. W. BACK

GROUP PSYCHOTHERAPY

GROUP PSYCHOTHERAPY

The application of psychotherapeutic principles with a group of people simultaneously is called group psychotherapy. Most commonly, group therapy involves a small number of participants (often 6–10), and one or two group therapists, but there are many variations in form and format. While there have been therapy groups in existence for most of the century, World War II and its aftermath brought group therapy into widespread use and recognition (Lifton, 1972; Phares, 1979). Most approaches that are used with individuals—and many that are not—are applied to group therapy.

There are both economic and therapeutic advantages to group treatment. Economically, therapist time spent and the cost of treatment can be reduced by group approaches. Therapeutic advantages lie in the possibilities that group therapy offers for personality change. Yalom (1970) identified 10 categories of curative factors present in group therapy: (a) imparting of information, or communication of instructions or advice by therapists or group members; (b) instillation of hope, which is especially powerful in group therapy, as each member can see the treatment progress made by every other member; (c) universality, or the discovery by each member that other members have similar feelings or problems; (d) altruism, or the feeling of being helpful or of being needed by other group members; (e) the corrective recapitulation of the primary family group, the experience of interacting in a therapeutic manner with a group similar in some ways to the structure of a family; (f) the development of socializing techniques, or improving interpersonal skills through interaction and feedback; (g) imitative behavior, or the opportunity for group members to observe and copy several models of appropriate behavior of others; (h) interpersonal learning, or the opportunity for testing a variety of behaviors with others; (i) group cohesiveness, or the solidarity and attractiveness of a group for its members; and (j) catharsis, or the ventilation of feelings with others in a safe environment.

Despite its advantages, group therapy has limitations. First, some members may be more reluctant to air intimate emotional issues than in individual therapy. Doing so may, in fact, put those members at risk for receiving feedback that exacerbates their problems, particularly when the issues discussed are those against which there are strong social proscriptions. Second, the process of group interaction may become so timeconsuming that individual concerns of group members are not dealt with, which complicates the therapist's role (Shertzer & Stone, 1974). Another limitation is that the behaviors appropriate to the protected, supervised group setting may not be appropriate in more natural settings; some group members may have trouble applying them in their own life situations. Shertzer and Stone (1974) also note that there is still disagreement about which problems can be better dealt with in group than in individual therapy.

Therapy groups differ in goals, composition, and techniques used. Some groups have specific goals, themes, or tasks, as for example groups formed to teach a certain skill (e.g., assertiveness training or social skills training groups) or to resolve a certain type of problem (e.g., groups for people with agoraphobia). Other groups have less stated structure and no established theme.

Some therapy groups are composed of specific types of individuals. These might be of a single diagnostic classification, such as alcoholism, or people with a specific life stress, such as the death of a child. Some, on the other hand, are more heterogeneous, with a wide range of problems to be dealt with therapeutically. Most groups have some degree of homogeneity. Each theoretical approach to group therapy may be time-limited or open-ended, and open or closed in accepting new members after the first meeting, and may vary in other ways as diverse as the personalities of the leaders and members. The widest variation among groups is in therapeutic techniques used. Some group therapists work with one group member at a time, while others work toward facilitating the interaction among the members.

This variation in technique is partially related to the fact that impetus for the growth of therapy groups as a medium of change came from two directions. One was the extension of principles of different types of individual therapy to groups, while the other was the development of T-groups and their related offshoots.

One of the earliest schools of individual psychotherapy to be applied to groups was the psychoanalytic model. Wolf (1968) pointed out extensions of classical psychoanalytic techniques to group contexts, providing a setting with multiple possibilities for interpersonal interaction. Another early group technique was Moreno's psychodrama approach (1957). Psychodrama is a therapeutic approach in which group members actually act out problems to gain new insights and awareness. Behavioral approaches to therapy have also been extended to groups. Lazarus (1968) points out that the group setting provides more opportunities for learning positive behavior and unlearning dysfunctional behavior than one therapist can provide in individual therapy.

The Gestalt and transactional analysis approaches to therapy have been extremely popular in group therapy. Perls (1951, 1973) applied his Gestalt approach to groups, usually by working with one group member at a time. Gestalt group therapists seek to integrate all aspects of the individual in a unified whole (Fagan & Shepherd, 1970). This integration provides observing members the opportunity to learn by identifying the conflicts of the other members with their own. Berne (1966) advocated a group approach as the

most efficient use of transactional analysis, because it allows transactions to be examined as they occur in the interpersonal context.

T-groups (training groups) began at the National Training Laboratories in Maine in the 1950s. These groups, born of an interest in Kurt Lewin's theoretical work in group dynamics (Marrow, 1969), were established to study and teach the effects of the group's experiences on its members (Bradford, Gibb, & Benne, 1964). Aronson (1972) described the main goals of T-groups as developing a willingness to examine one's behavior, learning more about people, becoming more interpersonally honest, working cooperatively, and solving conflicts logically and rationally. Encounter groups and sensitivity-training groups are similar approaches, with less structure and an emphasis on increasing self-awareness and personal growth (Shaffer & Galensky, 1974). Rogers (1970) has applied his client-centered approach to the context of encounter groups. Some encounter group leaders (Schutz, 1967) use a variety of planned exercises to mobilize the group process.

Other approaches to group therapy include art and dance therapy, body therapy groups, theme-centered interaction, and groups aimed at developing a variety of specific skills (Rudestam, 1982). A variety of self-help groups serve a therapeutic function, in addition to more traditional therapy groups. Some examples are Alcoholics Anonymous, the Synanon approach to treating drug addiction, and consciousness-raising groups.

One application of therapeutic principles which has been popular in recent years is the marathon group. Marathons are groups that last for extended periods of time, leading to fatigue, breakdown of psychological defenses, and intense interpersonal interaction (Bach, 1966). Bindrim (1968) introduced nudity as a further aid in lowering defenses in therapy groups.

Functions of the therapist in a group may involve facilitating member participation, interaction, and problem solving, focusing conversation, supporting upset members, mediating among members in conflict, and assuring that group rules are established and adhered to. The difficulty involved in understanding and managing group process issues, in addition to the emotional issues of each member, means that group leaders must be particularly well trained, sensitive, and competent.

There are ethical issues unique to group therapy. Group members are not bound by the same ethical constraints as are professionals. Group therapists must therefore be particularly sensitive to establishing clear standards for confidentiality among group members. Parloft (1970) emphasizes the importance of informed consent in groups. That is, group members should be informed as much as possible about the group prior to consenting to participate and should be accorded the freedom to choose whether to participate in any part of the group experience.

One question yet to be definitively answered concerns the efficiency of group therapy. Miles (1965) found that colleagues of managers who had participated in a T-group rated the participants as improving more in interpersonal skills than those who had not been in the groups. Lieberman (1976) found that members of sensitivity-encounter groups rated their own group-related changes as positive. Lieberman, Yalom, and Miles (1973) found that the results of sensitivity-encounter groups were generally positive when the group leaders were warm, supportive, and accepting, but observed that the possibility of negative effects on participants increased when leaders were more attacking and aggressive, and that many of these negative effects endured over time. Refinement of methods of evaluating therapeutic effects of groups will, hopefully, yield more information about whether groups are helpful and, if so, which characteristics of groups are likely to bring the most benefit.

REFERENCES

Aronson, E. (1980). *The social animal.* San Francisco: Freeman. (Original work published 1972)

Bach, G. R. (1966). The marathon group: Intense practice of intimate interaction. *Psychological Reports, 18,* 995–1002.

Bindrim, P. (1968). A report on a nude marathon: The effect of physical nudity upon the practice interaction in the marathon group. *Psychotherapy: Theory, Research, and Practice, 5,* 180–188.

Bradford, L. P., Gibb, J. R., & Benne, K. D. (1964). *T-group theory and laboratory method: Innovation in re-education.* New York: Wiley.

Fagan, M. J., & Shepherd, I. L. (1970). *Gestalt therapy now.* Palo Alto, CA: Science & Behavior Books.

Lazarus, A. A. (1968). Behavior therapy in groups. In G. M. Gazda (Ed.), *Basic approaches to psychotherapy and group counseling.* Springfield, IL: Thomas.

Lieberman, M. A. (1976). Change induction in small groups. In M. R. Rosenzweig & L. W. Porter (Eds.), *Annual Review of Psychology, 27.*

Lieberman, M. A., Yalom, I. D., & Miles, M. B. (1973). *Encounter groups: First facts.* New York: Basic Books.

Lifton, W. M. (1972). *Groups: Facilitating individual growth and societal change.* New York: Wiley.

Marrow, A. J. (1969). *The practical theorist: The life and work of Kurt Lewin.* New York: Basic Books.

Miles, M. (1965). Changes during and following laboratory training: A clinical experimental study. *Journal of Applied Behavior Science, 1,* 215–242.

Moreno, J. L. (1957). *The first book on group psychotherapy* (3rd ed.). Beacon, NY: Beacon House.

Parloff, M. B. (1970). Group therapy and the small-group field: An encounter. *International Journal of Group Psychotherapy, 20,* 267–304.

Perls, F. S. (1973). *The Gestalt approach.* Palo Alto, CA: Science & Behavior Books.

Perls, F. S., Hefferline, R. E., & Goodman, P. (1951). *Gestalt therapy.* New York: Dell.

Phares, E. J. (1979). *Clinical psychology: Concepts, methods, and profession.* Homewood, IL: Dorsey.

Rogers, C. R. (1970). *Carl Rogers on encounter groups.* New York: Harper & Row.

Rudestam, K. E. (1982). *Experiential groups in theory and practice.* Monterey, CA: Brooks/Cole.

Schutz, W. C. (1967). *Joy.* New York: Grove Press.

Shaffer, T., & Galensky, M. (1974). *Models of group therapy and sensitivity training.* Englewood Cliffs, NJ: Prentice-Hall.

Shertzer, B., & Stone, S. (1974). *Fundamentals of counseling.* Boston: Houghton Mifflin.

Wolf, A. (1968). Psychoanalysis in groups. In G. M. Gazda (Ed.), *Basic approaches to group psychotherapy and group counseling.* Springfield, IL: Thomas.

Yalom, I. D. (1975). *The theory and practice of group psychotherapy* (2nd ed.). New York: Basic Books.

T. S. BENNETT
Brain Inquiry Recovery Program

ASSERTIVENESS TRAINING

PSYCHOTHERAPY

GROWTH HORMONE ([GH]SOMATOTROPIN)

The human anterior pituitary gland contains 5 to 10 mg growth hormone (GH), which is synthesized and stored in cells called "somatotropes," located in the lateral wings of the gland. The human GH gene is on chromosome 17, and its mRNA transcript possesses five exons separated by four introns. The peptide contains 191 amino acids and has a plasma half-life of 20 minutes (Dinan, 1998). Growth hormone plays an important role in the regulation of growth and other trophic metabolic processes. The peripheral physiology of GH is not the focus of the current summary, but rather how GH function may inform the researcher about central nervous system (CNS) function and dysfunction.

One of the major limitations that has plagued psychiatric investigation in general has been the relative inaccessibility of its primary organ of focus, the brain. Growth hormone release by the pituitary gland is regulated by many of the monoamine and neuropeptide systems that act upon the hypothalamus and that are also involved in mood and anxiety regulation. The release of GH, either by a provocative stimulus or as a spontaneous release as part of a physiological process (e.g., sleep), has therefore been viewed as a potential window into the CNS. At least two major shortcomings have limited this approach: (a) Alterations that may be occurring at the hypothalamic-pituitary level may not necessarily be accompanied by parallel processes in other parts of the brain; and (b) Because psychoneuroendocrine regulation is complex, a host of confounding factors may obscure interpretation of data generated from GH studies.

With the recent development of neuroimaging technologies, the problems of inaccessibility are gradually being overcome. In an era in which direct measurement of different regions of interest in the CNS can be evaluated, the value of indirect markers as reflectors of CNS dysfunction, such as GH, has become increasingly questionable; the neuroscientific challenge will nevertheless remain to integrate fronto-limbic dysfunction (which current neuroimaging techniques are well equipped to detect) with hypothalamic-pituitary dysfunction, which, to date, is more readily apparent on psycho-neuroendocrine evaluation.

REGULATION OF GH SECRETION

Many CNS neurochemical systems play a role in the complex regulation of anterior pituitary GH release. The regulation of what is referred to as the "hypothalamic-pituitary-somatomedin" (HPS) axis occurs primarily through two main limbs: stimulation through the hypothalamic peptide growth hormone releasing factor (GRF) and inhibition through the 14 amino-acid peptide, somatostatin (SOM). Numerous factors impact upon these two limbs, and in fact, the degree to which neurotransmitter systems impact upon either limb may vary according to inter-species differences (see Uhde, Tancer, & Rubinow, 1992). It appears that clonidine, a widely studied α^2 adrenoceptor agonist, may produce its GH secretory effect in healthy control humans either through α^2-mediated stimulation of GRF and/or α^2-mediated inhibition of somatostatin release. Growth hormone secretion is inhibited by high plasma GH levels, as well as somatomedin-C, which is released by the liver in response to circulating GH. Other neurotransmitter systems that impact the regulation of GH response include the cholinergic, dopaminergic, GABAergic, HPA axis (specifically corticotrophin-releasing hormone), and serotonergic systems (for review, see Dinan, 1998). Age and phase of menstrual cycle may also influence the GH response to clonidine. Other factors that may confound GH response to clonidine include obesity, alcoholism, and postmenopausal status. Less clear-cut factors influencing GH response to GH secretagogues include heavy smoking, which may increase GH secretion; lifetime exposure to tricyclic antidepressants; and recent exposure to benzodiazepines.

POSSIBLE MECHANISMS FOR BLUNTED GH SECRETION TO GH SECRETAGOGUES IN ANXIETY AND MOOD DISORDERS

Blunted GH responses to GH secretagogues such as clonidine, desipramine, insulin tolerance test, and others, were thought to detect down-regulation of post-synaptic alpha-2 receptors following excessive central noradrenergic activity in major depressive disorder (Siever et al., 1982). That GH responses are blunted in response to both clonidine and growth hormone releasing factor (GRF) in panic disorder (PD) refuted the view that reduced GH response to clonidine simply reflects a specific alpha-2 abnormality. Uhde, Tancer, and Rubinow (1992) have reviewed the possible circumstances under which blunting of GH may occur. These includes: (a) reduced availability of pituitary GH stores secondary to reduced synthesis or excessive secretion (this option seems unlikely, as GH responses to the dopamine agonist, apomorphine, are exaggerated in PD); (b) overall hypersecretion of GH with secondary inhibition of GH secretion to secretory stimuli; (c) an abnormally enhanced negative feedback system (i.e., increased pituitary sensitivity to the inhibitory effects of GH or somatomedin-C); (d) subsensitivity of the pituitary to the secretory effect of GRF; (e) failure of clonidine to reduce the inhibitory effect of somatostatin neurons on the pituitary; and (f) abnormal function of a host of other factors enumerated above. It should be noted that blunted GH secretion is not only observed in PD and depression but also in generalized anxiety disorder and possibly social phobia. Growth hormone responses to GRF and clonidine in childhood depression also tend to be blunted. However, the abnormality is not observed in schizophrenia or obsessive-compulsive disorder.

NOCTURNAL GROWTH HORMONE SECRETION

Sleep onset represents a highly evolved, dynamic biological process, involving the reduction and ultimate cessation of noradrenergic and serotonergic neuronal activity; the onset of cholinergic bursts of firing from pontine nuclei; and the increased secretion of GH primarily through muscarinic inhibition of somatostatin (SOM), the GH secretagogue suppressant. During the early phases of sleep, increases of spontaneous GH secretion have been associated with slow-wave (delta) sleep, the former subsiding several hours following sleep onset. The elevations of corticotropin releasing factor (CRF) and cortisol increases that are frequently evident in mood disorders are inhibitory towards GH secretion and imply a CRF/GH releasing hormone (GHRH) ratio increase in adult depression (Holsboer, 1994).

Thus, adults with acute major depressive disorder (MDD) quite consistently hyposecrete GH around the time of sleep onset. Studies that followed depressed subjects into a drug-free recovery phase found persistence of sleep-related GH hyposecretion, suggesting that this may be a trait marker for MDD. Investigators have proposed that secretion of growth hormone at night may be phase-advanced in depression, such that secretion occurs just prior to sleep onset instead of during the first few hours of sleep. Of interest is that one group of investigators has reported that the phase-advanced GH peak is phase-delayed into the normal range after recovery from the depressive state, in contrast to the persistent, trait-like nature of the blunted nocturnal GH secretion in adult depression. The available data on sleep-related GH secretion in depressed children and adolescents are sparser and less consistent than in adults. Puig-Antich (1987) hypothesized that a serotonin deficit state with cholinergic dominance could lead to sleep-related GH hypersecretion in prepubertal depressives.

Investigators have argued that reduced GH responses to chemical or physiological stimuli in anxiety and mood disorders may represent a trait marker of vulnerability to mood and anxiety disorders. Coplan, Pine, Papp, and Gorman (1997) have presented evidence both in patients with PD and in unpredictably-reared non-human primates that the GH response to the GH secretagogue, clonidine, varies inversely with the degree of HPA axis activation. In certain instances, peripheral HPA axis function may be well compensated and appear normal, but elevations of extrahypothalamic CRF production and neurotransmission, in structures such as the amygdala, may take place and may only be evident in CSF, if at all. It is now well documented that elevations of extrahypothalamic CRF, either by injection or by detection in the CSF, is associated with a pattern of anxiety and depressive behaviors in animals strikingly similar to those observed in clinical disorders. The reduced GH response to secretory stimuli in clinical populations may provide an indirect, but as yet the most accurate, index of extrahypothalamic CRF overactivity.

REFERENCES

Coplan, J. D., Pine, D., Papp, L., & Gorman, J. M. (1997). A window on noradrenergic, hypothalamic-pituitary-adrenal axis and corticotropin releasing-factor function in anxiety and affective disorders: The growth hormone response to clonidine. *Psychopharmacology Bulletin, 33*(2), 193–204.

Dinan, T. G. (1998). Psychoneuroendocrinology of depression: Growth hormone. *The psychiatric clinics of North America: Psychoneuroendocrinology, 21*(2), 325–340.

Holsboer, F. (1994). Neuroendocrinology of mood disorders. In F. E. Bloom & D. J. Kupfer (Eds.), *Neuropsychopharmacology: The fourth generation of progress* (pp. 957–970). New York: Raven.

Puig-Antich, J. (1987). Affective disorders in children and adolescents: Diagnostic validity and psychobiology. In H. Y. Meltzer (Ed.), *Psychopharmacology: The third generation of progress* (pp. 843–859). New York: Raven.

Siever, L. J., Uhde, T. W., Silberman, E. K., Jimerson, D. C., Aloi, J. A., Post, R. M., & Murphy, D. L. (1982). Growth hormone response to clonidine as a probe of noradrenergic receptor responsiveness in affective disorder patients and controls. *Psychiatry Research, 6,* 171–183.

Uhde, T. W., Tancer, M. E., Rubinow, D. R., Roscow, D. B., Boulenger, J. P., Vittone, B., Gurguis, G., Geraci, M., & Black, B., Post, R. M. (1992). Evidence for hypothalamo-growth hormone dysfunction in panic disorder: Profile of growth hormone responses to clonidine, yohimbine, caffeine, glucose, GRF and TRH in panic disorder patients versus healthy volunteers. *Neuropsychopharmacology, 6*(2), 101–118.

J. D. COPLAN
Columbia University

HORMONES AND BEHAVIOR
PITUITARY
PITUITARY DISORDERS

GUILFORD, JOY PAUL (1897–1987)

Joy Paul Guilford received the BA and MA degrees from the University of Nebraska, the latter in 1919. His bachelor's work was interrupted by his army service in World War I. While a graduate student, he became familiar with Spearman's g factor in intelligence. While working for a brief time at the University of Nebraska's psychological clinic he became convinced that intelligence was not a monolithic global attribute but consisted of a number of different abilities.

Guilford received the PhD from Cornell University in 1927. While there, he worked with such eminent psychologists as Titchener, Helson, Dallenbach and Koffka. After brief stays at the Universities of Kansas and Illinois, Guilford returned to Nebraska until 1940. He then went to the University of Southern California until his retirement in 1962. His work at California was interrupted by service during World War II.

During his lifetime, he was an unusually productive researcher and writer, publishing numerous research articles, psychological tests, and books. His areas of investigation included traditional psychophysics, the autokinetic phenomena, attention, eye movements, scaling effects, and the phi phenomenon. His best known book was *Psychometric Methods,* used by students of psychology for decades. In a readable manner, the methods used by psychologists over the previous years were carefully explained.

In the middle 1930s Carl Jung's personality dimension of introversion-extraversion was widely discussed as one dimension of personality. Guilford demonstrated, using factoral analysis, that this was not a unitary factor but consisted of a complex composite of several personality attributes.

During his career, Guilford received many honors including presidency of the American Psychological Association (1949), the Distinguished Contribution Award (1964), and the Gold Medal Award from the American Psychological Foundation (1983).

R. W. LUNDIN
Wheaton, Illinois

GUTHRIE, EDWIN R. (1886–1959)

Edwin R. Guthrie received the PhD from the University of Pennsylvania in 1914. The remainder of his academic career was spent at the University of Washington until his retirement in 1956. In 1958, the year before his death, he was awarded the Gold Medal from the American Psychological Foundation.

Like John Watson, Guthrie maintained that psychology should be the study of observable behavior which was measurable and subject to proper experimental procedures. His first book, written in collaboration with Stevenson Smith, was entitled *General Psychology in Terms of Behavior.* Very much in the tradition of behaviorism, Guthrie was a learning theorist. His other books include *The Psychology of Learning, The Psychology of Human Conflict,* and in collaboration with A. L. Edwards, *Psychology: A First Course in Human Behavior.*

Guthrie is considered one of the most important learning theorists of the twentieth century. His theory is extremely simple. He starts out with one basic law of learning: What is being noticed becomes a signal for what is being done. Thus learning is simply a matter of an S-R (stimulus-response) association by contiguity. Further, a subprinciple states that when an S-R connection occurs, it reaches its full strength on the first trial (one trial learning), and will remain so indefinitely unless some succeeding event occurs to replace or destroy it. He accounts for improvement with practice simply by adding more and more S-R connection to a given performance.

The loss of behavior through either extinction or forgetting is accounted for by associative inhibition, which means that an incompatible response has been learned which interferes with the previous one. Thus no new learning principle is needed. A new

S-R connection occurs to replace the previous one. Forgetting is simply a matter of interference by succeeding associations.

Motivation and reward, according to Guthrie, are not essential to the learning process. In animal experimentation deprivation of food merely causes greater activity, thus allowing for the possibility of more new connections to be established. Reward is useful only because it allows the organism to move away from a situation so that previous learned associations will not be destroyed. Unlike other learning theorists such as B. F. Skinner or Clark Hull, who stressed the crucial role of reinforcement (reward) in the learning process, Guthrie maintained that learning occurs simply because S-R associations are established.

What many consider Guthrie's most important research in support of his theory was a study done with C. P. Horton using cats in a puzzle box. They demonstrated that extremely stereotyped responses were established when a cat entered a box, hit a pole, and then left the box via a door opposite the one of entry. They ob-

served that the way in which the cat hit or bumped the pole on the first trial was the same way it would do so on succeeding trials. If differences occurred, the stimulus situation somehow had changed.

Guthrie has been praised for the simplicity of his theory, which does not require numerous postulates, principles, and intervening variables (as does Hull's) to explain the results. It is straightforward and sticks with the observable events. On the other hand, his opponents claim he has tried to explain too much on the basis of too few principles. Furthermore, those who stress the importance of reinforcement (reward) as crucial to learning wonder how Guthrie can set forth a theory where the overwhelming experimental evidence supports a concept of reward. They feel that Guthrie dodged the issue of reward.

R. W. LUNDIN
Wheaton, Illinois

H

HABITUATION

Habituation is a relatively persistent waning of a response following continuous or (usually) repeated stimulation that is not followed by reinforcement. For some investigations it is an empirical result, while for others it is a hypothetical construct, depending on the depth and character of its study. Fatigue, drugs, adaptation, and injury, though they produce response decline, are not included under this term and are quite separate. Other terms are used in other contexts, however, for probably related phenomena.

The orienting reaction exhibits habituation's typical characteristics. When a strange, unidentified noise alarms a wild animal, it usually stops whatever it is doing, becomes motionless, and scans its surroundings in search of the sound source in preparation for flight. If only the usual rustling ensues, it is interpreted as absence of danger, and the animal shortly resumes its original activity. Subsequent similar noises, if uneventful, call forth similar but progressively weaker and shorter alerting responses, perhaps to finally eventuate in no outward sign of disturbance. The basic response or its rudiments can be seen in most species down to flatworms, and some investigators claim habituation in coelenterates and even protozoa. Different mechanisms are likely to be required to explain the similarity in results.

A second example, though considerably different in some respects, is essentially similar in others. Repeated severe coolings of a particular finger result in a progressive reduction of the associated cold pain. To the environmental physiologist this phenomenon is known as *specific habituation* when the response is restricted to the finger involved. *General habituation* is a change in the psychological set that results in a generalized diminution in response to the repeated stimulus. An example might be a reduced vasoconstriction outflow to all the periphery, although one particular finger was repeatedly cooled for several days. *Acclimatization* refers to the functional compensation that occurs over a period of days or weeks in response to a complex of environmental factors, as in seasonal or climatic changes. *Acclimation* refers to the same type of adjustment to a single environmental condition, as in controlled experiments.

The extent to which habituation mechanisms are involved in learning to like new foods that initially are unappealing, or in learning to tolerate and even become unaware of industrial sounds, odors, and other unpleasant stimulations, is a matter of speculation.

Habituation of the orienting response, the type most extensively studied, is of theoretical interest because it represents one of the most primitive types of learning: a persistent change in behavior in response to experience. Its functional significance to the animal lies in the fact that repetitive stimuli are usually uninformative and can be ignored, so the animal's attention can be reserved for significant or novel stimuli. Its interest for psychologists lies in its ubiquity in the animal kingdom ("sensitive" plants such as the Mimosa

also show diminished leaflet closing with repeated stimulation), and the similarity of its properties to those of associative learning.

Among habituation's main characteristics are the following: (a) After a long enough absence of stimulation, the originally strong but now diminished response will reappear at full strength (spontaneous recovery); (b) the more frequent and regular the eliciting stimulation, the faster the habituation; (c) the stronger the stimulation, the slower the habituation, although some near-threshold stimuli may not habituate, and very strong stimuli may elicit defensive responses that differ in characteristics from orienting responses; (d) additional stimulation beyond that which completely abolishes the original response (below-zero habituation) further prolongs habituation and delays spontaneous recovery; (e) habituation may generalize to other similar stimuli, and (f) presentation of another usually stronger—but sometimes much weaker—stimulus than is customary may restore the original response (i.e., cause dishabituation).

Several approaches have been taken to elucidate the nature of the neural mechanisms involved in short-term habituation. According to the synaptic depression model, sensory input activates small interneurons in the periphery of the reticular formation. They in turn activate those neurons at the reticular formation's core that evoke cortical arousal in higher mammals. But it is necessary to first demonstrate that synaptic depression is possible, and to this end a simpler animal model has been useful. The sea hare (*Aplysia*) is a shell-less mollusk that looks like a fast snail and possesses only a few easily identified ganglia. Habituation studies show that repeated stimulation of a single sensory neuron evokes progressively smaller excitation potentials in the postsynaptic membrane. No change occurs in the postsynaptic membrane itself: The decrease in the postsynaptic response occurs because progressively fewer quanta of the neurotransmitter acetylcholine are released into the synaptic cleft. It is presumed that something like the sea hare's synaptic depression also occurs in the reticular formation.

Sokolov proposed a match-mismatch model to explain habituation. He assumes that in higher mammals a stimulus elicits a neural representation of itself that is relatively permanent (engram). The neural consequences of subsequent stimuli are compared with the engram of the originally alerting stimulus; if the later stimulus matches the former, no reticular arousal occurs and habituation ensues.

One frequently finds in experimental work that the first response to the alerting stimulus is not the strongest; the magnitude of the next few responses may exceed that of the first, and only in subsequent trials does response strength diminish. One also finds that a habituated response can be rejuvenated (dishabituated) by a different, usually strong, stimulus (for example, a shock elsewhere on the body). Originally this dishabituation was thought to be merely a release of habituation, but it is now believed that another process, *sensitization,* underlies the augmented responding. Accordingly, the curve of responding that is usually seen is complex, having an initial rise and subsequent decline. Its shape is the result of the combined action of sensitization and habituation. Habituation becomes dominant after repeated stimulations, whereas sensitization remains at a constant level or declines. Some evidence points to the existence of neurons that only habituate and—in the opinion of some—markedly sensitize.

DISHABITUATION

Many stimuli instigate alerting responses that wane after the first occasion and may eventually disappear with successive stimulus experiences. This phenomenon, called habituation, can be removed or cancelled by dishabituation, if a different alerting stimulus is interpolated between habituation trials. Dishabituation may occur if the original stimulus is presented in conjunction with a previously irrelevant stimulus. It is manifest if the original stimulus again evokes the orienting response at nearly full strength on the trials following the interpolated trial. Some use the term "dishabituation" to indicate that the original response waned because of inhibition, and that the new stimulus or stimulus combination disinhibits the inhibited responses. Others believe that what some call dishabituation is actually a superimposed response, sensitization, which overrides the processes underlying the waning.

SENSITIZATION

Repeated presentations of a stimulus that elicits alerting responses may cause an increase, a decrease, or first an increase and later a decrease, in responding. With frequent stimulations the response generally wanes. The initial increase is known as sensitization. Thompson and Spencer (1966) have presented evidence for the independence of habituation and sensitization in both spinally transected and intact animals. Sensitization is thus an increase in arousal or in orienting and defensive arousals. Since the most likely final result is diminished responding, habituation eventually becomes stronger than sensitization. The empirical result is the sum of the algebraically combined strengths of the two opposing tendencies. A good deal of controversy exists in the theoretical as well as empirical aspects of sensitization regarding the equivalence of responses in widely different species, the parts of the nervous system involved in an intact organism's responses, and the time courses or unidirectionality of the underlying sensitization and habituation processes.

REFERENCES

Thompson, R. F., & Spencer, W. A. (1966). Habituation: A model phenomenon for the study of neuronal substrates of behavior. *Psychological Review, 173,* 16–43.

SUGGESTED READING

Eagan, C. J. (1963). Introduction and terminology: Habituation and peripheral tissue adaptations. *Federation Proceedings, 22,* 930–933.

Kandel, E. R. (1979). Small systems of neurons. *Scientific American, 241,* 66–85.

Sokolov, E. N. (1963). Higher neuron functions: The orienting reflex. *Annual Review of Physiology, 25,* 545–580.

Sokolov, E. N. (1963/1958). *Perception and the conditioned reflex.* New York: Macmillan.

A. J. RIOPELLE
Louisiana State University

ACCOMMODATION
ADAPTATION
FATIGUE
HOMEOSTASIS
INSTINCT

HALFWAY HOUSES

Halfway houses, often referred to as group homes or therapeutic communities, are locales where all activities and interactions may be viewed as having potentially healing, rehabilitative, and supportive properties and where all members may consciously or unconsciously contribute to therapy. Residents of these houses are halfway from institutionalization to independence. Halfway houses typically work to prepare individuals to move from institutionalized settings, where they are isolated from the community at large, to becoming able to function independently. Also, it is the goal of the halfway house to integrate or reintegrate their former residents into independently living members of their communities. This process is done with the aim that they may live in, interact with, and be a contributing member of the community, and be able to gain something from the community experience as well. In some cases, the halfway house may be the first referral source or an intermediary step before a person is institutionalized. This referral depends on the type of condition the individual is being referred for and the severity of their situation. Halfway houses are commonly affiliated with churches, private organizations, hospitals, or the government and may differ greatly in the number, gender, and age of residents they serve, as well as in the type of therapeutic approach and environmental conditions they offer residents.

HISTORY

For many years, there have been organizations and individuals that have sought to help people dealing with any number of situations and conditions that interfere with their adjustment to living and being functioning members of society. After World War II, homes were set up to help soldiers make the transition from war to living in their respective communities. During the 1960s, with the emphasis on deinstitutionalization of the mentally ill, advances made with psychotropic medications, and new community mental health legislation, the number of halfway houses increased greatly. As the emphasis on transitional facilities for the mentally ill grew, there was an increased amount of attention paid to helping individuals in the criminal justice system and with substance abuse problems make the transition from institutional life to becoming acclimated to the community. Today, there are halfway houses serving a variety of populations with a variety of issues.

TYPES

Halfway houses serve many different types of individuals coming from various situations and dealing with various conditions. The following is a list of the most frequently served populations within halfway houses.

Mentally Ill.

Residents are usually required to attend some type of treatment, whether it is on site or off. The staff insures that residents take their required prescription medication regularly and properly. A great deal of treatment focus is placed on social and vocational skills, particularly if the individual has been institutionalized for an extended period of time. Such individuals may have forgotten or never learned skills necessary to function independently. In some cases, aftercare for these clients is provided. This provides resources and support for individuals after they leave the house.

Substance abusers.

Individuals recovering from alcohol or other substance abuse are often sent to halfway houses after they have completed time in a residential treatment facility. Enrollment in a treatment program is mandatory and no drugs or alcohol are allowed to be used by the residents. Many of these residents have little family support, and the halfway house is a tool to facilitate their sobriety, provide support from people with similar problems, and help them to readjust to living in the community.

Criminal offenders.

Incarcerated individuals may be sent to halfway houses to serve out the remainder of their sentences if they have had good behavior, or they may be sent to halfway houses after they are released from prison. These homes can be for either adult or youth offenders. There is an emphasis on finding and maintaining a job. Sobriety is also usually required for these residents.

Troubled adolescents.

Children with severe behavioral problems, emotional problems, volatile home situations, and other problems are often sent to halfway houses. These children may remain residents until they can be provided with alternative, stable housing or until their behavior changes. Training children in social skills is a large component of these programs. The halfway house is staffed by personnel around the clock who monitor the children's schoolwork, chores, and recreation. These homes seek to provide children with a consistent, stable environment until more permanent arrangements can be made.

Developmentally disabled.

In halfway houses for the developmentally disabled, staff work to help the residents function independently. Residents learn how to manage their money, cook, clean, and utilize public transportation. Through activities with staff and each other, residents learn to develop more adaptive social behaviors. Some residents attain and maintain jobs while staying at the home. Many of the residents go on to live on their own or function well with minimal help from others.

METHODS

There are a variety of treatment modalities and techniques used in halfway houses. In fact, two different halfway houses serving the same population may approach the same goal in very different manners. Nevertheless, there are four basic theoretical approaches taken by halfway houses: democratization, communalism, permissiveness, and reality confrontation. Democratization refers to promoting staff and patients to be involved in the important decisions made in the running of the house. House administrations that subscribe to this approach believe that democratization may decrease resident dependence on the staff and foster independence and inventiveness by the residents. Halfway houses that follow a communalism model encourage staff and residents to take part in the activities of the home together. Cooking, chores, and recreational activities involve the residents and the staff. This interaction of staff and residents provides more opportunities to model and teach desired behaviors. Houses that follow the permissiveness model allow a greater expression of emotional and behavioral displays than most traditional settings before physical or behavioral restraints are used. In houses that apply the reality confrontation model, patients receive the same response to and consequence for their actions and behaviors as they would in the community.

Halfway house staff members also employ a number of techniques within these modalities to aid in the adjustment of their residents to community life. Group and individual therapy, 12-step programs, social skills training, development of financial management skills, social outings, job training, and moral support are used by many house staff to help foster the independence of their residents. Many houses use some type of reward system, whether a token economy, gaining of privileges as skills are mastered, or acquisition of rewards and privileges with seniority as one moves through the program of the house. These tools are used in many combinations, often depending on the population of residents and the philosophical orientation of the organization, to help the resident develop the skills necessary to become integrated into the community.

The ideals on which the halfway house model are built may seem quite laudable. Nonetheless, the efficacy of such programs has not yet been adequately demonstrated. There has been a wide array of studies producing various results. Several methodological issues, such as no control groups in research and lack of random assignment, have been raised in relation to studies done on halfway houses. Also, due to the various kinds of modalities of treatment and different populations served, it has been difficult to conduct research and determine effectiveness. More methodologically sound research should be conducted to tell us which methods are most effective and which methods work most effectively with certain types of individuals. Additionally, greater emphasis should be placed on using empirically supported methods in working with residents, instead of using antiquated methods that may not be appropriate for the population.

SUGGESTED READING

Bloor, M. J. (1986). Problems of therapeutic community practice in two halfway houses for disturbed adolescents: A comparative sociological study. *Journal of Adolescence, 9,* 29–48.

Cometa, M. S., Morrison, J. K., & Ziskoven, M. (1979). Halfway to where? A critique of research on psychiatric halfway houses. *Journal of Community Psychology, 7,* 23–27.

Grove, B. (1989). Therapeutic communities: Halfway home. In A. Brackx & C. Grinshaw (Eds.), *Mental health care in crisis.* London: Pluto Press.

Huberty, D. J. (1978). Innovations in the halfway house concept. *Alcohol Health & Research World, 2,* 13–19.

Moczydlowski, K. (1980). Predictors of success in a correctional halfway house for youthful and adult offenders. *Corrective and Social Psychiatry, 26,* 59–72.

Plotinsky, I. (1985). Conrad house: The halfway house as transitional residential facility. *Psychiatric Annals, 15,* 648–652.

Sarata, B. P. V. & Behrman, J. (1982). Group home parenting: an examination of the role. *Community Mental Health Journal, 18,* 274–285.

M. S. Coe
J. R. Ferrari
DePaul University

HALL, CALVIN S. (1909–1985)

Known for his investigations of dreams and books on personality theory, Calvin S. Hall decided to become a psychologist during his junior year at the University of Washington, while taking a course on psychological theories taught by Edwin Guthrie. Not permitted to enroll for his senior year because he refused to take required courses in military science, he transferred to the University of California at Berkeley. There his interest in theoretical psychology was nourished by Edward Tolman, and he was introduced to statistics and behavior genetics by Robert Tryon, who became his dissertation advisor.

For the next 15 years Hall's primary area of research was the inheritance of temperament in the rat. He obtained his first faculty appointment at the University of Oregon in the depths of the Great Depression. Three years later, in 1937, he became chairman of the department at Western Reserve University, where he remained for 20 years. He began to read Freud at 30, but his interest in dreams did not emerge until 6 years later when he began to collect dreams from college students.

After 2 years at Syracuse University, becoming weary of teaching, administration, and campus politics, Hall decided to devote the remainder of his life to writing and dream research. His writing has been about equally divided between books on psychological

theories and books on dreams. His chief contributions to the study of dreams are the application of quantitative content analysis to large samples of dreams, and a cognitive theory of dreams and dream symbolism. He believes that chance played the greatest role in shaping his personal and professional life.

Staff

HALL, G. STANLEY (1844–1924)

If William James is honored as the initial hero of modern psychology in America, G. Stanley Hall, his student, deserves to be honored as the founder and promoter of organized psychology as a science and profession. He founded the American Psychological Association in 1892, was its first president, and in 1887 founded the first psychological journal in America, the *American Journal of Psychology.* He also founded other journals: the *Pedagogical Seminary* (later the *Journal of Genetic Psychology*) in 1894, the *Journal of Religious Psychology* in 1904, and the *Journal of Applied Psychology* in 1917.

After study at Williams College, a year at the Union Theological Seminary, then a year of study in Germany in which he moved toward physiology, Hall returned to America jobless. To pay off his debts, he tutored some children in New York for a year, taught English and foreign languages (among other duties) at Antioch College, then accepted an instructorship in English at Harvard University. While occupying that post, he found time to work in the physiological laboratory of Henry P. Bowditch and to study psychology with William James, and was granted the PhD in psychology under their joint auspices in 1878. It was the first PhD in psychology earned in America, and only the 18th PhD granted at Harvard in all fields of study. Setting off again for Europe, Hall became the first of a succession of American students to seek out Wilhelm Wundt at Leipzig, and was there when Wundt's laboratory was founded.

His American career as a university psychologist began with his professorship in psychology and pedagogics, a title won after his second year at the new Johns Hopkins University, where he had gone in 1882. During his few years at Hopkins he had a number of students who became distinguished psychologists, among them W. H. Burnham, J. M. Cattell, John Dewey, Joseph Jastrow, and E. C. Sanford, four of whom were later presidents of the American Psychological Association. The laboratory that Hall founded was second only to a demonstration laboratory that William James had arranged earlier at Harvard.

Hall became the president of Clark University, which opened its doors in 1889, and he served there until his death in 1924. In the last decade of the 19th century, through 1898, of the 54 PhDs that were granted in psychology, 30 were students of Hall. He continued to turn out PhDs—a total of 81 from his department during his active years there. Two of these also became presidents of the American Psychological Association, William L. Bryan and Lewis M. Terman. Other prominent students from the Clark days were Arnold Gesell, important in child development, and Henry H. Goddard, known for his studies of mental retardation.

Hall had his hand in on many aspects of child development and education, and was widely sought as an adviser for new innovations. A promoter of new views, he invited Sigmund Freud to come to Clark University for a series of lectures in 1909, giving Freud his first public academic recognition and his only honorary degree.

Hall remains important primarily for what he did for the child study movement, with its many consequences for education and developmental psychology. His theoretical emphasis was upon the doctrine of recapitulation as promoted by Haeckel: Ontology recapitulates phylogeny. While the theory became discredited, it permitted Hall to call attention to adolescence as an important turning point in psychological growth. He thought of childhood essentially as an extention of embryological development. The long period of dependency and of assimilating knowledge and skills in maturing stages leads eventually to the flowering of independence at adolescence. Hall's two-volume *Adolescence* was influential in its day.

The focus on the child and the introduction of questionnaire methods, which soon led to a variety of tests other than merely intellectual ones, are more important contemporary residues from Hall's career than any basic theoretical ideas. His leadership and organizational and promotional skills were needed by the psychology of his day, and contemporary psychology is broader and more viable because of him.

E. R. HILGARD
Stanford University

HALLUCINATIONS

An hallucination is typically defined as a false sensory impression. The "false" part of this definition refers to the lack of an external set of referents that, to the evaluator, would explain and support the individual's description of the event. Dreaming is considered by some to be a common example of an hallucinatory experience, surrounded at the onset of sleep in some people by hypnogogic hallucinations and waking up with hypnopomic hallucinations (American Psychiatric Association, 1987; Kaplan & Sadock, 1985).

Various estimates place between one-eighth and two-thirds of the normal population as having had hallucinations while awake (Coleman, Butcher, & Carson, 1984; Parish, 1914; Posey & Losch, 1983). The phenomenon appears more frequent the more it is investigated, with tactile then auditory hallucinations the most common. The occurrence of hallucinations may not necessarily be related to psychopathology. Posey and Losch (1983) found confirmatory evidence for this from their 375 college subjects, based on interviews and MMPI results. These authors found that the most common auditory hallucinations were hearing a voice calling one's name aloud when alone (36%) and hearing one's own thoughts as if they were spoken aloud (39%).

Preschool children may experience hallucinations as part of their normal development. Schreier and Libow (1986) found that those 2 to 5 children experiencing phobic hallucinations were uniformly bright and independent.

For both normal and psychiatric persons, the typical phasing of hallucinations consists of: (a) startle reaction when confronted

with the sensory impression; (b) organization (coping); and (c) stabilization (Romme & Escher, 1989).

Culture appears to moderate the occurrence, quality, and frequency of hallucinations. Third World cultural groups—particularly Africans, West Indians, and South Asians—hallucinate more often than those in industrialized societies (Ndetei & Vadher, 1984). Within the United States, blacks and Hispanics report more auditory hallucinations than whites, which tends to lead to a higher risk of misdiagnosis in the direction of psychopathology (Mukherjee et al., 1983). Gender differences are not apparent from the literature.

In nonpsychiatric populations, hallucinations have been known to be caused by: (a) exhaustion, as in the last stage of the GAS cycle (Selye, 1980–1983); (b) sleep deprivation; (c) social isolation and rejection (Coleman et al., 1984); (d) a severe reactive depression; (e) amputation of limbs, as in the phantom limb experience with kinesthetic sensations; (f) prescribed medication (Kaplan & Sadock, 1985); and (g) a secondary outcome of substance intoxication by the hallucinogenics (particularly LSD, mescaline, and psilocybin) and other drugs (e.g., morphine, heroin, and cocaine) (de Morsier, 1969). Formication involves creeping sensations under the skin found with cocaine abusers.

In the organic brain syndromes, hallucinations may be caused by a variety of events (see reviews by Lezak, 1983; Strub & Black, 1981), including: (a) delirium; (b) tumors associated with increasing intracranial pressure; (c) temporal lobe lesions; (d) seizures of several types; (e) alcohol-related encephalopathy; (f) head injury, as in postcoma experiences and disorientation; and (g) irritation of various sensory pathways, such as the visual pathways' transversing the temporal lobes (causing Lilliputian hallucinations) or the olfactory pathways (causing hallucinations of distinctive odors such as burnt rubber).

Not all organic brain-induced hallucinations involve the perception of a separate reality. In organic hallucinosis, for example, the (usually auditory) hallucinations may arise within a full state of alertness and orientation. In Lilliputian hallucinations, the affected person knows the small figures are not real; they are not associated with delusions.

Support for cerebral insult as the cause of some hallucinations stems from lateralization data. Chamorro, Sacco, CieCierski, and Binder (1990) described the case of a 41-year-old woman with a subcortical CVA in alcohol withdrawal with visual hallucinations confined to the right side of space. De Morsier (1969) reported a case of visual hallucinations localized in the left half of the visual field associated with sensory-motor hemiparesis. Kahn, Clark, and Oyebode (1988) report on a 72-year-old female with unilateral auditory hallucinations related to deafness on the same side, which disappeared with a hearing aid. Tanabe and colleagues (1986) describes a case of verbal hallucinations lateralized to the right ear, associated with fluent aphasia and a CVA in the left superior temporal gyrus. Other studies that support a cerebral insult interpretation of hallucinations are presented in Table 1.

The major psychotic disorders are often associated with hallucinations (American Psychiatric Association, 1987). Vivid hallucinations can be seen in all the schizophrenic subtypes. Hallucinations are encountered within the affective disorders. In major

Table 1   Hallucinations Correlated with Cerebral Insult

Auditory Hallucinations

Reduced platelet MAO activity (Schildkraut et al., 1980)

Hypothyroidism (Pearce & Walbridge, 1991)

Alzheimer's disease (Burns, Jacoby, & Levy, 1990)

Atrophy of left superior temporal gyros (Barta et al., 1990)

Visual Hallucinations

Vascular insufficiency of temporo-parieto-occipital regions (Schneider & Crosby, 1980)

Lesion of right diencephalon (De Morsier, 1969)

Subcortical infarct interrupting striatocortical pathways (Chamorro et al., 1990)

Anterior cerebral artery occlusion (Nakajima, 1991)

Tactile and Other Hallucinations

Peduncular hallucinosis associated with paramedian thalamic infarction (Feinberg & Rapcsak, 1989)

Stereognostic hallucinations and haptic sensations associated with biparietal lesions (Stacy, 1987)

Table 2   Diminishing Auditory Hallucinations

Method	Condition	Reference
Relaxation tapes	Schizophrenics	Hustig et al. (1990)
Stimulating tapes	Schizophrenics	Hustig et al. (1990)
Increasing ambient noise levels (via hearing aid)	Anxiety and depression	Fenton and McRae (1989)
Stop-and-name technique (with occluded auditory input to ear)	Schizophrenics	Birchwood (1986)
Switching (concentration on visual stimulus)	Process schizophrenics	Heilbrun et al. (1986)
Holding (repeating words to ignore later words)	Reactive schizophrenics	Heilbrun et al. (1986)
Diversion strategies	Schizophrenics	Allen et al. (1985)
Satiation therapy (prolonged exposure to voice)	Obsessional thoughts	Glaister (1985)

depression, for example, the examiner using *DSM-III-R* criteria is asked to determine whether reported hallucinations are mood congruent or mood incongruent. Schizoaffective psychosis, a combination of thought disorder and affective psychosis, often has hallucinations as an associated feature.

Early work suggesting that different mental conditions involve different types of hallucinations is illustrated by Alpert and Silvers (1970). A total of 80 adult hallucinating inpatients who were either alcoholics or schizophrenics were studied. The differences in hallucinations between the two groups were as follows. In alcoholics: (a) the onset of the hallucinations in their illness was early; (b) the type of sound was nonverbal or consisted of unintelligible voices; (c) the perceived source was outside the body; (d) patterned visual stimulation decreased the frequency of hallucinations; (e) arousal increased the frequency; (f) delusions accompanied the hallucinations infrequently; and (g) patients were often eager to discuss the experiences. In contrast, in schizophrenics: (a) the onset was later; (b) voices were usually clear; (c) hallucinations were perceived to originate inside the body; (d & e) patterned visual stimulation and arousal created no change in frequency; (f) delusions were more frequent; and (g) patients were reluctant to share their hallucinatory experiences.

Hallucinations can be set off by multiple or indirectly combining events. Tactile (haptic) hallucinations can be secondary to schizophrenia, withdrawal from alcohol, or drug intoxication. Olfactory hallucinations (the false perception of smell), and gustatory hallucinations (the false perception of taste), are often experienced together in such conditions as temporal lobe epilepsy and schizophrenia. Reflex hallucinations involve irritation in one sense, creating an hallucination in another—for example, a toothache's setting off an auditory hallucination in a schizophrenic. Finally, kinesthetic hallucinations involve the sensation of altered states of body organs for which no receptor apparatus could explain the experience. This is found in psychotics and also in organics, as, for example, a burning sensation in the brain caused by schizophrenia or

a severe depression. The thalamic pain syndrome also can account for the perception.

For both normal and psychiatric populations, hallucinations may serve an adaptive function. Benjamin's (1989) 30 individuals with mental illness reported an integrated, interpersonally coherent and complementary relationship with their auditory hallucinations.

Hallucinations are ubiquitous and adaptive, occurring in normals and all the major psychiatric diagnostic categories. Speculation continues regarding etiology; for example, whether hallucinations associated with cerebral insult represent a release from inhibitory neural mechanisms. Psychological explanations, for example, that hallucinations represent intrapersonal and/or interpersonal dynamics that help the individual adjust to a changing and often threatening environment are just as valid. Both neurological and psychological theories are plagued with the lack of a direct method to measure hallucinations.

Interventions for hallucinations vary widely, from spontaneous recovery to invasive drug procedures, which frequently cause hallucinations themselves as a toxic side effect. Cognitive behavioral methods have generated some interest (Table 2). Investigation into this fascinating domain of human behavior is projected to continue as part of a heightened interest in altered states of consciousness.

REFERENCES

Allen, H., Halperin, J., & Friend, R. (1985). Removal and diversion tactics and the control of auditory hallucinations. *Behaviour Research & Therapy, 23,* 601–605.

Alpert, M., & Silvers, K. (1970). Perceptual characteristics distinguishing auditory hallucinations in schizophrenia and acute alcoholic psychoses. *American Journal of Psychiatry, 127,* 298–302.

American Psychiatric Association. (1987). *Diagnostic and statistical manual of mental disorders* (3rd ed., rev.). Washington, DC: Author.

Barta, P., Pearlson, G., Powers, R., & Richards, S. (1990). Auditory hallucinations and smaller superior temporal gyral volume in schizophrenia. *American Journal of Psychiatry, 147,* 1457–1462.

Benjamin, L. (1989). Is chronicity a function of the relationship between the person and the auditory hallucination? *Schizophrenia Bulletin, 15,* 291–310.

Birchwood, M. (1986). Control of auditory hallucinations through occlusion of monaural auditory input. *British Journal of Psychiatry, 149,* 104–107.

Burns, A., Jacoby, R., & Levy, R. (1990). Psychiatric phenomena in Alzheimer's disease: II. Disorders of perception. *British Journal of Psychiatry, 157,* 76–81.

Chamorro, A., Sacco, R., Ciecierski, K., & Binder, J. (1990). Visual hemineglect & hemihallucinations in a patient with a subcortical infarction. *Neurology, 40,* 1463–1464.

Coleman, J., Butcher, J., & Carson, R. (1984). *Abnormal psychology and modern life* (7th ed.). Glenview, IL: Scott, Foresman.

De Morsier, G. (1969). Studies of hallucinations. *Journal de Psychologie Normale et Pathologigue, 66,* 421–452.

Feinberg, W., & Rapcsak, S. (1989). "Peduncular hallucinosis" following paramedian thalamic infarction. *Neurology, 39,* 1535–1536.

Fenton, G., & McRae, D. (1989). Musical hallucinations in a deaf elderly woman. *British Journal of Psychiatry, 155,* 401–403.

Glaister, B. (1985). A case of auditory hallucinations treated by satiation. *Behaviour Research and Therapy, 23,* 213–215.

Heilbrun, A., Diller, R., Fleming, R., & Slade, L. (1986). Strategies of disattention and auditory hallucinations in schizophrenics. *Journal of Nervous Mental Diseases, 174,* 265–273.

Hustig, H., Tran, D., Hafner, & Miller, R. (1990). The effect of headphone music on persistent auditory hallucinations. *Behavioral Psychotherapy, 18,* 273–281.

Kahn, A., Clark, T., & Oyebode, F. (1988). Unilateral auditory hallucinations. *British Journal of Psychiatry, 152,* 297–298.

Kaplan, H. I., & Sadock, B. J. (Eds.). (1985). *Modern synopsis of comprehensive textbook of psychiatry* (4th ed.). Baltimore: Williams & Wilkins.

Lezak, M. D. (1983). *Neuropsychological assessment.* New York: Oxford University Press.

Mukherjee, S., et al. (1983). Misdiagnosis of schizophrenia in bipolar patients: A multiethnic comparison. *American Journal of Psychiatry, 140,* 1571–1574.

Nakajima, K. (1991). Visual hallucinations with anterior cerebral artery occlusion. *No to Shinkei (Brain and Nerves), 43,* 71–76.

Ndetei, D., & Vadher, A. (1984). A comparative cross-cultural study of the frequencies of hallucinations in schizophrenics. *Acta Psychiatrica Scandinavica, 70,* 545–549.

Parish, E. (1914). *Hallucinations and illusions.* London: Walter Scott.

Pearce, M., & Walbridge, D. (1991). Myxoedema madness: A case report. *International Journal of Geriatric Psychiatry, 6,* 189–190.

Posey, T., & Losch, M. (1983). Auditory hallucinations of hearing voices in 375 normal subjects. *Imagination, Cognition and Personality, 3,* 99–113.

Romme, M., & Escher, A. (1989). Hearing voices. *Schizophrenia Bulletin, 5,* 209–216.

Schildkraut, J., Orsvlak, P., Schatzberg, A. & Herzog, J. (1980). Platelet monoamine oxidase activity in subgroups of schizophrenic disorders. *Schizophrenia Bulletin, 6,* 220–225.

Schneider, R. & Crosby. (1980). Motion sickness: II. A clinical study based on surgery of cerebral hemisphere lesions. *Aviation, Space & Environmental Medicine, 51,* 65–73.

Schreier, H., & Libow, J. (1986). Acute phobic hallucinations in very young children. *Journal of the American Academy of Child Psychiatry, 25,* 574–578.

Selye, H. (Ed.). (1980–1983). *Selye's guide to stress research* (3 vols.). New York: Van Nostrand Reinhold.

Stacy, C. (1987). Complex haptic hallucinations & palinaptia. *Cortex, 23,* 337–340.

Strub, R., & Black, F. (1981). *Organic brain syndromes.* Philadelphia: Davis.

H. V. HALL
Honolulu, Hawaii

SCHIZOPHRENIA
HALLUCINOGENS
PERCEPTUAL DISTORTIONS

HALLUCINOGENIC DRUGS

Many drugs can produce hallucinations (e.g., LSD, scopolamine, phencyclidine, methamphetamine, bromides, alcohol withdrawal, corticosteroids), but only a few can do so without producing delirium, and those few, with LSD being the prototype, are termed "hallucinogens." Even LSD does not usually produce true hallucinations, since the user usually remains aware that his misperceptions are drug-induced pseudohallucinations, but this label has persisted. Hallucinogens are also called phantastica, psychedelics, and psychotomimetics. Sometimes, but not herein, phencyclidine ("PCP") and ketamine are called hallucinogens, but they are best considered to be in a class of their own—the dissociative anesthetics.

The hallucinogens fall into two broad chemical classes, indolealkylamines (e.g., lysergic acid diethylamide [abbreviated LSD from the original German name, Lyserg-Säure-Diäthylamid], psilocybin, ibogaine, and harmaline) and phenylalkylamines (e.g., mescaline, methylenedioxymethamphetamine [MDMA or "ecstasy"], and 4-methyl-2,5-dimethoxyamphetamine [DOM or "STP"]). Some are plant constituents (mescaline from the peyote cactus, psilocybin from *Psilocybe* mushrooms), while others are synthetic (MDMA; LSD is semisynthetic, since the lysergic acid moiety is derived from the ergot fungus). The most potent is LSD, with a typical oral dose of 100 micrograms. Some other hallucinogens are as powerful as LSD (mescaline is at least as powerful); in other words, they are capable of exerting effects that are as profound as those of LSD, though at a much higher dose (e.g., 200–400 milligrams of mescaline).

Most hallucinogens, including LSD, are believed to induce their hallucinogenic effects by directly activating certain subtypes of brain serotonin receptors, resulting in intensified glutamate release in several regions of the neocortex (Marek & Aghajanian, 1998). There is a significant correlation between hallucinogenic potencies in humans and the drugs' affinities and agonist potencies for these serotonin receptor subtypes in vitro (Glennon, 1996; Sanders-Bush, 1994). These same subtypes of serotonin receptors are blocked by some of the newer antipsychotics, and have been implicated in the pathogenesis of schizophrenia. A few hallucinogens, like MDMA, work primarily by releasing serotonin.

The psychological effects of LSD are unpredictable. They depend on the amount ingested and the user's personality, mood, expectations, and surroundings. Sensations and feelings are affected much more dramatically than somatic signs. The user may feel several different emotions (including euphoria) at once, or swing rapidly from one emotion to another. Visual delusions, distortions and pseudohallucinations usually occur. Colors, sounds, odors, and other sensations appear intensified, and pseudohallucinations of movements, forms, and events may follow. The user's perceptions of time and self are distorted, including feelings of time slowing, one's body changing shape (e.g., arms very long), and out-of-body experience. Sensations may seem to cross over ("synesthesia"), giving the user the feeling of hearing colors and seeing sounds. Old memories may be vividly recalled. Anxiety often occurs while using LSD and other hallucinogens, and some users experience terrifying thoughts, nightmarish feelings, despair, and fears of insanity, death, and losing control. Fatal accidents have occurred during LSD use. However, there are no documented toxic fatalities from LSD. The somatic effects of LSD are mainly sympathetic and relatively slight. They include dilated pupils, hyperthermia, increased heart rate and blood pressure, sweating, loss of appetite, restlessness, dry mouth, dizziness, and tremors.

Users refer to LSD and other hallucinogen experiences as "trips" and to the acute adverse experiences as "bad trips," though most hallucinogen trips have both pleasant and unpleasant aspects. LSD trips are long—typically they begin to clear after 8 to 12 hours. Most users of hallucinogens feel that their experiences have a mystical, perception-expanding, epiphanous character. Lasting benefits, if any, of the trips have not been scientifically demonstrated. The works of authors associated with hallucinogens (e.g., Aldous Huxley, Timothy Leary) were discussed in the Hallucinogenic Drugs article in the previous edition of this *Encyclopedia*.

LSD was synthesized at the Sandoz Company pharmaceutical-chemical research laboratories in Basel, Switzerland in 1938 by Albert Hofmann, who discovered its pharmacological properties in 1943, at first by accidentally ingesting a small amount, and then by self-experimentation (Hofmann, 1980). Hallucinogens did not be-

come popular until the 1960s. Their abuse declined in the 1970s, but persists. The 1997 National Household Survey on Drug Abuse by the Substance Abuse and Mental Health Services Administration estimates that 7.8% of the American household population aged 12 and older has used LSD at least once. Hallucinogens are usually taken orally. Illicit LSD is often supplied absorbed on small squares of paper, known as "blotter acid," which are printed with cartoons.

The hallucinogens are not known to produce overt brain damage, except MDMA, which damages brain serotonergic neurons in man and animals, and ibogaine and harmaline, both of which produce cerebellar Purkinje neuron degeneration, at least in rats. However, LSD and other hallucinogens may produce a subtle neurotoxicity not yet detected in experiments. There are two long-term disorders associated with LSD, which could possibly be caused by subtle damage to the brain—persistent psychosis and hallucinogen persisting perception disorder (HPPD; Abraham, Aldridge, & Gogia, 1996). A danger of LSD is that the user may suffer a devastating psychological experience, including recollections of suppressed memories, resulting in a long-lasting psychosis. Post-LSD psychoses are unpredictable, and sometimes follow a single dose, but are more common in people with prior psychopathology. Post-LSD psychoses resemble schizoaffective disorders and are frequently accompanied by visual disturbances. The extent of this problem with the other hallucinogens is not known. However, MDMA, which does not produce the profound sensory disruptions characteristic of LSD and mescaline, but instead produces primarily alterations in emotions and a feeling of empathy with others, is believed to be less likely to produce long-lasting psychoses (or HPPD). The most effective treatments for post-LSD psychoses are electroconvulsive therapy and lithium.

In the 1950s, flashbacks (spontaneous, usually unexpected recurrences of aspects of LSD experiences—often the bad experiences—without the LSD) began to be reported, sometimes months after LSD use. The work of Henry Abraham (Abraham et al., 1996) demonstrated that this syndrome is typically persistent and stable, rather than paroxysmal, and presents primarily with visual disturbances, including geometric pseudohallucinations, false motion in the peripheral fields, halos, flashes, and trails (afterimages) associated with moving objects. Thus, the term flashback has been supplanted by HPPD. The visual distractions are increased by several factors (including stress, darkness, and marijuana) and decreased by benzodiazepines.

Hallucinogens, with the exception of the amphetamines such as MDMA, are not addictive. The hallucinogenic amphetamines also differ from the other hallucinogens in that toxic fatalities due to hyperthermia have occurred with their use. MDMA fatalities have been reported associated with the "rave" party scene.

In studies conducted in the mid-1960s, when LSD was added to suspensions of human white blood cells in vitro, there was more chromosomal breakage than in the cells without LSD. However, later in vivo animal experiments and surveys of people who used or were given hallucinogens offered no evidence of genetic damage, birth defects, mutations, or cancer due to hallucinogens.

Use of peyote cactus in small amounts as a sacrament, only by Native American Church members, is legal. Otherwise, use of hallucinogens is prohibited; hallucinogens are categorized under the Controlled Substances Act as Schedule I drugs, which includes drugs with no currently accepted medical use and/or high potential for abuse. However, the supposed insightful, epiphanous quality of hallucinogen experiences, and the vivid recall of repressed memories that occurs during use, combined with the relative lack of somatic toxicity, have led to suggested psychotherapeutic uses of hallucinogens, especially in the treatment of mental illness, including substance addiction. Sandoz marketed LSD in 1949 as an adjunct in psychoanalysis. Medical use was halted in the 1960s due to the long-term adverse psychological effects outlined above and limited evidence of therapeutic benefit. Nonetheless, psychiatric methodology has greatly improved since then, and there is renewed interest in experimentally reexamining hallucinogens (especially those other than LSD, due to LSD's reputation to produce long-lasting psychoses and HPPD) in the therapy of alcoholism and other refractory diseases. For example, though ibogaine itself may not be used therapeutically in the US due to its neurotoxicity, studies of ibogaine analogs are continuing in animal models in the search for therapeutic agents that are not neurotoxic. Investigators are seeking to determine if it is possible to develop a therapeutic hallucinogen, novel or old, whose benefits outweigh its risks in selected patients.

REFERENCES

Abraham, H. D., Aldridge, A. M., & Gogia, P. (1996). The psychopharmacology of hallucinogens. *Neuropsychopharmacology, 14,* 285–298.

Glennon, R. A. (1996). Classical hallucinogens. In C. R. Schuster & M. J. Kuhar (eds.), *Pharmacological Aspects of Drug Dependence* (Handbook of experimental pharmacology, vol. 18; pp. 343–371). Berlin: Springer.

Hofmann, A. (1980). *LSD: My Problem Child.* New York: Mc-Graw-Hill.

Marek, G. J., & Aghajanian, G. K. (1998). Indoleamine and the phenethylamine hallucinogens: Mechanisms of psychotomimetic action. *Drug and Alcohol Dependence, 51,* 189–198.

Sanders-Bush, E. (1994). "Neurochemical evidence that hallucinogenic drugs are 5-HT$_{1C}$ receptor agonists: What next?" In G. C. Lin & R. A. Glennon (eds.), *Hallucinogens: An update* (National Institute on Drug Abuse Research Monograph No. 146, NIH Publication No. 94–3782; pp. 203–213). Washington: Government Printing Office.

SUGGESTED READING

Hanson, G. R., & Venturelli, P. J. (1997). *Drugs and Society* (5th ed.). Sudbury, MA: Jones and Bartlett.

Pellerin, C. (1996). *Trips: How Hallucinogens Work in Your Brain.* New York: Seven Stories.

J. Frankenheim
G. Lin
National Institutes of Health

AMPHETAMINE EFFECTS
MARIJUANA
NEUROCHEMISTRY
PSYCHOPHARMACOLOGY
STIMULANTS

HALO EFFECT

The halo effect is the tendency of a rater to evaluate an individual high on many traits because of a belief that the individual is high on one trait: The rated trait seems to have a spillover effect on other traits. The halo effect was first empirically supported by Thorndike in "A Constant Error on Psychological Ratings" (1920).

The halo effect is detrimental to rating systems because it masks the presence of individual variability across different rating scales. Many suggestions have been made to cope with it, as for instance rating all people on one trait before going to the next, varying the anchors of the scale, pooling raters with equal knowledge, and giving intensive training to the raters. The latter technique seems to be the most effective and frequently used approach to counter this effect.

Closely related to the halo effect is the so-called devil effect, whereby a rater evaluates an individual low on many traits because of a belief that the individual is low on one trait assumed to be critical. The halo (or devil) effect usually increases to the extent that the rated trait is vague, difficult to measure, or seen as a subset of another rated trait.

REFERENCES

Thorndike, E. L. (1920). A constant error on psychological ratings. *Journal of Applied Psychology, 4,* 25–29.

L. Berger
Clemson University

RATING SCALES

HANDEDNESS

Handedness refers to the dominance of one hand over the other for writing, manual skills, and activities. Hand preference, a complexity, also involves the eyes and speech. The left cerebral hemisphere of the brain controls the operation of the right hand, rightward eye turning, and speech, whereas the right hemisphere monitors the left hand, left eye turning, and spatial and temporal tasks (Figure 1).

It is estimated that 90% of the world's population prefers to use the right hand. The mystery of universal right-hand preference prompts many different theoretical explanations, such as: (a) Soldiers fight for survival with their weapons in their right hands and protect their hearts with shields in their left hands; (b) mothers bottle-feed their infants on their left arms in order to free their right

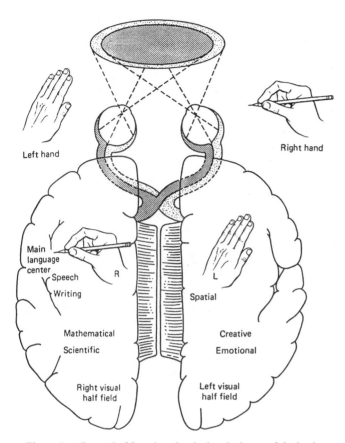

Figure 1.   Control of functions by the hemispheres of the brain.

speaking can interfere while one is simultaneously writing with the right hand (Restak, 1979). When we speak (using the left brain), we detect things in our right field of vision, but may miss something in the left field. People who are prone to move their eyes leftward (using the right brain) were reported to have almost twice as many psychosomatic symptoms as rightward movers (Restak, 1979).

The brain's left hemisphere also controls the movements of the right hand, and is the speech center of approximately 98% of right-handers and more than 50% of left-handers. The left brain then controls both written and spoken language. The preeminence of the left hemisphere for speech—a peculiarly human activity—is necessary for communication and ultimately for the survival of the human species. Specialization of the left brain for speech occurs as early as the fetal stage, and speech registers in the newborn just 12 hours after birth. These findings suggest that there is an inborn biological tendency for speech. Springer and Deutsch (1981) have speculated that symbolic speech evolved in the left hemisphere after the gesturing by the right hand provided a foundation for communication.

There is the possibility that right-handedness, like speech, is also genetic in origin, or that handedness is a product of learning, inasmuch as children learn to meet the expectations of a right-handed society by relying on that hand. Yet instead of either extreme, it may be a combination of hereditary potential coupled with environmental stimulation that accounts for handedness, though the question of how much each factor contributes remains unanswered.

One can tell that a person is employing the left hemisphere by watching to see if the eyes move rightward when talking. It is possible to discover the left-hander who is using the language center in the left brain when he or she writes holding the left hand in a hooked or inverted position—that is, when the left-hander thinks like a right-hander. (For typical writing postures, see Figure 2.) The

hands for work and other activities; (c) mothers place their infants on their left arms so they can hear the mothers' heartbeats; (d) the visceral distribution of the body favors the right side (Springer & Deutsch, 1981).

Right-hand dominance may be traced back to the cave dwellers. Animal precursors to humans were left-handed, according to anthropological evidence (Napier, 1980). There is conjecture that the evolutionary change from left-hand to right-hand dominance evolved when tools were invented: The operation of a tool incorporates an active right hand together with a supportive left hand.

We can see a parallel between the history of the human race and human development. Infants are known to employ two different grips. The one-year-old usually grips an object and performs an action with the right hand, while the left hand is used for a holding grip. The operating hand that eventually will be preferred may be discovered as early as 4 weeks of age, when the infant lying on the back assumes a fencing-like position. The head is turned to the preferred side, toward which the hand and arm are extended, while the opposite arm is crooked. Gesell (1950) spoke of this fencing position as fundamental to eye-hand coordination.

Gesell referred to an active eye and a subordinate eye. The right eye is usually dominant, and the visual stimuli in the right field of vision, including the right hand, are projected onto the left hemisphere of the brain. In other words, the right eye and right hand work together.

However, cooperation does not always exist. Kinsbourne reportedly found that several competing activities originating in the same hemisphere may interfere with one another. For example,

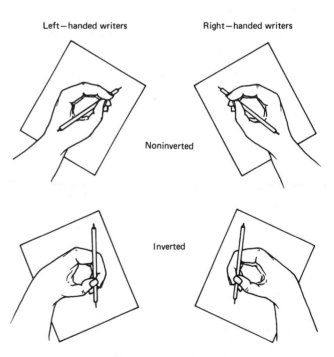

Figure 2.   Typical writing postures.

left-hander who speaks and moves the eyes leftward or who writes in a noninverted fashion is employing the right brain for both written and spoken language.

Since approximately 40% of left-handers have speech centers in their right brains, it is suggested that left- and right-handers perceive their respective environments differently. A small proportion of left-handers have speech centers in both sides of the brain. The bilateral distribution of speech in the brain may result in superior abilities for those left-handers. The close connection between intellectual and verbal abilities has been long established. Left-handers who have made their mark in history include Leonardo da Vinci, Michelangelo, Benjamin Franklin, Babe Ruth, and Harry Truman. Left-handers account for about 10% of the world's population and are growing in number. The growth may be due, in part, to the elimination of prejudices against left-handers (Barsley, 1979), and diminished attempts to change left-handedness by force.

If left-handness is a puzzle, ambidextrousness is a bigger riddle. Are there people who skillfully employ both hands equally well in all tasks? For example, a switch hitter in baseball will throw the ball more adeptly with one favored hand. It would appear that, even among the ambidextrous, one hand still prevails in certain tasks.

Instead of viewing people as strictly right- or left-handed, contemporary researchers view them as using predominantly the lead hand in certain activities and the opposite hand in others. Brown refers to 10 tests to determine which hand is the lead hand: writing; striking a match; sweeping a broom; drawing; taking a lid off a box; using a spoon, a knife, and scissors; throwing; and brushing the teeth (Brown, 1979).

REFERENCES

Barsley, M. (1979). *Left handed people.* North Hollywood, CA: Wilshire Books.

Brown, M. (1979). *Left handed: Right handed.* North Pomfret, VT: David & Charles.

Gesell, A. (1950). Infant vision. *Scientific American, 182,* 20–22.

Napier, J. (1980). *Hands.* New York: Pantheon.

Pines, M. (1973). *The brain changers.* New York: Harcourt Brace Jovanovich.

Restak, R. M. (1979). *The brain: The last frontier.* Garden City, NY: Doubleday.

Springer, S. P., & Deutsch, G. (1981). *Left brain, right brain.* San Francisco: Freeman.

SUGGESTED READING

Blakeslee, T. R. (1980). *The right brain.* Garden City, NY: Anchor Press/Doubleday.

Calder, N. (1970). *The mind of man.* New York: Viking Press.

Ornstein, R. E. (Ed.). (1973). *The nature of human consciousness: A book of readings.* San Francisco: Freeman.

Ornstein, R. E. (1977). *The psychology of consciousness* (2nd ed.). New York: Harcourt Brace Jovanovich. (Original work published 1972)

Samples, R. E. (1975). Learning with the whole brain. *Human Behavior, 4,* 16–23.

S. S. Brown
North Shore Community College

BRAIN LATERALITY
HUMAN DEVELOPMENT

HANDICAPS

A handicap is a constellation of physical, mental, psychological, and/or social properties or processes that complicate or compromise a person's adaptation, such that optimal development and functioning are not achieved. Although other terms such as disability or impairment are often used interchangeably, there has been a call for greater precision to decrease the stigmatization of individuals with various conditions. To that end, the World Health Organization (WHO) distinguishes the terms *impairment, disability,* and *handicap,* based on the manifestation of the disorder at the organic, whole person, and societal levels. Thus, handicap refers specifically to the effect of a condition on an individual's functioning in a particular setting or situation. For example, a paraplegic woman may be greatly handicapped on the dance floor, but she would not be handicapped at all in an office setting that is wheelchair accessible. A handicap is the limitation imposed by social and psychological reactions to the condition, both those of the disabled individual and those of others. We maintain that a disability does not necessarily imply a handicap.

To further understand the importance of this distinction, it is useful to consider handicaps that may be associated less with an impairment, defect, or disability than with an individual difference. For instance, consider individual differences in visual functioning. Individuals vary in terms of nearsightedness and farsightedness. Such visual impairment is often corrected with contact lenses or eyeglasses. An individual would be handicapped only if self-image were impaired, activity were restricted, visual information were distorted, or if others devalued the person for the impairment or prosthesis. At the same time, it is possible that none of these "handicaps" would enter into the individual's adaptation because vision problems are so common and so well accepted in our culture. It is easy to see how the same disability might be much more handicapping in a developing society where corrective lenses are unavailable.

Two major approaches to conceptualizing handicaps will illustrate the complexity of the transformation of a disability into a handicap. The dominant approach in both the professional and lay culture uses disease and illness metaphors to account for the individual differences or deviance represented by the disability. The disability is a negative property which sets the individual apart from "normal" people and requires medically oriented interventions such as diagnosis and treatment. Thus, there is something wrong with the individual who is seen as needing treatment aimed toward "curing," rehabilitating, or at least ameliorating the disability.

This medical orientation predominates in current professional practice and public policy. Its bias is inherent in most major classification systems currently available for categorizing disabilities and handicaps. For instance, the Federal Rehabilitation Act of 1973, Section 504, uses the term "handicap" to refer to a range of conditions including speech, hearing, visual, and orthopedic impairments, cerebral palsy, epilepsy, muscular dystrophy, multiple sclerosis, cancer, diabetes, heart diseases, mental retardation, emotional or psychiatric disorders, drug or alcohol addiction, and specific learning disabilities such as perceptual handicaps, dyslexia, minimal brain dysfunction, and developmental aphasia. Other dimensions critical to include in the classification of handicapping conditions are indications of severity (mild, moderate, severe, profound), as well as acknowledgement of common overlapping or co-existing disabilities, as implied in notions of the multiply handicapped individual. Further, the particular domain in which the handicap presents can be indicated in a classification schema, as in the concept of educational handicaps—conditions that interfere with a child's academic achievement but have limited impact in other settings, such as on the baseball field.

An alternative approach to conceptualizing handicaps considers the handicap a social construction rather than an inherent property or trait of the disabled individual. This approach maintains that a handicap is a social condition, created by society. A person's bodily or behavioral condition becomes a handicap only to the extent that other people, or the individuals themselves, define it as both distinctive and undesirable. This labeling implies unattractiveness, incompetence, or both. The result of this social definition is to create distinctive environments and behaviors which sequentially remove the person further and further from normal life patterns and, in time, convince all concerned that the person truly is handicapped.

Because most persons sense the serious social consequences of being different, they exert great effort to avoid being seen as different by those whom they value. When they are known to be different, they exert great effort to cover their differences—that is, to remove them from the focus of negative attention. These attempts to pass and cover, along with the substantial creations of society to cope with those who are different, provide extensive evidence for the need to examine handicaps as social conditions. Finally, this approach suggests directions for prevention and treatment of handicaps—directions that are antithetical to the current approaches of our educational and rehabilitation agencies, which require diagnosis or labeling in order to obtain services necessary to avoid turning a disability into a handicap.

Approaching handicaps as social constructions leads quickly to drawing parallels between handicapped persons and other minority or disadvantaged groups. Discrimination or prejudice against disabled individuals thus becomes a counterpart to racism and sexism as a powerful force in our society, whether in its individual, institutional, explicit, or implicit forms. Important implications for the development of disabled individuals and for the transformation of disabilities into handicaps are addressed by the 1980 Report of the Carnegie Council on Children, *The Unexpected Minority: Handicapped Children in America* (Gliedman & Roth, 1980).

The civil rights movement of the past three decades has recently made headway in increasing our society's awareness of and responsiveness to handicapped people. A variety of legislation and court decisions have moved our society in the direction of more humanitarian and pluralistic approaches to the disabled and handicapped. The Rehabilitation Act of 1973, the Education for All Handicapped Children Act (Public Law 94–142), and the Americans with Disabilities Act of 1994 represent this major thrust toward guaranteeing educational, civil, and human rights for handicapped individuals and specifying governmental obligations for ensuring advantages for their psychological as well as physical well-being. Under the Americans with Disabilities Act, failing fully to include individuals with disabilities is forbidden, with civil penalties for individuals and institutions that discriminate based on disability or handicap.

Concepts and policies such as *deinstitutionalization, mainstreaming, inclusion,* and *normalization* form the basis of these approaches. Deinstitutionalization refers to efforts to remove handicapped individuals from institutional and segregated settings and provide for their special needs in the community. This involves mainstreaming individuals into the least restrictive settings, thereby increasing their opportunity for optimal and normalized development. Inclusion is a newer version of mainstreaming which may include the disabled child from the onset, rather than separating the individual for some period of time and then reintegrating after some period of remediation. Normalization is a similar concept applied beyond educational settings, which emphasizes keeping disabled individuals fully integrated to the greatest possible extent, with the goal of normalizing their experiences.

SUGGESTED READING

Gleidman, J. and Roth W. (1980). *The unexpected minority: handicapped children in America.* NY: Harcourt Brace Jovavovitch.

Goffman, E. (1963). *Stigma: Notes on the Management of Spoiled Identity.* Englewood Cliffs, NY: Prentice Hall.

Marinelli, R. and Dell Orto, A. (1999). *The psychological and social impact of disability.* NY: Springer.

Seligman, M. and Darling, R. (1997). *Ordinary families, special children: A systems approach to childhood disability.* NY: Guilford.

Wright, B. (1960). *Physical disability: A psychological approach.* NY: Harper.

D. L. WERTLIEB
Tufts University

D. S. SPETTER
New England Medical Center

HAWTHORNE EFFECT

The Hawthorne effect is named for a series of studies conducted from the late 1920s through the 1930s at the Western Electric Company's Hawthorne Works near Chicago. Many textbooks cite these studies as central in the historical development of industrial/organizational psychology. Introductory textbooks and experimental methods texts discuss the Hawthorne effect, although only rarely is reasonable attention given to the overall scope of this research program. Stated in its simplest form, the Hawthorne effect suggests that any workplace change, such as a research study, makes people feel important and thereby improves their performance.

Much of the credit for the Hawthorne studies is often given to Roethlisberger and Dickson, who in 1939 published a major book describing the research. As described by them, the Hawthorne studies had five distinct research phases: the illumination experiments, the relay assembly test room experiments, the mass interviewing program, the bank wiring observation room experiments, and the program of personnel counseling (Cass & Zimmer, 1975).

The illumination experiments had the initial purpose of relating levels of lighting to worker productivity. A number of specific studies were done, but no clear functional relationship could be found between the two variables. Indeed, throughout these illumination studies, the researchers attempted to improve experimental control, apparently believing a well-designed study would answer their question.

The second major phase of the Hawthorne studies was an attempt at studying workers' performance under carefully controlled conditions. For this reason, five employees were selected and isolated in a separate room, along with a layout operator (i.e., a person who assigns work) and a research observer. In this setting a number of experiments were done, mostly focusing on differing schedules of rest breaks. Although it is often reported that all experimental conditions in the relay assembly test room led to improved production over the preceding condition, such an interpretation is misleading. Two individuals showed a general tendency to improve production; one showed steady production overall; but two others showed generally decreasing production and so were replaced by more "cooperative" employees. Clearly, the overall trend for improved production does not necessarily apply to individual workers.

At the completion of the relay assembly test room studies, the researchers began to realize that more was involved than the physical conditions of work. Specifically, it was apparent that the social impact of the research was far greater than the impact of changes in lighting or rest breaks. To clarify this issue, the mass interviewing program was begun. In the following years over 20,000 employees were interviewed.

The fourth phase of the Hawthorne studies grew out of the mass interviewing program. Given the importance of social groups in the workplace, the bank wiring observation room studies were designed as an intensive investigation of such groups. To do this, 14 men were observed and interviewed for over six months; this produced a wealth of data on work groups.

Finally, the fifth phase involved an extensive program of personnel counseling. Counselors were employed who could be approached by employees and confided in as impartial agents. With the opening of such communication channels, supervisors could be assisted in improving their behavior. In general, the researchers reported a number of improvements in intraorganizational communication.

A simplistic view of the Hawthorne effect is unwarranted.

Clearly, not everything the experimenters tried led to improved productivity, though the Hawthorne effect is often described in precisely such terms. What is clear, however, is that changes in lighting or rest breaks could not by themselves explain changes in employee performance.

Given the apparent complexity of the Hawthorne effect, a number of people have tried to clarify its nature. Kahn (1975) has pointed out that the Hawthorne effect cannot be counted on to emerge from all research studies. His analysis suggests that worker participation in important decisions plays a major role in eliciting the effect.

Another approach is taken by Parsons, who suggests that principles of operant conditioning and reinforcement can best explain the results of the Hawthorne studies (Parsons, 1974). In this view, day-to-day feedback is critical in shaping the behavior of workers, combined with an appropriate reward structure.

A third view of the Hawthorne studies was given by Bramel and Friend (1981), who suggest that traditional interpretations of these studies rely on the unjustified assumption of capitalist philosophy. Their analysis criticizes the studies from a socialist perspective and suggests that the traditional interpretation is a "myth."

In a recent paper, Gottfredson (1996) has shown that there are actually ways to increase the likelihood of obtaining the Hawthorne effect. In his work, he notes that many action researchers have the goal of bringing about positive changes in such measures as performance, and by using goals and feedback, and removing obstacles to performance, positive change is indeed more likely.

Regardless of one's personal theoretical orientation, it is clear that the Hawthorne studies constitute an important milestone in industrial/organizational psychology. Certainly, a wealth of data were collected, and while long recognized as not the "acme of perfection" (Blum, 1949), the studies are still important to consider.

REFERENCES

Bramel, D. and Friend, R. (1981). Hawthorne, the myth of the docile worker, and class bias in psychology. *American Psychologist, 36,* 867–878.

Blum, M. L. (1949). *Industrial psychology and its social foundations.* New York: Harper.

Cass, E. L. and Zimmer, F. G. (Eds.). (1975). *Man and work in society.* New York: Van Nostrand Reinhold.

Gottfredson, G. D. (1996). The Hawthorne misunderstanding (and how to get the Hawthorne effect in action research). *Journal of Research in Crime and Delinquency, 33*(1), 28–48.

Kahn, R. L. (1975). In search of the Hawthorne effect. In E. L. Cass and F. G. Zimmer (Eds.), *Man and work in society.* New York: Van Nostrand Reinhold.

Parsons, H. M. (1974). What happened at Hawthorne? *Science, 183,* 922–932.

Roethlisberger, F. J. and Dickson, W. J. (1939). *Management and the worker.* Cambridge, MA: Harvard University Press.

P. G. BENSON
New Mexico State University

INDUSTRIAL PSYCHOLOGY
ORGANIZATIONAL PSYCHOLOGY

HEALY, WILLIAM (1869–1963)

William Healy came to the United States from the United Kingdom as a child. He received his undergraduate education at Harvard College and also studied at the Harvard Medical School. He earned the degree of MD at the University of Chicago and took postgraduate work in Vienna, Berlin, and London. He held appointments in several hospitals and taught at the Northwestern University Medical School. From 1909 to 1917 he served as director of the Juvenile Psychopathic Institute in Chicago and from 1917 to 1946 as director of the Judge Baker Guidance Center in Boston.

Healy was actively involved in psychology as well as psychiatry. He developed performance tests to supplement the Stanford–Binet Intelligence Scale of which the Healy Picture Completion test is perhaps the most widely known and used. Healy made significant contributions to our understanding of delinquency and criminality and pioneered in the establishment of guidance clinics for problem children and disadvantaged youths. He was the author or coauthor of 14 books and many articles ranging over such topics as psychoanalysis, crime and delinquency, mental testing, and mortality.

P. E. LICHTENSTEIN

HEALTH PSYCHOLOGY

Drawing upon virtually every core field within psychology, health psychology links psychology to behavioral medicine, which is an interdisciplinary field concerned with the integration of behavioral and biomedical science knowledge, the development of behavioral intervention techniques relevant to health and illness, and the application of this knowledge to prevention, diagnosis, treatment, and rehabilitation.

Though health psychology as a distinct discipline is relatively new (it was recognized in 1980 by the establishment of Division 38, Health Psychology, in the American Psychological Association), its roots are as old and as varied as psychology itself. The first symposium on health psychology was held by the American Psychological Association in 1911, dealing with the role of psychology in medical education.

A major focus of health psychology is upon the training of health care personnel, accounting in part for the growth of behavioral science curricula and appointments of psychologists in medical schools and related settings. Because the field of health psychology is much older than its recognition as a subspecialty, there are a number of related disciplines which fall under this heading. Medical psychology, a subspecialty of clinical psychology, emphasizes professional practice and service delivery to patients with physical illness. Practitioners emphasize mental health related concerns, and they are frequently found in general or teaching hospitals, often as part of a consultation-liaison psychiatry service. The influence of psychotherapeutic intervention upon the course, outcome, and costs of a variety of physical illnesses is well documented. Initially, psychologists were frequently consulted by physicians for assistance in treating so-called "psychosomatic" illness, or diseases presumed to be caused by emotional or psychological factors such as asthma or nonspecific gynecological complaints. Because empirical investigations conducted by health psychologists failed to support a psychogenic etiology for many of the conditions which were hypothetically linked to psychopathology or personality, more integrated biopsychosocial conceptualizations of health and illness have largely replaced the psychosomatic model, recognizing the role of emotional or psychological factors in virtually all illness or health.

Health professionals across disciplines have recognized that the morbidity and mortality rates in the developed world are no longer related to the infectious diseases prevalent at the turn of the century. Instead, they are related to chronic disorders of our lifestyles. Thus, health care providers are more concerned with obesity, stress, and alcohol, tobacco, and substance abuse as contributors to declining health. Heart disease, asthma, HIV, hepatitis, Type II (adult-onset) diabetes, and cancer all are related to specific health behaviors. Furthermore, health professionals across disciplines are being called upon to address the "new morbidity" or problems which are heavily or primarily psychosocial in origin, such as child abuse, domestic violence, learning disorders, and stress disorders. These issues are not ultimately medical problems at all: They are behavior problems, requiring the alteration of characteristic response patterns and, thus, fall squarely within the province of psychology.

Changes in the health care delivery system in the US with the rise of managed care have pressured health providers to document the effectiveness of their interventions rather than relying on clinical lore and professional consensus to dictate practice parameters. Health psychologists are at the forefront in the assessment of health outcomes and the creation of treatment guidelines which are scientifically validated. In fact, it has been suggested that the only meaningful health outcomes are behavioral outcomes; that is, what is a treated individual capable of doing that he or she could not do without intervention (Johnson, 1994).

Pediatric psychology, another aspect of health psychology, was first described as a "marriage" between pediatricians and psychologists. Psychologists within this subfield work in close collaboration with pediatric health providers around meeting the developmental and health needs of children and families in service delivery, training, and research. Rehabilitation psychology is another specialization of psychologists in health care settings which finds health psychology a hospitable conceptual framework. Most often involved in assessing, counseling, or treating patients with chronic disorders or congenital or acquired physical disabilities, psychologists in rehabilitation settings contribute significantly to the profession and science of health psychology. Their collaboration with professionals in rehabilitation medicine and allied health services (e.g., nursing, physical therapy, occupational therapy) represents one of the major interdisciplinary links in the field.

Psychoneuroimmunology is the study of the relationships among psychological and behavioral factors and the body's ability to mount an immune response and effectively fight diseases. This field includes applications such as the relationship between environmental stress and a person's propensity to develop acute illnesses such as upper respiratory infections and viral illnesses, and the use of psychosocial and biobehavioral interventions such as meditation, stress management, and exercise to fight serious diseases such as cancer and HIV.

This account of health psychology has emphasized the professional or applied aspects of the field. Health psychology is far from immune to the tensions between applied and basic research which characterize psychology as a whole. Thus, research in health psychology finds its theoretical roots in social psychology (social support, attitudes and health beliefs, doctor-patient communication), clinical psychology (comorbidity of medical and psychological disorders, cognitive behavioral treatments to alter health behaviors, understanding and treating substance use and abuse), developmental psychology (parents with chronic health conditions, family factors and health outcomes), psychoanalytic psychology (the impact of illness or disability on the ego or sense of self, identity issues in persons with disfiguring health conditions), behavioral psychology (classical conditioning approaches to pain and symptom control, operant approaches to gastrointestinal disorders, health behavior change), cognitive psychology and neuropsychology (brain behavior relationships, iatragenic effects of medical treatments on learning, memory, and cognitive processing) and psychobiology/psychophysiology (biofeedback).

Among the major issues faced by health psychology is training. Until recently, relatively few psychologists have been trained explicitly as health psychologists. Rather, they were trained in the traditions of the varied specialties described above, and now function as health psychologists. An increasing number of predoctoral and postdoctoral training programs specializing in health psychology have been established. Exposure to health psychology at the undergraduate and predoctoral levels is more sporadic. The prospects for the continued development of health psychology are very good, given its relevance to one of our nation's most vital resources—the health of its people.

REFERENCE

Johnson, S. B. (1994). Health behavior and health status: concepts, methods, and applications. *Journal of Pediatric Psychology, 19*(2), 129–41.

SUGGESTED READINGS

Baum, A., & Posluszny, D. M. (1999). Health psychology: Mapping biobehavioral contributions to health and illness. *Annual Review of Psychology, 50,* 137–163.

Kaplan, R. M., & Sallis, J. F., Jr. (1993). *Health and human behavior.* New York: McGraw Hill.

Roberts, M. (1995). *Handbook of pediatric psychology* (2nd Ed.). New York: Guilford.

Wedding, D. (1990). *Behavior and medicine.* St. Louis: Mosby-Year.

D. S. SPETTER
Tufts University School of Medicine

D. WERTLIEB
Tufts University

BEHAVIORAL MEDICINE
PRIMARY PREVENTION OF PSYCHOPATHOLOGY

HEBB, D. O. (1904–1985)

During his first appointment, D.O. Hebb met the problem that determined the course of his later work. Some cases of large loss of brain tissue showed little effect on intelligence as measured by IQ tests or as seen in everyday life. How could one explain a high IQ with a damaged brain? The theory of cell assemblies was proposed as an answer, and this turned out to be relevant to other problems. Experiments confirmed the importance of early experience in the growth of mind and intelligence, and at maturity, the continued need of exposure to a normal sensory environment for mental health.

STAFF

HELMHOLTZ, HERMANN VON (1821–1894)

Hermann von Helmholtz was a German physicist. He received his medical degree in Berlin, then served 7 years as an army surgeon. He studied mathematics and physics, and formulated the mathematical foundation for the law of conservation of energy. After leaving the army, Helmholtz held academic appointments over the next 30 years at Bonn, Heidelberg, and Berlin, first as a physiologist and then as a physicist.

Helmholtz published in several areas of science; of special interest to psychologists are his investigations of the speed of the neural impulse, vision, and audition. Before Helmholtz, the neural impulse was thought to be instantaneous—too fast to be measured. Helmholtz provided the first measurement of the rate of conduction with experiments using frogs; he was less successful with humans. Helmholtz demonstrated that conduction is not instantaneous, and suggested that thought and movement follow one another at a measurable interval. His research was used by other scientists in experiments on reaction time.

Helmholtz invented the ophthalmoscope in the course of his work on vision and optics. *Physiological Optics* reported this work in three volumes. He extended the theory of color vision that had originated with Thomas Young in 1802; it became known as the Young-Helmholtz theory of color vision. His research on acoustical problems resulted in *On the Sensations of Tone*. Helmholtz's work in audition included perception of combined and individual tones, the nature of harmony and discord, and his resonance theory of hearing.

Although not a psychologist, Helmholtz contributed a great body of knowledge to sensory psychology. He influenced the experimental approach to psychological problems, and his work strongly supported the development of an empirical tradition, especially in perception and sensation.

N. A. HAYNIE

HERITABILITY OF PERSONALITY

Heritability of personality traits is one of the oldest, as well as one of the most hotly debated topics of modern psychology. The roots of such theorizing can probably be traced back several thousand years to Plato, whose famous "myth of metals" in *The Republic* presupposed genetic determinants of ability:

You, citizens, are all brothers, but the God who created you has put different metals into your composition—gold into those who are fit to be rulers, silver into those who are to act as their executives, and in those whose task it will be to cultivate the soil or manufacture goods he has mixed iron or brass. Most children resemble their parents. Yet occasionally a golden parent may beget a silver child or a silver parent a child of gold; indeed, any kind of parent may at times give birth to any kind of child.

It was the ardent belief during the 18th and 19th centuries that the individual was born as a blank slate (tabula rasa) on which the environment inscribed the elaborate and detailed architectural plans for the developing personality. The human psyche, untampered by the tendrils of evil, would blossom in kindness, virtuosity, and reason. The myth of the tabula rasa was epitomized by the charge of John Stuart Mill that "of all the vulgar modes of escaping from the consideration of the effect of social and moral influence on the human mind, the most vulgar is that of attributing the diversities of conduct and character to inherent natural differences."

The 20th century witnessed the stark realities of the human propensity to turpitude. Perhaps one of the derivatives of the tumultuous sociopolitical and cultural changes during the early decades of the 20th century was a need to look inward for answers to the baffling riddles of human behavior. The change in attitude toward genetics is reflected in a quip by Abraham Myerson (c. 1930): "Environmentalists seem to believe that if cats gave birth to kittens in a stove, the offspring would be biscuits."

The pioneer in this area was actually the British experimental psychologist Francis Galton (1822–1911). Galton posed the simple, straightforward prediction that any differences between identical (monozygotic, or MZ) twins must be attributable to environment, since genetic contribution had presumably been held constant. He further argued that differences between fraternal (dizygotic, or DZ) twins could be due to either heredity or environment. Galton's assumptions, while insightful, were not entirely correct.

One of the very earliest attempts to empirically examine twin sets with regards to mental and physical characteristics was the often cited study by Newman, Freeman, and Holzinger (1937). Fifty fraternal and fifty identical twins were compared on a battery of tests. The following is the widely quoted conclusion: "the physical characteristics are least affected by the environment; intelligence is affected more; educational achievement still more; and personality or temperament, if our tests can be relied upon, the most" (p. 192). In *The Biological Basis of Personality* Eysenck pointed out that not only are there serious questions about the reliability and validity of the personality instruments used by Newman, Freeman, and Holzinger, but the tests were designed for adults, not children. Despite the apparent drawbacks, the early research was certainly foundational and served heuristic purposes.

In a series of studies beginning in the early 1960s, Gottesman compared MZ and DZ twins on scale scores from the Minnesota Multiphasic Personality Inventory (MMPI). In one study (1963), a significant amount of variance was accounted for by heritability on the social introversion scale. This was especially true for the males. In a subsequent study (1965), the results were similar though not as strong. Gottesman (1966) concluded that the combined probability for both studies taken together indicates that the component of variance attributable to genetics in social introversion was highly significant ($p < .005$). Similarly, Scarr (1969) found that more than half of the within-family variance on social introversion-extroversion (measured by Gough's Adjective Checklist and the Fels Behavior Scales) in a large sample of twin girls was accounted for by genetics. There is substantial evidence to support Scarr's conclusion that "social introversion-extroversion is a basic dimension of responsiveness to the environment. Individual differences are observable in the first years of life; it is relatively stable over the developing years; twin studies find significant genetic contributions to it; and it is constantly rediscovered as a source of individual differences in behavior" (1969, p. 831).

A longitudinal study conducted by Dworkin, Burke, Maher, and Gottesman (1976, 1977) examined the stability from adolescence into adulthood of personality traits with significant heritability. For the adolescent subsample (part of which was a follow-up of the 1966 Gottesman study), the depression, psychopathic deviate, paranoia, and schizophrenia scales of the MMPI evidenced significant heritability. This pattern did not carry over into adulthood (average age at follow-up was 27.9 years), where hypomania, the K scale, and ego strength (a research scale) showed significant heritability. Only anxiety and dependency (research scales) demonstrated evidence of significant heritability at both ages. The results for the California Psychological Inventory are similar, with only the dominance scale capturing a significant amount of genetic variance at both ages. From these data it is apparent that, while there is a significant component of heritability in the fashioning of personality, there are also considerable changes with age in which specific traits manifest signs of heritability. The investigators posited several explanations for age effects in the heritability of personality traits, one of which is that changes in genetic variance are a function of gene regulation and genotype-environment interaction and correlation. It is also possible that development is inversely correlated with genetic influence on a trait. That is, since development is most accelerated during adolescence, more traits would be under genetic control during this period. It is also apparent that the potential influence of the environment on personality is at least in part a function of time: The longer the exposure to prepotent events, the greater the probability of influence by those events.

At least one important longitudinal study did find stability in the dimension of introversion-extroversion (Kagan & Moss, 1962). These investigators followed children from birth to adulthood, discovering that the tendency to be socially inhibited was quite stable from age 10 to adulthood. In fact, there was even evidence for stability in this dimension from age 3 onward.

There are several other sources of data suggesting a heritable component in a general personality dimension of introversion-extroversion. An ambitious attempt to examine genetic contributions to personality was made by Claridge, Canter, and Hume (1973). The sample of 44 pairs of MZ twins and 51 pairs of DZ twins was subjected to an extensive battery of personality, cognitive, and psycho-physiological tests. According to the personality questionnaires, MZ twins were significantly more alike on sociability, self-criticism, and intropunitiveness, the last two traits being attributable to variations in anxiety and extroversion.

In another study Fulker, Eysenck, and Zuckerman (1980) examined the genetic and environmental contributions to sensation seeking (the trait measured by Zuckerman's Sensation-Seeking Scale) in a sample of 422 pairs of twins. The investigators found that 58% of the variance in the overall sensation-seeking score, and 69% of the reliable variance (after correcting for test unreliability), were attributable to heredity. Fulker, Eysenck, and Zuckerman noted that this heritable component is quite high for a personality trait, and that it compares favorably with the research of Eaves and Eysenck (1975), who reported that 42% of the uncorrected and 60 to 70% of the reliable variation in extroversion in 837 pairs of adult twins was attributable to genetics. Eaves and Eysenck found that the unitary trait of extroversion provided more powerful discrimination with respect to genetic and environmental determinants than either of its components—sociability and impulsivity—taken separately. As they pointed out, these data do *not* suggest what genes are involved, only that "the segregation and recombination of alleles may be a primary cause of variation" in this personality trait (1975, p. 382). Whatever gene action does control the general trait of extroversion, Fulker (1981) noted that it appears to be primarily additive. He concluded an excellent review of the literature with the following observation: "The high heritability, once unreliability is removed, the absence of common family environment, and the similarity of genetic and environmental covariance structures suggests a high, if not total, degree of constitutional determination of reliable individual variation and provides strong support for a biological theory of the origin of these traits" (1981, p. 120).

If we assume that introversion-extroversion is influenced by some genetic factor, that factor could be specific or polygenic. Most gene-determined human variability derives from polygenic effects. This amounts to the simultaneous occurrence of numerous minor aberrations that, when all lumped together, are not individually detectable. In fact, they blend into a Gaussian distribution for that trait. A polygene is something like a Mendelian major gene; it has a small multiply mediated effect on trait variation relative to all the variation observed in that trait. The expression of certain traits depends much more on the cumulative pulling power of all genes concerned than on a few unspecific genes. Hence polygenes tend to be very sensitive to environmental factors (endogenous as well as exogenous). The principle alternative to polygenes are those disorders with specific gene etiologies. Huntington's chorea, for instance, is caused by one dominant gene, though as yet we are unable to trace the pathway from the gene to its behavioral expression. Phenylketonuria (PKU) is caused by two recessive alleles, wherein a specific congenital metabolic error exists. In the case of PKU, heterozygotes can be identified biochemically, whereas in Huntington's chorea the biochemical error is unknown and unaffected heterozygotes cannot be identified.

The cases of single-gene substitution are relatively straightfor-

ward. It sometimes happens, however, that a continuous distribution of genotypes results in discrete phenotypes for certain disorders. The disorder would appear to have a continuously distributed liability, and would be manifested when some variable exceeds a threshold. The phenotypic discontinuity is not genetic, arising only when the threshold is exceeded. There are many assorted quasi-continuous disorders, such as diabetes mellitus, ulcers, and cleft palate. Some theorize that schizophrenia falls in this category.

If we wish to maintain that a personality dimension such as introversion-extroversion has a genetic component, we are in effect saying that a specific genetically coded biochemical error exists that results in the behavior labeled as introversion or extroversion. The trait itself cannot be inherited. There must be some intermediary effect, such as a genetic code, which results in a biochemical error. Such a biochemical error may result in, for example, an imbalance of the autonomic nervous system (i.e., sympathetic or parasympathetic dominance). Given what is known about the behavioral manifestations of introversion and extroversion, it is highly unlikely that it could be tied to a specific gene or, for that matter, exclusively to heredity without regard to the environment.

While research on the heritable nature of certain personality traits has yielded highly interesting and encouraging results, these data should not be misinterpreted or alternative explanations overlooked. It was noted at the beginning that Galton made a fair assumption that MZ twins are genetically identical. This assumption is less a postulate of the laws of inheritance than a hypothesis (Darlington, 1954). Darlington pointed out that intrachromosomal genetic changes (gene mutations or chromosome errors at mitosis) may result in asymmetry. Indeed, it is even possible for two sperms to fertilize the halves of one egg.

A related issue is the determination of zygosity. The similarity method is the one typically used. This method includes several possible comparisons. Objective single-gene traits such as blood type and serum protein can be used. Morphologic features such as eye color, ear shape, and nose shape can be used, though these are less reliable. Ridge counts from fingerprints have also been used to determine zygosity. The ultimate test for zygosity is skin grafting, though this is obviously impractical for research purposes. The procedure typically employed in research is that of blood grouping, though some investigators (Eaves & Eysenck, 1975) have made use of a brief questionnaire that asks about similarity during childhood. In any event, monozygosity can be determined only with a specifiable probability, never with absolute certainty (McKusick, 1964).

A cogent criticism of the twin research concerns the evidence that MZ twins are reared in a more homogeneous environment than DZ twins (Scarr, 1965; Smith, 1965). That is, some of the variance in high MZ intragroup correlations may be accounted for by highly similar environments rather than genetics. This criticism obviously does not affect the adoptee studies that examined twins reared in different homes (Shields, 1962).

Finally, the relative contribution of genetic control over personality traits may well depend on the specificity of the traits or behaviors examined. Matheny and Dolan (1980) reported that "sociability was found to be an isolable and genetically influenced factor, but its relations with other factors of a social nature did not produce any evidence for a strong link between actions toward others and actions taken to be with others, a distinction between the quality and quantity of social interactions." Similarly, a study by Horn, Plomin, and Rosenman (1976) found certain aspects of sociability to be genetically influenced (conversational poise, compulsiveness, and social ease), while other aspects were more environmentally influenced (leadership confidence, impulse control, and social exhibitionism). The investigators concluded that while most definitions of sociability imply gregariousness or the need to be with people, their factor derived from genetic items was quite specific and limited to talking with strangers.

The question raised here boils down to what aspect of the organization of personality or of a particular trait of personality is genetically controlled. The problem we face is precisely that explored by the brilliant Russian-American geneticist Theodosius Dobzhansky—namely, separating genetic fixity from phenotypic plasticity. Dobzhansky maintained "that an essential feature of human evolution which has made our species unique has been the establishment of a genetically controlled plasticity of personality traits. This plasticity has made man educable and has made human culture and society possible" (1960, p. 52). Were we able to hold development constant, observed variance in personality traits would reflect genotypic variability. In reality, development is unique for every individual. Hence, variance in personality traits unequivocally reflects environmental factors. The question, then, is to what extent we inherit constitutional factors that influence the acquisition of certain personality traits. If something akin to parasympathetic dominance is inherited, there is in effect a predisposition to behavior patterns that are labeled "extroversion" (and the panoply of traits associated with it).

REFERENCES

Claridge, G. S., Canter, S., & Hume, W. I. (1973). *Personality differences and biological variations: A study of twins.* Oxford: Pergamon.

Darlington, C. D. (1954). Heredity and environment. Proceedings of the IX International Congress of Genetics. *Caryologia,* 370–381.

Dobzhansky, T. (1960). *The biological basis of freedom.* New York: Columbia University Press.

Dworkin, R. H., Burke, B. W., Maher, B. A., & Gottesman, I. I. (1977). Genetic influences on the organization and development of personality. *Developmental Psychology, 13,* 164–165.

Dworkin, R. H., Burke, B. W., Maher, B. A., & Gottesman, I. I. (1976). A longitudinal study of the genetics of personality. *Journal of Personality and Social Psychology, 34,* 510–518.

Eaves, L., & Eysenck, H. (1975). The nature of extraversion: A genetical analysis. *Journal of Personality and Social Psychology, 32,* 102–112.

Eysenck, H. J. (1967). *The biological basis of personality.* Springfield, IL: Thomas.

Fulker, D. W. (1981). The genetic and environmental architecture of psychoticism, extraversion and neuroticism. In H. Eysenck (Ed.), *A model for personality.* New York: Springer-Verlag.

Fulker, D. W., Eysenck, S. B. G., & Zuckerman, M. (1980). A genetic and environmental analysis of sensation seeking. *Journal of Research in Personality, 14,* 261–281.

Horn, J. M., Plomin, R., & Rosenman, R. (1976). Heritability of personality traits in adult male twins. *Behavior Genetics, 6,* 17–30.

Kagan, J., & Moss, H. A. (1962). *Birth to maturity.* New York: Wiley.

Matheny, A. P., & Dolan, A. B. (1980). A twin study of personality and temperament during middle childhood. *Journal of Research in Personality, 14,* 224–234.

Newman, H. H., Freeman, F. N., & Holzinger, K. J. (1937). *Twins.* Chicago: University of Chicago Press.

Plato. (1973). *The republic and other works.* Garden City, NY: Anchor Books.

Scarr, S. (1965). *The inheritance of sociability.* Presented at the annual meeting of the American Psychological Association.

Scarr, S. (1969). Social introversion-extraversion as a heritable response. *Child Development, 40,* 823–832.

Shields, J. (1962). *Monozygotic twins.* Oxford: Oxford University Press.

Smith, R. T. (1965). A comparison of socio-environmental factors in monozygotic and dyzygotic twins. In S. G. Vandenberg (Ed.), *Methods and goals in human behavior genetics.* New York: Academic.

R. A. PRENTKY
Justice Resource Institute

HERITABILITY

INSTINCT

HERMENEUTICS

Hermeneutics is a broad-based intellectual movement that has sought to redress the dominance of scientific modes of thinking within modern culture. Hermeneutic thinkers have attempted to critique the positivist worldview that takes natural science and mathematics as the standards by which all knowledge claims must be evaluated. The common thread that unites diverse hermeneutic positions is a humanistic opposition to scientism and positivism and the attempt to supply philosophical, cultural, and methodological correctives to objectivism and mechanism—the perspectives that have dominated the social sciences and mental health professions. Recently, the discussion of hermeneutic views has become widespread in the social sciences and the humanities. Clinical psychology and psychiatry have begun to feel the impact as the methods, theories, and philosophical underpinnings that have predominated within these disciplines have come under hermeneutically-inspired criticism.

The word "hermeneutic" derives originally from Hermes, the messenger of the Greek gods. It came to be used in the eighteenth century to refer to methods of Biblical and judicial interpretation (in other words, procedures that allowed ascertaining the meaning of various texts).

We owe to Dilthey (1989) our modern definition of hermeneutics. Dilthey contrasted the approaches of the natural sciences with what he termed the human sciences, *Geisteswissenschaften.* According to Dilthey the natural sciences seek to explain phenomena by objectifying them and subsuming them under general laws that allow for prediction (and sometimes for control). However, disciplines that study human beings, because of the nature of their subject matter, aim at understanding rather than explanation. For Dilthey, understanding of social and psychological reality is achieved through the interpretation of human action in a fashion analogous to textual interpretation. The behavior of another person is a text-analog that must be comprehended and elucidated by the interpreter.

Hermeneutic views are reflected in various approaches within the social sciences, especially those that emphasize the understanding of subjective meanings (*Verstehen*). The sociology of Weber, the phenomenological sociology of Schutz, Garfinkel's ethnomethodology, and the anthropology of Geertz are examples of approaches to the human sciences that have been influenced by hermeneutics. On the contemporary scene, hermeneutics has been used as a justification for employing qualitative methods utilized in naturalistic settings, as contrasted with the quantitative methods and the emphasis on controlled experimental study within mainstream behavioral science.

Within clinical psychology and psychiatry, hermeneutics has had great influence on the conceptualization of psychotherapy. Habermas and Ricouer, two philosophers, were among the first to reconceptualize psychotherapy (psychoanalysis) as a hermeneutic endeavor. Habermas argues that Freud's original conceptualization of psychoanalysis as an applied science fell prey to a "scientistic misunderstanding" of his creation that obscured its true status as a depth hermeneutic that is fundamentally analogous to the Socratic dialogue, wherein reasoned self-reflection can yield enlightenment and reprieve from the constraints and impairments of false opinion. Psychoanalysis, thus conceived, is a hermeneutical endeavor that allows for a decoding of the distortions that result from the activity of psychic defenses. Ricoeur (1970) also views psychoanalysis as an interpretive discipline whose subject matter is human intentionality, or in his phrase, "the semantics of desire." Human action is seen as a text-analog, more appropriate as an object of hermeneutic inquiry than the reductionistic explanatory efforts of mainstream behavioral science. Recent applications of hermeneutics to psychotherapy have extended the work of Habermas and Ricoeur and have been part of a postmodern trend in psychotherapy that abjures the epistemological criteria for truth that have characterized the Western tradition since the Greeks.

The writings of Schafer (1981) have radically revised Freud's metaphor of the psychoanalyst as a psychic archeologist in search of objective historical truth. Schafer has stated that psychoanalytic interpretation is fundamentally an act of narrative construction or reconstruction, akin to the constructions of literature, myth, and the visual arts. For Schafer there is no final test of truth to which such interpretative construction can be submitted.

In a similar vein, Spence provides a hermeneutic vision of psychoanalysis that contrasts two kinds of truth that can apply to therapeutic interpretations: historical and narrative. Historical truth is the conventional correspondence-based concept; the accurate reconstruction of events as they actually occurred. Narrative truth, in contrast, invokes criteria other than correspondence with objective fact. Interpretations are said to possess narrative truth if they meet the criteria of coherence, aesthetic appeal, and pragmatic efficacy in the context of therapy. Narrative truth makes no appeal to correspondence with reality, but rather suggests that validity is relative to what makes a patient's life understandable and produces therapeutic benefits.

A number of recent writers who have followed the trail blazed by Spence and Schafer (Gergen & Kaye, 1992; Neimeyer, 1993; White & Epston, 1990) have tended to move in a postmodern direction toward epistemological relativism and social constructionism. The postmodern trend within psychotherapy is opposed to attempts to privilege any therapeutic narrative, and further aims to dispense with truth as a criterion for the various conclusions reached by client and therapist over a course of therapeutic treatment. For postmodern therapists there is little authority an interpretation can possess beyond its power to reframe events such that people come to feel better about themselves or to act in "healthier" ways. As the constructivists would put it, the client's problem is "restoried," or made part of a new narrative that has the power to improve the client's problem. This is about all there is to therapy, and all therapists should be concerned with—to find the right narrative, the one that makes the problem better.

Postmodern perspectives have been criticized both from the perspective of mainstream science (Held, 1995) but also from a hermeneutic perspective (Woolfolk, 1998). The hermeneutic criticism of postmodern trends charges that they sacrifice a key historical aim of hermeneutics, that of establishing the validity of interpretation in intellectual realms where certainty is difficult to achieve. Although hermeneutics, along with postmodernism, recognizes that what is studied by the human sciences is often subjective and value-laden, its response is not a retreat to epistemological relativism. Rather, hermeneutics advocates interdisciplinary inquiry and methodological pluralism in the service of a richer, more complex, and, ultimately, more valid understanding of the human existence.

REFERENCES

Dilthey, W. (1989). *Selected works. Vol. 1.* in R. A. Makkreel & F. Rodi (Eds.) (R. A. Makkreel, M. Neville, & F. Schreiner, Trans.) Princeton: Princeton University Press.

Gergen, K. J., & Kaaye, J. (1992). Beyond narrative in the negotiation of therapeutic meaning. In S. McNamee & K. J. Gergen (Eds.), *Therapy as social construction* (pp. 166–185). Newbury Park, CA: Sage.

Held, B. S. (1995). *Back to reality: A critique of postmodern theory in psychotherapy.* New York: W. W. Norton.

Neimeyer, R. A. (1993). An appraisal of constructivist psychotherapies. *Journal of Consulting and Clinical Psychology, 61,* 221–234.

Ricoeur, P. (1970). *Freud and philosophy: An essay on interpretation.* (D. Savage, Trans.) New Haven: Yale University Press.

Schafer, R. (1981). *Narrative actions in psychoanalysis.* Worcester, MA: Clark University.

Spence, D. (1982). *Narrative truth and historical truth.* New York: W. W. Norton & Co.

White, M., & Epston, D. (1990). *Narrative means to therapeutic ends.* New York: W. W. Norton.

Woolfolk, R. L. (1998). *The cure of souls: Science, values, and psychotherapy.* San Francisco: Jossey-Bass.

R. L. WOOLFOLK
Rutgers University

HETEROSEXUALITY

SEXUAL BEHAVIOR

The idea that sex is strictly for reproduction has deep historical roots in Western culture. Early Christian writers such as Thomas Aquinas promoted the view of sex as sinful, justifiable only in marriage for the purpose of procreation. Greater knowledge, technical advances in contraception, media awareness, and legal decisions have allowed people to separate sexuality from procreation and make personal decisions regarding sexuality. Variations in ethnicity, acculturation, religious orthodoxy, and socioeconomic status account for great diversity in sexuality. Human sexual behaviors cluster primarily around kissing and touching, intercourse (vaginal and anal), oral-genital stimulation, and masturbation. Atypical sexual behaviors, those behaviors that fall outside this range, include noncoercive paraphilias such as fetishism, transvestism, sexual sadism, and sexual masochism, and coercive paraphilias such as exhibitionism, voyeurism, frotteurism, necrophilia, and zoophilia. Because paraphilic behaviors are typically a source of intense sexual pleasure, individuals are generally reluctant to seek treatment and psychotherapy has not proven to be highly effective.

SEXUAL RESPONSE

Stages

Masters and Johnson (1966) describe the physiological sexual response patterns of both men and women as occurring in four phases: excitement, plateau, orgasm, and resolution. The primary markers of the excitement phase in both sexes are increased myotonia (muscle tension), heart rate, blood pressure, and vasocongestion (blood engorgement) which leads to penile erection in males and engorgement of the clitoris, labia, and vagina (with lubrication) in females. The plateau phase is a period of high sexual arousal that prepares the body for potential orgasm. Orgasm is marked by peaks in blood pressure, heart rate, and respiration rate; involuntary muscle spasms throughout the body; and subjective feelings of intense pleasure. In males, orgasm generally occurs in two stages, (emission which refers to rhythmic muscular contractions which force semen into the ejaculatory ducts) and expulsion (which is the release or ejaculation of semen through the urethra). Contrary to Freud's assertion of two distinct types of orgasm in females, clitoral (the "infantile" orgasm) and vaginal (the "mature" orgasm), Masters and Johnson found no physiological differences in orgasm produced by vaginal versus clitoral stimulation. Other researchers note that intensity of orgasm and emotional satisfaction can differ dependent upon type of stimulation. Unlike males, some females (approximately 15%) are able to experience multiple (i.e., simultaneous) orgasms, and some women experience orgasm and perhaps ejaculation when the Grafenberg spot, an area along the anterior wall of the vagina, is stimulated. During the fourth stage, resolution, physiological responses return to the unaroused state. In males, there is a refractory period, a period of time in which it is physiologically impossible to achieve another orgasm. The length of the refractory period is highly variable and depends upon a number of factors including age, novelty of sexual situation, and frequency of sexual encounters. The extent to which aging affects sexual function depends largely on psychological, pharmacological, and illness-related factors. Normal age-related changes for men include greater physical stimulation to attain and maintain erections, less intense orgasms, reduced semen volume and ejaculatory force, and lengthened refractory period. In women, menopause (which occurs in most women around age 50) terminates fertility and leads to estrogen-deficient changes such as decreased vaginal lubrication, and decreases in the size and elasticity of the vagina and uterus.

Physiology

In males, about 95% of androgens (e.g., testosterone) are produced by the testes, and the remainder are produced by the outer adrenal glands. In females, androgens are produced by the ovaries and adrenal glands in quantities much lower than in males (about 20 to 40 times less; Rako, 1996). In both males and females, decreased testosterone levels due to, for example, orchidectomy (removal of testes) or oophorectomy (removal of ovaries) have been linked to impaired sexual desire. Exogenous testosterone has been successful in treating low sexual desire in males and females with abnormally low androgen levels. Raising testosterone levels above a normal range, however, has not been successful in enhancing sexual desire (Rako, 1996) and may lead to adverse side effects. In females, estrogens are predominately produced by the ovaries; in males they are produced in small quantities by the testes. Estrogens help maintain the elasticity of the vaginal lining and assist in vaginal lubrication. They have not been directly linked to sexual motivation in either males or females.

The cerebral cortex, the outer layer of the brain's cerebrum, controls higher mental processes such as sexual fantasies. Sexual arousal in males and females (and orgasm in some women) can occur strictly via brain imagery, in the absence of physical stimulation. At a subcortical level, the limbic system, in particular the hypothalamus, appears to play an important part in determining sexual responding. In males, blood flow into the penis is facilitated by innervation of the parasympathetic branch of the autonomic nervous system, and ejaculation by the sympathetic branch. In females, orgasm and possibly the initial stage of arousal appear to be facilitated by sympathetic nervous system activation.

The nerve endings that respond to touch are unevenly distributed throughout the body; locations most responsive to tactile pleasure are referred to as erogenous zones (e.g., genitals, buttocks, anus, breasts, thighs, neck, and ears). Although more men than women report being sexually aroused by visual stimuli, studies have demonstrated comparable physiological sexual responses to visual erotica. Smell and taste can act as powerful sexual stimulants, but it is unclear whether they play a biologically determined role in human sexual arousal. Animal studies have isolated various pheromones (sexual odors) that are related to sexual reproduction, but the findings from studies of this nature in humans are inconclusive.

SEXUAL DYSFUNCTION AND TREATMENT

Diseases of the neurological, vascular, and endocrine systems (e.g., diabetes, cancer, multiple sclerosis) can impair virtually any stage of the sexual response. Medications used to treat depression, high blood pressure, psychiatric disorders, and cancer, as well as numerous recreational drugs (e.g., barbiturates, narcotics, alcohol abuse, tobacco smoking) can interfere with sexual interest, arousal, and orgasm. Psychological factors contributing to impaired sexual function most commonly include anxiety, relationship concerns, negative attitudes about sex, religious inhibition, and fears of pregnancy (Masters & Johnson, 1970).

Low or absent sexual desire (hypoactive sexual desire) is the most common problem of couples going into sex therapy (Leiblum & Rosen, 1989) and the most difficult sexual problem to treat. Most treatments focus on increasing pleasure and decreasing anxiety along with couples therapy to resolve relationship problems and increase communication and intimacy. Testosterone's effectiveness in increasing sexual desire appears to be limited to men and women with abnormally low levels of testosterone. Sexual aversion disorder is an extreme, irrational fear or dislike of sexual activity.

Excitement-phase difficulties include female sexual arousal disorder (inhibition of the vasocongestive/lubrication response) and male erectile disorder. Erectile problems may be of organic (e.g., circulatory problems, neurological disorders, hormone imbalances) or psychogenic (e.g., performance anxiety) origin. The ability to have erections during REM sleep suggests the problem is psychological. Medical treatments include self-injections of drugs and vacuum devices that work to increase blood flow into the penis and, for men who have suffered permanent nerve or vascular damage, penile implants. Oral medications (e.g., Viagra), which work by relaxing smooth muscles so that blood can more readily flow into the penis, have recently become the most common treatment for erectile difficulties. Studies are underway to examine the effectiveness of such drugs in treating female arousal disorder. Psychogenic impotence has been successfully treated with therapy techniques such as sensate focus and systematic desensitization, which focus on decreasing anxiety and increasing pleasurable sensations.

Anorgasmia, the inability to attain orgasm, is the most common female dysfunction presented for sex therapy. Efficacious treatments for anorgasmia include directed masturbation, sensate focus, and desensitization. Premature ejaculation is defined as ejaculation early on in the sexual scenario and before the person wishes it. Successful treatment approaches include the "pause and squeeze" technique and the use of pharmacological agents which delay ejaculation. Dyspareunia, or pain during intercourse, occurs most commonly in females, and generally involves a combination of physical and psychological factors. Vaginismus is characterized by involuntary contractions of the muscles in the outer third of the vagina. Treatment involves repeated daily insertion of graduated dilators.

REFERENCES

Leiblum, S. R., & Rosen, R. C. (1989). *Principles and practice of sex therapy: An update for the 1990s.* New York: Guilford.

Masters, W., & Johnson, V. (1966). *Human sexual response.* Boston: Little, Brown.

Masters, W., & Johnson, V. (1970). *Human sexual inadequacy.* Boston: Little, Brown.

Rako, S. (1996). *The hormone of desire.* New York: Harmony.

C. M. MESTON
University of Texas, Austin

FEMALE SEXUALITY
MALE SEXUAL DYSFUNCTION
SEX THERAPY
SEXUAL DEVELOPMENT
SEXUALITY: ORIENTATION + IDENTITY

HIGHER ORDER CONDITIONING

Higher order conditioning refers to the use of the conditioned stimulus from one phase of an experiment (CS-1) as the uncondition stimulus (US) for further conditioning. In one demonstration reported by Pavlov, CS-1 was an auditory stimulus, while the original unconditioned stimulus was food and the conditioned response (CR) and unconditioned response (UR) were both salivation. When the CR to CS-1 had been firmly established, a black square (CS-2) was presented briefly before CS-1. On the tenth pairing of the black square and the auditory stimulus, a salivary response—about half as strong as the response to the auditory stimulus—occurred to the square. This is an example of higher order conditioning—specifically, a conditioned reflex of the second order (see Figure 1). Pavlov found third-order conditioning possible, but only with defense reflexes such as those in response to shock. Fourth-order reflexes could not be established in dogs.

Typically the higher order CRs were small in amplitude, long in latency, and had only a short life span. This last fact follows from the consideration that the higher order conditioning procedure is one in which the first-order CR is subjected to extinction: CS-1, now functioning as a US, occurs without reinforcement. Because

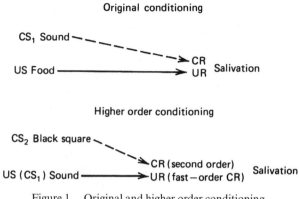

Figure 1.   Original and higher order conditioning.

of this, trials with the paired stimuli, following an early establishment of the secondary reflex, lead to its gradual disappearance.

The fact that higher order conditioning is a somewhat evanescent phenomenon does nothing to diminish its theoretical importance, which is that the reinforcement (US) in the higher order conditioning procedure obtains its reinforcing power as a result of learning. In modern terminology, the secondary conditioned reflex is established on the basis of a secondary reinforcement. The process of secondary reinforcement has been of much greater interest in the field of operant learning than in classical conditioning.

G. A. KIMBLE
Duke University

**CLASSICAL CONDITIONING
LEARNING THEORIES**

HILGARD, ERNEST R. (1905–   )

Ernest R. Hilgard graduated with honors in chemical engineering at the University of Illinois, and received the PhD (1930) in experimental psychology from Yale with a dissertation on conditioned human eyelid responses under Raymond Dodge. He became a teaching assistant and remained at Yale as an instructor from 1929 to 1933, when he accepted an invitation from Lewis M. Terman to join the faculty at Stanford University, where, except for World War II, he spent the rest of his career, becoming an emeritus professor in 1969. He held a joint appointment between the School of Humanities and the School of Education, served as executive head of the department of psychology from 1942 to 1950, and was dean of the graduate division from 1951 to 1955.

His research interests before World War II were primarily in psychology of learning and motivation, and during the war years he turned to social psychology in various agencies as a civilian in Washington. From 1957–1979, he headed a laboratory of hypnosis research within the department of psychology. He continued publishing and revising his more general books as well as publishing in the field of hypnosis. Later he turned to historical writing; his primary contribution to the field is *American Psychology: A Historical Survey.*

Hilgard was elected president of the American Psychological Association and is a member of the National Academy of Sciences, the National Academy of Education, the American Academy of Arts and Sciences, and the American Philosophical Society. He received the Gold Medal Award from the American Psychological Foundation in recognition of his lifetime contributions to psychology.

STAFF

HIPPOCAMPUS

Ever since Scoville and Milner's 1957 report of the patient H. M., who suffered a profound amnesia following bilateral surgical resection of the medial temporal lobe, it has been clear that the hippocampal region of the brain plays a critical role in memory. The hippocampus has since been prominent in efforts to explore the neural bases of memory, through investigations on anatomical pathways of the hippocampus, on the functional role of components of the hippocampal region in humans and animals, and on characterizations of the information encoded by firing patterns of hippocampal neurons. The combined findings gained from each of these directions constitute a framework for understanding the functional circuitry of the hippocampal memory system.

ANATOMY OF THE HIPPOCAMPUS

From the perspective of its role in cognition and memory, the hippocampal system is last in a long succession of stages of cortical representation (Van Hoesen, 1982). The hippocampus itself is composed of several distinct subdivisions and operates along with the immediately surrounding parahippocampal cortical region; together these structures comprise the hippocampal memory system. Neocortical areas that provide information to the hippocampal system include only the highest stages of each neocortical sensory system, plus multimodal and limbic cortical areas and the olfactory cortex. These inputs arrive in three main cortical subdivisions of the parahippocampal region: the perirhinal, parahippocampal, and entorhinal cortices. The cortical projections onto the parahippocampal region arrive in broad topographical gradients such that olfactory and prefrontal inputs terminate within rostral parts of the perirhinal and lateral entorhinal cortices, whereas parietal and temporal inputs terminate in more caudal parts of the perirhinal and lateral entorhinal cortices. Superficial layers of parts of the parahippocampal region then project onto the hippocampus itself at each of its main subdivisions.

The main flow of information through the hippocampus involves serial connections from the dentate gyrus to CA3 to CA1, and then to the subiculum (Amaral & Witter, 1989). The intrinsic hippocampal pathway partially preserves the topographical gradients of neocortical input, but there are also considerable divergence and associational connections, particularly at the CA3 step. Outputs of subiculum, and to a lesser extent CA1, are directed back to deep layers of the parahippocampal region, which in turn projects back onto the neocortical and olfactory areas that were the source of cortical inputs. Thus, the hippocampal system is organized for maximal convergence of the final outcomes of cortical processing, and is positioned to influence the nature of cortical representations based on an architecture ideal for the formation of associations among them.

HUMAN AMNESIA AND ANIMAL MODELS OF HIPPOCAMPAL FUNCTION

The early findings on H. M. emphasized the global nature of his impairment, an almost complete failure to learn all sorts of new verbal and nonverbal material (see Corkin, 1984; Cohen & Eichenbaum, 1993). Yet, H. M.'s remote autobiographical memories and his capacity for short-term memory were completely intact, leading to the initial view that the hippocampal region plays a specific role in the consolidation of short-term memories into long-term memory. More recent work with H. M. and other amnesic patients has shown conclusively that the impairment in acquiring long-term memories is also circumscribed to a particular type of memory expression. Despite profound impairment in conscious or explicit remembering of learned materials, amnesic patients retain aspects of experience that can be revealed in unconscious changes in speed or biases in performance. Thus, amnesics can normally acquire new motor, perceptual, and cognitive skills and demonstrate normal sensory adaptations and priming of perceptual stimuli; such implicit learning occurs despite the patients' inability to recall or recognize the learning materials or the events of the learning experience. Based on these distinctions, the kind of memory lost in amnesia has been called "declarative" or "explicit" memory, emphasizing the characteristic capacity for conscious and direct memory expression so devastated following damage to the hippocampal region. Conversely, the collection of capacities preserved in amnesia has been called "procedural" or "implicit" memory, emphasizing the finding that hippocampal-independent memories are characteristically revealed by unconscious and indirect means of expression.

Considerable success has been achieved in developing a nonhuman primate model of human amnesia, using a set of tasks that involve complex objects as memory cues (Mishkin, 1982). Following removal of the same medial temporal structures involved in H. M.'s surgery, monkeys are severely impaired on delayed recognition of objects and show poor retention of rapidly acquired object discriminations. Conversely, they have a preserved ability to acquire slowly-learned motor skill and pattern discrimination tasks. In addition, hippocampal damage results in impaired retention of object discriminations learned shortly before the lesion, but spares retention of similar discriminations learned long before the damage. These findings parallel the pattern of impaired and spared memory capacities observed in human amnesics, and have been exploited subsequently for investigations focused on which medial temporal lobe structures are critical to declarative memory.

The surgical resection performed on H. M. included, in addition to the hippocampus, both the amygdala and surrounding entorhinal and perirhinal cortices. Findings from experiments on monkeys and rats focused on more selective damage within the medial temporal lobe have shown that the amygdala does not play a critical role in declarative memory, but that the surrounding parahippocampal region may play an even more important role than the hippocampus itself. Selective damage to the hippocampus, or its selective disconnection from subcortical areas by a transection of the fornix, results in either no deficit or only a mild deficit in recognition memory for specific objects, whereas damage to the parahippocampal region results in a deficit as severe as removal of the entire hippocampal region. This dissociation has led some to propose functional distinctions between components of the hippocampal system; according to one model, the parahippocampal region acts as an intermediate-term buffer for convergent perceptual representations, whereas the hippocampus associates these representations into the network of long-term memories (Eichenbaum, Otto, & Cohen, 1994).

Studies of the nature of amnesia consequent to hippocampal damage in animals have generated several proposals about hippocampal function, each suggesting a specific form of hippocampal-dependent and hippocampal-independent memory. Perhaps the most prominent of these is the hypothesis that the hippocampus constitutes a cognitive map, a representation of allocentric space. This notion captures the multimodal nature of hippocampal inputs and accounts for a wealth of data indicating that animals with hippocampal damage are severely impaired on a variety of place-learning tasks. However, by its specificity for the spatial modality, this model does not incorporate all the findings of the more global impairment observed in human amnesics, and does not adequately account for impairments observed on some nonspatial learning tasks in animals with hippocampal damage.

A reconciliation of divergent views about the hippocampus may be possible if one considers a fundamental role for the hippocampus in the representation of relations among items in memory (Eichenbaum, 1997). A common thread that runs through all proposals about the hippocampus is involvement in comparison and manipulation of representations according to significant relationships among perceptually independent stimuli. Correspondingly, animals with hippocampal-system damage are impaired on learning an organization of items presented either at the same time, as in the learning of spatial or configurational relations, or sequentially, as required in episodic memory. By contrast, what characterizes each view of the learning capacities spared in animals with hippocampal system damage is the intact ability to learn the significance of individual stimuli, unrelated to other items in memory, and indeed such learning is not dependent on the hippocampus.

A fundamental property of relational representations is the flexibility with which such memory can be expressed. Thus, a memory representation that contains links among many items should support expression of memory for all items via access at any point in the network. Indeed, recent findings using both monkeys and rats have shown that animals with hippocampal damage are severely impaired when challenged to express memories in such a flexible way. In these experiments, animals are initially trained on discrimination and place-learning tasks that involve multiple items presented in specific configurations, then tested for their capacities to express memory when the same items are rearranged in novel ways. Even when the animals with hippocampal damage succeeded in learning the initial problems at a normal rate, they failed to use their memory representations flexibly in the rearranged condition.

The characterization of hippocampal-dependent memory as relational and flexible may link descriptions of amnesia in humans, primates, and rodents, and it goes a considerable distance toward identifying the fundamental properties of hippocampal-dependent declarative memory.

INFORMATION ENCODED BY HIPPOCAMPAL NEURONS

Complementary evidence on the nature of memory processing accomplished by the hippocampus has been derived from studies of the firing patterns of hippocampal neurons in behaving animals. As might be expected from the anatomical and neuropsychological evidence described above, cellular recordings at successive stages leading to the hippocampus should reveal increasing sensory convergence. At early stages of neocortical processing, neuronal activity is related to particular sensory or movement parameters, reflecting the encoding of particular features of the stimulus or behavioral output. At progressively higher neocortical processing stages the functional correlates become increasingly complicated and multimodal, and reflect conjunctions of the simpler features. Consistent with the view that the hippocampus is the ultimate stage of hierarchical processing, the functional correlates of hippocampal cells are supramodal in that they appear to encode the abstract stimulus configurations that are independent of any particular sensory input.

Most prominent among the functional types of hippocampal principal neurons are cells that fire selectively when a rat is in a particular location in its environment as defined by the spatial relations among multiple and multimodal stimuli (O'Keefe, 1976). Moreover, the firing of place cells is characteristically not dependent upon any particular stimulus element and is not affected even if all the stimuli are removed, so long as the animal behaves as if it is in the same environment. These properties parallel the neuropsychological findings that suggest the hippocampus is critical to memory for stimulus relations and for flexible memory expression.

The discovery of hippocampal place cells has been viewed as supporting the cognitive mapping hypothesis of hippocampal function. However, many reports of non-spatial behavioral correlates of hippocampal neuronal activity indicate that hippocampal representation is not limited to the encoding of spatial relations among distal cues. Perhaps the best counter-example is the finding that many hippocampal principal cells fire associated with conditioned motor responses in restrained rabbits. Even in freely moving rats, the activity of place cells is influenced by aspects of movement trajectories that are meaningful to the task at hand. Furthermore, during the performance of a variety of non-spatial tasks, hippocampal neuronal activity is determined by specific olfactory, visual, tactile, or auditory cues, and these encodings prominently reflect non-allocentric spatial, temporal, and other relations among the cues that guide performance (e.g., Wood, Dudchenko, & Eichenbaum, 1999). These findings extend the range of hippocampal coding to reflect the global involvement of the hippocampus in memory indicated by the neuropsychological studies, and serve to reinforce the conclusion that the hippocampus supports relational representations.

A comprehensive and consensual understanding of role of the hippocampal system in memory remains elusive. Consensus on its importance for declarative or explicit memory, derived from studies of human amnesia, has dictated the critical direction for further development of animal models. However, characterizations of declarative memory in terms of conscious recollection and explicit memory expression present a formidable challenge for animal models of declarative memory. By focusing on the fundamental properties of relational organization and representational flexibility it may indeed be possible to develop valid animal models of declarative memory. Consistent with this goal, findings from neuropsychological studies showing impairments following hippocampal damage on diverse tasks that involve learning and remembering stimulus relations, and using them flexibly, have converged with findings from electrophysiological studies showing that hippocampal principal cell-firing patterns reflect stimulus configurations and can be instantiated flexibly by any element of the overall pattern.

REFERENCES

Amaral, D. G., & Witter, M. P. (1989). The three-dimensional organization of the hippocampal formation: A review of anatomical data. *Neuroscience, 31,* 571–591.

Cohen, N. J., & Eichenbaum, H. (1993). *Memory, amnesia, and the hippocampal system.* Cambridge: M.I.T. Press.

Corkin, S. (1984). Lasting consequences of bilateral medial temporal lobectomy: Clinical course and experimental findings in H. M. *Sem. Neurol., 4,* 249-259.

Eichenbaum, H. (1997). Declarative memory. Insights from cognitive neurobiology. *Annual Review of Psychology, 48,* 547–572.

Eichenbaum, H., Otto, T., & Cohen, N. J. (1994). Two functional components of the hippocampal memory system. *Brain and Behavioral Sciences, 17,* 449–518.

Mishkin, M. (1982). A memory system in the monkey. *Philosophical Transactions of the Royal Society of London, B209,* 85–95.

O'Keefe, J. A. (1976). Place units in the hippocampus of the freely moving rat. *Experimental Neurology, 51,* 78–109.

Scoville, W. B., & Milner, B. (1957). Loss of recent memory after bilateral hippocampal lesions. *Journal of Neurology, Neurosurgery, & Psychiatry, 20,* 11–12.

Van Hoesen, G. W. (1982). The parahippocampal gyrus. New observations regarding its cortical connections in the monkey. *Trends in Neuroscience, 5,* 345–350.

Wood, E., Dudchenko, P. A., & Eichenbaum, H. (1999). The global record of memory in hippocampal neuronal activity. *Nature, 397,* 613–616.

H. EICHENBAUM
Boston University

BRAIN INJURIES
DECLARATIVE MEMORY
MEMORY

HIPPOCRATES (ca.460–ca.377 B.C.)

Hippocrates of Cos, the father of medicine, is the name under which we know Greek medical thought of his period; he himself may have written little. Medical practice then focused on the use of symptoms to classify the illness. Hippocrates described the etiology in terms of the four body humors and prescribed purgatives, baths, vapors, or special diets to change the balance of the humors. Surgery was used for external trauma such as fractures of limbs. Hippocrates said it was impossible to treat any part of the body without taking account of the whole body.

Hippocrates took the four elements according to Empedocles—earth, air, fire, and water—and developed his theory of disease with four corresponding bodily humors: black bile, blood, yellow bile, and phlegm. Too much bile could cause overheating of the brain and thus fear or terror (the flushed face was partial evidence), while too much phlegm could cause overcooling and thus anxiety and grief. His book *On the Sacred Disease* concerned epilepsy; after stating that it was really no more sacred than any other disease, Hippocrates described it as hereditary and due to an imbalance of humors, particularly blood and phlegm. He also described severe phobias and the depression of postpartum psychosis.

Hippocrates had a primitive typology as well. He noted that the apoplecticus (the short, thickset individual) tended to have seizures, whereas the phthisicus (the slender, frail person) would have tuberculosis. Thus he anticipated the pyknic and asthenic types of Kretschmer and the work of Sheldon. It was Galen, however, who developed Hippocrates' vague notions of humors affecting behavior into a complete theory of temperament or personality.

STAFF

HISTRIONIC PERSONALITY

In accord with the *Diagnostic and Statistical Manual of Mental Disorders* (3rd ed.), individuals with this personality disorder are best characterized by their lively and dramatic, albeit fickle behaviors; by their tendency to exaggerate life events so as to draw attention to themselves; and by their easy excitability and tendency to react emotionally to the slightest promptings. Craving novelty and stimulation, they are inclined to become bored quickly with routine matters and relationships. Impressionable and susceptible to fads and fashions, they are highly suggestible and are readily taken in by those who strike them as interesting or powerful. Quick to form friendships, they often become demanding and inconsiderate once the relationship is established. They seek to pursue a sociable, facile, and romantic lifestyle. Their persistent seeking of attention is notable, expressed often in seductively charming, if at times immaturely exhibitionistic and self-dramatizing behaviors. Many of their relationships prove frivolous and transient. Their intolerance of delay and inactivity frequently results in impulsive and hedonistic behaviors. Their thought processes are typically rather insubstantial, unreflected, and even scattered.

The label "histrionic" in *DSM-III* is relatively new, replacing the term "hysterical." As a concept, the classification of hysteria can be traced back to the early Greeks and Romans. In the mid-1840s the symptom picture of clinical hysteria was broadened to encompass a personality type—one especially prevalent, if not exclusively found, among women. Thus Griesinger in *Mental Pathology and Therapeutics* (1845) noted among histrionics' distinguishing characteristics a volatile humor, senseless caprices, immoderate sensitiveness, and an inclination to deception and jealousy. Von Feuchtersleben wrote in *Principles of Medical Psychology* (1847) that these women were sexually heightened, selfish, and "overprivileged with satiety and boredom." In *The Mental State of Hystericals* (1901), Janet made note of their exhibitionistic, flamboyant, and demanding behaviors. Kretschmer described them in *Hysteria* (1926) as possessing "an overlively and overidealistic sexuality . . . a rapidly vanishing elan of feelings . . . a theatrical pathos." Providing the first underpinnings to a psychoanalytic theory of character formation, Reich described the major features of the hysterical in *Charakteranalyse* (1933) as "disguised or undisguised coquetry . . . fickleness of reactions . . . strong suggestibility . . . an attitude of compliance followed by its opposite, swift deprecation." Synthesizing earlier formulations in line with a biosocial-learning theory, Millon listed the prime criteria for diagnosing the histrionic in his *Millon Clinical Multiaxial Inventory Manual* as follows:

1. *Fickle affectivity:* displays short-lived, dramatic, and superficial affects; reports tendency to be easily excited and as easily bored.

2. *Sociable self-image:* perceives self as gregarious, stimulating, and charming; attracts fleeting acquaintances and enjoys rapidly-paced social life.

3. *Interpersonal seductiveness:* actively solicits praise and manipulates others to gain attention and approval; exhibits self-dramatizing and childishly exhibitionistic behaviors.

4. *Cognitive dissociation:* integrates experiences poorly, which results in scattered learning and unexamined thought; reveals undependable, erratic, and flighty judgment.

5. *Immature stimulus-seeking behavior:* is intolerant of inactivity, leading to unreflected and impulsive responsiveness; describes penchant for momentary excitements, fleeting adventures, and short-sighted hedonism.

REFERENCES

Griesinger, W. (1867). *Mental pathology and therapeutics.* London: New Syndenham Society. (Original work published 1845)

Janet, P. (1901). *The mental state of hystericals: A study of mental stigmata and mental accidents.* New York: Putnam.

Kretschmer, E. (1926). *Hysteria.* New York: Nervous and Mental Disease.

Millon, T. (1977). *Millon clinical multiaxial inventory manual.* Minneapolis, MN: National Computer Systems.

Reich, W. (1949). *Charakteranalyse.* Leipzig, Germany: Sexpol Verlag. (Original work published 1933)

T. MILLON
University of Miami

*DIAGNOSTIC AND STATISTICAL MANUAL OF MENTAL
    DISORDERS (DSM-IV)*
**PERSONALITY DISORDERS
PERSONALITY TYPES**

HOBBES, THOMAS (1588–1679)

Educated at Oxford, Thomas Hobbes is considered the father of British empiricism and associationism. His psychology is set forth in two books, *Human Nature* (1651) and *Leviathan* (1651).

Influenced by Galileo's concept of motion, Hobbes concluded that psychological (mental) activities were motions in the nervous system resulting from motions in the external world. Thinking, therefore, was nothing more than movement excited in the brain. In this way he also accounted for action and emotion. In stating that everything in nature was motion, Hobbes tried to deny the existence of a mind separate from the body. Antagonistic to any theological interpretation of mind or soul, he reduced consciousness—like other mental activity—to motions of atoms in the brain. However, he offered no explanation as to the coexistence of these brain movements and mental activity; it simply happened. As a contemporary of René Descartes, Hobbes rejected the former's conception of an interaction between body and mind (soul) via the pineal gland. In stating his thesis of the coexistence of motions and mental activity, Hobbes was still left with some concept of a mind. He also rejected Descartes's notion that some ideas in the mind were inherited. Some mental activity was the residual of previous sensory experiences; for example, images and memory were mere decay of the original sensations.

Hobbes touched on the notion of the association of ideas, but left the details to be worked out by the later empiricists and associationists. He referred to the associations as "trains of thought" and described them as being of two types: one unguided or rambling, and the second orderly, as when a person associated two ideas that were appropriately related.

Hobbes also wrote of the passions and desires, which, though also motions, arose from within parts of the body other than the brain. He made it clear that passions could influence reason. They seemed to direct thought, but in so doing could distort logical thinking. In the end, the passions determined conduct. In stating that we seek pleasure and avoid pain, Hobbes was anticipating a psychological hedonism to be elaborated later by Julien La Mettrie and Jeremy Bentham.

Hobbes's psychology was derived from his concern for political and social conduct. In the *Leviathan* he wrote that man had originally lived in a state of mutual warfare; only calculated selfishness had produced cooperation in the establishment of a state or government. Without government, life would be "poor, nasty, brutish and short." On the basis of self-interest and fear of destruction, humans established government to control themselves.

Historians agree that Hobbes had little influence on his successor, John Locke, who really established the empirical movement. They also agree that Hobbes's writings were vague, unclear, and often contradictory.

R. W. LUNDIN
Wheaton, Illinois

HOLLINGWORTH, LETA S. (1886–1939)

Leta S. Hollingworth received the PhD in education at Columbia Teachers College, where she then taught for more than 20 years. Her interests centered upon children and individual and group differences. Her early work on subnormal children was summarized in *The Psychology of Subnormal Children* and *Special Talents and Defects*. She pointed out that children with serious problems may frequently be intellectually retarded; furthermore, they suffer emotionally and their emotional problems tend to increase during adolescence. Hollingworth's textbook *The Psychology of the Adolescent* was widely used.

Impressed by the fact that gifted children may also suffer from emotional problems, Hollingworth concentrated her attention in this area. She noted that very high intelligence may lead to isolation and consequently may disqualify the gifted for popular leadership. Hollingworth spoke eloquently for the gifted and wrote *Gifted Children*.

Working at a time when there were few women psychologists, Hollingworth set for herself high standards of scholarship and fully earned the respect of her colleagues.

P. E. LICHTENSTEIN

HOLT, EDWIN B. (1873–1946)

One of the early behaviorists, Edwin B. Holt received the PhD at Harvard in 1901 and remained there until 1917. After taking some time out for writing, he taught at Princeton from 1926 to 1936.

Holt felt strongly that psychology should study behavior, or what he called "the specific response relationship." However, unlike Watson's atomistic or "muscle twitch" psychology, Holt thought of a response system as involving a whole, or what Tolman later called "molar behavior." For example, rather than saying a man was walking step by step down the street, Holt would say he was walking to the grocery store. Thus there was a certain purpose in the behavior.

Holt was much concerned with psychological meaning. When one responded adequately to a thing, one got its meaning. When a response specified something, that constituted meaning. Our capacity to respond specifically to the world constituted knowledge. Thus Holt made his behaviorism into a cognitive psychology wherein the specific response relation was the essence of the event.

This notion also became the basic dynamic principle for Holt. He termed the dynamic principle "wish." In *The Freudian Wish and Its Place in Ethics* he said Freud had given psychology back its will. The wish as a specific response relation provided psychology with a notion of cause. Furthermore, the wish was to be regarded as a purpose. It was a cause of action wherein some mechanism of the body was set to carry out an act directed toward a goal.

Holt's psychology can be related to William McDougall's purposivism, Alfred Adler's teleology, and Edward Tolman's purposive behaviorism.

R. W. LUNDIN
Wheaton, Illinois

HOMEOSTASIS

Complex organisms must maintain relatively stable internal environments to survive and move freely through the changing and often adverse conditions which surround them. "Homeostasis" is the name given to this constancy in 1926 by W. B. Cannon, an American physiologist. Through his work on homeostasis, Cannon created a concept that has become a milestone in the history of ideas. It was the culmination of an approach begun some six decades earlier with the work of C. Bernard, the French physiologist who is considered to have established the foundations of scientific physiology. Bernard concluded that organisms have evolved toward a greater independence from the changing environment by developing, from the blood and bodily fluids, an internal environment held stable by its own adjustments (Robin, 1979). Cannon demonstrated that the activities of homeostasis, often simple if viewed each in isolation, are nevertheless orchestrated by remarkably complex regulatory processes involving the organism across physiological systems and levels of functioning.

Cannon (1925/1973) described his findings as instances of the maintenance of steady states in open systems. In 1926 he named this steady condition "homeostasis" (1926/1973) and offered a set of postulates regarding its nature which he later expanded upon (1929/1973), publishing an overview of homeostasis and the regulatory mechanisms identified up to that point. The body, he asserted, was able through homeostatic reactions to maintain stability in the fluid matrix surrounding the body cells, thus controlling body temperature, blood pressure, and other aspects of the internal environment necessary for life. Homeostasis was also maintained in the levels of supplies needed directly for cellular activities, including materials for energy and growth (glucose, protein, fat), water, sodium chloride, calcium, oxygen, and certain necessary internal secretions. Regulated by the nervous system and endocrine glands, bodily reactions at all levels of complexity were involved, from the speed with which cell metabolism proceeded and produced heat in cold weather, to increases and decreases in the complex processes giving rise to hunger and thirst, with impact on behaviors affecting energy and water intake.

Cannon's concept of homeostasis emerged as a complex statement regarding the existence, nature, and principles of self-regulating systems. He emphasized that complex living beings are open systems made up of changing and unstable components subjected continually to disturbing conditions precisely because they are open to their surroundings in so many ways. Thus, while themselves continuously tending toward change, they nevertheless must also maintain constancy with regard to the environment, so as to preserve circumstances favorable to life. Adjustments within such systems must be continuous and less than perfect. Homeostasis therefore describes a state that is relatively, rather than absolutely, stable.

The concept of the open system challenged all conventional views regarding the appropriate unit of analysis of an entity. If the heart, lungs, kidneys, and blood, for example, are parts of a self-regulating system, then their actions or functions cannot be understood by studying each alone. Full understanding comes only from knowledge of how each acts with reference to the others. The concept of the open system also challenged all conventional views of causality, substituting complex reciprocal determination for any notion of simple serial or linear causality. Homeostasis therefore offered a new perspective both for viewing the behavior of systems of many sorts and for understanding people as members of open systems.

Homeostasis has served as a cornerstone for a number of subsequent developments involving a system perspective of control and causality. Selye's work with stress and disease, and his discovery of the general adaptation syndrome, began with the insight that certain diseases and disorders might arise as the cost of the body's struggle to maintain homeostasis in the face of prolonged disruptive pressure (Selye 1956/1978). Selye's view of disease as derangement of homeostasis contributed to a view of health in which the role of medicine is to assist the homeostatic processes to return the organism to the constant state. Wiener's cybernetic theory (1948) attempted to formulate principles to account for self-regulation across biological and nonliving systems such as computers, a pursuit construed even more broadly in von Bertalanffy's general system theory (1968). In the 1950s Jackson (1968) began to explore applications of homeostasis to family interaction, identifying family systems in which apparently disturbed behaviors are homeostatic. His concept of family homeostasis provided impetus to the then emerging field of marital psychotherapy and contributed to such concepts as the double bind.

Homeostasis research continues to stimulate new perceptions in recent decades, by establishing that learning is central to homeostatic regulation of even physiological systems (Ramsay & Woods, 1997), demonstrating (to select one example of many) that homeostasis is involved in addictions in complex ways (Poulos & Cappell, 1991). In a series of experiments starting in the 1970s, Siegel (1988) showed that the development of increased morphine tolerance in rats involves a learning process. A body of subsequent research demonstrates that the increased levels of drug tolerance found in repeated drug administrations involve learned homeostatic efforts to restore normal functioning in the presence of many drugs that otherwise destabilize normal functioning. With repeated exposure to the drug, the organism learns to produce a pattern of offsetting physiological and behavioral responses that counteract its perturbing effects. Once learned, this pattern of homeostatic responses can be elicited in anticipation of or otherwise in the absence of the drug (Ramsay & Woods, 1997). Overall, Cannon's system concepts continue to play a central role in organizing our understanding of the nature of our interactions with our inner and outer environments.

REFERENCES

Bertalanffy, L. von. (1968). *General systems theory.* New York: Braziller.

Cannon, W. B. (1973/1925). Some general features of endocrine influence on metabolism. In L. L. Langley (Ed.), *Homeostasis.* Stroudsburg, PA: Dowden, Hutchinson.

Cannon, W. B. (1973/1926). Physiological regulation of normal states: Some tentative postulates concerning biological homeostasis. In L. L. Langley (Ed.), *Homeostasis.* Stroudsburg, PA: dowden, hutchinson & Ross.

Cannon, W. B. (1973/1926). Organization for physiological homeostasis. In L. L. Langley (Ed.), *Homeostasis.* Stroudsburg, PA: dowden, hutchinson & Ross.

Jackson, D. D. (Ed.) (1968). *Communication, family and marriage* (Vols. 1, 2) Palo Alto, CA: Science & Behavior books.

Poulos, C. X., & Cappell, H. (1991). Homeostatic theory of drug tolerance: A general model of physiological adaptation. *Psychological Review, 98*(3), 390–408.

Ramsay, D. S., & Woods, S. C. (1997). Biological consequences of drug administration implications for acute and chronic tolerance. *Psychological Review, 104*(1), 170–193.

Robin, E. D. (Ed.) (1979). *Claude Bernard and the internal environment: a memorial symposium.* New York: Dekker.

Seyle, H. (1978/1956). *Stress of life.* New York: McGraw-Hill.

Siegel, S. (1988). State dependent learning and morphine tolerance. *Behavioral Neuroscience, 102*(2), 228–232.

Wiener, N. (1948). *Cybernetics: Control and communication in the animal and the machine.* Cambridge, MA: M.I.T. Press.

SUGGESTED READING

Beishon, J., & Peters, G. (Eds.). (1972). *Systems behaviour.* New York: Open University Press/Harper & Row.

Langley, L. L. (Ed.) (1972). *Homeostasis: Origins of the concept.* Stroudsburg, Pa.: Dowden, Hutchinson & Ross.

Poulos, C. X., & Cappell, H. (1991). Homeostatic theory of drug tolerance: A general model of physiological adaptation. *Psychological Review, 98*(3), 390–408.

Ramsay, D. S., & Woods, S. C. (1997). Biological consequences of drug administration implications for acute and chronic tolerance. *Psychological Review, 104*(1), 170–193.

Siegel, S. (1988). State dependent learning and morphine tolerance. *Behavioral Neuroscience, 102*(2), 228–232.

ADAPTATION
GENERAL ADAPTATION SYNDROME
GENERAL SYSTEMS
MIND/BODY PROBLEM

HOMOSEXUALITY

Homosexuality refers to sexual behaviors, desires, attractions, and relationships among people of the same sex, as well as to the culture, identities, and communities associated with them. The earliest usage of "homosexual" listed in the *Oxford English Dictionary* was in 1897 by Havelock Ellis in his *Studies in the Psychology of Sex.* Other scholars, however, trace the term to two anonymous German pamphlets authored in 1869 by Hungarian Karl Maria Benkert. Although Benkert originally contrasted homosexual (an amalgam of Greek and Latin roots) to "normalsexual," heterosexual ultimately became the term for describing comparable phenomena between people of different sexes. The term bisexual is often used to describe persons with attractions to both men and women.

Homosexuality has often been assumed to be a monolithic construct. However, it actually encompasses many different phenomena that are often—but not always—related. At least five different aspects of homosexuality are relevant to this article. First, the term is used to describe specific behaviors; that is, individual sexual acts as well as sexual attractions and desires that occur at a given moment. Both homosexual and heterosexual behaviors are common throughout human societies (and in many other species), with all cultures regulating the conditions under which they are permitted.

In many of Papua New Guinea's indigenous societies, for example, males are expected to engage exclusively in homosexual behavior for several years during adolescence (data are generally lacking for female sexual behavior in these cultures). Later, they are expected to marry a female and engage in heterosexual behaviors with her. In some of these societies, adult males regularly return to homosexual behavior to initiate new generations of adolescent boys. Thus, appropriate male sexual behavior is defined according to the individual's age and societal events (e.g., the occurrence of rituals in which older males are called upon to initiate adolescents).

In the United States and most other industrialized Western societies, in contrast, cultural norms dictate that all individuals engage in heterosexual behavior within a socially approved dyad (usually recognized by the society through marriage). Nevertheless, society accepts to some degree that homosexual behavior occurs under certain circumstances, such as during adolescence or in sex-segregated institutions. Historically, for the most part, adult homosexual behavior outside of such institutions has been stigmatized.

Another usage of "homosexuality" refers to enduring patterns of attraction for sexual or romantic partners of one's own gender, whether or not these preferences are expressed behaviorally. An individual's ongoing attractions are not necessarily consistent with her or his specific sexual behaviors. Many people with primary attractions to others of their own gender report having heterosexual experiences, just as many people with heterosexual preferences have engaged in homosexual activity at some time. Some people remain celibate; they do not engage in sexual behavior with another person, sometimes for their entire lives. In cultures such as the contemporary United States, where heterosexuality and homosexuality are regarded as mutually exclusive categories and homosexual behavior is generally stigmatized, homosexual attractions are probably less likely to be acted upon than are heterosexual attractions.

A third aspect of homosexuality is psychological identity, a sense of self defined in terms of one's attractions. In the United States, people who have developed an identity as a homosexual person typically refer to themselves as "gay," with many women preferring the term "lesbian." Because heterosexuality has long been equated with normalcy, people with a heterosexual orientation have typically not developed personal identities based on their sexuality. Instead, social roles such as "husband," "wife," "father," and "mother" have fulfilled this function. Like other minority group members, however, people with primarily homosexual attractions have defined themselves in terms of what makes them different from the majority.

People arrive at a homosexual identity through various routes. Some individuals, for example, identify as gay only after multiple homosexual experiences, whereas others form a gay identity entirely on the basis of their romantic attractions without having engaged in homosexual behaviors. Not all people with homosexual attractions develop a gay or lesbian identity, and not all people who identify themselves as gay engage in homosexual acts. Many men, for example, regularly have sex with other men but never label themselves as gay or bisexual. And some women develop a lesbian identity primarily on the basis of feminist political values rather than erotic attractions.

A fourth aspect of homosexuality is participation in intimate, committed same-sex relationships and families. Societal stigma has often restricted opportunities for people of the same sex to form long-term relationships, and marriage between two people of the same sex is not recognized in any of the 50 states as of this writing. Indeed, the federal government and many states explicitly define legal marriage as heterosexual. Nevertheless, a large proportion of gay and lesbian people are committed life partners, with relationships lasting 20 years and longer not uncommon. A growing number of employers, organizations, and local governments now offer same-sex "domestic partners" some of the same benefits that they give heterosexual married couples. And same-sex couples now enjoy legal recognition in the Scandinavian countries and elsewhere.

In terms of psychological dynamics, heterosexual and homosexual relationships are highly similar. For example, no consistent differences have been observed between homosexual and heterosexual relationships in psychological adjustment or satisfaction. Despite their many similarities, heterosexual and homosexual relationships also differ in some respects. Perhaps the most significant difference is that antigay stigma denies same-sex couples the positive social support that heterosexual couples typically receive, and even forces many same-sex couples to keep their relationship at least partly hidden. In addition, because social norms are lacking for same-sex relationships, there is considerable diversity in the way that such couples define their relationship. Some adopt many conventions of heterosexual relationships, whereas others create new ways of being together. Partners in same-sex relationships may be less likely than those in heterosexual couples to assume gender-typed roles (i.e., one partner performing all the tasks that are stereotypically "men's work" and the other partner doing the "women's work"). Another difference is that same-sex couples may be more likely than heterosexual couples to directly discuss and negotiate the issue of sexual monogamy and to distinguish it from emotional fidelity. Lesbian couples appear more likely to be sexually exclusive than heterosexual couples, who in turn are more likely than gay male couples to be sexually monogamous.

Since the early 1990s, growing numbers of lesbians and gay men have chosen to become parents, often in the context of a committed same-sex relationship. Although there is no scientific basis for claims that lesbians make bad mothers or gay men make bad fathers, gay parents have often met with hostility from conservative segments of society and have even been denied custody of their own children. Nevertheless, lesbian and gay families are increasingly common.

Yet another phenomenon encompassed in "homosexuality" in the United States (and many other societies) is minority group membership. In the twentieth century, society increasingly came to regard gay people as a minority group, and individuals sharing a gay or lesbian identity developed visible communities similar to ethnic, religious, and cultural minorities. Empirical research indicates that gay men and lesbians in the United States manifest greater psychological adjustment to the extent that they identify with and feel part of such a community.

HOMOSEXUALITY IN HISTORICAL PERSPECTIVE

That the word homosexual was coined only in the nineteenth century suggests that our modern notions about it—encompassing the five types of phenomena described above—are historically recent. Homosexual behavior does not appear to be limited to any particular era of human history. Our contemporary understanding of such behavior and its relationship to a larger cosmology, however, have evolved fairly recently. Philosophers and historians in the social constructionist school (see below) have argued that homosexuality as an identity or membership in a community (with heterosexuality as its counterpart) has developed only within the past few centuries. Prior to this time, they suggest, individuals were not socially defined in terms of their sexual behaviors (homosexual or heterosexual). Anyone might engage in homosexual behavior, but such behavior did not bestow an identity or community.

Modern attitudes toward homosexuality have religious, legal, and medical underpinnings. Before the High Middle Ages, homosexual acts appear to have been widely tolerated or ignored by the Christian church throughout Europe. Beginning in the latter twelfth century, however, hostility toward homosexuality began to take root, and eventually spread throughout European religious and secular institutions. Condemnation of homosexual behavior as "unnatural," which received official expression in the writings of Thomas Aquinas and others, became widespread and has continued to the present day.

Religious teachings were incorporated into legal sanctions. Many of the early American colonies, for example, enacted stiff criminal penalties for sodomy (often described in Latin or obliquely in phrases such as "wickedness not to be named"). In the New Haven colony and elsewhere, male and female homosexual acts were punishable by death.

By the end of the nineteenth century, medicine and psychiatry were competing with religion and the law for jurisdiction over sexuality. As a consequence, discourse about homosexuality expanded from the realms of sin and crime to include that of pathology. This historical shift was generally considered progressive because a sick person was less blameful than a sinner or criminal. Even within medicine and psychiatry, however, homosexuality was not universally viewed as a pathology. Whereas Krafft-Ebing described it as a degenerative sickness in his *Psychopathia Sexualis,* Freud and Ellis both adopted more accepting stances. Ellis urged that homosexuality be treated as a normal variant of human behavior, like left-handedness. Although Freud believed that homosexuality represented a less than optimal outcome for psychosexual development, he nevertheless asserted in a 1935 letter that "it is nothing to be ashamed of, no vice, no degradation, it cannot be classified as an illness."

Despite the rise of psychiatry, the religious and legal perspectives remained influential. Homosexual relations continued to be condemned by most major religions and were illegal in the United States and most other countries. Twentieth century hostility toward homosexuality reached a tragic climax in Nazi Germany, where thousands of suspected homosexual men were imprisoned in concentration camps and forced to wear an inverted pink triangle as a badge of identity. Between 5,000 and 15,000 of those prisoners are estimated to have died in the camps.

American psychoanalysis, psychiatry, and psychology treated homosexuality as a form of psychopathology during much of the twentieth century. This view became wedded to official government policies during World War II, when psychiatrists and psychologists were employed in the U.S. military's war effort. Although homosexual recruits were often accepted during the early years of the war when the need for personnel was greatest, they were later expelled in a series of witch hunts during the war's waning years.

Ironically, the mass courts martial and discharges provided a major impetus for the development of lesbian and gay communities and the modern movement for gay rights. Socially ostracized, often unable to secure employment, and ineligible for benefits under the GI Bill because of their undesirable discharge as a "sexual psychopath," men and women ejected from the military for homosexuality often chose not to return to their hometowns. Instead, they settled in large cities such as San Francisco, Los Angeles, and New York, where they developed social networks and a community. Despite the relatively greater tolerance of those large urban centers, however, gay men and lesbians were routinely harassed and their meeting places were often raided by the police. In response, they organized politically. Groups such as the Mattachine Society in Los Angeles and the Daughters of Bilitis and the Society for Individual Rights in San Francisco worked to change societal attitudes and laws while also serving as safe havens for their members.

It was not until the 1970s that these small-scale efforts developed into the modern movement for gay and lesbian rights. The signal event occurred on June 27, 1969, when the police raided the Stonewall Inn, a gay bar in New York City that appealed to a largely young and nonwhite clientele that included drag queens (men dressed flamboyantly in women's clothes) and street people. Although such harassment was fairly routine, the patrons on that night did not acquiesce as usual. Instead, they attacked the police and the ensuing confrontation erupted into a riot that lasted for three nights. In the months and years immediately following what became known as the Stonewall Rebellion, the gay liberation movement flourished, influenced by the campaigns for racial, ethnic, and gender equality that had matured during the 1960s.

The psychiatric establishment was an early target of the new movement. Homosexuality had been included in the first *Diagnostic and Statistical Manual* (*DSM*) of the American Psychiatric Association, published in 1952. The diagnosis, however, was based on clinical impressions rather than empirical data from representative samples. The clinicians often were influenced by the American school of psychoanalysis, which rejected Freud's theory of inherent bisexuality and adopted the postulate that heterosexuality is innate (and homosexuality, therefore, is a pathological aberration).

Systematic empirical data for evaluating the diagnostic category were not available. Many military physicians and social scientists had recorded their observations that homosexual soldiers appeared to function as effectively as heterosexuals, but their reports remained largely hidden and ignored for decades until uncovered by Bérubé (1990). The first published study comparing the psychological functioning of a nonclinical sample of homosexuals with comparable heterosexuals was conducted by Hooker (1956). She administered projective tests to men who were members of a homosexual organization in southern California, and to a sample of heterosexual men matched for age, education, and IQ. A panel of experts, unaware of each participant's sexual orientation, judged most of the men in both groups to be free from psychopathology. Furthermore, based on Rorschach responses, they could not differentiate the homosexual men from the heterosexuals at a level better than chance. Hooker concluded from her study that homosexuality did not constitute a clinical entity and that it was not inherently associated with pathology.

Hooker's results subsequently were replicated in numerous empirical studies of men and women. Although some later investigations claimed to support the view of homosexuality as pathological, they were methodologically weak. Many relied on clinical or incarcerated samples, for example, or failed to safeguard the data collection procedures from possible biases by the investigators (e.g., having a man's psychological functioning evaluated by his own psychoanalyst, who was simultaneously treating him for his homosexuality). Others found differences between homosexual and heterosexual respondents on variables such as childhood experiences or family relationships, and then assumed that these differences indicated pathology among the homosexuals (even in the absence of observed differences in psychological functioning).

In 1973, the weight of empirical data, coupled with changing social mores and the development of a politically active gay community in the United States, led the Board of Directors of the American Psychiatric Association to remove homosexuality from the *DSM*. Their decision was supported in 1974 by a vote of the membership. Subsequently, a new diagnosis, "ego-dystonic homosexuality," was included in the *DSM*'s third edition in 1980. Ego-dystonic homosexuality was indicated by (a) a persistent lack of heterosexual arousal, which the patient experienced as interfering with initiation or maintenance of wanted heterosexual relationships, and (b) persistent distress from a sustained pattern of unwanted homosexual arousal.

The new diagnostic category, however, was criticized professionally on numerous grounds. It was viewed by many as a political compromise to appease the minority—mainly psychoanalysts—who still considered homosexuality a pathology. Others questioned the appropriateness of having a separate diagnosis that described the content of an individual's dysphoria. They argued that the psychological problems related to ego-dystonic homosexuality could be treated as well by other general diagnostic categories, and that the existence of the diagnosis perpetuated antigay stigma. In 1986, the diagnosis was removed entirely.

The movement to declassify homosexuality as a diagnosis has been strongly supported by the American Psychological Association (APA) since 1974. The APA has passed numerous resolutions supporting equal rights for lesbians and gay men in employment (including teaching and military service), child custody, and access to services. Similar positions have been adopted by other professional and academic groups.

HOW MANY PEOPLE ARE HOMOSEXUAL?

Because of the stigma that continues to be attached to homosexuality, as well as the difficulties of defining exactly who should be considered gay or homosexual, no accurate estimate exists for the number of gay people in the United States today. The figure of ten percent is widely quoted, based on studies conducted by Alfred Kinsey and his colleagues in the 1940s and 1950s. Kinsey, however, never assessed his respondents' psychological identity or community membership. Rather, he asked them about their sexual behavior and fantasies, and found that ten percent of the males in his sample were more or less exclusively homosexual in their behavior for at least three years between the ages of 16 and 55. For women, the corresponding figure was between two and six percent, depending upon their marital status.

Unfortunately, no studies comparable to Kinsey's have since been conducted in the United States. Current data about human sexual behavior in general, including homosexual behavior and identity, are lacking. Large-scale surveys conducted in North America and Europe throughout the 1980s and 1990s indicated that roughly one to ten percent of men and one to six percent of women (depending on the survey and the country) report having had sexual relations with another person of their own sex since puberty. Such behaviors are especially common during adolescence and early adulthood.

THE ORIGINS OF SEXUAL ORIENTATION

Before the 1970s, most scientific research on homosexuality aimed to discover its etiology. More recently, many researchers have recognized that the causes of heterosexuality are equally puzzling. Consequently, scientific inquiry now focuses on the broad question of the beginnings of sexual orientation.

Three competing perspectives can be identified within this area of research. Some researchers have approached homosexuality and heterosexuality as biological phenomena, and have sought to explain their origins in terms of genetic factors or prenatal exposure to specific hormones. Other researchers have attempted to understand sexual orientation as the product of experience. They have examined the role of early family relationships, classical conditioning, social learning throughout the life span, and similar factors in its development. These two perspectives were once pitted against each other in a "nature–nurture" debate. However, most researchers in this tradition now assume that biological and experiential variables are both important, although their relative importance in shaping adult sexual orientation remains unknown. Theorists favoring each type of explanation have been able to find at least some empirical support for their own theory and some empirical disconfirmation for competing views. As of this writing, no single account of the origins of sexual orientation—biological or experiential—has been empirically demonstrated to be valid and replicable.

Most researchers in these two traditions have shared the assumption that homosexuality and heterosexuality are universal characteristics of human beings. Some have even extended the concepts to other species. However, another perspective argues that the very concept of sexual orientation is specific to particular cultures and historical eras. According to this social constructionist paradigm, societies organize human sexual relations in a variety of ways. Although female-male, female-female, and male-male sexual acts occur in all societies, they do not necessarily endow the actors with an identity or social role that corresponds to Western notions of "heterosexuality" and "homosexuality." Because the phenomenon itself is culture-bound, any attempt to develop a universal explanation for the origins of sexual orientation—a position labeled "essentialism" by the constructionists—is fundamentally misguided.

Some scientists have sought a middle ground in this controversy. They have suggested that commonalities exist across cultures in patterns of sexual behavior and attraction, which probably have a biological basis to at least some extent. At the same time, they acknowledge that the meanings associated with these patterns vary widely among cultures, and that the differences must be understood in order to recognize which aspects of human sexuality are universal and which are culturally specific. In other words, "heterosexuals" and "homosexuals" may not exist in all human societies in the way that residents of Western industrialized cultures understand these concepts; but some (as yet unspecified) aspects of "heterosexuality" and "homosexuality" may indeed be universal.

Debates about the origins of sexual orientation have led to a more pluralistic view of human sexuality. Scientists are increasingly coming to appreciate that homosexuality and heterosexuality are not unitary phenomena, and that even in our own culture different people develop and express their sexual orientation in different ways. Based on these insights, no single theory seems likely to be able to explain the development of heterosexuality or homosexuality in all people. Indeed, some researchers have emphasized this view by framing their work in terms of *heterosexualities* and *homosexualities*.

BEHAVIORAL AND SOCIAL RESEARCH ON LESBIANS AND GAY MEN

Whether or not it is a universal human phenomenon, sexual orientation is experienced by most people in the United States and other western industrialized societies as a deeply-rooted and unchangeable part of themselves. Many adults report that they never made a conscious choice about their sexual orientation and that they have always felt the same type of sexual attractions and desires. There may be a sex difference in this regard, with men reporting more categorical and absolute definitions of their sexual orientation, but women more often reporting a more plastic and malleable sense of their sexuality over the life span.

When homosexuality was assumed to be a form of psychopathology, psychiatrists and psychologists often attempted to "cure" it; that is, to change homosexual people into heterosexuals. Even today, some psychotherapists and religious counselors try to change people in this way. The "success" of their techniques, however, is highly doubtful and the ethics of their treatments have been challenged by many mental health professionals and human rights advocates. In the late 1990s, the American Psychological Association and the American Psychiatric Association questioned the effectiveness and ethics of such treatments, and expressed doubts about the extent to which clients could provide true informed consent before undertaking them. Most mainstream therapists now attempt to help lesbian and gay clients to adjust successfully to their sexual orientation, to develop meaningful intimate relationships, and to cope with societal stigma.

Many gay men and lesbians seek a therapist's help in "coming out of the closet" ("coming out" for short); that is, accepting their homosexual orientation and disclosing it to others. Coming out can be especially difficult for people who have internalized society's negative stereotypes and attitudes toward homosexuality. Many psychotherapists now devote special attention to helping their gay clients to overcome this "internalized homophobia." Self-help groups exist in most cities and on many college campuses through which gay men and lesbians share their coming out experiences and develop positive feelings about themselves.

Just as the focus of psychotherapy with gay men and lesbians has changed in recent years, so too has the emphasis shifted in empirical research. Increasingly, scientific studies of homosexuality now address the problems and challenges faced by lesbians and gay men as a result of societal prejudice and discrimination. Perhaps the most important overall insight gained from such research is that gay men and lesbians constitute a highly diverse group. Apart from their sexual orientation, they are no more homogeneous than is the heterosexual population.

This diversity has been revealed in a large number of empirical studies that have failed to find significant differences between homosexual and heterosexual people on a wide range of characteristics. In studies that have employed noninstitutionalized samples and have included adequate safeguards against researcher bias, no consistent differences have been found for psychological adjustment, the capacity to form and maintain an intimate relationship, the ability to be a good parent, the likelihood of victimizing children or adults, or the ability to function in a group or organization. These studies also have effectively debunked many societal stereotypes about gay men and lesbians, such as the assumption that gay men are necessarily effeminate or lesbians masculine. At the same time, many studies have shown that society's prejudice against homosexuality can be a significant stressor for gay men and women, and may lead to psychological distress and maladaptive behaviors.

SEXUAL PREJUDICE

Antigay prejudice remains widespread in the United States. Nevertheless, heterosexuals' attitudes toward lesbians and gay men appear to have become somewhat more accepting since the Stonewall Rebellion. Although the majority of respondents in public opinion polls continue to regard homosexual behavior as wrong, moral condemnation has decreased dramatically since the early 1990s. In addition, growing numbers oppose discrimination in employment on the basis of sexual orientation.

Despite shifts in public opinion, discrimination in employment and housing on the basis of sexual orientation is not prohibited by federal law. However, laws forbidding such discrimination have been enacted in most major U.S. cities and in several states. Laws prohibiting consensual sex between two adults of the same sex (so-called sodomy laws) still exist in nearly one-half of the states.

Prejudice against lesbians and gay men has been called by several names. Most popular among them has been "homophobia," a term coined by psychologist George Weinberg in the late 1960s. Although it is widely used, this term can be misleading because it suggests that hostility toward gay men and lesbians represents a clinical pathology rather than a social phenomenon similar to racism and antisemitism.

Empirical research has identified several consistent correlates of heterosexuals' prejudice against lesbians and gay men. In contrast to those with favorable attitudes, individuals with more negative feelings tend to be older, less educated, male, and residents of rural areas or the midwestern or southern United States. They are more likely to attend religious services frequently, and to hold traditional beliefs about the proper social roles of men and women and restrictive views about sexual behavior. They also are less likely to have had a close relationship with an openly gay person.

During the 1980s, public recognition of the problem of violence against lesbians and gay men grew. Reports of beatings, sexual assaults, and murders became more common. Small-scale surveys with convenience samples indicated that many lesbians and gay men had experienced physical assault because of their sexual orientation. Still more lived in fear of such attacks, and many restricted their public activities to reduce their risk. In response to the violence, lesbians and gay men organized neighborhood patrols and service agencies in cities such as San Francisco and New York. In concert with members of racial and religious minorities, who also experienced an apparent upsurge in what have come to be called hate crimes, members of the gay community lobbied state and congressional representatives to enact legislation in response to the violence. The federal government and many states adopted laws mandating tabulation of hate crimes and imposing enhanced penalties for them.

Scientific understanding of the most effective ways to combat sexual prejudice is still in its early stages. Because such prejudice probably has many sources and serves different psychological functions for different individuals, a variety of strategies will probably be needed to change antigay attitudes. One of the most consistently noted sources for heterosexuals' attitude change is having personal contact with a lesbian or gay man, especially when such contact involves open discussion of sexual orientation.

Scientific views of homosexuality have changed dramatically since the 1960s, paralleling changes in the larger society. Psychology now regards homosexuality as a different, rather than pathological, form of sexuality. Psychology also recognizes the considerable diversity that exists among gay men and lesbians, and seeks to address the problems they face as a result of the stigma historically associated with homosexuality in the United States.

REFERENCES

Bayer, R. (1987). *Homosexuality and American psychiatry: The politics of diagnosis* (2nd Ed.). Princeton, NJ: Princeton University Press.

Bérubé, A. (1990). *Coming out under fire: The history of gay men and women in World War II.* New York: Free Press.

Cabaj, R. P., & Stein, T. S. (Eds.). (1996). *Textbook of homosexuality and mental health.* Washington, DC: American Psychiatric Press.

D'Emilio, J. (1983). Sexual politics, sexual communities: *The making of a homosexual minority in the United States, 1940–1970.* Chicago: University of Chicago Press.

Freud, S. (1951). A letter from Freud. *American Journal of Psychiatry, 107,* 786–787.

Herek, G. M. (2000). The psychology of sexual prejudice. *Current Directions in Psychological Science, 9,* 19–22.

Hooker, E. (1957). The adjustment of the male overt homosexual. *Journal of Projective Techniques, 21,* 18–31.

Kinsey, A. C., Pomeroy, W. B., & Martin, C. E. (1948). *Sexual behavior in the human male.* Philadelphia: W. B. Saunders.

Kinsey, A. C., Pomeroy, W. B., Martin, C. E., & Gebhard, P. H. (1953). *Sexual behavior in the human female.* Philadelphia: W. B. Saunders.

Weinberg, G. (1972). *Society and the healthy homosexual.* New York: St. Martin's.

G. M. HEREK
University of California, Davis

HETEROSEXUALITY
PREJUDICE AND DISCRIMINATION

HOPELESSNESS

Hopelessness refers to a psychological characteristic defined by pessimism or negative expectancies. Within cognitive therapeutic approaches, hopelessness is viewed as a set of negative cognitions about the future. These cognitions have been implicated as relevant for understanding a variety of psychological problems such as depression, suicide, schizophrenia, alcoholism, sociopathy, and physical illness.

Although historically hopelessness had been previously linked clinically to affective problems, it was the work of Aaron T. Beck at the University of Pennsylvania and the Philadelphia General Hospital that has resulted in the recent upsurge of interest in the concept (Beck, Weissman, Lester, & Trexler, 1974). Before Beck's involvement, the supposed nebulosity of the concept of hopelessness had deterred attempts at its objective measurement, thus limiting clinical research and applications. Based, however, on clinical observations and on research demonstrating associations between pessimism and self-harm (Cropley & Weckowicz, 1966), hopelessness has now been quantified using various specifically defined psychological tests. Furthermore, research has suggested that hopelessness may be composed of interrelated facets, representing negative feelings about the future, loss of motivation, and negative future expectancies.

Hopelessness is now regarded as the preeminent psychological predictor of suicide and its accompaniments, being linked in psychiatric patients to the presence of suicide intent, suicide ideation, and to subsequently completed suicides (Beck, Brown, & Steer, 1989). Findings in regard to hopelessness predicting eventual suicide have been replicated with samples of suicide ideators, depressives, and schizophrenics. Hopelessness, in fact, may be a more important predictor of suicidal intent than depression. Research has shown that when hopelessness is statistically controlled, previously significant associations between depression and suicide measures become nonsignificant. However, when depression is statistically held constant, previously significant associations between hopelessness and suicide measures remain significant (Dyer & Kreitman, 1984). Thus emerges the suggestion that hopelessness mediates the association of depression to suicide:

$$\text{Depression} \rightarrow \text{Hopelessness} \rightarrow \text{Suicide}$$

It should be noted, however, that although the relationship between hopelessness and suicide measures is significant, the association is far from perfect. Not all extremely hopeless people are suicidal, nor are all suicidal persons necessarily hopeless. Nevertheless, hopelessness represents an important clinical sign of suicidal potential.

REFERENCES

Beck, A. T., Brown, C., & Steer, R. A. (1989). Prediction of eventual suicide in psychiatric impatients by clinical ratings of hopelessness. *Journal of Consulting and Clinical Psychology, 57,* 309–310.

Beck, A. T., Weissman, A., Lester, D., & Trexler, L. (1974). The measurement of pessimism: The Hopelessness Scale. *Journal of Consulting and Clinical Psychology, 42,* 861–865.

Cropley, A. L., & Weckowicz, T. E. (1966). The dimensionality of clinical depression. *Australian Journal of Psychology, 18,* 18–25.

Dyer, J. A. T., & Kreitman, N. (1984). Hopelessness, depression and suicidal intent in parasuicide. *British Journal of Psychiatry, 144,* 127–133.

SUGGESTED READING

Beck, A. T. (1967). *Depression: Clinical, experimental, and theoretical aspects.* New York: Hoeber.

R. R. HOLDEN
Queen's University

DEPRESSION
LEARNED HELPLESSNESS
SUICIDE

HORMONES AND BEHAVIOR

Hormones are chemical substances synthesized and secreted by the endocrine glands. The hormones are transported by the blood supply until they reach a target organ and regulate its activity. Hormones function in communication within the body, integrating and regulating bodily activities and responses. Thus they have important effects on behavior in human and nonhuman animals.

THE HORMONES AND ENDOCRINE GLANDS

There are three principal types of hormones. Peptide hormones are chains of amino acids of varying length. Steroid hormones are built about a particular structure based on a four-ring, 17-carbon aromatic nucleus. Biogenic amines are amino acid derivatives of tyrosine that also can function as neurotransmitters.

The master control gland of the endocrine system is the pituitary gland, situated at the base of the brain just beneath the hypothalamus. The anterior pituitary secretes at least seven different peptide hormones. Adrenocorticotropin (ACTH) stimulates the secretion of steroid hormones by the adrenal cortex. Follicle-stimulating hormone (FSH) is a gonadotropin that promotes the growth of ovarian follicles and the secretion of estrogens in females and stimulates the formation of sperm in the male testis. Luteinizing hormone (LH) triggers ovulation and the formation of corpora lutea, modulates progesterone formation in females, and promotes the secretion of androgens in males. Prolactin functions in the mammary gland to initiate the secretion of milk and in the ovary in the maintenance of the corpora lutea and regulation of progesterone secretion. The other anterior pituitary hormones are somatotropin, or growth hormone, thyroid-stimulating hormone, and melanocyte-stimulating hormone. The posterior pituitary secretes vasopressin, or antidiuretic hormone, which elevates blood pressure and promotes the reabsorption of water, and oxytocin, which stimulates smooth muscle contraction as in the mammary glands and the female reproductive tract. Both are synthesized in the hypothalamus.

The pituitary gland is regulated by hormones from the hypothalamus. These are peptides that function to increase or decrease the secretion of pituitary hormones. The hypothalamic hormones include somatostatin, thyrotropin-releasing hormone, luteinizing hormone–releasing hormone, corticotropin-releasing hormone, growth hormone–releasing hormone, and prolactin-inhibiting hormone.

A variety of hormones are produced by the gonads and placenta. Estrogens, such as estradiol, function in the development and maintenance of the female reproductive tract, in the stimulation of the mammary glands, in the development of secondary sex characteristics, and in the regulation of behavior. Progestins, such as progesterone, often work in synergy with estrogens in affecting the female reproductive tract, mammary glands, and behavior. Androgens, such as testosterone, influence the development and maintenance of the male reproductive tract, secondary sex characteristics, and behavior.

The central part of the adrenal gland, the adrenal medulla, secretes epinephrine (adrenaline) and norepinephrine (noradrenaline), which function to mobilize bodily functions in times of emergency. The outer covering of the adrenal gland, the cortex, secretes at least 28 different steroids related to metabolism and resistance to infection. Other hormones are secreted in the thyroid gland, the parathyroid gland, and the pancreas.

PHYSIOLOGICAL CONTROL AND EFFECTS OF HORMONES

The body possesses exquisite mechanisms for the regulation of the formation and secretion of hormones. In a typical system, a hypothalamic-releasing hormone acts on the pituitary gland to stimulate the secretion of a peptide. The peptide travels via the bloodstream to increase the secretion of a hormone by the target gland. This hormone has at least two effects. One is the primary function for which it has evolved. The other is to feed back to the hypothalamus and/or pituitary to decrease the secretion of the hormones that started the process. Thus in the pituitary-adrenocortical system, for example, the hypothalamus secretes corticotropin-releasing hormone, which travels to the pituitary to stimulate the secretion of ACTH, which stimulates the secretion of cortisol by the adrenal cortex. The cortisol has its effects on target tissues and the liver and feeds back to decrease the secretion of corticotropin-releasing hormone and ACTH. The system works in a manner similar to that of the thermostat found in many homes. With a thermostat, cold temperatures cause movement in the thermostat, which turns on the heat; the heat warms the house but also feeds back on the thermostat to turn it off. For this reason, the hypothalamic-pituitary-target organ system sometimes is called a *hormonostat*.

Hormones are believed to have their effects at the level of the cell by affecting the formation of specific proteins. The hormone enters the cell and binds to a specific receptor molecule to form a hormone-receptor complex. The complex is then altered in such a way that it can enter the cell nucleus and bind to nuclear components to promote the transcription of specific messenger RNA (mRNA). The mRNA is translated into specific proteins, which have physiological effects.

METHODS

Two methods for determining the amount of hormone present in a system have been in common use. Bioassays are based on the assessment of the effects of the hormone in a physiological system in the body of an animal that has been standardized so that the amount of hormone present can be estimated from the amount of response in the system in relation to a known standard. Most assays are now done using laboratory methods of radioimmunoassay (RIA). The amount of hormone present can be determined by incubating radiolabeled hormone, the unlabeled sample, and specific antibodies to the hormone. These are more sensitive and accurate than bioassays.

Many methods have been used in relating hormones to behavior: Correlational and experimental methods are the most common. With correlational methods, the natural variation in the amount of hormone present is correlated with variation in behavior. This method has been commonly used in determining correlates of the estrous cycles of mammals. Laboratory rats have 4-day estrous cycles in which the unmated female ovulates once every 4 days. This cycle is regulated by fluctuating levels of hormones in the female's body. On the day of estrus, the female shows a decreased body temperature, decrease in food and water intake, decrease in body weight, increase in running activity, and she becomes sexually receptive. With the advent of RIA assays it has become possible to conduct correlational analyses with respect to specific hormones in a variety of systems with much greater sensitivity than previously was possible.

With experimental methods the amount of hormone present in the system is altered experimentally and the consequences for behavior are measured. Typically, this involves variations on the castration-replacement technique. In the case of the male, behavior is measured in the intact animal, and then the testes are removed. If the behavior is hormone dependent, it should decrease after castration. However, there are many reasons for which specific behaviors can decrease. Therefore, it is important to be able to restore the behavior with a restoration of the hormone levels.

An example of the use of these methods can be seen in studies of marking behavior in Mongolian gerbils (Thiessen, 1973). Gerbils have a scent gland on their undersides; they display a stereotyped marking pattern in which they rub this gland across prominent objects in their environment. Although both males and females show this pattern, it is more frequent in males. The correlational method can be used to show that females do more marking during estrus, when levels of estrogen and progesterone are elevated. The marking behavior of males decreases after castration and can be restored with the injection of androgens. Several related methods may be illustrated with this work. Because both the behavior and the gland change in unison with castration and replacement, it is possible that the behavior is a function of changes in the gland rather than of direct action of the hormone on the brain. However, by placing very small amounts of androgens in discrete loci in the preoptic area of the hypothalamic region, it was possible to restore the behavior without increasing gland size. Thus the hormone acts directly on the brain to affect behavior. Only androgens with a highly specific chemical structure are effective in the restoration of behavior. Thus the behavior can be seen to increase or decrease as a function of the presence of certain hormones with clearly defined structure at specific sites in the brain.

EFFECTS OF HORMONES IN ADULTS

The examples discussed above reveal the ways in which hormones act in adults to activate potential behavioral patterns. When the hormones are present, the behavior is displayed; when the hormones disappear, the behavior disappears. This reversibility of effect is characteristic of hormonal action in adults. The other element in this aspect of the system is the stimulus. The hormone does not trigger the behavior directly but sensitizes the animal to respond in the presence of specific stimuli. Thus presentation of a female to an intact male animal may produce mating behavior, whereas presentation of a male may produce aggression; both are influenced by the same hormones.

As noted above, hormones may affect behavior by acting either on peripheral targets, such as the scent glands of gerbils or the antlers of deer, or directly on neural mechanisms. Alternatively, hormones may alter sensitivity in sensory-perceptual systems (see Gandelman, 1983). For example, the receptive field of the pudendal nerve of female rats, which lies in the genital region, changes in relation to estrogen levels so that the female is sensitive to tactile stimulation over a larger bodily region when she is in estrus.

PERINATAL EFFECTS OF HORMONES

The generally reversible effects of hormones acting on adults can be contrasted with the more permanent effects early in life. Hormones acting early in life may affect the potential for behavior for the rest of an animal's life. Hormones acting during these periods are thought to have three important characteristics. First, their action is limited to clearly defined periods in the development of the organism. If the hormones are to have their effect they must be present during this critical period. Second, they are permanent and irreversible. That is, after the critical period, the potential for the hormones to work their effect is gone; once the change is effected, there is no going back. Third, the hormones affect systems that are not manifest at the time of occurrence of the hormone treatment but only later in life. Thus hormones acting early in life can affect adult reproductive behavior, aggressive behavior, and other systems not characteristic of the young animal.

There are two general rules for early hormone effects in mammals. First, if androgens are present during the sensitive period, the individual will develop the characteristics of a male, and female characteristics will be suppressed. Second, if androgens are absent during the sensitive period, the individual will develop the characteristics of a female, and male characteristics will fail to develop.

These effects can be illustrated with experiments done on laboratory rats, such as the classic experiment of Whalen and Edwards (1967). Normal adult male rats that have normal levels of androgens in their systems display behavioral patterns with receptive females that include mounting the female, vaginal intromissions, and ejaculations. Normal adult female rats with the appropriate hormones (estrogen and progesterone) present respond to males with a variety of responses, including lordosis, a posture that facilitates the intromission by males. Various groups were tested when they were given appropriate hormone injections as adults and partners of the appropriate sex. Control males or males that had received a sham operation neonatally showed normal male behavior but did not show normal female behavior, even when injected with estrogen and progesterone and presented with a male. Males that had been castrated within the first 5 days of life did not show normal male behavior even after hormones were provided when they were adult. However, when given estrogen and progesterone and presented with a vigorous male, these neonatally castrated males responded with the pattern of lordosis characteristic of normal females. Males that were castrated neonatally and given androgens soon after the castration acted like normal males, showing that the effects were due to the loss of hormones, not to extraneous causes. Similarly, both normal and sham-operated females displayed normal female, but not male, behavior in the test situation. However, when females had been ovariectomized and given androgen neonatally they displayed normal male, but not female, behavior. Thus neonatal removal of the gonad affected the males but not the females. Female behavior in mammals develops normally in the absence of gonadal hormones; male behavior and the suppression of female behavior require the hormones. In a sense, one can think of the female condition in rats as analogous to a default condition in a computer program.

There are many complications to this basic pattern—in birds it is the male condition that seems more like a default condition, and hormones are needed for the development of mechanisms supporting female behavior and suppressing the potential for male behavior. This seems correlated with the pattern of sex chromosomes: Males are XY in mammals, whereas females are XY in birds.

Although they can have some subtle feminizing effects under some conditions, estrogens generally act neonatally in the same manner as do androgens. Thus, in the experiment described above, there were groups of males and females that were gonadectomized and injected neonatally with estrogen rather than androgen. The results were the same as when androgen was given: The estrogen masculinized and defeminized the behavior. This has a number of implications. Why does not the normal female masculinize and defeminize herself? The primary reason is that a protein, α-fetoprotein, normally binds the estrogens so that they do not have these effects in the intact female. Indeed, it appears that androgens normally produce their effects by acting as estrogens. Because they are closely related steroid hormones, some androgens can be converted to estrogens by a process of aromatization. According to the aromatization hypothesis, this is normal for androgens acting perinatally. Thus those androgens that are not aromatizable to estrogens are generally ineffective in producing the perinatal effects.

Interestingly, the masculinization and defeminization effects are not mutually exclusive. Injection of androstenedione, a kind of androgen, to neonatally castrated male rats produces males that display both lordosis and intromission and ejaculation. This implies that male and female are two independent dimensions, not just the ends of a continuum.

The hormones of the males of a litter can have some effect on the females of the litter via the shared intrauterine blood supply. The timing of the critical period varies from species to species, being both prenatal and postnatal in laboratory rats and house mice, but completely prenatal in primates, including humans. The behavioral effects are correlated with anatomical changes in the brain attributable to early hormonal influence. Drugs, such as opioids, or stress on the mother can have demasculinizing and feminizing effects.

EARLY HORMONE EFFECTS IN HUMANS

Effects of early hormones in humans have been studied in relation to three syndromes. With progestin-induced hermaphroditism, female babies born to women who were administered progestins to maintain their pregnancies were masculinized. Congenital adrenal hyperplasia (CAH), also called the adrenogenital syndrome, is a hereditary disease caused by an enzyme deficit in the adrenal gland, so that a genetic female produces androgen instead of cortisone. With androgen insensitivity, or testicular feminization, a genetic male secretes testosterone, but, because of an enzyme deficiency, the target cells do not respond to it.

In all three cases, there is an ambiguity of gender and the individual may be assigned as either male or female. However, humans are quite different from other animals in various respects. In general, humans of ambiguous gender adopt the gender identity of the sex to which they are assigned and in which they are reared. Thus environmental effects are quite important.

Although individuals of ambiguous gender resulting from these three syndromes generally accept the gender to which they are assigned, various subtle effects of the early hormone abnormalities have been detected. In studies of the 1960s, the hormone-exposed females appeared more likely than other genetic females to prefer jeans to dresses and professional careers to homemaking. However, the culture has changed. In one study (Reinisch & Karow, 1977), progestin-exposed women given personality tests were found to be more independent, sensitive, self-assured, individualistic, and self-sufficient than other women. Subjects exposed to estrogen were more group oriented and group dependent. In another study, Ehrhardt and colleagues (1989) found rather minimal effects of exposure to diethylsilbestrol (DES); however, DES-exposed women showed less orientation toward parenting than did controls.

OTHER EFFECTS OF HORMONES IN HUMANS

Many other effects of hormones on human behavior have been reported. An important distinction in studies of human males, in parallel with that in other animals, is between motivation, desire, or libido, on the one hand, and capacity or performance on the other. Thus, in rats, estradiol benzoate (a form of estrogen) produces no facilitation of performance, as measured by penile reflexes measured in an ex-copula reflex testing apparatus, but some facilitation of copulatory behavior as displayed with a female, which includes motivational effects. By contrast, dihydrotestosterone facilitates ex-copula reflexes, but not copulation. Analogously, castrated and hypogonadal men show good erection to stimuli, but few spontaneous erections during the day. Thus castration decreases libido. With aging, by contrast, desire remains, but capacity deteriorates. Castration has been used as a treatment of sex offenders, but its effects do not justify such treatment (Heim, 1981).

During the 17th and 18th centuries, castrati, men who had been castrated before puberty to preserve their high-pitched voices, played an important role in opera. However, many psychological and physiological abnormalities were caused by this treatment, including abnormal fat deposition, abnormally long arms and legs, and probably disturbances in psychosexual orientation (Peschel & Peschel, 1987).

In other studies, men who were winners of doubles tennis matches had higher testosterone levels than did losers. There was no such difference when prizes were awarded by lottery. Recipients of medical degrees showed increases in testosterone several days later. In another study, testosterone was found to rise just before most matches; players with higher testosterone levels generally did better. After matches, the testosterone levels of the winners rose relative to those of the losers. There is some suggestion of a relationship between androgens and dominance-related behavior that may apply to such situations.

Studies of hormonal effects in human females have been especially controversial because of possible implications for gender issues. There have been many reports of changing mood, performance in cognitive tasks, sensory sensitivity, sexual activity, performance of tongue twisters, and making precise hand movements during different phases of the menstrual cycle. Although there have been many negative results, there is a sufficient number of studies with positive results to suggest that at least some of these effects are real and reliable.

Even more controversial has been research suggesting a hormonal basis for sexual orientation, including homosexuality. The results are not clear, but it is clear that if there is an important endocrine effect, it is embedded within a complex web of dynamic interactions among genetic, hormonal, environmental, and social factors.

SOME COMPLEXITIES OF HORMONE ACTION

As is apparent from the above, hormones do not simply trigger particular behavioral responses. Early hormone effects are mediated by changes in the nervous system that affect the potential and proclivity for certain behavioral patterns later in life. These may be expressed in the adult, something like a developer bringing out a photographic image, when conditions are appropriate. However, there is an elaborate network of determinants of the behavior.

Space can be an important influence on the effects of hormones. In studies of rhesus monkeys in small test enclosures, it was found that the copulatory behavior was not greatly influenced by the female's reproductive condition. However, in large enclosures, copulatory behavior did vary, decreasing during the female's luteal phase. Thus the spatial conditions of the test affect the effects of hormones on behavior.

In studies of red-deer stags, it was found that season was an important mediating influence. Castration abolished all rutting behavior and caused a drop in the dominance status of the male. When testosterone was injected in December, rutting behavior was restored. With testosterone in April or June, however, there was no immediate restoration of the rut. Thus testosterone plays a permissive role in rutting but is effective only at some times of year. By contrast, testosterone induced social aggressiveness at any time.

Individual differences and genetic effects are important. Male guinea pigs that showed individual differences in sexual behavior before castration all showed decreased sexual behavior after castration. After hormone replacement, not only was the behavior restored but so were the individual differences in behavior. Thus the locus of the individual differences seems to be in the soma, probably in the central nervous system. Similarly, early androgen treatment of female house mice of different strains increases levels of aggression but generally to the level characteristic of the males of the different strains.

The subtle nature of social modulation of hormone effects is especially apparent in the reproductive cycles of birds, such as the ring dove, a relative of the domestic pigeon. The cycle proceeds through a complete sequence, including nest building, courtship, copulation, incubation, and parental behavior. Through the entire cycle the behaviors of male and female are coordinated and synchronized into a pattern that results in the production of viable offspring. It is a complicated sequence in which the behavior of one partner may serve as the stimulus for a hormonal change in the other, with that hormonal change altering the second partner's behavior in a manner that may affect the first. Some of the changing behavioral proclivities through the cycle may be mimicked by implanting hormones into particular loci in the brain.

The dogma has been that once the vertebrate nervous system is formed, its structure is rather fixed. Recent hormone research has challenged that dogma. In songbirds such as canaries and zebra finches, there is a set of discrete brain regions that are critical to song production. There is even a lateralization of function. These structures are generally larger in males than in females. The sex differences in neuron number and size appear to be due to early effects of steroid hormones. However, testosterone treatment of adult females induces structural changes that involve a reorganization of synaptic connections among neurons. Thus, under some circumstances, the structure of the nervous system can be sensitive to hormones well into adulthood. Even more remarkably, there are cyclical anatomical changes in the brains of birds. The size of two of the nuclei implicated in the control of song in canaries is larger in spring, when birds are singing, than in fall and after several months of not singing. There appear to be increases and decreases in the number of synapses as part of an annual cycle of breeding and hormonal changes. These effects are hormonally mediated.

Plasticity of the nervous system in adults is not limited to birds. In a similar manner, motoneurons in the lumbar spinal cord of male rats show decreases in both soma size and dendritic length after castration and are restored by androgen treatment.

Hormones play a pivotal role in the integration and control of behavior in a wide range of species and situations. However, they do so only as part of very complex interactive systems, and thus simplistic interpretations of hormone effects are to be discouraged.

REFERENCES

Ehrhardt, A., Meyer-Bahlburg, H. F. L., Rosen, L. R., Feldman, J. F., Veridiano, N. P., Elkin, E. J., & McEwen, B. S. (1989). The development of gender-related behavior in females following prenatal exposure of diethylstilbestrol (DES). *Hormones and Behavior, 23,* 526–541.

Gandelman, R. (1983). Gonadal hormones and sensory function. *Neuroscience and Biobehavioral Reviews, 7,* 1–17.

Heim, N. (1981). Sexual behavior of castrated sex offenders. *Archives of Sexual Behavior, 10,* 11–19.

Peschel, E. R., & Peschel, R. E. (1987). Medical insights into the castrati in opera. *American Scientist, 75,* 578–583.

Reinisch, J. M., & Karow, W. G. (1977). Prenatal exposure to synthetic progestins and estrogens: Effects on human development. *Archives of Sexual Behavior, 6,* 257–288.

Thiessen, D. D. (1973). Footholds for survival. *American Scientist, 61,* 346–351.

SUGGESTED READING

Crews, D. (Ed.). (1987). *Psychobiology of reproductive behavior: An evolutionary perspective.* Englewood Cliffs, NJ: Prentice-Hall.

Hubbard, J. R., Kalimi, M. Y., & Witorsch, R. J. (1986). *Review of endocrinology and reproduction.* Richmond, VA: Renaissance.

D. A. DEWSBURY
University of Florida

HORNEY, KAREN D. (1885–1952)

Karen D. Horney received the MD from the University of Berlin in 1915. Horney was originally trained in Freudian psychoanalysis at the Berlin Psychoanalytical Institute. However, she eventually broke from the standard Freudian orthodoxy over the issue of female sexuality. In *New Ways in Psychoanalysis* she strongly criticized Freud's libido theory, stating that his stress on the sexual instinct was completely out of proportion. In 1932 she emigrated to the United States, where she practiced her new form of analysis in Chicago and New York.

Although Horney kept many of the basic Freudian concepts (repression, resistance, transference, free association), like other social analysts (Alfred Adler, Erich Fromm, Harry Stack Sullivan) she stressed the importance of social and environmental conditions in molding the personality. In her first book, *The Neurotic Personality of Our Times* (1937), she stressed one of her most important concepts: basic anxiety. This feeling of the child resulted from "being isolated and helpless in a potentially hostile world," and hence was not inherited but a product of culture and upbringing. Such anxiety was a primary condition for later personality difficulties. Out of this feeling arose a basic drive for safety or security: To be secure meant to be free from anxiety. Unlike Freud, Horney believed anxiety to be a striving force.

Through interaction with society humans also acquired other needs. In *Our Inner Conflicts* (1945), Horney divided these needs into three groups: (a) to move toward people (approach, affection); (b) to move against people (power, exploitation); and (c) to move away from people (restriction of one's life, self-sufficiency). These three forces could obviously come in conflict with one another. The normal person resolved the conflict by integrating them, or the conflicts could be resolved or avoided if a child were raised amid love and respect, feeling wanted and secure, and being surrounded by trust. When a person took one orientation to the exclusion of others, three types of personality might emerge, depending on the orientation: (a) the compliant type (moving toward people), (b) the hostility type (moving against people), and (c) the detached type (moving away from people).

Another of Horney's basic concepts—also related to the conflicts—was that of the idealized image. In actuality, this image was fictitious and illusory. Here there was a discrepancy between a person's self-image and the person's real self. Through this self-deception, one creates an image of what one believes or feels he or she ought to be: a saint, a mastermind, or a Casanova. This image expresses the fact that the person cannot tolerate his or her real self.

R. W. Lundin
Wheaton, Illinois

HORNEY'S THEORY

Although the writings of Karen Horney deal primarily with the causes and dynamics of neurosis, her work also represents a significant contribution to the area of personality theory.

In essence, Horney's theory involves a unique synthesis of Freudian and Adlerian ideas. Like Freud, she stresses the importance of powerful unconscious intrapsychic conflicts—a conception that Adler's holistic model specifically rejects. Yet she differs markedly from orthodox psychoanalysis in several respects: by dispensing with the construct of libido; by rejecting the assumption that all human beings are motivated by inborn illicit instincts such as incest and destructiveness; and by emphasizing the social, rather than the biological, determinants of personality.

CAUSES OF NEUROSIS

Every individual has the capacity and desire to develop individual potentialities in constructive ways and become a decent human being. Psychopathology occurs only if this innate force toward positive growth and self-realization is blocked by external social influences. Parents who are themselves neurotic are generally incapable of healthy love, benign care, and respect for the child's individuality. Instead, they tend to behave in pathogenic ways determined by their own neurotic needs such as domination, overprotectiveness, overindulgence, humiliation and derision, brutality, perfectionism, hypocrisy, inconsistency, partiality to other siblings, blind adoration, and/or neglect.

Whereas the healthy child develops a sense of belonging to a safe and nurturing family, the child reared by neurotic parents becomes profoundly insecure and apprehensive and views the world as unfriendly and frightening. Alleviating this intense basic anxiety now becomes the child's primary goal, one that overrides its innate healthy desires and needs. To this end, the child rejects warm and spontaneous dealings with other people in favor of manipulating them to his or her own advantage. Thus the healthy quest for self-realization is replaced by an all-out drive for safety—the hallmark of neurosis.

MOVING TOWARD, AGAINST, AND AWAY FROM PEOPLE

The neurotic striving for safety is accomplished by exaggerating one of the three main characteristics of basic anxiety: helplessness, aggressiveness, and detachment.

The neurotic solution of *helplessness* is typified by excessive desires for protection and exaggerated, hypocritical compliance with the wishes of others (moving toward people). Those who emphasize this orientation try to convert their seemingly inescapable inner weakness into an advantage by using it to evoke concern, care, and love from other people. Such individuals consciously profess a sincere interest in others, while repressing their intense selfishness, manipulativeness, hostility, and healthy self-assertion.

The neurotic solution of *aggressiveness* is typified by the belief that life is a Darwinian jungle where only the fittest survive (moving against people). Those who emphasize this orientation regard most other people as hostile and hypocritical and are likely to conclude that genuine affection is unattainable or even nonexistent. Such individuals repress their feelings of helplessness and need for love and may behave sadistically toward those who seem weak because this provides a threatening reminder of what they most dislike about themselves.

The neurotic solution of *detachment* is typified by avoiding intimate or even casual contacts with others (moving away from people). Those who emphasize this orientation strive to become completely and unrealistically self-sufficient, supporting this aim by overestimating their abilities and their differences from other people. Such individuals try never to allow anyone or anything to become indispensable. Thus they deny their healthy emotions and need for love, behaving much like a person in a hotel room who never removes the "Do Not Disturb" sign from the door.

Whereas the healthy person is free to move toward, against, or away from people as circumstances dictate, the three neurotic solutions are compulsive and inflexible. However, they are not mutually exclusive. In each instance, the two orientations that are consciously deemphasized remain powerful at an unconscious level and conflict with the dominant orientation. Thus the neurotic solution of compliance is maintained by repressing one's desires to be aggressive and detached as well as properly self-assertive, all of which conflict strongly (albeit unconsciously) with the manifest helplessness. Similarly, the neurotic solution of aggressiveness involves sharp inner conflicts with repressed wishes to be compliant and detached, and to obtain affection and love. And the neurotic solution of detachment conflicts with repressed desires to be dependent and aggressive, as well as the need for friendship and love. Thus Horney's model can be schematized as a triangle, with a given individual's dominant orientation at the apex and the two remaining orientations (which are primarily unconscious and conflict with the dominant orientation) at each of the corners.

THE IDEALIZED IMAGE

Those who suffer from neurosis repress not only their painful inner conflicts, but also the faults and weaknesses that they perceive—and despise—in themselves. Instead they form a conscious self-image that is exaggeratedly positive, and that reinforces the dominant neurotic solution. Thus the compliant, dependent, and manipulative individual may believe that he or she is outstandingly unselfish, helpful, and desirable; the individual who masks inner weakness by moving against people may conclude that he or she is destined to be an invincible leader or warrior; and the detached individual who unconsciously craves affection may decide that he or she is totally capable, self-sufficient, and has no need at all of other people.

This grandiose idealized image seems quite normal and realistic to its creator. The result is a vicious circle: The idealized image drives the individual to establish unattainable standards and goals that make ultimate defeat a certainty; this in turn increases the sufferer's self-contempt, intensifies the inner conflict between the fallible true self and the idealized image, increases the dependence on the idealized image, and furthers a compulsive and insatiable striving to bolster this unrealistic image by achieving glorious triumphs.

NEUROTIC CLAIMS

Those who suffer from neurosis often convert normal wishes into irrational claims that supposedly entitle them to the triumphs demanded by the idealized image. Thus a woman beset by severe but repressed self-doubts may consciously believe that any man upon whom she bestows her love must unfailingly return it. Or a man who unconsciously feels professionally (or socially) incompetent may expect to receive a better job (or someone's affection) without having to earn it or even ask for it.

THE TYRANNY OF THE SHOULD

The relentless inner demands that aim toward the actualization of the idealized image resemble the workings of a totalitarian police state, a quality Horney characterizes as "the tyranny of the should." Thus neurotic individuals may believe that they should be perfectly (and impossibly) successful, accurate, unselfish, or loving; that they should choose a particular job or mate; and so forth. These "shoulds" so dominate conscious thought and so obscure the repressed innate healthy drives, that the sufferer no longer is able to recognize what he or she truly needs and desires. To liberate drives toward self-realization that have been so thoroughly blocked and to enable the sufferer to replace the compulsive and painful striving toward unreachable goals with activities that are enjoyable and rewarding, typically requires formal psychotherapy.

SUGGESTED READING

Horney, K. (1945). *Our inner conflicts: A constructive theory of neurosis.* New York: Norton.

Horney, K. (1950). *Neurosis and human growth: The struggle toward self-realization.* New York: Norton.

R. B. EWEN
Miami, Florida

ADLERIAN PSYCHOTHERAPY
PSYCHOANALYSIS
SULLIVAN'S INTERPERSONAL THEORY

HOT LINE SERVICES

The telephone hot line offers members of a selected community free, immediate, and anonymous access to a counseling service, typically provided by a trained volunteer worker or paraprofessional. The original purpose of these telephone-based counseling services was to give help in emergency situations. One of their earliest uses, beginning in the 1950s, was in suicide prevention centers, though the effectiveness of this use is equivocal (Lester, 1974). Subsequently, their function and setting broadened to include the provision of information, referral, and empathic listening for even minor problems in community mental health and college counseling centers. On one college campus hot line, the problems mentioned most frequently by callers were dating, family, and loneliness (Tucker, Megenity, & Vigil, 1975).

The hot line has been understood as an application of technology that offsets the complexity and impersonality so common in a technological society. In particular, the telephone may offer certain unique features to a counseling process, such as caller and counselor anonymity and caller control (Williams & Douds, 1973).

Historically, however, the hot line was associated with the rise of community psychology, with its emphases on the social determinants of psychological problems and their prevention through social and community intervention. Reacting to a shortage of professional mental health workers and their inequitable availability according to social class; to the presence of medically oriented, largely custodial, and isolated mental health institutions; and to the predominance of intrapsychic models of individual pathology, a community psychology perspective emerged in the 1960s. It emphasized more effective employment of professionals in consultative and supervisory roles, together with the use of direct service of paraprofessionals indigenous to a target community. It also shifted to an active public health model aimed at reducing incidences, in part by teaching social competence and coping skills to populations at risk. As part of its goal of attaining comprehensive community service, the Community Mental Health Centers Act of 1963 required the inclusion of a 24-hour service (Garfield, 1974). The walk-in clinic and the telephone hot line readily lent themselves to this requirement and, generally, to the considerations critical to a community psychology.

In *Principles of Preventative Psychiatry,* Gerald Caplan provided a conceptual framework for therapeutic techniques that highlight the importance of the immediate availability and flexibility of a treatment modality like the telephone hot line. Drawing on psychoanalytic ego psychology and a public health model, Caplan advocated immediate and time-limited intervention in crisis situations as a strategy of prevention. A crisis is an accidentally or developmentally induced stressful situation during which an individual's typical coping abilities and resources are exceeded. Since an individual is believed to be less defended and more open to change during a crisis, brief intervention in such a period can avert a more damaging disorder. In this context, the telephone hot line evolved as a modality of crisis intervention. Through clarifying perceptions of the situation, facilitating expression of feeling, providing cognitive restructuring, mobilizing resources, and encouraging problem solving, the counselor attempts to relieve distress, restore previous functioning, and develop new coping techniques for future use.

REFERENCES

Caplan, G. (1974). *Principles of preventative psychiatry.* New York: Basic Books. (Original work published 1964)

Garfield, S. (1974). *Clinical psychology.* Chicago: Aldine.

Lester, D. (1974). Effects of suicide prevention centers on suicide rates in the U.S. *Health Service Reports, 89,* 37–39.

Tucker, B., Megenity, D., & Vigil, L. (1975). Anatomy of a campus crisis center. In R. Suinn & R. Weigel (Eds.), *The innovative psychological therapies: Critical and creative contributions.* New York: Harper & Row.

Williams, T., & Douds, J. (1973). The unique contribution of telephone therapy. In D. Lester & G. Brockopp (Eds.), *Telephone therapy and crisis intervention.* Springfield, IL: Thomas.

SUGGESTED READING

Lester, D., & Brockopp, G. (Eds.). (1973). *Telephone therapy and crisis intervention.* Springfield, IL: Thomas.

K. J. Shapiro
Psychologists for the Ethical Treatment of Animals

COUNSELING
DRUG REHABILITATION
SPOUSE ABUSE
SUICIDE PREVENTION
TIME-LIMITED PSYCHOTHERAPY

HOUSE-TREE-PERSON TEST

Pictorial symbols have existed prior to letters throughout the history of humanity. Although these pictographs had given clues as to the determination of their meaning, the first used as a recognized psychological test was the Baum Tree-Drawing Test developed 54 years ago. This test was developed by Koch, a Swiss vocational guidance counselor. Koch was said to have developed the test based on the influence of a colleague who was well versed in mythology, and from whom Koch conceptualized the idea that a person's basic personality could be determined from their tree sketch.

Additionally, a psychologist from Bern asserted that not only one's personality but abnormalities could also be ascertained, and the Baum Test began to be used in a wide variety of areas. At around the same time, Buck developed a test in which a house, a tree, and a person were drawn on paper: the House-Tree-Person Drawing Test (HTP). The Character Portrait Test also came out around this time. The Character Portrait Test measured intelligence from a developmental perspective and also had a position from which it was used to understand personality. For the most part, the major drawing tests used today were developed at the end of the 1940s.

Picture drawing may be utilized for both testing as well as therapy itself, similar to sandbox therapy. If we limit the discussion to task-picture drawing, then the HTP would be classified as a projective psychological test. Similar to the Rorschach Test, because there are no limitations in the theory it is necessary to consider the materials and way of thinking that form the basis at the time of analytic interpretation in actual clinical practice.

From the viewpoint of developmental psychology, as age advances, picture drawing goes through corresponding characteristic stages that can be both empirically and statistically understood. Personality development, maturity, retrogression, and pathology can therefore be examined by comparing actual age to that suggested by the drawings. In addition, the results of statistical studies have made it clear that various groups show peculiar characteristics in drawing pictures, and these can form a basis for analysis. Finally, the characteristics of pictures drawn and their correspondence with clinical symptoms or problematic behaviors can be examined for clinical validity. The above three uses are common, but because Koch conceived the Baum Test based on an understanding of the influence of myths and the use of spatial symbolism as a basis of explanation, a knowledge of symbolism, ethnology, archeology, and analytic psychiatry are integral to interpreting the picture drawing test. However, this makes it difficult for psychologists trained in the natural sciences to get a grasp on using the test.

Based on the work of picture drawing test specialists and others, various spatial diagrams related to the test have been published. However, quite apart from these specialists, Jung stated, "Symbols of trees are regarded as an archetypal inheritance born from the unconscious. Trees, like mandalas, express the personal development of the self." Machover, who utilized portrait drawing from the standpoint of psychoanalysis, explained, "Because people have so many external characteristics, choices are made in identification including projection and selection, thereby expressing the desires and conflicts of the drawer."

The interpretation of a single picture tends to become complicated, but for the combined House-Tree-Person test the meaning is divided between three pictures. "House" expresses thoughts and conditions regarding the family and household. "Tree" expresses the symbolic or unconscious self. Finally, "Person" tends to express the conscious self and perception of humanity.

It must be made clear from the outset that the pictures discussed here are not drawn from the point of view of art but in order to test personality. A variety of types of pictures including abstract, concrete, scenic, portrait, still life, free, and thematic pictures, may be used for such testing. In general there are two methods of personality testing: the "question method," which uses replies of "yes" or "no" to various questions regarding personality, and the "projection method," which studies individuals' responses to ink blots, vague pictures, and incomplete sentences. Drawing tests are regarded as belonging to the projection method.

The projection method is based on the idea that when people are faced with unclear or diverse stimuli or problems, in order to give them meaning, they project their own lifestyle or deep desires and conflicts onto them. For instance, it is well known that people in vague and complicated situations in daily life will express diverse and different behaviors and emotions under objectively identical conditions.

Requirements for tests falling under the theory of the projection method are: (a) the topic (stimulus) presented is either vague or unstructured; (b) the subject can react with a high degree of freedom; and (c) the results are interpreted as a projection of the subject's inner world. In contrast to the question method, the projection method is characterized by subjects being unable to control their responses because they do not know the meanings or methods of interpretation of the test.

Most projection method tests require subjects to use words in their responses, but the picture drawing test asks that pictures be drawn. However, since these are psychological tests, topics, forms, and tools must be specified so that statistical comparisons and verification can be performed. Consequently, it is a general rule to have a theory for the evaluation and interpretation of the drawing.

Subjects commonly used clinically for drawing tests include trees, people, families, and the combination house/tree/person. These tests are called the Baum, DAP, Family Drawing, and HTP test, respectively. The tests are performed using regulated sizes of paper and pencil thickness (sometimes crayons or colored pencils may be added) and an eraser, and the subject is asked to draw on the paper a house, a tree, and a person in whatever way they like. As a rule there is no time limit. Sometimes a simple explanation from the subject is required regarding what has been drawn.

In the HTP test the topics are a house, a tree, and a person without any specifications. Therefore, examinees are free to draw whatever they like, and because they are not sure how their character or psychological state will be judged using the pictures, they cannot disguise it. Accordingly, their inner state is to some extent inevitably revealed by the picture drawn.

Various factors must be dynamically interpreted in combination while also considering statistical research results for the interpretation of drawing tests. However, a general outline of the usual meanings of picture characteristics is as follows. In the analysis of form, the size of the picture, pressure of the pencil stroke, and detail of the drawing all express energy and activity. Disordered lines indicate emotional instability, and poor picture balance and a lack of relationship between picture elements show a lack of perception of reality and poor planning. Inappropriate gaps and missing elements show strong impulsiveness and conflict. Enumerated pictures show objectivity and a lack of perspective, and the strength of shadowing expresses anxiety.

In the analysis of content, pictures of houses tend to reflect the subject's recognition, feelings, and attitudes toward their own household or family. For example, subjects who depend strongly on their family draw far larger than actual houses, while those with conflicts or dissatisfaction draw peculiar buildings other than houses or draw their own house dilapidated at the edge of the paper. Pictures of trees tend to express the basic unconscious self of the subject. The trunk reflects vitality, the state of the ego, and how the subject feels about these things. Branches show the subject's relationship and adaptation to the environment, while roots reveal the relationship between the subject and reality. Those who are vital and well adapted tend to draw appropriately big, luxuriant trees. Character portraits are not limited to self portraits. This is because the examinee tends to be guarded, unlike the case for houses and trees. However, even if there is deliberate distortion, in some form self portraiture or perceptions of humanity can be considered to be expressed. Body parts can be interpreted as follows: the head is intelligence, imagination, and self control; the face, communication with others; the body, physical energy; the hands, ability to contact the outside world; and the feet, stability of the personality and attitude toward sex.

Recently an Integrated HTP has been developed in which the three items (house, tree, person) are all drawn on a single sheet of paper. This integrated HTP can make clear the strength of integration of the personality and abnormalities from the balance and presence or lack of relationships among the three pictures. Compared to other projection tests, the advantages of the drawing test are that there is no disadvantage due to level of verbal ability, that it can be applied to a wide range of people, and that it is impossible to create a verbal self-defense through rationalization or intellectualization. A subject who outwardly appears very optimistic and active and who boasts that "everything is going great" may draw an atrophied picture, while an introvert may show an unexpectedly lively and strongly active potential, and juvenile delinquents who are continually running away from home may draw a picture of a family group happily sharing a meal in an expression of their sadness. In this way the inner, psychological world that even the subject was unaware of can be expressed in drawings in ways that could not be anticipated from outer speech and behavior.

REFERENCES

Fukunishi, I., Misawa, N., & Kikuchi, M. (1997). Alexithymic characteristics in the synthetic House-Tree-Person (HTP) Drawing Test. *Perceptual and Motor Skills, 85,* 939–942.

Fukunishi, I. (1998). A truncated tree: Anxiety before living kidney transplantation in Japanese recipients. *Nephron, 79*(3), 375–376.

Kikuchi, M., & Fukunishi, I. (1999). Psychological problems of end-stage renal disease (ESRD) patients in cutting-edge medicine and liaison psychiatry. In M. Matsushita & I. Fukunishi (Eds.), *Psychiatric problems of organ transplantation, cancer, HIV, and genetic counseling* (pp. 159–167). Amsterdam: Elsevier.

I. FUKUNISHI
Tokyo Institute of Psychiatry

CLINICAL ASSESSMENT
PROJECTIVE TECHNIQUES
PSYCHOLOGICAL ASSESSMENT

HOVLAND, CARL I. (1912–1961)

Known for his research in the psychology of attitudes and the psychology of communication, Carl I. Hovland earned his reputation at the Yale Communication and Attitude Change Program, an institute that he founded. The BA and MA were earned at Northwestern University; Yale conferred the PhD upon him in 1936, the year he began his career at Yale as an instructor. During World War II Hovland served as chief psychologist and director of experimental studies in the office of the chief of staff of the War Department. His long tenure at Yale was interrupted at the height of his career by death from cancer.

While heading the Yale Studies in Attitude and Communication Program, Hovland with his associates published several important volumes, including *The Order (Presentation in Persuasion, Attitude Organization and Change, Communication and Persuasion, Experiments in Mass Communication,* and *Social Judgment: Assimilation and Contrast Effects in Communication and Attitude Change* Sherif & Hovland, 1961). Hovland's research team is credited with a number of contributions to psychology, among them being (a) the sleeper effect, (b) communicator credibility, (c) the preferred value of stating a conclusion, and (d) valuable effects due to the order of presenting propaganda.

W. S. SAHAKIAN

HULL, CLARK L. (1884–1952)

Clark L. Hull's most important contribution to psychology lies in his theory of learning, considered one of the most important learning theories of the 20th century.

He received the PhD in 1918 at the University of Wisconsin. Early in his career he was interested in the field of aptitude testing, an area he abandoned because he did not see much future in it. He then turned to the field of hypnosis and suggestibility. In 1929 he accepted an appointment as research professor at Yale University, a post he held until his retirement.

For most of his career Hull devoted himself to the development of a theory of learning along with experimental research to support it. In 1940, with a number of colleagues he published *A Mathematico-Deductive Theory of Rote Learning.* This was considered a masterpiece in theory construction, but it was so complicated that most psychologists failed to understand it. In 1943 he published the first complete statement of his theory of learning, *Principles of Behavior,* of which revisions followed in 1951 and 1952.

Hull's theory was basically an S-R (stimulus-response) theory and reflected some influences from the behavioristic ideas of John Watson. Hull was also influenced by Ivan Pavlov's work on the conditioned reflex, which he considered to be a simple form of learning on which more complex kinds of learning could be built.

Like B. F. Skinner, Hull stressed the importance of reinforcement if learning was to take place. Reinforcement was successful because it resulted in the reduction of drives. Thus the concept of drives and their reduction became an important aspect of Hull's theory. He considered the environmental influences on the organism as well: These were the input, while the responses the organism made were the output.

The formulation of a hypothetico-deductive theory of learning involved a series of postulates which should eventually be tested by experimentation. The final formulation of the theory consisted of 18 postulates and 12 corollaries, stated in both mathematical and verbal forms. Hull's theory also includes intervening variables, constructs that are assumed but never really subject to experimental verification.

Hull's theory was systematic and generated a great deal of research. Hull insisted on well-controlled experiments and on the quantification of the resulting data.

R. W. LUNDIN
Wheaton, Illinois

HUMAN DEVELOPMENT

Life-span developmental psychology proposes that human development occurs from conception to death and that it involves the intricate interweaving of biological, sociocultural, and psychological processes (Baltes, 1987; Thomae, 1979). With regard to individual development (ontogenesis), this theoretical approach focuses on: (a) how single individuals change over time (intra-individual change); (b) differences among individuals during different developmental periods (inter-individual variability); and (c) differences in individuals' patterns of change over time (inter-individual variability in intra-individual change). Moreover, life-span developmental psychologists agree on a set of core assumptions from which they study human development. In concert, these assumptions state that human development is a life-long process that involves continuity and discontinuity, multidirectionality, gains and losses, plasticity, and embeddedness in multiple contexts. These assumptions have resulted in specific developmental research methodologies and have made the study of human development a multidisciplinary endeavor rather than the domain of a single discipline (Baltes, 1987).

CONTINUITY AND DISCONTINUITY IN HUMAN DEVELOPMENT

Theorists of human development have debated two issues with respect to the nature of continuity and discontinuity. The first issue is whether there are certain age periods (e.g., early childhood) which hold primacy in human development, or whether development occurs at all stages of the life span. The second issue is whether development proceeds in a smooth, linear, and continuous manner or whether it proceeds through a series of discontinuous stages.

Based on comprehensive reviews of the empirical literature, several theorists have come to the conclusion that humans have a capacity for change across the entire life span (Brim & Kagan, 1980) and that "no age period holds supremacy in regulating the nature of development" (Baltes, 1987, p. 613). Furthermore, over the course of human development, and at all stages of the life span, both continuous (cumulative) and discontinuous (qualitatively different and innovative) processes are at work (Baltes, 1987; Lerner, 1984).

MULTIDIMENSIONALITY AND MULTIDIRECTIONALITY OF HUMAN DEVELOPMENT

Another core principle of human development is its multidimensionality and multidirectionality. Regardless of the domain of development, multiple dimensions are required to capture the complexity of behavioral changes over time. The sequencing of changes, the conditions influencing continuity and change, and the direction of changes (increasing or decreasing in complexity, frequency, or salience) tend to vary across dimensions within any domain. The multiple dimensions can and typically do vary in the directions of change and the pacing of those directional changes. For example, within the cognitive domain, some types of intellectual functioning remain stable or increase over most of the adult life span and into late life (e.g., vocabulary), whereas others show normative decline after the age of 60 or even earlier (e.g., complex problem solving). Only by examining multidirectional variations in the trajectories of change of multiple dimensions over time can the complexity of human development be elucidated.

GAINS AND LOSSES IN HUMAN DEVELOPMENT

The process of human development is not a simple movement toward higher efficiency, such as incremental growth. Rather, throughout life, development always consists of the joint occurrence of gain (growth) and loss (decline). In contrast to earlier views of human development that focused solely on processes that generated increasing capacity or complexity, life-span models of human development assert that in order to gain capacity in one dimension, loss must occur in another (Baltes, 1987). New adaptive capacities replace or subsume previously functional ones that have been lost. This principle presumes that some dimensions within any system grow and become more differentiated and adaptive, whereas others are simultaneously declining. In the second half of the life span, losses are likely to outpace gains in adaptive capacity, requiring the individual to engage in selective optimization with compensation (Baltes & Baltes, 1990). As reserve capacity and the range of plasticity decline in later life, older adults select more carefully the domains of functioning in which they try to maintain high efficacy and, when necessary, rely on compensatory mechanisms to adapt to the demands of the environment within those specialized domains.

PLASTICITY IN HUMAN DEVELOPMENT

The term "plasticity" refers to the " . . . processes by which one develops one's capacity to modify one's behavior to adjust to, or fit, the demands of a particular context" (Lerner, 1984, p. 10). This principle presumes the organism's capacity to influence the environment and itself in order to shape the course of its own development. Structural characteristics of the species both create the potential for and set the constraints on behavioral plasticity. Fundamental tasks for developmentalists are: (a) to identify the internal as well as the external conditions under which developmental processes can be altered to promote optimal development; and (b) to examine the range of plasticity (modifiability) in different domains of behavior and developmental changes in the possible range across the life span (Baltes et al., 1998).

CONTEXTUAL EMBEDDEDNESS OF HUMAN DEVELOPMENT

Two key propositions of the life-span perspective on human development are contextual embeddedness and dynamic interaction (Lerner, 1984). Contextual embeddedness is the idea that the key phenomena of human life exist at multiple levels (e.g., inner-biological, individual-psychological, social-sociological, cultural-historical, outer-physical/ecological). These levels do not operate independently; rather, variables and processes at all levels influence each other in reciprocal ways. Thus, the task of human developmentalists is to describe and explain how different levels interact and influence each other, and to optimize the parameters that affect these interactions and the resulting developmental trajectories (Baltes et al., 1998; Lerner, 1984).

A classic theoretical model for examining levels of environmental embeddedness was proposed by Bronfenbrenner (1979). In this model, development is seen as a joint function of the individual and all levels of his or her environment. The environment is conceived as a nested system of four structures, including: (a) the immediate setting surrounding the individual (microsystem); (b) interrelations among microsystems (mesosystem); (c) links between settings that include the individual and settings that affect the individual but do not include him or her directly (exosystem); and (d) societal and cultural influences on individuals (macrosystem).

A related point emphasized by life-span theorists is that individuals' development can also vary substantially in accordance with historical-cultural conditions. For example, Elder's (1974) research on children of the Great Depression illustrated the profound effects of a major historical event on individual development, but also showed that the nature of the effect varied depending on a person's age at the time—that is, the Great Depression affected members of different birth cohorts in different ways. In a similar way, Schaie (1996), in his ongoing cohort-sequential study on intellectual development across the adult life span, has shown conclusively that substantial generational (cohort) differences exist for different psychometric abilities.

MULTIDISCIPLINARY INQUIRY
Taken together, the basic principles of life-span development make multidisciplinary inquiry a necessity. Developmental changes in human behavior can be explained only by examining multiple levels of multiple dimensions (Bronfenbrenner, 1979). Therefore, the study of human development requires the inclusion of multiple levels of analysis of both internal and external contexts, leading to the inevitable necessity that development be examined at the biological, psychological, interpersonal, cultural, and historical levels of analysis. The openness of the life-span perspective to interdisciplinary posture implies that a "purist psychological view offers but a partial representation of behavioral development from conception to death" (Baltes, 1987, p. 613). The interplay among levels of inquiry can be understood only when multiple disciplines work together to examine developmental processes.

RESEARCH DESIGNS AND METHODS IN THE STUDY OF HUMAN DEVELOPMENT
Although theorists (Baltes, Reese, & Nesselroade, 1988) have argued that human development research requires observation over the "period of time during which the developmental phenomena of interest are thought to occur" (Schaie, 1983, p. 1), developmental research has mostly relied on cross-sectional comparisons of different age groups (Schaie, 1994). Cross-sectional studies are valuable in informing researchers about the possible magnitude and the pattern of age differences in a certain behavior at a given point in time, but they are limited in providing information about developmental changes. Schaie (1983) identified five rationales for the longitudinal study of behavioral development. Specifically, longitudinal studies permit: (a) the direct identification of intra-individual change; (b) the identification of inter-individual variability in intra-individual change; (c) the assessment of the interrelationships among different domains of intra-individual change; (d) the analysis of determinants or correlates of intra-individual change; and (e) the analysis of inter-individual variability in the determinants or correlates of intra-individual change.

These rationales have several implications. First, it is important to note that longitudinal studies are by design multivariate and that they draw on multiple data sources and, as much as possible, on variables from a person's natural environment (Block, 1993). Second, longitudinal studies do not conform to the rules for true experiments, because age is a person-attribute that cannot be experi-

mentally assigned. Consequently, longitudinal studies are subject to all the problems inherent in quasi-experimental designs as described by Campbell and Stanley (1967). Third, because longitudinal studies have traditionally been conducted with individuals from a single birth cohort, they confound time-of-measurement (period) and aging effects, and render estimates of age effects internally invalid (Schaie, 1983). In order to deal with this confounding and with the confounding of age and cohort that exists in cross-sectional research, Schaie (1983) has advocated the use of sequential study designs. Developmental psychologists find cohort-sequential designs of greatest interest because they explicitly differentiate intra-individual change within cohorts from inter-individual variability among cohorts.

CONCLUSION
Life-span developmental psychology has made great progress in the description, explanation, and optimization of human development across the whole life span. The use of longitudinal and sequential research designs (Schaie, 1983) has resulted in elaborate multivariate studies of behavioral development, showing that development occurs at all stages of the human life course, from conception to death. In general, human development is characterized by processes of continuity and discontinuity, multidirectionality, gains and losses, and modifiability (plasticity), and has as the ultimate goal the realization of a person's fullest potential (Lerner, 1984).

REFERENCES
Baltes, P. B. (1987). Theoretical propositions of life-span developmental psychology: On the dynamics between growth and decline. *Developmental Psychology, 23,* 611–626.

Baltes, P. B., & Baltes, M. M. (1990). Psychological perspectives on successful aging: The model of selective optimization with compensation. In P. B. Baltes & M. M. Baltes (Eds.), *Successful aging: Perspectives from the behavioral sciences* (pp. 1–34). New York: Cambridge University Press.

Baltes, P. B., Reese, H. W., & Nesselroade, J. R. (1988). *Life-span developmental psychology: Introduction to research methods.* Hillsdale, NJ: Erlbaum.

Block, J. (1993). Studying personality the long way. In D. C. Funder, R. D. Parke, C. Tomlinson-Keasey, & K. Widaman (Eds.), *Studying lives through time: Personality and development* (pp. 9–41). Washington, DC: American Psychological Association.

Brim, O. G., Jr., & Kagan, J. (Eds.). (1980). *Constancy and change in human development.* Cambridge, MA: Harvard University Press.

Bronfenbrenner, U. (1979). *The ecology of human development: Experiments by nature and design.* Cambridge, MA: Harvard University Press.

Campbell, D. T., & Stanley, J. C. (1967). *Experimental and quasi-experimental designs for research.* Chicago: Rand McNally.

Elder, G. H., Jr. (1974). *Children of the great depression.* Chicago: University of Chicago Press.

Lerner, R. M. (1984). *On the nature of human plasticity.* New York: Cambridge University Press.

Schaie, K. W. (1983). What can we learn from the longitudinal study of adult psychological development? In K. W. Schaie (Ed.), *Longitudinal studies of adult psychological development* (pp. 1–19). New York: Guilford.

Schaie, K. W. (1996). *Intellectual development in adulthood: The Seattle Longitudinal Study.* New York: Cambridge University Press.

Thomae, H. (1979). The concept of development and life-span developmental psychology. In P. B. Baltes & O. G. Brim, Jr. (Eds.), *Life-span development and behavior* (Vol. 2, pp. 282–312). New York: Academic.

S. H. Qualls
M. Diehl
L. M. Youngblade
University of Colorado

ADOLESCENT DEVELOPMENT
ADULT DEVELOPMENT
INFANT DEVELOPMENT
LIFE-SPAN DEVELOPMENT
THANATOLOGY

HUMAN INTELLIGENCE

DEFINITION OF INTELLIGENCE

Intelligence, according to *Webster's New World College Dictionary* (3rd ed.), is "the ability to learn or understand from experience, ability to acquire and retain knowledge; mental ability. . . ." (Neufeldt, 1997). Such a definition captures many facets of the nature of intelligence, but not necessarily those believed by experts to be key.

Two symposia have sought to ascertain the key features of intelligence according to experts in the field. Critical elements of the definition of intelligence, according to experts, are: (a) adaptation in order to meet the demands of the environment effectively; (b) elementary processes of perception and attention; (c) higher-level processes of abstract reasoning, mental representation, problem solving, and decision making; (d) ability to learn; and (e) effective behavior in response to problem situations.

Some experts, however, have been content to define intelligence operationally, simply as the intelligence quotient, or IQ (Boring, 1923). These definitions rely on tests such as those originated by Binet and Simon (1916) to measure judgmental abilities, or of Wechsler (1939) to measure verbal and performance abilities. Earlier tests proposed by Galton (1883) measured psychophysical abilities (such as sensitivity of hearing or touch). They proved to be less viable, in that they correlated neither with each other nor with success in educational settings.

Laypeople can also be asked to define intelligence, and it turns out that lay definitions differ from expert definitions in that they place somewhat more emphasis on social competence skills. In one study, for example, laypeople defined intelligence in terms of three broad classes of skills: (a) practical problem solving, (b) verbal ability, and (c) social competence. However, the way laypeople define intelligence does vary across occupations. For example, one study found that philosophy professors tend to stress critical and logical thinking very heavily, whereas physicists tend to place more value on precise mathematical thinking, the ability to relate physical phenomena to concepts of physics, and the ability to grasp quickly the laws of nature.

How people define intelligence also depends upon the culture in which they live. For example, Mallory Wober studied two tribes in Uganda. He found that the Baganda tended to associate intelligence with mental order, whereas the Batoro associated it with mental turmoil. Charles Super analyzed concepts of intelligence among the Kokwet of western Kenya. He found that intelligence meant a different thing for children versus adults. Intelligent children were viewed as responsible as well as quick in comprehension and effective in their management of interpersonal relationships. Intelligent adults were viewed as inventive, clever, and sometimes, wise and unselfish.

HERITABILITY AND MODIFIABILITY

Whatever human intelligence may be, the aspect of it that is measured as IQ is both partially heritable—with a heritability coefficient estimated at about .5 (albeit slightly lower in childhood and somewhat higher in adulthood)—and modifiable in at least some degree. Indeed, intelligence as measured by IQ tests has been rising steadily through most of the century (Neisser, 1998).

THEORIES OF INTELLIGENCE

Another approach to understanding intelligence is through a more elaborated theory. A theory, in contrast to a definition, must provide an explanatory framework and be testable. Theories have been of several different kinds.

Psychometric Theories

The most well-known theories are probably psychometric ones. Among these theories, the earliest major one is that of Spearman (1927), who proposed that intelligence comprises a general factor (*g*) of intelligence common to all intellectual tasks, as well as specific factors (*s*), each of which is unique to a given test of intelligence. His proposal was based on his finding of a "positive manifold" among intelligence tests: All tests seemed to be positively intercorrelated, suggesting the existence of a general factor. Spearman's theory still has many proponents today (e.g., Jensen, 1998). Thurstone (1938) disagreed with Spearman, arguing that the general factor was an artifact of the way Spearman analyzed his data. Thurstone suggested that seven primary mental abilities underlie intelligence: verbal comprehension, verbal fluency, number, spatial visualization, inductive reasoning, memory, and perceptual speed. More modern theorists, such as Cattell (1971) and Carroll (1993), have attempted to integrate these two kinds of views, suggesting that intelligence is best understood hierarchically, with a general factor at the top of the hierarchy and narrower factors below it. Cattell proposed two such factors: fluid intelligence, which is involved in reasoning with novel kinds of stimuli; and crystallized intelligence, or stored knowledge base.

Systems Theories

Some theories of intelligence have viewed intelligence as a system. By far the most well-known theory of this kind is that of Piaget (1972), according to which intelligence involves an equilibration between two processes: assimilation of new information to fit existing cognitive structures, and accommodation of existing cognitive structures to incorporate information that does not fit into preexisting cognitive structures. Sternberg (1985, 1997) has proposed that intelligence comprises three aspects: analytical abilities (used to analyze, evaluate, and critique), creative abilities (used to create, discover, and invent), and practical abilities (used to apply, implement, and use). Gardner (1983, 1999) has suggested instead that there are eight multiple intelligences—linguistic, logical-mathematical, spatial, musical, bodily-kinesthetic, naturalist, intrapersonal, and interpersonal—and perhaps existential and spiritual intelligences as well.

REFERENCES

Binet, A., & Simon, T. (1916). *The development of intelligence in children* (E. S. Kite, Trans.). Baltimore: Williams & Wilkins.

Boring, E. G. (1923). Intelligence as the tests test it. *New Republic, 35–37.*

Carroll, J. B. (1993). *Human cognitive abilities: A survey of factor-analytic studies.* New York: Cambridge University Press.

Cattell, R. B. (1971). *Abilities: Their structure, growth, and action.* Boston: Houghton-Mifflin.

Galton, F. (1883). *Inquiry into human faculty and its development.* London: Macmillan.

Gardner, H. (1983). *Frames of mind: The theory of multiple intelligences.* New York: Basic.

Gardner, H. (1999). Are there additional intelligences? The case for naturalist, spiritual, and existential intelligences. In J. Kane (Ed.), *Education, information, and transformation.* Englewood Cliffs, NJ: Prentice-Hall.

Jensen, R. B. (1998). *The g factor.* Greenwich, CT: Greenwood.

Neisser, U. (Ed.). (1998). *The rising curve.* Washington, DC: American Psychological Association.

Neufeldt, V. (Ed.). (1997). *Webster's New World College Dictionary* (3rd ed.). New York: Macmillan.

Piaget, J. (1972). *The psychology of intelligence.* Totowa, NJ: Littlefield Adams.

Spearman, C. (1927). *The abilities of man.* London: Macmillan.

Sternberg, R. J. (1985a). *Beyond IQ: A triarchic theory of human intelligence.* New York: Cambridge University Press.

Sternberg, R. J. (1997). *Successful intelligence.* New York: Plume.

Thurstone, L. L. (1938). *Primary mental abilities.* Chicago: University of Chicago Press.

Wechsler, D. (1939). *The measurement of adult intelligence.* Baltimore, MD: Williams & Wilkins.

R. J. STERNBERG
Yale University

ACTING + INTELLIGENCE
INTELLIGENCE MEASURES
INTELLIGENCE, SOCIAL POLICY, GENETIC CONTRIBUTION
STANFORD-BINET INTELLIGENCE SCALE
WECHSLER INTELLIGENCE TESTS

HUMAN LOCOMOTION

In the 18th century, the investigation of movement was based on the premise that upright stance and gait as well as differentiation of hand movements represented a basic requirement for human cultural development. These movements necessitate that the nervous system must function to automatically balance the body's center of mass over the feet during all motor activities. In other words, every movement must begin and end with a postural adjustment.

Analysis of human gait first became possible toward the end of the 19th century with the development of photographic recordings of running movements. Later, the technique for recording electrophysiological responses during locomotion was developed and was first used with cats.

The relative significance of reflexes on central rhythms and programming in locomotion has been addressed. The central mechanisms involved in locomotion are reflected in a di- or triphasic pattern of leg muscle activation following displacement of the feet that is thought to be programmed in its basic structure. Close similarities with the triphasic EMG pattern described for ballistic voluntary movements suggest that there is an underlying analogous neuronal mechanism. The EMG pattern is assumed to be evoked by a multisensory afferent input and generated by spinal interneuronal circuits that are closely connected with spinal locomotor centers. The extent to which the timing of the pattern can be modified by afferent input is not yet fully explored. A basic requirement of bipedal locomotion is that both legs act in a cooperative manner; each limb affects the strength of muscle activation and the time-space behavior of the other. There exists some evidence that this interlimb coordination is mediated by spinal interneuronal circuits, which are themselves under supraspinal (e.g., cerebral and cerebellar) control.

With regard to the reflex mechanisms, short-latency stretch reflexes in leg extensor muscles are profoundly modulated during gait mainly by presynaptic inhibition group I input and less by fusimotor influences. During large translational perturbations a significant contribution of this reflex has not yet been demonstrated. However, it may be involved in compensating for small ground irregularities at distinct phases of gait. Compensation for foot displacement during gait is provided by polysynaptic spinal reflexes, including an activation of synergistic muscle groups of both legs. These EMG responses are thought to be mediated predominantly by peripheral information from group I afferents (converging with different peripheral and supraspinal inputs onto common spinal interneurons) on a spinal pathway. These reflexes modulate the basic motor pattern of spinal interneuronal circuits underlying the respective motor task.

During recent years, increasing evidence has emerged of the importance of load receptor input in the control of bipedal stance and gait; yet we are still only beginning to understand the nature of this input and its interaction with other afferent inputs and control mechanisms. Vestibular and visual functions are mainly context-dependent and are essential when afferent input from other sources is reduced.

One of the first symptoms of a lesion within the central motor system is movement disorder, which is most characteristic during locomotion in patients with spasticity, cerebellar lesions, or Parkinson's disease. The clinical examination reveals typical changes in tendon-tap reflexes and muscle tone typical for one of the movement disorders. However, today we know that there exists only a weak relationship between the physical signs obtained during the clinical examination in a passive motor condition and the impaired neuronal mechanisms in operation during an active movement. By recording and analyzing electrophysiological and biomechanical parameters during a functional movement such as locomotion, the significance of, for example, impaired reflex behavior or pathophysiology of muscle tone and its contribution to the movement disorder can reliably be assessed. Consequently, an adequate treatment should not be restricted to the cosmetic therapy and correction of an isolated clinical parameter, but should be based on the pathophysiology and significance of the mechanisms underlying the disorder of functional movement that impairs the patient.

V. DIETZ
University Hospital Balgrist, Zürich, Switzerland

REFLEXES

HUMANISTIC PSYCHOLOGY

Humanistic psychology is both a social movement within psychology and an enduring perspective. Both aspects require attention and analysis. The concept of humanistic psychology implies a contrast with scientific psychology. (Whether the contrast is legitimate is an unsettled issue.) Humanistic psychology emerged as a movement and continues as a perspective, in contrast to the conception, promoted by American behaviorism from Watson to Hull and Skinner, of a scientific psychology that seemed to deny the validity of human experience, values, intentions, and meanings. Humanistic psychology in most of its manifestations gives priority to human experience, the meaningful life of the common-sense world with its tragic and comic aspects, that makes contact with its embodiments in works of art and documents of the humanities. Most of the proponents of humanistic psychology have been engaged in psychotherapy as a privileged window on human experience, and the humanistic movement has been heavily involved in the applied psychology of personal growth and change.

ANTECEDENTS

During the 1920s and 1930s, American psychology was dominated in its mainstream by dogmatic behaviorism, a positivistic view that regarded conscious human experience as out of bounds scientifically. Anthropomorphism—the unwarranted attribution of human characteristics to lower animals—became a sin charged even against psychologists who attributed human characteristics to human animals. In this unfriendly setting, a psychology of personality emerged in the late 1930s, heralded by two classic (and complementary) books: Gordon Allport's *Personality: A Psychological Interpretation,* and Henry Murray's *Explorations in Personality.* With exposure to phenomenological and pre-existential European models, Allport provided a broadly based framework for studying the mature ego (as Freud would have put it) and how it develops. Murray, trained in medicine, biochemistry, and embryology, brought a Freudian-Jungian orientation to bear on personality from a point of view that paid special attention to depths inaccessible to consciousness, from which both creativity and neurosis might erupt. Immediately after World War II, two other major theorists of personality issued important systematic books: Gardner Murphy's *Personality: A Biosocial Approach to Origins and Structure,* a brilliant integration that had rather little impact, perhaps because of its eclectic reasonableness; and George Kelly's *Psychology of Personal Constructs,* which also had little initial impact but was resurrected, especially in England after the cognitive revolution in psychology, for its original ideas about how people construe one another and the world.

Meanwhile mainstream behaviorism, in the later sophisticated version represented by Dollard and Miller (1950), tended to find common cause with psychoanalysis (the fortunes of which were then riding high), but was inherently in opposition to views of personality like Allport's and Kelly's, which rejected both the mechanistic premises of behaviorism and the biological reductionism of classical psychoanalysis. Personality psychology as it took shape after World War II was the base from which humanistic psychology emerged.

THE FOUNDING OF HUMANISTIC PSYCHOLOGY

In 1964, a conference at Old Saybrook, Connecticut, launched humanistic psychology as a social movement within psychology. Leading figures in the psychology of personality and in the humanistic disciplines participated: Allport, Murray, Murphy, and Kelly of the founding generation; Charlotte Bühler, representing a European tradition of research that was subsequently labeled "life-span development" (Bühler & Massarik, 1968); Jacques Barzun and René Dubos as humanists from literature and biological science; and Carl Rogers, Abraham Maslow, and Rollo May, who became the intellectual leaders of the movement. May subsequently described it (Gilbert, n.d.):

That conference developed out of the groundswell of protest against the theory of man of behaviorism on the one side and orthodox psychoanalysis on the other. That is why we are often called the Third Force. There was a feeling on all sides among different psychologists that neither of these two versions of psychology dealt with human beings as human. Nor did they deal with real problems of life. They left great numbers of people feeling alienated and empty. At that conference we discussed what the chief elements of humanistic psychology would be.*

Thus at its launching, both the creators of American personality psychology and the leaders of humanistic psychology in the next generation participated, and some proper humanists, too. The Third Force had not cast off anchor from scientific aspirations; rather, it sought to influence and correct the positivistic bias of psychological science as it then stood.

Rogers, Maslow, and May established the initial character of humanistic psychology and remained its most respected figures. In *Counseling and Psychotherapy,* Rogers introduced his conception of nondirective counseling, later to be reconceptualized as client-centered therapy. The view of human functioning that Rogers developed assumed intrinsic tendencies toward self-actualization that the vicissitudes of socialization could block, but that would predictably be released by the therapeutic relationship of unconditional positive regard, accurate empathic understanding, and honesty and integrity (Rogers, 1961). Abraham Maslow came from a background in the experimental study of primate behavior. Under the influence of Kurt Goldstein (a Gestalt-oriented neurologist, author of *The Organism* and *Human Nature in the Light of Psychopathology*), Maslow developed a hierarchical theory of human motivation in *Motivation and Personality.* Physiological needs call preemptively for satisfaction; then follow needs for safety, for love and belonging, and for esteem. These Maslow regarded as "deficiency needs." When the deficiency needs are provided for, the "being" motives of self-actualization can emerge. (See especially *The Farther Reaches of Human Nature.*) So both Rogers and Maslow embraced self-actualization as an empirical principle and as an ethical ideal. They aligned themselves with Rousseau's romantic view of human nature as intrinsically good but corrupted by society, as distinguished from Freud's Hobbesian view of human nature as problematic, tinged with intrinsic evil, and from the behaviorists' Lockean assumption of human plasticity under environmental programming.

Strongly influenced by the existential theologian Paul Tillich, Rollo May brought the European current of existentialism and phenomenology into humanistic psychology. His books *The Meaning of Anxiety* and *Man's Search for Himself* introduced American psychologists to ideas stemming from Kierkegaard and Heidegger, while in later popular works such as *Love and Will* he emphasized the inherently tragic aspects of the human condition. Rogers's emphasis on empathic understanding of the person's experiential world had been tagged as "phenomenological"; May on his part brought humanistic psychology into more direct contact with the phenomenological tradition of European philosophy.

With their Rousseauistic belief in human goodness, Rogers and Maslow defined the mainstream of humanistic psychology. May's

*Reprinted by permission, Association for Humanistic Psychology.

existential variant, with its tragic overtones, did not prevent humanistic psychology from becoming generally identified with the blandly optimistic view of human nature that has been an American propensity at least since Mary Baker Eddy and Norman Vincent Peale.

IMPACT OF THE COUNTERCULTURE

The founding of humanistic psychology as a Third Force essentially coincided with the emergence of the counterculture of the flower children and drug-oriented hippies as a phenomenon of the 1960s—proclaimed and promoted by Roszak (1968) and Reich (1970) and analyzed by the sociologist Rosabeth Kanter (1972) and the psychoanalytic culture critics Herbert Hendin (1975) and Christopher Lasch (1979).

In its psychological aspect, the counterculture had a number of features that established resonance with humanistic psychology. There was its individualism: the fulfillment of the individual as the center of value, virtually stripped of concern with interdependence and commitments to the lives of others (people should "do their own thing"). There was its sentimental belief in human perfectability, neglecting political and ethical modes of enhancing actual life among imperfect creatures at cross-purposes with themselves and others. There was its stress on the value of self-disclosure, or as Jourard put it in his title, *The Transparent Self.* In the language of the counterculture, one should "let it all hang out." Easy but superficial intimacy, sexual and otherwise, was sought in attempts to bypass the work required to develop and maintain caring personal relationships. There was emphasis on the here and now—a fecklessness about past and future which ill accords with self-control and the commitments to self and others that underlie planfulness, self-respect, and loving care. There was hedonism—"if it feels good, do it"—which is implied in life in the here and now with minimal baggage of moral commitments. Finally, there was irrationalism, manifested in disparagement of science and of rational problem solving, in reliance on intuition over evidence, in uncritical affinity with the occult, and in the celebration of drug-induced highs.

The founders of humanistic psychology were not antiscientific. They sought rather to correct the biases of behaviorism and psychoanalysis so as to produce a psychology truer to human life and more useful for its improvement. By historical coincidence, however, the humanistic movement was essentially captured by the counterculture. The survivors among the older generation of founders dropped out in dismay, and at least Maslow and May of the new leadership were ambivalent about the directions that humanistic psychology was taking. At the center of the new developments was the encounter group movement identified with the so-called human growth centers, especially the Esalen Institute at Big Sur in California, founded by Michael Murphy and Richard Price in 1962.

THE ENCOUNTER GROUP MOVEMENT

The focus of humanistic psychology during the 1960s and 1970s, the encounter group movement had several roots. One was the work of J. L. Moreno, a messianic Austrian psychiatrist who before

1920 was writing about psychological encounter and using the spontaneous theater of psychodrama (his term), which he subsequently promoted in America as a psychotherapeutic technique. Another was the sensitivity training originated by Kurt Lewin and his students. An emigré German psychologist, Lewin was an exponent of field theory in psychology. Through his own work and that of his students, he was virtually the father of modern American social psychology and developed the self-studying group, professionally facilitated but not led, as a technique for training people in human relations skills (Lewin, 1948). Sensitivity training became a movement in its own right, isolated from academic social psychology and more closely linked to industrial-organizational psychology as it developed. Aspects of this tradition got absorbed in the encounter group movement. A third influence was Gestalt therapy, represented at Esalen by its principal developer Fritz Perls (1969). Gestalt therapy is a group approach in which the therapist plays a very active part, using a variety of techniques including role playing to focus participants on holistic emotional experience of the here and now.

At Esalen the intensive group experiences orchestrated under these influences—typically, weekend marathon occurrences—also kept company with body-oriented techniques influenced by Reich (1949), forms of massage, and meditational techniques and yogic exercises influenced by Eastern religion. Watts (1961) had sponsored Eastern religion as an ideology for psychotherapists, and foreshadowed the mystical side of the humanistic movement. Definitive accounts of these developments are contained in Kurt Back's *Beyond Words* (Back was a student of Lewin), and in *The Intensive Group Experience,* edited by Max Rosenbaum and Alvin Snadowsky.

Encounter groups at Esalen and elsewhere were not regarded as psychotherapy. If they had been, statutory restrictions would have interfered. The human growth that they were supposed to promote was unregulated and, with minor exceptions, it was also unevaluated empirically. For a while the movement flourished, uncontrolled.

By the mid 1980s, the encounter group movement had faded into one minor component among others in the psychoculture. In retrospect, it can best be characterized by two antagonists: Carl Rogers, a founder of humanistic psychology and, in his middle years, an imaginative innovator in bringing scientific methods to bear on the fragile interchanges of counseling and psychotherapy; and Sigmund Koch, initially an experimental psychologist, later a humanistic critic of psychological scientism.

In a personal book commending encounter groups to the public as "one of the exciting developments of our time," Rogers wrote that "the encounter group or intensive group experience . . . is, I believe, one of our most successful modern inventions for dealing with the feeling of unreality, of impersonality, and of distance and separation that exists in so many people of our culture" (*On Encounter Groups,* p. 127).

In opposition, Koch (1971, p. 112) offered the following bill of indictment:

The group movement is the most extreme excursion thus far of man's talent for reducing, distorting, evading and vulgarizing his own reality. . . . It is adept at the image-making maneuver of evading human reality in the very process of seeking to discover and enhance it. It seeks to court spontaneity and authenticity by artifice; to combat instrumentalism instrumentally; to provide access to experience by reducing it to a packaged commodity; to engineer autonomy by group pressure; to liberate individuality by group shaping. . . . It can provide only a grotesque simulacrum of every noble quality it courts. It provides, in effect, a convenient psychic whorehouse for the purchase of a gamut of well-advertised existential "goodies": authenticity, freedom, wholeness, flexibility, community, love, joy. One enters for such liberating consummations but settles for psychic striptease.

Encounter groups and the panoply of techniques sponsored by the human growth centers, given psychological status by the ideas of Rogers and Maslow, continued into the 1980s without the quasireligious fervor that accompanied their heyday. Rogers's endorsement is understandable—encounter groups seemed to compensate for culturally engendered lack of meaning (faith), hope, and community (communion, *caritas,* charity)—the Pauline virtues of Christian tradition (Smith, 1978). But Koch's criticism also stands: The movement was responsive in remarkably shallow and sometimes meretricious terms.

TRANSPERSONAL PSYCHOLOGY

The irrationalist, mystical tendencies pressing from the counterculture found the boundaries of humanistic psychology confining. Within the humanistic movement, and not rejecting it, a conception of transpersonal psychology was developed (Tart, 1975) that frankly avowed its affinity to Sufi and other forms of mysticism and focused on supposed processes connecting individual consciousnesses to a larger spiritual ocean in which they participate, here echoing ideas suggested by Jung (*Two Essays on Analytical Psychology*). In transpersonal psychology the humanistic movement finally cast anchor from its founders' aspiration for a humanistic psychological science. Without apostolic authority, it seemed to be setting itself up as a latter-day religion. Indeed, the ideas and practices emerging in the humanistic psychology movement around 1970 seemed to echo those of the new sects and the burgeoning charismatic movement in the old denominations of traditional religion, as described in *The New Religious Consciousness,* edited by Bellah and Glock, and in Harrell's *All Things Are Possible: The Healing and Charismatic Revivals in Modern America.* Humanistic psychology as a social movement was responding to the cultural lack of faith, hope, and charity, as previously noted, but in so responding, it was presenting itself as a religion and losing touch with the science of psychology.

OTHER FACETS OF HUMANISTIC PSYCHOLOGY

The humanistic movement was not entirely absorbed in Esalen and encounter groups; other contemporary aspects should be noted. Among them was Frankl's logotherapy (1962), a religiously existentialist version of psychoanalysis rather similar to the approach taken by May—an account of the human predicament that emphasizes the human need to place death and suffering in a context of human meaning that can be lived with. Another is Giorgi's interpretation (1970) of the phenomenological philosophy of Merleau-Ponty: a philosophical humanistic psychology not caught up in the so-called touchy-feely aspects of the movement. Still another is Bakan's scholarly vision, *The Duality of Human Existence,* an interpretation of dialectically related principles of agency and communion that preceded the feminist revolt but continues to provide a useful commentary on the meanings of masculinity and femininity. These contributions were regarded by their authors and others as within the compass of humanistic psychology.

The movement produced its own critics. Particularly Richard Farson, a former student and close colleague of Rogers, who objected almost as strongly as Koch to the mindless fascination with therapeutic gimmickry that he saw as corrupting humanistic psychology (Farson, 1978). There have also been attempts to domesticate the movement and bring it into the fold of academic scientific psychology, while at the same time reforming academic psychology in a humanistic direction—especially Rychlak's *Psychology of Rigorous Humanism,* a philosophically grounded attack on the Lockean tradition of scientific psychology, with proposals for dialectical but rigorous alternatives. Psychologists have also tried to negotiate the conflicts between mechanistic behavioristic psychology and humanistic psychology, an unlikely venture that becomes feasible if the focus is upon therapeutic concerns. Abraham Wandersman and others edited a book, *Humanism and Behaviorism: Dialogue and Growth,* to which leading humanistic and behavioristic psychologists contributed, attempting to integrate the applied side of the humanistic/behavioristic dichotomy. But practical rapprochement does not resolve the underlying philosophical issues (Smith, 1978). On the behavioristic side, Bandura (1978) has stretched his social learning theory to accommodate central humanistic concerns in developing a theory of reciprocal determinism in which he manages to take into account self-control and personal initiatives in constituting one's environment.

SECULAR HUMANISM: A NEGLECTED VERSION OF HUMANISTIC PSYCHOLOGY

Humanistic psychology as a social movement systematically ignored a major strand of psychological thought with excellent humanistic credentials: the psychology of secular humanism (as named by its fundamentalist detractors). The concept of secular humanism is best understood within the existentialist tradition of humanistic thought. Pascal in the 17th century and Kierkegaard in the 19th defined a religious version of existentialism, influential in modern times on Rollo May and embraced by Ernest Becker (1973). Humankind—"man" in earlier parlance—is a "thinking reed," as Pascal put it, vulnerable, incomplete, and needing God's validation. In the contrasting secular humanist spirit of Shakespeare and Montaigne, Nietzsche in the 19th century and Sartre in the 20th proposed a mundane, Godless humanism, also existentialist in its concern with the responsibility entailed by human self-consciousness.

For the religious existentialist, an authentic appreciation of the human situation leads to acknowledgment of human insufficiency in the face of both death and life, alleviated only by willing submission to God. For the atheistic existentialist, in contrast, reliance on God means regression to childish dependence; human dignity requires the clear-headed acceptance of self-choosing existence in a neutral world. Human meaning is a human creation. The reli-

gious and the secular views cannot be reconciled, though both presuppose attentiveness to tragic ingredients of human existence ignored by mainstream humanistic psychology.

Humanism of the secular kind has been well represented in psychology, though not in the humanistic psychology movement. Among the founders of modern personality theory—and of the humanistic psychology movement—Murray (1981) made an explicit point of his secular humanism. The neo-Freudian psychoanalyst Erich Fromm expounded his version in two early classics, *Escape From Freedom,* a Marxist-psychoanalytic account of Nazism in historical perspective, and *Man for Himself,* an attempt to build humanistic ethics on a psychological basis. Still another example of secular humanism was offered by Isidor Chein in *The Science of Behavior and the Image of Man,* a critique of behaviorism and ambitious integration of psychoanalytic and phenomenological views of motivation and selfhood. Characteristically, however, Chein was not thought of as a humanistic psychologist by those in the movement.

To return, then, to the distinction between the humanistic movement and humanistic perspectives in psychology, consider the question posed initially: Need humanism in psychology be defined in opposition to psychological science?

HUMANISM AND SCIENCE IN PSYCHOLOGY

Since the turn of the century, a distinction introduced by the German philosopher Dilthey has echoed in various versions through modern social thought: the distinction between the natural and the mental or cultural sciences (*Naturwissenschaften* vs. *Geisteswissenschaften*), as elaborated by Max Weber in his methodological contrast between explanation and understanding (*Erklärung* vs. *Verstehen*), as partly clarified by British analytic philosophy and recently emphasized in the "dialectical hermeneutics" of Habermas (1971) and in the so-called rule/role psychology of Harré and Secord (1972). The contrast is between accounts in terms of causes and accounts in terms of reasons; between efficient causes and telic ones (in classical Aristotelian terms); between descriptive empirical lawfulness and normative regulation; and indeed, between *behavior* and *action* in a common reading of these terms. Perhaps the clearest phrasing of the distinction contrasts the perspective of *causal* understanding, traditionally from a standpoint external to the behaving person, with *interpretive* understanding, usually within the person's own perspective—a realm of feelings, meanings, intentions, and values.

The causal perspective, as it applies to human beings, finds continuity with the natural sciences of the physical and biological world. The interpretive perspective emphasizes the uniqueness of human beings as symbolizing, culture-bearing creatures who act in a frame of past and future; who can make sense or nonsense to themselves; and who are capable of deceiving themselves and others and of seeing through one another's deceptions. Both perspectives obviously apply to human beings.

When these perspectives are clearly drawn, they define a sharp polarity. The attempt to reduce one to the other can be carried out only by corrupting the everyday knowledge that we depend upon for grounding our science as well as the conduct of our daily lives.

One way of regarding the situation is to consider it as involving a true complementarity, akin to the prototypical relation between wave and quantum formulations in physics—both necessary, yet incapable of synthesis in an integrated theory. This may be the best our theorizing can do, but it is not only dissatisfying: it also gives us no help with the fact that in the phenomena of selfhood, the meanings or interpretations that we ascribe to our characteristics and actions are empirically important causal factors in what we do. This characteristically human consequence of the reflexivity of self-reference was the subject of extensive research on attribution theory by social psychologists during the 1960s and 1970s. In spite of the appearance of philosophical solecism, meanings and reasons do sometimes seem to act like causes (Smith, 1978). To the extent that this is the case, it can be argued that for the distinctively human world, interpretation and causal explanation must somehow be joined; that, indeed, the only satisfactory science of human experience and action must be one in which hermeneutic interpretation plays a central part conjoined with causal explanation.

DISTINCTIVE TASKS FOR HUMANISTIC PSYCHOLOGY

Scientific psychology has changed since the founding of the humanistic movement as a "Third Force." The cognitive revolution swept through psychology, legitimizing concern with experience or consciousness, and psychoanalysis was also substantially liberalized, even while falling from fashionable favor. As the movement falters—partly through its own countercultural excesses and partly in response to the changed situation in psychology—one may appropriately ask what special foci of attention continue to hold promise from a humanistic perspective. The suggestions offered here are concerned with humanistic aspects of psychological science, not of psychotherapeutic practice.

In the first place, a humanistic psychology has special responsibility to keep windows open on actual human experience. The special window afforded by the helping relationship of psychotherapy has played an enormous role in providing the basis for such understanding as we have attained of human psychology. The window provided by arts and letters has been much less used by psychologists, Murray (1981) being the outstanding exception. As psychotherapy becomes more technological and the new cognitive psychology occupies itself with flow charts of information processing, the need continues for close attention to human experience in the psychological studies.

Second, the attempt to understand the reflexive aspects of selfhood just alluded to poses a major challenge. Psychologists of personality, as reflected in the standard text by Hall and Lindzey (1978), have mostly framed their competing formulations in an ahistorical, culture-bound vein. If indeed the reflexiveness of selfhood implies that personality is substantially constituted by the symbolic/cultural content of our self-construals, then our theories of personality will have to be cast with more explicit attention to the historical and cultural context, if they are to be scientifically valid. As the anthropologist Clifford Geertz (1973) has remarked, if we wish to encounter humanity face to face, "the road to the general, to the revelatory simplicities of science, lies through a concern with the particular, the circumstantial, the concrete" (p. 53)—guided by theoretical concerns with the interplay of conceptual levels.

Two developments in psychological studies in the 1980s may especially inherit the mantle of humanistic psychology, in the spirit of humanistic science that characterized the founding generation. One is the resurrection of holistic personality study after the long drought of barren situationism (Tomkins, 1981). The comments made just previously bear upon directions that this renaissance might take. The other development is the interdisciplinary movement—in which psychology participates centrally—of life-span human development. As the movement has developed, the life-span approach has been explicitly concerned with the dialectical interplay between human lives in their social context and historical change. It has also called into question earlier assumptions about the stability of psychological characteristics and the determinative impact of early experience—perhaps incidental features of the movement, but nevertheless ones that align it with the sense, promoted by humanists in psychology, that people can and should do something about their lives (Brim, & Kagan, 1980; Lerner & Busch-Rossnagel, 1981).

REFERENCES

Allport, G. W. (1937). *Personality: A psychological interpretation.* New York: Holt.

Back, K. (1973). *Beyond words: The story of sensitivity training and the encounter movement.* New York: Russell Sage Foundation.

Bakan, D. (1966). *The duality of human existence.* Boston: Beacon Press.

Bandura, A. (1978). Learning and behavioral theories of aggression. In I. L. Kutash, S. B. Kutash, & L. B. Schlesinger (Eds.), *Violence: Perspectives on murder and aggression.* San Francisco: Jossey-Bass.

Becker, E. (1973). *Escape from evil.* New York: Free Press.

Bellah, R. N., & Glock, C. Y. (Eds.). (1976). *The new religious consciousness.* Berkeley, CA: University of California Press.

Brim, O. G., Jr., & Kagan, J. (Eds.). (1980). *Constancy and change in human development.* Cambridge, MA: Harvard University Press.

Bühler, C., & Massarik, F. (Eds.). (1968). *The course of human life: A study of goals in the humanistic perspective.* New York: Springer.

Chein, I. (1972). *The science of behavior and the image of man.* New York: Basic Books.

Dollard, J., & Miller, N. E. (1950). *Personality and psychotherapy: An analysis in terms of learning, thinking, and culture.* New York: McGraw-Hill.

Farson, R. (1978). The technology of humanism. *Journal of Humanistic Psychology, 18,* 5–35.

Frankl, V. E. (1980). *Man's search for meaning: An introduction to logotherapy.* New York: Simon & Schuster. (Original work published 1962)

Fromm, E. (1947). *Man for himself: An inquiry into the psychology of ethics.* New York: Holt, Rinehart & Winston.

Fromm, E. (1965). *Escape from freedom.* New York: Avon Books. (Original work published 1941)

Geertz, C. (1973). *The interpretation of cultures: Selected essays.* New York: Basic Books.

Gilbert, R. (Ed.). (April 4–6, 1975). *AHP theory conference, Tucson, Arizona* [Edited transcript]. San Francisco: Association for Humanistic Psychology.

Giorgi, A. (1970). *Psychology as a human science.* New York: Harper & Row.

Goldstein, K. (1947). *Human nature in the light of psychopathology.* Cambridge, MA: Harvard University Press.

Goldstein, K. (1959). *The organism: A holistic approach to biology derived from pathological data in man.* New York: American Book. (Original work published 1934)

Habermas, J. (1971). *Knowledge and human interests.* Boston: Beacon Press.

Hall, C. S., & Lindzey, G. (Eds.). (1978). *Theories of personality* (3rd ed.). New York: Wiley. (Original work published 1957)

Harré, R., & Secord, P. (1972). *The explanation of social behavior.* Oxford: Blackwell.

Harrell, D. E. (1976). *All things are possible: The healing and charismatic revivals in modern America.* Bloomington, IN: University of Indiana Press.

Hendin, H. (1975). *The age of sensation.* New York: Norton.

Jourard, S. M. (1971). *The transparent self.* New York: Van Nostrand Reinhold. (Original work published 1964)

Kanter, R. M. (1972). *Commitment and community.* Cambridge, MA: Harvard University Press.

Kelly, G. A. (1955). *The psychology of personal constructs.* New York: Norton.

Koch, S. (1971). The image of man implicit in encounter group theory. *Journal of Humanistic Psychology, 11*(2), 109–128.

Lasch, C. (1979). *The culture of narcissism: American life in an age of diminishing expectations.* New York: Norton.

Lerner, R. M., & Busch-Rossnagel, N. A. (Eds.). (1981). *Individuals as producers of their development: A life-span perspective.* New York: Academic.

Lewin, K. (1948). *Resolving social conflicts.* New York: Harper.

Maslow, A. H. (1954). *Motivation and personality.* New York: Harper & Brothers.

Maslow, A. H. (1969). The farther reaches of human nature. *Journal of Transpersonal Psychology, 1,* 1–9.

May, R. (1953). *Man's search for himself.* New York: Norton.

May, R. (1979). *The meaning of anxiety.* New York: Ronald Press. (Original work published 1950)

Murphy, G. (1947). *Personality: A biosocial approach to origins and structure.* New York: Harper.

Murray, H. A. (1962). *Explorations in personality: A clinical and experimental study of fifty men of college age.* New York: Oxford University Press. (Original work published 1938)

Murray, H. A. (1981). *Endeavors in psychology: Selections from the personology of Henry A. Murray.* (E. S. Shneidman, Ed.). New York: Harper.

Peris, F. S. (1969). *Gestalt therapy verbatim.* Layfayette, CA: Real People Press.

Rogers, C. R. (1942). *Counseling and psychotherapy.* Boston: Houghton Mifflin.

Rogers, C. R. (1961). *On becoming a person.* Boston: Houghton Mifflin.

Rosenbaum, M., & Snadowsky, A. (Eds.). (1976). *The intensive group experience.* New York: Free Press.

Roszak, T. (1968). *The making of a counter culture.* Garden City, NY: Doubleday Anchor.

Rychlak, J. (1977). *The psychology of rigorous humanism.* New York: Wiley Interscience.

Smith, M. B. (1978). Encounter groups and humanistic psychology. In K. W. Back (Ed.), *In search for community: Encounter groups and social change.* Boulder, CO: Westview Press.

Tart, C. T. (1975). *States of consciousness.* New York: Dutton.

Tomkins, S. (1981). The rise, fall, and resurrection of the study of personality. *Journal of Mind and Behavior, 2,* 443–452.

Wandersman, A., Poppen, P., & Ricks, D. (1976). *Humanism and behaviorism: Dialogue and growth.* New York: Pergamon.

SUGGESTED READING

Bugental, J. F. T. (1961). *The search for authenticity.* New York: Holt, Rinehart & Winston.

Child, I. L. (1973). *Humanistic psychology and the research tradition: Their several virtues.* New York: Wiley.

Royce, J. R., & Mos, L. P. (Eds.). (1981). *Humanistic psychology: Concepts and criticisms.* New York: Plenum.

Severin, F. (Ed.). (1965). *Humanistic viewpoints in psychology: A book of readings.* New York: McGraw-Hill.

Smith, M. B. (1974). *Humanizing social psychology.* San Francisco: Jossey-Bass.

M. B. Smith
University of California at Santa Cruz

BEHAVIORISM
FUNCTIONALISM
LIFE EVENTS
RELIGION AND PSYCHOLOGY

HUMOR

Humor has fascinated humanity since recorded history. Unfortunately, this timeless curiosity has not led to the persistent pursuit of crucial knowledge. Philosophers have left us with isolated and abstract speculations. Scientific investigators have likewise approached humor in bits and pieces, lacking both vigor and rigor in their efforts. As a result, there is no comprehensive network of facts about the development and purposes of humor in human existence. We have not progressed far from the armchair speculation of the philosopher. Much of the current interest in humor comes from the disciplined observations of the clinician, that peculiar mixture of philosopher and scientist, who attempts to use humor for treatment even while assembling speculations into a theory.

Few concepts in psychology can match the complexity of humor. The subject has been approached from its stimulus structure. Is humor simply one response and, if so, is it measured by inner or outer changes? What are the relationships between physiological responses, comprehension, production, and simple appreciation? Can humor be analyzed into different types, motivated by different purposes and therefore reflective of varying degrees of maturity and pathology? If a response is to be judged, how should this be done and who is to make the judgment: oneself, impartial observers, peers, or friends? How do physiological responses with their differing latencies, frequencies, and amplitudes relate to social judgments under varying degrees of stress? One way out of perennial ignorance would be through large-scale longitudinal studies of identified humorists for the initial purpose of gaining empirical facts as well as generating questions. The small-scaled study of the comedian as contrasted with the actor by Fisher and Fisher (1981) is a step in this direction.

What little speculative knowledge is available proceeds from trying to test in the lab what can hardly be measured anywhere. The clinician, more often than not a psychotherapist, constructs an intellectual map by looking for similarities and differences in treatment outcomes of patients with varying amounts of infrequent humor.

The writings of the most influential therapists have abundant references to the healing qualities of humor and often have made that process the assumed goal of treatment. However, explicit references to that state are rare in their case histories and theorizing. For example, the therapeutic interactions of Alfred Adler and Milton Erickson (together with such creative pupils as Jay Haley) are prime examples of the seeding and unfolding of the humorous attitude, yet direct references to humor itself are quite scarce.

Three psychologists who have been most vocal about the tactics and goals of humor are Albert Ellis, Harold Greenwald, and Walter O'Connell. Ellis (1978) uses self-contradiction, incongruity, and exaggeration to challenge negative assumptions of the patient as they unfold. Greenwald (Chapman & Foot, 1977) views therapy as an opportunity for playing with events formerly regarded as traumatic, to find ways of using the painful past for the enhancement of future enjoyment. The humorous attitude is the criterion of maturity in O'Connell's natural high therapy (Chapman & Foot, 1976, 1977), in which clients' well-practiced attempts to cling to guilt and discouragement for useless social influence (power) are subjected to the therapist's jocular dismay and comic over- and understatements of the patients' mistaken certainties.

Humorists-as-therapists, as a rule, see themselves as active guides (not stretcher bearers), demolishing by words and action an often cherished reality of patients who see themselves as worthless, isolated, and of no positive value in universal evolution. Humorous psychotherapists protect themselves from staff burnout by separating their inherent worth as persons and purposes in life from their success as therapists (measured by quieting symptoms and gaining status in the eyes of others). Humorous psychotherapy is conducted with respect for the patient's person, in spite of the therapist's disdain for the painful and paradoxical power of the patient's current discouragement. Psychotherapy is seen as a game in which an encouraging therapist vies with a discouraged client, showing the utmost respect for the personhood of both "athletes." The creativity involved in all ploys, even those which are subject to laughter, is the action of the game. In humorous psychotherapy there are no passive victims in the serious (but not grave) interactions. This model of humorous psychotherapy suits our quantum world made up of processes rather than things, not subject to perfect prediction and continuous control. Therefore it concurs with holistic medicine in which so-called patients become pupils, learning the theory and practice of self-control and self-enhancement while contributing to the development of similar states for others.

HUMOR IN THE LIBRARY

There are few source books for the curious to get an intellectual grip on the study of humor. Freud's two studies—*Jokes and Their Relation to the Unconscious* and *Humor*—set the theme for future scholars to follow. Unfortunately most researchers overlooked Freud's distinction between humor as the mature ability to repudiate one's suffering, and wit as the release of repressed drives or possible aimless play. Humor is not mentioned in personality theories, as a rule, any more than is death, the ultimate test of humor. However, Ledford Bischof in his first edition only (*Interpreting Personality Theories*) speculated on how 10 personality theorists might perceive the role of humor in human development. The best way to discover the work of both experimentalist and clinician is through the use of two special editions of a journal for psychotherapists and four texts for both clinicians and experimentalists: Warkentin, *Voices* (1969); Stern, *Voices* (1981); Chapman, and Foot (1976, 1977); Goldstein and McGhee (1972); Mindess and Turek (1979).

Overall there is little sustained crucial research with the complex mediational responses of wit and humor. Pioneering efforts have pointed out how readily humor is affected by the stimulus structure, the social setting, and the state of arousal which is itself influenced by memories and anticipation. Berlyne (1972) has studied arousal, curiosity, and exploratory behaviors on humor appreciation. McGhee (1972) extended the study of humor to the relationship between cognition and behavior, especially with children. Suls (1972) researched the relationships of the perception and resolution of incongruity and humor responses. Social functions of humor have been interests of Martineau (1972), Goodchilds (1972), and LaFave (1972). Goldstein (1972) has studied the saliency of the stimuli involved in humor as being of more importance than the repressed drives. Here we see one example of the general trend of confusing Freud's ideas of humor with those of wit and then finding wit to be far more complex than a mere signpost to the repressed. Once again, one must be wary of generalizations across researchers' work because of different definitions of humor and the measurements thereof.

Walter O'Connell (Chapman & Foot, 1976) has made the distinction between measures of wit and those of humor and researched stimulus, mediational state, and social setting variables.

Psychometric tests were devised to measure response preferences for humor as differentiated from hostile wit, resignation, and nonsense wit. Following Freud's ideas that humor represented the triumph of the pleasure principle and a sign of the invincibility of the ego, a series of 15 research studies were conducted to test sexual, adjustment, and treatment variables relating to wit and humor (Chapman & Foot, 1977). O'Connell found evidence of personality differences between the aggressive and competitive wit and the nonjudgmental optimistic humorist. He then turned to clinical inferences about the growth of humor. O'Connell believes that the sense of humor consists of the conviction of one's unconditional worth as a person (beyond the question of the success of one's behavior). In addition, the humorist feels like a universal, irreplaceable force in life, sharing similarities with others. The humorist realizes that words and numbers cannot capture and contain the spirit of life. The flow of life unites logically incompatible processes (e.g., sad/glad, male/female, sacred/profane, past/present, life/death).

HUMOR IN THE FUTURE

In spite of the divergence of approaches to research posed by the complexity of humor and lack of systematic experimentation over time, professional interest is accelerating rapidly. International Congresses on Humor and Laughter have convened at Cardiff, Wales (1976), Los Angeles (1979), and Washington, DC (1982). The well-circulated account (1976, 1981) of Norman Cousins's self-healing of a near fatal illness through massive doses of humor (and vitamin C) have called attention to the neglected dynamics of humor as a therapeutic agent. Freud's clinical insight into humor—almost totally neglected for 50 years—is receiving new life by being assimilated into new theories.

Humor as a stimulus for growth of self-esteem and optimistic belonging, as well as a reflection of those inner qualities, has a fruitful future. Pain reduction and prevention of violence toward self and others through humor raises questions about the mutual interplay of endorphins, immunology, and humor. Accounts of the success of humor in the rearing and treating of children and in the social defusing of riotous conditions opens the issue of humor intervention for the optimal functioning of homes, schools, churches, and all other facets of institutional living.

REFERENCES

Berlyne, D. E. (1972). Humor and its kin. In J. Goldstein & P. McGhee (Eds.), *The psychology of humor.* New York: Academic.

Bischof, L. (1964). *Interpreting personality theories.* New York: Harper & Row.

Chapman, A., & Foot, H. (Eds.). (1976). *Humour and laughter: Theory, research and applications.* London: Wiley.

Chapman, A., & Foot, H. (Eds.). (1977). *It's a funny thing, humour.* Oxford: Pergamon.

Ellis, A. (1978). Fun as psychotherapy. In A. Ellis & R. Grieger (Eds.), *Handbook of rational-emotive therapy.* New York: Springer.

Fisher, S., & Fisher, R. (1981). *Pretend the world is funny and forever: A psychological analysis of comedians, clowns, and actors.* Hillsdale, NJ: Erlbaum.

Freud, S. (1956). Humor. In *Collected papers* (Vol. 5). London: Hogarth. (Original work published 1928)

Freud, S. (1968/1905). Jokes and their relation to the unconscious. In *The standard edition of the complete psychological works of Sigmund Freud* (Vol. 8). London: Hogarth.

Goldstein, J., & McGhee, P. (Eds.). *The psychology of humor: Theoretical perspectives and empirical issues.* New York: Academic.

Goldstein, J., Suls, J., & Anthony, S. (1972). Enjoyment of specific types of humor content: Motivation or salience? In J. Goldstein & P. McGhee (Eds.), *The psychology of humor.* New York: Academic.

Goodchilds, J. (1972). On being witty: Causes, correlates, and consequences. In J. Goldstein & P. McGhee (Eds.), *The psychology of humor.* New York: Academic.

La Fave, L. (1972). Humor judgments as a function of reference groups and identification classes. In J. Goldstein & P. McGhee (Eds.), *The psychology of humor.* New York: Academic.

Martineau, W. (1972). A model of the social functions of humor. In J. Goldstein & P. McGhee (Eds.), *The psychology of humor.* New York: Academic.

McGhee, P. (1972). On the cognitive origins of incongruity humor: Fantasy assimilation versus reality assimilation. In J. Goldstein & P. McGhee (Eds.), *The psychology of humor.* New York: Academic Press.

Mindess, H., & Turek, J. (1979). *The study of humor.* Los Angeles: Antioch.

O'Connell, W. (1981). Natural high therapy. In R. J. Corsini (Ed.), *Handbook of innovative psychotherapies.* New York: Wiley.

Stern, M. (Ed.). (1981). Humor and illumination. *Voices: The Art and Science of Psychotherapy, 16*(4).

Warkentin, J. (Ed.). (1969). Humor in therapy. *Voices: The Art and Science of Psychotherapy. Journal of the American Academy of Psychotherapists, 5*(2).

W. E. O'CONNELL
Natural High Center

PSYCHOTHERAPY

HUNGER

MEALS

Meals are the fundamental unit expressing hunger. Although meal size and intermeal intervals can be affected by a wide range of physiological and environmental variables, the basic pattern persists. Thus, a description of the timing, size, and content of meals over any interval provides a complete description of what and how much we eat. Furthermore, abnormal meal size is the fundamental behavioral change in clinically disordered eating in anorexia nervosa, bulimia nervosa, and obesity. Therefore, the behavioral neuroscience of hunger addresses the control of meals and the subjective phenomena associated with them.

FOOD SELECTION AND MEAL INITIATION

Food selection and meal initiation are controlled mainly by conditioned (usually highly individuated) olfactory, visual, temporal, cognitive, and social stimuli. Two physiological signals, however, are also sufficient to control normal meal initiation. First of all, brief, transient declines in blood glucose supply signal the motivation to eat in both rats and humans (Campfield, 1997). These declines are not hypoglycemia (i.e., decreases in blood glucose that reduce cellular glucose supply), which rarely occurs spontaneously. Second, certain changes in liver metabolism that can occur between meals (e.g., in fatty acid oxidation) are sufficient to initiate eating in rats (Langhans, 1996). Gastric contractions are not adequate stimuli for meal initiation, and the referral of hunger pangs to the stomach appears to be an epiphenomenon.

MEAL SIZE

Controls of the maintenance of eating and of the termination of eating determine meal size. Taste, especially sweet taste, is the only known unconditioned oropharyngeal stimulus that can facilitate or inhibit eating once it has begun. Odors are of course crucial for flavor, but their contribution is conditioned. Numerous other conditioned stimuli associated with food may also help maintain eating once it has begun, including social facilitation.

Stomach volume, detected by mechanoreceptors in the gastric muscles, and small intestinal nutrient content, detected by chemoreceptors in the intestinal mucosa, are the most important unconditioned controls of meal termination or satiation (Smith, 1998). Information detected by these receptors reach the brain either via sensory fibers in the vagus or splanchnic nerves, or via an intermediate step involving the release of gut peptides. A number of peripheral peptides are involved, including gastrin-releasing peptide (GRP), cholecystokinin (CCK), glucagon, and amylin (Geary, 1999; Smith, 1998).

The feedback effects of taste on eating and the negative feedbacks produced by gastrointestinal signals appear to represent the most fundamental level of the neural hierarchy controlling eating, because they are initiated by preabsorptive stimuli and because brainstem neural networks are sufficient to mediate their behavioral effects. For these reasons they are called direct controls of meal size (Geary & Smith, 2000). It appears that indirect controls involving the forebrain act via descending projections that alter the stimulus-response characteristics of the underlying brainstem direct control networks.

HUNGER AND BODY WEIGHT

Increased levels of body fat normally tend to reduce meal size. This lipostatic control appears to be signaled by two hormones whose blood levels are correlated with body fat content: insulin and leptin (Rosenbaum, Leibel, & Hirsch, 1997; Schwartz, Woods, Porte, Seeley, & Baskin, 2000). Each enters the brain via active transport mechanisms and appears to act in the hypothalamus. The control of meal size and food intake by body fat can be dramatic or weak, depending on, for example, on genetic variation; on the availability, palatability, variety, and energy density of food; and, probably, on conditioning.

NEUROCHEMISTRY OF HUNGER

Neuropharmacological methods, including the measurement of neurochemicals at their site of action in awake, behaving animals, link many specific neurochemical systems in the brain to hunger (Elmquist, Elias, & Saper, 1999; Geary & Smith, 2000; Schwartz, Woods, Porte, Seeley, & Baskin, 2000).

Dopamine and endogenous opioids are neurotransmitters crucial for food reward, that is, for the maintenance of eating during meals, the production of pleasure, and the reinforcement of learning about food (Geary & Smith, 2000). They act in overlapping forebrain sites including the nucleus accumbens and amygdala. Neuropeptide Y (NPY) and norepinephrine (NE) also increase eating, apparently by increasing hunger rather than affecting reward. The paraventricular nucleus of the hypothalamus (PVN) is a site of action of both.

The most researched neurotransmitter that inhibits eating is serotonin (5-hydroxytryptamine, 5HT). 5HT participates in many aspects of eating, including food reward, CCK's satiating action, and conditioned preferences related to protein metabolism, and acts in several brain sites, including the PVN.

GENETICS OF HUNGER

Both spontaneous and experimental targeted mutations (knockouts) of single genes can lead to dramatic changes in eating and body weight in animals (Rosenbaum et al., 1997). For example, mutations of genes encoding either leptin or the CCK, 5HT, or leptin receptors all produce phenotypes of overeating and obesity. Emerging methods for reversible manipulations of genes in specific brain areas at any stage of development should soon produce dramatic advances in the genetics of eating.

Although human obesity has a genetic component, only extremely rare cases are due to single-gene mutations. Thus, another challenge for the genetics of hunger is the development of better methods for analysis of multiple-gene systems' phenotypes.

LEARNING

Except for the unconditioned effects of taste, all food identification, selection, and preference is learned. Very little, however, is known about the complex social and cultural conditioning that so dramatically influences human appetite, producing, for example, the paradoxical preference for capsaicin (chili; Rozin, 1986). Food's rewarding, satiating, metabolic, and toxic effects all support learning (Sclafani, 1997). A neutral flavor associated with a satiating food can simultaneously condition preference (so that the neutral flavor is preferred) and satiety (so that less food of that flavor is eaten). Conditioned aversions linking tastes with certain forms of illness are a dramatic example of a special biological preparedness: Only a single pairing of taste and illness is required, the taste-illness interval can be hours, and the learning is very resistant to extinction. A complex neural network involving the brainstem and the amygdala mediate this learning.

EATING DISORDERS

The behavioral neuroscience of eating has begun to contribute to analysis of human eating disorders. For example, it has been shown that patients with bulimia nervosa eat larger-than-normal meals under laboratory conditions, that the experimenter's instructions can induce binges, and that ingested food is less satiating for these patients than for unaffected individuals (Kissileff et al., 1996). The decreased satiety appears in part to be due to a decrease in CCK secretion, which, remarkably, recovers when eating behavior is normalized (Geracioti & Liddle, 1988). Bulimic patients are also especially sensitive to manipulations of brain 5HT that affect hunger (Geary & Smith, 2000).

REFERENCES

Campfield, L. A. (1997). Metabolic and hormonal controls of food intake: Highlights of the last 25 years. *Appetite, 29,* 135–152.

Elmquist, J. K., Elias, C. F., & Saper, C. B. (1999). From lesions to leptin: hypothalamic control of body weight. *Neuron, 22,* 221–232.

Geary, N. (1999). Effects of glucagon, insulin, amylin and CGRP on feeding. *Neuropeptides, 33,* 400–405.

Geary, N., & Smith, G. P. (2000). Appetite. In B. J. Sadock & V. A. Sadock (Eds.), *Comprehensive textbook of psychiatry* (7th ed., pp. 209–218). Philadelphia: Lippincott, Williams & Wilkens.

Geracioti, T. D., & Liddle, R. J. (1988). Impaired cholecystokinni secretion in bulimia nervosa. *New England Journal of Medicine, 319,* 683–688.

Kissileff, H. R., Wentzlaff, T. H., Guss, J. L., Walsh, B. T., Devlin, J. J., & Tornton, J. C. (1996). A direct measure of satiety disturbance in patients with bulimia nervosa. *Physiology and Behavior, 60,* 1077–1085.

Langhans, W. (1996). The role of the liver in the metabolic control of feeding. *Neuroscience and Biobehavioral Reviews, 20,* 145–153.

Rosenbaum, M., Leibel, R. L., & Hirsch, J. (1997). Medical progress: Obesity. *New England Journal of Medicine, 337,* 396–407.

Rozin, P. (1986). Food likes and dislikes. *Annual Review of Nutrition, 6,* 433–456.

Sclafani, A. (1997). Learned controls of ingestive behavior. *Appetite, 29,* 153–158.

Schwartz, M. J., Woods, S. C., Porte, D., Jr., Seeley, R. J., & Baskin, D. G. (2000). Central nervous system control of food intake. *Nature, 404,* 661–671.

Smith, G. P. (Ed.). (1998). *Satiation: From gut to brain.* New York: Oxford.

N. GEARY
Weill Medical College of Cornell University

APPETITE DISORDERS
EATING DISORDERS
OBESITY

HUNT, J. McVICKER (1906–1991)

Although tagged an environmentalist, J. McVicker Hunt prefers to call himself an interactionist. The environmentalist label stems from his work *Intelligence and Experience.* But Hunt is perhaps better known for the two-volume publication *Personality and Behavior Disorders* edited by him in 1944.

Hunt obtained the BA from the University of Nebraska before heading for Cornell University, where he was granted the PhD in 1933. He spent a decade going from instructor to associate professor at Brown University (1936–1946), and a year or two at Teachers College of Columbia University and at New York University, before settling down at the University of Illinois, where he stayed from 1951 until his retirement in 1974. He was also affiliated with the Institute of Welfare Research of the Community Service Society in New York from 1944 to 1951. He was president of the American Psychological Association in 1952.

STAFF

HUNTINGTON'S CHOREA

Huntington's chorea, also known as Huntington's disease, is a genetically determined disorder of the central nervous system, first described by George Huntington in 1872. Reliable estimates of its prevalence are not available because of the frequency with which it is misdiagnosed or concealed.

The first observable symptom is often a facial twitch, which gradually spreads to tremors and loss of voluntary control elsewhere. Locomotion, speech, and swallowing become more impaired and eventually impossible. Mood becomes depressed. Hallucinations, delusions, and other common symptoms may closely resemble schizophrenia and many Huntington's patients are misdiagnosed as having schizophrenia, especially in the early stages. In the later stages, however, the intellectual, memory, and movement disorders become much more severe than in schizophrenia.

The usual age of onset is 30 to 40, with some cases originating as early as 20 or as late as 60. When it has a childhood onset (rare), the symptoms are somewhat different and the deterioration more rapid. The disease is progressive, with the expected result being death about 15 years after onset. The cause of death is usually heart failure, inability to breathe, or pneumonia.

These behavioral symptoms are related to a progressive loss of cells in the basal ganglia of the brain. The symptoms can be mimicked in animals by injections of kainic acid (which kills cell bodies) into the basal ganglia (Mason, Sanberg, & Fibiger, 1978). There is also an associated decrease in the brain concentrations of the synaptic transmitters acetylcholine, GABA, serotonin, and glutamine, especially in the basal ganglia. The decline in these transmitters may lead to excessive activity of catecholamine synapses, through a loss of inhibition. Treatment often includes major tranquilizers (neuroleptics) or other drugs. However, none of the drugs yet tested retards the deteriorating course; at best they reduce the twitches and some other problems.

Because Huntington's disease is controlled by an autosomal dominant gene, males and females are equally affected, and anybody with one affected parent has a 50% chance of developing the disorder. However, genetic counseling is complicated by the late age of onset. A person may not know whether he or she has the condition until age 40 or more. Furthermore, it has been observed that an occasional early manifestation of the condition in males is a period of sexual promiscuity; thus, with many illegitimate births, no one even knows that the child is at risk.

There has been some interest in finding a way to detect Huntington's disease before it becomes symptomatic, largely for genetic counseling purposes. Klawans, Paulson, Riegel, and Barbeau (1972) administered L-dopa to 30 young adults at risk for Huntington's disease. (L-dopa aggravates symptoms once they become apparent.) Under the influence of L-dopa, 10 of the 30 developed temporary tremors resembling Huntington's disease. In an 8-year follow-up study, five of these 10 had developed the disease, while only one of the other 20 had done so (Klawans, Goetz, Paulson, & Barbeau, 1980). Thus this test shows promise of providing presymptomatic detection. However, some have questioned the ethics of the test, because it may lead to hopeless despair if it indicates the presence of the condition and because of the hypothetical possibility that the L-dopa test might actually accelerate the course of the disease.

REFERENCES

Klawans, H. L., Goetz, C. G., Paulson, G. W., & Barbeau, A. (1980). Levodopa and presymptomatic detection of Huntington's disease—Eight-year follow-up. *New England Journal of Medicine, 302,* 1090.

Klawans, H. L., Jr., Paulson, C. G., Riegel, S. P., & Barbeau, A. (1972). Use of L-dopa in the detection of presymptomatic Huntington's chorea. *New England Journal of Medicine, 286,* 1332.

Mason, S. T., Sanberg, P. R., & Fibiger, H. C. (1978). Kainic acid lesions of the striatum dissociate amphetamine and apomorphine stereotypy: Similarities to Huntington's chorea. *Science, 201,* 352–355.

SUGGESTED READING

Chase, T. N., Wexler, N. S., & Barbeau, A. (Eds.). (1979). Huntington's disease. *Advances in neurology* (Vol. 23). New York: Raven Press.

J. W. KALAT
North Carolina State University

ALZHEIMER'S DISEASE
CENTRAL NERVOUS SYSTEM

HUSSERL, EDMUND (1859–1938)

Edmund Husserl was the founder and most prominent exponent of a new philosophic movement, phenomenology, which found many followers, especially in continental Europe, and greatly influenced both the philosophical and psychological thought of the twentieth century. When Husserl began his academic studies, his main interest lay in mathematics and the natural sciences. He studied in Leipzig, Berlin, and Vienna, where he received the PhD in 1883. After serving briefly as an assistant in mathematics at the University of Berlin, he returned to Vienna to study philosophy under Franz Brentano.

Husserl's academic career began at the University of Halle in 1887, where he lectured for 14 years. Later he was professor at Göttingen and at Freiburg in Breisgau, where he died. He was active to the end in developing and improving his system. At the time of his death phenomenology had become a powerful movement, and Husserl had won recognition as one of the keenest intellects and most influential philosophers of the century. During his lifetime Husserl published six books, but left an enormous number of manuscripts from which dozens of volumes have been published posthumously and still more are currently being prepared for publication. Husserl's first exposition of phenomenology appeared in a 2-volume book *Logische Untersuchungen* (Logical Investigations), later revised and enlarged.

The point of departure of Husserl's phenomenology is two affirmations: (a) Philosophical inquiry cannot begin with anything but with phenomena of consciousness, because they are the only givens accessible to us, the only material at our immediate disposal; (b) only phenomena of consciousness can reveal to us what things essentially are. Thus Husserl's phenomenology is principally a systematic and full exploration of consciousness. The phenomena of consciousness are numerous and manifold: things, persons, events, experiences, memories, feelings, moods, thoughts, images, fantasies, mental constructs, and the like. Phenomenology explores them through a method especially adapted for this purpose, known as the phenomenological method. This method became the keystone of Husserl's entire philosophical system. Through its use Husserl hoped to reform philosophy and to establish a rigorously scientific philosophy which could provide a firm basis for all other sciences.

The phenomenological method consists of examining whatever is found in consciousness—all the data or phenomena of consciousness. The basic prerequisite for the successful practice of the method is freeing oneself from any preconceptions or presuppositions. It is imperative that in the exploration of consciousness all biases, theories, beliefs, and habitual modes of thinking be suspended or "bracketed," that is, put between "brackets," as Husserl described it, using an expression familiar in algebra. The ultimate goal of the phenomenological method is to reach and grasp the essences of things appearing in consciousness.

Phenomenology has profoundly affected psychology, in both theory and practice, especially in Germany and Austria. Husserl's intent was to bridge the psychology of his day with phenomenology by developing a new and special psychological discipline, which he called phenomenological psychology. Its goal was to study consciousness in its meaningful structure and function.

Among the eminent psychologists influenced by Husserl's ideas were David Katz, August Messer, Karl Bühler, and Albert Michotte. European psychologists sympathetic to Husserl's conception of psychology, emigrating to the United States in the 1930s, introduced American psychologists to phenomenology and helped form the so-called Third Force in American psychology.

H. MISIAK
Fordham University

HYMAN, STEVEN E.

Steven E. Hyman is director of the National Institute of Mental Health (NIMH), the component of the National Institutes of Health charged with generating the knowledge needed to understand, treat, and prevent mental illness. Under Hyman's leadership, NIMH has heightened the priority it gives to four broad areas: (a) fundamental research on brain, behavior, and genetics; (b) rapid translation of basic discoveries into research on mental disorders; (c) research that directly impacts the treatment of individuals with mental disorders, including clinical trials and studies of treatment and preventive interventions in real world settings; and (d) research on child development and childhood mental disorders. Hyman continues to direct an active research program in molecular neurobiology on the NIH campus (Bethesda, Maryland), focusing on how neurotransmitters, especially dopamine and glutamate, alter the expression of genes in the striatum and thereby produce long-term changes in neural function that can influence behavior.

Prior to his position at NIMH, Hyman was professor of psychiatry at Harvard Medical School and director of psychiatry research at Massachusetts General Hospital in Boston. He also taught neurobiology at Harvard Medical School and was the first faculty director of Harvard University's Interfaculty Initiative in Mind, Brain, and Behavior. In addition to his scientific writings, Hyman has authored and edited several widely used clinical texts. He serves on numerous review and advisory boards, including the Riken Brain Sciences Institute in Japan, the Max Planck Institute in Germany, and the Howard Hughes Medical Institute in the United States. Hyman received his BA from Yale in 1974 (summa cum laude), and his MA in 1976 from the University of Cambridge, where he was a Mellon fellow studying the history and philosophy of science. He received his MD from Harvard Medical School (cum laude) in 1980. Following an internship in medicine at Massachusetts General Hospital (MGH), a residency in psychiatry at McLean Hospital, and a clinical fellowship in neurology at MGH, he was postdoctoral fellow at Harvard in molecular biology.

STAFF

HYPERACTIVITY

The term "hyperactivity" refers to both a nonspecific symptom associated with a variety of medical and behavioral disorders, and a common psychopathological syndrome. There is considerable debate over appropriate use of the word, and a range of related terms are often treated interchangeably. These over-lapping concepts include overactivity, hyperkinesis, minimal brain dysfunction, Attention Deficit Disorder, and Attention-Deficit/Hyperactivity Disorder. This discussion will address hyperactivity as a descriptor, symptom, and syndrome, emphasizing the disorder currently called Attention-Deficit/Hyperactivity Disorder.

DESCRIPTOR

Activity level is an important developmental and temperamental dimension. It represents an individual difference among all animals, including human beings. Developmental change is expected, as captured in the contrast between a frisky young puppy and a sedentary older dog. Thus, a range of behavior is considered appropriate or within normal limits. Exceeding these limits in either statistical or clinical terms can be called "overactivity." A continuous form of movement, such as squirming, fidgeting, or foot tapping, rather than discrete or episodic movement with a clear beginning and end (such as a spasm or tic) is called hyperactivity.

One category of temperament is overall activity level: constitutionally-based qualities of responsiveness that are evident and relatively stable throughout life. Hyperactivity, as a statistical or clinical extreme, has particular implications for problems in development and adaptation that can contribute to a host of secondary difficulties for the individual.

SYMPTOM

When the normal limits of activity level are surpassed, hyperactivity becomes a potentially confusing term. A common, often primary, symptom, hyperactivity is observed in a variety of medical and behavioral disorders, including Bipolar Disorder (manic depression), Schizophrenia, autism, developmental disabilities, metabolic disorders, endocrine disorders (e.g., hyperthyroidism), toxic exposure (e.g., lead poisoning), and various other diseases and disorders of the brain (brain tumor, encephalitis, Parkinson's disease, etc.). Furthermore, hyperactivity is not in itself a cause for concern. Instead, experienced clinicians and researchers view it as a nonspecific symptom whose significance depends on demographic and situational factors and the presence of other physiological characteristics or behavioral symptoms.

SYNDROME

Despite the heterogeneity of conditions that include motor excess, there appears to be a set of factors that co-vary, which has resulted in the identification of a hyperactivity syndrome or disorder. Initially, defective moral regulation was presumed to cause hyperactivity. Later, the motor excess itself became central, and research focused first on brain damage and later on variability in neurological development in order to understand hyperactive children, and more recently, hyperactive adults.

Hyperactivity does not constitute a syndrome in the technical sense of the word, because the particular pattern of symptoms or characteristics does not form a unitary cluster, nor is there adequate evidence of common etiology—both sine qua non of a true syndrome. However, the disorder most closely associated with hyperactivity, and which is sometimes used synonomously, is Attention-Deficit/Hyperactivity Disorder (ADHD; American Psychiatric Association, 1994). The core symptoms are hyperactivity, distractibility, and impulsivity.

Russell Barkley (1997a, 1997b, 1998) has summarized the research on this disorder and developed a cohesive theory to understand both the disorder itself and the disability it creates. As a developmental disorder, ADHD is present from birth and symptoms manifest at a young age (before age 7). Symptoms are persistent rather than episodic and are present across situations. However, hyperactivity may be more obvious in settings where quiet, calm behavior are required and may go virtually unnoticed in unstructured settings where active behavior is allowed or encouraged, accounting for the difference in a child's presentation in the classroom, on the playground, and at home.

Prevalence estimates range from 3 to 7%. More boys than girls are affected, with a ratio of about 3:1. Differences in diagnostic criteria and problems in diagnostic reliability account for some of the cross-cultural variation in prevalence reports.

Attention-Deficit/Hyperactivity Disorder was conceptualized as a childhood disorder that one outgrew, until longitudinal research showed that, while some manifestations of the disorder may become less problematic when formal education is completed, the overall pattern persists in at least 30 to 50% of the affected population. In addition to the primary symptoms, individuals with ADHD are at increased risk for poor academic progress, suspension and expulsion from school, and poor interpersonal relationships. Increased rates of anxiety and depression, more aggressive and delinquent behavior, and increased rates of substance abuse also have been documented. Furthermore, adults with ADHD may have vocational difficulties, increased risk for motor vehicle accidents, and greater marital instability.

Specific etiology of ADHD remains unknown, although professional consensus leans toward biological explanations of the pathogenesis. Genetic, organic, and environmental hypotheses all have some support. Genetic perspectives are supported by the increased incidence of the disorder in relatives of those with ADHD and the over-representation of males, although intra-familial variability does not rule out psychological or behavioral transmission. Organic explanations are supported by observations of similar behavior in individuals with traumatic head injuries, and the prevalence of hyperactivity in some metabolic disorders, suggesting that an acquired illness or injury may contribute to the condition.

Environmental factors associated with ADHD-type symptoms include toxins such as lead, exposure to radiation, and specific medications. Although psychological hypotheses such as particular child-rearing patterns or learning patterns are less well accepted than other theories, these factors affect the course and outcome of the disorder.

Recently, Barkley and others have turned their attention to so-called executive functioning as the core deficit that causes ADHD. Barkley suggests that developmentally, certain types of self regulation, including regulation of motor behavior and sustained attention, ought to emerge with age. These skills do not adequately develop in people with ADHD. Neuroimaging findings, neuropsy-

chological tests, and laboratory tasks appear to provide converging evidence for this perspective, which identifies behavioral inhibition as the key deficit. However, given the range of factors that may contribute to ADHD and the high prevalence of the disorder, it is likely that the actual etiology is multifactorial. Furthermore, if the notion of multiple syndromes is borne out, multiple etiologies are likely to be revealed.

Consistent with the variation in etiological hypotheses, assessment and treatment of the disorder are wide-ranging and cross disciplinary lines with the educators, physicians, and mental health providers all claiming ownership of the disorder. Neuro-developmental, psychological, psychoeducational, and neuropsychological evaluations all are used to identify the disorder.

Several valid and reliable parent and teacher rating scales have been developed for identification of ADHD. Many children are identified by their teachers or pediatricians in the absence of a comprehensive assessment, and no data comparing the accuracy of each type of diagnosis are available because there is no definitive test that proves the presence of this disorder. Historically, devices measuring frequency of motor behavior were used when the emphasis on activity level superseded the appreciation of attention and impulsivity as hallmarks of the disorder.

Electroencephalographic and electrophysiological measures more closely associated with attentional and central nervous system arousal appear in clinical research, as do computer-based assessment tasks such as the Continuous Performance Test. Recent attention has turned toward specific neuropsychological assessment tools that may provide greater sensitivity and specificity than existing measures. However, none of these has sufficient reliability or validity to be the gold standard for diagnosis. Consequently, comprehensive multidisciplinary assessment, incorporating parent and teacher reports, cognitive and behavioral assessment, and norm-based rating scales, are particularly desirable in diagnosing ADHD.

Treatment with stimulant medications such as methylphenidate or dextroamphetamine is the most common, most effective, and yet controversial treatment for ADHD. However, it is generally recognized that medication alone, even for those who respond dramatically, is insufficient to address either the primary disorder or its disabling effects. Therefore a variety of cognitive, behavioral and psychoeducational interventions are necessary adjuncts to medication.

REFERENCES

American Psychiatric Association (1994). Diagnostic and statistical manual of mental disorders, (4th ed.). Washington, DC: Author.

Barkley, R. A. (1997a). Behavioral inhibition, sustained attention, and executive functions: Constructing a unifying theory of ADHD. *Psychological Bulletin, 121*(1), 65–94.

Barkley, R. A. (1997b). Attention deficit/hyperactivity disorder and the nature of self control. New York: Guilford Press.

Barkley, R. A. (1998). Attention deficit hyperactivity disorder: A handbook for diagnosis and treatment (2nd ed.). New York: Guilford Press.

Diagnosis and Treatment of Attention Deficit Hyperactivity Disorder (ADHD). NIN Consensus Statement, 1998, Nov. 16–18; 16(2): 1–37.

D. L. Wertlieb
Tufts University

D. S. Spetter
New England Medical Center

SCHOOL ADJUSTMENT
TEMPERAMENTS

HYPERTENSION

Hypertension, a disease affecting the cardiovascular system and commonly known as high blood pressure, is a major health problem. It is characterized by chronic elevation of diastolic and, typically, systolic blood pressure without demonstrable pathology of either the blood vessels or the heart. Hypertension is a primary cause of adult sickness, disability, and death in the United States, afflicting approximately 50 million persons. Additionally, it is one of the most important risk factors in the promotion of atherosclerotic diseases, kidney failure, congestive heart failure, coronary heart disease, heart attack, and stroke.

Blood pressure occurs on a continuum with no clear division between normal and elevated pressure. Further, the blood pressure values of concern to a practitioner vary as a function of a patient's history, age, sex, and environment. In general, however, blood pressure is regarded as high when the systolic pressure at rest consistently provides a measurement of 140 mm Hg (millimeters of mercury) or more, and the diastolic pressure is 90 mm Hg or more. Depending upon a variety of factors, a diagnosis of hypertension may or may not be applied when consistent readings above 140/90 (reported as one-forty over ninety) are obtained. Nevertheless, consistent readings above this level do warrant monitoring and perhaps remediation.

If remediation is selected, the treatment strategy depends upon the etiology of the malady. Primary or essential hypertension refers to an instance in which the cause is unknown, while secondary hypertension is the result of an identifiable antecedent such as malfunction of particular endocrine organs, coarctation of the aorta, pregnancy, or oral contraceptive medication. While secondary hypertension may be ameliorated via surgery or chemotherapy, this category accounts for a relatively small percentage of the cases.

In contrast to the low incidence of secondary hypertension, in about 80% of the patients evidencing hypertension there is no clear cause for the disease. Even though this type of hypertension is of unspecified etiology, it has been recognized for a long time that emotional factors, stress, and a fast-paced life-style have an elevating effect on blood pressure. Within this context, much research has been directed toward establishing effective behavioral treatments that may be employed alone or in conjunction with a variety of pharmacological regimens.

These behavioral treatments include progressive muscle relaxation, meditation, yoga exercises, autogenic training, biofeedback-assisted relaxation, blood pressure biofeedback, contingency managed aerobics, and diet, as well as strategies combining two or more of these programs.

SUGGESTED READING

Berkow, R. (Ed.). (1997). High blood pressure. In *The Merck manual of medical information* (pp. 112–118). Whitehouse Station, NJ: Merck Research Laboratories.

Boone, J. L., & Christiansen, J. F. (1997). Stress and disease. In M. D. Feldman & J. F. Christensen (Eds.), *Behavioral medicine in primary care.* Stamford, CT: Appleton & Lange.

W. W. Wenrich
University of North Texas

HYPNOSIS

It is difficult to give a satisfactory definition of hypnosis. Most authorities would agree that hypnosis occurs (a) within the context of a special hypnotist-subject relationship, during which (b) suggestions of distortions of cognition, perception, memory, and affect can be responded to by (c) some individuals who (d) are able to control (voluntarily) their levels of consciousness. Arguments about the nature of hypnosis depend on which of these four aspects is the focus of theory and research. Hypnosis appears to be characterized by the dissociative subject's ability to accept as reality suggested distortions of perception, cognition, and affect for a temporary period of time.

HISTORY OF HYPNOSIS

The modern history of hypnosis begins with Franz Anton Mesmer (1734–1815), who, like others before and since, tried to apply discoveries in physics, in this case, the principles of magnetism, to mental health. His patients gathered around the baquet, a tub of water filled with iron filings with protruding rods that were to be held by the patients, who in turn joined hands with other patients. The purple-robed Mesmer would then appear—often late—and proceed with the laying on of hands. The gathered ill became hypnotized, as evidenced by the crisis, or hysterical seizure, that rippled from those nearest the baquet to nearby neighbors throughout the crowd. Several ingenious experiments conducted in 1784 in Paris by a Royal Commission headed by Benjamin Franklin led to the rejection of Mesmer's animal magnetism theory. The alleged therapeutic cures were dismissed as "mere imagination."

James Braid in 1852 first introduced the term "hypnosis" from the Greek *hypnos* (to sleep). Jean Charcot (1882) considered hypnosis a manifestation of hysteria occurring only in women, although current research has shown that there are no sex differences in hypnotic responsivity. Charcot influenced the later development of dissociation theorizing by Pierre Janet and Morton Prince. Charcot also influenced Sigmund Freud, whose observations of the hypnotic abreaction in his famous case with Breuer were influential in his development of the concept of unconscious motivation. Freud later gave up hypnosis because he stated that he could not hypnotize everybody. He did not recognize (along with even some contemporary practitioners) that hypnosis was a characteristic of the individual rather than something done by a hypnotist/therapist. Hippolyte Bernheim (1886) saw hypnosis not as a characterological defect or dissociated system, but as a manifestation of suggestibility—a view carried forward by the first major research program in hypnosis conducted by Clark Hull at Yale in 1933. Unfortunately, suggestibility, as defined by Hull and others, shows little or no correlation with measured hypnotic responsivity.

Modern counterparts of all these developments still persist. These early differences help to place current controversies in perspective, including both the prevailing enthusiasm and skepticism toward hypnosis.

THE MEASUREMENT OF HYPNOSIS

A number of standardized scales testing responses to suggestions chosen by a consensus of experts, which have made it possible to measure hypnosis with high reliability and validity. The scales are based on objective behavioral ratings of responses to subjective suggestions that have been graded in difficulty. Examples are the *Stanford Hypnotic Susceptibility Scales* (*Forms A, B, and C*) and the tape-recorded, group-administered *Harvard Group Scale of Hypnotic Susceptibility, Form A*. About 30% of normal subjects and hospitalized psychiatric patients score in the high range of hypnotizability, while another 10–25% have very limited capacity to experience hypnosis. Once measured under properly stabilized conditions (the first such measurement may be somewhat unreliable because of the fears, misconceptions, and anxieties that often surround hypnosis), hypnotic responsiveness is unlikely to increase or decrease.

CHARACTERISTICS OF HYPNOSIS

The methodological sophistication of contemporary hypnosis research is considerable and contributes to general psychological theory. Hypnosis research has made contributions to the evaluation of various phenomena: subjective experience, verbal reports, the limits of human performance, attention and consciousness, factors involved in the social psychology of the psychological experiment, and clinical practice. Three illustrative areas can be summarized.

Trance Logic

One unique characteristic typically not found in unhypnotizable subjects who are asked to fake hypnosis is trance logic, or the ability to tolerate logical incongruities (Orne, 1970). For example, an hypnotized person is asked to hallucinate his friend Joe sitting in a chair on his left, when Joe is really sitting off to the right. The hypnotized individual will converse with the hallucination in a realistic way. When pushed by the experimenter, who points to the real Joe, the truly hypnotized subject remains quite comfortable in maintaining the duality of the real and hallucinated person. If prompted, he can easily determine which is the hallucination ("I tried to make them *both lift their* right hand in the air: The one on the left did, but I cannot control the real Joe") even while calmly maintaining the hallucination. Similarly, when asked to forget the number 6, the hypnotized subject may smile benignly but will not show any affective concern when, counting his fingers, he discovers

he has an extra digit. In contrast, using a special research methodology, subjects simulating hypnosis will cleverly find that they do have only 10 fingers. In the example of the hallucinated friend, a subject simulating hypnosis will deny that the real Joe exists, or the hallucinated Joe will disappear. This characteristic willingness to tolerate logical incongruity is the hallmark of the hypnotized person; similarly, it is not particularly troublesome for the hypnotized person to regress to, for example, seven years of age. At one level the hypnotized person knows reality exists, but at another level that reality can be suspended in an effortless absorption in a fantasy world. It must be stressed, however, that one's recollection of his or her experiences as a 7-year-old will have been contaminated by the contextual aspects of memory, and therefore it should not necessarily be expected that the hypnotized subject's regression accurately reproduces what happened when he or she was a child. While the distorted and confabulated material may be important therapeutically, there is a disturbing tendency for hypnosis to be used in forensic applications based on the faulty premise of accurate recall. Hypnotized subjects can lie under hypnosis just as easily as in the waking state.

Pain Control

Hypnosis can play an important role in pain control; hypnotic analgesia can best be understood in terms of at least two distinct processes. (a) Hypnosis can directly reduce pain at a sensory, physiological, or primary level. (Some recent evidence suggests that endorphins are not involved in hypnotically-induced pain control, as they are in other methods of pain control, including pain killing medications and acupuncture.) (b) Expectational or placebo-like effects can reduce pain, because of the special context in which hypnosis is induced, regardless of how hypnotizable the person is (Evans, 2000). Thus, there is only a modest correlation between the capacity for hypnosis and the capacity for pain control (and any other therapeutic intervention). This correlation is kept low by the impact of the nonspecific or placebo-like factors brought into play with patients who are psychologically ready to give up their symptoms if an intervention is appropriately legitimized.

The subject who is experiencing a profound analgesic effect can still report the objective pain stimulus conditions when the hypnotist addresses another part of the hypnotized subject's awareness (the so-called hidden observer, Hilgard, 1977). Some investigators argue this is evidence that the hypnotic experience is not real; these critics fail to recognize that people operate on multiple cognitive levels in many everyday situations.

Characteristics of the Hypnotizable Person

These characteristics of hypnosis (in which the hypnotized subject seems tuned to multiple cognitive pathways and is easily able to distort reality while remaining aware of its existence at other levels of awareness, coupled with the extreme stability of hypnotic performance even over several years) have led many investigators to speculate that only selected people are prone to experience hypnosis. The hypnotizable person is not gullible, hysterical, weak-willed, passive, prone to the placebo response nor to the control of the dominant hypnotist; instead, the person has the capacity to become totally absorbed in ongoing experiences, such as becoming lost in fantasy or identifying with the emotions of a character in a play or movie. He or she reports having had imaginary playmates as a youngster. The highly hypnotizable subject may turn up late for experimental appointments—a puzzling finding for those theorists who see hypnosis as little more than role-playing performed to please the hypnotist. The occasional lateness of the hypnotizable subject may stem from his or her capacity to give up reality testing in order to become absorbed in an ongoing activity.

Nevertheless, this ability to become lost in thought is not just a form of absentmindedness, nor is it a lapse in memory. Hypnotizable subjects may be able to manipulate memory at will. They can have posthypnotic amnesia by failing to use those normal retrieval strategies (e.g., temporal sequence, experience of success) that typically facilitate memory. However, this memory lapse is easily reversible, and high hypnotic subjects have superior memories, particularly for events of many years past. This cognitive flexibility is the hallmark of the hypnotizable person. The hypnotizable person naps and falls asleep quickly at night, and has other characteristics that cluster together to define an individual difference dimension involving the control of consciousness, or a basic individual difference in cognitive flexibility. This flexibility dimension suggests that the hypnotizable person should have an advantage in the treatment of habit disorders and specific symptoms. Hypnotizability is a significant prognostic index of recovery from psychiatric illness and of the ability to give up symptoms (Evans, 2000; Hilgard, 1977).

CLINICAL HYPNOSIS

Professional Training in Clinical Hypnosis

The use of hypnosis as an adjunctive treatment modality has been increasing rapidly as it becomes more accepted and training facilities improve. Hypnosis is a technique, not a science or a treatment. Its use must be integrated into the specialized skills of the professional in his or her own area of competence, like any adjunctive method. It is the skill and judgment of the therapist—what to treat, when not to treat, possible side effects and complications—that define the safety and efficacy of the technique. So-called hypnotechnicians and other groups that are quite active in many areas have the mistaken belief that mere hypnotic suggestion can cure a variety of disorders. Referring patients to such nonprofessionals is considered unethical and possibly dangerous.

Training opportunities are available in a number of universities and medical schools. Annual workshops limited to physicians, dentists, psychologists, nurses and psychiatric social workers are offered by two national hypnosis soceities: the American Society of Clinical Hypnosis and the Society for Clinical and Experimental Hypnosis. Both societies publish a journal on hypnosis. The American Psychological Association's Division 30, Psychological Hypnosis, also offers workshops, and the International Society of Hypnosis provides a forum for professional colleagues throughout the world.

Clinical Applications

Hypnosis has been used in the treatment of a wide variety of medical, psychological, and behavioral problems. Claims of dramatic clinical results have not usually been documented by careful studies. Hypnosis tends to be more effective in those conditions that have a clear-cut etiology, and is relatively less effective where there

are issues of psychodynamic or behavioral control. Thus, the use of hypnosis to control pain in cancer and burns, to modify chemotherapy-induced vomiting and nausea, and to ease the discomfort of invasive procedures (e.g., debridement, bone marrow procedures) shows great promise even with those of moderate hypnotizability. In contrast to its value with acute pain and anxiety, the use of hypnosis to treat chronic functional pain and other chronic conditions is less successful. In such cases, secondary gain or masked depression may control the symptoms, and hypnosis would usually be contraindicated, except as an initial therapeutic contact, until the quality of life issues are addressed. Similarly, it is difficult to treat habit disorders, particularly those that are easily partially reinforced (e.g., eating and weight disorders). However, hypnosis is especially useful in habit control when, for whatever reason, the patient is ready to give up a symptom and needs legitimization and often a dramatic intervention to justify change.

Hypnosis is useful in establishing whether patients have the resources to develop some kind of meaningful mind-body self-control and cognitive mastery over their symptoms. Thus pain patients who can produce a glove analgesia or who can hallucinate pain in another part of the body or imagine themselves pain free, are likely to have internal processes of self-control of the kind necessary in symptom relief once secondary gain or masked depression have been handled therapeutically.

Finally, hypnosis is a useful adjunct in behavioral interventions, particularly because fantasy and cognitive distortions can be produced quite readily during hypnosis as an adjunct to behavioral and cognitive therapies. The use of hypnosis to facilitate relaxation, aid ego strengthening, control anger and other negative emotions, uncover affect with age regression, develop imagery strategies, and facilitate symptom relief, is usually safe and effective.

SUMMARY

The clinical application of hypnosis as a specialized technique runs far ahead of our basic understanding of the nature of the hypnotic phenomena. Indeed, the role of social psychological variables and the interaction of the hypnotist-subject makes it difficult to study hypnosis, but with carefully controlled, methodologically sophisticated studies these mysteries may be unraveled. A comprehensive psychology of consciousness is probably needed to understand hypnosis. Hypnotic phenomena can provide paradigms for understanding important aspects of the psychopathology of everyday life (e.g., memory disorders from posthypnotic amnesia, pain control from studies of hypnotic analgesia, etc.). It is clear that some individuals can experience hypnosis and control different states of consciousness with flexibility. As understanding of these mechanisms grows, more sophisticated applications of hypnosis will be developed for clinical use.

REFERENCES

Evans, F. J. (2000). Hypnosis: An introduction. In *The use of hypnosis in surgery and anesthesiology.* New York: Charles T. Thomas.

Orne, M. T. (1959). The nature of hypnosis: Artifact and essence. *Journal of Abnormal Psychology, 46,* 213–225.

SUGGESTED READING

Burrows, G. D., & Dennerstein, L. (Eds.). (1980). *Handbook of hypnosis and psychosomatic medicine.* Holland: Elsevier.

Clarke, J. C., & Jackson, J. A. (1983). *Hypnosis and behavior therapy.* New York: Springer.

Crasilneck, H. B., & Hall, J. A. (1985). *Clinical hypnosis.* New York: Grune & Stratton.

Frankel, F. H. (1976). *Hypnosis: Trance as a coping mechanism.* New York: Plenum.

Gardner, G., & Olness, K. (1981). *Hypnosis and hypnotherapy with children.* New York: Grune & Stratton.

Hilgard, E. R. (1977). *Divided consciousness: Multiple controls in human thought and action.* New York: Harcourt, Brace & World.

Lynn, S. J., & Rhue, J. W. (1991). *Theories of hypnosis.* New York: Guilford.

Sheehan, P. W., & Perry, C. W. (1976). *Methodologies of hypnosis.* Hillsdale, NJ: Erlbaum.

Weitzenhoffer, A. M. (1953). *Hypnotism.* New York: Wiley.

F. J. Evans
Reading Hospital

HYPNOSIS AS A THERAPEUTIC TECHNIQUE
MEMORY
PAIN
PLACEBO
SLEEP

HYPNOSIS AS A THERAPEUTIC TECHNIQUE

Hypnosis is a procedure in which the use of suggestions presented by the therapist or researcher (or self, in the case of self-hypnosis) allows the hypnotized individual to experience changes in sensations, perceptions, thoughts, or behaviors. Hypnosis capitalizes upon an innate cognitive capacity that probably involves imaginative ability, the capacity to concentrate, and an effortless receptivity. Typically, an induction procedure is used to establish the context in which hypnotic suggestions are presented. Although hypnotic inductions vary, most involve suggestions for relaxation, calmness, and a sense of well-being. On the other hand, active-alert inductions that involve physical activity have also been shown to be effective in establishing responsiveness to suggestion.

The ability to respond to hypnotic suggestions is a stable personality trait that varies little over time or situations. This trait of hypnotic responsiveness is roughly normally distributed, with the largest number of individuals able to experience some but not all types of hypnotic suggestions. Hypnotic responsiveness peaks at about 9 to 11 years of age with a slight decrement in later years. A highly responsive subject will become hypnotized under a host of experimental conditions and therapeutic settings. A low hypnotizable person will not, despite his or her sincere efforts. This trait of

hypnotic responsiveness appears to be unrelated to other traits such as trust, interrogative suggestibility, and gullibility. Evidence exists that some highly dissociative individuals are also highly responsive to hypnosis, but for the general population, dissociativity and hypnotic responsiveness are minimally related, if at all.

Even highly hypnotizable subjects remain in control of their behavior when hypnotized, and typically continue to be aware of self and surroundings. On the other hand, a major component of the experience of hypnosis is a sense of involuntariness. Kenneth Bowers best described this paradox when he stated that "hypnotic responses can be purposeful without being enacted on purpose." Hypnosis can be thought of as an invitation to experience suggested alterations that the subject can then either accept or reject. While amnesia can occur during hypnosis, for the most part this occurs only when explicit suggestions for amnesia are given, and the amnesia is reversible.

Contrary to some popular depictions, hypnosis is not a panacea for recovering forgotten memories. Research indicates that memories recalled under hypnosis may or may not be accurate. Further, difficulty distinguishing true memory from suggested memory arises as a result of increased confidence in memories that can occur under hypnosis. Hypnosis appears to diminish ability to discriminate between fantasy and reality, and of course involves enhanced responsiveness to suggestions. Similarly, hypnotic age regression does not enable subjects to return to an earlier point in their life. Alterations in behaviors or speech following hypnotic age regression are no more childlike than those observed among adults role-playing as children.

Hypnosis is not a form of therapy per se but rather a technique that can be used within the context of therapy or as an adjunct to medical treatment. Hypnosis is effective for some individuals and for some problems. Thus hypnosis should be used only by a clinician or researcher who is familiar with the applications and limitations of hypnosis as well as being trained in the area for which hypnosis is being used.

It is well established that hypnosis can be a very effective tool for minimizing both acute and chronic pain for some individuals, and that this effect exceeds that of placebo. In 1996 a National Institute of Health Technology Assessment Panel Report found hypnosis to be a viable and effective intervention for alleviating pain with cancer and other chronic pain conditions. Hypnosis can also be effective for minimizing pain associated with burn treatment, surgical procedures, childbirth, and invasive medical diagnostic procedures. The use of hypnosis can allow the patient to respond in an active manner when faced with pain, can reduce the use of medication, and may facilitate medical compliance. Hypnotic suggestion can be used directly to alleviate the experience of pain, to alter the pain sensation, or to provide distraction from pain. Typically the client will eventually be taught to use self-hypnosis once the effective use of suggestion has been demonstrated.

There is evidence that the addition of hypnotic suggestion to behavioral treatment plans provides some advantage in treating habit disorders. Hypnotic suggestions that alter perceptions can be especially useful in these treatments. For individuals trying to quit smoking, hypnotic suggestions to increase the adversiveness of smoking and minimize withdrawal symptoms can be incorporated into a standard smoking cessation protocol. Similarly, treatment for obesity can incorporate suggestions for adverse reactions to unhealthy foods and an enhanced sense of self-control over eating behaviors. Augmenting treatment with hypnotic suggestions can also increase confidence in the ability to achieve one's goals and can lead to greater compliance with the selected treatment program. Meta-analytic studies suggest that the effects of treatments for obesity and pain (among others) may be enhanced by the inclusion of hypnosis.

One way in which hypnosis can be used in expressive psychotherapies is to help the patient modulate and work through particularly painful emotional experiences. Suggestions can help to productively direct emotional expression and thereby facilitate affect regulations in the service of cognitive mastery. Further, the use of hypnosis may increase access to painful primary process and symbolic material, as logical, critical thinking tends to be suspended. This allows the therapist and patient to develop creative approaches to solving problems in living, with an emphasis on self-efficacy. Again, because of enhanced receptivity to suggestion, it is important that the therapist be knowledgeable in working with the presenting issues, has a clear clinical formulation, and has the wherewithal to treat the patient with or without hypnosis.

It appears that for some patients, hypnosis can increase receptivity, enhance relatedness, and facilitate symptom resolution. This makes hypnosis a useful tool to be integrated into many forms of treatment for medical and psychological problems.

B. J. KING
M. R. NASH
University of Tennessee

HYPNOSIS
PSYCHOTHERAPY
PSYCHOTHERAPY TECHNICHES

HYPOTHALAMUS

The hypothalamus is a cluster of nuclei (or centers) in the brain which participates in the initiation and/or control of autonomic responses such as temperature regulation, increased blood pressure, sweating, and dilation of the pupils of the eyes.

The hypothalamus exerts this control by two separate mechanisms: (a) It influences the activity of other groups of cells, both autonomic and somatic, which lie in the brain stem and other positions of the central nervous system; and (b) it acts as the major nervous control center for the endocrine glands. There is, for instance, a "drinking center" in the hypothalamus which stimulates drinking behavior and releases an antidiuretic hormone that works toward preventing the body from excreting water. Thus the hypothalamus acts in two ways: neurally through other portions of the nervous system and directly in stimulating glandular activity.

Bard (1928) showed that, even with all brain tissue above the hypothalamus removed, cats could manifest full-fledged rage. These animals would spit, snarl, bite, claw, lash their tails, and manifest hair erection, blood pressure elevation, increased heart rate, sweating, and other autonomic effects. But if the hypothalamus, along with the brain tissue above it were removed, only incomplete components of rage could be evoked.

The hypothalamus takes part in controlling sexual behavior—a participation both neural and endocrine. Fisher, Magoun, and Ranson (1938) found that female cats with lesions in supraoptic nuclei of the anterior hypothalamus did not mate. The same thing was demonstrated in the female guinea pig (Brookhart, Dey, & Ranson, 1940).

The hypothalamus plays a crucial role in the body's temperature regulation and in the activity of the pituitary gland, sometimes called the master gland, since it plays a role in controlling other glands.

REFERENCES

Bard, P. A. (1928). A diencephalic mechanism for the expression of rage with special reference to the sympathetic nervous system. *American Journal of Physiology, 84,* 490–515.

Brookhart, J. M., Dey, F. L., & Ranson, S. W. (1940). Failure of ovarian hormones to cause mating reactions in spayed guinea pigs with hypothalamic lesions. *Proceedings of the Society of Experimental Biologists, 44,* 61–64.

Fisher, C., Magoun, H. W., & Ranson, S. W. (1938). Dystocia in diabetes insipidus. *American Journal of Obstetrics and Gynecology, 36,* 1–9.

S. H. BARTLEY
Memphis State University

LIMBIC SYSTEM

HYPOTHESIS TESTING, POWER

Hypothesis testing involves contrasting two rival hypotheses. The null hypothesis specifies that nothing unusual is happening. The alternative hypothesis specifies that something unusual is happening. For example, the null hypothesis might state that two groups have the same mean or that the correlation between two variables is zero. The alternative hypothesis can be directional or nondirectional. A directional hypothesis states the direction of the phenomenon; for example, group 1 has a larger mean than group 2 or the correlation is larger than zero. A nondirectional hypothesis does not specify the direction of the effect, but states that the effect does exist; for example, the two groups have different means or the correlation is not zero.

Statisticians begin by assuming that the null hypothesis is true and reject the null hypothesis only if the observed results are quite unlikely under this assumption. Based on some assumptions concerning the study, for example, a random sample and a normally distributed dependent variable, the researcher can calculate the probability of rejecting the null hypothesis when it is true (α) and the probability of rejecting the null hypothesis when the alternative hypothesis is true (the power of the test). Because the researcher wants to reach the correct conclusion, good studies are designed to have low α and high power. A correct null hypothesis is unlikely to be rejected if α is low, and a correct alternative hypothesis is likely to be concluded if power is high.

Researchers generally set the α level at .05. They reject the null hypothesis only if the sample results are in the extreme 5% of the range of possible outcomes if the null hypothesis were true. When the null hypothesis is rejected, the researcher concludes that the results are significant and specifies the significance probability—that is, the α associated with the outcome. For example, the researcher may conclude that the correlation is significant at $p < .05$, meaning that the null hypothesis of a zero correlation could be rejected with an α less than .05. A more extreme result has a smaller significance probability, such as $p < .001$.

Because the traditional approach is designed to keep α low, researchers must be careful to ensure that the power of their tests is reasonably high. Power estimations can be made before data are collected, and research studies with insufficient power can be redesigned to improve power. There are four principal strategies to increase power: increase α, specify directional hypotheses, increase the sample size, and increase the effect size.

Increasing α increases power. Researchers are more likely to reject the null hypothesis when α is higher, so they are more likely to conclude that a correct alternative hypothesis is true. However, increasing α increases the risk of rejecting a true null hypothesis, an error that should be avoided. Levels of α above .05 traditionally are considered unacceptable, but higher levels can be used when power is extremely important and the ramifications of falsely rejecting the null hypothesis are not too costly.

A second way to increase power is to specify directional hypotheses. This allows the researcher to concentrate the α risk at only those outcomes that are consistent with the directional hypothesis. For example, a test on a correlation coefficient using a nondirectional hypothesis and an α of .05 might reject the null hypothesis for observed correlations below $-.60$ or above $+.60$. Outcomes between $-.60$ and $+.60$ are expected to occur 95% of the time for that study, whereas outcomes outside of this range are expected only 5% of the time when the null hypothesis is true. If the researcher could specify a directional hypothesis, such as a positive correlation, the decision might be to reject the null hypothesis for all correlations above $+.55$, because 5% of the expected correlations under the null hypothesis exceed this value. If the observed correlation were .58, the researcher could not reject the null hypothesis in favor of the nondirectional hypothesis, but could reject the null hypothesis in favor of the directional hypothesis. By concentrating the α risk at one end of the possible set of outcomes, the researcher has a more powerful test. Unfortunately, if the directional hypothesis postulates the wrong direction, the researcher will not find significant results and will be in error. In the above example, if the observed correlations were $-.63$, the researcher could reject the null hypothesis in the nondirectional test, but could not do so for the directional test that has been tailored for positive relationships. Researchers specify directional hypotheses only when the opposite result is inconceivable based on previous research, theory, or logic. For example, if all previous research has demon-

strated a positive relationship between the two variables, the researcher would feel secure conducting a directional test.

A third way to increase power is to increase sample size. Statistics based on larger samples are more stable, allowing more precise estimation of population characteristics. This increased precision makes it more likely that correct alternative hypotheses are confirmed. In fact, research based on huge samples may have too much power because such studies may reject null hypotheses for trivial, although statistically significant, results. For example, a correlation of .02 may be significantly different from zero in a huge sample, but the relationship probably is too weak to be useful.

The effect size is the strength of the relationship being studied. Research on variables with large effect sizes has more power. For example, to demonstrate that different types of birds have different size eggs, one should compare ostriches and hummingbirds, with an enormous effect size, rather than compare chickens and ducks, with a smaller effect size. Studies investigating variables with a large effect size are more likely to reject the null hypothesis than studies designed to uncover small, more subtle effects. Researchers can select variables with strong relationships and choose ways to measure or control variables to maximize the effect size to have more powerful studies.

Researchers want studies with low α and high power so they are likely to reach accurate conclusions. They generally control α by not allowing it to exceed .05, and they have strategies to increase power. A well-designed study may have a larger α, a directional hypothesis, a large sample size, or a large effect size. The researcher considers all these options in designing a study that is likely to contribute meaningful information to the knowledge of psychology.

M. J. ALLEN
California State University, Bakersfield

RESEARCH METHODOLOGY
STATISTICS IN PSYCHOLOGY
STATISTICAL SIGNIFICANCE

HYSTERIA

The term "hysteria" has been used to describe a variety of maladaptive behavior patterns that have ranged in severity from a type of personality disorder (hysterical personality) to a form of psychosis (hysterical or factitious psychosis). However, hysteria has most frequently referred to a neurotic form of psychopathology subdivided into either the *conversion type* or the *dissociative type*. A third subtype known as *Briquet's disorder* was also occasionally included. Unfortunately, as noted by McDaniel in her chapter "Hysterical neurosis" (1978, p. 220), these various subtypes "share no common etiology, pathogenesis, epidemiology, clinical picture, or prognosis." Thus while it can be said that hysterical symptoms allow individuals to avoid unpleasant situations without assuming responsibility for their behavior, this hardly distinguishes them from other neurotic behavior patterns that serve the same purpose. Because the term "hysteria" refers to a heterogeneous group of symptom patterns and adds little discriminatory power to the diagnostic process, it has been essentially eliminated from the current classification system of psychiatric disorders presented in the American Psychiatric Association's *Diagnostic and Statistical Manual of Mental Disorders (Third Edition)*.

CURRENT NOSOLOGY OF HYSTERICAL-TYPE DISORDERS

The major types of hysteria have been broken down into more discrete and homogeneous groupings, each constituting an individual disorder and classified under two main *DSM-III* diagnostic categories: somatoform disorders and dissociative disorders. The term "somatoform" refers to those disorders in which physical symptoms are the chief complaint, yet no demonstrable physiological or disease mechanisms account for the symptoms. Three discrete disorders that had previously been labeled hysterical in nature have been identified: somatization disorder (previously Briquet's syndrome), conversion disorder (hysteria of the conversion type), and psychogenic pain disorder (previously considered a conversion symptom).

According to *DSM-III*, the essential features of a *somatization disorder* are "recurrent and multiple somatic complaints of several years' duration for which medical attention has been sought but which are apparently not due to any physical disorder. The disorder begins before the age of 30 and has a chronic but fluctuating course" (1980, p. 241). The early age of onset (typically in the teen years) and the multiple symptom picture without demonstrable organic pathology distinguish somatization disorders from other somatoform disorders.

In *conversion disorders* the symptom picture is much less varied and usually involves a single, predominant loss or alteration of physical functioning (paralysis, blindness, seizures, etc.) that is not under the person's voluntary control but also cannot be explained by pathophysiological processes. *DSM-III* views conversion disorders as somewhat unique among the somatoform disorders in that specific psychological mechanisms have been delineated to account for the symptoms. Typically, there is a temporal relationship between some environmental event and the abrupt appearance of the conversion symptom, which allows the individual to achieve both primary and secondary gain from the symptom. Primary gain is achieved when the symptom allows the person to temporarily avoid an unpleasant emotional conflict, while secondary gain is achieved through the symptom by gaining others' attention and support for being incapacitated and/or by allowing the person to avoid an aversive activity. While conversion disorders were fairly common around the turn of the century and provided the cornerstone for Freud's theory of psychopathology, they are now relatively uncommon and occur primarily among medically unsophisticated populations.

Psychogenic pain disorder was originally considered a form of hysterical neurosis of the conversion type, but is now a separate category in the current *DSM-III* nomenclature. *DSM-III* (1980, p. 247) describes the clinical picture of this disorder as consisting of "the complaint of pain, in the absence of adequate physical findings and in association with evidence of the etiological role of psychological factors." The psychological factors in psychogenic pain

are similar to those found in conversion disorders, but psychogenic pain is treated separately because it usually runs a much longer course than conversion symptoms and has different treatment implications. Behavioral approaches such as those described by Fordyce in *Behavioral Methods for Chronic Pain and Illness* have proven quite effective in dealing with psychogenic pain disorders.

Classification of hysteria of the dissociative type has been refined to include separate categories for psychogenic amnesia, psychogenic fugue, multiple personality, and sleepwalking, which are collectively grouped under dissociative disorders in *DSM-III*. *Dissociative disorders* are characterized by "a sudden, temporary alteration in the normally integrative functions of consciousness, identity, or motor behavior" (1980, p. 253), resulting in disturbances of memory, personal identity, and sense of reality. Although sleepwalking is formally listed under disorders of infancy, childhood, or adolescence in *DSM-III* because of its early age of onset, it shares the essential features of a dissociative disorder and is therefore considered here.

The *DSM-III* diagnostic criteria for *psychogenic amnesia* is a "sudden inability to recall important personal information that is too extensive to be explained by ordinary forgetfulness" and cannot be accounted for by an "Organic Mental Disorder" (1980, p. 255). The disturbance in recall is usually for a circumscribed period of time in which there is either a total or selective failure of recall for events that occurred during that period (typically, several hours following an emotionally traumatic experience). In rare cases an individual may develop a generalized amnesia that encompasses his or her entire life or a continuous amnesia in which the person cannot recall events after a specific point in time. It is believed that these forms of amnesia allow the person to avoid consciously acknowledging highly charged, emotionally painful events.

According to *DSM-III* (1980, p. 255), the essential feature of *psychogenic fugue* is "sudden, unexpected travel away from home or customary work locale with assumption of a new identity and an inability to recall one's previous identity." In fugue states there is an alteration of both motor behavior and identity. Such instances are quite rare except in times of war or natural disaster, and heavy alcohol use may be a predisposing factor. Usually the symptoms are of brief duration and recovery is rapid.

Although rare, *multiple personality* is perhaps the best known of the dissociative disorders, entailing the existence of two or more distinct personalities, each having its own complex make-up and social relationships. The individual's behavior is determined by the personality that is dominant at that particular moment. *DSM-III* notes that the various personalities are frequently quite discrepant, often represent opposites (e.g., one male and one female), and often go by different names. The clinical course of multiple personality tends to be more chronic than other dissociative disorders; childhood trauma and abuse appear to be the main predisposing factors. Classic examples of multiple personality in literature include *The Strange Case of Dr. Jekyll and Mr. Hyde; Three Faces of Eve;* and *Sybil*.

The last form of dissociative disorder to be considered here is sleepwalking. *Sleepwalking disorder* is typically a disturbance of childhood that involves repeated episodes of getting out of bed and walking about without full awareness or later recall. The episodes are usually brief, lasting a few minutes to a half hour, and seem to occur during periods of nondream sleep. According to *DSM-III,* the child has a blank facial expression; is able to see and walk around objects, but is fairly unresponsive to others' attempts to communicate or influence his or her behavior; and shows no residual mental impairment after the episode. It is estimated by the authors of *DSM-III* that 1 to 6% of children have episodes of sleepwalking at one time or another, but generally outgrow it by their 20s. The major differential diagnosis is complex-partial seizures (psychomotor epilepsy), which can also occur during sleep but which have evidence of abnormal brain-wave (EEG) activity.

REFERENCES

Fordyce, W. E. (1976). *Behavioral methods for chronic pain and illness.* St. Louis, MO: Mosby.

McDaniel, E. (1978). Hysterical neurosis. In G. Ballis, L. Wurmser, E. McDaniel, & R. Grenell (Eds.), *Clinical psychopathology.* Boston: Butterworth.

SUGGESTED READING

Coleman, J. C., Butcher, J. N., & Carson, R. C. (1980). *Abnormal psychology and modern life.* Oakland, NJ: Scott, Foresman.

Johnson, C. W., Snibbe, J. R., & Evans, L. A. (1975). *Basic psychopathology: A programmed text.* New York: Spectrum.

G. J. CHELUNE
The Cleveland Clinic Foundation

CONVERSION DISORDER

ICELAND, PSYCHOLOGY IN

Psychologists in Iceland have been trained in various countries. An undergraduate course in psychology was started at the University of Iceland in 1971, but post-graduate training in psychology had to take place abroad until 1999, when a post-graduate MA course in psychology began at the University of Iceland. Initially most Icelandic psychologists completed their training in Denmark, but later they sought their training in other countries (e.g., Norway, Sweden, Germany, France, England, Scotland, United States, Canada, Australia).

The Icelandic Psychological Association was established in 1954, and the current membership is 149. Within the association there are three divisions: clinical, educational, and rehabilitation psychology. The office of the IPA is housed at the Academics Union Bandalag Hàskòlamanna (BHM).

The profession of psychology in Iceland is regulated by law #40/1976, which protects the title and to some extent the function of psychologists. The accrediting committee of the Icelandic Psychological Society is consulted by the Ministry of Health, which is the awarding authority of accreditation for psychologists in Iceland. Only those who have the right to call themselves psychologists can apply for positions advertised for psychologists. Psychologists are permitted to practice psychotherapy.

Four specialties are recognized within psychology in Iceland and regulated by bylaw #158/1990: clinical psychology, rehabilitation psychology, educational psychology, and organizational/occupational psychology. Only those who have been accredited by the Ministry of Health to practice as psychologists can embark upon postgraduate training in one of these specialties; this training lasts four and a half years. During this time the trainee has to work under the supervision of a specialist within specified areas for a stipulated number of months. The trainee receives 120 hours of personal supervision from at least two specialists and 40 hours of group supervision (1 hour per week/40 hours per year). The trainee has to complete 300 hours of didactic training. Finally, the trainee has to conduct a research project and publish in a refereed journal before becoming recognized as a specialist in one of the areas above.

Most of the psychologists in Iceland are employed by the health, social, and school services. There are about ten psychologists working full time and about thirty part-time in private practice. The services rendered by psychologists and specialists in psychology in private practice are not reimbursed by the national health services, private insurance, or the social services. Patients are either self-referred or referred by a physician or the social services. Many practicing psychologists consult with corporations and industry.

E. Ö. Arnarson
University of Iceland, Reykjavik

IDENTITY FORMATION

There are numerous theoretical approaches that illuminate certain areas of identity development (i.e., Kagan's constructive-developmental approach or Blos's object relations approach), but Erikson's (1963, 1968) psychosocial approach to human development appeals to many professionals because of its utility in many professional arenas: clinical, theoretical, and empirical. Erikson's seminal work stressed the importance of history (personal and societal) and social contexts as influencing individuals' lives; consequently, he incorporated these ideas into his concept of identity formation in adolescence.

Erikson developed the construct of ego identity as an adaptive response to Freud's focus on neurotic personalities. He was interested in the development of healthy personalities and created a lifespan stage theory that addressed the development of the healthy ego. A healthy ego identity evolves through unconscious and conscious mechanisms interacting dynamically in a process of discovering the self. According to Erikson, there are certain key crises inherent in different periods of a person's life which are a direct reflection of the person's social maturity and societal expectations. The crises are then categorized into distinct psychosocial stages of development, at which times certain ego strengths emerge as resolutions of these crises.

A person integrates into his or her ego identity the resolution of the crises for each stage of development. Each stage of psychosocial development culminates in a balance of both syntonic and dystonic outcomes. A syntonic outcome is a positive experience through which the individual strives to attain and consequently maintain the experience in the overall ego structure. Receiving accolades for achievement in school from a significant teacher is an example of a syntonic experience. Conversely, a dystonic outcome is a negative experience whereby the individual strives to avoid and consequently rectify the experience in the overall ego structure. Being the recipient of a disparaging remark from a significant teacher is an example of a dystonic experience. Healthy psychological development occurs when the number of syntonic experiences outweighs dystonic experiences (Waterman, 1993).

Adolescence, the fifth stage of psychosocial development, is the crucial period during which identity formation occurs. It reflects the accumulative syntonic and dystonic outcomes of the prior four stages of development. Identity formation is an integration in the self of the prior outcomes of earlier stages of development. However, as Erikson noted, the formation of identity does not occur in a vacuum. The culture of society is crucial in how the adolescent integrates the prior stages of development. One's culture is shaped by the contexts in adolescents' lives. Hamachek (1985) uses a metaphor of ego growth rings, much like the growth rings of a tree, to facilitate an understanding of how an adolescent integrates the self in relation to contextual conditions when constructing an identity. Erikson's psychosocial stages of development are imbedded in a series of concentric circles such that the width between each ring of development identifies the context, both positive and negative, of growth. Development that is constricted by the environment and made up of mostly dystonic outcomes would show a shorter width in growth for a particular stage, while development that is enriched or expanded by the environment and made up of mostly syntonic outcomes would show a longer width in growth for a particular stage.

Identity development mirrors the outcomes achieved in various domains in a person's life. Erikson delineated the following identity domains where this mirroring or self-reflection occurs. These are: (a) vocation; (b) ideologies (religious, political and economic); (c) philosophy in life; (d) ethical capacity; (e) sexuality; (f) gender, ethnicity, culture, and nationality; and (g) "an all-inclusive human identity" (Erikson, 1968, p. 42). Through growth and integration in these domains, the adolescent's identity becomes integrated ideally forming a healthy and stable self.

Marcia (1980) applied Erikson's concepts of ego identity into two operational dimensions of *exploration* and *commitment*.

Exploration refers to a period of struggle or active questioning in arriving at various aspects of personal identity, such as vocational choice, religious beliefs, or attitudes about the role of a spouse or parenting in one's life. *Commitment* involves making a firm, unwavering decision in such areas and engaging in appropriate implementing activities (Waterman, 1993, p. 56).

Relative to these two dimensions of exploration and commitment, Marcia delineated four identity statuses that exist for an individual in later adolescence. These four statuses are as follows: (a) identity diffusion; (b) identity foreclosure; (c) moratorium; and (d) identity achievement. Identity Diffused adolescents have not committed to an internally consistent set of values and goals and exploration is superficial or absent. Identity Foreclosed adolescents have committed to a set of values and goals with little or no exploration present. Moratorium adolescents are in the process of committing to a set of values and goals as they are intensely exploring alternatives to their decisions. Identity Achieved adolescents have experienced a period of exploration (as in moratorium) and have come to an autonomous resolution of identity by committing to a set of values and goals (Patterson, Sochting, & Marcia, 1993; Marcia, 1993). Through the theoretical underpinnings of Erikson and the empirical applications of Marcia, it is readily apparent that the earlier stages of psychosocial growth profoundly affect early adolescents' potential to explore and commit to a set of values and goals consistent with their identity.

For even within a wider identity man meets man always in categories (be they adult and child, man and woman, employer and employee, leader and follower, majority and minority) and "human" interrelations can truly be only the expression of divided function and the concrete overcoming of the specific ambivalence inherent in them: that is why I came to reformulate the Golden Rule as one that commands us to always act in such a way that the identities of both the actor and the one acted upon are enhanced (Erikson, 1968, p. 316).

REFERENCES

Erikson, E. H. (1963). *Childhood and society* (2nd ed.). New York: Norton.

Erikson, E. H. (1968). *Identity: Youth and crisis.* New York: Norton.

Hamachek, D. E. (1985). The self's development and ego growth: Conceptual analysis and implications for counselors. *Journal of Counseling and Development, 64,* 136–142.

Marcia, J. E. (1980). Identity in adolescence. In J. Adelson (Ed.), *Handbook of adolescent psychology* (pp. 149–173). New York: Wiley.

Marcia, J. E. (1993). The ego identity status approach to ego identity. In J. E. Marcia, A. S. Waterman, D. R. Matteson, S. L. Archer, & J. L. Orlofsky (Eds.), *Ego identity: A handbook for psychosocial research* (pp. 3–21). New York: Springer-Verlag.

Patterson, S. J., Sochting, I., & Marcia, J. E. (1993). The inner space and beyond: Women and identity. In G. R. Adams, T. P. Gullotta, & R. Montemayor (Eds.), *Adolescent identity formation: Vol. 4. Advances in adolescent development* (pp. 9–24). Newbury Park, CA: Sage.

Waterman, A. S. (1993). Identity as an aspect of optimal psychological functioning. In G. R. Adams, T. P. Gullotta, & R. Montemayor (Eds.), *Adolescent identity formation: Vol. 4. Advances in adolescent development* (pp. 50–72). Newbury Park, CA: Sage.

K. McKinney
University of Wisconsin, Stevens Point

ERIKSONIAN DEVELOPMENTAL STAGES

IDIODYNAMICS SUPERSEDING PERSONALITY THEORY

There are three universes in the known cosmos: a universe of stellar bodies that, at one extreme, requires telescopic observation (astronomic), while, at the other extreme, there is the atomic universe of molecules and other particles (microscopic). Between these two realms exist the human idioverses of coherent events.

Concepts. Idiodynamics is the science of the Idioverse: the science of behavior from the standpoint of human individuals with a shared language (Rosenzweig, 1951, 1958b, 1986a, 1986b). The individual is conceived to be a population of experiential events, an idioverse. Events are the basic units of idiodynamics and are defined and observed phenomenologically. Though every idioverse is, in its entirety, unique, certain events form patterns that repeat at intervals, and these are known as "markers." Markers can be discovered through study of the data by a practiced observer. The events of any idioverse also have parameters that are shared with all other individuals universally (nomothetic) and, again, some events that may be shared by certain groups of individuals (demographic). The nomothetic and demographic parameters can usually be measured quantitatively and serve to distinguish individuals in essential, general respects. But the particular idioverse as a whole is unique. This uniqueness critically supplements the universal and group characteristics idiodynamically. While nomothetic and demographic

Table 1: Three Types of Explanatory and Predictive Norms

NOMOTHETIC (Universal)	FUNCTIONAL PRINCIPLES OF GENERAL PSYCHOLOGY CONSIDERED VALID BY AND LARGE.
DEMOGRAPHIC (Group)	STATISTICAL GENERALIZATIONS DERIVED FROM PARTICULAR CULTURES OR CLASSES OF INDIVIDUALS.
IDIODYNAMIC (Individual)	DISTINCTIVE MARKERS RECURRING IN A GIVEN, SINGLE POPULATION OF EVENTS (IDIOVERSE).

Note. Each type of norm not only involves a different mode of understanding but implies a cognate basis for predicting and/or controlling behavior.

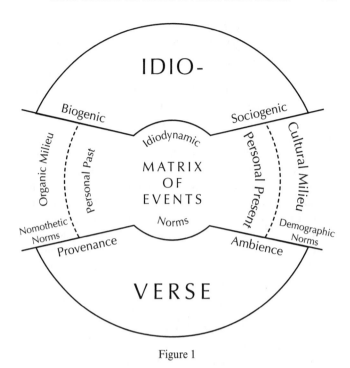

Figure 1

characteristics can be observed and measured in cross-section, the uniqueness of the idioverse ultimately depends upon longitudinal observation, over time. (See Rosenzweig, 1987, Hormuth, 1986 for general reviews of such methods, and see also the formulation of Larsen, 1989.) Fully to understand the idioverse requires that nomothetic, demographic, and idiodynamic characteristics be considered in their interrelationships (See Table 1).

In addition to these types of norms, there are three other conceptual triads in idiodynamics: three mandated postulates, three constitutive media of the idioverse, and three levels of communication (or creativity) which, taken together, reveal the message or messages of the idioverse (see Rosenzweig, 1986b).

Idiodynamics takes the events of individual experience at the very outset as the basic units of observation. In obtaining such data, three guiding principles or postulates prevail. (1) Response dominance: Unlike both general psychology and most clinical psychology, which adopt stimulus-response relationships as the empirical starting point, idiodynamics basically observes response-response relationships. The stimuli and responses are mutually definitive, i.e., the response often defines or helps to define the stimulus in the reaction. (2) Configuration dominance: This postulate complements the subordination of the stimulus to the response by subordinating the part to the whole. (3) Idioverse dominance: The universe of events (idioverse) replaces the person or subject as fundamental (i.e., the idioverse is postulated to be predominant in the conceptualization of behavior; Rosenzweig, 1951).

The idioverse has a core matrix; a biogenic medium on one side, and a sociogenic medium on the other contribute to the core matrix. These media overlap and converge at the matrix idiodynamically (see Figure 1).

There are also three levels of communication by which the idioverse can be meaningfully understood: the immediate or literal level, the intermediate or allusive, and the inframediate or intimate (Rosenzweig, 1986b). They correspond roughly to the three layers of meaning depicted in the fourteenth century by Dante Alighieri who delineated them to his friend con Grande, to whom he was dedicating the *Paradiso,* the third part of his *Divine Comedy.* Dante called these levels the literal, the allegoric, and the mystical (Haller, 1973). In the present formulation the first level is similar to Dante's; the second involves not only possible allegory but other modes of allusion; and the third, instead of being mystical, is disguised autobiography or otherwise intimate details. These levels are intuitively, if not deliberately, employed by creative writers like Melville and Hawthorne, but they should be recognized explicitly.

Origin and Development. Idiodynamics had its origin in three areas of empirical investigation: (1) the experimental redefinition of clinically derived psychoanalytic concepts; (2) the intensive study of individual mental patients by supplementing anamnesis with interviews and projective and psychometric methods of assessment; (3) the reconstruction of the life and work of creative writers and selected patients by an approach designated as "psychoarchaeology."

One early contribution of this program was a formulation by Rosenzweig, "The Experimental Situation as a Psychological Problem" (1933). It exhaustively examined the earlier methodological literature of experimental psychology vis-à-vis the evidence of the writer's current experimental research from the standpoint of the reciprocal interactions of the observer and the subject. These interactions were schematically classified. In accordance with this reciprocity, the terms "observer" and "subject" were replaced by "experimenter" and "experimentee." It was shown that in the early German literature just such a reciprocal terminology was employed—*Versuchsleiter* and *Versuchsperson.* The chief contribution of Rosenzweig's paper was a classification of the various typical, reciprocal interactions encountered in previous and current investigations. This advance in experimental psychodynamics and social psychology made little impact until about 20 years later when, in the 1950s, Rosenthal and others began to publish their independent findings on "experimental bias" and so on (Rosenthal, 1959, 1966).

The first formulation of the complementarity between experimenter and experimentee (Rosenzweig, 1933) was followed by three other similar formulations: "Some Implicit Common Factors in Psychotherapy" (Rosenzweig, 1936), in which Sherrington's neurological principle of the "final common pathway" was, without deliberate intent, applied to the very different field of psychological therapy; "Schools of Psychology: A Complementary Pattern" (Rosenzweig, 1937), in which the natural division of labor among the five then-current schools was shown to represent a complementary pattern in which a certain type of problem achieved acceptable resolution by methods and concepts appropriate to the problem emphasized; and "Converging Approaches to Personality: Murray, Allport, Lewin" (Rosenzweig, 1944). Each of these contributions stressed a different kind of complementarity though all were guided, implicitly if not explicitly, by an overriding principle.

Later it became evident that the principle of complementarity, which seemed so apt for the solution of the contending purviews in psychology, had somewhat earlier become a key to seemingly irreconcilable theories in the science of physics. In 1927 the principle of complementarity was formulated by Bohr as an alternative to Heisenberg's "indeterminacy" and as a new way of reconciling the conflicting conceptions of light as consisting of waves on one hand or particles on the other (Bohr, 1927). To Bohr, both formulations were justified and were equally correct once it was recognized that each was served by a different observational approach. Not all physicists were ready to embrace this solution of contradictory formulations, but Bohr applied it not only to the theory of light but to other problems in physics. By 1937, when Rosenzweig's paper on schools of psychology appeared, Bohr was simultaneously recommending that complementarity be extended beyond the physical to the natural sciences, including biology and psychology (Bohr, 1937).

Another basis for idiodynamics is the fact that psychology has developed historically and exists today as a coordinate composite of the other major sciences (Rosenzweig, 1958b). These sciences may be arranged not only in the traditional vertical hierarchy, but horizontally and complementarily, with the implication that each discipline is autonomous. It is not necessary, as is conventional, to reduce a discipline to a lower and more fundamental one, for example mental activity to neurology (i.e., neuroscience), which is supposed to have greater dignity or explanatory power. During the past century psychology has marshaled its forces in relation to physics as psychophysics, physiology as psychophysiology, biology as psychobiology, personality as psychodynamics (or psychoanalysis), sociology and anthropology as social psychology. If psychodynamics is now reconsidered, it is submitted that "idiodynamics" should supersede "psychodynamics." There is a unique self-consistency in this substitution because, in view of its position in the scientific gamut, psychodynamics—and, even more reasonably, idiodynamics—insists on remaining in its own (experiential) universe of discourse. Although from an unsympathetic standpoint this insistence might be regarded as problematically subjective, from the present overview subjectivity is both natural and proper. In the broadest sense of the term "behavioral," (for example, in the usage of Woodworth in 1958), idiodynamics would be phenomenologically behavioral. One thus recognizes that psychology is implicitly a composite discipline of coordinate members. In a comprehensive picture of what is *called* psychology, psychology embraces all the above coordinates complementarily. In the limited sense, "idiodynamics" supersedes conventional personality theory.

As discussed above, a critical distinction in idiodynamics is the threefold complementary way in which behavior may be alternatively explained: nomothetic, demographic, and idiodynamic (Table 1). These three modes are known as "norms." They were first designated as universal, group, and individual, and were illustrated by reviewing the role of association in the history of psychology (Rosenzweig, 1950). The principles of association were first described by the early Greek thinkers by reference to the categories of similarity, contiguity, and so on. Even in present-day theories of learning, such principles are used and are treated as universally valid. After Galton (1879–80), these categories became the basis for experimental studies of word-association conducted in Wundt's laboratory of experimental psychology in Leipzig (Trautscholdt, 1883). But even in that setting it was recognized early that certain groups of individuals, including mental patients of a given diagnosis, produced associations peculiar to or characteristic of the group. In these terms certain kinds of associations consistently produced by an individual helped to classify him or her as belonging to a given group (e.g., the clang associations of the manic patient). Finally, in Jung's research on complexes (Jung, 1918), the individual or individualized significance of certain word associations were seen as pointing to unique constellations of thoughts, images, and feelings in a particular person. This insight adumbrated the idiodynamic orientation. The association of ideas could be alternatively accounted for in one or another of these modes according to the objective of the application.

These three explanatory modes are now more appropriately designated as *nomothetic, demographic,* and *idiodynamic,* thus to avoid the quantitative inferences misleadingly emphasized in the earlier terminology. That confusion is evident in the writing of Gordon Allport (1937), who commended a new formulation of personality that implicitly equated each mode with the size of a population. In this way Allport tended to confound the idiodynamic with the idiographic (Rosenzweig & Fisher, 1997).

The idioverse (Figure 1) is conceptualized as a universe of experiential events that represents a given person at a particular time. It includes three milieus, two that persist through time and a third that is fluid and transitory, representing a personality at a given moment. From the one side, an organic (and genetic) milieu affects the idioverse biogenically; from the other, a cultural (or social) milieu contributes sociogenically; and both these relatively permanent transmitters overlap in the transitory matrix of the idioverse. In that matrix, determinants from the two persisting milieus flow through continuously, are generatively transformed, and provide the idiodynamic signals for a complete understanding of a given human event. While it endures, this vehicle—the matrix of the idioverse—is psychologically paramount, and its norms make the person who feels, thinks, and acts become intelligible to the prepared observer.

The three types of norms of Table 1 are to a considerable extent aligned with the three milieus shown in Figure 1, the biogenic tending to be used nomothetically; the sociogenic, demographically; and the matrix of the idioverse is allied with idiodynamic norms.

The temporal aspect of experience is crucial in idiodynamics. While in the matrix of the idioverse everything is of present tense, the biogenic milieu tends to stress derivation from the genetic past. These inputs interact with those from the cultural past, and all these inputs converge in the adaptively creative and future-oriented matrix of events. In that matrix, the personal present and personal past mingle in perception and memory.

Allport's stress on the idiographic (as contrasted with the nomothetic) was intended to underscore personal uniqueness, but his preoccupation with traits rather than events fell short of what is here intended by idiodynamic. It should be evident that the idiodynamic differs from the idiographic by referring not to a statistical N of 1 (with unique traits peculiar to it) but to a universe of numerous events (the idioverse). A unique dynamic organization through time distinguishes one person from another by providing an explanation of behavior in terms of a peculiar endowment and developmental history (Rosenzweig & Fisher, 1997).

There are three empirical ways in which idiodynamics has been and can be further implemented. The one that initiated the approach appeared as a systematic survey of the experimenter-experimentee interaction. It demonstrated that, in contrast to the situation in the impersonal sciences (physics, chemistry, etc.), the human psychological laboratory involves at least two interacting individuals. The particular characteristics and expectations of each individual must be taken into account. This caution applies to both the design of experiments and the interpretation of results. Implicit here is a form of relativity; not of space-time, to be sure, but an interpersonal reciprocity and complementarity that affects the process of observation. From this and subsequent work by other investigators, it is now clear that the interactive reorientation was a first step toward idiodynamics (Adair, 1973). But the possibilities are just beginning to be exploited.

The second way in which idiodynamics expresses itself is in experimental investigation involving quantitative measures to be achieved by self-reference; for example, the use of the experimenter's modal reaction times as a basis for clinically and experimentally evaluating his or her other responses. An early example appeared in Jung's complex indicators of the word-association method. Another example was reported in Rosenzweig's "The Investigation of Repression as an Instance of Experimental Idiodynamics" (1952), which studied memory in relation to affect.

The third empirical methodology is not in the strict sense experimental, but it can be as objectively valid as are field studies in biology. These procedures exploit the linguistic aspects of the idioverse. Such techniques are available in clinical psychology and other applied areas. They reveal the meanings inherent in the idioverse. The three above levels are recognized. The procedures by which these levels of communication are unraveled have been named "psychoarchaeology." The levels are studied concurrently, with the assumption that they will not necessarily be represented with equal strength in every production (see Rosenzweig, 1987, for a detailed example of psychoarchaeology).

Psychoarchaeology can be employed with documents such as psychotherapy transcripts, diaries, letters, and the data yielded by projective psychological techniques. But the most rewarding results are available in the imaginative productions of creative writers, the elite of whom are almost compulsively involved in veiled self-exposure (Rosenzweig, 1943). These authors employ the levels intuitively, endogenously to their artistry. In conducting research with such data, it is crucial to take into account not only the artistic productions themselves but the other available biographical evidence from the entire idioverse. Peculiar sensitivities of the organic or genetic milieu as well as recurrent modes of response to social encounters must be considered, for the levels express not only the coalescence of the three milieus of one particular idioverse but their interpenetration with other idioverses.

In practice this abstract sketch of the process of disclosure is often dramatically particularized. Secrets of the individual that shaped the unique experience—the very private life—may be discovered, including unknown facts of biography or history. The methodology also throws light on the intricate but elusive course of the creative process. Although the best examples of applied psychoanalysis demonstrate the possibilities of idiodynamics, a complete example of psychoarchaeology in its full potentiality has been recently published (Rosenzweig, 1999). But a fair approximation is available in "Sally Beauchamp's Career: A Psychoarchaeological Key to Morton Prince's Classic Case of Multiple Personality" (Rosenzweig, 1987).

REFERENCES

Adair, J. G. (1973). *The human subject: The social psychology of the psychological experiment.* Boston: Little, Brown.

Allport, G. W. (1937). *Personality: A psychological interpretation.* New York: Holt.

Bohr, N. (1927). The quantum postulate and the recent development of atomic theory. International Congress of Physics, Como, Italy. Bologna: Zanicelli, 1928. (An expanded version published in *Nature,* 1928, *121,* 580–590.)

Bohr, N. (1937). Causality and complementarity. *Philosophy of Science, 4,* 289–298.

Galton, F. (1879–80). Psychometric experiments. *Brain, 2,* 149–162.

Haller, R. S. (1973). *Literary criticism of Dante Alighieri.* Lincoln: University of Nebraska Press.

Hormuth, S. E. (1986). The sampling of experience in situ. *Journal of Personality, 54,* 262–293.

Jung, C. G. (1918). *Studies in word association.* London: Heinemann.

Larsen, R. J. (1989). A process approach to personality: Utilizing time as a facet of data. In D. Buss & N. Cantor (Eds.), *Personality psychology: Recent trends and emerging directions* (pp. 177–193). New York: Springer.

Rosenthal, R. (1959). The experimental induction of the defense mechanism of projection. *Journal of Projective Techniques, 23,* 357–364.

Rosenthal, R. (1966). *Experimenter effects in behavioral research.* New York: Appleton-Century-Crofts.

Rosenzweig, S. (1933). The experimental situation as a psychological problem. *Psychological Review, 40,* 337–354.

Rosenzweig, S. (1936). Some implicit common factors in diverse methods of psychotherapy. *The American Journal of Orthopsychiatry, 6*(3), 412–415.

Rosenzweig, S. (1937). Schools of psychology: A complementary pattern. *Philosophy of Science, 4*(1), 96–106.

Rosenzweig, S. (1943). The ghost of Henry James: A study in thematic apperception. *Character & Personality, 12,* 79–100. (Reprinted with a postscript in *Modern Criticism,* edited by W. Sutton & R. Foster, New York: Odyssey Press, 1963, 401–416).

Rosenzweig, S. (1944). Converging approaches to personality: Murray, Allport, Lewin. *Psychological Review, 51*(4), 248–256.

Rosenzweig, S. (1950). Norms and the individual in the psychologist's perspective. In M. L. Reymert (Ed.), *Feelings and emotions: The Mooseheart symposium* (pp. 327–335). New York: McGraw-Hill.

Rosenzweig, S. (1951). Idiodynamics in personality theory with special reference to projective methods. *Psychological Review, 58*(3), 213–223.

Rosenzweig, S. (1952). The investigation of repression as an instance of experimental idiodynamics. *Psychological Review, 59*(4), 339–345.

Rosenzweig, S. (1958b). The place of the individual and of idiodynamics in psychology: A dialogue. *Journal of Individual Psychology, 14,* 3–20.

Rosenzweig, S. (1986a). Background to idiodynamics. *The Clinical Psychologist, 39,* 83–89.

Rosenzweig, S. (1986b). Idiodynamics vis-à-vis psychology. *The American Psychologist, 41,* 241–245.

Rosenzweig, S. (1987). Sally Beauchamp's career: A psychoarchaeological key to Morton Prince's classic case of multiple personality. *Genetic, Social, and General Psychology Monographs, 113*(1), 5–60.

Rosenzweig, S. (2000). The anacalypsis of Melville's *Moby Dick.* In preparation.

Rosenzweig, S. & Fisher, S. (1997). "Idiographic" vis-à-vis "idiodynamic" in the historical perspective of personality theory: Remembering Gordon Allport, 1897–1997. *Journal of the History of the Behavioral Sciences, 33*(4), 405–419.

Trautscholdt, M. (1883). Experimentelle Untersuchungen über die Association der Vorstellungeu. *Philosophische Studien* (Wundt), *1,* 213–250.

Woodworth, R. S. (1958). *Dynamics of behavior.* New York: Holt.

SUGGESTED READING

Allport, G. W. (1961). *Pattern and growth in personality.* New York: Holt, Rinehart, & Winston.

Rosenzweig, S. (1958a). The idiocultural dimension of psychotherapy: Pre- and posthistory of the relations between Sigmund Freud and Josef Popper-Lynkeus. *Psychoanalysis and the Social Sciences, 5,* 9–50.

Silverman, I. (1977). *The human subject in the psychological laboratory.* New York: Pergamon.

S. ROSENZWEIG
Washington University, St. Louis

HERITABILITY OF PERSONALITY

IGF-I, INSULIN, BRAIN GLUCOSE, AND COGNITION

Activity of insulin-like proteins was discovered in 1957. The precise action of insulin-like growth factor I (IGF-I) remained poorly understood until the production in the 1980s of recombinant human IGF-I. This trophic factor has been well characterized, first as a factor mediating growth hormone action (Jones & Clemmons, 1995; Isaksson, Ohlsson, Nilsson, Isgaard, & Lindahl, 1991). IGF-I is found in high levels in the blood and is believed to originate mainly from the liver (Pankov, 1999). The detection of the IGF-I gene using molecular techniques showed its presence in several organs, including the brain (Rotwein, Burgess, Milbrandt, & Krause, 1988). Substantial evidence supports the importance of IGF-I and insulin in normal development and maintenance of adequate neuronal functions throughout the entire lifespan. The structure of IGF-I is quite similar to that of insulin (Isaksson et al., 1991). Interestingly, researchers have suggested that the level of insulin in the brain is quite low and that, in fact, IGF-I could act as insulin in the central nervous system. IGF-I has the capacity to bind to the entire IGF receptor family including the insulin receptor. High densities of binding sites for IGF-I and insulin are discretely and differentially distributed throughout the brain, with prominent levels localized to the hippocampus. IGF receptors are produced by numerous neuronal and non-neuronal cell types. IGF-I is a well established stimulant of cell growth, proliferation, and differentiation, and can stimulate glucose transport and prevent cell death (Doré, Kar, & Quirion, 1997a). These later effects are crucial for survival of post-mitotic neurons.

The authors have previously demonstrated that IGF and insulin receptors are tightly regulated and subject to rapid and chronic changes after a multitude of surgical and pharmacological lesions (Doré, Kar, Rowe, & Quirion, 1997; Doré, Krieger, Kar, & Quirion, 1996; Kar, Seto, Doré, Chabot, & Quirion, 1997). Both the IGF-I and insulin receptors possess similar tyrosine kinase activities, and binding of the ligand to the α-subunit of the receptor induces the autophosphorylation of the β-subunits. One of the key phosphoproteins is the insulin receptor substrate (IRS), which interacts directly with other intracellular signalling substrates.

IGF-I AND INSULIN RECEPTOR LEVELS IN COGNITION

No significant differences are found in IGF-I or insulin receptor levels in any sub-fields of the hippocampus of young versus aged rats (Doré, Kar, Rowe, et al., 1997). Furthermore, deficits in cognitive performance do not relate to alterations in the levels of these receptors in aged impaired (AI) compared to aged unimpaired (AU) rats. It thus appears that IGF-I and insulin receptor binding sites are not markedly altered during the normal aging process in rats, and cognitive deficits observed in the Morris water maze are not mirrored by changes in these markers. Accordingly, spatial learning deficits observed in the AI group are not due to alteration in IGFs and/or insulin receptor sites. However, these data do not rule out the potential of altered IGFs or insulin post-receptor signaling efficacy between AU and AI groups (discussed later). These results can also be related to those obtained in the human brain. No significant differences in the levels of IGF-I binding sites were reported in the human cerebral cortex with respect to age, postmortem delays, or medications (Crews, McElhaney, Freund, Ballinger, & Raizada, 1992). In contrast, specific IGF-I binding was increased in the cerebral cortex of Alzheimer's disease (AD) patients, possibly in response to decreased levels of IGF-I. It would thus appear that IGF-I receptor levels are not significantly altered with age in the rat and human brains, with possible changes being seen in a disease condition such as AD.

Regarding insulin receptors, an earlier study reported results similar in 22-month-old (compared to young) Wistar rats, with no significant changes being observed in any brain regions, except for a slight decrement in olfactory bulbs (Tchilian, Zhelezarov, Petkov, & Hadjiivanova, 1990). In contrast, insulin receptor binding was reported to be decreased in aged mouse brain homogenates (Zaia & Piantanelli, 1996). These differences are likely to be species-related. A study on the ontogenesis of the insulin receptor using synaptosomal membranes revealed a general decrease in the human cerebral cortex from development to adulthood (Potau, Escofet, & Martinez, 1991).

INSULIN AND/OR IGF-I RESISTANCE WITH AGING

In general, aging is associated with insulin resistance. Is it possible that neurons also become resistant (or somewhat diabetic) and their uptake of glucose is not as efficient to keep up with energy demand? In the periphery, previous studies showed age-related alterations in tyrosine kinase activity (Ruiz et al., 1992). Moreover, despite normal levels of insulin receptors in 20-month-old Wistar rats, it was shown that receptor autophosphorylation was reduced by 25%, in addition to decreased IRS-1 levels. Moreover, insulin-stimulated IRS-1 association with phosphatidyl-inositol 3-kinase (PI3-kinase) was decreased by 70% in the liver and 98% in muscles of 20- versus 2-month-old rats, with no change in PI3-kinase level; the phosphorylation of IRS-2 followed a similar pattern (Carvalho et al., 1996). Interestingly, insulin could not induce sodium/potassium-ATPase activation and plasma membrane hyperpolarization of certain cell types in aged Wistar rats (Frolkis, 1995). It was also demonstrated that peripheral insulin resistance in 24-month-old Wistar rats was accompanied by an impairment in insulin-sensitive glycosyl-phosphatidylinositol–dependent cellular signaling (Sanchez-Arias et al., 1993). One study divided 24- to 27-month-old Wistar rats into three groups having mild, moderate and severe reduction in maximal insulin-related kinase activity and found that deficits in the mild and moderate sub-groups could be reversed by extensive autophosphorylation (Nadiv, Cohen, & Zick, 1992). It remains to be established whether in aged rats differential alterations in these markers could be correlated with cognitive performance and comparable changes in the IGF-I receptor signaling pathway.

A study was also designed to assess whether cognitive deficits in aging could be partially overcome by increasing the availability of IGF-I in the brain (Markowska, Mooney, & Sonntag, 1998). Male rats of two ages (4 and 32 months) were preoperatively trained in behavioral tasks and subsequently implanted with mini-pumps to infuse IGF-I or a vehicle into the cerebral ventricles. Animals were retested at 2 and 4 weeks. IGF-I improved working memory in the repeated acquisition and object recognition tasks. An improvement was also observed in the place discrimination task, which as-

sesses reference memory. Moreover, injection of IGF-I antisense oligonucleotides in the inferior olive region elicited a complete inhibition of conditioned eye-blink learning in freely moving rats (Castro-Alamancos & Torres-Aleman, 1994). Furthermore, insulin treatment prevents deficits in water maze learning and long-term potentiation (LTP) in streptozotocin-diabetic rats (Biessels et al., 1998). Taken together, these data indicate a potentially important role for IGF-I (and insulin) in the reversal of age-related behavioral impairments in rodents.

The growth hormone (GH)/IGF-I axis is known to be involved in the aging of physiological functions. Recent studies indicate that the GH/IGF-I axis may also be associated with cognitive functioning. For example, Aleman and colleagues (1999) determined whether age-related decline in circulating IGF-I levels were correlated with cognitive performances. Twenty-five healthy older men with well-preserved functional ability participated in the study. Neuropsychological tests of general knowledge, vocabulary, basic visual perception, reading ability, visuoconstructive ability, perceptual-motor speed, mental tracking, and verbal long-term memory were administered. Performance on the last four tests declined with age, whereas the first four were not as sensitive to aging. Interestingly, the authors found that plasma IGF-I levels were significantly correlated with performances (controlled for education) on the Digit Symbol Substitution test and the Concept Shifting Task, two tests measuring perceptual-motor and mental processing speed. Subjects with higher IGF-I levels performed better on these tests. These data support the hypothesis that circulating IGF-I may play a role in the age-related decline of certain cognitive functions, especially those related to the speed of information processing (Aleman et al., 1999). In another recent study, Rollero and colleagues (1998) reported that plasma IGF-I levels were directly correlated with cognitive function as assessed using the Mini Mental State Examination, scores and IGF-I levels being lower in patients with the most advanced cognitive deterioration. This could be taken as an indication that plasma IGF-I levels may indicate cognitive abilities in aging.

IMPORTANCE OF CONTROLLING GLUCOSE HOMEOSTASIS

In aged rats and humans, impaired glucose regulation has been correlated with poor memory performance. Aged (22–24 months) and young (3 months) rats were assessed in a battery of behavioral tests that included tasks of learning and place navigation. Following evaluation, all animals were analyzed for their local glucose utilization. The decline in performance correlated significantly with the decrement in regional glucose utilization (Gage, Kelly, & Bjorklund, 1984). Moreover, performance in these two tests showed significant correlation with glucose use in brain regions associated with learning processes. These results suggest that learning impairments in aged rats may be related to decreases in glucose utilization.

Interestingly, intraperitoneal glucose injections result in improved learning performance (Long, Davis, Garofalo, Spangler, & Ingram, 1992). For example, effects of a pre-training intraperitoneal glucose injection on learning and memory were tested using the Morris water maze. Glucose injection before a block of trials enhanced spatial memory performance in mice (Li et al., 1998). In aged, cognitively-impaired Wistar rats, significantly-reduced cerebral glucose utilization was observed in various regions associated with learning and memory processes (Wree et al., 1991). Treatment of both neuronal and glial cultured cells with insulin and IGF-I induced a time- and dose-dependent increase in the steady state levels of glucose transporter mRNA (Werner et al., 1989). Severe decreases in brain insulin levels were also observed in aged rabbits, and the expression of the glucose transporters in the Wistar rat brain was altered during aging (Vannucci, 1994). Interestingly, herpes simplex virus vectors bearing a glucose transporter gene were found to protect neurons against a one-hour focal ischemic insult in rats (Lawrence et al., 1996), suggesting a possible treatment strategy to increase glucose transporter availability in the aged brain. Hence, in spite of apparently normal levels of IGF-I and insulin receptor sites in the AU and AI Long Evans rats (discussed earlier), alterations in related signaling pathways and glucose transporters could lead to decreased cognitive abilities. It is thus possible that altered cellular IGF and/or insulin responsiveness is a general feature of aging having functional significance in neurodegenerative diseases by affecting cognitive abilities. Interestingly, experimental desensitization of brain insulin receptors in aged Wistar rats induced abnormalities in glucose utilization, membrane phospholipids, and monoaminergic metabolism, resembling some of the disturbances seen in AD (Hoyer, Muller, & Plaschke, 1994). Links between the onset of AD and diabetes are thus possible because the latter is a risk factor in AD (Fanelli et al., 1995; Vanhanen et al., 1998).

Using rat hippocampal slices, the authors observed that IGF-I modulates potassium-evoked acetylcholine (ACh) release (Kar, Seto, Doré, Hanisch, & Quirion, 1997). These data suggest a direct role for IGF-I and its receptors in the regulation of transmitter release in the central nervous system. Recent evidence indicates that systemic glucose treatment enhances memory while producing a corresponding increase in hippocampal acetylcholine (ACh) release (Ragozzino, Pal, Unick, Stefani, & Gold, 1998). Unilateral intrahippocampal infusions of glucose were examined for enhanced spontaneous cognitive performance and corresponding increases in ACh release. Twelve minutes after a unilateral infusion of glucose, rats were tested in a cross maze for spontaneous alternation behavior with concurrent microdialysis collection. Glucose infusions significantly increased cognitive scores compared to controls, and behavioral testing resulted in increased ACh output in the hippocampus. These results suggest that glucose may enhance cognitive abilities by modulating ACh release. Accumulated evidence (Kar, Seto, Doré, Hanisch, et al., 1997; Knusel, Michel, Schwaber, & Hefti, 1990) suggest that IGF-I acts as a trophic factor as well as a rapid neuromodulator for selected populations of cholinergic neurons, and thus may be of relevance to certain degenerative diseases, particularly AD, in which decreased levels of cholinergic markers are associated with impairments in cognitive functions (Perry, 1986; Quirion, 1993; Selkoe, 1994). In support of a possible role for IGF in AD, it has recently been shown that IGF-I binding sites are increased in the cortical areas affected by this disease (Crews et al., 1992), and IGF-I can protect/rescue cultured hippocampal neurons against β-amyloid mediated toxicity (Doré, Kar, & Quirion, 1997b). Interestingly, glucose levels may also mod-

ulate the production and the toxicity of β-amyloid fragments (El Tamer, Raikoff, & Hanin, 1998; Hoyer et al., 1994; Mark, Pang, Geddes, Uchida, & Mattson, 1997), again associating the beneficial effect of IGF-I and brain glucose metabolism.

POTENTIAL THERAPEUTIC APPROACHES

It has been reported that intraventricular and subcutaneous supplementation of IGF-I protects the immature and adult brain against hypoxic-ischemic injury and ischemia (Hoffmann, Schaebitz, & Schwab, 1999; Loddick et al., 1998; Tagami et al., 1997; Zhu & Auer, 1994). Brain injury is often associated with increase in IGF levels (Gluckman et al., 1992; Sandberg Nordqvist et al., 1996) and IGF receptors (Bergstedt & Wieloch, 1993). IGF-I has been extensively used clinically (Lewis et al., 1993; Yuen & Mobley, 1995). It has been studied with respect to growth delay, diabetes, and catabolic disorders. Its safety has been well established, although some side-effects need to be considered, especially in relation to chronic use. One of the counter-indications is that IGF-I, due to its characteristic growth-promoting activities, could promote the progression of some tumors (Lewis et al., 1993; Lonning & Lien, 1995). Hence, the design of mimetics devoid of the side effects of IGF-I should be developed.

In that regard, a few strategies are worth considering. One relates to alterations of IGF-I–binding to IGF-binding proteins (IGFBP) in order to increase the level of IGF-I while the other is based on the design of non-peptidic mimetics. It is well known that the action of IGF-I is modulated by the IGFBPs (six different forms are well known; Jones & Clemmons, 1995), which form high-affinity complexes and under most circumstances inactivate IGF-I. It was recently suggested that displacement of this large pool of endogenous IGF-I from the binding proteins could elevate free IGF-I levels to elicit neuroprotective effects comparable to those produced by the administration of exogenous IGF-I (Loddick et al., 1998). It was shown that a human IGF-I analog (Leu[24,59,60] Ala[31]hIGF-I) with high affinity for IGF-binding proteins but no biological activity at the IGF-I receptors, increased the levels of free, bioavailable IGF-I in the brain. Intracerebroventricular administration of this analog up to one hour after an ischemic insult to the rat brain had a potent neuroprotective action comparable to that of IGF-I. This ligand also attenuated losses of pyramidal neurons in the hippocampus in a model of toxicity induced by quinolinic acid. Hence, this may represent a novel strategy to increase free IGF-I levels in the brain.

The second strategy is very challenging. It is based on the design of non-peptidic mimetics. Taking into consideration that large polypeptides such as IGF-I do not readily cross the blood-brain barrier, the development of a non-peptide mimic would be ideal. Recently, a team of researchers have shown the feasibility of this approach by developing L-783,281, a non-peptidyl mimic acting as an agonist on the insulin receptor (Zhang et al., 1999). A similar strategy could lead to the characterization of an IGF-I mimetic on the basis of similarities between the IGF-I and insulin receptors.

In conclusion, knowing the pleotropic actions of IGF-I and insulin on neuronal and non-neuronal cells following injuries, an IGF-I treatment could have therapeutic applications in a number of neurodegenerative disorders, in traumatic brain and spinal cord injuries, and in aging. Several clinical trials have suggested the potential beneficial effect of IGF-I in the nervous system, especially in amyotrophic lateral sclerosis (ALS; Lewis et al., 1993). The need to develop IGF mimetics is now imperative to directly assess the usefulness of IGF-I–like drugs in the treatment of neurodegenerative diseases. A better understanding of the links between IGF-I and brain glucose metabolism could also lead to the development of new drugs that would reduce memory loss in Alzheimer's disease and normal aging.

REFERENCES

Aleman, A., Verhaar, H. J., De Haan, E. H., De Vries, W. R., Samson, M. M., Drent, M. L., Van Der Veen, E. A., & Koppeschaar, H. P. (1999). Insulin-like growth factor-I and cognitive function in healthy older men. *Journal of Clinical Endocrinology and Metabolism*, 471–475.

Bergstedt, K., & Wieloch, T. (1993). Changes in insulin-like growth factor 1 receptor density after transient cerebral ischemia in the rat: Lack of protection against ischemic brain damage following injection of insulin-like growth factor 1. *Journal of Cerebral Blood Flow and Metabolism, 13*, 895–898.

Biessels, G. J., Kamal, A., Urban, I. J., Spruijt, B. M., Erkelens, D. W., & Gispen, W. H. (1998). Water maze learning and hippocampal synaptic plasticity in streptozotocin-diabetic rats: Effects of insulin treatment. *Brain Research, 800*, 125–135.

Carvalho, C. R., Brenelli, S. L., Silva, A. C., Nunes, A. L., Velloso, L. A., & Saad, M. J. (1996). Effect of aging on insulin receptor, insulin receptor substrate-1, and phosphatidylinositol 3-kinase in liver and muscle of rats. *Endocrinology, 137*, 151–159.

Castro-Alamancos, M. A., & Torres-Aleman, I. (1994). Learning of the conditioned eye-blink response is impaired by an antisense insulin-like growth factor I oligonucleotide. *Proceedings of the National Academy of Sciences, U.S.A., 91*, (10203–10207).

Crews, F. T., McElhaney, R., Freund, G., Ballinger, W. E., Jr., & Raizada, M. K. (1992). Insulin-like growth factor I receptor binding in brains of Alzheimer's and alcoholic patients. *Journal of Neurochemistry, 58*, 1205–1210.

Doré, S., Kar, S., & Quirion, R. (1997a). Rediscovering an old friend, IGF-I: Potential use in the treatment of neurodegenerative diseases. *Trends in Neuroscience, 20*, 326–331.

Doré, S., Kar, S., & Quirion, R. (1997b). Insulin-like growth factor I protects and rescues hippocampal neurons against beta-amyloid- and human amylin-induced toxicity. *Proceedings of the National Academy of Sciences, U.S.A., 94*, 4772–4777.

Doré, S., Kar, S., Rowe, W., & Quirion, R. (1997). Distribution and levels of [125I]IGF-I, [125I]IGF-II and [125I]insulin receptor binding sites in the hippocampus of aged memory-unimpaired and -impaired rats. *Neuroscience, 80*, 1033–1040.

Doré, S., Krieger, C., Kar, S., & Quirion, R. (1996). Distribution and levels of insulin-like growth factor (IGF-I and IGF-II) and insulin receptor binding sites in the spinal cords of amyotrophic lateral sclerosis (ALS) patients. *Molecular Brain Research, 41*, 128–133.

El Tamer, A., Raikoff, K., & Hanin, I. (1998). Effect of glucose-deprivation on amyloid precursor protein (APP) release from rat hippocampal slices. *Society for Neuroscience Abstracts, 24*, 1006.

Fanelli, C., Pampanelli, S., Calderone, S., Lepore, M., Annibale, B., Compagnucci, P., Brunetti, P., & Bolli, G. B. (1995). Effects of recent, short-term hyperglycemia on responses to hypoglycemia in humans: Relevance to the pathogenesis of hypoglycemia unawareness and hyperglycemia-induced insulin resistance. *Diabetes, 44*, 513–519.

Frolkis, V. V. (1995). The role of "invertors" (intracellular activators) in age-related changes in cell response to hormones. *Experimental Gerontology, 30*, 401–414.

Gage, F. H., Kelly, P. A., & Bjorklund, A. (1984). Regional changes in brain glucose metabolism reflect cognitive impairments in aged rats. *Journal of Neuroscience, 4*, 2856–2865.

Gluckman, P., Klempt, N., Guan, J., Mallard, C., Sirimanne, E., Dragunow, M., Klempt, M., Singh, K., Williams, C., & Nikolics, K. (1992). A role for IGF-1 in the rescue of CNS neurons following hypoxic-ischemic injury. *Biochemistry and Biophysical Research Communications, 182*, 593–599.

Hoffmann, T. T., Schaebitz, W. R., & Schwab, S. (1999). Reduction of infarction volume in rats after intraventricular and subcutaneous application of IGF-I. *Journal of Cerebral Blood Flow and Metabolism, 19*, S182.

Hoyer, S., Muller, D., & Plaschke, K. (1994). Desensitization of brain insulin receptor: Effect on glucose/energy and related metabolism. *Journal of Neural Transmission* (Suppl. 44), 259–268.

Isaksson, O. G., Ohlsson, C., Nilsson, A., Isgaard, J., & Lindahl, A. (1991). Regulation of cartilage growth by growth hormone and insulin-like growth factor I. *Pediatric Nephrology, 5*, 451–453.

Jones, J. I., & Clemmons, D. R. (1995). Insulin-like growth factors and their binding proteins: Biological actions. *Endocrine Reviews, 16*, 3–34.

Kar, S., Seto, D., Doré, S., Chabot, J. G., & Quirion, R. (1997). Systemic administration of kainic acid induces selective time dependent decrease in [125I]insulin-like growth factor I, [125I]insulin-like growth factor II and [125I]insulin receptor binding sites in adult rat hippocampal formation. *Neuroscience, 80*, 1041–1055.

Kar, S., Seto, D., Doré, S., Hanisch, U., & Quirion, R. (1997). Insulin-like growth factors-I and -II differentially regulate endogenous acetylcholine release from the rat hippocampal formation. *Proceedings of the National Academy of Sciences, U.S.A., 94*, 14054–14059.

Knusel, B., Michel, P. P., Schwaber, J. S., & Hefti, F. (1990). Selective and nonselective stimulation of central cholinergic and dopaminergic development in vitro by nerve growth factor, basic fibroblast growth factor, epidermal growth factor, insulin and the insulin-like growth factors I and II. *Journal of Neuroscience, 10*, 558–570.

Lawrence, M. S., Sun, G. H., Kunis, D. M., Saydam, T. C., Dash, R., Ho, D. Y., Sapolsky, R. M., & Steinberg, G. K. (1996). Overexpression of the glucose transporter gene with a herpes simplex viral vector protects striatal neurons against stroke. *Journal of Cerebral Blood Flow and Metabolism, 16,* 181–185.

Lewis, M. E., Neff, N. T., Contreras, P. C., Stong, D. B., Oppenheim, R. W., Grebow, P. E., & Vaught, J. L. (1993). Insulin-like growth factor-I: Potential for treatment of motor neuronal disorders. *Experimental Neurology, 124,* 73–88.

Li, A. J., Oomura, Y., Sasaki, K., Suzuki, K., Tooyama, I., Hanai, K., Kimura, H., & Hori, T. (1998). A single pre-training glucose injection induces memory facilitation in rodents performing various tasks: Contribution of acidic fibroblast growth factor. *Neuroscience, 85,* 785–794.

Loddick, S. A., Liu, X. J., Lu, Z. X., Liu, C., Behan, D. P., Chalmers, D. C., Foster, A. C., Vale, W. W., Ling, N., & De Souza, E. B. (1998). Displacement of insulin-like growth factors from their binding proteins as a potential treatment for stroke. *Proceedings of the National Academy of Sciences, U.S.A., 95,* 1894–1898.

Long, J. M., Davis, B. J., Garofalo, P., Spangler, E. L., & Ingram, D. K. (1992). Complex maze performance in young and aged rats: Response to glucose treatment and relationship to blood insulin and glucose. *Physiology and Behavior, 51,* 411–418.

Lonning, E., & Lien, E. A. (1995). Mechanisms of action of endocrine treatment in breast cancer. *Critical Reviews in Oncology/Hematology, 21,* 158–193.

Mark, R. J., Pang, Z., Geddes, J. W., Uchida, K., & Mattson, M. P. (1997). Amyloid beta-peptide impairs glucose transport in hippocampal and cortical neurons: Involvement of membrane lipid peroxidation. *Journal of Neuroscience, 17,* 1046–1054.

Markowska, A. L., Mooney, M., & Sonntag, W. E. (1998). Insulin-like growth factor-1 ameliorates age-related behavioral deficits. *Neuroscience, 87,* 559–569.

Nadiv, O., Cohen, O., & Zick, Y. (1992). Defects of insulin's signal transduction in old rat livers. *Endocrinology, 130,* 1515–1524.

Pankov, Y. A. (1999). Growth hormone and a partial mediator of its biological action, insulin-like growth factor I. *Biochemistry (Moscow), 64,* 1–7.

Perry, E. K. (1986). The cholinergic hypothesis—ten years on. *British Medical Bulletin, 42,* 63–69.

Potau, N., Escofet, M. A., & Martinez, M. C. (1991). Ontogenesis of insulin receptors in human cerebral cortex. *Journal of Endocrinological Investigation, 14,* 53–58.

Quirion, R. (1993). Cholinergic markers in Alzheimer disease and the autoregulation of acetylcholine release. *Journal of Psychiatry and Neuroscience, 18,* 226–234.

Ragozzino, M. E., Pal, S. N., Unick, K., Stefani, M. R., & Gold, P. E. (1998). Modulation of hippocampal acetylcholine release and spontaneous alternation scores by intrahippocampal glucose injections. *Journal of Neuroscience, 18,* 1595–1601.

Rollero, A., Murialdo, G., Fonzi, S., Garrone, S., Gianelli, M. V., Gazzerro, E., Barreca, A., & Polleri, A. (1998). Relationship between cognitive function, growth hormone and insulin-like growth factor I plasma levels in aged subjects. *Neuropsychobiology, 38,* 73–79.

Rotwein, P., Burgess, S. K., Milbrandt, J. D., & Krause, J. E. (1988). Differential expression of insulin-like growth factor genes in rat central nervous system. *Proceedings of the National Academy of Sciences, U.S.A., 85,* 265–269.

Ruiz, P., Pulido, J. A., Martinez, C., Carrascosa, J. M., Satrustegui, J., & Andres, A. (1992). Effect of aging on the kinetic characteristics of the insulin receptor autophosphorylation in rat adipocytes. *Archives of Biochemistry and Biophysics,* 231–238.

Sanchez-Arias, J. A., Sanchez-Gutierrez, J. C., Guadano, A., Alvarez, J. F., Samper, B., Mato, J. M., & Feliu, J. E. (1993). Changes in the insulin-sensitive glycosyl-phosphatidyl-inositol signalling system with aging in rat hepatocytes. *European Journal of Biochemistry, 211,* 431–436.

Sandberg Nordqvist, A. C., von Holst, H., Holmin, S., Sara, V. R., Bellander, B. M., & Schalling, M. (1996). Increase of insulin-like growth factor (IGF)-1, IGF binding protein-2 and -4 mRNAs following cerebral contusion. *Molecular Brain Research, 38,* 285–293.

Selkoe, D. J. (1994). Normal and abnormal biology of the beta-amyloid precursor protein. *Annual Review of Neuroscience, 17,* 489–517.

Tagami, M., Ikeda, K., Nara, Y., Fujino, H., Kubota, A., Numano, F., & Yamori, Y. (1997). Insulin-like growth factor-1 attenuates apoptosis in hippocampal neurons caused by cerebral ischemia and reperfusion in stroke-prone spontaneously hypertensive rats. *Laboratory Investigation, 76,* 613–617.

Tchilian, E. Z., Zhelezarov, I. E., Petkov, V. V., & Hadjiivanova, C. I. (1990). 125I-insulin binding is decreased in olfactory bulbs of aged rats. *Neuropeptides, 17,* 193–196.

Vanhanen, M., Koivisto, K., Kuusisto, J., Mykkanen, L., Helkala, E. L., Hanninen, T., Riekkinen, P., Sr., Soininen, H., & Laakso, M. (1998). Cognitive function in an elderly population with persistent impaired glucose tolerance. *Diabetes Care, 21,* 398–402.

Vannucci, S. J. (1994). Developmental expression of GLUT1 and GLUT3 glucose transporters in rat brain. *Journal of Neurochemistry, 62,* 240–246.

Werner, H., Raizada, M. K., Mudd, L. M., Foyt, H. L., Simpson, I. A., Roberts, C. T., Jr., & LeRoith, D. (1989). Regulation of rat brain/HepG2 glucose transporter gene expression by insulin and insulin-like growth factor-I in primary cultures of neuronal and glial cells. *Endocrinology, 125,* 314–320.

Wree, A., Kaever, C., Birgel, B., Schleicher, A., Horvath, E., & Zilles, K. (1991). Local cerebral glucose utilization in the brain of old, learning impaired rats. *Histochemistry, 95,* 591–603.

Yuen, E. C., & Mobley, W. C. (1995). Therapeutic applications of neurotrophic factors in disorders of motor neurons and peripheral nerves. *Molecular Medicine Today, 1,* 278–286.

Zaia, A., & Piantanelli, L. Insulin receptors in the brain cortex of aging mice (2000). *Mechanisms of Ageing and Development, 113,* 227–32.

Zhang, B., Salituro, G., Szalkowski, D., Li, Z., Zhang, Y., Royo, I., Vilella, D., Diez, M. T., Pelaez, F., Ruby, C., Kendall, R. L., Mao, X., Griffin, P., Calaycay, J., Zierath, J. R., Heck, J. V., Smith, R. G., & Moller, D. E. (1999). Discovery of a small molecule insulin mimetic with antidiabetic activity in mice. *Science, 284,* 974–977.

Zhu, C. Z., & Auer, R. N. (1994). Intraventricular administration of insulin and IGF-1 in transient forebrain ischemia. *Journal of Cerebral Blood Flow and Metabolism, 14,* 237–242.

S. Doré
Johns Hopkins University

R. Quirion
Douglas Hospital Research Center, Canada

MEMORY

IMAGERY

In everyday conversation an image is supposed to be some kind of mental experience, a picture in the mind's eye. Such a description is referred to as the picture metaphor, but imagery also refers to experiences in other perceptual areas, such as hearing, tasting, and kinesthesis. The experience described as an image is recognized to exist inside the person; it is an as-if experience, in that no physical stimuli corresponding to the image are present. The image is not projected outside, although people will occasionally refer to images—say, of other persons—by remarking, "I can see him as if he were standing right there." They of course know very well that he is not "right there." When people claim that they actually see nonpresent objects (e.g., pink elephants), they are said to be hallucinating. If present objects are misinterpreted, as when a rag is misperceived as a rat, we refer to illusions.

Images are commonly described as faint, fleeting, undetailed, and partial, but some people report having vivid, detailed images. Presumably people differ in the strength of their imagery, and certainly they differ in scores attained on various tests of imagery designed to measure the vividness or clarity of images in various sense areas. The tests are reasonably reliable in that the scores are stable enough, but what validity they may have is difficult to establish, since no one can share any other person's imagery. A simple test of imagery that nearly everyone can pass is to count the outside and inside corners of a block letter, such as F. The average person has no difficulty with such a task, which, it is commonly argued, cannot be accomplished without resorting to imagery. Certainly the average person asserts that he or she visualizes the F and simply counts the corners while going over them mentally.

In the early history of psychology Wundt (1879) considered images as one of the three basic elements of consciousness, along with sensations and feelings. Images were regarded as revived former sensory-perceptual experiences. They were commonly accepted as fundamental psychological phenomena whose reality could hardly be questioned. Some investigators like Sir Francis Galton thought that imagery was more functional for children than for sophisticated adults, some of whom claimed to have no imagery in responding to a Galton questionnaire.

Because of the personal, subjective nature of reported imagery, John B. Watson, the founder of behaviorism, in his book *Behaviorism* described images as "the ghosts of sensation," ruling them out of serious concern for a psychology that was supposed to rely on socially confirmable facts. Images lost favor as objects of study as long as behaviorism held sway, but began to enjoy a recovery of interest in the 1960s and 1970s as what has come to be called cognitive psychology began to capture the interest of psychologists. Imagery again began to play a role in the areas of learning, perception, thinking, and meaning.

One of the important causes of the revival of interest in imagery was the publication of Frances Yates's *The Art of Memory.* Yates described how the early Greeks and Romans practiced various mnemonic skills based on images of already known frames of reference such as the structure of one's house. One could remember long lists of items by imaging each item in one room after another. Following Yates's book, a large number of studies of mnemonics appeared. In the typical study, a subject would first learn a list of peg (or key) words, then later would associate a list of random words with each peg by imagining some interaction between the referents of the two words. By such a procedure lists of 50 or more words could be remembered after one hearing. The only limit appears to be that of allowing enough time for two images to be associated, which usually takes about 5 seconds.

Other investigators asked subjects to rate long lists of words for their imagery value on a scale from 1 to 7. If an image occurred quickly and clearly, a word such as "auto" might be rated 6 or 7. Abstract words such as "beauty" might rate 1 or 2, as images might be slow or vague or mixed-up in various ways. It was found that high-imagery words could be learned very quickly, in contrast with low-imagery words. More important, it was found that high-imagery words could be learned more quickly than high-meaning words. In such studies, words would be rated for both meaningfulness and imagery. The meaningfulness could then be held constant by selecting words of the same meaningfulness value but different imagery value. In learning such lists the learning efficiency depended upon the imagery value whereas in the control situation, with imagery held constant and meaningfulness varying, the learning did not appear to vary with meaningfulness. It could then be argued that imagery was more important than meaningfulness and that, indeed, it was a better index of *meaning* than the so-called meaningfulness measures. A catalogue of 925 common words has been developed by Paivio (1971) in which measures of imagery are presented.

In the area of perception, researchers began to demonstrate that if a person is busy with an auditory discrimination task, asking the person to indulge in auditory imagery will result in deterioration of the discrimination performance, while visual imagery would have no similar effect. If one asked for visual discrimination while the person was also engaged in either auditory or visual imagery, visual imagery would interfere, while auditory imagery would not. Such studies led to identifying imagery with brain centers involved in processing perceptual discrimination for different sensory inputs. In split-brain research it was discovered that the right hemisphere appears to be strongly involved in processing visual forms and structures, as compared with the well-known involvement of the left-brain with linguistic concerns. Considerable interest developed in studies where subjects imaged a rotating three-dimensional figure and compared it with possible samples of how the figure would look if rotated various numbers of degrees. It was discovered that mental rotation took approximately the same time as a physical rotation of a figure would, and the subjects were then judged to have been rotating the figure imaginally or mentally. Similar manipulations of images were introduced in studies where subjects were asked, for example, to visualize animals at different distances and compare their sizes with pictures of other objects or with other animals of different size, at the same or different distances. One might imagine walking up to an elephant until one got so close that the body size (as an image) would overflow—that is, one could not see all of the elephant any more because one was up too close. Subjects would estimate the distances of such overflows with reasonable validity and reliability.

Such studies have convinced researchers such as Kosslyn (1980) that images are real, functional capacities of people and not ephemeral epiphenomena. Of course, even if epiphenomenal, they could still prove useful if found to be consistently correlated with other variables such as instructions to image, rated imagery, and imagery test scores. Some cognitive psychologists interested in computer simulation of cognitive processes prefer to downgrade imagery as of little or no interest, however real, and put their trust in alleged mental constructions called "propositions." For them, the mind becomes populated with propositions and mechanisms for processing propositions to create information or knowledge. Supporters of mental imagery appear not to be impressed with the arguments of the propositionists and continue their research with images.

Defining images appropriately so that one could find some operational agreement appears to be difficult. The efforts thus far have not enjoyed much success, as they commonly employ references to mental experience that cannot be objectified. The 1939 experiment of W. J. Brogden offers some hope. Brogden paired tones and lights some 200 times for dogs who could only look and listen, and of whom nothing was required by way of action. Subsequent to such pairing, Brogden shocked the animals just after one of the two previous stimuli (either a light or a tone, not both) was presented. The animals quickly learned an avoidance response. Then the animals were tested with the other stimulus, to see if any reaction would occur. Brogden reported that on at least some test trials some dogs would respond to a signal to which they had not been trained to respond. He labeled his findings evidence for "sensory pre-conditioning." There appears to be no reason to insert the "pre" before "conditioning," except to locate the conditioning in the time sequence. What apparently happened was that the lights and tones had been associated with each other as reactions in the dogs' nervous systems. Such a demonstration suggests that a dog hearing the tone would also have a sensory-like reaction corresponding to a light. If the light had been conditioned to an avoidance reaction, the tone might now, via the light reaction, initiate the avoidance reaction.

On the basis of Brogden's experiment and other sensory-conditioning studies, we have a foundation for defining imagery as conditioned sensory reactions. Suppose one hears the Polish word *Jabko* while being shown an apple. It is conceivable that the sound of the word and the visual reaction in viewing the apple might become associated so that, on a future hearing of the word, the visual reaction of looking at an apple could also be activated. One would then see (have an image of) an apple. The image might not be a strong, vivid, detailed response because the actual apple is not there, but it might be identifiable as an apple.

Presumably the same kinds of events took place in Pavlov's laboratory when he conditioned his dogs to salivate to the sounds of bells. It is argued here that the bell would initiate an image of food and this image would then lead to salivation, if the dog happened to be hungry and not otherwise distracted. Such an interpretation suggests that imagery might be the potent activator in what William James called "ideo-motor action." James speculated that a thought of any action would tend to be followed by that action, if no other distracting thoughts intervened. The sight of a chair might be associated with the image of sitting and thus lead to the response of sitting down, assuming no contradictory conditions like being en route to the door. The imagery in such a case might be kinesthetic in nature and not easily recognized, even though acted upon. When we swing a baseball bat at an oncoming ball, we might have some kinesthetic imagery that amounts to "feeling right" with this particular pitch.

All imagery is difficult to describe in crisp, neat communication, just as are all internal reactions. We never can describe a bellyache or toothache sufficiently clearly to get all the sympathy we want. We do learn to describe some of our internal reactions like hunger and thirst, but a description like "I'm so hungry I could eat a horse" is clearly inappropriate and amounts to saying "I'm very hungry" or "I'm hungrier than usual." To actually describe how hungry one might be is probably impossible. To describe an apple seen in imagination is equally impossible, if any strict criteria are applied. The fact that we have trouble describing our images does not make them any less real than toothaches or other pains. But however real they may be, we must recognize that images are not likely to be good guides for all decisions. Describing a criminal to a police artist will compound a problem: You describe your image and the artist interprets your words with his imagery, which he then tries to translate on paper. The result rarely resembles the criminal or the person later apprehended for the crime.

In studies of so-called eidetic imagery it was once believed that children—or at least some children—enjoyed remarkable imagery that practically amounted to looking at the real thing. Haber (1979) has demonstrated, however, that children alleged to be eidetic were no more accurate than other children in describing previously viewed pictures. The verity value of imagery is still highly questionable. It is easy enough to ask anyone to imagine anything and then show the real thing and ask, "Is this exactly like you imagined?" Any positive answer is certainly questionable. Conditioned responses have long been recognized as varying from the unconditioned response. There is no reason why images should be any more precise as reproductions of a prior response. After all, the stimulus for the actual reaction is not present.

The practical value of imagery has been exploited in a number of ways in the last two decades. Perhaps the greatest exploitation has been in the area of behavior therapy, where clinical psychologists have asked patients to imagine the kinds of things that give them anxiety or create problems for them, then teach them to relax while imaging their (formerly) distressing situations. Thus if someone is afraid of high places, he can be conditioned to relax while first imagining reaching for a box on a high shelf, then getting onto a footstool to get a higher box, and so on. Eventually he might be able to relax regardless of how high up he imagined himself to be. With care and patience, such patients can be brought to relax in the presence of the real situations, after having the appropriate practice with imaginary threats. Transfer from the clinical office to the real world cannot be assumed, however, and practice in actual anxiety-provoking situations must be introduced.

Another interesting application of imagery has been in sports and skills such as dart-throwing, gymnastics, and basketball free throws. People who spend some time imagining going through successful motions apparently can improve their scores more than control groups who do not engage in mental practice (Richardson, 1969). Should such an advantage from mere imagining prove reliable, many additional areas could probably benefit. It remains to spell out the details of the imaging sessions that are actually beneficial.

REFERENCES

Haber, R. N. (1979). Twenty years of haunting eidetic imagery: Where is the ghost? *The Behavioral and Brain Sciences, 2,* 583–630.

Kosslyn, S. (1980). *Image and mind.* Cambridge, MA: Harvard University Press.

Paivio, A. (1971). *Imagery and verbal processes.* New York: Holt, Rinehart & Winston.

Richardson, A. (1969). *Mental imagery.* New York: Springer.

Watson, J. B. (1958) *Behaviorism.* New York: Norton. (Original work published 1925)

Yates, F. (1966). *The art of memory.* Chicago: University of Chicago Press.

B. R. Bugelski
State University of New York at Buffalo

IMITATIVE LEARNING

Imitation is commonly accepted as an innate tendency to mimic or copy others. The common expression "monkey see, monkey do" suggests that monkeys are especially prone to behave like others, but this tendency is presumed to be a human trait as well. As far as psychologists are concerned, the fact that there is a name for some

alleged phenomenon does not prove its existence, and there may be more appropriate explanations for imitative behavior. Imitation not only is alleged to cover routine activities as in children's play, but also is supposed to play a role in learning. When children play "Simon says . . ." they perform acts that they are perfectly able to do and no learning is required—or at least nothing new is being learned. The same is true if children behave aggressively after watching violence on television shows—they already know how to perform the responses involved; all that needs to be explained is the motivation. Mowrer (1960) has provided a suitable explanation of such modeling behavior. The model, if admired by the observer, engages in some behavior like kicking a "Bobo" doll. Later the observer, given the opportunity, also kicks the doll. According to Mowrer, watching the model is accompanied by positive emotional reactions that become conditioned to the features of the situation. When the doll is available, the positive emotional reactions are revived and the kicking behavior may ensue, enhancing the positive emotional reaction. The kicking is probably not a precise replication of how the model kicked. It is not necessarily the specific response, but the more general destructive pattern, that is "aped." Imitators of TV violence do not necessarily use the same equipment or the precise reactions of their models, either; the general destructive behavior is adequate to provide the pleasurable reactions.

In new learning situations it is an age-old practice for teachers to say, "Let me show you." They then perform some operation that the learner observes and tries to duplicate. Such learning is not understood any better by calling it imitation. It is learning by observation—a factor in all learning (Gibson, 1969). Whether there is a teacher or model or not, learning requires observation of the factors in a situation and response to such factors. Without a teacher, a learner may waste a lot of time observing wrong or irrelevant features. A teacher or model saves this time by pointing out or illustrating specific factors that must be observed and responded to. A passenger in a car may not learn much about driving a motor vehicle, but a teenage passenger hoping to become a driver may attend quite carefully to what the driver does and thereby learn a great deal. The learning in such cases, as in all learning, requires attending to the relevant factors long enough and/or frequently enough for associations to be formed. In some situations one can also learn by merely being told what to do without a demonstration. The demonstration may be helpful, if the situation is complicated enough to invite erroneous responses.

Miller and Dollard (1941) trained rats to follow other rats (previously trained alone) on a two-choice T-maze. The follower rats learned to make the correct turns more easily than rats without leaders. Dollard and Miller, however, also demonstrated that the rats could learn to take the opposite turn—a case of negative imitation. What the rats were learning was to use the leader rats as cues for their own responses. There was no innate imitation involved. Birds will arrive at a feeding station if they see other birds eating there. Again, this is not imitative behavior so much as responding to cues associated with eating in the past.

Imitation is not a special force or tool that operates independently to produce learning. We tend to do what we see others doing, if we also observe the satisfactory outcomes of their behavior. If we do not observe completely and carefully enough, as in magic shows, all our efforts at imitation will be useless. Learning requires the association of relevant stimuli with other stimuli or responses. Certainly we can learn by watching others; we always have.

REFERENCES

Gibson, E. J. (1969). *Principles of perceptual learning and development.* New York: Appleton-Century-Crofts.

Miller, N. E., & Dollard, J. (1941). *Social learning and imitation.* New Haven, CT: Yale University Press.

B. R. BUGELSKI
State University of New York at Buffalo

IMMUNOLOGICAL FUNCTIONING

The immune system represents a complex series of mechanisms whose principal function is to protect the organism from foreign substances that lead to disease; it may also be essential as a defense against cells that have undergone neoplastic transformation. The immune system comprises two major categories, the cellular and humoral immune systems, both of which involve the action of lymphocyte cells.

The principal components of the cellular system are macrophages and T-lymphocytes, the latter being thymus-derived or thymus-influenced. It is thought that the main function of T-cells is defense against certain microorganisms, intracellular bacterial pathogens, and viruses, and that it is responsible for delayed skin hypersensitivity, rejection of allografts, and antitumor actions. The T-lymphocytes can be subdivided into specific classes: regulatory and effector T-cells. The regulatory cells may be either helper or suppressor cells, whereas effector cells are responsible for the immune reactions. Macrophages are responsible for presenting the foreign particle (antigen) to the T-cell and may determine which cells will be stimulated by particular antigens. Moreover, macrophages may regulate the magnitude of the T-cell response by influencing cell division or differentiation. The major component of the humoral immune system is the B-cell, so designated because in birds they develop from the bursa of Fabricius and in mammals from the bone marrow. The immunological function of the B-lymphocytes is expressed through the production of antibodies or immunoglobulins (IgM, IgG, IgA, and IgE).

Prior to encountering an antigen, lymphocyte cells are committed to form only a single type of antibody. These cells react with the antigen through specific cell/surface–bound immunoglobulin molecules. T-cells may also act as helpers in antibody production by B-cells. Once the individual is exposed to a particular antigen, increased resistance to infection is exhibited upon reexposure to that antigen. In effect, having been exposed to an antigen, both T- and B-cells have a memory for that antigen, resulting in a relatively rapid and pronounced reaction to it. The memory appears to be specific and long-lasting and is associated with an increased number of specifically reactive T- and B-cells.

The occurrence of tolerance, essentially the opposite of the sensitization or memory effect, has also been noted in response to antigens. That is, with repeated exposure to a particular antigen, immune responsivity may decline. The fact that an animal's immune system does not react against its own tissue may be an instance of tolerance. Under some conditions this resistance fails, resulting in autoimmune diseases such as rheumatoid arthritis, myasthenia gravis, and systemic lupus erythematosus (Cunningham, 1978; Fudenberg, Stites, Caldwell, & Wells, 1980). In addition to a role for T-cells in immunosurveillance against cancer, it has been suggested that other effector cells, termed natural killer cells, may be fundamental to immune surveillance (Herberman & Ortaldo, 1981). It is thought that natural killer cells may react within a few hours to foreign substances, as opposed to the 5- to 7-day period for the primary response of T-cells and the 2- to 5-day response of sensitized T-cells. Accordingly, this type of broad-range defense may act as a temporary measure until the more potent and specific immune response is sufficiently potent.

Increasingly greater attention has been devoted to the possibility that immunological changes, and hence susceptibility to disease, may be influenced by psychological factors (Ader, 1981). Indeed, it has been demonstrated that stressful situations may alter immunological activity and increase susceptibility to some immunologically related diseases. It seems, however, that a variety of factors—including previous stress history, stress chronicity, as well as other experiential and organismic variables—will determine the immunological changes observed (Monjan, 1981). Moreover, the immune response may be subject to conditioning processes, such that the immunosuppressive effects of agents such as cyclophosphamide can be induced with cues that had been paired with the drug (Ader & Cohen, 1975).

Although immunological functioning was traditionally considered to be independent of central nervous system activity, it has been shown that manipulations that alter central nervous system functioning (e.g., lesion of the anterior hypothalamus) will affect immune responsivity (Stein, Schleifer, & Keller, 1981). Conversely, antigen administration appears to alter activity of neurons in some brain regions (Besedovsky, Sorkin, Felix, & Haas, 1977). Extensive documentation is also available indicating that hormonal changes have profound influence on immunological functioning (Maclean & Reichlin, 1981). Accordingly, it is certainly possible that the central nervous system manipulations influence immunological activity via alterations of hormonal secretion. Only limited data are available concerning the interrelationships among these various systems, and the way in which psychological variables come to influence the immune response remains to be fully elucidated.

REFERENCES

Ader, R. (1981). *Psychoneuroimmunology.* New York: Academic.

Ader, R., & Cohen, N. (1975). Behaviorally conditioned immunosuppression. *Psychosomatic Medicine, 37,* 333–340.

Besedovsky, H. O., Sorkin, E., Felix, D., & Haas, H. (1977). Hypothalamic changes during the immune response. *European Journal of Immunology, 7,* 325–328.

Cunningham, A. J. (1978). *Understanding immunology.* New York: Academic.

Fudenberg, H. H., Stites, D. P., Caldwell, J. L., & Wells, J. V. (1980). *Basic and clinical immunology.* Los Altos, CA: Large.

Herberman, R., & Ortaldo, J. R. (1981). Natural killer cells: The role in defenses against disease. *Science, 214,* 24–30.

Maclean, D., & Reichlin, S. (1981). Neuroendocrinology and the immune process. In R. Ader (Ed.), *Psychoneuroimmunology.* New York: Academic.

Monjan, A. A. (1981). Stress and immunologic competence: Studies in animals. In R. Ader (Ed.), *Psychoneuroimmunology.* New York: Academic.

Stein, M., Schleifer, S. J., & Keller, S. E. (1981). Hypothalamic influences on immune responses. In R. Ader (Ed.), *Psychoneuroimmunology.* New York: Academic.

H. ANISMAN
Carleton University

ACCOMMODATION
ADAPTATION
ADRENAL GLANDS
HOMEOSTASIS
PSYCHOPHYSIOLOGY

IMPLOSIVE THERAPY

A form of behavior therapy developed by Stampfl in the late 1950s, implosive therapy is based on the hypothesis that neurotic behavior—notably intense anxiety—develops as an avoidance mechanism for coping with a repressed traumatic experience, and that the relative success of avoidance enables the anxiety to persist. In implosive therapy, the patient's anxiety is increased and maintained at an almost intolerable level by imagining a series of provoking cues, described either by the therapist or by the patient with the therapist's assistance, until the anxiety dissipates. Proponents believe the technique reinforces anxiety control and extinguishes related public responses by depriving the anxiety of its avoidance function.

SUGGESTED READING

Frankel, A. S. (1970). Treatment of a multisymptomatic phobic by a self-directed, self-reinforced imagery technique: A case study. *Journal of Abnormal Psychology, 76,* 496–499.

Levis, Donald J. (1995). Decoding traumatic memory: Implosive theory of psychopathology. In William T. O'Donohue & Leonard Krasner (Eds.), *Theories of behavior therapy: Exploring behavior change.* Washington, DC: American Psychological Association.

Stampfl, T., & Levis, D. (1967). Essentials of implosive therapy: A learning theory-based psychodynamic behavioral therapy. *Journal of Abnormal Psychology, 72,* 496–503.

F. W. HANSEN
Lake Forest College

ANXIETY

IMPRESSION FORMATION

The origins of research on impression formation can be traced to an influential paper by Solomon Asch, "Forming impressions of personality" (1946). Two major issues were addressed in the paper. First, when forming an impression, the perceiver must somehow cope with what is often a heterogeneous set of facts about the other person. Asch was concerned with how people give meaning to their observations of others. The second problem was in knowing exactly what the perceiver's impression was. How does a researcher go about measuring something as intricate—and yet amorphous—as an impression?

MEASUREMENT OF IMPRESSIONS

A variety of approaches to the measurement problem have been employed. Asch was interested in preserving as much of the qualitative flavor of impressions as possible. He used three methods. One was to simply ask the perceiver to write out in a brief paragraph impressions about another person. The researcher would then evaluate these paragraphs to see if consistent themes emerged. A second approach was to ask the perceiver to make a list of words or phrases that came to mind when thinking about the other person. This method is a variation on the free association procedure and is evaluated in the same way as the first method.

The third technique was more structured. It provided the perceiver with a list of prechosen adjectives and asked him or her to place a check mark by the ones that applied to the other person. Although this procedure does not allow new perceiver-generated thoughts to emerge, it does produce a qualitative profile of the perceived person and has the advantage of simple and objective scoring.

In recent years, a fourth approach has gained dominance. Researchers have moved away from studying the more qualitative features of impression and toward simpler evaluative disposition. Overall impression is measured on a single-item rating scale defined by end labels such as "very favorable" and "very unfavorable." Most recent research on impression formation, then, has studied factors that affect the overall favorability of impressions.

THEORETICAL PERSPECTIVES

The main substantive concern raised by Asch was the importance of understanding how people cope with the diverse information items they receive about another person. This is sometimes referred to as the information integration problem. Two distinct theoretical perspectives have been advanced. The *Gestalt approach* argues that people adopt a configural strategy. They appraise the entire information array and arrive at a thematic interpretation that integrates all the disparate items into a coherent whole. This process often involves reinterpretation of some information items and the discounting of others.

The *cognitive algebra approach* argues that each item of information contributes independently to the overall impression. Unlike the Gestalt approach, this view assumes that the information items are not actively interrelated into a single meaningful configuration. Rather, the evaluative implications of each item are extracted at the time the item is first received and are combined with any preexisting evaluative response to yield the present evaluative impression of the other person. It is referred to as the cognitive algebra approach because information items can be combined through such algebraic rules as averaging, adding, or multiplying. Although these two theoretical perspectives are very different in their conceptual assumptions, they have proven equally adept at accounting for the primary empirical findings in the field.

RESEARCH FINDINGS

Most research in the area of impression formation has focused on first impressions. Subjects participating in the research are given a list of personality-trait adjectives and asked to form an impression of a hypothetical person who possesses that particular set of traits. The resulting impressions are found to be affected by a variety of characteristics of the information items.

When information items are presented sequentially, both *primacy* and *recency effects* have been observed. Primacy results when the early items in the sequence are attended to more closely than the later items. If the more positive items come at the beginning of the sequence, the overall impression will be more positive. Recency effects are found when people are asked to rate their impression repeatedly, following the presentation of each new information item. In this case the final overall impression will be more favorable if the more positive information items come at the end of the series.

After an overall impression is formed, subjects are sometimes asked to give a separate rating to one of the items in the set. In this case, *meaning shift effects* are reliably obtained. A particular trait such as "cooperative" is evaluated more positively (e.g., similar to "selfless") when the other traits in the set are positive. It receives a less favorable interpretation (e.g., similar to "compliant") when the remaining information is negative.

The number of items in the information set can be large in some cases and small in others. Substantial *set size effects* have been obtained in impression formation research. The basic influence of set size is to polarize impressions. This occurs even when the average affective value of the information is held constant. As the number of positive items increases, impressions become more favorable; as the number of negative items increases, impressions become more unfavorable.

LIMITATIONS

Impression formation research is but one of several approaches to the study of how people come to understand other people. Its strength derives from the relatively precise way in which stimulus factors such as primacy-recency and set size can be studied. The use of personality traits as stimulus items and favorability ratings as the response permits a great deal of experimental control to be imposed. It provides a test tube environment, free from the complexities and impurities found in more naturalistic impression settings. However, this research domain also has clear limitations.

Most studies in this area have used traits exclusively as the stimulus information provided the subject. It is possible that the findings would be very different if other kinds of person information were used (e.g., behaviors, social affiliations, physical appearance, and demographic features). However, the little research that has been conducted with nontrait stimuli suggests that this problem may not be a major concern. Phenomena such as primacy effects and set size effects appear to occur even when other types of stimulus items are used.

In this research area, the subjects are usually forewarned that they are to provide an impression rating after seeing the trait set. Consequently, they are undoubtedly actively developing their impression responses during the time they encounter the information items. Thus there is little or no role for memory in this impression formation task. In contrast, the development of impressions (even first impressions) in our everyday social encounters necessarily involves memory processes. It is presently unclear what changes in the Gestalt and cognitive algebra formulations would be required to accommodate memory for previous information.

SUGGESTED READING

Anderson, N. H. (1981). *Foundations of information integration theory.* New York: Academic.

Ostrom, T. M. (1977). Between theory and within theory conflict in explaining context effects in impression formation. *Journal of Experimental Social Psychology, 13,* 492–503.

Schneider, D., Hastorf, A., & Ellsworth, P. (1979). *Person perception* (2nd ed.). Reading, MA: Addison-Wesley.

T. OSTROM
Ohio State University

ATTITUDES
SOCIAL COGNITION

IMPRINTING

First used by Konrad Lorenz (1965), the term "imprinting" designates the process of rapid development of social attachments by young animals toward their mothers. The social attachments, as exemplified by the following response of ducklings in which they follow their mother wherever she goes and whenever she moves, are directed and confined to stimuli with which the young have specific appropriate experience at an appropriate time. The exact stimulus object to which the birds respond in this way maintains its capability of evoking the adient response (attachment) through much of the young animals' life. The innate social responses through the process of imprinting become altered, so that the originally great diversity of objects capable of eliciting attachment becomes restricted to only the class or classes of objects encountered during the limited acquisition period.

Spaulding (1873/1954), the first to describe the phenomenon, showed that the attachment need not be restricted to the mother, although it normally is. He noted that as soon as newly hatched chickens could walk, they would follow any moving stimulus. This promiscuity of following could be observed in visually naive chicks only during the first few days. He placed small hoods over their heads as soon as they hatched and removed them at different intervals. For up to 3 days the chicks would run to Spaulding, but the chicks whose hoods were removed after 4 days fled in terror.

The strength of the attachment can be seen in one or more of the following tests: (a) *recognition at reunion,* in which, after separation, more imprinted birds return to the imprinting stimulus than do control chicks; (b) *choice,* in which experimental and control birds are presented with a training and a control stimulus; (c) *distress at separation;* (d) *run to mother,* in which somewhat dispersed chicks are exposed to a novel, frightening stimulus, whereupon the imprinted but not the control chicks are expected to retreat to the training stimulus; and (e) *work for reunion,* in which the birds must perform an arbitrary response such as a bar press to obtain access to the training stimulus.

Lorenz and others distinguished imprinting from ordinary learning because: (a) imprinting can take place only during a limited critical period; (b) once imprinting is accomplished, forgetting does not occur; (c) conventional rewards are not necessary for imprinting; (d) certain responses to the imprinted stimulus may not appear until late in life, long after the imprinting took place; (e) imprinting occurs more readily when trials follow each other quickly than when they are widely spaced, contrary to most associative-learning experience; and (f) painful stimuli strengthen imprinting, whereas punishment usually results in the avoidance of the associated stimulus.

The term "critical period" has been weakened somewhat into "sensitive period," for the all-or-nothing character of the former term does not stand up to fact. Instead, there seems to be a quantitative rise and fall in the ease or strength of imprinting. Moreover, additional experiences may interfere with imprinting: Communally reared chicks may imprint on one another, and this fraternal imprinting may inhibit the maternal. Also, if fear responses develop naturally at a certain age to potential social stimuli, the termination of the sensitive period may be abrupt.

The belief that imprinting is irreversible is no longer widely held. It has been shown that attachment can be transferred to new stimuli. In addition, a number of species do not direct their adult social attachments strictly to the parental figure or to its species; again, the species of its broad companions may dominate. This observation is rather general and is the rationale for having domestic fowl rear clutches of wild birds in wildlife refuges, the young of which eventually are released and, presumably, carry on a normal reproductive life. Perhaps one way of looking at the persistence of early attachments is to note that primacy may be more effective than recency in the formation of the association.

The fixed action patterns of species that are imprinted to unusual objects remain unchanged. A human-imprinted ring dove shows the typical courtship rituals that would normally be used in courting a member of the opposite sex.

Object imprinting may be sex-related. Females of many groups of closely related species are often similar, particularly if they are rather drab; males, in contrast, have rather conspicuous markings that can act as releasers. The similarity of the females (absence of releasers) implies ease in accepting other species as sexual partners. The female is dependent with respect to her sexual behavior on the key sign stimulus of the male of her species. Accordingly, she is unlikely to court males of other species, even though she may have been raised with them.

Although much of the research on imprinting has been done with birds, a few observations suggest that similar processes occur in mammals. Sheep, horses, and other hoofed animals can be imprinted to humans, if a person assumes the parental role shortly after birth. Dogs are known to form close attachments to persons who care for them between the fourth and the sixth week of life. The pattern of treatment, nurturant or punishing, seems to be of little importance.

In *A General Introduction to Psychoanalysis,* Freud emphasized the importance of early childhood in the development of attachments. If these attachments fail to develop during the sensitive period, the child's well-being may be permanently impaired. Separation studies by Spitz (1945) and others have provided evidence for such irreparable damage.

REFERENCES

Lorenz, K. Z. (1965). *Evolution and modification of behavior.* Chicago: University of Chicago Press.

Spaulding, D. A. (1954). Instinct with original observation on young animals. *Macmillan Magazine, 27,* 282–283. (Original work published 1853)

Spitz, R. A. (1945). Hospitalism: An inquiry into the genesis of psychiatric conditions in early childhood. In *Psychoanalytic studies of the child* (Vol. 1). New York: International Universities Press.

SUGGESTED READING

Harlow, H. F., & Harlow, M. K. (1962). Social deprivation in monkeys. *Scientific American, 207,* 137–146.

Hess, E. H. (1959). Imprinting: An effect of early experience. *Science, 130,* 133–141.

Sluckin, W. (1965). *Imprinting and early learning.* Chicago: Aldine.

A. J. RIOPELLE
Louisiana State University

ETHOLOGY
LEARNING THEORIES

INCEST

The term "incest" is broadly construed to refer to sexual behavior between individuals who are related in any fashion except directly by marriage. Beyond this consensus, definitions found in various state laws and those proposed by experts differ along two dimensions: specific behaviors involved and specific relations of participants.

Some definitions list only vaginal and anal coitus as behaviors involved in incest, while others include oral-genital behaviors and even fondling or mutual exhibition of the genitalia. These differences, especially among surveys and other research reports, make it difficult to estimate the incidence of various types of incest, however defined. Furthermore, any collation of data is bound to be attenuated by a significant failure to report on the part of victims—a tendency that incest shares with rape. For this reason, it has been suggested that brother-sister incest occurs far more often than father-daughter incest, which has been traditionally regarded as the most common form. A comparison of recent surveys suggests that if incest is broadly defined to include casual types of sexual contact and if a large unselected sample is surveyed, then sibling incest will be the most common with a reported incidence of 10 to 15%. However, intercourse or attempted intercourse will be reported in less than 2% of the cases. Examples of such survey reports are in Hunt, *Sexual Behavior in the 1970's,* and Finkelhor, "Sex among siblings: A survey of prevalence, variety and effects."

On the other hand, if the researcher seeks out individuals who have already reported incest, then the father-daughter form is most common. Proportionately, coitus appears to occur more often in the father-daughter dyads than among siblings. The perennial belief that incest occurs primarily in lower class and rural communities is not supported by recent data such as that of Finkelhor (1980) and Hunt (1974). These investigations suggest that incest is somewhat more likely to occur in upper- and middle-class communities. The fact that the lower-class offender is more likely to come in contact with law enforcement agencies has distorted the overall picture.

The impact of incest, especially its long-term effects, has been generally thought to be malignant. Masters, Johnson, and Kolodny et al. (1982) suggest that incest can lead to "drug abuse, prostitution, suicide attempts, and a host of other problems [including] a variety of sexual problems." Recent data indicate that the effect of incest is not that simple. For example, Nelson (1981) found that the long-term reaction was more likely to be untoward if the incest occurred prior to age 10 and might actually be benign if it occurred after age 13. Nelson also reported that a negative effect was more likely if coitus had occurred, as opposed to other, more superficial forms of sexual contact. Tsai, Feldman-Summers, and Edgar (1979) found that a malignant outcome was more likely when the incestuous relationship lasted for a number of years, as opposed to relationships of relatively short duration.

Gebhard, Gagnon, Pomeroy, and Christenson (1965) summarize the man who has incest with a prepubescent victim as one who is "rather ineffectual, nonaggressive, dependent . . . drinks heavily, works sporadically, and is preoccupied with sexual matters." Men whose incestuous partners were adolescents are described as "conservative, moralistic, restrained, religiously devout, traditional, and uneducated." However, the institutionalized sex offenders who made up Gebhard's sample very probably constitute only a select minority of the prevalent group. It is also likely that Gebhard's samples are overweighted with lower–socioeconomic class offenders.

Almost every society regards incest, defined as sexual intercourse between members of the nuclear family, as taboo. Every state in this country has a statute punishing incest. In those states that have recently recodified laws dealing with sexual behavior, the victim must be a minor. However, incest in which the victim is an adult is extremely rare.

REFERENCES

Finkelhor, D. (1980). Sex among siblings: A survey of prevalence, variety and effects. *Archives of Sexual Behavior, 9,* 171–194.

Gebhard, P. H., Gagnon, J., Pomeroy, W., & Christenson, C. (1965). *Sex offenders: An analysis of types.* New York: Harper & Row.

Hunt, M. (1974). *Sexual behavior in the 1970's.* Chicago: Playboy Press.

Masters, W. H., Johnson, V. E., & Kolodny, R. C. (1982). *Human sexuality.* Boston: Little, Brown.

Nelson, J. A. (1981). The impact of incest: Factors in self-evaluation. In L. L. Constantine & F. M. Martinson (Eds.), *Children and sex.* Boston: Little, Brown.

Tsai, M., Feldman-Summers, S., & Edgar, M. (1979). Childhood molestation: Differential impacts on psychosexual functioning. *Journal of Abnormal Psychology, 88,* 407–417.

SUGGESTED READING

Constantine, L. C., & Martinson, F. M. (Eds.). (1981). *Children and sex.* Boston: Little, Brown.

Lester, D. (1975). *Unusual sexual behavior: The standard deviations.* Springfield, IL: Thomas.

E. E. LEVITT
Indiana University School of Medicine

CHILD ABUSE
SEXUAL DEVIATIONS

INDIA, PSYCHOLOGY IN

Metaphysical speculation is the characteristic achievement of the Indian philosophical system, and thus such speculation forms the basis of Indian psychology. Since psychology and metaphysics are identified together in Indian thinking, it is difficult to select an appropriate name for Indian psychology from among the psychological schools of the West. There seems to be no word more suitable than *Atman* (soul) psychology (Raju, 1953), which emerged as a result of introspective meditation through scientific methods of observation and experiment.

The beginnings of the study of psychology in India are in the *Vedic* literature, which presents elaborate systematic expositions of personality as a whole. The *Upanisads,* particularly the major *Upanisads,* reveal profound speculative insights with regard to consciousness, mind, knowledge, will, fear, and sleep. They include the celebrated view of *kosas* (zones) of personality, the fourfold division of conscious state, and the threefold levels of normal personality among many others. The later growth of psychological principles and theories was based on these *Upanisadic* endeavors.

Seminal contributions have been made by the Gita, regarding human nature, personality integration, inborn qualities, the problem of division and conflict, ways to resolve conflict, and many other issues related to personality. The schools of Hindu philosophy are replete with insightful and intuitive psychological theories. Buddhism and Jainism represent a view of personality and methods for its growth into a particular form of perfection. Jainism is created with supplying what is perhaps the most exhaustive Indian analysis of sensation. It recognizes the quality of mind and body, upholding a theory closely resembling parallelism. The various schools of Yoga, which help to reach a high level of consciousness through the transformation of psychic organism to go beyond the limits of ordinary human experience, are well known. A creative contribution has been made by Sri Aurobindo toward the understanding of human personality through what is called the system of Integral Yoga. The Yogic schools, whether in combination with the philosophical system or as independent disciplines, are the best sources for a reconstruction of Indian psychology in modern form (Sen, 1951).

Indian psychology has tried to tackle most of the problems of mental life discussed in modern psychological literature in the West. The psychology of thinking has received the greatest attention, and some of the subtle distinctions drawn in Buddhism, Jainism, and Brahmanism still merit careful study. The psychology of feeling was comparatively less developed in philosophical literature, though this defect was partially compensated for in the aesthetic literature. The psychology of willing, however, was fairly well developed in the interest of morality and religion, which dominated every philosophical system of India. In the Ayurvedic (medical) literature, a description is found of the physiological system as then known, the tradition having come down from the times of the *Atharva-veda,* and this is repeated in the Tantra and later Yoga literature. Naturally it is in the medical literature that one also finds a description of the etiology, symptoms, and treatment of the various types of mental diseases, generally divided into the two major classifications of insanity (*unmada*) and epilepsy (*apasmara;* Raju, 1953). An elaborate account of the various psychological theories embedded in Indian philosophical systems, from the Vedas down to the medieval period is given in various sources (refer Gergen, Gulerce, Lock, & Misra, 1996). Recently, Paranjpe (1996) has dealt with some basic psychological concepts derived from the Indian intellectual tradition. Taking specifically the nature and states of consciousness, self-identity, self-realization, and the nature of human suffering, Paranjpe (1996) discusses how the Indian contributions parallel, contrast, contradict, and complement certain well-known themes of Western psychology.

PSYCHOLOGY IN CONTEMPORARY INDIA: EDUCATION AND TRAINING

In 1915, more than 30 years before Indian independence in 1947, the foundations of scientific psychology were laid in India with the establishment of Department of Psychology at Calcutta University, the first of its kind in the country. Subsequently, departments of psychology started functioning at the universities of Mysore and Aligarh in 1924 and 1932, respectively. In 1946, Patna University started a full-fledged department of experimental and applied psychology. Since 1947, scientific psychology in India has grown rapidly through various phases (D. Sinha, 1986), and one finds a steady rise in the number of universities and many governmental and autonomous institutions now taking a keen interest in teaching and research in psychology. Graduate training in psychology is provided by 67 universities. In addition, it is taught in nearly 1400 colleges (Dalal, 1996), and is accepted and received with enthusiasm and recognized as an independent and useful field of study, research, and training. For the Senior School Certificate Examination of the Central Board of Secondary Education, and also in the majority of the State Boards of Examination in India, it is offered as an elective subject.

In undergraduate as well as postgraduate training, the central role is played by the university departments of psychology. During the years 1975–1977, the total enrollment in the university departments and the affiliated colleges at the master's level was 7,369; at the doctoral level during these years, it was 592. Compulsory courses offered, according to rank order, at master's level in the majority of the universities are: Research Methods, Social/Experimental/Psychological Measurement, Abnormal Physiological Systems, and Theories of Psychology. As electives, the following courses in rank order are offered: Industrial/Organizational Behavior, Clinical/Educational/Counseling, Guidance, Personality, and Psychological Testing. However, some new courses such as Biopsychology, Behavioral Genetics, Cognitive Processes, Psychology of Disadvantaged Children, and Social Change have also been introduced.

The Curriculum Development Centers Program was taken up by the University Grants Commission in order to promote excellence in teaching at the undergraduate and postgraduate levels. The Curriculum Development Center in Psychology (CDCP) was set up in 1986 with the objective of the creation of a modern curriculum that ensures social relevance and effective utilization of human resources. The curriculum development appropriately kept in view the role it would play in the task of nation development. The CDCP found that the current structure as described above did not offer much freedom to students to take up study areas where their interest has sufficiently grown. It also indicated the lack of application of the existing syllabi. In addition, the fact that many of the contents were borrowed from the countries that export textbooks and journals to India made psychology an inappropriate subject and resulted in an identity crisis and also a crisis of relevance, termed as the "first crisis" in psychology in India (D. Sinha, 1997).

The Center (Report of the Curriculum Development Center in Psychology, 1989) recommended that several vocational courses, in addition to core courses, be offered at the undergraduate level in order to enhance the link between study and useful application. At the master's level, during the first year courses of core nature are recommended and during second year the scope is expanded for specialization. Keeping in view the need of the community and the relevance of psychology for meeting the challenge of national development, many vocational courses have been recommended. Information is not available about the implementation of these recommendations and what shape courses have taken very recently. However, with the change in economic policy of the government and also the rapid and continuous transformation of the Indian society, many universities are either considering or have already introduced new professional programs in clinical psychology, counseling, human resource development, community development, and so on. Courses in psychology leading to the MPhil as an intermediary research degree are also offered by many universities to strengthen the research foundation of those who register for doctoral programs.

Psychology courses in India lack interdisciplinary and multidisciplinary orientation and sensitivity to sociocultural nuances of behavior and human functioning; in the process they have remained largely academic with not much experiential exposure. As a result, "high quality", "bright male students" keep away from psychology courses, which has been characterized as the "second crisis" (D. Sinha, 1997). Psychology courses are more popular among female students and some psychology departments have only female students.

Most of the research in psychology in India is conducted within the university departments, many of which are strongly research-oriented and eclectic in their theoretical approach. The doctoral investigations relate to a variety of areas and have been found to vary widely with regard to standards. Other institutes and organizations, in addition to universities, feature psychological research and have contributed substantially to this area.

Some organizations, particularly the Indian Council of Social Science Research, sponsor several foundation courses in social science research methods, and also a few data-processing and survey research courses to upgrade the research foundation of workers.

PSYCHOLOGISTS, PSYCHOLOGICAL SOCIETIES, AND INFORMATION SOURCES

Currently India has the largest number of psychologists outside the West and is considered a "publication giant" among all developing countries (Gilgin & Gilgin, 1987). By the end of the 1980s the number of psychologists was estimated to be between 4,000 and 4,500, which seems to be an underestimate (J. B. P. Sinha, 1993). Most of the psychologists work in academic institutions, and there is clear evidence that psychology in India is overwhelmingly an urban discipline. The analysis of 1994 data indicates that the most popular areas of study with Indian psychologists are industrial and organizational psychology, followed by social psychology. The fields of testing, personality, and clinical and educational psychology also continue to be popular areas of study (Dalal, 1996). However, rural, health, and cross-cultural psychology are emerging as new areas of interest. J. B. P. Sinha (1993) notes the work of front runners whose contributions "are impressive compared to the contributions of psychologists in any developing country and many developed countries. . . . They appear even more impressive in the face of the odds that the Indian psychologists have to cope with" (p. 145). Indian psychologists are widely quoted and have received substantial international recognition and occupied prestigious positions in international professional bodies.

There are currently eight national and four regional psychological organizations. In 1922, the Indian Psychoanalytic Society was founded, and the Indian Psychological Association was formed in 1925 with the objective "to coordinate researches, to publish works, and to standardize the curricula of studies." In 1925, psychology was included in the Indian Science Congress as one of its sections. In the same year, the *Indian Journal of Psychology,* an official publication of the Indian Psychological Association, and the oldest such journal, made its appearance. Among other active organizations are the Indian Association of Clinical Psychologists and the Indian Academy of Applied Psychology. Active regional organizations include the Bihar Psychological Association, Madras Psychology Society, and the Bombay Psychological Association. Membership in these groups is not large; national organizations number perhaps 300 to 400 members. A new association— The National Academy of Psychology—was established in 1989 to promote professional activities in the area of psychology.

During the past 50 years, the number of journals published in psychology has increased considerably to a present total of nearly 50 (Dalal, 1996). Among those published regularly are the *Indian Journal of Applied Psychology, Journal of Psychological Researches, Journal of Indian Psychology, Journal of Education and Psychology, Indian Psychological Review, Indian Journal of Experimental Psychology, Journal of Indian Academy of Applied Psychology, Indian Journal of Clinical Psychology, the NIMHANS Journal* and *Psychological Studies.* Some journals are published in regional languages. There are also journals of interdisciplinary nature that publish papers relating to psychological research. A new journal of international status, *Psychology and Developing Societies,* has also been launched. Further, *Indian Psychological Abstracts and Reviews* provides a forum for psychologists to articulate their views on contemporary issues in psychology and related disciplines in India.

RESEARCH

There has been a rapid growth in the volume of psychological research after 1960 and such areas as personality, clinical, and social psychology were most popular with research workers. After analyzing 12,374 research publications during 1980–95, Raina and Srivastava (in press) reported that the highest percentage of published studies were related to clinical psychology (22%), followed by social psychology (19%), personality (13%), organizational behavior (12%), general (9%), and educational psychology (9%). The number of publications in areas such as experimental psychology (6%), research methods (5%), developmental (3%), and physiological psychology (2%) were smaller.

A relatively clear picture based on comprehensive coverage of the entire field of psychological research in India may be obtained from the four surveys sponsored by the Indian Council of Social Science Research. The focus of most of the research is quite narrow, resulting in its isolation and fragmentation regarding knowledge and application, and lack of linkage with other social sciences for mutual learning and growth. The trend has now shifted to meaningful interaction with other social sciences and to steps toward psychology's further advancement as a discipline and profession. This phenomenon is reflected in the second survey of psychology in India. Psychological theories and data are being interpreted in terms of social, anthropological, and life-historical factors. Psychological study of social, ecological, economic, and political issues has resulted in the emergence of new disciplines such as political processes and behavior, psychology of work, communication and influence process, social issues, and psychological intervention for social change. In the recent past, a rapidly accelerating interest in interdisciplinary work has emerged, and such specializations as medical psychology, bioclinical psychology, pediatric psychology, clinical psychophysiology, and neuropsychology have become popular. It is also accepted throughout the discipline that "we need to build up a base for progressive neuroscientific advances" (Ramamurthi, 1985, p. 47).

Earlier work on methodology and research technology has been mainly in the area of test construction, validation, and factor analysis, with a little work on methods. However, later analysis revealed that work has also been done on such diverse items as mathematical models of human behavior and theory and methods of attitude measurement, including the assessment of behavioral dispositions, scaling, psychophysics, and multivariate statistical techniques. Attempts at conceptualization, reconceptualization, and measurement of psychological concepts, together with efforts to build or reformulate a middle-range theoretical framework, have also been made (Mukherjee, 1979). There is a trend toward utilizing psychology for conceptual and intervention insights and making the subject socially relevant. A keen interest has been evidenced in cross-cultural studies and in studying the impact of sociocultural disparities and traditional social disabilities on various behaviors. India offers fascinating challenges to social scientists because of the interesting, complex, and multifaceted nature of Indian society.

A significant development is a release of *Psychology in India* (Pandey, 1988), the third survey, presented in a three-volume set and providing a comprehensive review of Indian research in psychology over the 1980s, reflecting the diversity of research interests and evaluating the extent to which psychology as a discipline has been responsive to the Indian sociocultural context and reality. These volumes have been divided thematically and provide a focused treatment in the areas of theoretical, conceptual, and methodological importance and empirical reality. Included in these critical reviews are analytical frameworks highlighting research achievements, lacunae, potentialities, alternatives, and policy implications (Pandey, 1988).

The first volume in the series is devoted to personality development (including socialization) and the evolution of higher mental processes, identity, stress, anxiety, and perceptual and cognitive processes (including cross-cultural studies on cognitive style). The second volume focuses on basic and applied psychology. The areas covered in this volume include social cognition and attitudes, social influence processes, manipulative social behavior, power and control mechanisms, development and change, intergroup relations and social tension, dynamics of rural development, and the social psychology of education. The third volume includes chapters on basic and applied social psychology and focuses primarily on job attitudes and organizational effectiveness, employment satisfaction and commitment, motivation, the implications of organizational effectiveness in the Indian development context, attitudes and beliefs about mental health, definitions and classifications of mental illness, and the significance of sociocultural factors in the management of mental illness.

Based on the contributions in these volumes, Pandey (1988)

suggests that some "creative directions had emerged and probably psychology is not strictly standing at the crossroads" (p. 354). However, Dalal (1996) does not share this optimism and comments that "psychological research in India has not taken any discernible direction so far" (p. 231). J. B. P. Sinha (1993) drew a distinction between the bulk and the cutting edge of psychological research. Not much has changed in the mass-produced bulk of the research, which continues to be replicative and imitative. However, as a consequence of the long debate, some interdisciplinary themes in psychological research are identifiable among the most innovative researchers.

Some indication of the major shifts in psychological research in India can be observed by perusal of the fourth survey entitled *Psychology in India Revisited: Development in the Discipline* (Pandey, in press) covering research from 1983 to 1992. It covers the development of indigenous concepts, methods, theories and cross-cultural research. Relating psychological research to the Indian sociocultural context has been a major goal of the surveys. Employing an integrative and analytical framework emphasizing major trends emerging in the thematic area, each chapter presents theoretical and applied issues. The chapters of the fourth survey are organized into three volumes. The first volume, subtitled "Physiological Foundation and Human Cognition," consists of chapters relating to animal behavior; physiological foundations of behavior; perceptual, learning and memory processes; intelligence and cognitive processes; and language and behavioral processes. The second volume, "Personality and Health Psychology," contains chapters on such topics as consciousness; child and adolescent development; personality, self and life events; gender issues; health psychology and mental health; illness, and therapy. The third volume, subtitled "Applied Social and Organizational Psychology," consists of chapters about attitudes; social cognition and justice; social values; psychological dimensions of poverty and deprivation; ethnic minority identity; environment and behavior; motivation leadership; and human performance. The last chapter, "Emerging Trends" by the editor, critically examines changes and shifts in research subjects as well as strengths and weaknesses of the discipline as we enter the twenty-first century.

Psychologists in India have shown concern about the kind of psychology that India needs as a nation in this new millennium. They have advocated a shift in the agenda of psychological research, which in turn would require radical changes in the goals of scientific inquiry. They have also pleaded for the meeting of the two sides of the Indian psychologist, both professional and personal, so that research issues spring from each psychologist's heart and psychological inquiry defines their own existence within this culture. The emergence of psychology as a cultural science appears to be a real possibility (Dalal, 1996).

INDIGENIZATION OF PSYCHOLOGY

There is a growing realization (D. Sinha, 1986) that unless a move toward indigenization is seriously made and studies are conducted where 'Indianness' is not missing, the discipline will continue to play a very limited role in our national life. Psychologists in India tend to "create their own world and priorities which do not overlap with the real world outside. They continue to live in two parallel worlds, while investing their creative energy in activities other than professional ones" (Dalal, 1996, p. 236). In this context, Mukherjee (1979) rightly observed that "Psychology has to go native if it has to be creative and relevant to society" (p. 93). Efforts are underway in this direction to generate data and develop psychological principles and theories appropriate to the particular sociocultural climate of India (Adair, Puhan, & Vohra, 1993; Dash & Jain, 1999). However, the progress of such attempts is slow.

The indigenous, or culturally-rooted, psychology (D. Sinha, 1996) is a reaction to decontextualized psychology and its uncritical dependence on the Western system for concepts, models and theories, and viewing non-Western cultures and psychological functioning through the lens of Western norms. In recent years, Indian psychologists are showing definite signs of self-confidence. Research problems, methodology, and conceptual frameworks are beginning to look more mature, spontaneous, and driven by the immediate, sociocultural concerns and contents, and hence, have become more relevant to Indian society (Dash & Jain, 1999). These efforts to offer alternative cultural concepts have taken various forms, including theoretical and methodological innovations in social psychology and clinical and organizational contexts. Fruitful interface between indigenous Indian thought and psychological discourse is found in the *Guru-Chela* paradigm of therapy; the nuturant task style of leadership; analysis of self and personality; the reconceptualization of achievement; analysis of the Indian psyche, emotions, and senses of justice and morality; the concepts of well-being, development, and values; detachment; and methods of organizational intervention (Gergen, et al., 1996).

In recent years Indian psychologists have concentrated on problems of rural development and agro-economic growth, poverty, and deprivation. Many Indian psychologists have emphasized the collective and contextual features against the individual and textual features that characterize Western society. They have accordingly highlighted the need for exploring alternative models of development and a change in disciplinary perspective. This change is from its focus on self-contained individualism to the notion of a socially embedded person; from the reductionist analysis to holistic description, from quantitative statistical treatment of data to more qualitative understanding; from universal principles to cultural specificity; from cognitivist orientation to a constructionist approach; from scientific objectivity to understanding through subjectivity. In adopting these focal changes within the discipline, the psychological concepts will possibly show a shift towards social relevance and cultural appropriateness. Though there is a move towards the development of indigenous psychology in India, the progress has been rather slow. Also, it is only the result of a small group of innovators who are struggling to outgrow the foreign framework (J. B. P. Sinha, 1993). Their limited achievements in various areas of psychology have been meticulously mapped by reviewers (Pandey, 1988; Raina & Srivastava, 2000; D. Sinha, 1986).

REFERENCES

Adair, J. G., Puhan, B. N., & Vohra, N. (1993). Indigenization of psychology: Empirical assessment of progress in Indian research. *International Journal of Psychology, 28,* 140–169.

Dalal, A. K. (1996). A science in search of its identity: Twentieth century psychology in India. *Indian Psychological Abstracts and Reviews, 3,* 201–243.

Dash, U. N., & Jain, U. (1999). *Perspectives on psychology and social development.* New Delhi: Concept Publishing Company.

Gergen, K. J., Gulerce, A., Lock, A., & Misra, G. (1996). Psychological science in cultural context. *American Psychologist, 51,* 406–503.

Gilgin, A. R., & Gilgin, C. K. (Eds.). (1987). *Psychology in world perspective: International handbook of psychology.* Westport, CT: Greenwood Press.

Mukherjee, B. N. (1979). Psychological theory and research methods. In U. Pareek (Ed.), *A survey of research in psychology.* Bombay: Popular Prakashan.

Pandey, J. (Ed.). (1988). *Psychology in India: The state-of-the-art* (3 vols.). New Delhi: Sage.

Pandey, J. (Ed.). (in press). *Psychology in India revisited: Development in the discipline.* New Delhi: Sage.

Paranjpe, A. C. (1996). Some basic psychological concepts from the intellectual tradition of India. *Psychology and Developing Societies, 8,* 7–27.

Raina, M. K., & Srivastava, A. K. (2000). *Indigenization of knowledge: The case of educational psychology in India.* New Delhi: National Council of Educational Research and Training (mimeographed).

Raina, M. K., & Srivastava, A. K. (in press). Educational psychology in India: Its present status and future concerns. *International Journal of Group Tensions.*

Raju, P. T. (1953). Indian psychology. In H. Bhattacharya (Ed.), *The cultural heritage of India.* Calcutta: Ramakrishna Mission Institute of Culture.

Ramamurthi, S. (1985). Trends in neurosciences. *NIMHANS Journal, 3,* 45–49.

Report of the curriculum development centre in psychology. (1989). New Delhi: University Grants Commission.

Sen, I. (1951). The standpoint of India psychology. *Indian Journal of Psychology, 26,* 89–90.

Sinha, D. (1986). *Psychology in the third world country: The Indian experience.* New Delhi: Sage.

Sinha, D. (1996). Culturally-rooted psychology in India: Dangers and developments. *Interamerican Journal of Psychology, 30,* 99–110.

Sinha, D. (1997). Second crisis in psychology. *Bulletin of the National Academy of Psychology (India), 1,* 1–3.

Sinha, J. B. P. (1993). The bulk and the front of psychology in India. *Psychology and Developing Societies, 5,* 135–150.

M. K. RAINA
*National Council of Educational Research and Training,
Sri Aurobindo Marg, New Delhi, India*

INDIVIDUALISM

In common usage, individualism is defined as leading one's life in one's own way without regard for others. Individualism may be separated from individuality, which is the sum of the qualities that set one person apart from others. To individualize is to distinguish a person as different from others, whereas to individuate is to make a person individual or distinct. Individualism is also distinct from autonomy, which is the ability to understand what others expect in any given situation and what one's values are, and to be free to choose how to behave based on either or both. While individuality and autonomy are important aspects of healthy psychological development and health, individualism is not.

Based on the theorizing of Deutsch (1962) and Johnson and Johnson (1989), individualism may be defined as believing and behaving as if one's efforts and goal attainments are unrelated to or independent from the efforts toward goal attainment of others. Individualism is usually contrasted with cooperativeness and competitiveness. Cooperativeness may be defined as believing and behaving as if one's efforts and goal attainments are positively related to the efforts and goal attainments of others, or as if one can achieve one's goals if, and only if, the others with whom one is cooperatively linked obtain their goals. Competitiveness may be defined as believing and behaving as if one's efforts and goal attainments are negatively related to the efforts and goal attainments of others, or as if one can achieve one's goals if, and only if, the others with whom one is competitively linked fail to achieve their goals.

There is considerable research comparing the relative effects of individualism, cooperativeness, and competitiveness. These reviews have primarily been conducted by Johnson and Johnson and their colleagues (Johnson & Johnson, 1989, 1999). Individualism, compared with cooperativeness, tends to be related to: (a) lower beliefs that one is liked, accepted, supported, and assisted by others; (b) less seeking of information from others, and utilizing it for one's own benefit; (c) intrinsic and continuing motivation, and greater orientation toward extrinsic rewards; (d) less emotional involvement in efforts to achieve one's goals; (e) lower achievement; (f) lower ability to take the cognitive and less healthy processes for deriving conclusions about one's self-worth; (g) lower psychological health, as reflected in greater psychological pathology, delinquency, emotional immaturity, social maladjustment, self-alienation, self-rejection, lack of social participation, basic distrust of other people, pessimism, and inability to resolve conflicts between self-perceptions and adverse information about oneself; and (h) less liking for others and more negative interpersonal relationships. There has been very little research comparing individualism and competitiveness.

If the direct evidence is not very favorable toward individualism, the writings in personality and clinical psychology are even less so. The solitary human who avoids relationships and coalitions with others is considered abnormal. Humans are basically interdependent beings, biologically and socially. Effective socialization brings with it an awareness that one cannot achieve one's life goals alone; one needs other people's help and resources. Psychological health requires a realization that one's goals and the goals of others, one's efforts and the efforts of others, and one's success and the success of many different people, are all related and interdependent. Accurately perceiving the interdependence between yourself and others involves an awareness of sharing a common fate (both you and your fellow collaborators will receive the same outcome), mutual causation (achieving your goals depends on both your own efforts and those of collaborators), a long-term time perspective, and the skills, information, competencies, and talents of other people as well as oneself. Individuals who are high on individualism do not have a high degree of such awareness. Individualism often brings with it the following: (a) feelings of alienation, loneliness, isolation, inferiority, worthlessness, depression, and defeat; (b) attitudes reflecting low self-esteem, an emphasis on short-term gratification, and the conviction that no one cares about oneself or one's capabilities; and (c) relationships characterized by impulsiveness, fragmentation, withdrawal, and insensitivity to one's own and other's needs.

Every person needs to establish a coherent and integrated identity that differentiates one as a unique individual separate and distinct from all others. Although the ability to act independently, autonomy, and individuality are all important aspects of developing an identity, individualism is not. Paradoxically, it is out of collaborative and supportive relationships that encourage individuality that a mature identity is formed. Self-awareness, self-understanding, differentiating oneself from others, the internalization of values and self-approval, and social sensitivity are all acquired through encouraging and cooperative relationships, not through isolation or leading one's life in one's own way without regard for others.

REFERENCES

Deutsch, M. (1962). Cooperation and trust: Some theoretical notes. In M. Jones (Ed.), *Nebraska symposium on motivation.* Lincoln, NE: University of Nebraska Press.

Johnson, D. W., & Johnson, R. (1989). *Cooperation and competition: Theory and research.* Edina, MN: Interaction.

Johnson, D. W., & Johnson, R. (1999). *Learning together and alone: Cooperative, competitive, and individualistic learning* (5th ed.). Boston: Allyn & Bacon.

D. W. JOHNSON
R. T. JOHNSON
University of Minnesota

AVOIDANT PERSONALITY
COOPERATION /COMPETITION
DEINDIVIDUATION
SOCIAL ISOLATION

INDUSTRIAL CONSULTANTS

An industrial or management consultant provides an organization an independent, advisory service based on professional knowledge and skills relevant to solving the organization's practical management problems. *External consultants* are not part of the organization to which the service is provided; *internal consultants* are typically part of a corporate or headquarters human resource development staff who may provide consulting assistance to other parts of the organization. External consultants are brought in ad hoc to provide help on a particular problem or set of problems on a contractual basis. Such a relationship may develop into a more stable one in which the consultant is on a retainer, either providing periodic visits or serving on an on-call basis.

Several aspects of this definition require explication. First and most important, external consulting is an independent service, characterized by the detachment of the consultant. Thus, the consultant comes to the client organization with a fresh perspective; an impartial, external point of view; and no commitment to the organization other than to be helpful. Such independence enables the consultant both to see and to recommend solutions that members of the organization either do not see or regard as imprudent to recommend.

Second, the external consultant has no direct authority to make any changes in the organization; thus the consultant's role is always advisory. Consultants use a variety of strategies to help organizations utilize their expertise (Steele, 1973). Some consultants are strong advocates for the changes they recommend; others arrange circumstances so that the clients regard the changes as their own ideas; while still others offer a final report with recommendations that the client may or may not implement. Regardless of which strategy the consultant uses, implementation always rests with the client. Most consultants recognize the need for client involvement in the earliest possible stages of the consultancy.

Third, consultation is built on the professional knowledge and skill of the consultant. A psychologist becomes an industrial consultant by developing a considerable awareness and understanding of a broad range of industrial management processes and problems. This knowledge is applied to identifying problems, ascertaining the relevant information that bears on the problem, analyzing and synthesizing this information, offering various solutions, and recommending how a solution might be chosen and implemented. In this context, consulting is not providing set or preprogrammed solutions to management problems; rather, it is working with the client to develop innovative but feasible solutions based on a thorough analysis of data.

In general there are two types of industrial consultants: expert and process. An *expert consultant* has an extremely high degree of competence in a subject area directly relevant to the problems faced by the client. Expert consultants might be knowledgeable about illumination requirements on the factory floor, compensation systems, equipment design, or morale studies. Expert consultants listen to the client's request for information, attempt to clarify the need, and then provide the information with suggestions for implementation.

A *process consultant* (Schein, 1969) typically is brought in to help diagnose problems in the human relations area. The client may be concerned with absenteeism, high turnover, overt conflict between subunits, lower productivity, or employee morale. The initial focus of a process consultant is on assessment and diagnosis—on the collection of data and on integrating these data into a coherent pattern. Once the client and consultant agree on the diagnosis, they make a joint effort to consider alternative solutions to

remedy the problem. The choice of solution is always the client's, as is the implementation, although the consultant is actually engaged in facilitating the client's solution. Argyris (1970) has characterized this kind of intervention as involving three steps by the client: (a) receiving valid information; (b) choosing a course of action; and (c) committing to that course of action.

Process consultation is advocated over expert consultation because the former should lead to double-loop learning (Argyris & Schön, 1978), while expert consultation results in single-loop learning. In the latter, the organization learns to solve the immediate problems with which it was confronted, whereas in double-loop learning it learns to solve not only the immediate problem but also future problems of a similar type. Process consultation leads to a general increase in the problem-solving capacity of the organization.

Process consultation is the primary strategy of organization development (OD). Organization development has been defined as a planned, organization-wide effort, managed from the top, to increase organizational effectiveness and health through planned interventions in the organization's processes by using behavioral science (Beckhard, 1969). Among the several strategies of OD are team building (Dyer, 1977), management of intergroup relationships (Burke, 1982), survey-guided development (Bowers & Franklin, 1977), transition meetings (Mitchell, 1976), confrontation meetings (Beckhard, 1967), and coaching.

The rapid and successful growth of organizational consultation augers well for the future of this systematic and systemic approach to a still developing field.

REFERENCES

Argyris, C., & Schön, D. A. (1978). *Organizational learning: A theory of action perspective.* Reading, MA: Addison-Wesley.

Beckhard, R. (1967). The confrontation meeting. *Harvard Business Review, 45,* 149–155.

Beckhard, R. (1969). *Organization development: Strategies and models.* Reading, MA: Addison-Wesley.

Bowers, D. G., & Franklin, J. L. (1977). *Survey-guided development I: Data-based organizational change.* San Diego, CA: University Associates.

Burke, W. W. (1982). *Organization development: Principles and practices.* Boston: Little, Brown.

Dyer, W. E. (1977). *Teambuilding: Issues and alternatives.* Reading, MA: Addison-Wesley.

Mitchell, M. D. (1976). The transition meeting: A technique when changing managers. *Harvard Business Review, 54*(3), 13–16, 182–186.

Schein, E. H. (1969). *Process consultation.* Reading, MA: Addison-Wesley.

Steele, F. I. (1973). *Physical setting and organization development.* Reading, MA: Addison-Wesley.

L. D. GOODSTEIN
Washington, DC

LEADERSHIP TRAINING
ORGANIZATIONAL DIAGNOSIS
WORK EFFICIENCY

INDUSTRIAL PSYCHOLOGY

The branch of psychology concerned with the scientific study of behavior in the workplace and the application of psychological knowledge to that setting is known as industrial psychology. The field stresses both knowledge generation (research) and the application of that knowledge (practice) to better meet the needs of employees and employers.

Industrial psychology represents the merging of two disciplines of psychology to address behaviors in the workplace. One discipline is that of individual differences. Psychologists well grounded in the understanding of human abilities bring this knowledge to the workplace and focus upon the match of job demands to individual skills and abilities. The second focus flows from social psychology. This focus, best expressed by Lewin, is concerned with the attitudes and behaviors of people in social settings encountered in the workplace.

SELECTION AND PLACEMENT

One of the most important concerns of industrial psychologists is the selection of individuals to fill the various work roles in an organization and the placement of hired employees into jobs to create a good match of employees to jobs. To accomplish the selection and placement tasks, the following procedures are used by industrial psychologists.

Job Analysis

A job analysis is the study of the job requirements. It first involves a description of the duties and responsibilities of the person who holds the job. In addition, the job analysis goes beyond the simple description of what must be done to suggest the human characteristics necessary to accomplish the job successfully. It is absolutely necessary that the nature of the job be understood before any attempt is made to select or place persons in the job. In addition to selection, job analyses are essential for developing compensation systems and guiding career development and training programs.

Personnel Assessment

Once the job characteristics have been assessed, it is necessary to assess the characteristics of individuals so as to match persons with jobs. The industrial psychologist must choose methods for assessing job-relevant individual characteristics that: (a) are appropriate for the characteristic being assessed; and (b) possess acceptable psychometric properties of reliability and validity. Since standardized tests of skills, abilities, aptitudes, and interests often provide the best means of accomplishing these two objectives, the industrial psychologist must have a thorough knowledge of the variety of standardized tests available as well as the construction and evaluation of such tests. Situational interviews, assessment centers, biographical data, and a variety of other standardized measures are used to measure individual differences. Finally, it is the professional, ethical, and legal responsibility of the industrial psychologist to develop assessment procedures that are reliable, valid, and do not discriminate unfairly against any group.

Criterion Development

Once employees are on the job, methods of assessing their effectiveness must be developed. This task includes the classical criterion problem that has received considerable attention from industrial psychologists. The development of criteria first involves identifying those job behaviors or outcomes relevant to effective job-role accomplishment, and then developing valid and reliable ways to assess the dimensions identified.

Validation

The final step in the selection and placement process is to evaluate the fit between individual characteristics used for selection and the effectiveness of the employees on the jobs. This complex process is referred to as validation or the validity study.

PERFORMANCE APPRAISAL

Judgments about the effectiveness of employees' job performances often must be based on subjective evaluations obtained from other individuals. Although these judgments can be made by any of a number of individuals, the task of judging employees' performances is usually performed by their immediate supervisors. These evaluations serve a wide variety of functions. Performance evaluations can be used as criteria for validating selection systems. They are also used for determining raises and promotions, evaluating training effectiveness, and counseling employees about their performance on the job or their long-term career goals. For the latter, subordinates, peers, and supervisors often provide feedback in order to provide an employee with information about how his work and interactions are seen from many perspectives.

The establishment of appraisal systems requires that rating scales and procedures for using them be developed so that the rater can provide ratings that are as unbiased and accurate as possible. To accomplish this, the industrial psychologist is faced with complex issues of scale construction and the development of policies for rating procedures. Major advances have been made in this area. One of the most important involves scaling critical job behaviors and describing them in the job incumbent's own words.

TRAINING

When employees or potential employees do not possess the knowledge, skills, or abilities needed to perform their jobs, it often is decided to obtain such knowledge and skills through training rather than through employee selection. Industrial psychologists are involved in all four of the major phases of training. The first phase is a *needs analysis* that considers the present and near-future demands of the jobs in the organization and then, in a very real sense, inventories the extent to which the workforce possesses the knowledge and skills that are and will be needed. This analysis considers not only the present employees, but also estimates the losses of personnel through retirement and other forms of turnover during the time period of interest. Once the needs analysis is complete, the industrial psychologist *plans the training programs* to meet these needs. During this second phase, he or she applies what is known about human learning and the knowledge available about training methods to best facilitate the development of the knowledge and skills needed.

The third phase of the training process is the actual *training.* Industrial psychologists frequently are involved with conducting training. The ability to deliver training over the Web to create relatively high fidelity simulations with computers, and other recent advances are rapidly changing the nature of training. Finally, the *effectiveness of the training* should be assessed. It is the responsibility of industrial psychologists to attempt to build into training programs ways to assess their effectiveness.

WORK MOTIVATION

The industrial psychologist deals with motivation at three different levels. First of all, he or she must have a thorough knowledge of human motivation in general. Here there is a need to be aware of current theory and thinking related to motivation regardless of the setting.

At a more work-related level, at least four general motivationally oriented processes are applied by the industrial psychologist. *Incentive systems* development involves the association of valued rewards with behaviors that the employer wants to encourage. To use incentives effectively requires a thorough knowledge of what is valued by employees and the likely behavioral effects of making valued outcomes contingent upon performance. In addition, one must be aware of the relative value of the incentives in the marketplace. *Goal-setting* involves the establishment of standards for performance and feedback with respect to those standards. Participation in *decision making* or autonomy is predicated on the assumption that employees desire to have more say in what goes on at work. Industrial psychologists often have attempted to build participation into managerial/leadership training, performance appraisal, and other processes in work settings. The success of these procedures is mixed, and to a large extent it depends on whether one is interested in increasing performance or employee satisfaction.

Finally, within the work place industrial psychologists attempt to influence the motivation of employees through *job design.* In this case the goal is to design jobs so that job incumbents will believe that their needs can be met best by behaving in a way that meets the organization's goals. The design of motivationally-focused systems is to tailor the general motivational strategies to the particular organization setting, its culture, and the people in it. To do this, some combination of the four motivational processes is typically used.

JOB SATISFACTION

A great deal of effort has been expended by industrial psychologists to assess work attitudes. In particular, there is considerable interest in measuring employees' satisfaction with their jobs. Much earlier work was motivated by the assumption that the more satisfied people were with their work, the more productive they would be. In the face of repeated failures to show that this was true, later work with job satisfaction has stressed the value of a satisfied work force as an end in itself. Also, information about satisfaction has a great deal of diagnostic potential for the organization. With it, the organization can often identify problem areas and then take action to alleviate these problems.

Job satisfaction measures are most useful when they are a part of a regularly scheduled attitude survey repeated over time in the same organization. Periodic surveys provide feedback to employees on a regular basis, spotting trends in changes in attitudes, and for training supervisors abut the feelings of the people who work for them. Such surveys are also frequently used to assess the reactions of customers.

JOB DESIGN

Although job design has been briefly mentioned under work motivation, more space needs to be devoted to it, because of its relevance to industrial psychologists from a broader perspective than motivation. In particular, jobs must be designed to fit the abilities of the individuals who hold the jobs, as well as their motivation. Therefore, industrial psychologists tend to take one of two general approaches to job design. One is a motivational approach: Recent motivational emphasis has been on changing jobs so that they allow job incumbents more control, autonomy, feedback, and opportunity for involvement in their work. This point of view underlies the area known as job enrichment. With the increasing use of teams in the work setting, job design is also being raised to a level above that of the individual to include coordination, cooperation, helping, and other interpersonal behaviors.

The other orientation toward job design concentrates on individual abilities and attempts to design tasks in jobs to match, as closely as possible, the abilities of the jobholders. This field is known as human factors engineering or ergonomics. Human factors engineering has been strongly influenced by the information-processing capabilities of the interface between people and computers, and also by the technological advances in robotics. As a result, the field of human factors engineering has become less a subset of industrial psychology than of applied experimental psychology and industrial engineering.

SUGGESTED READING

Dipboye, R. L., Smith, C. S., & Howell, W. C. (1994). *Understanding industrial and organizational psychology: An integrated approach.* New York: Harcourt Brace.

Dunnette, M. D., & Hough, L. M. (Eds.). (1990–1994). *Handbook of industrial and organizational psychology* (Vol. 1–4). Palo Alto, CA: Consulting Psychologists Press.

D. R. ILGEN
Michigan State University

JOB ANALYSIS
PERSONNEL EVALUATION

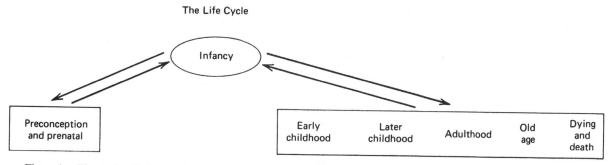

Figure 1.   The study of infancy takes on much greater significance when studied as an integral part of the entire life cycle.

INFANT DEVELOPMENT

Infant development is the study of infancy from the framework of the rest of the life course as illustrated in Figure 1. This broad approach investigates: (a) prenatal influences; (b) infant development as such; (c) infant influences on the rest of human life; and (d) the search for means for optimizing *both* infant and human development. Placing infancy in a life-span perspective converts it into an interdisciplinary field covering psychological, biological, and sociological developments in different cultures and over historical time.

DOES INFANT DEVELOPMENT INFLUENCE LATER LIFE?

The central assumption in life-span infancy is that some infant developments significantly alter the remainder of life. The search is for those critical developments whose influences extend beyond infancy into the entire human life course. Even though common sense tells us that there are many such early experiences, the scientific verification of such lifelong determinants is still being investigated and questioned. Students of personality, beginning with Sigmund Freud and others such as Adler (1927), present the major case for the occurrence of significant continuities from early to later life. In general, however, published observations have seriously questioned the psychoanalytic life-span predictions (Orlansky, 1949). Nevertheless, modern psychoanalysts such as Erikson (1963, 1980) and Bowlby (1980) continue to present long-term evidence that certain infant experiences such as love and trust have effects which significantly alter the course of human life. Psychohistorians such as De Mause (1974) provide historical support, dating back hundreds of years, that early infant experiences powerfully influence later adult personality and child-rearing practices.

The major evidence for diminishing the importance of early infant experiences in later life comes from research studies comparing the effects of early deprivation and later growth-promoting and enriching life experiences. These studies indicate that early deficits remain as defects only as long as the defective conditions continue to exert their detrimental influences on the growing person (Kagan, Kearsley, and Zelazo, 1978). Brim and Kagan (1980) conclude that "there are important growth changes across the life-span from birth until death, and the consequences of the events of early childhood are continually transformed by later experiences, making the course of human development more open than many have believed." There is, therefore, strong evidence that infant retardation

in some areas of development such as cognitive and motor development may be repaired by later sustained effort or change in life experiences.

On the other hand, although the influence of early infancy on later life may be modified, these findings do not mean that importance of infancy for later optimal development has been significantly diminished. It does indicate, however, the positive value that infant development has much more plasticity or openness to change than had previously been realized. The research by White (1971, 1975) provides evidence that infant development can: (a) withstand a considerable range of environmental diversities and still maintain its normal course of development; and (b) alter in positive ways the rate and the quality of development for both infancy and later childhood development. Finally, there is evidence for the wisdom of the old proverb "An ounce of prevention is worth a pound of cure," as documented by Albee and Joffe (1977) in their efforts to prevent the long-term consequences of early emotional difficulties, and by Kearsley and Siegal (1979) in their efforts to diagnose high risk and handicaps in infancy as early as possible. Instead of sustained and heroic remedial efforts such as in compensatory school programs as summarized by Zigler and Valentine (1979), early efforts toward optimizing the course of infant development may improve the quality of life during both infancy and the rest of the life span. Such efforts toward optimal infant development are seen in the area of mental health by Blehar (1980), and in the quality of home experiences as analyzed by White and his associates (1979, p. 183) in their final report of the Harvard Preschool Project:

After 20 years of research on the origins of human competence, we are convinced that much that shapes the final human product takes place during the first years of life. We are also convinced that the traditional failure of society to offer training and assistance to parents has several harmful consequences.

IMPROVEMENTS IN LIFE-SPAN RESEARCH

The acceptance of a life-span perspective has encouraged the expansion of infant influences into later development. New longitudinal research designs permit the more accurate tracking of those developmental processes suspected of influencing both early and later development, as detailed by Nesselroade and Baltes in *Longitudinal Research in the Study of Behavior and Development.*

Research is now also evaluating the effects on infant development of cultural and parental values as described by Leiderman, Tulkin, and Rosenfel (1977), and Field and associates (1981). It is now clear that: (a) development cannot be studied adequately in isolation of the context which gave it life; (b) that the environment alone cannot account for all the variability in human development; and (c) that a cross-cultural perspective is needed for avoiding the misconception that one's own culture offers the "natural and best way for rearing infants." Once it is appreciated that much of current development is a matter of social selection from a much broader horizon of human experiences, the awareness and potentialities for optimizing development across the entire course of life are greatly enhanced.

Life-span research is also increasingly studying multiple and interacting sets of related variables in a more realistic attempt to understand the enormous complexities of human development. Nearly all previous longitudinal research was limited to the effects of single variables such as infant activity level by Thomas and Chess (1977), attachment of infant to caretaker by Ainsworth and others (1978), and infant maturational schedules by Gesell, Ilg, and Ames (1974). While there is value in such specificity, it fails to do justice to the complex origins of human development and the changing nature of its environment. According to Lipsitt (1982), all attempts to explain human development with single-variable analysis have failed. Examples of increasingly multivariable approaches are *Infant and Environment* by Yarrow, Rubenstein, and Pedersen, and *The First Year of Life: Psychological and Medical Implications of Early Experience* by Shaffer and Dunn.

LIFE-SPAN INFANT INFLUENCES

During infancy the human being progresses from a primarily reflexive and predictable existence to a socially organized, emotionally expressive, and intellectually competent organism able to find solutions to simple problems prior to acting on them. In trying to understand these remarkably complex developmental feats, the life-span framework increases the odds for locating and cerebrating those processes that hold the greatest promise for optimizing all of human life.

Two prenatal factors most likely to have a life-span impact are genetic and nutritional influences. According to *Birth Defects*, published by the National Foundation-March of Dimes, one infant in 14 comes into this world with a significant mental or physical defect, and nearly half of all chronic childhood disabilities are caused by birth defects. In the United States alone about 250,000 babies are born with birth defects each year, and about 500,000 to 600,000 children and adults die each year as a result of such genetic disorders. The overall incidence of recognized genetic diseases is about 5% of all live births, and about 7–8% of the total U.S. population, according to the National Institute of General Medical Sciences. Furthermore, each human being carries five to eight recessive genes capable of producing genetic defects, in addition to possibly carrying late-appearing dominant genetic defects such as Huntington's chorea, Wilson's disease, and late-type diabetes mellitus. The detection, prevention, and (at times) treatment of potentially thousands of genetic defects is best accomplished through genetic counseling before, during, and after pregnancy.

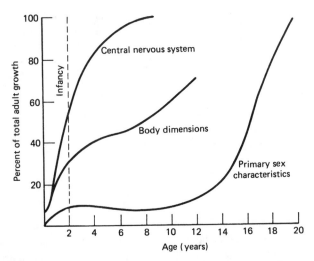

Figure 2. There are dramatic differences in developmental rates of the nervous system, body, and primary sexual characteristics. After J. A. Harris, *The Measurement of man* (Minneapolis: University of Minnesota Press, 1930).

Proper maternal nutrition before and after conception is the single most important factor in ensuring a healthy baby at birth and, possibly, throughout life itself. Montagu (1962) reports that every infant who was born dead or died within the first few days of life was born to a mother who had a poor diet during pregnancy, with the exception of those unborn suffering from major congenital defects. Furthermore, there is mounting evidence that the earlier the malnutrition, the more severe the resultant brain retardation and the more likely the occurrence of reduced intellectual functioning throughout the entire life span (Stein & Susser, 1976). The reason for lowered mental abilities becomes clear with the findings that prenatal malnutrition results in a 15–20% reduction in total brain cells found at birth (Brasel, 1974), and that 25% of the total adult number of brain cells are present at birth (Chase, 1976). Furthermore, if there is malnutrition both in the uterus and during the first six months after birth, there is an incredible 60% reduction in total brain cells. Since virtually all brain cell production ceases between 12 to 15 months of life, there is little time for the poorly developed brain to normalize (Winick, 1976).

The search for optimal infant development goes on in biological, social, and psychological domains. Figure 2 shows the general growth curves for the central nervous system, the body in general, and the primary sex organs. It indicates the need for giving a top priority to the development of the nervous system because: (a) it serves as the necessary foundation for learning, thinking, and emotional life; and (b) its development during infancy is extremely rapid. The rapidity of brain development within the nervous system is clearly depicted in Figure 3. Adult brain development is 25% by birth, 66% by six months, and 90–95% by age one year. In sum, optimal nutrition during pregnancy and infancy is a necessary but not sufficient condition for optimal brain development (optimal environmental stimulation is also needed), and optimal brain development is a necessary but not sufficient condition for optimal social and psychological development (optimal psychosocial interactions are also needed).

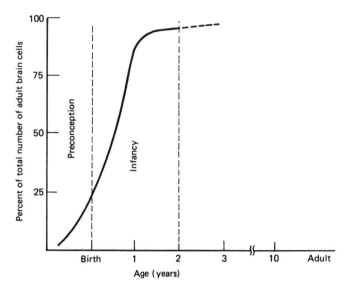

Figure 3. Human brain cell production is very rapid. Basically, all brain cell production ceases between 12 and 15 months. After P. T. Chase, from J. D. Lloyd-Still (Ed.), *Malnutrition and intellectual development* (Littleton, MA: Publishing Science Group, Inc., 1976).

Table 1. Normal Developmental Sequence[a]

Skills	Some Behavioral Landmarks and Expected Ages	
	Most Infants	All Infants
Mouthing objects	2 months	2 months
Visual inspection (momentary attention)	3 months	3 months
Hitting (having or striking object on a surface)	4 months	7 months
Shaking (side-to-side movements)	5 months	10 months
Examining (looking while manipulating)	6 months	10 months
Differentiated skills (pulling, turning, crumpling, depending on special characteristics of the objects)	7 months	10 months
Dropping and throwing	8–9 months	9–11 months
Naming	18 months	21 months

[a] From Užgiris and Hunt (1975).

As the search for optimal infant development and its effect on later life progresses, there may be need for reassurance that normal psychological development is being achieved. Table 1, based on the research of Užgiris and Hunt (1975), summarizes the expected developmental sequence of specific skills to be achieved by infants by specific ages. Note that there are numerous ways for deciding normal psychological development.

No one questions any longer the overwhelming power of experience on all domains of development: without stimulation, the infant becomes sick and dies; with stimulation, the infant survives and develops; with optimal stimulation (a process as yet not adequately defined), the infant flourishes (Hunt, 1979). Infant psychological development—the most researched of all domains—offers a rich reservoir of growth-enhancing developments which may form the much needed matrix for life-span development. One candidate for consideration as an essential lifelong development is the development of love from its symbiotic (parasitic) beginnings to self-love, to parent-child love, and to brotherly love (Fromm, 1956). Love is seen as the only way for developing caring and loving human beings (Otto, 1972), and as the translucent thread that runs through creation and life (Brenner, 1981).

Another possible lifelong development is the development of intelligence from reflex reactions to hypothetico-deductive logic, as analyzed by Piaget (1966) from infancy through adulthood. His work on the development of human abilities remains incomplete, because he believed that human intelligence existed beyond those forms being measured today. A third lifelong development might be that of perception, or how we pick up information from both within and without the body, from the newborn's readiness to respond to gross changes in taste, temperature, loudness, color hues, pressure, pain, odors, rhythms, movements, and location in space (Borstein & Kessen, 1979; Bower, 1979), through its development (Pick, 1979) and gradual decline beginning during the third decade of life (Pollack & Atkeson, 1978). A fourth lifelong development

might be social development from the first social recognition (a newborn, when held up and talked to, will gradually—with effort—establish human contact) as researched by Lamb and Sherrod (1981), to the socialization process which enables the infant to learn how to become human (Bandura, 1977).

Illustrative of optimal infant developmental models with possible life-span implications are those of Pikler (1971) on motor development, and White (1975) on the development of general competencies, particularly those of learning and thinking. Pikler's suggestions for learning motor skills, based on self-induced movements, are as follows:

1. *Nonrestrictive clothing and suitable space.* As soon as the infant can turn from back to side (about the third month), use a play area at least 50 by 50 inches; as soon as the baby can roll over, utilize a larger play area. When crawling and creeping make locomotion easy, use appropriately larger areas.

2. *Appropriate toys.* Beginning at age 8–10 weeks, toys are given which the infants can manipulate on their own without any assistance from adults.

3. *No direct help from caretakers.* Caretakers should not anticipate motor skills. Infants are not to be placed in expected positions even when anticipatory movements are demonstrated. Only the infant will decide when it is ready to assume a new position and practice and experiment with newly developing skills.

4. *Intensive infant-caretaker interactions.* The best moments for intensive relationships with infants are during bathing, feeding, and diapering. Caretakers, with no other adults present, focus completely on the infant's actions and reactions with no concern over time limits.

5. *Reciprocal treatment of toys.* After intensive interactions, the infant is placed in a play area with appropriate toys. Typically

Table 2.   Assisting Infant Competency[a]

Birth to 6 Weeks	6 Weeks to 3½ Months	3½ to 5½ Months	5½ to 8 Months	8 to 14 Months	14 to 24 Months
Place mobiles 12 in. from eyes and to extreme right 85% of the time; use colorful and contrasting colors; use oval designs with nose and eyes.	Place mirror about 7 in. from eyes; use crib devices which are semirigid and well constructed; place where they can be seen, hit, and manipulated.	Use cradel gym; respond to ongoing activities by talking and playing.	Increase interaction time, more talking and playing; read simple stories at bedtime; set up simple games such as hide-and-seek, stalking objects.	Create balance of attention among caretaker, infant, and objects; Ideal sequence: when infant is excited, provide immediate assistance, express a related idea or two, and leave.	A balance must be maintained among all developmental skills such as language, social, biological, and psychological development.

[a] Compiled from White (1975).

the infant will now "return the care and love it received" to its toys in a similar, intensive manner.

The infant competency model of White assumes that parenting is an enormously challenging—possibly the most difficult and rewarding—task in life. An ideal mother must understand the various developmental schedules and related sequences of developmental tasks, prepare and teach a tailored curriculum for the particular baby, design and construct a changing learning environment, and orchestrate effectively the changing needs and moods of the infant, herself, family, and society. Table 2 illustrates one infant-rearing practice for increasing specific skills from birth to the end of infancy. Such parents react to the infant only when doing so does not interfere with the infant's ongoing activities. They make infants feel that what the infants are doing is important and interesting to them also. They demonstrate and explain skills, but principally only at the infants' instigation. These parents are not "slaves" to their infants and do not devote the bulk of their time to rearing. They tend to be busy with other activities and provide help "on the fly of the moment" for periods lasting 10–30 seconds.

As described in *The Psychological Birth of the Human Infant* by Mahler, Pine, and Bergman, the process of separation and individuation takes about 30 months for the average infant. The baby gradually begins to "hatch" from mother's existence into an "I" and "not I" relationship. A loving caretaker gently pushes her infant away from her toward greater independence. This process of breaking away from old loves to find new ones has been described as necessary for adolescent separation from parental guidance (Bloom, 1980). Possibly this process of separation (saying "goodbye") and individuation (saying "hello") is the hub around which life begins, evolves, and ends.

REFERENCES

Adler, A. (1971/1927). *Practice and theory of individual psychology.* New York: Humanities Press.

Ainsworth, M. D., & Blehar, M. C. (1978). *Patterns of attachment: A psychological study of the strange situation.* Hillsdale, NJ: Erlbaum.

Albee, G. W., & Joffe, J. M. (1981/1977). *The primary prevention of psychopathology: The issues.* Hanover, NH: University Press of New England.

Bandura, A. (1977). *Social learning theory.* Englewood Cliffs, NJ: Prentice-Hall.

Blehar, M. (1980). *Development of mental health in infancy.* Washington, DC: U.S. Government Printing Office, NIMH [Monograph 3]. Science.

Bloom, M. V. (1980). *Adolescent parental separation.* New York: Gardner Press.

Bornstein, M. H., & Kessen, W. (1979). *Psychological development from infancy: Image to intention.* Hillsdale, NJ: Erlbaum.

Bower, T. G. R. (1979). *Human development.* San Francisco: Freeman.

Bowlby, J. (1980). *Attachment and loss:* Vol. 3. *Loss: Sadness and depression.* London: Hogarth. New York: Basic Books.

Brasel, J. A. (1974). Cellular changes in intrauterine malnutrition. In M. Winick (Ed.), *Nutrition and fetal development.* New York: Wiley.

Brenner, P. (1981). *Life is a shared creation.* Marina del Rey, CA: Devorss.

Brim, O. G., Jr., & Kagan, J. (Eds.). (1980). *Constancy and change in human development.* Cambridge, MA: Harvard University Press.

De Mause, L. (Ed.). (1974). *The history of childhood.* New York: Psychohistory Press.

Erikson, E. H. (1963/1950). *Childhood and society.* New York: Norton.

Erikson, E. H. (1980). *Identity and the life cycle.* New York: Norton.

Field, T. M., Sostek, A. M., Vietze, P., Leiderman, P. H. (Eds.). (1981). *Culture and early interactions.* Hillsdale, NJ: Erlbaum.

Fromm, E. (1956). *The art of loving.* New York: Harper.

Gesell, A., Ilg, F. L., & Ames, L. B. (1974). *Infant and child in the culture of today.* New York: Harper & Row.

Harris, J. A., et al. (1930). *The measurement of man.* Minneapolis, MN: University of Minnesota Press.

Hunt, J. M. (1979). Psychological development: Early experience. *Review of Psychology, 30,* 103–143.

Kagan, J., Kearsley, R., & Zelaso, P. R. (1978). *Infancy: Its place in human development.* Cambridge, MA: Harvard University Press.

Kearsley, R. B., & Siegel, I. E. (1979). *Infant at risk: Assessment of cognitive functioning.* Hillsdale, NJ: Erlbaum.

Lamb, M. E., & Sherrod, L. R. (Eds.). (1981). *Infant social cognition.* Hillsdale, NJ: Erlbaum.

Leiderman, P. H., Tulkin, S. R., & Rosenfeld, A. (1977). *Culture and infancy: Variations in the human experience.* New York: Academic.

Lipsitt, L. P. (1982). Infancy and life-span development. *Human Development, 25,* 41–48.

Mahler, M. S., Pine, F., & Bergman, A. (1975). *The psychological birth of the human infant: Symbiosis and individuation.* New York: Basic Books.

Montagu, A. (1962). *Prenatal influences.* Springfield, IL: Thomas.

Nesselroade, J. R., & Baltes, P. B. (Eds.). (1979). *Longitudinal research in the study of behavior and development.* New York: Academic.

Orlansky, H. (1949). Infant care and personality. *Psychological Review, 46,* 1–48.

Otto, H. A. (Ed.). (1972). *Love today: A new exploration.* New York: Association Press.

Piaget, J. (1966/1952/1936). *Origins of intelligence.* New York: International Universities Press.

Pick, A. D. (1979). Listening to melodies: Perceiving events. In A. D. Pick (Ed.), *Perception and its development: A tribute to Eleanor J. Gibson.* Hillsdale, NJ: Erlbaum.

Pollack, R. H., & Atkeson, B. M. (1978). A life-span approach to perceptual development. In P. B. Baltes (Ed.), *Life-span development and behavior* (Vol. 1). New York: Academic.

Shaffer, D., & Dunn, J. (Eds.). (1979). *The first year of life. Psychological and medical implications of early experience.* New York: Wiley.

Stein, Z., & Susser, M. (1976). Prenatal nutrition and mental competence. In J. D. Lloyd-Still (Ed.), *Malnutrition and intellectual development.* Littleton, MA: Publishing Science Group.

Thomas, A., & Chess, S. (1977). *Temperament and development.* New York: Brunner/Mazel.

Užgiris, I. C., & Hunt, J. McV. (1975). *Assessment in infancy: Ordinal scale of psychological development.* Chicago: University of Chicago Press.

White, B. L. (1971). *Human infants: Experience and psychological development.* Englewood Cliffs, NJ: Prentice-Hall.

White, B. L. (1975). *The first three years of life.* Englewood Cliffs, NJ: Prentice-Hall.

White, B. L., Kaban, B. T., & Attannucci, J. S. (1979). *The origins of human competence.* Lexington, MA: Heath.

Yarrow, L. J., Rubenstein, J. L., & Pederson, F. A. (1975). *Infant and environment: Early cognitive and motivational development.* Washington, DC: Hemisphere.

Zigler, E., & Valentine, J. (Eds.). (1979). *Project Head Start: A legacy of the war on poverty.* New York: Free Press.

SUGGESTED READING

Clarke, A. M., & Clarke, A. D. B. (1976). *Early experience: Myth and evidence.* New York: Free Press.

Freud, S. (1964). *The complete psychological works of Sigmund Freud* (Vols. 1–24). London: Hogarth.

Piaget, J., & Inhelder, B. (1969). *The psychology of the child.* New York: Basic Books.

Schaffer, H. R. (1977). *Mothering.* Cambridge, MA: Harvard University Press.

J. O. Lugo

EARLY CHILDHOOD DEVELOPMENT

INFANT PLAY BEHAVIOR

Research in the 1930s on social participation in young children revealed that play activities become increasingly social from the first few months of age through early childhood. Parten's classic study (1932) of preschoolers between 2 and 5 years of age led to the traditionally held view that social interaction develops through a sequence of stages. In the earliest stage, children show relatively little interaction when among peers, and their play is chiefly *solitary.* The next stage, *parallel* play, involves more socialized activity, since children play beside one another with similar materials, but do not interact substantially. After children reach 3 years of age, the most advanced stages of social participation begin to dominate. In *associative* play there is some sharing of materials and interaction, but play activities are not coordinated, while in *cooperative* play children act together in tasks that involve shared goals and rules.

A 30-year hiatus in research on early play development left the impression that although infants show some social interest by glancing, smiling, or vocalizing toward age mates, their predominant orientation when placed together is nonsocial. But as Mueller and Vandell have described in "Infant-infant interaction," a post-1970 resurgence of research attention to infant-infant encounters has revealed infants to be far more interested in and competent at social interaction with age mates than the traditional view describes—within obvious motor, cognitive, and linguistic limits, of course. It has also been discovered that children's social interactions become increasingly frequent and complex throughout the first 2 years. The present discussion focuses on the development of infant and toddler play between the approximate ages of 6 months and 3 years.

When studied in a social situation with age mates and/or adults (usually the mother, who is instructed not to initiate interaction), infants and toddlers engage in substantial amounts of nonsocial activity (solitary play and irrelevant behaviors) and parallel play, which may be regarded as marginally social. Although the occurrence of nonsocial activity does not decline appreciably during the second and third years, the incidence of social play increases and becomes the most frequent type of activity by about 24 months of age (Eckerman, Whatley, & Kutz, 1975; Sarafino, 1982b). Recent research has led to a reinterpretation of the role of nonsocial and marginally social behavior in children's play (Bakeman & Brownlee, 1980; Rubin, Maioni, & Hornung, 1976; Sarafino, 1982b). The results of these studies suggest that: (a) social participation develops gradually, beginning in infancy, and does not show a stage-wise progression in which play shifts with age from being chiefly solitary to mainly parallel and then to social; (b) parallel play functions in the stream of children's activities as a bridge from nonsocial to social behavior; and (c) after the age of 18 months or so, nonsocial behavior does not necessarily reflect an immature level of play in normal children.

DEVELOPMENTAL CHANGES IN THE CONTENT OF SOCIAL PLAY

Even in the first few months after birth, infants show an interest in age mates (Mueller & Vandell, 1979). When placed close together, infants gaze at—often for extended periods—and touch the pair mate. But truly social intent and interaction between peers does not seem to emerge until about 6 months when, for example, they smile at one another and in response to the other's vocalizations. Seven-month-olds approach and follow peers once they are able to locomote, and those aged 9 to 12 months show offer-and-take social exchanges and even game playing, such as peek-a-boo. When infants are between 6 and 12 months of age, most peer-peer interactions are simply brief, 2-unit sequences that end when the recipient of a socially directed behavior reacts with a social behavior; but their interchanges also include a substantial minority of sequences involving 3 or more units (Vandell, Wilson, & Buchanan, 1980).

During the second and third years, the content of children's play progressively shows more joint use of play materials, more conversation, and less orientation toward simply offering or taking possession of toys (Holmberg, 1980). Attempts have been made to evaluate infant and toddler social behavior for antisocial content (e.g., fighting, struggling over toys) and prosocial content (e.g., sharing, smiling); some have revealed high levels of agonistic interactions among infant peers that decreased with age, while others found very little antisocial behavior. Two methodological differences may be responsible for these contradictory findings: Higher levels of antisocial activity are found when children are observed (a) in play groups rather than dyads, and (b) unobtrusively (as via videotapes) rather than overtly, with adult monitors obviously watching and recording interactions (Mueller & Vandell, 1979; Sarafino, 1982b).

Social interchanges become increasingly complex in the second and third years. Not only do the sequences of behavior become more sustained, involving a greater number of units or turns taken per interchange, but each social act becomes more complicated by coordinating two or more behavioral elements, such as when a toddler simultaneously smiles, vocalizes, and waves at a peer (Holmberg, 1980; Mueller & Brenner, 1977). Studies with children after the second year of life have shown that, as their cognitive abilities improve, their play activities become increasingly complex, ab-

stract, and rule-based (Johnson, 1976; Parten, 1932; Rubin & Maioni, 1975).

FACTORS IN PLAY DEVELOPMENT

Research has identified several influential factors in infant and toddler social play.

Toys and Other Objects

The role of objects in social play seems to change with development. Studies with infants between 6 and 14 months have found that peer interaction does not depend on, but may be reduced by, the presence of toys (Jacobson, 1981; Vandell et al., 1980). In the second year, however, toys appear to promote interaction (Mueller & Vandell, 1979).

Peer-Peer Familiarity

Unfamiliar peers attract a considerable amount of social attention, particularly in infancy (Jacobson, 1981). But familiarity appears to affect the specific social activities that occur among infant peers–familiar infants are more likely than unfamiliar infants to seek close proximity, touch one another, and show positive rather than negative affect, such as smiling or laughing (Mueller & Vandell, 1979). Social participation by 3-year-olds also manifests an effect of familiarity, such that familiar peers show more associative and cooperative play and less onlooker behavior (watching but not interacting) than do unfamiliar peers (Doyle, Connolly, & Rivest, 1980).

Social Experience

Most American infants receive very little opportunity for social contact with peers, but when they do—even just for a few hours per week—their social competence is enhanced (Jacobson, 1981; Mueller & Vandell, 1979). In a review of studies comparing the social behavior of preschool children in day care versus age mates who were home-reared, Belsky and Steinberg (1978) reported that day-care children exhibit more interaction when placed with peers. Vlietstra (1981) compared the behavior of children who attended half-day versus full-day preschool and found that the full-day children showed more positive social interaction with peers.

Individual Differences

Substantial differences have been observed between individuals in their social activity with infant and toddler peers (Mueller & Vandell, 1979). Some infants tend to be more socially active than others, and these individual differences tend to persist into toddlerhood. However, children under 3 years of age generally show no gender differences in social activity (Eckerman et al., 1975; Holmberg, 1980; Vandell et al., 1980).

Parents and Teachers

When infants and toddlers are given the choice of interacting with a peer or their own mother in a free play situation, the children tend to direct more social attention toward the peer (Mueller & Vandell, 1979). Eckerman and colleagues (1975) found that in infancy the social acts toward the peer tend to be distal behaviors, such as looking or vocalizing. Then, during the second year of life, activities with peers increasingly involve play materials, while contact with the mother, by proximity seeking and touching, declines.

In day-care settings, teacher-child and child-child interactions occur frequently. Holmberg (1980) found that infants engage in far more interactions with teachers than peers, chiefly because the teachers do most of the initiating. The frequency of child-to-teacher and child-to-peer initiations increases during the second and third years of life, when peers show substantial increases in their joint use of play materials and their conversations. The number of interactions among peers equals the number involving teachers by about 3 years of age.

REFERENCES

Bakeman, R., & Brownlee, J. R. (1980). The strategic use of parallel play: A sequential analysis. *Child Development, 51,* 873–878.

Belsky, J., & Steinberg, L. D. (1978). The effects of day care: A critical review. *Child Development, 49,* 929–949.

Doyle, A., Connolly, J., & Rivest, L. (1980). The effect of playmate familiarity on the social interactions of young children. *Child Development, 51,* 217–223.

Eckerman, C. O., Whatley, J. L., & Kutz, S. L. (1975). Growth of social play with peers during the second year of life. *Developmental Psychology, 11,* 42–49.

Holmberg, M. C. (1980). The development of social interchange patterns from 12 to 42 months. *Child Development, 51,* 448–456.

Jacobson, J. L. (1981). The role of inanimate objects in early peer interaction. *Child Development, 52,* 618–626.

Johnson, J. E. (1976). Relations of divergent thinking and intelligence test scores with social and nonsocial make-believe play of preschool children. *Child Development, 47,* 1200–1203.

Mueller, E., & Brenner, J. (1977). The origins of social skills and interaction among playgroup toddlers. *Child Development, 48,* 854–861.

Mueller, E., & Vandell, D. (1979). Infant-infant interaction. In J. D. Osofsky (Ed.), *Handbook of infant development.* New York: Wiley.

Parten, M. B. (1932). Social participation among pre-school children. *Journal of Abnormal and Social Psychology, 27,* 243–269.

Rubin, K. H., & Maioni, T. L. (1975). Play preference and its relationship to egocentrism, popularity, and classification skills. *Merrill-Palmer Quarterly, 21,* 171–179.

Rubin, K. H., Maioni, T. L., & Hornung, M. (1976). Free play behaviors in middle- and lower-class preschoolers: Parten and Piaget revisited. *Child Development, 47,* 414–419.

Sarafino, E. P. (1982b). Peer-peer interaction among infants and toddlers with extensive day-care experience. Submitted for publication.

Vandell, D. L., Wilson, K. S., & Buchanan, N. R. (1980). Peer interaction in the first year of life: An examination of its structure, content, and sensitivity to toys. *Child Development, 51,* 481–488.

Vlietstra, A. G. (1981). Full versus half-day preschool attendance: Effects in young children as assessed by teacher ratings and behavioral observations. *Child Development, 52,* 603–610.

E. P. SARAFINO
The College of New Jersey

INFANT DEVELOPMENT
INFANT SOCIALIZATION

INFANT SOCIALIZATION

Don't you know that the beginning is the most important part of every work and that this is especially so with anything young and tender? For at that stage it's most plastic, and each thing assimilates itself to the model whose stamp anyone wishes to give it. (Socrates, in Plato's *Republic*)

Throughout recorded history mankind has been concerned with the rearing of the preverbal child. This is a time of high mortality, and those systems of infant care prevail that function best to provide survival for this vulnerable member of the species.

The term "infant", meaning "without language" in Latin, generally includes children from birth to 2 or 2½ years. Socialization is a more difficult concept to define succinctly, since it can be construed to cover a wide range of behavior. Socialization is the process by which the individual becomes a member of the family, culture, and society—a process that begins at birth and continues throughout the life cycle, involving a complex of formal and informal institutions. During infancy the baby's most immediate contacts translate and mediate the strictures of the society.

The infant as a particular object of socialization is important for several reasons. During the life span the first 18 months of life is the period of most rapid growth. Accordingly, environmental insults such as malnutrition and physical or emotional abuse are thought to have a more deleterious effect on the developing child than later in life, while according to many authorities, environmental enrichment during infancy may have equally long-lasting effects. Since at birth the infant has no prior experience with culture, one may attempt to assess the relative contribution of the environment to development. Many students have pursued the study of infant socialization in an attempt to tease out from the complex interdigitation of heredity and environment the relative contribution of each to the developing organism.

There is an unquestioned assumption that the experience of early life has import for the later development of the child and character of the adult. In the most extreme form there is the widely held belief that if we knew all the salient features of the optimal environment for the infant and young child we could, as social engineers, perfect society. To understand how an infant becomes a member of the society into which it was born, cultural anthropologists, sociologists, psychiatrists, and social, developmental, and cultural psychologists have all observed and made systematic studies of the process of socialization. Philosophers have examined the infant's growth, developed theories of epistemology, and postulated the becoming of mind, self, and society (Piaget, 1952; Mead, 1934).

Notions about the basic nature of the infant are implicit in all studies of socialization. The infant has frequently been portrayed as an asocial barbarian at birth who needs to be civilized and has been described as satanic, needing to have the devil exorcised. Aristotle and Locke attributed to the infant a tabula rasa on which the influence of environment is imprinted. More recently the infant has been characterized as being born with specific social attributes and is conceived as an active participant in the socialization process.

BACKGROUND

Research in socialization was spearheaded by social anthropologists interested in the relationship between culture and personality. In the early 1930s, under the aegis of Edward Sapir and John Dollard, a group of scholars from various disciplines began to focus on child rearing as a crucial element in the understanding of cultural transmission. A major impetus came with the publication of Freud's *Totem and Taboo,* and psychoanalysis joined hands with cultural anthropology.

Since the cornerstone of psychoanalytic theory rests on the outcome of the environmental mediation between the asocial drives of the infant and the demands of society, how an infant was fed, weaned, and toilet trained became critical issues for study. Psychologists added their brand of behaviorism, and a complex network of cross-cultural studies of socialization was launched.

Psychohistory, ecology, and ethology have been added to the list of diverse disciplines that contribute to understanding the developing infant. However, no matter what the discipline or procedure employed to collect data, the infant's accomplishments remain invariant, as do the basic cultural provisions made for the infant's survival.

Within the normal limits of any culture, given that the infant is healthy, socialization of the infant will not alter major transitions which occur in its growth toward becoming a fully functioning member of society. The infant will master the forces of gravity, stand upright, and free the hands for more refined activity. It will separate from the environment and develop a concept of self, gender, and permanence in that environment. It will form attachments and will acquire the language of its culture.

All cultures tend to the basic needs of the infant, since all infants are helpless at birth and cannot survive without nurturance. The infant will be fed, sheltered from lethal effects of the environment, and weaned from bottle or breast. It will learn to regulate excretory functions and begin to obey the rules of the culture. All cultures have prescriptions and proscriptions for the care and feeding of infants. According to Mead (National Film Board of Canada, 1959), any infant will become a member of the culture in which it is reared.

To simplify the complex concatenation of this rapidly growing organism within an ecological niche that in turn is in a constant state of flux, some obvious variables constrain the outcome of the socialization. The metamorphosis of the infant, and its gender and language provide the agents of its culture with the basic ingredients of socialization. These agents include the family, the father, the mother, siblings and peers, institutions, and of course the infant itself.

INVARIANT INFANT CHARACTERISTICS

Gender

One of the most salient characteristics determining the socialization of the infant in any culture is sex. From the moment of birth this will influence how it is treated by others, impose basic behavioral differences, identify its self-concept, and later determine its role . As early as one year, however, it is impossible to determine the relative contributions of socialization to the differences between the sexes.

At birth, males are on the average heavier and larger than females, and from age one have less subcutaneous fat than the female child. The male is more vulnerable to insult throughout life, and in the first month after birth, 25% more males than females die. As early as the second year, males engage in more rough-and-tumble play than do females. There is some indication that the female newborn is more sensitive to tactile stimuli than the male. There is also some indication that the female infant vocalizes more to her mother than does her male counterpart, and strong evidence that she acquires language earlier than the male infant. However, according to Maccoby and Jacklin (1974), there is no clear-cut evidence that mothers provide more verbal stimulation to their daughters than to their sons.

The foundations for socialization of sex-typed behavior are firmly entrenched even before birth. It is a common finding in the United States, and other countries as well, that male infants are preferred to female, particularly if a firstborn. From the moment of birth the sex of the infant will determine, in large measure, how he or she is handled. Adult males engage in rougher play with all infants than do females, and all adults are less restrained in their play with baby boys than with baby girls. Mothers are more concerned with the physical safety of their infant daughters than with that of their sons, and both parents encourage more gross motor activity in the male infant. Recent studies demonstrate clearly that in this culture, at least, we begin early to differentiate appropriate behavior on the basis of gender. In several studies adults were asked to play with infants and were told the sex of the child according to name and dress. All adults handed the nominal female infants dolls and soft toys, while the boys were given balls and blocks. Overall, the adult male behaves in a more stereotypic way toward infants, depending on the sex of the child, while the adult female's behavior is similar in most aspects toward both male and female infants.

One's gender identity is inseparable from one's self-concept. Money (1972) postulates that this identity is acquired between 2 and 3 years of age and that any attempt to alter this identity after this time will meet with resistance and result in psychological stress. By the age of 2½, infants know their own sex quite clearly and discriminate between male and female adults as well as peers.

Differential treatment of the infant based on gender may be more prevalent in this culture than in others. Barry and Paxson (1971) report few sex differences, and the coding system they developed does not include behavior that is sex-typed per se. The most frequent finding was that fathers spent more time with a son than with a daughter. Other cultures have well-developed sex roles and children are initiated into these roles when young. The nonreporting of this differential socialization in most descriptions of infancy in other cultures may be a function of the selection of behaviors reported.

Development

One obvious aspect of the socialization of the infant which differs from the older child and young adult is a rapidly changing behavior. Socially, emotionally, cognitively, structurally, and in motor skills the older toddler barely resembles the newborn. This rapidly changing organism presents the society of elders with a constant demand to adapt to its metamorphosis.

Within culture and between cultures temperamental differences between infants exist at birth. Newborns arrive with a set of preprogrammed reflexes, which during the course of the first year remain as the foundation for intentional skills such as holding and releasing, sitting, walking, smiling, and talking. These motor skills are considered to be specific, hereditary equipment, but any given culture imposes different restraints on their evolution in the newborn.

Large numbers of infants are swaddled, some infants are taught to sit, others are never allowed to crawl. In some cultures the infant is covered with a blanket and kept in a dark room for the first 3 months. Yet despite all these disparate practices the infant emerges from infancy as a competent, accomplished child, ready to sally forth into the next stage.

Language

Language is so embedded in culture that becoming a member of a language community is tantamount to socialization, but for the infant such socialization also involves the precursors of language. Data indicate that the infant is an active participant in its linguistic environment from birth. The infant demonstrates a fine ability to discriminate between language sounds. Condon and Sander (1974) have demonstrated that the newborn moves in rhythm in relation to the language sounds in the environment, but does not adjust in the same manner to nonlanguage sounds. They refer to this as one example of the earliest display of the infant's participation in cultural entrainment, long before becoming an active member of the language community.

Language involves a sound system, and the newborn infant comes into the world elegantly equipped to produce arresting noises. The infant's first communication, reflexive in nature, is the cry. The cry is universally aversive; adults learn quickly to facilitate the cessation of this aversive stimulus. According to Mead (1934), this is very basic to socialization, since the adult gives meaning to the infant's cry. The next step in the development of meaning is that crying and intonation become instrumental rather than reflexive.

In addition to the phonological aspects of language, language includes a system of semiotics as well as syntax. Semiotics refers to that aspect of language which conveys meaning to the sound system; syntax refers to the principles of combining words in grammatical sentences. The infant at first displays idiosyncratic and personalistic speech. Its speech must then become socialized,

as do other aspects of its behavior during the course of development.

Stern (1974) attests to the subtle communication between mother and infant. There appears to be an understanding of communication between the two. Mother and infant each respond to the other's gesture, and at this level the responding mother imparts meaning to the infant's gesture. At this early stage Mead (1934) does not impute intention to the baby. Mead contends that it is the other who gives the action meaning. It is the partial completion of acts as well as the results of these acts that form the basis of the mind, characteristic of the level of communication. This final level of activity is when both share in the understanding of the act. This knowledge is sophisticated, and the infant begins to reveal the nascent understanding of itself in relation to the environment; then the infant becomes unembedded from the environment. Language is a major vehicle through which the actor becomes aware of how significantly he or she is viewed by others and provides a basis for individuation, a cornerstone of socialization.

The infant cannot be taught language until there is sufficient and necessary development of the central nervous system. The ability to develop a symbol system will parallel the infant's mastery in the process of becoming unembedded and its knowledge that objects exist apart from itself. From the extensive observations of Piaget (1962) and Bower (1982), these are not competencies that can be taught, but they do depend on a responsive and supportive environment.

Language, since it represents mutual agreement, is a social contract that involves two or more persons. In different cultures different aspects of language may be stressed. The Baganda, Mixtec, and Japanese stress that the infant understand what it is told but not answer back to elders, while the Italians and Americans coach their infants to speak. In spite of these differences, this interaction between the maturing organism, now capable of language, and its language environment produces a language-competent child between 3 and 4 years of age.

Current evidence suggests that all individuals acquire language in much the same fashion, despite the vast variety and complexity of languages. Language is a part of one's culture and, much like the infant itself, it is both a product of socialization and an agent of the process.

AGENTS OF SOCIALIZATION

Father and Family

Mead (National Film Board of Canada, 1959) suggested that fathers were a biological necessity but a social accident. Sociologists refer to the family as a system that, of course, includes the father as a major component, but regarding socialization of the infant, the father's role is to support the mother. He has in the past been thought to have little influence on the infant per se.

Precipitated perhaps by the women's movement, an active interest in the male's nurturant activity has become a legitimate area of scientific inquiry. Parke (1979) and his coworkers initiated a methodical observation of fathers and their infants. Fathers do not differ in their behavior with the newborn, and older infants are as equally attached to their fathers as to their mothers. Lamb (1976) has suggested that fathers play a different but equally important role in the socialization of the infant. Fathers spend more time in unpredictable rough-and-tumble play with infants of both sexes, while on the other hand mothers play a more predictable and nurturant role. Lamb poses that the mother serves as an all-important source of security for the infant, while the father provides an exciting and challenging stimulus and serves to buttress the infant's burgeoning cognitive capacities. Cross-cultural data reveal father involvement with the infant to be limited, if not nonexistent, in many cultures. If fathers participate, they are more active in the rearing of their infant sons than of their daughters.

Mother

The major portion of infant socialization involves the mother-infant dyad. Under usual circumstances the mother assumes primary care for the infant during the newborn period. In cultures in which the infant is nursed, the mother-infant contact is determined in large part by the maturation of the infant's digestive system. As the infant matures and can ingest more milk and spend less time feeding, the mother may be released to take care of other tasks. In industrial countries such as the United States where bottle feeding often supplants breast feeding, there are a number of alternatives for infant care as well as different emphases on relationships with the infant.

The mother's relationship with the infant is determined by economic factors that impinge on her time, as well as by the space for family living and the number of others in the household. In many cultures in which the mother has limited time and space, the infant is strapped to the mother or another care-giver until the infant is able to walk. This confinement keeps the infant out of harm's way until he or she is considered old enough to obey commands. Therefore the mother's role in many cultures is to keep the baby fed and safe.

Minturn and Lambert (1964) report that U.S. mothers had more exclusive care of their infants than did mothers in six other cultures studied. Mothers in the United States also had more time and space available for the care of infants and had fewer children in the family.

For reasons mentioned earlier, the study of cross-cultural development has been on the wane; we have much more detailed information on infant socialization as a function of U.S. or British standards than we do for other cultures. Much of this detailed work has focused less on feeding, weaning, and toileting and more on subtle facets of mother–infant interaction. Mutual gaze, vocal play, and reciprocal games have been analyzed. Attachment has been a major focus of research, and with the older infant, the mother's organization of care and empathy with her infant have been major sources of investigation.

Certainly peek-a-boo is an almost universal contact with the young infant, but there are great differences in the emphasis of care. The mother may not have constant contact with the infant, but is probably the major interpreter of the culture for the infant. It is hard to imagine that a mother would engage in peek-a-boo in a culture that avoids eye contact or fears that the evil eye may endanger an infant's health; nor would she be involved with the complex visual games so well documented for mothers of infants in the United States.

In a culture that values independence, individuality, and self-reliance, the mother is more likely to foster behaviors in her infant that reflect these values: exploration, self-help skills, and early motor skills. Infant stimulation or education is considered important for later development. This is a characteristic value in both the United States and Russia, for example.

There has been a tacit assumption that during infancy the mother is the person responsible for socialization. Maternal deprivation has been thought of as detrimental to the infant's mental health, and multiple mothering has been questioned. Despite the extensive studies of Casler (1961), Rutter (1972, 1979), and Yarrow (1963), which have demonstrated that the purported ill effects of multiple mothering or other-than-mother care during infancy cannot be substantiated, there are still those professionals who question this data. Levi (1979), after a review of epidemiological data on suicide in adolescence and maladjustment in childhood, finds a hypothesis emerging that he considers worthy of testing. "Does the provision of frequent contact with one 'mother' during infancy and one 'mother and father' during childhood reduce the risk of disease in childhood and particularly suicide and maladjustment?" Menaker (1973) maintains that "the internalization of the communicative interaction between mother and child is the primary basis for all personality development, social action and ultimately for all we know as culture."

Peers

We know much less about the influence of infant's peers as agents of socialization than about other persons in the infant's environment. Anthropological studies document the use of other children to augment infant care, but little systematic review is available. Weisner and Gallimore (1977) ascertained from cross-cultural data that nonparental caregiving is either the norm or a significant factor in infant socialization. They found young female caretakers to be largely responsible for other-than-mother care. And from what we know about the development of the young child, being cared for by a child is likely to have different consequences than primary care by an adult.

We also know little about social interaction between infants and how this affects the developing child. Bridges in the early 1930s made systematic observations of infants in an orphanage. Unfortunately, they were kept in their cribs until almost a year old, so their interaction was necessarily limited to looking. Recently, there has been a resurgence of interest in peer relationships between infants, and we have data to support that infants do engage in social exchange. We know that relationships with age mates undergo a predictable alteration. Young infants (3 to 6 months) engage in mutual inspection and fingering. They may even engage in clumsy bouts of peek-a-boo. At 6 to 7 months the infant exchanges vocalizations and smiles. Crawlers will play follow the leader and chase the ball together. Infant games of the typical one-year-old involve a sender and receiver; one child gives toys and another collects. Later the game begins to be one of exchange. The importance of these exchanges is that they are observed with infants who have regularly spent time together, not with infants who meet for the first time. Furthermore, if the adults are intrusive, infants will rely on the adult for social interaction and will not develop elaborate relations with peers. Adult behavior may be more predictable than infant behavior, but given the opportunity, the infant does develop playmates. As yet we know little concerning how these relationships alter the developing child's world. We do know that infants cannot rear themselves and that adults are necessary in their lives, but infant peers may enhance their social development and be important for social facilitation, as we know to be the case for older children.

Infant

Traditionally, socialization studies have been limited to those conspicuous features of a child's environment considered to be the source of the child's current behavior and/or the cause of later personality structure. Bell (1968) questioned the naiveté of the notion that socialization is a process that only happens *to* the developing infant, stressing the importance of the infant's own contribution to the caretaking. Newborn infants are truly preadapted for social exchange. They would die without nurture, but are quite capable of either demanding or inveigling response to their needs. The newborn cry demands attention; the newborn response to attention is rewarding. They have a complex repertoire of responses that indicate to nurturing adults that the adults are vital to their care. They will quiet to the sound of the human voice and will search the human face; their arousal level depends on the sensitive handling by the caregiver. Their behaviors are truly social from the very beginning. The newborn teaches new parents how to parent; in the apt words of one authority, "of men and women he makes fathers and mothers" (Rheingold, 1968).

According to ethologists, the infant of any species that depends on adult care for survival possesses features that release parental behavior and assure care. Lorenz (Hess, 1970) refers to these qualities as babyishness, which includes such distinguishing features as a large bulbous forehead, lowered placement of overly large eyes, and a receding chin. Hess (1970) has studied the response of adult humans to baby pictures and found that pictures of the human infant release approach behavior in adults—more so in the adult female than in the male.

During the course of maturation the infant produces responses that universally promote a parental-filial bond. Bowlby (1958) lists these action patterns as crying, smiling, sucking, clinging, vocalizing, looking, and following. A vast amount of research has been done in the United States on the mother-infant dyad to evaluate the relative contribution of these behaviors to maternal response and vice versa. The baby does give the mother cues regarding her social interaction. In response to an overstimulating or implosive mother, an infant may turn away or arch the back. Brightening, smiling, and laughing indicate to responsive adults that the infant enjoys their company.

Older infants may in fact take the lead in prosocial behavior. Their first games involve sharing toys, or give-and-take; they share their world by pointing with the index finger and will spontaneously imitate the parental behavior of adults. This is apparently universal behavior and has been repeatedly reported by almost all child watchers.

Other-than-Mother Care

There is a natural relationship between the type of care given infants and a culture's economic structure. In those cultures dependent on the labor of women outside the home, alternative forms of care—other-than-mother care—become a necessity. In many cultures the infant is cared for by the mother until weaned. Until weaning, the relationships may be extraordinarily intimate, since the infant sleeps with the mother at night and is carried by her during the day while she works in the garden or fields. In many of these cultures child nurses, usually elder siblings or cousins, may have certain charge of the infant and weaning. In cultures in which women of the same family or clan share a common courtyard, it is not uncommon for many to be responsible for the care of the infant.

Care for the infant out of the home is not uncommon in many industrial nations. France, Sweden, Belgium, and Italy all provide government-sponsored infant care. Both Russia and China furnish extensive government-supported care and education for the infant. Israel's kibbutzim provide an excellent example of other-than-mother care for the infant, with the intent to alter traditional Western European socialization practices. Israel also has limited government-supported infant care in the Oriental Jewish settlements. The purpose of these infant programs is to socialize not only the infant into Israeli traditions but the entire family as well.

These diverse examples of infant care in groups share one common purpose: to supplant or augment the socializing function of the family. In Italy many babies spend time in the infant *nido* in order to learn to become a cooperative member of the group at an early age. Implicit in many of the guides for child rearing is the notion that the infant must learn early to be a member of the community and that group care fosters this learning. Infant care in Russia is organized to facilitate specific learning with emphasis on cooperation. Sidel (1972) describes the Chinese infant care, where babies learn to recite Communist doctrines as soon as they learn to speak. Infant programs for the Oriental Jew in Israel provide the infant with an environment that reflects the Israeli home with books and pictures that reflect a Western European lifestyle. Not only do these programs reflect the necessity of augmenting the family to educate or socialize the infant, but they also see the infant nurse as a special professional who is trained with specific skills necessary for the care and education of the infant.

As early as 1920, Watson (1925/1958) predicted the demise of the family in the United States. Contrary to those experts who claim that the family is the backbone of this country, Watson maintained that it was probably better for the young child to be cared for by persons with special training rather than for this important job to be left to the whims of the family. Needless to say, this has not been a popular position in the United States, where the family has been considered the appropriate authority on child rearing, and there is a strong belief that an infant should remain with the mother. There is a growing need for appropriate other-than-mother care in this country, but the government has not seen fit to regulate or support such care.

In both the United States and Great Britain infants are cared for in their own homes with "minders" (or babysitters), or formal or informal arrangements are made for infants to be cared for in another's home. This care provides surcease from the constant demands of infant care for the mother or allows her to obtain employment. The mother selects care she deems appropriate, and there is no programatic socialization as found in other countries.

SUMMARY

Socialization, when taken in its broadest sense, covers several topics not covered here but equally important. The entire area of the educative aspect of socialization has been left untouched. This includes the chronicles of infant care and the current surfeit of books on advice to parents (Wolfenstein & Mead, 1955). Freedman (1978) and his colleagues, on the basis of their data, propose that culture and inborn temperament may be closely intertwined. In contrast to Mead's earlier statement, perhaps the Japanese culture is product as well as producer of the Japanese infant, and perhaps it is easier for the Eskimo infant to become an Eskimo than to become a Bugandan adult. The annals of socialization research are long and productive, but there remain many unanswered and intriguing questions.

REFERENCES

Barry, H., III, & Paxson, L. M. (1971). Infancy and early childhood: Cross-cultural codes 2. *Ethnology, 10,* 466–493.

Bell, R. Q. (1968). A reinterpretation of the direction of effects and studies of socialization. *Psychological Review, 75,* 81–95.

Bower, T. G. R. (1982). *Development in infancy.* San Francisco: Freeman. (Original work published 1974)

Bowlby, J. (1958). The nature of the child's tie to his mother. *International Journal of Psycho-Analysis, 39,* 350–373.

Bridges, K. M. B. (1932). Emotional development in early infancy. *Child Development, 3,* 324–341.

Bridges, K. M. B. (1933). A study of social development in early infancy. *Child Development, 4,* 36–49.

Casler, L. (1961). Maternal deprivation: A critical review of the literature. *Monographs of the Society for Research in Child Development, 26*(80), serial no. 2.

Condon, W. S., & Sander, L. W. (1974). Neonate movement is synchronized with adult speech: Interactional participation and language acquisition. *Science, 183,* 99–101.

Freud, S. (1957). Totem and taboo and other works. *The standard edition of the complete psychological works of Sigmund Freud* (Vol. 13). London: Hogarth. (Original work published 1912)

Hess, E. H. (1970). Ethology and developmental psychology. In P. H. Mussen (Ed.), *Carmichael's manual of child psychology* (3rd ed., Vol. 1). New York: Wiley.

Lamb, M. E. (1976). Interactions between two-year-olds and their mothers and fathers. *Psychological Reports, 38,* 447–450.

Levi, L. (1979). *Psychosocial factors in preventive medicine* (DHEW [PHS] Publication No. 79-55071A).Washington, DC: U.S. Department of Health, Education and Welfare.

Lorenz, K. Z. (1970–1971). *Studies on animal behavior.* Cambridge, MA: Harvard University Press.

Maccoby, E. E., & Jacklin, C. N. (1974). *The psychology of sex differences.* Stanford, CA: Stanford University Press.

Mead, G. H. (1934). *Mind, self, and society: From the standpoint of a social behaviorist.* Chicago: University of Chicago Press.

National Film Board of Canada (Producer). (1959). *For families* [Film]. New York: McGraw-Hill Films.

Menaker, E. (1973). Social matrix: Mother and child. *Psychoanalytic Review, 60,* 45–58.

Minturn, L., & Lambert, W. W. (1964). *Mothers of six cultures: Antecedents of child rearing.* New York: Wiley.

Money, J., & Ehrhardt, A. (1972). *Man and woman, boy and girl: The differentiation and dimorphism of gender identity from conception to maturity.* Baltimore, MD: Johns Hopkins University Press.

Parke, R. D. (1979). Perspective on father-infant interaction. In J. Osofsky (Ed.), *The handbook of infant development.* New York: Wiley.

Piaget, J. (1962). The stages of the intellectual development of the child. *Bulletin of the Menninger Clinic, 26,* 120–145.

Piaget, J. (1966). *Origins of Intelligence.* New York: International Universities Press. (Original work published 1936)

Rheingold, H. (1968). Infancy. *International encyclopedia of the social sciences* (Vol. 7). New York: Crowell-Collier/Macmillan.

Rutter, M. (1972). *Maternal deprivation reassessed.* Baltimore: Penguin Education.

Rutter, M. (1979). Maternal deprivation, 1972–1978: New findings, new concepts, new approaches. *Child Development, 50,* 283–305.

Sidel, R. (1972). *Woman and child care in China: A first hand report.* New York: Hill & Wang.

Stern, D. (1974). Mother and infant at play: The dyadic interaction involving facial, vocal, and gaze behaviors. In M. Lewis & L. A. Rosenbloom (Eds.), *The effect of the infant on its caregiver.* New York: Wiley.

Watson, J. B. (1958). *Behaviorism.* New York: Norton. (Original work published 1925)

Weisner, T. S., & Gallimore, R. (1977). My brother's keeper: Child and sibling caretaking. *Current Anthropology, 18,* 169–190.

Wolfenstein, M., & Mead, M. (Eds.). (1955). *Childhood in contemporary cultures.* Chicago: University of Chicago Press.

Yarrow, L. J. (1963). Research in the dimensions of early child care. *Merrill-Palmer Quarterly, 8,* 101–114.

H. W. ROSS
San Diego State University

**EARLY CHILDHOOD DEVELOPMENT
INFANT DEVELOPMENT**

INFORMATION PROCESSING

Several crucial assumptions are shared by researchers who adopt the information-processing approach to the study of human behavior. The most important assumption is that behavior is determined by the internal flow of information within a person. Since this information flow is internal and invisible, special techniques and methodologies are used to allow inferences about this postulated flow. But all these techniques share the basic goal of information-processing research, which is to map internal information pathways.

The information-processing approach uses techniques in many ways similar to those used by engineers designing large systems. The human being is regarded as a complex system, and experimental psychologists try to discover what happens inside the "black box." However, engineers have a considerable advantage, since they can insert probes and meters within their black boxes, whereas psychologists cannot. Although some researchers use psychophysiological measures such as brain waves to peer into the black box, this technique cannot as yet plot the hypothetical information pathways inside the human. Thus the effort to understand internal information flow proceeds primarily by testing alternate representations based upon different arrangements of subsystems with different properties. It is not sufficient to create a model that will duplicate the behavior of human beings, although this is of course a necessary requirement for any information-processing model. A female singer and a tape recording made with the proper brand of tape might both be able to shatter a slender crystal goblet, but no one would claim that this duplication of behavior proves that the singer and the tape recorder produce auditory signals by the same internal processes. Thus the information-processing theorist must duplicate not only behavior but also the internal patterns of information flow before an acceptable explanation of human thought and action can be found.

Information-processing models differ in the number and arrangement of subsystems. Many possible arrangements are reasonable, so that theorists must try to show how their model is superior to other competing models. There is seldom complete agreement about which model is best, which can confuse the nonspecialist wishing to learn only a little about information-processing models. To avoid this problem, this entry discusses the general characteristics of information-processing models, rather than comparing particular models proposed by individual theorists. Even extremely good models are eventually replaced by newer theories or even by older theories that are reborn because of new data or new techniques (Kantowitz & Roediger, 1978).

The typical information-processing model represents the human cognitive system as a series of boxes connected by an assortment of arrows. The boxes represent subsystems that perform different functions and processes that route information to and from the various boxes. Each box represents a generalized kind of information transformation that goes on inside one's head. As the models become more refined, the level of detail represented by a box becomes finer. A box that represents a relatively fine level of detail is often called a stage of information processing (Sternberg, 1975; Taylor, 1976) or an isolable subsystem (Posner, 1978). The precise definition of a stage is mathematically sophisticated (Townsend, 1974), but we will not be far off if we think of it as corresponding to a single transformation of information. In general, the output of a stage will not match its input. For example, one common model of memory assumes that printed words received through the eyes get recoded into a format that is related to how the words sound when read aloud. This transformation occurs even though people were not asked to pronounce the words. So a visual input has been transformed into an auditory (i.e., acoustic or phonological) output. This kind of transformation is common in machines. A computer transforms punched holes in cards into electrical impulses. A telephone transforms electrical signals into air vibrations. So it is not surprising that the human information processor is capable of these kinds of internal information transformations.

Different arrangements of stages are required to model the flexibility of the human information processor. The simplest arrangement occurs when several stages are linked in a straight line with the output of one becoming the input of the succeeding stage. This is called serial processing because no stage can perform its own transformation of information until it receives the output of the preceding stage in the chain. This, of course, will not happen until that stage has received information from its preceding stage. So the stages are like a row of dominoes: Tipping the first one over starts a reaction that is communicated down the whole line of dominoes. Similarly, serial processing models require each stage to wait its turn before producing an output.

If a stage need not wait for other stages to finish, the arrangement is called parallel processing. In parallel processing several stages can access the same output simultaneously. Each parallel stage can proceed without having to wait for other parallel stages to complete their processing. An arrangement with both serial and parallel components is called hybrid processing. Hybrid processors are often more powerful than serial or parallel processors, but this extra power is gained by making the model more difficult to understand and analyze. Since many people find serial models easier to understand, most information-processing models are serial. (See Figure 1.)

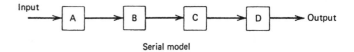

Serial model

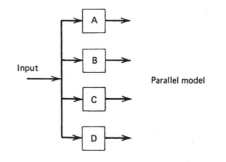

Parallel model

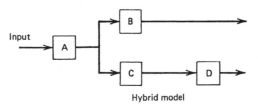

Hybrid model

Figure 1.   Serial, parallel, and hybrid models in human information processing.

Although we now have an excellent scheme for classifying the structure of a model into three categories—serial, parallel, and hybrid—structure alone cannot determine the predictions a model will generate. We must also know the price each stage demands for performing its transformation of information. This is called resource allocation or capacity. Capacity is a hypothetical construct that controls how efficiently a stage operates. In some models it is assumed that each stage has adequate capacity to do its own thing, regardless of how many other stages are operating and how complex these operations might be (Sternberg, 1969). Other models assume that capacity is limited, so that stages must compete for available processing resources (Kantowitz & Knight, 1976). In these models, a stage cannot always operate as efficiently as if it were the only stage in the system. Other stages may divert the necessary capacity. By cleverly selecting assumptions about capacity, it is possible to make serial systems mimic parallel systems, and vice versa (Townsend, 1974). Thus, to generate predictions for a model, we must specify both the structure of the model and its capacity assumptions. The best models of human information processing specify: (a) the number and configuration of internal processing stages; (b) the capacity requirements of individual stages; and (c) total availability of capacity and rules that govern distribution of capacity to individual stages.

REFERENCES

Kantowitz, B. H., & Knight, J. L. (1976). Testing tapping time-sharing: II. Auditory secondary tasks. *Acta Psychologica, 40,* 343–362.

Kantowitz, B. H., & Roediger, H. L. (1978). *Experimental psychology.* Chicago: Rand McNally.

Posner, M. I. (1978). *Chronometric explorations of mind.* Hillsdale, NJ: Erlbaum.

Sternberg, S. (1969). Memory scanning: Mental processes revealed by reaction time experiments. *American Scientist, 57,* 421–457.

Sternberg, S. (1975). Memory scanning: New findings and current controversies. *Quarterly Journal of Experimental Psychology, 27,* 1–32.

Taylor, D. A. (1976). Stage analysis of reaction time. *Psychological Bulletin, 83,* 161–191.

Townsend, J. T. (1974). Issues and models concerning the processing of a finite number of inputs. In B. H. Kantowitz (Ed.), *Human information processing.* Hillsdale, NJ: Erlbaum.

SUGGESTED READING

Allport, D. A., Antonis, B., & Reynolds, P. (1972). On the division of attention: A disproof of the single-channel hypothesis. *Quarterly Journal of Experimental Psychology, 24,* 225–235.

Broadbent, D. E. (1971). *Decision and stress.* New York: Academic.

Duncan, J. (1980). The demonstration of capacity limitation. *Cognitive Psychology, 12,* 75–96.

Kahneman, D. (1973). *Attention and effort.* Englewood Cliffs, NJ: Prentice-Hall.

Kantowitz, B. H. (Ed.). (1974). *Human information processing.* Hillsdale, NJ: Erlbaum.

Kinsbourne, M. (1981). Single-channel theory. In D. Holding (Ed.), *Human skills.* New York: Wiley.

Lane, D. (1981). Attention. In W. C. Howell & E. A. Fleishman (Eds.), *Human performance and productivity* (Vol. 2). Hillsdale, NJ: Erlbaum.

Navon, D., & Gopher, D. (1979). On the economy of the human processing system. *Psychological Review, 86,* 214–255.

B. H. KANTOWITZ
Battelle Institute

INFORMATION PROCESSING
LEARNING THEORIES

INGROUPS/OUTGROUPS

In his *Folkways* (1906/1911), the sociologist William Graham Sumner was able to consolidate a substantial ethnographic literature on group self-images and attitudes toward neighboring groups under the terms "ethnocentrism," "in-group," and "out-group." He described the interrelationships among these concepts (pp. 12–13):

> . . . a differentiation arises between ourselves, the we-group, or in-group, and everybody else, or the others' groups, out-groups. The insiders in a we-group are in a relation of peace, order, law, government, and industry to each other. Their relation to all outsiders, or others-groups, is one of war and plunder. . . . Sentiments are produced to correspond. Loyalty to the group, sacrifice for it, hatred and contempt for outsiders, brotherhood within, warlikeness without—all grow together. . . . Ethnocentrism is the technical name for this view of things in which one's own group is the center of everything, and all others are scaled and rated with reference to it.

In thus introducing the concept of ingroup-outgroup differentiation to the social sciences, Sumner set the stage for a long line of research on how group identification affects an individual's perceptions of and attitudes and behavior toward other persons and groups. An ingroup is generally defined as any social group or category of which an individual is identifiably a member. Technically, outgroups are any social groups to which the individual does *not* belong, but in practice particular outgroups are usually identified with reference to any specified ingroup (males-females, neighboring ethnic groups, competing nations, etc.). In accord with Sumner's thesis, the focus of investigation in this area has been the proposition that attitudes and behaviors are biased in favor of ingroup members over outgroup members. The preponderance of research evidence supports this proposition, although some important moderating variables have also been identified.

RESEARCH APPROACHES

The study of ingroup-outgroup attitudes and behavior has been the subject of multiple methodological approaches. Most of the systematic research in the area can be classified into three types—attitude surveys, field studies, and laboratory experiments—each of which has contributed somewhat differently to the understanding of ingroup biases.

Attitude Surveys

Much of the empirical data on intergroup attitudes and behaviors are based on surveys or opinion polls in which the unit is the modern nation-state or racial or ethnic subgroups within a state. Large-scale studies of this type have included Buchanan and Cantril's nine-nation UNESCO survey, *How Nations See Each Other;* Lambert and Klineberg's international comparative study of children's perceptions, *Children's Views of Foreign Peoples;* and Brewer and Campbell's survey of ethnic groups in East Africa, *Ethnocentrism and Intergroup Attitudes: East African Evidence.* By examining the differences between respondents' evaluations of their own and other groups, these studies have documented pervasive tendencies toward ingroup favoritism on a number of dimensions. Preference for ingroups over outgroups has been found on measures of affect (ratings of liking and trust for group members), evaluation (attributions of positive and negative characteristics to group members), and social distance (respondents' willingness to engage in interactions with group members at various levels of intimacy). Evaluative bias in favor of ingroups is not totally indiscriminate, however. It is obtained most consistently in attributions of positive character traits such as "moral," "peaceloving," "trustworthy," and "cooperative"; but on other evaluative dimensions ingroups are not always rated as higher than outgroups. There is also some evidence that groups occupying a minority status within a society adopt some (though not all) of the majority group's derogatory stereotypes in their self-image.

Field Studies

In 1954, Muzafer Sherif and his colleagues undertook one of the first field studies of the induction and reduction of ingroup-outgroup bias in the context of a boys' summer camp: *Intergroup Conflict and Cooperation: The Robber's Cave Experiment* (1961). In that study, 11-year-old boys were arbitrarily divided into two groups that were allowed to develop in isolation from each other over a period of eight days before being brought into contact under conditions designed to maximize competition and mutual frustration. The resulting intergroup hostility was documented with anecdotal evidence based on observation of overt behavior, supplemented by structured measures of sociometric preferences, evaluative trait ratings, and estimates of performance by group members during a competitive game. On each of these indicators, the boys revealed consistent biases favoring members of their own group over members of the outgroup. In general, ingroup solidarity was enhanced in the presence of conflict with an outgroup. Reductions in these biases were achieved when the nature of the relationship between the two groups was altered by the systematic introduction of superordinate (shared) goals that required cooperative interaction.

Since the Sherif study, most of the field experiments on ingroup-outgroup attitudes have been conducted in contexts involving pre-existing social groups, such as racial and ethnic groups, in desegregated settings. Much of this work has been designed to assess the so-called "contact hypothesis"—the idea that outgroup rejection and devaluation is exacerbated by segregation and lack of contact between members of different groups, and can be reduced by promoting intergroup interaction under favorable conditions. Empirical evidence indicates that contact per se is not sufficient to reduce awareness of ingroup-outgroup differentiation and attendant preferential biases. Consistent with Sherif's findings, significant changes in intergroup acceptance are obtained only under conditions that promote extensive cooperative interaction between members of the different groups. Even when cooperative acceptance is achieved, it is not clear whether its effects on attitudes toward outgroup members are limited to the immediate setting, or whether they will generalize to other members of the outgroup and other situations.

Laboratory Experiments

Whereas field research on ingroup-outgroup attitudes has focused on documenting the presence and extent of evaluative biases in favor of ingroups, laboratory research has been conducted to identify the minimal conditions under which ingroup-outgroup differentiation can be developed and can lead to preferential biases. Much of this research has employed a paradigm developed by Henri Tajfel (1978) and his colleagues at the University of Bristol to study ingroup-outgroup discrimination in a situation involving no face-to-face interaction among group members, anonymity of group membership, and an arbitrary basis for group differentiation. Even under these minimal conditions of group identification, significant ingroup bias is obtained in that subjects make point allocation decisions that favor individuals labeled as members of their own group over individuals labeled as members of the outgroup. Apparently any form of categorization into groups, even in the absence of information about similarity-dissimilarity among group members or any direct conflict between groups, is sufficient to generate ingroup favoritism. In general, any factors that serve to enhance the salience of category distinctions (such as minority status, differential treatment or status, or the presence of intergroup competition) tend to increase the degree of bias exhibited on both behavioral and attitudinal measures.

Because it concerns the relationship between intergroup behavior at the societal level and attitudes and perceptions at the individual level, the concept of ethnocentrism or ingroup bias provides a link between sociological theories of group relations and psychological theories of interpersonal attraction. In 1972 anthropologist Robert A. Levine and social psychologist Donald T. Campbell compiled an inventory of social science theories and derived propositions relevant to ingroup-outgroup attitudes in their book, *Ethnocentrism: Theories of Conflict, Ethnic Attitudes and Group Behavior.* Four theoretical perspectives have proved most influential in attempts to explain the pervasive tendency toward ingroup favoritism.

Realistic Group Conflict Theory

Sumner's thesis on the origin of ethnocentrism and intergroup hostility explicitly recognized the role of competition over scarce resources in the initiation and perpetuation of group differentiation and conflict. The differentiation of peoples into distinct groups originated, according to Sumner, in the context of the "conditions of the struggle for existence" that determine the size and internal organization of groups as well as the relationships between them. Sherif's summer camp experiment was based on similar premises, testing the assumption that interpersonal behaviors among individuals would be determined by the nature of the structural relationships between the groups to which they belonged. The presence of incompatible goals at the group level affected interpersonal relationships both within and between groups, strengthening evaluative preferences for ingroup members and creating negative attitudes and hostility toward outgroup members. When the structural relationship between groups was altered by the introduction of compatible (superordinate) goals, changes in the nature of interpersonal behaviors and attitudes between groups followed. The Sherif study is regarded as a major source of support for realistic group conflict theory predictions. The study was not, however, a complete experimental test of the theory, because no assessments of attitudes toward ingroup and outgroup were made prior to the introduction of intergroup competition. Thus the results of the study do not indicate clearly whether the presence of conflict or competition between groups is a necessary condition for the emergence of ingroup favoritism and outgroup hostility.

Psychoanalytic Theory

Whereas realistic group conflict theory places the origin of ingroup-outgroup discrimination in processes operating at the group level, psychoanalytically oriented theorists trace such biases to the needs and motives of individuals. Probably the most extensive treatment of the subject from a psychoanalytic perspective is represented in the *The Authoritarian Personality* by. Adorno, Frenkel-Brunswik, Levinson, and Sanford (1950). According to the theory behind the authoritarianism concept, generalized hatred and distrust toward outgroups—particularly prejudice against racial and religious minorities—derives from projection of repressed hostilities originating in childhood experiences with parental authority. In this view, then, derogation of outgroups relative to ingroups develops in the service of maintaining the individual ego or self-esteem.

Categorization Theory

While motivational theories such as group conflict and psychoanalytic theory are applicable to the intergroup relations of nation states, ethnic groups, and other long-standing social units in real-world settings, they do not readily account for the ingroup biases obtained under minimal conditions in many laboratory studies. In light of these findings, a number of theorists have sought to explain ingroup-outgroup biases in terms of the general cognitive processes by which human beings structure, simplify, and give meaning to their physical and social environment. In this view, intergroup perceptions derive from the same processes of classification and categorization that apply to the perception of physical objects. One perceptual phenomenon associated with category differentiation is the *assimilation-contrast* effect: when a classification (i.e., the introduction of category boundaries) is superimposed on a set of stimuli that vary systematically along some physical dimension, there is a strong tendency to accentuate intercategory differences

and intracategory similarities on that dimension. When extrapolated to social differentiation, this implies that members of the same social group will be seen as more similar to one another, and more different from members of other groups, than they actually are. Hence members of one's own group (ingroup) are perceived as generally similar to oneself, whereas members of outgroups are perceived as different. When combined with the positive effects of perceived similarity on interpersonal attraction, categorization and accentuation of category differences can account for some aspects of ingroup favoritism and outgroup rejection. However, there is a general tendency for ingroup bias to be more selective than would be expected based on categorization alone. Accentuation of differences in favor of the ingroup occurs readily for groups who occupy a superior position on the dimension of evaluation, but convergence or perceptual reduction of differences is often found for groups who hold an inferior position. In addition, there is evidence that the tendency to perceive homogenization within groups is greater for the perception of outgroups than it is for ingroups.

Social Identity Theory

A theory that combines the basic features of categorization theory with some aspects of motivational theories was developed by Henri Tajfel and John Turner (1979). In this perspective, the perceptual effects of category differentiation are coupled with a posited drive for "positive self-identity" and social comparison. An individual's social identity is presumed to be highly differentiated, based in part on membership in multiple significant social categories. When a particular category distinction is highly relevant or salient, the individual responds with respect to that aspect of social identity, acting toward others in terms of their group membership rather than their personal identities. At this level, the motivation for positive self-identity takes the form of a desire to differentiate the ingroup from the outgroup to the extent that favorable comparisons are available on dimensions relevant to the ingroup-outgroup distinction. Whereas realistic group conflict theory postulates that ingroup solidarity and identification are the product of intergroup competition, social identity theory reverses this causal ordering, suggesting that social competition is generated by group differentiation. Ingroup-outgroup differences provide the basis for accentuating social comparisons that favor the ingroup in the service of positive self-identity.

REFERENCES

Adorno, T. W., Frenkel-Brunswik, E., Levinson, D. J., & Sanford, R. N. (1950). *The authoritarian personality.* New York: Harper.

Brewer, M. B., & Campbell, D. T. (1976). *Ethnocentrism and intergroup attitudes: East African evidence.* New York: Halsted Press/Sage Publications.

Buchanan, W., & Cantril, H. (1953). *How nations see each other.* Urbana, IL: University of Illinois Press.

Lambert, W. E., & Klineberg, O. (1967). *Children's views of foreign peoples.* New York: Appleton-Century-Crofts.

Levine, R. A., & Campbell, D. T. (1972). *Ethnocentrism: Theories of conflict, ethnic attitudes and group behavior.* New York: Wiley.

Sherif, M., Harvey, O. J., White, B. J., Hood, W. R., & Sherif, C. W. (1961). *Intergroup conflict and cooperation: The Robber's Cave experiment.* Norman: University of Oklahoma Press.

Sumner, W. G. (1940/1906). *Folkways* (3rd ed.) New York: Ginn.

Tajfel, H. (Ed.). (1978). *Differentiation between social groups: Studies in the social psychology of intergroup relations.* London: Academic Press.

Tajfel, H., & Turner, J. C. (1979). An integrative theory of intergroup conflict. In W. Austin & S. Worchel (Eds.), *The social psychology of intergroup relations.* Monterey, CA: Brooks/Cole.

SUGGESTED READING

Billig, M. (1976). *Social psychology and intergroup relations.* London: Academic Press.

Brewer, M. B. (1979). In-group bias in the minimal intergroup situation: A cognitive-motivational analysis. *Psychological Bulletin, 86,* 307–324.

M. B. BREWER
University of California at Santa Barbara

TERRITORIALITY

INHIBITORY CONDITIONING

At the beginning of the 20th century, Ivan Pavlov developed the original model of conditioning. In his research, he conditioned dogs to salivate at the sound of a bell, by the repeated process of ringing the bell and then presenting food. His research showed that each time the bell and food were paired, the amount of saliva that the dog produced increased. Using the standard terminology, the bell is referred to as the conditioned stimulus (CS), the food is the unconditioned stimulus (US), the salivation in response to the ringing of the bell is called the conditioned response (CR), and each bell–food pairing is called a trial. In this study, Pavlov was interested in the processes that cause the CS to activate or "excite" the behavior of salivation. In this example, the CS is referred to as excitatory because it acts to elicit the CR. However, Pavlov was also interested in the processes that are responsible for the "inhibition" of responding. In inhibitory conditioning, the CS acts against the elicitation of a conditioned response.

The standard conditioned inhibition procedure involves two phases. In the first phase, a CS such as a tone is repeatedly paired with the presentation of a food US (T+ trials), until the subject shows a stable salivary response to the tone. As in the previous example, the tone can be considered excitatory because it elicits the CR of salivation. In the second phase of the procedure there are two types of learning trials that are randomly intermixed throughout the phase. One trial type is the same as that given in the first phase (T+ trials). The second trial type involves the simultaneous presentation of the tone and a second stimulus, such as a light. However, on these compound trials, no food is given (TL- trials).

At the beginning of this phase, the dog may salivate on both the T+ trials and the TL- trials. However, as the phase progresses, the dog will eventually stop salivating during the presentation of the compound stimulus, TL, while continuing to salivate during the presentation of the tone alone. Thus, the light may be considered inhibitory because it appears to act against the elicitation of a CR that would have normally been produced by the tone.

Although Pavlov discovered conditioned inhibition in the early 1900s, inhibitory conditioning did not command the serious attention of researchers until over 40 years later when Rescorla (1969) reintroduced the topic by arguing that the candidate inhibitor must pass both a "summation test" and a "retardation test" in order to be declared a true conditioned inhibitor. For the summation test, a third stimulus is employed. This new stimulus (say, a bell) has already been paired with a US, and is thus known to be excitatory. During the test, the candidate inhibitor (L) is presented in compound with the bell (BL- trials). The light is said to pass the summation test if it is successful in reducing the level of conditioned responding to the bell. In the retardation test, the candidate inhibitor (L) is paired with a US (L+ trials) and the rate at which the light acquires excitatory strength is observed (as measured by the development of conditioned responding). It is said to pass the retardation test if it acquires that strength more slowly than would a neutral or novel stimulus paired with the same US.

Rescorla maintained that a candidate inhibitor must pass both of these tests because a CS could pass either one of these tests alone and still not be a true conditioned inhibitor. For example, if it had only passed the summation test, one could argue that it was merely distracting the animal and drawing the animal's attention away from the excitatory stimulus. If it had only passed the retardation test, then one could argue that the training during the second phase served merely to cause the animal to ignore the stimulus. However, if it passed both tests, neither the "distracting" nor the "ignoring" explanation could work—a stimulus cannot be both distracting and ignored at the same time; it must be a true conditioned inhibitor with the ability to act against the elicitation of a conditioned response.

Rescorla's belief that a conditioned inhibitor must be able to pass these two special tests is reflective of the concept that excitation and inhibition are at different ends of a single continuum of associative strength. Excitation and inhibition were viewed by Rescorla and others as opposing associative processes that carried opposite signs and counteracted each other (Rescorla & Wagner, 1972). The summation and retardation tests were meant to capitalize on this opposition by pitting the two opposing processes against each other. However, some studies have suggested, and some theories argue, that inhibition is not the symmetric opposite of excitation and that they are not two mutually exclusive associative processes (Zimmer-Hart & Rescorla, 1974; Matzel, Gladstein, & Miller, 1988; Williams & Overmier, 1988). Still others have rebelled against the notion of inhibition itself, suggesting that what appear to be the effects of inhibition on conditioned responding are really the effects of varying amounts of excitation in combination with some principle of performance (Gibbon & Balsam, 1981; Miller & Schachtman, 1985). These theories explain the behavioral effect of a putative inhibitory CS in terms of a comparison of the

CS's relative strengths of excitation. For a review of this issue, see Williams, Overmier, and LoLordo, 1992.

While much is known about the neural systems involved in the expression of excitatory conditioning, particularly the expression of conditioned fear, relatively little is known about the structures of the brain that are responsible for the effects of conditioned inhibition training. However, recent studies using the fear-potentiated startle paradigm have shed some light on the neural mechanisms that may be involved (Falls & Davis, 1995; Falls, Bakken, & Heldt, 1997). In the basic fear-potentiated startle paradigm, excitatory conditioning is defined as an elevated startle amplitude in the presence of a light CS that has previously been paired with a shock US. Conditioned inhibition of fear-potentiated startle is produced by giving rats training in which L+ trials are randomly intermixed with trials in which a serial noise and light compound is presented without shock (N → L-). Following this training, the rats show significantly less startle to the light when it is preceded by the noise than when it is presented alone. Lesioning studies (Falls & Davis, 1995; Falls, Bakken, & Heldt, 1997) using this paradigm seem to suggest that conditioned inhibitors may act at the sensory structures that process the CS, the lateral or basolateral nuclei of the amygdala, or on the pathway that connects the central nucleus of the amygdala to the startle-reflex pathway.

REFERENCES

Falls, W. A., Bakken, K. T., & Heldt, S. A. (1997). Lesions of the perirhinal cortex interfere with conditioned excitation but not with conditioned inhibition of fear. *Behavioral Neuroscience, 111*(3), 476–486.

Falls, W. A., & Davis, M. (1995). Lesions of the central nucleus of the amygdala block conditioned excitation, but not conditioned inhibition of fear as measured with the fear-potentiated startle effect. *Behavioral Neuroscience, 109*(3), 379–387.

Gibbon, J., & Balsam, P. D. (1981). Spreading association in time. In C. M. Locurto, H. S. Terrace, & J. Gibbon (Eds.), *Autoshaping and conditioning theory* (pp. 219–253). San Diego, CA: Academic Press.

Matzel, L. D., Gladstein, L., & Miller, R. R. (1988). Conditioned excitation and conditioned inhibition are not mutually exclusive. *Learning & Motivation, 19*(2), 99–121.

Miller, R. R., & Schachtman, T. R. (1985). Conditioning context as an associative baseline: Implications for response generation and the nature of conditioned inhibition. In R. R. Miller & N. E. Spear (Eds.), *Information processing in animals: Conditioned inhibition* (pp. 51–88). Hillsdale, NJ: Erlbaum.

Rescorla, R. A. (1969). Pavlovian conditioned inhibition. *Psychological Bulletin, 72*(2), 77–94.

Rescorla, R. A., & Wagner, A. R. (1972). A theory of Pavlovian conditioning: Variations in the effectiveness of reinforcement and nonreinforcement. In A. H. Black & W. F. Prokasy (Eds.), *Classical conditioning: II. Theory and research* (pp. 64–99). New York: Appleton-Century-Crofts.

Williams, D. A., & Overmier, J. B. (1988). Some types of conditioned inhibitors carry collateral excitatory associations. *Learning & Motivation, 19*(4), 345–368.

Williams, D. A., Overmier, J. B., & LoLordo, V. M. (1992). A reevaluation of Rescorla's early dictums about Pavlovian conditioned inhibition. *Psychological Bulletin, 111*(2), 275–290.

Zimmer-Hart, C. L., & Rescorla, R. A. (1974). Extinction of Pavlovian conditioned inhibition. *Journal of Comparative & Physiological Psychology, 86*(5), 837–845.

J. McPhee
Florida Gulf Coast University

CLASSICAL CONDITIONING
OPERANT CONDITIONING

INSTINCT

The concept of instinct is a very old one, going back to antiquity and the writings of philosophers who were interested in the natural behavior and psychology of animals, including humans. When an act, perception, motive, or goal is said to be instinctive, that means the observer views it as being unlearned and caused by the organism's hereditary makeup. Instincts are often adaptive, in the sense that they aid in the survival of the individual and the species (courting, mating, nestbuilding, and rearing of young in birds, for example). In the early part of the twentieth century, as psychology was struggling to become a recognized science, so many different instincts were attributed to humans that the concept was thought to be unwieldy, and so lost favor in some quarters. Another, more important criticism of the concept of instinct was its antianalytic flavor. If a behavior or perception was labeled instinctive, there was no reason to experimentally analyze its development in the individual because it was thought to come directly from the genes (genes → species-typical behavior). As it became clearer that the genes must influence behavior through the nervous system, the developmental understanding of instinct became genes → nervous system → behavior.

Beginning in the 1920s and 1930s, the popularity of the instinct concept waned in psychology, especially as the so-called behaviorist school of thinking became dominant and much of behavior, perception, and motivation were thought to be learned or acquired rather than innate or instinctive. In the 1920s and 1930s, a small group of zoologists called ethologists became interested in the natural behavior of animals as observed in field settings, and they brought the instinct concept back into the scientific study of animals' perceptions, motives, and actions. They invented a whole new vocabulary for dealing with instinctive behavior: *Releasers* or *sign stimuli* were behavioral or anatomical features of other members of the species that innately triggered *fixed action patterns* (FAPs) that arose from special places in the nervous system that had been put there by genes. The motivational part was seen in the observation that, if the FAPs were not released by encountering the appropriate releaser they would "go off in a vacuum" (i.e., without being triggered by a sign stimulus). Since the ethologists were zoologists who were trained in the importance of natural selection in the evolution of species, they focused on the reproductive behavior of species, especially birds. They found that each species had their own special set of releasers and innate motor movements (FAPs), and the more closely related the species, the greater the similarity in their releasers and FAPs. In the hands of ethologists, the classical features of instinct were defined as:

1. species-typical or species-specific behaviors

2. not dependent on known forms of learning

3. adaptive (survival value)

4. responsive to a narrow range of sensory stimulation (sign stimuli or releasers) provided by other members of the species and not requiring prior exposure to such stimulation

5. largely or totally unmodifiable by the organism's experience

6. attributable to hereditary influences operating directly on the nervous system to prepare the animal to behave in an adaptive fashion

This was an imposing and precise list of defining features of instinct that motivated young, experimentally-oriented animal behaviorists (both zoologists and psychologists) to analyze instinctive behavior under laboratory conditions. What was learned is that behavior, perception, and motivation thought to be instinctive in the strict sense defined above was more influenced by an animal's prior experience than previously believed to be the case. For example, in the instance of gulls rearing their baby chicks, the chicks come to peck (FAP) at a spot (releaser) on the lower mandible of the parent and the parent regurgitates predigested food that the young eat. In studies by Hailman, it was found that the baby chicks are at first not accurate in their pecking response and only become so during a fairly protracted period of "practice." In studying the motor patterns involved in courtship displays in various species, Barlow and others observed a good bit of individual variability in the precision of the motor patterns within every species studied (thus, the *fixed* action pattern became the *modal* action pattern). And, in studying the instinctive perceptual response of newly hatched ducklings to the maternal assembly call of their own species, Gottlieb found that, in order for the ducklings' response to be species-specific, they had to have heard their own embryonic vocalizations. In the experimental cases in which the embryos were prevented from hearing their own vocalizations, the specificity of the posthatching response to the species maternal call was lost; they were as likely to respond to the maternal call of another species as they were to their own. In a similar vein, Miller found that the specificity of newly hatched ducklings' freezing response to the maternal alarm call was lost in the absence of their usual embryonic and postnatal experiences. In another remarkable case of a nonobvious prior experience preparing the developing animal to respond adaptively, Wallman found that preventing newly hatched chicks from seeing their own toes move by covering their feet with white taffeta cloths resulted in the chicks being nonresponsive to mealworms, their favorite food under usual conditions. The list goes on—what does it mean? How has it changed our understanding of instinct?

While there can be no doubt that animals exhibit species-typical and species-specific behavior that is adaptive and is often not dependent on known forms of learning such as associative learning or conditioning, that does not mean that the animals' prior experi-

ences, more broadly considered, are irrelevant. The classic concept of instinct was based on the notion that the epigenesis (development) of behavior, perception, and motivation is *predetermined;* namely, that genes give rise to structures that then function in unilinear manner (genetic activity → structure → function). As experiments on behavior, the nervous system, and genetic activity have shown, epigenesis is *probabilistic* rather than predetermined, in that the relation among genetic activity, structure, and function is bidirectional rather than unidirectional: (genetic activity ⇆ structure ⇆ function ⇆ environment). So, the present definition of instinctive behavior includes the prior experiences of the individual, broadly construed. Instinct is an outcome of the probabilistic epigenesis of behavior, perception, and motivation, based on the bidirectional coactions among the environment, function, structure, and genetic activity. Instinct is not a special class of behavior in terms of its determinants.

SUGGESTED READING

Barnett, S. A. (1998). Instinct. In G. Greenberg & M. M. Haraway (Eds.), *Comparative psychology: A handbook* (pp. 138–149). New York: Garland.

Birney, R. C., & Teevan, R. C. (Eds.). (1961). *Instinct.* Princeton, NJ: Van Nostrand.

Gottlieb, G. (1997). *Synthesizing nature-nurture: Prenatal roots of instinctive behavior.* Mahwah, NJ: Erlbaum.

Miller, D. B. (1997). The effects of nonobvious forms of experience on the development of instinctive behavior. In C. Dent-Read & P. Zukow-Goldring (Eds.), *Evolving explanations of development: Ecological approaches to organism-environment systems* (pp. 457–507). Washington, DC: American Psychological Association.

Spalding, D. A. (1954). Instinct. *British Journal of Animal Behaviour, 2,* 2–11.

G. GOTTLIEB
University of North Carolina, Chapel Hill

COMPARATIVE PSYCHOLOGY
EVOLUTION

INSTRUMENTAL CONDITIONING

Instrumental conditioning represents a form of behavioral change that depends on the temporal relationship (contingency) between a response and an environmental outcome. The response might correspond to pressing a bar, lifting a leg, turning a wheel, or navigating a maze. In the laboratory, the outcome is typically a biologically relevant event, such as food, water, or a frightening shock. Outside the laboratory, behavior can be modified by a variety of events, including social praise, access to a sexual partner, or a stimulus that has acquired value (e.g., money). Outcomes capable of modifying an organism's behavior are sometimes called reinforcers, and the process through which they influence behavior is known as reinforcement. Examples of an instrumental contin-

Table 1.   Criteria for instrumental and operant learning

Minimum Criteria
1. Instituting a relationship between the response and an outcome produces a change in behavior (performance).
2. The effect is neurally mediated.
3. The modification outlasts (extends beyond) the environmental contingencies used to induce it.
4. The behavioral modification depends on the temporal relationship between the response and the outcome.

Advanced Criteria
5. The nature of the behavioral change is not constrained (e.g., either an increase or decrease in the response can be established).
6. The nature of the reinforcer is not constrained (a variety of outcomes can be used to produce the behavioral effect).

gency include praising a child for waiting quietly or providing a food pellet to a rat whenever it presses a bar. According to Thorndike's law of effect, these contingencies should bring about a lasting change in behavior, leading the child to stand quietly and increasing the frequency with which the rat presses the bar.

It is clear that the timely application of a reinforcer can bring about a dramatic change in behavior. Anyone who has trained a pet using food as a reward, or attempted to influence a roommate's behavior through social reinforcement, has employed a form of instrumental conditioning. It is important to remember, however, that instituting a response-outcome relationship can sometimes affect performance in the absence of instrumental learning. For example, suppose a parent raises his or her voice and spanks a child every time the child teases a sibling. Soon, the parent's raising his or her voice is enough to stop the teasing. What has the child learned? The parent's hope is that sibling teasing (the response) will decline because it is associated with an aversive outcome (the parent's raised voice); but perhaps the raised voice is effective because it is associated with a spanking (pain), yielding a form of Pavlovian (classical) fear conditioning. In this case, the raised voice may temporarily suppress the performance of the unwanted behavior in the absence of instrumental learning.

Concerns of this sort have led learning theorists to develop formal criteria for instrumental learning (see Grau, Barstow, & Joynes, 1998, Table 1). Criterion 1 specifies the essential condition common to all definitions of instrumental learning: that it depends on the response-outcome relation. If the response-outcome relation matters, the behavioral change should not be observed in a yoked control group in which subjects receive the outcome independently of their behaviors. Because performing the response can alter its vigor through a peripheral modification (e.g., muscular exercise or fatigue), it is important to show that the behavioral change is neurally mediated (criterion 2). To demonstrate that the effect reflects a kind of learning, rather than a mechanical response to the current stimulation, the environmental contingency must have a lasting effect on behavior (criterion 3). If the behavioral effect disappears as soon as the reinforcer is removed, the behavioral modification may be better characterized as a performance effect rather than learning. Finally, we must show that learning depends on the temporal relationship between the response and the outcome (criterion 4). If the temporal relation is important, disrupting

response-outcome contiguity should undermine the acquisition of the instrumental response (Church, 1964).

Some instrumental behavior is biologically constrained by the organism's evolutionary history (Timberlake & Lucas, 1989). For example, consider the flexion response elicited by an aversive stimulus applied to the base of the foot. Because this response is organized by neurons within the spinal cord, it can be elicited in the absence of feedback from the brain. This reflex can be modified by imposing a response-outcome contingency: if shock is presented only when the limb is extended, the organism quickly learns to maintain its leg in a flexed (up) position. This modification of a reflexive behavior meets the minimum criteria (1–4) for instrumental conditioning (Grau et al., 1998). However, learning within the spinal cord appears biologically constrained. Given the same outcome, we cannot arbitrarily train subjects to exhibit either a flexion or an extension.

More sophisticated neural systems can support a greater range of flexibility. We could, for example, train a subject to lift or lower his or her hand using a variety of reinforcers (food, money, or shock). Such advanced forms of instrumental conditioning meet two additional criteria: Neither the nature of the behavioral change (criterion 5) nor the reinforcer (criterion 6) are constrained.

The term "instrumental conditioning" has its roots in the reflexive tradition of Thorndike, Konorski, and Hull (Hilgard & Marquis, 1940). From this perspective, instrumental learning reflects a form of elicited behavior, one that depends on the relationship established between a response and an outcome (Konorski & Miller, 1937). An alternative view was suggested by Skinner (1937, 1938), who noted that it is often difficult (or impossible) to specify the eliciting stimulus for advanced forms of instrumental behavior. He referred to this type of behavior as operant conditioning and argued that it is emitted, not elicited.

These historical facts continue to influence how the terms are used within the modern learning literature. Skinnerians focus on the experimental analysis of behavior and generally employ the term "operant conditioning," in which the emphasis is on emitted behavior and rate of responding. Those that follow in the tradition of Hull (1943) assume that response-outcome relations can affect elicited responses and that associative processes underlie complex instrumental behavior (Rescorla, 1991).

Because both instrumental and operant conditioning depend on the response-outcome relation, the terms are sometimes treated as synonymous. However, in cases in which the target response is elicited and/or an attempt is made to explain the behavior in terms of associative mechanisms, the term "instrumental conditioning" is more appropriate.

REFERENCES

Church, R. M. (1964). Systematic effect of random error in the yoked control design. *Psychological Bulletin, 62,* 122–131.

Grau, J. W., Barstow, D. G., & Joynes, R. L. (1998). Instrumental learning within the spinal cord: I. behavioral properties. *Behavioral Neuroscience, 112,* 1366–1386.

Hilgard, E. R., & Marquis, D. G. (1940). *Conditioning and learning.* New York: Appleton-Century-Crofts.

Hull, C. L. (1943). *Principles of behavior.* New York: Appleton-Century-Crofts.

Konorski, J. A., & Miller, S. M. (1937). On two types of conditioned reflex. *Journal of General Psychology, 16,* 264–273.

Skinner, B. F. (1937). Two types of conditioned reflex: A reply to Konorski and Miller. *Journal of General Psychology, 16,* 272–279.

Skinner, B. F. (1938). *The behavior of organisms.* Englewood Cliffs, N.J.: Prentice-Hall.

Thorndike, E. L. (1898). Animal intelligence: An experimental study of associative processes in animals. *Psychological Review., Monograph, 2* (8).

SUGGESTED READING

Hearst, E. (1975). The classical-instrumental distinction: Reflexes, voluntary behavior, and categories of associative learning. In W. K. Estes (Ed.), *Handbook of learning and cognitive processes: Conditioning and behavior theory* (pp. 181–223). Hillsdale, NJ: Erlbaum.

Rescorla, R. A. (1991). Associative relations in instrumental learning: The eighteenth Bartlett memorial lecture. *Quarterly Journal of Experimental Psychology, 43B,* 1–23.

Timberlake, W., & Lucas, G. A. (1989). Behavior systems and learning: From misbehavior to general principles. In S. B. Klein & R. R. Mowrer (Eds.), *Contemporary learning theories: Instrumental conditioning theory and the impact of biological constraints on learning* (pp. 237–275). Hillsdale, NJ: Erlbaum.

J. W. Grau
Texas A & M University

CLASSICAL CONDITIONING
OPERANT BEHAVIOR
OPERANT CONDITIONING
REINFORCEMENT
THORNDIKE'S LAW OF EFFECT

INTELLIGENCE MEASURES

Intelligence is a broad term referring to complex mental abilities of the individual. It is a term employed by lay persons to denote such qualities as quickness of mind, level of academic success, status on an occupational scale, or the attainment of eminence in a particular field of endeavor. Psychologists who measure intelligence have variously employed the term to indicate the amount of knowledge available and the speed with which new knowledge is acquired; the ability to adapt to new situations and to handle concepts, relationships, and abstract symbols; and even simply that phenomenon that intelligence tests measure. Validation studies of standardized tests of intelligence have demonstrated that they measure elements of mental abilities that appear to require intelligence, as the latter term is subjectively understood by scientists who study this human

characteristic. IQ scores derived from clinically administered individual intelligence tests can predict academic achievement for the top 90% of the general population who proceed through school in regular classes, while identifying individuals in the bottom 10% with IQs below 80 who may require specialized educational, psychological, or medical assistance.

It would be erroneous to think that intelligence is completely measured by current standardized tests of IQ. An IQ score is not the only measure of intelligence. It is merely the score earned by a person on a particular set of tasks or subtests on a test of measured intelligence, compared to the scores of those upon whom the test was normed (or standardized). Intelligence as the lay person understands it is more than the sum of the measured psychometric abilities tested by an IQ test. Intelligence also includes level of adaptive ability in such hard-to-measure but critically important characteristics as grades in school, performance at work, and success as a parent or, more generally, as a citizen. This is not contradictory, unless one insists upon the complete identity of intelligence merely with those aspects of intellectual ability that are currently measurable. As developed elsewhere in considerably more detail (Matarazzo, 1972, 1980), this section will use the term "intelligence" as a human characteristic best assessed by an index of the individual's *measured intelligence* (namely, an IQ score), plus an index of that same individual's *adaptive success* in everyday life (grades in school, standing on the occupational ladder, community achievement, and so on).

NONINTELLECTIVE FACTORS IN MEASURED INTELLIGENCE

The English psychologist Spearman (1904) demonstrated the presence of at least one *general factor* (g) in the degree of success demonstrated in classroom tests and tests of achievement requiring intellectual ability. Students who did well on arithmetic tests also seemed to do well on tests of vocabulary, geography, history, and other subjects. He also demonstrated the existence of *specific factors* (s) by showing that, despite this trend to perform at the same level on most tests, some individuals appeared to do exceptionally well in specific areas. Whether intelligence is basically a single ability (g), or an aggregate of numerous specific and different intellectual abilities (s), was debated by psychologists for three generations and still remains unresolved. What is known is that when large groups of persons are tested with a variety of intelligence or achievement tests, those who make high scores on one test tend to score high on others, while those who score low on one test also tend to score low on others. The evidence is equally strong that specific abilities exist above and beyond this general factor in measured intelligence.

Beginning in 1930, a third dimension of human intelligence was identified: Qualities of a person's individual level of intelligence that are reflected in his or her observed personality or temperament were unique to that individual and were as important as the measurable elements for understanding the person's level of adaptive success in everyday living. Subsequently, Wechsler termed these components *nonintellective factors* in general intelligence (1940). Wechsler found that existing tests of intelligence could measure only a portion of the capacities that enter into intelligent behavior. Even when dealing exclusively with measured intelligence, only 50 to 70% of intertest correlational variance (a statistical measure of individual differences in measured intelligence) could be accounted for after all measurable intellectual factors were eliminated; therefore, 30 to 50% of the total factor variance in individual differences in measured intelligence was unaccounted for. This meant that the remaining variance involved nonintellective factors and consisted of such components as drive, energy, impulsiveness, and so on (Wechsler, 1950). Since that time, a number of other nonintellective factors have been identified as crucial to the full assessment of an individual's intelligence, including: (a) motivation; (b) physical health; (c) level of aspiration; (d) anxiety; (e) level of maturation and personality integration; and (f) life history.

Since the introduction of the first test of measurable intelligence by Binet and Simon in 1905, all such tests have implicitly assumed the existence of a general or common factor in measured intelligence, along with specific and nonintellective factors. In addition to obtaining a sample of global intelligence, IQ and achievement tests have had as their purpose the prediction of future behavioral performance. Binet believed that, as an assessment instrument for gauging an individual's general intelligence, even his 1905 test assessed more than merely one's current ability to employ vocabulary, solve arithmetic problems, reproduce facts from memory, or manipulate objects manually. Anticipating Wechsler's more fully developed views, Binet believed that, above and beyond the mirroring of these cognitive abilities in intelligence tests, intricate components of the total personality such as reasoning and judgment are also present in one's score on an intelligence test. Nevertheless, Binet's main hope for the first successful test developed by him and Simon in 1905 was that it would serve as an objective yardstick for ascertaining which children were educable in the public schools, which ones needed extra or special education classes, and which were too intellectually retarded to benefit from regular schooling and therefore needed institutionalization. Not only did his test differentiate the educational approach needed by these three broad groups of children (regular classes, special education classes, and institutionalization), but in time his test proved capable of differentiating within each of these broad groupings.

Tables 1, 2, and 3 portray in specific and in summary fashion the results obtained from numerous studies on the validity of the IQ index. Table 1 can be used as a rough rule of thumb to assess the value of an IQ score in everyday living, while Table 2 shows the degree of usefulness of the IQ score when combined with a measure of adaptive behavior. As stressed previously, first Binet and later Wechsler concluded that intelligence is a quality of the total person and not a separate component that can be measured by IQ tests in isolation. A judgment of the level of one's intelligence requires the assessment of current adaptive performance in everyday living ascertained from a clinical history, existing environmental circumstances, and current behavior, as well as performance on a test of measurable intelligence. Since one's level of accomplishment is the result of both past and current experiences and abilities, it is susceptible to change when conditions in the individual or environment change. Such changes may result in a change (modest or major) in the individual's functional level of adaptive intelligence.

Table 1   Measured Intelligence and Education[a]

WAIS IQ[b]	Educational equivalent
125	Mean of persons receiving PhD and MD degrees
115	Mean of college graduates
105	Mean of high school graduates
100	Average total population
75	About 50/50 chance of reaching ninth grade

[a]From J. D. Matarazzo, 1972, *Wechsler's measurement and appraisal of adult intelligence* (5th ed.). Baltimore: Williams and Wilkins. Copyright Oxford University Press, New York. Reprinted by permission.
[b]These IQ values are averages only. Many individual exceptions can be found. For example, some college graduates have IQs of 100 or less, and many persons with IQs above 125 fail to complete high school.

Table 2   Exemplars of Validity Coefficients of IQ[a]

Exemplars	Correlation
IQ with adaptive behavior measure	
IQ × mental retardation	0.90
IQ × educational attainment (in years)	0.70
IQ × academic success (grade point)	0.50
IQ × occupational attainment	0.50
IQ × socioeconomic status	0.40
IQ × success on the job	0.20
Related variables	
IQ × independently judged prestige of one's occupation	0.95
IQ × parent's educational attainment	0.50

[a]From J. D. Matarazzo, 1972, *Wechsler's measurement and appraisal of adult intelligence* (5th ed.), p. 296. Baltimore: Williams and Wilkins. Copyright Oxford University Press, New York. Reprinted by permission.

The study carried out by Dillon and summarized in Table 3 provides an example of how well (but certainly not completely) an IQ score is able to predict the adaptive success of growing children, namely each child's subsequent level of school performance. Dillon gave an IQ test to the 2,600 seventh graders listed under the columns showing different IQ subgroupings in the first line of Table 3. As shown in the last line of that table, only 4% of the 400 seventh graders with an IQ below 85 progressed through grades 8 to 12 and graduation. Conversely, as shown in the last column of Table 3, 86% of the 400 youngsters whose IQ in Grade 7 was measured at 115 and above graduated from high school. Thus, anyone knowing a child's IQ in Grade 7 would have a reasonable idea of that child's chance of graduation from high school (see last row) 5 years before the child reached that age level. Armed with this information, youngsters in the lowest groups of measured intelligence shown in Table 3 could be encouraged to substitute drive (more hours of homework) for this relative deficiency in measured intelligence and thereby also graduate from high school with their classmates who in grade 7 scored relatively higher in these measurable aspects of intelligence. This was the major hope Binet had for his creation, and it remains the manner in which IQ tests are even today best used—namely, as guides for children and their parents to better help a willing youngster more effectively utilize intellectual potential.

Table 3   IQ and School Attrition as a Measure of Adaptive Behavior for 2600 Seventh Graders[a]

	Intelligence quotient				
	85	85–94	95–104	105–114	115+
All students in Grade 7	400	575	650	575	400
Remainder entering Grade 9	307	545	636	570	398
Remainder entering Grade 11	66	374	493	492	369
Remainder continuing to Graduation	14	309	412	437	344
Percent Grade 7	4%	54%	63%	76%	86%

[a]Adapted from H. J. Dillon, 1949, *Early school leavers: A major educational problem.* New York: National Child Labor Committee, and J. D. Matarazzo, 1972, *Wechsler's measurement and appraisal of adult intelligence* (5th ed.), p. 283. Baltimore: Williams and Wilkins. Copyright Oxford University Press, New York. Reprinted by permission.

INTELLIGENCE TESTS

Arithmetic skills, information, reasoning, manipulation of objects, vocabulary, and memory functions constitute some of the tasks employed in tests of measured intelligence, whether they are called primary grade achievement tests, Scholastic Aptitude Tests (SAT), or intelligence tests. The objective of each of these types of tests is to appraise overall performance so as to obtain an estimate of general intellectual potential. Numerous tests of these types can be combined to furnish a single measure of intelligence because of their functional equivalence. To obtain a person's IQ or relative standing, one can add together the results obtained from tests of apparently disparate abilities, because scores on such tests are known to be related (correlated), thus providing a measure of global intelligence.

The Stanford–Binet and the Wechsler Scales are individually administered tests widely used today by educational psychologists, industrial psychologists, and clinical psychologists whose day-to-day work involves an intensive clinical, school, or job-related investigation of a person's intellectual functioning. *Group* intelligence tests such as the Scholastic Achievement Test provide the advantage of administration to many persons at the same time. However, such tests are used primarily for purposes of classification and screening in schools, the military, employment settings, and hospitals and clinics that process large numbers of patients. Group-administered tests of intelligence do not provide sufficient clinical or personal data for the comprehensive assessment of a single person's intelligence. This latter is better obtained through use of individually administered tests; a review of the individual's levels of adaptive success in school, on the job, and in other aspects of daily living; plus his or her motivation to succeed and the opportunities available.

Prerequisite to a correct interpretation of an individual's IQ test score as one of the two components of intelligence is a knowledge of some basic characteristics of such IQ scores—specifically, knowledge of their norms, reliability, and validity. It is important in using an IQ test to be familiar with the complexities and subtleties of intelligence assessment through reading and clinical experience, so as to identify individual differences arising from any of a host of environmental circumstances, brain dysfunction, personality disturbance, and physical disability (Matarazzo, 1972, 1980).

Norms are the scores obtained from a large number of subjects during the process of standardizing a test. These multiple person-derived scores serve as a standard for comparison against which a single individual may be evaluated. If such a client differs in sex, race, or socioeconomic status from the group upon whom a test's norms were derived, then the test is not valid for this individual. Test norms are generally reported as mental ages, standard scores, or percentiles. A child's mental age (MA) is the age of all other children whose test performance he or she equals. In one early form of its measurement, an IQ was obtained by dividing the mental age by the chronological age (CA) and multiplying by 100:

$$IQ = \frac{MA}{CA} \times 100$$

Thus an 8-year-old who scores as well as an average 10-year-old on the individually administered Stanford–Binet Test has an MA of 10 and a CA of 8. His IQ in this case is 125.

The measurement of intelligence as reflected by IQ test scores reveals that individuals vary by degrees along a continuous scale. The distribution of such scores is portrayed graphically in Figure 1. A percentile is a score that divides the sample population into 100 parts. It tells the percentage of individuals found below a given score. Standard scores show an individual's distance from the mean in standard deviation units. In Figure 1, the mean IQ is arbitrarily set at 100. That number is merely a convention. The standard deviation (SD) is a measure of the variability of the IQ scores of many individuals around that mean. One finds approximately 68% of the IQ scores of individual persons within one standard deviation above and below the mean for the age (sex, and so on) group of which they are a member. In Figure 1, 50% of all persons shown earned an IQ score between 90 and 110, with 25% obtaining IQs below 90 and the remaining 25% earning scores above 110. The 25% of the population scoring below 90 has been classified progressively by psychologists as dull normal, borderline, and retarded, respectively. For better treatment and education of such individuals, the retarded classification was subsequently divided into subcategories of mild, moderate, severe, and profound retardation. The remaining 25% of the population scoring above 110 is classed as bright normal, superior, and very superior as measured on the Wechsler scales. Approximately 2% of the population is found in each of the extreme categories of very superior or retarded. Scores from an intelligence test are readily converted into any scale of units such as the Wechsler or Binet Scales, the Army General Clas-

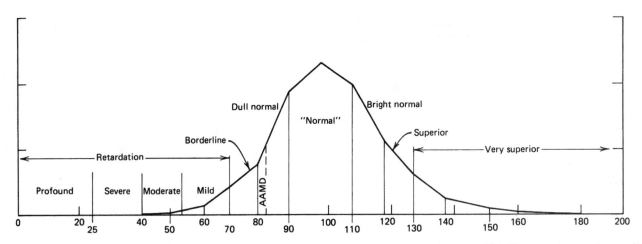

Figure 1.   The distribution of Wechsler Adult Intelligence Scale IQ categories. These categories of measured intelligence serve as only one of several indices of intelligence. A second, equally critical index is an estimate of the same person's adaptive intelligence in school, in the home, at work, and in the community. From J. D. Matarazzo, 1972, *Wechsler's Measurement and Appraisal of Adult Intelligence,* p. 124 (5th ed.). Baltimore: Williams and Wilkins. Copyright Oxford University Press, New York. Reprinted by permission.

sification Test, or the Scholastic Aptitude Test (which, for example, uses a mean of 500 and a standard deviation of 100).

Reliability refers to the consistency of a person's test score. It is usually obtained by comparing (correlating) the individual's test score with a second score, obtained by readministering the same test to that person, or with the score from an alternate form of the same test. *Validity* refers to whether the test used actually measures what it purports to measure: namely, what can be inferred from the test score by reference of it to something outside the test. Thus validity is commonly employed to describe the extent to which IQ test scores correlate with past or future measures of the individual's performance, such as scholastic achievement or success on a job. Tables 1, 2, and 3 provide examples of the extent (validity) to which scores on an IQ test correlate with indices in everyday living that are believed to be related to a person's level of intelligence. Such extratest measures of behavior as are enumerated in these tables are referred to as the criterion or criteria against which scores on an IQ test are validated.

Some objective measures of an individual's level of adaptive success have been developed (especially for children's levels of success in day-to-day living). One such measure assesses a child's level of skills in using eating utensils, toileting requirements, sensory and motor development, dressing and undressing, socialization, using a bus, traveling within the neighborhood, and so on. Correlations ranging from 0.58 to 0.95 have been reported between the score obtained from such adaptive behavior scales and an intelligence test on the same child, indicating that adaptive behavior and measured intelligence are correlated but not identical (Leland, Shellhaas, Nihira, & Foster, 1967). Experts agree that in the field of mental retardation, the use by a skilled professional of a client's IQ score, indications of socioadaptive behavior, and clinical history has improved the diagnosis of mental retardation to a level of validity more accurate than that of any other diagnosis in the field of psychopathology.

Like most tools, psychological assessment techniques can be used for a diversity of purposes, some destructive and some con-

structive, and their use cannot be separated from the training, competence, and ethical values of the psychologist. In the hands of a good clinician, the results of an IQ examination, when correlated with other information, are as useful as comparable laboratory data in the hands of a good surgeon, internist, accountant, or plumber. Most intelligence-test users use them wisely and humanely and—in conjunction with measures of adaptive success—in a manner that maximizes the potential of each individual taking the examination.

REFERENCES

Binet, A., & Simon, T. (1905). Application des methodes nouvelles au diagnostic intellectual chez des enfants normal et anormaux d'hospice et d'école primitive. *L'Année Psychologique, 11,* 245–336.

Binet, A., & Simon, T. (1905). Méthodes nouvelles pour le diagnostic du niveau intellectuel des anormaux. *L'Année Psychologique, 11,* 191–244.

Dillon, H. J. (1949). *Early school leavers: A major educational problem.* New York: National Child Labor Committee.

Matarazzo, J. D. (1972). *Wechsler's measurement and appraisal of adult intelligence* (5th ed.). Baltimore: Williams & Wilkins.

Matarazzo, J. D. (1980). Behavioral health and behavioral medicine: Frontiers for a new health psychology. *American Psychologist, 35,* 807–817.

Matarazzo, J. D. (1980). Psychological assessment of intelligence. *Comprehensive textbook of psychiatry/III.* Baltimore, MD: London: Williams & Wilkins.

Spearman, C. E. (1904). "General intelligence," objectively determined and measured. *American Journal of Psychology, 15,* 201–292.

Wechsler, D. (1940). Nonintellective factors in general intelligence. *Psychological Bulletin, 37,* 444–445.

Wechsler, D. (1950). Cognitive, conative, and nonintellective intelligence. *American Psychologist, 5*, 78–83.

J. D. MATARAZZO
Oregon Health Sciences University

D. R. DENVER
Quebec, Montreal, Canada

HUMAN INTELLIGENCE
MEASUREMENT
STANFORD–BINET INTELLIGENCE SCALE
WECHSLER INTELLIGENCE TESTS

INTELLIGENCE, SOCIAL POLICY & GENETIC CONTRIBUTION

The contribution of genetics to intelligence requires at the outset a definition of intelligence and the tests that measure (estimate) it. The genetic contribution is estimated from the distribution of raw scores on a test that is a reasonably valid measure of the construct, generally known as psychometric general intelligence.

Psychometric general intelligence can be defined uniquely. It is derived empirically by narrow, objective tests measuring a broad set of cognitive tasks that are positively intercorrelated. When standard psychometric methods are used, a general factor is defined from these intercorrelations that is highly replicable from one representative set of problem-solving tasks to another (Humphreys, 1994).

The general factor can be estimated validly by a number of broader-based problem-solving tests. The most accurate estimator is a test like a Wechsler (1988, 1974) that has varied content and requires widely different operations with that content. Tests with one type of content requiring complex operations, such as verbal, quantitative, or figural, are substantially valid and differ litte from each other in that respect.

Behavior geneticists estimate a statistic called heritability, which is the ratio of genetic variance in a test to the total variance of the test for a particular population at a particular period of time. Their data will shortly be discussed. Quantitative estimates may not be necessary to quiet endemic concerns of so many Americans about a genetic contribution. There is a perceived conflict with democratic values. Such concerns might be disconfirmed by seeing the consequences of a hypothetical heritability coefficient of 1.00. In addition to the heritability of 1.00, we shall assume a zero correlation between the respective intelligences of the parents.

Under these circumstances the correlation between distributions of the intelligence of one of the two parents and a single child would be .50. The average level of intelligence of the sample of children would be halfway to their mean from the mean for the parents. The error of estimate about the children's mean would be .866 of a unit standard deviation, indicating that their individual scores would be almost as widely scattered as the distribution of children in general. These numbers describe a phenomenon known as re-

gression to the mean. Regression provides, when produced by either genetics or culture, for major differences between a given parent and a given child.

When the intelligence of both parents is known, the score correlated is midparent intelligence. In this hypothetical example the standard deviation of the midparent distribution is reduced from 1.00 to .707. The estimate of children's mean intelligence is the same as their parents' midparent score. The children would still regress almost a third of the difference toward the children's mean and would be distributed about their regressed mean with a standard deviation of .707 of the unit value. In most cases there would be a substantial difference between a child's score and one of the two parents.

BEHAVIOR GENETICS DATA

An excellent source for these data is Plomin and Petrill (1997). Behavior geneticists divide variance into genetic, between-family (shared environment), and within-family (nonshared environment) components. Each of the three can be independently estimated by imposing appropriate constraints. The genetic variance is derived from information about family resemblances. The genetic contribution is not necessarily unitary, biologically. It may require nothing more than the structures and chemicals of the central nervous system and other more peripheral structures and chemicals of the body as a whole. Between-family variance includes, but is not limited to, socioeconomic differences. Sources of within-family variance include person-to-person interactions within the family and the environmental choices made by a developing child.

Themselves drawing from several published sources, Plomin and Petrill (1997) provided the source of the data we present in Table 1. Heritability of intelligence increases from about .4 in early childhood to .6 in the late teens and early adulthood. (It may continue to increase into old age). Between-family variance peaks in early childhood and drops to zero in early adulthood. Apparently the family environment is able to jump-start growing intelligence in the earlier ages, but genetic differences become increasingly important. Within-family variance increases somewhat with increasing maturity. Error is the estimate of measurement error in the test.

These behavior genetic results are paralleled by longitudinal research in which correlations between individual differences over many different intervals of time are computed (Humphreys, Davey, & Park, 1985; Humphreys & Davey, 1988; McCall, 1979). The intercorrelations that result from the annual measurement of general intelligence from early in life to the late teens form a quasi-simplex (Guttman, 1955). Correlations are high from year to year, but become increasingly lower as time between test and retest increases.

Table 1.   Contributions to Variance of Four Components at Two Age Levels

| Age Levels | Genetic | Environment | | Error |
		Shared	Nonshare	
Early Childhood	.40	.25	.25	.10
Late Teens and Early Adult	.60	.00	.35	.05

Neither Humphreys nor McCall explained the gradual change in individual differences that took place, but the data in Table 1 provide one. The explanation requires a gradual increase in genetic variance to the behavior on the test.

OBSERVED FAMILY RESEMBLANCES

The single parent-single child correlation may be as high as .50, but there is a good deal of scatter about values reported (Plomin & Petrill, 1997). These values represent the correlation for the cultural-genetic mix in the variance of the test used. The correlation between the two parents may also be as high as .50. Accepting these values, estimates of regression toward the children's mean of the children of one and two parents can be obtained. Very able parents in the distribution of single parents produce children who regress at least halfway back to the mean of their group. The correlation between midparent scores and single children is less than .60. The mean child regresses about .40 toward the children's mean.

It is known with certainty that the phenotypic scores of children on intelligence tests will be much closer to the mean, on average, than were their parents. Children will show substantial variability about the average expected. Correlations between children's intelligence and other relatives shrink as the difference in degree of relationship increases. On average the intelligence of the descendants of highly intelligent persons after several generations is merely average. Genetics does not produce a rigid class structure. The role that a child will play in society as an adult need not be determined by social class. It can be determined by genetics without violence to democratic values.

GENETICS AND RACE

A contribution of genetics to intelligence should not be discussed without a brief reference to race. There are cultural-genetic components to race differences in observed scores on intelligence tests. The reason is that biological and cultural differences do exist. The mix is not known, but two different statements about the mix can be made with confidence. There are no data meeting scientific standards that reject the hypothesis that the black-white difference is entirely cultural. There are also no data meeting the same standard that reject the hypothesis that the black-white difference is largely genetic in origin. Neither argument nor pontification will resolve the question. We do have quantitative estimates of nature and nurture on *individual* differences in intelligence.

INTELLIGENCE, GENETICS, AND SOCIAL POLICY

A heritability coefficient as high as the ones reported cannot harm a democratic society. Citizens can embrace a large genetic contribution to general intelligence and use it to follow democratic principles of equality of opportunity and equality under the law. Social institutions, however, can produce relatively rigid social classes or even castes that defeat these principles.

A single flat tax is being advocated as a way of simplifying the tax structure. The simplifying argument is appealing, but a graduated flat tax can be applied in successive strata of income. A reduction in inheritance taxes is advocated on the basis of saving family-owned businesses and family farms. Those reasons are appealing,

but accomplishing those goals does not require the same action for huge fortunes.

Change is being advocated in public education to help disadvantaged children by giving parents vouchers. The radical element in the proposal extends vouchers to all parents to help pay expenses in every primary and secondary school, both public and private. This legislation would be accompanied by the existing and still increasing costs of higher education. Economically segregated schooling would increase social class rigidity.

An economically entrenched upper class falls far short of producing the talent needed by a country to be competitive in business and industry, the arts, and science. The genetic mechanism produces talent almost at random throughout a given population. Social action should concentrate on finding talent and encouraging it. No matter how widely dispersed, talent can be located by a valid psychometric test of general intelligence. Locating is just the first step; encouragement requires social action to change existing and proposed policies.

REFERENCES

Guttman, L. (1955) A generalized simplex for factor analysis. *Psychometrika, 20,* 173–192.

Humphreys, L. G. (1994). Intelligence from the standpoint of a (pragmatic) behaviorist. *Psychological Inquiry, 5,* 179–192.

Humphreys, L. G., & Davey, T. C. (1988). Continuity in intellectual growth from 12 months to 9 years. *Intelligence, 12,* 183–197.

Humphreys, L. G., Davey, T. C., & Park, R. K. (1985). Longitudinal analysis of standing height and intelligence. *Child Development, 56,* 1465–1478.

McCall, R. B. (1979). Stability-instability in mental performance. In J. D. Osofsky (Ed.), *Handbook of infant development* (pp. 707–741). New York: Wiley.

Plomin, R., & Petrill, S. A. (1997). Genetics and intelligence: What's new? *Intelligence, 24,* 53–77.

Wechsler, D. (1958). *Measurement and appraisal of adult intelligence* (4th ed.). Baltimore: Williams and Wilkins.

Wechsler, D. (1974). *Manual for the Wechsler Intelligence Scale for Children-Revised.* New York: Psychological Corporation.

L. G. HUMPHREYS
S. STARK
University of Illinois

INTELLIGENCE MEASURES
CULTURE BIAS IN TESTS
CULTURE FAIR TESTS
MEASUREMENT

INTEREST INVENTORIES

Various methods for determining an individual's preferences for specific topics or activities are available, including direct observations of behavior, performance on ability tests, responses to projective test items, and self-report inventories. The last of these—inventories of interests in educational, social, recreational, and vocational activities—has stimulated a great amount of research and development. Beginning with the pioneering efforts of E. K. Strong, Jr., during the 1920s, the emphasis has been on measures of vocational interests, culminating in sophisticated, multivariable, computer-scored, and computer-interpreted inventories.

THE STRONG AND KUDER INVENTORIES

Two landmarks in the history of interest measurement were the Strong Vocational Interest Blank for Men (Strong, 1927) and the Kuder Preference Record (Kuder, 1939). These instruments and their successors have helped two generations of high school and college students become acquainted with career options and aware of their vocational interests. Such tests have also played a role, to some extent, in employee selection and classification in occupational contexts.

Publication of the first Strong Vocational Interest Blank for Men in 1927, and one for women in 1933, was followed by various revisions of each; in 1974 they were merged into the Strong–Campbell Interest Inventory, a restandardization of which was published in 1981. Further development of Kuder's inventories also occurred, represented by the publication of the Kuder Form A: Personal Preference Survey; Kuder Form C: Vocational Preference Record; Kuder Form DD: Occupational Interest Survey; and Kuder Form E: General Interest Survey.

The item format on the Strong–Campbell Interest Inventory requires examinees to indicate whether they like, dislike, or are indifferent to a list of occupations, school subjects, activities, amusements, and types of people. There is also a section on which examinees are asked to choose between two activities and another section on which they indicate whether each of 14 characteristics describes them. In contrast, the Kuder items are forced-choice triads, on which examinees indicate which of the three things they would most like and least like to do.

The Strong inventories were originally scored by the empirical procedure of comparing the examinee's item responses with the responses of specific occupational groups of people. Thus, scoring of the Strong inventories was normative, in contrast to the ipsative scoring of the original Kuder inventories. The Kuder Preference Record is scored on 10 interest scales, consisting of items having high correlations with one another but low correlations with the other scales. The forced-choice format of the Kuder inventories makes it impossible to score high or low on all scales. A typical score profile on the Kuder Preference Record consists of one or more high scores and one or more low scores, but mostly average scores. Both the Strong and Kuder inventories are also scored on special scales to determine if examinees followed the test directions carefully.

The Strong–Campbell Interest Inventory is scored both in the traditional empirical manner (162 occupational scales) and the Kuder interest cluster way (23 basic interest scales). By employing Holland's interest classification scheme (1972), the Strong–Campbell Interest Inventory is also scored on six general occupational themes. A further indication of the rapprochement between the methods of scoring the Strong and Kuder inventories is seen in the fact that the Kuder Form DD: Occupational Interest Survey is scored empirically by comparing the responses of examinees with those of specified occupational groups.

Research on the reliability of the Strong and Kuder inventories has found moderate to high short-term reliability coefficients and moderate long-term coefficients. Studies have also revealed appreciable validities for predicting occupational entry and persistence, but not performance within occupations. Like most inventories of interests and personality, the Strong–Campbell and Kuder instruments can be faked. It seems reasonable that they are more likely to be answered honestly in vocational counseling situations than when used for applicant selection.

OTHER INTEREST INVENTORIES

Although the Strong–Campbell and Kuder inventories dominate the field of interest measurement, there are many other entries. Noteworthy among these are factor-analyzed instruments such as the Guilford–Zimmerman Interest Inventory and the G-S-Z Interest Survey, as well as general interest surveys such as the California Occupational Preference Survey, the Jackson Vocational Interest Survey, and the Ohio Vocational Interest Survey. In addition, there are special inventories for children ("What I Like to Do," Career Awareness Inventory); for the disadvantaged (Geist Picture Interest Inventory); and for assessing interests in skilled trades (Minnesota Vocational Interest Inventory). Following Holland's theory (1973) of the relationships of interests to personality is the Vocational Preference Inventory. Also developed with reference to a specific theory of personality is the Hall Occupational Orientation Inventory.

COUNSELING WITH INTEREST INVENTORIES

Interest inventories have found their greatest use in vocational counseling. The modern approach is to use inventories in conjunction with other kinds of career educational materials to introduce young people to the world of work. Most high school students are not very knowledgeable about what specific jobs entail and are often unrealistic in their career choices. Consequently, vocational counselors must be prepared to educate as well as counsel. One distinction to be made clear to counselees is that interest is not the same as ability; a high score on an interest inventory scale should not be interpreted as indicating an ability to pursue related occupations. To minimize the tendency to overinterpret scores on interest inventories, such scores should be interpreted only in the light of other supporting and clarifying information about counselees. Thus, vocational counseling is most effective when scores on ability tests and interest inventories, as well as school grades and information on out-of-school activities, are available to counselors.

REFERENCES

Holland, J. L. (1970–1973). *The self-directed search.* Palo Alto, CA: Consulting Psychologists Press.

Holland, J. L. (1973). *Making vocational choices: A theory of careers.* Englewood Cliffs, NJ: Prentice-Hall.

Kuder, G. F. (1939). The stability of preference items. *Journal of Social Psychology, 10,* 41–50.

Strong, E. K. (1927). Differentiation of CPAs from other occupational groups. *Journal of Educational Psychology, 18,* 227–238.

L. R. AIKEN
Pepperdine University

CAREER COUNSELING
COUNSELING
JOB SATISFACTION
OCCUPATIONAL COUNSELING

INTERFERENCE

One of the earliest and most robust findings of experimental psychology is that two event representations in memory can compete with one another. If training on Task A precedes Task B, subsequent testing on Task B may yield impaired (i.e., proactive interference) or facilitated performance relative to control subjects who were not exposed to Task A. Conversely, subsequent testing on Task A may yield impairment (i.e., retroactive interference) or facilitation relative to control subjects who were not exposed to Task B. Such interference is commonly viewed as evidence of competition between the representations of Tasks A and B. Interference (and facilitation) has been observed across a wide variety of subjects (including human and nonhuman species) and tasks. Much of the memory research conducted over the last century has attempted to identify relevant variables (for excellent reviews, old but still relevant, see Postman & Underwood, 1973; Underwood, 1957). The following remarks apply equally to proactive and retroactive interference (and facilitation) except where otherwise noted.

INDEPENDENT VARIABLES

The most important variables in producing proactive and retroactive interference appear to be: (a) the amount of training on each task; (b) the temporal interval between training on the two tasks and between training on each task and testing; and (c) the similarity of the two tasks, the last of which appears central in determining whether interference or facilitation will be observed. Not surprisingly, more extensive training on a task makes it more apt to impact performance on another task and less apt to be impacted by training on another task. The closer in time the two tasks are to one another, the more apt they are to interact, producing interference (or facilitation) on the test task. Given a fixed interval between Task A and Task B training, the retention interval can be manipulated. Unlike the effects of most other independent variables on interference, which are symmetric between the proactive and retroactive cases, lengthening the retention interval decreases retroactive interference and enhances proactive interference, presumably because a significant portion of retroactive interference depends on a recency effect, and recency effects wane with increasing retention intervals (Postman, Stark, & Fraser, 1968). Task similarity appears

to be the prime determinant of whether interference or enhancement will be observed.

One of the most systematic attempts to summarize these relationships was by Osgood (1949). Although his principles were elegantly logical, research has found that only some of them are consistently supported. Let us conceptualize a task as consisting of an eliciting stimulus and an acquired response to that stimulus (e.g., in paired-associate learning, Task A eliciting stimulus = chair, response = banana; Task B eliciting stimulus = stool, response = car). Obviously, two tasks with the same eliciting stimuli and same responses are identical, reducing the Task A–Task B sequence to additional training on a single task; consequently, facilitation is anticipated and, of course, observed. Conversely, when the two eliciting stimuli are highly dissimilar and the two responses are also highly dissimilar, little interaction is expected and little is observed. The interesting cases are when the eliciting stimuli are similar and the responses are dissimilar (or incompatible) as in the above example from paired associate learning, and when the eliciting stimuli are dissimilar and the responses are similar. In the former case, interference is ordinarily observed. But in the latter case, the outcome can range from interference to facilitation, and we do not yet have a simple rule for anticipating which outcome will occur other than experience with prior similar situations.

THEORETICAL MECHANISMS

Several different theoretical accounts have been proposed to explain interference. Available evidence suggests that no single account will suffice (which is not to suggest that all proposed mechanisms contribute equally or even at all in each case). Accounts appear to fall into one of three categories (Miller, Greco, Marlin, & Balaz, 1985; Runquist, 1975): (a) competition for a limited capacity processing system at the time of acquisition (often called "processing interference"); (b) competition between tasks for representation in long-term memory over the Task B-test retention interval; and (c) competition for retrieval and response generation at the time of testing (often called "trace interference"). Processing interference appears to take place only when the two competing tasks occur close in time. With this type of interference, task similarity is relatively unimportant. (However, more interference can be expected if the two events use the same sensory modality than in different modalities because the limited processing capacity of organisms appears to be largely segregated by sensory modality.) The second mechanism assumes that the representations of the two task (or event) representations compete for a place in long-term memory rather than coexist with one another. This mechanism would only be relevant only when the two events are contrafactual (e.g., acquisition and extinction, or conditioning and counterconditioning). Many researchers deny that this second interference mechanism exists, preferring to attribute all evidence cited in support of this mechanism to trace interference. Trace interference has received the greatest amount of attention, and, not surprisingly, theorizing concerning it is most highly developed. The consistent finding concerning this third mechanism is that the greater the similarity between eliciting stimulus of the interfering task (including nominal, contextual, and temporal cues) and the test conditions, relative to the similarity between the eliciting stimulus of the target task and the test conditions, the greater interference will be (e.g., Bouton, 1993; Tulving & Thomson, 1973).

Generally speaking, temporal variables (i.e., processing interference) appear to have their greatest impact when the intervals separating Tasks A, B, and testing are relatively short (measured in seconds, e.g., Peterson & Peterson, 1959), whereas the impact of task similarity variables (trace interference) seems to be greatest at longer intervals (Runquist, 1975). This suggests that these variables act through fundamentally different mechanisms (Miller et al., 1985). Seemingly, most interference with short intervals separating Tasks A and B reflects competition between A and B for access to a limited capacity short-term memory. In contrast, interference with longer intervals reflects competition for retrieval and for response generation. These relationships have been well known for over thirty years. Contemporary research on interference (e.g., Matute & Pineno, 1998) has given rise to a plethora of hypothesized mechanisms, but they all appear to fall within the three families of accounts described above.

PERMANENCE

Interference effects in principle can be due either to a potentially reversible lapse in performance (an expression failure) or an irreversible absence of information (i.e., failure to acquire information or loss after acquisition). Each of the three types of mechanisms could, in principle, yield reversible or irreversible interference. But the three types of mechanisms are commonly thought to diverge sharply in terms of the interference that they produce being reversible or irreversible. The first and second types of interference are generally viewed as resulting in an irreversible absence from memory of the target task representation. In contrast, the third type of interference is usually viewed as yielding a failure to express information that is still retained in memory. Consistent with this view, interference observed with relatively long intervals between training on the two tasks often can be reversed without additional training on the target task. Spontaneous recovery from retroactive interference is one particularly clear case of this. Priming and variation in retrieval cues at test are other often successful means of obtaining recovery from interference; however, these demonstrations are less compelling evidence of a lapse (rather than an absence) of information, because they potentially tap into different representations of the target task than that which was assessed (and found wanting) originally.

AN APPLIED EXAMPLE

Interference theory is applicable to many practical situations. For example, one contemporary application of interference theory (and controversy in its explanation) is provided by demonstrations that eyewitness accounts of events are subject to retroactive interference, often originating with leading questions from attorneys. One view is that the representation of the original (target) event is irreversibly altered by the (subsequent) interfering event (in our terminology, mechanism type 2; e.g., Loftus, 1975). In contrast, an alternative view is that the representation of the original event is still present in memory but is less readily retrieved because of the interfering event (trace interference; e.g., McCloskey & Zaragoza, 1985).

REFERENCES

Bouton, M. E. (1993). Context, time, and memory retrieval in the interference paradigms of Pavlovian learning. *Psychological Bulletin, 114,* 80–99.

Loftus, E. F. (1975). Leading questions and the eyewitness report. *Cognitive Psychology, 7,* 560–572.

Matute, H., & Pineno, O. (1998). Stimulus competition in the absence of compound conditioning. *Animal Learning & Behavior, 26,* 3–14.

McCloskey, M., & Zaragoza, M. (1985). Misleading postevent information and memory for events: Arguments and evidence against memory impairment hypotheses. *Journal of Experimental Psychology: General, 114,* 3–18.

Miller, R. R., Greco, C., Marlin, N. A., & Balaz, M. A. (1985). Retroactive interference in rats: Independent effects of time and similarity of the interfering event with respect to acquisition. *Quarterly Journal of Experimental Psychology, 37B,* 81–100.

Osgood, C. E. (1949). The similarity paradox in human learning: A resolution. *Psychological Review, 56,* 132–143.

Peterson, L., & Peterson, M. J. (1959). Short-term retention of individual verbal items. *Journal of Experimental Psychology, 58,* 193–198.

Postman, L., Stark, K., & Fraser, J. (1968). Temporal changes in interference. *Journal of Verbal Learning and Verbal Behavior, 7,* 672–694.

Postman, L., & Underwood, B. J. (1973). Critical issues in interference theory. *Memory & Cognition, 1,* 19–40.

Runquist, W. N. (1975). Interference among memory traces. *Memory & Cognition, 3,* 143–159.

Tulving, E., & Thomson, D. M. (1973). Encoding specificity and retrieval processes in episodic memory. *Psychological Review, 80,* 352–373.

Underwood, B. J. (1957). Interference and forgetting. *Psychological Review, 64,* 49–60.

R. R. MILLER
State University of New York, Binghamton

FORGETTING
MEMORY

INTERNAL VALIDITY

Internal validity pertains to the degree of assurance that can be attributed to a suspected causal relationship between variables. An experiment has internal validity to the extent that observed effects can be attributed to independent variables and not some other extraneous factors.

An imputation of causality generally assumes that two variables—the cause and the effect—will covary, but before internal validity can be inferred, it must be demonstrated that A does indeed *cause* B, i.e., that the occurrence of A alone produces B. One could, for example, erroneously assume that home instruction in the performance of perceptual-motor tasks: (A) causes children to earn better grades in school (B) when, in fact, it is parental concern and attention (C) rather than the perceptual-motor training per se that produce the desired result.

Psychological experiments are particularly vulnerable to the misleading and unintended effects of adventitious variables, because they can rarely be performed within pristine confines such as a physics laboratory. Therefore, designing an experiment in such a way that when positive results ensue causality can be inferred has become a preoccupation of thoughtful researchers in psychology.

Internal validity can be contrasted with external validity, which refers to the generalizability of results beyond the specific context in which internal validity was obtained. For example, if it could be shown, under carefully controlled conditions, that overcrowding in cages causes aggressive behavior in white rats (internal validity), would this also hold true for humans living in a ghetto (external validity)?

Internal validity should be differentiated from construct validity, which is a theoretical explanation of a hypothesized cause-and-effect relationship. In most cases, however, if internal validity seems reasonably established, a researcher would want to formulate a conceptual framework or construct to account for the relationship. Also, internal validity should not be confused with internal consistency, which is a testing term relating to intercorrelations among a set of items.

The term *internal validity* was coined by Campbell and Stanley (1963), but philosophically, the issues addressed were recognized and dealt with by John Stuart Mill (1862), who believed that causal connections could be established provided observations were made in the proper manner. Mill's "Canons of Induction," arguably the forerunners of what is known today as experimental design, dealt with logical stratagems for instituting control over an experiment, which he designated the method of agreement, method of difference, joint method, and method of residues. He also introduced the concept of concomitant variations, which has now been supplanted by the statistical term *correlation*. Unfortunately, however, it is impossible to control every aspect of an experimental environment. A correlation, even if it is perfect, does not guarantee causation. Therefore, internal validity must be viewed as an ideal to be approximated rather than a goal to be attained.

In attempting to establish internal validity, it is necessary to verify the sequence of events. Obviously, if there is a relationship between A and B and A always precedes B, it is logical to assume that A causes B and not the reverse. Along with instituting as much environmental and situational control as possible, psychologists conducting research are concerned with selecting subjects in such a way as not to bias assignment to experimental and control groups. They also resort to sophisticated experimental designs such as covariance and counterbalancing to exert statistical controls over variable effects so that informed judgments about causal relationships can be made.

Often, however, the exigencies of psychological research with human beings result in flawed designs and it is then incumbent on the investigator to at least be cognizant of "threats" to internal validity. The following, in abbreviated form, is an analysis taken from Cook and Campbell (1979) of problems that can arise when conducting quasi-experimental or field research in psychology, all of which pose potential threats to internal validity.

1. Events can transpire during the time that has elapsed between two evaluations that can alter the subjects' reactions. For example, if the effect of a new drug on reducing anxiety is being tested but a tornado hits the locale during the interim between evaluations, measures of anxiety may be unduly influenced by the fear-inducing catastrophe.

2. By the same token, naturally occurring maturational changes over time can also produce effects that contaminate the experiment, i.e., improvement in perceptual-motor skills in children could be due to simple aging rather than training.

3. In research involving repeated testings, many exposures to the same instrument can produce a cumulative effect that contaminates the treatment being investigated, e.g., improvement in IQ due to an "enriched" environment could be a result of familiarity with the intelligence test.

4. Changes in the instruments used to make evaluations, whether mechanical or human, can produce effects other than the treatments being investigated; a spring can lose its elasticity and a rater can alter his or her orientation over time.

5. If the phenomenon of statistical regression (the tendency for higher and lower scores to revert toward the average on retesting) is ignored, an overly positive and misleading estimate of a relationship can be obtained, and consequently, erroneous conclusions about causality drawn.

6. An unintentional bias in allocating subjects to control and/or experimental groups can produce results that are related to these unsuspected but nonrandom assignments of cases. Differences among the groups due to selectivity rather than the treatments being investigated can then lead to unwarranted conclusions.

7. Any loss of cases during the conduct of an experiment as a result of drop out, illness, or even death can bias the results of an experiment if the attrition turns out to be nonrandom.

8. Uncertainty about whether A is caused by or is a result of B has an obvious bearing on internal validity. Does the football team play better because of larger crowds or do larger crowds come to the game because the team plays better?

9. Accidental and unwanted communication among treatment groups destroys the experimental naïveté of the subjects and can induce attitudes and expectations unrelated to the purpose of the research. Along the same lines, the experiment itself could generate compensatory rivalry, resentment, and demoralization in participant subjects and/or groups, all of which are not germane and could differentially affect the results.

10. Because experimenters do not operate in a vacuum, it sometimes happens that, for administrative or social reasons, groups receive compensatory treatment that tends to equalize effects and work against the achievement of valid results. For example, giving at least minimal therapy to a control group of patients who were to receive no therapy at all could be justified for humanitarian reasons but patently defeats the intent of the experiment.

There is no way to conduct a perfect experiment, i.e., one in which control is so complete that it would be impossible to explain away an effect or relationship as artifactual. Furthermore, the context in which psychological experiments are usually conducted makes them especially vulnerable to interpretive ambiguity and the drawing of erroneous conclusions. An intimate knowledge of the field and cognizance of the many pitfalls involved in quasi-experimental research can, however, help the psychologist to design an experiment that is more likely to permit genuine inferences about internal validity.

REFERENCES

Campbell, D. T., & Stanley, J. (1963). Experimental and quasi-experimental designs for research. In N. L. Gage (Ed.), *Handbook of research on teaching.* Chicago: Rand-McNally.

Cook, T. D., & Campbell, D. T. (1979). *Quasi-experimentation: Design and analysis issues for field settings.* Boston: Houghton Mifflin.

SUGGESTED READING

Mahoney, M. J. (1978). Experimental methods and outcome evaluations. *Journal of Clinical and Consulting Psychology, 46,* 660–672.

E. E. WAGNER
Forest Institute of Professional Psychology

EXPERIMENTAL DESIGNS
EXPERIMENTAL METHODS
HYPOTHESIS TESTING
RESEARCH METHODOLOGY
STATISTICAL SIGNIFICANCE

INTERNALIZATION

As described by Schafer (1968), internalization refers to processes by which one brings some aspect of the external world into one's private life, and by which that internal representation of the external world exerts an influence over one's thoughts and behavior. There are three types of internalizations. The first is introjection, which refers to an inner presence that is not viewed as being an integral part of oneself. A person might introject a feature of another person (e.g., a hostile or benevolent glance, a hand that spanks or caresses, etc.) or the entire person (e.g., an imaginary playmate). In other words, introjection is the style of identification that takes in part or all of another individual's persona as a sort of foreign body (Hales et al., 1994).

The second type of internalization is identification, which describes a change in different aspects of one's subjective self so that one resembles another person, who is taken as a role model. In other words, identification involves taking attributes of important others into one's own self; thus, he or she becomes like others by acquiring their attributes, which he or she can then modify (Hales et al., 1994). The assimilation process inherent in identification leads to, for example, a young child's modeling of traits exhibited by his or her parents as truly part of the self and not, in contrast to introjection, as an acquisition of foreign characteristics (Kaplan & Saddock, 1995).

The concepts of introjection and identification are often confused. Hales and colleagues (1994) note that the confusion stems from the fact that identification can be not only a primitive defense mechanism but also a psychologically healthy process that is vital for normal growth and development. Introjection is a primitive type of identification exhibited in response to a painful awareness of emotional or physical separation from important people in one's life, and so these persons are self-protectively taken into one's psyche (Kaplan & Saddock, 1995). For example, when a young child becomes angry towards a parent as a result of a spanking given for some transgression, the child may introject the image of the spanking hand and recall it when tempted to transgress again, or may spank smaller children in a similar way so as to feel closer to the parent whose love the child is fearful of losing. If instead the child models the parent's value system and applies it in a principled way to guide his or her own behavior even when the parent is absent, adapting the rules to fit specific circumstances, this process is identification. In identification, the characteristics of the other person are no longer memory-bound; rather, they are acquired as one's own traits—thus, there is depersonification. So, depending on its type, identification can be healthy, a part of normal maturation, or remain a primitive, sometimes pathological process of grafting onto oneself the attributes of others (Hales et al., 1994).

The last type of internalization is called incorporation, and this concept applies when a person views all or part of another as constituting all or part of themselves. The difference between identification and incorporation is close to the difference between wanting to be like somebody and wanting to be the *same* as somebody. Incorporation, in comparison to identification, is a more primitive process and is fundamentally unrealistic because it is practically impossible for one person to be the same as another person.

REFERENCES

Glass, D. C., Snyder, M. L., & Hollis, J. (1974). Time urgency and the Type A coronary-prone behavior pattern. *Journal of Applied Social Psychology, 4,* 125–140.

Glass, D. C. (1977). *Behavior patterns, stress, and coronary disease.* Hillsdale, N.J.: Erlbaum.

Hales, R. E., Yudofsky, S. C., & Talbott, J. A. (1994). *Textbook of psychiatry, 2nd ed.* (pp. 157–159). Washington, D.C.: American Psychiatric Press.

Jenkins, D., Rosenman, R. H., & Friedman, M. (1967). Development of an objective psychological test for the determination of the coronary-prone behavior pattern in employed men. *Journal of Chronic Diseases, 20,* 371–379.

Jenkins, C. D., Zysanski, S. J., & Rosenman, R. H. (1971). Progress toward validation of a computer-scored test for the Type

A coronary-prone behavior pattern. *Psychosomatic Medicine, 33,* 193–202.

Kaplan, H. I., & Saddock, B. J. (Eds.). (1995). *Comprehensive textbook of psychiatry,* 6th Ed. Vol. 2. Baltimore, Md: Williams & Wilkins, 1995, pp. 451–455 & 1444–1446.

Lovallo, W. R., & Pishkin, V. (1980). Performance of type A (coronary-prone) men during and after exposure to uncontrollable noise and task failure. *Journal of Personality and Social Psychology, 38,* 963–971.

MacDougall, J. M., Dembroski, T. M., Dimsdale, J. E., & Hackett, T. P. (1985). Components of type A, hostility, and anger-in: further relationships to angiographic findings. *Health Psychology, 4,* 137–152.

Matthews, K. A., & Brunson, B. I. (1979). Allocation of attention and the type A coronary-prone behavior pattern. *Journal of Personality and Social Psychology, 37,* 2081–2090.

W. Samuel
F. Simjee McClure
University of California, San Diego

COPING
IMITATIVE LEARNING

THE INTERNATIONAL CLASSIFICATION OF DISEASES

The International Statistical Classification of Diseases and Related Health Problems (ICD), under different names and changing auspices, has undergone 10 approximately decennial revisions reflecting advances in medical knowledge and changing emphases in public health. The tenth revision was published by the World Health Organization in 1992.

The first attempt to classify diseases systematically was made by François Bossier de Lacroix (1706–1777), better known as Sauvages, whose comprehensive treatise was published under the title *Nosologia Methodica.* A contemporary of Sauvages was the great methodologist Linnaeus (1707–1778), one of whose treatises was entitled *Genera Morborum.* The utility of a uniform classification of causes of death was so strongly recognized at the first International Statistical Congress, held in Brussels in 1853, that, it requested Dr. William Farr—the first medical statistician of the General Register Office of England and Wales—and Dr. Marc d'Espine of Geneva to prepare "a uniform nomenclature of causes of death applicable in all the countries."

At the next Congress in Paris in 1855, Farr and d'Espine submitted two separate lists based on very different principles. Farr's classification was arranged under five groups: epidemic diseases, constitutional (general) diseases, local diseases arranged according to anatomical site, developmental diseases, and diseases that are the direct result of violence. D'Espine classified diseases according to their nature (gouty, herpetic, haematic, etc.). The Congress adopted a compromise list of 139 rubrics, and further revi-

sions followed in 1874, 1880, and 1886. Although there was never any universal acceptance of this classification, the general arrangement, including the principle of classifying disease by anatomical site proposed by Farr, has survived as the taxonomic basis for the ICD.

The International Statistical Institute (ISI), which replaced the International Statistical Congress, at its meeting in Vienna in 1891 charged a committee chaired by Dr. Jacques Bertillon, Chief Statistician of the City of Paris, with the preparation of a classification of causes of death. The report of this committee was adopted in 1893 and included three different classifications, which represented a synthesis of English, German, and Swiss classifications. In 1898, the American Public Health Association at its meeting in Ottawa, Canada, recommended the adoption of the Bertillon Classification by registrars of Canada, Mexico, and the United States. The Association further suggested that the classification be revised every 10 years. International conferences for the revision of the classification were held in 1900, 1909, 1920, 1929, and 1938.

The International Health Conference, held in New York City in 1946, requested the Interim Commission of the World Health Organization (WHO) to prepare "The International Lists of Causes of Death" and to establish "The International Lists of Causes of Morbidity." The International Conference for the Sixth Revision of the International Lists of Causes of Death was convened in Paris by the government of France and WHO in April, 1948. The work on classification was then carried out by WHO, whose constitution includes the development of the classification as one of the Organization's basic normative functions. WHO leads the international cooperation of national committees on vital and health statistics. The seventh conference was held in Paris in 1955, and the 8th, 9th, and 10th revision conferences were held in Geneva at WHO in 1965, 1975, and 1989.

There had been an enormous growth of interest in the ICD. There was considerable pressure for greater clinical detail and for adaptation of the classification to make it more relevant for the evaluation of medical care. At the other end of the scale, there were representatives from countries and areas in which a detailed and sophisticated classification was irrelevant, but which, nevertheless, needed a classification based on the ICD in order to assess their progress in health care and in the control of disease. Over successive revisions, the use of the ICD has expanded to cover the entire spectrum of health data. It is presently used for the compilation of statistics on underlying and multiple causes of death, hospital and ambulatory care morbidity, epidemiological research, indexing of medical records, medical audit systems, planning and evaluation of health services, and, finally, economics: social security, health insurance, health costs, and reimbursement for care services.

It was realized during the preparation of the Ninth Revision that the ICD alone could not meet all these needs and that a "family" of disease and health-related classifications was required with the ICD. The family would have a core covering the needs for traditional mortality and morbidity statistics, while needs for more detailed, less detailed, or different classifications would be dealt with by other members of the family. Currently, for example, ICD is mainly used for recording mortality and morbidity (causes of death and diseases); whereas disability and functioning is recorded

Table 1 Different Presentations of ICD-10 Chapter V for Different Users.

Version	Feature	User
ICD-10 Main Volume	Short glossary definitions	Coders
ICD-10 Chapter V: Classification of Mental and Behavioral Disorders: Clinical Descriptions and Diagnostic Guidelines ("*blue book*")	Diagnostic guidelines and descriptions	Clinicians
The ICD-10 Classification of Mental and Behavioral Disorders: Diagnostic Criteria for Research ("*green book*")	Operational Criteria	Researchers
ICD-10 Classification of Mental and Behavioral Disorders: Primary Care version	Diagnostic and Management Guidelines	Primary Care Workers

with International Classification of Impairments, Disabilities, and Handicaps (ICIDH), which is currently undergoing revision. (Table 1)

The 10th Revision of the ICD was the product of a vast amount of activity both within WHO and around the world. The main innovation is the use of an alphanumeric coding scheme of one letter followed by three numbers at the four-character level. The three-character core, the four-character classification, and the short tabulation lists are integral parts of the ICD and are totally compatible with one another. Specialty-based adaptations represent another degree of relationship with the main body of the ICD. These usually bring together in a single, compact volume the sections or categories of the ICD that are relevant to a particular specialty. The four-character subcategories are retained with additional clinical detail being provided at the fifth, sixth, and even seventh character levels. Applications of the 10th Revision have been prepared for dermatology by the British Association of Dermatologists and for pediatrics by the Royal College of Pediatrics and Child Health. WHO has produced adaptations for oncology (for tumor registries), dentistry, stomatology, neurology, and a series of publications for mental and behavioral disorders.

The mental and behavioral disorder chapter has undergone major changes during the last three revisions. In 1957, Stengel's seminal report called for the need for operational definitions to overcome the problem of lack of agreement on the diagnosis of mental disorders among mental health professionals. Therefore, brief descriptions of the categories included in chapter V (mental disorders) were introduced in the ninth revision of the ICD in 1975. No other chapter includes such a glossary. These definitions were meant to assist the person making the diagnosis. Their inclusion in the ICD has been very useful, and it has stimulated the work on the definitions of criteria and rules concerning the classification of mental and behavioral disorders.

The ICD-10 for Mental and Behavioral Disorders chapter was successively reformulated following extensive work of various conferences and field trials. The products of these efforts represent a congruent set of related classifications intended for different users such as clinicians, researchers, and primary care workers (see Table 1). These include: (a) the ICD-10 Classification of Mental and Behavioral Disorders: Clinical Descriptions and Diagnostic Guidelines; (b) the ICD-10 Classification of Mental and Behavioral Disorders: Diagnostic Criteria for Research; and (c) a Primary Care version, which also included management guidelines for most common mental disorders frequently seen in general health care settings. In addition, there have been multi-axial representations of

the classification to record different aspects of adults' and children's mental disorders. The research version of ICD-10 contains operationally defined criteria that are quantifiable and linked to national adaptations of widely used classifications in the field such as the *Diagnostic and Statistical Manual* (*DSM*) of the American Psychiatric Association. The ICD-10 classification of mental and behavioral disorders represents a consensus base among mental health workers and, to the extent possible, represents the current scientific evidence for better describing the disease and disorder knowledge.

T. B. ÜSTÜN
A. L'HOURS
World Health Organization, Geneva

CLINICAL ASSESSMENT

DIAGNOSIS

INTERNATIONAL PSYCHOLOGY

Psychology has been an international enterprise since its beginning as a modern science over a century ago. When most psychologists use the term "international psychology," they are referring to various forms of organized psychology at the international level, including societies, congresses, journals, and other kinds of scientific and professional exchanges. Sometimes the term also designates the social psychology of international relations, or the comparative study of psychological processes across different nations and cultures, as in cross-cultural psychology. These last two meanings of international psychology are dealt with only briefly here.

SOCIAL PSYCHOLOGY OF INTERNATIONAL RELATIONS

The systematic use of psychological concepts and methods for the development of theory, research, and policy studies in international relations is a relatively new area of specialization within social psychology. Following World War II, various studies of national stereotypes, attitudes toward war and peace, nationalism, and international affairs made significant contributions to an improved understanding of international relations. Generally interdisciplinary in character, these social-psychological approaches deal with the problems of interaction among nations, often with a goal of reducing tension and promoting international cooperation.

Among the kinds of research that deal specifically with the international behavior of individuals are studies of national stereotypes or images, attitudes toward international affairs, of national ideology and how it is communicated, and of the effects of crossnational contacts upon individual or group behavior. The investigation of intergroup conflict and its resolution has been broadened to include both simulated and naturalistic studies of international negotiation. These and related aspects of psychology applied to international relations are discussed in detail by Kelman in *International Behavior: A Social Psychological Analysis* (1965).

INTERNATIONAL STUDY OF PSYCHOLOGICAL PROCESSES

Cross-cultural psychology has expanded greatly in the past twenty-five years. Cross-cultural, comparative approaches are particularly appealing for the study of sociocultural factors in any aspect of human development. The growing realization of parochial limitations in Western psychology, particularly within the United States, has stimulated the development of a new kind of comparative psychology, a comparative psychology of human behavior in markedly different natural settings, rather than a comparative psychology dealing with different animal species. International studies of personality development, cognitive development, and perceptual processes have become commonplace, in spite of the difficult methodological problems encountered in such research.

The most common type of cross-national or cross-cultural study involves only two cultures. Comparisons between two nations are generally very difficult to interpret, because many cultural differences are operating which might provide alternate explanations of the findings that cannot be ruled out. The inclusion of subcultural variation and social factors within each nation enhances the likelihood that interpretable results can be obtained. An example of such an international study comparing children studied over a six-year period in Mexico and the United States is given by Holtzman, Diaz-Guerrero, and Swartz in *Personality Development in Two Cultures* (1975). The intensive study of 800 children in an overlapping longitudinal design produced clear and uniform differences across the two cultures for many psychological dimensions and test scores, as well as a number of interactions between culture and age, sex, and social class. Six major hypotheses concerning personality differences between Mexicans and Americans were proposed by the authors.

International psychology is only one aspect of cross-cultural psychology, the latter encompassing a much wider range of comparative studies. The search for cultural variation and its consequences for psychological functioning may be limited to a study of cultures within one large multicultural nation, rather than international differences in culture. The first *Handbook of Cross-Cultural Psychology* was published in 1980–1981 in six volumes. Edited by Triandis and Lambert, the *Handbook* provides a comprehensive review of cross-cultural psychology, the underlying theoretical and systematic approaches, the methodological issues and techniques, the basic processes that have been studied comparatively, and special reviews of developmental psychology, social psychology, and psychopathology as studied from cross-cultural or international perspectives.

ORGANIZED PSYCHOLOGY AT THE INTERNATIONAL LEVEL

The first International Congress of Psychology was held in 1889, less than 10 years after the founding of the first laboratory of experimental psychology. The rapid exchange of new ideas and methods of research across the different countries of Europe and the Americas produced a truly international psychology with a predominantly Western orientation. Most of the early leading academicians received much of their training in Germany or Great Britain. A long and distinguished series of international congresses served psychology well, but there was clearly a need for an international organization to provide continuity between congresses held only every three or four years.

At the 13th International Congress of Psychology held in Stockholm in July 1951, the International Union of Psychological Science (IUPsyS) was formally established. The IUPsyS is the only international organization that has as its members national psychological societies rather than individuals. The eleven psychological societies that served as the charter members in 1951 were from Belgium, France, Germany, Great Britain, Italy, Japan, the Netherlands, Norway, Sweden, Switzerland, and the United States. By 1999 the Union had grown to 64 national societies, representing most of the psychologists on every continent in the world.

Organizing an international congress every four years is the most important activity of the Union. The 26th International Congress of Psychology, held in Montreal, Canada, in July 1996, attracted nearly 5,000 psychologists and guests who participated in over 400 symposia, workshops, and related scientific sessions—a total of nearly 1,700 individual presentations. The 27th Congress will be held in Stockholm, Sweden on July 23–28, 2000.

The major aims and objectives of the Union are to promote the exchange of ideas and scientific information among psychologists of different countries, to foster international exchange of scholars and students, to collaborate with other international and national organizations in promoting psychology as a science and profession, and to encourage international projects that will further the development of psychology. An example of such projects is the organization of advanced research training seminars for young psychologists held in proximity to the world congresses.

One of the most important projects of the Union in the past was the compilation and publication of the *International Directory of Psychologists*. The fourth edition (1985) of the *Directory* edited by Pawlik, lists over 32,000 psychologists from 48 different countries excluding the United States, where the American Psychological Association and the American Psychological Society already publish readily available directories of their members. In the past fifteen years the number of psychologists throughout the world has increased so rapidly that a single directory of individuals is no longer possible, even excluding the several hundred thousand psychologists in the United States. Efforts are now underway by the Union to publish specialized international directories of research institutions rather than directories of individuals.

In 1975, the three-volume *Trilingual Psychological Dictionary*, edited by Duijker and van Rijswijk, provided a standard technical vocabulary for translating psychological terms from English, French, or German into either of the other two languages. Since then, the publication of similar bilingual dictionaries for translation between English and another language have greatly expedited standardized translation of psychological works. A recent example is the *Concise Encyclopedia of Psychology* (1991), edited by Jing, which defines in Chinese the many technical terms in psychological science.

Another kind of publication promoting international psychology provides English summaries of articles and books published originally in a different language. The *German Journal of Psychology, French-Language Psychology,* and *Spanish-Language Psychology* have set the standard for exchange of scientific information across languages. Since nearly 90% of the articles and books in psychology are published originally in English, and since most psychologists can read English, *Psychological Abstracts* and its electronic version, PsycSCAN, provide readily available, English-language abstracts of articles in the leading psychological journals throughout the world.

Most international organizations in psychology have individuals rather than societies as members. The oldest is the International Association of Applied Psychology, founded in 1920 by Claparede. As in the case of IUPsyS, the International Association of Applied Psychology sponsors a world congress every four years. At the 24th International Congress of Applied Psychology in San Francisco in August 1998, applied psychologists from throughout the world participated in symposia, workshops, general sessions, and individual paper-reading sessions devoted to such fields as industrial, clinical, counseling, and school psychology; applied social or experimental psychology; and educational psychology, usually from an international or cross-cultural perspective. Between congresses, the association sponsors international projects and exchanges such as the International Test Commission. A number of special interest divisions within the association deal with more narrowly defined international issues in applied psychology.

Smaller international organizations also exist to meet the specialized international interests of psychologists. Illustrative of such organizations are the International Council of Psychology, the International Association for Cross-Cultural Psychology, the Interamerican Society of Psychology, the European Association of Experimental Social Psychologists, the International Association of French-Speaking Psychologists, and the International School Psychology Association.

The above associations are comprised almost entirely of psychologists. Some interdisciplinary associations have large numbers of psychologists as members. Leading examples of such associations are the International Brain Research Organization and the International Society for the Study of Behavioral Development.

The development and status of psychology in different countries and regions of the world vary considerably. As one would expect, the most highly developed scientific psychology exists in North America, Europe, and Japan. Rapid growth in the post-World War II period has also occurred in Australia, Brazil, and Mexico, with several other countries of Latin America and Asia close behind. Surveys of trends in the development and status of psychology throughout the world, as reviewed by Rosenzweig, editor of *International Psychological Science* (1992), suggest that there are well over half a million recognized psychologists throughout the world. The most rapid growth has occurred among practi-

tioners rather than research scientists. The greatest concentration exists in the United States and Canada, followed closely by Western Europe. If one could count all individuals engaged in some kind of psychological research or practice, the actual number would be far greater. International comparisons are complicated by the fact that some countries may require a doctoral degree for full membership in their national psychological societies and for most professional positions, while other countries may require only a professional certificate after five years of university work.

Psychology is a discipline cultivated mainly in the industrialized countries, although the developing countries are rapidly catching up. While the scientific principles of psychology are valid regardless of cultural boundaries and politics, the scientific status of psychology and its social relevance vary greatly throughout the world.

REFERENCES

Duijker, H. C. J., & van Rijswijk, M. J. (1975). *Trilingual psychological dictionary.* Vol. 1: English/French/German; Vol. 2: Français/Allemand/Anglais; Vol. 3: Deutsch/Englisch/Französisch. Bern: Hans Huber.

Holtzman, W. H., Diaz-Guerrero, R., & Swartz, J. D. (1975). *Personality development in two cultures.* Austin: University of Texas Press.

Jing, Q. C. (Ed.). (1991). *Concise encyclopedia of psychology.* Hunan, China: Hunan Educational Publishers.

Kelman, H. C. (Ed.). (1965). *International behavior: A social psychological analysis.* New York: Holt.

Pawlik, K. (Ed.). (1985). *International directory of psychologists.* Fourth Edition. Amsterdam: North Holland.

Rosenzweig, M. R. (Ed.). (1992). *International psychological science: Progress, problems, and prospects.* Washington, DC: American Psychological Association.

Triandis, H. & Lambert, W. (Eds.). (1980–81). *Handbook of cross-cultural psychology.* (6 volumes). Boston: Allyn & Bacon.

W. H. HOLTZMAN
University of Texas, Austin

CROSS-CULTURE PSYCHOLOGY: CULTURE-UNIVERSAL AND . . .
CROSS-CULTURAL PSYCHOLOGY: INTRODUCTION AND OVERVIEW

INTERPERSONAL ATTRACTION

As defined by social psychologists, interpersonal attraction refers to a favorable attitude toward, or feeling of liking for, another person. Most empirical research has focused on first impressions and initial encounters, although attraction between individuals in ongoing relationships is drawing increased attention. Initial impressions are found to guide a person's behavior toward another individual and may elicit from the other responses that are consistent with, and thus reinforce, the initial impression. As a general rule we are attracted to individuals who, we believe, possess favorable characteristics or qualities, and we dislike individuals to the extent that we perceive them to have unfavorable attributes.

PHYSICAL APPEARANCE

People of all ages tend to prefer physically attractive to physically unattractive individuals. Within a given culture or subculture there is considerable agreement in judgments of a person's physical attractiveness, but little is known about the particular attributes, or combinations of attributes, that define beauty. The physically attractive are perceived as being likely to possess such socially desirable personality traits as sensitivity, kindness, modesty, intelligence, and sociability; consistent with these stereotyped beliefs, physically attractive individuals are liked better than the physically unattractive. There is evidence, however, that physical appearance has a greater influence on the attraction of males to females than vice versa.

BEHAVIOR

Impressions are often based on observation of overt behavior in combination with the context in which the behavior occurs. Research on causal attribution has shown that the behavior of another person is frequently explained by attributing corresponding personality dispositions to the person. Thus, under appropriate circumstances, hostile acts are attributed to aggressiveness, helping to kindness, and so forth. These inferences are later reflected in liking or disliking for the person.

There is some evidence that liking is influenced by such nonverbal behaviors as smiling, eye contact, physical touch, and body posture. As to the effects of verbal behavior, much attention has been devoted to the intimacy of information disclosed by an individual. Contrary to early theorizing, the degree to which others disclose intimate information about themselves is found to have no systematic effects on attraction to them. The effects of self-disclosure appear to depend on the circumstances under which the information is disclosed and, most importantly, on whether the information disclosed is socially-desirable or undesirable.

SIMILARITY

Our attraction to other people increases as a direct function of the extent to which we perceive them to be similar to us in their opinions, interests, and personality characteristics. Numerous laboratory and field experiments have provided strong evidence in support of this conclusion. Several explanations have been offered for the similarity–attraction relationship.

One possibility is that a similar other confirms the appropriateness or desirability of our own opinions, interests, and personality traits. Expression of a similar opinion or indication of a similar interests may thus have positive reinforcement value, while a dissimilar opinion or a dissimilar personality trait may have negative reinforcement value. It has been argued that the positive reinforcement values of similar opinions, interests, and personality traits, and the negative reinforcement values of dissimilar opinions, interests, and personality traits become associated with the person who possesses these attributes by a process of classical conditioning.

Another possibility is that similarity affects attraction by virtue of the information it provides about the other person. Given that we usually value our own opinions, interests, and personality characteristics, a person who appears to share some of our attributes will naturally be perceived in a favorable light. This interpretation implies, and empirical research has confirmed, that we will prefer a dissimilar other whose opinions, interests, and personality traits we value positively, to a similar other who possesses attributes which we value negatively (in that person as well as in ourselves).

CONSEQUENCES OF ATTRACTION

The consequences of interpersonal attraction have received much less scrutiny than have its antecedents. Of course, in the context of ongoing relationships, antecedents and consequences cannot be easily separated. Thus interaction between individuals may increase the similarity of their opinions and interests, which in turn may affect liking and further interaction, and so on.

Many reactions to another person appear to be largely unaffected by the person's attractiveness. There is little evidence that attraction has systematic effects on attributions of responsibility for an accident or a crime, on responses to a request for assistance, or on cooperation and competition among individuals. On the other hand, attraction to another person generally produces a tendency to approach and affiliate with that person. To be sure, situational and personality factors greatly influence the forms this approach tendency will take. For example, a man is more likely to ask an attractive than an unattractive woman for a date, but only if he anticipates that she will respond favorably to his invitation. Anticipation of reciprocity also plays an important part in the disclosure of intimate information. Although people tend to disclose more intimate information to liked than to disliked others, intimate information is disclosed primarily when these other people are expected to be similarly revealing of their own thoughts and feelings.

SUGGESTED READING

Berscheid, E., & Walster, E. (1974). Physical attractiveness. In L. Berkowitz (Ed.), *Advances in experimental social psychology* (Vol. 7). New York: Academic.

Byrne, D. (1971). *The attraction paradigm.* New York: Academic.

Duck, S. W. (Ed.). (1977). *Theory and practice in interpersonal attraction.* London: Academic.

Huston, T. L. (Ed.). (1974). *Foundations of interpersonal attraction.* New York: Academic.

Huston, T. L., & Levinger, G. (1978). Interpersonal attraction and relationships. In M. R. Rosenzweig & L. W. Porter (Eds.), *Annual Review of Psychology, 29,* 115–156.

I. AJZEN
University of Massachusetts

ATTITUDES
LOVE
SPOUSE SELECTION
STEREOTYPING

INTERPERSONAL COMMUNICATION

Attempts at defining interpersonal communication date back to the Golden Age of Greece. Plato and Aristotle discussed communication in terms of rhetoric. However, several millennia later there is still no generally agreed upon scientific definition of communication. According to Webster's *New World Dictionary* (1966), "to communicate" is defined as "to impart, pass along, transmit," and "communication" is defined as "giving and receiving of information, signals or messages by talk, gestures, writing, etc." These definitions are helpful as orientations to this area of study, but lack sufficient detail or specificity for scientific purposes.

The notion of transmission of information has been applied to genetic materials as well as nonorganismic events. An individual might transfer information from one cognitive context to another in a form of intra-individual communication. Furthermore, categories representing intergroup, interorganizational, international, and (in science fiction) intergalactic communication could be developed. Interpersonal communication refers to the transfer of information by a source to a specific target. These communications typically occur in face-to-face interactions, although they may also occur by mail, telephone, television, the Internet, or other electronic means. Lasswell (1948) captured in one sentence much of the subject matter of human communication: "Who says what in what channel to whom with what effect?"

Electrical engineering principles were applied by Shannon and Weaver in 1949 to human communication. Figure 1 shows their model of the communication process. The mind of the communicator may be considered the source of the communication. Presumably, messages originate in the brain and are encoded for transmission to other people. The source must have a means of transmitting information, such as speech, gestures, or writing. The message is encoded and sent as a signal to a receiver, who must decode the message. Thus, the destination of a message is the mind of a target or receiver person.

This information model is helpful in examining some of the more important questions regarding interpersonal communication. It should be noted that the source may unintentionally communicate to others, as when nonverbal cues betray a liar. Of course, the source may not even be aware of a communication. For example, a person may communicate liking for another by maintaining a rather close physical proximity, but may be unaware of doing so.

Intentional communication may be examined in terms of the degree to which the interpretations of the source are accurately received by the target. For some communication theorists it is the sharing of interpretations and not just the exchange of information that lies at the heart of the communication process. Any interference with accurate transfer of information is referred to as noise in the system. Noise may be due to ambiguous encoding, problems with channels through which signals are transmitted, or faulty decoding by the target. If, for example, the source transmitted a message in German and the target understood only English, noise would be attributable to the target's inability to decode the communication. If two persons were talking over the telephone but could not hear each other because of static over the lines, noise would be located in the channels being used. One should not construe disagreement between two persons as necessarily caused by noise. A target may be able to take the viewpoint of the source and fully understand the interpretation communicated, but nevertheless disagree with it. Often persons believe they have not been understood, when in reality the target persons disagree with them.

There has often been confusion even among scientists in distinguishing between language and communication. To make the distinction, one must understand the differences between signs, signals, and symbols. Signs are environmental stimuli which the organism has associated with other events. For example a hunter may associate certain prints in the dirt as a sign that a deer has recently passed nearby. Signs are inflexibly and directly related to their associated events.

Signals are signs produced by living organisms. Most animals can use signals in their interaction with other animals. Thus, birds may emit love calls, insects may transmit odors, and monkeys may manifest threat gestures. Research by Gardner and Gardner (1969) has shown that chimpanzees can be taught to use complex signals often taught to deaf and/or mute humans. However, even the most intense training results in fewer than 400 signals learned by these higher primates. Nevertheless, the ability of these animals to communicate is clearly greater than previously thought possible.

A symbol, like a signal, has a referent. However, symbols do not necessarily refer to physical reality and may not have space-time

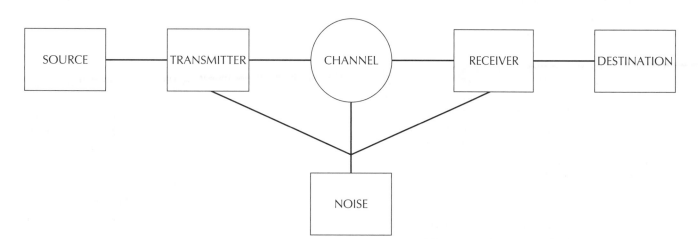

Figure 1.   A schematic of a communications system (after Shannon & Weaver. 1949).

relationships as their referents. Symbols derive their meaning from a community of users and not from a connection with a referent. The use of symbols allows the development of various abstract areas of knowledge such as history, literature, religion, art, and science. Furthermore, it provides the basis for the individual's construction of social reality, including a self. The available evidence (Gardner & Gardner, 1969) indicates that only humans use symbols. Chimpanzees appear to be confined to the existential moment and cannot escape their time-space coordinates. Although they can remember and signal what they did an hour ago, they cannot report what they did yesterday or reveal plans about the future. Thus, it appears that the symbol represents an important discontinuity in phylogenetic development between humans and all other forms of life.

Language is a means of information processing and is used to store, manipulate, create, and transmit information. No analysis of interpersonal communication among humans would be complete without a consideration of the symbolic aspects of language. Two important properties of symbols are that they may refer to classes of things, and they may have multiple meanings. Thus, errors in communication are both frequent and inevitable; that is, noise tends to be an inevitable feature of interpersonal communication.

Situations and relationships with others provide contexts within which persons can share interpretations of communication and hence reduce noise. The individual's definition of the social situation typically involves certain expectations about the behavior of others, the rules that define and regulate interactions, and guides to conduct. These expectations provide a frame of reference within which the person encodes and decodes information. For example, "Did you buy the pot?" means something different when communicated on a street corner between teenagers than when transmitted from a mother to a daughter.

Communication has a number of functions. It allows the coordination of behaviors of individuals in a group. Large corporations and government bureaucracies require a great deal of communication among employees at all levels in order to function at all. Interpersonal communication also allows for instruction, in which one individual helps another to learn skills or develop new frames of reference. Perhaps most important of all, communication functions as a means to influence others. Messages used for purposes of power and influence may be considered actions with as much impact as skeletal behaviors. Thus, communicative actions are sometimes referred to as speech acts.

Speech acts that refer to rewards and punishments take the form of threats or promises which may be contingent or noncontingent in form. A contingent threat specifies that a target must comply with some demand of the source or else suffer some cost to be inflicted by the threatener. A noncontingent threat announces the source's intention to impose some cost on the target without any demand for compliance being made. A contingent promise offers a reward, if the target complies with a request by the source. A noncontingent promise simply announces the source's intention to reward the target. Promises, unlike threats, carry a moral obligation of fulfillment by the source.

There are several speech acts that may be classified as means of information control. Persuasion represents a source's attempt to influence a target's decisions. Among the types of persuasive com-

munications are warnings, mendations, and activation of commitments. Warnings convey expectations of future negative events not controlled by the source, while mendations are predictions of positive events not controlled by the source. Activation of commitments consists of exhortations appealing to the normative values of the target in order to induce some related behavior by the target.

Another classification of speech acts refers to their function as self-presentational. Actors project certain identities to others and engage in various tactics to foster desired identities in the eyes of others. Among the more prominent speech acts devoted to impression management are accounts, entitlements, and enhancements. When a person does something that seems strange, untoward, or abnormal to others, an explanation is usually offered or demanded. The lack of an explanation leaves an unfavorable impression and may lead observers to blame and perhaps punish the actor. Accounts are explanations for untoward behavior and consist of excuses and justifications. Excuses are explanations that deny responsibility for negative effects of behavior. Excuses may deny intention to produce the effects, or may deny that the source had volitional control over the actions in question. Denials of intention refer to lack of foreknowledge, mistake, inadvertence, and accident. Denials of volition may refer to drugs, alcohol, physical disability, or mental illness (insanity). Justifications are explanations of actions that admit responsibility but offer legitimate reasons for them. For example, a person may justify spanking children as a way to teach them not to run out into the street. Justifications may appeal to authority, ideology, norms of justice, self-defense, or self-actualization.

Entitlements are speech acts in which the source attempts to take responsibility for positive events. Enhancements are attempts to embellish the value of the positive consequences. People want credit for positive consequences because they gain approbation and rewards for such actions. The more positive the consequences, the greater the credit; hence, actors are motivated to use enhancement tactics.

Gestures, visual contact, body orientation, and the use of interpersonal space may substitute for verbal communication or may serve as a context within which to interpret verbal communication. In many instances, nonverbal responses act as signals and do not convey symbolic forms of information. For example, eye contact may communicate hostility or love, or indicate that the source is acting deceitfully.

REFERENCES

Gardner, R. A., & Gardner, B. T. (1969). Teaching sign language to a chimpanzee. *Science, 165,* 664–672.

Lasswell, H. D. (1946). Describing the contents of communications. In B. L. Smith, H. D. Lasswell, & R. D. Casey (Eds.), *Propaganda, communication, and public opinion.* Princeton, NJ: Princeton University Press.

Shannon, C., & Weaver, W. (1949). *The mathematical theory of communication.* Urbana: University of Illinois Press.

J. T. TEDESCHI
State University of New York at Albany

INTERPERSONAL PERCEPTION

The impressions we form of other people serve as important bases for interpersonal interactions. Person perception is a complex topic and clearly different from space perception. The latter is concerned with how perceptions of physical reality are mediated and tends to focus on biochemistry, biophysics, and/or psychophysics; the researcher attempts to relate cognitive factors to physical ones through the pathways provided by the sensory apparatus of the organism. In person perception the observer is concerned with the interior psychological processes of stimulus persons: what are they feeling, what plans do they have for future action, what effects do they intend to produce in the environment, and what causes them to act the way they do? These questions have little to do with sensory mechanisms, but instead are answered by inferences or attributions made by the observer. In a way, person perception is a misnomer which perhaps would be better expressed as "person inferences." Much of the topic is currently referred to as attribution theory, or more generally as social cognition.

In his seminal work, *The Psychology of Interpersonal Relations,* Fritz Heider (1958) noted that there are three differences between the perceptions of objects and persons. First, persons are assumed to experience an interior life and objects are not. Each person experiences thoughts and emotions, and assumes that others do also. Second, objects are not perceived as causes of their own actions, whereas persons are often viewed as first causes. The concept of responsibility is inextricably interwoven with the notion that one acts for one's own interior reasons, rather than in response to the inexorable forces of the environment. Third, persons can deliberately manipulate and exploit the perceiver, while inanimate objects cannot. One purpose of person perception is to allow the observer to predict the probable actions of the stimulus person, so as to anticipate in planning his or her own actions.

The study of person perception is essentially an attempt to reconstruct the way the average person processes information about other people and the self. The observer is interested in answering the question of why the stimulus person acted as he or she did. Thus, the average person acts as a naive psychologist in seeking explanations for behavior. According to Heider (1958), causes for behavior are attributed to either the environment or the person. Environmental forces may be perceived to be so strong as to move actors around as if they were pawns on a chessboard. On the other hand, the person may be seen as the origin of action, even acting against strong environmental currents. When the action can be attributed to environmental causes, the actor is not held responsible for the positive or negative effects of his or her behavior, but when factors inside the actor are perceived as the origins, the actor is held accountable for the effects.

Much of the work done in the area of attributions is concerned with the rules that observers use in attributing cause to the environment or the person. For example, suppose an automobile swerves toward a sidewalk and runs over and kills a pedestrian. Is the death (an effect) attributable to environmental factors, such as a mechanical failure, or a reaction to another car that sideswiped the automobile and so caused the death? Or is the death attributable to deliberate intention to commit murder, or perhaps to the inebriated condition of the driver? Which of many potential causes actually produced the effect will determine how others react to the driver.

The tendency of observers is to accept the first sufficient cause as the reason for behavior. The impact of any particular cause in producing an effect is discounted, however, if other plausible causes are present. This discounting principle may lead to attributions to both environmental and person causes of behavior. Furthermore, the more effects the observer believes are associated with the actor's behavior, the more plausible causes there can be. Harold H. Kelley (1973), who proposed the discounting principle, also suggested an augmentation principle: the more costs the actor risks in order to act as he or she does, the more likely the observer is to attribute the behavior to person causes. Thus, the more embarrassment, pain, criticism, penalty, or punishment the actor suffers, the more likely an observer will attribute the behavior to something about the person. On the other hand, when the actor does what most other people would do in the same situation, observers would not believe they had learned anything much about this particular actor. The rule of thumb is that the more the actor's behavior deviates from what the observer believes most people would do, the more likely the action is associated with something peculiar about this actor. Of course, different observers may have different expectations about the so-called average or typical person, and hence may apply the augmentation principle somewhat differently.

An observer may observe an actor only once or may have multiple opportunities to witness behavior. Most attributional rules can be categorized as based on either a single observation or on multiple observations. Among the former are the following:

1. *Out-of-role behavior.* People are often rewarded for playing certain roles and meeting the expectations of others. For this reason, people tend to conform to role demands and expectations. When a person violates the norms governing a role, the out-of-role behavior is attributed to the person, who is apparently acting against environmental constraints. Out-of-role behavior can be construed as derivative from the augmentation principle. The person who is out of role has given up customary rewards and is apparently willing to accept negative reactions from others. The action must stem, therefore, from some inner personal factors.

2. *Noncommon effects.* An observer may mentally reconstruct the decision making of the actor in order to understand the choices made. Each choice alternative would presumably bring about desired effects for the decision maker. It may be assumed that the chosen alternative is preferred because it maximizes some value for the actor, at least as compared to the other alternatives. That is, some effect that is noncommon to the decision alternatives is the basis for the decision that is made, and that effect reveals something about the decision maker.

3. *Hedonic relevance.* When the actions of another person have some positive or negative impact on the observer, the latter has

a stronger tendency to attribute the behavior to personal causes. That is, the observer is more apt to make environmental attributions when the actor's behavior affects other people than when it affects the observer.

4. *Personalism.* When the observer experiences positive or negative effects from the actor's behavior, consideration will be given to whether those effects were specifically aimed at the observer. When the observer believes the behavior was directed at him or her (personally), the observer more confidently makes a person attribution.

Kelley (1973) has provided a model of the rules used by naive observers in making attributions after multiple observations of an actor. If the observer does not have a ready causal schema within which particular actions are analyzed, causes attributed, and responsibility assigned, he or she will rationally process the data available, much as a scientist would. Suppose, for example, that someone tells you they liked a particular movie. Is this reaction to the movie due to something about the person, or is it because the movie is really good (i.e., an environmental cause)? To answer this question, the observer can assemble all the information he or she has about the movie reviewer. According to Kelley (1973), the following principles will allow the observer to make attributions to the person and/or the environment:

1. *Consistency.* If the reviewer saw the movie more than once and liked it both times, it would seem unlikely that some personal factor such as a temporary mood or state of emotion, which would tend to fluctuate and change over time, could account for the reaction to the movie on both occasions. The movie is part of the physical environment, which is experienced as stable and relatively unchanging, and would seem a more likely cause of the reaction. Thus, consistency of reaction suggests a stable environmental cause, while inconsistent reactions suggest fluctuating personal causes.

2. *Distinctiveness.* If a reviewer likes all movies seen, one would tend to attribute the reaction to personal causes. After all, some movies are excellent, some are good, and then there are the others. A reviewer who does not have distinctive reactions to movies apparently does not react to the differences between them, hence appears to react more on the basis of internal personal factors. Generally speaking, then, the more distinctive the person's response, the more apt an observer is to make an environmental attribution, and the less distinctive the response, the more likely a personal attribution will be made.

3. *Consensus.* If a large number of people react in the same way to a situation, an environmental attribution will be made. However, if a person reacts in a manner different from most other people, a personal attribution is more likely. In the case of the movie reviewer, if a large number of people agree with the reviewer's reaction, it will be attributed to the film and not to anything about the reviewer. However, if the reviewer's reaction is idiosyncratic, the reaction will be attributed to something about the reviewer rather than to the film.

There is a tendency for divergences in attributions between actors and observers. Actors usually cannot do everything they most desire, but must act within the context of obtaining the best outcomes possible under the circumstances. As a result, actors tend to see their own actions as strongly constrained by the environment. On the other hand, as Heider (1958) has noted, behavior of the actor tends to engulf the perceptual field of the observer. This focus on the actor to the exclusion of the environment is referred to as the fundamental attribution error and leads observers to make stronger personal attributions than do actors. Also, of course, actors have more information about themselves and a wider context of attribution than do observers.

Jones and Davis (1965) have argued that once an observer makes an attribution to personal causes, a corresponding inference will be made from the characterization of the behavior that was observed and the motive that is inferred as underlying that behavior. The observer notes effects that occur in the environment and traces these back to the behavior of an actor. If the behavior is attributed to environmental factors, the information processing ceases. However, if a personal attribution is made, the observer assumes the actor intended the effects observed. Intent implies that the actor has foreknowledge of the effects and the ability to produce them. Intent refers to the effects and not to the behavior in question. If intent is attributed to the actor, a motive for the intention is inferred. The difference between intent and motive is that the former is an "in order to" reason and the latter a "because of" reason. That is, a forward-oriented reason that the behavior was emitted to produce the effects is an intention, whereas a motive is backward looking and gives a reason for wanting to produce those effects.

Correspondent inference assumes a commonality between the nature of a response and the motive attributed for it. For example, domineering people may have a power motive attributed to them. This theory, offered by Jones and Davis (1965), assumes that whenever an observer makes an attribution of cause to the person, a correspondent inference will be made. It must be further assumed that the identification and labeling of responses is unproblematic and is a given, much like the proximal energies of space perception. It can be argued, however, that an action cannot be identified apart from the goals assumed to guide the actor. For example, a man pulling and pushing a pump handle could be described as exercising his back and arm muscles or as pumping water into a trough. Which description is more "accurate" would depend on what the man's goals were believed to be.

Clearly, observers do form overall impressions of other people. Information is gathered from direct observations and from reports by other observers. The first impression of an actor tends to have a stronger impact than later information. This primacy effect may occur because earlier information serves as a context within which later information is interpreted. Some kinds of information are more central in forming overall impressions, and other information is more peripheral or unimportant. For example, describing someone as warm or cold has been shown to have more impact on overall impressions than to describe the stimulus person as polite or blunt. Anderson (1965) has proposed mathematical models of how observers process and weigh information provided (in adjectival form) about actors. How likable a person is may be more heavily weighted by some traits than others, and earlier information may be given more weight than later information. The primacy effect may be due to the discounting of later information or may occur by inattention after an early impression is formed. These ideas can be presented in the form of an algebraic weighted averaging model, which has received rather impressive support from empirical studies.

Social psychologists have had a traditional concern about the accuracy with which observers attribute emotional states and personality traits to actors. Observers have been presented idealized paintings, photographs, motion pictures, and live actors portraying various emotions, and have been asked to identify the emotion expressed. If one accepts the labels given to stimuli by scientists as the criterion, then observers are fairly accurate in identifying emotions from viewing only facial expression, hand movements, still photographs, and voice inflections. Furthermore, there is rather good agreement across very different cultures in making these attributions to identical stimuli. The latter finding has provided some support for the Darwinian belief that human expressions have evolved through the phyla. Viewing cues in social context allows observers in all cultures to provide more "accurate" labels of emotional states. But there is a criterion problem with much of this research: there is no satisfactory definition of what exactly an emotion is, hence it is not very clear how one identifies any particular state.

Observers tend to assume that other people will behave consistently over time. To attain a view of the world as orderly and predictable, the observer tries to maintain organized and meaningful impressions of other people. It might even be said that observers will invent some constancy to characterize others, such as underlying stable dispositions, so as to make sense out of the diversity of behavior. Each person tends to develop an implicit theory of personality in which certain kinds of traits and dispositions are viewed as being mutually associated or dissociated. For example, an observer who makes a correspondent inference that another person has a power motive may then construct, through a chain of inferences, a belief that the stimulus person has a series of other traits (strong, exploitative, aggressive, cold, impolite, etc.). While there may be some commonality of implicit personality theories within a given culture, there is considerable variation as well.

Observers will often cluster traits together as descriptive of a particular category of people. This picture in our heads is referred to as a stereotype. A social stereotype exists when a sizable group of people agree on the category-based cluster. A stereotype of Italians, for example, may include that they are musical and passionate. Presumably, if the only information an observer has regarding a given actor is that the individual is Italian, any future interaction between them may be based on the belief that the actor possesses the stereotypical traits. In this sense stereotypes help to organize perceptions and to provide a basis for predicting what strangers are likely to do. While there may be a grain of truth in some stereotypes, at least as they apply to entire groups of people, they tend to present an impoverished and inadequate basis for understanding and interacting with individuals.

An important stereotype recently investigated by social psychologists refers to beautiful women. It is generally believed that beautiful women have more dating opportunities and more socially desirable personalities, and are happier and more intelligent. Beautiful women may also have an advantage in job interviews and performance ratings. However, there is evidence that at higher levels of management, physical attractiveness is an asset for men but a handicap for women.

Most of the literature on interpersonal perception assumes that a stimulus person is inert and merely stands (as for a portrait), while the observer draws inferences from the behavior performed. However, the actor may have much to gain or lose from the impressions given off by behavior, and hence is motivated to affect them in some way. Thus, the actor may engage in one or more of a numerous assortment of possible impression management strategies to negotiate an identity in the eyes of the observer.

Impression management may be defensive in remedying a spoiled identity resulting from negative behaviors, or in warding off negative impressions in advance of behavior. For example, the actor may offer accounts or explanations for a problematic behavior. Such accounts may take the form of excuses, generally helping the observer to make environmental attributions for the behavior, or justifications that argue that the beneficial effects of the behavior outweigh the negative effects. Impression management behaviors may also be assertive in the sense that the actor tries to establish a preplanned identity in the eyes of the observer. For example, when positive effects are produced by behavior, the actor will try to get the observer to make a personal attribution. If a personal attribution is made, the actor will gain responsibility and credit for the positive effects, and is apt to gain approbation or other rewards for so doing.

Rules of decorum and demeanor often require that an observer accept an identity presented by another. To challenge that identity may be taken as an insult and generally would not lead to smooth interactions between the two parties. On the other hand, an observer cannot allow an actor to establish any identity whatsoever, since to do so would give control of the interaction to the actor. Thus, there is a tendency for people to negotiate their identities in front of one another.

The study of interpersonal perception has not yet incorporated the dynamic interaction proposed by impression management theory. The attribution process appears to be static and perhaps relies too much on rational models of information processing. Future focus is likely to examine strategies of impression management and how observers penetrate attempts to control their impressions in forming judgments of actors.

REFERENCES

Anderson, N. G. (1965). Averaging versus adding as a stimulus-combination rule in impression formation. *Journal of Experimental Psychology, 70,* 394–400.

Heider, F. (1958). *The psychology of interpersonal relations.* New York: Wiley.

Jones, E. E., & Davis, K. E. (1965). From acts to dispositions: The attribution process in person perception. In I. Berkowitz (Ed.), *Advances in experimental social psychology* (Vol. 2). New York: Academic Press.

Kelley, H. H. (1973). The process of causal attribution. *American Psychologist, 28,* 107–128.

J. T. TEDESCHI
State University of New York at Albany

INTERPERSONAL ATTRACTION
SOCIAL COGNITION
STEREOTYPING

INTERVIEWING (SELECTION)

Organizations rarely select members at random. Opportunities for employment or educational programs are typically given to those judged to merit them. Many procedures are used to assess merit, but few are used as widely as the selection interview. Interviews are nearly universal in employment settings, and they are included in the admissions procedures for many educational programs as well.

An interview is a conversation between a candidate and a person (or group) who makes or influences the selection decision. As a selection tool, its primary purpose is the assessment of candidate merit (either an overall assessment or the assessment of specified characteristics); however, it serves other purposes as well. It is a forum in which the employing organization or school can explain the nature of the organization, the details of the job or program, and what it expects of successful candidates. It also serves a public relations function, even for those ultimately rejected; an interviewer who gives an impression of fairness and consideration can create or preserve a favorable organizational image (Schmitt & Coyle, 1976).

Selection interviews are notoriously unreliable and invalid. As far back as 1922, Hollingworth demonstrated that a group of experienced interviewers made completely different ratings of candidates. Subsequent reviews of interview research have consistently confirmed the findings that reliabilities are poor and that interviewers' judgments do not generally predict future performance. Rarely have researchers even addressed the question of how validly specified candidate characteristics are assessed by interviewers.

Nevertheless, since interviews continue to be used widely, substantial research efforts have been directed toward finding principles for their improvement. Unfortunately, most of the studies have used simulated research, the simulations usually consisting of pieces of paper giving the interviewer information about candidates or candidate responses to questions. The defining ingredient of an actual interview, the interaction between the two people, is conspicuously absent from such simulations. Without that interaction, the applicability of the research to real interviews must be seriously questioned. Two studies reported by Gorman, Clover, and Doherty (1978) demonstrated clearly that the judgments interviewers make on the basis of paper information are quite different from those made when the same information is accompanied by face-to-face interaction.

Despite a generally gloomy picture of the value of selection in-

terviews, there are some positive research findings. Valid predictions were reported in selecting stockbrokers (Ghiselli, 1966); in managerial assessment centers (Grant & Bray, 1969); and in group interviews (Landy, 1976). Since interviews are sometimes valid, perhaps the emphasis in research should first be directed toward the identification of interviewers who make valid judgments and to find out what cues they observe (or overlook) in making their judgments.

However, people who must do interviewing cannot wait for such research results. Some suggestions seem appropriate, even without firm research foundations.

1. Use a structured interview specifically designed for the selection problem at hand. Thorough knowledge of the job or educational program permits planning an agenda explicitly directed toward relevant information.

2. Listen; don't talk too much. To get relevant information, the interviewer must allow the candidate to do most of the talking. Paradoxically, the greater the proportion of time the interviewer talks, the more favorably the interviewee is evaluated (Daniels & Otis, 1950).

3. Avoid premature judgments. Regardless of interview length, judgments are often formed very quickly. It may be helpful to keep seeking new information by keeping the candidate talking; it may also help to divide the interview into segments, each with its own task according to objective and evaluation. For a certain job, for example, one segment might be aimed at information about the candidate's ability to resolve disputes among other people; the segment might include planned questions, problem situations, and a behavioral expectations rating scale to complete before moving on to the next topic.

4. Avoid prejudicial questions. Some questions, whether intentionally or not, foster or imply prejudice—especially if used inconsistently. For example, an interviewer may want to know whether a candidate for a job will be flexible about staying overtime in emergencies, accepting spur-of-the-moment travel assignments, and so forth. If so, questions about the candidate's family obligations may seem reasonable. Some interviewers may consider such questions reasonable if the candidate is a woman, but not even think of them with a man. This clearly prejudges candidates on the basis of sex rather than on the basis of relevant information, and invites litigation.

Most legal and technical problems surrounding selection interviews can be avoided by using the standardized interviews tailored to the specific jobs or academic settings involved. Unfortunately, such standardization is not a common practice.

REFERENCES

Ghiselli, E. E. (1966). The validity of a personnel interview. *Personnel Psychology, 19,* 389–394.

Gorman, C. D., Clover, W. H., & Doherty, M. E. (1978). Can we learn anything about interviewing real people from "interviews" of paper people? Two studies of the external validity of

a paradigm. *Organizational Behavior and Human Performance,
22,* 165–192.

Grant, D. L., & Bray, D. W. (1969). Contributions of the interview
to assessment of management potential. *Journal of Applied Psychology, 53,* 24–34.

Hollingworth, H. L. (1922). *Judging human character.* New York:
Appleton.

Landy, F. J. (1976). The validity of the interview in police officer selection. *Journal of Applied Psychology, 61,* 193–198.

Schmitt, N., & Coyle, B. W. (1976). Applicant decisions in the employment interview. *Journal of Applied Psychology, 61,* 184–192.

R. M. GUION
Bowling Green State University

EXECUTIVE SELECTION
JOB EVALUATION

INTRINSIC MOTIVATION

The field of motivation is concerned with why and how people behave as they do. Intrinsic motivation is a type of motivation based in people's interests in activities that provide novelty and challenge. Intrinsically motivated behaviors are an expression of a person's *self* and do not depend on external reinforcements. Thus, the behaviors have what in attribution theory is referred to as an internal perceived locus of causality; people experience the causes of these behaviors as being within themselves (deCharms, 1968).

Throughout life, when in their healthiest states, people are active, curious, and involved; they display an eagerness to learn and explore. This natural, intrinsically motivated activity is critical for optimal development. It is through acting on their inherent interests that people acquire knowledge about themselves and their world.

Until the 1950s, theories of motivation, both in the empirical tradition (e.g., Hull, 1943) and the psychoanalytic tradition (Freud, 1962/1923), focused on physiological drives such as hunger, thirst, and sex, proposing that all behaviors are motivated by those drives and their derivatives. However, as various phenomena emerged that could not be explained by drive theories, White (1959) suggested that a full understanding of motivation required that psychological needs be considered a motivational basis for some behaviors. More specifically, he proposed an innate motivation for interacting effectively with the environment. Building on that initial statement, intrinsic motivation theorists (e.g., Deci & Ryan, 1985) have stated that the psychological needs for competence and autonomy underlie intrinsically motivated behaviors, which flourish in contexts that allow satisfaction of those needs.

Whereas drive theories implied that humans seek quiescence and prefer minimal stimulation, intrinsic motivation theories suggest that people enjoy excitement and desire an optimal level of stimulation. Accordingly, the structure of intrinsically motivated behavior involves an ongoing cycle in which people find stimulation and work toward quiescence, only to begin again, once they have achieved the quiescence, looking for a new stimulation. In other words, intrinsically motivated activity involves seeking and conquering optimal challenges.

Behaviors such as reading a book, solving puzzles, studying objects, exploring novel spaces, looking at paintings, and playing softball are intrinsically motivating for many people, but not necessarily for all, because intrinsic motivation is a property of the interaction between a person and an activity. For an individual to be intrinsically motivated for an activity, that individual must find the activity interesting.

Intrinsic motivation is typically contrasted with extrinsic motivation, which is the type of motivation that requires rewards or reinforcers. People are extrinsically motivated for an activity when they do it to earn money, to gain approval, to avoid censure, or to comply with social norms.

Numerous studies reviewed by Deci and Ryan (1985) have now confirmed that, relative to extrinsic motivation, intrinsic motivation leads to better conceptual learning, greater creativity, more cognitive flexibility, and enhanced well-being. Consequently, there has been great interest in the conditions that enhance versus diminish intrinsic motivation. Initially, the studies examined how extrinsic rewards affect intrinsic motivation, and a recent meta-analysis substantiated that tangible extrinsic rewards undermine intrinsic motivation for the rewarded activity (Deci, Koestner, & Ryan, 1999).

Additional studies with young children, teenagers, college students, and adults have revealed that other external events, such as directives, surveillance, deadlines, threats of punishment, and negative performance feedback also decrease intrinsic motivation. In contrast, ample evidence has verified that events such as offering choice, acknowledging people's feelings, and providing positive performance feedback enhance intrinsic motivation.

Deci and Ryan (1985) interpreted these results in terms of satisfaction versus thwarting of the basic needs for competence and autonomy. Specifically, people tend to interpret rewards, directives, deadlines, and threats as controllers of their behavior which thwart their need for autonomy; whereas people tend to experience choice and acknowledgments as supports for their autonomy. Similarly, positive feedback tends to satisfy people's basic need for competence, while negative feedback tends to thwart that need.

Further studies examined the general interpersonal context or ambience of a particular setting such as a classroom or workgroup. In that research, the significance of autonomy versus control for the maintenance of intrinsic motivation was also clearly observed. For example, investigators found that teachers who were more autonomy-supportive (in contrast to being controlling) catalyzed their students' intrinsic motivation and desire for challenge, and that managers who supported their subordinates' autonomy promoted motivation and satisfaction on the job (Deci & Ryan, 1991). In fact, people in positions of authority, including doctors, parents, and coaches, have also been found to influence the motivation and behaviors of their patients, children, and athletes depending on the degree to which they are autonomy-supportive versus controlling.

Finally, Deci and Ryan (1985) pointed out that external events such as rewards, feedback, and deadlines can be interpreted differently by different people. Specifically, many external events that have the potential to control behavior also convey positive competence information. If the controlling aspect is more salient, it will pressure people toward specific outcomes and undermine their intrinsic motivation; if the informational aspect is more salient, it will affirm their competence and enhance their intrinsic motivation. Whether the controlling or informational aspect is more salient depends on both the situation and the person.

If the interpersonal context or ambience within which rewards or feedback are administered is generally autonomy-supportive, the informational aspect of the rewards or feedback will tend to be more salient. For example, studies have shown that, although monetary rewards typically diminish intrinsic motivation, they can maintain or enhance it if they are administered in an autonomy-supportive context—in other words, if they convey competence within the context of choice.

In addition, some people are inclined to experience events such as rewards and feedback as more informational, whereas others are inclined to experience them as more controlling. Thus, individual differences can lead people to experience the same external event differently, so the event will have different effects on intrinsic motivation (Deci & Ryan, 1991).

To summarize, intrinsic motivation flourishes when people do interesting tasks and are able to satisfy their needs for competence and autonomy. Specific events in the interpersonal environment, such as the offer of rewards, the imposition of deadlines, and the provision of performance feedback, can directly influence people's need satisfaction and, accordingly, their intrinsic motivation. Further, the general interpersonal ambience can also impact their need satisfaction and intrinsic motivation both directly and by influencing how they experience external events. Finally, people differ in their tendencies to interpret events and environments in ways that can either support or thwart need satisfaction and thus affect intrinsic motivation.

Because intrinsic motivation is relevant in many walks of life and has been associated with more positive outcomes than extrinsic motivation, it seems important to be mindful of the ways we can support the autonomy and competence of our children, students, clients, employees, and patients.

REFERENCES

deCharms, R. (1968). *Personal causation.* New York: Academic.

Deci, E. L., Koestner, R., & Ryan, R. M. (1999). A meta-analytic review of experiments examining the effects of extrinsic rewards on intrinsic motivation. *Psychological Bulletin, 125,* 627–668.

Deci, E. L., & Ryan, R. M. (1985). *Intrinsic motivation and self-determination in human behavior.* New York: Plenum.

Deci, E. L., & Ryan, R. M. (1991). A motivational approach to self: Integration in personality. In R. Dienstbier (Ed.), *Nebraska symposium on motivation: Vol. 38. Perspectives on motivation* (pp. 237–288). Lincoln: University of Nebraska Press.

Freud, S. (1962). *The ego and the id.* New York: Norton. (Original work published 1923)

Hull, C. L. (1943). *Principles of behavior.* New York: Appleton-Century-Crofts.

White, R. W. (1959). Motivation reconsidered. *Psychological Review, 66,* 297–333.

E. L. DECI
University of Rochester

MOTIVATION
SELF-DETERMINATION

INTROSPECTION

Introspection (literally, looking inward), a popular methodology of psychologists toward the end of the 19th and in the early decades of the 20th centuries, is a method of inquiry in psychology in which subjects attempt to examine the contents and processes of their consciousness. Introspection was used in the study of a range of psychological processes, including memory, learning, thinking, problem solving, dream analysis, and perception.

The method of introspection was not a simple reflection on experience. Subjects were rigorously trained in the process of examining, describing, and reporting immediate sensory experience in response to systematic questioning. Edward Bradford Titchener defined the conditions for optimum introspective observation: Subjects should be unbiased and should prevent other associations from influencing the report of the immediate experience. In addition, subjects should be alert, free from distractions, healthy, fresh and free from fatigue, and interested in the experience under study.

Introspection was the principal method of the structuralist school led by Wilhelm Wundt in Germany and Titchener in America, which defined psychology as the study of conscious experience. Structuralists sought to break down experience into its component parts or elementary sensations. Sensation was considered primary, with perceptual processes being viewed as secondary organizing activities. A subjective understanding of consciousness and the contents of mind was the goal of structuralist psychology.

This view was opposed by the members of the Gestalt school who rejected the assumption of primary elements of experience in favor of innate organizational propensities and a holistic view of perception. Introspective analysis they claimed could reveal nothing because phenomena were experienced as patterns, rather than simply the sum of their parts. The functionalist school represented by John Dewey also opposed the subjective introspective approach, emphasizing instead the importance of systematic, objective demonstration, and experimental testing of theory. The behaviorists, such as J. B. Watson, condemned introspection as qualitative and unreliable and opposed the consideration of all notions of subjective experience and questions of consciousness, emphasizing only observable behavior analyzed in terms of measurable stimuli and responses.

SUGGESTED READING

Titchener, E. B. (1909). *Lectures on the experimental psychology of the thought process.* New York: Macmillan.

Titchener, E. B. (1923). *A textbook of psychology.* New York: Macmillan. (Original work published 1910)

Wundt, W. (1897). *Outline of psychology.* Leipzig, Germany: Engelmann.

Wundt, W. (1897). *Principles of psychology,* Leipzig, Germany: Engelmann.

R. C. ADAM-TEREM
Kapiolani Medical Center, Honolulu

STRUCTURALISM
FUNCTIONALISM
GESTALT PSYCHOLOGY

INTROVERSION-EXTRAVERSION

Jung (1921/1971) coined the terms "introversion" and "extraversion" to refer to two different psychological types. By introversion, Jung meant a turning inward of the libido (psychic energy), whereas extraversion referred to a directing outward of the libido. Note that either term can be spelled with an "o" or an "a" (i.e., either as above or as intraversion and extroversion). Although inconsistent, introversion and extraversion are the spellings used with the Myers-Briggs Type Indicator (MBTI), which is a popular personality assessment instrument based on Jung's type theory.

An introvert's mind, emotions, attention, and so on are turned inward toward himself or herself. Jung believed that the introvert directs the libido inward because of inferiority feelings, an idea reminiscent of Adler. Particularly during stressful periods, introverts tend to withdraw into themselves, to avoid others, and to be self-absorbed. With a bent toward self-sufficiency, the introvert's essential stimulation is from within, from his or her inner world of thoughts and reflections. Introverts are frequently reserved and difficult to get to know: they tend to bottle up their emotions and they need privacy.

In contrast, extraverts orient primarily to the outer world, focusing their perceptions and judgments on people and things. Extraverts draw energy from other people and external experiences, tend to express their emotions, need relationships more than privacy, and are usually friendly, talkative, and easy to get to know. Extraverts may seem shallow to introverts, whereas introverts may seem withdrawn to extraverts.

On the MBTI, the E-I or extraversion-introversion index is one of four dichotomous scales. The other three are sensing-intuition (S-N), thinking-feeling (T-F), and judgment-perception (J-P).

REFERENCE

Jung, C. G. (1971). *Psychological types.* In *The collected works of C. G. Jung* (Vol. 6), Bollinger Series XX. Princeton, NJ: Princeton University Press.

SUGGESTED READING

Myers, I. B., & Myers, P. B. (1980). *Gifts differing.* Palo Alto, CA: Consulting Psychologists Press.

B. M. THORNE
Mississippi State University

EXTRAVERSION AND INTROVERSION: CONCEPTS OF
PERSONALITY TYPES

IRRITABLE BOWEL SYNDROME

Irritable bowel syndrome (IBS) is one of several functional bowel disorders. In IBS, abdominal discomfort or pain is associated with defecation, change in bowel habits, and disordered defecations (Thompson et al., 2000a, 2000b). The clinical presentation and the severity of the disorder are often influenced by environmental, psychological, and social factors.

Irritable bowel syndrome is one of the most common gastrointestinal (GI) disorders seen in primary care and is also the most common disorder seen in gastroenterology practice (Mitchel & Drossman, 1987). Population-based surveys in western countries have shown prevalence rates of 10 to 20%. The prevalence of IBS decreases with age and is higher in females (female to male ratio 2:1), and no ethnic differences are reported (Drossman et al., 1993).

The pathophysiological mechanism of IBS is still unknown. Several physiological and psychosocial factors may contribute to the development of patients' symptoms and illness.

PHYSIOLOGICAL CONTRIBUTIONS

A variety of physiological factors may contribute to the clinical features of IBS. Patients with IBS have exaggerated intestinal motor activity in response to intrinsic (e.g., meals, intraluminal distention) or environmental (e.g., psychological stress) stimuli. This could explain postprandial or stress-related symptoms such as diarrhea. Also, with rectal balloon distention, IBS patients experience pain and urge to defecate at lower distention volumes than do controls. This suggests that they also have lower thresholds for rectal sensation and pain (Mertz, Nabiloff, Munakata, Niazi, & Mayer, 1995). The phenomenon of altered pain perception and visceral hypersensitivity in IBS patients has also been described in other parts of the GI tract (e.g., small intestine and colon). This supports the role of hypersensitivity in the pathogenesis of the disorder (Mayer & Raybould, 1995; Rao, 1996). Nevertheless, no single physiological mechanism can fully explain the variable clinical presentations of IBS (diarrhea, constipation, pain, bloating, etc.). It is likely that the experience of symptoms results from dysregulation of the bi-directional communication system between the gut and the brain (i.e., the brain-gut axis) including the enteric nerve terminals, spinal cord, and the brain (Mayer & Raybould, 1995).

Recent studies using functional brain imaging (positron emission tomography [PET], functional magnetic resonance imaging

[fMRI]) in patients with IBS and healthy controls have shown differences in regional brain activity in response to intraluminal balloon distention (Silverman et al., 1997; Mertz et al., 2000; Ringel et al., 2000). This finding emphasizes the role of the central nervous system (CNS) in modulating gut physiology and conscious perception of visceral sensation and pain in IBS. Previous studies have shown clearly that the gut is physiologically responsive to stressful stimuli and emotions. Psychological and environmental stressors may cause prolonged motor abnormalities (Rao, Hatfield, Suls, and Chamberlain, 1998) and reduction in the threshold at which individuals experience gastrointestinal sensations. Moreover, other studies have shown that stressors (e.g., life stress, abuse, etc.) can also affect the patients' symptom perception (i.e., sensation intensity/severity), illness behavior, and treatment outcome (Drossman, Whitehead, & Camilleri, 1997; Drossman, Li, Leserman, Toomey, & Hu, 1996).

PSYCHOSOCIAL CONTRIBUTIONS

Several psychological and social factors have a role in the development and course of IBS. Early life experience such as living with a family member who suffers from GI symptoms or living with familial dysfunctions (e.g., divorce, death, conflicts) are significantly more common in patients with IBS as compared to either the general population or to patients with IBS as compared to either the general population or to patients with other (i.e., organic) gastrointestinal disorders (Lowman, Drossman, Cramer, & McKee, 1987; Whitehead et al., 1994). Recent stressful life events (such as the breakup of a close relationship) can precede the development of symptoms and are associated with an increased number of physician visits (Whitehead, Crowell, Robinson, Heller, & Schuster, 1992; Creed, Craig, & Farmer, 1988).

Comorbid effective disorders, psychiatric illnesses, and personality disturbances are also more prevalent in IBS patients when compared to the rates of those disorders in normal populations. Approximately 50% of IBS patients have a current psychiatric disorder as determined by structured psychiatric interviews (Drossman, Creed, et al., 2000). The most common types use anxiety, Panic Disorder, depressive disorders, Posttraumatic Stress Disorder, and somatization disorders. Sexual and physical abuse is reported in 44 to 55% of IBS patients seen in tertiary care settings (Drossman, Talley, Olden, Leserman, & Barreiro, 1995). It represents a higher prevalence when compared to patients with organic GI disorders.

A maladaptive or poorer coping style, such as catastrophizing or perceived ineffectiveness, may up-regulate the patient's symptom experience and contribute to the development of more severe symptomatology, increased health-seeking, and illness behavior (Drossman, Li, Leserman, Toomey, & Hu, 1997; Drossman, Li, Leserman, Keefe, Hu, & Toomey, 2000). Therefore, greater psychological disturbances and life stress, and a higher frequency of abuse history, are seen in IBS patients at referral centers and among patients who frequently seek medical care (Drossman et al., 2000; Gaynes & Drossman, 1999). These influencing factors are also associated with more severe symptoms, poorer daily function, and poorer health outcome. It is important to note that although psy-

chosocial factors are common and may have a prominent role in the expression of IBS, they only modify illness experience and behaviors; they do not cause IBS (Drossman et al., 2000). Moreover, the psychological and personality profiles of people with IBS who do not seek health care are no different than those of the general population (Drossman et al., 1988; Whitehead, Bosmajian, Zonderman, Costa, & Schuster, 1988).

Since both physiological and psychological factors contribute to the patient's symptoms and illness, the disorder is better understood by an integrative biopsychosocial model of illness and disease (Drossman, 1998). Consistent with the biopsychosocial model, psychosocial issues are considered to be essential components of the clinical presentation of the disorder in addition to physiological (biological) factors. Addressing all of these issues is essential for establishing a more comprehensive and effective approach for the diagnosis and management of patients with IBS.

DIAGNOSIS

There are no biological markers for IBS. The disorder is recognized by a cluster of clinical symptoms. A positive diagnosis is based on identifying specific symptoms consistent with the disorder using symptom-based criteria and a modest effort to exclude other diseases (Drossman, Whitehead, & Camilleri, 1997; Drossman, 1999). For IBS this includes abdominal pain associated with a change in the consistency or frequency of stools and relieved with defecation. Associated symptoms can include bloating or a feeling of distention, presence of mucus in stool, urgency, and feeling of incomplete evacuation. Irritable bowel syndrome may be diarrhea-predominant, constipation-predominant, or a combination of both at varying times.

Several symptom-based criteria have been developed for the diagnosis of IBS. The original Manning criteria were developed in 1978 (Manning, Thomson, Heaton, & Morris, 1978). A more comprehensive set of criteria, the Rome criteria, has recently been developed by a multinational working team (Thompson et al., 2000a, 2000b).

TREATMENT

Once a positive diagnosis of IBS has been made, an effective physician-patient relationship should be established. This includes appropriate reassurance and patient education about the condition and its consequences (Drossman, 1999; Drossman & Thompson, 1992). The physician's and patient's acknowledgment of the relevance and interrelations of physiological and psychosocial factors to the patient's symptoms, and the acceptance of the need to address both of them, are essential aspects of the treatment program.

The treatment approach depends on the severity of the disorder. This can be determined by the intensity and constancy of the symptoms, the nature of the physiological disturbances (i.e., diarrhea or constipation), the degree of psychosocial difficulties, and the frequency of health care use (Drossman, Whitehead, & Camilleri, 1997; Drossman, Li, et al., 1995; Drossman, Whitehead, Toner, et al., 2000).

Only 30% of IBS patients see physicians for their symptoms. Health care seeking is influenced by social and cultural factors, the presence and severity of pain, and psychosocial disturbances (Drossman, Whitehead, & Camilleri, 1997; Drossman, Creed, et al., 2000). Of the patients who do see physicians, the majority (75%) have mild symptoms. These patients vary in the frequency and severity of their symptoms, and in the degree to which the symptoms interfere with their daily activities. The majority of these patients will usually require no more than reassurance, education, and dietary/lifestyle changes. Patients with moderate symptoms (about 20%) may additionally require pharmacologic and/or behavioral treatments depending on the symptom severity and the degree of the psychological distress. Only 5% of IBS patients have severe symptoms. These are often more constant and associated with psychological disorders (e.g., depression) and chronically disturbed daily functioning. These patients often require additional psychopharmacologic (e.g., antidepressant) treatment and/or psychological (e.g., cognitive-behavioral) treatment.

Medication Treatments

As noted, most patients with IBS require no prescribed medications. They usually will benefit from dietary changes, recommendations for lifestyle changes, and encouragement of health-promoting behaviors. Short-term medication treatment can be prescribed during exacerbations. Consistent with the biopsychosocial model it is important to view medication therapy as part of a more comprehensive management plan.

Gut-directed medications (e.g., anticholinergics, prokinetics, etc.) can be used to relieve specific symptoms such as pain, diarrhea, and constipation (Camilleri, 1999). Some new medications directed to reduce gut sensitivity are currently under clinical trial. These include 5HT3 (Mangel & Northcutt, 1999; Camilleri et al., 1999) and 5HT4 antagonists, and kappa opioid antagonists (Dapoigny, Abitbol, & Freitag, 1995). Medications with central/psychotrophic effects (e.g., antidepressants) can be used to treat comorbid affective or psychiatric disorders (e.g., depression, anxiety). In addition, low doses of antidepressants are also effective in alleviating chronic or severe abdominal pain. These neuro-modulatory and analgesic properties of antidepressants are independent of their psychotrophic effects. In fact, patients may improve using medication at lower doses and a shorter time interval than that used for patients with psychiatric disorders (Clouse, 1994; Jackson et al., 2000). Tricyclic agents such as desipramine (50–150mg) or amitriptyline (25–100mg) have been best studied and appear to be effective in controlling IBS symptoms. However, serotonin reuptake inhibitors may be preferred in older patients or in those having constipation because they have little or no anticholinergic effect.

Psychological treatments

Psychological treatments are usually recommended for patients with disabling symptoms (e.g., major depression), abuse history with maladjustment to the current illness, and somatization with multiple consultations across specialties (Thompson et al., 2000a, 2000b). Several psychological treatments have been used in patients with IBS. These include psychotherapeutic treatments such as cognitive-behavioral therapy (CBT) and dynamic psychotherapy; hypnotherapy; and relaxation training (Drossman, Creed, et

al., 2000). The psychotherapeutic approach emphasizes the importance of identifying both the patient's specific concerns and the illness model associated with his or her GI symptoms, and understanding the interaction between physical/physiological factors and psychosocial factors. Treatment involves applying the various techniques in the fashion that best integrates these contributing features. The relaxation training approach involves teaching the patient techniques to reduce arousal and anxiety, and to control bowel symptoms. At times, the optimal approach may involve a combination of different treatment methods.

Psychological treatments appear superior to conventional medical treatment in reducing psychological distress, improving copying, and reducing some bowel symptoms (Guthrie, Creed, Dawson, & Tomenson, 1991). However, no one specific treatment approach or type was found to be superior (Drossman, Creed, et al., 2000).

In conclusion, an effective treatment program requires an integrated diagnostic and treatment approach that addresses both the biological and the psychological aspects of the illness (adopting a biopsychosocial approach). Unfortunately, patients and physicians tend to focus on the physiological aspects of the illness, and many patients are skeptical and resistant to psychological referral or therapy. Establishing a team that combines conventional medical treatment (by primary physician or gastroenterologist) and individual psychological treatment (by a psychologist interested in functional GI disorders) can increase the patient's compliance with and motivation toward the treatment. Such an approach can significantly contribute to the success of the treatment in IBS patients.

REFERENCES

Camilleri, M. (1999). Clinical evidence to support current therapies of irritable bowel syndrome. *Alimentary Pharmacological Therapy, 13*(Suppl. 2), 48–53.

Camilleri, M., Mayer, E. A., Drossman, D. A., et al. (1999). Improvement in pain and bowel function in female irritable bowel patients with alosetron, a 5HT3-receptor antagonist. *Alimentary Pharmacological Therapy, 13,* 610.

Clouse, R. E. (1994). Antidepressants for functional gastrointestinal syndromes. *Digestive Disorder Science, 39,* 2352–2363.

Creed, F. H., Craig, T., & Farmer, R. G. (1988). Functional abdominal pain, psychiatric illness and life events. *Gut, 29,* 235–242.

Dapoigny, M., Abitbol, J. L., & Freitag, B. (1995). Efficacy of peripheral kappa agonist, fedotozine, vs. placebo in treatment of irritable bowel syndrome: A multicenter dose-response study. *Digestive Disorder Science, 40,* 2244–2249.

Drossman, D. A. (1998). Gastrointestinal illness and the biopsychosocial model. *Psychosomatic Medicine, 60,* 258–267.

Drossman, D. A. (1999). [Review of the article "An integrated approach to the irritable bowel syndrome"]. *Alimentary Pharmacological Therapy, 13*(Suppl. 2), 3–14.

Drossman, D. A., Creed, F. H., Olden, K. W., Svedlund, J., Toner, B. B., & Whitehead, W. E. (2000). Psychosocial aspects of the functional gastrointestinal disorders. In D. A. Drossman,

E. Corazziari, N. J. Talley, W. G. Thompson, & W. E. White-head (Eds.), *Rome II. The functional gastrointestinal disorders: Diagnosis, pathophysiology, and treatment.* McLean, VA: Degnon and Associates.

Drossman, D. A., Li, Z., Andruzzi, E., Temple, R., Talley, N. J., Thompson, W. G., Whitehead, W. E., Janssens, J., Funch-Jensen, P., Corazziari, E., Richter, J. E., & Koch, G. G. (1993). Householder survey or functional GI disorders: Prevalence, sociodemography, and health impact. *Digestive Disorder Science, 38,* 1569–1580.

Drossman, D. A., Li, Z., Leserman, J., Keefe, F. J., Hu, Y. J., and Toomey, T. C. (2000). Effects of coping on health outcome among female patients with gastrointestinal disorders. *Psychosomatic Medicine, 62,* 309–317.

Drossman, D. A., Li, Z., Leserman, J., Toomey, T. C., & Hu, Y. J. B. (1996). Health status by GI diagnosis and in relation to abuse history. *Gastroenterology, 110,* 999–1007.

Drossman, D. A., Li, Z., Leserman, J., Toomey, T., & Hu, Y. (1997). Association of coping pattern and abuse history: A prospective study. *Gastroenterology, 112,* 724.

Drossman, D. A., Li, Z., Toner, B. B., Diamant, N. E., Creed, F. H., Thompson, D., Read, N. W., Babbs, C., Barreiro, M., Bank, L., Whitehead, W. E., Schuster, M. M., & Guthrie, E. A. (1995). Functional bowel disorders: A multinational comparison of health status and diagnosis, and development of an illness severity index. *Digestive Disorder Science, 40,* 986–995.

Drossman, D. A., McKee, D. C., Sandler, R. S., Mitchell, C. M., Lowman, B. C., Burger, A. L., & Cramer, E. M. (1988). Psychosocial factors in the irritable bowel syndrome: A multivariate study of patients and nonpatients with irritable bowel syndrome. *Gastroenterology, 95,* 701–708.

Drossman, D. A., Talley, N. J., Olden, K. W., Leserman, J., & Barreiro, M. A. (1995). Sexual and physical abuse and gastrointestinal illness: Review and recommendations. *Annals of Internal Medicine, 123,* 782–794.

Drossman, D. A., & Thompson, W. G. (1992). The irritable bowel syndrome: Review and graduated, multicomponent treatment approach. *Annals of Internal Medicine, 116,* 1009–1016.

Drossman, D. A., Whitehead, W. E., & Camilleri, M. (1997). Irritable bowel syndrome: A technical review for practice guideline development. *Gastroenterology, 112,* 2120–2137.

Drossman, D. A., Whitehead, W. E., Toner, B. B., Diamant, N. E., Hu, Y. J. B., Bangdiwala, S. I., and Jia, H. (2000). What determines the severity among patients with painful functional bowel disorders? *American Journal of Gastroenterology, 95*(4):974–980.

Gaynes, B., & Drossman, D. A. (1999). The role of psychosocial factors in irritable bowel syndrome. In P. J. Whorwell & L. A. Houghton (Eds.), *Bailliere's clinical gastroenterology international practice and research 13*(3), 437–452.

Guthrie, E., Creed, F., Dawson, D., & Tomenson, B. (1991). A controlled trial of psychological treatment for the irritable bowel syndrome. *Gastroenterology, 100,* 450–451.

Jackson, J. L., O'Malley, P. G., Tomkins, G., Balden, E., Santoro, J., Kroenke, K. (2000). Treatment of functional gastrointestinal disorders with antidepressant medications: a meta-analysis. *American Journal of Medicine, 108,* 65–72.

Lowman, B. C., Drossman, D. A., Cramer, E. M., & McKee, D. C. (1987). Recollection of childhood events in adults with irritable bowel syndrome. *Journal of Clinical Gastroenterology, 9,* 324–330.

Mangel, A. W., & Northcutt, A. R. (1999). The safety and efficacy of alosetron, a 5-HT3 receptor antagonist in female irritable bowel syndrome patients. *Alimentary Pharmacological Therapy, 13*(Suppl. 2), 77–82.

Manning, A. P., Thompson, W. G., Heaton, K. W., & Morris, A. F. (1978). Towards positive diagnosis of irritable bowel syndrome. *British Journal of Medicine, 2,* 653–654.

Mayer, E. A., & Raybould, H. E. (1995). Role of visceral afferent mechanisms in functional bowel disorders. *Gastroenterology, 99,* 1688–1701.

Mertz, H., Morgan, V., Tanner, G., Pickens, D., Price, R., Shyr, Y. U., Kessler, R. (2000). Regional cerebral activation in irritable bowel syndrome and control subjects with painful and nonpainful rectal distention. *Gastroenterology, 118,* 842–848.

Mertz, H., Nabiloff, B., Munakata, J., Niazi, N., & Mayer, E. A. (1995). Altered rectal perception is a biological marker of patients with irritable bowel syndrome. *Gastroenterology, 109,* 40–52.

Mertz, H., Tanner, W. G., Kessler, D., Price, R., & Pickens, D. (1998). Functional MRI measurement of brain activity during rectal distention in normal volunteers and patients with irritable bowel syndrome. *Gastroenterology, 114*(4), A803.

Mitchel, C. A., & Drossman, D. A. (1987). Survey of the AGA membership relating to patients with functional gastrointestinal disorders. *Gastroenterology, 92,* 1282–1284.

Rao, S. S. (1996). Visceral hyperalgesia: The key for unraveling functional gastrointestinal disorders. *Digestive Disorders, 14,* 271–275.

Rao, S. S., Hatfield, R. A., Suls, J. M., Chamberlain, M. J. (1998). Psychological and physical stress induce differential effects on human colonic motility. *American Journal of Gastroenterology, 93,* 985–990.

Ringel, Y., Drossman, D. A., Turkington, T. G., Hawk, T. C., Bradshaw, B., Coleman, R. E., Whitehead, W. E. (2000). Dysfunction of the motivational-affective pain system in patients with IBS: PET imaging in response to rectal balloon distension. *Gastroenterology, 118*(4), A444.

Silverman, D. H., Munakata, J. A., Ennes, H., Mandelkern, M. A., Hoh, C. K., & Mayer, E. A. (1997). Regional cerebral activity in normal and pathological perception of visceral pain. *Gastroenterology, 112*(1), 64–72.

Thompson, W. G., Longstreth, G. F., Drossman, D. A., Heaton, K. W., Irvine, E. J., & Mueller-Lissner, S. A. (2000a). Functional bowel disorders. In D. A. Drossman, E. Corazziari, N. J.

Talley, W. G. Thompson, & W. E. Whitehead (Eds.), *Rome II. The functional gastrointestinal disorders: Diagnosis, pathophysiology, and treatment.* McLean, VA: Degnon and Associates.

Thompson, W. G., Longstreth, G. F., Drossman, D. A., Heaton, K. W., Irvine, E. J., & Mueller-Lissner, S. A. (2000b). Functional abdominal pain. In D. A. Drossman, E. Corazziari, N. J. Talley, W. G. Thompson, & W. E. Whitehead (Eds.), *Rome II. The functional gastrointestinal disorders: Diagnosis, pathophysiology, and treatment.* McLean, VA: Degnon and Associates.

Whitehead, W. E., Bosmajian, L., Zonderman, A., Costa, P., & Schuster, M. M. (1988). Symptoms of psychologic distress associated with irritable bowel syndrome: Comparison of community and medical clinic samples. *Gastroenterology, 95,* 709–714.

Whitehead, W. E., Crowell, M. D., Heller, B. R., Robinson, J. C., Schuster, M. M., & Horn, S. (1994). Modeling and reinforcement of the sick role during childhood predicts adult illness behavior. *Psychosomatic Medicine, 56,* 541–550.

Whitehead, W. E., Crowell, M. D., Robinson, J. C., Heller, B. R., & Schuster, M. M. (1992). Effects of stressful life events on bowel symptoms: Subjects with irritable bowel syndrome compared to subjects without bowel dysfunction. *Gut, 33,* 825–830.

Y. RINGEL
D. A. DROSSMAN
University of North Carolina

BIOFEEDBACK
CONVERSION DISORDER
ENURESIS
NEUROPSYCHOLOGY
PSYCHOSOMATICS
TOILET TRAINING
TYPE A PERSONALITY

ISOMORPHISM

In psychology, the term "isomorphism" is identified with the classical Berlin school of Gestalt psychology. The concept was used by Gestalt theorists to characterize their particular approach to the mind/brain problem; they argued that the objective brain processes underlying and correlated with particular phenomenological experiences are isomorphic with (that is, have functionally the same form and structure as) those subjective experiences.

The etymology of isomorphism makes the term appropriate for such a theory. The Greek root "iso-" means *same, equal,* or *identical,* and "morph-" means *form, shape, organization,* or *structure.* What the Gestalt psychologists intended to convey with their idea of isomorphism is that the Gestalt properties—the form, shape, organization, and structure—of biophysical, electrochemical processes in the brain that underlie subjective cognitive experiences are identical to the Gestalt properties—the form, shape, organization, and structure—of the experiences themselves. This proposal contrasted sharply with the relatively inert connectionistic mind/

brain theories that prevailed during the first half of the 20th century, which viewed the brain more as a giant switchboard of interconnected, insulated switches and wires than as a dynamic system of interdependent electrochemical biological processes that constitute a complex interactive field.

Because such a dynamic, interactive field conception of brain function and activity was radically different from the much more static and mechanistic view of the brain that was implicitly taken for granted by the majority of psychologists of the time, the Gestalt idea of isomorphism was generally not well understood. One recent Gestalt theorist, Henle (1984, p. 317), wrote, "I know of no concept in psychology that has been more misunderstood, indeed more distorted, than isomorphism."

One reason for such distortion or misunderstanding is that the term had been used, long before the Gestalt psychologists adopted it, in such fields as chemistry, crystallography, and mathematics—in a way that typically implied a piecemeal orientation that is totally foreign to the Gestalt conception. Thus, in mathematical set theory, two groups of items are isomorphic if there is a perfect correspondence between the two sets such that there is a one-to-one identity between them; that is, each item in the first set can be paired one-for-one with an item in the second set.

Such one-to-one correspondence between two isomorphic processes or phenomena is contrary to the Gestalt approach. For example, two dotted circles, one composed of twenty dots along its circumference and another of twenty-two dots, are isomorphic in the Gestalt sense of having the identical functional form; the number of dots composing each circle is immaterial as long as there are enough of them to specify the shape reasonably clearly. What is crucial is precisely the form or shape or structure itself, not the number of elements that happen to make up its "parts." Thinking in terms of one-to-one correspondence of dots on the circumference of the two circles is a piecemeal, disconnected caricature which ignores the dynamic characteristics of the continuity of the trajectory of the circumference of a circle, of the equidistance of each part of the circumference from the center, and so on that make up the essential Gestalt or configuration of a circle. Two circles, whatever the number of "elements" composing them and irrespective of their color or size, are isomorphic simply because they both are circles: both display the circular shape. Comparably, two squares are isomorphic even if they are made up of different "elements," or are of different sizes, brightnesses, or colors. Further, although the notes of a particular melody are totally different when that melody is played in different keys, the sequences of notes are isomorphic and are still the same melody—and variations on the melody remain isomorphic as long as the basic melody is still recognizable (even if some variations might contain many more notes than others).

The first reference to brain processes that are isomorphic in the Gestalt sense to perceptual processes occurred in a 1912 paper on apparent motion by Wertheimer that is generally considered to have launched the Gestalt school. The reference concerns processes in the brain that are presumed to correspond to one version of the "phi phenomenon," or the perception of motion when there is in fact no motion in the physical stimulus. Assume, say, two short vertical lines, and , each about one inch long, separated horizontally by about one inch. If is exposed for a few seconds, then disappears, and a brief fraction of a second later is exposed, it may appear to the observer that what was shown was not two different lines successively exposed, but a single line that moved from location x to location y. If the sequence is continued, so that a very short time after disappears is exposed again, and then reappears almost immediately after goes off, and so on, as long as the distance and time relations are appropriate, the result is that a single line is seen as moving consistently back and forth. If the time between the removal of one line and the appearance of the other is too long, the observer experiences two stationary lines in two different places being successively exposed; if the time interval is too short (or if there is overlap in the time that both lines are exposed), the observer reports two stationary lines being exposed in two different places.

What happens in the brain under the conditions in which a single moving line is seen in such an experiment? Wertheimer argued that virtually every mind/brain theory assumes that there must be excitation of particular parts of the visual cortex when the observer sees the lines, one area of excitation that corresponds to , and another nearby that corresponds to . Furthermore (and here is where Gestalt theory deviates from other mind/brain theories) when motion is perceived, *there must be some kind of a "short circuit"* between the brain area corresponding to and the nearby area corresponding to ; this *"short circuit" is the brain process that is isomorphic* with the experience of a single moving line. The Gestalt properties of the process in the brain must somehow correspond with the Gestalt properties of seeing a single moving line rather than two separated, stationary, isolated lines.

Wertheimer's fairly rudimentary theoretical conception was elaborated in much greater detail by two of Wertheimer's Gestalt colleagues, Koffka (in his massive 1935 book, *Principles of Gestalt Psychology*) and especially Köhler (in extensive biopsychological and perceptual experiments; 1929). Köhler and his collaborators generated some rather surprising predictions from the theory, and managed to validate these predictions experimentally. An entire monograph was devoted to what Köhler and Wallach (1994) called figural after-effects, a set of perceived distortions of figures that are generated by prolonged prior observation of other figures.

Assume, for example, that the perceived distance between two points in the visual field, x and y, is isomorphic with the electrical resistance between their corresponding locations in the visual cortex, X and Y. If the resistance is greater, the brain processes X and Y are functionally far apart, and the perceived distance between the corresponding points in the visual field, x and y, should be greater; if the functional distance (that is, the electrical resistance) between the two brain processes X and Y is small, then the perceived distance between their experienced isomorphic counterparts, x and y, should also be small.

Now if some way can be found to change the resistance between two points in the visual cortex, then such a change should result in a corresponding change in the isomorphic visual experience. It is well known that any excitatory process that continues for some time in neural tissue will generate a process that inhibits the continuation of that excitatory process; every continuing excitation generates its own inhibition. According to the theory of isomor-

phism, this inhibition is "satiation," or an increase in electrochemical resistance. One way to generate enhanced resistance between two points in the visual cortex, therefore, is to excite it with an appropriate visual stimulus. If, then, the brain area corresponding to the space between two points in the visual field is stimulated for some time by a figure exposed visually in that space, this should increase the satiation or resistance in the space, and the same two points in the visual field should therefore appear farther apart than before. A wide variety of experiments testing this kind of prediction were performed by Köhler and Wallach, and such distortions were indeed corroborated.

Consider the configuration in Figure 1. There are three components in the pattern. The × marked "F" is a fixation point, on which observers are to keep their eyes fixed all the time. The four small squares marked "T" are the "test" pattern, where what is in question is the perceived distance between the left upper and lower squares in comparison with the perceived distance between the right upper and lower squares. The three rectangles marked "I" are the "inspection figure," or the pattern that is inspected for a prolonged period of time so as to increase the satiation in, or the resistance of, the corresponding parts of the visual cortex.

The procedure is as follows. First the "T" or test pattern is presented (with the fixation point). One of the vertical pairs of squares is adjusted until the left-hand pair appears to the observer to be exactly as far apart vertically as the right-hand pair. The test pattern is then removed, and replaced by the "I" or inspection pattern (with the same fixation point, to assure alteration of the resistance of the appropriate portion of the visual cortex), and the observer stares at this pattern for a period of one or two minutes. During this time, according to the theory of isomorphism, parts of the visual cortex that are stimulated by the images of the inspection pattern should become satiated and increase in resistance to further electrical activity. For the pattern in Figure 1, the resistance in the area between the brain processes corresponding to the left-hand pair of squares should increase, as it should in the areas just above the top square, and just below the bottom square, in the right-hand pair. Thereafter, the I pattern is removed, and the same T pattern is exposed once more. According to the prediction of the theory of isomorphism, since the resistance in the area between the two left-hand squares has been increased by exposure of the inspection figure in that area, the two squares should now look farther apart than they did before. That is indeed the result: Now the two right-hand squares are perceived as decidedly closer together than the two left-hand squares.

A large number of experiments of this kind (not only in vision but in other sense modalities, such as kinesthesis) made the theory of isomorphism widely discussed by the middle of the 20th century. In the early 1950s, two prominent neuroscientists, Lashley and Sperry (and their collaborators), performed some radical animal experiments in an effort to disprove the theory (1951, 1955). They experimentally altered the electrical properties of the visual cortex of cats and monkeys by making incisions in their brains and inserting insulating material into the cuts, or by placing gold foil or tantalum wire (excellent electrical conductors) directly on the surface or into the substance of the animals' visual cortices. Such disturbance in the electrochemical, biophysical characteristics of the brain, they argued, should interfere profoundly with the continued performance of visual discriminations that the animals had learned previously—if Köhler's specific theory of isomorphism was indeed correct. But none of these massive alterations in the visual brain medium produced any change in the animals' ability to make the visual discriminations they had learned previous to the surgical insults.

Köhler responded by pointing out various technical flaws in these experiments, and by arguing that the local changes in the electrical characteristics of the altered brains should redistribute and reorganize their field properties almost instantaneously, and that hence no disturbance in visually-guided performance would be expected. Neither Lashley nor Sperry rebutted these arguments, but Karl Pribram (1984), another prominent neuropsychologist, performed a variant on the Lashley-Sperry studies late in the 1950s. He altered the electrical activity of some monkeys' visual brains by irritating them with a cream of aluminum hydroxide; once again, there was no interference with the retention of previously-learned visual discriminations—but Köhler's point that natural physical field processes would almost immediately redistribute the change produced by local irritation was not addressed by Pribram's experiment either.

Interest in the Gestalt isomorphism hypothesis appears to have waned during the 1960s and 1970s; discussions of it in books about perception and about physiological psychology became rare by the 1980s. The predominant view by the late 1980s and early 1990s among neuroscientists about how the brain functions left no room for processes as dynamic, interactive, field-theoretical and systems-oriented as the Gestalt view of isomorphism.

The theory was neither definitively proven nor completely refuted by empirical data; neuropsychological researchers appear simply to have lost interest in the hypothesis, and have gone on to study other issues. Nevertheless, the Gestalt theory of physical processes in the brain that are functionally isomorphic with processes in subjective experience remains among the more ingenious efforts to come to grips with the recurring fundamental question of the relation between mind and brain.

REFERENCES

Henle, M. (1984). Isomorphism: Setting the record straight. *Psychological Research, 46,* 317–327.

Koffka, K. (1935). *Principles of Gestalt psychology.* New York: Harcourt, Brace.

Köhler, W. (1929). *Gestalt psychology.* New York: Liveright.

Köhler, W., & Wallach, H. (1944). Figural after-effects. *Proceedings of the American Philosophical Society, 88,* 269–357.

Lashley, K. S., Chow, K. L., & Semmes, J. (1951). An examination of the electrical field theory of cerebral integration. *Psychological Review, 58,* 123–136.

Pribram, K. H. (1984). What is iso and what is morphic in isomorphism? *Psychological Research, 46,* 329–332.

Sperry, R. W., & Miner, N. (1955). Pattern perception following insertion of mica plates into visual cortex. *Journal of Comparative and Physiological Psychology, 48,* 463–469.

Sperry, R. W., Miner, N., & Myers, R. E. (1955). Visual pattern perception following subpial slicing and tantalum wire implantations in the visual cortex. *Journal of Comparative and Physiological Psychology, 48,* 50–58.

Wertheimer, M. (1912). Experimentelle studien über das sehen von Bewegung. *Zeitschrift für Psychologie, 60,* 321–378.

M. WERTHEIMER
University of Colorado, Boulder

BRAIN
FORM-SHAPE PERCEPTION
GESTALT PSYCHOLOGY
ILLUSIONS
IMAGERY
MIND-BODY PROBLEM
PERCEPTUAL ORGANIZATION
SPLIT-BRAIN RESEARCH

ISRAEL, PSYCHOLOGY IN

The total area of Israel is about 8000 square miles, and its population is 4,000,000, of whom about 3,300,000 are Jewish. The State of Israel was established in May 1948. Following a 15-month War of Independence, Israel embarked upon a painstaking process of building the country and absorbing numerous and varied waves of Jewish immigration. The initial immigrants consisted of European Jews, the survivors of the Nazi concentration camps, followed by Jewish refugees from Moslem countries, who were forced to leave their homes as a consequence of the Israeli-Arab war. Israel's population doubled in the first four years of its existence, and continued to grow rapidly in the following years.

Three classes of problems have exerted a decisive influence on Israel and its people:

1. Problems of defense and a continuously stressful environment stemming from the ever-present threat of war with the Arab nations, including major wars in 1956, 1967, and 1973.

2. Economic problems caused by the need to maintain large and well-equipped armed forces in a country poor in resources and continuously absorbing massive immigration.

3. Social problems caused by the need to absorb and integrate immigrant populations of diverse cultural backgrounds from about 100 countries.

These problems have shaped the norms, attitudes, expectations, and behavior of the Israeli people and, by necessity, have had important implications for the development of psychology and psychologists' functions in Israel.

PAST AND PRESENT

The scope of psychological activity in the preindependence period was very limited. The rapid growth of the new state and the massive immigration created numerous and urgent needs for psychological services that could not be provided within the existing facilities. The shortage of professionals was gradually remedied by immigrant psychologists, primarily of Anglo-Saxon origin, and by young Israelis who returned from specialized training elsewhere. At the end of the 1950s, the Israeli psychological community consisted of about 200 psychologists active in continuously expanding psychological services in the areas of health, education, welfare, and social research.

The first psychology department was opened at the Hebrew University in 1957. Three additional departments were established at Bar-Ilan (1958), Tel-Aviv (1966), and Haifa (1966) universities. Psychology courses are also taught at the youngest Israeli university (Beer-Sheva), at the Israeli Institute of Technology (Technion), and in various university departments other than psychology. It is of interest to note that while psychology departments were established and directed by psychologists who came from, or were trained in other countries, by the end of 1982 all departments were chaired by Israeli-born psychologists who had received at least part of their training in that country.

Psychology is one of the most popular subjects of study at Israeli universities. Because of the large number of applicants, strict selection procedures for admission to B.A. programs are used. The general curriculum is similar across the various departments and includes: a three year B.A. program that requires about 60 semester credits in psychology; a two- to four-year M.A. program, which concentrates on one particular area and requires an additional 40 semester credits, a thesis, and a final examination; and a Ph.D. program, in which the emphasis is on a large-scale independent and original thesis with little course work. In 1982, there were approximately 900 B.A., 700 M.A., and 100 Ph.D. candidates.

Israel's psychological community as of 1982 included 2,000 practitioners, of whom 1700 were members of the Israel Psychological Association (IPA). The IPA has four sectors—clinical psychology, school psychology, rehabilitation psychology, and social vocational psychology. Membership is voluntary, but in 1977 the Parliament passed "The Psychologists' Law," which defines psychologists' functions and certification standards. The law is implemented by the Minister of Health, who is assisted by "the Psychologists' Council"—which provides consultation on issues related to the practice of psychologists in Israel, such as approval of working places and professional ethics. The IPA is one of the most active professional organizations in Israel.

In summary, then, the transition of Israeli psychology from past to present has been characterized by a dramatic expansion of psychological activity, coinciding with the rapid development of the country. Israeli psychologists are actively involved in the provision of a wide spectrum of psychological services as well as in extensive basic and applied research in all areas of psychology (Amir & Ben-Ari, 1981; Kugelmass, 1976; Sanua, 1971; Winnik, 1977).

PSYCHOLOGICAL RESEARCH

In spite of its youth, the psychological research carried out in Israel has reached impressive proportions. The bulk of research is pursued by psychologists in departments of psychology, as well as in schools of education, medicine, social work, business administration, and so on. In addition, a number of research institutes outside the universities employ psychologists on their research teams. The most famous is the Israel Institute of Applied Social Research, which is involved in a variety of studies on large samples of the Israeli adult population. These issues include problems of immigration, social structure, cultural patterns, consumer preferences, communication, and industrial sociology and psychology. The Henrietta Szold National Institute for Research in the Behavioral Sciences is mainly concerned with problems of education, welfare, and community. Since 1949, the institute has published *Megamot*, the behavioral science quarterly. Several public and private research institutes employ psychologists in such areas as education, social psychology, marketing, and psychological research.

The research carried out by Israeli psychologists is derived from a variety of theoretical approaches and covers all areas of psychology in both its basic and applied aspects. The contribution of this research is reflected in an impressive body of published work in Hebrew as well as in internationally renowned professional journals. In addition, the Israeli research community places heavy emphasis on continuous contact and exchange of information with the international psychological community. To this end, departments of psychology organize frequent international conferences, host short- and long-term visitors, and enable their staff members to participate in highly flexible sabbatical programs.

Along with the universal research areas of psychology, increasing attention has been directed to research problems unique to the Israeli reality.

Immigration and Cultural Variation

The problems created by the "ingathering of the exiles" have been of central concern to Israeli leaders and the general public. The two major immigrant groups, the World War II survivors and the refugees from the Moslem countries, were in tremendous need of help and guidance. Most important, the social, economical, and technological gap between these two groups created two distinct subgroups in the Israeli Jewish population—the European or Western group and the Eastern or Oriental group. Different problems of adjustment were presented by the immigrant populations from the free Western countries and the U.S.S.R.

This situation has given rise to extensive social and behavioral research aimed at elucidating causes and finding solutions. Along with social anthropological studies of the cultural and behavioral patterns of the various subgroups, there was an urgent need to seek solutions to problems of ethnic tensions, language and communication difficulties, intergroup contact, and the like. The multichild demographic structure of the immigrant populations from Asian and African countries, and their status of "culturally disadvantaged," presented the challenge of integrating and assimilating the younger generations and preparing them for the status of equal rights, as well as acting as adequately functioning citizens. With this background, large-scale research on problems of interethnic integration and enrichment of the culturally disadvantaged has been carried out. This research has resulted in the development of novel teaching and enrichment methods, part of which have been employed outside of Israel as well.

In addition to the two Jewish subgroups, Israel includes a variety of other cultural and ethnic groups—Moslem and Christian Arabs, Druze, and Bedouins. This cultural diversity has provided a natural laboratory for cross-cultural research on socialization patterns, cognitive and perceptual functioning, environmental impact on development, and so forth. Another question posed by the Israeli reality is that of Arab-Israeli relations. The Israeli Arabs constitute a minority in a country dominated by a Jewish majority and in a practically continuous state of war with its Arab neighbors. This situation has stimulated the investigation of questions concerned with the relationship between the two nations and ways to improve it. These questions acquired increased importance in light of the Israeli-Egyptian peace treaty (Amir et al., in press; Klein & Eshel, 1980; Greenbaum & Kugelmass, 1980; Beit-Hallahmi, 1972; Feuerstein et al., 1980).

Stress

In a country faced by a continuous threat of war, the investigation of the effects of stress is of special concern. This concern was intensified by the trauma of the sudden outbreak of the Yom Kippur War and the large number of its casualties. The public and scientific interest in the problems of psychological stress and ways of coping effectively culminated in the organization of two international conferences on psychological stress and adjustment in time of war and peace, in 1975 and 1978. In 1979, the Institute for the Research of Psychological Stress, one of the first of its kind in the world, was opened at Haifa University. Research topics include the assessment of the physiological and cognitive effects of stress and ways of human coping with stress. The institute provides consultation and services on the topic to various agencies, such as the military, the Ministry of Defense, and the Ministry of Health. (Milgram, 1978; Spielberger et al., 1982).

Holocaust

An additional area of research and clinical work of particular relevance to the Israeli situation concerns the effects of the Holocaust. This issue is related to the area of stress, but its uniqueness stems from the extent and the intensity of the national trauma of the Jewish people, of whom six million were exterminated by the Nazis during World War II. Many of the concentration camp survivors came to Israel to live with the haunting memories of their horrid past. The psychological problems faced by these individuals and their families, including Israeli-born generations, have motivated psychologists and other researchers to study the problem and search for ways of treatment and assistance.

The Kibbutz

Probably the best known Israeli social institution is the Kibbutz, with its unique social structure, communal economy, and child-rearing practices. Although kibbutz members constitute only 3% of the total population, their influence in politics, economy, education, social life, and the army by far exceeds their small proportion. The structure of the kibbutz has attracted the attention and interest of the scientific community in Israel and the world at large. Anthropological and psychological research of kibbutz psychodynamics made its appearance in the early 1950s. In later years,

systematic research followed, dealing with kibbutz socialization patterns, child-rearing practices, cognitive development, personality structure, interpersonal relationships, sex roles, and other questions and issues of interest. In 1976, the Institute for Research of the Kibbutz and the Cooperative Idea was established at Haifa University. The institute coordinates research activities and compiles literature related to the kibbutz movement and cooperative enterprises in general. The basis of the work of the institute is the belief of its founders, most of whom are kibbutz members, that the kibbutz provides an example of an alternative lifestyle based on principles of cooperation and equality, of direct democracy and mutual help. The kibbutz experience has important implications for problems of the wider society, such as child-rearing, old age, education, and rural industry (Beit-Hallahmi, 1977; Shur et al., 1981).

APPLIED PSYCHOLOGY

The following descriptions of applied areas of psychology in Israel are presented according to the professional sections to which they belong.

Clinical Psychology

Clinical psychology constituted the launching platform for psychological activities in Israel. In a war-torn country characterized also by mass immigration, the traditional role of the clinical psychologist was assigned a central place, and clinical psychology services have been rapidly developed by governmental agencies, such as the Ministry of Health.

The activities of clinical psychologists span a wide range of tasks and responsibilities. The majority of clinical psychologists are employed by two agencies—the Ministry of Health and the Kupat Holim Workers' Sick Fund. These agencies operate psychiatric hospitals, psychiatric wards in general hospitals, and community mental health clinics for children and adults, where about 300 clinical psychologists work in consultation, counseling, diagnosis, and psychotherapy. Additional governmental and public agencies that employ clinical psychologists include Hadassah, several municipalities, the Social Welfare Ministry, the police, prisons, the Youth Immigration Agency, and student counseling centers.

Until the last decade, there was relatively little private clinical practice in Israel. One of the phenomena accompanying the development of psychology in Israel has been the growth in the number of private treatment institutes as well as in the number of individuals seeking treatment at these institutes. However, the number of clinical psychologists engaged solely in private practice is still low.

The area of clinical psychology and psychotherapy in Israel covers a broad range of theoretical and treatment approaches. The clinical psychology scene includes the Israel Institute of Psychoanalysis, the Adlerian Institute, and the Israeli Association for Behavioral Therapy, as well as practitioners who apply the principles of Jungian psychotherapy, less orthodox dynamic methods, Gestalt, TA, various methods of family and group therapy, and so on. This pluralism and eclecticism reflect the variety of sources, within and outside Israel, from which Israeli psychologists have derived their professional knowledge.

Clinical psychology has remained one of the most popular areas of study in Israeli universities and has become an integral part of all psychotherapeutic settings and mental health systems (Shanan & Weiss, 1963; Sharni & Zemet, 1981; Berman, 1981).

School Psychology

About one million children, aged 4 to 18, are registered in the Israeli school system. School attendance between the ages of 5 and 16 is mandatory and free. The Israeli educational system is probably the best example of a traditional institution that has been shaped by the needs and problems of the society at large. In the face of enormous adjustment and integration problems created by the "ingathering of the exiles," schools have increasingly assumed, in addition to their conventional functions of education and academic achievement, the complex and difficult role of socialization and integration of youths from diverse cultural and socioeconomic backgrounds into one cohesive nation. Consequently one of the major features of the system has been the creation of specialized educational frameworks geared to the needs and problems of the various school populations. The special education frameworks include classes or schools for the mentally retarded and emotionally disturbed, classes and schools for gifted children, and various programs for the culturally disadvantaged. The central task of the school psychologist within this framework is to diagnose and direct children to the appropriate educational settings. School psychological services are provided by the local municipality under the supervision of the Ministry of Education. The practitioners are usually based in a clinic and make frequent visits to the schools.

School psychology in Israel has undergone a rapid expansion in its scope and quality of activity. At the end of the 1960s, school psychological services were scarce, but in 1970 there were 160 school psychologists in 32 centers, and by 1982 the number had grown to 800 psychologists operating in 120 centers and reaching most Israeli schools.

In addition to their direct work with individual children and their function of diagnosis and early problem identification, school psychologists in Israel are involved in therapeutic interventions with pupils and their parents. The treatment is usually short-term and involves parent counseling and family therapy, as well as mental health consultation for teachers, principals, and other educational personnel.

The theoretical approaches underlying school psychologists' work are varied, but in general they apply models of primary and secondary preventive intervention in an attempt to aid pupils in improving their cognitive and emotional functioning. Some psychologists view school as an organization and employ the principles of organization development; others treat school as a basis for providing psychological services for the community as a whole.

Within the model of prevention and intervention in times of crisis, school psychologists are involved in the preparation of pupils and teachers for effective coping in family or emergency/war crisis situations. In addition, school psychologists are actively engaged in research and assessment of problems raised within the educational system (Benyamini & Klein, 1970; Raviv, 1979; Raviv et al., 1981).

Industrial and Rehabilitation Psychology

These are the two newest branches of Israeli psychology that developed as a direct consequence of the country's needs. The rapid growth of Israel's industry and the introduction of American managerial approaches required professional guidance in areas of human relations, workers' morale, methods of increasing productivity and efficiency, organizational development, and human factors engineering. The industrial psychology sector combines psychologists from several disciplines, including vocational counseling, industrial psychology, human relations, and human factors engineering. These specialists are employed by several private institutes of vocational counseling and personnel selection, the Ministry of Labor, the army, industry, and the Israel Institute of Productivity.

Rehabilitation psychology services are provided along with other types of psychological services within the various professional settings surveyed in preceding sections and are mainly directed toward two populations—handicapped individuals and war casualties, including wounded and disabled soldiers and their families.

Military Psychology

The Israeli Defense Forces (IDF) employ a wide variety of psychological services, through two separate bodies. The Military Psychology Unit is headed by the chief psychologist of IDF and serves as the consulting and executive body of the Manpower Wing on issues concerned with psychological research and consultation. The functions performed by the unit's psychologists include diagnosis, personnel selection, development and improvement of training programs, assessment of organizational climate, leadership effectiveness and performance, guidance and consultation to various IDF units, and crisis intervention. An important aspect of the military psychologist's role is concern with soldiers' morale, particularly in times of war and crisis. The second framework that utilizes psychologists is the Medical Corps Unit; in addition to psychiatrists, it employs clinical psychologists in mental health–related work. This unit is headed by a clinical psychologist instead of the psychiatrist who held this position in the past.

In addition to the functions performed in the field, military psychologists engage in extensive applied research concerned with IDF-raised problems.

In an army whose strength and fighting superiority stem from the quality of its soldiers rather than the quantity, the work carried out by military psychologists is of critical importance. Undoubtedly these professionals have made an immense contribution to the unique makeup of the Israeli army (Greenbaum et al., 1977; Babad & Salomon, 1978).

REFERENCES

Amir, Y., & Ben-Ari, R. (1981). Psychology and society in Israel. *International Journal of Psychology, 16,* 239–247.

Amir, Y., Sharan, S., & Ben-Ari, R. (in press). *School integration: Cross cultural perspectives.* Hillsdale, NJ: Erlbaum.

Babad, E. Y., & Salomon, G. (1978). Professional dilemmas of the psychologist in an organizational emergency. *American Psychologist, 33,* 840–846.

Beit-Hallahmi, B. (1972). Some psychosocial and cultural factors in the Arab-Israeli conflict: A review of the literature. *Journal of Conflict Resolution, 16,* 269–280.

Beit-Hallahmi, B., & Rabin, A. I. (1977). The Kibbutz as a social experiment and as a child-rearing laboratory. *American Psychologist, 32,* 532–541.

Benyamini, K., & Klein, Z. (1970). The educational system and mental health. In A. Jarus, J. Marcus, J. Oren, & H. Rapaport (Eds.), *Children and families in Israel: Some mental health perspectives.* New York: Gordon & Breach.

Berman, E. (1981). Growing pains of professional clinical psychology: A report from Israel. *The Clinical Psychologist, 34,* 6–8.

Feuerstein, R., Rand, Y., Hoffman, M. B., & Miller, R. (1980). *Instrumental enrichment: An intervention program for cognitive modifiability.* Baltimore: University Park Press.

Greenbaum, C. W., & Kugelmass, S. (1980). Human development and socialization in cross-cultural perspective: Issues arising from research in Israel. In N. Warren (Ed.), *Studies in cross-cultural psychology* (Vol. 2). London: Academic.

Greenbaum, C. W., Rogovsky, I., & Shalit, B. (1977). The military psychologist during war-time: A model based on action research and crisis intervention. *Journal of Applied Behavioral Science, 13,* 7–21.

Klein, Z., & Eshel, Y. (1980). *Integrating Jerusalem schools.* New York: Academic.

Kugelmass, S. (1976). Israel. In V. S. Sexton & H. Misiak (Eds.), *Psychology around the world.* Bakersfield, CA: Brooks.

Milgram, N. A. (1978). Psychological stress and adjustment in time of war and peace: The Israeli experience as presented in two conferences. *Israel Annals of Psychiatry and Related Disciplines, 16,* 327–338.

Raviv, A. (1979). Reflections on the role of the school psychologist in Israel. *Professional Psychology, 10,* 820–826.

Raviv, A., Wiesner, E., & Bar-Tal, D. (1981). *Survey of psychologists in school psychological services: Research report* (in Hebrew). Jerusalem: Ministry of Education and Culture.

Sanua, V. D. (1971). Psychology in action. *American Psychologist, 26,* 602–605.

Shanan, J., & Weiss, A. A. (1963). Clinical psychology in Israel. *Israel Annals of Psychiatry and Related Disciplines, 1,* 107–111.

Sharni, S., & Zemet, R. (1981). Clinical psychologists as part of the mental health services in the Ministry of Health in Israel. Their tasks, contributions, and prospectives. *The Israel Annals Of Psychiatry and Related Disciplines, 18,* 237–245.

Shur, S., Beit-Hallahmi, B., Blasi, J. R., & Rapin, A. (Eds.). (1981). *The kibbutz: A bibliography of scientific and professional publications in English.* Darby, PA: Norewood Editions.

Spielberger, C. D., Sarason, I. G., & Milgram, N. A. (1982). *Stress and anxiety* (Vol. 8). Washington, DC: Washington Hemisphere.

Winnik, H. Z. (1977). Milestones in the development of psychoanalysis in Israel. *Israel Annals of Psychiatry and Related Disciplines, 15,* 85–91.

A. RAVIV
Tel Aviv University

ITALY, PSYCHOLOGY IN

In Italy, interest in psychology was officially recognized by the academic world in 1878 when the University of Messina (Sicily) authorized Sergi to give the first course in this new discipline. Sergi opened the first laboratory of experimental psychology at the University of Rome 10 years later. During these years, a Polish student of Wundt, Ferdinando Kiesow, was invited to teach at the University of Turin; at the same time, physiologist Angelo Mosso became involved in psychological issues, such as fear and fatigue.

Early in this century, interest in the new discipline spread among several groups of psychiatrists and neurologists working in different parts of the country. The shift from an originally philosophical to a more naturalistic and biologically-oriented interest was gradually achieved and became apparent at the 1923 National Congress on Psychology in Florence. Since 1915, a number of psychophysiological studies have been aimed at identifying psychological characteristics of aircraft pilots (Agostino Gemelli). During the period of Fascism, from approximately 1925 to 1945, psychology as well as other humanistic sciences were opposed for political reasons.

The "official" idealistic philosophy considered psychology an ancillary discipline, and marginal space was left for its development. In fact, during these two decades, very few laboratories continued their work; the Institute of Psychology at the Catholic University of Milan, directed by Gemelli, was for many years dedicated to the psychology of perception, language, and experimental phonetics. In Rome, Mario Ponzo devoted his work to problems of perception and subsequently became interested in career counseling for adolescents.

In addition, several small groups of researchers were active in Florence, including Enzo Bonaventura, originally interested in perceptual illusion and then in developmental psychology; in Padua, Cesare Musatti continued the tradition of Benussi in studying perception from a Gestalt viewpoint; and in Rome, Sante De Sanctis published the first Italian book of "work psychology." After World War II, the demand for professional competence was greatly increased in several branches of psychology. In particular, educational, clinical, and industrial psychology developed quickly in the context of the reorganization of Italian society. A few notes on the way in which each of these branches has developed in the past 30 years will help to understand the Italian psychology of today.

Clinical psychology was gradually, but consistently, pervaded by psychoanalysis in all of its various approaches. The orthodox Freudian school still represented the largest group of clinicians. Their efforts as well as those of Jungian psychologists were initially concentrated on training psychotherapists. At the same time, a remarkable number of original and translated publications pervaded Italian culture; they greatly exceeded the limits of professional interest. Prominent figures in this area were Musatti, Fornari, Gaddini, and Ossicini.

In the past 10 years, the influence of psychoanalytic thinking has also increased in the academic world, through the teaching of Leonardo Ancona, Gustavo Iacono, Lidia De Rita, Sergio Molinari, and Renzo Canestrari. Three more recent developments derived from the original nucleus: family therapy (Selvini, Andolfi, and Malagoli), group psychotherapy (Spaltro), and group dynamics, particularly oriented toward interaction within institutions (Carli, Trentini, Spaltro, Manoukian, and De Maria).

In the 1970s, both clinical and social psychology were strongly influenced by the antipsychiatry movement, and this impact produced important and concrete changes in the organization of psychiatric treatment, as well as a remarkable influence of the psychological approach in the area of Italian psychiatry (Basaglia and Jervis). Only recently has there been increasing interest in therapeutic techniques based on behavior (Meazzini) and Gestalt principles (Francescato). Industrial reorganization following World War II led to the introduction of industrial psychology in personnel selection, training techniques, and management (Spaltro).

Despite considerable demand for industrial psychology, there seems to have been little growth in this area, and the teaching of work psychology is practically nonexistent at the university level. Social psychology started from the classical experimental approach, and made contributions in the area of interpersonal perception, small group dynamics, perception of stereotypes, and aggressive behavior (De Grada, Iacono, Amerio, Palmonari, and Caprara). Social psychologists primarily devoted their activities to inducing change in public institutions (such as schools) and, particularly, to the integration of physically and mentally handicapped children, the organization of public health services, the application of new laws for psychiatric assistance within the social environment, and more recently, the organization of social activity for the elderly. The application of social psychology (Francescato and Laicardi) has been particularly effective in community psychology. Educational psychology has received widespread attention over the past three decades, and psychological services in the schools have offered the greatest opportunity for work. In spite of this, for a number of social and political reasons, contributions to the development of this applicative branch of psychology have been impeded.

Developmental psychology has been studied at the experimental level, particularly with reference to Piagetian thinking; however, little impact has been seen in the field of normal or pathological child development. An important exception is the area of communicative abilities in children, for which there have been theoretical contributions, together with interesting applications for normal and special education (Antinucci, Volterra, Camaioni, Gobbo, and D'odorico). This is probably the result of the long interest of experimental psychologists in a variety of cognitive problems.

Studies on visual perception are the oldest and clearest example of this trend. For many decades, the phenomenological approach to visual perception was investigated by a large number of researchers (Musatti, Metelli, Kanitza, and Luccio). More recently,

this has been extended to psychophysiological aspects, with substantial cooperation by physiological laboratories (Bertini, Mecacci, Berlucchi, Marzi, and Rizzolatti). Research in psycholinguistics and in communication has resulted in many important findings (Parisi, Castelfranchi, and d'Arcais). In the last 10 years intense activity in artificial intelligence has been developed by Parisi.

A joint effort of psychologists, neurologists, and physiologists led to important finds in the field of neuropsychology (which, together with cognitive psychology is the best known and most productive field of research in Italy) as well as the establishment of a promotional group for clinical applications (De Renzi, Vignolo, Umiltá, Pizzamiglio, Spinnler, Gainotti, Denes, Basso, and Bisiach). In the broad area of brain sciences, there are few, but important, psychobiological laboratories in Italy (Bovet, Oliverio, Renzi, and Robustelli).

The psychological community is represented by the Societá Italiana di Psicologia Scientifica, founded in 1954, which publishes the *Psicologia Italiana* (formerly *Rivista di Psicologia*, 1955). Scientific and professional discussions can be found in a number of journals: *Achivio di Psicologia Neurologia e Psichiatria* (1939), *Bollettino di Psicologia Applicata* (1954), *Rivista di Psicoanalisi* (1955), *Orientamento Scolastico e Professionale* (1961), *Psicologia e Lavoro* (1968), *Psicologia Analitica* (1971), *Giornale Italiano di Psicologia* (1974), *Psicologia Contemporanea* (1975), *Storia e Critica della Psicologia* (1977), *Ricerche di Psicologia* (1977), *Terapia Familiare* (1977), and *Giornale Storico di Psicologia Dinamica* (1977).

For about 25 years after World War II formal training of psychologists was centered in postgraduate schools in various parts of Italy: Milan, Padua, Turin, Bologna, and Rome. Connections with the original matrices of psychology were present in this training. Access to postgraduate schools was available to students who came either from philosophy or from medicine. The situation changed completely in 1971 when two undergraduate faculties of psychology opened, one in Rome and the other in Padua. Since then, the training of Italian psychologists has become quite similar to that in most Western countries. Specific studies of the discipline begin at the university; currently there are several programs for doctoral and postdoctoral training. In addition, the past three decades have seen a considerable increase in the teaching of psychology as part of the curricula of other faculties, such as education, law, fine arts, engineering, history, literature, and medicine.

L. PIZZAMIGLIO
Universita Degli Studie de Roma, Rome

ITARD, JEAN MARIE-GASPARD (1775–1838)

Jean Marie-Gaspard Itard acquired a medical education through practice. He was a pioneer in the field of otology and author of a 2-volume work on diseases of the ear. He was also a pioneer in the study of mental deficiency having attempted to train Victor the so-called wild boy of Averyron. While his efforts with Victor met with little success, he developed methods that proved useful in training retardates. For many years, Itard worked with deaf-mutes, and his studies provided a sound basis for modern methods of treating the deaf.

P. E. Lichtenstein

ITEM ANALYSIS

The major purpose of item analysis is to provide information on the extent to which the individual items that comprise a test are functioning in a desirable manner. The resulting information can then be used to improve the reliability and validity of the test by editing or discarding poor items. An item analysis of an achievement test may also provide diagnostic information on what examinees know and do not know, serving as a basis for instructional planning and curriculum revision.

Item analysis information may be either rational (judgmental) or empirical (statistical). A rational item analysis entails careful inspection of each item to determine whether its content is accurate, congruent with the test specifications, free of cultural or other bias, and not contrary to standard item-writing guidelines. This approach is characteristic of item analyses of criterion-referenced achievement tests, but it can also be applied to norm-referenced tests.

Traditionally, empirical item analysis has involved the calculation of one or more statistical measures of item functioning, including an item difficulty index, an item discrimination (validity) index, and some measure of the functioning of distracters. The difficulty index (p) of an item is computed quite simply as the proportion of respondents who answer the item correctly. The optimum difficulty index varies with the purposes of the test and the type of item. If a test is designed to select only the most highly qualified applicants, then the mean p value of the items should be fairly low; if it is designed to screen out only the very poorest applicants, then a high mean value of p is best. The optimum mean value of p varies inversely with the number of response options, ranging from .85 for two-choice items to .50 for open-ended items (Lord, 1952). The p values for acceptable items fall within a fairly narrow range around the optimum mean p, say ±.20, or even less for a peaked test designed to measure efficiently within a fairly narrow range of ability.

The procedure for determining an index of the ability of an item to discriminate among examinees who obtain different scores on a criterion variable depends on the nature of the criterion and the type of test. The usual internal criterion for an achievement test is total scores on the test itself, which are rank-ordered and divided into upper (U) and lower (L) groups. In the case of a norm-referenced test, these two groups usually consist of examinees in the top 27% and the bottom 27% on the distribution of total test scores. Then the discrimination index (D) for each item is computed as $D = p_U - p_L$, where p_U and p_L are the proportions of examinees in the top and bottom groups, respectively, who answer the item correctly. With an external criterion such as performance ratings or school marks, the item discrimination index is computed as the point-biserial correlation (r_{pb}) between item scores (0s and 1s) and scores on the criterion. The closer either D or r_{pb} is to 1.00, the more valid is the item as a discriminator between high and lower performers on the criterion. Depending on the size of the group of respondents on whom the indexes are computed, D or r_{pb} values as low as .20 may be adequate for judging items as acceptable. Selecting items on the basis of D tends to yield an internally consistent, homogeneous test, but selecting items on the basis of r_{pb} usually results in a less homogeneous test having greater validity for predicting an external criterion.

Item analyses of teacher-made classroom tests are usually conducted on the test as a whole, but separate item analyses may be conducted on different item subsets or subtests. When a test is being designed to measure several abilities, item analyses should reveal that the items composing a subtest of a specific ability are highly interrelated (have high D or r_{pb} values) but that the correlations among subtests are low. Then there is some assurance that the various subtests are measuring different abilities or aptitudes.

Determination of the discriminative power of items on a criterion-referenced test involves a bit more work than for norm-referenced tests. Popham (1981) described two procedures: (a) pretest versus posttest differences; and (b) uninstructed versus instructed group differences. In the first method, the same group of examinees is tested before and after they are instructed on the test material. The differences between the proportions of examinees who answer an item correctly before and after instruction constitute the item discrimination index. The second method entails using two different groups, one instructed and one not instructed in the test material. The difference in the proportions of those in the instructed group and those in the uninstructed group who get the item right is the discrimination index for the item.

Although an item analysis of a multiple-choice test focuses on the difficulty and discrimination indexes of individual items, inspection of responses to the incorrect options (distracters) is also informative. In general, each distracter should be equally attractive to examinees who know the right answer and those who do not know it. Consequently, on a well-constructed test item, one would expect approximately equal numbers of examinees to select each of the distracters. Furthermore, the ratio of the number of respondents in the upper group on the criterion measure to those in the lower group should be approximately equal for all distracters.

Another statistical index that may be computed in analyzing test items for gender or racial bias is a measure of differential item functioning (DIF; Camilli & Shepard, 1994; Holland & Wainer, 1993). Furthermore, in addition to the traditional, or classical, item analysis procedure described in the preceding paragraphs, measures of item difficulty and discrimination may be obtained from item characteristic curves and item response models. On an item characteristic curve (ICC), the proportion of respondents selecting the keyed answer is plotted against their scores on an internal (total test) or external (e.g., scholastic achievement or occupational performance) criterion. The difficulty level of the item is the criterion score at which 50% of the respondents selected the correct (keyed) answer, and the discrimination index is the slope of the item characteristic curve at the 50% point.

In item response theory (IRT), which is an extension of the item characteristic curve approach, the proportion of respondents selecting the keyed response is plotted against estimates of their scores (θs) on a latent ability continuum. In the most general, three-parameter, IRT model, difficulty (a), discrimination (b), and guessing (c) parameters are estimated for the item. In the two-parameter IRT model, difficulty and discrimination parameters are estimated, and in the one-parameter (Rasch) model, only the difficulty parameter is estimated. Unlike the classical item analysis procedure in which the values of the item difficulty and discrimination indexes vary with the particular sample of respondents, the values of the item parameters obtained in IRT methodology are, at least in theory, independent of the particular sample of respondents on which they are determined.

REFERENCES

Camilli, G., & Shepard, L. A. (1994). *Methods for identifying biased test items.* Newbury Park, CA: Sage.

Holland, P. W., & Wainer, H. (Eds.). (1993). *Differential item functioning: Theory and practice.* Hillsdale, NJ: Erlbaum.

Lord, F. M. (1952). The relation of the reliability of multiple-choice tests to the distribution of item difficulties. *Psychometrika, 17,* 181–194.

Popham, W. J. (1981). *Modern educational measurement.* Englewood Cliffs, NJ: Prentice Hall.

L. R. AIKEN
Pepperdine University

STATISTICS AND PSYCHOLOGY

IVERSEN, SUE

Sue Iversen was born and reared in Buckinghamshire, a rural area of Southern England. After high school she went on to study natural sciences in Cambridge in 1958. She read zoology at the advanced level with a special interest in brain function and behaviour. Her mentor at the time was the ethologist Robert Hinde, and he encouraged her to move to the nearby Department of Experimental Psychology, where she could study the relationship between brain and behavior with experimental techniques, for her graduate work.

Iversen's PhD work with Larry Weiskrantz focused on the behavioral effects of surgical lesions to the temporal and frontal lobes of monkeys. The special emphasis of this work was an attempt to replicate in monkeys the global amnesia, reported by Milner a few years earlier, to follow bilateral medial temporal lesions in man. After Cambridge Iversen spent a postdoctoral year with Mortimer Mishkin at the National Institutes of Health (NIH), continuing studies of the frontal lobe in the monkey, followed by a year in the Department of Pharmacology of Harvard Medical School with Peter Dews. This year was of particular significance because it opened her eyes to quantitative behavioral techniques and introduced her to the emerging field of psychopharmacology.

Iversen returned to Cambridge in late 1966 to work as a re-

search assistant to Weiskrantz, but this plan was aborted when he moved soon afterwards to Oxford. Disaster turned to good fortune, however, when Oliver Zangwill, the head of the Cambridge laboratory, offered Iversen the vacant post and the chance (at the age of 27) to run a substantial research laboratory and train graduate students. Sixteen fruitful years followed in Cambridge with the opportunity to continue with lesion studies in monkeys and to introduce behavioral pharmacology to the lab. Many wonderful students and postdocs passed through the lab over those years, most of whom have remained in science and have gone on to be international authorities in behavioral neuroscience.

In 1983, Iversen and her husband (Leslie) left Cambridge to establish a neuroscience research center for the American pharmaceutical company Merck Co. The pharmaceutical industry demanded new and far-ranging skills and quite different management of science when compared with the university setting. Although she was rewarded by the change of job, the new mid-career challenge and the 10 years spent in industry, Iversen, having been told by a friend at Cambridge that one probably should not stay for more than 10 years in one job, decided in 1993 to apply for the position of chair of the Department of Experimental Psychology at Oxford. She was appointed and has spent the ensuing years nurturing a distinguished research and teaching department with a strong international neuroscience presence.

The various research themes of the earlier parts of her career are already established at Oxford: further work on dopamine systems of the nucleus accumbens, the development of new behavioral paradigms for evaluating psychotropic drugs, and an abiding interest in the pathophysiology of schizophrenia. Iversen's focus on clinical projects involving neuropsychology is increasing. Projects on the psychological deficits following left and right temporal-lobe resections for epilepsy, on the earliest neuropsychological impairments in Alzheimer's disease, and on neuropsychological trait disorders in manic depressive disorder, are all in progress. In Oxford, as in many centers worldwide, functional magnetic resonance imaging (fMRI) is rapidly emerging as a powerful technique for studying the brain-behavior relationship in man. Iversen also has projects underway on the integration of auditory and visual cues in speech perception and on reading of the Chinese language, with collaborations in Hong Kong and Shanghai.

Iversen has published more than 300 articles in reference journals; has co-authored *Behavioural Pharmacology* (a monograph) with L. L. Iversen; has co-edited with L. L. Iversen and S. Snyder 20 volumes of the *Handbook of Psychopharmacology;* and has co-edited monographs for Oxford University Press on Psychopharmacology (Recent Advances and Future Prospects) Cognitive Neurochemistry, and Multiple Cholecystokinin Receptors in the Central Nervous System.

From such an eclectic research output, it is difficult to select the more significant themes. However, the early work on 6-hydoroxydopamine (with Creese) received considerable attention, as did the 1975 publication (Kelly, Seviour, & Iversen), "Amphetamine and apomorphine responses in the rat following 6-OHDA lesions of the nucleus accumbens septi and corpus striatum," which demonstrated that dopamine depletion from the nucleus accumbens abolished the locomotor arousal induced by d-amphetamine.

The dopamine receptors of the nucleus accumbens remain of considerable interest, a paper (with Canales) will appear in 2000 reporting that, with local infusion techniques, co-activation of DA2/D3 and DA1 receptors are required for the expression of locomotor arousal.

It is interesting that old findings take on new significance as science moves on. A particular example is the 1970 Iversen and Mishkin paper ("Preseverative interference in monkeys following selective lesions of the inferior prefrontal convexity") defining in the monkey the role of the inferior prefrontal convexity for performance on an auditory go/no-go task. Only within the last decade has attention returned to sectors of the prefrontal cortex typified by the work of Goldman-Rakic and Petrides using lesions and recording (in monkeys) and brain imaging (in man). In their rather different theories of frontal lobe function, cortex ventral to sulcus principalis is recognized to serve a distinct role in online processing of information. The 1970 paper is only now regularly cited.

Iversen's career has been quite varied by any standard. She has been associated with many professional societies and granting agencies, and with government science policy. She is currently Pro–Vice Chancellor for Research at Oxford University.

STAFF

J

JAMES, WILLIAM (1842–1910)

An American philosopher and psychologist, William James was educated in Europe, England, and America. Frequent trips abroad made James a man of the world. Although he was supported and encouraged to pursue a scientific education, James suffered physical illnesses, indecision, and depression throughout his early years. Finally he earned his medical degree from Harvard in 1869 and took a teaching position there in 1872. From 1875 to 1876 James taught the first psychology course in an American university at Harvard. He was given funds for laboratory and demonstration equipment for the course in 1875 the same year that Wilhelm Wundt established his psychology laboratory in Leipzig.

After 12 years of work, in 1890 James published *The Principles of Psychology,* a major contribution to the field. Dissatisfied with his work, he decided that he had nothing else to offer psychology. He left the Harvard psychological laboratory and the course work to Hugo Munsterberg, and concentrated on philosophy for the remaining 20 years of his life. In the 1890s James became America's leading philosopher.

James is considered America's greatest psychologist because of his brilliant clarity of scientific writing and his view of the human mind as functional, adaptive mental processes, in opposition to Wundt's structural analysis of consciousness into elements. The concept of functionalism in James's psychology became the central principle of American functional psychology: the study of living persons as they adapt to their environment.

James treated psychology as a natural, biological science. Mental processes he believed to be functional activities of living creatures attempting to adapt and maintain themselves in a world of nature. The function of consciousness was to guide persons toward adaptation for survival. James emphasized the nonrational aspects of human nature, in addition to the reasonable. He described mental life as always changing—a total experience that flows as a unit, a stream of consciousness. His most famous theoretical contribution concerned emotions. He stated that the physical response of arousal preceded the appearance of emotion—that *because of* the bodily changes such as increased heart rate or muscle tension, the person experienced emotion. The example of this chain of events was "see the bear, run, and *then* feel afraid." A simultaneous discovery of this theory by the Danish physiologist Carl Lange led to its designation as the *James-Lange theory.*

James believed that mental and emotional activities should be studied as processes, and not as the static elements of consciousness being taught by the structural psychologists of that time. Because of the dynamic nature of his theories and views, James' psychology was named *functionalism.* With G. Stanley Hall and James M. Cattell, James anticipated the school of functional psychology at the University of Chicago under John Dewey and James Rowland Angell. James's *The Principles of Psychology* influenced thousands of students. He is one of the most important psychologists the United States has ever produced.

N. A. HAYNIE

JAMES-LANGE THEORY OF EMOTIONS

The James-Lange theory of emotions has been the subject of considerable scientific debate since its publication by James in *Principles of Psychology* (1890). Portions of James' theory had been formulated by the Danish physiologist Lange in 1885. James combined his views with those of Lange, and credited Lange in the name of the theory. It offers a physiological explanation of the constitution, organization, and conditioning of the coarser emotions such as grief, fear, rage, and love in which "everyone recognizes strong organic reverberations," and the subtler emotions, or "those whose organic reverberations are less obvious and strong," such as moral, intellectual, and aesthetic feelings (James, 1890, p. 449).

The general causes of the emotions are assumed to be internal, physiological, nervous processes and not mental or psychological processes. The moods, affections, and emotions which persons experience are "constituted and made up of those bodily changes which we ordinarily call their expression or consequence" (James, 1890, p. 452). A purely disembodied emotion—for example, the emotion of fear without a quickened heart beat, sharp breathing, or weakened limbs—would be a nonentity for this theory. The emotions are the result of organic changes which occur in the body as a reflex effect of an exciting object or fact confronting the person.

There are three factors in the sequence of an emotional experience: (a) the perception of an exciting fact or object; (b) a bodily expression such as weeping, striking out, or fleeing; and (c) a mental affection or emotion, such as feeling afraid or angry. Many theories of emotion, as well as common sense, place the bodily expressions of weeping, striking out, or fleeing after the emotion of anger or fear. The James-Lange theory alters this sequence, placing bodily expressions between the perception of the exciting fact and the emotion. In everyday terms, this means we cry and then feel sad rather than feeling sad and then crying. "The bodily changes follow directly the perception of the exciting fact . . . our feeling the same as they occur is the emotion" (James, 1890, p. 449; italics in original).

The debate which has surrounded the theory involves the relative importance of central nervous system processes and social environmental factors in the production of emotion (Pribram, 1981). Centralists (including James and Lange) have argued that there are discrete physiological changes for each emotion (Scheff, 1979; Kemper, 1978). Peripheralists argue that there is no discrete physiological change for each emotion (Cannon, 1927; Schachter & Singer, 1962); rather, there is only a bodily state of arousal modified by factors in the social environment. The experimental evidence is inconclusive (Scheft, 1979; Kemper, 1978).

Sartre, in *Sketch for a Theory of the Emotions* (1939), critically evaluated the James-Lange theory from a phenomenological perspective and rejected it on several grounds. First, behavior, physiological or expressive, is not emotion, nor is emotion the awareness of that behavior. Second, the body does not call out its own interpretations, which are given in the field of consciousness of the person. Third, the bodily disturbances present in emotion are disorders of the most ordinary kind and are not the causes of emotion. They ratify emotion's existence for the person and give emotion its believability, but are not its causes. Fourth, to have considered only the biological body independent of the lived body—and the person's consciousness of the body—as the source of emotion was to treat the body as a thing and to locate emotion in disorders of the body. Emotion as a part of the person's lived experiences in the life world has not been given adequate attention by either the centralist or the peripheralist followers of the James-Lange theory.

The James-Lange theory of emotions remains a viable theory today. The factors isolated by the theory are not disputed. Controversy remains over the ordering of the sequence of the factors and on the emphasis to be given to strictly physiological—as opposed to social and psychological—factors and processes (see Barbalet, 1998). However, the historical character of emotional experience suggests that cultural and structural factors strongly influence how emotions are felt and expressed (see Newton, 1998).

REFERENCES

Barbalet, J. A. (1998). *Emotion, social theory, and social structure: A macrosociological approach.* New York: Cambridge University Press.

Newton, T. (1998). The sociogenesis of emotion: A historical sociology? In G. Bendelow and S. J. Williams (Eds.), *Emotions in social life: Critical themes and contemporary issues* (pp. 60–80). London: Routledge.

N. K. DENZIN
University of Illinois

EMOTIONS
SURPRISE

JAMISON, KAY REDFIELD

Kay Redfield Jamison is professor of psychiatry at the Johns Hopkins University School of Medicine. She is the coauthor of the standard medical text on manic-depressive illness, which was chosen in 1990 as the Most Outstanding Book in Biomedical Sciences by the American Association of Publishers, and author of *Touched with Fire: Manic-Depressive Illness and the Artistic Temperament.*

She is the author or coauthor of five books and approximately 100 scientific publications about mood disorders, suicide, psychotherapy, and lithium. Her memoir about her own experiences with manic-depressive illness, *An Unquiet Mind,* was selected by the Boston Globe, Entertainment Weekly, and the Seattle Post Intelligencer as one of the best books of 1995. *An Unquiet Mind,* currently under development as a feature film, was on the New York Times Bestseller List for more than five months.

Jamison did her undergraduate and graduate studies at the University of California, Los Angeles, where she was a National Science Foundation Research Fellow, University of California Cook Scholar, John F. Kennedy Scholar, United States Public Health Service Predoctoral Research Fellow, and UCLA Graduate Woman of the Year. She also studied zoology and neurophysiology at the University of St. Andrews in Scotland.

Jamison, formerly the director of the UCLA Affective Disorders Clinic, was selected as UCLA Woman of Science and has been cited as one of the "Best Doctors in the United States." She is recipient of the American Suicide Foundation Research Award, the UCLA Distinguished Alumnus Award, the Fawcett Humanitarian Award from the National Depressive and Manic-Depressive Association, the Steven V. Logan Award for Research into Brain Disorders from the National Alliance for the Mentally Ill, the William Styron Award from the National Mental Health Association, and the McGovern Award for excellence in medical communication. She was selected as one of five individuals for the public television series "Great Minds of Medicine," and chosen by Time magazine as a "Hero of Medicine."

Jamison was a member of the first National Advisory Council for Human Genome Research, and is currently the clinical director for the Dana Consortium on the Genetic Basis of Manic-Depressive Illness, as well as the Chair of the Genome Action Coalition, a coalition of more than 125 patient groups and pharmaceutical and biotechnology companies. She also serves on the National Committee for Basic Sciences at UCLA, and is the executive producer and writer for a series of award-winning public television specials about manic-depressive illness and the arts.

Jamison is Honorary Professor of English at the University of St. Andrews in Scotland. Her most recent book is *Night Falls Fast: Understanding Suicide.*

STAFF

JANET, PIERRE (1859–1947)

Pierre Janet received his doctor of letters from the University of Paris in 1889. Becoming a pupil of Jean Charcot, he worked in Charcot's neurological laboratory and clinic at Salpêtrière, the Parisian hospital for insane women. He took over as director of the laboratory from Charcot in 1890 and finished his degree in medicine while working there until 1894. Under Janet's direction the emphasis of the laboratory work changed from neurological to psychological. In 1895 Janet went to the Sorbonne, and from 1920 to 1936 he was at the Collège de France.

Janet was a systematic psychopathologist. Although he worked under Charcot, who was primarily a neurologist, Janet rejected the opinion that the hysteria of the patients at Salpêtrière was a physiological disorder. He classified hysteria as a mental disorder instead and his preferred treatment was hypnosis, which he used especially for the problems of memory impairment and fixed ideas. He developed a system of psychology and psychopathology that he called "psychologie de la conduite" (psychology of conduct or behavior). His chief effort at reporting this work was *The Major Symptoms of Hysteria.*

A decrease in psychic energy was a central belief in Janet's explanation of mental disorders. He taught that a healthy personality was one that had a stable psychic energy level supporting an integrated system of ideas and emotions; in contrast, fluctuations in psychic energy and lowered mental tension caused insufficient energy to cope with problems, leading to neurosis. Hysteric patients had a weakness, characterized by exaggerated suggestibility, faulty memory, and fixed ideas. Hysterical personalities lacked integration: Their minds could dissociate into conscious and unconscious processes, so that multiple personalities in one individual could result. Janet believed that the fixed ideas of the hysteric narrowed conscious attention and forced unacceptable mental ideas into the unconscious realm, where they were converted into symbolic symptoms. This belief closely resembled Sigmund Freud's, and a controversy arose between the two about which of them first used the concept of the unconscious.

Janet wrote 15 other books and many articles. He published in the *Journal de la Psychologie,* which he founded with Georges Dumas in 1904 and which Janet edited until 1937.

N. A. HAYNIE

JANIS, IRVING LESTER (1918–1990)

Irving Lester Janis received the BS degree from the University of Chicago and the PhD from Columbia University in 1948. During World War II he was a senior social scientist analyst with the Special War Policies Unit of the Department of State. In 1940 he joined the faculty of Yale University for a long tenure. He published *Air War and Emotional Stress* and *Communication and Persuasion* in collaboration with Hovland and Kelley. Then followed *Personality and Persuasability* and *Victims of Group-Think.*

According to the Janis-Feisrabend hypothesis, an argument is most effective when the pro side is advanced before the negative. In other experimental studies Janis demonstrated that a positive relationship exists between high persuasability and low self-esteem, also between persuasability and feelings of inadequacy. Finally, he demonstrated experimentally that hostile individuals are less susceptible to persuasion.

R. W. LUNDIN
Wheaton, Illinois

JAPAN, PSYCHOLOGY IN

The Japanese term *shinrigaku* was coined and first used in Japanese literature in 1878 as a translation of the English phrase "mental philosophy," and later was adopted formally as the word for *psychology.* Thus psychology in Japan started with the borrowing and translating of concepts, notions, and theories from the Europeans in the late nineteenth century.

The European influence continued to dominate psychology in Japan until the end of World War II in 1945. Among those best known and most influential in prewar Japanese psychology were the Experimentalists (Helmholtz, Hering, and Ebbinghaus), the Gestaltists (Weltheimer and Köhler), and the Introspectionists (Wundt, and his American disciples, Tichener and James). Also well known were the classic Behaviorists (Watson and Pavlov) and the more contemporary Neobehaviorists (Tolman and Hull). European dominance affected psychology-related institutions as well. For example, following the European tradition, departments of psychology were established in the faculty of literature at every university, and a literature degree was conferred on these students. This tradition remains in a number of the older Japanese universities—the highest degree equivalent to the PhD degree in psychology still is a LittD degree.

Two significant trends characterize postwar Japanese psychology: *Americanization* in teaching and research, and *popularization* of psychology for the lay public.

In the 1950s, opportunities were opened for young Japanese psychologists and graduate students in psychology to pursue graduate studies in the United States as part of various exchange programs, or on scholarships, fellowships, and assistantships available from U.S. institutions. Many earned these advanced degrees in psychology and returned to Japan to teach, with an acquired and strongly affirmative sense of methodologies, styles, and directions unique to contemporary American psychology. As a result, the use of computers, for instance, was first introduced and became more commonplace in psychology in the early 1960s than in other areas of the social sciences. The first-hand experiences of the U.S.-educated Japanese psychologists have exerted a great influence on the introduction of new statistical methods, such as multivariate analysis, in addition to classic quantitative analytic methods, into the research environment in Japan.

Also in the early 1950s, psychology became a subject of great interest among the lay public. Several publishers contributed to awakening the popular interest in psychology, as they found a promising mass market for psychological writings. The Iwanami Publishing Company, for example, published seven books related to psychology during the 1950s, all in inexpensive soft-cover forms directed to mass consumption. These early "enlightening" psychological books included Shimizu's *Social Psychology* (1951), Miyagi's *Introduction to Psychology* (1952), Murakami's *Abnormal Psychology* (1952), Sagara's *What is the Memory?* (1950) and *Gestalt Psychology* (1952), Imada's *Contemporary Psychology* (1958), and Minami's *Introduction to Social Psychology* (1958). These authors were recognized as the forerunners and founders of modern postwar psychology in Japan, not only serving to fill in the knowledge gap resulting from disruption by World War II, but also contributing to the bridge between the ivory-tower/laboratory psychologists and the lay public. Today many TV stations broadcast educational programs on psychology.

THE "GREAT LEAP FORWARD"

In 1958, one great step was taken in an effort to unify psychology-related disciplines by defining the common concepts and standardizing their usage in Japanese. After three years of joint efforts by four editors (Umezu, Sagara, Miyagi, and Yoda) and a total of 184 contributors, *The Heibonsha Encyclopedia of Psychology* was published. This encyclopedia includes more than 7,000 entries, covering 14 major areas in psychology: history; methodology; behavior; learning; emotion; perception; language and thinking; personality; social psychology; culture; applied psychology; developmental psychology; physiological psychology; and psychological testing and measurement. The encyclopedia was sufficiently comprehensive and up to date at the time it was published that it contributed a great deal to the enhancement of psychology in Japan.

In addition to normal usage of the encyclopedia, it also had a unique use—the standardization of the terminology in psychology. Each entry in the encyclopedia is accompanied by English, German, and French translations whenever possible. These translations are needed for Japanese users to identify the "original" foreign term from which the Japanese translation was derived. Most technical concepts used by the Japanese are of foreign origin, such as "cognition," translated as *ninchi*, or "perception," as *chikaku*. And the fact that one "original" foreign term will have more than one Japanese translation is likely to cause conceptual confusion and semantic ambiguity. With the publication of the *Heibonsha Encyclopedia*, such confusion and ambiguity were reduced, if not totally eliminated; each entry in the encyclopedia, as given in Japanese, has been accepted as *the* only "authoritative" terminology for use by the Japanese.

In 1981, 28 years after its initial publication, a second, enlarged edition of *The Heibonsha Encyclopedia of Psychology* appeared. The number of entries increased to 8,000 and the number of contributors increased from 184 to 292, with 97% of the content completely rewritten. The editorial board also changed: In place of the four editors of the first edition, 14 associated editors collaborated under the direction of four editors-in-chief for the second edition. These associate editors are, by and large, recognized as leading psychologists representative of one or more areas of psychology in Japan, and are internationally known for their frequent contributions to international or foreign psychological journals. They are Hiroshi Azuma (educational psychology), Takeo Umemoto (learning), Tadasu Ōyama (perception), Shigeo Kashiwagi (industrial psychology), Jūrō Kawachi (learning), Morio Saji (developmental psychology), Toshirō Suenaga (social psychology), Taketoshi Takuma (personality), Tadashi Hidano (developmental psychology), Tamotsu Fujinaga (developmental psychology), Yoshiaki Maeda (perception), Kazuo Miyake (educational psychology), Fumio Mugishima (criminal psychology), and Masaaki Yoshida (perception). One of their most significant contributions was the inclusion of the new vocabulary of mathematical psychology, cognitive psychol-

ogy, cross-cultural psychology, attribution theory, helping behavior, and the like, which came into common use in the 1960s and 1970s. The new vocabulary helps to reduce the time and knowledge gaps that might previously have existed in the profession at large.

PSYCHOLOGICAL ASSOCIATIONS

Psychology is one of the most important behavioral and social science disciplines in Japan. Eight major psychological associations maintain their representation in Division I of the Science Council of Japan, whose function is akin to that of the Social Science Council in the United States or the Academy of Sciences in the Soviet Union.

The Japanese Psychological Association is the largest, with 4,200 members (as of November 1982); it publishes *Shinrigaku Kenkyū* (the *Japanese Journal of Psychology*), a bimonthly journal with the text in Japanese and summaries in English, and *Japanese Psychological Research,* an English-language quarterly.

The Japanese Association for Educational Psychology had a membership of 3,200 as of 1982. The association publishes two journals in Japanese with summaries in English: *Kyōikushinrigakū Kenkyū* (the *Japanese Journal of Educational Psychology,* a quarterly) and *Kyōiku-shinrigaku Kenkyū Nempō* (the *Annual Report of Educational Psychology in Japan*).

In 1982, the Japanese Association of Clinical Psychology had 1,000 members. It publishes a quarterly journal in Japanese, *Rinshō-shinrigaku Kenkyū* (the *Japanese Journal of Clinical Psychology*).

The Japan Association of Applied Psychology, with 992 members as of 1982, publishes the Japanese annals with English summaries, *Ōyō-shinrigaku Kenkyū* (the *Japanese Journal of Applied Psychology*).

The Japanese Association of Criminal Psychology showed a membership of 730 in 1982, and publishes a biannual Japanese journal, *Hanzai-shinrigaku Kenkyū* (the *Japanese Journal of Criminal Psychology*), which contains summaries in English.

The Japanese Society of Social Psychology, which had 700 members as of 1982, publishes *Nempō Shakai-shinrigaku* (the *Annals of Social Psychology*) in Japanese.

The Japanese Group Dynamics Association had 547 members in 1982, and publishes a biannual journal in Japanese with English summaries, *Jikken Shakai-shinrigaku Kenkyū* (the *Japanese Journal of Experimental Social Psychology*).

The Japan Society for Animal Psychology, with 459 members as of 1982, publishes a biannual Japanese journal with English summaries, *Dōbutsu-shinrigaku Nempō* (the *Annals of Animal Psychology*).

These eight psychological associations constitute the core of psychology in Japan, and many psychologists hold a membership in two or more associations simultaneously. A growing number of Japanese psychologists also join foreign and international psychological associations, such as the American Psychological Association and the International Association for Cross-cultural Psychology, as their research objectives and collaborative efforts extend beyond national boundaries.

TOWARD GREATER INTERNATIONALIZATION

Although science has no national boundaries, the divisions and boundaries imposed by languages present a serious problem for the Japanese. Their language is a unique disadvantage for Japanese psychologists and their profession, as they lack a common means of international communication as long as they use only Japanese. Except for those who have been educated in another country or who have been doing collaborative research with "foreign" colleagues for many years, most Japanese are handicapped by an inability to write in a foreign language. Their output thus is limited to consumption by other Japanese, despite its potential international value and importance.

However, the Japanese are trying, through various means, to disseminate the results of their scientific labors to psychologists in other countries. In addition to *Japanese Psychological Research,* published in English by the Japanese Psychological Association, and the *Annual Report of Educational Psychology in Japan,* published in English by the Japanese Association for Educational Psychology, some universities publish their own psychological journals in English. These include *Psychologia* (Department of Psychology, Kyoto University), the *Tōhoku Psychologia Folia* (Department of Psychology, Tōhoku University), and the *Journal of Child Development* (Department of Educational Psychology, Waseda University).

There are also a growing number of publications by Japanese psychologists in both foreign and international psychological journals. In reviewing the trends in cross-cultural psychology in Japan between 1960 and 1979, Watanabe and Otsuka (1979) list 86 English-language journal articles of which a Japanese is either the author or a coauthor. These articles appeared in the *Journal of Social Psychology,* the *Journal of Cross-cultural Psychology,* the *International Journal of Psychology,* the *Journal of Personality and Social Psychology,* the *Journal of Verbal Learning and Verbal Behavior,* the *Japanese Psychological Research,* and *Psychologia,* all of which are prestigious international, foreign, or local journals.

Most internationally active Japanese psychologists are involved in cross-cultural research, and have their reports published in foreign and international journals. Among these psychologists are Hiroshi Azuma (child development and educational testing), Kitao Abe (human behavior under disaster), Hiroshi Akuto (communication behavior and attitude measurement), Tarō Indō (mathematical psychology), Sumiko Iwao (communication behavior and culture), Saburo Iwawaki (perception and personality), Tadasu Ōyama (perception and color symbolism), Shigeo Kashiwagi (factor analysis and graphic rotation schemes), Akio Kikuchi (interpersonal behavior and cross-cultural psychology), Yasumasa Tanaka (subjective culture analysis and cross-cultural psychology), Bien Tsujioka (personality test and measurement), Masanao Toda (mathematical psychology and game theory), Chikio Hayashi (social psychological survey and quantification theory), Akira Hoshino (personality development and cross-cultural psychology), Jyūji Misumi (group dynamics and leadership theory), and Kazuo Yamamoto (personality and mental health).

These and other Japanese psychologists have taught and/or conducted their research in the United States, Europe, or elsewhere in Asia. Many were, or currently are, involved in cross-cultural research of scientific value and practical importance in alleviating the ethnocentrism that affects the psychological discipline in general. The number of such internationally oriented psychologists is not very large as yet, considering the membership of the Japanese Psychological Association (4,200), perhaps partly because of the linguistic handicap, and partly because of the insular mentality of the Japanese as a whole. Nonetheless the "open door" is a consistent policy of the Japanese Psychological Association. Consequently, while the Association continues to award fellowships to junior Japanese psychologists who wish to do their research and studies in other countries, there is also an increasing number of researchers and students visiting Japan from the United States, Europe, and Asia. If we take into consideration the relatively short period of time since the end of World War II, and the limited financial basis on which such international personal exchanges are made possible, the internationalization of psychology in Japan may be regarded as fairly satisfactory.

MOVEMENT TOWARD INTERDISCIPLINARY AREAS

The postwar development of psychology in Japan is the subject of continuous examination and review. Developments in group dynamics and small-group psychology were fully reviewed in English in *Social Psychology in Japan* (Misumi, 1972), for example. The most comprehensive review of the current state of affairs in psychology in Japan can be found in *Trends in Modern Psychology, 1946–1980,* edited by Tadashi Hidano in collaboration with some 45 psychologists and reporting the current developments in the area each author represents, ranging from perception, learning, and test theories to clinical, industrial, criminal, social, and cross-cultural psychologies.

More and more psychologists seem to be becoming interested and actually involved in interdisciplinary research. Such interdisciplinary research areas include communications, political values and behaviors, war and peace, culture change and acculturation, and environmental protection and disaster control, most of which are related to important social issues embedded in Japanese society. Attempts to apply psychological methodologies and theories to the analysis and solution of these real social issues are also clearly seen. It may be premature to suggest that this widespread interest in the interdisciplinary research will persist long enough to characterize psychology in Japan. But it can certainly be said that the concept of an "interdisciplinary approach," first coined in the United States in the early 1950s and brought to Japan in the 1960s (Tanaka, 1969), now seems to have begun to bear fruit in terms of psychology in Japan. This might remind us that the very concept of "psychology" was introduced to Japan from Europe in the nineteenth century, and this has constituted the basis upon which psychology has been continuing to grow so remarkably through the twentieth century, and perhaps beyond.

REFERENCES

Imada, M. (1958). *Gendai no shinrigaku (Modern psychology).* Tokyo: Iwanami.

Minami, H. (1958). *Shakai-shinrigaku nyūmon (Introduction to social-psychology).* Tokyo: Iwanami.

Misumi, J. (Ed.). (1972). *Social psychology in Japan.* Tokyo: Japanese Society of Social Psychology.

Miyagi, O. (1952). *Shinrigaku nyūmon (Introduction to psychology).* Tokyo: Iwanami.

Murakami, H. (1952). *Ljō-shinrigaku (Abnormal psychology).* Tokyo: Iwanami.

Sagara, M. (1950). *Kioku towa nanika (What is the memory?)* Tokyo: Iwanami.

Shimizu, I. (1951). *Shakai-shinrigaku (Social psychology).* Tokyo: Iwanami.

Tanaka, Y. (1969). *The behavioral sciences: The science of humans in an age of information.* Tokyo: Chikuma Shobō (in Japanese).

Watanabe, F., & Ōtsuka, K. (1979). Nihon ni okeru Ibunkakan Shinrigaku no Kenkyū Dōkō 1960–1979. (The trends in cross-cultural psychological research in Japan, 1960–1979). *Shinrigaku Hyōron, 22*(3), 247–277.

Y. TANAKA
Gakushuin University, Tokyo

JASPERS, KARL (1883-1967)

Karl Jaspers was born in 1883 in Oldenburg, Germany. He was a sickly child for whom an early death had been forecast. Throughout his life, Jaspers was never well. This may partially explain his immense commitment to his work. He excelled in all three fields he pursued: psychiatry, psychology, and philosophy. His prolific work attests to his determination to make the most of what had been predicted to be a "short life."

After medical studies in Berlin, Göttingen, and Heidelberg, Jaspers obtained his MD degree from the latter university in 1908. Between 1909 and 1915, he served as an assistant at the psychiatric clinic of Heidelberg, an outstanding center of psychiatric research in Germany. In 1913, the same year Jaspers' *Allgemeine Psychiatrie* (General Psychopathology) appeared, he succeeded with his habilitation in psychology at the University of Heidelberg, obtaining the venia docendi (right to teach) psychology and psychopathology. Three years later, he was promoted to professor extraordinarius for psychology (associate professor), and in 1922 he became ordinarius (full professor) for philosophy. The Nazis dismissed Jaspers from Heidelberg University in 1937 and a year later stopped him from publishing. Having criticized the political regime and living with his Jewish wife, Jaspers suffered grave injustices during the Hitler years. Their scheduled pickup for extermination was foiled by the arrival of the Allied Forces. Once the Americans occupied Heidelberg in 1945, Jaspers was reinstated as university professor, becoming the first post-WWII Rector Magnificus.

In 1948, Jaspers accepted the psychology chair at the University of Basel, Switzerland. He wanted to shield his wife from the reminders of their Nazi nightmare, and he treasured the opportunity to teach where Nietzsche had taught. Later he became a Swiss citizen. Among numerous great honors (honorary doctorates and honorary memberships in professional societies and national academies on either side of the ocean), Jaspers received the International Peace Prize and the order "Pour le Merit." Jaspers died in Basel in 1967, on his wife's 90th birthday. There is a Karl Jaspers Society of North America.

The work of Jaspers contributed to all three of his disciplines: psychology, psychiatry, and philosophy, at times addressing overlapping topics. Jaspers' exploration of man on a psychological level is transparent towards his philosophical understanding of man, which he saw founded in the thinking of Kant, Kierkegaard, and Nietzsche. Selected key concepts and issues in Jaspers' work include the structure of Dasein; acquiring existence; communications with our fellow men and ourselves; Selbsterhellung (enlightenment of oneself); Grenzsituation (borderline situation, like death, guilt, or an accidental event); freedom and responsibility; experience of transcendence; man's thinking at the core of the subject-object split; and the limitation of man's thinking.

Jaspers' philosophical thinking, both existential and phenome-

Table 1.   World Images and Orientations

I. From the OBJECT's side: THE WORLD IMAGES	II. From the SUBJECT's side: THE ORIENTATIONS Orientation, as Disposition towards a Specific Worldview

A. THE SENSORY-SPATIAL WORLD IMAGE
  1. the world of nature
  2. the world of technology
	A. OBJECT-RELATED ORIENTATIONS
	  1. active orientation
	  2. contemplative orientation
	    a) intuitive orientation
	    b) esthetic orientation
	    c) rational orientation
	  3. mystical orientation

B. THE EMOTIONAL-CULTURAL WORLD IMAGE
  1. cultures
  2. human personalities
  3. psychomythology
	B. SELF-REFLECTIVE ORIENTATION
	  1. contemplative self-reflection
	  2. active self-reflection:
	    a) pleasure orientation
	    b) ascetic orientation
	    c) self-formulation orientation
	  3. reflexive and unmediated: the moment

C. THE METAPHYSICAL WORLD IMAGE
  1. unmediated wholeness
  2. the split between the present world and the world beyond
  3. the levels of reality
	C. ENTHUSIASTIC ORIENTATION
	  —difference from mystical orientation
	  —self-sacrifice
	  —enthusiastic orientation as love

nological, permeated his psychiatric and psychological work. He was the first social and medical scientist to propose a clear, systematic methodology for phenomenological research in psychology and psychopathology. Jaspers' *General Psychopathology* has retained its relevance. His psychological and psychiatric understanding of man never became separated from his vision of human existence in the world, and in transcendence of the world. Jaspers set high standards for psychotherapy and for the therapist. He demanded that the client be treated from the broader standpoint of the wholeness of human existence and not merely from the narrow perspective of psychopathology or other stated problems. Jaspers was highly protective of the clients and of their values. He warned about the implications political systems and sociological conditions might have on psychotherapy (conformist therapists). Jaspers disdained therapeutic approaches which take on the character of religious sects as well as the notion of therapy as a secularized form of religion. He cautioned that the psychological atmosphere can be noxious. There is the danger that the patient's psychological reality can become, egocentrically, the final goal of therapy. Psychotherapy has to remain merely a path.

Having survived the Third Reich, Jaspers remained interested in how it was possible that extreme atrocities had been committed in Germany. In his inquiry into the question of guilt (1978), he stated that everybody's immoral acts contribute to the development of a public atmosphere which fosters obscurity, vagueness, and confusion. According to Jaspers, it is the psychological atmosphere that makes evil possible. He may be the only psychologist who ever dared address this rather intangible concept of "atmosphere" which is difficult to subject to scientific scrutiny.

Jaspers' major contribution to psychology in his book *Psychologie der Weltanschauung* (1971, not published in English). In this work he delineates his personality typology based on an individual's mode of perceiving, understanding, and relating to the world, which also governs how a person integrates life experiences as well as new information. All of these functions participate in the construction of a person's life philosophy.

Jaspers' typology of Weltanschauung is based on the interplay of two components, a subject- and object-related one. An individual's style of relating to the world is understood as the subject's orientation. The object, namely the world, appears to this person in the image most compatible with the individual's world affinity. Jaspers distinguished between three types of world images and between three types of subjective orientations. Both groups can be delineated into further subdivisions.

WORLD IMAGES

Although the person perceives the image as an objective presentation of the world reality, it actually is a representation of reality modified or even distorted by a person's bias filters. New information is assimilated selectively based on a person's predisposition within the framework of the existing preferred image, resulting in a psychologically congruent but biased worldview that diminishes the fullness of the object.

The three world images describe an objective world reality which reflects the aspects of the sensory-physical, emotional-psychological, and the metaphysical dimensions of the world. In line with individual differences (interest-related affinities, perceptual filters), individuals perceive self-congruent world images.

1. The sensory-spatial world image represents the view of the physical world, encompassing concerns with nature and technology.

2. The psychocultural world image is human-factor oriented. It includes the objective world of culture, personality based individual experience (as an object), and beyond both, the world images projected by psychomythology.

3. The metaphysical world image questions the one reality we recognize as the one we believe to know. It offers dimensions beyond the given reality, permits a split between this world and a world beyond, and opens up the possibility of different levels of reality. It poses questions and, in answering some, spans the gap from attributing relativity to what is "known to be real," to setting the "unknown" as an absolute. The ever-changing philosophical world image fits here.

ORIENTATIONS

The three subjective orientations reveal a personal style of orientation, operation, and attitude. One is straightforwardly object-related, one relates to the object via a distancing self-reflective loop, and the last one overcomes the subject-object dichotomy on the level of anticipatory synthesis.

The Object-Related Orientation

The object related orientation branches into three subtypes, which include the active, the contemplative, and the mystical orientation.

The Active Orientation

The person with an active orientation seeks to change the world; he or she has a sense of reality and is able to weigh strengths and possibilities, but is never satisfied. There is always an either/or. The active orientation can be a playful orientation if the involvement is not serious. It can lead to an empty form of filling empty time. The erotic orientation falls into this category. However, when erotics and sexuality connect, a reality component gets involved, and often biological consequences follow.

The Contemplative Orientation

Interest is the key word. Objects do not call for activity. They are here to be contemplated and accepted for what they are. The contemplative object relation is characterized by viewing and contemplating, not creating or governing, by seeing, not owning.

A. Intuitive Orientation: The intuitive person envisions and accepts joyfully, experiences fullness and no boundaries. When becoming immersed in an object which holds a relatedness, clear differentiations of subject and object are suspended.

B. Esthetic Orientation: Isolation is the key word for the esthetic orientation. Unity and totality may be experienced as contemplation takes place, but the person remains uninvolved. What is seen, heard, or partaken in may be experienced as a merely sensual impression or as a cosmic expression. Whether the object appears in the form of a direct sensual input of as a symbolic message, it will always, in some way, remain formalized, never to responsibly involve the person. Art, or metaphysics in this orientation, becomes a way to move away from the reality of existence.

C. Rational Orientation: Objects become frozen within rational boundaries. The total reality, especially what is alive, keeps losing out to the killing fixations of intellectualization. Formalization creates abstractions of reality; it dogmatizes and forces what was alive into identical concepts and repeatable conditions.

The Mystical Orientation

The mystical orientation is comparable to the intuitive one, but reaches far beyond. Subject and object merge without split, polarity, or tension. All is one. Mystics often speak in images because specific realities can rarely satisfy the total unity to be expressed. Messages regarding their world experiences refer equally to fullness or to total emptiness.

The Self-Reflective Orientation

Contemplative Self-Reflection

This person does not live in the moment or the immediate present, but instead lives in a mediated, reflected postpresent reality, comparing notes between what was experienced without involvement and what anticipatory fantasy had projected. An involving experience can occur only when projection and reality coincide. Normally, living is flat, secondary, preknown and lived, as it is intellectually confirmed to have coincided with projections. When anticipations are not met, life disappoints. Experiences are never overwhelming. Since experience builds on memory, the memory can be enhanced and mediated if it is not satisfactory. Faith is experienced in buffering reflection. Self-pity, respect, or disdain for oneself are the passive psychic states of this type of existence. This type person cries out of pity with himself or herself, rather than spontaneously in response to an ongoing situation or event.

Active Self-Reflection

Active self-reflectors not only watch themselves, they also actively participate in developing what shall be. They never "are." They remain in a state of becoming, focused on becoming their authentic self, which remains an unending task. Pleasure and asceticism are the two elements used for self-formation.

A. Pleasure Orientation: The pleasure orientation is not directed at pleasure as an object, but at the self in the mode of experiencing pleasure. This orientation is relatively passive, limiting its activity to reflecting. Pleasure is not experienced in its immediacy, it is felt when reflecting on the pleasure, be it in music, other sensual experiences, or even pain. The immediate is seen as naive, reflective pleasure as refined. Because the person is never involved in the object's immediacy, but only in the reflected experience, more and more objects of pleasure have to be sought.

B. Ascetic Orientation: While the pleasure orientation seeks events, situations, impressions, and activities, the ascetic orientation does the opposite: It avoids. It denies the self: marriage, success, status, meat, and wine, among others. Whatever is pleasant and cannot be avoided must not be enjoyed. The ascetic as well as the pleasure seeker are not enslaved by things. The pleasure seeker is not attached to the object, merely to experiencing pleasure. The ascetic is not dominated by the objects, but shielded from pleasure through distancing and uninvolvement. Active asceticism (fasting, waking, self-flagellation, and so on) can lead to a sense of power over reality. While others have to accept fate and pain, the ascetics create their own, subject to their own will, which can lead to a sense of extreme power. Ascetics may gain a sense of having overcome reality, finding a form of masochistic pleasure which was not sought at the outset.

C. Self-Formation Orientation: This person accepts an ideal image of self and, in reflective thinking, tries to adjust the self that is confronted during daily reality to the ideal self. Only if the ideal realistically connects with the person's potential is the development authentic. Otherwise, a sham development results. The various types of self-formation achievers range from fully developed individuals to a type of "saint" who tries to negate whatever his or her genuine reality would have been.

The Unmediated Orientation: The Moment

This person lives in the real, current world, in the fullness and immediacy of the moment, its depth, and its creative powers. Decisions are made at the moment and the anxiety of the moment is tolerated.

The Enthusiastic Orientation

Enthusiasm is a moving process. Enthusiasts are striving, carried by drive and yearning, anticipating the fulfillment with what is yet to come and restlessly moving towards it. Totally dedicated to the cause, they will, if necessary, sacrifice their individuality. Limits are overcome; values are recognized which are beyond earthly values. The enthusiastic person works from a metaphysical foundation, is involved in its depth and does not have to adhere to normal categories of usefulness, success, or basic reality. The source of the underlying ideas could be art, philosophy, science, or religion. Enthusiasm offers a power of unity and synthesis. It makes it possible to become oneself by giving oneself up. Man knowingly takes chances and gains a sense of freedom from it.

The enthusiastic orientation has to be understood in its differentiation from the fanatic as well as from the mystical one. The fanatic is fixated, authoritarian, without respect for his fellow men, isolated and stuck without a developmental process. In contrast, the enthusiastic orientation moves in the direction of oneness and unity which mysticism has already achieved. Mysticism is a state of fulfillment. Enthusiasm remains in the process of being on the way.

REFERENCES AND BIBLIOGRAPHY

Jaspers, K. (1971, 6th edition [1919]). *Die Psychologie der Weltanschauung.* Berlin, New York: Springer.

Jaspers, K. (1963). Die phänomenologische Forschungsrichtung in der Psychopathologie [1912] in: Gesammelte Schriften zur Psychopathologie. Berlin, Göttingen, Heidelberg: Springer.

Jaspers, K. (1967). *Schicksal und Wille.* München: Piper.

Jaspers, K. (1963, 7th ed. [1913/1973 9th edition]). *General psychopathology.* Chicago: University of Chicago Press.

Jaspers, K. (1978 [1947]). *The question of German guilt.* Westport, CT: Greenwood Press.

Jaspers, K. (1977). *Strindbergh and Van Gogh.* (O. Grunow & D. Woloshin transl.) Tucson, AZ: University of Arizona Press.

Jaspers, K. (1975, 4th ed.). *The nature of psychotherapy: a critical appraisal.* (J. Hoenig & M. W. Hamilton transl.). Chicago: University of Chicago Press.

Jaspers, K. (1971). *Philosophy of existence.* (R. F. Grabau transl.). Philadelphia: University of Pennsylvania Press.

Jaspers, K. (1969, Vol. I; 1970, Vol. II; 1971, Vol. III) *Philosophy.* (E. B. Ashton transl.). Chicago: University of Chicago Press.

Jaspers, K. & Bultmann, R. (1958 [1954]). *Myth and Christianity.* New York: Farrar, Straus & Giroux.

Saner, H. (1979, 5th ed.). Karl Jaspers in *Selbstzeugnissen und Bilddokumenten.* Hamburg: Rowohlt.

E. WICK
St John's University

JASTROW, JOSEPH (1863–1944)

Joseph Jastrow came to the United States as a young man and received the PhD at Johns Hopkins University in 1886. Historians consider this to be the first PhD granted in psychology as such. While at Johns Hopkins, Jastrow was a colleague of G. Stanley Hall. In 1888 he went to the University of Wisconsin, where he established the first psychological laboratory. The remainder of his career was spent at Wisconsin until his retirement in 1927.

Jastrow's early work was in the field of psychophysics. An early paper published with C. S. Peirce described a new way to determine the difference limen (the point of just noticeable difference in discriminating a sensation). Previously, the difference limen had been defined as the point at which judgments of correct responses were at the level of 50%, half right and half wrong. Jastrow argued that the point of 50% was mere chance, so the subject was really not able to make a proper discrimination. He suggested the criterion be raised to 75% correct—better than chance, but still a fine discrimination in which some error was made.

Jastrow is best known for his books that popularized psychology, including *The Subconscious* and *The House that Freud Built.* In *Fact and Fable* he wrote on the occult, psychic research, mental telepathy, spiritualism, hypnosis, and dreams of the blind. Jastrow was at least in part a believer in psychic phenomena. In *The House that Freud Built* he attacked Freudian theory, likening it to a house built of playing cards that could easily be demolished by appropriate arguments. Although Jastrow was not a behaviorist in any interpretation of the term, his book was one of the early attacks on Freudian theory and was followed by many from other authors in a more behavioristic tone.

R. W. LUNDIN
Wheaton, Illinois

JENSEN, ARTHUR R.

One of the most visible educational and differential psychologists in the past half-century, Jensen is professor emeritus of educational psychology in the Graduate School of Education, University of California, Berkeley. During the forty years of his tenure at Berkeley, he was been a prolific researcher in the psychology of human learning, individual differences in cognitive abilities, psychometrics, behavioral genetics, and mental chronometry, and his activity has continued since his official retirement in 1994. His work, published in seven books and some 400 articles in scientific and professional journals, has placed him among the most frequently cited figures in contemporary psychology, and his name has become one of the "-isms" in our language. The Random House and Webster's Unabridged Dictionaries contain the following entry:

Jen-sen-ism (jen'se niz'em), *n.* the theory that an individual's IQ is largely due to heredity, including racial heritage. [1965–1970]; after Arthur R. Jensen (born 1923), U.S. educational psychologist, who proposed such a theory; see -ism]
—**Jen'sen-ist, Jen'sen-ite'**, *n., adj.*

Jensen was born and attended public schools in San Diego, CA. As a teenager his chief interests were herpetology and classical music. After graduating from high school and playing clarinet for one season in the San Diego Symphony, he gave up his ambition for a musical career and majored in psychology, with as many courses in biology and physiology, receiving his BA from the University of California, Berkeley in 1945. Music, however, has remained his chief avocation, which he has continued to pursue with nearly as much enthusiasm as he has pursued his profession of psychology. After obtaining a master's degree in psychology at San Diego State University (1952) while teaching high school biology and physiology, he went to Teachers College, Columbia University to study educational and clinical psychology, and served for three years as a research assistant to his major professor and mentor, P. M. Symonds. Symonds was a prolific scholar in dynamic psychology and projective techniques, with whom Jensen also coauthored a book based on their research with projective techniques, *From Adolescent to Adult* (1961). Jensen's PhD dissertation *Aggression in Fantasy and Overt Behavior* (1955), examined the validity of the Thematic Apperception Test for discriminating individual differences in degree and types of aggressive behavior in high school students. During his year's clinical internship at the University of Maryland's Psychiatric Institute in Baltimore (1955–56), Jensen became disillusioned with the methods of Freudian and dynamic psychology, which seemed to him more literary than scientific. He was strongly attracted to the objective, quantitative, and experimental research on personality being developed by the eminent

British psychologist H. J. Eysenck in the University of London's Institute of Psychiatry. The award of an NIMH postdoctoral fellowship made it possible for Jensen to spend two years (1956–58) in Eysenck's laboratory. This was an experience Jensen has claimed as the predominant influence in all of his subsequent career, more because of Eysenck's philosophy of science as applied to psychology than for the particular substantive content of Eysenck's own research. Eysenck was then the leading active exponent of the "London School" of psychology established by Galton and Spearman, the founders of psychometrics, differential psychology, and behavioral genetics, and their writings had great appeal for Jensen, whose future ambition it became to advance the scientific aims of the London School.

Appointed assistant professor of educational psychology in the University of California, Berkeley in 1958, Jensen was advanced in 1966 to full professor and research psychologist in the Institute of Human Learning. Meanwhile, Jensen had returned to Eysenck's lab on a Guggenheim fellowship during his first sabbatical (1964) and also spent a year (1966–67) as a fellow in the Center for Advanced Study in the Behavioral Sciences.

After a decade of research resulting in some thirty publications on the experimental psychology of human learning, Jensen turned to the study of individual differences in scholastic performance, especially the problems of the culturally disadvantaged, including minority groups such as Mexican-Americans and Blacks. His now-classic 124-page article "How Much Can We Boost IQ and Scholastic Achievement?", which appeared in the *Harvard Educational Review* (Spring, 1969), was immediately sensationalized in the general media and followed a storm of protest by many social scientists and political commentators, mainly because the article dealt in part with Black-White differences in IQ and scholastic achievement and suggested as a research hypothesis that genetic as well as environmental factors are involved in racial differences, just as they are in individual differences, the evidence for which was comprehensively reviewed in Jensen's article. These events are detailed in the preface of Jensen's *Genetics and Education* (1972). He has spent much of his subsequent career responding to the criticisms of his heresy by subjecting each of the main issues to rigorous empirical investigations, using the techniques of experimental psychology, psychometrics, and behavioral genetics in the tradition of the London School. This research was presented in numerous journal articles and was summarized in *Educability and Group Differences* (1973) and in his later books. Jensen views group differences essentially as aggregated individual differences and therefore as involving mainly the same genetic and environmental causal factors rather than characteristics that are sui generis or unique to any particular group. Jensen's tome, *Bias in Mental Testing* (1980) remains the most comprehensive examination ever made of the question of psychometric test bias claimed to be due to cultural differences associated with social class, race, and sex for the tests most commonly used in schools and colleges, in employment, and in the Armed Forces. Jensen's investigation led to the conclusion, which has not since been contradicted by evidence, that "The most widely used standardized tests of mental ability . . . are, by and large, *not* biased against any native-born English-speaking minority groups. . . (p. ix)." Jensen's *Straight Talk About Mental Tests* (1981) summarized the issues in the debate for a lay audience. In 1971, to further his research on the nature of individual and group differences related to educational performance, Jensen founded the Institute for the Study of Educational Differences.

The next two decades of Jensen's research were devoted to the use of mental chronometry as a means for analyzing the elemental features of general mental ability, or psychometric *g*, which reflects the highest-order common factor (or the first principal component) of a large battery of diverse psychometric tests of various mental abilities. Measuring reaction times in a wide variety of elementary cognitive tasks that are so simple that response times (RT) were less than one second for college students, Jensen established that individual differences in speed of information processing in RT tasks that involved such elemental processes as stimulus apprehension, discrimination, retrieval of information from short-term and long-term memory, and the like, were correlated with IQ, and more specifically, with the *g* factor of psychometric test batteries. The speed of information processing and the trial-to-trial consistency of RTs (that is, a low degree of intraindividual variability in RT) were related to individual differences in psychometric *g*. This finding led Jensen to investigations of the physical correlates of the *g* factor by what he termed the "method of correlated vectors," whereby the column vector of *g* loadings of each of a large battery of psychometric tests is correlated with the corresponding column vector of those tests correlations with some nonpsychometric physical measure, usually some property of the brain. A number of such variables were found to show positive correlations between these vectors, and the correlations are invariably higher for the *g* factor than for any other significant factors that can be extracted from a test battery. Some of the nonpsychometric variables that show correlations with psychometric *g* are the assortative mating coefficient (i.e., the spouse correlation), the genetic heritability of test scores, inbreeding depression of test scores in the offspring of cousin mating, various features of the latency and amplitude of the brain's evoked electrical potentials, brain intracellular pH level, cortical glucose metabolic rate during mental activity, and nerve conduction velocity in a brain tract (retina to visual cortex). Jensen believes that *g*, more than any other psychometric factor, reflects the physical basis of human intelligence, a view most comprehensively spelled out in his book *The g Factor: The Science of Mental Ability* (1998).

Critical commentaries on Jensen's contributions to psychology by 27 experts in the relevant fields are *Arthur Jensen: Consensus and Controversy,* edited by Modgil and Modgil (1987), and a special issue of the journal *Intelligence* (Vol. 26, No. 3, 1998), which includes Jensen's bibliography.

STAFF

JOB ANALYSIS

The design of research and psychological programs in organizations often requires knowledge of aspects of the jobs people do. The process by which this knowledge is acquired is *job analysis;* a *job description* is the record of the results of the analysis. Sometimes these terms are used interchangeably. Job analyses and the resulting descriptions vary widely in detail, standardization, and rigor. Where only a general understanding of the job is needed, casual procedures and general information may suffice. Where research or managerial programs are to be developed on the basis of job information, more comprehensive data are needed; the job description may take on the characteristics of a research report.

PURPOSES

Fundamentally, jobs are analyzed to answer two kinds of questions: (a) What is done on the job; and (b) what resources are needed to do it? Answers to the first question may describe work outcomes or accomplishments, tasks or responsibilities, work methods and procedures, and other job-related behavior common to all the people who do the job. A comprehensive study of a job may also provide information about diversity in the procedures followed or about possible but unexpected and even undesirable consequences of actions at work. Answers to the second question may describe physical resources (e.g., tools, equipment, or materials), social or organizational resources (supervisory or coworker interactions, staff services), or the personal resources of the worker (skills, knowledge areas, abilities, or other personal characteristics—often abbreviated as SKAPs—needed for effective performance). Answers to the two questions are not independent. If good material is particularly necessary to good performance, the worker may be responsible for evaluating incoming material or for working around minor defects.

Job descriptions provide the basis for many kinds of research and practical program planning. Examples of their use are found in job design, development of training programs, career counseling, job evaluation, and identification of job knowledge, skill, or of more abstract constructs to be assessed in personnel selection.

METHODS OF ANALYSIS

The most comprehensive job analyses use several methods and combine different sources of information. Information may come from documents, from job incumbents, from the inferences of a job analyst, or from other people; the methods of developing the information from any of these sources are limited only by the resourcefulness of the analyst. The number of distinguishable methods of job analysis is therefore large; however, most methods may be subsumed under five broad categories.

Self-Report

The incumbent is the basic source—often the only source—of job information; some job descriptions are no more than the incumbent's report based on a somewhat introspective look at what is done. Incumbents may be asked to develop such descriptions individually or in small groups or to complete diaries, other records of activities, standard questionnaires, or inventories. One variation on this theme is the report of the job analyst who tries out the job, but this is limited to relatively simple tasks.

Direct Observation

Some jobs can be studied by watching the incumbents do their work. Observational aids such as cameras or stop watches may be used, and the observations may be taken in planned time samples. This method is informative for jobs consisting of easily observed physical activity and short work cycles, but is not very helpful for jobs that are basically cognitive in nature.

Document Searches

Peace officers file reports of incidents in which they are involved. Complaint registers may be available for them and for people in other service occupations. Memoranda may report on unusual but important activities and achievements. Medical records may identify health or safety hazards in the work environment or in work methods. Prior job descriptions may exist. Such documents may provide information that might be overlooked when following other methods.

Interviews

Incumbents, supervisors, or other workers with related activities can be interviewed, singly or in groups, to identify broad categories of job characteristics and details within the categories. Interviews in the early stages of analysis may be open and unstructured; if the analysis is to include several different jobs, standard interview forms may be needed.

One special approach that works well in group interviews was developed by Flanagan in "The critical incident technique." Employees or others can be asked to identify critical incidents-examples of particularly effective or ineffective performance. The description includes the chain of events leading up to the incident and the subsequent effects. From a collection of incidents, much can be learned about safety hazards, influences on judgments, or personal characteristics related to the quality of performance. The technique is particularly well adapted to jobs in which much that is important about the job is not readily apparent to others.

Survey Methods

When many jobs are to be studied or when many people working under the same job title may have variations of the basic job, questionnaires and job inventories can be used to collect information ordinarily developed by the other methods. The development of an inventory may require observation and interviewing; if it is to be widely or frequently used, it may also require a trial and revision before undertaking the full scale survey. McCormick (1979) described procedures for developing such inventories, as well as some general inventories (e.g., the Position Analysis Questionnaire, the Clerical Task Inventory, and the Executive Position Description Inventory) that are widely available.

REFERENCES

Flanagan, J. C. (1954). The critical incident technique. *Psychological Bulletin, 51,* 327–358.

McCormick, E. J. (1979). *Job analysis: Methods and applications.* New York: Amacom.

SUGGESTED READING

Levine, E. L., Ash, R. A., & Bennett, N. (1980). Exploratory comparative study of four job analysis methods. *Journal of Applied Psychology, 65,* 524–535.

McCormick, E. J. (1976). Job and task analysis. In M. D. Dunnette (Ed.), *Handbook of industrial and organizational psychology.* Chicago: Rand McNally.

Prien, E. P. (1977). The function of job analysis in content validation. *Personnel Psychology, 30,* 167–174.

R. M. Guion
Bowling Green State University

APPLIED RESEARCH
CAREER DEVELOPMENT
INDUSTRIAL PSYCHOLOGY
JOB EVALUATION

JOB EVALUATION

People with different jobs receive different pay. The fact of pay differentials is usually accepted as fair, although different justifications for them may sometimes be based on contradictory values. For example, pay differences based on need would lead to greatly different wage structures from those based on investments such as educational preparation or levels of responsibility. In most organizations in industrial societies, relative pay differences are usually considered equitable if they reflect relative differences in relative worth to the organization. The process of measuring differences in the relative worth of jobs is called job evaluation.

There are many different methods of job evaluation. A common approach can be described in five steps: (a) Job descriptions are provided to members of a job evaluation committee; (b) a set of characteristics or dimensions along which jobs differ, the so-called compensable factors, are developed by or presented to the committee; (c) on the basis of the job descriptions, committee members rate or otherwise evaluate each job on each dimension and reach a consensus on the ratings; (d) all ratings for a job are summed and weighted according to an accepted formula to provide a measure of job worth; and (e) the sums are translated into pay rates. The basic value judgments are identified in the second and fourth steps: the designation of the compensable factors and the relative weights assigned to them.

BASIC JUDGMENTS

Someone, or some group, must decide which job characteristics should be used as a basis for compensation. Examples of compensable factors found in some programs include: (a) job demands for creativity; (b) extent of education, training, or experience required; (c) intellectual level demanded; (d) amount of physical exertion; (e) level of communication; (f) consequences of error; (g) level of responsibility (frequently subdivided by area of responsibility); (h) degree of independence of action; (i) time period of discre-

tionary action; (j) scope of influence of job activities; (k) working conditions; and (l) risk of sickness or injury. A given job evaluation program may use fewer or more factors; it might even be restricted to the single factor of overall worth. Definitions of factors may be broad in some programs and narrowly precise in others. Whatever the nature of the final list of compensable factors, it must be established and there must be consensus on the relative weights. Without consensus, acceptance of the resulting pay plan is not likely. It follows that these judgments should be reached collaboratively by people representing different levels and functions in the organization. If there is a union, there should be union representation. If there is no union, the principle of worker representation or participation is still important.

Job evaluation committees usually work from brief, narrative job descriptions containing enough information for each committee member to have a general, but not a detailed, understanding of all the jobs to be evaluated. It is not likely that the raters can absorb the highly detailed job information necessary for a complete understanding of each of a large set of jobs. A combination of different perceptions of the compensable factors, different ways of rating, and different understandings of the jobs may result in greater differences in ratings for a particular job on a particular dimension. Such differences are resolved by group discussion or often by negotiation. The result is a measure of the job characteristic that is highly subjective, sometimes even political, and subject to substantial measurement error.

An ideal job analysis procedure would provide direct measurement of each compensable factor for each job; committee ratings could be eliminated. Some job evaluation plans approach the ideal. For example, Elizur (1980) developed descriptive scales for seven job characteristics which were then embedded in a larger job survey. Incumbents completed the descriptive survey and their responses were verified by their supervisors. More complex job component systems were described by McCormick (1979); however, Schwab (1980) questioned the reliabilities of these procedures.

WAGE SETTING

Job evaluation as such identifies the relative worth of jobs within a set studied. The translation of abstract indices of relative worth into actual pay scales ordinarily requires the use of key jobs—jobs found throughout a community or industry with reasonably uniform pay scales. Uniformity exists because the market forces of labor supply and demand have stabilized. For such jobs, a curve can be statistically established to show how relative worth measures are related to the pay rates for the key jobs. The same curve may then be used for other jobs to establish pay rates that will be seen as equitable.

COMPARABLE WORTH

Law in the United States has established that men and women doing the same jobs should have the same pay. An extension of the principle is that people doing work of comparable worth should receive equal (or comparable) pay. Livernash (1980) stressed that job evaluation systems must be used or developed to handle this issue of equity. However, Blumrosen (1979) argued that, historically, women have been segregated in a small number of occupations and that the oversupply in such jobs has depressed their wages. If such jobs are included among the key jobs, traditional job evaluation perpetuates the effects of prior wage discrimination. The issue points up the need to avoid an uncritical use of key jobs in the transformation of relative worth statements to wage rates.

REFERENCES

Blumrosen, R. G. (1979). Wage discrimination, job segregation, and Title VII of the Civil Rights Act of 1964. *University of Michigan Journal of Law Reform, 12,* 397–502.

Livernash, E. R. (Ed.). (1980). *Comparable worth: Issues and alternatives.* Washington, DC: Equal Employment Advisory Council.

SUGGESTED READING

Bureau of National Affairs. (1981). *The comparable worth issue.* Washington, DC: Author.

Otis, J. L., & Leukart, R. H. (1954). *Job evaluation: A basis for sound wage administration.* Englewood Cliffs, NJ: Prentice-Hall.

Treiman, D. J., & Hartmann, H. I. (1981). *Women, work, and wages: Equal pay for jobs of equal value.* Washington, DC: National Academy Press.

R. M. Guion
Bowling Green State University

APPLIED RESEARCH
INDUSTRIAL PSYCHOLOGY
JOB ANALYSIS

JOB SATISFACTION

Over the years since the early 1930s, psychologists have endeavored to determine the components of job satisfaction—that quality or combination of qualities that has escaped precise definition because, as the late Edwin E. Ghiselli and his collaborator, Clarence W. Brown, pointed out in *Personnel and Industrial Psychology,* it has many different points of reference, and few workers are satisfied with all aspects of their jobs. "The overall measurement of job satisfaction may obscure differences in degree of satisfaction in specific areas. . . . The satisfactions the worker derives from his job are not only many and varied but are also highly sensitive to change. . . . [T]here is considerable variation in satisfaction from day to day and from week to week" (1955, p. 430).

In his *Psychology of Careers,* Super described satisfaction with one's work as the most important outcome of successful vocational planning. He found job satisfaction to be a function of occupational level within broad classes of occupations—for example,

manual and nonmanual. Within each class, workers at the higher levels expressed greater satisfaction with their work than did workers at the lower levels. Super's work also indicated that satisfaction shows cyclical changes with age; workers were less satisfied at ages 25 to 34 and 45 to 54 than at other ages. These differences might be related to the different stages of vocational development described by Super.

Hoppock, whose landmark study, *Job Satisfaction,* was published in 1935, more recently pointed out (1975) that there is now a great deal of evidence that satisfied workers are found in all occupations and that some workers in repetitive and manual jobs are better satisfied than some in more creative occupations.

Kuder (1977) found that the best indicator of satisfaction or dissatisfaction with one's work was the response to the question, "If you had your choice, which of the following would you choose, if each paid the same: The job you have now; the same kind of work but with some changes in the working conditions or people you work with; a different kind of work entirely?" Those who said they would choose a different kind of work entirely were clearly the most dissatisfied and were more likely than satisfied workers to receive higher Kuder Occupational Interest Survey scores on occupations other than their own.

With the social unrest and changing mores of the 1960s and early 1970s, the theme of worker alienation became widespread. Poor morale, especially among blue collar workers, was said to be rampant in the American workplace, accompanied by apathy, absenteeism, and even industrial sabotage. The U.S. Department of Health, Education, and Welfare appointed a special task force to investigate and report on the situation. The report, *Work in America* (Special Task Force, 1973), immediately became the object of both praise and criticism. Among the critics was Harold Wool, a senior economist at the Research Center of the National Planning Association. Although Wool conceded that job satisfaction was alive but might not be so well, he also expressed the opinion that, in its "zeal to advance the cause of 'humanization of work,'" the report suffered from "overgeneralization concerning the extent and nature of work dissatisfaction and from overstatement of the potentials of work redesign as a primary solution to work-related ills" (1975, p. 158). He contended that a review of available research— some 2,000 surveys of job satisfaction conducted in the United States over a period of several decades—revealed that few people expressed extreme satisfaction with their jobs, but still fewer reported extreme dissatisfaction, while the greatest number described themselves as "pretty satisfied."

Sociologist H. Roy Kaplan (1975) questioned some of the assumptions of the report that were presented as fact. He pointed out that considerable sociological evidence indicates that "many people do not seek greater opportunities for creativity and responsibility," but instead prefer security, good wages, good working conditions, and so on. Furthermore, work may not be a central interest for all workers.

On the other hand, support for the ideas expressed in the report could be found in books such as *Working* by Terkel and *Where Have All the Robots Gone?* by Sheppard and Herrick. In *Varieties of Work Experience,* Stewart and Cantor related problems of alienation and loss of job satisfaction to workers' lack of control over their product in both industrial and bureaucratic settings.

The status of job satisfaction in America was brought into focus again as the result of a survey conducted by Staines and Quinn (1979) of the Survey Research Center of the University of Michigan. Job satisfaction was measured with a set of general questions and a set of questions about specific aspects of job and employment conditions. Both indexes were combined to yield an overall index, which showed an appreciable drop in overall satisfaction between 1973 and 1977, although there had been no change between comparable surveys in 1969 and 1973. The general index showed a slight but significant decline, and the specific index showed a marked decline for five of six areas—comfort, challenge, financial rewards, resource adequacy, and promotions; only relations with coworkers showed no decline. Although the decline affected all demographic and occupational classes, there were some differences. Thus, men showed a greater decline than did women, and older workers also showed a decline. The decline was about the same for white and black workers, but black workers remained less satisfied than whites. Satisfaction was down in all educational categories, but more so among workers with college degrees. Those in the lower skilled occupations showed more decline than those in the higher skilled occupations, as Super had found years earlier (Staines & Quinn, 1979).

A number of investigators have speculated that declining job satisfaction can be traced to a growing gap between job expectations and the realities of the job situation. As workers acquire more education, they want the opportunity to make greater use of their talents and training, and more intrinsic satisfaction from their work. Others have questioned whether more satisfied workers are also more productive workers. Opinion remains divided, as do the results of research. The reasons for the differences in findings and explanations may be, as Ghiselli pointed out, the many different points of reference from which the concept of job satisfaction is approached by both workers and scholars.

REFERENCES

Ghiselli, E. E., & Brown, C. W. (1955). *Personnel and industrial psychology.* New York: McGraw-Hill.

Hoppock, R. (1935). *Job satisfaction.* New York: Harper.

Kaplan, H. R. (1975). How *do* workers view their work in America? *Vocational Guidance Quarterly, 24,* 165–168.

Kuder, F. (1977). *Activity interests and occupational choice.* Chicago: Science Research Associates.

Sheppard, H. L., & Herrick, N. Q. (1972). *Where have all the robots gone? Worker dissatisfaction in the '70's.* New York: Free Press.

Special Task Force, U.S. Department of Health, Education and Welfare. (1973). *Work in America.* Cambridge, MA: MIT Press.

Staines, G. L., & Quinn, R. P. (1979). American workers evaluate the quality of their jobs. *Monthly Labor Review, 102,* 3–12.

Stewart, P. L., & Cantor, M. G. (1974). *Varieties of work experience.* New York: Wiley.

Super, D. E. (1957). *Psychology of careers.* New York: Harper.

Terkel, S. (1974). *Working.* New York: Pantheon.

Wool, H. (1975). What's wrong with work in America?—A review essay. *Vocational Guidance Quarterly, 24,* 155–164.

E. E. DIAMOND
Evanston, Illinois

EXIT INTERVIEWS
JOB ANALYSIS
JOB EVALUATION

JONES, MARY COVER (1896–1987)

Mary Cover Jones was an undergraduate at Vassar and received the PhD from Columbia. Most of her career was spent at the Institute of Human Development of the University of California at Berkeley. Much of her later work on longitudinal studies of development was in collaboration with her husband, Harold E. Jones.

Her name is most prominent, however, as the first researcher to remove a fear in a child, the case of Peter. On a weekend trip to New York during her last semester at Vassar, she attended a lecture by John Watson in which he discussed and showed movies of the fear conditioning of Little Albert. By the time Jones became a graduate student at Columbia, Watson had been expelled by Johns Hopkins for his sensationally publicized divorce and was working with the J. Walter Thompson Advertising Agency in New York. Since Jones had been a classmate and friend of his second wife, Rosalie Raynor Watson, Jones was able to obtain Watson's advice on most Saturday afternoons throughout the project. The therapeutic experiments were carried on in the children's home where, as it happened, Jones lived with her husband and daughter. The project ended with the article, "A laboratory study of fear."

Since a single case study was unacceptable as a dissertation, Jones extended Watson's studies of developmental activities to a larger and more representative sample. Her comparison of observations of 300 normal babies was accepted. In 1936, with Barbara Burks, she published an extended monograph on the topic.

STAFF

JUDD, LEWIS L.

Born in Los Angeles, California, Lewis L. Judd received his MD degree with honors and was elected to Alpha Omega Alpha at the University of California, Los Angeles School of Medicine. He completed his medical internship, psychiatry residency, and fellowship in child psychiatry at the UCLA Center for Health Sciences. Prior to his appointment at the University of California, San Diego (UCSD), he joined the UCLA faculty, rising to associate professor as director of education in child psychiatry.

In 1977 Judd was appointed chair of the Department of Psychiatry UCSD and the Mary Gilman Marston Professor of Psychiatry. Under his leadership, the UCSD Department of Psychiatry has emerged as one of the nation's meritorious academic departments with extensive and high-quality programs in research, education and training, and clinical care. The department is known for its excellence in basic cellular and molecular biology and translational research in clinical neuroscience, psychobiology, neuropsychopharmacology, brain imaging, molecular genetics, and neuropsychology, as well as for its research and training programs in the severe mental disorders throughout the entire life cycle. The department at UCSD is one of the few departments in the country with four separate National Institute of Mental Health (NIMH)–funded Mental Health Clinical Research Centers (MHCRCs) in mood disorders, late onset psychoses, neurobehavioral aspects of HIV infection, and services research to children and adolescents. It also has one of the first Mental Illness Research and Education Centers (MIRECs) awarded by the Department of Veterans Affairs. Although it is not one of the largest departments of psychiatry in the country, it is among the most active scientifically in terms of research funding, peer-reviewed publications, and eminence of faculty. In addition to chairing the department, Judd has served as psychiatrist-in-chief at UCSD, chief of psychiatry services at the Veterans Affairs' San Diego Health Care System, chair of the executive committee of the UCSD Medical Center, and president of the medical staff.

Judd is an expert in biological psychiatry and clinical psychopharmacology, and his extensive research contributions include investigations into the effects of psychopharmacological agents on both brain mechanisms and symptom patterns of depression, Manic Depressive Disorder, and schizophrenia. Since returning from NIMH he continues to be scientifically active, publishing broadly in the scientific literature on mood and anxiety disorders and their treatment as well as in mental health economics and societal consequences of the mental disorders. He is a national leader and spokesperson for the essential role of empirical science in psychiatry and has been an important national force for equitable treatment of the mentally ill in national health-care reform.

At the time of his appointment in 1987, Judd was one of the first active clinical researchers to be named director of NIMH. During his tenure at NIMH his initiatives included developing and implementing the following research plans: National Plan for Schizophrenia Research, The Decade of the Brain Research Plan, The National Plan for Research in Child and Adolescent Mental Disorders, and the National Research Plan to Improve Services for Severe Mental Disorders. While Judd was director, the number of new research programs and the increases in the annual NIMH budget substantially exceeded that achieved during any other comparable period in NIMH's 40-year history. Judd was also the leader of the Decade of the Brain effort within the executive branch of the federal government. Upon leaving NIMH, he was very influential and central in the transfer of NIMH back to its original home at the National Institutes of Health (NIH).

Judd was elected vice president of the American Psychiatric Association (APA) from 1992 to 1994, and president of the International College of Neuropsychopharmacology (CINP) from 1994 to 1996. In 1997 he was elected vice president of the World Federation of Societies of Biological Psychiatry (WFSBP), a federation that includes more than 50 national societies of biological psychiatry. He is one of the United States' most active leaders in international psychiatry and neuroscience, consulting and facilitating the implementation of Decade of the Brain efforts in all the countries of the European Community, in Switzerland, and in others, each of which has developed its own Decade of the Brain efforts on behalf of patients with mental, addictive, and neurological disorders.

Judd has been the recipient of the Distinguished Service Award for the National Alliance for the Mentally Ill (NAMI), the Award of Distinction for National Leadership in Child and Adolescent Mental Disorders from the National Mental Health Association (NMHA), and the William C. Menninger Memorial Award for Achievement in the Science of Mental Health from the American College of Physicians. He has also been elected to the Institute of Medicine (IOM) of the National Academy of Sciences and has received an honorary Doctor of Science degree from the Medical College of Ohio for national leadership in brain research. He received the Distinguished Service Award (1999) from the American College of Psychiatrists and the first prize (1999–2000) of the Anna-Monika Award for research in depression.

STAFF

JUDGMENT AND DECISION MAKING

The area of judgment and decision making has been an active one for mathematicians, statisticians, economists, and especially for psychologists who attempt to prescribe how decisions should be made, to describe systematically the variables that affect decision making, and to formulate strategies and principles aid and support for decisions in a variety of situations. The prescriptive or normative approach to decision making has a long history, dating back to the 17th- and 18th-century mathematicians who advised gamblers in the French court. The descriptive approach to decision making has developed within the framework of behavioral science during the last 30 years. The cognitive approach to decision making has been closely related to the rapid development of cognitive psychology, especially the information processing studies in the early 1970s. Both the organizational approach and the decision support-system approach to decision making are more recent developments in an increasing interest in solving practical issues in the context of organizational change and technological innovation, using psychological principles of judgment and decision making. Obviously, judgment and decision making play a significant role in one's attempts to deal with the environment. Thus they have become important psychological subjects in research and applications to improve decision effectiveness.

Studies on judgment and decision making may be divided into four decision categories: the behavioral, the cognitive, the organizational, and the decision support-systems categories. Each has its own theoretical perspective and methodology for analyzing decision-making behaviors and building its models.

BEHAVIORAL DECISION APPROACH: UTILITY AND PROBABILITY

Although the idea of utility and probability has a long history, dating back about 400 or more years, the modern history of decision analysis theories started with von Neumann and Morgenstern, who published *Theory of Games and Economic Behavior* (1947), establishing risky choice as a topic of psychological study. Savage (1954) provided a set of axioms, with the simultaneous measurement of both the utility and the probability of an outcome that expanded the utility theory. In the meantime, Edwards (1954) introduced the Bayesian approach to psychological studies on judgment and decision making, which takes base rate, prior odds, posterior odds, and the likelihood ratio into consideration and is a normative model based on probability theory. Edwards (1961) also introduced the idea of subjective probabilities and the maximization of subjective expected utility that have become a descriptive model of decision-making psychology. Some static models are founded on the assumption that people choose among courses of action on the basis of two variables: the value associated with action outcomes, and the likelihood that certain actions will lead to the valued outcome. Von Winterfeldt and Edwards (1986) argued that when faced with complex tasks involving multiple value dimensions, individuals need a multi-attribute utility theory to break down the evaluation task into attributes to make single-attribute evaluations. The trade-offs among attributes are then quantified as importance weights for attributes to reaggregate into an overall task evaluation in decision making. Three classes of techniques are proved to be effective for multi-attribute utility analysis: the simple multi-attribute rating technique for value measurement, the indifference methods for value measurement, and the lottery-based methods for utility measurement.

COGNITIVE AND DECISION PROCESS APPROACH

Because many decisions involve uncertainty, a number of studies have focused on the assessment of probabilities under various situations. The probabilities for some events should be interpreted as degrees of confidence. For a large set of probability assessments, a kind of validity can be examined (i.e., a calibration can be made) in terms of the real probability that certain events occur. A general finding is that people often assess the probability with overconfidence, which is related to the difficulty of the task, especially in general knowledge tasks. Some other experiments have been devoted to the conservatism in information processing in decision making and showed that conservatism could be attributed to either the failure in perceiving the data-gathering process accurately or the failure in combining information improperly. Some diagnostic systems were designed to overcome the deficiency of the conservatism in decision making.

In addition to overconfidence and conservatism, cognitive bias and heuristics are widely noted in a number of studies (see Kahneman, Slovic, & Tversky, 1982). Typical bias and heuristics include representativeness (insensitivity to prior probability of outcomes, sample size, predictability, and statistical misconceptions); availability (biases due to the retrievability of instances, the effectiveness of a search set, the imaginability, and illusory correlation); and

anchoring (insufficient adjustment, biases in evaluating conjunctive and disjunctive events and in assessing subjective probability distributions; Slovic, Lichtenstein, & Fischhoff, 1988). In recent years, emotions, framing effects, and risky and uncertain choice are among the active areas of research on judgment and decision making (Mellers, Schwartz, & Cooke, 1998).

The decision-making process is characterized largely by the heuristics and cognitive strategies the decision maker adopts. Various kinds of cognitive strategies are classified in decision-making studies, depending on subjects' knowledge structure and the information structure of decisions. Decision makers use the additive difference model, the elimination-by-aspects model (Kahneman et al., 1982), and intuitive and analytic strategies (Wang, 1990). To elicit cognitive strategies in the decision process, process-tracing techniques were developed, including simultaneous verbal protocols and information search measurement. Both reliability and validity of the process-tracing techniques in understanding human information processing are demonstrated in many studies (Ericsson & Simon, 1980; Svenson, 1979; Wang, 1990).

ORGANIZATIONAL APPROACH

Judgment and decision making also are extensively studied in the organizational context (Stevenson, Busemeyer, & Naylor, 1991). In a study on decision making and administrative organizations, Simon (1976) emphasized the importance of fact and value premises in decision making and defined the notion of bounded rationality in relation to choice behavior in organizations. This has had a significant impact on organizational decision making. Another area in the organizational approach to judgment and decision making is group decision making. The two popular topics in this area are groupthink and group risk taking in decision making. Janis (1977) defined groupthink as a collective pattern of defensive avoidance in which the members use their collective cognitive resources to develop rationalizations supporting shared illusions in decision making. At the organizational level, much attention has been paid to participation and influence-power-sharing in decision making. In a 3-year field study of 129 large companies in eight countries, Heller and Wilpert (1981) developed a model of influence-power-sharing and skill utilization in organizational decision making and the method of group feedback analysis. Wang (1989) further proposed a process model of organizational decision making, illustrating the effects of influence-power-sharing on both competence use and managerial transparency (two-way communication and sound psychological climate for goal purposing), which in turn lead to changes in decision effectiveness. In addition to organizational decision making, strategic decision making has been a focus of research. It has its roots in business policy and strategic management and is concerned with understanding and improving decisions about organizational strategies (Taylor, 1992).

DECISION SUPPORT-SYSTEMS APPROACH

In the area of decision aid and decision support, various kinds of decision support-systems have been developed for unstructured decision tasks. To support decisions, the decision problems must be structured, which includes identifying the problem, developing an overall analytic structure, and structuring value trees (von Winterfeldt & Edwards, 1986). An important task in designing decision support systems is to develop decision modeling and decision support information. Some useful types of decision modeling include (a) causal models, focusing on the causal relationships among different decision factors; (b) mathematical models, developing some mathematical formulas for the quantitative relations of key indicators for decisions; (c) operational research models, producing powerful standard models for management decisions (e.g., allocation, queuing, and competitive models); and (d) heuristic models, attempting to derive suboptimal solutions (a satisficing approach; Cooke & Slack, 1984). In a series of experiments on the effects of decision support information, Wang and Zhong (1992) demonstrated that the type of decision support information greatly affected subjects' information search patterns and modified their cognitive strategies during the decision-making process. A multilevel decision support model was proposed with the compatibility between types of user knowledge networks and levels of decision support as its key concept.

CONCLUSIONS

With recent research on decisions, errors and biases, and real world violations of rational choice theory, many psychologists now recognize the need for behavioral assumptions in exploring more efficient, adaptive, satisfying decision making. The trend of research into judgment and decision making is to develop frameworks that make connections with research on cognition, emotions, and social and organizational factors (Mellers et al., 1998).

REFERENCES

Cooke, S., & Slack, N. (1984). *Making management decisions.* London: Prentice-Hall.

Edwards, W. (1954). The theory of decision making. *Psychological Bulletin, 51,* 380–417.

Edwards, W. (1961). Behavior decision theory. *Annual Review of Psychology, 12,* 473–498.

Ericsson, K. A., & Simon, H. A. (1980). Verbal reports as data. *Psychological Review, 87,* 215–251.

Heller, F. A., & Wilpert, B. (1981). *Competence and power in managerial decision making.* Chichester, UK: Wiley.

Janis, I. L. (1977). *Decision making: A psychological analysis of conflict, choice, and commitment.* New York: Free Press.

Kahneman, D., Slovic, P., & Tversky, A. (Eds.). (1982). *Judgment under certainty: Heuristics and biases.* Cambridge, MA: Cambridge University Press.

Mellers, B. A., Schwartz, A., & Cooke, A. D. J. (1998). Judgment and decision making. *Annual Review of Psychology, 49,* pp. 447–477.

von Neumann, J., & Morgenstern, O. (1947). *Theory of games and economic behavior.* Princeton, NJ: Princeton University Press.

Savage, L. J. (1954). *The foundation of statistics.* New York: Wiley.

Simon, H. A. (1976). *Administrative behavior.* New York: Macmillan.

Slovic, P., Lichtenstein, S., & Fischhoff, S. (1988). Decision making. In R. C. Atkinson, R. J. Herrnstein, G. Lindzey, & R. D. Luce (Eds.), *Stenvens' handbook of experimental psychology* (Vol. 2, chap. 10). New York: Wiley.

Stevenson, M. K., Busemeyer, J. R., & Naylor, J. C. (1991). Judgment and decision-making theory. In M. D. Dunnette & L. M. Hough (Eds.), *Handbook of industrial psychology* (Vol. 1, pp. 283–374). Palo Alto, CA: Consulting Psychologists Press.

Svenson, O. (1979). Process descriptions of decision making. *Organizational Behavior and Human Performance, 23,* 86–112.

Taylor, R. N. (1992). Strategic decision making. In M. D. Dunnette & L. M. Hough (Eds.), *Handbook of industrial and organizational psychology* (2nd ed., Vol. 3, pp. 961–1007). Palo Alto, CA: Consulting Psychologists Press.

von Winterfeldt, D., & Edwards, W. (1986). *Decision analysis and behavioral research.* Cambridge, UK: Cambridge University Press.

Wang, Z. M. (1989). The human-computer interface hierarchy model and strategies in system development. *Ergonomics, 32*(11), 1391–1400.

Wang, Z. M. (1990). Information structures and cognitive strategies in decision-making on systems development. *Ergonomics, 33*(7), 907–916.

Wang, Z. M., & Zhong, J. A. (1992). The effects of decision support information on decision making patterns in systems development. *Ergonomics, 35.*

Z. M. Wang
Zheijang University, China

CLUSTER ANALYSIS
ECOLOGICAL VALIDITY
NONPARAMETRIC STATISTICAL TESTS
PARAMETRIC STATISTICAL TESTS

JUNG, CARL (1875–1961)

Carl Jung was a Swiss psychoanalyst and the founder of analytical psychology. Born and raised in Switzerland in an unhappy family, he learned early to depend upon his own inner resources for guidance and encouragement. He graduated in 1900 with a medical degree from the University of Basel. He was appointed to the University of Zurich psychiatric clinic to work under Eugen Bleuler, noted for his interest in schizophrenia. Jung also studied with Pierre Janet, the French clinical psychologist known for his work in hysteria and multiple personality. In 1905 Jung was a lecturer in psychiatry at the University of Basel, but after several years he resigned to concentrate on private practice, research, and writing. From 1932 to 1942 he was professor at the Federal Polytechnical University of Zurich. Illness forced his resignation; his last years were spent in writing and publishing books about analytic psychology.

Jung read Sigmund Freud's *The Interpretation of Dreams* in 1900 and met Freud in 1907. In 1909 he accompanied Freud to Clark University in America, at which they both delivered lectures. In 1911 Jung became president of the International Psychoanalytic Association with Freud's complete endorsement. However, Jung's interpretations and theories of psychoanalysis, the unconscious, and the libido differed from Freud's. After Jung published *Psychology of the Unconscious,* dissent and disagreement grew between him and Freud, and in 1914 their relationship ended. Thereafter, Jung's theory and practice was known as analytical psychology.

In 1913 Jung suffered an inner turmoil that lasted for about 3 years. Like Freud, he used self-analysis through dream interpretations to resolve his emotional distress. It was a time of creativity and growth, leading to Jung's unique approach to personality theory. Jung came to appreciate the myths and symbols of humankind throughout the centuries. He made several field trips in the 1920s to study preliterate peoples in Africa and the southwestern United States, their myths, folkways, religions, and more.

Jung's basic difference from Freud's psychoanalytic theory concerned the libido: Freud insisted upon its sexual energy, whereas Jung regarded it as a generalized life energy. A second difference was with Freud's deterministic view of the influences of childhood on the personality. Jung believed that personality can change later in life and is shaped by future goals and aspirations.

Jung's personality system included three levels of the *psyche,* or mind: (a) the conscious, or *ego;* (b) the *personal unconscious,* forgotten and repressed experiences sometimes formed into complexes; and (c) the deeper *collective unconscious,* containing the cumulative experiences of previous generations, including animal heritage. The collective or transpersonal unconscious forms the basis of personality and is its most powerful influence. It is a storehouse of universal evolutionary and latent memory traces inherited from man's ancestral past.

The components of the collective unconscious Jung called *archetypes.* There are numerous archetypes, including energy, the hero, the earth mother, death, birth and rebirth, unity, the child, God, and demon. Some archetypes are identified as separate systems within the personality: the *persona,* or masked public personality; the *anima* and *animus,* or bisexual characteristics; the *shadow,* or animal-like, part of human nature; and the *self,* which, composed of all parts of the unconscious, strives for unity and equilibrium as expressed in the symbol of the circle, the mandala. The self attempts to achieve integration, self-actualization, and harmony of the personality.

Jung is probably best known for his descriptions of the orientations of the personality, *extraversion* and *introversion,* published in *Psychological Types* (1921). He also identified four psychological functions: thinking, feeling, sensing, and intuiting. Research has been generated about these dimensions of personality, although scientific psychology has ignored Jung's work.

Jung has been influential and inspirational to other disciplines, such as art, literature, film making, religion, anthropology, and history. He published prolifically, but many of his works did not appear in English until after 1965. Only a few days before his death, Jung finished his own chapter and the drafts of his disciples' chapters for *Man and His Symbols,* a book that has popularized and explained Jung's use of dream analysis and his theories of universal symbolic representations of man's deeper nature.

N. A. HAYNIE

JUST NOTICEABLE DIFFERENCE

The concept of just noticeable difference (jnd), also known as the difference threshold or difference limen (Latin for threshold), derives from early work in the area of classical psychophysics conducted in the mid-nineteenth century. This work was highlighted by the research of Weber (1795–1878), a German physiologist, whose experimental investigations focused on tactile stimulation and the determination of sensory thresholds. Weber's seminal work in this area was extended and elaborated upon by German philosopher and mathematician Fechner (1801–1887) who coined the term "psychophyics" to refer to this area of experimental psychology and, in 1860, published the first textbook on psychophysics, which laid out the basic goals of this emerging discipline and the scientific methods which were to be employed to advance knowledge in this area (Watson, 1973).

A primary focus of classical psychophysics was on investigating the relationships between different types of physical stimuli and the sensations they evoked in human (and animal) subjects and in assessing the ultimate sensory capabilities of the organism. Of specific interest was determining thresholds for the detectabilty of stimuli. Much of the early research in this area focused on the determination of absolute thresholds. While investigators employed various experimental methods, depending on the specific nature of the research, subjects in such studies were typically presented with some stimulus (e.g., auditory, visual, tactile) of very low (and undetectable) intensity. This was then followed by a graded presentation of test stimuli, at increasing levels of stimulus intensity, with the subject's task being to indicate when they were able to detect the stimulus. Presentations of stimuli were continued until a stimulus intensity was reached where the stimulus was reported as present. Since subjects in such studies were often found to be quite variable regarding the level of stimulus intensity required for detectability on different trials, experiments most often provided subjects with a number of stimulus presentation trials, with each subject's absolute threshold being considered as that level of stimulation where the subject reported the stimulus as being present 50% of the time.

While experiments like these were designed to determine absolute thresholds (e.g., the smallest amount of sensory stimulation required for detectibility), other studies, specifically relevant to the present topic, focused on the issue of differential sensitivity or difference thresholds. Here, the primary research questions were: To what extent must the intensity of one physical stimulus differ from the intensity of a second physical stimulus for subjects to distinguish one from another? What is the smallest increment in stimulus intensity that is detectable? Studies of difference thresholds often employed experimental methods similar to those used in determining absolute thresholds. For example, subjects might be provided with a standard stimulus of a given weight, which could be used for purposes of comparison (the standard stimulus), and then be presented with a graded series of test stimuli which differed from the standard stimulus along the weight dimension. The subject's task would be to indicate whether a test stimulus was the same or heavier (or lighter depending on the nature of the specific study) than the standard stimulus. The primary focus of these studies was on determining the smallest increment in weight necessary for subject's to perceive the test stimulus as different from the standard stimulus (50% of the time). This threshold for the detection of differences in physical stimuli has been referred to by a variety of terms: difference threshold, difference or differential limen, least perceptible difference, and just noticeable difference. The term "just noticeable difference," typically abbreviated "jnd," is the one most widely accepted in the psychophysics literature. Formally, the jnd can be defined as the magnitude of change in a stimulus necessary for it to be perceived as different from another stimulus, as the smallest detectable difference between two stimuli (Levine & Shefner, 1981). Early work related to just noticeable differences in sensation was subsequently extended by attempting to characterize, quantitatively, the precise nature of the relationship between increases in the magnitude of physical stimuli and just noticeable differences in detectability. Indeed, one of the first general laws of psychology dealt with the degree to which the intensity of a stimulus must be increased beyond that of a comparison stimulus for the difference between the two to be detectable. Here, Weber's Law (which was actually popularized by Fechner) states that the amount of increase in stimulation that results in a just noticeable difference is a constant proportion of the standard stimulus. Thus, a heavy stimulus must be increased by a larger increment in weight for one to notice a difference between the two objects than a lighter stimulus, where a smaller increment in weight may result in the detectability of a difference.

It should be noted that remnants of this early interest in the concepts of absolute and difference thresholds are reflected in the psychological literature even today, although the concept of threshold has to some extent fallen into disrepute (apart from its value in assessing the capacity of sensory systems). This is due, in part, to the influence of contemporary cognitive psychology and current views of the individual as an active processor of information. Specifically, it would seem that notions of thresholds have been largely supplanted by concepts derived from signal detection theory (see Green & Swets, 1974) where it is assumed that detectability of stimuli is determined not only by the sensory capacities of the individual, but also by the nature of the response criteria one adopts in responding to detectability tasks (Levine & Shefner, 1981).

REFERENCES

Green, D., & Swets, J. A. (1974). *Signal detection theory and psychophysics.* Huntington, NY: Krieger.

Levine, M. W., & Shefner, J. M. (1981). *Fundamentals of sensation and perception.* Reading, MA: Addison-Wesley.

Watson, C. S. (1973). Psychophysics. In B. B. Wolman (Ed.), *Handbook of general psychology* (pp. 275–305). New York: Wiley.

J. H. JOHNSON
University of Florida

PERCEPTION
PSYCHOPHYSICS

JUVENILE DELINQUENCY

Juvenile delinquency is usually defined as legally prohibited behavior committed by a juvenile. The exact age at which delinquency applies depends on state law. Children under the age of 8 are usually not remanded to a detention home or youth house, but ordinarily are placed in a shelter facility. Depending on the severity of the delinquent behavior, a youngster might be considered either a juvenile delinquent or a JINS (juvenile in need of supervision). Behavior of the latter category—such as loitering, truancy, running away, trespassing, and incorrigibility—would not be considered criminal if committed by an adult. Juvenile delinquency includes criminal offenses such as breaking and entering, burglary, shoplifting, arson, rape, and homicide.

A special report in *U.S. News and World Report* of December 14, 1981, notes that one-third of all major crimes are committed by people under 20 years of age. No ethnic, religious, racial groups, or socioeconomic levels are free from the apparently rapidly rising tide of juvenile problems.

Adler in *The Problem Child* identifies three situations that can lead to problems. Children born sickly and physically weak experience their bodies as a burden and find life oppressive. As a result they are more interested in their own persons than in others and show egotistical traits that hamper the development of social feelings. A second situation is that of spoiled children who become dependent and want to be supported by others. Adler estimated that in his time these children constituted perhaps 50 to 60% of all children. The third situation is that of hated children, including the illegitimate, the unwanted, orphans, and those who have not learned to be interested in their fellow humans. In all three categories there is something amiss with the children's social feelings.

REFERENCES

Adler, A. (1963). *The problem child.* New York: Capricorn Books. (Original work published 1930)

SUGGESTED READING

Ansbacher, H. L., & Ansbacher, R. R. (Eds.). *The individual psychology of Alfred Adler.*

Coleman, J., Butcher, J., & Carson, R. (1984). *Abnormal psychology and modern life* (7th ed.). Glenview, IL: Scott, Foresman.

Lombardi, D. (1975). *Search for significance.* Chicago: Nelson-Hall.

D. N. LOMBARDI
Seton Hall University

AGGRESSION
ENVIRONMENTAL PSYCHOLOGY

K

KAGAN, JEROME

Jerome Kagan received his Bachelor of Science degree from Rutgers University in 1950 and the PhD in psychology from Yale University in 1954. After a term of teaching at Ohio State University, he was inducted into the United States Army during the Korean War. Following discharge from the Army in 1957, Kagan became senior scientist at the Fels Research Institute in Yellow Springs, OH, where his major work involved analyzing a large corpus of longitudinal data on children who were followed from birth to adolescence and assessed again when they were young adults. The results of this work, in collaboration with Howard Moss, revealed that preservation of individual differences in this relatively typical middle-class sample did not emerge until after six or seven years of age. A summary of the project was published in a book entitled *Birth to Maturity,* which won the Hofheimer Prize of the American Psychiatric Association.

Kagan went to Harvard in 1964 as professor of psychology with the hope of building a graduate program in developmental psychology within the Arts and Sciences faculty. After 36 years of teaching at Harvard, Kagan will retire from teaching responsibilities in June of 2000 but will continue as a research professor.

Kagan's work at Harvard can be divided into three phases. The first studies probed the maturation of a small number of fundamental human competences that emerge in all children during the first two years of life. These include recognition memory at three to four months, the ability to retrieve the past between seven and 12 months, awareness of self in the middle of the second year, and, finally, a moral sense which emerges toward the end of the second year. These discoveries were summarized in the books *Change and Continuity in Infancy* and *The Second Year.*

Kagan spent a sabbatical year in 1972–73 working in an isolated Mayan Indian village in Northwest Guatemala. His observations of infants and children in this isolated site motivated him to challenge the view, which was popular among many American developmental psychologists in the early 1970s, that lack of variety in visual and auditory stimulation during the first year of life could permanently compromise the child's cognitive development. The infants in this village were deprived of a great deal of stimulation because of cultural mores, but the older children were cognitively and affectively competent. This discovery supported Kagan's growing belief that the basic human competences mature in all children under all but the most aversive conditions.

The second phase of research involved an extensive study of the effects of daycare on young infants in collaboration with P. Zelazo and R. Kearsley. Because large numbers of American mothers with young children were entering the workforce, Congress was considering, during the early 1970s, establishing daycare centers even though it was not clear whether these experiences would be harmful to young infants. The project revealed minimal differences between infants raised in a daycare center and those raised at home. However, the data also revealed the existence of stable tempera-mental differences among infants, whether they were raised in a daycare center or at home. This finding provided the incentive for the third phase of work at Harvard.

Kagan has been working for over 20 years on the temperamental categories called "behaviorally inhibited" and "behaviorally uninhibited" to the unfamiliar. The evidence has revealed that four-month-old infants who show a combination of vigorous motor activity and irritability to unfamiliar stimulation, presumably due to low thresholds of excitability in limbic areas, are prone to become shy, fearful, timid children. Infants who show the complementary characteristics of minimal motor activity and minimal irritability to stimulation are biased to become sociable, relatively fearless children. These qualities show modest preservation through ten years of age.

Kagan has received a reasonable number of honors, including the Distinguished Scientist Award for Research from the American Psychological Association and the Society for Research in Child Development; Kenneth Craik Award of St. Johns College, Cambridge University; Wilbur Cross Medal from Yale University; the C. Anderson Aldrich Award of the American Academy of Pediatrics; and the G. Stanley Hall Award given by Division 7 of the American Psychological Association. Kagan is a member of the Institute of Medicine of the National Academy of Sciences and a fellow of the American Academy of Arts and Sciences. Kagan's scholarship is marked by a probing skepticism toward premises that are in accord with the deep ethical biases of Western society but fail the criterion of sound empirical support. His recent book entitled *Three Seductive Ideas* contains an analysis of three such pleasing assumptions.

STAFF

KANDEL, ERIC R.

Eric R. Kandel was born in Vienna, Austria, and immigrated to the United States in 1939. He received a BA at Harvard College in 1952 and an MD at the New York University School of Medicine in 1956. After internship, Kandel did three years of postdoctoral research in the Laboratory of Neurophysiology at the National Institutes of Health (NIH), working on the cell biology of the hippocampus. From 1960 to 1962 and from 1963 to 1964 he took residency training in psychiatry at the Massachusetts Mental Health Center, Harvard Medical School. He spent 1962 to 1963 as a National Science Foundation postdoctoral fellow at the Institute Marey in Paris, working on the marine snail Aplysia with Ladislav Tauc. Kandel then returned to the Harvard Medical School in 1963 as a faculty member of the Department of Psychiatry. In 1965, Kandel moved to New York University as associate professor and in 1968 attained the rank of professor. In 1974, he was recruited to the College of Physicians and Surgeons of Columbia University as the founding director of the Center for Neurobiology and Behavior. He became a university professor in 1983 and a senior investigator of the Howard Hughes Medical Institute a year later. In addition to being a professor in psychiatry, physiology, and cellular biophysics, Kandel is currently a professor in the Department of Biochemistry and Molecular Biophysics at Columbia.

Until the late 1950s, investigations of learning and memory storage were dominated by behavioral approaches that tended to treat the brain as a black box. To overcome the technical obstacles that had previously kept the study of learning beyond the reach of a cell and molecular biological analysis, Kandel turned to a simple invertebrate animal, the marine snail "Aplysia," in an attempt to use the large, readily identifiable neurons of this animal to work out elementary neural circuits that could be modified by learning. In this animal, Kandel and his colleagues were able to describe a simple behavior, the gill-withdrawal reflex, to analyze its neural circuit in terms of its constituent nerve cells, and to discover elements in the circuit that were modifiable by learning. By developing a cell and molecular biological approach to these simple forms of learning in Aplysia and then using genetics to extend this approach to more complex forms of learning in the mouse, Kandel opened up the molecular study of long-term synaptic plasticity and its relation to learning and memory storage.

In Aplysia, Kandel and his colleagues analyzed three simple forms of learning: habituation, sensitization, and associative classical conditioning. They thereby established the first important links between cellular and molecular events in individual neurons and behavior of the whole organism. Specifically, Kandel and Vincent Castellucci provided the first direct evidence that learning leads to changes in the strength of specific synaptic connections and that the persistence of these changes contributes to memory storage. Moreover, Kandel found that the same synaptic connections could be modulated in opposite ways by different learning processes and could participate in the storage of different forms of memory. The same synaptic connection could be depressed by habituation and facilitated by sensitization and classical conditioning.

Kandel next discovered that, whereas short-term memory involves alterations in the strength of pre-existing connections, long-term memory involves structural changes. To analyze both the short- and long-term memory storage mechanisms in molecular terms, Kandel focused on behavioral sensitization. Sensitization is a form of learning in which an animal learns to strengthen its reflex responses to previously neutral stimuli following the repeated presentation of an aversive stimulus. Kandel, Castellucci, Tom Carew, and William Frost found that an aversive stimulus to the tail of Aplysia activates serotonergic and other modulatory systems that lead to short- and long-term memory for sensitization. These forms of memory are mirrored by the short- and long-term strengthening of the synaptic connections between the sensory and motor neurons that mediate this reflex. This direct monosynaptic component was examined not only in the intact animal, but also in a single sensory neuron cultured with its target postsynaptic motor neuron. At this cultured synapse, Kandel, Pier Giorgio Montarolo, and Samuel Schacher found that one pulse of serotonin, the key transmitter released in vivo by modulatory neurons activated by

the sensitizing tail stimuli, induced short-term facilitation lasting only minutes by activating the two intracellular signaling pathways: (a) cyclic AMP and the cyclic AMP-dependent protein kinase, and (b) protein kinase C. In contrast, 5 spaced pulses of serotonin elicited a long-term facilitation lasting several days. With 5 pulses of serotonin, the cAMP-dependent protein kinase recruits still another signaling pathway, the MAP kinase as pathway with the result that both translocate to the nucleus. Here they activate a transcription factor CREB-1 leading to the induction of a set of immediate-response genes that activate effector genes, resulting in the growth of new synaptic connections. In the course of this work, Kandel made the surprising discovery that long-term memory is normally constrained by a set of genetic inhibitory processes (memory suppressor genes) that determine the ease with which short-term memory is converted to long-term memory. One particularly dramatic inhibitory constraint is an inhibitory transcription factor called CREB-2. CREB-2 acts to inhibit the actions of the activator CREB-1 and therefore blocks long-term facilitation. Removal of the repressor gave rise to immediate long-term facilitation. The same PKA, CREB-1, CREB-2 pathway has been identified in Drosophila using a completely different strategy.

Kandel and colleagues Craig Bailey and David Glanzman next discovered that long-term but not short-term memory is associated with growth (or retraction) of synaptic connections made by the sensory neuron. There is an increase in the number of synaptic contacts with behavioral sensitization as well as with serotonin. The growth process is associated with a down-regulation at the membrane of a set of immunoglobulin-related cell adhesion molecules (apCAMs) homologous to the vertebrate neural cell adhesion molecule NCAM. Conversely, there is a decrease in the number of synaptic contacts with long-term memory for habituation.

The requirement for transcription during long-lasting forms of synaptic plasticity has raised the question of whether the critical cellular unit of synaptic plasticity is the cell and its nucleus or the synapse. If it is the synapse, then there must be a set of mechanisms that allows the products of gene expression to alter synaptic strength at some synapses independently of others made by the same cell. To address this question, Kelsey Martin, Andrea Casadio, and Kandel have developed a new culture system consisting of a single Aplysia sensory neuron with a bifurcated neuron making synaptic contact with two spatially-separated target motor neurons. By perfusing serotonin onto the synaptic connections made on only one of the motor neurons, Kandel and his colleagues have found that a single axonal branch is able to undergo both short-term and long-term synapse-specific facilitation. The long-term synapse-specific facilitation produced by repeated local exposure to serotonin involves the growth of new synaptic connections at the serotonin-treated, but not at the untreated, branch. These studies also made the interesting finding that the establishment of long-term synapse-specific facilitation requires local protein synthesis. This led Kandel to examine protein synthesis in the sensory neuron axons deprived of their cell bodies.

The ability to construct genetically modified mice provided Kandel and his colleagues an opportunity to ask the question: Does the same signaling pathway play a role in plasticity and in explicit forms of memory storage in the mammalian brain? Complex explicit forms of memory are concerned with a memory for facts and events and require the medial temporal lobe and a structure lying deep to it called the hippocampus. Study of these mutant mice by Kandel and colleagues Seth Grant, Tom O'Dell, and Mark Mayford, and by Tonegawa and his laboratory, soon showed that genetic manipulation of any one of several kinases, including Ca2+/calmodulin-dependent protein kinase IIa (CaMKIIa) and the tyrosine kinase fyn, interferes with long-term potentiation (LTP), an activity-dependent form of synaptic plasticity in the hippocampus as well as with behavioral explicit memory.

Prior to Kandel's entry into the field, studies of LTP in the hippocampus had focused primarily on an early, transient phase (E-LTP) that lasts about an hour. Study of both amnesic patients and experimental animals has revealed, however, that the role of the hippocampus in memory storage extends from weeks to months, suggesting that a longer-lasting form of hippocampal synaptic plasticity may be required for LTP. Together with Frey and Huang, Kandel explored the major synaptic pathways in the hippocampus—the perforant pathway, the mossy fiber pathway, and the Schaffer collateral pathway. They found that in all three pathways, a single train gives rise to conventional LTP that lasts one or more hours. This is the sort of LTP that has been studied by others. It does not require new protein synthesis and it is mediated by phosphorylation—the addition of a phosphate group to proteins—mediated by CaM kinase IIa, fyn, and other second-messenger kinases. By contrast, repeated trains bring out the novel, late phase of LTP (L-LTP) which requires new RNA and protein synthesis, and is triggered by the cAMP-dependent protein kinase (PKA). In contrast to E-LTP, which lasts only an hour, the late phase of LTP (L-LTP) lasts unchanged for up to 10 hrs in hippocampal slices.

To address the question of how this late phase of LTP maps onto long-term memory, Abel and Kandel expressed a transgene that specifically inhibits the cyclic AMP-dependent protein kinase, and found that although these genetically modified animals had a perfectly normal early phase of LTP in the Schaffer collateral pathway, they have a selective defect in the late phase of LTP (L-LTP). Moreover, these animals learn normally and have perfectly good short-term memory, but have a selective defect in long-term memory. Earlier studies by Silva and his colleagues had shown a similar outcome using a knockout of several isoforms of CREB. The correlation between long-term memory and the late phase of LTP in the Schaffer collateral pathway in the R(AB) transgenic mice suggests not only that L-LTP maps onto long-term memory, but also that the Schaffer collateral pathway is an important component of the system that stores long-term memory.

The studies in Drosophila, Aplysia, and mice taken together with parallel studies in Drosophila by Benzer, Quinn, Davis, and Tully suggest that these quite different types of memory processes, involving distinct neuronal systems for storage, share a common set of molecular mechanisms for the consolidation of short-term to long-term memory.

Since LTP is an artificially induced change in synaptic strength produced by electrical stimulation at high frequency of synaptic pathways, it became important to address the question: Is this form of synaptic plasticity relevant physiologically? If so, how does it affect the normal processing of information for memory storage in the hippocampus? The first insight into the physiological function of LTP in information processing has emerged from studies of the place cells in the hippocampus by Kandel in collaboration with Robert Muller and Alex Rotenberg, and independently by Tonegawa and Matt Wilson. Kandel and Mayford had earlier found that mice that express a constitutively active form of the calcium/calmodulin-dependent protein kinase have a defect in a certain component of LTP and in spatial memory. Together with Rotenberg and Muller, Kandel now found that these mice also have a defect in the ability of the pyramidal cells to represent space. In wild-type mice a field is formed in a new environment within minutes, and once formed it is stable in that environment for days. Mutant mice form normal fields, but every time the mouse is removed from a space and then reintroduced into the same space, those cells that were previously active in that space form different fields. This instability of place cells in the mutant mice is reminiscent of the memory defect in H. M. and other patients with lesions of the medial temporal lobe. Even after these patients repeatedly entered a new space, they acted as if they had never entered it before. These discoveries by the Kandel and the Tonegawa laboratories provided the first evidence that LTP is important for fine-tuning the appropriate properties of place cells that are necessary for the maintenance of a coherent spatial map.

Finally, Mayford and Kandel have developed methods for regional and regulated expression of transgenes restricted to specific regions of the mouse forebrain. In collaborative experiments with Tonegawa and Kandel's former post-doc, Joe Tsien, these methods have now been extended to obtain region-specific expression restricted to the CA1 region. These new methods should allow a detailed dissection of the specific regions in the medial lobe system essential for the various components of explicit memory storage.

By these means, Kandel and his colleagues have helped to demystify the study of simple forms of learning and memory storage in both invertebrates and mice, and to place them squarely within the context of modern cell and molecular biology.

For these achievements, Kandel was elected to membership in the National Academy of Sciences in 1974. He also is a corresponding member of the Academy of Science and Literature, Mainz, Germany (1988) and the German Academy of Science, Leopoldina; and a foreign associate of the French Academy of Sciences. He has received honorary degrees from Jewish Theological Seminary, Hahnemann University, State University of New York–Stony Brook, Johns Hopkins University, Mount Sinai Medical Center, Northwestern University, University of Vienna, and University of Edinburgh.

Kandel has been honored with the Henry L. Moses Research Award; the Lester N. Hofheimer Prize for Research; the Lucy G. Moses Prize for Research in Basic Neurology; the Solomon A. Berson Medical Alumni Achievement Award in Basic Science; the Karl Spencer Lashley Prize in Neurobiology; The Dickson Prize in Biology and Medicine; the New York Academy of Sciences Award in Biological and Medical Sciences; the Albert Lasker Basic Medical Research Award; the Lewis S. Rosenstiel Award for Distinguished Work in Basic Medical Research; the Howard Crosby Warren Medal; the American Association of Medical Colleges Award for Distinguished Research in the Biomedical Sciences; the

Special Presidential Commendation of the American Psychiatric Association; the Gairdner International Award for Outstanding Achievement in Medical Science; the National Medal of Science; the J. Murray Luck Award for Scientific Reviewing; the Gold Medal for Scientific Merit; the Distinguished Service Award of the American Psychiatric Association; the Award in Basic Science of the American College of Physicians; the Pasarow Foundation Award in Neuroscience; the Diploma Internacional Cajal; the Bristol Myers Squibb Award for Distinguished Achievement in Neuroscience Research; the John P. McGovern Lectureship Award in Behavioral Neuroscience; the Warren Triennial Prize; the Jean-Louis Signoret's Prize on Memory; the Harvey Prize of the Technion in Israel; the F. O. Schmitt Medal and Prize in Neuroscience; the Isaac Ray Decade of Excellence Award; the Mayor's Award for Excellence in Science and Technology; the Stevens Triennial Prize; the New York Academy of Medicine Award; the Gerard Prize for Outstanding Achievement in Neuroscience; the Charles A. Dana Award for Pioneering Achievement in Health; and the Wolf Prize in Biology and Medicine.

STAFF

KANT, IMMANUEL (1724–1804)

Educated at Königsberg, Immanual Kant spent most of his career as a professor of philosophy there. One of the most influential philosophers of the 18th century, he dominated philosophy for generations thereafter. His *Critique of Pure Reason* (1781) and his *Anthroponomy* (1798) contain what implications his philosophy had for psychology.

Kant represented the viewpoint of the German rational philosophers. He had read the British empiricists—in particular David Hume—and agreed that known objects were phenomena of consciousness and not realities independent of the mind. He disagreed with the empiricist argument that knowledge amounted to nothing more than mere bundles of sensation. For Kant, knowledge was characterized by a priori principles. Consciousness of time and extension in space were real enough, but not the result of mere bodily sensations. The way humans perceived the world was already predetermined. Thus Kant advanced a nativistic conception of space perception.

Kant rejected the mind as mental substance. Mental processes could not be measured, since they had only the dimension of time and not space. Psychology could never be an experimental science. He did not reject a conception of mind as such, but considered it a means whereby concepts could be known. The mind ordered perceptual phenomena through innate principles. The mind was active and took the material from the world and ordered it into conceptual phenomena. "Apperception" was the term Kant used for the mind's perceiving, assimilating, and interpreting new experiences. This was all part of the nativism which stressed certain inborn ways of knowing and perceiving that which was true and not dependent only on sensations.

The presupposition that perceptions could not be broken down into divisible forms became a basic premise of Gestalt psychology of the 20th century. Kant's nativism also was taken up by Gestalt psychologists in what they referred to as the "primitive organization of experience." This meant that we tend to perceive things in natural ways not dependent on previous experience or learning. This is related also to Noam Chomsky's linguistic theory. Other reflections of nativism in perception are found in the work of the animal ethologists, and in experiments with perception of infants that propose that certain perceptions of depth are innate.

R. W. LUNDIN
Wheaton, Illinois

KASLOW, FLORENCE W.

Florence W. Kaslow is an internationally known and respected teacher, supervisor, consultant, therapist, guest lecturer, and workshop leader. A PhD from Bryn Mawr College (1969), she is in independent practice as a therapist, mediator, coach, and family business consultant in Palm Beach Gardens, Florida. She is also director of the Florida Couples and Family Institute; an adjunct professor of medical psychology, Department of Psychiatry, at Duke University Medical School in Durham, North Carolina; and a visiting professor of psychology at Florida Institute of Technology in Melbourne, Florida. She was a lecturer in the Department of Psychiatry at Harvard University Medical School in 1992 and 1997.

Kaslow is board certified in clinical, family, and forensic psychology from the American Board of Professional Psychology (ABPP), and in sexology from the American Board of Sexology. She is a fellow of numerous American Psychological Association (APA) Divisions, the American Association for Marriage and Family Therapy (AAMFT), and other organizations. She has served as a site visitor for both organizations and has traveled throughout the United States, Argentina, Austria, Brazil, Canada, England, Finland, Germany, Hungary, Israel, Japan, Mexico, Norway, Poland, Russia, South Africa, and Sweden, doing workshops and guest lecturing on a variety of relationship-focused topics. She served as first president of the International Family Therapy Association (1987–1990) and continues to serve as a member-at-large on its board of directors. Currently she is president of the International Academy of Family Psychology (1998–2002), and of the American Board of Family Psychology of ABPP (1996–2000).

Kaslow was a professor and chief of the forensic psychology/psychiatry section at Hahnemann Medical University in Philadelphia from 1973 to 1980. While there, she initiated and served as co-director of the PhD/JD program in psychology and law, which Hahnemann co-sponsored with Villanova Law School. She was the first president of the American Board of Forensic Psychology, from 1977 to 1980, and of the American Academy of Forensic Psychologists. She has been a board member of APA Division 41 (Psychology and Law) and is a past president of both Division 43 (Family Psychology) and Division 46 (Media Psychology). She has served on the APA Committee on International Relations in Psychology (CIRP), and is a member of the Family Firm Institute's International Committee.

She is a past editor of the *Journal of Marital and Family Ther-*

apy, and is currently on the editorial boards of JMFT and such other journals as *Psychotherapy, Contemporary Family Therapy, Journal of Divorce, Mediation Quarterly, Child Clinical Psychology, Journal of Family Psychology,* and *Journal of Family Psychotherapy.* She was editor of the family law issues in the Family Therapy Practice section of the *American Journal of Family Therapy* for many years. She has edited, authored, or co-authored 18 books and has contributed chapters to over 50 others. Over 150 of her articles have been published in professional journals in the United States and abroad.

Kaslow served as first president of the Florida Association of Professional Family Mediators (1984–1986). She conducts training workshops for potential mediators in the United States and abroad, and was a board member and treasurer of the (National) Academy of Family Mediators (1985–1987).

From 1973 to 1996 Kaslow was a consultant to various Departments of Psychiatry of the U.S. Navy and Air Force, training residents and other mental health personnel in understanding and treating military families. Some of this work is reflected in her books, *The Military Family: Dynamics and Treatment,* co-edited with Admiral Richard Ridenour, MD (1984), and in *The Military Family in Peace and War* (1993).

Other recent books include *Voices in Family Psychology, Vols. I and II* (1990); *Projective Genograms* (1995); *Handbook of Relational Diagnosis and Dysfunctional Family Patterns* (1996); *Painful Partings: Divorce and Its Aftermath,* with Dr. L. L. Schwartz (1997); *Handbook of Couple and Family Forensic Issues* (1999); and *Together Through Thick and Thin: A Multinational Picture of Long Term Marriages* (with Dr. S. Sharlin and Ms. H. Hammerschmidt) (in press).

Dr. Kaslow has received numerous honors, including:

- 1985   Who's Who in America (Continuous since)
- 1986   Family Psychologist of the Year Award/APA Division of Family Psychology
- 1987   Election to the National Academies of Practice as a Distinguished Practitioner in Psychology
- 1989   APA's Distinguished Contribution to Applied Psychology Award
- 1991   AAMFT's Outstanding Contribution to the Field of Family Therapy Award
- 1992   APA's Council of International Relations in Psychology (CIRP) Award for distinguished contribution to international psychology in the arena of practice
- 1994   ABPP's Award for Outstanding Contribution and Distinguished Service to the Profession
- 1995   Who's Who in the World
- 2000   APA's Award for Distinguished Contributions to the International Advancement of Psychology

Dr. Kaslow has made numerous guest appearances on national and local television and radio programs. Since August 1993 she has been featured on a weekly *Voice of America* (VOA) show entitled "Psychological Issues," which is beamed by satellite to many coun-

tries, as an acknowledged media expert she has trained other professionals in media presentation preparation and techniques.

Dr. Kaslow has served as a Book Series editor for both Brunner/Mazel (now a subdivision of Taylor & Francis), John Wiley & Sons, Inc, & A.P.A.

KAZDIN, ALAN E.

Alan E. Kazdin completed his BA at San Jose State University in 1967 and in 1970 received his doctorate in psychology (clinical/experimental psychopathology) from Northwestern University, where he remained as an assistant professor for one year. In 1971 he took a position as assistant professor of psychology at the Pennsylvania State University, where he remained until 1979. In 1980, he became professor of child psychiatry at the University of Pittsburgh School of Medicine, where he directed an inpatient treatment service for disturbed children. In 1989, he moved to Yale University, where he has been professor and chairman of psychology and director of the Yale Child Conduct Clinic, an outpatient treatment service for children and families.

From 1974 through 1978, he worked on a project for the National Academy of Sciences to document the evolution of scientific findings and theoretical approaches leading to the development of behavior modification. The product was published in a book, *History of Behavior Modification: Experimental Foundations of Contemporary Research.* This was the only large-scale historical effort to chart the development of behavior modification. In 1977 and 78, he spent a year at the Center for Advanced Study in the Behavioral Sciences (Stanford, CA) and collaborated with a group of colleagues (S. Agras, N. Azrin, W. Mischel, S. Rachman, and G. T. Wilson) on the status, accomplishments, and limitations of behavior therapy. Two of the products of this collaboration were *Evaluation of Behavior Therapy: Issues, Evidence, and Research Strategies* and *Behavior Therapy: Toward an Applied Clinical Science.*

Kazdin has served as editor for a number professional journals, including *Behavior Therapy* (1979–1983), *Journal of Consulting and Clinical Psychology* (1985–1990), *Psychological Assessment* (1989–1991), *Clinical Psychology: Science and Practice* (1994–1998), and *Current Directions in Psychological Science* (1999–   ). He has served on the editorial boards of over 40 journals. He has also edited an annual book series on *Advances in Clinical Child Psychology* (1977–1992, with B. Lahey) and a book series on *Developmental Clinical Psychology and Psychiatry* (1983–1998). In addition, he was editor-in-chief of the *Encyclopedia of Psychology* (2000), an 8-volume work, under the auspices of the American Psychological Association and Oxford University Press.

He has received several honors, notably a Research Scientist Award and a MERIT Award from the National Institute of Mental Health; an Award for Distinguished Scientific Contribution to Clinical Psychology (1992), an Award for Distinguished Professional Contribution to Clinical Child Psychology (1995), and a Distinguished Scientist Award (1999) from the American Psychological Association; and an Award for Outstanding Research Contribution by an Individual (1998) from the Association for Advancement of Behavior Therapy. He has served as president for the Association for Advancement of Behavior Therapy (1977–1978).

His research has focused primarily on the development of behavioral and cognitive-behavioral interventions. During his graduate training, he worked in a treatment and rehabilitation facility for emotionally disturbed and mentally retarded children, adolescents, and adults, and was given the task to develop interventions. This contributed to his interest in behavioral interventions in home, school, institutions, and the community at large. This interest was reflected in subsequent writings, including *The Token Economy* and *Behavior Modification in Applied Settings*.

At the Pennsylvania State University his research focused on interventions for children in the schools and institutions for the mentally retarded and for adults with social withdrawal and anxiety. When he moved to the University of Pittsburgh School of Medicine, his research focused more exclusively on childhood psychopathology. He began a series of studies on depression and antisocial behavior in clinically referred youths. The studies led to additional work on suicidality, hopelessness, child abuse, fire setting, and anxiety disorders.

The majority of Kazdin's work has focused on treatment of aggressive and antisocial children referred for inpatient or outpatient treatment. This work has spanned a period of approximately 20 years. A series of studies evaluated the effectiveness of problem-solving skills training and parent management training with children (ages 2–13), the factors that contribute to therapeutic change, and more recently models of delivering treatment to optimize treatment effectiveness. Among the main findings are that variants of treatment produce clinically important change in such children at home and at school and that multiple factors predict treatment outcomes including severity and scope of child dysfunction, parent psychopathology stress, and socioeconomic disadvantage. Several factors that influence outcome, including parent perceptions of treatment, parent relationship with the therapist, and stress during the course of treatment, are of special interest because efforts to address these in therapy are likely to influence participation in and adherence to treatment and clinical outcomes. His writings have focused on evaluation of child and adolescent psychotherapy more broadly including recent works lamenting the paucity of theory, the endless proliferation of unevaluated treatments (550+), and the need for different ways of conducting treatment research. These are outlined in papers and a recent book, *Psychotherapy for Children and Adolescents: Directions for Research and Practice*.

Over the years, Kazdin's writings and research program have generated over 500 publications, including over 30 authored or edited books. Many of these writings have focused on methodology and research design. During graduate training, he imprinted on the notion that the answers to critical research questions depend quite heavily on the methods and statistics used to evaluate them. His writings have attempted to elaborate the practices, methods, and foibles of the ways in which research is planned, executed, and reported. This emphasis is illustrated in *Single-Case Research Designs: Methods for Clinical and Applied Settings, Research Design in Clinical Psychology,* and *Methodological Issues and Strategies in Clinical Research*. Kazdin's contributions reflect the melding of intervention research with these interests in evaluation methodology more generally. Key to this is his emphasis on the importance of

evaluation in intervention work, whether in research or clinical practice.

STAFF

KELLER, FRED S. (1899–1996)

Fred S. Keller received the BS from Tufts College, the MA and PhD (1931) from Harvard University. He taught psychology at Colgate University from 1931 to 1938, and at Columbia University from 1938 to 1964, when he became professor emeritus. On leave from Columbia in 1961, he taught at the University of São Paulo, in Brazil. In 1964, he helped to organize the psychology department at the new University of Brasília. He spent the next 3 years at Arizona State University, and in 1968, he went to Western Michigan University for 5 years, which were interrupted by short appointments at Texas Christian University and Colorado State. From 1974 to 1976 he was at Georgetown University's Center for Personalized Instruction. In 1990 he became an adjunct research professor at the University of North Carolina at Chapel Hill.

His contributions to psychology include *Principles of Psychology* (with W. N. Schoenfeld), *The Definition of Psychology, Learning (Reinforcement Theory), Summers and Sabbaticals, Pedagogue's Progress,* and *The Keller Plan Handbook: PSI* (with J. G. Sherman). He has published approximately 80 papers on learning, training, or education.

His honors include the Certificate of Merit from President Truman in 1948; several honorary degrees (Long Island University, Colgate University, Western Michigan University, and the University of Brasília) and awards from various organizations in the United States and abroad (Brazil, Canada, China/Taiwan, Mexico, Peru, and Venezuela).

STAFF

KELLY, GEORGE A. (1905–1967)

George A. Kelly attended four different colleges (and spent an exchange year at Edinburgh), receiving the PhD from the State University of Iowa in 1931. He spent most of his career building the clinical psychology program at Ohio State University with the assistance of Julian Rotter.

Kelly's theory of personal constructs is a broad, inclusive personality theory based upon the notion that each individual attempts to anticipate and control his or her environment. Behavior is conceptualized as a question. Will mother spank me if I have a piece of cake as a snack, or can I talk her into just a scolding? Is Jeff as nice as he seems, or does he have a mean streak? Only by experiencing the world can individuals obtain answers that become their personal constructs, their view of the world.

Personal constructs specific to the individual and created by the individual can be exemplified by the following: A spanking is: (a) to the parent, a corrective action that benefits the child; (b) to the child, an unfortunate part of a random world that must be tolerated; (c) to a social worker, a cruel and ineffective punishment; (d) to a preacher, an extension of divine judgment to a sinful earth. Each point of view, each personal construct, approximates truth. To understand the world, one must be able to understand the points of view of others. Set down in a formal postulate with 11 corollaries in his 1955 book, Kelly's theory is difficult to classify and to contrast with other views. Sechrest (1977) describes it as having lots of second cousins, but no siblings.

Kelly always sought to develop a therapeutic technique, but had very little contact with severe pathology. Although known for his innovative fixed-role therapy (in which the client tries on a role much as one tries on new clothing at the store), Kelly used that technique for only a few selected clients. In his counseling, he was as flexible and varied in technique as was Carl Jung.

C. S. PEYSER
The University of the South

KILTS, CLINTON D.

Clinton D. Kilts received his BS degree (with high honors) from Michigan State University in 1973, majoring in zoology and minoring in Chemistry. Following a brief work experience in the pharmaceutical development and product testing business, Kilts applied for and was granted admission to the graduate training program in pharmacology and toxicology at Michigan State University. This career decision was based upon a perceived impact of pharmaceutics and the holistic scientific nature of the training program. Kilts was awarded his PhD in pharmacology and toxicology in 1979, then completed a postdoctoral training program in neuropharmacology under the mentorship of George Breese at the University of North Carolina. This postgraduate training experience emphasized further development in the quantitative analysis of drugs and neurotransmitters using gas chromatography/mass spectrometry (GC/MS) in the emerging technique of high-performance liquid chromatography/electrochemistry (HPLC/EC). A report describing a novel quantitative HPLC/EC analytic procedure in neurochemistry published during this time was recognized as a citation classic.

Kilts joined the faculty of Duke University in 1981. He began his academic career as a member of the Department of Psychiatry and organized and directed a clinical psychopharmacology laboratory that provided an analysis and consultation service in therapeutic and toxicological drug monitoring. He later joined the faculty of the Department of Pharmacology. Major accomplishments during his time at Duke included the further contribution of novel methods and approaches in neurochemistry and drug monitoring. Major accomplishments also included a careful and comprehensive description of the pharmacology, regulation, anatomy, and stress reactivity of dopamine-containing neurons innervating the rodent amygdaloid complex. Consistent research funding from the National Institute of Mental Health (NIMH) and the Scottish Rite Schizophrenia Research Foundation has enabled his research efforts.

Kilts' work in this area was recognized for its thorough nature and critical approach. During this time, Kilts also initiated a research program focusing on the development of animal genetic models of cognitive/behavioral deficits associated with schizophrenia. He rose to the rank of associate professor while at Duke and left to join the faculty at the Department of Psychiatry and Behavioral Sciences at the Emory University School of Medicine in 1992. In his last year at Duke, Kilts developed a research program in human functional brain imaging that better suited his evolving interest in a systems neuroscience approach to clinical problem solving. Since joining Emory University, he has expanded his relationship with the Emory Center for Positron Emission Tomography (PET), first as a user, later as the associate director for psychiatry, and most recently as the acting director of the Emory Center for PET. This technology proved well suited to Kilts' interest in systems and behavioral neuroscience. Broadly defined, this imaging technology was applied to the acquisition of new knowledge related to the neural correlates of social behavior. As a psychopharmacologist, Kilts' research in PET stressed its application to understanding both the basis of treatment response for psychiatric disorders and the basis of addiction processes. His own research has focused on imaging drug-motivational states associated with addiction and defining the neural processing underlying the pharmacotherapy of schizophrenia, Attention-Deficit/Hyperactivity Disorder, and social anxiety. In these associations with the Emory Center for PET, an expanding and necessary role in mentoring junior faculty and fellows in the use of functional imaging technology was undertaken. Most recently, PET and functional magnetic resonance imaging (fMRI) technology have been established as a converging point for Kilts' mutual interests in behavioral neuroscience and genetics. Kilts is a newly elected member of the American College of Neuropsychopharmacology.

STAFF

KINDLING

Kindling is the development of full-blown seizures to repeated subthreshold stimulation of the brain. In the classical sense it involves intracerebral electrical stimulation of various areas of brain, most typically the amygdala, with electric currents that are below those required to produce a local afterdischarge (AD). However, with repeated stimulation, the afterdischarge threshold is decreased (brain excitability is increased) and ADs begin to emerge with increasing duration and complexity, and to spread to other areas of the brain. This process is accompanied by a behavior seizure stage progression through stage I (behavioral arrest), stage II (head nodding and chewing movements), stage III (unilateral forepaw clonus), stage IV (bilateral forepaw clonus with rearing), stage V (rearing and falling), and, following sufficient numbers of stimulation, stage VI (major motor seizures in the absence of exogenous electrophysiological stimulation) (a true model of spontaneous epileptogenesis).

Kindling is obviously a model of seizure evolution and progression from triggered to spontaneous seizures. However, from the outset, Goddard and Douglas also described kindling as a model for neuronal learning and memory as the brain was showing increasing and long-lasting increases in responsivity to repetition of the same stimulus over time. This was apparent using a variety of electrophysiological and behavioral endpoints including lowering of the initial AD threshold, increasing AD duration and complexity, increasing spread to other areas of the brain, the concomitant progression of behavioral seizure stages evolution culminating in full-blown triggered seizures, and eventually spontaneous major motor seizures.

Much investigation has revealed a host of biochemical and structural changes associated with both the lasting kindled memory trace and shorter-lived compensatory or endogenous anticonvulsant mechanisms. Both of these processes involve a spatiotemporal evolving set of changes in first and second messenger systems, as well as in growth factors, immediate early genes (IEGs), and late effector genes (LEGs) ultimately associated with changes in neuronal excitability and the balance of neurotrophic and apoptotic processes. Thus, kindling appears to be a useful model for studying the complex cascade of changes in gene expression mediating biochemical and microstructural changes associated with neuronal learning and memory.

However, since seizure endpoints are not a common manifestation of most psychiatric illnesses, kindling must be considered a nonhomologous model and an analogy for related processes that are likely to occur in other neuroanatomical and biochemical systems that might be more pertinent to behavioral pathology short of a full-blown seizure endpoint. In this manner, the kindling analogy is used to help further characterize one course of the unipolar and bipolar illness which typically involves the occurrence of early stressors that are initially insufficient to precipitate a full-blown affective episode, but that, with stressor recurrence (parallel to repeated electrical stimulation kindling), may trigger an episode of depression or mania. With sufficient occurrence of these triggered affective episodes, they, too, may begin to occur in the absence of obvious psychosocial precipitants. The data of Kessing and Bolwig and colleagues have validated one of the many predictions based on the kindling model, in that the number of prior hospitalizations for depressive episodes is directly proportional to the vulnerability to a recurrence, as assessed by both incidence and latency to relapse.

Another potential use of the kindling model in conceptualizing some elements of neuropsychiatric disorders is in the realm of loss of therapeutic efficacy to a drug treatment via a tolerance mechanism. Initially, administration of anticonvulsants before each amygdala-kindled seizure is typically associated with a marked reduction or complete suppression of seizure manifestations, depending on the drug. However, with repeated drug administration prior to (but not after) each kindled stimulation, seizures eventually break through most pharmacological interventions based on pharmacodynamic (and not pharmacokinetic) alterations associated with the contingent tolerance.

Loss of efficacy via tolerance has increasingly been recognized as a problem in the treatment of a variety of neuropsychiatric illnesses, including trigeminal neuralgia, Panic Disorder, epilepsy, and the recurrent affective disorders. To the extent that there is parallelism between tolerance mechanisms across these diverse

syndromes, manipulations that are found to slow the development of tolerance to the anticonvulsant effects of drugs on amygdala-kindled seizures may provide hints to some of the molecular mechanisms involved and the maneuvers that may be assessed and directly tested in the clinical situation.

The data from the preclinical anticonvulsant tolerance studies of Weiss and associates suggest that tolerance is slowed by: use of higher rather than lower or only marginally effective doses; use of stable rather than escalating doses; use of higher potency drugs, such as valproate instead of carbamazepine or lamotrigine; initiating treatment early in the course of kindled seizure expression rather than late in its course; using combination strategies, such as combining carbamazepine and valproate at doses that for each alone would be associated with more rapid tolerance development.

In terms of approaching treatment when tolerance has already occurred, switching to drugs with different mechanisms of action may be most appropriate because these differently acting drugs are often not associated with cross-tolerance to the initial drug. When tolerance has occurred, returning to a previously effective agent after a period of time off that drug may also be helpful. Tolerance has been associated with the loss of selective endogenous anticonvulsant adaptations and with progression of the primary pathological processes of kindling. Hypothetically, a period of time off a drug would allow the endogenous compensatory adaptations to reemerge; this may be associated with renewed responsivity. Again, each of these potential approaches deserves consideration for its applicability to the clinical realm, and direct tests of the predictive validity of the model are needed. Some preliminary data are already supportive of some of the factors that might show loss of efficacy, such as the fact that lithium carbonate treatment instituted earlier in the course of bipolar illness is much more likely to be effective than when instituted later in the course of illness, after multiple episodes have occurred.

In summary, the development of kindled seizures to a previously subthreshold stimulation most clearly is a model of epileptogenesis, but may also be pertinent for considering molecular mechanisms and pharmacological interventions involved in the progression and treatment of a variety of other neuropsychiatric syndromes. Because the model is not behaviorally homologous for most of these syndromes, one must be particularly cautious about the direct inferences derived. The model would appear to be most useful in the area of conceptualization of mechanisms and interventions underlying syndrome progression and in its heuristic value toward new approaches to treatment and prevention.

SUGGESTED READING

Adamec, R. E. (1990). Does kindling model anything clinically relevant? *Biological Psychiatry, 27,* 249–279.

Clark, M., Post, R. M., Weiss, S. R., Cain, C. J., & Nakajima, T. (1991). Regional expression of c-fos mRNA in rat brain during the evolution of amygdala kindled seizures. *Brain Research and Molecular Brain Research, 11,* 55–64.

Goddard, G. V., McIntyre, D. C., & Leech, C. K. (1969). A permanent change in brain function resulting from daily electrical stimulation. *Experiments in Neurology, 25,* 295–330.

Goddard, G. V., & Douglas, R. M. (1975). Does the engram of kindling model the engram of normal long term memory? *Canadian Journal of Neurological Science, 2,* 385–394.

Kessing, L. V., Andersen, P. K., Mortensen, P. B., & Bolwig, T. G. (1998). Recurrence in affective disorder: I. Case register study. *British Journal of Psychiatry, 172,* 23–28.

Corcoran, M. E., & Moshe, S. L. (Eds.). (1998). *Kindling* (5th ed.). New York: Plenum.

McNamara, J. O. (1988). Pursuit of the mechanisms of kindling. *Trends in Neurological Science, 1,* 33–36.

Post, R. M., & Weiss, S. R. B. (1994). Kindling: Implications for the course and treatment of affective disorders. In K. Modigh, O. H. Robak, & T. Vestergaard (Eds.), *Anticonvulsants in psychiatry* (pp. 113–137). Stroud, UK: Wrightson Biomedical.

Post, R. M., & Weiss, S. R. B. (1996). A speculative model of affective illness cyclicity based on patterns of drug tolerance observed in amygdala-kindled seizures. *Molecular Neurobiology, 13,* 33–60.

Post, R. M., Weiss, S. R. B., Ketter, T. A., Denicoff, K. D., George, M. S., Frye, M. A., Smith, M. A., & Leverich, G. S. (1997). The kindling model: Implications for the etiology and treatment of mood disorders. *Current Review of Mood and Anxiety Disorders, 1,* 113–126.

Racine, R. (1978). Kindling: The first decade. *Neurosurgery, 3,* 234–252.

Sato, M., Racine, R. J., & McIntyre, D. C. (1990). Kindling: Basic mechanisms and clinical validity. *Electroencephalography and Clinical Neurophysiology, 76,* 459–472.

Weiss, S. R., & Post, R. M. (1994). Caveats in the use of the kindling model of affective disorders. *Toxicology and Indicators of Health, 10,* 421–447.

Weiss, S. R., & Post, R. M. (1998). Kindling: Separate vs. shared mechanisms in affective disorders and epilepsy. *Neuropsychobiology, 38,* 167–180.

R. M. POST
National Institute of Mental Health

KINSEY, ALFRED C. (1894–1956)

Alfred C. Kinsey received the BS from Bowdoin College. He received the ScD in biology from Harvard in 1920. His entire career was spent in the zoology department of Indiana University.

Kinsey's first study was of the behavior of birds in the rain. He published several biology texts, including one on research methodology. By 1938 he was the leading authority on the gall wasps of Mexico and Central America. His research had important implications for evolutionary theory.

While teaching a course at Indiana on marriage problems in the 1930s, he turned to the study of sexual behavior because of the lack of adequate information. His initial interviews were with individuals living in the central United States. His work showed sufficient promise that both the National Research Council and the Rockefeller Foundation supported more extensive surveys of sexual behavior. The Institute for Sex Research, affiliated with Indiana University, was founded in 1947. The next year the results of the research on males was published, followed by *Sexual Behavior in the Human Female* in 1953.

Authored by Kinsey and three colleagues, these works became popularly known as "the Kinsey reports." They provided the only quantified, thorough description of a large number of diverse human self-reports of sexual experience. Kinsey found a far wider variation in experience than anticipated. The data also put to rest many misconceptions about childhood sexuality, homosexuality, and the sexual arousal of females.

C. S. PEYSER
The University of the South

KINSEY INSTITUTE

The Kinsey Institute for Research in Sex, Gender and Reproduction is a not-for-profit corporation closely associated with Indiana University, Bloomington. It is the oldest continuously operating institution in the United States, and perhaps the world, focusing on sexuality research; the archiving of art, literature, and scientific materials on sexuality; and public and academic sexuality education.

ALFRED C. KINSEY AND THE ESTABLISHMENT OF THE INSTITUTE FOR SEX RESEARCH

The Institute for Sex Research, its original name, was established in 1947 by Alfred C. Kinsey, ScD (1894–1956), a professor of zoology and eminent entomologist known for his studies of gall wasps; and Herman B Wells, president of Indiana University (Christenson, 1971; Gathorne-Hardy, 1998). Its primary purpose was to protect confidential interviews from the jeopardy inherent in being archived in a state-owned university. Later, this protection extended to the unique archives of books, diaries, personal papers, arts, artifacts, and ephemera started by Kinsey as a research resource of historical, legal, and scientific information regarding sexuality.

The Institute's origins trace back to 1938, when Kinsey began to prepare lectures for a course on marriage requested by the Association of Women Students (Christenson, 1971). The scant data then available on human sexuality focused primarily on clinical populations, case studies of unusual behavior or opinion based on individual experience. Kinsey began questioning students about their sex lives in order to have some data on which to base his lectures about the biological aspects of sex and marriage. By that September, the first 50 questionnaires had been collected and the course was an immediate success. Kinsey quickly developed a 350-question face-to-face interview, the answers to which were encoded to protect subjects' confidentiality. The data collection, which began with students attending the marriage class, eventually extended to individuals from around the United States. Of more than

17,000 interviews conducted by the Institute from 1938 to 1956 (the original goal was 100,000 histories), 8,000 were done by Kinsey himself (Gebhard & Johnson, 1979). His application of social science techniques to the empirical documentation of sexual behavior was revolutionary (Reinisch, 1998).

In 1940, in response to pressure from Indiana politicians and the community, Kinsey was forced to choose between continuing the sexuality research and teaching the marriage course. He chose the research, abandoning his entomological studies and the popular course. By 1941, research support from the National Research Council's Committee for Research in the Problems of Sex, then being funded by the Rockefeller Foundation, permitted the assembly of a full-time multidisciplinary research team: biologist Clyde Martin, 1941; psychologist Wardell Pomeroy, 1943; and anthropologist Paul Gebhard, 1946 (Reinisch & Harter, 1994).

Following the establishment of the Institute to which Kinsey sold his developing library and art collections for one dollar, *Sexual Behavior in the Human Male* (Kinsey, Pomeroy, & Martin, 1948), based upon 5300 interviews with American men, was released by the medical publisher W. B. Saunders. This dry, academic tome, written for physicians and scientists, became a national and international bestseller, translated into a dozen languages. Publication of *Sexual Behavior in the Human Female* (Kinsey, Pomeroy, Martin, & Gebhard, 1953), reporting on 5940 American women, was also a national and international success. The samples described in the two "Kinsey Reports" can most accurately be characterized as primarily white, middle class, college-educated, and under 35 years of age, although the samples did include some older subjects and those of color. The data addressed many taboo subjects, including masturbation, extramarital relations, same-sex interactions, bisexual behavior, oral-genital sex, and prostitution, and they challenged contemporary views of rare or abnormal behavior by revealing that large portions of both American men and women had engaged in many of these activities. These data were still relied upon in the mid 1980s, when the emergence of AIDS demanded information on sexual behavior that was available nowhere else (Institute of Medicine/National Academy of Sciences, 1986).

The volume on female behavior caused a major public, religious, and political furor, perhaps because American society was not ready to see women as sexual beings. Congressman Carroll Reece's committee investigating tax-exempt foundations for their possible support of unAmerican activities targeted the Rockefeller Foundation for its funding of the Institute. The Congressional Record during this period contains a member's comment that anyone who studied the sexual behavior of Americans was paving the way for a communist takeover of the United States. In 1954, in order to protect its tax-exempt status, the Rockefeller Foundation withdrew its funding of all sex-related research including Kinsey's. To sustain the work, proceeds from the "Kinsey Reports" originally earmarked for an Institute endowment were used to pay staff salaries. Coincident with congressional pressure were legal expenses resulting from seizures by the U.S. Customs Service of sexually explicit materials shipped to the Institute's archives from around the world. In 1957, after Kinsey's death, the Institute's battle for the right to import erotic materials for scientific research

was won by eminent civil liberties attorney Harriet Pilpell in the landmark decision *United States v. 31 Photographs*. Kinsey's death at 62 of cardiac failure following pneumonia on August 25, 1956, was perhaps hastened by the necessity of coping with a voracious press, the conservative backlash, financial stress, and Kinsey's exhausting workdays.

THE LOW-PROFILE 1960S AND 1970S

Following Kinsey's death, the university chose Gebhard as director. For the next two decades, in response to the controversy that had surrounded the Institute, a lower public profile was maintained. The staff focused primarily on further analysis of the 18,000 interviews, publication of books from the database, and organization and expansion of the collections. *Pregnancy, Birth, and Abortion* (Gebhard et al., 1958), and *Sex Offenders: An Analysis of Types* (Gebhard et al., 1965) were published from the database, while books addressing erotic art and Victorian sexual culture were produced by both the staff and outside scholars. From the mid-1960s through the 1970s, research relating to the sociology of sexuality (Gagnon & Simon, 1973) and sexual morality (Klassen, Williams, & Levitt, 1989) and the psychological and social aspects of homosexuality (Bell & Weinberg, 1978) reflected the interests of the research staff. NIMH supported some library services and a directory, thesaurus, index, bibliographies; in addition, catalogues of sex-related materials and research were compiled.

EXPANSION OF THE KINSEY INSTITUTE FOR RESEARCH IN SEX, GENDER, AND REPRODUCTION

In 1981 the university mandated that the Institute be overseen by an independent board of trustees. They conducted an international search and, following Gebhard's retirement, in 1982 appointed June Machover Reinisch, a developmental biopsychologist, as the third director. Incorporating Reinisch's scientific interests and the recommendations of the trustees and outside consultants, the Institute's research program was expanded to include biomedical and psychobiological issues. Both to honor its founder and mark its broadened mission, in 1983 the Institute was renamed The Kinsey Institute for Research in Sex, Gender, and Reproduction. New research included two large cohort studies examining the long-term consequences of maternal hormone and drug treatment during pregnancy on the sexual and psychosexual development of offspring (Reinisch, Mortensen, & Sanders, 1993). The database compiled from these two linked studies represents the largest ever constructed in this area. The commitment to sexual behavior research was maintained with studies on high-risk sexual behavior related to transmission of AIDS and other STDs (Reinisch, Hill, Sanders, & Ziemba-Davis, 1995). A series of multidisciplinary international research symposia was convened at the Institute beginning in 1983, from which the Kinsey Institute Series of volumes (Oxford University Press) was published, addressing *Masculinity/Femininity* (1990), *Adolescence and Puberty* (1990), *Homosexuality/Heterosexuality* (1987), and *AIDS and Sex* (1990).

The Institute's research and public outreach suggested the persistence of many myths and misinformation about sexuality and reproduction in our society. In response, a nationally representative survey of Americans empirically confirmed pangenerational ignorance regarding many sexuality and reproductive issues (Reinisch, Sanders, Hill, & Ziemba-Davis, 1991). Based upon the 1982 mandate of the Institute's trustees and university administrators to raise the Institute's public profile, and since the Institute's research was largely supported by public funds, mechanisms were sought to provide the public with scientific information on sex, gender, and reproduction. An internationally syndicated newspaper column, "The Kinsey Report," was launched in 1984 to respond to the public's questions. Published thrice weekly for nine years, more than 2,900 questions sent by readers from around the world were answered using current research findings. In 1990, the Institute produced its third bestseller and first book specifically designed for the general public (Reinisch with Beasley, 1990), *The Kinsey Institute New Report on Sex.* It has also been published in Taiwanese, French, German, Japanese, Korean, Chinese, British, and Spanish editions.

Central to the Institute's work are its collections of tens of thousands of print items, private papers and diaries, photographs, fine art objects, artifacts, popular ephemera, various data archives, films, and videotapes (Reinisch, 1993). These archives provide scholars with diverse materials encompassing all aspects of human sexuality from all eras, regions, and cultures. In addition to their continued growth, the years from 1982 to 1993 included appointment of the first curators for the collections and establishment of full-time library technical and information services. Beginning in the mid-1980s, a three-fold expansion and renovation of the facilities was initiated and completed, including storage, preservation, and exhibition areas for the library and archives and laboratory and office space. Staff was tripled; patron workspace expanded and climate controls, stacks, archival storage, and a new art gallery were installed. The process of inputting the library and archives catalogs online was begun.

RECENT YEARS

In 1993, Stephanie A. Sanders, a psychologist and the Institute's associate director, was appointed interim director upon Reinisch's retirement, election to the board of trustees, and appointment as first Director Emerita. The Institute's education, archival, and patron service programs continued to be built and major studies on high-risk sexual behavior (Sanders & Reinisch, 1999) and the effects of prenatal drug exposure on adult behavior (Reinisch, Sanders, Mortensen, & Rubin, 1995) were completed. In 1995, John Bancroft, a British psychiatrist and renowned sex researcher, was appointed as the fourth director. The Institute's research again underwent a change of direction, emphasizing study of the spectrum of sexual functioning, behavioral response to hormonal contraception, and sexuality research methodology. The first Kinsey Institute-associated clinics addressing sexual problems and menstrual cycle related problems were established in collaboration with Indiana University. A continuation of the symposium series began in 1995 with meetings on Researching Sexual Behavior: Methodological Issues (Bancroft, 1997), followed by The Role of Theory in Sex Research (Bancroft, 1999), and Sexuality in Midlife and Beyond. Renovation and expansion of the collections facilities continued and computerization of library catalogs was completed. Today active involvement in and future planning of graduate and professional education programs are underway.

Surviving more than five often turbulent decades, during which it was regularly under attack from societal forces demanding silence on sexual issues, The Kinsey Institute has remained the premiere academic research institute focused on the interdisciplinary study of sex, gender, and reproduction. It continues to develop and maintain extraordinary archives for a wide variety of artistic, cultural, and scientific materials related to human sexuality, which remain an unparalleled resource for future generations of scholars, students, and professionals.

REFERENCES

Bancroft, J. (Ed.). (1997). *Researching sexual behavior: Methodological issues.* Bloomington: Indiana University Press.

Bancroft, J. (Ed.). (1999). *The role of theory in sex research.* Bloomington: Indiana University Press.

Bell, A. P., & Weinberg, M. S. (1978). *Homosexualities: A study of diversity among men and women.* New York: Simon & Schuster.

Christenson, C. V. (1971). *Kinsey: A biography.* Bloomington: Indiana University Press.

Gagnon, J., & Simon, W. (1973). *Sexual conduct: The social sources of human sexuality.* Chicago: Aldine.

Gathorne-Hardy, J. (1998). *Alfred C. Kinsey: Sex the measure of all things—A biography.* London: Chatto & Windus.

Gebhard, P. H., Gagnon, J. H., Pomeroy, W. B., & Christenson, C. V. (1965). *Sex offenders: An analysis of types.* New York: Harper & Row.

Gebhard, P. H., & Johnson, A. B. (1979). *The Kinsey data: Marginal tabulations of the 1938–1963 interviews conducted by the Institute for Sex Research.* Philadelphia: Saunders.

Gebhard, P. H., Pomeroy, W. B., Martin, C. E., & Christenson, C. V. (1958). *Pregnancy, birth and abortion.* New York: Harper Brothers.

Institute of Medicine/Nation Academy of Sciences. (1986). *Confronting AIDS: Directions for public health, health care, and research.* Washington, DC: National Academy Press.

Kinsey, A. C., Pomeroy, W. D., & Martin, C. E. (1948). *Sexual behavior in the human male.* Philadelphia: Saunders.

Kinsey, A. C., Pomeroy, W. D., Martin, C. E., & Gebhard, P. H. (1953). *Sexual behavior in the human female.* Philadelphia: Saunders.

Klassen, A. D., Williams, C. J., & Levitt, E. E. (1989). *Sex and morality in the U.S.: An empirical enquiry under the auspices of the Kinsey Institute.* Middletown, CT: Wesleyan University Press.

Reinisch, J. M. (1993). *Preface: George Platt Lynes—A personal perspective.* In J. Crump, *George Platt Lynes.* New York: Bullfinch Press, Little Brown.

Reinisch, J. M. (1998). Hoist on another's petard: The misreading of Kinsey's caveats. *Sexualities, 1,* 88–91.

Reinisch, J. M., with Beasley, R. (1990). *The Kinsey Institute new report on sex: What you must know to be sexually literate.* New York: St. Martin's Press.

Reinisch, J. M., & Harter, M. H. (1994). Alfred C. Kinsey. In V. Bullough & B. Bullough (Eds.), *Human sexuality: An encyclopedia.* New York: Garland.

Reinisch, J. M., Hill, C. A., Sanders, S. A., & Ziemba-Davis, M. (1995). High-risk sexual behavior at a midwest university: A confirmatory survey. *Family Planning Perspectives, 27*(2), 79–82.

Reinisch, J. M., Mortensen, E. L., & Sanders, S. A. (1993). The Prenatal Development Project. *Acta Psychiatrica Scandinavica:* Suppl. 370, 54–61.

Reinisch, J. M., Sanders, S. A., Hill, C. A., & Ziemba-Davis, M. (1991). Perceptions about sexual behavior: Findings from a national sex knowledge survey—United States, 1989. *Morbidity and Mortality Weekly Report, 40,* 249–252.

Reinisch, J. M., Sanders, S. A., Mortensen, E. L., & Rubin, D. B. (1995). In utero exposure to phenobarbital and intelligence deficits in adult men. *Journal of the American Medical Association, 274,* 1518–1525.

Sanders, S. A., & Reinisch, J. M. (1999). Would you say you had sex if . . . ? *Journal of the American Medical Association, 281,* 275–277.

J. M. REINISCH
The Kinsey Institute for Research in Sex, Gender, and Reproduction
Indiana University, Bloomington

ALFRED C. KINSEY
HOMOSEXUALITY
SEXUAL DEVELOPMENT
SEXUALITY

KINTSCH, WALTER

Walter Kintsch is a professor of psychology and director of the Institute of Cognitive Science at the University of Colorado. Kintsch grew up in a German-speaking community in Romania. During World War II his family moved as refugees to Austria. He became a teacher and taught elementary school in a one-room mountaintop school, and during those years learned much about teaching and learning. Eventually, however, he decided to go to Vienna to study psychology; but fate intervened in the form of a Fulbright Scholarship to study in the United States at the University of Kansas. Ed Wike, a professor at Kansas who was at the peak of his research activity at that time, took Kintsch under his wing and introduced him to the experimental method and behavioristic theory. After a year of running his own experiments and absorbing Hull's *Principles of Behavior,* Kintsch returned to Austria with an MA from Kansas and enrolled at the University of Vienna. He had not been in Vienna long, however, before Wike offered him a research assistantship at Kansas, and Kintsch returned to the United States to stay.

In graduate school at Kansas, Kintsch received sound training in the experimental method, statistics, and the animal-learning literature of the day, as well as a broad exposure to important ideas in psychology—Heider, Scheerer, Wright, and Baldwin were professors at KU at that time. He also found two patient mathematics professors who were willing to tutor him in probability theory and stochastic processes. His dissertation in 1960 under the direction of Wike was on Hullian theory: drive-reward interaction, a study performed with rats in a straight alley runway.

By this time, however, Kintsch's interests had turned toward the new mathematical psychology, and he managed to obtain a National Institute of Mental Health postdoctoral fellowship to study with Bill Estes at Indiana University. Estes taught Kintsch a great deal and set an example to which Kintsch aspired thereafter. Kintsch's first job was at the University of Missouri, where he was again extremely fortunate to encounter George Collier and David Premack, who became both friends and mentors who taught him by their own examples what research and the intellectual life were all about. During the Missouri years, Kintsch spent summers with the mathematical psychology group organized by Estes, Suppes, and Atkinson at Stanford. Eventually, he moved to the University of California at Riverside, and then to Stanford as a visiting professor. In 1968 he became Professor of Psychology at the University of Colorado in Boulder, where he has remained since.

Kintsch's first important publication was an effort to integrate conflicting traditions—the all-or-none learning theory of Estes and the verbal-learning work of Underwood. He showed that a two-stage Markov model of the Estes variety could account for apparently conflicting paired-associate data. Markov models, however, turned out to be a fascinating but short-lived fad because they could not deal with the complexities of learning and memory that researchers had begun to address in the 1960s. Kintsch began to work on free recall and recognition memory of word lists, and quickly noticed that meaning is an overriding factor in memory studies. Experimental subjects always tried to imbue with meaning the lists of unrelated words they were asked to remember, often making memorable stories of them, which led Kintsch to wonder: Why not study memory for stories directly? Thus, Kintsch turned to text analysis, text processing, and text memory. Helped by a skiing accident, which immobilized him for many months, in 1974 he was able to put together his initial studies on a psychology of text comprehension in book form (*The Representation of Meaning in Memory*). This book became one of the foundations of the modern psychology of text and discourse comprehension.

While Kintsch's early work was strongly influenced by the way linguists and logicians analyze texts, a 1978 paper in the *Psychological Review* in collaboration with Dutch linguist Teun van Dijk was a breakthrough, in that it introduced the idea of a psychological process model of text comprehension. The very productive collaboration between van Dijk and Kintsch lasted for over a decade and eventually resulted in the influential book *Strategies of Discourse Comprehension* in 1983. In 1988, in another *Psychological Review* paper, Kintsch developed the idea that discourse comprehension initially proceeds on the basis of inexact and context-insensitive construction rules that require a contextual integration process to complete. For instance, relevant as well as irrelevant knowledge items will be activated in the initial phases of comprehension, but irrelevant items will be suppressed quickly, usually without their having reached consciousness. This construction-integration model has become the basis of Kintsch's subsequent work, leading up to his monograph *Comprehension: A Paradigm for Cognition* in 1998.

Currently, Kintsch is investigating latent semantic analysis (LSA) as the foundation for a psychological semantics. Latent semantic analysis is a statistical technique developed by Colorado psychologist Tom Landauer that automatically constructs a high-dimensional semantic space from a large corpus of text. Words and texts can be represented as vectors in this semantic space, and hence can be readily compared. By the combination of LSA with the construction-integration model of text comprehension, powerful results can be obtained, with respect both to semantic theory and to a wide variety of other applications.

Kintsch has been the director of the Institute of Cognitive Science at the University of Colorado since 1983. He has also served his discipline as chair of the Psychonomic Society, the Cognitive Science Society, and Division 3 of the American Psychological Association, and as the editor of the *Journal of Verbal Learning and Verbal Behavior* and the *Psychological Review.* He is a member of the National Academy of Education and received the Distinguished Scientific Contribution Award of the American Psychological Association in 1992.

STAFF

KLOPFER, BRUNO (1900–1971)

Bruno Klopfer, during his youth, enjoyed sailing, mountain climbing, and skiing. His education was interrupted for a time by World War I. Later he returned to the University of Munich, where he received the PhD at the age of 22; his dissertation was entitled "The psychology of inhibition."

Klopfer and his family spent 1933 and 1934 in Switzerland, then emigrated to the United States, where Klopfer taught at Columbia University for 13 years. During this time he established his first regular workshop in projective techniques in New York State. Later he added other workshops in California and other parts of the country. Joining the staff at UCLA, he remained there until his retirement in 1963.

Klopfer started dealing with Jungian psychology as an intellectual task; gradually, it became his philosophy of life. His specialty in his later years was Jungian analysis and the teaching of Jungian theory and practice. This tended to replace the Rorschach as his primary interest.

He was editor of the *Journal of Personality Assessment* for 36 years and developed it from an obscure newsletter into a major professional organ. He himself was a prolific writer and a tremendous stimulant to his students and colleagues. His major work was

The Rorschach Technique, first published in 1942 with Douglas Kelly and revised in 1962 with H. H. Davidson; it became the single most authoritative source on the Rorschach test. He received tributes from the Division of Clinical Psychology of the American Psychological Association, from the Society for Personality Assessment, and from the Analytical Psychology Club of New York.

W. G. KLOPFER

KOCH, SIGMUND (1917–1996)

Sigmund Koch studied at New York University, the University of Iowa, and Duke University (PhD, 1942). He was the university professor of psychology and philosophy at Boston University, he held senior appointments at the University of Texas, Austin, and at Duke. He taught at University College, London (as a Fulbright professor), at Clark University, and at the University of North Carolina. In the mid-1960s he was director of the Ford Foundation Program in the Humanities and Arts, and in the early 1970s he served as academic vice-president of Boston University.

Koch's persisting interests were in theoretical and philosophical foundations of psychology. Early on, he did theoretico-experimental work in learning and motivation. His later interests were in the analysis of inquiry, the theory of value and of language, and the empirical study of art. His critical writings were influential in liberating psychology from the hegemony of behaviorism. He was also known for his view that psychology is not a coherent science, but rather a collectivity of discrete and often incommensurable *psychological studies,* many of which require methods more like those of the humanities than the natural sciences. Also significant were his *perceptual theory of definition,* offered as an antidote to the muddles of "operationism," and his early priority in repairing the neglect by motivational theory of *intrinsic motivation* via his concept of objective *value properties.*

Koch directed and edited the American Psychological Association/NSF-sponsored study of the status of psychology at mid-century which resulted in the six-volume study *Psychology: A Study of a Science.* With D. E. Leary he edited a second large study, *A Century of Psychology as Science.* He was also president of three divisions of the American Psychological Association: General Psychology, Philosophical Psychology (twice), and Psychology and the Arts.

STAFF

KOFFKA, KURT (1886–1941)

Kurt Koffka, except for a year at Edinburgh, studied at Berlin's university. His 1908 PhD under Carl Stumpf was based on a dissertation on rhythm. He assisted Otto Külpe at Würzburg and Friedrich Schumann at Frankfurt. When the Nazis came to power he left the faculty at Giessen, emigrated to the United States, and accepted a position at Smith College.

Koffka was Wertheimer's second subject for his classic 1912 paper on the Phi Phenomena (apparent movement, as in motion pictures). Along with Max Wertheimer and Wolfgang Köhler, Koffka was a founder of the Gestalt psychology movement; of the three, he was particularly noted for his extensive publications. The Gestalt movement—a reaction against Wundt and (later) behaviorism—emphasized perceptual processes and the necessity for dealing with behavior in all its complexity (an holistic, emergent approach) as opposed to attempts to analyze behavior by components.

Prior to becoming Wertheimer's assistant in 1911, Koffka had done research on imagery and thought. He was responsible for applying Gestalt principles to developmental psychology. For him, learning was the same as perceptual reorganization, particularly a goal-directed tendency to restore equilibrium of perceptions (*Prägnanz*).

The most comprehensive—albeit difficult—exposition of the Gestalt approach is Koffka's *Principles of Gestalt Psychology*. In his last years his research primarily concerned color vision and perceptual organization. His basic position on the nature/nurture question was a further development of Stern's convergence theory: Psychological development is a collaboration of inner (hereditary) and outer (learned) conditions.

C. S. Peyser
The University of the South

KOHLBERG, LAWRENCE (1927–1987)

Lawrence Kohlberg is best known for his research on the moral development in children. He received the BA degree and the PhD from the University of Chicago in 1958. The following year, he went to Yale University and remained there until 1961. After several interim appointments he went to Harvard in 1967. His principal work was *Essays on Moral Development* (two volumes).

Following the lines of Piaget, Kohlberg stated that children followed moral development in three stages: (a) In the preconditioned level children's moral development followed from external standards; (b) in the conventional level morality is basically one of the following correct rules; and (c) in the conventional level morality is basically one of the shared standards of rights and duties. Each of these levels comprised two stages of orientation. The first is characterized by obedience and punishment and naive eogism; the second by "good boy" and authority; the third combined legalism and conscience. Like Piaget's theory, Kohlberg's is one of cognitive development. His results were achieved by 20 years of longitudinal study.

R. W. Lundin
Wheaton, Illinois

KÖHLER, WOLFGANG (1887–1967)

Wolfgang Köhler studied at Tübingen, Bonn, and Berlin. He received the PhD under Carl Stumpf at Berlin in 1909 for a dissertation on psychoacoustics. During the years from 1913 to 1920 he was director of the Prussian Academy of Sciences station at Tenerife in the Canary Islands. With the rise of Nazism, he left his position at Berlin for the United States, where he taught at Swarthmore and Dartmouth. He was president of the American Psychological Association in 1959.

Köhler was Wertheimer's first subject for his classic 1912 paper on the Phi Phenomena (apparent movement, as in motion pictures). Along with Wertheimer and Koffka, Köhler was a founder of the Gestalt psychology movement, of which he was particularly noted as the public spokesman.

The Gestalt movement was a reaction against Wundt and behaviorism. It emphasized perceptual processes and the necessity for dealing with behavior in all its emergent complexity, rather than attempting to analyze it by components.

Köhler's *The Mentality of Apes* (1917) established the applicability of the Gestalt to animal behavior. Based upon his work at Tenetrife, the book focuses on insightful or "aha!" solutions to problems. Most of the problems were *Ümweg*, or roundabout solutions. In the simplest case the desired object of food was placed on the other side of a fence at the end of an alley. If the ape conceptualized the Gestalt, it turned back down the alley, went around to the other side of the fence, and obtained the goal.

In another problem Köhler placed a banana outside a cage at a distance that could not be directly reached by arm. The chimpanzees invariably placed the stick beyond the fruit and knocked the fruit within reach. Although some required several trials to become proficient at the task, their intention or Gestalt was clear from the first successful attempt with the stick. Sultan, one of the brighter chimpanzees, has become known for his solving of the 2- and 3-stick problems. In these cases a single stick was not long enough to reach the fruit; rather, the smaller bamboo rod had to be inserted inside the larger hollow rod to create a longer stick. When the banana was within reach by a single stick, Sultan usually stopped using the extended stick. Other problems required tearing a branch off a small tree to obtain the stick, or piling boxes under fruit suspended from the ceiling.

Köhler also did work on relational or transposition learning at Tenerife. Chickens were taught to peck grain from the darker of two adjacent gray sheets. Then the sheets were changed, so that the lighter of the two was the same shade as the darker had been during training. The birds still pecked on the (even) darker gray, thus demonstrating that they had learned a relationship rather than a specific shade of gray.

Köhler also published important work on time error. In the United States he was primarily a defender of the principles of the Gestalt movement.

C. S. Peyser
The University of the South

KOOB, GEORGE F.

George F. Koob is a professor and the director of the Division of Psychopharmacology in the Department of Neuropharmacology at The Scripps Research Institute, and adjunct professor of psychology and psychiatry at the University of California, San Diego (UCSD). Koob received his BS degree in zoology in 1969 from Pennsylvania State University and his PhD in behavioral physiology in 1972 from The Johns Hopkins University. He began his postdoctoral studies in neurophysiology, neurochemistry, and psychopharmacology at Walter Reed Army Institute of Research in 1972; he continued his postdoctoral fellowship with Susan D. Iversen at the Department of Experimental Psychology and Leslie Iversen at the Medical Research Council Neurochemical Pharmacology Unit at the University of Cambridge, England. He has maintained an active collaboration since 1977 with Le Moal and Stinus at the Universite de Bordeaux II in Bordeaux, France.

An authority on the neurobiology of emotional behavior, addiction, and stress, Koob has published over 500 scientific papers and has received funding for his research from the National Institutes of Health (NIH) including the National Institute on Drug Abuse and the National Institute on Alcohol Abuse and Alcoholism (NIAAA), where he is a merit awardee. His current research is focused on exploring the neurobiological basis for the neuroadaptation associated with drug dependence and stress. He currently serves on the editorial boards of 16 scientific journals and has been the U.S. editor-in-chief for the journal *Pharmacology, Biochemistry and Behavior* since 1994. He is the director of the NIAAA Alcohol Research Center at The Scripps Research Institute. He won the Daniel Efron Award for excellence in research from the American College of Neuropsychopharmacology.

Koob's research interests include the behavioral neurobiology of emotion, reward and stress. The theoretical constructs of emotion, reward, and stress have long been associated with neurobiological substrates in the basal forebrain. While the anatomical connections of the emotional system have been defined and elaborated, the neurochemistry and neuropharmacology of emotional function is an area of growing interest. Particularly exciting is the increasing number of pharmacological tools available for exaggerating or blocking the action of central neurotransmitters.

Koob's current work focuses on afferent and efferent connections of the basal forebrain (extended amygdala) in the region of the nucleus accumbens, bed nucleus of the stria terminalis, and central nucleus of the amygdala, a region that his work has shown to have increasing importance in motor activation, reinforcement mechanisms, drug self-administration, and the neuroadaptation associated with drug dependence. This work includes characterization of the role of catecholamines and opioid and other peptidergic systems in behavioral activation and in opiate, stimulant, and alcohol reinforcement.

Koob's work with neuropeptides includes the characterization of behavioral functions in the central nervous system (CNS) for corticotropin-releasing factor. This hypothalamic releasing factor, which has classical hormonal functions as part of the hypothalamic pituitary adrenal axis, is located in extrahypothalamic brain structures and may be an important component of the function of the limbic system. Recent use of specific corticotropin-releasing factor antagonists suggests that endogenous brain corticotropin-releasing factors may be involved in specific behavioral responses to stress, and even in the psychopathology of anxiety and affective disorders. Koob also is characterizing functional roles for other stress-related neurotransmitters/neuroregulators such as neuropeptide Y and neuroactive steroids.

These studies provide not only basic research knowledge about the function of specific neurotransmitters in specific neuroanatomical sites in emotional behavior, but also provide significant information about the CNS action of drugs and the neuropharmacological basis of psychopathology.

Koob has taught an extensive series of undergraduate courses related to brain, behavior, neurochemistry, and psychopathology in the Department of Psychology at UCSD. These courses include "Drugs, Addiction, and Mental Disorders" (drugs of abuse and psychotherapeutic drugs), "Drugs and Behavior" (neuropsychopharmacology of psychoactive drugs), and "Impulse Control Disorders" (social psychology of self-regulation, addiction, and psychiatric concepts of drug and nondrug impulse control disorders and pathology). He also teaches a graduate course in psychopharmacology and has participated in numerous neuroscience graduate program courses as a lecturer. He has won six Excellence in Teaching awards and two Professor of the Year awards at UCSD.

At The Scripps Research Institute, Koob has trained 40 postdoctoral fellows and 9 predoctoral fellows in his psychopharmacology laboratory. He is director of a National Institute on Alcohol Abuse and Alcoholism postdoctoral training program ("Neuropsychopharmacology: Multidisciplinary Training") and serves on the executive committee for the neuroscience program at UCSD.

STAFF

KOREA, PSYCHOLOGY IN

Psychology in Korea is continuing its rapid growth in terms of membership size, organization, and academic and professional activities.

THE KOREAN PSYCHOLOGICAL ASSOCIATION

In late 1992, the last time the state of psychology in Korea was reported in this volume, the membership of the Korean Psychological Association stood at 542, of whom 43% held a doctorate (See Table 1). By the end of August 1999, the Association's membership stood at 1,479, including 50 nonvoting members. This means that the membership more than doubled within less than 7 years. Although the level of doctorate holders decreased from previous 43% (as of 1992) to 38.5%, this decrease is due to a large influx of MA degree holders, who were drawn in to register as KPA members as a result of election engineering. Since 1999, the Association president is elected by an electoral college rather than by the general meeting of members.

The Association, as before, remains the sole organization representing psychologists that is active in Korea. Since 1992, the Association added two new divisions, health psychology and psychology of women, increasing the total number of divisions from eight to ten (health psychology, developmental psychology, experimental and cognitive psychology, counseling and psychotherapy,

Table 1.   The Makeup of Korean Psychological Association Membership

As of	Membership size	BA	MA	Ph.D. (%)
July, 1969	113	63	47	3 (2.6%)
May, 1990	398	15	238	145 (36.0%)
November, 1992	542	22	285	235 (43.0%)
August, 1999	1,479	62	759	560 (38.5%)

psychology of women, social psychology and personality, clinical psychology, industrial and organizational psychology, biological and physiological psychology, and social issues). Personality was added to the division of social psychology. The largest of the divisions in terms of membership is counseling and psychotherapy (2,335), and the next largest is clinical (588), followed by developmental (300), industrial and organizational (148), experimental and cognitive (140), women (140), social and personality (127), social issues (99), and health (96), in that order. (These figures include both full members and affiliate members.)

Each of the divisions publishes its own journal, most of them biannually. The Association's editorial committee publishes the 11th journal, namely *Korean Journal of Psychology: General,* published annually. In addition, the Association publishes bimonthly newsletters.

One significant move has been a recent procurement of an Association office through the contributions of individual members of the Association. It will serve as the permanent site of all communications directed to the Korean Psychological Association. (Mailing address: Korean Psychological Association, 702–13 Yoksam-dong, Kang'nam-Ku, (Songchi Heights Officetel I-917), Seoul 135–080, Korea. Phone: Country code-02–567–0102; Fax: 02–567–0103.)

In 1996 the Association celebrated its fiftieth anniversary, and as a part of the event, a book was compiled detailing its history, organization, and activities. The volume also contains complete lists of the names and affiliations of members, and titles of articles published in KPA journals to date.

RESTRUCTURING OF UNIVERSITIES

The number of departments related to psychology grew from 27 (21 departments of psychology, 3 departments of educational psychology, and 3 departments of industrial psychology) in 1993 to 32 in 1999, an increase of 5 departments. The 32 comprise 24 departments of psychology, 2 departments of educational psychology, 5 departments of industrial psychology, and one department of rehabilitation psychology. However, a much more important change affecting psychology departments in Korea is in process. Beginning in 1998, a wave of "restructuring" swept over the universities in Korea. One feature of the restructuring has been a creation of faculties (or divisions), each of which subsume several academic departments. As a consequence, the prospect is that most of the 32 departments related to psychology will disappear by the end of 1999 except about 6 (those at Kyungbuk National University, Pu-san National University, Seoul National University, Chonnam National University, Tagu Hyosung Catholic University, and Sungsim Women's University), according to the latest survey.

This change is not expected to lead to a reduction of psychology faculty members, but it forces faculty members to teach fewer courses. Students admitted to a faculty will be required to choose their area of concentration at the end of the first year in the college or later. This change, which affected most departments of psychology in 1999, is not expected to affect psychology in Korea adversely in all instances because more often than not psychology emerges as the most popular major, attracting more students than the competing academic disciplines.

Another feature of the restructuring is a drastic reduction of credit points required for a concentration. The number of credits required to be a psychology major is halved to a level around 36 credit points. A third feature of restructuring is accommodating of non-Korean psychologists as faculty members. This is not a change restricted to departments of psychology. At this time of writing, universities are discussing the need of opening faculty positions to foreign scholars, but specific plans have yet to be developed. The restructuring process will force the universities to adopt global standards when evaluating faculty performances, which in turn will mean application of more stringent requirements for hiring and promotion of faculty members.

SUGGESTED READING

Korean Psychological Association (Ed.). (1996). The 50-year history of the Korean Psychological Association. Seoul: Kyo'yukgwahaksa. (in Korean)

J.-H. CHA
Seoul National University

KOSLOW, S. H.

Stephen H. Koslow is the first director of the Office on Neuroinformatics, and an associate director of the National Institutes of Mental Health (NIMH); he was appointed to this position in 1999. He also serves as the coordinator for the multi-agency Human Brain Project. He received his BS from Columbia University in New York in 1962. His training as a scientist began at the University of Chicago, where he received a PhD in 1967 in the biological sciences from the Department of Pharmacology, specializing in neuropsychopharmacology. His interest in the cellular mechanisms governing neuronal activity and drug action led him to further training at the Department of Pharmacology at the Karolinska Institute in Stockholm, Sweden. For two years (1968–1969) he was a Swedish Medical Research Council postdoctoral fellow. During this fellowship he learned and applied neurochemical techniques to single vertebrate neurons, and investigated the plasticity of the nervous system to form new functional synapses by heterologus nerve transplants. Koslow returned to the United States in 1970 as a staff fellow in the Laboratory of Preclinical Pharmacology, NIMH. In 1973, he received a tenured position at NIMH as a pharmacologist and was appointed head of the research unit on the neurobiological applications of mass spectrometry. During this period he developed techniques that expanded the use of gas chromatography–mass spectrometry to quantitative analysis. This technique, single ion monitoring, was developed and used to measure femtomole concentration of neurotransmitters and metabolites in micro-dissected brain nuclei.

Since 1975, Koslow has served in various programmatic science administration positions in the extramural programs of NIMH, each with greater responsibility and scope than the last. His responsibilities included the support and stimulation of research in the area of biological psychiatry and neuroscience. Additionally, he was project director and a principal investigator in the Collaborative Program on the Psychobiology of Depression—Biological Studies, a 6-center experimental clinical research program testing the extant hypotheses on the biological basis of depression and the mechanism of antidepressant action.

Koslow's major efforts and accomplishments at NIMH are in the area of neuroscience. In 1982 he was appointed the director of the first neuroscience Research branch responsible for supporting and stimulating a wide range of neuroscience research. He was responsible for initiating new research programs in a number of nascent areas. These included human brain imaging using noninvasive methods, and the application of the theories and formulations of chaos and non-linearity to the understanding of complicated brain processes. In a similar manner, he developed and actively supported molecular and cellular approaches toward understanding brain function as well as initiating activities on systems research, cognition, neurodevelopment, and neuroimmunology.

During the 1990s (the decade of the brain), Koslow helped to establish and served on the initial organizing committee for the National Library of Congress Lecture Series on the Decade of the Brain. Koslow created the NIMH report to Congress on "research opportunities for neuroscience in this decade and into the next millennium" (DHHS pub. no. 89–1580, 1988). This report clearly articulated the research opportunities and the challenge ahead, specifically identifying 50 important questions to answer during that decade. It was during this period that the division of neuroscience was formed at NIMH and Koslow appointed as its director.

In 1993, Koslow initiated the multi-agency initiative on the Human Brain Project (HBP), and serves as the chair of the Federal Interagency Coordinating Committee on the HBP (FICC-HBP). The HBP initiative was created to establish an enabling electronic communication computer base, distributed database, and knowledge-management system for the neuroscience community. The HBP was initiated as a result of a study commissioned by Koslow to the Institute of Medicine (IOM), National Academy of Sciences to examine the issue of the convergence of new computer capabilities and exponential growth of neuroscience research. The IOM study and report recommended the establishment of a brain mapping initiative to develop three-dimensional computerized maps and models of the structure, function, connectivity, pharmacology, and molecular biology of the nervous system across developmental stages and reflecting both normal and disease states. To ensure the participation of the world neuroscience community in the HBP/neu-

roinformatics goals. Koslow initiated a number of international initiatives. In 1995 he established and co-chaired a neuroinformatics committee within the United States and the European Commission—Biotechnology Task Force. In addition working with the White House Office on Science and Technology, he established and chaired the neuroinformatics subgroup of the biological working group of the megascience forum of the Organization for Economic Cooperation and Development.

Koslow has served on a number of important national and international panels and committees, including the President's Commission on Mental Health Research Task Panel (1978); the Public Health Service AIDS Prevention Neuroscience and Behavioral Workgroup (1988–1990); and the PHS Indo-U.S. Cooperation in Science and Technology, serving as the U.S. chair of the Working Group on Mental Health, Substance Abuse, and Neurosciences (1991). Koslow is an active member of a number of scientific societies, and is a fellow of the American Association for the Advancement of Science and the American College of Neuropsychopharmacology. Koslow has received numerous awards in recognition of his accomplishments, including a Public Health Service Special Recognition Award, two NIH Director's Awards, two Alcohol, Drug Abuse, and Mental Health Administration Administrator's Awards for Meritorious Achievement, and the Alumni Achievement Award from the University of Chicago Club of Washington. He serves on the editorial board of numerous neuroscience journals, and consults for a number of private organizations, businesses, and foreign governments. Koslow has 72 publications in referred journals and 20 invited chapters in books, and has edited 13 books.

STAFF

KRAEPELIN, EMIL (1855–1926)

At the time Emil Kraepelin entered the medical scene in the latter part of the 19th century, the classification of mental disorders was in a state of confusion. His interest in psychiatry began when he was still in medical school. For a time he was associated with Wilhelm Wundt at the University of Leipzig. At that time Wundt was concerned with the new psychology and was experimenting with sensory functions and the analysis of states of consciousness. It was against this background of scientific investigation that Kraepelin approached the problem of mental disorders. He believed that one should take a scientific approach to mental disorders, since they were predetermined. It seemed to him that a person who was mentally disturbed might naturally recover or might not.

Through careful observation of many patients and statistical tabulation of symptoms, he came to the conclusion that there were two major mental disorders: dementia praecox and the manic-depressive psychosis. He further divided these disorders into various subtypes: Dementia praecox could be subdivided into the hebephrenic, catatonic, and paranoid, while the manic-depressive psychosis had many more subdivisions, depending on the regularity or irregularity of the cycles of mania and depression. As a result, he became known as the "great classifier" of mental disorders.

In 1883 he published the first edition of his *Clinical Psychiatry;* the ninth edition appeared in 1927, the year after his death. Kraepelin's classifications were the culmination of efforts of various psychiatrists both in France and Germany for over a generation. Through his efforts the study, diagnosis, and prognosis of outcome of mental disorders became a legitimate branch of medicine. By and large, Kraepelin considered the causes of these disorders to be predetermined and basically of a biological nature. Physiological factors and malfunctions of various body organs seemed to be the important factors, rather than the psychological causes proposed by many from the French schools and by Sigmund Freud.

R. W. LUNDIN
Wheaton, Illinois

KRAFFT-EBING, RICHARD VON (1840–1902)

Richard von Krafft-Ebing held positions in psychiatry at the universities of Strasbourg, Graz, and Vienna. He published extensively on hypnosis, criminology, and sexual behavior. His basic psychiatry text was considered by many to be undistinguished, yet it is credited with influencing Carl Jung to choose psychiatry as a medical specialty.

In his early work Krafft-Ebing inoculated general paresis patients with syphilis. Since they did not contract the disease, they must have had it previously. In this fashion he demonstrated the link between syphilis and general paresis prior to the serological tests such as the Wassermann used today. At the Moscow International Congress of 1897 he made popular the phrase "civilization and syphilization."

Psychopathia Sexualis is Krafft-Ebing's best-known work. First published in 1886, it went through a dozen editions and many translations. Krafft-Ebing took a purely constitutional approach. All sexual variations are based upon genetic defects, although masturbation can hasten or even produce disorders. True to the German ideas of the time, he considered anything other than marital coitus for the purpose of procreation a perversion. A male was expected to have orgasm during coitus, but not a female. Krafft-Ebing discussed sexual perversions ranging from lust murder to fetish and masturbation with equal condemnation. His writings influenced the work of Sigmund Freud.

C. S. PEYSER
The University of the South

KRASNER, LEONARD (1924–   )

Krasner attended the City College of New York. After three years in military service during World War II, he received the PhD from Columbia University as a clinical psychologist.

Influenced by the experimental orientation of the faculty, particularly Fred Keller, Krasner's research efforts focused on the development of a behavioral approach in clinical psychology. Working with Leonard Ullmann, Krasner edited two volumes bringing together virtually all of the then extant research and applications

in behavior modification: *Case Studies in Behavior Modification* (1963) and *Research in Behavior Modification* (1965). Ullmann and Krasner then published the first text in abnormal psychology to offer a systematic behavioral model: *A Psychological Approach to Abnormal Psychology.* The two authors then further developed and broadened their behavioral/social learning model in *Behavior Influence and Personality: The Social Matrix of Human Action.*

Krasner has also published reports on studies in verbal conditioning, token economy, placebo effect, social responsibility, values, behavior therapy, clinical psychology, and other related areas. Later he broadened his behavioral approach in *Environmental Design and Human Behavior: A Psychology of the Individual in Society,* which describes the research, training, community, and school applications of himself and his colleagues and students.

STAFF

KRISHNAN, K. RANGA RAMA (1956–   )

K. Ranga Rama Krishnan was born in Madras, India, in 1956. He was educated in the Indian school system and earned a PUC (premedical) from Loyola College in Madras in 1973. In 1978, he received his MBBS in medicine from Madras Medical College. After working in several clinics around the world, Krishnan became a resident in psychiatry (chief, 1981–1983) and a postdoctoral fellow (1983–1984) in neurobiology at Duke University Medical Center; he remained on the faculty in the Department of Psychiatry and Behavioral Sciences there, becoming professor in 1995 and chair of the department in 1998.

Krishnan's work has focused primarily on neurobiological dysfunctions associated with mood disorders and Alzheimer's disease. He has collaborated with investigators in several disciplines to conduct investigations employing magnetic resonance imaging (MRI) and Magnetic Resonance Spectroscopy (MRS) to the study of the brains of patients with these diseases. A major effort of this collaboration has been to investigate the structural changes that occur among depressed elderly humans; this research has been published in scholarly journals in multiple disciplines.

Krishnan has received numerous awards for his research investigations. In 1984, he was a Laughlin Fellow of the American College of Psychiatry; in 1988, he received the Rafaelsen Award from the International College of Neuropsychopharmacology. He has served as a member of several different scientific review groups for the National Institute of Mental Health (NIMH). He is the recipient (1996–1998) of a Distinguished Investigator Award from the National Alliance for Research on Schizophrenia and Depression for a genetic imaging study of Bipolar Disorder.

While engaged in extensive research activities, Krishnan has maintained an active clinical practice. His clinical reputation is such that he is referred patients with difficult problems from all over the world. He is considered to be especially skillful at diagnostic differentiation of complex clinical problems.

STAFF

KUDER OCCUPATIONAL INTEREST SURVEY

The Kuder Occupational Interest Survey was developed in 1966 by Frederic Kuder. It consists of 300 occupationally relevant activities arranged in triad form. Persons taking the survey mark one most-preferred and one least-preferred activity for each of the 100 triads. These responses are then compared with those of representative members of 126 occupational groups and 48 college-major groups. Scores are reported in the form of correlations, or the degree to which the individual's responses and those of persons in each of the occupational or college-major criterion groups are similar. Occupational scales are representative of the range of occupations described in various U.S. Department of Labor publications and of the occupational hierarchy from professional to skilled trades occupations. College-major scales are representative of majors offered in colleges throughout the United States.

Scores are reported in rank order, separately for occupations and college majors, and separately for scales that have been developed on responses from female and male groups respectively. (For 39 of the occupations and college majors, twin scales—separate scales representing men and women in the same occupation or college major—have been developed. The reason for separate development by sex is that women and men—even those in the same occupation—differ significantly in their responses to a number of the survey items.) Scores on all scales are reported to all respondents, regardless of sex. Respondents are advised to consider their high and low scores on all scales in making occupational and educational plans and decisions, and are told that no occupation or field of study should be considered appropriate only for women or men exclusively.

Interpretive materials containing illustrative cases help both client and counselor to better understand and make use of the scores. The *General Manual* (Kuder & Diamond, 1979/1966) provides information on technical development, interpretation, and use, and on such characteristics as validity, reliability, and homogeneity of the scales. It also describes the criterion groups used in collecting the responses that formed the bases for the scales. It should be noted that, although the original scales were developed in 1966, new scales are developed periodically. A revised form was published in 1985.

REFERENCES

Kuder, F., & Diamond, E. E. (1979). *General manual, Occupational Interest Survey* (2nd ed.). Chicago: Science Research Associates.

SUGGESTED READING

Anastasi, A. (1982). *Psychological testing* (5th ed.). New York: Macmillan.

Kuder, F. (1977). *Activity interests and occupational choice.* Chicago: Science Research Associates.

E. E. Diamond
Evanston, Illinois

VOCATIONAL INTEREST MEASUREMENT

KUPFER, DAVID J.

David J. Kupfer was born in New York City on February 14, 1941. He received his bachelor (magna cum laude) and MD degrees from Yale University. Following an internship at Montefiore Hospital Center in New York in 1966, he was appointed a clinical fellow in psychiatry at Yale University School of Medicine. In 1967, he became a clinical associate at the National Institute of Mental Health (NIMH) and was assigned as a ward administrator in the laboratory of clinical psychobiology under F. Snyder. While at NIMH, he also completed a diploma course in community psychiatry at the Washington School of Psychiatry. In 1969, Kupfer continued his postgraduate training at the Dana Psychiatric Clinic of Yale-New Haven Hospital, serving as a team supervisor and becoming assistant professor of psychiatry and director of the outpatient division within a year. These experiences established an appreciation for the potential to gain insight into important diagnostic and treatment issues by expanding psychiatric research to include psychobiological, psychosocial, and epidemiological perspectives.

In 1971, Kupfer received an NIMH Research Career Development Award and became a faculty member of Yale's prestigious Biological Training Program in Psychiatry, where he continued his studies on mood disorders. In 1973, he joined the University of Pittsburgh School of Medicine as an associate professor of psychiatry and director of research and research training at Western Psychiatric Institute and Clinic (WPIC). Within two years, he was promoted to professor. He became chairman of the department of psychiatry in 1983. In 1994 he became the Thomas Detre Chair in psychiatry. At Pittsburgh he helped develop a model of service delivery system that provided a disorder-based focus for patient care. Not only did this model facilitate clinical research, but it also improved the quality of patient care and training. It has become a model that many other major research and clinical institutions have followed.

During both the 1970s and 1980s, Kupfer has stimulated psychiatric research within the University of Pittsburgh and nationwide. As Thomas Detre Professor, and chairman of the department of psychiatry, and director of research at WPIC, he oversees the coordination and expansion of investigations among the department's over 175 faculty members. He has promoted widespread collaborations between clinical investigators in psychiatry and those in more basic neurosciences. These studies are not limited to depression and other mood disorders, but encompass virtually every psychiatric disorder and every age group, from infants to the "oldest old."

Under Kupfer's direction, WPIC has become one of the nation's preeminent university-based psychiatric centers as evidenced by the quality and number of publications as well as the amount of peer-reviewed federal funding for mental health research. Since 1977, he has been the principal investigator and chief architect of an NIMH-funded Mental Health Clinical Research Center (MHCRC) for the Study of Affective Disorders, one of the first and most successful MHCRCs. This large, core-supported program fosters research at WPIC directed toward understanding the etiology, epidemiology, and treatment of mood disorders. In recent years, the MHCRC has remarkably advanced the field by innovative work in statistical design and methods, as well as by focusing increasingly on children, the elderly, and at-risk family members. The new Stanley Center for the Innovative Treatment of Bipolar Disorder has substantially increased the level of investigative effort in furthering treatment research on bipolar disorders.

Kupfer has been the recipient of numerous scholarships and research awards. He has received the A. E. Bennett Research Award in Clinical Science of the Society for Biological Psychiatry (1975), the Anna-Monika Foundation Prize sponsored by the German government for scientists who have contributed to advancing knowledge in the treatment of depression (1977), the Daniel H. Efron Award of the American College of Neuropsychopharmacology (1979), the Twenty-Sixth Annual Award of the Institute of Pennsylvania Hospital in Memory of Edward A. Strecker, MD (1989), the William R. McAlpin, Jr. Research Achievement Award sponsored by the National Mental Health Association (1990), the 1993 American Psychiatric Association Award for Research in Psychiatry, the First Isaac Ray Decade of Excellence Award (1994), the Twelfth Annual Edward J. Sachar Award (1996), the 1996 Gerald Klerman Lifetime Research Award (jointly with Ellen Frank), the Institute of Medicine's 1998 Rhoda and Bernard Sarnat International Prize in Mental Health, the American Psychopathologi-

cal Association's 1999 Joseph Zubin Award (jointly with Ellen Frank), and membership in the Institute of Medicine of the National Academy of Sciences (1990).

A prolific writer, Kupfer has authored or coauthored a combination of more than 700 articles, books, and book chapters. Kupfer's research has focused primarily on long-term treatment strategies for recurrent mood disorders, the pathogenesis of depression, and the relationship between biological rhythms, sleep, and depression.

Kupfer also sits on the editorial boards of the *Archives of General Psychiatry, European Archives of Psychiatry and Clinical Neuroscience, Journal of Affective Disorders, Journal of Clinical Psychopharmacology, Neuropsychobiology,* and *Psychiatry Research.*

Kupfer has served as president of the American College of Neuropsychopharmacology and the Society for Biological Psychiatry, a member of the Council of Research of the American Psychiatric Association, and is a fellow of the American College of Neuropsychopharmacology, the American Psychiatric Association, and the Academy of Behavioral Medical Research.

STAFF

L

LAMARCK, JEAN-BAPTISTE DE MONET DE (1744–1829)

Jean-Baptiste de Monet de Lamarck started his career as a botanist by developing a new method for identifying plants, and made the first effort to formulate a natural method of classification for the vegetable kingdom. He recognized the importance of environmental influences, especially climate, for vegetable development. For these efforts he was elected to the Académie des Sciences in 1779. His most important institutional affiliation was with the Jardin du Roi, an important scientific center at the time.

As his interests turned to zoology, he became affiliated with the Musée d'Histoire Naturelle as professor of "insects and worms." In this field he developed a classification system for invertebrates.

Out of these zoological interests Lamarck developed the theory of evolution that he first presented in 1800 in a public lecture. In the statement of his theory he presumed four laws. The first concerned the natural tendency toward increasing organic complexities. The second dealt with why new organs evolve by indirect environmental influences. The third was the use-disuse principle, which accounted for changes in an organ as a result of the acquisition of new habits or the disappearance of organs that were no longer useful. The last law dealt directly with the inheritance of acquired characteristics, which Lamarck thought to be necessary to explain cumulative changes and the emergence of new structures. At the time, this belief became so widely accepted that any proof of its validity seemed unnecessary.

Lamarck's theory went unchallenged for over 50 years, until Charles Darwin published his *Origin of Species by Means of Natural Selection* in 1859. Still, Lamarck's theory did not suddenly die out: it became the basis for Herbert Spencer's theory of the inheritance of associated ideas, which appeared late in the 19th century. In the late 1930s William McDougall attempted to prove Lamarck's theory in his experiments at Duke University by breeding successive generations of rats who had learned an escape problem. The work of Carl Jung reflected Lamarckian ideas in the theory of the archetypes that developed generation after generation in man's collective unconscious. However, most biologists and other natural scientists have abandoned Lamarck's theory in favor of Darwin's.

R. W. LUNDIN
Wheaton, Illinois

LANG, PETER

Peter Lang is a graduate research professor, the highest professorial rank at the University of Florida, which is awarded only to distinguished scholars. He holds appointments in the departments of psychology, clinical and health psychology, and neuroscience. He is the director of the NIMH Center for the Study of Emotion and Attention, a Basic Behavioral Science Research Center supported by the National Institutes of Health. He is the director of the Fear and Anxiety Disorders Clinic at the University Health Center and a member of the Faculty Advisory Board of the University of Florida Brain Institute.

Lang previously held the Clark Leonard Hull Professorial Chair at the University of Wisconsin, Madison, and has held visiting appointments at several European universities. He is a fellow of the American Association for the Advancement of Science, the Divisions of Physiological and Comparative Psychology and Clinical Psychology of the American Psychological Association, a fellow of the Academy of Behavioral Medicine Research, and a charter fellow of the American Psychological Society. He has served on the boards of directors of the Association for the Advancement of Behavior Therapy and the Scientific Advisory Board of the Anxiety Disorders Association of America, and is a former president of the Society for Psychophysiological Research.

The millennial International Congress of Psychology in Stockholm selected Lang as a keynote speaker, as did the European Conference on Psychosomatic Research, Oslo, 2000. The American Psychological Association previously named him a Distinguished Scientist Lecturer, supporting a special University lecture tour. Lang is a highly sought-after speaker for many scholarly societies, representing disciplines as diverse as education, neuroscience, medicine, psychiatry, and sports science. His broad service to psychology includes serving as action editor for the *Journal of Personality and Social Psychology,* and *Psychophysiology* (guest editor for a special European issue). Lang has served on the editorial boards of the *Journal of Behavior Therapy and Experimental Psychiatry; Journal of Applied Behavioral Analysis; Psychotherapy: Theory, Research, and Practice; Clinical Behavior Therapy Review; Journal of Psychopathology and Behavioral Assessment; Psychophysiology; Journal of Anxiety Disorders;* and *Cognition and Emotion.* He served on the National Research Council's Space Biology and Medicine Panel, organized by the National Science Foundation to evaluate behavioral research in extraterrestrial environments, and is a frequent member of NIH, NSF, and VA research review committees.

The National Institute of Mental Health has funded Lang's research continuously for over thirty years, and he has received many other research grant awards from NASA, NIA, and NATO, and private research foundations. His published work includes more than 180 research papers, many of which have subsequently appeared in edited collections. A quantitative analysis of psychological research papers in the 1990s that appeared in the *APS Observer* listed Lang among the top ten psychologists with greatest impact on the field. He has highly influential research programs in both basic and applied studies, and has collaborated in many multisite investigations, both national and international. His research areas of interest include basic studies in emotion and cognition, applications in fear and anxiety, psychophysiology, and neural imaging.

The first PhD student trained by Lang (at the University of Pittsburgh) won the American Institute of Research prize for the best thesis on mental health submitted that year in this country. He has since mentored a distinguished series of graduate and postdoctoral students who have gone on to be outstanding researchers, presidents of scientific societies, directors of clinical training, chairs of departments of psychology, and recipients of scientific awards. Lang has received a Career Development Award from NIMH, and the prestigious MERIT award from NIMH for his project on the psychophysiology of fear and anxiety. He has received faculty research awards from the Universities of Wisconsin and Florida. He has received the Award for Distinguished Contributions to Psychophysiology from the Society for Psychophysiological Research, the Distinguished Scientist Award from the Society for a Science of Clinical Psychology, and the Distinguished Scientific Contribution Award from the American Psychological Association. Lang's outstanding scholarship and international scientific stature have been recognized by honorary doctoral degrees from the University of Uppsala in Sweden and the University of Tübingen in Germany.

Lang's primary scholarly interest is the study of human emotion, with a particular focus on fear and anxiety. He was a seminal investigator in the field of behavior therapy, and his early research on the desensitization of fear was a key part of that method's primary experimental foundation. He subsequently contributed importantly to several areas of research in psychophysiology, exploring the limits in humans of learned control over cardiovascular responses, studying cortical reactivity in attention and action, and developing a new theory of emotional imagery that integrated physiological and information processing perspectives.

Lang's early emphasis on multiple response measurement in the study of affect had wide influence both on basic studies of emotion and on research in psychopathology. In this view, emotion is a construct defined by measures in three response domains: (a) evaluative report and expressive language; (b) overt actions; and (c) patterns of physiological reactivity. Because these three systems are often independently modified, and only modestly correlated, comprehensive emotion analysis cannot be accomplished if only one system is assessed (e.g., reports of emotional experience). Lang contends that two primary goals of emotion theory should be to account for response system concordance and discordance and to relate system output and organization to mediating brain structures.

Current work in Lang's laboratory explores the motivational determinants of emotion, using methods based on research in cognitive science, and guided by neurophysiological studies from the animal laboratory. A key discovery was the finding that the reflexive response to an incidental startle probe (e.g., a brief [50 ms] noise burst), presented while human participants attend to a foreground event, is systematically modulated according to the emotional quality of that foreground. Thus, for example, when an affectively positive (pleasant) scene or event is viewed, the probe startle reflex is partially inhibited; however, if the scene is affectively negative (unpleasant), the reflex is potentiated. A major early component of the startle reflex—the eyeblink—is readily measured by electromyographic recording from the orbicularis occuli muscle. Using this response, a primary dimension of emotional perception known as affective valence is readily measured. The method is founded on an obligatory (nonvoluntary) reflex circuit, and does not depend on human intention or verbal report. Research has demonstrated that the effect is independent of startle probe modality (auditory, visual, or tactile), and general for negatively and positively valenced percepts, regardless of whether they are prompted by pictures, sounds, or text. Furthermore, modulation in both directions (inhibition or potentiation) is enhanced when the appropriate stimulus type (pleasant or unpleasant) are judged to be more emotionally arousing.

Lang uses the startle reflex to probe emotional states in humans, and evaluate individual differences. Related studies explore the neural circuitry of emotional perception, using high-density electroencephalography and functional magnetic resonance imaging (fMRI) of the brain. Standardized emotional stimuli developed in this work are widely used in research laboratories throughout the world. In addition to its contributions to basic research on emotion, Lang's research program has important applications—in understanding the anxiety disorders and other psychopathology, in interpreting the emotional effects of media, and in determining how emotional images may influence the viewing society.

STAFF

LANGE, CARL GEORG (1834–1900)

A Danish physician and psychologist, Carl Georg Lange was professor of pathological anatomy at the University of Copenhagen for most of his life.

Lange is best known for his theory of emotion, which he published in 1885, a year after a very similar theory had been set forth by the American philosopher and psychologist William James. The two men came to similar conclusions quite independently of each other, but while there were some differences, the similarities were so great that the theory has long been identified as the James-Lange theory of emotions.

Lange distinguished emotion from passion, which James did not. For Lange, emotions included joy, sorrow, fear, and anger, while passions referred to love, hate, and admiration. Thus his theory applied only to the emotions. Also, his theory was more limited in formulation than that of James. But for both men the emotional experience followed the perception of internal physiological processes. An earlier theory, prevalent at the time, stated the reverse: The emotional experience preceded the physiological processes. For Lange, the emotion arose out of a perception of the activity of the circulatory system. James had related the emotion to a perception of visceral activity, as well as to body movement such as running from a feared object.

After reading Lange's paper on emotion, James republished his original theory with amplifications in his *Principles of Psychology* (1890). In 1922 Knight Dunlap edited Lange's book *The Emotions,* in which he gave credit to both James and Lange.

R. W. LUNDIN
Wheaton, Illinois

LANGUAGE ACQUISITION

In one of the most amazing of human feats, infants born into the world master a complex linguistic system within a relatively short amount of time. Abilities relevant to language acquisition are present early in life. Experimental evidence indicates that newborns are able to recognize their mother's voice from in utero exposure (De-Casper & Fifer, 1980), and are even able to recognize a particular story that was read to them in utero, probably on the basis of prosodic or other acoustic cues (DeCasper & Spence, 1986). In the first half-year of life, infants are able to discriminate both phonetic contrasts that occur and those that do not occur in their native language, but before the first year is up, generally lose the ability to distinguish contrasts not relevant to their native language (Werker & Tess, 1984). At the same time during this first year, infants are learning to distinguish additional characteristics of their native language, such as the prosodic structure and legal combinations of phonemes (Jusczyk, Friederici, Wessels, Svenkerud, & Jusczyk, 1993).

Language production starts in the first year of life with cooing and babbling, which increases in complexity and mirrors the prosodic patterns of the native language. Children start producing words around their first birthday. Initially, productive vocabulary acquisition is slow. Then at around 18 months, a burst in vocabulary acquisition occurs. In English, early words tend to be common nouns. With increasing vocabulary size, verbs and adjectives begin to increase in number, followed by growth in grammatical function words—that is, words like prepositions and articles (Bates et al., 1994). This early noun dominance is not found in all languages (Tardif, 1996). What words and word classes will be acquired early is probably a function of frequency and saliency in parental input, as well as their phonological or morphological complexity.

There may be constraints or principles that guide children in the acquisition of word meaning. For example, children tend to generalize the meanings of nouns on the basis of similar shape (e.g., calling the moon 'ball'), and sometimes on similar function. When confronted with a new word, children appear to be constrained in what they consider as possible referents for that word, tending to assign it to a novel object or to an object or part of an object for which they do not already have a name. An outline of the development and use of such principles, and how this development corresponds to nominal vocabulary growth, is given in Golinkoff, Mervis, and Hirsh-Pasek (1994).

Grammatically, children start off producing single-word utterances. With increasing age, utterances increase in length (generally measured in terms of number of morphemes—that is, meaningful units, rather than words per se) and sophistication. Early multiword speech tends to leave out unstressed and grammatical elements, although comprehension studies show that children do know what grammatical words are appropriate in a sentence frame (Gerken & McIntosh, 1993), and even children at the one word stage have mastery of grammatical devices such as word order in comprehension (Hirsh-Pasek, & Golinkoff, 1996). Grammatical sophistication increases with age, with predictable patterns of mastery on structures such as negation, questions, passives, and relative clauses.

THEORETICAL ORIENTATIONS

Because language learning occurs so quickly, and with such apparent ease, researchers such as Chomsky and Fodor have proposed that language learning is fundamentally different from other cognitive processes, and involves an innate, language-specific component. Much of this claim revolves around the mastery of the grammar, or syntax, of language. Theorists from this camp claim that the linguistic input that a child receives does not contain enough information to allow a child to deduce the grammatical structure of the language correctly. Thus, some innate contribution is necessary to enable the child to overcome this poverty of the stimulus. One particularly influential innate language-specific theory is parameter setting, which proposes that an infant is born with a set of switches, or parameters, that code all possible linguistic variation. These parameters begin with a default setting. Linguistic input then triggers these parameters to be set to the value appropriate for that language. Setting the parameter then grants mastery of particular syntactic structures of that language. This mastery may encompass other structures than those represented in the trigger input. Thus, through the combination of the innate parameters and triggers from the linguistic input, grammatical mastery is achieved.

In contrast to the above viewpoint, other researchers see language acquisition as an issue of general learning. According to this view, children bring general learning processes to language, and apply these to the input, which contains enough information for the child to figure out the grammar. Indeed, there is ample accumulating evidence that the linguistic input that children receive is not nearly as impoverished as innatists portray, and children appear to be sensitive to this information. For example, there are differences in phonetic and acoustic properties between content words and grammatical function words that may allow infants to distinguish between them (Morgan, Shi, & Allopenna, 1996). In addition, there is a high (although imperfect) correlation between prosodic units and syntactic units in speech. It has been demonstrated that during the first year of life, infants become sensitive to the prosodic cues that coincide with clause and phrase level boundaries (see Jusczyk, 1997). These prosodic cues may be exaggerated in speech directed to infants. There is also evidence that children can use general learning mechanisms to rapidly acquire knowledge about the speech stream. For example, with as little as two minutes of exposure to novel connected speech, infants can use statistical properties (i.e., what sequences are more likely to be heard together) present in the input to parse the speech stream (Saffran, Aslin, & Newport, 1996). Proponents of the general learning mechanism approach postulate that these and other types of information allow children to bootstrap up from the input to the grammar (see Hirsh-Pasek & Golinkoff, 1996).

REFERENCES

Bates, E., Marchman, V., Thal, D., Fenson, L., Dale, P., Reznick, J. S., Reilly, J., & Hartung, J. (1994). Developmental and stylistic variation in the composition of early vocabulary. *Journal of Child Language, 21,* 85–123.

DeCasper, A. J., & Fifer, W. P. (1980). Of human bonding: Newborns prefer their mother's voices. *Science, 208,* 1174–1176.

DeCasper, A. J., & Spence, M. J. (1986). Prenatal maternal speech influences newborns' perception of speech sounds. *Infant Behavior and Development, 9,* 133–150.

Gerken, L., & McIntosh, B. J. (1993). Interplay of function morphemes and prosody in early language. *Developmental Psychology, 29,* 448–457.

Golinkoff, R. M., Mervis, C. B., & Hirsh-Pasek, K. (1994). Early object labels: The case for a developmental lexical principles framework. *Journal of Child Language, 21,* 125–155.

Hirsh-Pasek, K., & Golinkoff, R. M. (1996). *The origins of grammar.* Cambridge, MA: MIT Press.

Jusczyk, P. W. (1997). *The discovery of spoken language.* Cambridge, MA: MIT Press.

Jusczyk, P. W., Friederici, A. D., Wessels, J., Svenkerud, V. Y., & Jusczyk, A. M. (1993). Infants' sensitivity to the sound patterns of native language words. *Journal of Memory and Language, 32,* 402–420.

Morgan, J. L., Shi, R., & Allopenna, P. (1996). Perceptual bases of rudimentary grammatical categories: Toward a broader conceptualization of bootstrapping. In J. L. Morgan and K. Demuth (Eds.), *Signal to syntax.* Mahwah, NJ: Erlbaum.

Saffran, J. R., Aslin, R. N., & Newport, E. L. (1996). Statistical learning by 8-month-old infants. *Science, 274,* 1926–1928.

Tardif, T. (1996). Nouns are not always learned before verbs: Evidence from Mandarin speakers early vocabularies. *Developmental Psychology, 32,* 492–504.

Werker, J. F., & Tess, R. C. (1984). Cross-language speech perception: Evidence for perceptual reorganization during the first year of life. *Infant Behavior and Development, 7,* 49–63.

J. L. McDonald
Louisiana State University

LANGUAGE DEVELOPMENT
SPEECH DEVELOPMENT

LANGUAGE DEVELOPMENT

Learning language is a lifelong process, beginning in the first months of life and continuing throughout adulthood. The most rapid learning occurs during early childhood, as by age 6 children have mastered the basic pronunciation, grammar, and more than 90% of the basic vocabulary of their native language. They use this mastery to communicate a wide variety of needs, wishes, ideas, and concerns.

THEORIES OF LANGUAGE DEVELOPMENT

Two quite different theories have been proposed to explain the human ability to learn language. One, originally proposed by Skinner in *Verbal Behavior,* suggests that children learn to talk through classical and operant conditioning. For instance, if Daddy says "Daddy" over and over when he plays with his infant, and if he grins whenever the baby says "dada," the infant will learn the word. This theory helps explain why one child might be much more skilled with language than another. It also can explain why groups of children, on average, have different language abilities. For instance, girls, children from small families, and middle- and upper-class children tend to be superior in language ability to their opposites.

The second theory, proposed by Chomsky in *Language and the Mind* and by McNeill in *The Acquisition of Language,* argues that language learning is largely innate. Just as a child walks when sufficient maturation occurs, so a child talks when the child's brain is ready. It is as if there were a language acquisition device (LAD) in the mind already programmed with the underlying linguistic rules. Only a minimal amount of specific language information is needed to learn whatever language the child's parents speak. This theory helps explain why children all over the world follow similar sequences of language development.

While both theories have their adherents, a third perspective on language development seems more firmly grounded in research. This theory holds that the interaction between infant and caregiver, and between one person and another, is the heart of language learning. That humans are innately sensitized to learn language is shown by evidence from deaf as well as hearing infants, for the deaf master sign language at the same rate, and in the same sequence, as hearing children master speech. At the same time, the specific responsiveness of other people has great influence on language mastery, from the fine-tuned play of mother and infant to the precise verbal and nonverbal communication between one adult and another. Thus the interaction of person and environment produces language.

ASPECTS OF LANGUAGE

Four separate aspects of language development have been studied: phonology (the sounds); syntax (the underlying structure); semantics (the meanings of words and phrases); and pragmatics (the practical communication skills).

Phonology

From the moment of birth, infants communicate with various cries, indicating hunger, pain, need for attention, and so forth. By 3 months, infants laugh and "coo," emitting vowel-like sounds of pleasure, and from 6 to 12 months they babble a variety of sounds, particularly the /d/, /m/, /p/, /n/, and /b/. At first these early communications are reflexive—even deaf babies babble—rather than deliberate attempts to communicate with sound. However, infants gradually become more intentional and responsive in their noise-making. They babble in response to talk and then wait for a reply, long before the content of the reply is understood. At about 12 months, when they finally connect the usual sounds that they babble, such as dada, mama, papa, nana, and baba, with specific people and objects in their lives, they are speaking their first words. From this point on, the sounds they produce come closer to standard speech, although many 5-year-olds still have some articulation problems.

After puberty, it becomes much more difficult for people to learn to produce sounds they have not practiced in childhood. Consequently, adults who learn another language almost always speak with an accent that reflects their mother tongue.

Semantics

Even before they begin to speak, infants understand the meanings of words: "No!" makes many an infant pause and "Mommy" or "Daddy" triggers looking for the designated parent. By 18 months, most children have a speaking vocabulary of a dozen or more words and seem to comprehend far more. At about age 2, many children undergo a language explosion as new words and phrases enter the vocabulary rapidly. Some children spend much of their time asking "what that," and seem limited only by their caregivers' patience as they attempt to learn the name of every object in their environment.

However, correct use of a word in one context does not guarantee that a child will use it correctly in another. Young children typically use "no" to mean any negation ("I no come"), and "doggie" to mean any four-legged animal. While semantic understanding proceeds rapidly in early childhood, certain common words are troublesome because they demand more cognitive sophistication than young children possess; "because" and "although," "here" and "there," and "yesterday" and "today" may be misused by a child who otherwise seems quite skilled with words.

In our culture, at almost every age the complexity and precision of a person's vocabulary is probably the best single indicator of intellectual ability and education. Semantics is one aspect of language that shows documented improvement throughout adulthood, at least until old age, especially for people such as writers and scholars who spend their lives trying to use words creatively and precisely.

Syntax

Children demonstrate some understanding of the structure of language when they first put two words together to make a sentence, an event that usually occurs between 18 months and 2 years. These two-word sentences show the child's comprehension of word order as an important grammatical tool: Toddlers say "more juice" and "go play," rather than "juice more" and "play go."

Syntactical understanding improves with age in a regular sequence. For example, children learn to form the plural before the past tense. As they learn the rules, children overregularize the language, talking for instance of "mouses" or "foots." Preschoolers show an impressive grasp of much of the syntax of their mother tongue, but during middle childhood, adolescence, and adulthood people become progressively better at understanding and applying the formal rules of syntax.

Pragmatics

A person's ability to communicate with language involves far more than acceptable phonology, semantics, and syntax: It involves tailoring the form of the message to fit the needs of the audience. Accordingly, people speak one way on the street and another way in the classroom, one way to a boss and another way to a baby. Pragmatics is the study of these differences.

Gestures and body language play a large role in pragmatics and are evident in the first months of life, as infants wave their arms in excitement or avert their gazes to indicate that they do not want to play. It is hard to know how much of this is intentional, but when a one-year-old raises her arms to be picked up or points his finger at a desired toy—especially when either gesture is accompanied by an insistent grunt—the message is clear.

Skill in communication develops throughout life. For instance, until about age 7 many young children are unaware that their own idiosyncratic experiences and vocabulary are not understood by others. Given the misunderstandings common among adults, it is obvious that pragmatics is a lifelong task.

REFERENCES

Chomsky, N. (1968). *Language and the mind.* New York: Harcourt, Brace & World.

McNeill, D. (1970). *The acquisition of language: The study of developmental psycholinguistics.* New York: Harper & Row.

Skinner, B. F. (1957). *Verbal behavior.* New York: Appleton-Century-Crofts.

SUGGESTED READING

Dale, P. S. (1976). *Language development: Structure and function* (2nd ed.). New York: Holt.

De Villiers, J. G., & de Villiers, P. A. (1978). *Language acquisition.* Cambridge, MA: Harvard University Press.

Meadow, K. P. (1980). *Deafness and child development.* Berkeley, CA: University of California Press.

K. S. BERGER
City University of New York

BIOLOGICAL RHYTHMS
SPEECH DEVELOPMENT

LANGUAGE IN GREAT APES

The issue of mental continuity is a major one stimulating research investigating language in great apes. Do the cognitive and linguistic abilities of humans as well as morphological structures exhibit continuity with nonhuman animals? Are humans unique because they have souls or minds while infrahumans do not? In what does the uniqueness of homo sapiens lie? Many argue that to have a mind or to be capable of thought depends upon language; for some philosophers, mind is identical with the ability to use language. If an infrahuman can be shown to have language, are humans still unique? These issues set the stage for ape language research.

There were early attempts to teach apes to produce words vocally (Ristau & Robbins, 1982). Suffice it to say that after extensive training apes could never say more than "papa," "up," and "cup." Subsequent research indicated that apes may lack the necessary physiologic machinery to produce something akin to human speech.

The pioneering work of Gardner and Gardner (1980) took advantage of the apes' natural tendencies to use manual gestures. Their first chimpanzee, a female named Washoe, learned to produce over 130 hand signs after 4 years of training. A second project with much younger chimpanzees showed much faster rates of learning. Patterson (1980) has taught gorillas to produce hand signs as well as understand spoken English. Terrace and his associates (1979) have used videotape extensively in the data collection process and have gathered a large corpus of the hand signs of the chimpanzee Nim. There are also two nonsigning projects using artificial visual designs: Savage-Rumbaugh and Rumbaugh (1980) have used a computer-based lexigram system, while Premack (1976) has taught chimpanzees to use haphazardly shaped plastic chips that are wordlike in function.

The signing projects have the advantage that the full repertoire of vocabulary items is available to the apes at all times. The major disadvantage concerns recording the apes' productions. Terrace and his associates are the only ones to have done the laborious and detailed analysis of the apes' productions and so-called conversations. The Nim project apparently placed great emphasis on drills and had too many trainers. The main conclusions reached by the investigators of that project were that the productions of Nim—and presumably those of other apes—are not linguistic, primarily because of a lack of grammar. The apes' use of signing is unlike humans' in several respects: Their communications are short in length; they become highly repetitive as length increases; the apes imitate much prior signing by their human trainers; and apparently their productions lack spontaneity. Critics reply that Nim's poor performances may result from the use of drills in training and also from the large number of trainers, which created a situation in which strong social bonds were not maintained. The importance of a strong positive social relationship between the ape and the trainer is emphasized in most projects, since such bonds obviously exist for humans in the initial acquisition of language.

From all these studies one can conclude that signs and items in the artificial lexicons do, on some occasions, operate as if they represent objects or events in the real world. Yet there is no convincing evidence that apes' utterances are grammatical. Further, the rate of acquisition for the apes is dramatically lower than that of human children; the average length of utterance is short; and the apes seem to repeat much and not add to what has just been communicated to them. It is thus difficult to conclude that the apes' productions bear more than a rudimentary similarity to human language. However, one would probably find it difficult to describe the production of young children as linguistic, if we did not know that these children will grow into language-using adults. And the ape language projects do indicate cognitive abilities and possible mental states in the apes.

REFERENCES

Gardner, B. T., & Gardner, R. A. (1980). Two comparative psychologists look at language acquisition. In K. E. Nelson (Ed.), *Children's language* (Vol. 2). New York: Gardner Press.

Patterson, F. (1980). Creative and innovative uses of language by a gorilla: A case study. In K. E. Nelson (Ed.), *Children's language* (Vol. 2). New York: Gardner Press.

Premack, D. (1976). *Intelligence in ape and man.* Hillsdale, NJ: Erlbaum.

Ristau, C. A., & Robbins, D. (1982). Language in great apes: A critical review. In J. S. Rosenblatt (Ed.), *Advances in the study of behavior.* New York: Academic.

Savage-Rumbaugh, E. S., Rumbaugh, D. M., & Boysen, S. (1980). Do apes use language? *American Scientist, 68,* 49–61.

Terrace, H. S. (1979). *Nim: A chimpanzee who learned sign language.* New York: Knopf.

D. ROBBINS
Fordham University

ANIMAL COMMUNICATION

LASHLEY, KARL (1890–1958)

One of the early behaviorists in psychology in the United States, Karl Lashley is best known for his work on localization of brain functions and his discoveries of how imprecise and generalized the functions of the brain can be. He was a student of John B. Watson at Johns Hopkins University, where he got the PhD in 1915. He was on the staff of the universities of Minnesota (1917–1926), Chicago (1929–1935), Harvard (1935–1952), and the Yerkes Laboratory of Primate Biology.

His behavioristic interpretation of consciousness put him in general agreement with the ideas of Watson. He had no use for the concept of consciousness or the method of introspection. Watson considered the brain a "mystery box," while Lashley was interested in digging—quite literally—into the brain to find out the nature of its functions.

As a result of his own research and that done with Shepard I. Franz, Lashley formulated two principles of brain functioning: mass action and equipotentiality. To illustrate the principle of *mass action,* Lashley taught cats to escape from a puzzle box, then removed various parts of the cortex of the animals' brains. After the cats had recovered from the operation, they were placed back in the box. He found that the cats could no longer perform the acquired task, but with further training they could relearn the task even in cases in which both frontal lobes had been removed. On the basis of this experiment and many others, the principle of mass action indicated that learning was not dependent on specific neural connections in the brain but on the brain as a whole. The rate of relearning turned out to be a function of the total mass of brain tissue involved.

The principle of *equipotentiality* stated that each part of the brain was just as important as any other. If some parts of the brain were removed, other parts could carry on their functions. For example, when the visual area of rats' brains was removed, although they lost patterning, the rats could still discriminate differences in light intensity and could follow light.

Lashley's major publication was *Brain Mechanisms and Intelligence.*

R. W. LUNDIN
Wheaton, Illinois

LATE-LIFE FORGETTING

There is considerable public concern that memory loss signals the beginning of Alzheimer's disease or senility. Early diagnosis, combined with intervention and family support, can assist older adults with memory loss to function and to manage life on a daily basis in the least restrictive setting.

The first task for the health professional faced by a patient concerned about memory loss is to ascertain whether the symptoms are indicative of dementia or whether they are the result of the normal decline in cognitive abilities associated with the aging process. Even if there is a diagnosis of dementia (defined by the American Psychiatric Association as a loss of intellectual abilities of sufficient severity to interfere with social or occupational functioning), it is important to determine whether the dementia is reversible or not. If the cause is determined promptly, some dementias are reversible, because an almost limitless array of diseases and behavioral disorders can result in a dementing process. Lezak (1983) points out that memory loss serves as a starting point for differentiating individuals with normal forgetting from those who do not warrant a diagnosis of dementia.

Two types of memory impairments are described by LaRue (1982) to distinguish between normal and nonnormal forgetting. Originally, these were labeled benign senescent forgetfulness and malignant senescent forgetfulness. Benign forgetfulness was characterized by memory failures limited to relatively unimportant facts but included the ability to recall these at a later time. Most of the forgotten aspects were part of the remote rather than recent past, and the individual was usually aware of the memory loss and could compensate for it. In some ways, this type of forgetting is not unlike the "absentminded professor" stereotype. In contrast, malignant forgetfulness of old age included distortion of memories, reduced retention time, and difficulties in remembering recent events and experience. In addition, disorientation to place, time, and eventually person also occurred. On the face of it, this seemed to be a straightforward distinction between types of forgetfulness. Critics have speculated whether benign and malignant senescent forgetfulness are points on a continuum rather than separate conditions.

There have been attempts to define changes in memory associated with normal aging. A National Institute of Mental Health work group was established in 1986 to study and encourage research and communication in this area. This group published diagnostic criteria for what they termed age-associated memory impairment (AAMI). The criteria for AAMI required the presence of memory complaints based on a gradual onset of memory loss in adults 50 years and older functioning within an acceptable intel-

lectual level (specifically defined by the criteria). To meet the criteria of AAMI, individuals must perform 1 standard deviation (SD) below the average established for younger adults on tests of recent memory. In addition, a number of criteria exclude an individual from meeting the AAMI category. These include the presence of dementia, alcohol dependence, depression, certain neurological disorders, and other medical disorders. Current use of psychotropic drugs also would disqualify an individual from meeting the diagnostic criteria. AAMI, it was argued, was designed to describe older adults who have memory problems but who do not suffer from a neurological impairment. It was assumed that AAMI is a normal consequence of aging in a proportion of older individuals.

Blackford and LaRue (1989) take some issue with the measurement aspects of AAMI. They recommended that there should be two categories within AAMI: age-consistent memory impairment and late-life forgetfulness. The criteria for age-consistent memory impairment include performance on 75% of memory tests used that are with +1 SD of the mean established for that participant's age.

The criteria for late-life forgetting requires performance on 50% or more of the tests given that are within 1 to 2 SD below the mean established for that age. The exclusion criteria for each of these subcategories is somewhat similar to those stated previously for age-associated memory impairments. All these categories apply to individuals between the ages of 50 to 79 so that individuals 80 and above are excluded.

Smith and others (1991) studied age-associated memory impairment, age-consistent memory impairment, and late-life forgetting by testing 523 cognitively normal older adults living in the community. The researchers did not seek out individuals who complained of memory problems. In fact, they specifically selected participants who did not present memory complaints. After excluding those participants who did not meet criteria (e.g., those who were taking psychotropic medications or had histories of alcohol abuse or who had medical, neurological, or other relevant disorders), they found that 98% of members in one group and 77% of members in another group met criteria for age-associated memory impairments as suggested by the National Institute of Mental Health. The researchers concluded that age-related changes in memory should avoid the implication of disability suggested by the term "impairment." They believe that a better term would be "age-associated memory decline." They also recommended that more effort be expended at developing normative data for individuals of advanced age, including the old-old. Finally, the researchers recommended that a specific memory battery be used rather than permitting researchers to select from a range of testing instruments. Smith and coworkers (1991) point out that there is wide variability in the diagnosis of early or probable dementia and the use of the term "impairment" suggests abnormality and disease. They counter that the true meaning of scoring 1 SD below that of younger individuals in decline of memory functions has not been determined. In the meantime, it might be best not to label such declines as pathological.

Some more recent developments include the addition of a listing titled "age related cognitive decline" in DSM-IV. This is found under "other conditions that may be a focus of clinical attention." The condition refers to declines in cognitive functioning as a result of the aging process and includes those changes that are within normal limits given the person's age. Another recent development is the *Guidelines for the Evaluation of Dementia and Age Related Cognitive Decline* which were passed in 1998 by the American Psychological Association's Council of Representatives. They can be found in the December 1998 issue of the *American Psychologist*. The entire area of memory status for older adults is undergoing considerable research and the definitive answers are not yet available.

REFERENCES

Blackford, R. C., & LaRue, A. (1989). Criteria for diagnosing age associated memory impairment: Proposed, improvements from the field. *Developmental Neuropsychology, 5,* 295–306.

LaRue, A. (1982). Memory loss and aging. *Psychiatric Clinics of North America, 5,* 89–103.

Lezak, M. D. (1983). *Neuropsychological assessment,* (2nd ed.). New York: Oxford University Press.

Smith G., Ivnik, R. R., Peterson, R. C., Malec, J. F., Kokmen, E., & Tangalos, E. (1991). Age associated memory impairment diagnoses: Problems of reliability and concerns for terminology. *Psychology and Aging, 6,* 551–558.

N. ABELES
Michigan State University

AGING: PHYSIOLOGICAL AND BEHAVIORAL CONCOMITANTS
ALZHEIMER'S DISEASE

LATE-LIFE PSYCHOSIS

The number of elderly persons with psychosis will increase with the increasing geriatric population. The factors leading to this increase include comorbid physical illnesses, age-related pharmacokinetic and pharmacodynamic changes, social isolation, sensory deficits, cognitive changes, polypharmacy, and substance abuse. Other possible risk factors include age-related deterioration of cortical areas and neurochemical changes, genetic predisposition, certain premorbid personalities like schizotypal and paranoid types, and female gender.

The diagnostic categories commonly associated with psychosis in the elderly (see *DSM-IV*) include delirium, Schizophrenia, Delusional Disorder, mood disorder, dementia, substance abuse, medical conditions, neurological conditions, and drug-induced psychosis.

The Epidemiologic Catchment Area Study showed a six-month prevalence for schizophrenia and schizophreniform disorders, ranging from 0.2% to 0.9% at three sites; cognitive impairment, including organic psychosis, ranged from 16.8%–23%. In a study of 57 patients with Alzheimer's disease, 63% developed psychotic symptoms. The prevalence of delirium is reported to be 11% to 24%

in elderly patients on hospital admission, but much higher in postsurgical patients.

Structural abnormalities in the brain have been reported in elderly patients with psychotic disorders. The structural changes have included white matter hyperintensities and focal brain disease of vascular origin. Two thirds of the subjects with late onset psychotic disorders had abnormal brain imaging studies and 50% of the subjects had white matter lesions greater than 5 cm^2 and/or lacunar infarctions.

DELIRIUM

Delirium is an acute state characterized by changes in cognition and consciousness, often accompanied by psychotic symptoms, predominantly visual hallucinations, and paranoid delusions. Delirium may be superimposed on other neuropsychiatric conditions such as Schizophrenia, mood disorders, or dementia, complicating the diagnosis. Clouded consciousness, poor attention span, and a fluctuating course during the day are differentiating features that help in the diagnosis. Early recognition and treatment of the underlying cause are important to reduce the high morbidity and mortality. Common causes of delirium in the elderly include infections, especially urinary tract and upper respiratory; drugs, especially anticholinergic; electrolyte imbalance; arrythmias; and myocardial infarction. Other causes include transient ischemic attacks, cerebrovascular accidents, structural brain lesions such as tumors, and withdrawal from prescription medications (such as benzodiazepines) and substances of potential abuse (such as alcohol). Disruption of the cerebral metabolism and neurotransmission, particularly of the dopamine and GABA pathways, have been implicated in the pathophysiology of delirium. In some cases, persistent cognitive deficits may reflect a concurrent dementing illness.

SCHIZOPHRENIA

Schizophrenia may continue into old age (Early Onset Schizophrenia—EOS) or its first episode may occur in patients older than 45 (Late Onset Schizophrenia—LOS). Approximately 15% of all patients with schizophrenia may have onset of symptoms after the age of 45. Even though the clinical presentation of both EOS and LOS may be the same, there are some differences between the two. LOS is more common in women, has fewer negative symptoms, and tends to respond to lower doses of antipsychotic medication than EOS. MRI study of the comparative size of thalami found them to be larger in LOS than EOS.

Symptoms of EOS do not usually worsen with age, but tend to become less severe and may not require ongoing antipsychotic medications. Both positive and negative symptoms improve in about 20% of patients, remain relatively unchanged in 60% of patients, and worsen in only 20% of patients.

DELUSIONAL DISORDER

As per *DSM-IV,* patients with Delusional Disorder reveal persistent delusions without prominent hallucinations in the absence of dementia, schizophrenia, or mood disorders. Age of onset is later in women. The delusions are nonbizarre and usually circumscribed. Certain premorbid personality disorders (e.g., schizotypal, paranoid), early life trauma, hearing loss, immigration status, and socioeconomic status have been reported to be associated with Delusional Disorder. Patients are generally resistant to treatment.

MOOD DISORDER WITH PSYCHOSIS

Mania and depression in the elderly can be associated with psychotic symptoms such as delusions and hallucinations, which are usually mood congruent. In one study, 36% of patients being treated for depression were observed to have delusions. Elderly patients with psychotic depression are at increased risk for relapse and have more persistent symptoms, suicide attempts, hospitalizations, comorbidity, and financial dependency.

DEMENTIA WITH PSYCHOSIS

Psychotic symptoms can occur in dementia secondary to various etiologies, including Alzheimer's Disease, Vascular Dementia, Alcohol-Related Dementia, Parkinson's Disease, Dementia with Lewy Bodies, and Huntington's Disease. By far, Alzheimer's Disease is the most common cause of dementia, and more than 50% of patients manifest psychotic symptoms during the course of the illness. A survey of Alzheimer's literature found median percentages of 28% for the occurrence of hallucinations, 44% for agitation, 24% for verbal aggression, 34% for disturbed ideation (delusions), and 18% for wandering. Visual hallucinations are common in Dementia with Lewy Bodies.

Detailed discussion of late life psychotic disorder due to medical or neurological conditions, substance abuse, and prescription drugs is beyond the scope of this article and may be found elsewhere.

TREATMENT OF LATE-LIFE PSYCHOSIS

A thorough psychiatric history and assessment of underlying medical conditions and concomitant medications are essential before initiation of treatment. Social, behavioral, and environmental interventions should be considered before pharmacotherapy. Antipsychotic drugs constitute the mainstay of treatment for psychotic disorders in the elderly. Other treatment options include cholinesterase inhibitor drugs for patients with Alzheimer's Dementia, electroconvulsive therapy for elderly depressed patients with psychosis, mood stabilizers, benzodiazepines, and buspirone.

Age-related pharmacokinetic and pharmacodynamic factors, comorbid medical illnesses, and concurrent medications increase the vulnerability for side effects and drug interactions in this population. The geriatric psychopharmacology maxim "start low and go slow" should be followed in the use of these medications. Generally, the appropriate starting dose of antipsychotics in the elderly is 25% of the adult dose. Total daily maintenance may be up to 30–50% of the adult dose. Some patients may require higher doses because of genetic variability of CYP 450 metabolism. Antipsychotic medications in the elderly, as with younger individuals, can require six weeks or longer for optimum therapeutic effects. The dose of antipsychotic medication for an older schizophrenic patient tends to correlate inversely with current age and with age at onset of illness. Dose requirements often decrease over time with chronically ill schizophrenic patients. Patients with a diagnosis of Dementia generally require smaller doses of antipsychotics than do patients with Schizophrenia.

Conventional Antipsychotics

The use of conventional antipsychotics is limited because of their increased potential for tardive dyskinesia (TD), extrapyramidal symptoms (EPS), and anticholinergic and cardiovascular side effects. The advantages include the availability of parenteral preparation for rapid control of agitation and long-acting, injectable preparations for haloperidol and fluphenazine.

Atypical Antipsychotics

The atypical agents have been found to be as efficacious as conventional agents in reducing positive symptoms, more efficacious in reducing negative symptoms, and to have a much safer side effect profile. The currently marketed atypical agents are clozapine, risperidone, olanzapine, and quetiapine.

Clozapine has moderate to good efficacy and very low rate of EPS, but has significant other side effects including delirium, somnolence, orthostasis/falls, agranulocytosis/leukopenia, and cardiac effects. Currently, clozapine remains the only antipsychotic medication with clear demonstrated efficacy in the treatment of refractory Schizophrenia. The recommended starting dose of clozapine in the elderly is 6.25–12.5mg/day.

Risperidone is the most widely studied atypical agent in the elderly. Published reports include case series, retrospective, and open label studies in Schizophrenia and controlled trials in dementia. A recent, thorough review has been conducted by Madhusoodanan and colleagues (1999). All reported good efficacy. The most frequent side effects reported include sedation, dose dependent EPS, dizziness, and postural hypotension. The advantages include negligible anticholinergic effects, low incidence of EPS and TD (at low doses), and efficacy for positive and negative symptoms. The starting dose for elderly patients in 0.5 mg once or twice daily. The average dose for Schizophrenia is 2–3 mg per day and for Dementia, 1 mg/day.

Olanzapine studies in the elderly are limited. Results of Dementia studies range from no difference to superior efficacy from placebo. The effective dose range in dementia appears to be 5–10 mg/day. Olanzapine has been found to be safe and effective in Schizophrenia studies, and the mean dose was about 8–10 mg/day. The side effects include sedation, weight gain, mild anticholinergic effects, mild dizziness, and orthostasis. The advantages include low incidence of EPS and good effect on positive and negative symptoms.

Quetiapine is the least studied atypical agent in the elderly. A published report on elderly patients with psychotic disorders indicate significant improvement in symptom severity. The mean daily dose was 100 mg/day. Since this was a heterogeneous diagnostic group, doses may vary for specific psychiatric conditions. The mean daily dose at discharge for elderly psychotic patients who responded in a case series was 325 ± 189mg/day. The common adverse effects were somnolence, dizziness, and postural hypotension. Advantages include negligible EPS and minimal anticholinergic effects, with good effectiveness on positive and negative symptoms.

CONCLUSION

The new atypical antipsychotic agents offer significant advantages over conventional agents in the treatment of psychosis in the elderly. Long-term efficacy and safety studies and head-to-head comparison studies of the atypicals are needed to draw more definitive conclusions. Antipsychotic drugs form part of a comprehensive treatment plan which should include psychosocial, behavioral, and environmental interventions in the management of late life psychosis.

REFERENCES

American Psychiatric Association. (1994). *Diagnostic and Statistical Manual of Mental Disorders* (4th ed.). Washington, DC: Author.

American Psychiatric Association (1997). Practice guidelines for the treatment of patients with schizophrenia. *American Journal of Psychiatry, 154* (4 suppl.) 1–63.

Belitsky, R., & McGlashan, T. H. (1993). At issue: The manifestations of schizophrenia in late life: A dearth of data. *Schizophrenia Bulletin, 19,* 683–685.

Brown, F. W. (1993). The neurobiology of late-life psychosis. *Crit. Rev. Neurobiol., 7,* 275–289.

Corey-Bloom, J., Jernigan, T., Archibald, S., Harris, M. J., & Jeste, D. V. (1995). Quantitative magnetic resonance imaging in late-life schizophrenia. *American Journal of Psychiatry, 152,* 447–449.

Gurian, B. S., Wexler, D., & Baker, E. H. (1992). Late-life paranoia: Possible association with early trauma and infertility. *International Journal of Geriatric Psychiatry, 7,* 277–284.

Gustafson, Y., Berggren, D., Brannskrom, B., Bucht, G., Norberg, A., Hanssen, L. I., & Winblad, B. (1988). Acute confusional states in elderly patients treated for femoral neck fracture. *Journal of American Geriatric Society, 36,* 525–530.

Harris, M. J., & Jeste, D. V. (1988). Late onset schizophrenia: An overview. *Schizophrenia Bulletin, 14,* 39–55.

Janicak, P. G., Easton, M., Comaty, J. E. (1989). Efficacy of ECT in psychotic and non psychotic depression. *Convulsive Therapy, 5,* 314–320.

Jeste, D. V., Eastham, J. H., Lacro, J. P., Gierz, M., Field, M. G., & Harris, M. J. (1996). Management of late-life psychosis. *Journal of Clinical Psychiatry, 57* (Suppl. 3) 39–45.

Jeste, D. V., Harris, M. J., Krull, A., Kuck, J., McAdams, L. A., & Heaton, R. (1995). Clinical and neuropsychological characteristics of patients with late onset schizophrenia. *American Journal of Psychiatry, 152,* 722–730.

Jeste, D. V., Lacro, J. P., Gilbert, P. L., Kline, J., & Kline, N. (1993). Treatment of late life schizophrenia with neuroleptics. *Schizophrenia Bulletin, 19,* 817–830.

Katz, I., Jeste, D. V., Mintzer, J. E., Clyde, C., Napolitano, J., & Brecher, M. (1999). Comparison of risperidone and placebo for psychosis and behavioral disturbances associated with dementia. A randomized double blind trial. *Journal of Clinical Psychiatry, 60,* 107–115.

Kaufer, D. I., Cummings, J. L., & Christine, D. (1996). Effect of tacrine on behavioral symptoms in Alzheimer's disease: An open label study. *Journal of Geriatric Psychiatry and Neurology, 9,* 1–6.

Kotrla, K. J., Chacko, R. C., Harper, R. G., & Doody, R. (1995). Clinical variables associated with psychosis in Alzheimer's disease. *American Journal of Psychiatry, 152,* 1377–1379.

Lacro, J. P., & Jeste, D. V. (1997). Geriatric psychosis. *Psychiatric Quarterly, 68,* 247–260.

Lesser, I. M., Jeste, D. V., Boone, K. B., Harris, M. J., Miller, B. L., Heaton, R. K., & Hill-Gutierrez, E. (1992). Late onset psychotic disorder, not otherwise specified: Clinical and neuro imaging findings. *Biological Psychiatry, 31,* 419–423.

Lipowski, Z. (1989). Delirium in the elderly patient. *New England Journal of Medicine, 320,* 578–582.

Madhusoodanan, S., Alcantara, A., & Brenner, R. (2000). Efficacy and tolerability of quetiapine in geropsychiatric patients—A case series. *Journal of Geriatric Psychiatry and Neurology, 13,* 28–32.

Madhusoodanan, S., Brecher, M., Brenner, R., Kasckow, J., Kunik, M., & Negron, A. E. (1999). Risperidone in the treatment of elderly patients with psychotic disorders. *American Journal of Geriatric Psychiatry, 7,* 132–138.

Madhusoodanan, S., Brenner, R., Araujo, L., & Abaza, A. (1995). Efficacy of risperidone treatment for psychosis associated with schizophrenia, schizoaffective disorder, bipolar disorder or senile dementia in 11 geriatric patients: A case series. *Journal of Clinical Psychiatry, 56,* 514–518.

Madhusoodanan, S., Brenner, R., & Cohen, C. I. (1999). Role of atypical antipsychotics in the treatment of psychosis and agitation associated with dementia. *CNS Drugs, 12*(2), 135–150.

Madhusoodanan, S., Brenner, R., Suresh, P., Concepcion, N. M., Florita, C. D., Menon, G., Kaur, A., Nunez, G., & Reddy, H. (2000). Efficacy and tolerability of olanzapine in elderly patients with psychotic disorders: A prospective study. *Annals of Clinical Psychiatry, 12* (1), 11–18.

Madhusoodanan, S., Suresh, P., Brenner, R. (1999). Experience with atypical antipsychotics risperidone and olanzapine in the elderly. *Annals of Clinical Psychiatry, 11, (3),* 113–118.

McManus, D. Q., Arvanitis, L. A., & Kowalcyk, B. B. (1999). Quetiepine, a novel antipsychotic: Experience in elderly patients with psychotic disorders. *Journal of Clinical Psychiatry, 60* (5), 292–298.

Myers, J. K., Weissman, M. M., & Tischler, G. (1984). Six month prevalence of psychiatric disorders in three communities. *Archives of General Psychiatry, 41,* 959–970.

Nelson, J. C., Conwell, Y., Kim, K., & Mazure, C. (1989). Age at onset in late-life delusional depression. *American Journal of Psychiatry, 146,* 785–786.

Pearlson, G., & Rabins, P. (1988). The late-onset psychoses: Possible risk factors. *Psychiatric Clinics of North America, 11,* 15–32.

Rosen, J., Bohan, S., & Gershon, S. (1990). Antipsychotics in the elderly. *Acta Psychiatric Scandinavia,* (Suppl 358), 170–175.

Sajatovic, M., Madhusoodanan, S., & Buckley, P. (2000). Schizophrenia in the elderly: Guidelines for its recognition and treatment. *CNS Drugs, 13*(2), 103–115.

Sajatovic, M., Perez, D., Brescan, D., & Ramirez, L. F. (1998). Olanzapine therapy in elderly patients with schizophrenia. *Psychopharmacology Bulletin, 34*(4) 819–23.

Satterlee, W. G., Reams, S. G., Burns, P. R., Hamilton, S., Tran, P. V., & Tollefson, G. D. (1995). A clinical update on olanzapine treatment in schizophrenia and in elderly Alzheimer's disease patients (abstract). *Psychopharmacology Bulletin, 31,* 534.

Street, J., Clark, W. S., Mitan, S., Tamura, R., Kadem, D., Sanger, T., Gannon, K. S., & Tollefson, G. D. (1998, December 14–18). Olanzapine in the treatment of psychosis and behavioral disturbances associated with Alzheimer's disease. American College of Neuropsychopharmacology 37th Annual meeting. Las Croabas, Puerto Rico, *Scientific abstracts, 223.*

Targum, S. D., & Abbott, J. L. (1999). Psychoses in the elderly: A spectrum of disorders. *Journal of Clinical Psychiatry, 60*(Suppl 8), 4–10.

Tariot, P. N. (1996). Treatment strategies for agitation and psychosis in dementia. *Journal of Clinical Psychiatry, 57*(Suppl 14), 21–29.

Thorpe, L. (1997). The treatment of psychotic disorders in late life. *Canadian Journal of Psychiatry, 42*(suppl. 1), 195–275.

S. Madhusoodanan
St. John's Episcopal Hospital

R. Brenner
St. John's Episcopal Hospital

C. I. Cohen
State University of New York, Brooklyn

AGING: BEHAVIOR CHANGES
ALZHEIMER'S DISEASE
DEMENTIA
GERIATRIC PSYCHOLOGY
LIFE-SPAN DEVELOPMENT
PARKINSON'S DISEASE

LATENT INHIBITION

Latent inhibition (LI) is demonstrated when a previously exposed, unattended stimulus is less effective in a new learning situation than a novel stimulus. The term "latent inhibition" dates back to Lubow and Moore (1959), who intended to design a classical conditioning analog of latent learning. As such, the LI effect was "latent" in that it was not exhibited in the stimulus preexposure phase, but rather in the subsequent test phase. "Inhibition" simply reflected the fact that the effect was manifest as a *retardation* of learning. Since that first demonstration of LI over forty years ago, there have been hundreds of experiments which relate to the phenomenon. Latent inhibition has been found to be extremely robust, appearing in all mammalian species that have been tested and across many different learning paradigms.

The ubiquitous nature of LI suggests some adaptive advantage. Indeed, LI appears to protect the organism from associating irrelevant stimuli with other events. It helps to partition the important from the unimportant, and thus to economize on processing capacity by selectively biasing the organism to more fully process new inputs as opposed to old, inconsequential ones. Latent Inhibition, which has been described in terms of the conditioning of inattention, adaptively modulates functional stimulus novelty, and guards against an information processing overload.

Although the term "latent inhibition" is meant to be entirely descriptive, it has been subject to a number of theoretical interpretations, of which there are two major classes. One class of theory holds that nonreinforced or inconsequential stimulus preexposure results in reduced associability for that stimulus. In other words, the preexposed stimulus is less capable of entering into new associations than a novel stimulus. The loss of associability has been attributed to a variety of mechanisms which reduce attention (see Lubow, 1989 for a review), which then must be reacquired in order for learning to proceed normally.

Alternatively, it has been proposed that LI is a result of *retrieval failure* rather than acquisition failure. Such a hypothesis proposes that, following stimulus preexposure, the acquisition of the new association to the old stimulus proceeds normally. However, in the test stage, at least in three-stage procedures, two competing associations may be retrieved, an earlier stimulus-no consequence association from the preexposure stage and/or the stimulus-unconditioned stimulus association of the acquisition stage. In normal LI, the nonpreexposed group performs better than the preexposed group because there is only the second association to be retrieved, whereas the preexposed group performs poorly because both the first and second associations, which are in competition, are retrieved.

Irrespective of the outcome of the continuing debate as to whether LI represents a failure of association or retrieval interference, the robustness of the basic effect, and the orderly manner in which LI is modulated by experimental variables, requires theoretical consideration. Amongst those variables that consistently have been shown to modulate the size of the LI effect, and perhaps the most important theoretically, is that of context-change. (Context refers to those environmental stimuli which are relatively constant during the course of an experiment.) In virtually all LI studies, the context, unless specifically an experimental variable, remains the same in the stimulus preexposure and test phases. However, if context is changed from the preexposure to the test phase, then LI is drastically reduced or abolished. In addition, for context and stimulus preexposure to be effective in producing LI, the two must be preexposed conjointly. Context preexposure after preexposure of the stimulus in that same context (context extinction procedure) has little or no effect on LI. Preexposure of the context prior to stimulus preexposure in the same context increases the magnitude of LI.

The various stimulus preexposure-context effects have been used to develop a theory of the conditioning of inattention and its modulation by context effects to account for both LI in normals and its attenuation in schizophrenics. The theory proposes that normal LI is manifest when the preexposure context reappears in test and sets the occasion for eliciting the stimulus-no consequence association that was acquired during preexposure. As such, the context limits the access of the previously exposed irrelevant stimulus to working-memory. In addition, it has been proposed that, in schizophrenia, there is a breakdown in the relationship between the preexposed stimulus and the context, such that the context no longer sets the occasion for the expression of the stimulus-no consequence association. Consequently, working memory is inundated with experimentally familiar but phenomenally novel stimuli, each competing for the limited resources required for efficient information processing. This description fits well with the symptoms of schizophrenia, particularly high distractibility, as well as with research findings.

Indeed, the assumption that the same attentional process that produces LI in normal subjects is dysfunctional in schizophrenics has stimulated considerable research in this area. Evidence to support this contention comes from several sources, including the parallel effects of dopamine activity associated with schizophrenia and with LI. There are strong data which indicate that dopamine agonists and antagonists modulate LI in rats and in normal humans. Dopamine agonists such as amphetamine abolish LI, while dopamine antagonists, such as haloperidol and other neuroleptics, produce a super-LI effect. In addition, manipulations of putative dopamine pathways in the brain have the expected effects on LI. Thus, hippocampal and septal lesions interfere with the development of LI, as do lesions of the nucleus accumbens. This literature has been extensively reviewed (Gray, Feldon, Rawlins, Hemsley, & Smith, 1990; Gray, 1998; Weiner & Feldon, 1997). With human subjects, there is some evidence that nonmedicated schizophrenics show reduced LI compared to medicated schizophrenics and normals, while there are no differences in the amount of LI in the latter two groups. Finally, symptomatically normal subjects who score high on psychotic-prone or schizotypal scales also exhibit reduced LI compared to low psychotic-prone/low schizotypal subjects. Lubow and Gewirtz (1995) have reviewed the modulation of LI effects in these groups.

In addition to LI illustrating a fundamental strategy of information processing and providing a useful tool for examining attentional dysfunctions in certain pathological groups, such as schizophrenics, LI has also been used to explain why certain therapies are not as effective as might be expected. A recent analysis of conditioned alcohol aversion treatments suggests that LI may account for the relative ineffectiveness of these therapies. On the other hand, LI procedures may be useful in counteracting some of the undesirable side effects which frequently accompany radiation and chemotherapies for cancer, such as food aversion, for example. Finally, LI research has suggested techniques that may be efficacious in the prophylactic treatment of certain fears and phobias. Many of the practical applications of LI have recently been reviewed (Lubow, 1997).

In summary, the basic LI phenomenon represents some output of a selective attention process which results in learning to ignore irrelevant stimuli. It has become an important tool for understanding information processing in general, as well as attentional dysfunctions, and it has implications for a variety of practical problems.

REFERENCES

Gray, J. A. (1998). Integrating schizophrenia. *Schizophrenia Bulletin, 24,* 249–266.

Gray, J. A., Feldon, J., Rawlins, J. N. P., Hemsley, D. R., & Smith, A. D. (1990). The neuropsychology of schizophrenia. *Behavioral and Brain Sciences, 14,* 1–84.

Lubow, R. E. (1989). *Latent inhibition and conditioned attention theory.* New York: Cambridge University Press.

Lubow, R. E. (1997). Latent inhibition and behavior pathology. In W. D. O'Donohue (Ed.), *Learning and behavior therapy* (pp. 107–121). Boston: Allyn and Bacon.

Lubow, R. E., & Gewirtz, J. (1995). Latent inhibition in humans: Data, theory, and implications for schizophrenia. *Psychological Bulletin, 117,* 87–103.

Lubow, R. E., & Moore, A. U. (1959). Latent inhibition: The effect of non-reinforced preexposure to the conditioned stimulus. *Journal of Comparative and Physiological Psychology, 52,* 415–419.

Weiner, I., & Feldon, J. (1997). The switching model of latent inhibition: An update of neural substrates. *Behavioral Brain Research, 88,* 11–26.

R. E. Lubow
Tel Aviv University

INFORMATION PROCESSING

LATERAL DOMINANCE

Lateral dominance is the use of one side of the body more often or more skillfully than the other in unilateral activities. The most obvious example of lateral dominance is more frequent or skillful use of one hand over the other. Lateral dominance is associated with asymmetrical organization of the functions of the two cerebral hemispheres, although the relationship is not exact.

The majority of people are right-handed, although there is considerable variation in the discrepancy between the efficiency, force, and frequency of use of the right hand as opposed to the left. Questionnaires are sometimes used as tests for handedness, but more accurate and descriptive behavioral methods include observation of the individual performing such tasks as writing, throwing, and cutting (Reitan, *Manual*).

The preference for the use of one foot or one eye over the other, while not as frequently studied as handedness, is as important a part of lateral dominance. While most right-handed people are also right-footed and right-eyed, there are many whose eye/hand/foot lateral dominance is mixed. Such tasks as stepping on something and kicking differentiate right-footed from left-footed individuals, while tasks such as looking through a telescope and sighting a rifle are used to evaluate eye dominance (Reitan, *Manual*).

While environmental factors probably play a large part in determining lateral dominance, some studies suggest that there may be hereditary influences as well (Chamberlain, 1928; Springer & Deutsch, 1981; Hécaen & de Ajuriaguerra, 1964).

Some lateral dominance apparently exists in many nonhuman animals (Collins, 1968, 1969; Warren, Abplanalp, & Warren, 1967). Cats, monkeys, and mice often show a preference for use of one limb over the other.

REFERENCES

Chamberlain, H. D. (1928). The inheritance of left-handedness. *Journal of Heredity, 19,* 557–559.

Collins, R. L. (1968). On the inheritance of handedness: I. Laterality in inbred mice. *Journal of Heredity, 59,* 9–12.

Collins, R. L. (1969). On the inheritance of handedness: II. Selection for sinistrality in mice. *Journal of Heredity, 60,* 117–119.

Hécaen, H., & de Ajuriaguerra, J. (1964). *Lefthandedness: Manual superiority and cerebral dominance.* New York: Grune & Stratton.

Reitan, R. M. (n.d.). *Manual for administration of neuropsychological test battery for adults and children.* Seattle, WA: Neuropsychology Laboratory.

Springer, S. P., & Deutsch, G. (1981). *Left brain, right brain.* San Francisco: Freeman.

Warren, J. M., Abplanalp, J. M., & Warren, H. B. (1967). The development of handedness in cats and rhesus monkeys. In H. W. Stevenson, E. H. Hess, & H. L. Reingold (Eds.), *Early behavior: Comparative and developmental approaches.* New York: Wiley.

T. S. BENNETT
Brain Inquiry Recovery Program

BRAIN LATERALITY
NEUROPSYCHOLOGY
PSYCHOPHYSIOLOGY: OVERVIEW
SPLIT-BRAIN RESEARCH

LATIN AMERICA, PSYCHOLOGY IN

Psychology is a growing science and profession in the first (or industrialized) world, the second (or communist) world, and the third (or developing) world. In Latin America, psychology in a broad sense has existed since 1566, when the first mental hospital in the Americas was founded in Mexico City. At the present time, psychology is an academic discipline and a profession with many social functions. Only the most important features of psychology in Latin America are discussed here. The reader is referred to Ardila's various publications for further information.

Psychology began in Latin America as part of philosophy. Later, it was considered a complement to medicine and education. The first laboratory of experimental psychology in Latin America was founded in Argentina in 1898. The earliest training programs began in 1946 and 1948 in Colombia, Chile, and Guatemala.

Three main cultural influences have taken root in Latin America as far as psychology is concerned—psychoanalysis, behaviorism, and what is called "French" psychology. In the early stages of development, psychology was taught by medical doctors trained in Freudian psychoanalysis, and this tradition still remains, especially in Argentina. The second influence, behaviorism, came to Latin America in the 1960s and 1970s and continues to be influential in most of these nations. What is called French psychology is a mixture of psychoanalysis, Marxism, linguistics, and anthropology. The three influences are not sequential, but represent different emphases.

Mexico and Brazil in the 1980s are the leaders in psychology in Latin America. Research, training programs, and professional applications exist in the majority of the countries. Psychologists in Chile, Argentina, Colombia, Panama, Venezuela, Cuba, Peru, Bolivia, Puerto Rico, and other Latin American countries have made important contributions.

The situation of psychology varies from country to country. Latin America is a large area, with more than 20 nations in different stages of development. The name "Latin America" refers to the whole of the American continents, with the exception of the United States and Canada. The Latin American countries are heterogeneous, inhabited by Indians, whites, blacks, and Chinese. They speak Spanish, Portuguese, French, or English, in addition to a large number of native dialects. The culture is a mix of European, Indo-American, and African traditions.

Science is not a major cultural value in Latin America (Ardila, 1982b). The humanities, literature, and art are positively evaluated, but science and technology do not receive much esteem.

In some of the pre-Columbian cultures, much philosophical and psychological thinking went on; the Mayas, Incas, and Aztecs were concerned with the nature of human beings and their place in the world. During the colonial period, philosophical ideas cultivated in Europe were brought to Latin America by the Spanish and the Portuguese. Philosophical psychology, based on the ideas of Aristotle and St. Thomas Aquinas concerning the soul and its functions, was studied at the Latin American universities of the period.

DEVELOPMENT

The first mental hospital in the Americas was founded in Mexico City in 1566, by Bernardino Alvarez. This event can be considered the beginning of psychology in Mexico and the rest of Latin America. The scientific origins, on the other hand, can be traced to the founding of the first laboratory of experimental psychology, in

Buenos Aires, by Horacio Pinero (1869–1919) in 1898. Soon laboratories opened in Brazil and Mexico. In other countries, the majority of psychological laboratories were founded around 1965.

During the last decades of the nineteenth century and the beginning of the twentieth century, positivism was quite influential in Chile, Argentina, and Mexico, and it helped in the development of the sciences, particularly biology, psychology, and sociology.

José Ingenieros (1877–1925), a psychologist, philosopher, and socialist leader, helped to introduce positivism in Argentina. Ingenieros was the author of the earliest system of psychology postulated by a Latin American; he called it *genetic psychology* and presented it in 1910. The system was based on the objective, behavioral approach, and evolutionism. According to Ingenieros, psychology is a natural science, devoted to the study of psychic functions of living organisms; its method is behavioral observation, and does not have anything to do with the soul. Psychological functions adapt the organism to the environment and are elementary processes of all living beings.

Enrique Mouchet (1886–1977) was another pioneer of psychology. He directed the Institute of Psychology of the University of Buenos Aires, founded the first journal of psychology in Latin America, and did important experimental research on perception. Mouchet wanted to convert his institute into the main center for psychological research in the Spanish-speaking world.

In Brazil, Waclaw Radecki (1887–1953) had a decisive influence. He was a Polish psychologist who worked in Brazil, Uruguay, and Argentina in experimental psychology. Radecki was much involved in the new psychology and organized the First Latin American Congress of Psychology in Montevideo in 1950.

Ezequiel A. Chávez (1868–1946) taught experimental and educational psychology in Mexico, translated Titchener's work into Spanish, and played an important role in the development of psychology in Mexico.

Other pioneers were Emilio Mira y López (1896–1964), who did work in psychometrics in Brazil; Walter Blumenfeld (1882–1967), a German who worked in Peru in measurement and psychometrics; and Béla Székely (1892–1955), who was born in Hungary, and who worked in psychoanalysis.

THE NEW PROFESSION

The professionalization of psychology is relatively new in Latin America, beginning about 1946. A majority of training programs began in the 1960s and 1970s. Psychology emerged as a profession in the context of psychoanalysis, and the first professors of psychology were psychiatrists. The new profession had to overcome many obstacles to attain an independent role and to take its proper place in society.

In Mexico, a graduate program was started in 1937, and the first professional program in that country was initiated in 1958. That same year saw the creation of the first psychology programs in Argentina, at the University of Litoral (Rosario) and at the University of Buenos Aires. A decade and a half later, psychology graduate programs were established in Brazil, Mexico, Venezuela, and Colombia. By the 1980s, there were professional programs in practically all Latin American countries.

Psychology in Latin America follows what is called the Latin American training model (Ardila, 1978a): a five-year professional training after high school graduation. Training is given in all areas of psychology and related disciplines (sociology, anthropology, physiology, mathematics). This training is both theoretical and practical; at the end of the five-year period the student must write a thesis to receive the degree of "psychologist" or "licenciate in psychology." The title enables the holder to work in any area of psychology—educational, industrial, clinical, experimental.

The training is similar to the Boulder model in the United States, in that it is both scientific and professional. However, no graduate work is required. The majority of Latin American psychologists have studied five years, and relatively few have masters' or Ph.D. degrees, which must be obtained in the United States or Europe.

ORGANIZATIONS

Latin American psychologists have organized many associations, with different aims. There are also associations that go beyond the national boundaries. The main group is the Interamerican Society of Psychology (SIP), with members from the United States, Canada, and Latin America. The SIP was founded in 1951 in Mexico City. It organizes the Interamerican Congresses of Psychology, which usually are very well attended. It also publishes *Revista Interamericana de Psicología/Interamerican Journal of Psychology,* with articles in Spanish, Portuguese, and English; and a newsletter called *The Interamerican Psychologist.* Another journal is *Spanish-Language Psychology,* containing summaries in English of all psychological literature originally published in Spanish.

There are three Latin American associations of psychologists, devoted to the analysis of behavior, to social psychology, and to physiological psychology. The Latin American Association for the Analysis and Modification of Behavior (ALAMOC) has 800 members and organizes the Latin American Congresses for the Analysis and Modification of Behavior; it also publishes a journal entitled *Aprendizaje y Comportamiento/Learning and Behavior.* The Latin American Association for Social Psychology (ALAPSO) is active in the promotion of research and applications of social psychology. The Latin American Society for Psychophysiology has encouraged work in this area, in different countries.

Usually in each Latin American country there are one or more societies concerned with work on professional problems and on training problems in psychology. Some are more scientifically oriented than others. Although not all psychologists belong to a national association, there is a trend to take the association into consideration in all issues related to psychology and to its role in society.

Many journals of psychology are published in Latin America. The majority have irregular publication dates. A number of new journals are started each year. Currently (1980s), the main journals published regularly are: *Revista Latinoamericana de Psicología* (Colombia), *Revista Interamericana de Psicología* (SIP journal), *Revista Argentina de Psicología* (Argentina), *Arquivos Brasileiros de Psicología* (Brazil), *Revista del Hospital Psiquiátrico de la Habana* (Cuba), *Enseñanza e Investigación en Psicología* (Mexico), *Re-*

vista de Psicología Clínica (Peru), Revista Chilena de Psicología (Chile), Psicología (Venezuela), and Aprendizaje y Comportamiento (ALAMOC journal).

RESEARCH

Scientific research is encouraged in all psychology training programs in Latin America. To receive a degree, students have to write a thesis, usually of an experimental nature.

Research in psychology is carried out in Brazil, Mexico, Puerto Rico, Cuba, Venezuela, Colombia, Bolivia, Peru, and many other countries. The main areas of study are social psychology and the experimental analysis of behavior. In many cases, research is sponsored by the government, by the university, by private national foundations, or by international foundations. In each country, a government organization, similar to the National Science Foundation in the United States, sponsors science.

It is impossible to write a short summary of psychological research in Latin America. The reader is referred to the previously cited publications for further information. Centers such as the National University of Mexico, the Institute of Psychology of the University of São Paulo, the Interdisciplinary Center for Research in Mathematical and Experimental Psychology (Buenos Aires), the Laboratory for Sensory Investigations (Buenos Aires), the School of Psychology of the Central University of Venezuela (Caracas), the Caribbean Center for Advanced Studies (San Juan), the Faculty of Psychology of the University of Havana, and other centers, are doing research of high caliber.

The research project by Holtzman, Díaz-Guerrero, and Swartz (1975) on personality development in Mexico and the United States has been considered the most important investigation to be carried out by Latin American psychologists. A sample of the work on operant conditioning can be found in Ardila (1974), and of the work on social psychology in Marin (1975).

Besides operant conditioning and social psychology, Latin American psychologists have also worked on perception, cognition, psychophysiology, developmental psychology, comparative psychology, history of psychology, political psychology, clinical psychology, industrial and organizational psychology, educational problems, and many other areas of contemporary psychology.

CONCLUSIONS

Psychology is one of the most popular fields of study in Latin America (Heineken, 1979), as is also the case in many other regions of the world. Training centers exist in practically all the countries of Latin America. The Latin American model is similar to the European training model. Research is in progress in many areas, especially in the experimental analysis of behavior and in social psychology. Applications of psychology to clinical problems, and in educational, industrial, and social fields, have grown very rapidly in recent years.

REFERENCES

Ardila, R. (Ed.). (1974). El análisis experimental del comportamiento, la contribución latinoamericana. Mexico, D.F.: Trillas.

Ardila, R. (Ed.). (1978). La profesión del psicólogo. Mexico, D.F.: Trillas.

Ardila, R. (1978). Behavior modification in Latin America. In M. Hersen, R. M. Eisler, & P. M. Miller (Eds.), Progress in behavior modification (Vol. 6). New York: Academic.

Heineken, E. (1979). Zur Lage der Psychologie in Lateinamerika. Psychologische Rundschau, 30, 257–268.

Holtzman, W. H., Diaz-Guerrero, R., & Swartz, J. (1975). Personality development in two cultures. Austin, TX: University of Texas Press.

Marín, G. (Ed.). (1975). La psicología social en Latino américa. Mexico, D.F.: Trillas.

R. Ardila
National University of Colombia, Bogotá

LAW OF PARSIMONY

The law or principle of parsimony is concerned with the evaluation of theoretical propositions within science. The principle holds that the simplest of alternative theoretical accounts is to be accepted whenever the alternatives are equally consistent with empirical data.

Scientists have learned that unnecessarily complicated theoretical explanations are much more likely to be found to be in error than simpler ones. Analogically, the more embellishments that ones gives a lie, the more likely it is to be detected; the simplest lies are generally the most effective.

The high degree of acceptability of the parsimony principle among scientists can be accounted for, historically, in terms of the experiences that scientists have had with respect to the simplicity variable in their theorizing. It seldom takes a fledgling scientist very long to see the use of the principle of parsimony.

HISTORY

Adaptation of the principle of parsimony to psychological problems was accomplished by the British comparative psychologist C. Lloyd Morgan. Morgan's (1899) position is usually represented by the following widely quoted statement: "In no case may we interpret an action as the outcome of the exercise of a higher psychical faculty, if it can be interpreted as the outcome of the exercise of one which stands lower in the psychological scale" (p. 59). This position has come to be known as Lloyd Morgan's canon; an earlier, more general, and much more picturesque name for the law of parsimony is Occam's razor. The operational use to which such a razor is put should be self-evident.

Lloyd Morgan's canon was intended to refer to explanatory accounts of animal behavior, especially unusual feats of animals too often attributed to humanlike capabilities. A common example is a dog's habit of carrying a newspaper through a rail fence by holding it in a horizontal position. There is a strong tendency for pet owners to attribute this kind of behavior to high intelligence or learning ability, a tendency called anthropomorphism. Application of the principle of parsimony to such behaviors requires that simpler explanations, such as conditioning, be accorded a higher degree of acceptance as long as they can explain all of the relevant data equally well. Questioning a less parsimonious account does not amount to a denial of it, rather it represents a kind of working position that guards against the premature acceptance of unnecessarily complex theories and encourages a more vigorous search for new empirical evidence that may require acceptance of the more complex account. Newbury (1954) provided an early extensive treatment of the many ramifications of Lloyd Morgan's canon as a methodological principle within psychology.

APPLICABILITY

It is important to recognize the wide range of conditions under which the parsimony principle can be applied. Perhaps the most significant dimension here is that of theoretical versus real-life setting. In the former case, little damage of a practical sort is likely to be suffered if a serious error is made—that is, if the more complex theoretical account is erroneously accepted. As a matter of fact, it is just such active seeking of error in the testing of hypothesis that is the hallmark of the experimental method. This is not so in the latter case, unfortunately. Here life-and-death decisions may well be involved, for example, in the realm of military affairs, and a great many lives may be needlessly sacrificed when some more complex account is mistakenly accepted and acted on. Less dramatically, but in an essentially similar manner, crucial social, political, and economic decisions often revolve around the acceptance or rejection of differentially complex theoretical accounts, relating directly to social policies (e.g., early interventions such as the Head Start program). Acceptance of complex but faulty hypotheses can have drastic consequences. It is thus crucial that parsimonious theoretical filters be carefully applied to alternative interpretations of fundamental issues. Unfortunately, it is in these areas rather than in the strictly theoretical (academic) ones that decision makers are least likely to be knowledgeable and experienced with respect to application of the parsimony principle. Hence, it is important that those who are so experienced (scientists and academicians) contribute as much as possible to the decision making, as is regularly done—for example, by forming special committees of the National Research Council (NRC).

NRC COMMITTEE ON ENHANCEMENT OF HUMAN PERFORMANCE

An especially good example of how the principle of parsimony operates in the evaluation of complex theoretical propositions is afforded by the functioning of one such NRC committee. As the world's largest training institution, the U.S. Army has been necessarily sensitive to claims for enhancement of human performance made for many diverse instructional programs. Such proposals range from the use of meditation and altered mental states to sports psychology techniques intended to prepare one for performance under intense pressure. They have all had strong advocacy of one kind or another within the military community. However, most of them did not originate within the scientific community, so that the usual testing and evaluation techniques were not readily applied.

Besieged by such a variety of highly touted programs that obviously needed thorough scientific evaluation, the army recognized the need for behavioral as well as the traditional engineering (hardware) evaluations and in 1984 formally asked the National Academy of Sciences for help. A special committee of 13 psychologists was established under the auspices of the NRC. In its first phase, the committee analyzed the degree of scientific support for a number of unconventional, New Age techniques; its initial report was published by the National Academy Press in 1988 and proved to be, relatively, a best-seller.

In the second phase of its work, the committee proceeded to investigate mainly some more basic issues of performance enhancement. A number of unsuspected relationships were uncovered; for example, it was shown that certain factors that were associated with relatively poor training performance, such as distributed rather than massed practice and the use of irregular conditions in training, were nonetheless associated with *superior* subsequent (after training) performance. Little positive support was found for several popular techniques such as meditation (beyond the conventional effects of relaxation) or subliminal tapes.

These bits and pieces selected from a wide-scale attack on the performance problem can do little more than suggest the no-nonsense flavor of what was, in effect, a far-reaching application of the parsimony principle to a set of important behavioral problems, but they do appear to constitute deep-seated support for the scientific use of the parsimony principle.

More details of the important second phase of the NRC committee work are available in an informal interim report (Bjork & Druckman, 1991) as well as the official report itself (National Research Council, 1991).

REFERENCES

Bjork, R., & Druckman, D. (1991). How do you improve human performance? *American Psychological Society Observer, 4,* 13–15.

Morgan, C. L. (1899). *Introduction to comparative psychology* (2nd ed.). London: Scott.

National Research Council. (1991). *In the mind's eye: Enhancing human performances.* Washington, DC: National Academy.

Newberry, E. (1954). Current interpretation and significance of Lloyd Morgan's canon. *Psychological Bulletin, 51,* 70–74.

M. H. MARX
N. Hutchinson Island, Florida

OPERATIONAL DEFINITION

LAZARUS, ARNOLD A.

Arnold A. Lazarus was born and educated in Johannesburg, South Africa. He attended the University of the Witwatersrand in Johannesburg. In 1957 he was awarded an MA in experimental psychology and in 1960 he obtained a PhD in clinical psychology. Lazarus's doctoral dissertation contained a number of "firsts." It was the first time that systematic desensitization had been conducted in groups. It was also the first formal study that used objective indices of avoidance (e.g., how high would an acrophobic individual climb up a fire escape before and after therapy?). Lazarus went into full-time private practice and was a part-time lecturer at the Witwatersrand Medical School.

In 1963, he accepted an invitation from the department of psychology at Stanford University and joined their faculty as a visiting assistant professor. He returned to South Africa in 1964 where he continued his psychotherapy practice and part-time teaching. He immigrated to the United States in 1966 and was the director of the Behavior Therapy Institute in Sausalito, CA. In 1967 he joined the faculty of Temple University Medical School as a full professor. From 1970 to 1972 he was a visiting professor at Yale University and director of clinical training, and in 1972 he accepted an offer from Rutgers University where he received the rank of distinguished professor of psychology. After chairing the department of psychology at Rutgers' University College for two years, he moved to the Graduate School of Applied and Professional Psychology, where he taught from 1974 to 1998 and then retired as a distinguished professor emeritus of psychology. In addition to his private practice, he now works with his son C. N. Lazarus and is the president of the Center for Multimodal Psychological Services in Princeton, NJ. He also serves on the editorial boards of 12 scientific journals.

A former president of several professional associations and societies, Lazarus has received many honors and awards for his contributions to clinical theory and therapy. These include the Distinguished Psychologist Award from APA's Division of Psychotherapy, the Distinguished Professional Contributions Award from APA's Division of Clinical Psychology, the Distinguished Service Award from the American Board of Professional Psychology, and two Lifetime Achievement Awards, one from the California Psychological Association and the other from the Association for Advancement of Behavior Therapy. Lazarus is also the recipient of the first Annual Cummings PSYCHE Award. He has been inducted, as a charter member, into the National Academies of Practice as a distinguished practitioner in psychology.

With 16 books and over 200 professional and scientific articles to his credit, Lazarus is widely recognized as an international authority on effective and efficient psychotherapy and has given innumerable talks and workshops in the US and abroad. In addition to his academic and scholarly activities, as a licensed psychologist and a diplomate of the American Board of Professional Psychology, he has maintained an active psychotherapy practice since 1959.

He coined the terms "behavior therapy" and "behavior therapist," which first appeared in a professional publication (1958) and went on to innovate and develop many behavior therapy techniques. In his book *Behavior Therapy and Beyond* (1971) he stressed the need to add cognitive factors to the usual behavioral repertoire—this book is arguably one of the first on cognitive-behavior therapy and became a citation classic.

He has developed a broad-based and systematic approach he calls "multimodal therapy," which has been described by C. M. Franks, founder and first president of the Association for Advancement of Behavior Therapy, as "behavior therapy in one of its most advanced forms." His multimodal approach is humanistic, systematic, brief and yet comprehensive, and emphasizes flexibility

as a central process. He has written that an effective therapist is an "authentic chameleon" who adapts his methods to suit the needs of each individual. Lazarus is an innovator in couples therapy, group therapy, sex therapy, and the clinical use of mental imagery. He is listed in *Who's Who in America* and in *Who's Who in The World.*

STAFF

LEADERSHIP STYLES

Behavioral scientists have been involved in the study of leadership since the 1930s. One aim of these efforts has been to understand how leaders influence followers and gain their cooperation and commitment. Over the last 70 years, the study of various leadership styles has undergone a series of transformations, riding the waves of change in social science, assumptions about the nature of leadership, and the way businesses function.

EARLY EFFORTS

Initial leadership research took place in an era influenced by the scientific management precept that there is one best way to accomplish a given objective. Also dominant was the idea that leadership is an ephemeral quality of great men whose personal attributes made them natural leaders. Research was not directly concerned with understanding leadership styles; it was a quest to identify the characteristics that differentiated leaders from followers and effective leaders from ineffective leaders. This line of inquiry waned as research suggested that personality traits and intelligence play only a small role in leadership effectivness.

The earliest studies of leadership styles (defined as the manner by which individuals in position of authority influenced group activity) were conducted by Lewin and colleagues in the late 1930s. In these experiments there was little concern about personal characteristics and attributes; the focus was on how leaders influenced and directed groups. Three unique leadership styles were identified: an authoritarian style (directing group activity through unilateral decision making and personal control), a democratic style (involving group members in decision making processes), and a laissez-faire style (passive and disengaged, exerting little influence). Consistent with the tenets of scientific management, these researchers sought the most effective style and concluded that the democratic style led to higher member satisfaction and involvement. However, no single style was the best in terms of performance and task accomplishment.

THE BEHAVIORIST INFLUENCE

The rise of behaviorism to the dominant view in psychology guided leadership research during the 1940s and 1950s toward the study of leader behaviors. Two independent programs of research (at Ohio State University and University of Michigan) converged in the identification of two basic dimensions of leader behavior. One dimension, known as initiating structure or task-centered, was task-oriented in nature and emphasized the use of position power for the planning, coordination, improvement, and monitoring of group performance. The other dimension, labeled consideration or employee-centered, was relational or people-oriented and emphasized the well being, personal growth needs, and contributions of group members. These twin pillars of leadership behavior proved highly robust, appearing ubiquitously in several subsequent streams of research on leaders behaviors (see Bass, 1990).

Focus returned to the issue of leadership styles in the late 1950s and 1960s, as researchers began considering the effectiveness of various combinations of task-oriented and people-oriented behaviors. Influential was Blake and Mouton's (1964) managerial grid, which identified managers' styles as located on a plane defined by the two dimensions of concern for task performance and concern for people. It was argued that the optimal style was a high-high team management style, the area defined by high concern for performance and high concern for people. Although there is some support for this position, the high-high style is not necessarily the most effective in every management situation (Bass, 1990).

THE HUMANISTIC INFLUENCE

The late 1950s and early 1960s bore witness to the growth of a humanistic movement in psychology, which emphasized the personal growth and self-actualization needs of individuals. Definitive of this era was McGregor's (1960) popular Theory X and Theory Y models of leadership, which contrasted underlying views of human nature. Theory X managers, the model holds, see their employees as passive, self-interested, and lazy, and thus lead with a task-oriented style to motivate and keep followers on task. Theory Y managers, conversely, view employees as self-motivated and desiring to contribute to the organization, and thus lead with a people-oriented style in an effort to arrange conditions to tap their employees' potential and personal growth needs. Consistent with the humanistic influence of the time, McGregor and others argued for the superiority of a people-oriented leadership style. This was very popular in the practice of management, but research efforts led to conflicting results: In some studies, a task-oriented style appeared superior, while a people-oriented style was more effective in others. Perhaps the most important long-term effect of this era of thinking about leadership styles was the recognition that leadership requires both a forceful and directive component and an enabling component that takes account of the needs of those being influenced.

THE RISE OF CONTINGENCY THEORIES

The vestiges of scientific management and the one-best-way assumption gave way to a new and more complex level of thinking about leadership styles in the mid-1960s. Parallel to this was growing debate in psychology regarding whether personal characteristics or situational characteristics were the more powerful determinants of behavior, with situationists gaining most support. Fiedler's (1964) contingency model spawned a new breed of prescriptive leadership style theories by suggesting that the reason previous research had failed to identify a universally best leadership style is that the effectiveness of a given style depends on the context in which it takes place.

Building on the research of the 1950s, Fiedler's model portrayed leaders as motivated primarily by either task accomplishment or the development of supportive relationships with group members. Leadership situations could be defined on a continuum of favorability, depending on the degree of group dependability, task clarity, and the leader's formal power. Task-motivated leaders are said to perform best in extreme conditions of high or low situational favorability; relationship-motivated leaders were said to perform best in the moderately favorable conditions. The theory has been extensively evaluated (Peters, Hartke, & Pohlman, 1985), and this body of research generally supports it. The historical significance of this is validation of the idea that the optimal leadership style depends on the situational context. Interestingly, Fiedler's successful Leader Match training program uses his theory to teach leaders how to change their leadership situations to match their leadership styles, reflecting Fiedler's scholarly roots in behaviorism and emphasis on situational causality.

The late 1960s and early 1970s witnessed the advancement of several contingency leadership theories. At the same time, there was a growing person-situation debate in psychology, with each side presenting strong evidence for its position. Accordingly, situational leadership theory, path-goal theory, and the normative decision theory each prescribed that leaders alter their styles to suit the conditions of changing situations.

Hersey and Blanchard's (1969) situational leadership theory extended Blake and Mouton's managerial grid approach by incorporating the group's maturity level as a situational variable. The theory suggests that a leader's style should emphasize task-oriented or relations-oriented behaviors, depending on how willing and able the group is to perform the task. Groups are seen as maturing in a life cycle from unable and unwilling, to unable and willing, to able and unwilling, and finally to able and willing. The prescribed leadership styles are, respectively, a task-oriented *telling* style, a task- and relation-oriented *selling* style, a relation-oriented *participating* style, and finally, a *delegating* style of low task- and relation-oriented behaviors. This theory has been highly criticized because of conceptual ambiguities, lack of a logical or empirical foundation for the group maturity life cycle construct, and little empirical validity evidence (see review in Bass, 1990). Nonetheless, the model has been immensely popular in practice and has served as the basis of many leadership training programs.

House's (1971) path-goal theory was based on variables that represent situational factors, follower characteristics, and several moderator variables. The theory assumes that motivation and performance are enhanced when a leader helps group members understand how their personal needs can be met through contributing to the organization or group (a goal) and helps to clarify strategies for members to achieve this (a path). To summarize this complex model, task-oriented behaviors are prescribed when the path is unclear and not recommended when the path is apparent. People-oriented behaviors are prescribed when the path is aversive or boring. Research suggests that employee job satisfaction and motivation can be enhanced by following path-goal theory's prescriptions, but performance may be only marginally affected.

A good deal of leadership research has been concerned with decision making. The normative decision theory of Vroom and Yetton (1974) specified which decision-making style—autocratic, consultation, or democratic—is likely to lead to higher decision quality and follower acceptance under various situational contingencies. In this model, managers must make a series of judgments about their situations, such as the amount of relevant knowledge they and subordinates have, the likelihood of followers to accept an autocratic decision, likelihood of follower cooperation, extent of disagreement among followers regarding alternatives, and the degree of task ambiguity. Plotting the answers to these questions in a flow chart leads to a recommended decision-making style. The latest version of the theory takes into account the relative importance of the various situational variables and includes an additional decision-making style—delegating responsibility to subordinates. Of all the contingency theories, Vroom's theory has garnered the strongest empirical support.

Although the contingency theories differ in content, they have a common theme. Each assumes that there is no universal leadership style that is superior for all tasks and situations. This implies that highly effective leaders must adapt to changing conditions by having a well-rounded repertoire of available responses, ranging from task-oriented forceful to people-oriented enabling styles, and from autocratic to participative decision-making methods.

A NEW PARADIGM: TRANSFORMATIONAL LEADERSHIP

The 1970s saw dramatic changes both in the study of leadership and, more broadly, in the field of psychology. The cognitive revolution had dethroned behaviorism and brought information processing models of human behavior to the fore. There was also growing interest in an interactionist position that viewed the person and the situation as reciprocally influential. Although not directly concerned with leadership styles, Graen and colleagues advanced the vertical dyad linkage model that defined the individual group member–leader dyadic relationship as the context of influence processes.

The 1970s also witnessed discussion about the differences between leaders and managers (Zaleznick, 1977). A fundamental distinction was made relegating management to routine supervisory activities that kept an organization on a steady path and encouraged stability and continuity. Leadership, on the other hand, was glamorized as the force that dramatically altered the orientation, vision, culture, and sometimes even the mission of organizations through fundamental change. In the same period, House (1977) proposed a theory of charismatic leadership to describe how some leaders (e.g., John F. Kennedy) were unusually inspirational and influential, capable of persuading followers to identify with them and to internalize their beliefs and values. Peters and Waterman's (1982) widely read *In Search of Excellence* detailed how inspirational visionary leaders of highly successful businesses established strong organizational cultures by aligned employee commitment with the leader's personal vision and ideology. A stage was set for explaining how leaders can inspire performance beyond expectation by transforming followers' values, needs, beliefs, and attitudes. Dissatisfied with the inability of previous leadership theory to account for higher order revolutions in organizations, Bass (1985) helped shape a new paradigm with his theory of transformational leadership.

According to Bass, prior research was concerned with transactional leadership—how leaders appeal to followers' self-interests by setting goals, clarifying desired outcomes, providing feedback, and exchanging rewards for effort and accomplishments. For these purposes, task-oriented and people-oriented behaviors, directive and participative decision-making styles, and the like were well suited. Yet the transactional paradigm was insufficient for explaining how leaders motivate followers to move beyond self-interests to rally around collective values, celebrate a new vision for the future, and elevate performance to extraordinary levels. These outcomes were argued to result from a transformational leadership style. Recent formulations specify transformational leadership to involve idealized influence (integrity, subordinating self-interest to the needs of others, sharing risks with followers, and setting challenging goals); inspirational motivation (imbuing followers' work with a meaningful sense of purpose and contribution); intellectual stimulation (framing problems in a new perspective, questioning basic assumptions, advancing a compelling future vision); and individualized consideration (treating followers as unique individuals, understanding their needs and abilities, facilitating their personal development).

The transformational leadership style is not seen by Bass as supplanting a transactional style. Rather, it is intended to augment the effects of transactional approaches, and empirical data suggest that it does indeed do so. A wealth of data indicate that transformational leadership is more strongly linked to organizational performance and effectiveness than is a transactional style. Moreover, this appears to be a culturally universal phenomenon.

Originally, charismatic and transformational leadership styles were discussed as necessary in situations of crisis and emergency, but later theorizing stressed that they enhance performance in virtually all situations and occasions. In this sense, this way of thinking about leadership styles bears resemblance to the earliest work in the area in its one-best-way prescriptive theme. It was, however, urged that although publicly-noted transformational leaders are often great men or great women, all business managers have the capacity to develop a more transformational style of leading.

A LOOK TO THE FUTURE

The 1990s were a time of unprecedented change in organizational life. Rapid technological innovation, the competitiveness of increasingly global markets, growing demographic diversity in the labor pool, and a move toward flatter organizational structures all continue to challenge organizations to rethink radically the way they function. One thing sure to remain constant during these times of chaos is the need for leadership. However, the way leadership is played out in the organizations of tomorrow may take on a dramatic new look.

Modern realities are calling forth new models of leadership, models that move away from the idea of leadership as a property of a single influential person to a more relational perspective that views leadership as a shared social process in which group members are reciprocally influential in creating meaning and purpose (Drath & Palus, 1994; Rost, 1991). As Fiat Auto president and CEO Roberto Testore put it, "For too long we have had a model of leadership founded on the power of the person. . . . To get the leadership we want requires a cultural change—away from the individualistic model toward a team approach" (Csoka, 1997, p. 7). It is not yet clear what the next face of leadership will look like. Nor is it certain that existing leadership theory will be adequate. The future promises to be a fertile time for reconceptualizing the role of leadership and influence, how and by whom it is enacted, and how organizations can bring people together in the creation and pursuit of a common purpose.

REFERENCES

Bass, B. M. (1985). *Leadership and performance beyond expectations.* New York: Free Press.

Bass, B. M. (1990). *Bass and Stogdill's handbook of leadership: Theory, research, and managerial applications* (3rd ed.). New York: Free Press.

Blake, R. R., & Mouton, J. S. (1964). *The managerial grid.* San Francisco: Gulf.

Csoka, L. S. (1997). *Bridging the leadership gap.* New York: The Conference Board.

Drath, W. H., & Palus, C. J. (1994). *Making common sense: Leadership as meaning-making in a community of practice.* Greensboro, NC: Center for Creative Leadership.

Fiedler, F. (1964). A contingency model of leadership effectiveness. In L. Berkowitz (Ed.), *Advances in experimental social psychology.* New York: Academic.

Hersey, P., & Blanchard, K. (1969). Life cycle theory of leadership. *Training and Development Journal, 2,* 6–34.

House, R. J. (1971). A path-goal theory of leader effectiveness. *Administrative Science Quarterly, 16,* 321–339.

House, R. J. (1977). A 1976 theory of charismatic leadership. In J. G. Hunt & L. L. Larson (Eds.), *Leadership: The cutting edge* (pp. 189–204). Carbondale, IL: Southern Illinois University Press.

McGregor, D. (1960). *The human side of enterprise.* New York: McGraw-Hill.

Peters, L. H., Hartke, D. D., & Pohlman, J. T. (1985). Fiedler's contingency theory of leadership: An application of the meta-analysis procedures of Schmidt and Hunter. *Psychological Bulletin, 97,* 274–285.

Peters, T. J., & Waterman, R. H. (1982). *In search of excellence: Lessons from America's best-run companies.* New York: Harper & Row.

Rost, J. C. (1991). *Leadership for the 21st century.* New York: Praeger.

Vroom, V. H., & Yetton, P. W. (1974). *Leadership and decision-making.* New York: Wiley.

Zaleznick, A. (1977). Managers and leaders: Are they different? *Harvard Business Review, 55*(5), 67–80.

R. B. Kaiser
D. L. DeVries
Kaplan DeVries, Inc.

ORGANIZATIONAL PSYCHOLOGY

LEADERSHIP TRAINING

Leadership is the social influence process that creates shared norms and values, provides groups with a collective purpose, and directs group efforts toward the realization of common goals. The importance of leadership in the modern global economy is widely recognized; yet a recent survey indicates that nearly half of *Fortune* 1,000 companies regard their leadership capacities as fair to poor (Csoka, 1997). Accordingly, leadership training and development for managers is a booming enterprise, an approximately $40 billion-a-year industry in the United States alone (Walter, 1996). A quantitative review of the impact of managerial development interventions, however, suggests that traditional approaches may be minimally effective (Burke & Day, 1986). Similarly, the survey of *Fortune* companies just mentioned suggests that the content and delivery of leadership training is largely outdated, focusing more on classroom approaches to functional business and traditional management skills and less on leadership per se.

This review covers the field of leadership training broadly and focuses on some of the more promising methods and tools. It is structured around three key steps in creating leadership training systems: (a) identifying training needs; (b) selecting from alternative training methods and techniques; and (c) evaluating the impact of training.

IDENTIFICATION OF TRAINING NEEDS

Leadership development efforts, like all training initiatives, should be informed by a needs analysis. This includes an assessment of the organization's leadership needs and an analysis of prospective trainees' capacities to meet those needs. There are many ways of identifying organizational leadership needs, such as through succession planning, performance reviews, and culture and satisfaction surveys. Recent surveys indicate that forward-looking companies are increasingly linking leadership development efforts with organizational culture and strategic business needs (Walter, 1996).

The managerial job is more complex than most occupations, which make it unusually difficult to assess the leadership development needs of managers. Nonetheless, these needs can be identified systematically as part of a formal succession plan, through career planning, and with a variety of diagnostic tools (see review in Clark & Clark, 1990) such as 360-degree/multi-rater feedback systems. Despite frequently outsourcing the development and delivery of leadership training programs, organizations rarely use these content-experienced professionals to help identify training needs (Walter, 1996). It is ironic that training needs are rarely explicitly identified through a formal method, given that knowing what needs to be developed is the cornerstone of the whole process. This is surely one reason so few leadership training programs have been demonstrated to improve leadership effectiveness.

Organizations noted for exemplary leadership development practices are creating leadership competency models—defining qualities and characteristics of their outstanding leaders—against which to assess individual development needs. Executives from a variety of firms generally agree on the widespread need for such leadership basics as self-awareness and understanding of leadership styles, team dynamics, developing employee motivation, and inspiring enhanced performance.

METHODS AND TECHNIQUES

A bewildering array of approaches is used to develop organizational leadership. One way to bring order to the diversity of methods is to draw a distinction between formal training programs and techniques that capitalize on job experiences.

Leadership Training Programs

Formal training programs are the dominant approach used in leadership development. These programs occur away from the immediate worksite and take many forms, ranging from afternoon workshops, to week-long courses, to multiyear university programs. Human resource professionals and consultants typically deliver these programs, but some innovative companies (e.g., Ameritech, Ford Motor Company, General Electric) have senior management conduct the activities (Tichy & Cohen, 1997). Many companies' human resource departments offer workshops and courses, while some standard-setting firms (e.g., General Electric, McDonald's, Motorola) have developed their own managerial training centers and corporate universities. By far the most common are short courses focused on specifically defined topics delivered in a classroom environment. These courses range from those designed and delivered in-house through the human resource department, to commercially available programs offered by independent training and development organizations.

The substantive content of leadership training programs is varied, although for the majority of programs it consists of functional business and general management skills (Csoka, 1997). Rare is training content focused on leadership fundamentals such as self-awareness and personal insight; character and personal growth; communication and interpersonal skills; group process and team dynamics; and the application of certain leadership theories (e.g., Bass's transformational leadership theory, Fiedler's contingency theory).

Training designers are encouraged to make use of principles from learning and development theory when matching training content with delivery methods (e.g., Kolb's 4-state learning model, Knowles' andragogy theory of adult learning, Argyris's double-loop learning, neo-Piagetian constructive-development theory). However, there is little empirical research to inform this process. Notwithstanding the danger in blind adherence to tradition, the following techniques are often used to: (a) teach technical skills (lectures, demonstrations, procedural manuals, videotapes, equipment simulators, and interactive computer tutorials); (b) impart conceptual and administrative skills (cases, exercises, business games, simulations, and videotapes); and (c) develop interpersonal skills (lectures, case discussion, videotapes, role playing, and group exercises).

Most training programs are designed with sequenced combinations of different techniques. For example, one publicly available program designed to raise self-awareness of leadership skills includes a lecture presentation of leadership theory; 360-degree feedback and personality inventories for identifying personal strengths and weaknesses; a complex 2-day business game simulation followed by group discussion for illustrating how strengths and weaknesses played out; and time with trainers to set goals and chart an action plan for personal development.

No matter what technique is used, it should be designed with an understanding of motivation in mind, such as goal-setting theory (Locke & Latham, 1984). This increases the likelihood that the training content will be put into practice and will lead to a sustained improvement in performance. Of the numerous and varied techniques used in leadership training, two are highlighted: behavior role modeling and business simulations (for comprehensive reviews of techniques, see Bass, 1990; Wexley & Latham, 1991; Druckman, Singer, & Van Cott, 1997).

Behavior role modeling, based explicitly on social learning theory, is a technique used to develop interpersonal and self-management skills. The rationale is that informing managers of the need to behave differently is unlikely to lead to behavior change unless they have working mental models for how to perform alternative behaviors. In a typical behavior role modeling exercise, trainees are presented with a discussion about the target behaviors and their relevance to performance in a specific and challenging interpersonal matter (e.g., addressing a subordinate's performance deficiencies); they then observe a role model demonstrate the target behaviors. Trainees are next given a chance to practice the behaviors in role-play exercises. Afterward, trainers and other trainees provide constructive feedback about the performance and how it may be enhanced. This is one of the most well-researched leadership development techniques, and empirical data suggest that it is often effective (Burke & Day, 1986).

Business simulations are designed to provide a context-rich learning environment for assessing current managerial and leadership skills as well as an opportunity to work on strategic, interpersonal, decision-making, influence, and general leadership skills. The centerpiece to a simulation is a hypothetical multidivision organization in which trainees assume managerial roles and are responsible for making strategic and operational decisions over the course of a few days. Embedded within the simulation are several—often more than can be addressed—issues and problems that provide considerable challenge for participants. After the simulation, participants receive feedback from observers and engage in group discussions to understand better their performance, gain insight into strengths and weaknesses, and review learning. Research evidence to date indicates that simulations may facilitate skill development—albeit modestly so.

Learning from Experience

Pioneering studies in the 1980s found that many senior executives believed they grew most as leaders in dealing with varied and challenging on-the-job experiences, rather than in formal training programs (McCall, Lombardo, & Morrison, 1988). These unplanned real-time developments happened informally and haphazardly as job demands would tax or exceed the manager's leadership skills. Successful executives learned through adapting to these stretch situations by recognizing their personal limitations and working on a stronger and more differentiated skill set. Reflecting on these experiences appeared to be key to development and learning important lessons. Over the last decade, innovative strategies have been sought for capitalizing more systematically on the learning opportunities afforded by in vivo job experiences. Three of the more common and promising are discussed.

Inspired by research revealing a link between the breadth and diversity of challenging job assignments early in a manager's career and rapid career progression at AT&T (Howard & Bray, 1988), some organizations are customizing *special assignments* to develop leadership talent. However, there is very little research evidence that might suggest the optimal design and use of special assignments. Important is the careful identification of the challenges and learning opportunities provided by the assignment and a logical linkage to the manager's developmental needs and career planning. Some companies are involving managers themselves in creating specific learning objectives and planning assignments to fill their leadership skill gaps. These companies are also keeping track of skills developed through special assignments and using this data to inform succession planning and individual career counseling.

One of the oldest methods of using experience as a developmental tool is *job rotation*. In job-rotation, managers are given a series of work assignments in different organizational departments and subunits. Research evidence suggests that this technique can enhance leadership skill and knowledge (Druckman et al., 1997). Specific benefits important for skills in establishing a vision and crafting strategy include increased understanding of unique problems facing different units, knowledge of subtle interdependent linkages between units, and frameworks for understanding problems from multiple perspectives. One potential drawback to job rotation is the potential lost productivity incurred while rotated managers cycle through learning curves in new departments.

Formal mentoring programs—which involve having a more experienced manager form a developmental relationship with a less experienced protégé—are increasingly being used in organizations. Further, a good deal of research suggests involvement in mentoring relationships can assist in adjustment to change (e.g., a promotion, job rotation, special assignments) and lead to rapid career advancement (Druckman et al., 1997). Ideally, mentors serve two roles, one of socioemotional support through acceptance, counseling, and encouraging the protégé, and one of career facilitator through providing challenging assignments, sponsorship, and sharing skills. Research suggests that mentoring programs may be most effective when participation is voluntary, mentors get to choose their protégés, and role expectations are clarified at the outset (Druckman et al., 1997)

EMERGING TRENDS

The hottest trend in leadership development is undoubtedly the use of *360-degree/multi-rater feedback*. This process extends traditional performance appraisal techniques by employing survey methodology to gather ratings of a target manager's performance from him- or herself and his or her peers and subordinates in addition to the typical evaluations by superiors. Assessments from the full circle of constituents are then fed back, providing managers an opportunity to calibrate systematically self-perceptions of leadership with the perceptions held by key coworkers. The power of 360-degree feedback is in its systematic and regular use as a means of informing and tracking leadership development needs. There is an abundance of commercially available feedback instruments and many companies are designing their own around competency models and existing leadership theory.

Executive coaching is another rapidly growing approach used to expand senior managers' repertoire of leadership skills. This technique involves an ongoing relationship between an individual executive and a helping professional (typically from outside the organization). The work is one-on-one, tailored to the leader's particular developmental needs, and takes place over an extended period of time— ranging from weeks to even years. Coaching usually involves four interrelated steps: determining the leader's unique profile of strengths and developmental needs; making sense of the profile with the leader; establishing goals to address limiting aspects of his or her leadership; and counsel as the leader enacts a developmental action plan. Coaching services vary greatly in scope and depth, with some focused on solving immediate concrete problems or developing a specific skill, and others designed to foster growth in more fundamental aspects of character. The value of executive coaching is being affirmed by the marketplace, but little more than anecdotal evidence supports its value.

Action learning is a technique developed in Europe as a way to achieve synergy by combining formal training programs with experiential methods. This technique extends over time and involves field work on real organizational issues interspersed with classroom training seminars. In a program setting, concepts for leading more effectively are explained to managers who then engage in group discussions exploring how the concepts can be applied in their jobs. Trainees set goals and return to the workplace to implement the new skills and behaviors. They return periodically to the classroom to report their experiences and work with facilitators and other trainees to refine their goals and strategies for applying the concepts. Action learning is being used increasingly in United States (e.g., General Electric, Motorola, Ford Motor Company) as a technique to develop leadership competencies in large groups of managers (Tichy & Cohen, 1997). Participants of action learning report great value in it, although systematic evaluation of its impact is lacking in the published literature.

The explosion of possibilities made possible with advances in information technology is beginning to have an effect on leadership training. For example, the Internet and E-mail have made it possible to receive 360-degree feedback on-line and to access information and training in a specific area in which a manager needs to improve to solve a current problem (just-in-time learning; Johnson-Cramer, 1997). In the future, state-of-the-art leadership training will likely leverage computer technology to augment existing training content and delivery methods in a more sophisticated, integrated, and efficient system.

IMPACT EVALUATION

Reviews of the leadership training literature almost universally reach the conclusion that there is a scarcity of meaningful research on the impact of these interventions. Reviewers note that too little is known about how leadership development takes place, including which personal and contextual factors are crucial to ensuring successful training outcomes. This is unfortunate for many reasons, especially because evaluation research can provide valuable feedback for double-loop learning and the opportunity to update and fine-tune training activities. It also suggests that the consumers of the multibillion-dollar leadership training industry take it as an article of faith that they are getting their money's worth.

Burke and Day's (1986) exhaustive review of management training impact studies led them to conclude that the majority were poorly designed and used minimally important outcome criteria. In terms of Kirkpatrick's four levels of training-evaluation criteria, most management training studies focused on the two lowest levels, namely, trainees' affective reactions and learning tests that assess changes in knowledge. Neglected were the bottom-line criteria of improved job performance and enhanced organizational performance. Methodological weakness and a lack of scientific rigor are other problems with most evaluation research. This is so despite the availability of sophisticated methods appropriate for field studies that allow for stronger conclusions about how (and how well) the training works and the economic value it has to the organization (see an excellent example in Morrow, Jarrett, & Rupinski, 1997).

In an era of stricter budgetary accountability in organizational life, practitioners and scholars alike are taking greater stock in the importance of evaluating the effects of leadership training. Encouraging are two recent studies of the impact of transformational leadership training programs. One field experiment causally linked a program designed around principles from transformational leadership theory and goal-setting theory to enhanced subordinate perceptions of leaders' performance, an increase in subordinates' organizational commitment, and improved branch-level financial performance in one region of a large Canadian banking institution (Barling, Weber, & Kelloway, 1996). The other, which is the first documented true field experiment of the effects of transformational leadership training, was conducted within the Israeli Defense Forces (Dvir, Eden, Avolio, & Shamir, 1999). This study demonstrated that participation in a transformational leadership training program caused leaders to have a more positive impact on subordinates' development than did participation in a more traditional group dynamics training program. The transformational leadership training also led to higher unit performance on the battlefield.

It is instructive to note that organizations regarded as standard-setters in leadership development report that they consistently conduct some type of impact and evaluation research (Fulmer & Wagner, 1999), although the results of these studies rarely appear in public-domain publications. Also noteworthy is a recent policy decision by the Center for Leadership Studies at the State University of New York at Binghamton insisting that all organizations that request their training services must also consent to conducting impact evaluation research.

Taken together, these recent trends paint a promising picture for the future of leadership training research and, ultimately, practice. These examples demonstrate the availability and application of sophisticated methodological designs that allow for causal inferences and rely on important performance criteria as outcome measures. This trend may be a major force in establishing accountability in the leadership training industry, a pressure that should improve the quality of these services.

Especially when considering the complexity of social influence, developing the leadership talent of managers may best be viewed as a necessarily ongoing and iterative sequence of life-long learning. Stated simply, leadership development is a process and not an event. Thus, lectures and seminars, 360-degree feedback, off-site programs and courses, simulations and games, and various developmental job experiences all play important roles in an individual's growth as a leader over time. Each may be judiciously employed at stages appropriate to the developmental level of the person as revealed through a needs analysis.

REFERENCES

Barling, J., Weber, T., & Kelloway, K. E. (1996). Effects of transformational leadership training on attitudinal and financial outcomes: A field experiment. *Journal of Applied Psychology, 81,* 827–832.

Bass, B. M. (1990). *Bass and Stogdill's handbook of leadership: Theory, research, and managerial applications* (3rd ed.). New York: Free Press.

Burke, M. J., & Day, R. R. (1986). A cumulative study of the effectiveness of managerial training. *Journal of Applied Psychology, 71,* 232–246.

Clark, K. E., & Clark, M. B. (1990). *Measures of leadership.* West Orange, NJ: Leadership Library of America.

Csoka, L. S. (1997). *Bridging the leadership gap.* New York: The Conference Board.

Dvir, T., Eden, D., Avolio, B. J., & Shamir, B. (1999, May). *Impact of transformational leadership training on follower development and performance: A field experiment.* Paper presented at the annual meeting of the Society for Industrial and Organizational Psychology, Atlanta, GA.

Druckman, D., Singer, J. E., & Van Cott, H. (1997). *Enhancing organizational performance.* Washington, DC: National Academy Press.

Fulmer, R. M., & Wagner, S. (1999). Leadership: Lessons from the best. *Training and Development, 53,* 29–32.

Howard, A., & Bray, D. W. (1988). *Managerial lives in transition: Advancing age and changing times.* New York: Guilford.

Johnson-Cramer, M. (1997). "Just-in-time" learning in executive development: A literature review. *Executive Development Roundtable.* Boston: Boston University School of Management.

Locke, E. A., & Latham, G. P. (1984). *Goal-setting: A motivational technique that works.* Englewood Cliffs, NJ: Princeton.

McCall, M., & Lombardo, M., & Morison, A. M. (1988). *The lessons of experience: How successful executives develop on the job.* Lexington, MA: Lexington Books.

Morrow, C. C., Jarrett, M. Q., & Rupinski, M. T. (1997). An investigation of the effect and economic utility of corporate-wide training. *Personnel Psychology, 50,* 91–119.

Tichy, N. M., & Cohen, E. (1997). *The leadership engine: How winning companies build leaders at every level.* New York: Harper Business.

Walter, G. M. (1996). *Corporate practices in management develop-ment.* New York: The Conference Board.

Wexley, K. N., & Latham, G. P. (1991). *Developing and training hu-man resources in organizations.* Glenview, IL: Scott Foresman.

R. B. KAISER
D. L. DEVRIES
Kaplan DeVries, Inc.

ORGANIZATIONAL PSYCHOLOGY

LEARNED HELPLESSNESS

Learned helplessness was first described by psychologists studying animal learning. Researchers immobilized a dog and exposed it to a series of electric shocks, painful but not damaging, that could be neither avoided nor escaped. Twenty-four hours later, the dog was placed in a situation in which electric shock could be terminated by a simple response. The dog did not make this response; instead, it just sat and passively endured the shock. This behavior was in marked contrast to dogs in a control group that reacted vigorously to the shock and learned readily how to turn it off.

These investigators proposed that the dog had learned to be helpless. When originally exposed to uncontrollable shock, it learned that nothing it did mattered. The shocks came and went in-dependently of the dog's behaviors. They hypothesized that this learning of response-outcome independence was represented cog-nitively as an expectation of future helplessness that was general-ized to new situations to produce a variety of deficits: motivational, cognitive, and emotional. The deficits that follow in the wake of un-controllability have come to be known as the *learned helplessness phenomenon,* and their cognitive explanation as the *learned help-lessness model.*

Much of the early interest in learned helplessness stemmed from its clash with traditional stimulus-response theories of learn-ing. Alternative accounts of learned helplessness were proposed by theorists who saw no need to invoke mentalistic constructs, and many of these alternatives emphasized an incompatible motor re-sponse learned when animals were first exposed to uncontrollable shock. This response was presumably generalized to the second situation, where it interfered with performance at the test task. Said another way, the learned helplessness phenomenon is pro-duced by an inappropriate response learned in the original situa-tion rather than an inappropriate expectation (of response-outcome independence). For example, perhaps the dogs learned that holding still when shocked somehow decreased pain. If so, then they hold still in the second situation as well, because this re-sponse was previously reinforced.

Maier, Seligman, and others conducted a series of studies test-ing between the learned helplessness model and the incompatible motor response alternatives. Several lines of research implied that expectations were operative. Perhaps the most compelling argu-ment comes from the so-called *triadic design,* a three-group exper-imental design which shows that the uncontrollability of shocks is responsible for ensuing deficits. Animals in one group are exposed to shock that they are able to terminate by making some response. Animals in a second group are yoked to those in the first group, ex-posed to the identical shocks, the only difference being that ani-mals in the first group control their offset whereas those in the sec-ond do not. Animals in a third group are exposed to no shock at all in the original situation. All animals are then given the same test task.

Animals with control over the initial shocks typically show no helplessness when subsequently tested. They act just like animals with no prior exposure to shock. Animals without control become helpless. Whether or not shocks are controllable is not a property of the shocks specifically, but rather of the relationship between the animal and the shocks. That animals are sensitive to the link be-tween responses and outcomes implies that they must be able to de-tect and represent the relevant contingencies. A cognitive explana-tion of this ability is more parsimonious than one phrased in terms of incompatible motor responses.

Also arguing in favor of a cognitive interpretation of helpless-ness effects are studies showing that an animal can be "immu-nized" against the debilitating effects of uncontrollability by first exposing it to controllable events. Presumably, the animal learns during immunization that events can be controlled, and this expec-tation is sustained during exposure to uncontrollable events, pre-cluding learned helplessness. Other studies show that learned help-lessness deficits can be undone by forcibly exposing a helpless animal to the contingency between behavior and outcome. In other words, the animal is forced to make an appropriate response at the test task, by pushing or pulling it into action. After several such tri-als, the animal notices that escape is possible and begins to respond on its own. Again, the presumed process at work is a cognitive one. The animal's expectation of response-outcome independence is challenged during the "therapy" experience, and hence learning occurs.

Psychologists interested in humans, and particularly human problems, were quick to see the parallels between learned helpless-ness as produced by uncontrollable events in the laboratory and maladaptive passivity as it exists in the real world. Thus began sev-eral lines of research looking at learned helplessness in people.

In one line of work, helplessness in people was produced in the laboratory much as it was in animals, by exposing them to uncon-trollable events and seeing the effects on their motivation, cogni-tion, and emotion. Unsolvable problems were usually substituted for uncontrollable electric shocks, but the critical aspects of the phenomenon remained: Following uncontrollability, people show a variety of deficits. Other studies further attested to the similarity between the animal phenomenon and what was produced in the human laboratory. Uncontrollable bad events made anxiety and depression more likely. Previous exposure to controllable events immunized people against learned helplessness. Similarly, forcible exposure to contingencies reversed helplessness deficits.

In another line of work, researchers proposed various failures of adaptation as analogous to learned helplessness and investi-gated the similarity between these failures and learned helplessness on various fronts. Especially popular was Seligman's proposal that reactive depression and learned helplessness shared critical features: causes, symptoms, consequences, treatments, and preventions.

As these lines of work were pursued, it became clear—in all cases—that the original learned helplessness explanation was an oversimplification when applied to people. Most generally, it failed to account for the range of reactions that people displayed in response to uncontrollable events. Some people indeed showed pervasive deficits, as the model hypothesized, that were general across time and situation, whereas others did not. Further, failures of adaptation that the learned helplessness model was supposed to explain, such as depression, were sometimes characterized by a striking loss of self-esteem, about which the model was silent.

In an attempt to resolve these discrepancies, Abramson, Seligman, and Teasdale reformulated the helplessness model as it applied to people. The contrary findings could be explained by proposing that when people encounter an uncontrollable (bad) event, they ask themselves why it happened. The nature of their answer sets the parameters for the helplessness that follows. If their causal attribution is stable ("it's going to last forever"), then induced helplessness is long-lasting; if unstable, then it is transient. If their causal attribution is global ("it's going to undermine everything"), then induced helplessness will be widespread; if specific, then it is correspondingly circumscribed. Finally, if the causal attribution is internal ("it's all my fault"), the individual's self-esteem drops following uncontrollability; if external, self-esteem is left intact.

These hypotheses comprise the *attributional reformulation* of helplessness theory. This new theory left the original model in place, because uncontrollable events were still hypothesized to produce deficits when they gave rise to an expectation of response-outcome independence. However, the nature of these deficits was now said to be influenced by the causal attribution offered by the individual.

In some cases, the situation itself provides the explanation made by the person, and the extensive social psychology literature on causal attributions documents many situational influences on the process. In other cases, the person relies on his or her habitual way of making sense of events that occur, what is called one's *explanatory style*. All things being equal, people tend to offer similar sorts of explanations for disparate bad (or good) events. Explanatory style is therefore a distal influence on helplessness and the failures of adaptation that involve helplessness.

According to the attributional reformulation, explanatory style in and of itself is, therefore, not a cause of problems but rather a risk factor. Given uncontrollable events and the lack of a clear situational demand on the proffered attribution for uncontrollability, explanatory style should influence how the person responds. Helplessness will be long-lasting or transient, widespread or circumscribed, damaging to self-esteem or not, all in accordance with the individual's explanatory style.

Explanatory style has been extensively studied in its own right, and it proves to have an array of correlates. People who explain bad events with internal, stable, and global causes show passivity; poor problem solving; depression; anxiety; failure in academic, athletic, and vocational realms; social estrangement; morbidity; and even mortality. Explanatory style can be highly stable, sometimes over decades. The self-fulfilling nature of explanatory style—and help-

lessness per se—explains this stability. At the same time, explanatory style can and does change in response to ongoing life events. Cognitive therapy, for example, can move explanatory style in an optimistic direction.

SUGGESTED READING

Abramson, L. Y., Seligman, M. E. P., & Teasdale, J. D. (1978). Learned helplessness in humans: Critique and reformulation. *Journal of Abnormal Psychology, 87,* 49–74.

Buchanan, G. M., & Seligman, M. E. P. (Eds.). (1995). *Explanatory style.* Hillsdale, NJ: Erlbaum.

Maier, S. F., & Seligman, M. E. P. (1976). Learned helplessness: Theory and evidence. *Journal of Experimental Psychology: General, 105,* 3–46.

Peterson, C., Maier, S. F., & Seligman, M. E. P. (1993). *Learned helplessness: A theory for the age of personal control.* New York: Oxford University Press.

Seligman, M. E. P. (1975). *Helplessness: On depression, development, and death.* San Francisco: Freeman.

Seligman, M. E. P. (1990). *Learned optimism.* New York: Knopf.

C. PETERSON
University of Michigan

ANXIETY
DEPRESSION

LEARNING AND CONDITIONING MODELS OF PERSONALITY

Learning and conditioning models of personality are based on the principles of behaviorism, founded by Watson in 1913. Early behaviorists focused solely on observable behavior—behavior that could be measured, predicted, and ultimately controlled. Personality, according to Watson, was the end product of people's habit systems. In other words, over time, people learn or are conditioned to respond to environmental stimuli in predictable ways. Because people have unique past experiences that shape how they typically respond to various stimuli, each person ultimately develops a different personality.

Behaviorists embraced the principles of learning theory as the key to understanding personality. While not denying the role of heredity, they saw its importance as far secondary to the power of learning experiences or conditioning. Both classical and operant conditioning principles were considered essential in explaining the development, maintenance, and alteration of human personality patterns.

Classical conditioning, first described by Pavlov, the famous Russian physiologist, demonstrated that animals could be made to respond to stimuli in their environment by pairing these stimuli with other events. As nearly every psychology student knows, Pavlov's dogs began to salivate to the sound of a bell, even though no meat powder was presented. In the same way, according to the behaviorists, stimuli and events that people experience are often inadvertently paired with other aspects of their environment. Thus, many stimulus-response associations come to influence human behavior. Ultimately, people's preferences for food, clothing, friends, mates, and so on are determined by classical conditioning principles.

About the same time that Pavlov was describing classical conditioning in Russia, American psychologists, most notably Thorndike, were investigating another type of learning through association. Thorndike formulated the law of effect, which proposed that behaviors that lead to satisfying consequences are more likely to be repeated, and conversely ones that are followed by unsatisfying consequences, are less likely to be repeated. Later, Skinner outlined the principles of operant conditioning, demonstrating how reinforcement and punishment shaped and controlled behavior. Skinner described in detail how, through exposure to various reinforcement processes or schedules, people's behaviors could be molded or shaped into complex behavioral patterns. Skinner viewed personality traits as groups of specific responses that come to be associated with certain kinds of situations. Consider, for example, a person who in social settings says little, never expresses opinions, always agrees, never interrupts, and avoids attention. According to Skinner, it is the aggregate of these particular responses that tells us that this person is submissive. Skinner would say that these responses go together because they are functionally similar in their social consequences and are the result of this person being consistently reinforced in the past for yielding to others, or perhaps punished for asserting himself or herself.

The conditioning model offers similar explanations for so-called irrational personality characteristics, such as phobias and paranoid behavior. Behaviorists assert that such dysfunctional attributes are explained by past conditioning. For example, a person with a social phobia may have learned that the only way to escape the ridicule and embarrassment he received at home is to avoid social contact as much as possible (negative reinforcement). A man suffering from paranoid delusions may believe he has thwarted a plan to capture him by staying at home all the time, thereby rewarding the irrational behavior.

Another assumption of the conditioning model of personality is that behavior can be changed or modified by systematically applying various conditioning strategies. Some of these, such as systematic desensitization and aversion therapy, are based on classical conditioning. Systematic desensitization, for example, is used to treat phobias by pairing images of the feared object with a relaxation response. In aversion therapy, therapists attempt to rid their clients of undesirable behavior by pairing aversive images with the behavior. Others, such as token economies and biofeedback, stem from operant conditioning. In token economies, for example, delinquent youngsters in institutional settings are rewarded for following rules with points or tokens that can be exchanged for candy or privileges.

The early behaviorist position on personality development was confined to measurable, observable behaviors. Later, however, other learning theorists, most notably Bandura and Rotter, expanded this position to include cognitive and social features. They developed their own social learning theories of personality. Although built on the behaviorist foundation, these theories expanded its basic concepts to include such nonobservable behaviors as thoughts, values, expectancies, and individual perceptions.

Bandura argued that there were both internal and external determinants of behavior, and that behavior was not explained exclusively by either or by a simple combination. Instead, Bandura proposed the concept of reciprocal determinism to explain personality. First, Bandura asserted that because human beings can think and regulate their own behavior, they are not simply pawns of environmental influence. Second, Bandura proposed that many aspects of personality development involve the interaction of people with others in social contexts. Thus, according to Bandura, an adequate theory of personality must take into account the social settings in which behavior is initially acquired and in which it is maintained. Through this reciprocal determinism process, people influence their destinies by controlling environmental forces and, in turn, are controlled by these same forces.

Consider the following example for clarification. Someone you dislike asks you to play golf. Initially, your internal expectation of having an unenjoyable day would likely cause you to reject the invitation. But, what if this person tells you that the game is at a private, exclusive golf club that you've always dreamed of playing? Suddenly, the external inducement is powerful enough to determine your behavior and you agree to play. Now, you imagine having one of your most fulfilling golf games ever. At the course, your host compliments your game and lauds your golf swing. You actually look forward to playing with him again. Thus, the behavior in this case has changed your expectations, which will affect future behavior, and so on.

Thus, a major distinction between social learning theory and behaviorist conditioning theory is the added emphasis on cognitive, or internal, facilitators of human personality. Bandura, for example, argued that most human behavior is self-regulated, or performed without external reinforcements and punishments. Self-regulation occurs through internal rewards like feelings of accomplishment, self-imposed goals, and self-punishment for not meeting personal standards.

Rotter, like Bandura, argued that basic conditioning principles were too limited to explain complex human behavior. According to Rotter's social learning theory, the explanation of personality must take into account such cognitive variables as perceptions, expectancies, and values. Rotter believed that the key to predicting what a person will do in any situation depends on his behavioral potential for each option. In a nutshell, a person's behavioral potential, or likelihood of a given response occurring in a particular situation, depends on that person's internal calculation of (a) the probability that an action will result in a given reinforcer and (b) the value that reinforcer has for the person. If the odds of being reinforced for a particular course of action are viewed as slim, or if the expected behavior is not highly desired, the behavior potential is weak. Of course, a person's expectancies are tied to past outcomes in similar situations. Naturally, different people with different histories of experiences in similar situations, and with different feelings about the value of similar rewards, will likely respond in different ways in the same situation. This, of course, is what is known as differences in personality.

Perhaps social learning theory's most important contribution to understanding personality is the concept of observational learning or modeling. These theories emphasize that learning is not limited to classical or operant conditioning. People also learn by observing, reading, or hearing about other people's behavior. However, the acquisition of learning by observation does not always lead to performing the learned behavior. Whether or not the behavior is performed is determined by a person's internal expectation of reinforcements. By observing how others are rewarded or punished for their actions, people develop cognitive expectancies about behavioral outcomes and about what they must do to achieve desirable outcomes and avoid undesirable ones.

The learning and conditioning models of personality have their strengths and weaknesses. Among the strengths are their solid foundation on empirical research. Skinner, Bandura, and Rotter's descriptions of human personality are based on empirical research findings. Another strength lies in the development of useful behavioral change procedures which use baseline data and objective criteria to determine their effectiveness. A common criticism of this model is that it is too narrow in its description of human personality, leaving out such important factors as free will and the role of heredity. Also, people have criticized behavior therapists' reduction of everything into observable behavior, and suggest that the positive effects of behavior therapy are short-lived. Nevertheless, learning and conditioning models of personality remain alive and well today. In fact, the social learning models of Bandura and Rotter appear to be more popular than ever.

SUGGESTED READING

Bandura, A. (1977). *Social learning theory.* Englewood Cliffs, NJ: Prentice Hall.

Bandura, A. (1986). *Social foundations of thought and action: A social cognitive theory.* Englewood Cliffs, NJ: Prentice Hall.

Burger, J. (1990). *Personality.* Belmont, CA.: Wadsworth.

Rotter, J. B. (1954). *Social learning and clinical psychology.* Englewood Cliffs, NJ: Prentice Hall.

Rotter, J. B. (1982). *The development and applications of social learning theory: Selected papers.* New York: Praeger.

Rotter, J. B., Chance, J. E., & Phares, E. J. (Eds.). (1972). *Applications of a social learning theory of personality.* New York: Holt, Rinehart & Winston.

Skinner, B. F. (1953). *Science and human behavior.* New York: Macmillan.

Skinner, B. F. (1968). *Beyond freedom and dignity.* New York: Bantam.

Skinner, B. F. (1974). *About behaviorism.* New York: Vintage Books.

Thorndike, E. L. (1911). *Animal intelligence: Experimental studies.* New York: Macmillan.

Watson, J. B. (1924/1970). *Behaviorism.* New York: Norton.

T. M. KELLEY
Wayne State University

BEHAVIORISM
CLASSICAL CONDITIONING
PERSONALITY THEORIES
SOCIAL LEARNING THEORIES

LEARNING DISABILITIES

If an individual does not benefit from a regular education program and is not socially disadvantaged, intellectually limited, or pedagogically deprived, and shows no evidence for hard sign neurophysiological dysfunction, that individual is characterized as learning disabled. If an individual has difficulty communicating either expressively or receptively and cannot read or do mathematics within the criterion range established by the school district, that individual is similarly considered to be learning disabled.

The lack of precision in evidence for this characterization of the learning disabled reflects the confusion found in clinical and educational settings. Concern over learning disabilities is widespread and has become a major field of interest in neurology, education, psychology, and medicine. The heterogeneity of disciplines concerned with the problem is precipitated by the heterogeneity of the symptomology presented. The disability may be specific to reading or generalized to all cognitive areas. It may be present with or without behavioral, social, or motor problems. In short, learning disabilities are idiosyncratic: Each case is symptom-specific. Major concerns for any professional are the appropriate diagnostic and remedial/compensatory program.

Although learning and especially reading disabilities were recognized prior to the 20th century, Samuel T. Orton's article " 'Word-blindness' in school children," which appeared in 1925 in the *Archives of Neurology and Psychiatry,* was the first formalized attempt to see in neurological dysfunction—or more precisely, mixed cortical lateral dominance—the source for disorders in writing and understanding printed text. Although some of his early notions about the consequences of mixed lateral dominance have been challenged, Orton did provide a formalized framework for describing alexia, agraphia, difficulties in recognizing words, slow and deliberate speech, stuttering, and apraxia or abnormal clumsiness. While there is a high correlation of learning disabilities in children with mixed or crossed dominance characteristics, this is now recognized as unlikely to be the cause of all learning disabilities, given the wide range of symptomology evidenced.

FREQUENCY

Estimates of the frequency of learning disabilities vary dramatically because of the lack of precise definition, but the following guidelines seem to hold internationally for the literate population: 2 to 4% show signs of severe disability in interpreting text, communicating verbally, and writing, while another 3 to 5% show substantial difficulty with specific areas like reading (dyslexia), writing (dysgraphia), and math (dyscalcula). On the other hand, readers who do poorly because of intellectual limitations or poor skill acquisition can account for as much as 15% of the population; though candidates for remedial aid, they are not considered learning disabled. Loose criteria like reading greater than 2 years below appropriate expected reading grade level also hinder the accumulations of more accurate statistics on frequency. Learning disabilities are known to be distributed equally across age, socioeconomic status, intellectual levels, and throughout all literate cultures. Although traditionally 90% of the learning disabled were males, this trend is expected to change through better screening procedures and changing emphasis on developmental differences between males and females.

PRIMARY CHARACTERISTICS

In line with the limits of specifying the disability as expressed previously, the following characteristics may or may not be present in any one individual. First, there may be difficulties with receptive or expressive language. *Receptive* language difficulties include trouble in understanding certain speech sounds like the endings of words, in comprehending written text or spoken words, and in discriminating words in text. *Expressive* language difficulties include misnaming objects, perseverating thoughts, deliberate speech as shown by pauses after every word, and agraphia or difficulty writing words and thoughts.

There may also be verbal and nonverbal thought disruption (nonpsychopathological). *Verbal* thought disruption includes receptive and expressive language disorders, failure to comprehend concrete and/or (more frequently) abstract words, and failure to recognize the connection between successive words in sentences and sentences in paragraphs. *Nonverbal* thought disruption includes a reluctance and failure to complete work, general confusion caused by classroom routine, a tendency to be easily distracted by others, and confusion in directions, left-right orientation, and spatial order.

Memory deficits, especially in short-term memory, can be found in many learning disabled persons. Here words just read must be reviewed because they and their meaning are forgotten. Recognition span for words and letters is found to be two or three, rather than five or six as in normal learning groups. *Perceptual* and *cognitive deficits* such as reversal and poor discrimination of letters, failure to group and categorize similar items, and poor problem-solving skills are common. When perceptual or cognitive deficits are identified, they should be separated from attentional deficits or the failure to stay on tasks to completion. While the latter deficits are susceptible to behavioral change, the former are not, but the perceptual and cognitive deficits may be eliminated as the attentional deficits are remediated. Frequent and erratic eye movement patterns are found among the learning disabled, but these are now attributed to the difficulty encountered with cognitive tasks rather than to aberrant motor activity.

SECONDARY CHARACTERISTICS

In addition to the frequently occurring perceptual, cognitive, linguistic, and neurological dysfunctions, the learning disabled frequently show signs of social and emotional disorders as well. Because most of these children get separated in some way for at least some time during each day from their regular classroom activity, they begin to feel different. Knowing they cannot do tasks such as reading as well as others can, plus a continued lack of success, further enhance negative feelings about themselves. It is not unusual for the learning disabled adult or child to have a poor self-image, self-concept, and self-esteem; to lack the will to pursue tasks because of the difficulties present; to show numerous psychosomatic disorders; and to withdraw from social contact. Others may overcompensate by becoming disruptive in whatever class they are in, being quarrelsome toward peers or classmates, and delinquent toward society. These social and emotional difficulties can present added complexity to getting the child on task. Hyperactivity is frequent among the learning disabled, which also proves disruptive to staying on task. Behavior training has been found to be effective if the hyperactive behavior is nonorganic; otherwise both Ritalin and Pemoline (Cylert) prove effective and do not interfere intellectually.

PROFESSIONAL COOPERATION

Because of the complexity of the syndromes evidenced in learning disorders, it is especially important to remove professional isolation. An interprofessional assessment would include a history of the individual and family; a physical and neurological exam; a psychological assessment including an intellectual, perceptual, and personality profile; and an educational program development. This cooperation can best guarantee that the assessment will reveal areas of strength and weakness. It is not unusual for a teacher to recognize a difficulty such as classroom disruption and attempt to change behavior that is the result of a learning problem. For both teacher and student, success is quite unlikely. Similarly, stomach cramps and headache occurring prior to school starting time are likely to be treated medically, while the cause is an avoidance of further unsuccessful experience at school.

PROGNOSIS: GOOD

In 1977 Public Law 94-142 was put into effect. A landmark event, it guaranteed equal educational opportunity to all handicapped aged zero to 21 years. The law also defined learning disabilities as a handicap and mandated that the states and their subdivisions provide the necessary services. Although implementation was a slow process owing to politics, economics, and refining issues, more learning disabled are being identified and receiving necessary services than ever before.

Because of the law, early detection of high-risk children is enhancing knowledge of remediation and compensation; new directions are being taken toward implosive verbal exposure; and alternate means of communication such as oral reports are being encouraged. Similarly, counseling toward appropriate career goals and college curricula aimed at the learning disabled student are becoming more frequent.

REFERENCES

Orton, S. T. (1925). "Word-blindness" in school children. *Archives of Neurology and Psychiatry, 14,* 582–615.

SUGGESTED READING

Adamson, W. C., & Adamson, K. K. (Eds.). (1979). *A handbook for specific learning disabilities.* New York: Gardner Press.

Gaddes, W. H. (1980). *Learning disabilities and brain function: A neuropsychological approach.* New York: Springer-Verlag.

Knights, R. M., & Bakker, D. (1976). *The neuropsychology of learning disorders.* Baltimore: University Park Press.

Myklebust, H. (Ed.). (1968). *Progress in learning disabilities* (Vol. 1). New York: Grune & Stratton.

Orton, S. T. (1937). *Reading, writing, and speech problems in children.* New York: Norton.

D. F. FISHER
Churchville, Maryland

SCHOOL LEARNING

LEARNING THEORIES

The field of learning studies those factors that produce long-lasting changes in the behavior of the individual as a result of experience. The task of learning theory is to formulate principles that encompass the findings of such studies. Learning principles provide explanations of current behavior and predictions of future behavior within the limits of uncertainty about future environments. Basic learning processes are identified through laboratory investigations, usually with nonhuman animals. The resulting principles may be applied to matters of general societal concern, such as education in the classroom and remediation of abnormal behavior.

At the behavioral level, the central problem for learning theory is to identify the conditions that are essential to change the way in which the environment guides behavior. At the subbehavioral level, the central problem is to identify the processes that underlie these changes. The major goal of learning theory is to formulate a principle of selection by the environment—that is, a *principle of reinforcement*—whereby experience changes individual behavior. A principle of reinforcement makes the same contribution to understanding differences among individuals as does the principle of natural selection to differences among species. Selection by the individual environment and by the ancestral environment are interdependent because the processes summarized by a principle of reinforcement are themselves products of natural selection.

The search for a principle of reinforcement uses two complementary laboratory procedures—Pavlovian (or classical) conditioning and operant (or instrumental) conditioning. In their most basic forms, both procedures study learning through the use of reflexes. Reflexes are environment-behavior relations that result from natural selection. In the Pavlovian procedure, a stimulus (such as the onset of a tone) precedes the elicitation of a reflexive response (such as the elicitation of salivation by food). In the operant procedure, a behavior—instead of a stimulus—precedes the elicitation of a response. For example, pressing a lever might be followed by food, which again evokes salivation. The Pavlovian and operant procedures have each identified two conditions that are necessary for learning—contiguity and discrepancy. Contiguity means that the stimulus (e.g., the tone) or the behavior (e.g., lever pressing) must occur *immediately* before the elicited response (e.g., salivation) if it is to be affected by the learning process (Gormezano & Kehoe, 1981). That is, the tone or lever-pressing must occur just

prior to the food if the tone is to guide salivation or if the sight of the lever is to increase its guidance of lever pressing (and salivation). The eliciting stimulus that brings about these changes is termed a reinforcing stimulus, or reinforcer. Discrepancy means that the reinforcer (food, in the example) must evoke a behavior (salivation) that differs in degree or kind from the behavior that is otherwise occurring (Kamin, 1969). For example, if a light accompanies a tone that was previously paired with food and food continues to be given immediately after the light-tone compound stimulus, then the light does *not* acquire the ability to evoke salivation. The light-food relation meets the contiguity requirement, but it does not meet the discrepancy requirement: The learner is already salivating during the tone when the food is presented. Thus, no change, or discrepancy, in salivation is produced by the food. In such cases, conditioning to the light is said to be blocked by prior conditioning to the tone.

Although there is general agreement about the two conditions required for learning, learning theories differ in their approaches to identifying the processes that underlie these changes. Two main approaches may be identified—an associationist approach and a biobehavioral approach. In the associationist approach, behavioral changes are assumed to reflect the strength of underlying associations. For example, blocking is inferred to occur because the discrepancy between maximum associative strength supported by the reinforcer and the existing strength of association between the tone and the reinforcer is too small to support additional conditioning to the light. The nature of the underlying associations is often inferred from tests conducted after original conditioning. As an example, suppose that lever-pressing is first followed by food, which strengthens pressing using the operant procedure. Then food is separately paired with a noxious stimulus using a Pavlovian procedure. When later tested, lever-pressing is reduced in strength, even though lever-pressing itself was never followed by the noxious stimulus. On the basis of these behavioral observations, the learner is inferred to have formed a response-reinforcer association (i.e., a lever pressing-food association) during the original operant procedure (see Colwill & Rescorla, 1986). The pairing of the food with the noxious stimulus is said to devalue the reinforcer, thereby weakening the response-reinforcer association. Note that the association itself is not directly observed, but is inferred from behavioral tests alone. The associationist approach in learning theory is a specific instance of an inferred-process approach, which is a common theoretical stance in psychology. Historically, most learning theories have been of this type, ranging from the earlier comprehensive learning theories of Tolman, Hull, and Spence to the later more specialized and quantitative theories of Estes (see Estes et al., 1954).

In the biobehavioral approach to learning theory, statements about underlying processes are not based on inferences from behavior but on direct observations of the biological processes that mediate the relationships observed at the behavioral level. Thus, a biobehavioral approach represents a synthesis of behavioral research with neuroscience. Learning theorists that pursue a biobehavioral approach do not believe that behavioral observations sufficiently constrain inferences about underlying processes to make such speculations worthwhile: A given observation at the behavioral level may be the product of many combinations of diverse underlying processes. In the field of learning, the behavior-analytic theory of Skinner is most receptive to a biobehavioral approach: "Between the stimulating action of the environment and the response of the organism, . . . only brain science can fill these gaps. In doing so, it completes the account; it does not give a different account of the same thing" (Skinner, 1953, p. 18). Behavior analysis seeks to uncover orderly functional relations between observed environmental and behavioral events and avoids inferences about the processes that mediate these relations. However, many learning theorists found a science that was silent on the mediating processes intellectually unsatisfying. Moreover, some phenomena—such as blocking—could not be completely understood on the basis of behavioral observations alone. In a biobehavioral approach, blocking is attributed to directly measured inhibitory effects of a stimulus that has been paired with a reinforcer on the neural systems of reinforcement (Schultz, 1997). Before the development of modern neuroscience, the inferred-processes approach might have been justified as an effort to identify the processes that filled the "gap." However, given the rapid advances in neuroscience, reliance on inferences from behavior instead of direct observations of the neural processes themselves seems imprudent. Theories of learning will increasingly integrate behavioral and neuroscientific research, which satisfies the need to specify the processes that mediate environment-behavior relations while simultaneously avoiding the temptations to logical circularity that plague inferred-process theories (e.g., Donahoe & Palmer, 1994).

REFERENCES

Colwill, R. M., & Rescorla, R. A. (1986). Associative structures in instrumental learning. In G. H. Bower (Ed.), *The psychology of learning and motivation* (Vol. 20, pp. 55–104). New York: Academic.

Donahoe, J. W., & Palmer, D. C. (1994). *Learning and complex behavior.* Boston: Allyn & Bacon.

Estes, W. K., Koch, S., MacCorquodale, K., Meehl, P. E., Mueller, C. G., Jr., Schoenfeld, W. N., & Verplanck, W. S. (Eds.). (1954). *Modern learning theory.* New York: Appleton-Century-Crofts.

Gormezano, I., & Kehoe, J. E. (1981). Classical conditioning and the law of contiguity. In P. Harzem & M. D. Zeiler (Eds.), *Predictability, correlation, and contiguity* (pp. 1–45). New York: Wiley.

Kamin, L. J. (1969). Predictability, surprise, attention, and conditioning. In B. A. Campbell & R. M. Church (Eds.), *Punishment and aversive behavior* (pp. 279–296). New York: Appleton-Century-Crofts.

Schultz, W. (1997). Adaptive dopaminergic neurons report the appetitive value of environmental stimuli. In J. W. Donahoe & V. P. Dorsel (Eds.), *Neural-network models of cognition* (pp. 317–335). Amsterdam: Elsevier Science Press.

Skinner, B. F. (1953). *Science and human behavior.* New York: Macmillan.

J. W. Donahoe
University of Massachusetts

CLASSICAL CONDITIONING
OPERANT CONDITIONING
REINFORCEMENT

LEITER INTERNATIONAL PERFORMANCE SCALE (LIPS)

The Leiter International Performance Scale (LIPS; Leiter, 1959) is an individually administered intelligence test that is being increasingly used as a general measure of intelligence in situations in which a so-called culture fair test is needed.

The LIPS is completely nonlanguage and instructions are given in pantomime. Test materials consist of approximately 200 one-inch cubical blocks, a response frame, and paper stimulus strips. The examiner places a stimulus strip on the response frame and the subject simply places a series of blocks in the response frame to coincide with the problem presented on the stimulus strip. The test consists of problems in matching colors, duplicating designs, matching shades of gray, estimating the number of dots in a given area, recognizing form, numerical reasoning problems, and so forth. The test uses number, perceptual, and abstract reasoning tasks, but no verbal material at all.

The basic version of the LIPS is suitable for testing persons from 2 through 18 years of mental age. Adults are considered to have an average mental age of less than 18 years on this device. A later version of the test developed by Grace Arthur in 1949—the "Arthur Adaptation of the Leiter"—is considered suitable for testing children between the ages of three and eight.

The reliability coefficients of the LIPS range in the low 90s. Relatively little data are available regarding validity. Despite its popular use as a culture fair test, some studies indicate that so-called culturally deprived persons may actually have more difficulty on this type of a test than they might on a Wechsler Intelligence Scale. Duvall and Maloney (1978), for example, demonstrated that culturally deprived adults actually scored significantly lower on the Leiter than they did on the Wechsler Adult Intelligence Scale. As with all psychological tests, caution should be used in interpreting test results.

REFERENCES

Duvall, S., & Maloney, M. P. (1978). A comparison of the WAIS and Leiter International Performance Scale in a large urban community mental health setting. *Psychological Reports, 43,* 235–238.

Leiter, R. G. (1969). Part I of the manual for the 1948 revision of the Leiter International Performance Scale: Evidence of the reliability and validity of the Leiter tests. *Psychological Service Center Journal, 11,* 1–72. (Original work published 1959)

M. P. Maloney
Pasadena, California

CULTURAL BIAS IN TESTS
INTELLIGENCE MEASURES
NONVERBAL INTELLIGENCE TESTS

LEWIN, KURT (1890–1947)

Kurt Lewin received the PhD from the University of Berlin in 1914. Among his early associates were two of the Gestalt psychologists, Max Wertheimer and Wolfgang Köhler. Some psychologists consider Lewin's system to be an extension of the Gestalt movement.

Lewin considered his system to be a *topological and vectoral psychology*. He took the terms "topology" and "vector" from mathematics. Topology investigates the properties of space. But topology was not enough: He needed a concept of force or vector.

Lewin began his system of psychology with the concept of *life space*. This was a psychological field, the space in which a person moved. This constituted the totality of facts that determined the behavior of an individual at any one time. Behavior was a function of life space at any moment: $B = fL$. L was a psychological field and not necessarily a physical one. The life space included oneself and other people and objects as one perceived them.

The life space was divided into regions by boundaries. Each region might be considered a psychological fact. The boundaries had several dimensions such as nearness/remoteness. This could be illustrated by a college student wanting to be a physician: The region of setting up practice as a physician is quite remote from the present situation. Other regions which must be passed through might include graduating from college, entering medical school, graduating from medical school, internship, and finally setting up practice. Another dimension of boundaries was firmness/weakness. Some boundaries were easy to cross, while others, such as passing a qualifying examination could be firm and difficult.

When a person passed from one region to another, movement occurred that had direction. In such movement one followed a pathway. Here Lewin invented a kind of geometry that he called hodological space. The characteristics of a given path varied according to the situation, and the direction depended on the properties of the entire field.

On the dynamic side, Lewin postulated a concept of tension. Tension occurred when needs arose. Needs could be either psychological or physiological.

Objects in the life space also had valences—plus or minus, depending on whether they were attractive or repulsive. Often a life space might contain several regions in which several valences existed at the same time. A conflict could occur between two objects both of which had a positive valence, or in a case in which two objects were equally repulsive, but a person had to choose between the two. The vector or force constituted the push which directed a person toward or away from a goal. This force was correlated with the valence of the object.

In his later years Lewin directed his attention to problems of social psychology. A major research effort (Lewin, Lippitt, & White, 1939) related to various social climates and aggression. Lewin also developed the concept of group dynamics, an application to the group that he borrowed from his earlier individual psychology. Just as the person in his life space constituted the psychological field, so the group and its environment constituted the social field. The group was characterized by a dynamic interdependence of its members. One's status depended on one's region as it related to other regions (members of the group). The group was subject to cohesive and disruptive forces. Disruptive forces arose out of too-strong barriers between members, which hampered communication. The group constituted a field of forces and individuals were attracted or repelled, depending on the kinds of valences existing in the group.

R. W. LUNDIN
Wheaton, Illinois

LIBIDO

"Libido is a term used in the theory of the instincts for describing the dynamic manifestation of sexuality." Thus Freud began his 1923 encyclopedia article on the libido theory. He had used the term "libido" as early as 1894. His major theoretical treatise, *Three Essays on the Theory of Sexuality* (1905, p. 255), placed libido at the center of his theories of development and psychopathology. In his *New Introductory Lectures on Psychoanalysis* (1933, p. 95), Freud introduced his review and current synthesis of libido theory, noting that "the theory of instincts is so to say our mythology." Even in his later years libido remained a central construct in psychoanalytic theory, one side of the basic, pervasive, and instinctual dualism: sex and aggression, life and death. The metapsychology of libido's vicissitudes and reorganizations over the course of development through the psychosexual stages—oral, anal, phallic, latency, and genital—formed the core of early psychoanalytic theories of developmental psychology, psychopathology, and clinical practice.

Libido theory is among the most far-reaching and controversial notions in psychoanalysis. Now as then, libido refers to the sexual biological instinct, drive, or psychic energy. However, whereas libido was not typically discussed in general physician's offices in Freud's era, modern internists and specialty physicians recognize the importance of healthy sexual functioning as an important indicator of overall health and quality of life. Thus, the term libido may also be used to refer to sexual instincts and sexual desire more generally.

Freud himself had strong allegiance and high hopes for biological causation and explanation, but still broadened his notion of libido to include the sensual as well as the more basic sexual aspects of life. Nonetheless, the relative emphasis upon biological versus social or psychological description still characterizes the ongoing controversy over libido theory. As early as 1916, Jung in his *Psychology of the Unconscious*, attacked Freud's theory of libido, arguing that sexuality was only a variant of a more primal, undifferentiated form of psychic energy. In Jung's view, furthermore, sexuality emerged and predominated only in puberty, much later than in Freud's theory, with its focus on infancy and early childhood manifestations of libidinal expression and development. Rapaport replaced the libido concept with a more general, nonspecific drive energy as he cast traditional and id-oriented psychoanalysis into more general ego psychology. The growing concern with the bankruptcy of hydraulic, thermodynamic, and drive discharge models led to the elimination of or de-emphasis of libido theory in many recent psychoanalytic reformulations. Klein, one of the most recent and influential systematizers of psychoanalysis, remarked that "in fact, the uncritical acceptance of libido theory with the newer current of ego psychology brings into sharp relief one of the focal dilemmas confronting psychoanalysis" (Klein, 1976, p. 147).

Aside from ongoing controversy over what role, if any, libido plays in psychoanalytic psychology, or with any other theory of behavior or pathology, two abiding domains or concepts derived from libido theory remain useful, especially when their metapsychological nature is appreciated and respected. One domain is the qualitative properties of libido (or any instinctual energy) which serve as structure, process, and organization for the so-called drive. Schafer notes that through variation in degree of anticathexis, cathexis, or hypercathexis of libido, we may posit dreams, symptoms, jokes, rituals, pathology, relationships, therapeutic effects, and so on—the concerns of psychoanalysis. He lists seven qualities of libido (Schafer, 1976, pp. 80–81):

1. direction (sexual gratification),

2. urgency or peremptoriness (unremitting pressure for discharge),

3. mobility (readiness to divert itself into indirect channels when direct channels are blocked),

4. dischargeability (its being reduced in quantity, hence in impetus, following certain activities),

5. bindability (its being maintained in a fixed or blocked position by opposing energy),

6. transformability (loss of its properties of direction, peremptoriness, probability), and

7. dischargeability (a loss known as desexuatization or deinstinctualization), fusibility (its capacity to blend with the energy of aggressive impulses/energy)*

The second useful domain of concepts derived from libido theory are those of the developmental progressions of psychosexuality and object relations. In the theory of infantile sexuality, Freud described the maturation and successive reorganization of libido through the oral stage (birth to about 18 months), anal stage (18 to 36 months), phallic stage (three to five years), latency stage (middle childhood), and genital stage (adolescence and adulthood). Libidinal gratification was associated with sensuality or activity focused about each of the so-called erotogenic body zones implied in the stage sequence. Particular qualities of character and pathology were associated with the successes, failures, and compromises at each mutually influential step of the developmental process. A related progression of libido from autoerotism (gratification through one's own body) to narcissism (love of one's "self") and object love (gratification through investment and involvement with other people) complements the psychosexual progression, contributing yet another of the major developmental lines which form the framework for psychoanalytic diagnostic classification.

The scientific status of libido theory and its derived constructs remains to be established by empirical research, an effort abandoned by many in the belief that it is not researchable. Greater understanding will undoubtedly emerge with the coming of improved technology and conceptualization. Until then libido theory remains an influential—though controversial—girder in the framework which guides a major portion of applied psychology: psychoanalysis.

REFERENCES

Freud, S. (1905). Three essays on the theory of sexuality. In J., Strachey (1973). *The standard edition of the complete psychological works of Sigmund Freud* (Vol. 7). London: Hogarth Press.

Freud, S. (1923). In J. Strachey, (1973). *The standard edition of the complete psychological works of Sigmund Freud* (Vol. 18). London: Hogarth Press.

Freud, S. (1933). New introductory lectures on psychoanalysis. In J., Strachey (1973). *The standard edition of the complete psychological works of Sigmund Freud* (Vol. 23). London: Hogarth Press.

Jung, C. (1993). *The basic writings of C. G. Jung.* New York: Modern Library.

Klein, G. S. (1976). *Psychoanalytic theory: An exploration of essentials.* New York: International Universities Press.

Nagera, H. (1990). *Basic psychoanalytic concepts on the libido theory.* London: Karnac Books.

Schafer, R. (1976). *New language of psychoanalysis.* New Haven, CT: Yale University Press.

D. L. WERTLIEB
Tufts University

PSYCHOANALYSIS
SEXUAL DEVELOPMENT

LIE DETECTION

An instrument that monitors one or more involuntary physiological variables from a person under interrogation is popularly called a lie detector. The most common instrument for this purpose, the polygraph, normally monitors breathing movements, relative blood pressure, and electrodermal responses (which are related to the sweating of the palms). Some examiners now use some form of voice stress analyzer, the most common of which measures the amount of low frequency (10hz) warble present in the speaking voice. Voice analyzers do not require attachments to the subject and therefore can be used covertly, even over the telephone. It is popularly believed that these or other instruments can identify lying by detecting some response or pattern of responses that is specific to deception—a so-called Pinocchio response or pattern of reaction that (nearly) everyone shows when lying but does not show when answering truthfully. That our species should have acquired such a maladaptive response tendency through natural selection seems implausible on evolutionary grounds, and although such claims have been made from time to time, no specific lie response has yet been objectively demonstrated.

*From R. Schafer, *New language for psychoanalysis* (New Haven: Yale University Press, 1976). ∀ Yale University Press. Reprinted with permission.

All one can determine from the polygraph chart is that the subject was relatively more disturbed or aroused by one question than by another; one cannot determine why the subject was aroused—whether the question elicited, for example, guilt, fear, or anger. Polygraph responses that are indistinguishable from spontaneous ones can be elicited by biting one's tongue or clenching the toes. In the case of the voice analyzers, pronouncing different phonemes (e.g., the different numerals) will yield different degrees of associated voice stress.

The examiner must therefore try to infer deception from the difference in reaction elicited by different types of questions. For many years, the standard question format was that of the relevant/irrelevant (R/I) test. Relevant questions (e.g., "Did you take the $1000 from the safe?") were intermixed with irrelevant questions (e.g., "Did you eat breakfast this morning?"). If the subject appeared to be more disturbed by the relevant than by the irrelevant questions, he or she was diagnosed as deceptive. Because most innocent persons are also likely to be disturbed by the accusatory relevant questions, however, the R/I test produced a high rate of false-positive errors.

Since the 1950s, most examiners have come to use some form of control question format, in which a third type of question is added to the list. Control questions refer in a general way to prior misdeeds of the subject. In the case of a theft investigation, for example, a control question might be, "Before last year, had you ever taken anything that didn't belong to you?" The objective is to find 2 or 3 questions to which (in the opinion of the examiner) the subject's answer is untruthful or, at least, about which the subject is uncertain that his or her answer is truthful. The theory of the control question test is that an innocent person, able to answer the relevant questions truthfully, will be more disturbed by these control questions and show stronger physiological reactions to them, whereas the guilty person will react most strongly to the relevant questions. In another test, the directed lie test which has become popular recently, the suspect is directed to lie in answering each control question deceptively.

A different method of polygraphic interrogation, the guilty knowledge test, or GKT, attempts to determine whether the suspect recognizes facts or images about the crime that would be known only to someone who had been present at the scene. The GKT consists of a series of multiple-choice questions such as: "The killer wore a ski mask. If you are the killer, you will know the color of the mask. Was it: Brown? Blue? Red? Black? Yellow? Green?" In the GKT, the subject's physiological responses to the incorrect alternatives serve as controls. If he or she responds differentially to the correct alternatives, then guilty knowledge can be inferred. The GKT is used extensively by police investigators in Israel and in Japan but seldom in the United States.

By 1981 there were probably 6,000 polygraph examiners and perhaps 2,000 voice stress analysts practicing in the United States, and at least one million lie detector tests were being administered annually. Most of these tests were administered for employers in the private sector for screening job applicants, for periodic testing of employees, or for deciding which of several suspected employees was guilty of some specific theft or other misconduct. At the same time, the lie detector was in heavy use by police and federal agencies. In 1988, the federal Employee Polygraph Protection Act was signed, prohibiting most employers in the private sector from requiring employees or job applicants to submit to lie detector testing. However, police departments, the FBI, the CIA, the National Security Agency, the Secret Service, the military services, and other federal agencies continue to rely on polygraph screening of employees.

Most city police departments still employ polygraph or voice stress tests as an aid in deciding which criminal suspects should be released and which should be prosecuted. The lie detector test is very effective in inducing confessions or damaging admissions, at least from unsophisticated suspects. In perhaps 14 states, polygraph evidence is admissible in criminal trials when both sides have so stipulated prior to testing. This normally happens when the prosecution's case is so weak that they offer to drop the charges if the defendant passes the lie detector. The defendant must stipulate, however, that the test results can be used against him or her in court, should he or she fail the test. In its 1993 Daubert decision, the Supreme Court ruled that federal judges must at least hold evidentiary hearings whenever lie detector (or other allegedly scientific evidence) is proffered. Such hearings to date have almost invariably led to the exclusion of polygraph test results. In its 1998 Scheffer decision, the Supreme Court ruled that the per se exclusion of polygraph evidence does not violate the defendant's sixth amendment right to present a defense.

ACCURACY OF LIE DETECTION

Polygraph and voice stress examiners claim very high rates of accuracy, ranging typically from 95 to 99%, but these claims have not been supported by credible research. Because one cannot simulate in the laboratory the emotional concerns of employees or criminal suspects being interrogated in real life, studies of lie detector validity must be done in the field situation. Interrogation of criminal suspects who have failed polygraph tests produces confessions in perhaps 20% of cases, thus verifying the test that produced the confession. Such confessions sometimes clear other suspects in the same case. To determine the accuracy of diagnoses based just on the polygraph recordings, the charts from such verified tests are then scored by a different examiner than the one who administered the test.

However, suspects who fail the polygraph and then confess may not be representative of guilty suspects generally. Moreover, because testing of multiple suspects normally ceases after one suspect has been diagnosed as deceptive, suspects verified as innocent by another's confession will usually have been tested prior to the suspect who confessed and their charts scored as truthful. Therefore, field studies based on charts verified by polygraph-induced confessions must necessarily overestimate the validity of the polygraph, because they exclude charts both from guilty suspects who passed the test and from innocent suspects who failed the test. By 1998, four such studies of polygraph accuracy had been published in scientific journals. Where chance accuracy would lead to 50% correct classification, the average accuracy obtained in these studies of lie detection methods was 73%.

It is important to examine the fate of the truthful or innocent subjects separately, since the consequences of failing a lie detector test in real life can be very serious. In the four mentioned studies, the charts of the innocent suspects were scored as deceptive in 39.5% of the cases, indicating that the lie detector tests are strongly biased against the truthful person. The accuracy of the GKT has not yet been adequately studied in real life applications. Laboratory studies agree, however, in showing that the GKT is highly accurate in identifying innocent suspects and, with 6 or more questions, in identifying guilty suspects as well.

SUGGESTED READING

Gale, A. (Ed.).(1988). *The polygraph test: Lies, truth, and science.* London: Sage.

Iacono, W. G., & Lykken, D. T. (1997). The scientific status of research on polygraph techniques: The case against polygraph tests. In D. L. Faigman, D. Kaye, M. J. Saks, & J. Sanders (Eds.), *Modern scientific evidence: The law and science of expert testimony.* (pp. 582–618, 627–629, 631–633) St. Paul, MN: West.

Iacono, W. G., & Lykken, D. T. (1997). The validity of the lie detector: Two surveys of scientific opinion. *Journal of Applied Psychology, 82,* 426–433.

Lykken, D. T. A tremor in the blood: Uses and abuses of the lie detector. New York: Plenum.

D. LYKKEN
University of Minnesota

ANXIETY
FORENSIC PSYCHOLOGY

LIÉBEAULT, AMBROISE-AUGUSTE (1823–1904)

Amboise-Auguste Liébeault spent most of his life as a quiet, hardworking country doctor in the provinces of France. While in medical school he had had some acquaintance with hypnosis. In 1864 he settled in the city of Nancy. Here he treated the peasants in a kindly way and became known to them as "le bon père" (the good father). He told his patients that if they wished to be treated with drugs they would have to pay, but if they allowed him to hypnotize them as a treatment for their symptoms, there would be no fee. He established a clinic that consisted of two rooms in a corner of his garden.

The work of Liébeault and that of James Braid, an English physician, marked a unique event in the history of psychology and medicine. Hypnosis was not only a new way of treating people with certain ailments, but it marked the beginnings of psychotherapy.

In 1882 Liébeault became acquainted with Hippolyte Bernheim, a well known physician of the time. Liébeault taught Bernheim the hypnotic technique and together they published a text on the subject. Treating patients with hypnosis, they became known as the Nancy School, in rivalry with another center in Paris, headed by Jean Charcot, also using the hypnotic technique.

Liébeault and Bernheim used the method of suggesting sleep to induce the hypnotic trance. While under hypnosis the patients were presented with new attitudes and beliefs that they accepted without question. Thus they were told that they would be well and rid of their symptoms. It is clear now that many of the patients were suffering from hysterical symptoms such as functional blindness, deafness, and paralysis. In a number of cases the symptoms returned, so the hypnotic suggestions had only a transitory influence; but in other cases the cure seemed permanent.

By the turn of the century the Nancy School came under the influence of the autosuggestion proposed by Emile Coué, who advised his patients to tell themselves, "Every day in every way I am feeling better and better." Thus a distinction was made between the "Old Nancy School" of Liébeault and Bernheim, and the "New Nancy School" of Coué.

Interpretations as to the nature of hypnosis and hysteria differed between the Nancy School and the Paris School. Charcot in Paris regarded hypnosis as a pathological physiological state and related it to inadequate functioning of the nervous system, which manifested itself in the form of hysteria. Liébeault and Bernheim did not agree, feeling that there was nothing basically wrong with the nervous system of hysterics, and that the whole matter revolved around the matter of suggestion.

R. W. LUNDIN
Wheaton, Illinois

LIFE EVENTS

Researchers have long been interested in understanding how individuals and environments affect each other, primarily so as to describe and explain age-related behavior and individual differences. One focus has been to study life events. A life event is "indicative of, or requires a significant change in, the ongoing life patterns of the individual" (Holmes & Masuda, 1974). These events can occur in a variety of domains (family, health, work) and may be age-graded (school, marriage, retirement), history-graded (war and depression), or non-normative (illness and divorce). Most of the adolescent and adult literature reflects a sociological tradition of assessing the impact of life events as transitions between major roles, age grades, status gains and losses, and so forth (Brim, 1966; Hill & Mattessich, 1980; Neugarten & Hagestad, 1976; Riley, 1976; Rosow, 1976).

When an event is shared by many people of the same age, the probability of its occurrence is high, and the stage for anticipatory socialization is set. These normative events have been classified by some researchers (Brim & Ryff, 1980) as biological, social, or physical, referring to the environs. Others (Bond & Rosen, 1980; Lazarus, 1980) have preferred to apply models of stress to classify life events and speak of social, psychological, and physiological reactions to harmful, threatening, or challenging phenomena. Here the definition of life events is restricted to personal catastrophes with chronically ill, acutely ill, or pathological individuals as the focus of study. Regardless of approach, individuals usually are asked to rate the amount of stress or behavioral change associated with lists of life events, which are then analyzed to determine their timing, sequencing, and clustering.

Elder's work (1974) on the impact of the Great Depression on men who experienced this event at different times in the life cycle catapulted an interest in life event research. He reported that younger men were more negatively affected by the Depression than older men, because the former did not have an opportunity to establish careers and evidenced a higher rate of career instability throughout their lives. This pattern was reversed in the case of lower-class men, reflecting a historical pattern of age discrimination in unskilled occupations.

Other investigators (Back, 1965; Chiriboga, 1978; Lowenthal, Thurnher, & Chiriboga, 1975; Uhlenberg, 1979) have been interested in age, sex, and cohort differences in exposure to and content of life events. For example, younger adults generally report more exposure to life events than older persons and experience more positive stresses, while older adults report more negative stresses. Older women appear to have fewer resources than do men for dealing with high levels of stress. Younger cohorts experience divorce more often than older cohorts, while older cohorts report a more rapid exit from the labor market than younger cohorts.

Several theorists have suggested that there is an underlying structure to adult life. Levinson (1978) has proposed a universal sequence of periods and transitions in human development within which life events have their impacts. The primary task of stable periods is to build a life structure by making certain choices and striving to attain certain goals. The primary tasks of the transition periods are to terminate the existing life structure and initiate a new one by reappraising old choices and goals and moving toward new ones. As a result of this sequence of periods and transitions, different life events may be important at different points in the life cycle. To illustrate: A first marriage was found to be less stressful when entered after education had been completed and a job obtained (Hogan, 1978); serious adaptation problems resulted when retirement and widowhood clustered; and work was the most salient source of stress for men, while for women it was health and family (Lowenthal et al., 1975).

It appears that there may be a relationship between affective positivity and control over life events (Bulman & Wortman, 1977; Langer & Rodin, 1976; Rodin & Langer, 1977). When events are regarded positively, people tend to assume they had influence or control over those events (Bradley, 1978; Langer, 1977). Others (Lazarus, Kanner, & Folkman, 1980) have suggested that generating positive feeling states may enhance an individual's capacity to adapt to stress. Also, the absence of negatively related events is correlated with adjustment (Fontana et al., 1979). And when people engage in selfselected activities that they perceive as positive, they tend to report a more favorable outlook toward the specific events and the quality of their lives in general (Reich & Zautra, 1981).

Research on children's reactions to life events is sparse, so normative patterns are not yet known. However, three stressful life events—changing residence, changing schools, and family crises such as divorce and the death of a parent—have been studied consistently, producing equivocal findings (Deutsch, 1982; Kellam et al., 1975). Data (Rutter, 1979) also show that, for children, stresses experienced singly or even in sequence are not as problematic as those experienced in combination; further, boys more than girls are damaged by family disruption and discord. Negative emotional reactions have been found to increase with age, especially in the areas of health and family, while positive emotional reactions were reported to be associated with life events reflecting interactions with parents and peers (Deutsch, 1982). The study of the impact of life events on children promises insight into the social-psychological adaptation process. Perhaps stresses do not have to become potentiated throughout life into adulthood until old age, when they appear to reduce.

REFERENCES

Back, K. W. (1965). Meaning of time in later life. *Journal of Genetic Psychology, 109,* 9–25.

Bond, L., & Rosen, J. (Eds.). (1980). *Primary prevention of psychopathology: Competence and coping during adulthood.* Hanover, NH: University Press of New England.

Bradley, G. (1978). Self-serving biases in the attribution process: A reexamination of the fact or fiction question. *Journal of Personality and Social Psychology, 36,* 56–71.

Brim, O. G., Jr. (1966). Socialization through the life cycle. In O. G. Brim, Jr., & S. Wheeler (Eds.), *Socialization after childhood: Two essays.* New York: Wiley.

Brim, O. G., Jr., & Ryff, C. D. (1980). On the properties of life events. In P. B. Baltes & O. G. Brim, Jr. (Eds.), *Life-span development and behavior* (Vol. 3). New York: Academic.

Bulman, R. J., & Wortman, C. B. (1977). Attributions of blame and coping in the "real world": Severe accident victims react to their lot. *Journal of Personality and Social Psychology, 35,* 351–363.

Chiriboga, D. (1978, November). *Life events and metamodels: A life span study.* Presented at the meeting of the Gerontological Society, Dallas, TX.

Deutsch, F. (1982). Toward knowledge about children's views of life events. *Journal of Genetic Psychology.*

Elder, G. H., Jr. (1974). *Children of the great depression.* Chicago: University of Chicago Press.

Fontana, A. F., Hughes, L. A., Marcus, J. L., & Dowds, B. N. (1979). Subjective evaluation of life events. *Journal of Consulting and Clinical Psychology, 47,* 906–911.

Hill, R., & Mattessich, P. (1980). Family development theory and lifespan development. In P. B. Baltes & O. G. Brim, Jr. (Eds.), *Lifespan development and behavior* (Vol. 3). New York: Academic.

Hogan, D. P. (1978). The variable order of events in the life course. *American Sociological Review, 43,* 573–586.

Holmes, T. H., & Masuda, M. (1974). Life changes and illness susceptibility. In B. S. Dohrenwend & B. P. Dohrenwend (Eds.), *Stressful life events: Their nature and effects.* New York: Wiley.

Kellam, S. G., Branch, J. D., Argalwal, K. C., & Ensminger, M. E. (1975). *Mental health and going to school.* Chicago: University of Chicago Press.

Langer, E. J., & Rodin, J. (1976). The effects of choice and en-hanced personal responsibility for the aged: A field experiment in an institutional setting. *Journal of Personality and Social Psychology, 34,* 191–198.

Lazarus, R. S. (1980). The stress and coping paradigm. In L. A. Bond & J. C. Rosen (Eds.), *Competence and coping during adulthood.* Hanover, NH: University Press of New England.

Lazarus, R. S., Kanner, A. D., & Folkman, S. (1980). Emotions: A cognitive phenomenological analysis. In R. Plutchik & H. Kellerman (Eds.), *Theories of emotion.* New York: Academic.

Levinson, D. J., Darrow, C. N., Klein, E. B., Levinson, M. H., & McKee, B. (1978). *The seasons of a man's life.* New York: Knopf.

Lowenthal, M. F., Thurnher, M., & Chiriboga, D. (1975). *Four stages of life: A comparative study of women and men facing transitions.* San Francisco: Jossey-Bass.

Neugarten, B. L., & Hagestad, G. O. (1976). Age and the life course. In R. H. Binstock & E. Shanas (Eds.), *Handbook of aging and the social sciences.* New York: Van Nostrand Reinhold.

Reich, J. W., & Zautra, A. (1981). Life events and personal causation: Some relationships with satisfaction and distress. *Journal of Personality and Social Psychology, 41,* 1002–1012.

Riley, M. W. (1976). Age strata in social systems. In R. H. Bistock & E. Shanas (Eds.), *Handbook of aging and the social sciences.* New York: Van Nostrand Reinhold.

Rodin, J., & Langer, E. J. (1977). Long-term effects of control-relevant intervention with the institutionalized aged. *Journal of Personality and Social Psychology, 35,* 897–902.

Rosow, I. (1976). Status and role change through the life span. In R. H. Binstock & E. Shanas (Eds.), *Handbook of aging and the social sciences.* New York: Van Nostrand Reinhold.

Rutter, M. (1979). Protective factors in children's responses to stress and disadvantage. In M. W. Kent & J. E. Rolf (Eds.), *Primary prevention of pathology: Vol. 3. Social competence in children.* Hanover, NH: University Press of New England.

Uhlenberg, P. (1979). Demographic change and problems of the aged. In M. W. Riley (Ed.), *Aging from birth to death: Interdisciplinary perspectives.* Boulder, CO: Westview Press.

F. DEUTSCH
San Diego State University

ENVIRONMENTAL PSYCHOLOGY
SURPRISE

LIFE-SPAN DEVELOPMENT

The point where change occurs throughout the life cycle is critical. Traditional approaches to human development have emphasized change from birth to adolescence, stability in adulthood, and decline in old age (Baltes, Reese, & Lipsitt, 1980). By 1940, developmental investigations of infancy, childhood, and adolescence were commonplace, yet studies of age-related changes in adulthood were just beginning (Havighurst, 1973). Sears and Feldman (1973) have captured the flavor of some of the most important of these adult changes. They indicate that the next 5 to 6 decades are every bit as important, not only to those passing through them but also to their children, who have to live with parents and grandparents. The changes in body, personality, and abilities may be great during these later decades. Strong developmental tasks are imposed by marriage and parenthood, by the waxing and waning of physical prowess and of some intellectual capacities, by the children's exit from the nest, by the achievement of an occupational plateau, and by retirement and the prospect of death.

A number of stage-crisis theories have been developed to explain the change adults undergo, the best-known being Erikson's and, in the popular literature, Sheehy's *Passages.* Many theorists and researchers, however, have not been satisfied with the stage-crisis approaches to adult development (e.g., Neugarten's changing rhythm of the life cycle perspective; Neugarten, 1980). To obtain a more accurate view of adult development, many experts believe that the study of life events adds valuable information (Datan & Ginsburg, 1975; Hultsch & Deutsch, 1981; Riley, 1979). Hultsch and Deutsch (1981) point out that our lives are punctuated by transitions defined by various events. Particular emphasis is placed on the stressful nature of these events. Events typically thought of as positive (marriage or being promoted at work), as well as events usually perceived as negative (death of spouse, being fired from work), are potentially stressful. Factors that can mediate such stressful life events include internal resources (physical health, intellectual abilities) and external resources (income, social supports). Adaptation involves the use of coping strategies that result in behavioral change.

Broadly speaking, there are two theoretical approaches to the study of personality development, one focusing on similarities and the other on differences. The stage theories of Sheehy, Gould, Levinson, Freud, and Erikson all attempt to describe the universals—not the individual variation—in development. It may be helpful to think about the comments of Neugarten (1980): "We have found great trouble clustering people into age brackets that are characterized by particular conflicts; the conflicts won't stay put, and neither will the people." In an extensive investigation of a random sample of 500 men at midlife, Farrell and Rosenberg (1981) concluded that while some studies have found middle age to be the apex of satisfaction and effectiveness, others found it to be a period of identity crisis and discontent. They indicate that both their research design and findings suggest a more complex model (than the universal stage model), one anchored in the idea that individuals are active agents in interpreting, shaping, and altering their own reality. They not only experience internal and external changes, but give meaning to them. The meaning given shows a wide range of variation.

In a recent discussion of life stress, Sarason (1980) has called attention to the wide array of individual differences in the frequency and preoccupying characteristics of stress-related cognitions. While the most adaptive response to stress is a task orientation that directs a person's attention to the task at hand rather than to emotional reactions, some individuals are task-oriented while others are not. The adaptive value of being able to set aside temporarily strong emotions in order to deal with a problematic situation is reflected in Vaillant's Grant study (1977). In reporting college student adjustments over a 30-year period after leaving school, Vaillant found that pervasive personal preoccupations are maladaptive in both work and marriage. Some individuals in the Grant study showed strong personal preoccupations, others did not.

Sarason (1980) emphasizes that the ability to set aside unproductive worries and preoccupations is crucial to functioning under stress. How stress is handled depends on the individual and the situation, so an interactional approach is required that incorporates both individual differences and situational factors (Lazarus & Launier, 1978). Both of these are going on in an individual when stress appears. The experience includes available social supports and what the person brings to the situation, as well as such tendencies as anticipating stress, being obsessive, or feeling secure or competent. At least five factors influence how an individual will respond to life stress, according to Sarason (1980):

1. The nature of the task or stress.
2. The skills available to perform the task or handle the stress.
3. Personality characteristics.
4. Social supports available to the person experiencing stress.
5. The person's history of stress-arousing experiences and events.

But while adults are likely to experience one or more highly stressful events during their lives, an increasing number of individuals are reaching late adulthood in a healthier manner than in the past. Fries (1980) has developed a provocative view of aging and health care that suggests adults should carefully examine the traditional view that they should anticipate a population that is ever older, ever more feeble, and ever more expensive to care for. His predictions suggest that the number of very old persons will not increase, that the average period of diminished physical vigor will decrease, that chronic disease will occupy a smaller proportion of the typical life span, and that the need for medical care in later life will decrease.

REFERENCES

Baltes, P. B., Reese, H. W., & Lipsitt, L. P. (1980). Life-span developmental psychology. *Annual Review of Psychology, 31,* 65–110.

Datan, N., & Ginsberg, L. H. (Eds.). (1975). *Life-span developmental psychology: Normative life crises.* New York: Academic. Press.

Farrell, M. P., & Rosenberg, S. D. (1981). *Men at midlife.* Boston: Auburn House.

Fries, J. F. (1980). Aging, natural death, and the compression of morbidity. *New England Journal of Medicine, 303,* 130–135.

Havighurst, R. J. (1973). History of developmental psychology: Socialization and personality development through the lifespan. In P. B. Baites & K. W. Schaie (Eds.), *Life-span developmental psychology.* New York: Academic.

Hultsch, D. F., & Deutsch, F. (1981). *Adult development and aging: A life-span perspective.* New York: McGraw-Hill.

Lazarus, R. S., & Launier, R. (1978). Stress-related transactions between person and environment. In L. A. Pervin & M. Lewis (Eds.), *Perspectives in interactional psychology.* New York: Plenum.

Neugarten, B. L. (1980). Must everything be midlife crisis? *Prime Time.*

Riley, M. W. (Ed.). (1979). *Aging from birth to death: Interdisciplinary perspectives.* Boulder, CO: Westview Press.

Sarason, I. G. (1980). Life stress, self-preoccupation, and social supports. In I. G. Sarason & C. D. Spielberger (Eds.), *Stress and anxiety.* Washington, DC: Hemisphere.

Sears, R. R., & Feldman, S. S. (Eds.). (1973). *The seven ages of man.* Los Altos, CA: Kaufmann.

Sheehy, G. (1976). *Passages: Predictable crises of adult life.* New York: Dutton.

Vaillant, G. E. (1977). *Adaptation to life.* Boston: Little, Brown.

J. W. SANTROCK
University of Texas at Dallas

ADOLESCENT DEVELOPMENT
ADULT DEVELOPMENT
AGING: BEHAVIOR CHANGES
HUMAN DEVELOPMENT

LIKERT, RENSIS (1903–1981)

Rensis Likert began college at the University of Michigan in engineering, but ended up getting the BA in sociology and economics. The PhD was conferred by Columbia University in 1932; his landmark dissertation, "A technique for the measurement of attitudes," was published in *Archives of Psychology.* This dissertation was the basis for development of the Likert Scale, a standard tool of social scientists.

After a brief teaching stint at New York University, Likert worked for the Life Insurance Sales Research Bureau, where his findings from interviews and paper-and-pencil questionnaires resulted in the series *Morale and Agency Management* (with J. M. Willits), a comparative study of the 10 best and 10 mediocre insurance agencies. This study presaged his continuing interest and findings in organizational leadership.

In late 1939 Likert was hired by the Division of Program Surveys in the Bureau of Agricultural Economics, where he developed techniques for interviewing, coding, and sampling techniques fundamental to social science research today. His government work during World War II included Office of War Information studies concerning public attitudes, public experiences, and behavior. His collaboration with Iowa State University led to a method of sampling households that has become known as probability sampling. He and others conducted extensive studies concerning war bonds, alien nationals, and the effects of wartime bombing.

In 1946, with several of his cross-discipline colleagues from those government projects, he was invited to the University of

Michigan to establish the Survey Research Center. With the addition of three more centers, it is now called the Institute for Social Research. Likert directed this institute until his retirement in 1970. During that time two of his major books, *New Patterns of Management* and *The Human Organization,* were published. Another book, *New Ways of Managing Conflict,* coauthored with his wife, Jane Gibson Likert, was published in 1976. These books—and more than 100 journal articles—presented his metatheoretical statement of participative management, and continued the refinement of conclusions that had begun with his insurance agency work and engaged Likert's attention throughout his life. Upon retiring from the university, he organized a consulting firm that bears his name—Rensis Likert Associates—in which he worked vigorously until his death in 1981, applying research findings in management and organizational areas.

STAFF

LIKERT SCALING

Likert scaling derives its name from its inventor, Rensis Likert, who first developed this approach to attitude surveys. Likert explained the benefits of his new approach in his article, "A technique for the measurement of attitudes" (1932). The prime advantages of his technique were that it was much quicker to develop and adopt than the previously used Thurstone technique, which required the use of judges and extensive item evaluation. Further, the Likert scaling approach does not necessitate the use of negative items, a benefit that explains its widespread industrial applications.

The Likert technique consists of a series of statements to which one responds using a scale of possible answers: Strongly Agree (5), Agree (4), Neither Agree nor Disagree (3), Disagree (2), and Strongly Disagree (1). This five-point Likert Scale can be expanded to seven or more steps with a modification of the adverbs (Strongly, Moderately, Mildly). The five- and seven-point scales are the most common forms in use.

Modifications of the Likert Scale include the forced-choice Likert approach (no neutral category) and the Faces approach developed by Kunin in "The construction of a new type of attitude measure" (1955), which uses faces scaled from a smile to a frown for illiterate respondents.

The reliability of the Likert Scales are in the 0.90 range, and the scales' results correlate approximately 0.80 with the Thurstone technique.

REFERENCES

Kunin, T. (1955). The construction of a new type of attitude measure. *Personnel Psychology, 8,* 65–78.

Likert, R. (1932). A technique for the measurement of attitudes. *Archives of Psychology, 140,* 1–55.

L. BERGER
Clemson University

RATING SCALES
THURSTONE SCALING

LIMBIC SYSTEM

In 1952, MacLean coined the term "limbic system" to refer both to a medial part of the cortex that enveloped the brainstem and to subcortical structures that were tightly associated with this region (1952). He based this grouping not only on its anatomic location but also on evidence that this region was well-developed only in mammals, was phylogenetically older than the more peripheral neocortex, and appeared to be important in emotional and social behavior (1990). The limbic, or paleomammalian, system of the brain is shown in Figure 1 in relation to higher cortical (or neo-mammalian) and deeper brain (or reptilian) structures. MacLean's subdivisions of the limbic system (1990) include the amygdalar, septal, and thalamocingulate divisions shown in Figure 2. Extensive pre-clinical and clinical observations have suggested that the limbic system is critical in learning, memory, emotions, social behaviors, and autonomic responses. This essay will briefly review the definition and anatomy of the limbic system, outline the history of the limbic system concept, describe the three limbic subdivisions, and critically discuss evidence for and against the limbic system construct.

DEFINITION AND ANATOMY

The limbic system as proposed by MacLean was considered to subserve emotions and included a group of medially located cortical and subcortical regions. Although there is no clear consensus, the following regions are generally considered part of the limbic system. The cortical structures include the cingulate gyrus, subcallosal gyrus, hippocampus, and olfactory cortex. Subcortical regions include the amygdala, septum pellucidum, epithalamus

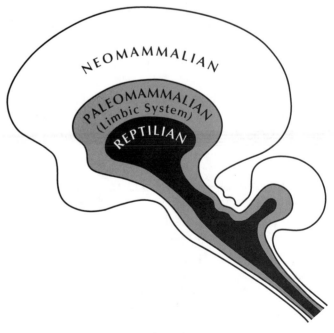

Figure 1.

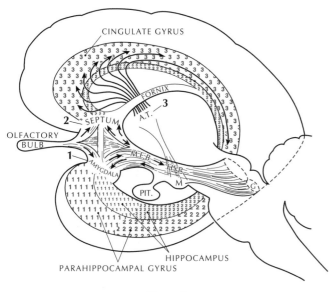

CINGULATE GYRUS

FORNIX

SEPTUM

OLFACTORY BULB

AMYGDALA

M.F.B.

HYP.

PIT.

M

A.T.

G.

HIPPOCAMPUS

PARAHIPPOCAMPAL GYRUS

Figure 2.

limbic structures he initially called the "visceral brain" (MacLean, 1990, p. 266). He went on to say that the visceral brain "eludes the grasp of the intellect because its animalistic and primitive structure makes it impossible to communicate in verbal terms" and thus "providing a clue to understanding the difference between what we 'feel' and what we 'know.'" While MacLean meant the term "visceral" in reference to its 16th-century meaning of "strong inward feelings" rather than to hollow organs, glands, and blood vessels, as is commonly meant in physiological terminology, he later referred to the visceral brain (i.e., rhinencephalon) as the limbic system so as to avoid any confusion (MacLean, 1990, p. 266).

MACLEAN'S PROPOSED LIMBIC SUBDIVISIONS (1990)

Amygdalar Division
MacLean emphasizes that this region is involved in self-preservation behaviors such as those required in the search for food, including fighting and self-defense. Stimulation of this area in humans may produce fear and anxiety.

Septal Division
The septal region may subserve behaviors related to sexual function and procreation. MacLean emphasizes that septal stimulation in humans can produce pleasurable sensations and in animals can elicit social grooming as well as genital tumescence.

Thalamocingulate Division
This region represents the phylogenetically newest subdivision of the limbic system. It is present in mammals but not in reptiles, even in rudimentary form. Several typical mammalian social behaviors are associated with this area, including extensive mother-infant bonding, infant crying, and play. Lesions of this region in non-human mammals often produce social apathy; even mothers will neglect their young.

In addition to these social functions, the cingulate, particularly its anterior extent, is believed to be important in selective attention and pain.

EVIDENCE FOR THE LIMBIC SYSTEM CONSTRUCT
Extensive evidence from animal literature, pre-clinical work, study of epilepsy patients, and functional imaging studies suggest the limbic structures are important in emotional behavior. What is questioned regarding the limbic system's role in emotion is the extent to which limbic regions and associated brainstem structures alone are important in emotions and whether the limbic system acts as a unified network. Much of the evidence for the limbic system construct as a unified network important in emotions has come from the study of psychomotor seizures. For example, epileptogenic activity during encephalograms in nongeneralizing psychomotor seizures appears to be self-contained in limbic regions (Jasper, 1964). Further, electrical stimulation of limbic regions in awake patients just prior to neurosurgery produces emotional responses ranging from fear to sadness to happiness (Penfield & Jasper, 1954). Some recent functional imaging studies in humans also support the notion of a limbic system concept. For example, people with depression appear to show blunted limbic activation in

(habenula), anterior thalamic nuclei, hypothalamus, and parts of the basal ganglia (Swanson, 1987). As well, several closely linked cortical structures that appear important in emotional behavior are also considered part of this circuit and are often referred to as paralimbic. These regions include the anterior temporal polar cortex, medial-posterior orbitofrontal cortex, and insular cortex (Mesulam & Mufson, 1982).

HISTORICAL PERSPECTIVES
In 1878, Broca described the "great limbic lobe" of the brain as a large cerebral convolution that lies medially and envelops the brainstem (Broca, 1878). In his comparative neuroanatomical work, he found that this great limbic lobe appeared to be common to all mammals (Broca, 1878; MacLean, 1990). In 1900, Shafer suggested that the limbic cortex was the phylogenetically oldest part of the cortex (Schaffer, 1900). Dating from Broca, the limbic lobe was thought to be important in olfaction due to its strong interconnections with the olfactory cortex and was referred to most often as the rhinencephalon (smell brain). As smell was not considered extremely important in human function, the rhinencephalon was greatly ignored for several decades (MacLean, 1990). Papez, in 1937, proposed that the rhinencephalon was important not only in olfaction but was in emotional behavior. Papez's now classic paper went largely unnoticed for more than a decade until MacLean discovered it in the course of looking for literature confirming his findings that the rhinencephalon's medial temporal lobe structures, such as the hippocampus, might be the source of epileptogenic foci in psychomotor epilepsy, a condition in which subjects experienced a vast array of emotions but subsequently lacked memory for these experiences (MacLean, 1990, p. 351). After meeting with Papez, MacLean elaborated extensively on Papez's proposal, suggesting that while our intellectual functions appear to be mediated by the newest and most highly developed parts of the brain, "our affective behavior continues to be dominated by a relatively crude and primitive system" that lies in

neuropsychological tasks (facial emotion recognition, the Stroop Interference task) or following pharmacological challenges with drugs that act mainly through limbic networks (intravenous procaine), while there are no activation differences in tasks that are mediated through more cortical circuits (Wisconsin Card Sorting, face identity matching, spatial matching) (George, Ketter, & Post, 1994). Further, functional brain imaging studies of emotion, particularly sadness, show that the anterior portion of the limbic system appears to act in a coordinated fashion (George et al., 1995, Ketter et al., 1996, Lane, Reiman, Ahern, Schwartz, & Davidson, 1997). Another example in which the anterior limbic system appears to act in a coordinated fashion occurs in patients with Posttraumatic Stress Disorder (PTSD) (Hamner, Lorberbaum, & George, 1999). For example, Rauch and colleagues (1996) have described activation of anterior limbic and paralimbic regions secondary to psychological stimuli, reminiscent of the original trauma in PTSD patients.

There is also evidence supporting the limbic system's ancient origins relative to the neocortex or, at the very least, that its cortical tissue is less well-defined than neocortical tissue (Rose, 1926). The inner limbic cortical structures are the hippocampus and olfactory cortex. These structures are called allocortex and have one to three layers. The outer limbic cortical structures are the cingulate gyrus, subcallosal gyrus, posterior-medial orbitofrontal cortex, insula, and anterior temporal polar region. These structures are called mesocortex and consist of three to five indistinct layers. The more peripheral neocortex is called isocortex and is made up of six well-defined layers.

EVIDENCE AGAINST THE LIMBIC SYSTEM CONSTRUCT

Critics of the limbic system construct (LeDoux, 1996; Kotter & Meyer, 1992; Swanson, 1987) point out that no two authorities can agree on which structures should be included in the limbic system. Also, limbic structures are connected with virtually all areas of the brain, so critics argue that one should then perhaps call the whole brain the limbic system. Further, concerning the definition of the limbic system as a phylogenetically older part of the brain that is well-developed only in mammals, some authors believe that even reptiles have a neocortex—although small. Moreover, if the limbic system is defined functionally as that part of the brain involved in emotion, there is evidence suggesting that the neocortex may be important in regulation and recognition of emotions and that limbic regions such as the hippocampus and cingulate are important in functions other than emotion, such as memory, cognition, and selective attention.

CONCLUSIONS

Extensive pre-clinical and clinical observations have suggested that the limbic system structures as originally suggested by Papez (1937) and then MacLean (1949, 1952) are critical in emotional behavior. These structures have also been found to be important in social behavior, cognition, and autonomic responses. The limbic system, however, has extensive direct interconnections with all brain regions, and the extent to which the limbic system functions as a network itself remains to be determined. Thus, the full utility

of referring to these structures as participating in a coordinated system remains to be seen. Perhaps the limbic system concept will lose its heuristic appeal as we improve our definitions of emotional states, and the roles of discrete structures and small circuits important in motivation (Kalivas, Churchill, & Romanides, 1999), fear (LeDoux, 1996), and other emotional behaviors. Alternatively, as some imaging studies suggest, we may actually confirm that emotional behaviors do not arise from the activity of single brain regions, but instead emerge from the coordinated action of many connected structures. The exciting notion is that with new techniques in functional imaging and noninvasive regional brain stimulation, the next few years will allow for direct testing of the limbic system construct, which has provided researchers over the last half-century with a critical starting point in searching for brain structures important in emotion. Broca's limbic lobe, initially thought to be important by some only in olfaction, is certainly no longer ignored.

REFERENCES

Broca, P. (1878). Anatomie comparee des circonvolutions cerebrales. Le grand lobe limbique et la scissure limbique dans la serie des mammiferes. *Review of Anthropology, 1*(2), 456–498.

George, M. S., Ketter, T. A., & Post, R. M. (1994). Activation studies in mood disorders. *Psychiatric Annals, 24*(12), 648–652.

George, M. S., Ketter, T. A., Parekh, P. I., Horwitz, B., Herscovitch, P., & Post, R. M. (1995). Brain activity during transient sadness and happiness in healthy women. *American Journal of Psychiatry, 152*(3), 341–351.

Hamner, M. B., Lorberbaum, J. P., & George, M. S. (1999). Potential role of the anterior cingulate cortex in PTSD: Review and hypothesis. *Depression and Anxiety, 9,* 1–14.

Jasper, H. H. (1964). Some physiological mechanisms involved in epileptic automatisms. *Epilepsia, 5,* 1–20.

Kalivas, P. W., Churchill, L., & Romanides, A. (1999). Involvement of the pallidal-thalamocortical circuit in adaptive behavior. *Annals of the New York Academy of Science, 29*(877), 64–70.

Ketter, T. A., Andreason, P. J., George, M. S., Lee, C., Gill, D. S., Parekh, P. I., Willis, M. W., Herscovitch, P., & Post, R. M. (1996). Anterior paralimbic mediation of procaine-induced emotional and psychosensory experiences. *Archives of General Psychiatry, 53*(1), 59–69.

Kotter, R., & Meyer, N. (1992). The limbic system: A review of its empirical foundation. *Behavioural Brain Research, 52,* 105–127.

Lane, R. D., Reiman, E. M., Ahern, G. L., Schwartz, G. E., & Davidson, R. J. (1997). Neuroanatomical correlates of happiness, sadness, and disgust. *American Journal of Psychiatry, 154*(7), 926–933.

LeDoux, J. (1996). *The emotional brain.* New York: Simon & Schuster.

MacLean, P. D. (1952). Some psychiatric implications of physiological studies on frontotemporal portion of limbic system (visceral brain). *Electroencephalographic Clinical Neurophysiology, 4,* 407–418.

MacLean, P. D. (1990). *The triune brain in evolution: Role in paleo-cerebral functions.* New York: Plenum.

MacLean, P. D., & Arellano, Z. (1950). Basal lead studies in epileptic automatisms. *Electroencephalographic Clinical Neurophysiology, 2,* 1–16.

Mesulam, M. M., & Mufson, E. J. (1982). Insula of the old world monkey: I. Architectonics in the insula-orbito-temporal component of the paralimbic brain. *Journal of Comparative Neurology, 212,* 1–22.

Papez, J. W. (1937). A proposed mechanism of emotion. *Archives of Neurological Psychiatry, 38,* 725–743.

Penfield, W., & Jasper, H. (1954). *Epilepsy and the functional anatomy of the human brain.* Boston: Little, Brown.

Rauch, S. L., van der Kolk, B. A., Fisler, R. E., Alpert, N. M., Orr, S. P., Savage, C. R., Fischman, A. J., Jenike, M. A., & Pitman, R. K. (1996). A symptom provocation study of posttraumatic stress disorder using positron emission tomography and script-driven imagery. *Archives of General Psychiatry, 53,* 380–387.

Rose, M. (1926). Uber das histogenetische Prinzip der Einteilung der Grosshirnrinde. *Journal of Psychological Neurology, 35,* 65–173.

Shafer, E. A. (1900). The cerebral cortex. In E. A. Shafer (Ed.), *Textbook of physiology* (Vol. 2). Edinburgh: Young J Pentland.

M. B. HAMNER
J. P. LORBERBAUM
M. S. GEORGE
Medical University of South Carolina

BRAIN EVOLUTION
CENTRAL NERVOUS SYSTEM

LINDZEY, GARDNER (1920–   )

Lindzey received the B.A. from the Pennsylvania State University and the PhD (1949) from Harvard. He was professor of psychology at Syracuse, Harvard, Minnesota, and Texas before becoming president and director of the Center for Advanced Study in the Behavioral Sciences (1975–1989). He was president of the American Psychological Association (1966–1967) and is a member of the American Academy of Arts and Sciences, the American Philosophical Society, the National Academy of Sciences and the Institute of Medicine.

He is perhaps best known for his contributions to the fields of personality, social psychology, and behavior genetics. Author or editor of more than 20 books and 100 technical articles, his most widely cited books are *Theories of Personality* (with C. S. Hall), three editions of the *Handbook of Social Psychology,* and four editions of the *History of Psychology in Autobiography. Theories of Personality* was the first book of its kind, leading the way for many others and for courses designed after this landmark publication.

STAFF

LINEHAN, MARSHA M.

Marsha Linehan is a professor of psychology and of psychiatry and behavioral sciences at the University of Washington, and director of the Behavioral Research and Therapy Clinics, a consortium of research projects developing new treatments and evaluating their efficacy for severely disordered and multidiagnostic populations. Her primary research is in the application of cognitive and behavioral models to suicidal behaviors, drug abuse, and Borderline Personality Disorder. She is also working to develop effective models for transferring efficacious treatments from research to the clinical community.

Linehan received her PhD in experimental-personality psychology in 1971 from Loyola University in Chicago. She then completed a clinical internship at the Suicide Prevention and Crisis Clinic in Buffalo, New York, and a post-doctoral fellowship in behavior modification at SUNY at Stony Brook. She was on the faculty at The Catholic University, Washington, DC, before going to the University of Washington.

Linehan is currently president-elect of the Association for the Advancement of Behavior Therapy, is on the editorial boards of several journals, and has published numerous articles on suicidal behaviors, drug abuse, behavior therapy, and behavioral assessment. A fellow of the American Psychological Association and the American Psychopathology Association, and a diplomat of the American Board of Behavioral Psychology, she has received several awards recognizing her clinical and research contributions, including the Dublin award for lifetime achievement in suicidal behaviors, the American Foundation of Suicide Prevention award for Distinguished Research in Suicide, the American Association of Applied and Preventive Psychology award for Distinguished Contributions to the Practice of Psychology, and the Association for the Advancement of Behavior Therapy award for contribution to clinical activities. She has written three books, including two treatment manuals: *Cognitive-Behavioral Treatment for Borderline Personality Disorder,* and *Skills Training Manual for Treating Borderline Personality Disorder.*

LOBOTOMY

A lobotomy is the cutting (-tomy) of connections between lobes of the brain or between a lobe of the brain and another area, such as the thalamus. The word often refers to a specific type of brain operation—the prefrontal lobotomy—in which prefrontal neural areas are separated from the thalamus. Lobotomy and prefrontal lobotomy are sometimes used synonymously with a more general term, psychosurgery, which refers to a brain operation designed to treat an otherwise intractable mental disturbance.

Trepanning—the primitive technique of opening the skull to release evil spirits causing mental aberration—is thought to be a forerunner of psychosurgery. In more modern times, despite a few published accounts of psychosurgery before 1935, the credit (or discredit) for initiating its widespread use is accorded the Portuguese neurologist, Egas Moniz (1874–1955).

In 1935, Moniz, who already had a reputation as a gifted scientist, attended the Second International Neurological Conference in London. There, he heard a paper by Carlyle Jacobsen on the effects of frontal lobe damage on learning in chimpanzees. Moniz apparently was most intrigued by Jacobsen's comment on the increased manageability of one of the chimps following the surgery. Soon after the conference, under Moniz's direction, Almeida Lima performed the first prefrontal operations, which Moniz called prefrontal leucotomies because they cut white (leuco-) matter or fiber tracts. Moniz also invented the term "psychosurgery."

In 1936, Moniz published a report of the results from his first 20 patients. Moniz claimed that seven were cured, seven were improved, and six were not improved. From this small beginning, the lobotomy became a widely used treatment for mental patients, and in 1949, Moniz shared the Nobel Prize in Physiology or Medicine for his contribution to the treatment of mental illness.

Walter Freeman, a neurosurgeon, and James Watts, a neuropsychiatrist, were leading practitioners of the operation. Freeman and Watts preferred the term "lobotomy" to Moniz's "leucotomy," because lobotomy suggested more than just the destruction of white matter. Of the two men, Freeman was more of a showman, and the two separated in 1947. By the time of his retirement in 1970, Freeman had been associated with more than 3,500 psychosurgical operations.

One variation of the lobotomy that Freeman popularized approached the brain through the back of the eye socket. This was called the transorbital lobotomy, and Freeman first used an icepick as his surgical tool, with electroconvulsive shock for anesthesia. Because of its simplicity, the transorbital approach undoubtedly increased the incidence of psychosurgery. The operation was sometimes performed as an office procedure by psychiatrists, and the patient was able to return home a few hours after the operation.

The lobotomy in particular, and psychosurgery in general, reached a peak in the late 1940s and declined rapidly in the mid-1950s, with the introduction of the first pharmacological agents that effectively treated severe mental disorders. It is difficult to evaluate the effects of the prefrontal lobotomy. Operations were performed by a variety of methods (e.g., the transorbital lobotomy, orbital undercutting in which the frontal lobes were elevated so that fibers beneath them could be cut, implantation of radioactive yttrium seeds) on a variety of patients with different diagnoses (e.g., people with Schizophrenia, Bipolar Disorder, and Obsessive-Compulsive Disorder). Recovery was often assessed mainly in terms of patient manageability, ignoring changes in affect, motivation, planning ability, and so on.

Although many clinical studies reported high percentages of postoperative improvement, without sham operated or unoperated controls in many cases, it is possible that the improvement occurred either as a placebo effect or spontaneously. The Columbia-Greystone Project was probably the most frequently cited evaluation of psychosurgery. Organized in 1947, project reports were published in 1949 and 1952. In the study, a relatively small number of psychosurgical and unoperated control patients were compared on a large battery of psychological tests. In general, the study produced little evidence either to indict or to praise psychosurgery, which continued at a high level for a few years after publication of the results.

Although the extensive use of lobotomies declined after 1955 and such operations are rarely performed today, the use of psychosurgery has continued at a low level. Changes in psychosurgery in the 1950s and 1960s included the use of stereotaxic procedures (a stereotaxic instrument holds the head in a standard position and permits accurate placement of damage in brain areas that cannot be directly visualized). Stereotaxic surgery led to a change in the brain areas targeted for destruction. Instead of frontal lobe damage, surgeons became interested in the selective destruction of portions of the limbic system, including the amygdala, thalamic nuclei having limbic connections, and portions of the hypothalamus.

Changes have also been made in the techniques used to produce the psychosurgical damage. In the early days of psychosurgery, most of the damage was accomplished with knives of different shapes and sizes. With the advent of stereotaxic surgery, brain areas began to be destroyed with electric current, radio-frequency waves, freezing probes, ultrasound, compression, and neurotoxins.

In summary, lobotomy as a form of psychosurgery was an attempt to alter behavior beneficially in psychiatric patients. The rationale for particular operations often came rather loosely from neuropsychological animal research. The lobotomy and specifically the prefrontal lobotomy were most used at a time before the introduction of effective pharmacological agents.

SUGGESTED READING

Finger, S. (1994). *Origins of neuroscience: A history of explorations into brain function.* New York: Oxford University Press.

Valenstein, E. S. (1973). *Brain control: A critical examination of brain stimulation and psychosurgery.* New York: Wiley.

Valenstein, E. S. (Ed.). (1980). *The psychosurgery debate: Scientific, legal, and ethical perspectives.* San Francisco: Freeman.

B. M. THORNE
Mississippi State University

PSYCHOSURGERY

LOCKE, JOHN (1632–1704)

Although John Locke lived in the 17th century, his writings expressed more the spirit of the 18th. He was the first of the British empiricists and bridged the gap between the rational continental philosophers such as Descartes, Leibnitz, and Spinoza and a new attitude toward knowledge that was fostered in the empirical tradition to follow.

Locke was educated at Oxford, he dabbled in medicine but never received a degree in that subject. He spent most of his life in politics and minor government offices. At the age of 58 he published his most famous work, *An Essay Concerning Human Understanding.* This was revised several times; the fourth edition (1670) was of particular importance because it first introduced Locke's notion of the association of ideas.

In the *Essay* Locke stated that all ideas came from experience. At birth the human mind could be considered analogous to a clean slate, a tabula rasa. Here he opposed Descartes, who considered some ideas inborn. For Locke the mind was basically passive and could do only two things. First, it could receive experiences from the outside world, which involved the act of sensing which was the primary source of knowledge. Second, the mind could reflect upon itself. It was through this process of reflection—what we today call introspection—that humans engaged in the process called thinking. Ideas could be simple or complex, as in merely sensing a color or combining a number of senses into a complex idea.

Ideas also had *primary* and *secondary* qualities. The primary qualities were inseparable from the object, and included movement, extension, shape, solidarity. The secondary qualities resided in the mind as experiences of the real world, such as touch, taste, smell, vision, and hearing; they were known apart from the object.

Locke had no doubt about the existence of a real world (though his successors George Berkeley and David Hume questioned this). However, Locke realized he could never know that real world's substance. He argued that he could not experience the qualities of things without there being something behind them, but that something was "I know not what."

Locke was the first in a long tradition to write about the association of ideas. He exemplified the significance of association in his affirmation of the "man born blind and suddenly made to see." Such a man could not identify a cube by sight, if he had not experienced it also through the sense of touch: These two experiences had to be associated.

His great significance for psychology is that he started an empirical tradition. The fact that things exist as a basic reality is a presupposition of all science. Furthermore, the concept of association introduced by him is the basis for many current psychological theories.

R. W. LUNDIN
Wheaton, Illinois

LOCUS OF CONTROL

Locus of control refers to a set of beliefs about the relationship between behavior and the subsequent occurrence of rewards and punishments. The more precise phrase for these beliefs about locus of control is *internal versus external control of reinforcement (I-E)*. Whenever reinforcements (either positive or negative) are perceived by the individual as being the result of his or her own behavior, efforts, or relatively permanent characteristics, we have an example of an *internal* belief. *External* beliefs, in contrast, involve perceptions that reinforcements occur as the result of luck, chance, fate, or the interventions of powerful others, or else are simply unpredictable because of the complexity of events. Beliefs about locus of control or I-E are not either/or but may fall anywhere along a dimension marked by external beliefs at the one extreme and internal ones at the other.

The I-E concept was first outlined by Rotter in 1966. He not only defined the concept but also described a social learning theory framework in which it could be incorporated. In addition, he reported a considerable amount of psychometric data and construct validity studies on a personality inventory, the *I-E Scale,* designed to measure the concept. Since that time, literally thousands of studies have been published which report on various aspects of I-E. It

may well be true that I-E has been the subject of as many empirical studies as any other individual differences concept in personality psychology.

The reasons for the popularity of any concept are never entirely clear. In the case of I-E, however, at least three possibilities suggest themselves. First, the concept grew out of a social learning theory context. Such a theoretical framework has been very popular in psychology: The late 1960s and the 1970s, when I-E was at its zenith, were no exception. Second, a short, objective scale is available to measure I-E. Third, the I-E notion arose in an era of civil rights turmoil and disillusionment over U.S. involvement in an unpopular Asian war. In succeeding years, concern has continued over issues of pollution, over-population, unresponsive government, political corruption, generation gaps, and so on. In short, I-E touched upon vibrant social phenomena involving matters of personal control that were important to many people.

THEORETICAL BACKGROUND

Many who employ the locus of control concept do so without considering how the concept fits into a larger scheme of factors that affect behavior. Such people sometimes use the concept as if it were the only determinant of behavior in a given situation. Such a simplistic use has sometimes led to failures in prediction, frustration over the small amount of variance accounted for by I-E, or difficulty in generalizing from one study to the next. But I–E was originally conceptualized as only one variable in a larger social learning theory scheme. This theory, first articulated by Rotter in *Social Learning and Clinical Psychology,* described several variables which act in concert to produce a behavior in a given situation: (a) expectancies; (b) reinforcement values; and (c) the psychological situation. Any behavior occurs because of expectancies that it will achieve the goal toward which it is directed and because of the value of that goal. The specific situation influences both the magnitude of one's expectancies and the value of the goal.

I-E is regarded as a generalized expectancy regarding how best to categorize situations that present the individual with a problem to be solved. Most human social situations confront us with problems, regardless of the specific needs involved (sexual, achievement, etc.). By categorizing situations as fitting somewhere along the I-E dimension, we feel that we can better cope with them. Locus of control, then, is a generalized expectancy or belief as to the optimum way in which the relationship between one's behavior and the subsequent occurrence of reward and punishment should be viewed.

In any given situation the expectancy that a specific behavior will lead to a particular outcome is determined by three variables. First, there are specific expectancies for the success of a given behavior based on previous experience in the same situation. Second, there are generalized expectancies for success based on experience generalized from related situations. Third, there are numerous problem-solving generalized expectancies, of which I-E is but one example. These three variables all interact to determine one's expectancy for the success of the behavior in question. Amount of previous experience in the situation determines the relative influence of each variable. Novel situations especially call forth generalized expectancies.

Situations which are quite familiar will more likely lead us to rely on expectancies based on that specific past experience.

THE BEGINNINGS OF THE I-E CONCEPT

The first I-E study was carried out by Phares (1957). The goal was to determine the differential effects on expectancies of reinforcement in skill and chance situations. Phares discovered that changes in expectancy following success or failure were greater in situations involving a person's skill than in situations where correct performance is chiefly dependent on luck. While this study did not succeed in showing strong individual differences effects, it did set the stage for the subsequent development of the I-E Scale.

Although locus of control is usually thought of as a generalized personality characteristic, it is evident that some situations are so compelling that they engender reactions regardless of existing I-E beliefs. A good example would be the sense of personal helplessness which developed in prisoners of Nazi concentration camps, as so vividly described by Bettelheim in *The Informed Heart.* Thus, regardless of personality considerations, the important situational effects of beliefs about lack of control or predictability must be noted.

MEASURING I-E

The most widely used device to measure locus of control as a generalized personality characteristic is the *I-E Scale.* The scale was introduced in a 1966 *Psychological Monographs* report by Rotter. The scale evolved out of efforts by Liverant, Seeman, Crowne, and James in collaboration with Rotter. The scale consists of 23 forced-choice items along with six filler items to help disguise the purpose of the test. An item similar to ones on the I-E Scale is as follows:

1. It is silly to think one can really change another's basic attitudes.

2. When I am right I can convince others.

Rotter's original data showed little evidence that the scale was anything but unidimensional. Since then, however, considerable evidence has begun to accumulate about the multidimensional nature of I-E. Furthermore, a variety of additional scales have been developed to measure specific areas of I-E beliefs (health care, politics, etc.). Many of these are adult scales, but children's scales have also appeared. Lefcourt's *Locus of Control: Current Trends in Theory and Research,* and Phares' *Locus of Control in Personality,* survey a number of these scales. Indeed, issues of measurement have become so prominent in I-E research that an entire volume, *Research with the Locus of Control Construct: Vol. 1. Assessment Methods,* has been edited by Lefcourt.

RELATIONSHIPS BETWEEN I-E AND PERSONA CONTROL

An internal belief orientation would seem to imply that an individual would adopt a more active and controlling posture toward the environment. In fact, a great deal of evidence exists to support this observation. The existence of this evidence speaks as much as anything else to the validity of the I-E Scale since the bulk of the research has employed that scale.

In the realm of health and body care, a variety of evidence supports the foregoing notion. One of the earliest pieces of I-E research demonstrated that internal tuberculosis patients possessed more information about their physical condition and sought more such information from physicians and nurses than did their external counterparts. It has also been noted that internal smokers are somewhat more likely to heed warnings to give up the habit as compared to external smokers. Similarly, there tends to be a relationship between internal beliefs and prophylactic dental behavior, effective involvement in weight reduction programs, acceptance of preventive medical shots, participation in physical fitness activities, and cooperation with a variety of medically advised regimens. Even the use of seat belts in autos is more typical of internals. All this evidence suggests a modest but reliable relationship between internal beliefs and taking active steps to protect one's health. There is even evidence to suggest that internal females are more likely to practice effective birth control than are external females. Given the complex, multi-determined nature of the foregoing behavior, it is impressive that a general, nonspecific personality variable can show such relationships.

In many ways, internals seem more competent than externals. Perhaps this stems from their more active efforts to acquire information that will enable them to have the effects on their environment that they believe they can have. They seek more information than externals, and they use it more effectively.

Internals are better at paying attention to information-relevant cues and more adept at discovering the principles necessary to solve problems. Thus, it is not surprising that they describe themselves as more active, striving, achieving, powerful, independent, and effective.

When others seek to exercise interpersonal influence, internals would be expected to be more resisting than externals; at least an internal's acceptance should be more thoughtful and analytical rather than simply reflexive. A variety of studies have supported this expectation. The evidence comes from conformity situations, subtle influence conditions, and others. To the extent that verbal conditioning represents an influence situation, the evidence is supportive here too, as we find that externals are more readily conditioned, whereas internals are more resistant to this kind of subtle influence. Similar results emerge when considering attitude change. Externals seem unusually susceptible, especially when confronted with sources of high prestige.

In the realm of social activism, the picture is rather complex. Initially, evidence suggested that internals were more likely to be active in sociopolitical endeavors, particularly when they valued the goals involved. With greater politicization of the country, however, evidence began to accumulate that certain externals were adopting a more activist stance. It is likely that, over the years, the meaning of externality has changed somewhat, so that it no longer automatically implies a passive, fatalistic belief structure.

Equally complex are relationships between I-E and both helping and attribution of responsibility.

Internals seem inclined to believe that we are all responsible for our own situations or behavior. As a result, they often appear less sympathetic when it comes to offering aid to people in trouble. Yet other evidence suggests that in face-to-face helping situations, internals are quick to offer assistance. Perhaps their greater competence and self-confidence are responsible. In any case, the relationships here are complex and probably are greatly affected by the specific situation.

When achievement is studied, the results are again highly complex. In children, academic success is related to internal beliefs, but in college students, the relationship wanes or else becomes inconsistent. Similarly, in the case of need for achievement, relationships are quite inconsistent and often clouded by sex differences. In a related area, it has been found that internal children are more able to defer immediate gratification in favor of delayed rewards. Similarly, since externals more often attribute their performance to other factors, they cannot fully experience the sense of pride and satisfaction that stems from achievement and is such an integral part of the achievement syndrome.

Much research has focused on relationships between I-E and adjustment. The general conclusion is that general maladjustment—as well as specific problems such as anxiety, depression, schizophrenia, and sometimes alcohol and drug abuse—are all associated with an external orientation.

More recent work has been directed toward the possibility that some externals adopt their beliefs as a defensive response. That is, they do not "really" believe the world is organized in an external fashion. Rather, their external beliefs represent a kind of defensive rationalization to account for their failures or anticipated lack of success. What this line of research suggests is that the beliefs of some externals are congruent with their previous experience or history of reinforcement, while the beliefs of others are defensive attempts to minimize the debilitating effects that failure otherwise would have.

ANTECEDENTS OF I-E

Perhaps the most serious gap in the locus of control literature is the systematic study of how I-E beliefs develop. However, some relationships have been noted in a broad fashion. For example, parents who are warm, protective, positive, and nurturant in their child-rearing practices tend to produce internally oriented children. Consistency of parental reinforcement, discipline, and standards are also linked to the development of internality. Research also suggests that lower socioeconomic status is associated with external beliefs. Racial and ethnic groups that have little access to power and mobility likewise show more external belief systems. Some evidence also suggests that certain cultures may more or less directly teach external beliefs.

CHANGES IN I-E

In general, experiences that stimulate lowered expectancies for personal control will affect I-E scores. For example, as the child attains increasing personal mastery over the environment, internal beliefs usually grow. In contrast, "leaving the nest" may (at least temporarily) foster a decline in those beliefs. Aging often brings with it a sense of loss of personal control through declining health, dwindling financial resources, and the like. It is necessary to examine I-E changes both as short-term responses to transitory influences and as long-term responses to what appear to be stable alterations in life circumstances. A number of investigators have recently attempted to show how specific training experiences as well as therapy programs can help induce internal orientations.

REFERENCES

Bettelheim, B. (1960). *The informed heart.* New York: Macmillan.

Lefcourt, H. M. (1979). Locus of control and coping with life's events. In F. Staub (Ed.), *Personality.* Englewood Cliffs, NJ: Prentice-Hall.

Lefcourt, H. M. (1981, 1983). *Research with the locus of control construct* (Vols. 1, 2). New York: Academic.

Phares, E. J. (1957). Expectancy changes in skill and chance situations. *Journal of Abnormal and Social Psychology, 54,* 339–342.

Phares, E. J. (1976). *Locus of control in personality.* Morristown, NJ: General Learning Press.

Rotter, J. B. (1966). Generalized expectancies for internal versus external control of reinforcement. *Psychological Monographs, 80* (1, Entire No. 609), 1–28.

Rotter, J. B. (1980). *Social learning and clinical psychology.* New York: Johnson Reprint. (Original work published 1954)

SUGGESTED READING

Lefcourt, H. M. (1966). Internal versus external control of reinforcement: A review. *Psychological Bulletin, 65,* 206–220.

Phares, E. J. (1979). Defensiveness and perceived control. In L. C. Perimutter & R. A. Monty (Eds.), *Choice and perceived control.* Hillsdale, NJ: Erlbaum.

Phares, E. J. (1978). Locus of control. In H. London and J. Exner (Eds.), *Dimensions of personality.* New York: Wiley Interscience.

Rotter, J. B. (1975). Some problems and misconceptions related to the construct of internal versus external control of reinforcement. *Journal of Consulting and Clinical Psychology, 43,* 56–67.

Rotter, J. B., Chance, J. E., & Phares, E. J. (Eds.). (1972). *Applications of a social learning theory of personality.* New York: Holt, Rinehart & Winston.

Strickland, B. R. (1977). Internal versus external control of reinforcement. In T. Blass (Ed.), *Personality variables in social behavior.* Hillsdale, NJ: Erlbaum.

E. J. PHARES
Kansas State University

OBEDIENCE
PEER INFLUENCES
SOCIAL CLIMATE RESEARCH

LOGICAL POSITIVISM

"Logical positivism" is the name given to an approach to the philosophy of science developed in the 1920s and 1930s in Vienna and Berlin (for review see Ayer, 1959; Brown, 1977; Kockelmans, 1968;

Kraft, 1953; Reichenbach, 1951; Suppe, 1974). Indeed, these philosophers, scientists, and mathematicians can be credited with starting the field we now call philosophy of science.

Although the Vienna Circle of Schlick and the Berlin school of Reichenbach were rife with their own internal controversies and subtle debates, as the chief proponents of logical positivism they zealously pursued a common goal: to rid philosophy of the excesses of metaphysical idealism by clarifying philosophical language. This philosophical project called for strict logical and empirical criteria for assigning meaning to terms and truth value to propositions. The logical criteria were those of deductive logic as supplied in the *Principia Mathematica* (Whitehead & Russell, 1913); and the empirical criteria were those assumed, on a particular misreading of Wittgenstein's (1921/1961) *Tractatus,* to be established in the natural sciences. Toulmin (1969) described how the members of the Vienna Circle mistook Wittgenstein's imprecise claims about "atomic facts" as implying that science contained a language of facts independent of theoretical assumptions and presuppositions, and Bloor (1983) and others have provided corrective antipositivist readings of Wittgenstein.

The problem situation of the logical positivists was how to set philosophy straight by making philosophy conform to the propositional calculus of deductive logic and the meaning criteria of naive empiricist epistemology. The vehicle for accomplishing this was a retrospective analysis of developments in the physical sciences. In order to correct philosophy and set it on "the sure path of science," the positivist movement concluded that it was necessary to *justify* scientific practice philosophically. Reichenbach even coined the distinction between the context of justification and the context of discovery to emphasize that the context of justification is most important. The primary concern of philosophy of science was the context of justification in which one could show, via a reconstruction of the history of theory change and development, that scientists' products (i.e., their theories) changed and developed in a pattern consistent with logical reasoning. Reichenbach made the logic of discovery and the logic of justification symmetrical, and thereby argued that philosophy of science need only concern itself with the context of justification, because new discoveries could always be given a logical and rational account after the fact (Curd, 1980; Nickles, 1980). From the logical positivist perspective, science is the set of theoretical and empirical propositions devised by physicists, chemists, and biologists to describe the world and explain its physical processes. Science differs from non-science by adhering both to logical truth as supplied in the propositional calculus and to empirical truth as rendered by the verification criterion of meaning.

Overall, the logical positivists were not enthusiastic about psychology, and they rejected, as what they called "psychologism," any attempts to base science on psychological principles. Attempts to base the authority of deductive logic on so-called natural habits of mind or psychological processes were rejected as psychologism. In order for the truths of logic and mathematics to command the high philosophical status of clear and certain truth (also trans-historical and universal), it was necessary that these truths be objectively true. By definition, objective truth meant truth independent of subjective experience. Consequently, any attempt to base the truths of logic and mathematics on a study of cognitive contents and/or pro-

cesses undermined their privileged status and authority (Notturno, 1985). Because many of the logical positivists identified psychology with subjective experience, psychology was divorced from the pursuit of objective truth. Epistemologically speaking, the positivist program assumed that the relationship between human perception and the world was virtually uncomplicated, with basic facts being given in direct observation. When taken literally, this account suggested that distortions of observation due to cognitive limitations and biases of the observer did not occur. Psychologically speaking, the scientist or at least the collective community of scientists was conceived as a perfect information-processing device capable of isomorphic inputs and outputs. Moreover, the claim was made that the language of science could be neatly bifurcated into distinct and non-overlapping sets: (a) basic statements about the world or the language of direct observation (e.g., blue, hard, hot); and (b) theoretical terms (e.g., wavelength, density, kinetic energy), which, when introduced, had to be linked to observational terms via explicit correspondence rules (i.e., operational definitions).

Under these assumptions the project of logical reconstruction consisted of demonstrating how new scientific knowledge was achieved through the accumulation of more extensive and accurate observations coupled with rigorous application of deductive logic. Scientific theories were reconstructed as if they were axiomatic systems like the postulates of pure geometry, their only difference being that they also had empirical content. The history of science was reconstructed as if it followed the rules of logic (Nagel, 1960). In the later, more developed form of logical positivism known as logical empiricism, the historical picture that emerged was a reconstruction of scientific development in which both rationality, as adherence to deductive logic, and progress, as movement toward ever more comprehensive theories, were inevitable (Feigl, 1970; Hempel, 1965; Nagel, 1961).

The logical positivists and logical empiricists accomplished their reconstruction of science by ignoring many of the particulars of what individual scientists might have done, said, and thought (Toulmin, 1953). For example, Feigl (1969) reflected on the project of the Vienna Circle as follows: "It must be kept in mind that all this is a logical reconstruction. It was never intended to be an account of the origin and development of scientific theories" (p. 17). Science as described by the logical positivists and logical empiricists was an abstraction, a set of propositions often taken out of historical context and only loosely tied to people called scientists. Further, their sampling of historical episodes of theory change and theory development was restricted in range, and often overlooked important details of the historical record that might have cast serious doubt on their particular reconstruction.

The logical positivist program constrained philosophy of science to the task of justifying scientific practice by addressing and attempting to resolve the logical problems of confirmation, induction, explanation, theory reduction, and so on—all of which could be adjudicated as analytical, philosophical problems independent of practicing scientists and the messy details of individual lives. Whether scientists past or present actually behaved in the manner described by this logical reconstruction was deemed irrelevant to the paramount task of establishing that science in the abstract somehow proceeded along logical lines and therefore made valid claims to Truth.

Thus, by focusing on an abstraction called science, the project of logical reconstruction could be carried forward without entertaining the sort of evidence that might be provided by detailed sociological and psychological studies of scientists' actual practices. As subsequent work in the history of science eventually showed, it is a bitter irony that the philosophical movement that promised to rid philosophy of speculative idealism only reinstated a kind of idealism in the logical reconstruction of science without scientists.

Much of psychology itself was judged by the logical positivists to be defective and in need of the purification that logical positivism offered (Bergmann, 1940; Carnap, (1932/1959); Feigl, 1945). To complicate matters further, the positivist prescriptions for philosophy were widely taken as prescriptions for science. Philosophy of science became philosophy *for* science, evident in the often tacit but nevertheless dogmatic adoption of major tenets of positivist philosophy by empirically oriented sociologists (for review see Bryant, 1985; Giddens, 1978) and psychologists (for review see Koch, 1959–1963; Toulmin & Leary, 1985), who apparently overlooked the anti-dogmatic stance of most members of the Vienna Circle (Ayer, 1984). Smith's (1986) study of leading behaviorists in the 1930s and 1940s raises doubts about the direct connection between their views and those of the logical positivists, but he also noted that by the 1950s, logical empiricism was widely accepted as the standard account of science among psychologists in general. Although some of the logical positivists and logical empiricists advocated types of behaviorism at times, Smith has shown that it is clearly incorrect to call Skinner a logical positivist.

REFERENCES

Ayer, A. J. (1984). The Vienna Circle. In A. J. Ayer (Ed.), *Freedom and morality and other essays* (pp. 159–177). Oxford: Clarendon Press.

Ayer, A. J. (Ed.). (1959). *Logical positivism.* New York: Free Press.

Bergmann, G. (1940). On some methodological problems of psychology. *Philosophy of Science, 7,* 205–219.

Bloor, D. (1983). *Wittgenstein: A social theory of knowledge.* New York: Columbia University Press.

Bryant, C. G. A. (1985). *Positivism in social theory and research.* New York: St Martin's Press.

Carnap, R. (1959). Psychology in physical language. In A. J. Ayer (Ed.), *Logical positivism* (pp. 165–198). New York: Free Press. (Original work published in 1932)

Curd, M. V. (1980). The logic of discovery: An analysis of three approaches. In T. Nickles (Ed.), *Scientific discovery, logic, and rationality* (pp. 201–219). Dordrecht: D. Reidel.

Feigl, H. (1945). Operationism and scientific method. *Psychological Review, 52,* 250–259.

Feigl, H. (1969). The origin and spirit of logical positivism. In P. Achinstein & S. F. Barker (Eds.), *The legacy of logical positivism* (pp. 3–23). Baltimore: Johns Hopkins.

Feigl, H. (1970). The 'orthodox' view of theories. In M. Radner & S. Winokur (Eds.), *Minnesota studies in philosophy of science IV* (pp. 3–16). Minneapolis: University of Minnesota Press.

Giddens, A. (1978). Positivism and its critics. In T. Bottomore & R. Nisbet (Eds.), *A history of sociological analysis* (pp. 237–285). New York: Basic Books.

Hempel, C. G. (1965). *Aspects of scientific explanation.* New York: Free Press.

Koch, S. (Ed.). (1959–1963). *Psychology: A study of a science* (6 vols.). New York: McGraw-Hill.

Kockelmans, J. (Ed.). (1968). *Philosophy of science: The historical background.* New York: Free Press.

Kraft, V. (1953). *The Vienna Circle.* New York: Philosophical Library.

Nagel, E. (1960). The meaning of reduction in the natural sciences. In A. Danto & S. Morgenbesser (Eds.), *Philosophy of science* (pp. 288–312). New York: World Publishing Company.

Nagel, E. (1961). *The structure of science.* New York: Harcourt, Brace, & World.

Nickles, T. (1980). Introductory essay: Scientific discovery and the future of philosophy of science. In T. Nickles (Ed.), *Scientific discovery, logic, and rationality* (pp. 1–59). Dordrecht: D. Reidel.

Notturno, M. A. (1985). *Objectivity, rationality and the third realm: Justification and the grounds of psychologism.* Dordrecht: Martinus Nijhoff.

Reichenbach, H. (1951). *The rise of scientific philosophy.* Berkeley: University of California Press.

Smith, L. D. (1986). *Behaviorism and logical positivism: A reassessment of the alliance.* Stanford: Stanford University Press.

Suppe, F. (1974). The search for philosophic understanding of scientific theories. In F. Suppe (Ed.), *The structure of scientific theories* (pp. 3–235). Urbana, IL: University of Illinois Press.

Toulmin, S. E. (1953). *Philosophy of science.* London: Hutchinson.

Toulmin, S. E. (1969). From logical analysis to conceptual history. In P. Achinstein & S. F. Barker (Eds.), *The legacy of logical positivism* (pp. 25–53). Baltimore: Johns Hopkins University Press.

Toulmin, S. E., & Leary, D. E. (1985). The cult of empiricism in psychology, and beyond. In S. Koch & D. E. Leary (Eds.), *A century of psychology as science* (pp. 594–617). New York: McGraw-Hill.

Whitehead, A. N., & Russell, B. (1913). *Principia mathematica.* Cambridge: Cambridge University Press.

Wittgenstein, L. (1961). *Tractatus logico-philosophicus.* London: Routledge & Kegan Paul. (Original work published in 1921)

AUTHOR NOTE

Support for this work was provided by a Centers of Excellence Grant from the State of Tennessee to the Department of Psychology of the University of Memphis.

Correspondence concerning this article should be addressed to Arthur C. Houts, Department of Psychology, Campus Box 5286400, University of Memphis, Memphis, TN 38152-6400. Electronic mail may be sent to ahouts@cc.memphis.edu.

A. C. Houts
University of Memphis

LONELINESS

Loneliness constitutes a destructive form of self-perception. The lonely feel left out, forgotten, unneeded, and ignored. It seems likely that thoughts concerning the loss of the past and those in it, and the high regard for others as shown by illogical beliefs such as "I must be included," "I must be loved," and "I must not be alone," provide unreasonable demands on the individual. Such demands usually go unfulfilled, causing individuals to feel more isolated and to interpret their present condition as catastrophic.

ORIGINS OF LONELINESS: THE IMPERATIVES

The *neurological imperative* dictates an optimal range of stimulation in the physical, cultural, and interpersonal environments. There are also qualitative constraints: there must be meaningful human interaction, the lack of which accounts for feelings of loneliness in a crowd. The *psychological imperative* cautions against being rejected or left out, which will lead to feelings of being unloved and rejected, which lead in turn to feelings of guilt for self-mistreatment because previously valued close contacts have been lost. Parental loss may be viewed as rejection and increase the likelihood of loneliness in children. The *social imperative* dictates that if we are excluded from the group, we will not get what we need and what we want out of life. Such exclusion is viewed as a challenge to basic motives seeking safety and the satisfaction of physical and reproductive needs. Witness the lonely elderly who become obsessed with reminiscence of past actions and experiences with others. The *cognitive imperative* mandates that we be able to send and receive messages so as to survive in society. Barriers to communication like a foreign language lead to feelings of isolation, while a loss of intellect (e.g., organic brain disease) impairs reminiscence and creativity.

Loss and Loneliness

Illness and death rates are higher for the single, widowed, and divorced. These higher rates may result from reduced endorphin, the body's natural immunizers. Endorphin production seems to fluctuate with emotional well-being and depression. Alternatively, the higher illness and death rates could be due to some illogical self-fulfilling expectation of members of these groups based on a perceived lack of deserving happiness, of deserving only loneliness. Whatever the cause, an important contributor to loneliness is a sense of *loss* or *separation* from someone or something in the past once viewed as the essence for survival.

Volition and Loneliness

Another component of loneliness is *control*. Having control over any given social situation decides the difference between feeling lonely and being alone. A voluntary walk in the countryside can be a pleasant pastoral interlude, but being abandoned in the same location can be a horrible anxiety-producing experience. Lack of control is the essence of loneliness. Hermits, martyrs, scientists, artists, and explorers are motivated and productive in their alone-

ness, but the abandoned, deserted, widowed, divorced, and isolates like criminals become harassed and depressed by their seclusion.

COUNTERING LONELINESS

Loneliness provokes a broad spectrum of reactions. Some accept loneliness as deserved and seek isolation; others attempt to escape feeling lonely by frenetic work habits; still others try to compensate for loneliness by the accumulation of possessions (e.g., clothes, pets, cars), or even through exhibitionist behavior (e.g., being the class clown, acting). Productive ways of countering feelings of loneliness are highly individualistic, but may be placed in the following framework: first, attempt to reduce the irrational beliefs that tend to accumulate regarding the catastrophe, unfairness, and self-depreciating aspects of being alone; second, assume a personal motivation for the feeling by acting instead of obsessing, one can dissipate the feelings; third, substitute reliance on oneself for reliance and support provided by the consensus of others; fourth, work to believe that the lonely condition will probably not last forever.

SUGGESTED READING

Hartog, J., Audy, J. R., & Cohen, Y. A. (Eds.). (1980). *The anatomy of loneliness.* New York: International Universities Press.

Peplau, L. A., & Perlman, D. (1982). *Loneliness: A source book of current theory, research and therapy.* New York: Wiley.

D. F. FISHER
U.S. Army Human Engineering Laboaratory

INTERPERSONAL ATTRACTION
LOVE

LONG TERM POTENTIATION

Virtually all ideas about memory hold dear the central notion that learning relies on the modification of synaptic function. In recent years considerable attention has focused on one particular form of use-dependent synaptic plasticity known as long term potentiation (LTP), which was first discovered by Terje Lomo. Lomo observed that repetitive high-frequency electrical stimulations of the pathway from the cortex to the hippocampus resulted in a steeper rise time of the excitatory synaptic potential as well as recruitment of spike activity from a greater number of cells. Moreover, these changes in synaptic and cellular responses to subsequent single shocks lasted several hours, suggesting the possibility of a lasting memory mechanism.

Two key properties of LTP are notable. First, LTP is specific to those synapses activated during stimulation. Other neighboring synapses, even on the same neurons, are not altered. This phenomenon parallels the natural specificity of human memories, and would be a key requirement of any useful cellular memory mechanism. The property of specificity may be key to the storage capacity of brain structures because each cell can participate in the representation of multiple memories composed from distinct subsets of its synaptic inputs.

Second, LTP is associative in that potentiation characteristically occurs across multiple inputs that are stimulated simultaneously. The property of associativity is consistent with Hebb's (1949) postulate that increasing synaptic efficacy requires both the repeated activation of a presynaptic element and its participation in the success in firing the postsynaptic cell, as indeed occurs in associative LTP when several inputs are simultaneously active.

Considerable evidence has accumulated revealing the cellular and molecular mechanisms that mediate the properties of different forms of LTP, as well as its cousin, synaptic plasticity mechanism (called long term depression), in both the hippocampus and the neocortex (Bear, 1996; Bliss & Collingridge, 1993; Madison, Malenka, & Nicoll, 1991; Malenka, 1994).

LTP AND MEMORY: IS THERE A CONNECTION?

As Stevens (1996) once put it, the mechanism of LTP is so attractive that it would be a shame if LTP turned out not to be a memory device. But there should be no doubt about the fact that LTP is not memory; it is a laboratory phenomenon never observed in nature. The best we can hope for is that LTP and memory share some of their physiological and molecular bases. In recent years evidence from two general strategies have emerged to provide supporting connections between LTP and memory.

Behavioral LTP

One strategy is to determine whether learning produces changes in synaptic physiology similar to the increases in synaptic and cellular responses that occur after LTP. Recently, Rogan, Staubli, and LeDoux (1997) offered the most compelling evidence to date that these aspects of LTP result from natural learning. In this case the circuit under study was the pathway from the medial geniculate nucleus of the thalamus to the lateral amygdala nucleus that is part of the critical circuit for auditory fear-conditioning. These investigators found that repeated pairings of auditory stimuli and foot shocks train rats to fear the tones. Furthermore, this learning experience alters evoked sensory responses to the tones in the same way as LTP does in that pathway. Thus, in rats with properly timed tone-shock pairings, tones produce evoked potentials of greater slope and amplitude, just as do electrical stimulus trains applied to this pathway. No enhancement of field potentials was observed with unpaired tone and foot shock presentations, even though this conditioning control leads to as much of a behavioral response (freezing) as paired presentations, because even the unpaired control rats learn to freeze to the environmental context where shocks are received. Furthermore, this behavioral LTP is enduring, lasting at least a few days, as long as the behavioral response during extinction trials.

Blocking LTP and Memory

Perhaps the most compelling and straightforward data on a potential connection between the molecular basis of LTP and memory has come from experiments in which a drug is used to block LTP and, correspondingly, prevent learning. These studies were based on the observations that induction of the most prominent form of hippocampal LTP is dependent on a specific glutamate receptor known as the N-methyl-D-aspartate (NMDA) receptor, and that drugs such as D-2-amino-5-phosphonovalerate (AP5) selectively block the NMDA receptor and prevent hippocampal LTP, while sparing normal synaptic transmission. Thus, to the extent that the role of the NMDA receptor is fully selective to plasticity, one might predict these drugs would indeed block new learning without affecting non-learning performance or retention of learning normally accomplished prior to drug treatment.

Consistent with these predictions, some of the strongest evidence supporting a connection between LTP and memory has come from demonstrations that a drug-induced blockade of hippocampal NMDA receptors prevents hippocampal dependent spatial learning (Morris, Anderson, Lynch, & Baudry, 1986). Additional experiments showed no effect of AP5 on retention of the same spatial learning when training was accomplished prior to drug treatment; this would be fully predicted, because NMDA receptors are viewed as required for only the induction of LTP and not for its maintenance. In addition, targeted genetic manipulations have now shown that knocking out NMDA receptors (McHugh, Blum, Tsien, Tonegawa, & Wilson, 1997) or later stages in the cascade of molecular triggers for maintenance of LTP (e.g., Silva, Paylor, Wehner, & Tonegawa, 1992), also results in severe memory impairments. These studies have also shown some restrictions on the role of NMDA receptor–mediated LTP in spatial memory. Recent experiments have indicated that blocking NMDA-dependent LTP does not necessarily prevent the encoding of a new spatial environment (Bannerman, Good, Butcher, Ramsay, & Morris, 1995). However, NMDA-dependent LTP may be necessary to remembering new episodes within a familiar space (Steele & Morris, 1999).

REFERENCES:

Bannerman, D. M., Good, M. A., Butcher, S. P., Ramsay, M., & Morris, R. G. M. (1995). Prior experience and N-methyl-D-aspartate receptor blockade dissociate components of spatial learning in the watermaze. *Nature, 378,* 182–186.

Bear, M. F. (1996). A synaptic basis for memory storage in the cerebral cortex. *93,* 13453–13459.

Bliss, T. V. P., & Collingridge, G. L. (1993). A synaptic model of memory: Long-term potentiation in the hippocampus. *Nature, 361,* 31–39.

Hebb, D. O. (1949). *The organization of behavior.* New York: Wiley.

Madison, D. V., Malenka, R. C., & Nicoll, R. A. (1991). Mechanisms underlying long-term potentiation of synaptic transmission. *Annual Review of Neuroscience, 14,* 379–397.

Malenka, R. C. (1994). Synaptic plasticity in the hippocampus: LTP and LTD. *Cell, 78,* 535–538.

McHugh, T. J., Blum, K. I., Tsien, J. Z., Tonegawa, S., & Wilson, M. A. (1996). Impaired hippocampal representation of space in CA1-specific NMDAR1 knockout mice. *Cell, 87,* 1339–1349.

Morris, R. G. M., Anderson, E., Lynch, G. S., & Baudry, M. (1986). Selective impairment of learning and blockade of long term potentiation by an N-methyl-D-aspartate receptor anatagonist, AP5. *Nature, 319,* 774–776.

Rogan, M. T., Staubli, U. V., & LeDoux, J. E. (1997). Fear conditioning induces associative long-term potentiation in the amygdala. *Nature, 390,* 604–607.

Silva, A. J., Paylor, C. F. R., Wehner, J. W., & Tonegawa, S. (1992). Impaired spatial learning in a-calcium-calmodulin kinase II mutant mice. *Science, 257,* 206–211.

Stevens, C. F. (1996). Strengths and weaknesses in memory. *Nature, 381,* 471–472.

Steele, R. J., & Morris, R. G. M. (1999). Delay dependent impairment in matching-to-place task with chronic and intrahippocampal infusion of the NMDA-antagonist D-AP5. *Hippocampus, 9,* 118–136.

H. EICHENBAUM
Boston University

LEARNING THEORIES
MEMORY

LONGITUDINAL STUDIES

Longitudinal studies represent a research design wherein individuals or groups are observed or repeatedly assessed over a considerable period of time in order to assess change. The longitudinal study is an important research method in developmental psychology, where time-related phenomena are under investigation. Often the intent is to study behavioral or physiological changes that may occur in subjects as they grow older. Two major approaches have been employed to investigate the time-related trajectory of change: cross-sectional and longitudinal designs. Cross-sectional studies measure a given dependent variable (e.g., IQ) on several different age cohorts. In this type of study, one may measure IQ on groups that were, say, 4, 7, 10, and 12 years old. Longitudinal investigations repeatedly assess the dependent variable on the same cohort of subjects over time (e.g., when they are 4, 7, 10, and 12 years of age). Narrowly defined, a longitudinal study is any investigation where repeated measurements are recorded on the same subjects over time. However, the term "longitudinal" is typically not used for studies where the time span is less than several months or years.

Longitudinal studies have a long history in various specialties of psychology as well as in many other fields, ranging from health to sociometric status. The late 19th century is generally cited as the time when psychology began to seriously employ longitudinal research. However, the classic study of infants by Tiedemann, entitled *Beobachtungen über die Entwicklung der Seelenfähigkeit bei Kindern,* was published in 1787. Early work using longitudinal studies significantly influenced the nature of developmental psychology.

One major strength of longitudinal designs is that researchers are able to follow the same subjects over the period of the study. This permits examination of change in the same individuals as they develop or decline. Consequently, longitudinal investigations permit more direct inferences regarding development than cross-sectional studies. Longitudinal studies with multiple measures such as the examples noted above (i.e., assessments at ages 4, 7, 10, and 12), are also preferred because of strong statistical power in determining the trajectory of a change over time.

Longitudinal designs also present certain methodological difficulties. Since the subjects are measured repeatedly, it is possible that changes may be observed which are partially due to the effects of repeated assessment reliability and the continuing attention or "Hawthorne effect" over time. Another potential problem is subject attrition: Because longitudinal studies often continue for an extended period of time, a certain number of subjects may be lost for a variety of reasons (death, moving, refusal to continue). As with most experimental designs, most problems associated with longitudinal studies can be successfully circumvented by ingenious researchers. Such studies remain an important research strategy in psychology, although not frequently undertaken because of the time and expense involved.

SUGGESTED READING

DeShon, R. P., Ployhard, R. E., & Sacco, J. M. (1998). The estimation of reliability in longitudinal models. *International Journal of Behavioral Development, 22,* 493–515.

Gelfand, D. M., Jenson, W. R., & Drew, C. J. (1997). *Understanding child behavior disorders.* Fort Worth, TX: Harcourt Brace.

Maassen, G. H., Goossens, F. A., & Bokhorst, J. (1998). Ratings as validation of sociometric status determined by nominations in longitudinal research. *Social Behavior and Personality, 26,* 259–274.

Maxwell, S. E. (1998). Longitudinal designs in randomized group comparisons: When will intermediate observations increase statistical power? *Psychological Methods, 3,* 275–290.

C. J. DREW
University of Utah

EXPERIMENTAL DESIGNS
RESEARCH METHODOLOGY

LOOSE ASSOCIATIONS

The most important source of data for assessing patients with psychiatric disorders is speech behavior during a clinical interview. One critical component of this assessment is the patient's ability to produce coherent conversational discourse.

The sine qua non of disrupted discourse coherence consists of loose associations. A synonymous term currently used is "derailment." Loose associations or derailments are suspected when the listener has significant difficulty following or tracking continuous, conversational speech. The overall intention or focus of the utterance is obscure, and the speaker seems to shift idiosyncratically from one frame of reference to another. (Andreasen, 1979a). A typical case of loose associations is illustrated in the following:

Interviewer: Tell me about where you live.
Patient: I live in one place and then another place. They're black and white you know. That's why I love Christmas and stuff because, you know, it's different colors. I used to live in Brooklyn. (Hoffman, Kirstein, Stopek, & Ciccheti, 1982)

Here the patient seems to respond to the interviewer's prompt but then abruptly switches to a Christmas motif that fails to elaborate on the "where I live" theme and does not, in itself, make a point. Of note is that each of the sentences, when considered separately, is quite ordinary and grammatical. Deviance reflects the juxtaposition of phrases and sentences.

A more complex form of loose associations is illustrated by the following (Hoffman, 1986):

Interviewer: Did you ever try to hurt yourself?
Patient: I cut myself once when I was in the kitchen trying to please David. I was scared for life because if David didn't want me then no man would. (Hoffman, 1986)

Here the patient seems to be talking about two frames of reference, the first pertaining to cutting herself, presumably while preparing food, and the second pertaining to reasons for being suicidal. Shift between the two frames of reference are expressed without warning to the listener. In other words, the patient did not state, "I never intentionally hurt myself but I was so upset about David that . . . " These shifts of frame ordinarily help the listener to make the transition from one frame of reference to another (Hoffman et al., 1982).

Most typically, loose associations are produced by patients with schizophrenia. However, some patients with aphasia or brain disturbances secondary to drug intoxication or organic encephalopathy may also produce such language disturbances. A related language difficulty is referred to as "flight of ideas," and is typically associated with patients with mania or amphetamine-induced states. Some researchers have not distinguished flight of ideas from loose associations (Andreasen, 1979a), but there is some empirical evidence that the two terms refer to distinct phenomena (Hoffman, Stopek, & Andreasen, 1986). In the case of flight of ideas, conversational speech yields unannounced and disruptive shifts in frame of reference, but is also accompanied by rapid production of speech. Most importantly, the speaker in the former case seems to retain the ability to flesh out particular themes or topics within a particular frame of reference. In contrast, looseness of associations suggests a sustained inability to fully and coherently elaborate on any theme or topic. Although the presence of these language difficulties favors some psychiatric diagnoses over others, they, in themselves, are not diagnostic of a specific disorder. For instance, it has been well established that some apparently normal speakers occasionally produce loose associations (Andreasen, 1979b; Hoffman et al., 1986).

There is some research exploring the cognitive and/or neurobiological basis of loose associations. Some recent studies have suggested that alterations in semantic processing produce loose associations and related language disturbances in patients with schizophrenia (Goldberg et al., 1998; Spitzer, 1997). Another recent study of regional cerebral blood flow using positron emission tomography suggested that these language difficulties arise from an imbalance of regional cerebral activation, with reduced activation in inferior frontal and cingulate brain regions combined with excessive activation in hippocampal regions (McGuire et al., 1998). Additional research of the neurocognitive basis of loose associations is needed.

REFERENCES

Andreasen, N. C. (1979a). Thought, language, and communication disorders: I. Clinical assessment, definition of terms, and evaluation of their reliability. *Archives of General Psychiatry, 36,* 1315–1321.

Andreasen, N. C. (1979b). Thought, language, and communication disorders: II. Diagnostic signficance. *Archives of General Psychiatry, 36,* 1325–1330.

Goldberg, T. E., Aloia, M. S., Gourovitch, M. L., Missar, D., Pickar, D., & Weinberger, D. R. (1998). Cognitive substrates of thought disorder: I. the semantic system. *American Journal of Psychiatry, 155,* 1671–1676.

Hoffman, R. E. (1986). Verbal hallucinations and language production processes in schizophrenia. *Behavior and Brain Science, 9,* 503–548.

Hoffman, R. E., Kirstein, L., Stopek, S., & Cichetti, D. (1982). Apprehending schizophrenic discourse: A structural analysis of the listener's task. *Brain Language, 15,* 207–233.

Hoffman, R. E., Stopek, S., & Andreasen, N. C. (1986). A comparative study of manic versus schizophrenic speech disorganization. *Archives of General Psychiatry, 43,* 831–838.

McGuire, P. K., Quested, D. J., Spence, S. A., Murray, R. M., Frith, C. D., & Liddle, P. F. (1998). Pathophysiology of 'positive' thought disorder in schizophrenia. *British Journal of Psychiatry, 173,* 231–235.

Spitzer, M. (1997). A cognitive neuroscience view of schizophrenic thought disorder. *Schizophrenia Bulletin, 23,* 29–50.

R. E. HOFFMAN
Yale University

CLINICAL ASSESSMENT

LORENZ, KONRAD (1903–1989)

Along with Tinbergen, Konrad Lorenz is generally considered one of the founders of ethology. He received the MD then the PhD (1933), both from the University of Vienna. During this early period, he set up many of his hypotheses on animal behavior, such as imprinting, innate releasing mechanism, and fixed action patterns.

Lorenz's methods were not always conventional. He never did a formal experiment, and his descriptive observations were often anecdotal. He infuriated his more conventional colleagues by saying, "If I have one good example, I don't give a fig for statistics." By this he meant that if he had seen an animal do something striking, he did not need to see a lot of other animals do the same thing to confirm what he already knew. His doctrine of imprinting is still a focus of research interest after a half century. Lorenz loved animals and kept an enormous variety, including jackdaws, geese, dogs, and fish.

In 1973 he received the Nobel Prize, which he shared with Niko Tinbergen and Karl von Friwsch. One of his later theories has been subject to considerable debate, namely, that of innate aggression. According to Lorenz, aggression involves stored instinctive energy and needs to be discharged. Then follows a refactory phase to build up the energy that has been flushed much like the flushing and refilling of a toilet.

Lorenz authored many articles (only one with Tinbergen) and books. Some of his books are *King Soloman's Ring: New Light on Animal Ways, Evolution and Modification of Behavior, On Aggression,* and *Civilized Man's Eight Deadly Sins.*

R. W. LUNDIN
Wheaton, Illinois

LOVE

Recently social scientists have begun a systematic gathering of information about love. For reviews of research in this area, see Duck and Gilmore (1981), *Personal Relationships,* Volumes 1–3; Hatfield and Rapson (1993), *Love, Sex, and Intimacy: Their Psychology, Biology and History,* or Hatfield and Rapson (1995), *Love and Sex: Cross-Cultural Perspectives.*

WHAT IS LOVE?

Most researchers agree that love comes in a variety of of forms. People generally assume that love encompasses two kinds of emotions: passionate love (which they label "infatuation") and companionate love (which they label "fondness"). Scientists find that most young people understand the difference between being in love and loving someone. When besotted lovers hear the dreaded mantra "I love you, but I'm not *in love* with you," generally their hearts sink. Men and women in a variety of nations, single or married, homosexual or heterosexual, appear to understand this distinction (Fehr, 1993).

Hatfield and Rapson (1993), too, distinguish between passionate love and companionate love. Passionate love is an intensely emotional state identified with a confusion of feelings: tenderness, sexuality, elation, pain, anxiety, relief, altruism, and jealousy. It is defined (p. 5) as:

A state of intense longing for union with another. A complex functional whole including appraisals or appreciations, subjective feelings, expressions, patterned physiological processes, action tendencies, and instrumental behaviors. Reciprocated love (union with the other) is associated with fulfillment and ecstasy; unrequited love (separation) is associated with emptiness, anxiety, or despair. A state of profound physiological arousal.

The Passionate Love Scale was designed to assess the cognitive, physiological, and behavioral incidents of such love (Hatfield &

Sprecher, 1986). This entry is concerned with this form of love. Companionate love, on the other hand, is a less intense emotion, combining feelings of friendly affection and deep attachment. It is characterized by friendship, understanding, and a concern for the welfare of the other. Companionate love is "the affection people feel for those with whom their lives are deeply entwined" (Hatfield & Rapson, 1993, p. 9).

Others have proposed a variety of definitions and typologies of love. Sternberg (1998) proposed a triangular theory of love. He argued that different kinds of love differ in how much of three different components—passion, intimacy, and the decision/commitment to stay together—they possess. Passionate love (infatuation), for example, involves intense passionate arousal but little intimacy or commitment. Companionate love involves less passion and far more intimacy and commitment. The most complete form of love is consummate love—which requires passion, intimacy, and commitment.

IS PASSIONATE LOVE A CULTURAL UNIVERSAL?

Since Darwin's classic treatise (1871) on *The Descent of Man and Selection in Relation to Sex,* scientists have debated the universality and nonuniversality of romantic love. At one time, scientists assumed that passionate love was primarily a Western phenomenon. Today, most anthropologists assume that passionate love is a cultural universal. Anthropologists Jankowiak and Fischer (1992), for example, drew a sharp distinction between "romantic passion" and "simple lust." In order to determine the worldwide frequency of romantic love, they selected a sampling of tribal societies from the *Standard Cross-Cultural Sample.* They found that in almost all of these far-flung societies, young lovers talked about passionate love, recounted tales of love, sang love songs, and talked about the longings and anguish of infatuation. When passionate affections clashed with parents' or elders' wishes, young people often eloped. The authors concluded that romantic love is indeed a pan-human characteristic. Cross-cultural researchers, anthropologists, and historians, however, point out that there is cultural variability in the commonality of such feelings.

DO MEN AND WOMEN IN DIFFERENT CULTURES DIFFER IN THEIR VIEWS OF LOVE?

Culture has been found to have a significant impact on how men and women view passionate love. Shaver, Wu, and Schwartz (1991) interviewed young people in America, Italy, and the People's Republic of China about their emotional experiences. In all cultures, men and women identified the same emotions as basic, prototypic emotions—these were joy/happiness, love/attraction, fear, anger/hate, and sadness/depression. They also agreed on whether the various emotions should be labeled as positive experiences (such as joy) or negative ones (such as fear, anger, or sadness). They agreed completely, except for one emotion—love. Americans and Italians tended to equate love with happiness—both passionate and companionate love were assumed to be intensely positive experiences. Chinese students, however, had a darker view of passion. In China there were few "happy love" ideographs. Passionate love tended to be associated with sadness, pain, and heartache. Chinese men and women generally associated passionate love with such ideographs as infatuation, unrequited love, nostalgia, and sorrowful love.

WHAT DO MEN AND WOMEN DESIRE IN ROMANTIC PARTNERS, SEXUAL PARTNERS, AND MATES?

Throughout the world, young men and women desire many of the same things in a mate. In a cross-cultural study, Buss (1994) asked over 10,000 men and women from thirty-seven countries, located on six continents and five islands to indicate what they valued in mates. The thirty-seven cultures represented a tremendous diversity of geographic, cultural, political, ethnic, religious, racial, economic, and linguistic groups. Buss discovered that love was of utmost importance. High on the list of things men and women cared about were character, emotional stability and maturity, a pleasing disposition, education and intelligence, health, sociability, a desire for home and children, refinement, good looks, and ambition.

Scientists have documented that a major determinant of sexual chemistry is physical attractiveness. There are three reasons why people find the attractive so appealing: (a) Good looks are in and of themselves aesthetically pleasing; (b) There is prestige associated with being seen with an attractive partner; (c) In accordance with the stereotype that "beautiful is good," most people assume that the beautiful possess socially desirable personality traits and lead happier and more successful lives than do unattractive persons. Indeed, this latter stereotype may be correct and attractiveness may be a marker for "evolutionary fitness". Of course, although almost everyone is attracted to good-looking partners, most people have to settle for partners whose physical attractiveness matches their own.

People also tend to fall in love with people who are similar to themselves in attitude, religious affiliation, values, interests, and education. There are several explanations for this phenomenon. First, people are more likely to encounter similar than dissimilar others: People of the same socioeconomic status tend to live in the same neighborhoods, go to the same schools, join the same clubs. Second, there are social pressures to interact with similar others: People are discouraged from falling in love with people from different socioeconomic, racial, ethnic, or religious backgrounds, or with those who are of an "unsuitable" age. Finally, in cost/benefit terms, it is more rewarding (and less costly) to interact with others who confirm our beliefs about reality.

Some researchers have argued that people tend to fall in love with those who complement them in certain ways, as suggested by the maxim "Opposites attract." Some scientists argue that people fall in love with those who complete and/or complement their own personalities and needs. However, researchers have been unable to replicate these findings. The data indicate that people tend to select mates who possess similar, rather than complementary, personalities and needs.

Proximity is perhaps the most important determinant of who people end up choosing as friends, lovers, and spouses. People often end up marrying mates who live only a few blocks away. Generally, the closer people are to others, the more chance they have to become familiar with them; knowledge quite often leads to attraction and love. In addition, when people are in close proximity to others, there are more chances to be in rewarding situations with them. Needless to say, people are attracted to others who provide them with rewarding experiences.

DO MEN AND WOMEN DESIRE THE SAME THING IN MATES?

Many sociobiologists argue that there should be major differences in what men and women desire in romantic partners and mates. An animal's "fitness," they point out, depends on how successful it is in transmitting its genes to subsequent generations. Thus, it is to both the male and female evolutionary advantage to produce as many progeny as possible. Men and women differ, however, in their "ideal" reproductive strategies: Men seek quantity while women seek quality in a mate if they are to maximize reproductive outcomes. This logic led Buss (1994) to propose a "sexual strategies theory" of human mating. Men and women, he argues, are genetically programmed to desire different traits in potential mates. Men prefer women who are physically attractive, healthy, and young, and they desire sexual encounters with a variety of partners. Women seek out men who possess status, power, and money; men who are willing to make a commitment, are kind and considerate; and who like children. They are hesitant to risk sexual encounters. Evolutionary psychologists have collected considerable evidence in support of these hypotheses.

Many anthropologists, historians, sociologists, and psychologists have sharply criticized the evolutionary approach. Sociobiologists themselves acknowledge that probably the main way in which humans differ from other species is in their unrivaled ability to adapt—to change themselves and their worlds. In different times and places, men and women have been forced to adapt to very different social realities. Men and women possess different attitudes, these critics continue, not because they are propelled by ancient genetic codes, but because they are responding to different sociocultural realities. Critics point out that for most of human history, men and women who desired passionate liaisons or indulged in casual sex were likely to face very different consequences. As Smuts (1991) observes:

In a variety of cultures, women have had their genitals cut out or sewn together to discourage sexual activity; their movements curtailed by mutilation of the feet, the threat of rape, and confinement to guarded harems; their noses bitten off in culturally sanctioned responses to adultery. Because of these and other similar practices, women associate sex with danger (p. 29).

Smuts points out that evidence from nonhuman primates and from women in societies with relatively few coercive constraints on female sexual behavior, such as the ¡Kung San or modern Scandinavia, makes it clear that under permissive conditions women are far more active and assertive sexually and far more excited by sexual variety.

IS PASSIONATE LOVE AN INTENSELY PLEASURABLE OR AN INTENSELY PAINFUL EXPERIENCE?

For centuries, theorists have bitterly disagreed over the true nature of passionate love. Is it an intensely pleasurable experience or an intensely painful one? Reinforcement theorists argue that passionate love can be explained by the same reinforcement principles that explain interpersonal attraction in general. They argue that the more potent the rewards people receive from others, the more they will love them. Thus, they insist that passionate love is stimulated by intensely positive experiences and dampened by intensely negative ones.

A minority of theorists take the opposite tack. Stoller (1979) in *Sexual Excitement* (p. 6) argues:

My theory is as follows: ... It is hostility—the desire, overt or hidden, to harm another person—that generates and enhances sexual excitement. The absence of hostility leads to sexual indifference and boredom. The following ... contribute to sexual excitement in general: hostility, mystery, risk, illusion, revenge, reversal of trauma or frustration to triumph, safety factors, and dehumanization (fetishization). Two unpleasant thoughts: first, when one tabulates the factors that produce sexual excitement, exuberance—pure joyous pleasure—is for most people at the bottom of the list, rarely found outside fiction. Second, I would guess that only in the rare people who can indefinitely contain sexual excitement and love within the same relationship do hostility and secrecy play insignificant parts in producing excitement.

Finally, most social psychologists (Hatfield & Rapson, 1993, 1995) agree that both pleasure and pain can fuel passion. They would endorse the adage "The opposite of love is not hate but indifference."

The evidence suggests that for most people love is associated with both pleasure and pain and may be stimulated by either.

There are physiological reasons why love might be linked to both pleasure and pain. Physiologically, love, delight, and pain have one thing in common—they are intensely arousing. Joy, passion, excitement, anger, envy, and hate all produce a sympathetic response in the nervous system. This is evidenced by the "symptoms" associated with all these emotions: a flushed face, sweaty palms, weak knees, butterflies in the stomach, dizziness, a pounding heart, trembling hands, and accelerated breathing. For this reason, theorists point out that either delight or pain (or a combination of the two) should have the potential to fuel a passionate experience.

An abundance of evidence supports the common-sense contention that, under the right conditions, intensely positive experiences such as euphoria, sexual fantasizing, an understanding partner, or general excitement can fuel passion. But there is also some evidence for the more intriguing contention that under the right conditions, anxiety and fear, jealousy, loneliness, anger, or even grief can fuel passion.

For example, one study (Dutton & Aron, 1974) discovered a close link between fear and sexual attraction. The investigators compared reactions of young men crossing two bridges in North Vancouver. The first bridge, the Capilano Canyon Suspension Bridge, is a 450-foot-long, five-foot-wide span that tilts, sways, and wobbles over a 230-foot-drop to rocks and shallow rapids below. The other bridge, a bit farther upstream, is a solid, safe structure. As each young man crossed the bridge, a good-looking college woman approached him. She explained that she was doing a class project and asked if he would fill out a questionnaire for her. When the man had finished, the woman offered to explain her project when she had more time. She wrote her telephone number on a small piece of paper, so the man could call her if he wanted more information. The men who called the coed were the men who met her under frightening conditions. (Nine of the 33 men on the suspension bridge called her; only two of the men on the solid bridge called.) This research suggests that people may sometimes passionately love others not in spite of the difficulties others cause them, but because of them.

Recently, more laboratory research indicates that under the right conditions any state of intense arousal can be interpreted as the stirrings of desire—even if it is the result of an irrelevant experience such as listening to a comedy routine, jogging, or listening to a description of a mob mutilating and killing a missionary. Strange as it sounds, then, evidence suggests that adrenaline makes the heart grow fonder. Delight is surely the most common stimulant of passionate love, but anxiety and fear sometimes play a part.

HOW CAN PEOPLE TELL IF SOMEONE LOVES THEM?

There are several tell-tale body signs. Lovers give away their feelings by several body signs, including special attention to physical appearance ("preening" gestures). People who love each other tend to spend a great deal of time gazing into each other's eyes. They also want to touch each other and tend to stand close. Perhaps most obvious of all, when people love someone, they want to spend a great deal of time with the other person and want to do things for him or her.

Love and intimacy are relatively unexplored topics and will be exciting areas of work for future psychologists and social psychologists.

REFERENCES

Buss, D. M. (1994). *The evolution of desire.* New York: Basic Books.

Darwin, C. (1871). *The descent of man and selection in relation to sex.* London: Murray.

Duck, S., & Gilmour, R. (Eds.). (1981). *Personal Relationships* (Vols. 1–3). New York: Academic Press.

Dutton, D., & Aron, A. (1974). Some evidence for heightened sexual attraction under conditions of high anxiety. *Journal of Personality and Social Psychology, 30,* 510–517.

Fehr, B. (1993). How do I love thee? Let me consult my prototype. In S. Duck (Ed.). *Individuals in relationships: Understanding Relationship Processes Series* (Vol. 1), (pp. 87–120). Newbury Park: Sage.

Hatfield, E., & Rapson, R. L. (1993). *Love, sex, and intimacy: Their psychology, biology, and history.* New York: Harper Collins.

Hatfield, E., & Rapson, R. L. (1995). *Love and sex: Cross-cultural perspectives.* New York: Allyn and Bacon.

Hatfield, E., & Sprecher, S. (1986a). Measuring passionate love in intimate relations. *Journal of Adolescence, 9,* 383–410.

Jankowiak, W. R., & Fischer, E. F. (1992). A cross-cultural perspective on romantic love. *Ethology, 31,* 149–155.

Shaver, P. R., Wu, S., & Schwartz, J. C. (1991). Cross-cultural similarities and differences in emotion and its representation: A prototype approach. In M. S. Clark (Ed.), *Review of personality and social psychology* (Vol. 13, pp. 175–212). Beverly Hills, CA: Sage Publications.

Smuts, B. (1991). Gender differences in sexuality. In D. A. Counts, J. K. Brown, & J. C. Campbell, (Eds.), *Sanctions and sanctuary: Cultural perspectives on the beating of wives* (pp. 29–30). Boulder, CO: Westview Press.

Sternberg, R. J. (1998). *Cupid's arrow: The course of love through time.* Cambridge, England: Cambridge Press.

Stoller, R. (1979). *Sexual excitement: The dynamics of erotic life.* New York: Pantheon.

SUGGESTED READINGS

Buss, D. M. (1994). *The evolution of desire.* New York: Basic Books.

Hatfield, E., & Rapson, R. L. (1993). *Love, sex, and intimacy: Their psychology, biology, and history.* New York: Harper Collins.

Hatfield, E., & Rapson, R. L. (1995). *Love and sex: Cross-cultural perspectives.* New York: Allyn and Bacon.

E. Hatfield
R. L. Rapson
University of Hawaii

INTERPERSONAL ATTRACTION
SPOUSE SELECTION

LURIA, ALEXANDER R. (1902–   )

Alexander Luria graduated from the University of Kazan, U.S.S.R. He received the degrees of MD, EdD, and DMed from the University of Moscow, where he later became a professor in the Department of Psychology and head of the Department of Neuropsychology.

Luria had a broad background in psychoneurology and carried out research on aphasia, the restoration of functions following brain trauma, speech, and higher cortical functions. He developed theories of language disorders and of the functions of the frontal lobe. He believed that mental functions are complex functional systems which cannot be localized in isolated cell groups or narrow regions of the cortex. Rather, the cell groups must be organized in systems of zones working in concert, each performing its role in the complex system.

Since many of his works have been available in English, Luria is well known in the United States. In the 1920s he studied human conflict, using hand movements and associative responses into which a conflict situation was introduced. This work was summarized in *The Nature of Human Conflicts.*

Staff

LURIA-NEBRASKA NEUROPSYCHOLOGICAL BATTERY

The Luria-Nebraska Neuropsychological Battery is a neuropsychological assessment battery based on the psychological procedures originated by the Russian neuropsychologist Alexander R. Luria, and subsequently reorganized by Charles J. Golden (1978) and his associates into a standardized battery of Luria's tests for the purpose of clinical neurodiagnosis. Luria, like the English neurologist J. Hughlings Jackson and his fellow Russian L. S. Vygotsky, believed that brain-behavior relationships could not be explained satisfactorily by either the localizationist or the equipotentialist theories of brain function. Instead, Luria conceived of behavior as the result of the interactions between all areas of the brain, and favored the use of simple test procedures which reflected relatively noncomplicated patterns of brain interactions, so that functional systems of the brain could be more precisely investigated.

Recognition of Luria in the United States came with the publication of *Higher Cortical Functions in Man* (1962) and *The Working Brain* (1973). Detailed information on Luria's test procedures became available with Anne-Lise Christensen's (1979) *Luria's Neuropsychological Investigation.* Luria's testing methods were not immediately accepted by American clinical neuropsychologists because of the absence of a standardized, quantitative scoring system and of experimental evidence supporting the validity of the test procedures. In addition, Luria's procedures appeared to rely heavily upon clinical judgment rather than objective, verifiable data.

To remedy the psychometric deficits of the Luria techniques, Golden and his colleagues transformed Luria's test items into standardized test procedures with objective scoring systems, and a battery that allowed a clinical evaluation on a quantitative level, like most American tests, as well as a qualitative level, as urged by Luria. The standardized version of Luria's tests assesses major areas of neuropsychological performance, including motor, tactile, and visual skills; auditory abilities; expressive and receptive speech functions; reading, writing, and arithmetic abilities; spatial skills; and memory and intelligence.

DESCRIPTION OF THE BATTERY

There are 269 items in the standardized Luria battery, initially referred to as the Luria-South Dakota Neuropsychological Test Battery. Each item is a test of a specific aspect of neuropsychological functioning. Subgroups of items exist which represent performance in the content area implied by the name of the scale, as, for example, the motor functions scale. The names of the scales of the Luria-Nebraska Neuropsychological Battery are as follows:

1. Motor functions
2. Rhythm (acoustico-motor) functions
3. Tactile (higher cutaneous and kinesthetic) functions
4. Visual (spatial) functions
5. Receptive speech
6. Expressive speech
7. Writing functions

8. Reading skills
9. Arithmetical skills
10. Memory
11. Intellectual processes

Form II of this battery added a twelfth scale, Intermediate Memory, which assesses delayed recall of 10 of the previously administered Memory items.

There are five summary scales, based on some of the items of the clinical scales:

1. Pathognomonic. This scale consists of simple items rarely missed by normals and is highly indicative of brain dysfunction.

2. Right hemisphere. This scale measures the motor and tactile functioning of the left side of the body.

3. Left hemisphere. This scale measures the motor and tactile functioning of the right side of the body.

4. Profile Elevation. This scale measures the level of present functioning or degree of behavioral compensation.

5. Impairment. This scale measures the degree of overall impairment.

Since the original publication of this battery, other scales have been developed, including eight localization scales (Frontal, Sensorimotor, Parietal-Occipital, and Temporal scales for each brain hemisphere) and 28 separate factor scales. A 66-item list of qualitative descriptors of test performance is also provided to aid the examiner in evaluating the nature of performance errors.

An impaired performance on any of the scales is determined by comparison with a critical level, which is calculated for each patient with age and education corrections. If a scale exceeds the critical level, the possibility of impairment on that scale is suggested. Two or more scales exceeding the critical level are suggestive of brain damage.

A short form of this battery has been proposed to be used with elderly patients.

The Luria-Nebraska is administered by psychologists as well as by psychology technicians trained in the administration and scoring procedures of the battery. The testing time averages about 2 1/2 hours.

NEUROPSYCHOLOGICAL STUDIES

Several validity studies of the Luria-Nebraska have been completed using normal, brain-damaged, and schizophrenic patients. In 1978, Golden, Hammeke, and Purisch reported the first validity study of the Luria, examining the test items with 50 brain-damaged and 50 control subjects. Of the 269 Luria items, 252 were found to discriminate significantly at the 0.05 level or better, with the remaining 17 items significant at the 0.02 level.

Hammeke, Golden and Purisch (1978) also studied the 14 scales of the Luria Battery with 50 brain-damaged and 50 controls. The diagnostic accuracy of the scales with the brain-damaged subjects ranged from 64% for the Arithmetic Scale to 86% for the Expres-

sive Speech Scale. The hit rates with the normal subjects ranged from 74% for the Expressive Speech Scale to 96% for the Memory Scale. A discriminant analysis using the 14 scaled scores correctly classified all 50 control patients and 43 of the brain-damaged patients, yielding an overall hit rate of 93%.

Cross-validation of the standardized Luria was reported by Golden and colleagues (1981b), utilizing 87 patients with localized lesions and 30 control patients. A Luria-Nebraska summary score led to an 74% accuracy rate for determining brain damage. The two hemisphere scales yielded a lateralization hit rate of 78%, whereas the highest localization scale led to a lateralization hit rate of 92% and a localization hit rate of 84%.

The effectiveness of the Luria-Nebraska was compared with the Halstead-Reitan Neuropsychological Battery, recognized as the most widely used standardized battery. Both test batteries were administered to 48 brain-damaged and 60 normal patients. The results showed a high degree of relationship (all Rs>0.71, p<0.05) between the 14 Luria-Nebraska scale scores and the major 14 scores of the Halstead-Reitan. Discriminant analysis found both batteries equally effective in identifying the brain-damaged, with hit rates over 85% (Golden et al., 1981a).

Critique of this battery has noted that it is comprised of test items from Luria's work but it does not necessarily represent Luria's clinical and qualitative methodology of testing hypotheses concerning a patient's neuropsychological functions or deficits. Support for the battery, on the other hand, has identified the standardization and empirical aspects of this battery as its strongest assets (Anastasi, 1982). Although the validity of this battery with neurologically impaired patients has been confirmed by a number of studies by Golden and his associates, others have been unable to replicate these validation findings.

A concise review of this battery is presented in Lezak's (1995) *Neuropsychological Assessment,* with concerns about the battery's norms, scale specificity, validation studies, and lateralization capabilities.

REFERENCES

Anastasi, A. (1982). *Psychological testing (5th ed.).* New York: Macmillan.

Christensen, Anne-Lise. (1979). *Luria's neuropsychological investigation (2nd ed.).* Copenhagen, Denmark: Munksgaard.

Golden, C. J., Hammeke, T. A., & Purisch, A. D. (1978). Diagnostic validity of a standardized neuropsychological battery derived from Luria's Neuropsychological Tests. *Journal of Consulting and Clinical Psychology, 46,* 1258–1265.

Golden, C. J., Kane, R., Sweet, J., Moses, J. A., Cardellino, J. P., Templeton, R., Vicente, P., & Graber, B. (1981a). Relationship of the Halstead-Reitan Neuropsychological Battery to the Luria-Nebraska Neuropsychological Battery. *Journal of Consulting and Clinical Psychology, 49,* 410–417.

Golden, C. J., Moses, J. A., Fishburne, F. J., Engum, E., Lewis, G. P., Wisniewski, A. M., Conley, F. K., Berg, R. A. & Graber, B. (1981b). Cross-validation of the Luria-Nebraska Neuropsychological Battery for the presence, lateralization, and localization of brain damage. *Journal of Consulting and Clinical Psychology, 49,* 491–507.

Golden, C. J., Purisch, A. D., & Hammeke, T. A. (1985). *Luria-Nebraska Neuropsychological Battery: Forms I and II.* Los Angeles: Western Psychological Services.

Hammeke, T. A., Golden, C. J., & Purisch, A. D. (1978). A standardized, short, and comprehensive neuropsychological test battery based on the Luria neuropsychological evaluation. *International Journal of Neuroscience, 8,* 135–141.

Lezak, M. D. (1995). *Neuropsychological assessment (3rd ed.).* New York: Oxford University.

Luria, A. R. (1962). *Higher cortical functions in man.* New York: Basic Books.

Luria, A. R. (1973). *The working brain.* New York: Basic Books.

Moses, J. A., Jr., & Purisch, A. D. (1997). The evolution of the Luria-Nebraska Neuropsychology Battery. In G. Goldstein & T. M. Incagnoli (Eds.), *Contemporary approaches to neuropsychological assessment* (pp. 131–170). New York: Plenum.

W. T. Tsushima
Straub Clinic and Hospital

CLINICAL ASSESSMENT
TESTING METHODS